Europe Since Waterloo

ROBERT ERGANG, Ph.D.

Europe

since Waterloo

D C. HEATH AND COMPANY BOSTON

Maps designed and executed
by THEODORE R. MILLER

Library of Congress
Catalog Card number 54-7862

5 L 7

PREFACE

THE PERIOD covered by this volume is but a moment of history. But it is a crowded moment, one vibrant with events. The old assertion that "there is nothing new under the sun" certainly does not apply literally to it. Even the most pessimistic must admit that it produced new things, some of which are so revolutionary as to transform the face of Europe. Many of the events and their causes are so complex, so intricate as to tax the most acute understanding. No historian dealing with the last century and a half will come away with the feeling that he has rendered it justice. I hope, however, that this volume will make some contribution to an understanding of the period.

"History," wrote David Hume in the eighteenth century, "is a collection of facts which are multiplying without end; and if they are to be made intelligible, they must, in some way, be abridged." Abridgment remains the eternal problem. It arises with especial force in the preparation of a general history. What is to be included? What left out? Selection, arrangement, and emphasis of fact are determined in large part by the preconceptions, preferences, and aims of the historian. This naturally gives rise to differences of opinion. The question of including the chapter "The Age of Romanticism" evoked from friends as many negative as affirmative answers. The same is true of the section, "The Beginnings of Modern Medicine." Each teacher will decide for himself whether to include the work of Jenner, Lister, and Pasteur as well as that of Bismarck, Cavour, and Gladstone.

A hearty "thank you" to Professor David Gaines of the College of the City of New York who was not only ready at all times to give me the benefit of his wide knowledge, but who also read most of the chapters in typescript and made many excellent suggestions for their improvement. I am also grateful for the cheerful assistance and cooperation of the staff of D. C. Heath and Company. Finally, there is the standing debt to my wife, Mildred Overbeck Ergang, for typing the manuscript, but above all for her faith and encouragement. The responsibility for the shortcomings of the book is entirely my own.

ROBERT ERGANG

New York City

TABLE OF CONTENTS

vii

LIST OF ILLUSTRATIONS

LIST OF MAPS

Europe Since Waterloo

CHAPTER ONE

The French Revolution and Napoleon

THE OLD REGIME WHEN powerful rulers with central administrative systems replaced feudalism at the beginning of the modern age,
absolute monarchy became the general mode of government in the
larger states of Europe. The foundation on which monarchs reared
their absolutism was the theory of divine right, that is, that "legitimate
monarchs derive their authority from, and are responsible to, God
alone." This theory had been asserted in the Middle Ages against the
claims of the papacy; now it was pressed into use again as a buttress
for despotic rule. Obedience to the king's commands became a religious
duty and disobedience was nothing less than defiance of the law of God.
It was James I who carried the dogma to its extreme logical conclusion
in England and Louis XIV who insisted upon it most literally in
France. "He who has given kings to the world," the Grand Monarque
stated, "willed it that they be respected as His lieutenants, reserving
for Himself the sole right to examine their conduct. It is His will that
whoever is born a subject should obey without question."

Through a series of struggles the British Parliament had by 1689
established its supremacy over kings; but in the Continental states the
sway of absolute monarchy continued. In France the king ruled arbitrarily, making no distinction between his own income and that of the
state. French kings recklessly squandered the money tax collectors
squeezed from an overburdened people. The many wars of Louis XIV
and his lavish expenditures at Versailles had been followed by the
apathetic prodigality of Louis XV. Under the weak but well-meaning
new king, Louis XVI, the debt leaped enormously; the interest on the
debt had increased until it absorbed three fifths of the annual revenue.

The *ancien régime* or old regime, as the order in prerevolutionary

3

France is commonly called, was characterized by many evils and weaknesses. Among these were confusion and incompetence in administration, favoritism before the law, and excessive regulation of industry and commerce. There was little uniformity in the machinery of government. The bewildering variety of overlapping administrative divisions and subdivisions made the French administration a masterpiece of red tape and confusion. The confusion was particularly evident in legal affairs. Justice was administered not only in the name of the king, but also in that of the Church, the feudal seigneurs, and of certain communes. On the eve of the Revolution there were more than three hundred distinct codes of law in force in the various parts of France. The same confusion existed in the realm of internal commerce. Although there was a group of thirteen provinces in central France in which internal trade could move freely, each of the nineteen other provinces had its own tariffs and raised customs barriers which separated one province from another, just as nations are today separated by tariff boundaries. There were also many different standards of weights and measures. In short, at a time when French commerce and industry were experiencing a remarkable growth, they found themselves hampered at every turn.

Under the old regime society was still, after the feudal manner, divided into three classes or estates: the clergy, the nobility, and the Third Estate. Of these the first two, comprising only a little more than 2 per cent of the nation, were the privileged classes. The highest rank in the social order was held by the great ecclesiastics, almost all of whom were drawn from the nobility. Many bishops and abbots enjoyed large incomes from the landed estates of the Church and from the tithe (a tax on agricultural products), but were exempt from some of the direct taxes and able to redeem themselves cheaply from the others. On the other hand, many of the parish priests, upon whom fell the burden of the work, were grossly underpaid.

The nobles were the largest privileged class. Not only had they ceased as a class to perform any useful functions; they had also lost faith in themselves and were largely addicted to frivolity and vice. Nevertheless, they still retained most of the privileges the nobility had enjoyed in the Middle Ages. In England these privileges had gradually been whittled down since the middle of the seventeenth century, but no similar change had taken place in France. Although the nobles were not entirely exempt from direct taxation as they had once been, they were wholly free from the taille (a tax on land or on income) and managed to evade other taxes. The nobles also enjoyed such privileges as exclusive hunting rights and freedom from billeting troops, and most of the higher offices in the army and in the Church were reserved for their younger sons. Finally, the French seigneurs could still collect from the peasants feudal dues in money, in kind, and in various forms of compulsory labor, despite the fact that the government had largely taken over the duty of protecting the peasants.

Ranged against this old order were the lower clergy and the Third Estate, which constituted the bulk of the nation. Within the Third Estate it was the members of the upper middle class, more particularly the professional men and the great merchants, industrialists, and financiers, who took the lead in demanding reform. Regarding themselves as equals of the clergy and nobility in wealth, education, and culture, they demanded social equality, equal taxation for all, and an equal opportunity to obtain the higher offices in the Church, the army, and the navy. They further demanded a curb on the royal expenditures, which by undermining the credit of the state were threatening the security of all loans and investments. The royal prerogatives, they believed, could be best limited by a constitution. Finally, they desired greater freedom of thought and economic freedom. As for the peasants, their demands were purely economic. First, they desired a reform of the inequitable system of taxation which permitted the privileged classes to evade most of the taxes and placed the heaviest burden upon the Third Estate. How heavy the burden was can be seen from the fact that in some districts the peasants paid out more than half their income in taxes. Second, they wanted freedom from the vexatious feudal dues which they still had to pay, even though they were landowners. Their demands as a whole had the sympathetic support of the lower clerics, who had little liking for an order that accorded them but miserable stipends while their titled superiors lived in luxury. In short, there was a widespread longing for a new state of things based on justice and freedom.

REVOLUTIONARY MUTTERINGS

The discontent of the middle classes and the masses with the old order and their longing for a new one did not remain inarticulate. Toward the middle of the eighteenth century there appeared upon the scene a group of publicists, known as the *philosophes*, who gave voice both to the grievances and the aspirations of the people. Prominent among them were Voltaire, Rousseau, Montesquieu, and Diderot. There have been few eras in history when literary men exercised so great an influence upon the minds and actions of men as did this group. Their books and pamphlets were probably read more eagerly than the gazettes of the time. While some of them were content with repeated denunciations of existing conditions, thereby making the people more conscious of the evils of the old regime, others presented a positive creed of reform. Among the theories they preached, two are especially important because of their profound influence on modern thought. Neither was original with the philosophes, both having previously been expounded by John Locke and by others before him. The first was that life, liberty, and property are inherent and inalienable rights of man. The inference was that if man does not enjoy these rights there is but one way to regain them and that is by a reconstitution of society.

Equally important was the social contract theory, that is, that government rightfully rests upon the consent of the governed. Sovereignty belongs to the people, not to the king. The natural corollary of this idea is that any government which flouts the will of the people may be abolished. It was not, however, the purpose of the philosophes to preach revolution. They wished only to change the existing state system, not to erect a new one. Rousseau himself had regarded his ideas as applicable only in a small republic such as his native city of Geneva. For a time the philosophes hoped that a small group of rulers, known as the "enlightened despots," would translate some of their ideas into action. Even Voltaire regarded them as the only possible source of progress and reform. But although the enlightened despots did make many proposals, very few of these proposals were carried out.

What the philosophes did do was to offer the French people a justification for leveling the old order and erecting the new. As the Abbé Siéyès stated it, "The French have something better to follow than history: they have principles." "It was impossible," Ségur wrote in his *Mémoires,* "that we should not receive with enthusiasm the hopes which men of genius held out to us of a future where humanity, tolerance, and liberty would reign instead of the errors, follies, and prejudices which had so long enslaved and embittered the world. We were soothed by the seductive dreams of a philosophy that sought to assure the happiness of the race. Voltaire charmed our intelligence, and Rousseau touched our hearts."

A further stimulus was given to revolutionary ideas in France by the successful revolt of the British colonies and the establishment of a republic in America. At the end of the war French soldiers who had given the United States substantial aid in the struggle for independence returned home full of enthusiasm for the new freedom. Returned officers, among them Lafayette, became leaders of the revolutionary movement at home. In general, the success of the American Revolution appeared to many to demonstrate the truth of the democratic doctrine of natural rights. But the cost of the intervention was, so to speak, the straw which broke the financial back of the French state and necessitated the calling of the Estates-General that inaugurated the French Revolution.

Although the people were deeply dissatisfied with the old order, they had clung to the hope that the monarchy would of itself initiate a reform movement. Hence, when Louis XV died in 1774, they hailed the accession of Louis XVI and confidently looked to him for better things. The new king, a good-hearted and well-meaning person, did at first raise expectations of change by dismissing some of the unpopular ministers and appointing as controller general M. Turgot, whose very name was a pledge of reform. Turgot at once addressed himself to the task and within a few months succeeded in restoring the national credit by reducing expenditures, revising the collection of taxes, converting the *corvées* (road taxes) into money payments to be levied on all classes alike, removing barriers to commerce, establishing free trade in corn, and suppressing the guilds which had hampered industry. But as his reforms meant the curtailment of personal advantage he called down upon himself the hostility of the privileged classes, particularly of the court party led by Marie Antoinette. Soon the court clique was demanding his dismissal. It was a great opportunity for Louis XVI to save the monarchy by carrying through the changes in the face of opposition. But he lacked the courage to do so. Giving way to the clamors of the court party, he dismissed Turgot in 1776 and permitted most of his work to be undone. Jacques Necker, the next minister of finance, sought to introduce improvements somewhat more slowly. Again the efforts shattered on the rock of the king's irresolution and the opposition of the privileged classes. In 1781 Necker went the way of Turgot.

During the decade of the eighties the spirit of revolt gradually gained strength. Beginning in 1785 France was visited by a series of bad harvests caused by floods, drought, and hailstorms. Bread was so scarce that bread riots occurred in many cities. To make matters worse, an industrial crisis was precipitated in 1788, largely as a result of a commercial treaty with England. This treaty, by greatly reducing the tariffs, opened the country to a flood of English goods which sold for less than the corresponding home products, causing great distress to businessmen and workingmen alike. More and more people came to regard the system of government as the cause of their troubles, and they did not hesitate to vent their feelings. Seditious remarks were everywhere to be heard and tumultuous gatherings became more frequent. A placard placed on the queen's box at the Italian opera read, "Tremble, tyrants! Your reign is ending!" Had the privileged classes consented to pay their proportionate share of the taxes, the budget might well have been balanced and the government's financial crisis solved. Since they refused to do this, the king was finally compelled to convoke the Estates-General. It was a measure of desperation, for this body had not met since 1614.

REVOLUTION BECOMES A REALITY

When the Estates-General met at Versailles on May 5, 1789, most of the delegates were determined that it should be more than a consultative gathering. The king, it is true, shared the feeling that reforms were necessary, but he did not intend to part with any of his power. The privileged classes, and in particular the court party, were still opposed to any concessions, and even Necker hoped to keep the changes within narrow limits. All of them underestimated the determination of the deputies of the Third Estate to assert the principle of the sovereignty of the people. These deputies were resolved to make this sovereignty a reality through constitutional government. The test came when the method of voting was discussed. If the Estates voted as units, the vote of the two upper Estates (clergy and nobles) could defeat any move the Third Estate might make. However, if the deputies voted as individuals, the six hundred members of the Third Estate could hope for a majority against the combined vote of the other two. When the king ordered them to vote "by order," they held firmly to their demand to be allowed to vote "by head."

Finally, on June 17, after many of the parish priests had passed to the side of the Third Estate, the commoners and curates joined in declaring themselves the National Assembly. Several days later when the king locked the doors of the assembly hall against them, the members of the National Assembly swore not to disband until they had drawn up a constitution for France. Thus the French Revolution was born.

The king retreated before this show of determination, but within a few weeks rumors became current that he was preparing a military coup against the Assembly. Support was given to these rumors by the fact that troops, mostly German and Swiss mercenaries, were being concentrated at Versailles. When on July 11 the king took the further step of dismissing Necker, who had been reappointed, excitement ran high in Paris. Mobs began to surge through the streets. On the morning of the 14th the populace took cannon and muskets from the Invalides and marched on to storm the Bastille, the famous old fortress that had long been used as a prison. The capture of its small garrison, whose weapons were obsolete, was no great military achievement. Nor did the pillage and slaughter of the helpless garrison, which followed the surrender, cover the mob with glory. Nevertheless, the capture and destruction of this emblem of Bourbon despotism was important politically, for it symbolized the end of arbitrary rule and the dawn of an era of freedom. During the succeeding weeks the fever spread all over France. Everywhere revolutionary bands rose up against the old order. Tollgates were demolished, many chateaux of the nobility were burned, and the hated manorial records which listed the feudal dues the peasants owed were consigned to the flames. Many of the reactionary nobles, seeing their traditional world collapse about them, began to flee beyond the borders of France where, as *émigrés,* they endeavored to stir up foreign intervention.

When a report on the disorder in the provinces reached the Assembly on August 3, it roused the members to action. "What is the cause of the evil which is agitating the provinces?" asked the Duc de Noailles. Then, after showing that the violence and chaos arose from the fact that the people were uncertain as to whether or not the old feudal bonds were to be perpetuated or abolished, he concluded with a proposal to abolish them at once. The result was that the deputies vied with one another throughout the feverish night of August 4, 1789, in annulling traditional obligations and social privileges. Dawn on the morning of August 5 saw serfdom, tithes, the seignioral corvées, the exclusive right of the nobles to hunt and fish, and the manorial courts abolished. The rest of the dues were declared redeemable for money, but were finally abolished without compensation in 1793. Furthermore, the principle of equal taxation for all was proclaimed, the sale of judicial and municipal offices was abolished, and all citizens, without distinction, were declared eligible for any office, whether civil, military, or ecclesiastical.

Having made the rights of all Frenchmen equal, the Assembly proceeded to declare what these rights were. This was done in the so-called Declaration of the Rights of Man, adopted on August 27, and probably the most notable document of the Revolution. Its authors intended that its general principles should serve as a statement of the rights not only of Frenchmen but of all mankind. "We wish," said M. Dupont, "to make a declaration of rights for all men, for all time, and for all countries, and thus serve as an example for the world." "Men," the declaration proclaimed, "are born and remain free and equal in rights. . . . The source of all sovereignty is essentially in the nation. . . . Liberty consists in the power to do anything that does not injure others. . . . Law is the expression of the general will. . . . Free communication of thought and opinion is one of the most precious rights of man. . . . No one should be disturbed on account of his opinions, even religious, provided their manifestation does not derange the public order established by law. . . . All citizens, being equal in the eyes of the law, are equally admissible to all dignities, places, and public employment according to their capacity, and without further distinction other than their virtue and talents." Thus it collected in a few short aphorisms the doctrines scattered through the teachings of the philosophes, particularly of Rousseau. It repudiated the abuses existing in France under the old regime and implied the reforms necessary to end them. Because of its general and abstract tone it has been styled "purely philosophical," with Bentham going so far as to term it "the *ne plus ultra* of metaphysics." Nevertheless, it has vitally influenced liberal and democratic thought to this day and has served as the model for similar declarations. The very generality of its ideas has made it the symbol of democratic aspiration.

Two years later the Declaration was used as a preface for the Constitution of 1791, which was believed by its framers to be a masterpiece of political wisdom. The new constitution can best be characterized as a compromise between the idea of absolute monarchy and that of the sovereignty of the people. It provided for a unicameral Legislative Assembly with authority to pass laws, levy taxes, and control expenditures. Frenchmen who paid a certain sum in taxes were classified as active citizens and entitled to vote, while those who paid less were styled "passive" and could not vote. This failure to carry out the promise of the Declaration of Rights indicated that the propertied classes feared the masses might get out of hand. The executive power remained in the hands of the king, who was allowed only a suspensive veto. He could not select his ministers from the legislature; nor could he dissolve the latter to allow the voters to decide any differences. Actually the new constitution, in sharply separating the executive and the legislative, rendered the smooth functioning of the government difficult.

The new constitution, the abolition of feudalism, and the Declaration of Rights were not the only reforms and changes introduced by the National Constituent Assembly during this "moderate" phase of the French Revolution. It also abolished the thirty-two old provinces and redivided France into eighty-three departments, with a large degree of self-government for these and the smaller units (arrondissements, cantons, and communes). Another reform accomplished a thorough reorganization of the judicial power. Whereas in the past judges had purchased their positions and were able to pass them down to their sons, thenceforth all judges were to be elected for a period of two to four years. Moreover, for the first time in the history of modern France the jury was introduced for criminal cases. Previously the judge had rendered decisions in all cases.

But the National Constituent Assembly failed to offer an effective solution of the financial problem which had occasioned the summoning of the Estates-General. As the financial situation had grown more critical the Assembly had nationalized the properties of the Church and decided to sell them. But instead of selling them directly for money, the Assembly resorted to the expedient of issuing paper money (assignats) with the former church lands as security. Persons possessing assignats could not turn them in for gold, but could use them to buy these lands. The temptation to issue more assignats at every crisis was great and the Assembly was unable to resist it. The result was that they gradually declined from a par value of 100 francs to 82 francs in 1791 and to less than one franc in 1796. In confiscating the property of the Church, the National Assembly had assumed the duty of paying the clergy. This led to the Civil Constitution of the Clergy (1790), which provided that bishops and priests were henceforth to be elected like other state officials. All the clergy were asked to take an oath to support the measure, but only a few did. After the pope denounced it, opposition to the Civil Constitution of the Clergy grew until in many cases it became opposition to the Revolution.

THE GROWING DEMAND FOR A REPUBLIC

Despite Louis' feeble efforts to block reforms, Mirabeau, his principal minister, had managed to maintain a measure of harmony between the king and the Assembly. But Mirabeau's untimely death in April, 1791, dispelled all hope of a permanent compromise. Having signed the Civil Constitution of the Clergy which made all priests civil servants, the pious Louis now regretted the step. He believed that it imperiled not only his own salvation but also that of his subjects. The only way out, as he saw it, was flight. He would join the émigré nobles who had left France and set up their headquarters across the border in Germany. On the night of June 20, 1791, the royal family secretly set out for the frontier in a closed carriage. Near the border Louis grew careless, put his head out of the window, and was recognized. Return to Paris followed for the royal pair. The unsuccessful attempt to leave the country undermined such faith as the reformers still had in the king. Few people had previously considered a republic possible in so large a country as France, but now the demand for one was openly voiced.

On September 14, 1791, the king solemnly swore to uphold the constitution, and on October 1 the Legislative Assembly held its first session. Two days earlier Maximilien Robespierre had said, "The Revolution is finished." But the future leader of the Jacobin dictatorship could not have been more wrong. For one thing, the king failed to cooperate wholeheartedly with the Legislative Assembly. For another, French nobles who had become émigrés carried on a ceaseless agitation against the new government. They finally succeeded in inducing the rulers of

Austria and Prussia to issue the famous Declaration of Pillnitz (August, 1791), which declared that the reestablishment of order and absolute monarchy in France was the concern of all the rulers of Europe. All this nourished the suspicion that Louis was conspiring with foreign monarchs against his own people.

During this period certain groups or clubs became influential centers of political agitation, the two most prominent ones being the Jacobin and Cordelier Clubs. The Jacobin Club derived its name from the fact that during the early days of the Revolution it had held its meetings in the convent of the Jacobin Friars. The members of both clubs had been quite moderate in their opinions at first but had grown increasingly radical as the conservative members dropped out. While the Cordelier Club was limited to Paris, the Jacobins gradually organized affiliated clubs in more than 2000 cities and villages. In time the Jacobin Club became so powerful as to rival the Legislative Assembly in influence. Both clubs began to exert pressure on the Assembly for the establishment of a republic. Outstanding leaders of the clubs were Danton, Marat, and Robespierre. As a result of their efforts and those of other leaders, the revolutionary spirit grew among the people. Various symbols of liberty and democracy, such as the *bonnet rouge* (red cap worn by emancipated slaves in ancient times) and the tricolor cockade (symbol of revolution), were displayed by the populace. Knee breeches (*culottes*) came to be regarded as a symbol of aristocracy and were discarded in favor of long trousers previously worn only by workingmen. Throughout France, but especially among the lower classes in Paris, a vigorous democratic feeling was manifesting itself.

The fate of the monarchy was sealed by the so-called Brunswick Manifesto. When Francis II of Austria refused to disperse the émigrés who had collected armed forces along the eastern border of France, the Legislative Assembly declared war on April 20, 1792. Most of the parties in the Assembly had desired war as a means of achieving their respective aims. While those who supported the monarchy thought the war would enable the king to recover his lost authority, many republicans believed that war would further discredit monarchical government and open the way for the establishment of a republic. But Robespierre and his Jacobin followers opposed war on the ground that only the rich and powerful benefit from it. Frederick William II of Prussia soon joined Francis II in the war, and the Austro-Prussian forces administered a series of reverses to the poorly drilled, poorly equipped French forces. After the Austro-Prussian forces had invaded France, the duke of Brunswick, commander of the joint forces, issued the Brunswick Manifesto (July 11, 1792), which ordered the French to restore complete liberty of action to Louis XVI at once and threatened with summary punishment anyone who should dare to resist the advance of the invading armies. More than this, it announced that Paris would be completely destroyed "if the least violence or outrage be offered to their Majesties, the king, queen and royal family."

Instead of intimidating the French the manifesto only made them more determined to resist. Many were now convinced that Louis was in treasonable correspondence with the enemy. On August 10, 1792, the feelings of the Parisian populace exploded in a formidable insurrection. On the morning of that day a large crowd invaded the Tuileries, forcing the king and his family to seek safety in the hall of the Legislative Assembly. After the mob had sacked the Tuileries, its representatives demanded that the Assembly dethrone the king. The Assembly responded by suspending the king and issuing a decree for the election of a National Convention to draw up a new constitution.

THE FIRST FRENCH REPUBLIC

The National Convention, elected by universal manhood suffrage in an atmosphere of terror, met on September 20, 1792, and on the following day decreed that "royalty is abolished in France." The fact that France was now a republic was brought out the next day when it was decided that all public documents should henceforth be dated from "the first year of the French republic." In December of the same year *EXECUTE* Louis XVI was put on trial before the Convention, and on January 15, 1793, the Convention voted that "Louis Capet" was guilty "of conspiracy against the liberty of the nation and of a criminal attack upon the safety of the state." The vote was almost unanimous, although a number of deputies abstained. The death penalty was then voted by a small majority and Louis was guillotined on January 21.

The execution of the king shocked all Europe, but it did demonstrate that even a king could in effect commit treason against the nation. A few days later the Convention in a decree referred to the "new crime" as *lèse nation*. It was a new thought to a Europe long cautioned to avoid *lèse majesté*.

The king having been put away, the Convention addressed itself to the task of discarding everything that smacked of royalty. All titles of nobility and also the terms "Monsieur" and "Madame" were abolished, "Citizen" and "Citizeness" becoming the proper mode of address. The old Gregorian calendar with its saints' days and religious festivals gave way to the revolutionary calendar, which designated September 22, 1792, as the first day of the year one. This new calendar divided the year into twelve months of thirty days, and set aside the five or six days necessary to complete the year as national holidays (*Sans-Culottides*).

Among the more lasting achievements of the Convention were the steps it took toward doing away with the legal confusion that existed in France by having a committee prepare the first draft of a civil code. However, it remained for Napoleon to carry this work to completion. Another solid accomplishment of the Convention was the enactment of laws providing for the extension of primary and secondary education and the creation of a number of technical schools. In 1793 an attempt was also made to de-Christianize France. It began with the consecration of the cathedral of Notre Dame to the worship of the Goddess of Reason, after which all the churches of Paris were closed. Other parts of France followed this example, many churches being closed or converted into Temples of Reason. But the French people were not in sympathy with the attempt and it was gradually abandoned.

The machinery set up by the National Convention to deal with both the domestic and foreign enemies of the republic included a Committee of General Security, a Committee of Public Safety, and a Revolutionary Tribunal. The Committee of General Security was entrusted with the task of maintaining internal order. In its line of duty it arrested those suspected of opposition to the republic. Such suspects were tried by the Revolutionary Tribunal, an extraordinary criminal court. There was no appeal from its sentences. The most important organ was the Committee of Public Safety, the members of which were chosen by the Convention. At first it had charge of foreign affairs and of the army, but its power and authority gradually increased until it had virtually complete direction of the state.

Of the greatest urgency was the need for effective military forces. On September 20, 1792, the day on which the National Convention first met, the French had offered determined resistance to the invading Austro-Prussian forces at Valmy. Although the French did not win a military victory, they did gain a moral victory by refusing to give way. The courageous stand of the French astonished the invaders. Already harried by disease, famine, and heavy rains, the invaders realized that they were now opposed by a united people. This caused them to turn back and recross the Rhine. Although the immediate danger was over, the need for trained armies was still great, for the French government was practically without friends in Europe. The Committee of Public Safety moved quickly and audaciously. A general call for troops was sounded with hundreds of thousands responding. Then Lazare Carnot, a member of the Committee, performed the herculean task of equipping and drilling them with such dispatch and efficiency that he earned for himself the title of "Organizer of Victory." After Valmy other nations had gradually joined the coalition against France, so that by the spring of 1793 it consisted of Spain, Portugal, Naples, and England, in addition to Austria and Prussia. For the forces of this coalition Carnot's armies were more than a match.

The success of the republican armies caused the members of the National Convention to hurl a challenge at the existing order in Europe. They would bestow the republican blessings on the other European states. In December, 1792, the Convention issued a proclamation which stated that the French nation would "never lay down its arms until the sovereignty and liberty of the people on whose territories the French armies shall have entered, shall be established." It promised "the suppression of all established authorities . . . the abolition of the tithe, of feudalism, of seignioral rights . . . of real and personal servitude . . . and generally of all privileges." In other words, the Convention proclaimed a great crusade against all governments which did not recognize and embody the sovereignty of the people. As the revolutionary wars spread, the French armies planted the seeds of democracy all over the continent of Europe.

While the French armies were trying to establish democratic government in the neighboring countries, democracy was rapidly declining at home. The changes which the Revolution had inaugurated were too sudden and too sweeping for a people without experience in democracy. More and more the management of both local and national affairs fell into the hands of politicians and political clubs. In the Convention power was gradually absorbed by the Jacobins, who sought to retain their power by terrorizing the opposition, a technique which culminated in the Reign of Terror. The Law of Suspects (September 17, 1793), which was so vague that almost anyone could be arrested under its provisions, permitted the ruling clique to fill the prisons. After trials that were travesties of justice, prisoners were condemned to death in batches. A steady procession of condemned passed through the streets of Paris to the two guillotines which had been erected in public squares. Among those who ascended the steps of the scaffolds were Marie Antoinette, Madame Roland, the astronomer Bailly, and Danton. In the succeeding weeks more and more victims were sent to the guillotine. The forty-nine days during which the Reign of Terror was at its height saw 1,376 heads drop into the baskets. Even the members of the Convention no longer felt safe. Finally they combined to send Robespierre to the guillotine on July 27, 1794.

After Robespierre's death a reaction set in and a milder regime began. Before the end of 1794 even the Law of Suspects was repealed and the Jacobin Club of Paris was closed. Under the provisions of the Constitution of 1795 the executive power was vested in a Directory of five members and the National Convention was dissolved (October 26, 1795) to make room for the new legislative councils: the Council of

Elders and the Council of Five Hundred. The new government was faced with the task of quelling the prevailing anarchy and disorder. The greater part of the French clerics, refusing to accept the Civil Constitution of the Clergy, were in open rebellion against the state; in the western part of France, the Vendée, civil war was raging between the government and the people; and in many districts robber bands were systematically pillaging the country. Everywhere respect for law was at a low ebb. Instead of improving, conditions became worse under the Directory. Weary of foreign war and internal strife, the French people wished nothing so much as peace, peace with honor abroad, peace with the Church, and the restoration of order and security at home.

NAPOLEON'S OPPORTUNITY

In this desire of the French people for peace with honor abroad and for order at home Napoleon Bonaparte saw his great opportunity. During the early part of the Revolution, Edmund Burke, the English philosopher, had said that if the republican experiment in France should fail it would be followed by the rise of "the most complete arbitrary power that has ever appeared on earth." This prediction was fulfilled at least in part in the career of Napoleon. In 1795, when the mob tried to storm the hall in which the National Convention was sitting, Napoleon demonstrated that he was its master. The propertied class, financiers, and commercial men remembered this and later threw themselves into his arms because they thought he could give them the stability they needed to make the most of their economic opportunities. Soon after he saved the Convention, Napoleon won a series of military victories in Italy (1796–1797) with a lightning-like swiftness that put his name on the lips of every Frenchman. So glaring was the contrast between the failure of the government at home and his successes in Italy that he could well pose as the victorious general who could provide the happy ending to the revolutionary melodrama. Although the Egyptian expedition that followed was a failure, he managed to gloss it over so completely as to give it the appearance of success.

While Napoleon was in Egypt, the corrupt and incompetent Directory succeeded in discrediting itself completely. The time seemed propitious for a *coup d'état* and Bonaparte gathered a group of conspirators about himself to plot one. After a rumor was circulated that the republic was in danger, the conspirators who were members of the Council of Elders managed (November 9, 1799) to get a resolution passed to transfer the sessions of both Councils to St. Cloud and gave General Bonaparte command of the troops that were to protect the Councils. The next day Napoleon made a somewhat incoherent speech before the Elders, but

left to address the Council of Five Hundred when some of the Elders
who were not party to the conspiracy became suspicious. Upon entering the hall where the Council of Five Hundred was in session he was
greeted with shouts of "Down with the dictator, down with the tyrant!"
In the pandemonium which ensued Napoleon was, according to an eyewitness, pushed and jostled and finally carried out by his men in a
fainting state. But his brother Lucien, who was president of the Council,
saved the day. He harangued the troops outside and finally succeeded
in having them drive the members of the Council out of the hall. That
evening a group of conspirators from both houses met and voted the
abolition of the Directory, appointed three provisional consuls (Napoleon, Siéyès, and Roger Ducos) to exercise the executive power, and
adjourned the sessions of the two houses for a period of four months.
Thus was achieved the coup d'état of the 18th and 19th Brumaire (November 9–10, 1799) which raised Napoleon to power. No uprising occurred in Paris, for the people approved the change.

Once Bonaparte had put his feet on the lower rungs of the ladder of
power, he poised himself for a further ascent. Under his supervision
a new constitution, the Constitution of the Year VIII, was hastily drawn
up, published in December, 1799, and adopted by a plebiscite. The government for which it provided was still republican in name, but monarchical in fact. The executive power was vested in three consuls, to be
elected for ten years, but the First Consul, Napoleon Bonaparte, exercised the real power. Two chambers, the Tribunate and the Legislative
Body, constituted the legislature, but had no power to take the initiative. No bill could be discussed or voted that had not been drawn up
and submitted by the First Consul. Even after a bill was voted it did
not go into force until it was promulgated by the First Consul. Thus,
while acknowledging that the people are the source of all power, Napoleon embodied in himself their professed sovereignty. As despotic power
was essential to his purposes, he bridled the press, stamped out political
debate, and gradually freed himself more and more from political
checks. Espionage and secret police became familiar agencies of his
government.

But if Napoleon discarded the idea of liberty as being demonstrably
bad for discipline, he did save a large measure of equality and did succeed in restoring order. He stamped out the bands of brigands who
were terrorizing many districts of France, brought to an end the civil
war in the Vendée, which had long vexed the revolutionary governments, and propitiated the monarchists and the Roman Catholic Church
by permitting many émigré nobles and priests to return to France. Thus
Napoleon repaired the major divisions in French society caused by the
Revolution.

THE FIRST FRENCH REPUBLIC

When Napoleon took up the task of bringing permanent peace to Europe, he found it rather more difficult than the restoration of order at home. After offers of peace to England and Austria, made largely for purposes of home consumption, were rejected, he decided to establish peace by means of the sword. In May, 1800, he quietly slipped out of Paris, took the hazardous route over the Great St. Bernard Pass with the main portion of his army, and routed the Austrians at Marengo. Having eliminated Austria from the coalition against him, he succeeded in winning over Tsar Paul of Russia by skillful flattery, and in 1802 terminated the hostilities with England by the treaty of Amiens. Thus within two years after his assumption of power he had managed to establish a semblance of peace. Though not yet wearing the imperial crown, he was already the most commanding figure in Europe.

THE FIRST EMPIRE IN FRANCE

In the ensuing months the First Consul devoted himself to a reorganization of internal affairs in France. Seldom has a country been in greater need of administrative powers and seldom have such powers been so ably exercised. In 1801 he signed a concordat with the pope which, by recognizing the Catholic faith as the religion of the majority of the French people and restoring freedom of worship to all Catholics, healed the breach the Civil Constitution of the Clergy had opened.[1] He further promoted such improvements as the construction of roads, the building of canals, and the expansion of harbor facilities, largely for military purposes. This period also saw the completion of the Civil Code, or Code Napoleon, on which committees had been at work since the time of the National Constituent Assembly. This orderly and systematic code put an end to the confusion and overlapping that had characterized French law. Its completion is probably the most celebrated of Napoleon's achievements. At St. Helena he himself said, "My real glory is not my having won forty battles. . . . What will never be effaced, what will endure forever, is the Civil Code." Other changes and improvements which he inaugurated were restoration of order in the national finances, reform of the tax system, establishment of the Bank of France, founding of the Legion of Honor, and reorganization of the educational system. These reforms increased still further the popularity

[1] The price the Church paid was high, for Napoleon used the priesthood as a satellite of his rule. In the catechism used during the period of the empire one may read, "Q. What are especially our duties towards our Emperor Napoleon I? A. We owe him especially love, respect, obedience, fidelity, and military service; we ought to pay the taxes ordained for the defense of the Empire and for his throne, and to offer up fervent prayers for his safety and the prosperity of his State. Q. Why are we bound to perform these duties towards our Emperor? A. Because God by loading our Emperor with gifts, both in peace and in war, has established him our sovereign and His own image upon the earth. In honoring and serving our Emperor thus, we are honoring and serving God himself."

he had won by his military victories, so that the proposal that he be made consul for life was carried in 1802 by an overwhelming majority. Two years later the people voted him the title of "Emperor of the French" and he was crowned in the cathedral of Notre Dame on December 2, 1804, with imposing ceremonies.

But the peace proved to be only a truce. War had begun again in 1803, and Napoleon was once more confronted by a strong coalition which, besides England, included Russia, Sweden, Austria, and Prussia. The war was studded with such notable victories as Austerlitz (1805), Jena and Auerstadt (1806), and Friedland (1807), which eliminated Austria from the list of great powers and made Prussia virtually a French province. When Portugal refused to support his Continental System, by means of which he hoped to ruin England,[2] Napoleon sent an army into that country. Then he tricked both the Spanish king and the heir apparent into resigning the rights to the Spanish throne and proclaimed his brother Joseph king of Spain. As the people refused to accept a Bonaparte as ruler, Napoleon found it necessary to lead an army into Spain. Having marched into Madrid and placed his brother on the throne, he believed that the Spanish question was settled. In 1809 he had another war with Austria, culminating in the hard-fought victory of Wagram. The speedy defeat of Austria raised him to the height of his power. His empire, extending from the North Sea to the Bay of Naples and eastward to the Adriatic, included Belgium, Holland, and the German territories on the left bank of the Rhine; Austria and Prussia were tributary to him; his brother Joseph was king of Spain, his brother Jerome king of Westphalia, and his brother-in-law, Murat, king of Naples. The tsar, too, seemed to accept his dominance. In short, the Emperor of the French appeared to be master of continental Europe.

The Napoleonic Empire was established exclusively by force and maintained by force. Ruthless police and spy systems which reached into every corner of his domain reported to Napoleon not only what the people were doing but also what they were saying. Any opposition to his rule was mercilessly stamped out. There was, however, a bright side to his conquests. Wherever his armies went they liquidated the accumulation of outworn institutions, leveled feudalism and class privilege, abolished guilds, and inaugurated far-reaching social reforms. Wherever his power made itself felt the laws of the Napoleonic Code

---

[2] Since he had no navy that could challenge the British supremacy on the sea, Napoleon hoped to weaken his most determined enemy by closing all Continental markets to her goods. He inaugurated the so-called Continental System with the Berlin Decree (November 21, 1806), which forbade the European states to trade in goods coming from England or her colonies. No British ship was to be admitted to any Continental port. To enforce the blockade Napoleon needed the support of all the Continental nations. This he failed to get. The struggle with England dominated the entire period from 1807 to 1814.

were to a greater or lesser extent established, sweeping away barbarous punishments and ancient perversions of justice and establishing equality before the law. In Italy, Holland, Belgium, and the German territories the effect of the Code was direct and lasting. It also exerted an important influence on the later legislation of Prussia, central and southern Germany, Spain, and Switzerland. Yet these benefits did not offset the humiliation the vanquished suffered.

No sooner had Napoleon's empire reached its greatest extent than it began to fall to pieces. Ironically, Napoleon himself was the most active agent in releasing the force which was to level the empire and cause his overthrow. This was the spirit of nationalism. In building his empire he had made a conscious appeal to it, not only in France but elsewhere. In Prussian Poland, for example, he had created the grand duchy of Warsaw for the deliberate purpose of enlisting Polish national sentiment on his side. Again, he had joined many of the small states of Italy into a kingdom for which he revived the ancient name of Kingdom of Italy. In Germany, too, he stimulated a desire for national unity. Soon the national sentiment which Napoleon had nurtured in a number of countries turned against him. Peoples instead of governments began to rise against his rule. The first concrete demonstration of the revived national spirit was made by the Spaniards when they rebelled against him in 1808. The vigor of their uprising proclaimed to the world that in the spirit of nationalism Napoleon had awakened a force more formidable than the disciplined armies he had repeatedly vanquished. Encouraged by the success of the Spaniards, the people of Prussia and northern Germany began the task of national regeneration in order to strengthen themselves for the inevitable struggle.

The opportunity of the nations to free themselves from the yoke came with the disastrous invasion of Russia in 1812. Determined to bring Tsar Alexander I to his knees for defying the Continental System, Napoleon collected an army of more than five hundred thousand men, the largest yet seen in civilized warfare. The major part of the army was, however, made up of soldiers from subject nations in which the national spirit was stirring. Hardly had the Grand Army crossed the Russian frontier when the soldiers began to desert in large numbers. Napoleon did reach Moscow, but was forced to retreat and on the way back most of his remaining troops fell prey to snipers, starvation, and the bitter cold of the Russian winter.

The destruction of Napoleon's army was the signal for a general uprising against him. Alexander I, having achieved his object of driving Napoleon and his army out of Russia, determined to become the "liberator of Europe." In February, 1813, he was joined by Prussia, and later in the same year Austria cast its lot with the allies. Although

THE EMPI

AREAS IN WHICH TRADE WITH THE BRITISH WAS PROHIBITED

THE
CONTINENTAL
SYSTEM
1809

NAPOLEON'S EMPIRE, 1810

DEPENDENT STATES

ALLIED STATES

NORWAY SWEDEN

DENMARK

PRUSSIA

RUSSIA

GREAT
BRITAIN

G.D.
POLAND

CONFED.
OF
RHINE

AUSTRIA

FRANCE

ITALY

OTTOMAN
EMPIRE

PORT.

SPAIN

NAPLES

Edinburgh

NORTH

SEA

York

ENGLAND

HOLLAN

Amsterdam

London

Antw

Brussels

Boulogne

Cherbourg

Amiens

USHANT

SEINE R.

Paris

Valmy

Lunévi

Versailles

Fontainebleau

Orleans

Nantes

LOIRE R.

FRANCE

Rochefort

Lyons

Bordeaux

GARONNE R.

RHONE R.

Avignon

CAPE
FINISTERRE

Coruña

GALICIA

San
Sebastian

Orthèz

Toulouse

Mar-
seilles

Oporto

DOURO R.

Burgos

EBRO R.

Saragossa

Almeida

Salamanca

Ciudad
Rodrigo

Madrid

Barcelona

PORTUGAL

Talavera

SPAIN

Lisbon

TAGUS R.

Elvas

Ocaña

MAJORCA

MINORCA

Albuera

GUADIANA R.

Valencia

IVIZA

BALEARIC IS.

GUADALQUIVIR R.

Seville

MURCIA

M

E

D

I

Cadiz

ANDALUSIA

CAPE
TRAFALGAR

GIBRALTAR (BR)

Ceuta (SP)

Algiers

ALGERIA
(OTT)

TRM

MOROCCO

NAPOLEON

Napoleon managed to win several victories with new armies he had hastily recruited, he was decisively defeated at Leipzig in the so-called "Battle of the Nations." At the news of his defeat his far-flung empire collapsed like a house of cards until little more than the France of Louis XVI remained. A brief campaign in the early spring of 1814 resulted in the capture of Paris by the allies and in Napoleon's abdication. When he retired to the island of Elba in the Mediterranean, it appeared as if the wars that had desolated Europe for a generation were at an end.

In the treaty that followed, known as the First Peace of Paris, France was treated very generously. The allies left the country larger in extent than it had been at the beginning of the war, the boundaries set being those of 1792. No indemnities were exacted and the French were required to return but a small part of the works of art Napoleon had collected after his military triumphs. However, the treaty settled only the boundaries of France; the territorial problems of the other European states were referred to a congress scheduled to meet at Vienna.

DEMOCRACY AND NATIONALISM

The most significant achievement of the French Revolution was the abolition of the remaining economic and social aspects of feudalism, but it also gave impetus to the development of democracy and nationalism, two of the major forces that shaped the history of the nineteenth century. The idea of a republic was not in the minds of the men who wrote the *cahiers* (lists of grievances and suggestions for reform) of 1789. Their demands were for the abolition of privilege and for a better administration. This is true also of the members of the National Constituent Assembly. No one dreamed at that time of dethroning the king. At most the members of the Assembly wished to change the absolute monarchy into a constitutional one. Republican sentiment was largely limited to a few intellectuals who had absorbed from the writings of Rousseau the doctrine of popular sovereignty. Continuance of the monarchical sentiment depended largely on the conduct of Louis XVI. Unfortunately he committed almost every error it was possible for him to commit. Even calm and moderate citizens were shocked by his conduct, with the general result that reverence for the theory of divine right was almost completely destroyed.

After the king was temporarily suspended by the Assembly (June, 1791) the revolutionary groups no longer exercised any restraint in exciting popular feeling against him. The more extreme newspapers openly stated their republican views, republican pamphlets were distributed in large numbers, and republican orators harangued the masses. In September, 1791, after he had formally accepted the constitution, Louis enjoyed a brief period of popularity, but the situation was rendered hopeless by his refusal to cooperate with the Legislative Assembly.

The attempt to establish democratic government failed because the French people lacked training in the management of their public affairs. Chaos and disorganization followed upon the proclamation of a republic. The new institutions of self-government were pushed aside in favor of centralized controls which were necessary successfully to wage foreign war, and a despotism exercised by a succession of small groups became the order of the day. But the failure to establish democracy at home did not prevent the French people from preaching the gospel of Liberty, Equality, and Fraternity to other peoples. In this way they scattered the seeds of liberty over Europe.

Although despotism reached its culmination under Napoleon, he did preserve the idea of equality, the democratic land system established by the National Assembly, and some semblance of republican forms. The establishment of a great military empire embracing half of Europe did not abate the zeal of the French for political liberty; nor did it obliterate the democratic ideas that had been proclaimed. Napoleon's soldiers were still apostles of these ideas, and even Napoleon's enemies borrowed them from the French. When the Spanish patriots set up a new constitution in 1812 they turned to the French Revolution for their model. Again, when the German patriots staged their national uprising against Napoleon in 1813, they demanded the political liberty "for which the French had made them yearn." Thus the French Revolution and the era of Napoleon opened the way for the struggle for democratic principles which characterized the nineteenth century.

The second major force to which the French Revolution gave impetus is nationalism; in fact, nationalism as an all-pervading group consciousness dates from the French Revolution. During this period Frenchmen realized for the first time their essential oneness. The growth of national feeling became evident during the early stages of the Revolution when the Estates-General adopted the name National Assembly. As Louis XVI discredited himself, loyalty to the nation replaced loyalty to the monarchy. The use of *patrie* as applied to the whole of France and of *nation* as embracing all the French people became ever more frequent. With the establishment of the republic the national idea developed a force theretofore unknown. The mighty shout of *Vive la nation* sounded from one end of France to the other. In the wars that followed, the French demonstrated what a people inspired by the national idea, the idea of oneness, can achieve. During these years the French soldiers fought not for pay, for loot, or for a king, but for *la patrie* in a sense that had not been revealed before. The national enthusiasm they evinced soon infected the peoples of other countries.

During the period from 1792 to 1815 the idea of nationalism and national patriotism was either carried into other countries by the French or developed as a reaction against the rule of Napoleon. While the national idea was carried directly into Italy and Poland, it appeared as a defense reaction in Germany and Spain. After Napoleon's fall the forces of nationalism, liberalism, and democracy became matters of great concern to the Congress of Vienna; but its efforts to stem the tide were unavailing.

CHAPTER TWO

The Congress of Vienna and After

WHO ATTENDED   IN the fall of 1814 diplomatists began to gather in Vienna for what was to be the most important international congress held up to that time. It was not, however, as is often stated, a "peace congress," for peace had already been made in Paris on May 30, 1814. The task which confronted the assembly was the establishment of "a real and durable settlement" after nearly a quarter century of wars. During the months before it met, Europe was vibrant with hope. Men believed that there would really be an arrangement which would end the recurrent wars and encourage the growth of representative institutions. The victorious powers encouraged this optimism by announcing their purpose as "the reconstruction of the social order" and "the regeneration of the political system of Europe." But the high hopes and expectations were not fulfilled. Such a shrewd observer as Friedrich von Gentz, secretary of the Congress, wrote almost at the very beginning, "I think I can assert with assurance that it will bring none of the advantages that Europe had the good nature to expect from this assemblage." Four months later he made bold to state its real purpose. "The high-sounding phrases," he wrote, "were at best produced to calm the people and to invest this solemn assembly with a dignified and sublime appearance. The true aim of the Congress consisted, however, in the division among the victors of the spoils." [1]

All that was most brilliant in Europe found its way to Vienna, the one important exception being the exiled former French emperor, who was neither invited nor expected. Not only did the leading statesmen come, but a number were accompanied by the rulers themselves, among

---

[1] Cited in Paul R. Sweet, *Friedrich von Gentz* (1941), p. 192.

whom were two emperors, Alexander I of Russia and Francis I of Austria, and four kings, those of Prussia, Bavaria, Denmark, and Württemberg. "There is literally a royal mob here," the Prince de Ligne wrote. "Everybody is crying out, 'Peace! justice! balance of power! indemnity!' As for me, I am a looker-on. All the indemnity I shall ask for is a new hat; I have worn mine out in taking it off to sovereigns whom I meet at the corner of every street." In addition to the sovereigns there were representatives from every European power except Turkey. It has been estimated that some two hundred and seven states or would-be states sent one or more delegates. Each of the great powers was represented by four or more ministers plenipotentiary. The principal representative of Austria was Klemens von Metternich, upon whom the Austrian emperor had bestowed the title of prince in 1813. Great Britain's mission was headed first by Lord Castlereagh and later by the Duke of Wellington. Among the chief representatives of the other states were Prince von Hardenberg for Prussia, Prince Czartoryski and Count Nesselrode for Russia, and Talleyrand for France. Pope Pius VII had sent as his representative Cardinal Consalvi, who kept in touch with everything and was tirelessly active in winning friends for the Roman Curia.

Besides those who had official business at Vienna, the Congress attracted hosts of visitors from every country of Europe. For the European aristocracy the Congress was a grand celebration to mark the end of a period of bad times. Others who thronged to the Austrian capital included pleasure-seekers, musicians, actresses, salesmen, courtesans, and social parasites of every kind. The city presented, as Gentz put it, "an overwhelming spectacle."

By all odds the most important figure was Metternich (1773–1859), who regarded himself as the apostle of conservatism. When the French Revolution broke out in 1789 there had been great enthusiasm at Strasbourg, where he was a student at the university, over what was believed to be the dawn of a new era; but the political and social upheaval left him cold. His thoughts and emotions were too firmly rooted in the old order to find the doctrines of liberty, equality, and fraternity attractive. In the Revolution he saw only anarchy, nothing more. Thus, as a youth standing on the threshold of his career he had already become a relentless foe of the ideas of 1789. It was his marriage to Princess Eleonore von Kaunitz, granddaughter of the great diplomatist of the eighteenth century, that opened the way for his career. Thereafter he was appointed, in succession, Austrian representative to Dresden and Berlin, and in 1806 ambassador to France. During his stay in Paris he made the most of his opportunity to study Napoleon at first hand, gaining a knowledge of him such as few others had. It did not take him long to decide that Napoleon's hold on France depended on continuous military glory and was therefore insecure.

Accordingly, Metternich addressed himself with infinite patience and imperturbable temper to the task of making ready for the hour when Europe would strike off the shackles of the conqueror. To his government he wrote, "We must confine our system entirely to maneuver, evasion, and compliance. In this way alone can we hope possibly to maintain our existence until the day of general deliverance." When he saw that Napoleon was lost, he eagerly rushed to the assistance of the allies. Later he liked nothing better than to pose as the conqueror of the "great conqueror." But even though the "Corsican Ogre" had been dethroned, the revolutionary principles which his armies had spread throughout Europe were still dynamic. To vanquish these became the task to which Metternich devoted the next thirty-four years of his life. "Fate has laid upon me," he said, "the duty of restraining, as far as my powers will allow, a generation whose destiny seems to be that of losing itself on the slope which will surely lead to its ruin." Chosen as acting president of the Congress, he fought the revolutionary principles with every weapon at his command. The year 1814 marks the beginning of the European ascendancy which he held until 1848, by which time he himself appears to have realized that he was fighting a losing battle. Besides a splendid physique, urbane manners, and a conversational facility which enabled him to impress everyone, he possessed diplomatic talents of a high order. Not all his contemporaries, however, shared the general opinion of him; one observer at the Congress wrote, "Too often Metternich's weakness and indecision are called astuteness."

Among the guests at Vienna, Alexander I of Russia (1777–1825) unquestionably took first place. His character was so complex that even among contemporaries there was little agreement regarding it. All were charmed by his tall and handsome presence, his conversational ease, and his perfect courtesy. But the man behind this exterior was an enigma which observers interpreted according to their prejudices. While Napoleon called him "a shifty Byzantine" and described him as "unimaginably false," Castlereagh said, "Either he is sincere or hypocrisy certainly assumed a more abominable garb than she ever yet was clothed in." This enigmatic quality was attributable largely to what has been styled "the double-working of his mental mechanism," which in turn was the result of the contradictory influences of his early life. His grandmother, Catherine II, who supervised his education, had chosen as his tutors Count Saltykov, who instructed him in the traditions of the Russian military autocracy, and the Swiss Jacobin La

Harpe, who inculcated in him an enthusiasm for the ideas of Rousseau and the principles of the French Revolution. In addition there was in Alexander a strain of religious mysticism which fostered a desire to establish permanent peace in Europe on a religious basis. It was the struggle of these influences for mastery over his mind that made him seem now the despot who, though believing sincerely in his divine right to rule, posed as the champion of the natural rights of man; now the militarist who, despite his passion for armies and military life, regarded it as his God-given mission to establish perpetual peace; and again the libertine who, with a private life that shocked even the free society of his time, spoke to his contemporaries in tones of religious exaltation.

A third important figure at the Congress, and one of the most conspicuous figures of the period since 1789, was Talleyrand (1754–1838). Before coming to Vienna as the representative of Louis XVIII he had been a priest, the bishop of Autun, a member of the National Assembly, an émigré who spent two and a half years in North America, and minister of foreign affairs under the Directory. When he saw Napoleon's star rising he had attached himself to the young Corsican and had served as foreign minister during both the Consulate and the empire. Although friction gradually developed between them, Napoleon found him too useful to be spared. In 1807 he resigned as minister on the plea of ill-health and thereafter worked almost openly for Napoleon's downfall. Napoleon, who knew this, is reported to have said to him on one occasion, "If you received your deserts, I would smash you like a bit of glass"; but he did nothing. Later Napoleon regretted that he had not ordered the execution of Talleyrand.

As a reward for advocating the restoration of the Bourbons Talleyrand was appointed representative of the French government at Vienna. At this time he was in his sixty-first year and at the height of his extraordinary career. For his task he was equipped with an easy bearing, ingratiating manners, a clear intelligence, quickness in repartee, and a great fund of ironical humor. Gouverneur Morris described him in his diary as possessing "a sarcastic and subtle wit, joined with immense tact." At all times his features wore an imperturbable calm. His impassivity, in fact, was such that Marshal Lannes is reported to have said, "If someone kicked Talleyrand's backside while he was talking to you, his face would not move a muscle." He was a master of duplicity and chicane. Lamartine said with considerable truth that he "served the strong, despised the maladroit, and abandoned the unfortunate," and Napoleon's parting words to him in 1814 were, "You would betray your own father." His defense was that he may have abandoned individuals but he had always served

France conscientiously. Scheduled to play only a minor role at Vienna, he soon managed by audacious and masterly intrigue to share with Metternich the chief influence in the deliberations.

THE CONGRESS DANCED

The formal opening of the Congress had been fixed for August 1, 1814, but was put off to October 1; in fact, the formal opening never took place. Strictly speaking, the Congress of Vienna never met. The credentials of the representatives were never verified, no authoritative list of accredited members was published, and there were no sessions to which all the ministers plenipotentiary were invited. What is actually meant when Metternich is referred to as the president of the Congress, and Gentz as its secretary, is that they were president and secretary of a small group of statesmen that drew up the settlement. When the ministers of Prussia, Russia, Great Britain, and Austria — the same group that had conducted the diplomacy of the coalition against Napoleon — arrived in Vienna about the middle of September, they at once assumed the function of making the final decisions on all questions. Thus these ministers constituted themselves the real Congress. When Metternich informed Talleyrand of the arrangement, the latter countered by reminding him that at the signing of the treaty of Paris the allied powers had numbered eight, including France, Spain, Portugal, and Sweden. Thereafter he continued to insist that these eight had equal rights in preparing the deliberations of the Congress. But no sooner was he admitted to the main council than he left Spain, Portugal, and Sweden to shift for themselves. Nevertheless the minor states were not entirely without a voice. Although the major decisions were made by the five powers, some of the work was delegated to committees in which both the major and the minor states had representation.

Very early the social affairs, which have sarcastically been called the main business of the Congress, had also started on an unprecedented scale. "Never before," La Garde wrote, "have such important and complicated interests been discussed amidst so much gaiety and dissipation." As host, Emperor Francis regarded it as his duty to see that the guests had the best possible time. He provided a continuous round of balls and banquets, fêtes and festivities. The daily expense of the entertainments has been reckoned by some at fifty thousand gulden (about $25,000), and by others at double that amount. In any case, it seriously strained the slender resources of the Austrian treasury. Hunting and sleighing parties, military parades and spectacles, fireworks, celebrations to commemorate such historic events as the battle of Leipzig, and scores of other diversions were staged to amuse the motley throng. There was also a great deal of gambling, though it was not pursued with as much frenzy as it would have been in an earlier period. In the theatres one could hear the operas of Mozart, the dramas of Schiller, and the comedies of Kotzebue. There were also many concerts, one of which was directed by Beethoven. Nor did the diversions stop here. Foreign diplomatists, native noblemen, and leaders of the financial world vied with one another in the splendor of their entertainments.

The most popular form of amusement was dancing. "People danced on every occasion and at every place. Every court dinner, concert, or reception ended with a dance." The favorite was the masked balls. Some of them were attended by as many as four thousand persons. What lent them particular glamour was the fact that the stranger behind the mask might be the ruler of a great country, for, says La Garde, "rulers, generals, and statesmen mingled in the crowd with persons of very inferior rank." In the light of this plethora of dances one can understand the classic remark of the Prince de Ligne, "The Congress dances but accomplishes nothing." Another contemporary wrote, "The emperors dance, the kings dance, Metternich dances, Castlereagh dances. Only the Prince de Talleyrand does not dance." Since he had a club foot, Talleyrand had to be content to play whist and to add copiously to the *chronique scandaleuse* of the time.

THE RETURN OF NAPOLEON

While the Congress was dancing, dissension broke out among the representatives of the five powers, who were trying to distribute the spoils. So long as actual warfare against Napoleon was going on, the necessity of defeating the common enemy had created at least a semblance of unity by pushing individual aims into the background. But no sooner was victory achieved than divergences of interest became apparent. By the time the Congress met, each of the powers was determined to override all opposition in order to achieve its particular object. Soon Castlereagh could write home, "I have watched every day the astonishing tenacity with which all the powers cling to the smallest point of separate interest."

The representatives managed to adjust most of the differences more or less satisfactorily, but one of them proved to be so serious that it threatened to break up the Congress. The moment Tsar Alexander had succeeded in driving Napoleon out of Russia he had conceived the ambition not only of liberating Europe from the Napoleonic tyranny but also of becoming the ruler of the whole of Poland. When the Congress assembled he put his hand on the map of Poland and declared emphatically, "C'est à moi!" He was determined to yield only to force. To the Princess Bagration, his favorite of the moment, he said, "Poland is ours! I hold it with 200,000 men. We shall see who will drive us out." [2] In his ambition he had Prussia as an ally. Before the Congress assembled, the rulers of the two states had entered into a compact whereby Prussia agreed to surrender its portion of Poland in return for compensation elsewhere. What Frederick William III demanded was the whole of Saxony. Like the Russians, the Prussians had already occupied the territory they claimed. Austria, however, was firmly opposed to any such aggrandizement of two states on her immediate borders; nor was she alone in her stand. She had the support of Great Britain and most of the lesser states of Germany; moreover, Talleyrand soon joined her. Feeling between the two factions gradually rose so high that Austria, Great Britain, and France agreed to resist the demands of Russia and Prussia by force if necessary. When the rulers of Russia and Prussia realized the seriousness of the situation, they moderated their demands and the whole question was settled by a compromise.

The dissension among the great powers had its repercussion in the return of Napoleon. The fallen conqueror had been watching intently the course of events at Vienna and in France. He knew that the rule of the gouty and unprepossessing Louis XVIII was unpopular, and when news of the dissensions at Vienna reached him he decided that the hour was propitious for an attempt to regain his throne. Sailing from Elba on February 25, 1815, with a guard of eleven hundred men, he landed at Cannes on March 1 and began his dramatic march to Paris. This news startled the gathering at Vienna and at once reestablished cordial unity. Great Britain, Austria, Prussia, and Russia immediately renewed the treaty of Chaumont, which had been concluded in March, 1814, whereby they bound themselves to continue fighting until their common object was attained. All agreed that whatever the future might produce or whatever policy they might be forced to pursue, they would have no dealings with Napoleon.

When the Italian diplomatist, Count Pozzo di Borgo, heard that Napoleon had left Elba, he prophesied that if the former emperor dared to set foot in France he would be hanged on the first tree. But he was wrong. The mistakes of the Bourbons had done much to allay any hostile feelings the people harbored against the "Little Corporal." As the march toward Paris progressed, peasants, soldiers, and Frenchmen of all kinds flocked to his standard in even greater numbers. The magnetism of his personality proved so irresistible that Marshal Ney, who

[2] *Les Dessous du Congrés de Vienne*, ed. H. M. Weil, I (1917), 206.

Legend:

	1810	1815	
KINGDOM OF PRUSSIA			RECOVERED OR ACQUIRED
KINGDOM OF SARDINIA			"
AUSTRIAN EMPIRE			"
RUSSIAN EMPIRE			"
UNITED KINGDOM			

BOUNDARY OF GERMAN CONFEDERATION

UNITED KINGDOM

NORTH SEA

ENGLAND

London

KINGDOM OF THE NETHER-LANDS

Amsterdam

NET

RHINE

BELGIUM (IND. 1830)

LU.

Lille

ENGLISH CHANNEL

Rouen

SEINE R.

Reims

Metz

Paris

Rennes

Orleans

Dijon

ATLANTIC OCEAN

Nantes

LOIRE R.

FRANCE

BAY OF BISCAY

Angoulême

Geneva

SAVOY

Lyons

Bordeaux

RHONE R.

Coruña

Toulouse

Burgos

EBRO R.

Saragossa

Mar-seilles

Oporto

Salamanca

Barcelona

PORTUGAL

SPAIN

Madrid

TAGUS R.

Lisbon

Valencia

BALEARIC IS. (SP).

Cordova

Seville

Granada

MEDIT

Tangier (SP)

GIBRALTAR (BR)

Ceuta (SP)

Algiers

ALGERIA

TRM

DENMARK

SCHLESWIG
HOLSTEIN
HELIGO-
LAND
(BR)
OLDEN-
BURG

MECKLEN-
BURG

KINGDOM OF
SWEDEN AND NORWAY

BALTIC SEA

Memel

LITHUANIA

Vilna

Minsk

Danzig

Grodno

RUSSIAN

Hamburg
Bremen
HANOVER

Berlin

PRUSSIA

POSEN

VISTULA R.

Warsaw

KINGDOM OF
POLAND

Kalisch

EMPIRE

WEST-
PHALIA

Cologne

HESSE

SAXON
STATES

SAXONY
Dresden

ODER R.

SILESIA

Lublin

ORRAINE

BADEN

WÜRT-
TEMBERG

Prague

BOHEMIA

MORAVIA

Cracow

GALICIA

DNIESTER R.

Munich

BAVARIA

AUSTRIA

Vienna

Pressburg

DANUBE R.

Budapest

HUNGARY

AUSTRIAN

EMPIRE

MOLDAVIA

SWITZ.

VALAIS

TYROL

CARNIOLA

DRAVA R.

CROATIA

SLAVONIA

SAVA R.

WALLACHIA

Bucharest

PIEDMONT
OF
Turin

LOMBARDY

VENETIA

Venice
ISTRIA

DALMATIA

Belgrade

DANUBE R.

PARMA

PO R.

Bologna

MODENA

BOSNIA

SERBIA

BULGARIA

Sarajevo

Sofia

KINGDOM OF
SARDINIA

GENOA

TUSCANY

PAPAL
STATES

ADRIATIC

HERZE-
GOVINA

MONTE-
NEGRO

OTTOMAN

ELBA I.

CORSICA
(FR)

Rome

SEA

Cattaro

EMPIRE

SARDINIA

Naples

KINGDOM
OF
NAPLES
(TWO SICILIES)

Salonica

Janina

AEGEAN
SEA

CORFU

IONIAN
ISLANDS
(BR. PROT.)

Athens

Palermo

SICILY

GREECE
(IND. 1830)

ERRANEAN

SEA

TUNIS

MALTA
(BR)

300 MILES

upon being commissioned to arrest him had vowed to bring him back to Paris in an iron cage, joined forces with him. On the evening of March 20 Bonaparte re-entered Paris without firing a shot and took up his abode in the Tuileries, from which Louis XVIII had fled only a few hours before. What the returned emperor needed, above all, was peace in order to reorganize his government and his army. Seeing, however, that all avenues to peace were closed, he hastily prepared to meet the advancing armies of the allies. The issue was soon decided. He succeeded in winning two indecisive victories; then came Waterloo on June 18, 1815, after which he was carried off to fret himself to death in helpless and hopeless inactivity on St. Helena, a tiny island of forty-seven square miles in the South Atlantic.

DECISIONS OF THE CONGRESS

By the time the Second Peace of Paris [3] was concluded, the Congress had finished its work and embodied its main decisions in a Final Act which was signed on June 9, 1815, nine days before the battle of Waterloo. Since nationalism had been an important factor in the overthrow of the Napoleonic tyranny, it might have been expected that the national idea would play a part in the settlement. But Metternich could hardly approve a principle which menaced the very existence of the conglomerate state he represented. Nor did the other statesmen, eager to acquire territory, respect it. Territories and populations were shifted from one ruler to another without any consideration for the wishes of the people. Nor did the settlement satisfy the desires of those who expected their sacrifices in the war against Napoleon to be rewarded by the establishment of representative institutions. In short, the settlement wholly disregarded the claims of nationalism and democracy. Even if the diplomatists had wanted to make a settlement on the basis of a theory or principle, they would have been prevented from doing so by the treaties that had been concluded during the struggle against Napoleon. For example, the allies had guaranteed to Austria, in return for its adherence to the coalition, the restoration of its empire to the proportions of 1805. By the same token Sweden had been promised Norway. Thus the territorial arrangements of the Congress were in large part dictated by the necessity of keeping pledges made before it met.

The primary duty of the assembled diplomatists, as they conceived it, was to set up a stable order after a period of confusion and devas-

---

[3] By the Second Peace of Paris (November 20, 1815) the boundaries of France were reduced to the limits of 1790, an indemnity of 700 million francs ($140 million) was imposed by the allies, and France was compelled to return the art treasures Napoleon had taken from foreign capitals. Finally, an allied army of occupation was to occupy the northern provinces for a period of five years.

tating wars. Believing that the old system of divine right government had made for order and stability, they sought to restore prerevolutionary conditions so far as possible. The first step was to enthrone again the old absolute dynasties. Next, they endeavored to make the world safe for kings by adopting measures to prevent revolutionary ideas from again exerting influence. The major problem was to keep the French from breaking out and running rampant over Europe again. The means devised to prevent this occurrence was a system of buffer states along the borders of France. One such state was created by joining the Austrian Netherlands (modern Belgium) to the Dutch Netherlands to form a kingdom under the rule of the house of Orange. On the eastern border Prussia was given extensive territories along the Rhine and was further strengthened by the addition of almost half of the kingdom of Saxony. This added enough to Prussia's stature to make her a formidable competitor of Austria in Germany as well as a buffer state against France.

In general, the diplomatists endeavored to safeguard the individual dynasties by the establishment of a balance of power. Not only did each of the great powers refuse to permit its rivals to grow unless it received territorial compensation itself, but the group as such made every effort to distribute the gains equally between the various powers. The Swedish king, for example, was made ruler of Norway by way of compensation for the loss of Finland, which was annexed by Russia. Russia was also given most of the Polish territory formerly held by Prussia and Austria. This, added to the Polish territory Russia already had, formed a new kingdom of Poland under the rule of the tsar. By way of compensation for the loss of its Polish territory and of the Austrian Netherlands, Austria received Lombardy and Venetia. This allotment of the rich regions of Lombardy and Venetia to Austria blasted the hopes for independence and unity that Napoleon had raised in Italy. In general, the Congress made short work of Napoleonic Italy. The papal territories were returned to the Pope, the Bourbons were restored to the throne of Naples (kingdom of the Two Sicilies), Nice and Genoa were joined with the kingdom of Piedmont, and petty despots were set up in Parma, Modena, and Tuscany. Italy became once more "a mere geographical expression," as it had been in the eighteenth century. Nowhere did the Congress ignore the claims of nationality more completely.

In Germany, too, the settlement showed that its authors were far more influenced by the desire to provide security against the dangers of the past than to anticipate the evolution of the future. Prince von Hardenberg and Baron von Humboldt, the Prussian representatives at the Congress, favored the establishment of a strong national government in Germany, and were supported by the representatives of some of the smaller German states. But the nationalist element in Germany was still not strong enough to prevail. Metternich could hardly be expected to promote a trend that was a threat to the very existence of his multi-national state. He regarded any such move as an "infamous thing." The French, too, did not want to see a national state in Germany. The very idea was a nightmare to Talleyrand. He wrote to Louis XVIII about the Prussian representatives, "German unity, that is their slogan, their doctrine, their religion, carried even to fanaticism."

Through the absorption of many minor principalities by their larger neighbors the map of Germany had become less complex, but there were still thirty-nine states. These were joined by the Congress in a loose confederation, called the Germanic Confederation (*Deutscher Bund*). Each state remained independent, almost the only restriction being that no state could enter into an alliance with a foreign power against any other state of the confederation. The only organ of the confederation was a Diet composed of representatives appointed by the rulers of the member states. Since the Austrian emperor was made the permanent president of this Diet, Austria became the recognized head of the confederation. In its constitution the object of the Germanic Confederation was stated as "the maintenance of the exterior and interior security of Germany, the independence and inviolability of the member states." Actually, however, it existed for very little else than to impose upon the minor states Metternich's reactionary policies.[4]

The British, who had largely financed the campaigns against Napoleon through subsidies and loans, made a number of additions to their extensive colonial empire. From the Dutch they received Cape Colony in South Africa, Ceylon in the Indian Ocean, and a part of Guiana in South America. Other additions included Helgoland from Denmark, and Malta and various small islands in the East and West Indies from France.

TWO ALLIANCES

Having achieved a settlement, the powers determined that it should be lasting. Like King Canute, they were resolved that the tide should not rise beyond the allotted mark. To insure this further object was the next problem. Alexander I, under the influence of a surge of religious mysticism, drafted a document which proposed that the rulers pledge themselves to act together in accordance with the precepts of the Christian religion. It was an attempt to establish an all-embracing international system on the principles of "Christian justice, charity, and peace." The mystical document, which constituted the Holy Alliance,

[4] Only the German states of the Austrian Empire were admitted into the confederation.

was issued in the name of the tsar of Russia, the king of Prussia, and the emperor of Austria. All European rulers were asked to join except the sultan, who could hardly be expected to pledge observance to the principles of the Christian religion. To the statesmen of Europe the scheme appeared visionary and impracticable, Castlereagh calling it "a piece of sublime mysticism and nonsense" and Metternich styling it "a loud-sounding nothing." Nevertheless, they humored the tsar and in due course all the invited rulers joined except the Pope and George III. But if the Holy Alliance affected the actions of any ruler as much as a hair's breadth, the fact has escaped the notice of historians. After the death of Alexander in 1825 it was conveniently forgotten.

If the Holy Alliance was the dream of a mystic, the Quadruple Alliance, signed in November, 1815, was a substantial diplomatic fact. By it Austria, Prussia, Russia, and Great Britain bound themselves to maintain the arrangements of Paris and Vienna for a period of twenty years. In a more specific sense they aimed to preserve the territorial boundaries they had set, to insure the perpetual exclusion of Bonaparte and his dynasty from the French throne, to combat the principles of the Revolution, and to prevent any future revolutionary uprisings. What is perhaps more important, the treaty introduced a new system for administering the affairs of Europe, that is, the Congress System. In a final article the four powers agreed that they would meet at fixed periods "for the purpose of consulting upon their common interests, and for the consideration of the measures which at each of these periods shall be considered the most salutary for the peace and prosperity of Nations, and for the maintenance of the Peace of Europe." During the succeeding period a series of congresses were held, at which the affairs of Europe were discussed and plans were laid for maintaining the *status quo*.

TROUBLE IN GERMANY AND SPAIN

The first of the congresses, attended by many of the statesmen who had been at Vienna, met at Aix-la-Chapelle, the ancient city of Charlemagne, on October 1, 1818. The question of whether the armies of occupation might safely be withdrawn from France was unanimously decided in the affirmative. France was also admitted, though rather reluctantly, to the deliberations. Consequently the Quadruple Alliance became, as it were, a Quintuple Alliance. The problem of the admission of France opened up the wider problem of the future of the Confederation of Europe, and a project was put forward for a union of the five powers for the express purpose of putting down any uprising against the *status quo*. But the proposal shattered on the rock of English opposition. Otherwise outward harmony prevailed among the powers. Metternich, jubilant because he was gaining greater control over Tsar Alexander I, was moved to write, "I have never seen a prettier little congress."

Despite Metternich's optimism, manifestations of discontent soon occurred which taught the powers that it was far easier to make a settlement than to maintain it. The first manifestations appeared in Germany. Many German patriots attributed her misfortunes under Napoleon's rule to the division of the country into small states. They hoped that the Congress of Vienna would prevent such misfortunes in the future by setting up a strong national state. The failure of the Congress to do this doomed their hopes, but did not extinguish their desires or silence their demands. Some of the bolder spirits, particularly of the middle classes, organized movements dedicated to the achievement of liberty and national unity. Among these movements were the *Burschenschaften* (student associations) whose aims were proclaimed in their slogan, "Honor, liberty, fatherland." The first *Burschenschaft* was formed at the University of Jena in 1815 and within two years similar organizations were started at fifteen other universities. In 1817 a call was sent out for a general meeting to cement the union of the *Burschenschaften* and on October 18 about five hundred members gathered at the Wartburg castle, famous as having been the temporary abode of Luther, to celebrate the third anniversary of Napoleon's defeat at Leipzig and the 300th anniversary of the Protestant Reformation. That evening a large bonfire was built and some of the students, in a moment of exaltation, burned books and pamphlets by authors who were opposed to the idea of German unity.

Metternich, upon receiving greatly exaggerated accounts of the Wartburg Festival, announced the existence in the universities of a widespread conspiracy against the *status quo*. His fears were confirmed when in March, 1819, the student Carl Sand, moved by particular fervor for liberty and unity, traveled to Mannheim and stabbed the playwright Kotzebue to death because he believed that the playwright's dispatches to Alexander I were forcing the tsar into the reactionary arms of Metternich. At the instigation of Metternich representatives of the German princes convened at Carlsbad to devise repressive measures, measures which were later adopted by the Diet of the Germanic Confederation. The Carlsbad Decrees established a rigid censorship of the press, sharply circumscribed the freedom of the universities, and decreed the suppression of all student societies. Not only were the *Burschenschaften* officially dissolved, but the display of their colors — red, black, and gold — was also forbidden even in such combinations as red waistcoats, black coats, and yellow or gold straw hats. At the same time a number of teachers were banned from the universities. Among these was Ernst Moritz Arndt whose songs and poems had helped to fire national enthusiasm during the War of Liberation. Government agents kept careful watch over all professors who were suspected of liberal or nationalist tendencies.

Metternich regarded the Carlsbad Decrees with great pride. "A grand example of vigor," he wrote, "has just been given in Germany, one which must resound in every corner of Europe." But if he thought he had stamped out liberalism and nationalism he was deceiving himself. The student associations, including the *Burschenschaften,* were soon revived in secret and many of them became much more revolutionary than before.

Early in 1820 the powers were confronted with a more serious problem, a revolt against the reactionary government in Spain. When the Bourbon Ferdinand VII, whom one historian has aptly described as "cowardly in adversity and in prosperity tyrannical," was reseated on the Spanish throne after Napoleon's downfall in 1814, he immediately stamped out everything that savored of representative institutions. The liberal constitution was abolished, all decrees issued during his exile were declared null and void, the Inquisition was reestablished, and the publication of all papers and periodicals, except the official *Gaceta,* was prohibited. Known liberals no less than radicals were hunted down and summarily imprisoned or executed. In short, Ferdinand imposed on Spain restrictions more severe than it had known in the eighteenth century.

But the king was unable to apprehend all those who cherished liberal opinions. Despite everything, secret societies fomented rebellion against his reactionary policy. After several attempts at insurrection had proved abortive, the standard of revolt was raised in January, 1820, by a portion of the army which Ferdinand was assembling at Cadiz for the purpose of forcing submission on the rebellious colonies in America. When the towns gave their support to the revolutionists, Ferdinand realized that resistance would be futile and in March, 1820, took the oath of allegiance to the new constitution.

The news that a revolt had flared up in Spain caused Metternich and his friends much anxiety, but they made no move to intervene. When in July, 1820, however, insurrectionists compelled King Ferdinand I of Naples to introduce the very liberal Spanish constitution of 1812, Metternich convoked a meeting of the powers for the purpose of deciding what course of action was to be taken. At the congress, which met at Troppau on October 20, 1820, Alexander I of Russia completely recanted his liberalism, saying to Metternich, "You are right! It is a malady of human nature which we must cure." Then the tsar, Metternich, and the Prussian representative drew up the famous statement which asserted that the three powers would never recognize the right of a people to revolt against its ruler. But the English representative remained aloof. Thus a serious breach was opened in the ranks of the great powers.

Two further congresses were held, one at Laibach (January, 1821) and the other at Verona (October, 1822). At the former the representatives of Austria, Russia, and Prussia decided to send an army into Naples for the purpose of reestablishing absolute monarchy. King Ferdinand I of Naples, who was present, assured the congress that the Neapolitan army would offer little resistance. "You may," he said, "dress it in blue or green or in red, but whichever you do it will run." Soon an Austrian army had moved into Naples and restored Ferdinand.

At the last conference the question of the Spanish revolt overshadowed all others. Tsar Alexander I proposed to lead an army into Spain for the purpose of abolishing the constitution. But while the representatives of France, Prussia, and Austria favored intervention in Spain, they were determined under no circumstances to permit a Russian army to march through Germany and France. Even more important was the opposition of Great Britain to the proposed intervention. British foreign minister Canning advised the congress that his government would rather withdraw from the "concert of Europe" than consent to a joint intervention in Spain. Austria, Russia, and Prussia did, however, individually give France, which was at the time controlled by the ultra-royalists, a free hand. In April, 1823, a French army marched into Spain, abolished the constitution, and restored the absolute rule of Ferdinand VII, who immediately proceeded to inaugurate that policy of reactionary terrorism which has made his name execrated in Spain to the present day.

At the very time that the European powers were stifling attempts to change the *status quo* in the Old World, the new-world colonies of both Spain and Portugal were in revolt. The question of adopting common measures to force the rebellious colonies into submission had been broached at the Congress of Verona but no decision was reached. As in the case of intervention in Spain the chief obstacle in the path of common action against the colonies was Great Britain. During the Napoleonic period a considerable trade between Great Britain and the revolting colonies had developed, and the British were not inclined to destroy this trade by a restoration of the old Spanish colonial system. Hence, when Ferdinand of Spain in December, 1823, summoned the European powers to a congress on Spanish America, Canning flatly refused to send an English representative. In the preceding year the United States of America had already recognized the independence of Colombia,

The Return of the Royal Family to Paris, June 25, 1791
(from the Bibliothèque Nationale, Paris)

The Return from Russia, after the painting by Géricault

A contemporary caricature of the great Wellington and the little Napoleon

A caricature of Louis Philippe entitled "The Pear"

Prince Metternich, from the painting by Lawrence

Talleyrand in his old age, from an old print

Chile, Argentina, and Mexico. Then at the beginning of December, 1823, President Monroe had delivered a message to Congress known as the Monroe Doctrine, which challenged the claims of the European powers to regulate the affairs of the world. He declared that the United States would consider any attempt on the part of the European powers "to extend their system to any portion of this hemisphere as dangerous to our peace and safety." When, in addition, the British government acknowledged the independence of Colombia, Mexico, and Argentina the following year, Metternich and his group were compelled to abandon whatever hope they may have cherished of establishing their system in the New World. Even Spain made no further attempts to force submission on its former colonies.

The refusal of England to send a representative to the congress on the Spanish-American colonies shook to its very foundations the hegemony of the great powers. Thenceforth the "concert of Europe" was frankly an alliance of Austria, Russia, and Prussia for the defense of autocracy.

NATIONAL UPRISINGS

While the "concert of Europe" lasted it had effectively curbed, or at least driven underground, the forces of nationalism and democracy. But the demand for popular liberties which the French Revolution had created and the sentiment of nationalism which had been stirred by the Revolutionary and Napoleonic Wars were too powerful to be repressed for any length of time. Despite the efforts of Metternich these forces once more asserted themselves, making his "wisdom" appear like foolishness. Fostered for a decade by underground movements, they now gave rise to open demands for a new order. On the one hand, national sentiment engendered revolts which resulted in the establishment of new nation-states, and, on the other, the demand for political liberty caused widespread agitation throughout Europe, achieving distinct successes in France and England.

It was in Greece that nationalism won its first triumph. The Greeks had been subject to Turkish rule since the capture of Constantinople in 1453. On the whole they had not been ill-treated, but it was galling to their pride to be a subject people. The spirit of the French Revolution stirred the sentiment of nationality in Greece to vigorous life. After the fall of Napoleon Greek representatives appealed to the Congress of Vienna for the right of self-determination, but the appeal was rejected. It became clear that if the Greeks would win their independence they must act on the principles enunciated by Lord Byron in the lines:

Hereditary bondsmen! Know ye not
Who would be free themselves must strike the blow?

In 1814 a group of Greek patriots had founded the *Hetairia Philike* (association of friends) for the avowed purpose of expelling the Turk from Europe. Most of the Greeks who were living in other countries joined the association and zealously worked to strengthen the cause. In 1820 the chiefs of the *Hetairia* raised the standard of revolt in northern Greece in the expectation that they would receive aid from Alexander I of Russia. As the protector of the Greek Orthodox religion the tsar was inclined to intervene, but the reactionary in him stifled the voice of his religion. Consequently the sultan, Mahmoud II, was able to smother the northern uprising.

Meanwhile, however, the Greeks of the southern peninsula had risen in full revolt. Greek guerrilla bands went about massacring every Turk they could seize. This method of warfare was so successful that by the end of 1821 the entire peninsula, excepting a few fortresses, was swept clean of Turks, and on January 1, 1822, the Greek National Assembly at Epidaurus proclaimed the independence of Greece. The sultan struck back by laying violent hands on every Greek within reach. In his blind fury he seized the Greek Patriarch of Constantinople as he was emerging from his service on Easter Sunday and hanged him in his priestly robes at the gate of the archepiscopal palace. This deed, followed by the execution of other officials of the Greek Orthodox Church and by the massacre on the island of Chios, where no less than 27,000 Greeks were put to the sword, sent a thrill of horror through Europe and aroused much sympathy for the Greeks (Philhellenism). When Lord Byron's sacrifices for Greek independence and finally his death at Missolonghi (1824) strengthened this philhellenic sentiment, the recognition of Greek independence became certain.

In 1825 Tsar Nicholas I, upon succeeding his brother to the throne, immediately took up the Greek cause. He was joined by England and France, which were determined not to permit the Russians to gain a predominant influence in the Turkish Empire. When the sultan refused to accept an armistice as a preliminary to a final settlement the allies put on a show of force. On October 20, 1827, the allied fleet sailed into the Bay of Navarino and in four hours transformed the Turko-Egyptian fleet which was anchored there into a mass of battered and burning wreckage. Even after the defeat of Navarino the sultan stubbornly continued the war another two years. It was necessary for both the French and the Russians to send armies to Greece, and not until the Russian army took Adrianople in 1829 and threatened to march on Constantinople did the Turkish government make peace overtures. The treaty which recognized the independence of Greece was signed at Adrianople on September 14, 1829.[5]

The Greek War of Independence was followed in 1830 by a national uprising in Belgium, which had been joined to the Dutch Netherlands under the scepter of King William I as a barrier against French ambition. From the first many Belgians, indignant at being treated merely as an "addition" to the Dutch kingdom, had offered strong opposition to Dutch rule. They particularly resented the fact that they were given the same representation in the Estates-General as the Dutch, although Belgium had three fifths of the total population of the new kingdom. Moreover, there was also religious friction, the Dutch being largely Protestant and the Belgians largely Roman Catholic. But it was, above all, the policy of the government, particularly of the king, that caused the failure of the union. Although hard-working and well-meaning, William I was tactless and self-willed. His determination to preserve the union led him to measures which completely alienated the Belgians. In 1819 a knowledge of Dutch was demanded from all candidates for public office, and in 1822 Dutch was made the official language for all public and official acts except in the Walloon districts. As a result the Dutch managed to acquire an almost complete monopoly of public offices by 1830.

The uprising began on the 25th of August, 1830, in Brussels. On the evening of that day Amber's *La Muette de Portici*, an opera based on the story of the 1647 revolt of Naples against Spain, was performed in a Brussels opera house. When the revolutionary scene in the play was reached the audience, carried away by a sudden burst of enthusiasm, took up the refrain of the song, which ends with the words:

> My country gave me life
> I will give my country liberty.

Singing the refrain, many members of the audience went forth into the street where they were joined by the crowd assembled there. The lower elements of the mob looted the shops of gunsmiths and pillaged the houses of Dutch ministers. Rioting and plundering continued throughout the night. The next day a group of the chief citizens of Brussels, determined to permit no mob rule, met at the Hôtel de Ville to enroll a strong citizen force to restore order. This achieved, they appointed a Council of Regency for a separate administration of the Belgian provinces, adopted the tricolor of Brabant (red, yellow, and black) as their official flag, and then sent a deputation to propose to King William that separate governments be set up for Belgium and Holland, the former to be

---

[5] At first Greece was a republic, but in 1832 it became a kingdom when Otto of Bavaria accepted an invitation to become king.

administered by the king's eldest son, the prince of Orange, as viceroy.

After treating the deputation with contempt, William dispatched an army to Brussels. But this force encountered determined resistance. From almost every house and from behind numerous barricades the revolutionaries fired on the Dutch troops until the latter were finally compelled to retreat in order to save themselves from annihilation. King William, panic-stricken at this failure, now announced that he was ready to grant the demands and at once sent the prince of Orange to Antwerp. The concessions came too late. On the very day on which the prince reached Antwerp a provisional government at Brussels declared Belgium independent, and all the Belgian provinces rose in support of this declaration.

Meanwhile Prussia had massed an army on the frontier ready to go to William's assistance, and Russia, though occupied elsewhere, announced its willingness to send a large force to quell the revolt. But Louis Philippe, who had become king of France as a result of the July Revolution, declared that no power had the right to interfere in the internal affairs of another. Finally, at the invitation of the king of the Netherlands, who was certain that they would not undo the work of the Congress of Vienna, the five great powers met November 4 in London to settle the question. The conference at once ordered cessation of hostilities and before the end of the year recognized the independence of the Belgian people. On the recommendation of the powers the Belgians elected a constitutional monarch under the title of Leopold I.[6] This settlement was not, however, to the liking of William I. He not only refused to recognize it, but also broke off the armistice and sent the prince of Orange with thirty-six thousand troops over the frontier into Belgium. It became necessary for the French to send a large army into Belgium and for an Anglo-French squadron to blockade the Dutch coast in order to compel King William to withdraw his troops. Not until 1839 did he finally acquiesce to the will of the powers.

While new kingdoms were being established in Greece and Belgium, a nationalist uprising in Poland resulted in the abolition of the kingdom that had been set up by the Congress of Vienna under Russian rule. Tsar Alexander I, who assumed the title of king of Poland, had in 1815 granted the Poles a constitution that was as liberal as any in Europe, and infinitely more liberal than the government of Russia itself. It assured them religious freedom, liberty of the press, and freedom from arbitrary arrest. Furthermore, the Poles were permitted to keep their flag, their coinage, and their army, with its distinctive organization and uniforms. But as Alexander's ardor for liberalism cooled he began to restrict more and more the rights and freedom he had granted the

[6] Leopold was a member of the German house of Saxe-Coburg.

Poles, causing them increasing discontent. Tsar Nicholas I, who succeeded his brother in 1825, at first tried conciliation, but after an attempt was made to assassinate him in 1829 adopted a policy of repression which caused the Poles to revolt in 1830.

The uprising, which began in Warsaw at the end of November, soon spread over the whole kingdom. When Nicholas refused to negotiate with the rebels, the Polish Diet declared the Romanov rule at an end and set up a provisional government. At first the Polish army, though far inferior in numbers, achieved several successes against the Russians. Unfortunately, however, dissensions within the Polish ranks soon weakened them, with the result that the revolt ended with the capture of Warsaw in September, 1831. Nicholas I decreed in a special ukase that "Poland shall henceforth be a part of the [Russian] empire and form one nation with Russia." Thenceforth the rule of Poland was entrusted entirely to Russian officials. Those leaders of the revolt whom he was able to apprehend were sent to a miserable exile in Siberia; others, who managed to escape, continued their agitation for Polish independence.

CHAPTER THREE

The Struggle for Democratic Principles

A T the same time that the principle of nationality was asserting itself in Greece, Belgium, and Poland, the ferment of the democratic
idea was working in other European states. Representative institutions had fared badly in the period since Napoleon's fall, but the demand for political liberty was so insistent that the powers, however
severe their methods of repression, were unable to silence it. The new
industrialism based on the use of power machinery, which had begun
in England in the eighteenth century and was being introduced into
the Continental countries, was raising two classes to a new importance,
the middle class and the factory workers. For several generations the
middle class had been gradually gaining control of the channels of
industry, trade, science, and public opinion, but it still had only a
small share in shaping political destinies. What it demanded was a
reconstruction of the governments which would extend the suffrage,
and consequently political power, to the members of this class. Although
active political thought was as yet largely limited to the middle class,
the desire for representative government was becoming widespread
among the masses too. The achievement of parliamentary institutions
in all the countries of Europe still lay in the future, but the year 1830
marks the beginning of an era. The parliamentary system established
in Belgium in that year embodied not only a wide franchise, but also
ministerial responsibility to parliament. The most terrifying shock,
however, to the supporters of conservatism was the appearance of a
new revolution in France.

THE REVOLUTION OF 1830 IN FRANCE

During the Revolution of 1789 the *bourgeoisie* had assumed the leadership in the attack on the old order and had succeeded in shattering it, but their advent to political power was postponed, first by the rise of Napoleon, then by the return of the Bourbons. After Waterloo, gouty and cynical Louis XVIII had returned in the wake of the allied armies to take up again the reins of government he had dropped so suddenly when Napoleon reappeared in 1814. The aged king was endowed with sufficient political judgment to realize that he must accept certain legacies of the revolutionary and Napoleonic period. Like Charles II of England he had no wish to go back into exile or, as a contemporary put it, "he had in him a very firm desire to die upon the throne." Hence he decided to reconcile revolution and counterrevolution. He did, it is true, speak of himself as king by the grace of God. He also restored the white flag of the Bourbons, which had for centuries been the symbol of royal absolutism. On the other hand, he retained the administrative, judicial, fiscal, and educational systems of the Napoleonic Empire, confirmed the confiscation of the property of the émigrés, and upheld the toleration of non-Catholics.

As proof of his spirit of moderation Louis had already in 1814 granted a "Charter of Liberties" as a means of winning the affections of his subjects. This charter guaranteed equality before the law, individual liberty, freedom of opinion, equal admissibility to all public offices, inviolability of property, and freedom of the press. But the charter did affirm that "all authority in France rests in the king." While making provisions for a parliament of two houses (Chamber of Peers and Chamber of Deputies) it did not take into consideration the great mass of the population which had become politically conscious and which during the revolutionary period had for a time played an important part in the affairs of state. The members of the upper house were nominated by the king and those of the Chamber of Deputies were elected on so narrow a franchise that only about 200,000 of a population numbering about thirty million could vote.[1] This legislature could not initiate legislation, but could only approve or disapprove of bills drawn up by the crown.

Even though the charter administered a setback to democratic ideas, it did establish a constitutional monarchy in theory and was acceptable to a majority of Frenchmen. But the members of the old nobility who had come back with the king opposed it from the start. Napoleon had urged these émigrés to return and be forgiven. The number, however,

---

[1] Suffrage was restricted to males over thirty paying not less than 300 francs a year in direct taxes.

who had made peace with the man who was to them the embodiment of the Revolution was small. Now with the return of Louis XVIII they hoped to come back into what they regarded as their own. These ultra-royalists, so called because they were more reactionary than the king, expected nothing less than the restoration of their privileges and their property. They saw no reason why the revolutionary era should not be forgotten, its accomplishments ignored, and the *ancien régime* restored in all its phases. Their ringleader was none other than the count of Artois, brother of the king and heir to the throne. In their efforts to wean the French people from the revolutionary ideas, the ultra-royalists organized widespread propagandist activities in which they employed books, pamphlets, and tracts as well as the spoken word.

Louis XVIII knew that if he gave the ultras a free hand it would cost him his throne; hence, he curbed their activities and their influence. "If these gentlemen are allowed to do as they like," he said, "they will finally apply their purge to me." After 1820 he did permit the adoption of an occasional reactionary measure, but the reaction did not go so far as to effect any important changes in the constitution. In 1824, however, his restraining hand was removed by death and he was succeeded by the count of Artois as Charles X.

If Charles had possessed the tact and prudence of his predecessor, the Bourbon monarchy might have continued on the French throne for a long time. Unfortunately he was dull-witted, obstinate, and tactless. He was so eager to restore autocratic rule that he did not stop to consider the opposition. "The French have desired a Charter," he said to one of his ministers; "they now have one and I do not think of taking it away, but this Charter cannot possibly prevent me from having my way." Unheedful of the warning his brother had uttered, "Do not forget that you must preserve the throne for your son and grandson," Charles began to propose reactionary legislation to the Chambers. Among the first bills was one which gave to the nobles an indemnity of a thousand million francs for the land they had lost during the Revolution. When further reactionary measures followed, even the moderate royalists became alarmed and opposition in the Chambers stiffened. The king reacted by ordering the election of a new Chamber of Deputies in the hope that it would be more reactionary, but a thoroughly aroused electorate returned a decisive majority of liberals. This still did not shake the king's determination. In his blind obstinacy he published the so-called July Ordinances (July 26, 1830), which established a strict censorship of the press, dissolved the newly-elected Chamber of Deputies, and restricted the franchise for the new elections. He was so certain of his position that he took no military precautions against a revolt.

A group of Paris journalists at once protested against the high-handed absolutism, declaring the ordinances illegal and calling upon the French people to resist. It is doubtful whether the journalists advocated more than legal resistance, but Paris mobs at once precipitated an uprising. "Long live liberty! Down with the Bourbons!" became the rallying cry as angry crowds tore up the cobblestones and built barricades in the narrow streets. General Marmont, to whom was entrusted the task of quelling the uprising, did not have enough troops to achieve his purpose; nor was he certain of their loyalty to the king's cause. The insurgents fought the soldiers with a fierce determination. They did not stop at pouring volleys of gunfire from every window but also dropped paving stones, and even furniture, on the soldiers from the roofs or upper stories. When several regiments deserted to the insurgents on July 29, Marmont withdrew the rest of his troops. In a desperate effort to save something from the wreckage Charles X offered to withdraw the hated ordinances, but when this availed him nothing he abdicated and set out for his last exile.

Most of the insurgents who had fought the king's soldiers wanted a republic, but such leading politicians as Talleyrand and Thiers felt that the time was not propitious. They feared that the establishment of a republic might rouse the reactionary states to military intervention. Consequently Louis Philippe, duke of Orleans, who posed as a prince of democratic beliefs and was therefore acceptable to the middle class, was put forward as a candidate for the throne of Charles X. On July 30, 1830, he was invested with the title of Lieutenant-General of the kingdom, but as soon as the legislature met he was enthroned as Louis Philippe I, king of the French. The principal feature of the change was that divine right was done away with as a feature of the kingship. Whereas Charles X had been "king of the French by the grace of God," Louis Philippe was "king of the French by the will of the people." There could be no more talk of a constitution granted by the grace of the crown.

All the fighting in the so-called July Revolution had been confined to Paris. Outside the French capital there had been no general discontent. The period being one of a rapid increase in wealth after the exhaustion of the Napoleonic Wars, the rest of France willingly acquiesced in the change of rulers.

PARLIAMENTARY REFORM IN BRITAIN

The repercussions of the French Revolution of 1830 were felt in many parts of Europe. During the subsequent months the people of a number of German states succeeded in wringing constitutions from their rulers, Greece became a parliamentary monarchy, and the system of popular elections of the Great Councils was extended in Switzerland. The revolution in France also intensified democratic feeling in Great Britain, giving rise to a general demand for parliamentary reform. Although the British government was theoretically a representative government at the beginning of the nineteenth century, it actually represented only a small section of the people. The House of Lords was for the most part made up of an hereditary aristocracy, and the House of Commons consisted of landed gentry, rich merchants, and wealthy financiers. It was impossible for a small freeholder, a lawyer of moderate income, or even a poor country gentleman to become a member of the House of Commons, for according to a law that had been passed early in the eighteenth century only such as possessed an estate worth at least £300 a year were eligible.

A more serious grievance was the obsolete machinery of parliamentary elections. Originally the House of Commons had been made up of two members from each county and two from each important town. But although the rise of the factory system had by the early nineteenth century caused a considerable shift in the population, the list of represented towns was practically the same as it had been in the fifteenth century. Many boroughs which in the fifteenth and sixteenth centuries had been flourishing market towns or seaports had since dwindled to a few dozen inhabitants, or in some cases had disappeared entirely; nevertheless, the landlord who owned the land on which the town had formerly stood still exercised the right to send representatives to Parliament. Such constituencies were known as "rotten boroughs." Other constituencies were known as "pocket boroughs" because their owners could "put their hands in their pockets and take out the appointment of members of Parliament to represent them." On the other hand, such great industrial cities as Manchester, Leeds, and Birmingham had no representatives whatever. A classic example of a rotten borough was Old Sarum, on the site of which one house remained in 1776, and none at all in 1792. Another borough still represented in Parliament was Dunwich, which had long since disappeared beneath the North Sea. The duke of Northumberland controlled no fewer than eleven seats, and several other landlords each had the appointment of half a dozen members. Thus more than three hundred out of 658 members of the House of Commons were chosen by a small group of influential nobles or by the ministers who were in office at the time of the election.

Even in most of the boroughs which had retained a considerable population the right to vote was restricted to a small number of persons. In some all male citizens residing within the limits of the borough could vote; in others all "pot-wallopers" (pot-boilers or those who had a hearth where they could cook their meals) had the right of franchise;

but in most the electorate was limited to a few. In some cases the mayor and the town corporation nominated the representatives in Parliament. According to one estimate [2] the 421 members of the House of Commons who sat for cities, towns, and universities represented only 84,000 electors. The natural result was corruption. In the boroughs with a small electorate a patron could almost always secure the election of his candidate by substantial money payments. Borough seats were even advertised for sale in the papers and were bought by rich merchants and industrialists. Thomas Holcroft, the dramatist, cynically recommended the purchase of a certain seat which had been put up for sale because, as he put it, there would be "no tormenting claims of insolent electors to evade; no tinkers' wives to kiss."

During the long wars the people had been buoyed up by the hope that the termination of the great struggle would bring an era of prosperity. But when peace was at last concluded, conditions became worse instead of better. Nations that had previously been dependent on British exports greatly curtailed their purchases either because they were beginning to manufacture goods they had previously bought or because they were too impoverished to buy. Even the sales at home were greatly reduced by the cessation of war orders. As a result economic distress became general among the poorer classes. Factories closed down and the numbers of the unemployed grew by leaps and bounds, the volume of unemployment being further increased by the disbandment of the army and the reduction of the navy. Wages fell so low that even those who had work could barely exist, for the price of grain was kept artificially high by a landlord Parliament. Becoming panic-stricken at the prospect of an inrush of cheap foreign grain, the landlord Parliament in 1815 passed a new Corn Law which excluded foreign grain unless — and this was unlikely — the price of home-grown grain rose to eighty shillings a quarter (eight bushels). A series of poor harvests during the subsequent years inflicted the most cruel sufferings on the masses and increased the number of paupers to an alarming degree. More and more the people began to feel that if they had representation in Parliament all could be changed.

Naturally the aristocrats who controlled Parliament were opposed to any reform whatsoever. The French Revolution with its attacks on privilege had filled the English upper classes with a horror of any change in the direction of democracy. As a result the members of the Tory party, which had practically monopolized political power since 1792, stood almost unanimously in opposition to the demand for parliamentary reform. Their creed, like that of Metternich, was, "Let nothing be changed," or as the duke of York expressed it, "Any change, at

[2] Veitch, *The Genesis of Parliamentary Reform* (1913), p. 2.

any time, for any purpose, is much to be deprecated." Thus the government had no remedy to propose for the grievances of the people except stern repression.

Nor did the general suffering evoke any sympathy from the sovereign; in fact, he had lost all contact with his people. George III being blind, deaf, and insane, his eldest son of the same name had been regent since 1811. The regent, a disreputable and dissolute fop whose behavior scandalized his people, was in no way competent to deal with the problems of the day. Shelley wrote in his "England in 1819":

> An old, mad, blind, despised and dying king,
>   Princes, the dregs of their dull race, who flow
> Through public scorn, mud from a muddy spring,
>   Rulers who neither see nor feel nor know.

The regent had all the vices of Louis XV and, in addition, the vacillating incompetence of Louis XVI. His misdoings often sorely tried the ministers who had to act in his name. No monarch of modern times dragged the British crown into greater disrepute. He was so little respected that moderate newspapers openly jeered him. Even so gentle a critic as Charles Lamb joined the chorus of denunciation in a poem entitled "The Triumph of the Whale," which reads in part:

> Not a fatter fish than he
> Flounders round the polar sea.
> See his blubber — at his gills
> What a world of drink he swills.
>
> By his bulk and by his size,
> By his oily qualities,
> _   This (or else my eyesight fails),
> This should be the Prince of Whales.

When George III died in 1820, the regent succeeded him as George IV. The fact that he was king wrought little change in his conduct. His continued profligacy and his attempt to divorce the eccentric Queen Caroline gradually robbed him of such power and prestige as he still possessed.

Meanwhile, the working classes were clamoring more and more loudly for reform. Some even resorted to rioting. During the years after the fall of Napoleon there were a number of demonstrations, none of them serious. The government regarded these incidents not as the manifestations of poverty and hardships but as indications that the country was on the verge of revolution. The remedy of the ministers was repression, and one of the measures to which they took recourse was the suspension of the Habeas Corpus Act in March, 1817, so that the authorities could imprison suspects without charge or trial. Such measures did not, however, allay the discontent or demonstrations. On August 16, 1819, a crowd of about fifty thousand people, which had gathered in St. Peter's Field, Manchester, to listen to a radical orator, was dispersed by a cavalry charge with the loss of one life and injuries to about forty persons. This incident, known as the Massacre of Peterloo, inspired Shelley to write his "Mask of Anarchy," in which he urged the people to

> Rise like lions after slumber
> In unvanquishable number
> Shake your chains to earth, like dew,
> Which in sleep have fall'n on you;
> Ye are many, they are few.

Still the government continued its repressive measures. In 1819 Parliament passed the notorious Six Acts which, among other things, prohibited all public meetings except those summoned by authority of the government, barred the drilling of civilians, and permitted the government to suppress all newspapers it regarded as undesirable. In short, Parliament sought to muzzle all except the governing classes.

The turn of events which brought about the triumph of reform came in 1830. Previously the middle and lower classes had failed to combine, but the Revolution of 1830 in France stimulated the two to draw together in a national crusade against the political privileges of the aristocracy. Furthermore, in 1830 George IV died, unregretted by his people, and was succeeded by his brother William IV, a kindly old man of limited intelligence but of more liberal views. The general election which followed the accession of the new sovereign gave the Whigs a majority in Parliament for the first time in many years. By this time the demand for reform had become so insistent and the passions of the people so heated that it was regarded unsafe to permit the new king to drive through the streets of London. Even a number of statesmen began to realize that the persistent refusal to grant reforms was more likely to hasten than to avert a revolution similar to that which had taken place in France. When in 1830 the duke of Wellington, who had insisted that "no better system could be devised by the wit of man" than the existing system of parliamentary representation, was displaced as prime minister by Earl Grey, a consistent advocate of reform since 1792, the latter at once took steps toward making the desired change a reality. A committee was appointed to draft a reform bill and in March, 1831, it was introduced into the House of Commons. For many months a bitter contest waged about it. It was not made law until June 7, 1832, and then only after it had been rejected by one House of Commons, passed by a new one, rejected by the Lords, and finally passed by them when the king threatened to create enough new peers to insure its passage.

Despite the enthusiasm it aroused among the people the Reform Bill of 1832 was a very moderate measure. It did, it is true, greatly increase the number of voters; however, those whom it enfranchised were largely of the middle classes. In the towns political power was vested in the merchants, manufacturers, and prosperous shopkeepers; in the country in the landowners and big farmers. It did nothing for the agricultural laborers, nor did it benefit the industrial workers. In giving the franchise to every tenant of a premise worth £10 a year it excluded most workmen, for but few paid as much as that in rent. But the bill did terminate the control of the House of Commons by a few great families. It also abolished the rotten boroughs. The very small constituencies lost both their representatives; others had their representation reduced to one member. The seats set free were redistributed among the more populous counties and among the larger towns that had hitherto been unrepresented. Finally, the bill made the franchise uniform. Whereas before 1832 every English borough had its own rules regarding the franchise, the qualifications were now the same in all. Thus the Reform Bill of 1832, though it did not inaugurate democratic government, was an important step forward.

THE SPIRIT OF 1848

On the Continent the political history of the period from 1830 to 1848 is largely a record of steadily growing discontent and increasing political agitation. The revolutionary movements of 1830 had shaken the political order erected in 1815, but it was far from overthrown. Censorship of newspapers and books, surveillance of the universities, prohibition of meetings, and repression of all liberal movements continued in many Continental states as before. Meanwhile the discontent was growing. The demands were either for written constitutions or, where such constitutions already existed, for an extension of the franchise. The factory system by concentrating workingmen in great centers made it easier for the apostles of these ideas to carry on propaganda among the working class. Secret clubs, newspapers, pamphlets, and books, together with the spread of popular education, enabled the disseminators of democracy to reach a larger section of the masses than ever before. Consequently the democratic movement gathered strength with each passing year.

In German politics the Austrian government still exercised a controlling influence. Old age was beginning to tell on Metternich's powers of statecraft, but he was no less determined to preserve his autocratic system. At the end of 1847 he denounced to the Diet of the Germanic Confederation "the misguided attempts of factions to supersede the monarchical principle by the modern idea of the sovereignty of the people." Despite everything he could do, the elements of opposition were becoming more determined in Hungary, Bohemia, and the Italian provinces under Austrian rule as well as in the purely German states. In the German states many writers and poets were turning their talents to stirring up revolution. Prominent among them was Georg Herweg (1817–1875), often called "the standard bearer of the Revolution of 1848." In his poems, which were received with great enthusiasm, he preached hatred of despotism and called upon the people to rise against "the paralysing encumbrance of autocracy." The first stanza of his poem, "Dare to Be Free," reads:

> My people, hearken, 'tis the drum;
>   Let wrath sweep all thy fear away;
> Dare to be free, whate'er may come,
>   If only for a single day.

Metternich himself saw the discontent growing; he even felt revolution to be imminent. "The world is very sick," he wrote to a friend in January, 1848; "the one thing certain is that there will be tremendous changes." Yet he did not think of yielding in the slightest degree.

In 1848 the flood waters which had been slowly rising for decades burst their restraining dikes, inundating Europe with a revolutionary movement such as it had not seen since the French Revolution of 1789. Revolutions exploded in every direction. In one respect they were all alike: they were all motivated by the desire for political liberty. In every case the revolutionists either demanded the establishment of a constitution which would afford the people a share in the government or, if a constitution existed, they aimed at widening the element of popular control. In some countries the democratic movement was closely associated with the national movement. Both were, in fact, often the result of the same impulses. Every national group that was under "foreign" rule sought self-government as well as constitutional government. In Italy the two were so closely interwoven that it is impossible to separate them. The same was true in Germany.

THE REVOLUTION OF 1848 IN FRANCE

Early in January of 1848 anti-Austrian riots broke out in Lombardy, and about the middle of the month an insurrection in Naples compelled

Ferdinand II to grant a constitution. But the real signal for the widespread uprisings in Central Europe was the so-called February Revolution in France.

Louis Philippe, upon becoming king of the French in 1830, had replaced the white flag of the Bourbons with the tricolor of the Revolution and had carefully avoided the pomp and ceremony of his predecessors. In accepting the throne from the "representatives of the people" he recognized the right of the people to impose a constitution on him. The revised charter abolished the king's power to issue ordinances and to suspend laws, broadened the suffrage, and decreed the responsibility of the ministers to the Chambers. It appeared to please Louis Philippe to be known as "the citizen king" and he could often be seen walking the streets of Paris with a green umbrella under his arm. On these walks he would stop to shake hands with workmen and converse with them. At other times he would appear on the balcony of his palace to sing the *Marseillaise* with the crowd, beating time with his hands and feet.

But in reality his government was not as democratic as it appeared. It was not "broadbased on the will of the people." At most it was a government by and for the well-to-do middle classes. Although the suffrage had been widened by lowering the property qualification, only a small part of the population enjoyed the privilege of voting. The proportion of the enfranchised has been estimated as less than one in a hundred and fifty. In brief, the government was "an aristocratic creation with a democratic appearance." Louis Philippe's democratic bearing was simply play-acting; at heart he was an absolutist. He was determined to be the head of the state in fact as well as in name, and he succeeded by various subterfuges in evading to a large degree the constitutional restrictions he had accepted in theory. Thus, while publicly accepting the principle that every minister must have the support of the Chambers, he conspired to make certain that they would support only those ministers who accepted the larger outlines of his policy. M. Guizot, who was Louis Philippe's prime minister during the last years of his reign, flouted the will of the people, but managed to hold the support of a parliamentary majority through the judicious allocation of public offices and the granting of lucrative favors to influential electors.

From the first the working classes had regarded themselves as deceived by the settlement of 1830. Although they had borne the brunt of the fighting against the soldiers of Charles X, the bourgeoisie had reaped all the advantages. Now the working classes demanded further reforms and were joined in their demands by many middle-class intellectuals. In general, the opposition to the government was composed of two groups, the republicans and socialists. Both demanded universal suffrage. But while to the former this was merely the means for establishing a republic, the latter regarded it as the first step toward a wider social reorganization (see Chapter 5). This was particularly true after the publication of Louis Blanc's *Organization of Labor* in 1839. Whereas the works of such early socialist writers as Saint-Simon and Fourier had exercised but little influence on the masses, this small book made a deep impression on them. The chief practical idea advanced by the book was the establishment of *ateliers nationaux* (national workshops) which would be administered by the members and in time lead to the elimination of private capitalism.

Having few legitimate means of expressing their demands, both the republicans and the socialists formed secret societies in which republican desires and revolutionary opinions were fomented and spread. As early as 1833 one such society, *Société des Droits de l'Homme* (Society of the Rights of Man) had sixty thousand members. Although the government prosecuted these societies, it was unable to stamp them out, for as soon as one was destroyed another was formed. Newspapers were also founded to win support for reform. By means of the secret societies and the press the opposition kept antagonism to the monarchy alive and active in most of the larger cities of France. There were occasional riots. Some of the more frantic members of the opposition went so far as to form conspiracies against the life of the king. No fewer than ten attempts to assassinate him were made. Louis Philippe himself was courageous enough to joke about them, saying that he was the only game which enjoyed no closed season in the year.

After Guizot was made prime minister, the demands for reform became more insistent year after year, but the king and he set their faces against any change. Guizot vehemently denounced the "blind and hostile" passions of the reformers and Louis Philippe said emphatically in 1847, "There will be no reform; I do not wish it. If the deputies vote it, the peers will veto it, and even if the peers should favor it my veto still remains." By this time even the bourgeoisie began to realize that the king and the prime minister were getting beyond their control, and many of them joined the opposition in the demand for reform.[3] In 1847 all the parties of the opposition, including the liberal monarchists, the republicans, and the socialists, united in a great campaign for an extension of the franchise and the abolition of the shameless corruption. Banquets

[3] Another reason for the rising opposition of the middle class was the pusillanimous foreign policy of the government. This policy may roughly be summed up as "peace at any price." After the part France had played in international affairs during the Napoleonic Empire, Frenchmen regarded this policy as humiliating. "Even among those who are in the most intimate personal relation to the king," Heinrich Heine, who was in France at the time, wrote, "his disposition to yield to foreign powers is greatly blamed."

were organized in various of the larger cities to give opposition speakers an opportunity to present the cause of reform. Between July and December of 1847, about seventy of these banquets were held, the guests numbering about 170,000. Finally, deputies of the opposition laid plans for a great banquet and street procession to be held in Paris on February 22, 1848. Guizot, upon being apprised of the plans, forbade them. The deputies yielded and the government appeared to have triumphed. The news that the deputies would not hold the banquet overwhelmed the king with joy. To Salvandy, one of his ministers, he said jubilantly, "Yesterday you told me we were walking over a volcano! They have given up the banquet, my friend; yes, they have given it up! Didn't I tell you it would all end in smoke!"

The king's jubilation was short-lived. The opposition deputies had, indeed, given up their plans, but the announcement had come too late. On February 22 great crowds poured into the streets singing the *Marseillaise* and crying, "Down with Guizot! Long live Reform!" Toward evening some of the gunshops were looted and a few barricades were raised. The National Guard, called out to restore order, openly proclaimed its sympathy with the insurgents by refusing to march against them. On the 23rd the situation assumed a more serious character as the National Guard joined in the fighting against the regular troops. This defection of the National Guard had such an unnerving effect on the king that he dismissed Guizot. The mobs quieted somewhat and it seemed as if the danger were past. But that evening a crowd gathered in front of Guizot's house. When somebody fired a pistol either purposely or accidentally, the troops guarding the house replied with a volley. Fifty-two persons fell dead or wounded and the mob immediately put the corpses on wagons which were hauled about the city with cries of vengeance. The next morning *Reformé,* a radical sheet, urged, "Louis Philippe lets the people be shot down as Charles X did. Let us send him after his predecessor." That day a large crowd appeared before the Tuileries. Seeing that it was too late to check the storm of popular passion, Louis Philippe abdicated in favor of his grandson and departed in disguise for England.

The revolutionists now proclaimed France a republic and chose a provisional government composed of republicans and socialists which ordered the election of a National Assembly to draft a new constitution. Meanwhile, the artisans of Paris were out of work and their families had no food. To calm the fears and passion of the people the provisional government decreed on February 25 the *droit au travail* (right to work) which Louis Blanc had demanded in his writings. "The Government of the French Republic," the proclamation read, "engages to guarantee the subsistence of a workman by his labor. It engages to guarantee work to all citizens." For this purpose "national workshops" were to be established.[4] On the 28th the Minister of Public Works informed the unemployed of Paris, who then numbered no more than seven or eight thousand, that they would be given work at certain designated places. Not only was the work at hand insufficient for the unemployed of Paris, but as word of the project was noised about workmen from the provinces flocked to Paris in large numbers, so that by March 2 the applicants for work numbered fifteen thousand. Since the government could not find work for all, it simply paid each applicant one and a half francs a day (later only one franc). This handing out of gratuities caused many workingmen to leave their jobs in order to join the ranks of the "unemployed." One franc a day as a gratuity, it appears, proved more attractive to them than regular employment with a larger income. By the middle of April there were no fewer than 60,000 enrolled in the "national workshops" and by the end of May, 115,000. It was clear that a prolongation of the experiment would not only put a severe drain on the national finances but also cause a serious dislocation of industry.

When the National Assembly, elected by universal suffrage, met at Paris in May, 1848, the delegates proved to be much more conservative than the provisional government. By this time property owners all over France were so apprehensive of socialism that a middle-class army was organized to restore order. Next, the Assembly turned to the problem of the more than a hundred thousand dole-supported idlers. On June 21 it issued a proclamation which summarily dismissed all unmarried men under twenty-five and all others who refused to work at their trade under private employers. The others were to be drafted as quickly as possible for work in the provinces. The workmen at once protested. When their protests went unheeded a terrible insurrection broke out on the 23rd. "Bread or lead" was the cry with which they went into battle. Only after four days of the bloodiest street fighting Paris has known did General Cavaignac, who was appointed military dictator, succeed in putting down the uprising. Estimates of the total number of killed and wounded on both sides run as high as ten thousand. So great was the Assembly's anxiety for the future that Cavaignac's powers were extended for four months. Meanwhile, the National Assembly drafted the new constitution, which vested the executive power in a president and provided for a single legislative body, both to be elected by male suffrage. The man the French people elected president in December, 1848, by an overwhelming majority was Louis Napoleon, nephew of

[4] Lamartine, who was probably the most outstanding figure during the first days of the provisional government, says that the *ateliers nationaux* were not the work of Louis Blanc, who was a member of the provisional government, but were "inspired by the spirit of his adversaries." See Lamartine, *Histoire de la Révolution de 1848*, II (1849), 120.

the first Napoleon.[5] Thus France emerged from the storms of 1848 with a republican constitution based on universal suffrage.

THE REVOLUTIONS IN AUSTRIA, ITALY, AND PRUSSIA

The February Revolution in Paris served as a wind which fanned the embers of discontent into a flame of revolution throughout Central Europe. In Germany the news of Louis Philippe's overthrow at once caused the people of many states to demand freedom of speech and of the press, the right of suffrage, and a constitutional form of government. Baden, one of the most liberal of the German states, was the first to yield to the demands of the people, granting them freedom of the press, an elected parliament, and other reforms. This initial success of the "democrats" in Baden led the governments of Hanover, Württemberg, and other states hastily to grant the demands of the people.

It was in Vienna, the very citadel of reaction, that the reactionary forces were for a time completely routed. Soon after the arrival of the news from Paris a placard appeared on one of the city gates with the words, "In a month Prince Metternich will be overthrown! Long live constitutional Austria!" Early in March the university students raised the cry, "Rather a constitutional hell than an absolutist heaven!" — although Austria was in no sense a heaven. On March 13 they were joined by the artisans of the city, and the streets of Vienna were soon in an uproar. In trying to protect the government buildings from being looted by the mob, soldiers fired a volley which cost several lives. Barricades were erected and hand-to-hand fighting took place. Meanwhile deputation after deputation urged concessions upon the government. Toward evening the crowds gathered about the emperor's palace shouting, "Down with Metternich!" Much to his amazement Metternich found himself opposed not only by the street mobs, but also by many aristocrats and by a powerful faction at court. Realizing that the jig was up, Metternich resigned. After personally announcing his resignation to a deputation, he made his escape from Austria, taking refuge in England. "The last beam of the old system has given way," reported the *London Times,* "or, to speak more respectfully of so experienced a statesman, Prince Metternich has been compelled to retire from a contest which he can no longer wage with the world, or even with the public opinion of the pacific inhabitants of Lower Austria." The revolutionary party soon gained the upper hand, so that the emperor was obliged to promise reforms. He announced the abolition of the censorship, the appointment of liberal ministers, and the summoning of a diet. Vienna believed his promises and proceeded to make holiday.

[5] For a more detailed discussion of the election see p. 131.

The uprising in Vienna was only one of many revolts in the Austrian Empire. In Bohemia the revolution had broken out even earlier than in Vienna. On March 11 a great meeting of "young Czechs" in Prague decided to send to the emperor a petition embodying demands for a responsible ministry and for the recognition of the equality of the Czech and German languages. Harassed on all sides, the emperor accepted the demands. Actually he was only waiting for an opportunity to disavow the reforms he had been compelled to accept. In Hungary, where there had long been a movement for a separate administration, the news of Metternich's fall had an effect that was electric. A mass meeting held in Budapest, the Hungarian capital, demanded a constitution and a parliament along English lines. The emperor acceded to these wishes and the Magyars were satisfied. But, having gained constitutional and national rights for themselves, the Magyars refused them to the Croatians, Serbs, and Rumanians under their rule. In consequence war broke out between the Hungarians and the subject peoples. It was more than Emperor Ferdinand I, whose health was none too robust, could stand. Feeling that the arduous duties of government should be in younger and stronger hands, he abdicated on December 1, 1848, in favor of his nephew, Francis Joseph, a young man of eighteen who was to rule until 1916.

In Italy also, where the friction between the populace and the Austrian authorities had been increasing, the fall of Metternich was the spark which set off an explosion. On March 18 barricades were raised in Milan. Most of the male population, some armed only with stones, sticks, bottles, and tiles, joined in attacking the Austrian garrison of thirteen thousand men and finally forced it to evacuate the city. In Venice Daniele Manin, a lawyer, led the people in proclaiming a republic and in forcing the withdrawal of the Austrian army and fleet from before the city. All over Lombardy and Venetia municipalities followed the example of Milan and Venice. In the duchies of Parma and Modena the ruling dukes fled, while in Tuscany the grand duke joined in the war against Austria to save his throne. Early in April Charles Albert, the king of Piedmont, lent Lombardy and Venetia his assistance, and by the early summer of 1848 nearly all of northern Italy was freed from the Austrian yoke. The empire of the Habsburgs seemed everywhere to be on the point of dissolution.

In Prussia the revolt was no less successful. Frederick William IV, who had become king in 1840, showed little regard for the claims of the people. At his coronation he had declared emphatically that he ruled by the grace of God and "would never do homage to the idea of a general popular representation." During the succeeding years various local outbreaks occurred and the temper of the people became so threatening that in February, 1847, the king sought to satisfy his subjects by summoning a United Prussian Parliament which was to advise him in the framing of new laws. But the king, who expected the assembly to be docile, was to have a rude awakening. No sooner did the representatives meet than they demanded a written constitution with a parliamentary system on English lines. The irate monarch answered by dissolving the assembly (June, 1847). This only postponed the crisis. On the arrival of the tidings of Louis Philippe's fall disturbances broke out in Berlin. Meetings were held at which excited Berliners demanded freedom of speech and of the press, full equality in civil and political rights, and the establishment of trial by jury, all of which were to be embodied in a written constitution. At the news of Metternich's fall riots broke out and there were sharp contests between the people and the soldiers. To avoid further disturbances the king promised reforms. For a time it seemed as if the reactionary forces had been routed everywhere in Germany.

THE FRANKFORT ASSEMBLY

Toward the end of March about five hundred leaders who were determined to establish both democracy and unity in Germany met at Frankfort on the Main, constituted themselves a provisional parliament, and called for the election of a National Assembly to draw up a constitution for a united Germany. This move was made without consulting the rulers of the German states, but was sanctioned by the Diet of the Germanic Confederation before it dissolved itself. The Assembly, chosen by universal suffrage at the ratio of one deputy for each 50,000 voters, convened in the Church of St. Paul in Frankfort on May 18. It was composed almost entirely of members of the middle class, the only representative of the working classes being a Silesian peasant. Its purpose, as stated by its president, was "to frame a constitution for the whole of Germany." "We derive our authority for this task," he said, "from the sovereignty of the people. . . . Germany desires to be one, a single state, ruled by the will of the people."

For the first time in modern German history elected representatives had the opportunity to decide the political future of the German people. Since the Habsburg and Hohenzollern rulers were beset with internal troubles, there was no threat of force to coerce the Assembly. Nor was there any competition from other national bodies, for the Diet of the Germanic Confederation had ceded its powers to the Frankfort Assembly. Prompt and decisive action was, however, necessary if the Assembly was to achieve its goal. Unfortunately much precious time was wasted in reaching a compromise between the various ideas represented.

One of the major problems was whether a Habsburg or a Hohenzollern was to be the head of the new state and whether the non-German nationalities of the Austrian Empire should be included. While the Assembly was listening to interminable harangues and speeches, the reactionary rulers of some of the German states were strengthening their position in preparation for the time when they would reassert themselves.

At last in January, 1849, the new constitution, representing a compromise between the idea of national unity and the particularist interests, was ready. It provided for a federation of democratic states, with the final authority resting in an all-German assembly chosen by universal manhood suffrage. The executive power was to be vested in an emperor who was to govern by means of a responsible ministry.

But the Assembly still had not settled the question whether a Habsburg or Hohenzollern was to become emperor of the new state. Finally the Habsburgs excluded themselves by asserting that the territories under their rule were indivisible, and the Assembly decided that the Hohenzollern king of Prussia was to be hereditary emperor. On April 3, 1849, a delegation offered the crown to Frederick William IV. In his reply the Prussian king said that he could not accept a crown "without the free assent of the crowned heads, the princes, and the free towns." His real feelings are expressed in a letter (December 13, 1848) to his ambassador in London who had urged him to accept the imperial crown if it should be offered to him. Frederick William IV wrote in part:

The crown which a Hohenzollern could accept, if circumstances rendered such a thing possible at all, is not one created by an Assembly born of revolutionary seed, even if offered with princely approval. No, it must be a crown set with the seal of the Almighty, one which makes him who assumes it, after the sacred annointment, 'Sovereign by Grace of God.' . . . But the crown you unfortunately mean dishonors one inexpressibly, stinking as it does of the Revolution of 1848.

The refusal of Frederick William IV doomed the first practical attempt by the German people to found a united German state. During the succeeding weeks public support of the Assembly began to crumble away rapidly. Twenty-eight German states did accept the constitution, but the four kings (Bavaria, Württemberg, Hanover, and Saxony) were determined not to abdicate any of their sovereign rights. This, together with the withdrawal of the Austrian deputies from the Assembly, alarmed Frederick William to such an extent that he absolutely declined the imperial crown on April 28. Thereafter the Frankfort Assembly gradually dissolved, some of its members being recalled and others withdrawing voluntarily.

THE REACTION

By this time the revolutionary movement had spent its force in the various states of Central Europe. Frederick William IV, who had previously formed a reactionary ministry and closed most of the liberal clubs in Prussia, now felt himself strong enough (April 27, 1849) to dissolve the Prussian Parliament because it had disagreed with him. Later he said that the revolution was "only a comedy he had been made to play." After the Prussian troops had quelled the insurrections in Prussia they were sent to overpower the republican forces in other states. Many who had participated in the struggle for democratic principles fled for their lives to neighboring countries. In Switzerland alone there were no fewer than eleven thousand German refugees, many of whom eventually migrated to America. Parliaments were dispersed and those leaders of the struggle for political freedom who did not escape were imprisoned. It was a sad blow to the development of constitutional liberty.

Meanwhile the old order was also restored in the Austrian Empire. In Prague a new uprising had taken place (June, 1848) because the Habsburg emperor had failed to carry out his promises to inaugurate reforms. This time the emperor did not try to mollify the Czechs with further promises; he sent a military force to crush the uprising. This victory stiffened the back of the government against the popular movement in all the Austrian territories. When the populace of Vienna staged another insurrection (October, 1848) against a government that was becoming more and more reactionary, Austrian troops bombarded the city into submission. Early in 1849 the Hungarian constitution was abolished and Hungary was reabsorbed into the Austrian Empire. Hungarian patriots under the leadership of Louis Kossuth fought desperately for the independence of their country and even forced the Austrian troops to retire from Budapest with heavy losses. But in answer to an appeal from the Habsburg government the autocratic Tsar Nicholas I sent a Russian force to help crush the republic. Kossuth and some of his followers managed to leave the country, but many other patriots suffered death, and all the leaders had their property confiscated. Thus Hungary relapsed to her former state as a province in the Austrian Empire.

During the spring and summer of 1849 the Italian provinces also had to submit. Charles Albert of Piedmont was defeated so decisively at Novara (March 23, 1849) that there could be no more thought of continuing the struggle. On the same day the weary king abdicated his throne in favor of his son, Victor Emmanuel, in the hope that the latter would obtain a more favorable peace from the Austrians. Lombardy had previously been reoccupied by Austrian troops and Venice capitulated in August after a heroic defense. Finally Tuscany was reoccupied and reactionary governments were reestablished in Parma and Modena. Thus Italy found herself once more parcelled out and dependent upon foreign powers.

Although the reaction of 1849 shattered many hopes, it did not completely rout the forces of progress. In Piedmont Victor Emmanuel maintained the liberal constitution his father had granted in 1848, and in Prussia Frederick William IV promulgated a constitution in 1850. Even the Habsburg government could not return to the old hidebound system in its entirety. Unequal taxation, the provisional administration of the nobility, and the seignioral rights of the nobility were not restored. In many states the memory of the uprisings of 1848 gradually influenced the princes to grant further concessions. Before two decades passed the Habsburgs themselves gave way to reform, and by 1880 practically every state of the Continent except Russia was governed under a written constitution.

CHAPTER FOUR

The Coming of the Machine

AT the beginning of the eighteenth century the textile industry was, by and large, the one considerable industry in England; and that was still in the domestic stage. Textiles were for the most part woven in the cottages of workers, whose main employment was agriculture. The weaver usually owned a few acres of land, a cow, and two or three pigs. In the summer he devoted most of his attention to the land, but in the winter or bad weather he would sit at his loom and weave. The yarn was usually spun by the women after they had finished their household duties and during the long winter evenings. They employed only the old spinning wheel that had been used for centuries. The process was so simple that even the children of the household could assist in it. Capitalist merchants distributed the raw materials, collected the finished products, and paid the weaver for his work. Most weavers owned their looms, with only a minority renting them from capitalists. The hours of work of both the weaver and the members of his family were long and the income small. In most cases, however, spinning and weaving only supplemented the income from the land. Such families were largely self-sufficient; they raised and cured their own meat, grew their own vegetables, cut their own fuel, and made their own clothes. The number of those who were completely separated from the land and dependent solely on wages for a living was comparatively small.

All this was to be changed during the course of the eighteenth century and the early decades of the nineteenth. From a predominantly agricultural country with the greater part of the industry carried on in the houses of the workers, England was transformed into an industrial nation in which the factory supplanted the home as the producing unit.

68

More than this, from a sparsely populated land with a rural civilization at the beginning of the eighteenth century, England gradually changed to a land of teeming industrial cities with an urbanized civilization. The change was effected by machinery. Machines were not, of course, first invented in the eighteenth century; in some form or other they had been in use since the Middle Ages. As early as the fourteenth century, for example, machines driven by both horse and water power were used in Italy to manufacture silk. But whereas machinery had earlier been a subordinate factor in industry, it became the central factor during the period beginning with the eighteenth century.

The process of mechanizing industry and commerce, often called the Industrial Revolution,[1] was not sudden or catastrophic. The changes came slowly, in some cases almost imperceptibly. Each invention was not an isolated miracle, but a new link in the long chain of industrial evolution. Nor can the changes be confined to a short period. They did not, as many historians formerly believed, begin with the accession of George III in 1760 and end with the accession of Queen Victoria in 1837. From a shadowy start in the earlier centuries they gathered momentum in the eighteenth century and continued with accelerated speed through the nineteenth and twentieth centuries. The fact that almost seven hundred patents were taken out in England between 1617 and 1760 shows the increasing interest in machinery.

Machines were invented to satisfy the growing demands of new markets. If merchants were to make the most of the opportunities offered by these markets, it was essential to increase output and reduce prices. So pressing was the need for certain machines that premiums were offered to inventors. Although many of the resulting feverish investigations produced nothing, others were highly successful. In all this development Great Britain took the lead. There were several reasons for this. First, British expansion had opened foreign markets which were ready to absorb more and cheaper goods. There was in India, for example, an almost unlimited market for cotton goods and, in fact, for cheap goods of all kinds. Second, Britain possessed the enormous advantage of having an ample supply of coal and iron, the two materials most necessary for the building of machinery. Finally, the British rose to the situation by producing a series of important inventions.

The application of machinery to manufacture was most rapid and most complete in the case of cotton goods. The first important advance was made by Kay's flying shuttle, patented in 1733, which could be

---

[1] The use of the term "Industrial Revolution" is in a sense misleading because the word "revolution" is generally applied to political changes of a sudden and explosive nature. The forces which brought about the mechanization of industry and commerce are still at work today, and we are still going through adjustments that were started in the eighteenth century and even earlier.

jerked to and fro through the warp with one hand, thus permitting the weaver to work faster and to weave wider cloth. A weaver using the flying shuttle could keep seven or eight hand spinners busy. When it was widely introduced into the cotton industry about 1760, the flying shuttle caused a scarcity of thread and turned the attention of many persons to the problem of improving the method of spinning. One result was that in 1764 James Hargreaves invented the spinning jenny (from "gin," meaning engine), a spinning frame on which at first eight and later more than a hundred spindles could be worked at once by one person, even a child. Five years later Richard Arkwright patented the water frame, which by means of rollers produced finer and stronger yarn than could be made with the spinning jenny. A decade later Samuel Crompton combined the principles of the jenny and the water frame in his "mule," which made possible the spinning of still finer and stronger thread. By this time the spinners were producing more thread than the weavers could use, but the balance was again restored when in 1789 Edmund Cartwright, a clergyman, patented a power loom that could weave. Crude at first, it was gradually improved until by 1815 it was a really practical machine.

Meanwhile other inventions were accelerating the output of the cotton industry. One was a cylindrical press which could print more calico in one day than a hundred men had previously been able to print with their wooden blocks. Another was a new method of bleaching by means of chlorine gas. By this method cotton textiles which had formerly required treatment in the open for six months could be bleached in a few days. Even the preparation of the raw cotton was speeded up through the invention of the cotton gin in 1793 by Eli Whitney, an American. As a result of the introduction of these new machines, the imports of raw cotton rose from four million pounds in 1764 to more than three hundred million in 1833, and the number of power looms increased from two thousand in 1813 to about fifty thousand in 1830. The woolen industry, older and less enterprising than the cotton industry, resisted the introduction of power machinery longer, but even there the change proceeded rapidly after it once started. The same was true of the linen industry. By 1830 power machinery was rapidly displacing hand labor in both industries.

If the iron industry had not in the meantime developed to meet the demands upon it, the introduction of machinery on so extensive a scale would have been impossible. At the beginning of the eighteenth century the iron industry was in a state of decadence because of a scarcity of fuel. The use of charcoal in its manufacture had exhausted the English forests to such an extent that the government had to limit the iron industry in order to assure itself a supply of timber for ships. The obvious remedy was to discover a process which would permit the use of coal for smelting. Although many experiments were undertaken, it remained for Abraham Darby to work out a method of smelting iron with coal and lime (1709). After further work he succeeded in converting coal into coke, which replaced charcoal. Other difficulties in production were removed about 1760 when John Smeaton invented a blast furnace, and in 1783 when Henry Cort patented a method of producing iron bars by rolling instead of hammering. Soon the quality was further improved by a method called "puddling," which burned out many of the impurities. Iron became so plentiful and so low in cost that it was applied to new uses. How greatly the production increased can be seen from the fact that from sixty-eight thousand tons in 1788 it grew to nearly one and a half million tons in 1839. In addition, considerable quantities of iron ore were imported. A significant advance was made in 1856 when Sir Henry Bessemer of Sheffield discovered a way of quickly turning pig iron into steel by removing the carbon and silica. By the Bessemer process steel could be manufactured at such a low price that it could be used in place of iron.

During the last quarter of the eighteenth century further progress in the use of machinery was made possible by the application of a new source of power. Steam was harnessed by a line of inventors and soon replaced wind power and water power almost completely. Although philosophers and scientists had studied the expansive power of steam since ancient times, no practical use was made of it until the seventeenth century, when a steam pump was constructed for the purpose of drawing water out of mines. This steam pump, called a "fire engine," was greatly improved by Thomas Newcomen early in the eighteenth century; but it was still only a pump. The application of steam to the driving of machinery was the contribution of James Watt, a maker of scientific instruments in Glasgow. Called upon in 1763 to repair a Newcomen engine, he first became interested in improving it as a pump by constructing a separate condenser, and then continued his experiments until he was able to produce a double-acting engine with a continuous rotative action (1782). Manufacturers were not slow to see the advantages of the new engine, for it offered them a continuous supply of power, while water power was largely dependent on the amount of water in the rivers and millponds.[2] Furthermore, the manufacturers were now able to set up their machinery wherever there was a supply of coal, and by 1800 industries were fast gravitating toward the coal fields.

All these improvements vastly increased production, but without

---

[2] Watt himself did not stop at inventing the steam engine. In partnership with the capitalist Matthew Boulton he organized a firm for the manufacture of the engine at Birmingham.

commensurate improvements in modes of transportation it would have been impossible to collect raw materials or to distribute finished goods. Since most of the rivers of England and Scotland were not navigable, the common mode of transportation at the opening of the eighteenth century was carts and carriages or horseback. There were some good roads, particularly those of the turnpike trusts, but most of the highways were in such a poor state that heavy goods could be carried on them only in dry or freezing weather. Even late in the century Arthur Young reported that most English roads were "execrable." Therefore, the first step in providing better transportation was to build better roads. Though much was done in this respect during the second half of the century, it was not until near its close that two Scottish engineers, Telford and Macadam, made some real contributions to the science of road building. Soon "macadamized" roads (roads with a foundation of larger stones covered with smaller stones and finished with crushed stones) were being built throughout Great Britain. In the meantime other promoters were feverishly building canals. The first real canal was built in 1761 for the duke of Bridgewater and ran from his coal mines at Worsley to the city of Manchester, a distance of seven miles. This canal, by halving the price of coal at Manchester, led to the adoption of bolder plans for canals. From 1790 to 1794 Parliament passed no fewer than eighty-nine canal acts. By 1815 much of Great Britain was covered with a network of connecting waterways.

In the next decade, however, canal transport was threatened by the steam locomotive. After Watt adapted the steam engine to turning machinery, various attempts were made to use this engine for purposes of locomotion. As early as 1784 William Murdock, an associate of the Watt-Boulton firm, constructed a model locomotive which ran eight miles an hour. After him others took up the work of development. In 1813, for example, William Hedley patented his *Puffing Billy,* which could draw eight wagons of coal at a speed of almost five miles an hour. But it is to George Stephenson more than to any other man that the modern railroad is due. First of all, he improved the *Puffing Billy* so that it had a top speed of fifteen miles an hour. Then he persuaded the directors to use it on the Stockton-Darlington railroad in 1825. Five years later when the directors of the new Manchester to Liverpool railroad offered a prize of £500 for the best locomotive, Stephenson entered his famous *Rocket* and won the competition with ease. His little engine attained the then astounding speed of almost thirty miles an hour. The Manchester to Liverpool line may be regarded as the first of the modern railroads. Its success encouraged others to form similar companies, with the result that thousands of men were soon engaged in laying rails in many parts of England. The first rails, made of wood, were soon replaced by cast-iron rails, and these in turn by wrought-iron rails. So widespread was the activity after 1830 that by 1848 the main railroad system of modern England was not only planned but in large part constructed. Originally intended only for the transportation of freight, railroads soon began to carry passengers also. The first carriages were nothing more than the bodies of stagecoaches placed on trucks. Third-class carriages had neither covering nor seating accommodations. However, when the railroad companies realized that the carrying of passengers was profitable, they built more comfortable carriages on springs, with glass windows and with lights for night travel.

While Stephenson was busy improving the locomotive, others were occupied with the problem of how to propel boats by steam. As early as 1802 a steamboat, equipped with a Watt engine which turned a paddle wheel, was used for towing on the Forth and Clyde Canal in Scotland; but it was abandoned after a short time because the canal owners feared it might damage the banks of the canal. Five years latei Robert Fulton made steam navigation a commercial success on the Hudson in America with a steamboat for which Watt and Boulton designed the engine. The first regular steamboat service in Great Britain was inaugurated in 1812 on the Clyde between Glasgow and Greenock by a boat called the *Comet* with an engine of only three horsepower. This was soon followed by larger boats which Coleridge described as

> Those trim skiffs unknown of yore,
> On winding Lakes and Rivers wide,
> That ask no aid of Sail or Oar,
> That fear no spite of wind or tide.

In 1819 the first steamship, the *Savannah*, crossed the Atlantic from the United States to England in twenty-nine days with the help of sails. However, progress in adapting steam to ocean transport was not as rapid as the development of the steam locomotive. It was not until 1838 that two steamers, the *Sirius* and the *Great Western*, crossed the Atlantic without sails, in eighteen and fifteen days respectively. In fact, until about 1870 sailing vessels competed quite successfully with steamships, for they were almost as fast as the latter, equally comfortable, and could carry goods more cheaply. After 1870 steamships demonstrated their superiority. Although the early ones were made of wood, experiments with iron steamers began in the decade of the thirties, and in 1843 the first iron steamship crossed the Atlantic.

THE FACTORY AND ITS SOCIAL EFFECTS

The invention of machinery and the application of power led inevitably to the rise of the factory system. There had been factories in which many workers congregated in the Continental countries as well as in England ever since the Middle Ages. They had, however, been the exception. What power machinery ushered in was the factory *system;* in other words, a general network of factories. First of all, such machines as Crompton's mule and Cartwright's power loom were too large to use in a cottage, even if water or steam power were available. Moreover, the use of power made it more economical to concentrate many machines under one roof. Above all, the new machines were too expensive for the average worker to afford. This situation gave rise to a new class of capitalist manufacturers. Country gentlemen, wealthy farmers, rich shopkeepers, and others who had capital or could borrow it now bought machinery and built factories. Whereas previously the capitalists had provided domestic workers with raw materials and sold the finished product, now, with the invention of power machinery, they gained control of the *means* of production as well.

The factory system spelled the doom of domestic industry, although hand workers were not entirely displaced. In 1825 there were still a quarter of a million hand weavers, but most of them were already reduced to a pitiable state. Their battle was hopeless, for the average weaver with his hand loom could not compete with power machinery. It became increasingly necessary for the workers to leave their villages and flock to the factories. There, all they had to sell was their labor, and this they had to do at terms prescribed by the employers, most of whom were interested only in profits for themselves. Since the government was under the spell of laissez-faire ideas and did not supervise the factories, the conditions under which most workers labored were abominable. The new factories were often poorly constructed, badly ventilated, poorly lighted, full of dust and dirt, and lacking in sanitary arrangements. At that, conditions were not much worse than they had been in many of the cottages of the domestic workers.

More galling to the workers were the long hours and the strict discipline of the factory. Where the machines were kept running day and night the usual working period was twelve hours for each shift. If there was only one shift, a thirteen- to sixteen-hour day was not unusual, and this for six days in the week and fifty-two weeks in the year. Such hours, it is true, were not uncommon in domestic industry. But under the old system the artisan worked in his own home at his own time. When work was slack, he could take days off for amusement. In the new factories, however, his time was rigidly regulated. He was summoned to the shop by a bell at a fixed time and, once there, was subject to a strict discipline which imposed fines for tardiness, talking and whistling, opening windows, and many other "misdemeanors." This discipline gave a

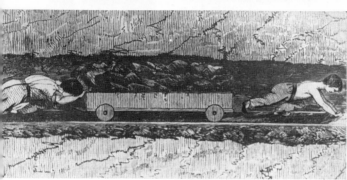

Stevenson's first railroad,
built for the mining district
of Hetton

Child labor in an English coal mine

The improved power loom, c. 1813

"DeWitt Clinton," an early American locomotive

Mendelssohn and his sister Fanny

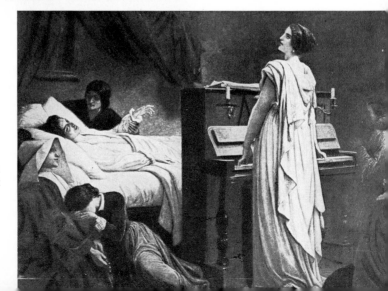

George Sand, by Delacroix
(Louvre Museum)

Liberty on the Barricade, by Eugè
Delacroix. This painting was inspir
by the French Revolution of 18
(Louvre Museum).

Death of Chopin, from
the painting by Felix
Joseph Barrias

sense of drudgery to factory work. Furthermore, the life of the worker lost whatever range and diversity it may have had. Previously he had been able to turn from craftsmanship to agriculture, or vice versa. Now his work was limited to only one process. Life became a monotonous routine.

The new towns which grew up about the manufacturing centers were largely slums from the day they were built. In the words of a contemporary, "These towns have been created with the utmost disregard of everything except the immediate advantages of the speculative builder." To fill the demand for living quarters, flimsy structures were quickly built, often back to back to make the most of the allotted ground, and without proper ventilation and drainage. Refuse was simply thrown outside, where it soon accumulated in heaps that were excellent breeding places for flies and other vermin. In most of the new towns the streets were not paved, nor were there any sewers to carry away the rain water. Of 850 houses which composed one district of Manchester in 1832, a total of 128 were reported as being out of repair, 177 as being damp, 112 as being in need of proper drainage, and 326 as wanting privies. A scarcity of even such houses often caused several families to crowd into accommodations designed for one. One-tenth of the population of Manchester lived in cellars, and in one district of Dorset each house had an average of thirty-six occupants. Such overcrowding and lack of sanitation bred disease and epidemics. Tuberculosis was common, and smallpox, typhoid fever, and even cholera were by no means rare. As one historian put it, "The faster the towns grew, the faster grew the death rate." One prolific source of disease was contaminated water. A commission appointed to study the state of towns in 1844 reported that of the fifty large towns it had examined "there was scarcely one in which the drainage was good and only six in which the water supply was good; in forty-two the drainage and in thirty-one the water supply was decidedly bad."

Thus, for most workers, "home" was a barren place. A contemporary physician wrote in 1833,

The houses of great numbers of the laboring community in the manufacturing districts present many of the traces of savage life — filthy, unfurnished, deprived of all the accessories to decency or comfort. What little furniture is found in them is of the rudest and most common sort, and very often in fragments — one or two rush-bottomed chairs, a deal table, a few stools, broken earthenware, such as dishes, teacups, etc., one or more tin kettles and cans, a few knives and forks, a piece of broken iron serving as a poker, a bedstead or not, as the case may happen to be, blankets and sheets in the strict meaning of the words unknown — their place often being made up of sacking, a heap of flocks [wool and cotton refuse] or a bundle of straw supplying the want of a proper bedstead and feather bed.[3]

In Manchester two thousand families were without beds. It is not surprising that the standard of morality among people who lived such bare lives and who lacked even the most elementary education was low. After long hours of work, both men and women turned to gin mills and other public houses for diversion. A report on the conditions among textile workers in 1840 states, "The people are as ignorant as ever and, in proportion to their numbers, more immoral. There is more profanity, more Sabbath-breaking, and more immorality than formerly. Their language is awfully depraved. Bastardy is greater than ever, even since the Poor Law Amendment Act. At any holiday time the public houses will be thronged with girls ready for the lowest excesses."[4]

Another outstanding evil of the early factory system was child labor. Being the least able to protect himself, the child suffered most from the absence of industrial regulations. Child labor had, of course, been widespread before the invention of power machinery, but its evils were aggravated by the factory system. There has, it is true, been a tendency on the part of many writers to exaggerate the evils of the conditions under which children worked; yet the actual facts are appalling enough. The first factories, dependent on water power, were built along streams in districts having only a scattered population, hence a scarcity of labor. Since the work of attending some of the machines was so simple and since child labor was so cheap, millowners saw in child labor a solution of the labor scarcity problem. Many of the children were paupers from the workhouses or poorhouses, the authorities of which often paid the millowners as much as £5 a head to take the children off their hands. How the children were treated depended entirely on the will of their masters, for their status at best was little higher than that of slaves. As a rule they received no pay, and their labor was limited only by physical exhaustion.

These "apprentice children," as they were called, were so frequently mistreated that Parliament passed a law in 1802 to curb the abuses. By this time, however, the employers had found a new source of child labor. The change from water power to steam power after the invention of Watt's rotary engine made it possible to build factories in towns where the labor supply was more plentiful. Here the wages of adults were so low that parents were often forced to send their children to work to add a few pence to the family income. Children, because of the small wages they received, could often find employment much more

---

[3] P. Gaskell, *The Manufacturing Population of England* (1833), p. 133.
[4] *Parliamentary Papers*, XXIV (1840), 76.

easily than their parents. Sometimes parents were even given employment only on condition that they send their children to the same mill.

Thus began the child labor known as "free labor." Long hours and an early age of employment were universal. The children, many of whom started to work at the age of five or six, began work at six in the morning and did not leave the mills until seven or eight at night. Most of those employed in textile factories were "piecers," that is, they attended the spinning machines and when a thread broke they joined the ends together. This work, which required constant alertness through the long hours, together with the noise of the machinery and the dirt and dust of the mills, put a severe strain on the health of the young workers. But conditions in other industries, particularly in the coal mines, were worse. In many mines boys, harnessed to trucks by a girdle round the waist, drew coal along low galleries, while girls were used to open and close the trap doors that ventilated the mines. Often the children were kept at their work by overseers who used a strap to spur them on to greater effort. How exhausting and even crippling this work was can be seen from the following description:

Many women and girls were compelled to spend Sunday, their one day of leisure, in bed, to recuperate and prepare for the labours of the following week. While this fatigue was sometimes traceable to occasional rushes of extra severity, in some districts it was so common among all workers as to suggest a continuous and general excess of labour, as a result of which health was impaired, disease promoted, and old age and death anticipated. An extraordinary muscular development, the outcome of their labour, which amounted almost to deformity in numerous instances, rendered "young people" capable of "prodigious muscular exertion"; but after a few years it was found that their strength diminished, leaving them as adults "pallid, stunted in growth, short of breath, sometimes thin, and often crooked and crippled." [5]

In such systems of child labor there was, of course, no room for education; in fact, the ruling class questioned whether education would make a child better fitted for the employment "to which his rank in society had destined him." The result was widespread ignorance and illiteracy: according to the report of a factory inspector in 1842, hardly one male out of fifty in South Wales could read.

EARLY FACTORY LEGISLATION

It was not an easy task for reformers to rid juvenile labor of its worst abuses. Public opinion of the eighteenth century saw nothing wrong with children working; in fact, there was a widespread belief

[5] Pinchbeck, *Women Workers and the Industrial Revolution*, pp. 259 f.

that it kept them out of mischief. Writing in 1833, P. Gaskell, a physician, stated, "The employment of children in manufactories ought not to be looked upon as an evil, till the present moral and domestic habits of the population are completely reorganized. So long as home education is not found for them, and they are left to live as savages, they are to some extent better situated when engaged in light labor." [6] Even many parents denounced attempts to shorten the hours because of the loss to the family income.

At last, however, the evils were such that the national conscience was shocked and Parliament appointed commissions to inquire into the conditions under which women as well as children were working in factories and mines. The reports of these commissions gave rise to a strong movement for control of working conditions and regulation of working hours by the government. In 1802 Parliament passed the first Factory Act, concerning child labor, and there were further acts in 1819, 1825, and 1831. But none of these proved effective because no proper means were provided for their enforcement. The first act that had any considerable effect was passed in 1833. It restricted the working hours of children between nine and twelve to forty-eight a week and provided for their attendance at school for two hours daily; persons under eighteen were to work no more than twelve hours a day and sixty-nine a week; and, most important, salaried inspectors were appointed to see that these provisions were carried out. After a number of convictions took place, most factory owners were careful not to flout the act too openly. The Mines Act of 1842 forbade the employment underground of any females or of male children under ten. Finally, in 1847 the Ten Hours Bill limited the work of all young persons between nine and eighteen to ten hours a day.

If public opinion was at first opposed to shorter hours for children, it was even more vigorously opposed to shorter hours for adults. The argument used most frequently was that the ignorant working people did not know how to use their leisure, that any limitation of hours would only lead to increased drunkenness and vice. Slowly the working classes realized that since the government was unwilling to take a hand in the matter, they must rely on themselves. Their only hope was in combining, particularly in trade unions, as a means of achieving an improvement of their condition. Combinations of workmen, however, were prohibited by the Combination Acts of 1799 and 1800, which made liable to imprisonment at hard labor any workman who combined with another for the purpose of gaining an increase in wages or a decrease in hours.[7] In other words, the Combination Acts placed the workingman

[6] Gaskell, *op. cit.*, p. 209.
[7] The acts did not apply to Scotland.

at the mercy of his employers. There remained to him only two ways of protesting: one was to wreck the establishments of those masters who were unfair, the other to agitate for a repeal of the laws that prevented him from combining with his fellow workers. At various times some resorted to rioting and violence, as in 1808 when Parliament refused the appeal of the cotton weavers for a minimum wage. In subsequent years, Parliament made the destruction of machines a capital offense.

Only a few extremists, however, resorted to terrorism; more widespread was the agitation for a reform of the government which refused to interest itself in industrial conditions. Despite prohibitions and repression, large numbers of workmen combined in secret. The weavers and spinners of Dewsbury, for instance, had a union which in 1819 counted five thousand members. Nor were the union agitations in vain. As time passed, more and more government leaders realized that repression was not the solution. Toward the end of the first quarter of the century, Francis Place, a retired tailor who believed that much of the discontent of the time was due to the Combination Acts, organized a campaign for their repeal, and actually succeeded in 1824. It was the first important victory for the working class in the post-Napoleonic period. When repeal was followed by a number of strikes for higher wages and shorter hours, and some of the strikes were accompanied by considerable disorder and violence, Parliament limited the rights of combinations in 1825 and prescribed penalties for violence, threats, intimidation, and molesting either employers or fellow workmen. However, combinations for mutual benefit or discussion were no longer illegal and the number of unions increased quickly, although improvements came slowly. Not until 1850 did a sixty-hour week for men become legal in the textile industries, and only in 1867 was this extended to all workshops and factories. Higher wages came still more slowly. Not until the abolition in 1870 of the "truck system," whereby the workman was paid not in cash but in goods which he had to sell at a loss, did his economic condition show real improvement.

THE MACHINE AND BRITISH AGRICULTURE

While industry and commerce were being mechanized, important changes took place both in the distribution and the size of the British population. First of all, there was a movement from the country to the towns. As industry became concentrated more and more in towns and cities, many villagers migrated to these industrial centers in search of work. In 1790 the number of country laborers was double that of the town laborers. By the middle of the nineteenth century the position

was reversed. The population of Manchester, for example, increased
75 per cent in the first two decades of the nineteenth century. Aside
from this shift, there was a net increase in the total population. While
the population of Scotland increased but slowly, that of England and
Wales doubled during the eighty years from 1750 to 1830. During the
first half of the nineteenth century the population increased from ten
and a half million to almost twenty-one million. This unparalleled increase called for a greater yield of agricultural products. Some idea of
the growing demand may be gained from the fact that, whereas England had previously been able to export a surplus of cereals, the 1770's
saw the country obliged to import increasingly large amounts of foodstuffs, not only of cereals but also of "butcher's meat"; and this importation was often difficult because of the repeated wars of the time.
Thus an increased production of agricultural commodities was necessary if Great Britain were to meet the needs of a growing industrial
population.

One step in this direction was the improvement of agricultural technique. Since the great demand made farming profitable, many farmers
became interested in better methods, with the result that the happy-go-
lucky traditional methods gradually gave way to more scientific methods. The great pioneer of the improvement of tillage was Jethro Tull
(1674–1741), a lawyer. After observing improved methods in France
and the Netherlands, Tull, upon his return to Britain, began a series of
experiments on a farm of his own. He gave the results to his countrymen
in his *New Horse-hoeing Husbandry* (1731). Plants, he stated, could
not obtain the maximum nourishment unless the soil was broken into
the greatest number of particles, a task for which he advocated the use
of the horse hoe, forerunner of the modern cultivator. In order to operate this hoe it was necessary to plant the seed in rows with a fair
space between them instead of sowing broadcast. To eliminate the
tediousness of doing this job by hand, he invented the seed drill (1701),
which laid the seed tidily in furrows. After he had pointed the way,
others invented new implements or improved the old ones. For example,
the cumbrous plows in general use up to that time were made lighter
and improved in form. Before the end of the eighteenth century crude
machines for harvesting and threshing, which previously had been a
matter of arduous labor by many hands, made their appearance. The
so-called Scotch reaper, invented about 1794, could gather as much
grain as seven men using sickles. Other reapers were soon put on the
market, some of which were operated by hand and others by horses.
The first machine which embodied many of the essential principles of
the modern reaper was that patented in 1834 by Cyrus H. McCormick,
an American. The first threshing machines were stationary and of sub-

stantial construction, but by the early years of the nineteenth century portable threshers came into wider use. The machine age had also come to agriculture.

While some farmers were improving agricultural technique through machinery, others were busy trying to increase the productivity of the soil through the use of new fertilizers and the rotation of crops. It had always been necessary to permit the land to lie fallow every third year after two grain crops had been raised on it, but enterprising farmers now discovered that with a proper rotation of crops the fallow year could be eliminated. The best of the new schemes was the so-called Norfolk system, which prescribed the sowing of wheat, turnips, barley, clover or rye grass, and back to wheat again. The growing of turnips, clover, and other roots and grasses meant not only an extra crop but also larger grain crops, for the root crops and grasses restored the fertility, particularly the nitrates, that had been taken from the soil by the grain. Moreover, if the root crops and grasses were stored for the winter, the farmer could keep more stock. Because of the serious difficulty of feeding cattle during the winter, it had previously been customary to slaughter most of them in the fall. Since this difficulty was now removed, by spring the farmer had a larger supply of manure to fertilize his fields.

Still other experimenters were improving livestock by selective breeding. Sheep had been raised primarily for wool, the mutton being a secondary product. The favorite type of sheep was small in frame, long-legged, and hardy enough to live on the scantiest food. But with the increasing demand for meat in the industrial towns, sheep raisers began to experiment in crossing different breeds for the purpose of developing fatter, more meaty, and less bony animals. The great pioneer in this matter was Robert Bakewell (1725–1795), whose New Leicesters produced as much wool as the old sheep, yielded much more meat, and matured in two years as compared with three or four for other breeds. Bakewell also met with success in breeding cattle in which the valuable joints were well developed and in producing a smaller but stronger and hardier horse than the large draft horse of England. His success raised up a host of imitators, and as a result the sheep and cattle of Great Britain were greatly improved by the end of the eighteenth century. Experiments were also conducted to increase the production of milk. By the beginning of the nineteenth century the daily yield of a prime dairy cow was increased through selective breeding from four to six, and in some cases as much as nine, gallons. Although pork formed a large proportion of the meat consumed by the rural inhabitants, much less attention was paid to the improvement of the breed of pigs than to sheep and cattle until about the middle of the nineteenth century. The Chinese pig, which reached England in the eighteenth century, was then used to impart early maturity and delicacy of flesh to the coarse and scraggy native breeds.

One result of improved farming was that the pace of enclosure, or fencing in for private use, of open fields, commons, and waste lands was accelerated, for the new methods could be put into practice only where the farms had already been enclosed. The process of enclosure had been going on for centuries, covering millions of acres; but as late as 1795 no less than 1.2 million acres in England were still being farmed on the open-field system, and there were an additional 7.8 million acres of commons, uncultivated land, or waste. Under the open-field system scattered strips in open fields were allotted to the small peasant cultivators. These strips, separated by balks (ridges of turf thrown up with the plow), were too narrow for cross-harrowing, and the balks were fruitful seed plots for weeds. Such new crops as turnips and clover could be raised only with the consent of all landholders; hence, one conservative or obstinate farmer could thwart the ambition of twenty enterprising farmers. Opportunities for selective breeding, too, were absent so long as the cattle of the community grazed together in meadows or stubble fields. With advances in agricultural methods these conditions became more and more intolerable to progressive farmers, and they wished to sweep away the medieval arrangements which obstructed the improvements that would greatly increase their income. When the prices of agricultural products rose during the Revolutionary and Napoleonic Wars, the incentives became even greater. During the years from 1797 to 1820 Parliament passed no less than 1727 private enclosure acts as well as a general enclosure act in 1801.[8] At the same time that they were consolidating scattered strips, many landlords also enclosed the wastes and the common pasture lands. By the middle of the nineteenth century this whole process was practically completed.

Enclosure put much waste land under cultivation, but, on the other hand, it caused much temporary suffering to the small cultivator. In some parishes, it is true, the small farmers were carefully protected, but in others they fared badly. Some lost their holdings entirely because they lacked expert advice to prove their legal rights. Even those who received their just dues were required within a given time to put hedges round their land and make provisions for roads, an expense which was so great that many had to sell out to wealthier neighbors.

[8] Enclosure might be carried out either by mutual consent or, if that could not be obtained, by private act of Parliament. The fact that the signatures on the petitions sent to Parliament for a bill of enclosure had to represent four-fifths of the land to be enclosed did not preclude injustice. "Those who owned the last fifth were often fairly numerous, sometimes they were the majority. Some petitions bore two or three names only, some could be found bearing but a single name." Mantoux, *The Industrial Revolution in the Eighteenth Century* (1928), p. 170.

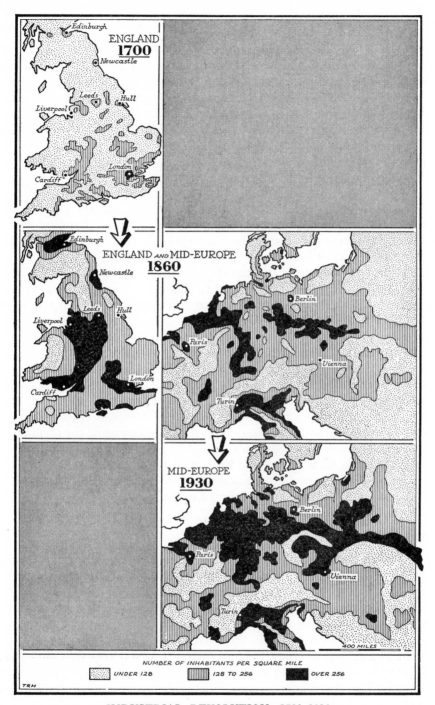

NUMBER OF INHABITANTS PER SQUARE MILE

UNDER 128   128 TO 256   OVER 256

INDUSTRIAL REVOLUTION, 1700–1930

Furthermore, when the commons and wastes were enclosed, the small proprietor not only lost the pasture for his cow or geese, but had to buy coal to replace the wood and turf he had gathered there. He was often unable to subsist solely on the remaining products of his arable land. Unfortunately, just at the time these changes came upon the small farmer he was also deprived, through the rise of the factory system, of the income from spinning, weaving, lacemaking, or some other form of manufacture which had supplemented his income from the land. The times were against him in almost every respect.

When during the years from 1815 to 1830 an agricultural depression was added to all these troubles, it spelled the doom of the yeoman. He could not purchase the expensive implements or the marl and other fertilizers that were necessary if he was to get the most from his land, and he could not buy blooded rams or bulls to improve his stock. Therefore he could not compete in the market with the fine grain and prime livestock of the large farmers who had the capital to produce these things. The result was that the yeoman almost disappeared in many parts of England by the middle of the nineteenth century. Some few managed to rent large farms after selling their small plots, or migrated to the new manufacturing towns or British overseas possessions; but the majority were reduced to the status of agricultural laborers at pitiful wages. Although agricultural wages did rise during the war period from 1793 to 1815, there was a similar sharp rise in general prices, which caused misery to thousands. As a result of this upheaval attendant upon the period of enclosures, three distinct agricultural classes emerged: the great landowners who collected high rents, the great tenant farmers who carried on agriculture on a capitalistic basis, and the laborer who worked for wages on the big new farms. Enclosures and machinery had completely changed the social structure of rural England.

FRANCE ADOPTS THE MACHINE

Mechanization of industry, commerce, and agriculture was not limited to Great Britain. The first of the large Continental countries to apply the new machinery to manufacturing processes was France. During the decade before the outbreak of the French Revolution machines and sketches of machines were smuggled out of Britain, despite all the efforts of the British to retain their monopoly. Enterprising Frenchmen went to England to study the new methods of smelting iron with coke instead of charcoal, and as a result the famous Creusot works were founded in 1781. Various types of English textile machines were also introduced. But the tempo of industrial change was much slower than in Great Britain; for example, in 1815 only about fifteen French establishments used steam engines, and these were mostly pumping engines for mines. The reasons for the slowness of change were many, among them the difficulty of obtaining machines, the survival of the gilds, and the troubles of the Revolution. But the most important reason was the fact that France did not have the abundance of cheap coal that was to be found in Great Britain. Only a few districts had coal deposits and these were not near iron deposits, as they were in Britain. Since no cheap mode of transportation had as yet been found, coal, when transported to the iron districts, cost several times as much in France as in England. In 1816 the total output of coal in France was less than a million tons as compared with sixteen million tons in Great Britain.

On the eve of the French Revolution industry was still largely controlled by the gilds under an elaborate set of regulations. The code of regulations filled no fewer than eight large volumes. In minutely prescribing the details of manufacture, these regulations discouraged the introduction of new techniques. But the National Constituent Assembly in March, 1791, abolished the gild restrictions [9] and opened the way for the wider introduction of machinery. During the period from 1815 to 1848 progress was still slow but nevertheless considerable. After 1825 Great Britain permitted the export of many varieties of machines. The importation of machine tools even permitted the French to produce their own machines after 1830. In addition, the inventive genius of the French people became active. Whereas the number of inventions patented during the Napoleonic period had not exceeded a hundred a year, no less than two thousand patents were issued in 1844. All this made for technical progress and industrial expansion. The output of pig iron almost tripled during the years from 1821 to 1847. The value of chemical products in 1847 was more than ten times as great as in 1814. Nearly thirty thousand kilometers of good roads were made between 1814 and 1848, nine hundred bridges built, and almost three thousand kilometers of canals opened to navigation.

When the steam locomotive first appeared, the French showed little interest in it because they had a magnificent network of highways, rivers, and canals. This vast system of transportation and communication had been developed by Napoleon to permit him to transport his troops quickly and easily to any part of Europe. After Napoleon's fall, France lacked the necessary leadership to start new developments, and commerce languished. While Britain and the United States were building railways, France hesitated. In 1830 a Parisian sought a concession

---

[9] Although the measure did not expressly abolish the gilds, it abolished the reason for their existence by declaring that any person was "free to do such business, exercise such profession, art or trade as he may choose."

to build a railway from Paris to Marseilles, but stagecoach owners, horse breeders, and canal bargemen objected so vigorously that the project was dropped. Not until the decade of the forties was a comprehensive plan of railroad building launched. The first important railway, running from Paris to Marseilles, was opened for traffic in 1843.

The most striking development in France was in the cotton industry, which had come into existence only in the eighteenth century. Soon after the three spinning machines — Hargreaves' spinning jenny, Arkwright's water frame, and Crompton's mule — were invented, they were smuggled out of England, and the outbreak of the Revolution saw them in actual operation in a number of factories in France. After 1815 progress was quickened, with the result that there were three and one-half million spindles at work in 1847. Some idea of the expansion may be gained from the fact that France imported five and one-half times as much raw cotton in 1847 as in 1814. Nevertheless, the process of mechanization did not reach the completeness it attained in the cotton industry across the Channel. Small establishments in which hand labor predominated still persisted, and even in the textile mills the use of steam power was on a small scale at the middle of the century. Most mills were still operated by water power, and some were even run by the power of horses and oxen. Steam power was first applied in mining and in metal works, and only slowly put to use in the textile industry.

In general, the industrial and commercial development of France lagged far behind that of Great Britain even at the middle of the century. A census taken in 1851 shows that 57 per cent of the people were still engaged in agriculture and only 25 per cent in industry. Of the latter only about one out of four was employed in *la grande industrie;* the rest were still in the handicraft stage. At this time the French output of iron and steel was less than a quarter of that of Great Britain, and most of the iron was still smelted in little charcoal furnaces scattered over the country, with less than one out of four using coke. French industry was, however, to make great strides during the next two decades. By 1871 it was using 26,146 steam engines with a horsepower of 316,000. The mileage of railroads increased fivefold from about two thousand miles in 1850 to about ten thousand in 1870, while the railroad freight service increased almost tenfold from 1850 to 1870. By making coal transportation cheaper the railroads stimulated the development of the iron and steel industry. So great was the progress of French industry generally that Napoleon III, thinking it could compete with British industry, concluded the so-called Cobden Treaty in 1860 (see p. 144).

Industrial changes in France were accompanied by the same evils that characterized the mechanization of industry in Great Britain; in fact, all countries in which the factory system was introduced show a remarkable uniformity of development. The hours of labor were often excessive, the wages low, and the working conditions lamentable. The normal working day in most industries was about fourteen hours, with longer hours not infrequent. During the early decades of the century the government did little to protect the working class.[10] A law passed in 1791 had declared associations of workers to be illegal, thereby giving the employer the advantage in any dispute over wages. But, as in England, workmen formed labor unions in defiance of the law. Paris, for example, had 132 unions in 1823, most of them organized as benefit societies. During the succeeding decades these unions had their ups and downs. At times the officials closed their eyes to their existence, and at other times ruthlessly suppressed them. It was not until 1864 that the Combination Acts were repealed and strikes became legal. By this time wages had risen considerably and working conditions improved. According to one historian, during the two decades from 1850 to 1870 wages rose about 41 per cent in the provinces and 32 per cent in Paris.[11]

In France the development of agriculture was in the opposite direction from that which English agriculture took. Whereas in England the small farms were absorbed by the large ones, in France the large estates were broken up into small holdings. This process, which had begun long before 1789, was accelerated during the revolutionary and Napoleonic periods. After the abolition of feudal dues and manorial rights in August, 1789, the peasants were given every opportunity to acquire small farms. Some achieved this by simply proclaiming themselves owners of their holdings when the landlords emigrated. Others purchased at low prices the small farms into which much of the land confiscated from the crown, the émigrés, and the Church was divided. Once established, the small farm was perpetuated by the provisions of the Napoleonic Code, which required the division of the land among all the children of a deceased proprietor, without distinction of age or sex. Hence it is not surprising that in 1862 more than half of the farms had an average area of twelve and a half acres or less and that only 4.77 per cent had an area of a hundred acres or more. Also, technical progress was slow, partly because the industrial development did not, as in England, call for an increased yield from the land, and partly because the average peasant was too poor and too conservative to adopt improved techniques. Nevertheless, the peasant succeeded in supplying most of the agricultural needs of the nation. While Great Britain became in-

10 An important exception to this statement was the prohibition of night work for young people in 1803, twenty-two years before it was prohibited in Great Britain, and then only in cotton mills. Furthermore, after 1813 no children under ten were permitted to work in mines, which also antedated similar British legislation by many years.
11 See Knowles, *Economic Development in the Nineteenth Century* (1932), p. 147.

creasingly dependent upon imported foodstuffs in the nineteenth century, France in 1870 imported only 5 per cent of its needs.

THE INTRODUCTION OF POWER MACHINERY INTO GERMANY

The mechanization of industry came comparatively late in Germany. In 1815 the German states were as a whole far more rural in character than was France. There were a few trading towns of some size, like Hamburg and Frankfurt, but no city comparable to Paris. The largest was Berlin, with a population of a little more than one hundred fifty thousand. Of the 1,016 towns only eighteen had more than ten thousand inhabitants, and 73.5 per cent of the population was classed as definitely rural. The unit of production was the small shop, in which journeyman and apprentice worked with the master after the old fashion. In most industries the gilds still played an important role. Theoretically, it is true, their power had been broken, but in many states the gild regulations continued in force. Methods of trade were also backward. As a rule the craftsman sold his goods directly to the consumer, both peasants and townsmen dealing with one another at the weekly markets and fairs. In short, economically, most Germans were still living in the Middle Ages.

There were a number of reasons for the tardiness of Germany's development. First of all, the political division was an obstacle to commerce and industry. Each of the thirty-nine states into which Germany was divided was, so to speak, a law unto itself in economic matters. Trade was obstructed not only by the tariff barriers which the petty governments had raised as a means of revenue, but also by the differences in the systems of coinage, weights, and measures. Nor was there such a thing as common law, each state, large or small, having its own laws. So long as the states remained separate units, any great industrial development could hardly be expected. Second, German markets were not sufficiently large to absorb the products of large-scale production. In the case of England, industry was fostered by foreign markets, especially in colonies settled by the English people; but the German manufacturer had no such outlets for his wares. Third, the home market was still further limited by the difficulties of transportation. Germany as a whole was extraordinarily ill-provided with roads, and the Napoleonic Wars had wrought havoc with the ones it had. After the wars the roads were so bad that it was difficult, and at times impossible, to move even food supplies except in the dry seasons.

Finally, the German manufacturer was hampered by the lack of free capital, which is a requisite for modern industrial production. Germany had not, like England, reaped the advantages of a profitable foreign trade, and it had suffered much from the devastating effects of the Napoleonic Wars. It was a poor country in almost every sense. Even the small well-to-do class possessed comparatively little capital that could be used in industrial enterprises because their wealth was largely in land. There was also a lack of banking and credit facilities. The so-called banks of Germany were, in fact, only places for money changing, and credit facilities were still in an elementary stage. During the first decade and a half after the war there was little if any progress. Some historians regard this period as one of economic retrogression. The historian Sombart wrote, "I believe it will not be amiss to assume that the economic condition of the people was worse in 1830 than in 1802."

After 1830 a movement began, slowly at first but gaining momentum after 1850. In this development Prussia took the lead. As early as the first decade of the nineteenth century the Prussian government freed the serfs and thus created a supply of free labor. During the same period it abolished the gild restrictions, thereby establishing an industrial freedom which permitted each person to choose his own trade. However, power machinery was introduced very slowly. In 1846, for example, less than 4 per cent of the cotton looms of Prussia were driven by power. Industrial development along factory lines got under way after the middle of the century. Up to 1850 coke-smelting furnaces were rare, but thereafter improved methods were introduced fairly rapidly. Though private capitalists had previously built a few short lines, the railway era was also inaugurated by the Prussian state in 1848, when work began on the state-owned railway running from Berlin toward the Russian border and projected primarily for military purposes.

The Prussian state did not stop at developing its own economic resources; it also took an important step toward the economic unification of Germany by establishing the *Zollverein* or Customs Union. When it went into force on January 1, 1834, the *Zollverein* included eighteen states with a total population of more than twenty-three millions. During the subsequent period the membership was extended until it included most of the German states. Within the framework of the *Zollverein* traffic between the states was made free from customs barriers of every kind. The aims of the union included the establishment of uniform coinage, weights, and measures, which was accomplished after the member states achieved political unity in the North German Confederation (1867). The *Zollverein* proved to be a potent stimulant to industrial development, particularly after 1850.[12] For example, the consumption of raw cotton in all of Germany rose from about 28,000

---

[12] It is impossible to say how much of the industrial progress of Germany before 1871 was due to the creation of the *Zollverein* and how much to the improvement of roads, the coming of railways, and other factors.

tons in 1851 to about 50,000 tons in 1865, while the annual consumption of silk increased from 300 tons in 1840 to 950 tons in 1870. A beginning was also made in the systematic exploitation of the natural resources of coal and iron. The production of iron ore quadrupled during the two decades from 1850 to 1870, and the production of coal increased from three million tons in 1846 to eighteen and a half million in 1867, and to nearly thirty million by 1871. During this period the first modern credit banks appeared, and the railroads were extended until Germany had a system of 11,501 miles by 1870. All this, however, was only preliminary to the great era of industrial expansion which came after the creation of the German Empire in 1871 and which made Germany one of the great industrial nations of the world.

In the other countries of Europe the mechanization of industry made more or less progress during the nineteenth century. The one country which kept pace with England in the first half was Belgium. Not only had the gild restrictions been broken down by the beginning of the century, but Belgium also had an abundant supply of iron and coal, particularly the latter. During the first half of the century it produced more coal than France. Great strides were also made in the development of the metallurgical industries. Before the middle of the century Belgium was sending machines to Holland, Russia, and Germany. On the other hand, in Russia, Spain, Italy, and the Scandinavian countries mechanization of industry on a wider scale was introduced only toward the end of the nineteenth and the early decades of the twentieth centuries.

CHAPTER FIVE

The Birth of Modern Socialism

WHAT IS SOCIALISM? SIDE by side with the new industry there arose a movement called "socialism," which aimed at redressing the social evils created in part by power machinery and the factory system. Although the word "socialism" is in everyday use, there is no clear, precise definition of it. Not that definitions are lacking; on the contrary, there are so many that they are bewildering in their variety, and sometimes so vague and contradictory as to deprive it of all real meaning. This situation is due to its many aspects. Writers have described socialism as a way of life, a class struggle, the obliteration of class hatreds and class distinctions, an attitude toward life, a form of society, practical Christianity, a science, the antithesis of capitalism, a program of action, the opposite of individualism, and many other concepts.[1] Hostile critics have called it "a plan that people often enthusiastically advocate when poor, which automatically ceases to interest them when they become wealthy," and "an attempt to legislate unsuccessful men into success by legislating successful men out of it." In brief, "What is socialism?" is a question to which there are many answers, according to the context or the education and prejudices of the person interrogated.

Nor is the confusion of meaning limited to those outside socialist ranks; it is equally prevalent among professed adherents. Controversies between socialists have often been so heated that one observer stated in *Punch* (February 18, 1925), "A scientist suggests dissipating icebergs with heat bombs. Personally we think it would be cheaper to land two socialists on the things and let them discuss what socialism really means." Perhaps an even greater diversity prevails among the

---

[1] In 1892 the Parisian *Le Figaro* published 600 separate definitions, and D. Griffiths' *What Is Socialism?* (1924) contains 263 separate definitions.

various socialist groups regarding aims and methods. Some would achieve a state in which the individual is given the greatest possible opportunity for self-expression; others would establish a society in which individual differences are sharply curbed. As for methods, they vary from the most gentle evolution to the most violent revolution. As the British historian Ramsay Muir put it, "Socialism is a chameleonlike creed."

Although the range of subjects grouped under the word "socialism" is too vast to be brought within the four corners of any comprehensive definition, it is possible to dispel much of the confusion surrounding the term by stating what the different forms of socialism have in common. This will at least enable one to distinguish it from other movements or influences. First, the problem all socialists have sought and are seeking to solve is primarily economic. In a more specific sense socialism has to do primarily with the production and distribution of wealth. All other considerations are secondary. Political power, for example, is coveted by socialists only as a means of setting up an economic system. Second, every form of modern socialism is in one sense or another a protest against or a condemnation of the economic system called "capitalism." This system, socialists state, has not only failed to effect a just distribution of wealth but has given rise to a conflict of interests between the employer and the employee. Third, all modern socialists agree that capitalism must be replaced by a new economic order. Although there has been no agreement as to the precise form this new order is to take, all socialists unite on one point: private property in land and industrial capital must be transformed into social or collective property. This idea of collective ownership is the core of socialism. Thus it is in its essence a movement toward the collective ownership and administration of land and industrial capital.

The idea of collective or common ownership of the means of production is very much older than socialism as an organized movement. It has, in fact, been widely held that common ownership preceded the institution of private property in the evolution of the human race.[2] One form in which the idea has survived is the myth of a Golden Age, of a time when men had all things in common and when slavery, injustice, and cruelty did not exist. Throughout history the bitter experience of the actual has caused men to seek refuge in dreams of a rosy past or of an ideal commonwealth in the future. Plato, for instance, stirred by the conflicts and disorders of his time, set up such a state in his *Republic*. But common ownership did not remain entirely in the realm of imaginative literature. Certain of the early Christian groups seem to have

---

[2] There is no agreement among anthropologists as to the earliest form of economic association.

put the idea into practice. Of one group it is stated in Acts 2:44, "And all that believed were together and had all things in common." This experiment was but a preparation for the coming of the millennium, the Christian version of a return to the Golden Age. When the millennium was not ushered in, common ownership disappeared after a brief time.

Throughout the Middle Ages heaven was the ideal community, but at the beginning of modern times Sir Thomas More, influenced to some extent by Plato's *Republic,* drew a picture of an earthly paradise in his *Utopia* (1516). Sensitive and sympathetic, More was grieved by the economic evils he saw about him — individual greed, the luxury of the nobility and gentry, and the consequent poverty, unemployment, and demoralization of the masses. His remedy for all this was common instead of private property. Thus he has Raphael Hythloday, the discoverer of Utopia, say, "I must freely own that as long as there is any property, and while money is the standard of all things, I cannot think that a nation can be governed either justly or happily; not justly because the best things will fall to the share of the worst men; nor happily, because all things will be divided among a few, the rest being left to be absolutely miserable." So far as practical results were concerned, More was but a voice crying in the wilderness. Even among his friends, his *Utopia* excited interest chiefly as an imaginative romance.

During the period after the appearance of *Utopia* there were scattered utterances of that theoretical socialism which sees in private property the root of all evil, and in its abolition the only cure; but it was not until the eighteenth century that the writers pursuing this theme became numerous. Outstanding in England was William Godwin (1756–1836). In his chief work, *Enquiry Concerning Political Justice,* published in 1793, he surveyed with a keen sense of social misery the evils of contemporary society, including the extreme inequality of wealth, the wretchedness of the poor, and the oppression on the part of the rich. These evils, he stated, are susceptible of cure, and the cure is the abolition of private property. His ideal society is complete anarchism, that is, a society on an individualistic basis, without a state organization. This new order, based on the idea of the innate goodness of man, was not to be established by violence but must come slowly through education; more specifically, "through the propaganda work of a small intellectual aristocracy."

In France some decades earlier Rousseau had revived the myth of the Golden Age, teaching that in the original state of nature all men had been free and equal and had owned all things in common. But the institution of private property had ended this state of felicity, and its concomitant evils beset society. Others after him developed his ideas. During the French Revolution François Émile Babeuf (1760–1797), inspired at least in part by the writings of Rousseau, propounded a definite scheme for a socialist society and even attempted to establish it (1796). Starting from the thesis that the aim of society is the happiness of all, he developed a plan according to which the state was to inherit all property until community of property was established. However, the French Revolution was too individualistic a movement to favor such ideas; when Babeuf sought to found a government that would carry out his principles, he was arrested and executed.

PRE-MARXIAN SOCIALISM

With exception of Babeuf, the socialist writers up to the end of the eighteenth century were all theorists; socialism as an organized and continuous movement dates only from the first quarter of the nineteenth century. Not until then did it become a systematic attempt to do something about the plight of the working classes. Distinct schools of socialist thought now appeared simultaneously in both France and Britain, and the words "socialist" and "socialism" were coined.[3]

A number of circumstances contributed to making socialism an organized movement. One of these was undoubtedly the evils of the new industrialism. Although conditions of poverty and misery had existed for centuries, they were brought into strong relief after Waterloo. The prosperity of the preceding decades disappeared with the coming of peace, and in its place stalked unemployment, depression, and distress, which aggravated the sufferings of the working classes. The inevitable consequence was not only widespread discontent, particularly in England, but also a heightening of the contrast between the working classes and the new class of rich industrialists. A further influence was the general ferment that was started by the French Revolution and expressed itself in various forms of economic and social reorganization. In France the advocates of socialism commonly regarded their plans as the completion of the work of the Revolution.

To regard socialism as being, in the first instance, a working-class movement is to misunderstand its character and its history. It made its appearance from above as a campaign in behalf of the workers. Its founders and leaders were not of the proletariat. This is true as well of Marx, Engels, and other leading spirits of later nineteenth-century socialism as of the men who set the movement going. These leaders saw the upward progress of the few and the helpless depression of the masses, the wealth at one end of the social order and the poverty at

---

[3] The word "socialist" was coined in England about 1825. Its earliest known use in print is in the *Cooperative Magazine,* November, 1827. The word "socialism" was coined independently in France about 1830 by Pierre Leroux, a writer of the Saint-Simonian school. See Shadwell, *The Socialist Movement* (1925), I, 13–19.

the other. They realized that the laborer was getting only a fraction of the wealth he was creating. A number of sensitive minds were not only convinced that the existing social order was unjust but were also filled with an ardent desire to relieve the situation. They began to cast about for a remedy, for the plan of a more harmonious economic order, one which would insure "the greatest happiness of the greatest number." Their motive was primarily sympathy, not self-interest. The ideas they propounded took root very slowly among the working classes; in fact, the working classes were induced, and then with some difficulty, to take up the ideas for themselves only during the last quarter of the nineteenth century.

It is indicative of the fermentative nature of the age that organized socialism was born simultaneously but quite independently in France and Great Britain. After Babeuf's futile attempt, socialism was submerged for a time but reappeared soon after the Revolution in the writings of Comte Claude Henri de Saint-Simon (1760–1825). A younger member of an old and famous French family, which claimed Charlemagne as an ancestor, he was full of reforming schemes from his youth onward. It is reported that in his teens he instructed his valet to awaken him early every morning with the words, "Arise, monsieur le comte, for you have great things to do." At the age of seventeen he went to America, where he served under Washington in the War of Independence. Upon his return to France he dedicated himself, as he later said, "to study the march of the human spirit and afterward to work for the perfecting of civilization." His early works, the first of which appeared in 1802, were largely scientific. It was not until some years later that he set his mind completely on "the amelioration of the lot of humanity." His plan for the reorganization of society was published in 1817 under the title *L'industrie,* and was further developed in later writings, the most important of which is probably his *Nouveau Christianisme,* published in the year of his death. The socialism in his plan was mild and philanthropic, the use of force being expressly repudiated. The essence of his proposal was the establishment of an industrialist state directed by modern science. In this state the right of inheritance was to be abolished because it transmits social privileges from one generation to another without consideration of merit. He did not, however, believe in the natural equality of man, for in the new society every man was to be employed according to his ability and rewarded according to his capacity. Having developed his plan, he made incessant but futile appeals to those in power, including Louis XVIII, to assist him in carrying it out.

Saint-Simon was not a systematic thinker, but his speculations did stimulate the minds of others. After his death, his disciples founded a school in which his doctrines were systematized and developed. Certain of his disciples even attempted to realize his preachings in select communistic societies. For a time the school attracted many artists, industrialists, and men of letters, but its success was short-lived. Soon dissensions developed among the disciples themselves and, when some of them tried to graft the principle of free love onto Saint-Simonism, the school became the object of ridicule and attack, with the result that it ceased to exert any appreciable influence. Nevertheless, the ideas of Saint-Simon continued to fertilize socialist thought long after the dissolution of the Saint-Simonian school.

Almost contemporaneously with Saint-Simon another Frenchman, Charles Fourier (1772–1837), was formulating a scheme for the reorganization of society. As a young man he, too, was convinced that the existing organization of society was a disastrous failure. The reason for this failure he found in the idea, popularized by Rousseau, that man had departed too far from nature. As a proof of his contention he pointed to the harmony and order of the universe as contrasted with the confusion in society. The obvious remedy was, of course, a return to nature, to an existence in which the natural passions and impulses have free play. His plan for realizing this involved the establishment of small groups, or "phalanxes," each comprising a self-sufficient community of sixteen hundred to two thousand persons. One square league of land was to be assigned to each phalanx, and the members of each group were to live together in a group of buildings called the phalanstery, for which Fourier drew the plans. In these communities marriage, which Fourier regarded as enslaving woman, was to be replaced by the "law of passionate attraction." Every member of the phalanx must work but would be free to choose his occupation or occupations according to his tastes or aptitudes. No one was to work to excess and all labor was to be made pleasant. "The labor is itself of the nature of a fête," Fourier stated; "brightly colored tents afford shelter from the rays of the sun or from rain; flags and banners, ornamented with the devices of the series, representing their triumphs in industry, indicate the parties at work. Tasteful kiosks are erected at convenient distances and are supplied with exquisite pastry and sparkling wine. The laborers go to the field and return again accompanied by the strains of music and the sweet singing of the youthful choirs." Private property was not to be abolished, but for his work each individual was to receive the minimum of subsistence. Any surplus was to be divided in the proportion of five-twelfths to labor, four-twelfths to capital, and three-twelfths to talent. Such was the utopian plan which, Fourier was convinced, would usher in the Golden Age of mankind.

Although there is much that is puerile in his idea, it had a wide vogue.

Soon after the publication in 1822 of his *Traité de l'Association Domestique Agricole,* the most important of his works, the nucleus of the so-called Associative School was formed by a few disciples. During the subsequent period this school grew in importance until in 1848 it had a membership of about thirty-seven hundred, including Louis Napoleon, the future emperor of the French. As early as 1832 one of Fourier's disciples attempted to establish a phalanx near Rambouillet, but the enterprise was abandoned for lack of the necessary capital before it was even set in operation. Near the middle of the century the plan was the object of experiment in a number of countries, above all in the United States of America. The promise of freedom and the simple life attracted for a time such eminent figures as Albert Brisbane, Horace Greeley, Ralph Waldo Emerson, Margaret Fuller, Nathaniel Hawthorne, and James Russell Lowell. More than thirty different Fourierist communities were established in America, only one of them lasting more than five or six years. Among the larger ones were the North American Phalanx (1843–1854), founded in New Jersey by Albert Brisbane, and the Wisconsin Phalanx (1844–1850). The most famous of all was undoubtedly Brook Farm (1841–1847), near Boston, which counted many distinguished men and women among its members.

The socialism of Fourier and Saint-Simon was largely imaginative and utopian, with only a remote connection with actual conditions. Louis Blanc (1811–1882) was the first to try to make use of the contemporary political machinery to achieve the ends of socialism. Blanc, a journalist, author, and politician, published his celebrated work, *The Organization of Labor,* in 1840. He began by denouncing the existing competitive system and then proceeded to propose measures for getting rid of it. As the first step, he advocated a political reform which would establish the state on a thoroughly democratic basis. Then the state would provide *ateliers sociaux* (social workshops) — farms for agriculturists, factories for workmen, shops for tradesmen — which would gradually and without shock replace workshops owned by individuals. The means for founding the workshops were to be provided by the state, which was also to draw up regulations for their operation. But once the workshops were set in motion, they were to be turned over to the workmen, who could choose their own directors and managers and decide on the division of the profits. The idea carried such great appeal that as early as 1846 there were widespread demands for its establishment. During the Revolution of 1848 these demands became so insistent that the provisional government yielded (see p. 61). The experiment, however, was not made to prove the practicability of Blanc's suggestions but to discredit them. In other words, it was but a travesty of his proposals and not in the least what he advocated. The national workshops were simply a relief scheme to provide work for the unemployed.

In Britain many rivulets contributed to make up the main stream of socialism. The most important was undoubtedly the influence of Robert Owen (1771–1858), who was not only the patron saint of English socialism as such but also the father of the cooperative movement. Furthermore, he was a pioneer in advocating factory legislation and democratic education, and also the originator of the nursery school or kindergarten. As a young man he became manager of a Manchester cotton mill employing five hundred persons, but he did not become a public figure until after 1800, in which year he and his partners bought the famous New Lanark Mills in Scotland. The purchase of these mills, the largest and best equipped in Great Britain, appeared to be an excellent investment, but to Owen they were less valuable as a means of making money than as an opportunity to put into practice certain social ideas that had been crystallizing in his mind. The two thousand people who worked in the mills at New Lanark, Owen said, were "a collection of the most ignorant and destitute from all parts of Scotland . . . and much addicted to theft, drunkenness and falsehood with all their concomitant evils." To raise these people from their destitution and moral degradation became the primary object of Owen's endeavors.

What Owen set out to create was not a model factory but a model social and industrial community. His experiment was based on the conviction that man is to a large extent the product of his environment; in other words, man will be good or bad to the degree in which his environment is good or bad. The necessary thing, as he saw it, to change the character of the people at New Lanark was to establish a right physical, moral, and social environment. To this end he built model dwellings with adjacent gardens and rented them to his employees at cost. He also opened shops in which commodities of good quality could be purchased at wholesale prices. Another innovation was a common dining hall in which the workers could get good food at reasonable prices. He further instituted model workshops with adequate lighting and good ventilation, reduced the hours of labor to ten a day, put an end to the brutal system of pauper apprentices from foundling homes, employed no children under ten, and limited the work for children under thirteen to six hours a day. Acting on the belief that training, in order to be really effective, must begin in infancy, he provided both infant and regular schools in which every child was given the best education circumstances permitted. Not only book learning but also nature studies, games, singing, dancing, and military drill occupied important places. The schools became so famous that educators from all parts of Great Britain and distinguished visitors from all over Europe and America flocked to New Lanark to see for themselves. All in all, the improvements produced a good effect upon the employees. They began to take a personal interest in their work, with the result that the mills prospered.

Thus far Owen was but a successful reformer of the factory system. However, he was gradually to change from an enlightened employer seeking to ameliorate the lot of his employees into an avowed enemy of the capitalist system. His success at New Lanark led him to propose to the government during the period of economic depression after 1815 that all the unemployed be gathered into self-supporting "Villages of Cooperation," which were also to be centers of social improvement and progressive education on the model of New Lanark. His plan was seriously discussed both in Parliament and in the press, but not adopted. Meanwhile, he was also pressing other employers to follow the example he had set at New Lanark. In addition, he was carrying on a crusade for industrial legislation which would prohibit children under ten from working in factories, regulate the hours of work, and set up a system of factory inspection. Little came of all his efforts.[4] Slowly the realization was forced upon him that the employers would never of their own efforts improve the conditions of the workers, that nothing short of the abolition of the system of capitalism could achieve this. Thereafter he began with apostolic fervor to preach the abstract principle that character is formed by environment. All mankind was to be divided into small communities of from five hundred to three thousand persons, and each community was to be settled on land which it was to cultivate for its own support, manufacturing everything for its own needs. In these communities labor was to be moderate for all, and everyone was to be guaranteed the means of subsistence. Every evil spirit of gain was to be exorcised, all inducements to vice were to be removed, and man's character was to be trained in goodness and truth, so that all would live together in peace and happiness. In short, Owen's means for becoming the savior of society were similar to those proposed by Fourier.

Owen preached his new gospel in letters, pamphlets, and periodicals; he addressed himself to the government at home and to the ruling powers of other European countries; he even sent out itinerary lecturers to various parts of Great Britain to expound the virtues of his plan. His ideas were at first received with interest and in some circles with applause. The *Times* (London), for example, spoke of "his enlightened zeal in the cause of humanity." But in 1817 Owen did irretrievable harm to his cause by his declaration of war against organized religion, after he became convinced that all religious sects were obstacles to his

---

[4] He did succeed in inducing the elder Sir Robert Peel to introduce a child labor bill in 1815. It was not until 1819 that a Factory Act was passed, but it fell far short of what Owen demanded.

plans for the regeneration of mankind because they taught the innate sinfulness of man. Although his fierce attack did not undermine his popularity among the working classes, it did cause the supporters of the existing religions to turn away in pious horror. Thenceforth, anyone who disagreed with him could conveniently, though not justly, hurl the epithet of "atheist" at him. When the newspapers turned against him, it became clear even to Owen's trusting optimism that neither the government nor any members of the governing class would sponsor his plan.

All this, however, only made him more determined to try it himself. In 1824 he heard that the Rappists, a German religious colony that had migrated to North America, wished to sell their land on the Wabash River in southwestern Indiana in order to move westward. Owen sailed to America at once, bought the Rappist village with 20,000 acres of land, and established a communist colony there under the name of New Harmony. He was certain that in the "fresh, democratic and uncorrupted air" of North America his colony would flourish and thus prove the feasibility of his ideas beyond any question of doubt. But difficulties soon developed among the heterogeneous collection of colonists over the idea of communism, and in 1828 Owen, after having spent large sums on the project, severed his connections with it because he felt that the colonists had deserted his principles.

Undiscouraged by the failure of New Harmony, Owen founded three other colonies at various times in England, Scotland, and Ireland, all of which repeated the earlier failure. Although most of his practical measures after New Lanark failed, his ideas remained as the leaven of many movements for social reform. Almost all the younger working-class leaders of his time and of the succeeding period were deeply influenced by his teachings. Friedrich Engels said of him, "Every social movement, every real advance in England on behalf of workers links itself on to the name of Robert Owen."

KARL MARX

The first phase of socialism may be said to have closed with the year 1848. In France both the Saint-Simonian and Fourierist schools had passed the peak of their influence by this time, and the fiasco of the national workshops served to discredit the state collectivism of Louis Blanc. After the Revolution of 1848 French socialism was almost completely submerged by the great reactionary movement which characterized the Second Empire. In England, too, socialism suffered a temporary setback. As one experiment after another foundered, the socialist forces were diverted into *Chartism* on the political side and into trade union-ism on the industrial side. So complete was its eclipse in both France and England that certain writers believed that socialism had been utterly destroyed. But it was soon to be revived in an even more vigorous form, that of Marxian socialism. Whereas the socialism of the first period had been hopeful and peaceful, Marxian socialism, by and large, was to be militant and aggressive. Instead of looking to voluntary cooperation of all classes as a means of introducing the new order, it preached class war. Again, whereas utopian socialism was content with vast impracticable schemes, Marxian socialism entered into the political arena to contest for control of the political forces. Other influences, it is true, asserted themselves at various times, but the Marxian creed remained the dominant one, and Marx the dominant figure.

Few men have been the object of such unsparing condemnation or such unalloyed admiration as Karl Marx. He has always been regarded with an almost religious frenzy; by some he has been regarded as a proletarian deity and by others as the offspring of satan. The truth lies somewhere between the two extremes. He was born at Trier (Treves) in Rhenish Prussia on May 5, 1818. His father was a lawyer of Jewish extraction who accepted the Protestant faith about a year before Karl's birth, after a government edict left the Jews no choice but to be baptized or to forgo all official positions and activities. Later, when Karl was about six, the entire family, including his mother, one brother, and five sisters, were received into the national Protestant Church. Neither religion seems to have appealed to young Marx, for he soon became hostile to everything connected with religion, and particularly with Judaism. He entered the University of Berlin, then at the height of its influence, and threw himself with enthusiasm into the study of history, geography, law, literature, art, and philosophy, devoting his best efforts to the last. The influence of Hegel was paramount in the university, and Marx became so deeply imbued with Hegelian ideas that they influenced his mental processes during all his subsequent life. Even the obscurities of his literary style can be traced to Hegel. It was from Hegel, above all, that he derived the evolutionary view of history which became a basic factor in his philosophy.

Rejecting the idea of a career in law, Marx decided to become a teacher of philosophy in one of the Prussian universities. But the fact that he was a leading member of a group of young intellectuals, known as the Young Hegelians, who interpreted Hegel in a "radical" manner, discredited him in the eyes of the reactionary Prussian government and closed the door on his ambition. He turned to journalism and became in 1842 contributor and, a few months later, editor of the *Rheinische Zeitung,* which under his editorship vigorously attacked the political reaction in Prussia. After the censors suppressed the paper in 1843, he married his childhood sweetheart, Jenny von Westphalen,[5] daughter of a high government official of noble birth, and they moved to Paris.

Marx's sojourn in Paris determined the course of his future career. Up to this time he was simply a democrat, with political ideas not unlike those of the German middle-class liberals who desired, above all, a unified Germany under a system of political democracy. But in France he came into contact with various socialist theories. He accepted none of them as a whole but scrutinized them all, fitting individual ideas into his own philosophic conceptions. He even decided that certain ideas of Hegel must be reversed. Whereas Hegel taught that only ideas are real, Marx decided that it was the material facts that were real and that they controlled the ideas. He was still intent upon accomplishing a democratic revolution in Germany, but as he progressed along the path of anticapitalism he decided that the revolution could not be limited to one country. In Paris he also met Friedrich Engels, and there began their extraordinary friendship. Both men, it appears, had been proceeding toward the same general conclusions. Although the exact intellectual relationship between them has yet to be accurately determined, the two minds complemented each other. From the time they met until Marx's death the two friends worked together in such a close collaboration that their labors are impossible to separate. The generous and self-effacing Engels also aided his friend financially, enabling him to carry on the research for his later writings. Of the two men, however, Marx was the mastermind.

Before many years, Marx and Engels had laid down the revolutionary principles upon which both Marxian socialism and communism are based. Their various polemical works attracted the attention of the League of the Just, an organization of exiled and emigrant German workers, with branches in many European cities. This organization was renamed the Communist League in 1847, and Marx and Engels were invited to draw up a "confession of faith" for it. The result was the *Communist Manifesto*,[6] which contains all the typical Marxian doctrines except that of surplus value, which was not elaborated until later. Short, concise, eloquent, and full of striking phrases, the *Communist Manifesto* has been a most influential pamphlet. In the words of one historian, "It gave direction and a philosophy to what had been before little more than an inchoate protest against injustice. It began the long process of welding together the scattered groups of the disinherited into an organized and influential party. It freed socialism from

---

[5] Marx's wife was to be a helper and companion to him in the truest sense of the words, sharing his hardships with a cheerfulness that was characteristic of her disposition. Of the six children born to the couple only three girls grew up.
[6] Because the word "socialism" was widely used in connection with utopian socialism, Marx preferred to have his teachings called "communism."

its earlier situation of a doctrine cherished by conspirators in defiance of government and gave to it at once a purpose and an historic background." [7] After publication the *Manifesto* was translated and distributed among most of the peoples of the world. In 1888 Engels declared that it had become "the common program of many millions of workers of all countries from Siberia to California." Some of its statements have become almost proverbial, such as the famous one, "The proletarians have nothing to lose but their chains; they have a world to win."

The ink on the *Communist Manifesto* had hardly dried when the February Revolution of 1848 broke out in Paris and was followed by uprisings in many parts of Europe. During the revolutions of 1848 both Marx and Engels traveled up and down Europe encouraging the revolutionists. Finally Marx went to Cologne, where he became the editor of the short-lived paper, the *Neue Rheinische Zeitung*. When censorship troubles put an end to the paper's existence, he returned to Paris and thence to London, which was then a place of refuge for the most distinguished exiles of Europe. There, with the exception of one or two brief intervals, he remained for the rest of his life.

Creatively, this last was the most fruitful period of Marx's life. Besides writing the *Eighteenth Brumaire of Louis Bonaparte* (1852) and the *Critique of Political Economy* (1859), he spent many years in collecting and systematizing the material for his great work, *Das Kapital* (*Capital*). During much of this period life was for him a constant struggle against poverty. His only regular income from 1851 to 1860 came from the weekly newsletter he wrote for the *New York Tribune,* which hardly covered his rent. At times the family was forced to live on bread and potatoes for days on end. How poor Marx was can be seen from the fact that in 1852 he had to pawn his only overcoat to get money for writing-paper. His mother is credited with the remark that "it would have been far better if Karl had made some Capital instead of writing about it." In the sixties his financial situation improved considerably. The family not only received several small legacies but Engels was able to increase his financial aid.

Finally, in 1867, the first volume of *Das Kapital,* often called "the bible of socialism," appeared in print. Its cumbrous and involved style, abstruse reasoning, and ambiguous statements do not make for easy reading; hence, it is more often discussed than read. Nevertheless, it has had a tremendous influence. Like the Bible it has become a book of texts broadcast in every quarter of the world. But Marx was not to finish his masterpiece. After the publication of the first volume his health began to fail, and during the last twelve years of his life he

[7] H. J. Laski, *Karl Marx: an Essay* (1922), pp. 14 f.

struggled almost uninterruptedly against various forms of illness. The loss of his devoted wife on December 2, 1881, was a severe blow, and on March 14, 1883, he died. Engels, who was destined to outlive his friend by twelve years, spent this time editing the last two volumes of *Das Kapital*. Marx's studies on surplus value were edited and published in four volumes by Karl Kautsky, a disciple.

MARXIAN SOCIALISM

Most of the doctrines Karl Marx preached did not originate with him, nor did he claim any originality for them. Many of them were, so to speak, "in the air" during the early decades of the nineteenth century, and a number of writers before him had developed one or more of them. Sismondi (1773–1842), in his *New Principles of Political Economy* (1819), for example, anticipated nearly all the main points in Marx's indictment of the capitalist system. Some writers had even stated certain ideas more clearly and more energetically than he. But what Marx did was to take a number of distinct ideas and in a masterly way combine them into a system. He united three streams of thought — the German metaphysical, the English economic, and the French political revolutionary — and the system as a whole has not only an air of originality but a virility that is unusual in any phase of human culture. Marx's primary concern, however, was not the development of a body of theory. The main object upon which all his thinking converged was the liberation of the working class from the capitalist system. "Marx was above all a revolutionary," Engels said at the grave of his friend; and Marx himself wrote in 1875, "Every step of real movement is worth a dozen programs." His theoretical system was, above all, a working philosophy, a plan of action, a weapon for the fight against the existing order. It is only in this light that his ideas can be understood.

Any attempt to state the essentials of the Marxian system is fraught with difficulties because of the complexity of the doctrines. Marx did not state his doctrines in a definitive or finished form. He himself states in the *Communist Manifesto* that his theories "only express in general terms the circumstances of an actually existing class struggle, of an historical movement going on under our own eyes." Moreover, he adopted inconsistent and even contradictory points of view according to the changing circumstances. As Spargo put it, "Marx was nothing if not an opportunist." In consequence, the most contradictory doctrines have been derived from his writings. Socialists of many hues appeal to them to find support for their sectarian beliefs, just as various religious sects appeal to the Bible.

The core of Marxism is an analysis of society from the economic point of view. Like the earlier socialists Marx asserted that the social evils he saw about him were caused by the existing economic system, and principally by the inefficient and inadequate distribution of the products of the workers' industry. The one thing common to all commodities, he declared, is labor; hence, labor is the only source of value.[8] Since labor creates all value, the worker has a claim to the whole product of his labor. As Marx put it, "All wealth is due to labor, and therefore to the laborer all wealth is due." In a primitive state of society the worker owned his own tools and kept the whole product of his labor, but under capitalism he receives only a small part of the value he creates, just enough for his subsistence. The rest, which Marx called "surplus value," is taken by the capitalists for their own enrichment. Thus the capitalist system, according to Marx, is a gigantic scheme for exploiting the worker, at whose expense it flourishes. Upon the basis of this analysis he built his system of social reform. The practical solution is to make it impossible for capitalists to exploit the workers, this to be done by establishing "collective ownership of all means of production, distribution, and exchange." In other words, the proletariat must get command of the tools of production, distribution, and exchange and then construct an economic and political order organized in the best interests of all members of society.[9]

History provides, Marx stated, the philosophical justification of his program of action. According to his theory of history, generally known as the "materialistic conception of history," the order of society in each stage of social evolution has been determined by economic factors. In other words, idealism, religion, culture, and civilization are at bottom the products of economic conditions.[10] Not only did he assert that economic conditions are the determinants of social evolution; he further stated that the social changes caused by the economic conditions invariably come about in a particular way, that is, by means of class struggle. This idea is stated in the first sentence of the *Communist Manifesto*, which reads, "The history of all hitherto existing society is the history of class struggles." The struggles are caused by the mode of production. Since the class which owns the means of production is in

[8] Thorstein Veblen, in *Quarterly Journal of Economics,* XX (1906), 584, says, "He offers no adequate proof of his labor-value theory." Among others, Adam Smith and David Ricardo also believed that labor supplied the common denominator of value. This theory, Veblen states, "has for the most part been given up by latter-day socialist writers."

[9] There is no agreement among socialists as to the form this ownership should take. Some of the different forms would be state ownership, municipal or local ownership, group or trade ownership, and universal ownership.

[10] Insistence upon the economic as the sole determining factor in history is, of course, demonstrably false. As Marx did not set down his philosophy of history in a clear or complete form, it is not at all certain that he meant to eliminate all other factors completely. After Marx's death Engels urged that his friend had not held the extreme view. In any case, Marx did call attention to the economic factor in social changes.

a dominant position, it exploits the other classes. This exploitation generates antagonism, which gradually increases until it bursts the existing order. The means of production in the Middle Ages, for example, was land, and the nobles who owned the land controlled both government and society. The early centuries of modern times saw a new class, the bourgeoisie, rise to importance. With the advent of power machinery this class became the dominant one because it owned the means of production and exchange in the form of money, machines, and industries. But just as the feudal class was supplanted by the bourgeoisie, so the bourgeoisie will in the course of time be superseded by the mass of the people, the proletariat, and the capitalist system will disappear.

Marx did not rest content with predicting the coming of the proletarian order; he also sought to show that its coming is inevitable. As he put it in *Das Kapital*, the new order is coming "with the inevitability of a law of Nature." "What the bourgeoisie produces, above all," the *Communist Manifesto* states, "is its own gravediggers. Its fall and the victory of the proletariat are equally inevitable." It is in the nature of capitalist competition that each capitalist will try to make his industry larger and that the smaller concerns will succumb in the competition. In other words, the rich will become richer and the poor poorer. All capital will gradually be concentrated in the hands of fewer and fewer capitalists. Conversely, more and more petty capitalists will be forced into the ranks of the proletariat. As the proletariat grows in strength and as the antagonism between capitalist and worker increases, individual proletarians will discover that their struggle is not one of individual against individual but of proletariat against capitalists. The mass of the proletariat will develop a working-class consciousness and will ultimately rise up against the exploiters to establish the temporary "dictatorship of the proletariat" as a prelude to the "classless society," which was Marx's ultimate ideal. The latter will be the last stage in social evolution. When the land and the means of production, distribution, and exchange are owned by all collectively, both the exploited and the exploiters will disappear. Since at this time there will be only one class, the class struggles, which are characteristic of all past historical epochs, will cease.

Although the coming of the new order is inevitable, the workers can facilitate and hasten its coming. They must organize against the existing system. The *Communist Manifesto* closes with the words, "The proletarians have nothing to lose but their chains. They have a world to win. Working men of all countries, unite!" Just what the workers are to do after they have united is a subject of dispute. Marx himself spent so much effort in trying to show the inevitability of the new order that he intimated the necessary course of action only in general terms.

In his earlier years he confidently preached violent revolution because he believed that the bourgeoisie was ripe for destruction. Thus he stated in the *Communist Manifesto* that the proletarian aims "cannot be attained without the violent overthrow of the whole existing order." Again, he wrote in the *Neue Rheinische Zeitung* (May 19, 1849), "We are ruthless and want no consideration from the bourgeoisie. When our time comes, revolutionary terrorism will not be sugar-coated. . . . There is but one way of simplifying, shortening, and concentrating the death agony of the old society as well as the bloody labor of the world's new birth — revolutionary terror." But the older and wiser Marx found it necessary to abate some of his earlier enthusiasm. After the failures of 1848–1849 he gradually realized that progress must necessarily be slow, and he inclined somewhat toward less violent methods. To his friend Kugelmann he deprecated the fact that many socialists were adamant revolutionists, stating that "they treat with contempt any idea of making use of the legislature for anything, as, e.g., for shortening the hours of labor." Even the cooperative societies, which he had ridiculed in 1848, he later praised as a step in the direction of associated free labor.

Many of Marx's ideas have not stood the test of criticism, and some of his predictions have failed to materialize. Many socialist groups have discarded some of his teachings and modified others. Marx the theorist, the dogmatist, has been pushed into the background to some extent by Marx the leader, the tactician. What has been most effective is his general attitude, his hostility toward the capitalist system, and his ability to envisage an alternative to this system. For multitudes of workers this general attitude was, and still is, enough. Here is a prophet who denounced in scathing terms the system that brought them only toil and poverty, and who also gave them hope for the future. He told them that their present condition is not permanent, that a better state of things is inevitable because history is working in their favor. They, the workers, are the next in succession to be the rulers and controllers. It is up to them to carry on energetically and unceasingly the working-class struggle and thereby hasten the coming of the new order. Thus Marxism became for many a gospel of salvation.

ORGANIZED MARXIAN SOCIALISM

If a definite date is to be set for the beginning of Marxian socialism as an international movement, it is the year 1864. Marx and Engels had already sounded the international note in the *Communist Manifesto* when they called upon the "proletarians of all countries" to unite. They were convinced at that time that the capitalist system had outlived its usefulness and would be violently overthrown in a year or two. But when the revolutionary movements of 1848–1849 collapsed, Marx realized that conditions for victory had not fully matured. Consequently, he sought, apart from his writing, to organize an association which would spread his ideas around the world. This aim was achieved in a very limited sense with the founding at London in 1864 of the International Working Men's Association, commonly known as the "First International." Although the association at first endeavored to exclude Marx as "bourgeois," he soon achieved pre-eminence over it and established his teachings as the militant creed. The four great congresses which the First International held during the years 1866–1869 filled the governments and the capitalists with alarm. But the life of the association was destined to be short because dissension broke out among the members. Among others, Michael Bakunin, an anarchist who demanded that the destruction of the state should be the object of the proletarian revolution, fiercely contested Marx's leadership.[11] The Franco-Prussian War, which broke out in 1870, widened the split into several groups. In 1873 a feeble attempt was made to hold another congress, and finally in 1876 the First International expired.

After the demise of the First International socialism developed largely along national lines. In one country after another its propaganda took root and grew into organizations which soon became a political force in national politics. The first party was organized in Germany. There Ferdinand Lassalle (1825–1864), member of a well-to-do, middle-class Jewish family, went about disseminating socialism with great enthusiasm. He was able to organize the Universal German Working Men's Association in 1863 on principles derived largely from Louis Blanc. Although he was killed the next year in a duel over a love affair, his disciples carried on the organization. In 1869 a group of Marxists founded a rival organization, but after competing a few years the two fused in 1875 to form the Social Democratic party.[12] Some idea of this party's growth may be gained from the fact that the number of votes cast for socialist candidates for the Reichstag increased from 3.2 per cent of the total in 1871 to 34.8 per cent in 1912, despite the fact that socialist organizations were illegal in Germany from 1878 to 1890. In 1912 the Social Democratic party was the largest in the Reichstag, with 110 members out of a total of 397.

---

[11] Anarchism as such is often defined as "the social doctrine of the abolition of government of man by man, and the constitution of society without government." Most anarchists accepted this political view, but there was no general agreement among them in regard to economic and social views. Some desired an absolute freedom for the individual in all his relations, while others advocated a society based upon a cooperative organization of production. Bakunin supported the latter view. After the expulsion of Bakunin from the Second International, anarchists remained outside socialism as an organized movement.
[12] In 1891 the Social Democratic party adopted a Marxian program, known as the Erfurt program.

In France socialism became a political force somewhat later than in Germany. Although Jules Guesde founded a socialist party in 1879, it was some years before the first socialists entered the Chamber of Deputies. In the decade of the nineties there were no less than five French socialist parties, the most important of which was the Independent Socialist party, founded in 1893 by Jean Jaurès. Finally in 1905 the two major ones coalesced, with the result that fifty-two socialist members were elected to the Chamber of Deputies in 1906. By 1914 the number had grown to one hundred and two.

Meanwhile, parties had also been organized in other countries. In 1884 a group of London intellectuals founded the Fabian Society for the purpose of promoting the spread of socialist ideas. The Fabians did not try to form a political party, nor was their platform basically Marxian. In fact, they rejected the Marxian dogmas of class war, revolution, and the dictatorship of the proletariat. Their purpose was to achieve social reforms by parliamentary means. Notable members of this society were George Bernard Shaw and, later, H. G. Wells. In the same year as the Fabian Society there was founded the Social Democratic Federation, which was superseded by the Independent Labor party in 1893. Primarily a political organization, the latter party also advocated socialism through parliamentary action. In 1900 English socialism assumed political importance when two socialist members were elected to the House of Commons; a decade later the number rose to forty-two. After 1880 parties were also organized in Italy, Russia, Hungary, Switzerland, Holland, Belgium, Sweden, and other European countries. Before long Marxian slogans and Marxian doctrines were heard in almost every manufacturing center of Europe. In the early decades of the twentieth century Marxian principles were to inspire the Russian Revolution and were also to undermine the influence of Confucius among large sections of the population of China.

Nor was international socialism dead during this period. It had suffered only a brief eclipse after the collapse of the First International. In 1889 the Second International was organized at Paris amidst a "hubbub" of conflicting opinions. Actually it was a loose federation of national parties rather than an international association in the true sense of the word. Besides the national differences, there was also a division of opinion in regard to the means that were to be employed and the ends that were to be gained. While the so-called Left Wing adhered to the idea of violent revolution and the dictatorship of the proletariat, the Right Wing revised the Marxian doctrine on these points. The members of the Right Wing, known as Revisionists, were ready to compromise with the liberal democratic parties in order to gain legislation which would improve the condition of the working classes within the framework of existing institutions. This policy of reform, as opposed to the policy of revolution, led to rifts within the various national groups, thus greatly weakening the cause of socialism. When the First World War broke out in 1914, the Second International foundered on the rock of nationalism. The loyalty of the constituent groups to the national state proved much stronger than their loyalty to international socialism. Not only the German socialists but the other national groups, including the French, English, and Belgian, gave their support to their respective governments. In demonstrating that national interests took precedence over socialist dogma, those who cooperated did much to disarm hostile opposition to socialism.

CHAPTER SIX

The Age of Romanticism

THE MEANING OF ROMANTICISM I N the history of thought, literature, and the fine arts the first half of the nineteenth century is often
called the Age of Romanticism. There were, to be sure, other powerful
influences at work, but romanticism was the dominant one, at least in
literature and the fine arts. Since it represented a multiplicity of divergent, in some instances even conflicting, forces, the term has come to
be used in a very general sense. There appears to be agreement on one
point only, namely, that the existence of romanticism is an historical
fact. Studying the inner history of the movement rather than its outward forms is the only way by which one can arrive at some understanding of its meaning and importance.

In a broad sense romanticism was a reaction against the forms and
conventions of the eighteenth century, more particularly as they were
prescribed by the philosophy of the Enlightenment and the aesthetics of
neoclassicism. The Enlightenment told the people exactly how to think,
feel, and behave; and the canons of neoclassicism set down hard and
fast rules which the poet, playwright, or artist must observe if he would
succeed in producing a perfect composition. Keats said of the neoclassical poets that they

> were closely wed
> To musty laws lined out with wretched rule
> And compass vile: so that ye taught a school
> Of dolts to smooth, inlay, and clip, and fit,
> Till, like the certain wands of Jacob's wit,
> Their verses tallied.

The general result was that rules, formulas, and conventions reigned
supreme in literature, in the fine arts, and in society generally. Romanti-

cism represents a revolt against classical restraint, intellectual discipline, and artificial standards. The new movement did not, of course, oppose everything for which the past had stood. Since literary romanticism, for example, proceeded from neoclassicism, the two have much in common. A writer or an artist is never exclusively romantic or exclusively classical. Pope was not wholly unromantic, and Wordsworth was not entirely free of classicism. This accounts for the fact that much has been written about the classicism of the romanticists and the romanticism of the classicists. The difference between romanticism and neoclassicism is, accordingly, largely a matter of emphasis.

One of the major differences is that romanticism emphasized feeling and imagination while the Enlightenment and neoclassicism stressed the importance of reason. During the Age of Reason both feeling and imagination were kept under the close restraint of taste and decorum. A cultured person was compelled by good taste to check his feelings and imagination as "something plebeian and uncultured." Matthew Prior has aptly described such people as

> Without Love, Hatred, Joy or Fear,
>   They led — a kind of — as it were:
> Nor Wish'd, nor Car'd, nor Laugh'd, nor Cry'd:
>   And so they liv'd; and so they dy'd.

Lord Chesterfield told his son that he had not laughed since he had the use of his reason. It is reported that Fontenelle never laughed, ran, or wept. The same restraint that was exercised in polite society held true also in literature and the fine arts; only such sentiments were permitted as could be suitably displayed in a drawing room.

Against the hampering restrictions of reason the romanticists asserted the rights of feeling and imagination. Feeling, they said, is more important than reason. "The heart," Novalis stated, "is the key to the world," or, as Goethe put it, "Feeling is everything." Mme. de Staël asserted that feeling far surpasses reason as a means of arriving at the truth, and Lamartine stated that man is really himself only "under the stress of powerful feeling." Man must, therefore, discard artificial standards in the expression of feelings and follow the promptings of the heart. In the words of one literary historian, "It now became reasonable to be irrational, and conventional to flout convention." At the same time imagination, which had been discredited by Locke's empiricism and held in check by the neoclassical temper, was freed from its shackles. Believing that genius must be untrammeled, the romanticist followed his imagination wherever it led him. Thus it may be said that if a work of literature or art exhibits the sovereignty of reason, with measure, harmony, and symmetry in its representation, it may be called classical; if, on the other hand, it is characterized by the dominance of feeling and imagination it may be styled romantic.

Since feeling and imagination differ in each person, romanticism necessarily involves the accentuation of the personal or individual. This has led some critics to style romanticism as "the liberation of personality" or "the emancipation of the ego." The general tendency of the Age of Reason in every domain had been toward a standardization which prescribed the avoidance of local variations and individual diversities. The individual was subordinated to the general or universal. The rules of the neoclassicists, for example, demanded that the subject matter of literature be limited to that which is universal in human experience. In contradistinction, romanticism emphasized the particular, the personal. It ceased to be contrary to good taste to exploit one's own personality; in fact, it became the object to produce literature and art which should be the peculiar expression of one's self. This accentuation of the individual was the artistic equivalent of the individualist political thought that expressed itself in the struggle for democratic principles, and more particularly in the demand for personal freedom.

Accentuation of the personal accounts for the diversity of subjects treated in romantic literature and art. Reacting against the rules and conventionalities of the preceding age, the various romanticists let their imaginations roam far and wide. The novel, the improbable was more interesting to them than the probable. Among their various interests were the primitive, the grotesque, the supernatural, the infinite, the exotic, the medieval, the pastoral, the startling — anything, in fact, that was different.

The origins of romanticism can quite obviously be traced to no one figure and to no one specific movement. Stirrings are to be seen in various religious movements of the late seventeenth and early eighteenth centuries. In both the Roman Catholic and the Protestant churches religious feeling had given way to a mere acceptance of certain dogmas and an unquestioning obedience to ecclesiastical authority. As this external churchism increased, religion gradually became as cold in its formality as was the literature of the time. In Protestant Germany the reaction against arid dogmatism and ecclesiasticism appeared in the form of Pietism, which stressed the inner spirit rather than outward conformity, setting a high value on that emotional exaltation which is the hallmark of romanticism. Reason it belittled as presumptuous and misleading. Pietists also strongly asserted the value and dignity of the individual human soul, with emphasis on God's love for the individual rather than for mankind as a whole. According to Pietist teachings a mystical union of the soul with God was the deepest experience a person could seek.

An even clearer protest against the Age of Reason was voiced in England by the Quakers, Baptists, and Methodists. Most widespread in its influence was Methodism, which was in a sense an offspring of Pietism. Although John Wesley's conversion to "the religion of the heart" was due to a number of influences, the determining impulse came from his association with a group of Moravian Brethren in London. The Methodist movement which resulted from this conversion rekindled again, after a period of religious apathy, a sense of religious ardor and enthusiasm in England. It brought the feelings once more into repute. Methodist preachers proclaimed their message with such fervent enthusiasm that outbreaks of collective hysteria often resulted. The hymns of Methodism were also of a high emotional character; much, for example, was made of the "rapturous joy of salvation," as in the hymn,

> O the rapturous height
> Of the holy delight
> Which I felt in the life-giving blood!

The Wesleys also sounded a deep personal note by stressing God's interest in every human being, as contrasted with the Calvinistic doctrine that only a limited number are to be saved. They preached redemption for every individual:

> Let every soul be Jesus' guest;
> Ye need not one be left behind.

They stressed the supreme value of the individual soul, its preciousness in the sight of God. As the opening line of Charles Wesley's most famous hymn phrases it, "Jesus, Lover of my soul." Thus, popular religion helped to feed the stream of sentimentalism and individualism that was to flow into literature and the fine arts.

In the Roman Catholic fold the wider reaction did not come until after the goddess of reason had been enthroned in the cathedral of Notre Dame in 1793 and had been found wanting. It was Chateaubriand's *Le Génie du Christianisme* (*The Spirit of Christianity*), published in four volumes in 1802, which heralded the advent of a sentimental Catholicism. Chateaubriand's conception of Christianity was the reverse of that held by the eighteenth-century rationalists. The religion which they saw simply as a collection of theological dogmas, he saw as a living creed, an aesthetic force. Whereas Voltaire had declared Christianity to be ridiculous, Chateaubriand sought to show that it was sublime. He told his readers that even though they might have doubts about certain Christian dogmas, they might at least admire the sublimity of Christianity and seek in it satisfaction for their religious emotions. Written in a language of great charm and dignity, *Le Génie du Christianisme* was, as it were, the vindication of the rights of religious sentiment after an age of skepticism and unbelief. How much it did to reestablish the popularity of religion in France, particularly in the salons where it had been frowned upon, can be seen from such statements as that of Madame Hamelin, who wrote, "What! Is that Christianity! Why, Christianity is perfectly delightful!"

TRENDS WITHIN ROMANTICISM

Although romanticism left no area of life untouched, it found its widest expression in literature. One of the major trends was a "return to nature" as a means of escape from civilized life. This idea was not original with the romanticists. Poets and philosophers since the dawn of civilization had been writing about the beauties of nature and the happiness to be derived from communion with it. Earlier neoclassicists had, it is true, showed a decided preference for city life as contrasted with life in the country. "When a man is tired of London," Dr. Johnson said, "he is tired of life." Life in the country, without society, without coffeehouses, without news, they regarded as dreary and monotonous. Isabella in Dryden's *The Wild Gallant* speaks the general sentiment, "I cannot abide to be in the country, like a wild beast in the wilderness." But in the eighteenth century, as the feeling spread that man had gotten too far from nature, the back-to-nature movement became an important element in the works even of the neoclassicists. The nature, however, to which they would return was thoroughly subordinate to human needs, a nature conditioned by man. Their interest was confined to French, English, and Italian gardens with their formal designs, well-rolled walks, rose arbors, and clipped hedges. It was, as Cowper put it,

> Nature in her cultivated trim
> Dressed to his taste.

The romanticists' love of nature was not for the familiar and the cultivated, but for the wild and the primitive. What interested them, above all, were the spiritual potencies of nature. They looked back longingly from the vexations of civilization to an imaginary primeval innocence, a state in which man was happy and virtuous. As a contrast to the "degenerate" men of their age, they transformed primitive man into the good child of nature. He was supremely happy because he obeyed only the pure impulses implanted in him by nature. For the romanticists this primitive state became the new ethical and social standard. They would cultivate not only the simplicity but the native instincts and emotional qualities of primitive man.

Among the primitive peoples whom they specifically idealized were the American Indians, the natives of Africa, and the South Sea Islanders. The theories evolved about them by the sedentary romanticists were not wholly products of the imagination. To some extent they were based on the reports of explorers who extolled the virtues of the untutored savage. Although the Age of Reason gave little encouragement to the belief in the essential goodness of man, the second half of the eighteenth century saw a new crop of stories depicting primitive life in glowing colors. During this period many expeditions, among them those of Captain Cook to Australia and New Zealand, went out to discover or rediscover various parts of the earth inhabited by primitive races. In the reports of the members of these expeditions there were many accounts of the happy, carefree life of splendid races of savages. Lord Edward FitzGerald, for example, reported from New Brunswick in 1788, "Savages have all the real happiness of life, without any of those inconveniences, or ridiculous obstacles to it, which custom has introduced among us. . . . I have seen human nature under almost all its forms, but the wilder it is, the more virtuous." Romanticists were not slow to make the most of such reports. A play entitled *The Indians,* which appeared in London in 1790, has Ononthio, a venerable Indian chieftain, say, "Away with your culture and refinement! . . . Enjoy the freedom and simplicity of nature. Be guileless! Be an Indian!"

Another phase of the "return to nature" is seen in the exaltation in literature of the life and joys of the common people. Great literature had seldom been concerned with the life of the ordinary man. Even Shakespeare had chosen kings, heroes, and conquerors as his prominent characters. The apostle of reason regarded the masses as inferior to the cultured classes because they were led by their emotions. Voltaire, for example, referred to the common people as the "vile canaille" and Prévost regarded them as too stupid to be depicted in literature. To the romanticists, however, the lowly classes, like primitive man, were a repository of goodness because they had been far less exposed to the corruptions of culture and civilization than the other classes.[1] In fiction and drama princes and princesses were banished, and their places filled with plain men and women.

A direct consequence of the exaltation of the common folk was that folk poetry came to be regarded by some romanticists as the only true poetry because it was the spontaneous expression of the natural impulses of man. For the same reason, legend and myth were also held in high regard. Numerous poets, particularly in Germany, were in-

[1] The enthusiasm for the lowly classes resulted in more than sentimental literature. It also played a part in the launching of various humanitarian movements. The romantic current, for example, which caused the Negro to be regarded as a noble savage was a powerful factor in antislavery propaganda.

spired to write in the manner of the folk song, so that much of the lyric poetry of the period is characterized by spontaneity, directness, and simplicity. Another result was the collecting of folk poetry, folk tales, and fairy tales. Among the earliest of the collections were Percy's *Reliques of Ancient English Poetry* (1765) and Herder's *Volkslieder* (1778–1779). In 1812 the Grimm brothers published their incomparable collection of folk and fairy tales.

A further expression of romanticism was the cult of the Middle Ages. Like the worship of the primitive it was a reaction against the Age of Reason. The rationalists had regarded the medieval period with disdain; it was to them the Dark Ages, a period of barbarism and superstition, a gap in the history of culture. Hume, for example, in his *History of England* (1754–1762) treated the period with studied contempt. Furthermore, while such great writers of the age of Louis XIV as Molière, Racine, and Corneille had simply ignored the period, Voltaire stated that the early Middle Ages were as little worthy of study as the doings of wolves and bears. Many romanticists, on the other hand, went to the opposite extreme. For them the Middle Ages were, so to speak, the Golden Age. There they saw more justice, more happiness, more variety, more color, more romance, and more adventure. This side of romanticism became prominent in Germany and England earlier than in France. Novalis (whose real name was Friedrich von Hardenberg) and other German romanticists praised the Middle Ages as the age of spiritual unity, of profound humanitarianism, of joy in poverty. In England the poems and novels of Sir Walter Scott shed a glamour on the period. The cult did not start in France until after the Restoration, but it was there that medievalism became almost a mania. Young men wore their hair long à la Charlemagne, grew beards à la Barbarossa, and sought to organize companies to revive the tournament. For the ladies, headdresses à la St. Louis and jewelry in the medieval style became fashionable. Masked balls were staged in medieval dress, and plays, operas, and novels were built around medieval subjects.

Although much has been made of the romanticists' "return to the Middle Ages," it was not actually a return. The medievalism they tried to revive had never existed. Their purpose in singing the praises of the period was not so much to depict it as it really was, but to escape from the hard realities of the present. Therefore they imagined a dreamland of feudal towers and visored knights, a world in which the strong protected the weak, and all women were gentle and all men chivalrous. Nothing, for example, could be more misleading than Scott's portrayal of certain phases of medieval life. There was, however, another side to the interest in the Middle Ages. Certain historians of the period did open the way for a genuine appreciation of medieval civilization by protesting against its neglect and by advocating a calm, fair-minded, and sympathetic approach. "If the past is approached in this way," Herder wrote, "our age will soon open its eyes. We will learn to appreciate periods we now despise."

LITERARY ROMANTICISM

Literary romanticism reached its greatest development during the first half of the nineteenth century. It was Rousseau in France during the eighteenth century who was able to combine the many wisps of romantic feeling, of individualism, and of subjective appreciation of nature into a highly influential theory. The romantic movement as such may be said to have started with his *New Héloise*. Having voiced his sentimental love of nature in this book, Rousseau proceeded to sentimentalize educational theory in *Émile,* theology in the *Savoyard Vicar,* and politics in the *Social Contract*. After Rousseau the progress of romanticism in France was checked by the French Revolution, which found its spiritual home largely in the republics of Greece and Rome.

During the last decades of the eighteenth century and the first years of the nineteenth the main current of romanticism is to be found in Germany. The father of German romanticism was Johann Gottfried Herder (1744–1803), who expressed a high estimation of the irrational, the spontaneous, the natural, and the individual, as well as of the Middle Ages and of folk poetry, which latter he regarded as "the true expression of feeling." Among those who came under his influence was a group of writers of the movement known as *Sturm und Drang* (Storm and Stress). The literature this group produced is characterized by its glorification of unbridled individualism. Some of its outstanding literary works are Goethe's *Goetz von Berlichingen* (1773), a drama in which a robber knight of the sixteenth century is idealized as the champion of individual freedom; his *Sorrows of Werther* (1774), a morbidly sentimental novel in which the hero commits suicide as a protest against socially controlled love; and Schiller's *The Robbers* (1781), a drama which breathes defiance to authority. After writing these works, both Goethe and Schiller reverted to classicism, leaving romanticism to such lesser figures as August and Friedrich Schlegel, Tieck, Novalis, Fichte, and Schleiermacher. It is to this group that the name "Romantic School" is generally applied. Probably the most important characteristic of these writers is their extravagant glorification of the Middle Ages. Feudalism, chivalry, the crusades, and medieval folk songs were all tinted with a romantic hue.

Not until the early decades of the nineteenth century did the romantic spirit finally triumph in France. The writer who played a prominent part in establishing the French movement was Chateaubriand (1768–1848). His *Génie du Christianisme* was instrumental in reviving interest not only in Christianity but also in an idealized Middle Ages. In *Atala*,[2] *René*, and *Les Natchez*, three tales inspired by his travels in North America, he glorified nature and pictured the American Indian as a "noble savage."

The greatest name in the French movement is Victor Hugo (1802–1885). He carried the romantic tradition of Chateaubriand to its loftiest heights. Until 1827 Hugo was neither decisively a classicist nor a romanticist, but in that year he published *Cromwell*, his first drama, in the preface of which he repudiated the traditions of neoclassicism and embraced all the romantic ideas and aspirations which had been current since the beginning of the century. He at once became the leader of the movement. When opponents ridiculed his drama by stating that only a playwright who adheres to the rules of neoclassicism can produce a dramatic masterpiece, Hugo's answer was *Hernani* (1830), his most famous drama. This play made romanticism the vogue for years to come. In 1831 he published the novel *Notre Dame de Paris* (*The Hunchback of Notre Dame*), which is probably the most successful single work of the period. The intensity of its emotional reconstruction of medieval life stirred men's hearts to the depths. Of Hugo's works this and his later *Les Misérables* are probably the best known outside France.

Meanwhile the movement had also been running its course in England. There was a romantic tone to Gray's "Elegy Written in a Country Churchyard" (1751), Percy's *Reliques* (1765), and Macpherson's *Ossian* (1760–1763), but romanticism did not become the dominant trend until the nineteenth century. English romanticism was neither so intense nor so comprehensive as its counterparts in France and Germany. Its triumphs were largely restricted to poetry. The drama of the period is scanty and feeble, and in the novel the outstanding figure is Sir Walter Scott. Even in poetry the new spirit was more evolutionary than revolutionary. Nevertheless, English romanticism is an expression of the same desire for freedom from the restraining forces of reason, the same assertion of the rights of feeling and imagination, the same interest in unspoiled nature that characterized the romantic literature of France and Germany.

The beginning of the age of romanticism in England is usually dated from the publication in 1798 of *Lyrical Ballads*, a collection of poems by William Wordsworth (1770–1850) and Samuel Taylor Coleridge (1772–1834). In his preface to the second edition (1800) Wordsworth

---

[2] As an idealized picture of the American Indian, *Atala* is the forerunner of James Fenimore Cooper's *Leatherstocking Tales*.

set forth his ideas of poetry. As to subject, his purpose was "to choose incidents and situations from common life." "Humble and rustic life was generally chosen," he wrote, "because in that condition the essential passions of the heart find a better soil in which they can attain their maturity, are under less restraint, and speak a plainer and more emphatic language." Regarding style, Wordsworth declared that the language of poetry ought to be "the language really used by men." This was a protest against the practice, common among poets of the preceding periods, of referring to things by circumlocution rather than by their ordinary names. Thus a deer was "the sportive tenant of the spicy lawn," or a hen "the tame villatic fowl." When Coleridge joined with Wordsworth in producing *Lyrical Ballads*, it was decided that he would give reality to the unreal, the supernatural, and the fantastic. The fruit of this idea was "The Rime of the Ancient Mariner" which thrills with its images of horror and supernatural beauty.

Another member of the romantic school was George Gordon, Lord Byron (1788–1824). Although an avowed admirer of the neoclassicist, he was more dependent on romantic material than any contemporary writer. His paramount interest was his own passions and sorrows, an interest which bulks so large that his poetry has been styled "the memorial of the imperious and colossal egotism." Byron's turbulent soul found relief in the wilder aspects of nature, more particularly in mountain peaks and the sea.

> Are not the mountains, waves, and skies, a part
> Of me and of my soul, as I of them?
> Is not the love of these deep in my heart
> With a pure passion? Should I not contemn
> All objects, if compared with these.

Byron early won fame with the first two cantos of *Childe Harold* (1812). For some years he continued to write poetry, including the remaining two cantos of *Childe Harold* and also *Don Juan* (1819), which ranks as one of the great satirical poems in English. But he longed to be in the thick of the fray where liberty was waging war against autocracy. In 1824 he went as a volunteer to aid the Greeks in their struggle for independence, and while drilling troops at Missolonghi he contracted a fever and died.

Percy Bysshe Shelley (1792–1822) is in some respects the greatest of English lyric poets. Two passions, those for nature and for humanity, characterize almost everything he wrote. *Prometheus Unbound* is a magnificent drama of the generation of humanity, with Prometheus symbolizing man. For Shelley as for Wordsworth nature is the incarnation of the divine. Some of the best examples of his nature poetry are "The Cloud," "To a Skylark," and "Ode to the West Wind." In 1822, at the height of his powers, he drowned in the gulf of Spezzia off the northwest coast of Italy.

The last of the eager band which set itself to rescue English poetry from the artificiality of neoclassicism was John Keats (1795–1821). Up to the age of twenty he gave little promise of poetic greatness, but when he died of tuberculosis five years later he left behind him poetry which ranks with the greatest in the language. The keynote of his work is to be found in the opening line of *Endymion* (1818), "A thing of beauty is a joy forever." With the supreme sensitiveness of his imagination he caught up the beauty about him, "as a lake takes color and shadows from the sky," and crystallized it in his verses. His longer poems tend to fatigue the eye with their luxuriant wealth of imagery, but his odes are among the imperishable things of English verse. Of these, "To a Nightingale" is by many regarded as his masterpiece. "No one else in English poetry save Shakespeare," Matthew Arnold said, "has in expression quite the fascinating felicity of Keats, his perfection of loveliness."

Romantic trends also manifested themselves in Spain, Russia, and Italy, but in none of these countries did they have any real vitality. The most important aspect of Spanish romanticism was the revival of Spain's past. Perhaps the only genuine romanticist in Russia was Lermontov (1814–1841), generally regarded as being, next to Pushkin, the greatest Russian poet of the nineteenth century. His most important poetical work was *The Demon* (1838), an epic of which a portion was set to music by Rubinstein. He was also a novelist, who in *A Hero of Our Times* (1839) wrote one of the great prose works of Russian literature. In Italy classicism was more strongly entrenched than in the other countries, for the Italians were always conscious of being the heirs of the ancient Romans. All that romanticism was able to achieve was the liberation of classicism from some of its more conventional restrictions. The chief figure was Alessandro Manzone (1785–1873), a poet, novelist, and dramatist who represented a movement that was above all religious. In a spirit akin to that of Chateaubriand he stressed the sublimity of Christianity. His "Sacred Hymns" are among the most beautiful lyrics ever offered to Christianity; and his *I Promessi Sposi* (The Betrothed), with its portrayal of feudal Italy crushed by foreign oppression, is the best prose work of Italian romanticism. The latter has been translated into almost every language of the civilized world.

ROMANTICISM IN ARCHITECTURE AND PAINTING

In architecture the romantic tendency manifested itself by a revival of the Gothic style. During the early part of the eighteenth century the name "Gothic," whether applied to architecture or to literature, was a term of disparagement, even of contempt. It was most commonly used as a synonym for "barbarous." But as the eighteenth century advanced, a reversal of valuation took place. The term "Gothic" gradually ceased to be one of reproach and became one of admiration. In England, where there had been a limited survival of Gothic, Horace Walpole heralded the revival about the middle of the century by his *Castle of Otranto* and by the neogothic architecture of his house, Strawberry Hill. In Germany several decades later, Goethe hailed Gothic architecture in *Von deutscher Baukunst* (1773) as being at once the glory and peculiar expression of the Germanic spirit. The real revival did not come until after 1820, when medievalism was in the air of all Europe. By this time literary romanticists had painted the medieval period in roseate hues, and some, like Friedrich Schlegel and Chateaubriand, had sung the beauties of Gothic architecture.

Like the literary and musical romanticists, the romantic architects desired their work to be "expressive," that is, to express certain emotions; and for this, Gothic appeared to be more appropriate than other styles. In France the new enthusiasm expressed itself at first not so much in the erection of new buildings as in the restoration of medieval structures. The Gothic structural theories, which were revised and developed by Viollet-le-Duc, were applied only later in the nineteenth century. In Germany, too, there was considerable restoration and reconstruction, the new buildings in a pure Gothic style being limited to a few churches. It was in England, however, that the Gothic revival had the greatest effect. Its most important landmark is the group of Parliament buildings in London, constructed after the Old Westminster Palace had burned down in 1834. In the succeeding period the Victorian Gothic became supreme. Not only churches and houses but also railroad stations and hotels were built in this manner.

In the meantime, the spirit of romanticism had also asserted itself in painting. In neoclassical painting, as in neoclassical poetry, the classical ideal had been replaced by hard and fast rules which restricted emotional expression and the scope of the imagination. The romantic painter, however, accentuated spontaneity rather than restraint. For him the beauty was not in the subject matter, harmony, or unity, but in depth of feeling. He demanded freedom not only in his choice of subject but also in his way of treating it. He expressed his own personality in his art instead of endeavoring to realize an extraneous and impersonal ideal. Although romanticism in painting first became a definitely self-conscious movement in France during the third decade of the nineteenth century, it had an important precursor in Goya (1746–1828), the Spanish artist. Spanish life in all its picturesque diversity was his subject, with each individual work reflecting a personal reaction.

Although the romantic element is prominent in Goya's art, he did not become the leader of the new movement. The leadership fell to two Frenchmen, Theodore Géricault (1791–1824) and Eugène Delacroix (1799–1863). Géricault's work, though still marked by considerable classic reserve, is the expression of his personal feelings. He always gave first place to his "story" and in telling it made full use of its dramatic possibilities. His first important pictures, painted in 1812 and the succeeding years, recorded various phases of the end of the Napoleonic epic, as, for example, *Wounded Soldiers in a Cart* and *The Return from Russia*. But his best historical work is *The Raft of the Medusa* (1818), now in the Louvre. The picture was exhibited in the salon of 1819 and immediately evoked much criticism from neoclassicists, who denounced both the subject and the treatment. Thus began the struggle between these two schools of painting in France. The picture itself is, according to a modern critic, "a masterpiece of dramatic vigor and vivid characterization, of wide and deep human interest."

The greatest painter of the romantic school was Eugène Delacroix, who brought to the dull and stiff painting of the period "a trumpet flourish of color and freedom of line." To find his equal as a colorist one must go back to Rubens and the great Venetian painters. Considerably bolder than Géricault, Delacroix freed himself more completely from the conventional rules and types of painting. In choosing his subjects he permitted his imagination to roam up and down the vistas of history. He was particularly fascinated by the Middle Ages, as can be seen from his *Entrance of the Crusaders into Constantinople* and *Templars Carrying Off Rowena*, which last is based on Scott's *Ivanhoe*. He also came under the spell of the Orient, which enchanted so many of the romanticists. Above all, he sought to depict the spirit of his age, particularly its passion for liberty, as for example in *Liberty Leading the People* inspired by the Revolution of 1830. Hence he has justly been styled "the painter of the soul of his age." The picture which caused the greatest sensation was his *Massacre of Scio* (1824), which represents scenes from the massacre on the island of Chios, an episode in the Greek struggle for freedom from Turkish rule. Its appearance immediately evoked a tirade of abuse from the neoclassicists, Baron Gros exclaiming, "It is the massacre of painting." On the other hand, this bold plea for liberty on behalf of both Greeks and painters won him much applause and made him the leader of the Romantic School of painting.

ROMANTICISM IN MUSIC

The characteristics of musical romanticism were basically those of literary romanticism. Both proceeded from, and in some respects repre-

sented a reaction to, classicism. In classical music, as in classical literature, beauty of form was the primary aim, everything else being secondary. Emotional content was carefully subordinated to form. The
attitude of the classical composers toward their work tended to be detached and impersonal, even craftsmanlike. The compositions of Johann
Sebastian Bach, the leading spirit of the school, are "monuments of abstract beauty, rather than messages, pleas or illustrations." Haydn and
Mozart, in their symphonies and quartets, are almost as impersonal as
Bach was in his preludes and fugues.

In romantic music, on the other hand, emotional content is first and
form is subordinate. Consequently, objectivity of expression gave way
to a subjective tendency. In other words, untrammeled self-expression
became the primary interest of the romantic composers. Each one attempted to express himself in a unique manner. One would illustrate
a poem, another would depict the moods of nature, while a third would
sing of his loves, sorrows, or desires. In any case, each composition
bears the unmistakable stamp of the composer's personality. The new
trend is already visible in Beethoven, who, although he is generally regarded as one of the greatest of the classicists, demonstrated in some
of his works how music can be the language of personal feeling and
individual passion. Among these works are the *Egmont* and *Coriolanus*
overtures, the slow movement of the *G-major Concerto,* and the later
quartets. Noteworthy also is the *Pastoral Symphony,* in which he
depicts rustic dances, shepherds' songs, and bird notes of the countryside.

The first of the composers for whom romanticism was the dominant
note is Franz Schubert (1797–1828). Probably no other great composer
worked with such ease as he. At his death he left more than eleven hundred compositions. So fertile was his mind that his only labor appears
to have been the writing down of the ideas. Every emotion, wherever it
originated, suggested to him some musical idea. All his music — symphonies and quartets as well as songs and piano pieces — is characterized by a persistent lyricism. Liszt said that when listening to Schubert's music one is impelled to exclaim, "How poetical, how beautiful,
how intensely Schubert." In larger forms he left such works as the
Unfinished Symphony and the *B-flat Trio,* but the sphere in which he
was supreme was song writing. He has rightly been styled "the father
of the song." His fund of melodies was so inexhaustible that he could
hardly find enough verses to set to music. The number of his recorded
titles is nearly 500, and he wrote no less than 144 of the melodies in
one year (1815), eight of them on one day. Among the best one might
include *Hark, Hark, the Lark; Who is Sylvia?; Am Meer; Du bist die
Ruh;* and *Heidenröslein.* Schubert died at the early age of thirty-two

after a life of such poverty that he was often unable to buy music paper. He received as little as twenty cents for some of the songs on which publishers have since grown rich.

If Schubert was the first out-and-out romanticist, Robert Schumann (1810–1856) was the first with whom the romantic ideal in music attained self-consciousness. He promoted romantic conceptions not only as a composer but also as a critic. In 1834 he assisted in founding, and for ten years edited, the *Neue Zeitschrift für Musik,* a journal which had as its principal aim the advancement of romanticism in music. To him, music was the language in which he expressed his moods, his sympathies, and his literary devotions; it was also the medium for making characterizations and portraits of his friends. Most of the works he wrote before the age of thirty were for the piano; thereafter he devoted his attention chiefly to vocal and instrumental music. His symphonies are by some regarded as the most notable contributions to this class since Beethoven.

An even more singular instance of a musician who gave to his works an intense personal flavor is Frédéric Chopin (1809–1849), the Polish pianist and composer. Schumann styled him "the boldest and proudest poetic spirit of the time." Although he composed a number of works in which he used the orchestra, and also some chamber music, he was first and last a composer for the piano. His compositions have a characteristic finesse, grace, and tenderness. In them he expressed all the ills of his soul, particularly his deep discontent with a world that appeared to him cold and discordant. Most of his work is also marked by a distinctly national spirit, voicing all the griefs of his downtrodden Poland. After spending his early life in Poland, at the age of twenty-two he left Warsaw for Paris, where he became a favorite in the circle which included Liszt, Berlioz, Balzac, and George Sand. Few outside this circle recognized his greatness at the time. The income from his concerts and compositions was so small that he had to give lessons to support himself. One critic wrote of his music, "Like the fugues of Bach, the symphonies of Beethoven, the songs of Schubert, and the music dramas of Wagner, Chopin's piano pieces touch the high-water mark in their kind."

Another outstanding figure of the age of romanticism is Felix Mendelssohn (1809–1847). A classicist by tradition, training, and taste, he is romantic in his tone painting, in his interest in picturesque detail, and in his depiction of nature. He was, as Wagner said, a landscape painter of the first order. This can be seen in the *Hebrides Overture,* which was inspired by the scenery of Scotland, more particularly by Fingal's Cave, under which title the overture is also known. Born of wealthy parents, he knew none of the poverty and deep sorrow which often inspire great music. As Goethe put it,

> Who ne'er with tears hath broken bread,
> Who never through the night's dark hours
> Sat hopeless, weeping on his bed,
> He knows ye not, ye heavenly powers.

Nevertheless, if tragic power is absent from Mendelssohn's music, he ranks high among the composers of music in a happy vein, as, for example, the overture to *A Midsummer Night's Dream.* The two completed oratorios, *Saint Paul* and *Elijah,* rising above all others that had been written in Germany since Haydn's *Creation,* awakened a new interest in this form of music. Other compositions which have remained favorites are the violin concerto, *Hymn of Praise,* and certain of the *Songs without Words* for the piano, particularly the "Spring Song" and the "Spinning Song."

The tendency to make instrumental music illustrative of definite conceptions, which manifested itself in the works of the early romanticists, advanced a step in program music.[3] The members of the program school used music as a wider medium of description or analysis. They did not stop at depicting merely a mood; they attempted actually to relate events or tell a story in music. Musical realism was advanced to the imitation of sounds connected with the theme of the composition. The crudest kinds were the imitation of birds singing, the roll of thunder, cannon firing, or the clang of bells. This idea was not new. It had already been applied in such works as Schumann's *Carnaval* and Mendelssohn's *Hebrides.* But with the members of this school it became a recognized principle. The first two important exponents were Hector Berlioz (1803–1869), the French composer, and Franz Liszt (1811–1886), the Hungarian pianist and composer. The former founded the school with his *Symphonie Fantastique* and the cantata, *The Death of Sardanapalus,* both of which are distinguished by the concreteness of their imagery, a wealth of detail, and a descriptive literalness. The first of these two works depicts the adventures of a hero who is none other than the composer himself. Thus the composition is, so to speak, an autobiography in music. Berlioz is acknowledged as one of the fathers of modern orchestration because he was one of the first composers who accurately gauged the qualities and characteristics of each individual instrument.

Liszt also stands high in the exactitude and intensity of his expression. A prolific composer, he continued for some thirty-five years to write symphonies, songs, pianoforte pieces, masses, psalms, and ora-

[3] It is called program music because the composer furnishes a preface or "program" explaining the music. Liszt defined "program" as "any preface in intelligible language added to a piece of instrumental music, by means of which the composer intends to guard the listener against a wrong poetical interpretation."

torios. His later life was spent largely in applying to instrumental music the principles he had learned from Berlioz. His work viewed as a whole is unequal. Apart from his songs, certain pianoforte pieces, and certain of the *Hungarian Rhapsodies,* his instrumental works have not achieved great popularity. A distinctive characteristic of his music is the national spirit which pervades it. As Schumann's music represents the soul of Germany, and Chopin's that of Poland, Liszt's music typifies the spirit of the Magyars. His influence on pianoforte music was great. "Above all, we owe to Listz," Saint-Saëns wrote, "the introduction on the piano of orchestral effects and of sonority, so far as these are possible on that instrument." His largest works are his *Dante* and *Faust* symphonies, in both of which he displays a strong dramatic sense.

By the middle of the century the tide had turned against literary romanticism, and a quarter century later the romantic spirit had also ceased to be the controlling force in music and painting. The spirit of romanticism did not, of course, cease to wield considerable influence in literature and the fine arts, but the movement as such had run its course. Having enlarged the emotional capacities of literature and the fine arts by its triumph over the traditional and artificial, romanticism in turn became artificial. Just as the earlier age had become tired of the regularity of classicism, so the mid-century public became weary of the grotesqueness, extravagance, and emotionalism of romanticism. A new era, characterized by analytic objectivity, by the growing dominion of science, and by an ever-increasing realism, had begun. But the romantic movement had accomplished its work; it had demolished tradition and given the world great works of literature, music, architecture, and painting. Even today its influence is still active to a greater or lesser extent in the various fields.

CHAPTER SEVEN

The Second Empire in France

THE NAPOLEONIC LEGEND W HEN Napoleon was sent to St. Helena after Waterloo, it seemed certain that an epoch had closed, that neither he nor any of his family would occupy the French throne again. But the fall of the First Empire proved to be merely the prologue to "the strange romance of the Second Empire's rise." Before four decades had passed, the Second Napoleonic Empire became an established fact. The man who established it was Louis Napoleon, nephew of the great emperor.

Few careers have been so adventurous as his. He was born in 1808 as the son of Hortense de Beauharnais, daughter of the Empress Josephine by her first marriage, and of Louis Bonaparte, king of Holland and brother of the Emperor Napoleon. After Waterloo, his mother settled in Switzerland and there Louis Napoleon, a dull-witted boy, remained until early manhood. He was carefully educated in the Napoleonic cult by his mother and early became acutely conscious of his relationship to the first Napoleon. At the age of thirteen, for example, he wrote, "Whenever I do wrong I think of the Great Man, and I seem to feel his spirit within me, urging me to keep myself worthy of the name of Napoleon." Inspired by the example of his uncle, he took a special interest in horsemanship, gymnastics, and military science, particularly artillery. In 1829 he went to Italy, where he took up arms against Austrian rule in the struggle for Italian unity. Two years later he left Italy and with his mother crossed into France; but Louis Philippe, who had not yet been a year on the throne, wanted no Bonapartes in France, so mother and son went into exile again. Since he could not stay in France, Louis Napoleon decided to make himself known to the French public by his pen. Early in 1832 he published his *Reveries Politiques,* in which he proclaimed himself a candidate for the imperial heritage. When the feeble life of the duke of Reichstadt (also known as L'Aiglon), the son of Napoleon Bonaparte, flickered out in July of the same year, Louis Napoleon became the leader of the Bonapartist cause and strengthened the conviction that he was destined to restore the Napoleonic Empire.

The time was propitious for a revival of the Bonaparte cause. When the heavy pall of Metternich's tyranny settled upon Europe and the dreams of a golden age faded, many hearts, inspired by the Napoleonic legend, turned again to the man of St. Helena. In a conscious effort to influence posterity Napoleon not only dictated a glorified account of his campaigns, but also represented himself as the unselfish friend of peace, liberty, and national rights. "I sowed liberty with both hands," he wrote, "wherever I instituted the Civil Code." He even went so far as to compare his "martyrdom" on St. Helena with the sufferings of Christ. The result was that the oppression and bloodshed of his rule were soon forgotten and he came to be regarded as "the friend and savior of his people." In France poets began to celebrate his military victories in ardent verse, and the liberal press began to weave about him a halo of divinity. He became the object of hero worship such as he had not enjoyed even in France during the period of his actual rule. The government of Louis Philippe, instead of trying to destroy this legendary ideal, fostered it as a means of strengthening its own position. On May 5, 1831, the tenth anniversary of Napoleon's death, his statue was restored to its pinnacle on the Vendome column. Steps were also taken to obtain the permission of the British government for the transfer of his remains to France, in fulfillment of his wish, "I desire that my ashes repose on the banks of the Seine in the midst of the French people whom I have loved so dearly." How this affected public opinion can be seen from a statement by Heinrich Heine, who was in Paris during these years. "Toujours lui," he wrote, "Napoleon, and Napoleon yet again! He has been the constant subject of daily discourse since his posthumous return was announced."

Louis Napoleon realized the immense possibilities latent in the legend and made the most of it. He decided in 1836 to make a bid for the crown. The plan was to win over the garrison at Strasbourg, which was known to have Bonapartist leanings, and then march victoriously to Paris. But the attempt to suborn the garrison failed and he was arrested. Louis Philippe quietly sent the pretender to America instead of prosecuting him and thereby attracting public attention to him. After several months in the New World, Louis Napoleon returned to Europe and in 1840 made a second attempt to seize the throne. With a few armed followers and a vulture to play the part of the Napoleonic eagle he landed at Boulogne, where the garrison was supposed to be friendly.

But the soldiers refused to join the "expedition to Paris" and he was arrested a second time. Now he was condemned to imprisonment for life in the fortress of Ham, situated about seventy miles north of Paris. He entered the gates of the fortress on the very same day on which the remains of the first Napoleon were laid to rest with much pomp and ceremony under the dome of the Invalides.

Even his imprisonment did not weaken Louis Napoleon's faith in his destiny. Instead of giving himself up to despair, he pursued a course of reading which did much to repair the defective education of his youth. In later years he himself often referred jestingly to his education in the "University of Ham." During his stay at Ham he also wrote a number of pamphlets, among them *The Extinction of Pauperism*, which advocated that the government settle the poor in agricultural colonies on reclaimed waste lands. This pamphlet won him so much support among the French masses that Louis Blanc paid him a visit at Ham. In 1846, while workmen were making repairs in the fortress, Louis Napoleon shaved off his moustache and whiskers, donned a wig and the garb of a mason, and then with a plank over his shoulder to conceal his face walked out of the gates unrecognized by the sentinels. He quickly crossed into Belgium and continued on to London, where he quietly awaited his hour of destiny.

Upon receiving the tidings of the February Revolution (1848) and the abdication of Louis Philippe, Louis Napoleon immediately hastened to Paris "to put himself at the disposal of the Republic," but the provisional government was not pleased at his presence and "politely" requested him to leave the country. In his absence, however, friends organized propaganda on his behalf, using the Napoleonic legend to further their purpose. The Bonapartists worked so hard that in June he was elected deputy to the National Assembly by four departments. However, he resigned his seat and cleverly chose to remain in exile. When thirteen seats were vacated in September, he was elected to no less than five of them. This time he decided to accept. His first speech before the Assembly was hesitating and bad. This turned out to be fortunate for him because it disarmed the vigilance of his foes. In the words of an American who was in Paris at the time, "They believed him a man of no mind or talent, and each party thought they could use him for their own ends."

When the time came to select candidates for the presidency, Louis Napoleon announced his candidature. As his guiding principle in the campaign he chose the maxim his mother left him as a kind of political testament, "The role of the Bonapartes is to pose as friends of everybody; they are the mediators, the conciliators." He made himself accessible to men of every political color, but by carefully keeping himself free from party entanglements steered clear of the rocks upon which so many political barks had shattered. His name spread like wildfire, particularly among the bourgeoisie, many of whom feared socialism. To them the name of Napoleon was a guarantee against social chaos; they believed that as the first Napoleon had saved France from the Jacobins, the second would save it from the socialists. To many of the bourgeoisie also the name stood for order at home and glory abroad. Even Victor Hugo lent his support by stating that "the name of Napoleon Bonaparte means order, force, and glory." "There is one name," he said, "which sums up all the memories of the past, all the hopes of the future; it is the name of Napoleon, of the man most beloved by the people." [1] As the time for the election neared, it became increasingly apparent that his only formidable competitor was General Cavaignac, whose bloody repression of the recent uprisings in Paris had made him unpopular with the working classes. Thus all the odds were in favor of the man who bore the famous name. In the election, which was held in December, 1848, the victory of Louis Napoleon was so overwhelming that even his most ardent supporters were astounded. He received no less than five million votes against a total of one million for Cavaignac.

PREPARATION FOR EMPIRE

In December, 1848, the new president took the oath of office. His appearance was not impressive. Of medium height, with a long body and short legs, he looked better on horseback than on foot. His nose was aquiline, and he had the high forehead and well-shaped head of the great emperor but lacked the latter's round, firm chin. It was to cover this "defect" that he wore the chin whisker which became known as the "imperial." His eyes were so dull and his face so inexpressive that Veuillot styled him "the eyeless sphinx." In general he was so devoid of the dash and animation characteristic of the French that scandal-mongers decided that a Dutch admiral was his real father. Despite his unimpressive personality he was not, however, the negligible figure the politicians thought him to be. Before many months had passed, they were to realize that appearances are often deceiving. In taking the oath of office the new president said of his own accord, "I shall regard as enemies of my country anyone who shall attempt by illegal means to change what France herself has established." He may have been sincere at the moment, but before many years passed he was to violate this promise. Despite his apparent acceptance of the republic, he was still obsessed with the idea of restoring the Napoleonic Empire. In mak-

[1] Later, when his personal ambitions were disappointed, he dubbed Louis Napoleon "Napoleon the Little."

ing the necessary preparations for its establishment he played his cards
with great skill.

The constitution drafted by the National Assembly limited the president's term of office to four years, immediate re-election being carefully
ruled out. Consequently it became the aim of Louis Napoleon to change
the constitution in such a way that he could continue in office at the
expiration of the four years. The attempt to bring about this change
stirred a bitter conflict between the president and the Assembly. Fear
of socialism had impelled the people to elect a conservative Assembly;
nevertheless, it contained but few Bonapartists. Of its 750 members
about two-thirds were monarchists who dreamed of the restoration of
either the Bourbon or the Orleanist line. Most of the rest were republicans, either moderate or "red." Only about seventy were sincerely attached to the Bonaparte cause. Thus Napoleon had no real party in the
Assembly, a situation which finally proved to be a distinct advantage to
him. Largely influenced by middle-class feeling, the Assembly on its
own initiative passed laws which limited the freedom of the press and
suspended the right of public meeting. In May, 1850, it also abolished
universal suffrage by passing a law which decreed that three years' residence in a district was a necessary qualification for voting. As it deprived more than three million migratory workmen and laborers, or
about one-third of the electorate, of the right of suffrage, this law excited much bitterness.

Meanwhile the president was using all the arts at his command to
win the favor of the people. He made ostentatious journeys through
the provinces, visiting especially those centers in which his supporters
were in the minority. On these tours there was much feasting and
speechmaking. In speaking to the members of the middle class he would
refer to the need of "order in the streets," and in addressing the masses
he was studiously careful to stress "the sovereignty of the people." At
the same time he was also increasing his popularity with the army by
bestowing orders and honors with a lavish hand, by staging a series
of banquets for the officers, and by distributing champagne, sausages,
and cigars to the men in the ranks. In return the troops were secretly
encouraged to shout "Vive Napoléon," and even "Vive l'Empereur,"
when he passed. Nor did he overlook the Roman Catholic Church,
which wielded great influence over the masses. Besides flattering the
clergy at every opportunity, he supported the passage of the *Loi Falloux*
(1850), named after the Minister of Public Education, which restored
control over education to the ecclesiastical authorities. As a further
means of winning support he sent a French garrison to Rome in 1849
to protect the interests of the pope. All the while, however, he was careful to repudiate the idea of a show of force with such statements as,

"The man who has been elected by six million voters carries out the will of the people and does not betray them."

By 1851 Louis Napoleon felt so certain of the support of the masses that he urged upon the Assembly the necessity of revising the constitution. When the Assembly refused, he countered with a demand for the repeal of the act limiting the right of suffrage. The Assembly's refusal to readmit to suffrage the three million citizens disfranchised in 1849 greatly strengthened the president's position by giving him the opportunity to pose as the champion of the rights of the people. All other means of keeping himself in office having failed, he decided on a coup d'état. His first step was to gather all the administrative threads into the hands of a few individuals, among them his half brother de Morny and his friend Persigny. All the arrangements were made with great secrecy and, when they were ready, carried out with extraordinary precision and skill. During the night of December 1, 1851, the prefect of police sent out his subordinates to arrest seventy-eight prominent military and civil leaders in Paris, including eighteen members of the Assembly who had led the opposition to the president's plan for extending his term of office. The morning of December 2 — it was the anniversary of Austerlitz, the most brilliant of Napoleon's victories — saw all seventy-eight behind prison bars and the streets placarded with a proclamation announcing the dissolution of the Assembly and the reestablishment of universal suffrage. It also proclaimed the advent of a new political system with the authority vested solely in the president, whose term was extended to ten years.

As a precaution against an uprising the president had stationed troops at every point of vantage in the city, but there was little excitement in Paris. The Parisians, upon reading the proclamation, shrugged their shoulders and turned to their daily tasks. Business was conducted as usual, the courts held their regular sittings, and the theaters were crowded. The next afternoon there was a feeble attempt at insurrection. A few barricades were raised, but on the 4th the uprising was decisively repressed by the troops, with a total loss on both sides of about two hundred men. Some two hundred deputies who attempted to hold a meeting were promptly dispersed, and order again prevailed in Paris. In the provinces resistance was somewhat more determined. Even there the opposition collapsed after more than twenty thousand men were imprisoned or sentenced to banishment.

On December 21 Louis Napoleon asked the nation to approve the coup d'état and to delegate to him the powers necessary to revise the constitution. Almost seven and a half million Frenchmen voted in the affirmative, less than seven hundred thousand casting negative votes. The new constitution, published in January, 1852, vested almost abso-

lute power in the president, although the government retained the name
of republic. In the president's hands were placed the supreme command
of the army and navy, the right to initiate legislation, and the right to
declare war and conclude treaties of peace, of alliance, or of commerce.
All ministers were chosen by him and were responsible solely to him. In
short, he was emperor in everything but name, and soon even the name
was accorded him. In November, 1852, nearly eight million Frenchmen
voted in favor of reviving the imperial dignity, less than a quarter million voting against it. On December 2, 1852, the fiftieth anniversary
of the coronation of the great emperor, Louis Napoleon was proclaimed
emperor of the French under the title of Napoleon III. Thus his great
desire was achieved. The Second Empire was an established fact.

CONSOLIDATION OF THE EMPIRE

The glamour of Napoleon's name, coupled with the exploitation of
the Napoleonic legend and the persistence, audacity, and skill of an
adventurer who had an unshakable faith in his destiny, had triumphed.
For the next eighteen years the nephew of the great emperor was to
rule France. The absolutist regime of Napoleon III rested mainly on
the army, but it did have the support of the majority of the nation.
The clergy were happy over their control of education, the bourgeoisie
applauded the restoration of order, the peasants blessed the name of
Napoleon as a guarantee against socialism, and even the working class
resigned itself to dreams of future utopias. There were still, of course,
opposition groups, including the royalists and the republicans, but the
government at once took steps to deprive them of all means of making
their opposition felt. The constitution had already limited the functions
of the only elected body, the Chamber of Deputies, to passing the laws
prepared by a Council of State, the members of which were appointed
by the emperor. But even the deliberations of the Chamber of Deputies
were forbidden publication except in the dry summaries published by
the presiding officer, himself nominated by the emperor.

Efforts to curb the liberal opposition to the new regime were made
soon after the establishment of the Second Empire. By executive decree
many workingmen's associations were dissolved for alleged socialism,
the use of the motto "Liberty, Equality, Fraternity" was forbidden,
and the National Guard was disbanded. The government also effectively
muzzled the press by declaring that no political or economic journal
could thenceforth be started except by permission of the proper authorities, nor could an established journal change proprietorship, management, or editorship without official sanction. Official permission was
necessary even for the publication of pictures or drawings, however in-

significant. The publication of "false" news, even though it was done in good faith, was made a misdemeanor. Any newspaper was liable to summary suspension by executive decree. In short, only such journals survived as the government decided to tolerate. Furthermore, the government broke up the republican societies, or at least drove them underground, by prohibiting all associations and meetings that were not expressly sanctioned. Even the educational system was made subservient to government interests. Not only did the officials prescribe the curricula, but they also kept a careful watch over the instruction lest liberal ideas be propagated in the classroom. Thus, with a rigidly controlled system of education and a muzzled press, all political life outside official channels was effectively paralyzed.

As emperor, it became imperative for Napoleon III to have direct heirs; hence, he began to look about for a princess to marry. Negotiations were opened for the hand, first, of a Swedish princess and then of an English princess. But he was rebuffed in both instances. Believing that further negotiations for a royal marriage would have similar results, he decided to contract a marriage which would flatter the democratic sentiments of his people. Eugénie de Montijo, the lady of his choice, though not of royal blood, was extremely beautiful. Eighteen years younger than her prospective husband, she was the daughter of one of the few Spanish nobles who had supported the cause of King Joseph Napoleon, and she had spent much of her life in France. In announcing the marriage to his ministers Napoleon III pretended to despise a royal marriage and concluded his statement with the words, "I have preferred to take a woman I love and respect rather than an unknown wife." The civil marriage took place at the Tuileries on the evening of January 29, 1853, and the next day the couple went to the cathedral of Notre Dame for the religious ceremony. They rode in the carriage especially built for the wedding of Napoleon I and Marie Louise. The emperor's choice was on the whole quite popular with the people, the general opinion being that the emperor "can tell a pretty woman when he sees one."

With the entrance of an empress into the Tuileries the imperial court began to revive the splendors of the First Empire and was soon more glittering than any other court in Europe. France began once more to set the tone of the social life of Europe and of its fashions. Many high offices were revived, and "hosts of equerries, chamberlains, aides-de-camp, secretaries, and maids of honor" were appointed. There were many state banquets and balls, either masked or fancy dress. At one of the latter in 1853 knee breeches reappeared. All court functions were regulated by a rigid etiquette, which was relaxed only on rare occasions, such as that on which a duchess performed a cancan dance. The emperor himself did not appear to enjoy most of the gaiety. He spoke very little, smiled seldom, and often yawned, leaving it to the court chamberlain to announce to the guests, "It is the emperor's wish that you amuse yourselves." So far as he was attentive to his guests it was largely to beautiful women. Extremely susceptible to feminine charms, he continued his amorous intrigues even after his marriage.

But there were vastly more important factors than the glamorous court in making the empire popular. What probably contributed more than anything else was the fact that the age was one of unprecedented material prosperity. Not that the government had in the first instance created this prosperity, but it did foster it with all the means at its command. For example, it drew up schemes for the advancement of credit and founded institutions to mobilize the capital necessary for the expansion of industry and commerce, such as the Crédit Mobilier which backed railroads and mines. As early as December, 1852, it founded the Crédit Foncier de France, a bank which advanced loans to property owners up to half of the value of their property. Moreover, the Bank of France was authorized to make loans on securities deposited with it. With the aid of such loans, in addition to those furnished by private institutions, the railroads tripled their mileage in a few years, steamship lines were founded for overseas trade, and canals were built to facilitate internal commerce. To the bourgeoisie all this meant an increased income which permitted them to live luxuriously. "Luxury and comfort," the Prussian ambassador wrote, "have reappeared as if by magic."

The prosperity was not limited to the middle class; the nation as a whole shared in it. Much poverty still existed, it is true, but the industrial expansion gave employment to many thousands who had lived on the brink of starvation. The peasant, too, reaped material benefits in that the improved means of transportation offered him access to wider markets. The emperor himself, perhaps to keep the masses, particularly the proletariat, from asserting political claims, endeavored to better their condition in many ways. Together with the empress he founded hospitals and convalescent homes for workmen, societies for the relief of the poor, homes for orphans, and centers for the distribution of free medicine. He also opened the door to future old-age pensions and sickness and accident insurance by subsidizing societies connected with these aims.

Public works inaugurated by the government also provided employment for many thousands. Fine boulevards were built and many improvements made in Marseilles, Lyons, and other cities; nowhere else, however, was the rebuilding done on so large a scale as in Paris. The first Napoleon had already been much disturbed because his capital presented such a shabby appearance, but it remained for his nephew to make it "the capital of capitals." The man chosen to supervise the work was Baron Haussmann (1809–1891), prefect of the Seine. Under his direction entire districts took on a new appearance. The work was motivated by military as well as by aesthetic and humane reasons. Open spaces were left about the palaces and other public buildings so that they could be more easily defended in case of uprisings. The narrow and crooked streets, which had been so useful to insurgents for barricades, gave way to spacious boulevards on which troops could move quickly and easily. Thenceforth it became practically impossible for insurgents to raise barricades against the troops. But the improvements did not stop here. A new water supply, a system of sewers, new bridges, and many buildings were constructed. Central markets were built, the Bois de Boulogne was transformed into one of the finest public parks of Europe, and many small parks were laid out. Foreigners came in droves to see the marvels of the new Paris, and even the Parisians applauded the work despite the fact that they and future generations had to bear the burden of debt which the changes entailed. The Parisian, says M. de la Gorce, "admired the reorganized and enlarged police service, the better organized street commissions, the macadamized roads that replaced the old pavements, the improved and developed water service, the public travel by means of the omnibuses beginning to traverse every quarter. . . . He was amazed at the interminable lines of gas jets on either side of the regular streets. . . . Even the least enthusiastic was lured into forgetting present cares in admiration of this Paris of Napoleon."

WAR IN THE CRIMEA AND ITALY

Shortly before the proclamation of the Second Empire, Louis Napoleon had sought to calm the fears of Europe generally and France in particular that the name of Napoleon stood for war and conquest. In October, 1852, he said at a public banquet in Bordeaux, "There is a fear to which I ought to reply. In a spirit of distrust people say: the Empire is war. But I say: the Empire is peace." He failed, however, to adhere to this policy. There was always before him the example of the first Napoleon. De Tocqueville said of Napoleon III, "His opinions, his theories, his maxims, even his plots are all borrowed, and from the most dangerous of models. It would be well for him if he would utterly forget all his uncle's history." But he could not forget. The memory of his uncle's victories and conquests, added to his desire to raise the prestige of his government, caused him to adopt an aggressive policy which led to a series of wars exhausting to France and disastrous to his dynasty.

The first of these was the Crimean War, which broke out in 1854. The basic cause was, in brief, the plan of Tsar Nicholas I to extend his control over the European dominions of Turkey. To this end he approached the British ambassador with the suggestion that, as Turkey was "a very sick man," it might be well to dismember the Turkish Empire. Although the tsar was willing to let Great Britain take Egypt and Crete, the British saw in Russia's plan to dominate the Dardanelles a threat to their maritime interests in the Near East. Thenceforth for a long time the preservation of the Turkish Empire was a major interest of British statesmen. Napoleon III, seeing an advantage in a British alliance, at once drew closer to Great Britain. He also had a grudge against Nicholas because the tsar, regarding him as an upstart ruler, refused to address him as "Monsieur mon frère." The immediate cause of the war was the dispute over the holy places in Palestine, which was a part of the Turkish Empire. As a pretext for a quarrel with Turkey the tsar demanded that the Greek rather than the Roman Catholic Church should have the custody of these places. When the Turks, at the suggestion of the British, adopted a conciliatory attitude, the tsar found a further pretext for a quarrel in claiming a protectorate over the Greek Church throughout the Turkish Empire on the basis of a vague clause in the treaty of Kuchuk-Kainarji (1774). After the diplomatists of England, France, Russia, Austria, and Turkey had almost exhausted themselves by their efforts to effect a peaceful settlement of the dispute, the tsar delivered an ultimatum to Turkey, and when it was rejected sent an army to occupy the Danubian principalities of Moldavia and Wallachia (later joined as Rumania). The tsar hoped that the war would be limited to Russia and Turkey, but in March, 1854, both France and England declared war on Russia and were joined by Sardinia (Piedmont) in January, 1855.

In the meantime Nicholas had decided to cross the Danube, take Silistra, and move on to Constantinople. The French and British at once began to form a military expedition for the purpose of thwarting the plan, but before this expedition reached Turkey the Turks had forced the Russians to lift the siege of Silistra and to retire across the Danube. It appeared as if the war were over, with the decision a draw; but the British public refused to be satisfied with anything less than a decisive victory. The Russian fleet was a great menace to British maritime interests as well as to Turkey. This fleet was stationed at the great naval base of Sevastopol, which occupied the most commanding position on the Black Sea. As the French government was still intent on glory and prestige, the allies decided to send the expedition which had landed in Turkey to the Crimea to capture and destroy Sevastopol and the Russian fleet. "Sevastopol delenda est" [2] became the new slogan. At the beginning of September, 1854, the combined French and English fleets of warships and transports, carrying about sixty thousand soldiers, appeared off the west coast of the Crimea and landed the soldiers unopposed about twenty-five miles north of Sevastopol. The Russians, expecting only a naval attack, had neglected the defenses on the land side, but the allied command dallied so long that they had time to strengthen their bastions. Consequently the allies, although they won a number of victories, failed to take Sevastopol that fall as they had planned. The three most famous battles were fought at the Alma River, Balaklava, and Inkermann. It was at Balaklava, a small seaport eight miles from Sevastopol, that the Light Brigade, through a misunderstanding of the orders of Lord Raglan, the British commander in chief, was ordered to charge the Russian artillery at the extremity of the valley (October 25, 1854), with disastrous results. This "drama of gallant error" became the inspiration for Tennyson's well-known poem "The Charge of the Light Brigade."

Winter, which set in earlier than usual that year, found the allies unprepared for cold weather. Both the French and the English had ordered warm clothing, foodstuffs, and drugs from home, but they were a long time arriving. In consequence the season was one of horrors. If the plight of the French was sad, that of the British was worse. Not only had their commissary become so disorganized during forty years of peace that it functioned poorly, but a violent storm which wrecked twenty-one British supply ships laden with clothing, food, and hospital stores caused an acute shortage. Most of the British troops were forced to subsist on biscuit and salt pork, and at times even that was scarce. Within a short time the summer uniforms of the men were in tatters, which exposed their limbs to the icy gales. Nor had they any shelter except wretched tents swept by an unremitting wind, or miserable caves dug in the rocky soil. Hence, disease proved far more disastrous than the guns of the Russians. Scurvy became so prevalent that in some regiments hardly a man escaped; dysentery, aggravated by the salt rations, swept the ranks; and cholera, which had already broken out before the troops landed, spread rapidly. To make matters worse, there were no hospitals to care for the sick and wounded. Dr. Hall, chief British medical officer in the Crimea, reported that such hospital tents as he possessed had "no fire to warm them, the snow drifting in every space, the floor a perfect slough." Many of the wounded had to lie on the ground until they were transported to Scutari on the Bosporus. Even such indispensable supplies as soap, castor oil, and opium deriva-

[2] Sevastopol must be destroyed.

tives were lacking for a time. The result was, as Lord Raglan himself put it, that the men died like flies. It has been calculated that four to five times as many men died from disease as were killed in battle.

By the middle of February the worst was over. Clothing, food, and medical supplies arrived in sufficient quantities. Florence Nightingale took command of the hospital system and with the help of her band of nurses and lady volunteers established order and comfort where chaos and "pestilential filth" had reigned supreme. She thereby laid the foundations of modern scientific nursing and inspired the organization of the Red Cross in 1864. Fresh troops also arrived from France and Great Britain and were reinforced by a Turkish army and men from Sardinia, so that the task of taking Sevastopol could be resumed in the spring with some promise of success. But the great fortress, gallantly and ably defended, held out until September 8, 1855, before it surrendered. Although the British still wished to continue the war after that date, France, which had done the lion's share of the fighting, was weary; and when Russia offered to make peace, the war came to an end. Just how many lives it cost has never been ascertained with any degree of accuracy. Most historians estimate the number of casualties at about a quarter million.[3]

The peace congress opened in Paris on February 25, 1856, under the presidency of Napoleon III. Only the belligerents and Austria were represented at first, but later Prussia was also asked to send delegates. Every day there were receptions, fêtes, or military reviews; at night there was usually a state dinner followed by a ball, a gala performance at the opera, or some other entertainment. Business meetings were held only every other day. After some weeks of deliberation the treaty was signed on March 30. On the whole, it made no drastic changes, nor did it levy an indemnity on Russia. As de Bourqueney remarked, "When one reads the treaty of March 30, no apparent sign reveals who is victor and who is vanquished." Only one territorial change was made: a strip of Bessarabia was detached from Russia and added to Moldavia. The principal business of the congress was its effort to check the advance of Russia into Turkey. To this end the powers guaranteed the independence and territorial integrity of the Ottoman Empire and renounced any right of intervention in its internal affairs, a stipulation aimed primarily at Russia's claim to be protector of the Greek Orthodox Christians. Furthermore, the Black Sea was neutralized. Its waters and ports were thrown open to the mercantile marine of every nation. "The maintenance and establishment upon its coasts of military-maritime arse-

---

[3] According to Arnaud (*Second Republic and Napoleon III*, p. 121) the French "lost in all nearly 100,000 dead, of whom 75,000 had been carried off by sickness." The English losses reached a total of 20,000, of whom 16,000 died of sickness; the Sardinians 2,000, nearly all of whom were victims of disease; the Turks 30,000; and the Russians 110,000.

nals" by Russia was interdicted, and no warships were to appear on it except the light vessels necessary to police the coasts Other provisions of the treaty guaranteed the self-government of Moldavia and Wallachia "under the suzerainty of Turkey" and declared the Danube open to navigation.

During the years immediately after the Congress of Paris Napoleon III was at the zenith of his career. The congress itself was in the nature of a triumph for him. Not only had he been honored in having his capital chosen as the seat of the deliberations, but he himself stood at the gathering as the most influential man in Europe. In other words, the upstart of yesterday had become the recognized arbiter in Europe. Sovereigns far and wide began to seek his favor, and distinguished visitors from many countries flocked to his court. As France itself was prosperous and generally contented, the future of the imperial family seemed secure. Popular opinion even attributed to the emperor many blessings for which he was in no way responsible. While the congress was in session the position of the dynasty was further strengthened by the birth of an heir, announced to the people with a salute of one hundred and one guns. "I am delighted to affirm," Marshal Pelissier said in a despatch from Sevastopol, "that no star ever shone so brilliantly as that of the emperor. This peace signed above the cradle of a child is a most fortunate omen." Anyone who had pointed out the smallest cloud on the horizon would have been regarded as an alarmist.

But Napoleon III was not content with his successes. Just when the French people thought he was returning to the program of "the empire is peace," he was secretly conspiring to deliver Italy from the rule of Austria. It was but natural that he should be sympathetic with Italian aspirations for independence and unity. Was not Italy the land of his ancestors? Had not his uncle greatly advanced the cause of independence, and even national unity, in Italy? Very early in life he had arrived at the conviction that it was his providential mission not only to reestablish Napoleonic rule in France but also to assure the independence of Italy. This conviction he had demonstrated as a young man by taking an active part in the struggle against Austria. At the Congress of Paris, Cavour, prime minister of Sardinia and the architect of Italian unity, played skillfully on Napoleon's sympathies. As a further means of binding him to the Italian cause he sent his cousin, the Countess Castiglione, to France "to flirt with the emperor, seduce him if necessary." This dazzling beauty was more than Napoleon could resist and for some months he remained under her spell. However, the incident which drove him completely into the Italian camp was the attempted assassination of the imperial couple by an Italian named Felice Orsini. As the emperor and the empress were driving to the opera on the night of January 14, 1858, Orsini threw a bomb which wounded 150 persons, killed ten, and demolished the imperial carriage; but both Napoleon and Eugénie escaped with a few scratches. Testimony at the trial convinced the emperor that his life would not be safe until he actively supported the Italian cause, and thus added the motive of self-preservation to the others. Soon thereafter he arranged a meeting with Cavour at Plombières, a watering place in the Vosges, for an exchange of views on the Italian question.

At Plombières, Cavour managed to extract from the emperor a promise to support the liberation of northern Italy from Austria by force of arms in return for the cession of Nice and Savoy to France. The war, which broke out in 1859, was short and bloody. On June 4 the allies defeated the Austrians at Magenta and on the 24th routed a superior Austrian force at Solferino. Suddenly, in the full tide of success, Napoleon decided to withdraw from the war. Without consulting his ally, Victor Emmanuel II of Sardinia, he requested an interview with Francis Joseph of Austria and on the eleventh of July concluded an armistice with him at Villafranca. By the terms of the treaty of Zurich Lombardy was annexed to Sardinia, but Venetia still remained under Austrian sovereignty.

Napoleon III, despite his desertion at a crucial moment, did render a notable service to the cause of Italian independence and unity, for without the help of French arms Sardinia would have been unable to lift the dead weight of Austrian rule from Lombardy. But his intervention damaged his prestige both in France and in Europe generally. In working for the establishment of a single greater Italy, a plan which involved the seizure of the lands of the pope, he outraged the views of the French clericals, theretofore his warmest supporters. Again, by suddenly withdrawing from the war he alienated those liberals who favored the cause of Italian independence. In Europe generally his sudden shift from Italy to the side of Austria lost him the trust of the powers and deprived him of his dominant place in European politics.

THE DECLINE OF THE EMPIRE

Napoleon's intervention in the affairs of Italy marks the beginning of the decline which was to end in his abdication and exile. More and more, Frenchmen began to doubt whether the taciturn man with the sphinx-like exterior really possessed the superior ability that had been ascribed to him. Ironically, the emperor himself, in trying to repair the damage his unfortunate Italian policy had done to his prestige, embarked on ventures which provoked further opposition. Among these was his policy of free trade. Ever since the time of Colbert, France had been pro-

THE SECOND EMPIRE IN FRANCE

tectionist. Napoleon I had even tried to close all French ports to British goods. Louis Napoleon, however, had as early as his imprisonment at Ham declared himself in favor of free trade. From the time he became emperor he had been carrying on negotiations with England for a commercial treaty, though the agreement finally signed in January, 1860, was not so much a free trade treaty as a general reduction of tariffs. By the Cobden Treaty, so called after Richard Cobden, the English champion of free trade, Napoleon obtained for France valuable concessions in the lowering of British duties on wines, silks, and fashion goods, as well as manufactures of all sorts, in return for opening the French markets to British goods. The result was that within a short time the French markets were swamped with English goods, and the French manufacturers were complaining loudly that their interests were being sacrificed for those of English industry. Thus, while pleasing certain sections of the French people, particularly the wine growers, the emperor had made formidable enemies among the industrial classes.

Another venture that contributed to the decline of his popularity and prestige was his Mexican expedition. When the Mexican Congress voted (1859) to suspend the payment of all foreign debts for a few years, Great Britain, France, and Spain decided in 1861 to send a joint expedition for the purpose of enforcing the claims of Mexico's European creditors. They were careful, however, to renounce all plans of conquest and all designs against the government. Accordingly Great Britain and Spain withdrew their troops from Mexico as soon as their object had been achieved, but before long it became evident that the French had other plans. To appease the clerical party at home, to please the empress, and to advance the commercial interests of France, Napoleon decided to overthrow the existing anticlerical government in Mexico, restore to the Church the lands this government had confiscated, and establish a new government under the rule of a foreign prince. The plan succeeded so well that by the middle of 1863 a Mexican assembly under the protection of the French troops offered the Mexican throne to Archduke Maximilian of Austria, brother of Emperor Francis Joseph. Maximilian, urged by his wife Carlota and by Napoleon III, accepted after a long hesitation and was maintained on the Mexican throne for several years by the French troops. But when the Civil War in the United States came to an end in 1865, the government of the United States, acting on the policy of the Monroe Doctrine, demanded the withdrawal of the French army, and enforced the request by sending a force of fifty thousand to the Rio Grande. After long negotiations Napoleon finally withdrew his troops in 1867, leaving the unfortunate Maximilian to the mercy of the Mexicans, who forthwith took him captive and executed him. Thus ended a venture which cost thousands of lives, enormous sums of money, and was a new blow to the emperor's prestige.

Meanwhile Napoleon III, feeling that he was losing the support of the Catholic and conservative elements at home, endeavored to gain the support of the liberals by a series of measures which ushered in the so-called Liberal Empire. In August, 1859, he proclaimed an amnesty for all political offenders, permitting all those who had been proscribed to return to France. Some few, including Victor Hugo, refused the amnesty, but the majority returned to swell the opposition to the imperial regime. The following year saw Napoleon introduce some constitutional changes in the direction of parliamentary government. In November, 1860, he gave the Chamber of Deputies the privilege of drawing up an address in answer to the speech from the throne. In other words, he gave the deputies the opportunity to express their opinion of the way in which the government was being conducted. Next he accorded the deputies the right to criticize the government at any time and also authorized the publication in full of the debates in the Chamber of Deputies. Two laws of the year 1868 relaxed the restrictions on the press and permitted the holding of meetings for the discussion of agricultural, industrial, scientific, and literary questions. Finally, in 1869 the ministers who conducted the government were made responsible to the Chamber of Deputies. These changes, however, served only to strengthen the opposition. As one of the deputies put it, "The emperor is providing his enemies with rods which they can use to beat him."

The emperor's response to the opposition was at last to turn the other cheek. He was definitely losing heart. The disease with which he had been afflicted for some years was probably sapping his moral as well as his physical strength and thus robbing him of the will necessary to control the course of events. When he acted at all, it was on the impulse of the moment. Meanwhile, the empress was manifesting a growing disposition to meddle in affairs of state. Having had her way in the Mexican affair, she began to interfere in other matters. Toward the end she even attended most of the meetings of the Council of Ministers, taking an active part in the discussions. Seeing the imperial structure crumbling, she decided that a bold stroke was necessary to save the throne for her son. Hence, she urged the rapidly failing emperor along the path toward war with Prussia. When the war came in 1870, it shattered the fabric of the empire at a single stroke and forced the imperial family into exile. Napoleon III died in 1873, but his wife, a pathetic figure in her later years, was to live until 1920.

Napoleon III has been variously judged by historians because he was a blend of manifold contradictions. He was at the same time an adventurer and an idealist, a selfish politician and a person of generous ideas, a daring conspirator and a vacillating victor. On the good side, his courtesy was instinctive, his sphinxlike exterior hid a benevolent soul, and his generosity to his supporters was incontestable. "One cannot know him," Queen Victoria said, "without seeing that there is much amiability and kindness in him. He is gifted with a powerful self-control, great calmness, one might even say, great gentleness." But the better qualities of the man do not condone the weaknesses of the sovereign. Since he inherited not merely the name but the ambitions of the first Napoleon, he naturally challenges comparison. Such a comparison, however, tends to dwarf Napoleon III. Cobden found him ignorant of even the ABC's of political economy; in generalship he showed himself a tyro; and for the wily statecraft of Cavour and Bismarck he was a mere plaything. As one historian has put it, he assumed the mantle of his uncle but found it very much too large for him. His chief talents were undoubtedly those of the dreamer and the conspirator. These he displayed in the plans and intrigues which procured his elevation to the throne. Thereafter his weaknesses, especially his inability to think deeply and clearly and his vacillation, tended to stand out more and more prominently, ultimately proving fatal to his rule.

FRENCH CULTURE

Louis Napoleon and Eugénie were not enthusiastic patrons of literature and the arts; if so, they might have found relief from their boredom. The reports of those who had opportunity to know both the emperor and the empress are unanimous on this point. Dr. Barthez wrote, "The emperor is not artistic. . . . He knows nothing of painting and scarcely cares for it." He was not only unmusical but had an actual aversion to music. A contemporary, who knew the empress intimately, wrote, "She was certainly intelligent; but her education had been neglected, and she cared for no intellectual employment or artistic occupation. She hated music; she had no taste for the fine arts; even a well-written play at the Théâtre Français did not amuse her." The imperial couple's deficiency is easier to understand if one remembers that most of the contemporary men of letters belonged to the political opposition.

The prevailing literary trend during the Second Empire was toward realism. Romanticism as a movement had largely spent itself by the middle of the century. Men had grown tired of the gorgeous pageants of historical romance, of vague speculations, and of poetical raptures. They longed for a return to everyday things, the concrete, and the contemporary. This, realism offered them. It has been defined as "the cult of the concrete fact," or in Gautier's words, "the exact imitation of nature as it is." The influence which probably did most to stimulate its development was the scientific spirit. Realism flourished especially in the realm of fiction, where authors began to write novels of contemporary manners in a style of supposedly impersonal and objective sincerity.

Honoré de Balzac (1799–1850) is regarded by most literary historians as the father of realism, and by many as the greatest French novelist of all time. He seized upon the new spirit engendered by science, collected a vast fund of detail from observing contemporary life, and then embodied it in his novels. Balzac was not a born writer, however. He learned his trade largely by experiment. At the age of twenty he turned his back on a legal career, rented a garret in Paris, and began to write. The ten romances he wrote for publishers of cheap books displayed so little ability that he was afterwards unwilling to have his name connected with them. The year 1830, in which he published *La Peau de Chagrin,* marks the beginning of his success. His labors during the decade which followed were little short of herculean. Sitting at his desk from twelve to eighteen hours a day without rest, he frequently did not leave his house for an entire week. Some of his best works were published during this period, among them *Eugénie Grandet* and *Le Père Goriot.* He also conceived the idea of a series of novels to present a picture of French society under the First Empire, the Restoration, and the July Monarchy, which when completed were grouped under the title *La Comédie Humaine (The Human Comedy).* Balzac was supreme in depicting the life of the middle and working classes. Love is subordinated to such other passions as envy and jealousy, and all of his characters are motivated, above all, by a desire for wealth.

The first great triumph of the realist movement was Flaubert's *Madame Bovary* (1857). This veracious study of middle-class provincial manners which is the author's masterpiece presents Emma Bovary in every detail of her life and milieu. The life of Flaubert is extraordinary in that he cared neither for honors nor wealth. No fiction writer ever stood more firmly on the motto, "Art for art's sake." He believed that since art is an end in itself, its creator must adhere to objective truth.

In art, as in literature, realism was the dominant trend during the Second Empire. The realists returned from the high coloring and careless drawing of the romanticists to landscapes and scenes from everyday life. Their first aim was not to depict the obvious, but to confer on painted objects the quality of existence and vitality. One of the clearest examples is to be found in a small group of landscape painters known as the Barbizon School. The two outstanding members of this school were Jean Baptiste Corot (1796–1875) and Jean François Millet

(1814–1875). It was Corot above all who breathed new life into landscape painting. No painter has depicted the full mystery of the morning so suggestively; nor has anyone surpassed him in expressing the charm of the twilight hour when the world turns from work to rest. At his death he left some six hundred paintings of which the best known probably is *The Dance of the Nymphs*. Millet is the great painter of the peasant life of France. His paintings, emphasizing as they do the somber and the tragic, the drudgery and the weariness of peasant life, have a strong emotional appeal. His better-known paintings include *The Gleaners, The Sowers, The Man with the Hoe, The Lot of Women,* and *The Angelus*. When asked why he restricted himself to scenes from peasant life, he answered, "To tell the truth, peasant subjects suit my nature best, for I must confess, at the risk of your taking me for a socialist, that the human side is what touches me most in art."

CHAPTER EIGHT

The Triumph of Nationalism in Italy and Germany

PREPARATIONS FOR ITALIAN UNITY АT the outbreak of the French Revolution Italy was what it had been for more than a thousand years, a patchwork of small states jealous of, if not actively hostile to, one another. Never since the days of the Roman Empire had the peninsula been effectively united under one rule. It remained for Napoleon to level the barriers of local rivalries and bring to Italy at least a good administration and an approach to political unity.[1] Moreover, he awakened in the minds of Italian patriots the conviction that the salvation of Italy lay in national unity. At St. Helena he still insisted that "Italy is one nation. The unity of manners, of language, of literature, must at some future date reunite her inhabitants under a single government."

Another half century was to pass, however, before the prophecy was fulfilled. The diplomatists who disposed of the fortunes of Europe at Vienna in 1815 made short work of Napoleonic Italy. It was divided into nine states with governments that were all reactionary and despotic. When the Congress adjourned, Italy was, in the words of Metternich, "simply a geographical expression." Almost all the princes who ruled over the Italian states were Austrian puppets: Austrian dukes ruled in Tuscany and Modena, an Austrian archduchess in Parma, and Austrian viceroys in Lombardy and Venetia. Metternich further entered into an alliance with the King of Naples and came to an understanding with the pope, which virtually put their political affairs under Austrian direction. "The baton of Metternich," Mazzini wrote, "gov-

[1] He condensed the fifteen states into three.

149

erns and directs all the petty tyrants of Italy." The only one who was not dependent on Austria was the king of Sardinia-Piedmont.

Though the diplomatists at Vienna did thus divide Italy, they did not succeed in quenching the national spirit Napoleon had roused. During the years after the Congress the desire for some kind of unity grew stronger, particularly in the south. This desire vented itself in sporadic insurrections which were promptly suppressed by Austrian soldiers. After every such uprising the Austrian government ruthlessly crushed all outward symptoms of opposition or independence. But the severity of these measures only gave sustenance to the spirit of nationalism. On the surface the Austrians continued to exercise their dominion, while underground systematic preparations were being made for the *risorgimento* (resurrection). An important factor in the agitation was the secret societies, the largest of which was the Carbonari, or Charcoal Burners. It has been estimated that by the year 1820 the membership in these societies numbered well over 100,000, drawn from all social classes. Under the watchwords "freedom and independence" the Carbonari were ceaselessly active in exciting opposition and revolution against foreign rule. But the abortive revolutions of 1820 and 1831, which they actively promoted, largely discredited them.

Another important factor in bringing about the *risorgimento* was the impassioned leadership of idealists and intellectuals. They kept the hope for an independent and united Italy alive even when their fortunes were at lowest ebb. The greatest of these, and the inspirer of most of the rest, was Giuseppe Mazzini (1805–1872). He is one of the three men to whom above all others the attainment of Italian unity was due. George Meredith, the English poet, said of them,

> Cavour, Mazzini, Garibaldi: Three:
> Her Brain, her Soul, her Sword.

Born in Genoa, Mazzini studied law as a young man and read widely in the writings of democratic thinkers. His radical leanings soon aroused the suspicion of the authorities, and in 1830 he was arrested because he was a "thinker." In explanation of the arrest the governor said to Mazzini's father, "He is gifted with talent and is too fond of walking by himself at night absorbed in thought. We don't like young people to think unless we know the subject of their thoughts." Although the authorities failed to substantiate a definite case against him, he was banished from the country upon his release. But he did not give himself up to despair. Firmly putting all personal interests aside, he thenceforth devoted himself to the cause of independence and unity. His faith in the ultimate realization of his dream inspired him to struggle on through a life filled with disaster and shattered hopes.

While he was in prison Mazzini had already resolved on the initial step. Having lost faith in Carbonarism, whose leaders were largely men of advanced years, he decided to entrust the cause of Italy to youthful minds and hands. "Place the young at the head of the insurgent masses," he said. "You do not know what strength is latent in those young bands, what magic influence the voice of the young has on the crowd; you will find in them a host of apostles for the new religion." Accordingly he organized among the Italian exiles in Marseilles a society called Young Italy (1832). Friends established the first lodge at Genoa, and from there it spread rapidly through all northern and central Italy, attracting mostly students, young professional men, and youths of the mercantile classes. Within two years the membership grew to more than fifty thousand. According to its statutes, "Young Italy is a brotherhood of Italians who believe in a Law of Progress and Duty and are convinced that Italy is destined to become one nation. They join this association in the firm intent of consecrating both thought and action to the great aim of reconstructing Italy as one important sovereign nation of free men and equals." The banner of the organization bore on one side the words "Unity and Independence" and on the reverse "Liberty, Equality, Humanity." Members undertook to disseminate the national idea regardless of sacrifices and hardships, even at the risk of their own lives. Soon the leaven of freedom and unity had permeated every part of Italy. Kindred spirits in other countries hailed the work, with the result that societies called Young Poland, Young Germany, and Young Switzerland were formed on the model of Young Italy.

Besides founding and directing the activities of Young Italy, Mazzini also exercised great influence through his writings. He wrote many fervent articles and pamphlets which, though immediately banned by the government, were smuggled into Italy in bales of merchandise and even on occasion in packets of sausages. Passed from hand to hand, they were widely read, particularly by the educated classes. Mazzini regarded the political division of Italy and of other parts of Europe as artificial. He believed that before all else the states of Europe must be remodeled to conform as far as possible to the principle of nationality. But he did not regard the nation as an end in itself; it was to him "the God-appointed instrument for the welfare of the race," the means of a wider service to humanity. Each nation has "its special mission to execute" and only as a nation can a people contribute its due quota to the general welfare of mankind. "Nationality is sacred to me," he wrote, "because I see in it the instrument of labor for the well-being and progress of all men. Countries are the workshops of humanity. A nation's life is not her own, but a force and a function in the universal scheme of things." Although the principles for which he contended were universally applicable, his more immediate concern was with his native country. The Italian people must attain freedom and unity, not for any selfish purpose but rather so that the Italian nationality could make its contribution to humanity at large. Furthermore, the new Italy must be a republic. This was not primarily because Mazzini hated tyrants but because he regarded a republic as the only form of government consistent with the dignity of a people.

Italian patriots, however, were not all of one mind as to the form of government they desired. Many shrank from Mazzini's conclusion that it must be a democratic republic. They wished a more moderate program. Among them were those who hoped to see Italy united under a limited monarchy and who therefore championed the cause of the king of Sardinia-Piedmont. A third major group was composed of those who rejected the idea of a fusion into a single state but hoped for a federation of the princely states under the presidency of the pope. In 1846 it seemed as if the aspirations of this group were about to be fulfilled when a new and liberal-minded pope ascended the throne as Pius IX. He strengthened the hopes of his followers by granting a list of liberal concessions unprecedented in modern Italy. Starting with an amnesty for political prisoners, he issued edicts removing some of the restrictions from the press, reforming the laws, relieving the Jews of some of their disabilities, conferring municipal government on Rome, and summoning an advisory council composed almost exclusively of laymen. He further increased his stature as a national hero by his hostility to Austria and by signing with Piedmont and Tuscany a customs treaty which could have been the beginning of a federal union of all Italy. But when he saw that the people would be satisfied with nothing less than a constitutional government, he began to retreat. Further reforms, he believed, would be incompatible with papal sovereignty. During the revolution of 1848, which saw the establishment of a short-lived republic in Rome and the flight of the pope to Gaeta, Pius repented of his liberalism and became a confirmed reactionary.

If the patriots differed in regard to the government of the new Italy, they were, however, at one in the conviction that unity, whatever form it might take, could be achieved only through expulsion of the Austrians. This and the attainment of political liberty were the aim of the uprisings of 1848. As early as January of that year the Sicilians rose in arms and compelled their king to grant a constitution. Some weeks later the news of the revolutions in France and Austria was the signal for a general uprising. After the Austrian garrisons were driven out of most of Lombardy and Venetia, Charles Albert of Sardinia-Piedmont initiated liberal reforms and joined in the war against the foreigner. The pressure of popular demand also forced the rulers of Tuscany,

Naples, and the Papal States to send troops. In the spring of 1848 it seemed as if the national forces would march to complete victory; but dissension soon divided them. Local jealousies and diverse political theories doomed any cordial cooperation. Naples and the Papal States withdrew their troops, and the army of Charles Albert was defeated in 1848 and again at Novara in 1849. By the summer of 1849 the Austrians were masters of the situation, and the puppet princes were creeping back to the thrones from which they had fled. The uprising had failed completely, and the achievement of independence and unity seemed farther off than ever. Nevertheless, the efforts had not been entirely in vain. While the revolutions did shatter the hopes of the republicans and of those who looked to the papacy to unite Italy, they also raised the house of Savoy in the patriots' esteem. The brave stand which Charles Albert, and after him his son, Victor Emmanuel II, made against the Austrians won many hearts. More and more the patriots began to look to the ruler of Piedmont as their natural leader. Even Gioberti, the stoutest champion of an Italian federation under the presidency of the pope, now stated, "Except the young sovereign who rules Piedmont, I see no one in Italy who can undertake our emancipation."

CAVOUR AND ITALIAN UNITY

After 1848 the building of Italian unity became essentially the task of the government of Piedmont. Victor Emmanuel, it is true, was not a statesman of the first rank, but he did possess much practical wisdom. He retained the constitution his father had granted and resolutely set himself to heal the wounds his country had suffered in the war. Above all, he had the wisdom to summon to his side a man who was to play the major role in the drama of unification, Count Camillo di Cavour (1810–1861). A Piedmontese nobleman by birth, Cavour had as a young man served for some years in the Engineers Corps of the Sardinian army but had been obliged to resign his commission in 1831 because of his liberal principles. The next decade and a half he spent managing the family estates and preparing himself for a higher service. Already an ardent advocate of constitutional government, he was often seen during his visits to England in the gallery of the House of Commons, listening raptly to the debates and studying the rules of procedure. In 1847 he took a definite political step when with several others he founded a journal called *Il Risorgimento*, devoted to securing a constitution for Piedmont. His articles in this journal exercised great influence on the king as well as on public opinion. In February, 1848, Charles Albert granted the constitution and, in June, Cavour took a seat in the parliament elected under its provisions. Two years later he was appointed

UNIFICATION OF ITALY

minister of agriculture and commerce, and in 1852 he became prime minister. From then until his death in 1861, except for two short intervals, he remained prime minister and virtual dictator of the kingdom.

Cavour at once threw himself heart and soul into the work of regenerating Piedmont and achieving Italian unity. The former he believed to be a necessary preliminary to the latter. "Piedmont," he said, "must begin by raising herself, by establishing in Europe, as well as in Italy, a position and credit equal to her ambition." Despite much opposition he made great progress in a comparatively short time. His first reforms concerned military affairs. He saw that if Piedmont were to unite Italy, it must prepare for a new war; hence, he reorganized the army, built new fortresses or strengthened old ones, and generally increased the military resources. He also gave much attention to the development of industry and commerce: he built numerous railways, made provisions to tunnel the Alps, and established a line of steamboats between Genoa and America. Furthermore, he negotiated commercial treaties with France, England, Belgium, Holland, and Switzerland. In short, he launched Piedmont on a career of rapid commercial progress. Ecclesiastical reform provoked even more opposition than his other changes. Believing that Piedmont had too many ecclesiastics, the ratio being one to every 214 inhabitants, he suppressed all religious orders that were not engaged in nursing, preaching, or public teaching. He also abolished the special privileges of the clergy and established civil marriage. In all this he was actuated by no feeling of hostility to the clergy; his motives were solely political.

Cavour saw that, although Piedmont was growing stronger, it could not expel Austria from Italy without foreign assistance. He was therefore intent upon gaining the support of one of the great powers. When the Crimean War broke out in 1854, he made the most of the opportunity by prevailing upon France and Great Britain to accept Piedmont as an ally. It was, in the words of William Roscoe Thayer, "one of the most brilliant strokes of statecraft in the nineteenth century." By sending an army to the Crimea, Piedmont established a strong claim to equality with other states, which was recognized by the admission of representatives of Piedmont to the Congress of Paris. Cavour, who personally attended the congress, improved the situation by informal discussions on the condition of Italy and by denouncing the influence and misgovernment of Austria in the peninsula. His most sympathetic listener was Napoleon III, but the latter hesitated to act because the clerical party in France was violently opposed to any step that might endanger the pope's temporal power. But the aforementioned attack on Napoleon's life by the fanatical Italian patriot Orsini bore fruit in a secret meeting of Napoleon and Cavour at Plombières in the summer of 1858. Napoleon III promised to aid in expelling the Austrians, after which the northern and central portions of Italy were to be ceded to Piedmont, while France was to be rewarded with Savoy and Nice.

It was now Cavour's task to maneuver Austria into a declaration of war. By supremely adroit, if quite unscrupulous, diplomacy he provoked Austria into insisting that Piedmont should disarm; and when the latter refused, the former declared war (April 19, 1859). The war was short and decisive. In the summer of 1859 the combined forces of France and Piedmont inflicted a severe defeat on the Austrians at Magenta (June 4) and again at Solferino (June 24). It seemed as if Austria were about to be expelled completely from Italy. Suddenly, however, Napoleon III stopped short and, without consulting his ally, concluded the armistice of Villafranca (July 8) with the Emperor Francis Joseph. By the terms of the treaty which was signed at Zurich on November 10, 1859, Lombardy was annexed to Piedmont, but Venetia remained under Austrian rule.

To Cavour the news of the armistice was a cruel blow. Just when it seemed as if his hopes for a free Italy were about to be accomplished, they were, as he believed, completely shattered. He tried to insist that Victor Emmanuel continue the fight against Austria alone, and when the king refused, Cavour resigned his premiership in a fit of rage. But the situation was not so bad as he thought, and after a retirement of a few months he returned to take up the struggle again. Stirred by the vigor of Piedmontese leadership, Tuscany, Modena, Parma, and Romagna (the northern part of the Papal States) had in the meantime revolted against their rulers and unanimously declared for union with Piedmont. While the government of Great Britain declared decidedly in favor of carrying out the wishes of these states, Napoleon III insisted that he could not permit so large an aggrandizement of Piedmont without compensation for France. Accordingly Cavour reluctantly arranged to gain Napoleon's consent by the surrender of Savoy and Nice. Victor Emmanuel then accepted the annexation of the four Italian states, and on April 2, 1860, an enlarged parliament, representing nearly half the population of the peninsula, met at Turin.

The next step was taken not by Cavour or Victor Emmanuel but by Giuseppe Garibaldi (1807–1882), the knight errant of Italian unification. Few lives of the nineteenth century were as adventurous as his. As a young man he joined the society of Young Italy and participated in an attempted insurrection at Genoa in 1833. Condemned to death, he managed to escape the country and in 1834 went to South America, where he plunged at once into several revolutionary wars. There he gained the expert knowledge of guerrilla fighting that was to serve him so well in the conquest of Sicily and Naples. When the news reached him in 1847 of the ferment in Italy, he embarked at once for his native land. The year 1848 saw him taking an active part in the short-lived Roman republic. Troops sent by Napoleon III to protect the interests of the pope drove the republicans out of the city and compelled Garibaldi to flee for his life a second time. This time he sailed for New York where, working at first as a candlemaker and later as a trading skipper, he accumulated the small fortune which enabled him in 1854 to purchase the island of Caprera off the coast of Italy and build a home.

From this island home he carefully watched the growing opposition to Bourbon rule in the kingdom of Naples. When he believed that the time was ripe for expelling the Bourbons from the southern kingdom, he collected at Genoa a thousand "Red Shirts," so called because of the color of their uniform, and in May, 1860, landed his expedition in Sicily. The opposition he met was overcome so quickly that he was master of the island in a few weeks, after which he crossed to the mainland and advanced almost unopposed on Naples. At his approach Francis II fled, and Garibaldi entered the capital amidst the joyful acclaim of the populace. After a plebiscite declared for annexation by an almost unanimous vote, Victor Emmanuel II with Garibaldi at his side rode into Naples early in November to make the annexation official. Garibaldi now felt that his work was done. Refusing all honors and rewards, he withdrew to his island.

Meanwhile the rest of the Papal States, excepting Rome and a small district around it, had also been occupied by Piedmontese troops. On February 18, 1861, the first national parliament representing the north and the south met at Turin. Amid fervent enthusiasm the united kingdom of Italy was proclaimed on March 17, and Victor Emmanuel II was officially styled "by the grace of God and the will of the nation king of Italy." The more difficult part of the work of unification was over. Only Venetia and Rome were still outside the new kingdom. Cavour was not to witness the consummation of his plans. Prematurely worn out by his strenuous labors, he died on June 6, 1861.

Before his death Cavour had urged his compatriots not to rest content until both Venetia and Rome were an integral part of the national state. "The star of Italy," he said, "is Rome; that is our polar star. The Eternal City, around which twenty-five centuries have accumulated all the glories of the world, must be the capital of Italy." In the attainment of this goal Prussia was to be an important factor. When Bismarck made ready to crush Austria in 1866 (see p. 164), he concluded an alliance with Italy, whose reward for fighting on Prussia's side was to be Venetia. The Italians were defeated by the Austrians both on land and on sea; but the Prussian victory at (Sadowa) Königgrätz (July 3, 1866) was so overwhelming that Prussia won the war, and the new kingdom of Italy received Venetia. Four years later the acquisition of Rome was made possible by the exigencies of the Franco-Prussian War. When the Prussians invaded France in 1870, Napoleon III found it necessary to withdraw from Rome the French troops which had upheld the temporal power of the pope since 1849. In July, 1871, Victor Emmanuel entered the Eternal City with the cheers of the people. In 1872 Rome was made the capital of the Italian kingdom. The dream of Cavour and the Italian patriots, which a quarter of a century earlier had provoked smiles in the diplomatic circles of Europe, was fulfilled.

THE WHETTING OF THE PRUSSIAN SWORD

The collapse of the revolutionary movement in 1849 was a great disappointment to the liberals of Germany. Little progress had been made toward the establishment of representative government and Germany still remained split into some three dozen states, the rulers of which clung tenaciously to their independent sovereignty. But some of the expectations were to rise again, and in little more than two decades a large measure of unity was to be achieved.

The driving force needed for this accomplishment came not from Austria but from Prussia. Prussia, in fact, had already taken the first step toward the practical realization of the goal in the establishment of the Zollverein or customs union which bound most of Germany outside Austria into a single commercial unit. In the eighteenth century each ruler of the some three hundred states had levied such customs and excise duties as he pleased, thereby crippling inland trade as a whole. On the Rhine, for example, there were thirty customs stations between Strasbourg and the Dutch frontier. The situation was somewhat improved by the drastic reduction of the number of states during the Napoleonic period, but there still remained thirty-nine of them and consequently thirty-nine customs boundaries. A merchant traveling from Hamburg to Austria still had to traverse ten states. Although the idea of a customs union had been discussed a number of times by the Austrian government, nothing came of the negotiations. Finally Prussia reformed its own tariffs and took up the task of constructing a Zollverein. On January 1, 1834, it went into force, and included eighteen states with a total population of more than twenty-three millions. As the term of the treaties which established it was only eight years, the Prussian government encountered some difficulties in renewing it over the opposition of Austria. Yet the Zollverein continued to function and even gained new members. Thus most of Germany was unified for purposes of trade and commerce long before political unity was achieved.

A contemporary wrote in 1840 that the Zollverein "has subdued much local feeling and habit and has replaced them by a wider and stronger element of German nationality."

A new era opened when Frederick William IV was succeeded by his brother William, first as regent in 1858 and, upon Frederick William's death in 1861, as King William I. The new king, who was already in his sixty-fourth year, had little love for liberal institutions. At his coronation he crowned himself with the words, "I receive this crown from the hands of God." His one enthusiasm was for the army. He was convinced that Prussia could reassert its claims to leadership in Germany only if it had a large army to support these claims. Like Frederick the Great he believed that "diplomacy without arms is music without instruments." To assist him in this task he chose as minister of war General von Roon (1803–1879), one of the great military organizers of the nineteenth century, and as chief of the general staff General von Moltke (1800–1891). But the liberals in the lower house of the Prussian Assembly could see no apparent use for a large army except to keep them in subjection. They believed that Prussia would sooner gain the support of the smaller German states, and with it the leadership in Germany, by adopting democratic principles of government. Although the bill which provided for a far-reaching reorganization and enlargement of the army was passed by the upper house, it was rejected by an overwhelming majority in the Chamber of Deputies. The king in his determination to carry out the reorganization dissolved the Assembly, but the new elections returned an even larger majority of liberals to the lower house. So great was William's despair over the continued opposition of the lower house that he considered abdication. Von Roon, however, felt that the situation was far from hopeless. For some years he had known and admired a man who shared his conviction that Prussia must have a strong army if it would achieve leadership. This man, he was certain, would be able to carry out the military program in spite of the opposition. The man was Bismarck.

Otto Edward Leopold von Bismarck was born on April 1, 1815, at Schönhausen in Brandenburg. His mother was a commoner, but on his father's side he came of a family of country gentry (Junker). At the age of seventeen he went to Göttingen, and later to Berlin, to study law and political science. As a student he was noted rather for his ability to consume great quantities of beer and for his readiness to engage in duels than for diligence in academic pursuits. Yet he cannot have neglected his studies entirely, for at the proper time he received his degree in law, passed the necessary examinations with credit, and entered the Prussian civil service as official reporter in one of the Berlin courts. Finding his duties distasteful, he withdrew at the age of twenty-four to assume the administration of his father's Pomeranian estates and for eight years devoted himself to grain growing and sheep raising. In addition, as a means of relieving the monotony of country life, he played hard, rode hard, and drank hard. Tales of his practical jokes, daredevil exploits, and wild revels soon circulated widely, earning for him the name of "the mad Junker." Only his more intimate friends knew that after a day of strenuous physical exertion his exuberant vitality enabled him to read history and philosophy far into the night.

Bismarck entered the arena of public life in 1847 when he was chosen delegate to the United Diet which Frederick William IV unwillingly summoned to still the cries of the liberals. In that assembly Bismarck was an imposing figure. Of herculean stature, with a massive head and large gray eyes loking out from under shaggy brows, he seemed the living embodiment of primeval Teutonism. During several sittings he held his peace but then began to state his opinions publicly. The political creed to which he adhered for the rest of his life had already taken form in his mind. Its essence was his belief that Prussia under the autocratic rule of the Hohenzollern must take its place as the leading state of Germany. Many statesmen have started their careers at one political pole and ended at the other, but not so Bismarck. At times he modified his views, but he never changed them radically. Viewing constitutional government and popular representation — in fact, everything the liberals had struggled and died for since 1789 — with unrelenting scorn, he entered the lists as the champion of the "divine right" of the Hohenzollern. So vigorously did he oppose the diminution of the royal prerogative by so much as a hair's breadth that he was styled "more royalist than the king." When in the spring of 1848 the Diet voted to thank Frederick William IV for promising his people a constitution, Bismarck was one of a minority of two who opposed the resolution. Thereafter he used every opportunity to state his reactionary views. Though he was naturally very sensitive, he always displayed perfect self-control. In the words of one of his biographers, "His brain worked as if packed in ice, when feelings within were red hot." On one occasion when the liberal deputies hissed him and shouted so loudly that he could not continue speaking, Bismarck calmly took a newspaper out of his pocket, read it until order was restored, and then continued his address.

During the succeeding years his plans for the aggrandizement of Prussia took a more developed form. Previously he had regarded Austria with a friendly eye and had even voted with the Austrophils. To him, as to most conservatives, Austria was the ideal state because it was the center of resistance against the advance of liberalism. But now he gradually came to the conclusion that Prussia could grow strong only by crushing Austria. "There will be no other way," he wrote in 1856, "to set the clock of our development at the right hour." The Habsburg government was quite willing to remain on friendly terms with Prussia so long as the latter was satisfied with a secondary place, but it manifested no willingness to resign its domination of the smaller states. At Frankfort, where he went in 1851 to attend the Diet of the Germanic Confederation as the Prussian representative, Bismarck became disgusted with the subservient attitude of the smaller states toward Austria, and showed at once that humility was not his role. Upon discovering that the Austrian member alone smoked at the sittings of the committee on military affairs, he took out a cigar and lighted it. Again, when Count von Thurn, the Austrian president of the Frankfort Diet, received him in his shirt sleeves, Bismarck at once took off his own coat. Trifling incidents, it is true, but significant nevertheless of the coming struggle for power. The next step of the Prussian representative was the conversion of the king to his way of thinking. To this end he frequently traveled to Berlin for personal chats with Frederick William IV. Furthermore, in his dispatches and in all places where caution did not prescribe silence he untiringly reiterated his conviction that the basic principle of any union of the German states must be the exclusion of Austria.

Gradually Bismarck's attitude became so pronounced that the Prussian government, which was not yet ready to challenge Austria's supremacy in Germany, "promoted" him to the position of ambassador to Russia (1859). Bismarck himself, realizing only too well the reason for the change, asserted that he had been "put on ice." But he had no intention of remaining in cold storage permanently. During his three years in St. Petersburg (now Leningrad) and also during his subsequent stay in Paris (1862), Bismarck was in communication with von Roon, the Prussian minister of war. Finally on September 18, 1862, he received from von Roon the following telegram, "There's danger in delay. Hasten!" Starting on the homeward journey at once, Bismarck arrived in Berlin on the morning of the 20th and that same afternoon induced King William I to tear up the abdication he had drafted. "I succeeded in convincing him," Bismarck later wrote, "that, so far as he was concerned, it was not a question of Liberal or Conservative, of this or that shade, but rather of monarchical rule versus parliamentary government, and that the latter must be avoided at all costs, even if by a period of dictatorship." The next day the official government newspaper announced the appointment of Bismarck as president of the ministry.

BLOOD AND IRON

The appointment of Bismarck was, of course, a direct challenge to the liberals; and because they held a majority in the Prussian Assembly, statesmen in the various chancelleries made bets whether he would last three weeks or three months. But they greatly underestimated his staying powers. Having taken up his residence in the Wilhelmstrasse, he remained there for twenty-eight years. In the conflict which followed his appointment the minister-president quickly showed the deputies that he would not permit "a sheet of paper," as he called the Prussian constitution, to stand in the way of the military reforms which von Roon and von Moltke had projected. He told the angry liberals that the decision as to the strength of the army rested not upon them but upon the royal prerogative. On September 30 he sounded the keynote of the future Prussian policy in an address to the finance committee of the lower house. "Germany," he declared, "looks not to the liberalism of Prussia, but to its power. . . . The great questions of the time cannot be solved by speeches and parliamentary majorities — that was the mistake of 1848 and 1849 — but by blood and iron." When the lower house continued to refuse to vote the army budget, Bismarck simply collected the necessary taxes and pushed forward the reorganization. For four years he continued to flout the will of the lower house and the vast body of public opinion which supported it. As a result he became the most hated person in Prussia. But it appeared to trouble him little. He even joked about his plight, writing that he was "the most vigorously and best hated person in the country."

While he was securing the efficiency of the Prussian army, Bismarck also made certain that Austria would be without foreign allies in the event of an Austro-Prussian war. During his three years at St. Petersburg he had taken great pains to create a friendly feeling between Russia and Prussia, and in 1863 he supplemented these efforts by offering the tsar help in putting down the Polish insurrection. He further successfully hoodwinked Napoleon III into remaining neutral by dropping hints at the famous interview at Biarritz (September 30, 1865) of possible "compensations" to France in the event of a Prussian victory over Austria.

All things being propitious, Bismarck needed only a pretext for war. He had not far to seek, for one was at hand in the so-called Schleswig-Holstein question which had been reopened by the death of Frederick VII, king of Denmark, in 1863. It remained only for Bismarck to make war inevitable and to make it appear as if Prussia were being forced into hostilities. The latter was necessary to overcome the scruples of King William, who was averse to war with a German power. "If you only knew," Bismarck wrote to a friend shortly before the war, "what a terrible struggle it was to convince His Majesty that we must fight." Never did Bismarck demonstrate greater diplomatic skill than in the conduct of the Schleswig-Holstein question. Like a magician he permitted his opponents and the Prussian public to see only the cards he wanted them to see. While he was publicly feigning willingness to submit the question to arbitration, under cover he manipulated the factors in such a way as to foredoom any attempt at arbitration. At all times he was careful to give the impression that Austria refused to be conciliated. Deftly he shifted from argument to argument until the preparations for war were complete and the struggle could begin. He himself was proud of his work. In his later years he said, "Schleswig-Holstein, that is the campaign, politically speaking, of which I am proudest."

The Schleswig-Holstein question with all its side issues and ramifications was the bugbear of nineteenth-century diplomatists. To Lord Palmerston it appeared "more intricate than any sphinx's riddle, and more difficult to unravel than any Gordian knot." He is also reported to have remarked jokingly that only three persons had ever understood it: the Prince Consort, a German professor, and he himself; but the first was dead, the German professor had been driven insane by its complexities, and he himself had forgotten what he once knew about it. The barest outline must suffice here. The question centered about the two duchies which lay just south of Denmark, with Holstein adjoining Germany, and Schleswig contiguous to Denmark. Both had long been attached to the crown of Denmark, but the union was solely in the person of the ruler, who in addition to being king of Denmark was also duke of both Schleswig and Holstein. The Danes, influenced by the rising spirit of nationalism, were eager to merge the duchies, particularly Schleswig, with Denmark. At the same time the Germans were no less desirous of bringing them under German rule.

Eventually the entire question was submitted to a congress of powers which convened in London in 1852. This congress drafted the so-called London Protocol, granting the duchies a measure of autonomy but decreeing that they should remain attached to the crown of Denmark. But the Danes refused to be satisfied with anything short of the complete absorption of Schleswig into their state. In March, 1863, when the powers were occupied with the Polish insurrection, Frederick VII declared Schleswig incorporated with Denmark. Although the German states protested at once, the Danish parliament voted a joint constitution for Denmark and Schleswig on November 14. Frederick died the next day but his successor, Christian IX, signed the new constitution.

Bismarck, who had set his mind on annexing the duchies to Prussia, at once demanded that the Danish government abandon the measures it had taken. When the Danes refused to abrogate the constitution, he induced Austria by means of artful diplomacy to join Prussia in occupying the duchies. The Danes fought desperately but had to give way and cede the duchies. Having acquired them, Austria and Prussia had to decide who was to rule them. A temporary agreement was finally reached in the Convention of Gastein (August, 1865), according to which Prussia assumed control of Schleswig, and Austria of Holstein. This arrangement, Bismarck was certain, would provide ample opportunity for further straining of relations between the rival powers. He did not miscalculate, for Austria soon began encouraging the claims of the young duke of Augustenburg, who maintained that he was the rightful heir to the duchies. This was enough to permit Bismarck to style the conduct of Austria "an alliance with revolution," and order the Prussian army to occupy Holstein. As the Prussian forces entered the duchy, the Austrians withdrew, but they appealed to the Diet of the Germanic Confederation for aid. This caused a rupture of relations between the two states, and on June 15, 1866, the Prussian troops began their march.

The war over the hegemony of Germany, which had been brewing ever since Frederick the Great took Silesia, had finally broken out. It was, as the name "Seven Weeks' War" indicates, of but short duration. Actually the fighting lasted only five weeks and three days. Neither Austria nor Prussia fought alone. While nearly all the states of the Germanic Confederation supported Austria, Prussia had Italy as an ally. From the first the advantages were on the side of Prussia. The Austrian army was inferior not only in organization and leadership but also in weapons, for the Prussians were armed with a new rifle called the "needle gun" which fired six times as fast as the Austrian rifle. In less than two weeks one Prussian army crushed the resistance in Saxony, Hanover, and Hesse-Cassel, while another moved southward into Bohemia to engage the imperial forces. The decisive battle was fought on July 3, 1866, at Sadowa (Königgrätz). There in a fierce struggle the Austrian army was routed so completely that the government sued for peace.

In the terms of peace which he offered to a vanquished foe Bismarck showed himself a far-sighted diplomatist. Having wrested the German hegemony from Austria, he was careful not to make his demands so severe that they would stir a desire for vengeance. He wished to end the age-long quarrel and if possible secure Austria as an ally. Hence, despite the clamors of the military party, he stood firm in his refusal to annex any Austrian territory, thereby rendering possible a speedy reconciliation of the belligerents. By the terms of the treaty of peace signed at Prague in August, 1866, Austria was compelled only to pay a small indemnity and to transfer her rights in Schleswig-Holstein to Prussia. She had to consent, however, to the dissolution of the Germanic Confederation and the formation of "a new organization of Germany without the participation of the empire of Austria." Thus was Austria excluded from all participation in German politics. Separate treaties of peace were signed with the south German states, but in the north Hanover, Hesse-Cassel, Nassau, and the free city of Frankfort were annexed to Prussia. In all, Prussia acquired nearly twenty-five thousand square miles of territory and nearly five million new subjects.

The "new organization of Germany" to which the treaty of Prague referred was the North German Confederation, embracing all German states north of the River Main. The constitution of the confederation, drawn up by Bismarck, ingeniously preserved the independence of the princes and at the same time established the supremacy of the king of Prussia. While each state was left to manage its own domestic affairs, the control of foreign policy and of questions of national defense was placed in the hands of the central executive, the king of Prussia, whose headship of the confederation was made hereditary. Under these provisions the state armies were henceforth armed and organized on the Prussian model and under Prussian direction. The legislative functions were vested in a federal council (Bundesrat) composed of the representatives of the various governments and in a diet (Bundestag) elected by the people as a whole. Here at last were the beginnings of a strong federal state in Germany.

The rapid and overwhelming success of Bismarck's schemes made him as popular in Prussia as he had previously been unpopular.[2] He became the hero of the hour, the man who by unifying north Germany had realized at least in large part a long-felt desire of many Germans. Honors were heaped upon him and he was cheered by enthusiastic crowds whenever he appeared in public. But Bismarck did not permit this popularity to turn his head. He knew it was merely the vulgar admiration of success. "Had I failed," he said, "the old women would have cursed me and swept me into the gutter with their brooms." He immediately seized the opportunity to offer the liberals in the Prussian Assembly the hand of friendship, and they grasped it with enthusiasm. Not only did the old liberals support a bill of indemnity for the sums Bismarck had unconstitutionally spent, but they also formed a new national liberal group to support his policies. There was no longer any need for him to ride roughshod over the opposition of the Assembly; he had only to make his desires known and they were promptly carried out. Thus the needle gun had at Sadowa destroyed Prussian liberalism as well as the Austrian army.

[2] For example, Rudolf von Ihering, the celebrated jurist and historian, wrote when war was declared with Austria, "Never probably has a war been engineered with such revolting shamelessness and alarming recklessness." After Prussia's victory over Austria he said, "I bow to the genius of a Bismarck. . . . For such a man of action I would give a hundred men of impotent honor."

THE FRANCO-PRUSSIAN WAR

Bismarck's work of unifying Germany under the leadership of Prussia was not finished. There still remained the problem of creating a sense of common interests between the south German states and the North German Confederation as a means of drawing the former into the confederation. The problem appeared to be anything but easy, for the south German states showed no inclination to exchange their independent sovereignty for Prussian rule. However, forces outside Germany unexpectedly came to Bismarck's aid, so that he was able before another five years to achieve the unity of all German states except those ruled by the Austrian Habsburgs. Napoleon III had not calculated on the proficiency of the Prussian army. Believing that the struggle between Prussia and Austria would be long and indecisive, he had planned to intervene on the Prussian side at the right moment in return for a substantial annexation of territory on the left bank of the Rhine. But the speedy and overwhelming Prussian victory thwarted his plans. Before the treaty of Prague was signed, he had already begun to demand territory on France's eastern frontier as "compensation" for having remained neutral. This would have meant the cession of territory belonging to the south German states. Although Bismarck was determined not to yield an inch of land, he nevertheless encouraged Count Benedetti, the French ambassador, to put the demands in writing. Upon receiving them, Bismarck at once communicated them to the south German states. It was enough to cause the latter to throw themselves into the arms of Prussia. Secret treaties were arranged in which Prussia guaranteed them their territory and they promised to put their armies under Prussian control in case of war. Germany, except Austria, was now one in a military sense. The surest means of welding the states together politically, Bismarck believed, would be a joint war against a common enemy. To bring on this war at the right moment, with France as the aggressor, now became the principal goal of his strivings.

When the time came for Bismarck to answer the French demand, he declared point-blank that any cession of German territory was out of the question. This still left open to Napoleon III the possibility of obtaining non-German territory as a means of bolstering his tottering prestige. Accordingly Benedetti offered Prussia permission to incorporate the south German states in the German Confederation if Prussia would assist her in acquiring Belgium. Again requesting the proposals in writing, Bismarck was to use them as effectively as he had the earlier ones. He published them in the London *Times* on the eve of the Franco-Prussian War, thereby definitely assuring the neutrality of Great Britain. When Napoleon III failed to gain support for the plan of seizing Belgium, he decided that if he could not take territory he might at least buy some. He offered to pay ninety million francs for Luxembourg. Although the Dutch, to whom it belonged, were ready to sell it at this price, Bismarck would agree only to its conversion into a neutral state. He was careful, however, to conduct the whole affair without provoking the French too much. Though he believed a contest with France to be inevitable, he had to wait until the military party at Berlin was ready. When Napoleon himself renounced the scheme, it appeared as if the war cloud was lifted from Europe, but fresh provocation was soon to be supplied by the question of the Hohenzollern candidature for the vacant Spanish throne.

After several candidates had refused the throne, which had been vacated in 1868 when Queen Isabella was deposed by a revolution, Bismarck, it appears, managed to procure the offer for Prince Leopold of Hohenzollern-Sigmaringen, a member of a south German branch of the Prussian royal house. This prince, oddly enough, was a nearer blood relative of Napoleon III than of William I; nevertheless, the French emperor did not regard him as a proper candidate. Twice Leopold refused the offer. When, however, it was renewed in 1870, he accepted it. No sooner did the news reach Paris than the French government instructed Benedetti to demand a withdrawal from William I. This the king refused, but the air cleared again when Leopold himself reversed his action. The fact that a Hohenzollern prince had renounced the Spanish throne "at a mere gesture of displeasure" from Paris was a not inconsiderable diplomatic triumph for the French and, conversely, a rebuff for Bismarck. Napoleon III himself was willing to drop the matter at this point, but the empress and the French foreign minister, the duc de Gramont, were not satisfied. The latter immediately ordered Benedetti to obtain from the Prussian king a promise that he would at no future time consent to have a member of the Hohenzollern family become a candidate for the Spanish throne. William, who was taking a holiday at the watering place of Ems when Benedetti presented the demand, naturally refused to give the desired pledge. When the persistent ambassador sought yet another interview, he was told that any further negotiations must be carried on with the king's ministers. There had, however, been nothing offensive in the conduct of either party.

Having given his answer William ordered his aide-de-camp to inform Bismarck by telegram of what had taken place (July 13). At the time Bismarck received this telegram, which has since been known as the Ems telegram, he was dining with von Roon and von Moltke. All three, bent as they were on war, became greatly depressed, for it seemed as if the favorable moment for a conflict had passed. Von Moltke was particularly eager for war because he wished to put in effect the plans he

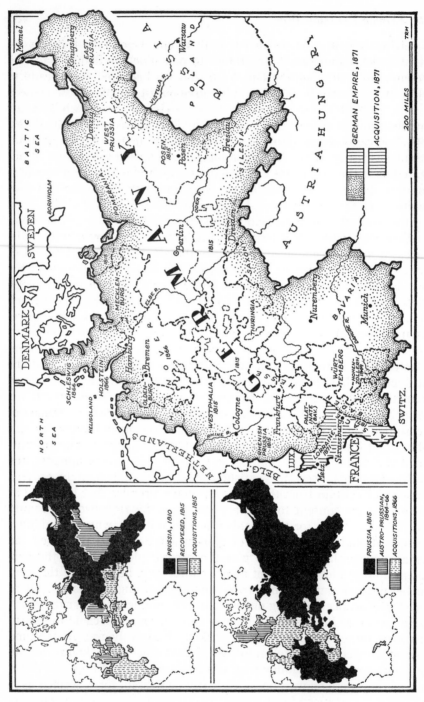

THE GROWTH OF PRUSSIA IN THE NINETEENTH CENTURY AND THE UNIFICATION OF GERMANY

had drawn up for an invasion of France. But after a time Bismarck took a pencil and began to edit the telegram. When he had finished his version, which he hoped would "have the effect of a red rag upon the Gallic bull," he sent it to be published in an extra evening edition of the official newspaper. The result was exactly what he desired. While, on the one hand, it left with the German people the impression that the French ambassador had been insolent, on the other it led the French to believe that their ambassador had been insulted. Indignation flared up in both countries. In Paris the populace as well as the ministers and deputies clamored for war so loudly that the advocates of peace could not be heard. Only Napoleon III still hesitated. Finally he, too, gave way and war was formally declared on July 19, 1870.

The French people had been told by the minister of war that everything was in readiness "down to the last button on the last gaiter of the last soldier." According to Benedetti, the people received "with transports of enthusiasm" the news that war had been declared. In Paris the streets resounded with the cry, "To Berlin." Many Parisians were so certain of speedy victory that they wagered the French troops would celebrate the Fête Napoleon (August 15) in Berlin. Actually there had been little preparation for war. The troops, upon being mobilized, were found to be in want of almost everything. Not only were clothing and food supplies lacking; in many places there were cannon without ammunition. The French armies were in general decidedly inferior to the Prussian forces in arms,[3] in generalship, and even in numbers. Moreover, when Napoleon III began to look to other nations for assistance, he found himself isolated by Prussian diplomacy. Having previously flattered himself that the cooperation of Austria would paralyze south Germany, he suddenly awoke to find that Austria dared not aid him for fear of Russia, whose friendship had been secured by Bismarck. Even Italy, upon whose help Napoleon had firmly relied, disappointed him; instead of coming to his aid, the new kingdom seized the opportunity to complete its unification by occupying Rome as soon as the French garrison stationed there was withdrawn. "On the morning of August 6," the French prime minister wrote, "France stood alone."

The result was that France was soon prostrate at Prussia's feet. A series of Prussian victories during the first month at Wörth, Colombières, Mars-la-Tour, and Gravelotte shut up one French army under the command of Marshal Bazaine in Metz. When a second army under Marshal McMahon set out to bring aid to the blockaded force, it was surrounded in an unfavorable position at Sedan. The battle began on the morning of September 1, and on the next day the entire French

---

[3] The one exception to this statement was the French Chassepot breech-loading rifle which, in the words of von Roon, was "far superior to the unimproved needle gun, as we found to our cost."

army, together with Napoleon III who accompanied it, surrendered to the Prussians. The news of the disaster caused the empire to collapse like a house of cards. In Paris a group of republicans proclaimed a republic, and a provisional government was hastily formed to take charge of affairs. The leaders were ready to make peace but not at Bismarck's price. So the struggle continued during the fall and winter. On October 27 Bazaine's great army in Metz surrendered and in the following January Paris fell. By the treaty of Frankfort, signed in May, 1871, France was required not only to pay an indemnity of five billion francs but also to cede Alsace, including Strasbourg, and part of Lorraine, including Metz, to the new German Empire. Although both had been wrested from the Holy Roman Empire by Louis XIV, the French refused to be reconciled to their loss. Bismarck himself later confessed that the territorial settlement had been unwise. "I do not," he stated, "want too many Frenchmen in my house." His plan was to annex only Alsace, which was largely German by blood and language. For weeks he opposed the annexation of Lorraine but finally permitted himself to be overruled by the military party.

Besides surrendering Alsace and part of Lorraine, France earlier had to submit to the humiliation of having King William proclaimed German emperor in the Hall of Mirrors at Versailles. The war in which troops from the south German states fought side by side with those of the North German Confederation raised the sentiment for German unity to such a pitch that it swept away whatever dislike of joining with the northern states still existed in the south. It only remained for Bismarck to negotiate the terms of a political union. He allowed the southern states, particularly Bavaria, more home rule than the northern states possessed. Everything else being arranged, William formally assumed the imperial dignity at Versailles on January 18, 1871, becoming Emperor William I. Thus was accomplished the task Bismarck had set for himself. The policy of blood and iron had worked out as he had predicted. All of Germany, except the German provinces of Austria, was united under the hegemony of Prussia. As a reward for his services Bismarck was raised to the rank of prince and appointed chancellor of the new empire.

Napoleon III moving out of Mexico, from a cartoon published in 1867

Napoleon III reproving Bismarck for supporting the candidature of Leopold of Hohenzollern, a cartoon from *Punchinello*, 1870

Empress Eugénie at the opening of the Suez Canal, 1869

Dreyfus on Devil's Island, from a drawing by Carrier

Victor Emmanuel II of Italy

Gambetta proclaiming the Third French Republic in 1870

Garibaldi, from an old print

CHAPTER NINE

The Third Republic in France

W HEN the government of Napoleon III declared war on Prussia in 1870, it sealed its own doom. Before the emperor left Paris to take command of the army, he issued a bombastic proclamation which began with the words, "Frenchmen! There are in the lives of peoples solemn moments where national honor, violently excited, imposes itself as an irresistible force, dominates all interests, and takes in hand the direction of the destinies of the country. One of these decisive hours has just sounded for France." Little did he realize that the war would in a short time lead to the capitulation at Sedan. Less than four months before this memorable battle nearly 7.5 million votes had been cast in support of his government against an opposition of 1.5 million. But the disaster at Sedan destroyed his prestige as completely as Waterloo had discredited Napoleon I. In handing his sword to the Germans he vacated his throne.

On September 3 the Empress Eugénie received the first news of the disaster in a laconic telegram which read, "The army is defeated and captive. I myself am prisoner. Napoleon." News of the full extent of the catastrophe was not made public until midnight of that day. It struck Paris like a thunderbolt, crushing the high hopes the people cherished of capturing Berlin in a few days. "The boulevards," the American minister to France wrote, "were thronged by masses of excited men filled with rage and indignation." At the meeting of the Corps Législatif shortly after noon on Sunday, September 4, it was proposed that a committee be appointed on the question of establishing a "Government of National Defense." But the assembly was not permitted to make the final decision. While the session was in progress, an indiscriminate mob of men, women, and children invaded the hall, singing the Marseillaise, and shouting "Vive la république." Leon Gambetta and Jules Favre, two popular republican leaders, tried to restore order, but finally gave way to the demand of the mob, led the motley throng to the Hôtel de Ville, and there proclaiming France a republic, set up a provisional government.

Thus the Second Empire fell as ignominiously at Paris as it had fallen disastrously at Sedan. For the third time in less than a century a republic had been proclaimed. Good-humored crowds had carried through a revolution unmarred by bloody incidents. But those who rejoiced over the establishment of the republic appeared oblivious to the fact that one French army was on its way to internment in Germany and the other was surrounded in Metz. Never was public opinion more optimistic than in that hour. Had not the First Republic raised fourteen armies in the midst of national distress to defeat a coalition that included the whole of Europe! The Parisian masses were certain that the Third Republic could repeat this achievement, and their faith was bolstered by their leaders. Jules Ferry, the Minister of Foreign Affairs, announced that France to get peace would not surrender "an inch of her territory or a stone of her fortresses." Gambetta, who was Minister of War, chose as his slogan the phrase, "Guerre à outrance" (war to the bitter end).

Meanwhile the Germans were moving inexorably forward. On September 19 they closed their lines around Paris, which was gradually isolated so completely that it could communicate with the provinces only by balloons and carrier pigeons. But the Parisians held out bravely. After doing all he could to prepare Paris for a siege, Gambetta on October 8 made his dramatic escape in a balloon which carried him safely over the German lines. During the next few weeks, working with the fury of a madman, he succeeded in collecting and equipping a force of 600,000 men, a feat which commanded the admiration even of General von Moltke. The new levies, however, lacked the training and discipline successfully to oppose the best army in Europe. Meanwhile even the seasoned French troops were unable to breach the German ring around Metz, and on October 27 this army of more than 170,000 surrendered. By this time the situation in Paris was critical. Food was so scarce that horses, mules, dogs, and even cats had been standard fare for some time. The sufferings from hunger were multiplied by the bitter cold and a scarcity of fuel. Smallpox had claimed the lives of more than 60,000 people. Finally Jules Favre, the Vice-President of the Government, realizing that there was no longer any hope of military success, concluded an armistice with the Germans on January 28.

Since Bismarck refused to make peace with the provisional government, which was self-constituted, elections for a National Assembly were held on February 8, 1871. When the Assembly which now became the *de facto* government met at Bordeaux on February 13, it was found that of six hundred deputies only two hundred were republican, the rest having strong monarchist sympathies. Ordinarily the cause of the republic would have been hopeless, but the monarchists, almost evenly divided between Legitimists (supporters of the Bourbons) and Orleanists (supporters of the Orleans branch), were unable to agree on a candidate. Each group appears to have preferred the establishment of a republic to the success of the rival monarchist party. Hence the republic was inaugurated as a sort of least common denominator. The new government, according to a phrase current at the time, was "a republic without republicans."

The first task of the Assembly was to negotiate peace with Germany. Adolphe Thiers, upon whom the Assembly had conferred the title of "Chief of the Executive Power," went to negotiate directly with Bismarck. Although he contested point after point of the demands, he was able to gain but few concessions. Bismarck exacted his price, which included the cession of the whole of Alsace except Belfort, the eastern part of Lorraine, the payment of five billion francs as indemnity, and the occupation of France by German troops until the final installments of the indemnity were paid. The treaty was officially signed at Frankfort on May 10, 1871.

The conclusion of peace with Germany did not terminate the misfortunes of France. Even before the end of the war with Prussia, civil war broke out between the Commune of Paris and the government of the National Assembly. Friction between the two was caused by a number of factors. First, the people of Paris were unhappy over the way the siege had been conducted by the provisional government. Second, the Parisians, who were ardent republicans, feared that the National Assembly, which was predominantly monarchist, would proclaim a monarchy at the first propitious moment. Third, Parisians resented the decision of the Assembly to sit at Versailles, where it did not have to fear the temper of the Paris mobs. The Parisians regarded it as an insult of the first order that, after sustaining a tremendous siege and endeavoring to hold high the honor of France, their city had to give way to a small sleepy town that had been a Bourbon stronghold.

The immediate cause of the outbreak of hostilities was the attempt of the Assembly to seize the artillery of the National Guard. Earlier Bismarck had requested that the Guard surrender their arms, but when Thiers informed him that any attempt to disarm them would cause serious trouble, the request was withdrawn. When the feelings of the mobs against the Assembly ran high, the latter sent General Lecomte to remove the cannon, but surging crowds gathered to stop the removal. Having tried everything possible to make the crowds give way, General Lecomte ordered his soldiers to fire on them. The soldiers refused. Revolutionary leaders at once seized Lecomte and shot him. As the troops that were loyal to the Versailles government withdrew, the insurgents occupied most of the western forts, and on March 27 they declared Paris to be an autonomous Commune. Three days later the government of the Commune of Paris decreed that "the employees of the various departments of government will hereafter treat as null and void orders or communications emanating from the government of Versailles or its adherents."

The Versailles government, having failed in a last attempt to solve the difficulties by conciliation, decided to subdue the city by force. The damage Paris suffered in the second siege, which saw Frenchmen pitted against Frenchmen, exceeded that inflicted by the Germans. When the Versailles troops after a six weeks' siege finally forced their way into the capital on May 21, humanity seemed to vanish completely. The succeeding "Bloody Week" witnessed a fearful destruction of life and property. In falling back, the defenders murdered their hostages; the soldiers of Versailles in turn shot down all they took fighting. Among those shot in cold blood by the insurgents was the Archbishop of Paris. Incendiarism was also added to the horrors of slaughter. On the night of May 25–26 orders were given to set fire to parts of the city. In the ensuing holocaust the Tuileries, the Hôtel de Ville, the Louvre Library, and other historic buildings were destroyed by the flames. After the suppression of the Commune, courts-martial were appointed to try the large number of prisoners. The number of death sentences was small; but thousands were deported to penal colonies, and other thousands were sentenced to hard labor.

The insurrection having been put down, France was finally at peace, but the German army of occupation was still in France. In order to get it out of the country France had to pay in full the war indemnity of five billion francs. Under the leadership of Thiers this was done with amazing celerity. Bismarck had hoped to cripple France economically for a decade, but in September, 1873, the last installment freed French soil from the invader. For this achievement Thiers was acclaimed by the French people as "The Liberator of the Territory." To prevent a recurrence of the German invasion a law was passed in July, 1872, instituting compulsory military service. What the law actually did was to establish in France the Prussian system which had been so successful against all opponents. In a few years the frontier was refortified and the new military system was firmly established, so that France appeared more formidable than ever. So surprising was her recovery that Germany became alarmed and seriously considered striking her down before she could grow too strong.

Meanwhile, the monarchists had cooperated halfheartedly in the hope that an opportunity to restore the monarchy would present itself. When Thiers, a liberal monarchist, gradually became convinced that a republic was the only possible form of government for France, the monarchists realized that he must first be unseated if a restoration were to be effected. Accordingly, they forced his resignation in May, 1873. They then agreed to back the Count of Chambord, who chose the title of Henry V. He refused, however, to accept the tricolor, insisting on the old Bourbon banner. This caused the Orleanists to withdraw their support. The republic was saved.

But the National Assembly, though it had failed to restore the monarchy, was still unwilling to establish a republic by drawing up a constitution. This state of affairs might have continued indefinitely if the Bonapartists had not begun to agitate for a plebiscite. The Right Center, which had never recognized the republic, in alarm now joined the republicans in drafting a constitution which was a compromise between republican and monarchical principles. This constitution not only lasted longer than the two previous republican constitutions but also became less monarchical in character with the passing of time. It was not a single document; it was a series of separate laws and therefore lacked the clear-cut definition of earlier French constitutions.

The constitution of 1875 provided, first of all, for a bicameral legislature composed of the Chamber of Deputies and the Senate. The members of the former, some six hundred in number, were to be elected for four years by direct popular vote on the basis of universal manhood suffrage. The Senate, on the other hand, was to consist of some three hundred members, one third appointed for life and the rest chosen for a nine-year term by electoral colleges meeting in the various departments.[1] Each house had the power to initiate and amend laws and to reject proposals of the other house. A further law provided that the president of the republic should be elected for a term of seven years by the Chamber and the Senate united as the National Assembly.[2] He was given wide powers in initiating legislation, was head of the army and navy, appointed state officials, exercised the power of pardon, and negotiated treaties. But his powers were exercised through ministers who were responsible to the legislature. In other words, the law provided that all acts of the president must be countersigned by one or more ministers. Thus a "parliamentary" and not a "presidential" republic like the United States was set up.

[1] The appointment of further life senators was abolished in 1884.
[2] The first president was Marshal MacMahon, who resigned in 1879, and Jules Grévy was elected his successor.

VICISSITUDES OF THE REPUBLIC

Under the Third Republic France had no political parties in the American sense but only small factions. Groups would be formed in support of a principle such as royalism or clericalism or about some personality. While some of these small groups had a fairly long life, others were made and unmade by the shifting kaleidoscope of politics and by the rise and fall of specific leaders. No cabinet could take office until it had combined enough of these factions to make up a majority in parliament. Often one or more factions of such a combination would withdraw because of some disagreement and then the entire coalition would collapse. The result was political instability. During the forty years from 1874 to 1915 no fewer than fifty-two cabinets passed in review. Thus the average life of a cabinet was less than nine months; some lasted only a few weeks. The instability was, however, more apparent than real, for nearly every cabinet contained a number of members from its predecessor.

In the first elections after the new constitution went into effect, the republicans secured a large majority in the Chamber of Deputies, but in the Senate the monarchists were still the strongest group. Only in 1878, after a bitter contest, did the republicans succeed in gaining control of the Senate. The monarchists, however, did not relinquish the idea of a restoration, nor did other groups abate their hostility toward the republic. During the next decades a series of incidents occurred which, though disconnected, involved a struggle of the republicans against the reactionary and disruptive forces represented by the monarchists, the clericals,[3] and the military party. Although the republic managed to weather the storm, its strength was subjected to a real test.

One of these incidents was the Boulanger affair of 1888–1889, which was an attempt to establish a dictatorship. The affair was made possible by the burning desire for revenge and the hope of winning back Alsace-Lorraine. Since the republic appeared to have no plans to regain the lost provinces, many were ready to pin their hopes on an individual. This gave General Georges Boulanger his opportunity. Big, handsome, a good speaker, and a striking figure on horseback, he drew men to him with his debonair charm rather than through outstanding ability. Lady Randolph Churchill, at whose house he dined on several occasions, wrote, "Boulanger, notwithstanding a military bearing, a fierce mustache and, to French ideas, a handsome face, gave an impression of a man not quite sure of himself. . . . He seemed unable to rise above his

[3] In the first elections under the new constitution the monarchists' campaign against the republicans found strong support in the ranks of the Catholic or clerical party, causing Gambetta to coin the slogan, "Clericalism, that is our enemy."

middle-class origin and early surroundings. . . . He was banal in conversation, and I cannot think of anything of interest he said to me." This was the man whose name was on everybody's lips. "Le brav' Général" sedulously cultivated his popularity by making frequent public appearances riding his famous black horse and attired in an immaculate uniform adorned with decorations.

Boulanger had not won his rank of general on the field of battle but by lobbying for many years in public offices and anterooms. Appointed Minister of War in 1886, he had made the most of the opportunity to gain the support of the soldiers by improving their living conditions and by advocating a reduction of the period of service. As his popularity increased, he obtained the support of several newspapers which suggested at various times that he was the man to restore France's self-respect by leading her in a war of revenge against Germany. Soon he became the focus of every discontent. To gain further support he promised each group what it desired. The great moment arrived in January, 1889, when a Paris constituency elected him to the Chamber by a large majority over the government candidate. His popularity had reached a point at which he would only have had to say the word to start an insurrection in his favor. But he disliked the idea of a *coup d'état*. "In six months," he said, "I can get power by constitutional methods." The popular clamor became so loud that it was obvious he must be discredited if the republic was to be saved. In this desperate situation the republicans contrived to have rumors reach him of his imminent arrest for conspiring against the safety of the state. These rumors robbed the brave general of his courage, and he fled into exile. His lack of valor cost him much of his popularity. In 1891 he wrote the end of the episode when he committed suicide in Belgium.

In 1892 the republic was shaken by the so-called Panama scandal. Some years earlier the Panama Canal Company had been formed to construct a canal across the Isthmus of Panama. The leading spirit of the enterprise was Ferdinand de Lesseps (1805–1894), who had successfully completed the Suez Canal. In Panama, however, the company encountered unforeseen difficulties which quickly exhausted its capital. To overcome the shortage a plan was projected to sell bonds with a lucky lottery number attached to some. The law required that the project be authorized by parliament, but sentiment in the Chamber was unfavorable. To smooth the passage of the bill, agents of the company paid bribes to various deputies and members of the cabinet, with the result that the bond sale was authorized. Seven months later the company was bankrupt. For four years the government succeeded in stifling demands for an inquiry. Finally attacks by the opposition made it impossible to postpone the investigation any longer. Then came the revelation that ministers and members of parliament had accepted bribes. The disclosures were the more formidable because those who had done so were with few exceptions republicans. The affair was never totally concluded or elucidated, and in the end only one minister was convicted. But the sordid story convinced many people that politics under the republic was a profession unworthy of honest citizens.

THE DREYFUS AFFAIR

The repercussions of the Panama scandal were mild compared with those of the Dreyfus affair. The exceptional character of this case lies in the fact that it speedily transcended the personality of Captain Dreyfus and extended to the national policy of France. Fiercely contesting factions took form, causing sharp divisions in society and politics and nearly shattering the republic. All this was over the conviction of one individual, Alfred Dreyfus, who was of Jewish extraction and a captain in the French artillery. Only the barest outlines of the long and complicated story can be presented here. In December, 1894, Dreyfus was convicted on circumstantial evidence by a court-martial of having delivered to a foreign power, presumably Germany or her agents, secret documents concerning the national defense. The sentence was expulsion from the army and imprisonment for life. Dreyfus was then publicly degraded, with every detail of ignominy and humiliation. Before a large detachment of the army the lace, buttons, and other ornaments were torn from his uniform, and his sword was broken. He bore all this with amazing self-command, meanwhile loudly protesting his innocence. After this humiliation he was deported to Devil's Island off the coast of French Guiana, where he was kept in solitary confinement.

Most of those who knew about the case regarded it as closed, but there were some to whom Dreyfus' protestations carried conviction, and with his family and personal friends they did not cease their efforts to prove his innocence. Moreover, these efforts were supported by the German minister, who remonstrated against the degradation of Dreyfus and issued an official denial that any German representative had in any way been in contact with him. In 1895 Major Picquart, who had been present at the trial and was later made the head of the intelligence division of the General Staff, quietly carried on investigations and before long became convinced that the handwriting of the incriminating document was not that of Captain Dreyfus but of a certain Major Esterhazy. His superiors, however, refused to hear of Dreyfus' innocence and in their determination to prevent a reopening of the case had Picquart removed from his position. Gradually the newspapers took up the question with ardor, ranging themselves on one side or the other. The result

was a division of the French people into Dreyfusites and anti-Dreyfusites. While the Dreyfusites were accused of being traitors corrupted by
Jewish money, the anti-Dreyfusites were charged with anti-Semitism
and with maintaining a loose alliance between "the sword and the holy-
water sprinkler (le sabre et le goupillon)."

In a general way those who were against Dreyfus were classed with
the right; those who believed in his innocence with the left. While
military men, authoritarians, monarchists, and to a large extent clericals
made the maintenance of the conviction a point of honor, the republican
groups were moved by a desire to see justice done. Many men of intellect, including the novelist Émile Zola, demanded revision. In 1898
Zola, who did not know Captain Dreyfus personally, published his
famous letter, "J'Accuse," which was addressed to the president of the
republic. He charged the highest military authorities with the crime of
deliberately causing the imprisonment and torture of a fellow officer
whom they knew to be innocent. Zola was tried for seditious libel and
sentenced to a year's imprisonment, which he escaped only by fleeing to
England.

As the battle raged, one cabinet after another fell in trying to mediate
the problem. Finally in June, 1899, the *Cour de Cassation,* the highest
tribunal in France, annulled the conviction and ordered a new trial by
court-martial. Dreyfus was brought back to France, retried, and again
convicted. This time he was sentenced to ten years' imprisonment [4] but
was pardoned ten days later. But the Dreyfusites were still not satisfied.
After further investigations Dreyfus in 1906 was solemnly absolved
of all guilt and decorated with the Legion of Honor. Picquart was rein-
stated and later became Minister of War in the cabinet of M. Clemenceau. Zola had died in 1902, but in 1908 his remains were removed to
the Panthéon as a kind of canonization for his defense of justice. Thus
ended a great domestic crisis which for a time had threatened to rend
the Third Republic asunder.

PROBLEMS OF CHURCH AND STATE

Before the Dreyfus case had been settled, a new controversy broke
out between church and state. In the fall of 1900 premier Waldeck-
Rousseau fired the opening gun by stating in a speech at Toulouse that
the growing power of the religious orders (the orders of monks and
nuns) constituted a real peril to the republic. Under the Second Empire
the Roman Catholic Church had occupied a very favorable and influential position, particularly during the later years after Napoleon III had

[4] It is noteworthy that one of the two officers who voted for acquittal was the Com-
mandant de Breon, an ardent Roman Catholic.

strengthened his alliance with the church in the hope of bolstering his tottering throne. To the growing strength of the church the republicans had replied by making the separation of church and state one of the principal planks in their program. When the Third Republic was founded, the very men who had subscribed to this program became the most ardent supporters of the new regime; hence the church regarded the new state with fear and suspicion. In general, the church was anything but favorable to those principles of the French Revolution by which the government of the Third Republic professed to be guided. Consequently certain orders had frequently exerted their influence against the government and had been a pivot for antirepublican movements.

Having become masters of the situation, the republican leaders began to consider retaliatory measures. The first move came in the field of education, which was largely controlled by the church. After passing a law in 1880 making instruction free in all primary schools, the government in the following year passed another act making education compulsory and secular. The first article of the law of 1881 read, "Religious instruction shall no longer be given in the public primary schools." An attempt was also made to incorporate the following provision in the law: "No one shall be allowed to direct an establishment of education, public or private, of any order or grade, nor to teach in a school, if he belongs to a nonauthorized congregation." The measure was passed in the Chamber of Deputies but was rejected in the Senate. The government did, however, take steps to enforce the laws which already existed against unauthorized religious communities, with the result that the activities of certain orders were restricted.

During the papacy of Leo XIII (1878–1903) relations between church and state improved greatly. In the encyclical *Inter Innumeras* (1892) the pope declared that the civil power comes from God, and that it is the duty of all good Catholics to support the government under which they live. This statement not only cleared the way for French Catholics to rally to the republic but also demolished the claim that the doctrines of the church were inimical to the republican form of government. For a time anticlerical measures almost disappeared from the legislative program of the republicans.

But just at the moment when the reconciliation was becoming more and more a reality, the Dreyfus affair generated a tempest which caused many Frenchmen to believe that the church had never ceased its opposition to the republic. Consequently in 1900 a move against unauthorized associations was launched. Since the measure of 1881 had failed, religious associations had grown rapidly both in numbers and in wealth, a growth which was regarded by their historic rivals, the parochial clergy, with an unfriendly eye, and by the government with alarm. In 1901 a bill forbidding members of unauthorized orders to teach in any school was introduced and passed with little opposition. During the succeeding years the government rigorously enforced the Associations Law against those orders that failed to ask for authorization or to whom authorization was refused. Tens of thousands of monks and nuns were forced to leave institutions, which were then closed. After the death of Leo XIII in 1903, friction developed between the new pope, Pius X, and the French government over the visit of president Loubet of France to the king of Italy. The Vatican, which had not recognized the Italian government, regarded the visit as an insult to the pope. When the pope protested, the French government replied by withdrawing its ambassador to the Vatican. Soon thereafter relations were embittered by the treatment accorded by Vatican authorities to two French bishops who had shown loyalty to the republic. The government took the part of the bishops, and to punish the Vatican for interfering with French prelates in violation of the concordat of 1802, definitely broke off diplomatic relations.

These events caused a widespread demand for a complete separation of church and state. A further step in this direction was taken in 1904 by a law which provided that all teaching by religious orders, even those authorized, should cease within ten years. Thenceforth the state was to have a monopoly of the education of the young and could instruct them in republican traditions. This was, however, only preliminary to the Separation Law which was passed in December, 1905. In abrogating the concordat of 1802, this law relieved the state from paying the salaries of the clergy. A system of pensions was provided for clergymen with many years of service. As for the property of the church, it was stipulated that the various religions should form "Associations of Worship" which were to be the custodians of the church buildings. Just before the law became operative (December 8, 1906) the pope denounced it and refused to permit Catholics to form Associations of Worship. In January, 1907, a supplementary law was passed which prescribed that the use of church property should be regulated by contracts between the priests and the prefects or mayors. Thus church and state in France were formally separated after a more or less close union of fourteen centuries.

ECONOMIC DEVELOPMENT

After the establishment of the Third Republic the tempo of industrial progress continued to be slow compared with that of her neighbors. One reason for this was the fact that French industry specialized largely in the production of such luxury articles as perfumes, chinaware, laces, silks, embroideries, and fine wines rather than of articles that lent themselves more easily to mass machine production. Another reason was that French industries did not develop along big business lines. Whereas in Britain the bulk of the exports were produced by a few large industries, in France the average business firm was small, very often a family enterprise. The little shop with five or six employees continued to outnumber all other manufacturing establishments at the ratio of about eight to one. In 1896 there were more than half a million establishments employing five or less employees, while all others numbered about 67,000. Of these almost 50,000 employed twenty or less employees and about 10,000 fifty or less. Only 352 establishments had more than five hundred employees.

The average business firm consisted of one head and two employees or assistants. Many of the "manufacturers" were peasants who cultivated their little plots of land in the summer and during the winter produced ribbons, laces, brushes, combs, knives, and baskets. The system, prevalent in Britain during the early stages of the introduction of power machinery, whereby capitalists provided the materials and sold the finished products, continued in many districts of France. In the Amiens district, which produced many umbrellas and ladies' shoes, the town manufacturer furnished ready-cut materials and collected the finished products after paying the peasants for their work. For a time the peasant manufacturers were quite prosperous. It was, in fact, their savings which provided a large part of the indemnity paid to Germany in 1871.

Gradually, however, the use of power machinery became more widespread, especially in the heavy industries. Thus the use of power machinery in manufacturing and mining increased from 336,000 horsepower in 1875 to 3.5 million horsepower in 1913. It was introduced even in many home industries. In some districts peasants banded together to harness streams and to purchase engines. In 1898, for example, the silk-weaving peasants at Croix Russe cooperated in providing electric power for their industry. At St. Etienne, a center for the manufacture of silk ribbons, in 1904 no less than 18,000 power looms belonged to peasant manufacturers. In the textile industry in general the horsepower employed rose from 172,999 in 1890 to 434,529 in 1902 resulting in greatly increased production. The same was true in other industries. From 1891 to 1906 the production of iron increased 71 per cent in quantity and 73 per cent in value. But whereas Britain produced 7.5 million tons in 1913, and Germany 17 million, the French output was only 5 million. The production of coal rose from 13 million tons in 1870 to 41 million tons in 1913. This was a far cry from the 292 million tons of coal produced in Britain and the 279 million tons mined in Germany. French industry was, in fact, hampered throughout the period of the Third Republic by the difficulty of obtaining a sufficient supply of cheap coal for industrial purposes.

An American industrial commission which visited France in 1916 reported:

Some of the plants visited in central and southern France were thoroughly modern and well equipped with the best machine-tools and satisfactory labor-saving devices. . . . The general impression was formed, however, that modern machine-tools and labor-saving devices are not used in France to the same extent as in this country in plants of corresponding importance. This does not necessarily imply a lack of progressive management. The manufacturing conditions in many of the plants are very difficult. The demand which these factories supply is comparatively small, and it is therefore necessary to manufacture a wide range of products instead of concentrating upon a limited standard output.

France also fell behind in the construction of railroads. The decade of the fifties had been a period of vigorous expansion, so that by 1860 there were almost 6000 miles. Realizing the folly of competitive railroad building, the government consolidated all the small companies into six large ones. Five of the major ones radiated out from Paris and the sixth was in the south of France. As each company was given a monopoly in its district there was no incentive to build branch lines and the government found it necessary to guarantee the companies a profit in order to stimulate interest in the construction of branch and subsidiary lines. Nevertheless France had less railway mileage than either Great Britain or Germany in 1870. Even Belgium outstripped France in proportion to area.

During the Franco-Prussian War the railroads functioned so poorly that many Frenchmen became convinced that the slowness and inefficiency of the railroads was one of the major causes of the defeat. A period of feverish building followed, but the government again had to guarantee the companies a profit. Since most of the companies were earning substantial profits this did not appear to involve heavy financial obligations, but in the eighties when trade declined it became an expensive venture for the government.[5]

In matters of social legislation France also lagged behind Britain and Germany. Just before its collapse the government of the Second Empire had presented a comprehensive factory law to parliament, but before any action could be taken the Franco-Prussian War broke out. Thus

[5] The railway situation later became so acute that they were nationalized in 1938.

the task of passing new labor legislation was left to the Third Republic. After months of debate a new factory act was finally passed in 1874 which raised the minimum age of child workers to twelve, prohibited night work for female workers under twenty-one, and established for the first time a corps of factory inspectors. In 1892 the working day for women was limited to eleven hours and for children to ten hours; men, however, were still permitted to work twelve hours. A weekly day of rest was also assured to women and children in 1892. Four years later the ten-hour day was set as the legal maximum and in 1906 the privilege of a day of rest was extended to all workers in industry and commerce.

Trade unions were tolerated during the early years of the Third Republic so long as they did not cause serious disturbances. Their membership grew with the expansion of industry. In 1884 unions were given legal status and thereafter became an important influence in the passage of social legislation. The first workmen's compensation act was passed in 1894, the first measure to provide old-age relief became law in 1905, and in 1910 the first steps were taken to provide unemployment insurance. Although social legislation was much further advanced in Britain and Germany, the Third Republic did make considerable progress by 1914.

FRENCH CULTURE

After the establishment of the Third Republic Paris remained the center of European culture. It boasted not only the best plays and the best operas, but also the best bookshops and art museums. Moreover, the Parisian bourgeoisie was the most cultured in the world. The development of French cultural life was in some respects similar to that of French politics. While the political pendulum swung back and forth between revolution and reaction, republic and empire, civil and foreign wars, French culture — and particularly painting — oscillated between the classic and romantic, the realist and naturalist, the impressionist and post-impressionist schools. In literature, and especially in the novel, the first decade of the republic saw a group of writers push the doctrine of realism to its extreme and call it "le naturalisme." Naturalism was concerned with a more scrupulous exactness in observation, with common and precise details of everyday life, and with "the average man."

One of the outstanding members of the school was Guy de Maupassant (1850–1893), a Norman who deliberately educated himself for the profession of letters. To his command of expression he added a mastery of storytelling which is in some respects unrivaled. His fame rests principally on his 212 short stories, in which he surveys a wide range of subjects, including the peasants of Normandy, the society of the Riviera, and the bureaucracy of Paris. But he also wrote a number of novels, the most remarkable being *Une Vie* (1883) and *Pierre et Jean* (1888). It was Maupassant's purpose to depict life as it is — or rather, as he saw it — without seeking its meaning. Through his art he transfers to the mind's eye exactly the scene he wishes to call up. He makes the reader see a specific room, house, or street. It is verbal photography carried to perfection. Although his stories are as readable as anything in modern literature, they are for the most part gloomy, brutal, and full of obsessions of sex. In other words, they deal with the vices rather than with the virtues of men.

The high priest of naturalism was Émile Zola (1840–1902). In 1867 he published the novel *Thérèse Raquin;* then projected a plan to depict French life and society during the Second Empire in a number of volumes. It is upon this series, known as the Rougon-Macquart series (1871–1893), that Zola's reputation chiefly rests. Although the earlier volumes enjoyed considerable success, it was *L'Assommoir* (1877) which made the author's fame and fortune. He became the most read and most discussed novelist in France. *Nana,* which is probably his best known work, was published in 1880. Toward the end of his life he planned a new cycle entitled *The Four Gospels,* of which only three were completed: *Fécondité, Travail,* and *Vérité,* the last dealing with the Dreyfus case. Because of his attacks on the church, the judicial system, and the army, Zola was widely denounced.

The most versatile literary figure of the period was Anatole France (1844–1924) who touched practically every form of literature, including the essay, the novel, the short story, the nouvelle, poetry, drama, history, biography, reflective writing, satire, and criticism. One reason for his reputation is his supreme mastery of the French language. *The Crime of Sylvester Bonnard,* in 1881, proclaimed the rise of a storyteller of the first magnitude. Other important volumes are *Thaïs* (1890), *The Red Lily* (1894), and *Penguin Island* (1908). He was elected to the French Academy in 1896 and was awarded the Nobel prize in literature in 1921.

One of the most striking proofs of the versatility of France in the nineteenth century is provided by the French painters. Probably never before in history has one city harbored so many great painters as Paris during the late sixties and the ensuing period. We have Delacroix, Ingres, Millet, Daumier, Corot, and Courbet, and also Manet, Degas, Monet, Renoir, Cézanne, Gauguin, and van Gogh, in addition to many lesser figures. At the opening of the Universal Exhibition at Paris in 1889 the foreign artists who attended it unanimously voted the French school the foremost in the world. The same act of homage was repeated on a number of occasions in subsequent years. In 1897 a British writer stated, "Paris is still the world's emporium of art, the maelstrom, as it is often said, that sucks in men and women of all nationalities. . . . Nowhere else is art the subject of so much discussion, whether in clubs and cafés, or in journals and reviews. Nowhere else are exhibitions so frequent and so numerous."

Most of the great masters of the French school were at some time or other revolutionaries, as French painting moved rapidly from classicism and romanticism to realism, naturalism, and impressionism. The major trend during the period from the Franco-Prussian War to the First World War was impressionism, which has been defined as "realism which has taken light as its subject." The impressionists sought to present "instantaneous vision" of the whole picture, as opposed to the "consecutive vision" which sees the picture "piece by piece." More particularly, impressionism connotes the study of light out of doors and its effect on the atmosphere and landscape. The man generally regarded as the father of the impressionist school is Édouard Manet (1832–1883). He taught painters to open their eyes and see the light and air in the world around them. In this sense he was the most original painter of the second half of the nineteenth century. Among his better known works are *Boy with the Sword, The Balcony, Woman with Parrot, Portrait of Émile Zola,* and *Olympia.*

The most famous of the impressionist painters and the one who by his talents did the most to spread the theories of the movement was Claude Monet (1840–1926). It was one of his canvases entitled *Impression: Soleil Levant,* which gave the name to the movement in 1874. He was a tireless painter of landscape and would sally forth at dawn with twenty canvases so as to be able to paint the same object from the same point of view but under different light conditions. Famous among this type of paintings are his *Peupliers* (1891), the series of poplars on a river bank, and *Les Nympheas* (1899), one of the most interesting and original of the water lily series. Perhaps the best known of his paintings is the façade of the cathedral of Rouen.

Two masters often classed with the impressionists are Auguste Renoir (1841–1919) and Paul Cézanne (1839–1906). Both were associated for a time with leaders of the impressionist movement but gradually struck out into independent paths which carried them far from the impressionist camp. Renoir was a tireless workman who painted every kind of subject, including portraits, genre, landscapes, nudes, marine scenes, and above all, flower pieces and still life. To appreciate the beauty of his coloring one must see the originals, for they photograph poorly. His master portrait of the early period is *The Charpentier*

Family, now in the Metropolitan Museum of Art. He possessed singular skill in depicting not only facial expression but flesh color and skin texture. Some of his better known canvases are *Déjeuners des Canotiers, Bal au Moulin de la Galette, Petite Danseuse, The Terrace,* and *The Sleeping Woman.* Cézanne, like Renoir, would permit nothing to interfere with his work. He was, in fact, too engrossed to attend his mother's funeral. His work is distinguished by the fact that he subdued or ignored local color to gain an enduring effect. Toward the end of his life buyers were paying fantastic sums for his paintings.

Another outstanding artist of the period was Edgar Degas (1834–1917) who differed from the impressionists in that he disliked outdoor painting. His favorite subjects were race horses, laundresses, milliners, women at their toilets, and ballet dancers. It was his portrayal of ballet dancers which made him world famous. His obvious superiority over his contemporaries lay in his mastery of form and movement. His ballet girls float, leap, and gyrate marvelously. In 1873 he took a trip to the United States, where he painted *The Cotton Market in New Orleans,* now in the Metropolitan Museum.

An artist known for the excitement and turbulence of his color is Paul Gauguin (1848–1903). For the first half of his life he lived an undistinguished existence in France, but then decided to go off to a tropical island where he could devote himself entirely to his art. He went to Tahiti and later to the Marquesas Isles. Living in native fashion he tried, in his own words, to set on canvas "the primal innocence, the enigmatic mystery of life as it was lived in Eden." He continued for the rest of his life to paint brilliant canvases which richly express the life of the South Seas. There is something in Gauguin that is reminiscent of Rousseau, and to a lesser extent of Walt Whitman and Thoreau. Like Rousseau, he felt that civilization is largely sham and deceit, and that peace can be found only in unspoiled nature. The plot of Somerset Maugham's *The Moon and Sixpence* is based on his life.

The name of Gauguin is often associated with another bizarre character, Vincent van Gogh (1853–1890). A Hollander by birth, he was for a time an evangelical missionary in the Belgian coal fields; then turned his burning faith from religion to art. His first pictures were sombre, but after he settled in France, his colors became exuberant. In five years van Gogh painted almost 700 canvases. He worked with fury and violence, literally splashing his canvases with brilliant colors. He suffered a mental breakdown, but continued to paint feverishly in the asylum. He himself said in a lucid moment: "I have risked my life for my work, and for it I have lost my reason." After a year his condition improved so greatly that he was released and not long thereafter committed suicide near Paris. During his life he sold only two paintings, receiving about $4 for one and about $80 for the other. In 1935 one of his landscapes sold for $50,000.

In sculpture one master towers above all others. He is Auguste Rodin (1840–1917). His daring, vision, and originality opened new worlds of art. One day while he was studying the art of sculpture young Rodin saw an old shepherd with a flat nose and an anguished face. He used this shepherd as the model for his *Man with the Broken Nose,* but when he sought to exhibit the work in the Salon of 1864, it was rejected. Academic rules prescribed physical perfection as the supreme object of the sculptor's art. Rodin's bust, which threw down the gauntlet to this ideal, is now regarded by many critics as his greatest work. During the succeeding years he chiseled the *Age of Bronze,* also known as *The Man Who Awakens to Nature,* which is so true to life that some critics declared it to be a cast. Among famous works include his *Eve, Minerva, Statue of Victor Hugo,* and *The Burghers of Calais.* Probably his best known work is *The Thinker,* a great bronze figure in front of the Panthéon in Paris. It was the union in Rodin of the sculptor and the psychologist which distinguished him from other artists. Not since the Greeks had a sculptor so felicitously combined nature and intellectuality. With equal mastery he could portray the entire scale of human sentiment, from terror and anger to tenderness and voluptuousness. Rodin himself ascribed his success to the study of nature.

In France music made extraordinary advances in originality, technical mastery, and subtlety of expression after the Franco-Prussian War. More than this, every field of musical activity began to reflect the feeling of national consciousness which the war had awakened. Thus the music no less than the literature of the period became a mirror of national characteristics. During the first half of the century French music had been dominated largely by the opera, but the change in public taste, which had started with the establishment of orchestras and chamber-music societies, continued during the second half of the century. A distinguished group, among them Bizet, Gounod, Saint-Saëns, Debussy, and Franck, produced a wealth of music which exercised an influence upon the entire civilized world.

Two musicians who stand in the front rank of French composers are Alexandre César Bizet (1838–1875) and Charles Gounod (1818–1893). Both are largely remembered for one great composition. Bizet's great work is *Carmen,* based on the novel by Prosper Mérimée. When it was first performed in 1875 the audience was indifferent. Only after Bizet's death did it achieve great popularity. The work with which Gounod conquered the public is *Faust,* based on Goethe's drama. Its production in 1859 marked a definite triumph for its composer after his earlier operas had failed to evoke enthusiasm. Of the works he wrote during the years that followed *Romeo and Juliet* (1867) ranks next to *Faust* and is to be found in the repertoire of many opera houses. The best known of his religious works is undoubtedly his *Ave Maria*.

Another composer who helped to place France in the front rank of musical nations was Camille Saint-Saëns (1835–1921). From boyhood until his death at eighty-six he composed almost incessantly. Only a few of his many compositions have stood the test of time. To operagoers he is known as the author of *Samson et Dalila*. No French opera, with the exception of Gounod's *Faust* and Bizet's *Carmen*, was more popular in France during the two decades after 1890. In the United States the role of Samson was repeatedly performed by the great Enrico Caruso. In the realm of symphonic music Saint-Saëns achieved distinction with his *Third Symphony in C Minor*. During the years after the Franco-Prussian War he composed a series of symphonic poems of which *Phaéton, Le Rouet d'Omphale, La Jeunesse d'Hercule,* and *La Danse Macabre* are the best known. Noteworthy also are his piano concertos, of which the *Warsaw Concerto* has enjoyed considerable popularity.

César Franck (1822–1890) occupies a unique position in music. Though regarded as the founder of the modern French school of symphonic music, Franck was born at Liége in Belgium and later became a Frenchman by naturalization. No genius ever asked less. He supported his family by serving as church organist and by giving lessons. Even at the age of sixty he taught eight to ten hours a day, carrying on the work of composition in his spare time. His operas, which have been largely forgotten, were disappointments. The two oratorios, *Redemption* and *The Beatitudes,* are among his best-known compositions. Masterpieces of his last years include *Violin Sonata, Symphony in D Minor, String Quartet,* and a number of chorales for the organ. Few great musicians obtained less popular recognition during their life. It was only in his last year that the public began to show some appreciation of his work, his *Violin Sonata* then being successfully played all over Europe and the United States. The same year his *String Quartet* was greeted with a storm of applause which moved the composer to say to a pupil quite naively, "There, you see, the public is beginning to understand me."

The development of music was also deeply influenced by Claude Debussy (1862–1916), whose basic aim it was to give sheer and unadulterated sensuous pleasure to the most delicately developed musical perception. His first important work was the orchestral prelude to *The Afternoon of a Faun* (1891). This together with his nocturnes and some thirty songs made him known to a small circle of French music lovers.

Not until he completed his opera, *Pelléas et Mélisande* (1902), one of the great landmarks in the history of opera, did he become famous outside France. He spent most of the rest of his life in a futile effort to write a successor. His many beautiful preludes, often touched with humor as *Golliwog's Cakewalk,* made him the greatest innovator in piano music since Chopin.

CHAPTER TEN

Hohenzollern Germany

THE GOVERNMENT OF
THE NEW EMPIRE
T HE proclamation of the German Empire in the Hall of Mirrors at Versailles on January 18, 1871, was an outstanding event in the history of the nineteenth century, for it added another great power to the family of European nations. The new empire embraced twenty-two states, the three free cities of Lübeck, Bremen, and Hamburg, and the imperial provinces of Alsace and Lorraine. The states varied in size from the kingdom of Prussia with an area of 114,-000 square miles to the principality of Schaumburg-Lippe with less than 131 square miles. Four of them were kingdoms,[1] six were grand duchies, five were duchies, and seven were principalities. The federal system that was established sought as far as possible to unify the country without depriving the rulers of the individual states of too much authority. Consequently the powers of the imperial government were specifically listed. They included matters relating to the army and navy, customs, weights, measures, banking, coinage, postal and telegraph service, foreign trade, and the mercantile marine. On the other hand, the states could determine their own forms of government, settle all questions of internal administration, draw up their own police regulations, frame laws regarding the tenure of land, and control education within their boundaries. The sphere of authority which was left to the states was, however, gradually reduced, particularly by the civil code, which went into effect January 1, 1900.

The constitution of the new empire was simply a revision of the constitution of the North German Confederation. It vested the legislative functions in two bodies, the Bundesrat (Federal Council) and the

[1] Prussia, Bavaria, Saxony, and Württemberg.

Reichstag (Imperial Diet). The former was composed of fifty-eight members who represented the governments of the states; [2] the latter consisted of 397 members elected by universal manhood suffrage for a period of three (later five) years, each member representing an electoral district of approximately 100,000 inhabitants. The Reichstag, since all laws required its consent, appeared to possess considerable power, but in reality its chief function was to consider bills prepared by the chancellor and the Bundesrat. It possessed no control over the administration or the executive except so far as it could refuse to grant supplies. Even this power was not so great as it might appear, for revenue laws, once passed, became permanent and could be changed only with the consent of the Bundesrat. If a Reichstag refused to pass a bill, the government could always secure a majority by dissolving the recalcitrant chamber and appealing to the country. The Reichstag could not consider a bill until it had been passed by the Bundesrat; even any amendments it might suggest were subject to the veto of the upper house. Thus the Reichstag, the only agency of the people, was merely a kind of debating club that had little power to enforce its will.

The executive head of the empire was the king of Prussia,[3] who received the hereditary title of *Deutscher Kaiser* or German emperor. He had charge of the foreign relations of the empire, was commander in chief of the army and navy, and had the right to appoint the chancellor, who was his chief assistant, and such other imperial officials as were not appointed by the Bundesrat.[4] On the other hand, he had no veto; nor could he declare war unless it was purely defensive. An offensive war he could declare only with the consent of the Bundesrat. Nevertheless the range of his powers was wide. Through the chancellor, who presided over the Bundesrat and introduced the bills for its consideration, he controlled the seventeen Prussian votes. These enabled him to veto any constitutional amendments, since only fourteen votes were necessary to prevent any change of the constitution. Although the emperor and his chancellor were usually able to control enough votes to hold a majority in the Bundesrat, the other states did combine to defeat Prussian proposals on a number of occasions. In 1877, for example, the Bundesrat decided that Leipzig was to be the seat of the imperial court of appeal, instead of Berlin, as the Prussian government had desired.

Having launched the new ship of state Bismarck, as imperial chancellor, took charge of the tiller to guide it on its course. Whereas Cavour

[2] The number of votes accorded to each state varied according to the size of each. While the smaller had one, two, or three votes, Saxony and Württemberg had four each, Bavaria had six, and Prussia had seventeen.

[3] Prussia comprised about three fifths of the territory and about two thirds of the population of the new empire.

[4] There was no cabinet in the sense of the British cabinet. The chancellor simply appointed administrative functionaries to whom he assigned the duties of cabinet ministers.

was struck down by death in the maturity of his powers, even before the work of Italian unification culminated in the annexation of Venetia and the transfer of the capital to Rome, Bismarck survived the establishment of German unity by nearly twenty-eight years, for nineteen of which he remained chief minister. Down to the day of his retirement he labored strenuously, regarding nothing that promised to further his object as too trifling. That object always remained the same: the aggrandizement and consolidation of Germany under the leadership and control of the Prussian monarchy. William I, already seventy-four at the time the empire was founded, was no longer capable of doing the work required of a ruler; hence he gave his chancellor considerable freedom in the management of affairs. As a diplomatist Bismarck proved himself to be not only the most powerful but also the ablest force in Europe. His influence surpassed even that which Metternich had wielded from 1815 to 1848. Lord Russell's statement that "at St. Petersburg Bismarck's word is gospel, as well as at Paris and Rome," applied with equal truth to Vienna, Madrid, and Constantinople. On the other hand, in dealing with domestic problems he met more opposition, and even his most ardent admirer would hardly insist that his home policy was an unqualified success.

The political parties with which Bismarck had to deal during the early years of the new empire were five in number. Originally, during the conflict over the Army Bill, the members of the Prussian legislature had separated into two hostile groups, the Conservatives and the Liberals. The former were recruited mainly from the Junkers or great landowners and were the upholders of militarism, class distinctions, and strong monarchy; the Liberals came largely from the towns and sought to establish German unity on the basis of liberal principles. It was over the opposition of this party that Bismarck had ridden roughshod in 1862 on the question of military reform. But after the defeat of Austria in 1866 a number of the Liberals who were less dogmatic and doctrinaire than the rest separated themselves to form the National Liberal Party, which supported Bismarck in his efforts to complete unification. Similarly a number of Conservatives who were less reactionary than their fellows left the old party to organize the Free Conservative Party. All four parties continued to exist after the founding of the empire. To these a fifth, the Center Party, which was intent upon advancing policies favorable to the Catholic church, was added during the first session of the Reichstag.

During his early years as chancellor Bismarck drew his main support from the Free Conservatives and National Liberals. At no time, however, did he identify himself permanently with any political group. Busch reports that he said in 1881, "While I have been minister, I have never belonged to any party, whether liberal or conservative. My party consists solely of the king and myself." In order to carry his measures it became necessary for him at times to ally himself temporarily with a party or, better, a combination of parties, often of mutually discordant parties. To effect such a combination he had to give as well as receive. If he believed a measure necessary, he would go into the parliamentary market place, as it were, and offer certain concessions in return for support. At some time or another every party in the Reichstag supported or opposed him according to the measure of the moment. That he should have any opposition whatever often irked him greatly, for he believed that the government had a right to the support of the deputies. He conceded them the right to criticize details of policies but insisted that the government alone must determine the policies. His theory, then, was that the prosperity and happiness of a people can best be attained by a government whose right to act is not, in the last analysis, dependent on the popular will.

As chancellor, Bismarck's first care was to rivet the German states together more firmly. This he did by consolidating the various institutions of the empire. One of the first achievements of his government was the establishment of a common currency and a common standard of weights and measures. Gradually all the postal and telegraph systems, except those of Bavaria and Württemberg, were merged. By 1874 the Prussian military system was functioning in all the states except Bavaria, Saxony, and Württemberg, which had retained the right to organize their own military forces. In 1876 legal procedure was made uniform throughout the empire and a supreme court of appeal (*Reichsgericht*) was established at Leipzig; the following year saw the codification of criminal law; but the crowning achievement of the legal reform, the civil code, was not put in force until 1900. Bismarck endeavored also to unify the railways; but as some of the states were unwilling to merge their systems into one great national organization, he had to content himself with one that embraced the railways of Prussia and a few neighboring states.

THE KULTURKAMPF

While Bismarck was trying to weld the German states together more firmly, a conflict broke out which tended to divide the people into two hostile religious groups. Known as the *Kulturkampf,* it was basically a renewal of the medieval contest between church and state. Bismarck himself said, "It is the old struggle between king and priest, a struggle for power as old as the human race." Its immediate causes were the doctrine of papal infallibility and the efforts of the Catholics to regain for the pope the temporal power he had lost. In 1870, just when Rome itself was about to be added to the kingdom of Italy and the pope to become "the prisoner of the Vatican," the Vatican Council voted the dogma that the pope, when he speaks *ex cathedra* to settle some point of faith and morals, is infallible and that the decisions he makes at such times are in themselves unalterable even by the common consent of the church. Most of the German Catholics accepted the new dogma at once, but a small group, including a number of distinguished men known as the Old Catholics, refused. When they remained adamant in their refusal, the pope finally excommunicated them and requested the Prussian government to remove them from their positions in state schools and universities and from their offices as priests and religious preachers. But the Prussian government, having no desire to compel the acceptance of a dogma in which it saw a threat to the authority of the state, would not comply.

Furthermore, there was a strong feeling in the Catholic districts that the new empire should intervene at once in Italian affairs for the purpose of restoring the pope's temporal power. When the support was not at once given, the Catholics constituted themselves into a party to win it. This party, which its members called the "Constitutional Party," became more generally known as "The Center" because its members occupied the seats in the center of the assembly hall. As early as February 18, 1871, it showed its real character by urging the emperor to undertake at once "the restoration of the rights and freedom of the Holy Father." In the elections a fortnight later for the first Reichstag the Center Party, aided by the exertions of the Catholic clergy, managed to gain sixty-three seats.

The appearance of the Center Party greatly disturbed the Iron Chancellor, who regarded it as the "mobilization of the church against the state" and a serious threat to the religious peace of Germany. A party founded on a confessional basis, he said, was "the most monstrous phenomenon in politics." So in 1871 he entered into a conflict with the Catholic hierarchy which was to be fought out mainly in Prussia but which also affected Germany as a whole. He was confident he would not be defeated in the struggle. Alluding to the humiliation of Henry IV before Gregory VII at Canossa (1077) he exclaimed, "Do not fear; we will not go to Canossa either in body or in spirit."

The opening gun was fired by the Reichstag in 1871 when it passed the famous *Kanzelparagraph* (pulpit paragraph), which made it a penal offense for priests to use their pulpits for inciting opposition to the government. In the next year a second imperial statute decreed that all foreign Jesuits must leave the country, and native Jesuits were prohibited from developing any activity as an order. Then the Prussian diet discharged its salvo at the church. In 1873 Dr. Adalbert Falk, the minister of public worship and education, framed the first of the laws which later became known as the May Laws because they were generally passed in the month of May, although in different years. In general they aimed to restrict the disciplinary power of the church over its members and to put the education and installation of the clergy under government control. By the first laws, converts were compelled to obtain the consent of a magistrate before changing from one church to another; all ecclesiastical seminaries were placed under state control; and candidates for the priesthood were required to spend three years in a German university and to pass an examination in philosophy, history, philology, and German. These laws were supplemented by others which stipulated that all clergymen who did not obey the previous laws were to be suspended from office and that vacant dioceses were to be administered by the state. Finally as a means of limiting ecclesiastical authority a civil ceremony was made compulsory for marriage.

But the laws failed to accomplish their object. Although a few clergymen submitted, the majority refused to obey, declaring that human laws ought not to be obeyed if contrary to the laws of God. For their refusal priests and bishops were fined, deprived of their salaries, imprisoned, or exiled. Monasteries were suppressed and their members dispersed. Of the Jesuits alone more than eight hundred were compelled to leave Germany. By the year 1877 eight of the twelve Prussian bishoprics and more than four hundred curacies were vacant. It was all to no avail.

In politics Bismarck met with equal failure in trying to bring the clerical opposition to its knees. In the elections of 1874 the Center Party managed to carry no less than ninety-four seats. More than this, Bismarck had lost the support of many Conservatives who, though Protestant, were averse to any attack on established religion; and signs of disaffection were also becoming manifest among the National Liberals because the chancellor, after accepting their support through the years, had done little to help them carry out their own program. Thus Bismarck's embarrassment in the Reichstag was steadily increasing, a situation that was particularly serious to him because he had projected plans of an economic and social nature which could be realized only with the help of the Center Party. He wished, first, to inaugurate a protectionist policy for the twofold purpose of protecting German industry and agriculture and of increasing the imperial revenues. Second, he was determined to repress the socialist movement, which he regarded as a greater menace to the peace of Germany than the claims of the Catholic church.

Consequently he began to beat a retreat despite his vow that he would "not go to Canossa." This retreat was made easier by the accession to the papal throne of Leo XIII (February 20, 1878), who adopted a conciliatory attitude. After a series of conversations between papal and German representatives the government laid down its arms little by little. Bismarck himself said regarding the May Laws, "We can always wring the necks of the chickens we have ourselves hatched." In return for the support of the government policies by the Center Party most of the May Laws were gradually suspended and finally repealed. Vacant bishoprics and curacies were filled, sequestrated revenues were returned to the clergy, and, in general, religious peace was restored. Later Bismarck tried to disavow responsibility for the *Kulturkampf* by attributing it to his colleagues, especially to Falk, his loyal servant. His arguments, however, carry no conviction. They are but an illustration of a singular intellectual foible he possessed, which Prince Hohenlohe described as follows: "He will not admit his own share in anything that has failed." More plausible is Bismarck's statement that "the course of our policy was not determined by religious considerations but purely by the desire to establish as firmly as possible the unity won on the battlefield."

THE STRUGGLE WITH SOCIALISM

The struggle with socialism fills the second decade of Bismarck's chancellorship much as the conflict with the Catholics filled the first. In 1848 socialism still had no strong foothold in Germany. Six years earlier a German writer had said, "Germany need not fear socialism, for unlike France and England she has no proletariat to speak of." But as industry began to flourish after 1848, the seeds of socialism, sown by the writings of Karl Marx and other socialists, began to sprout. In 1862 Ferdinand Lassalle (1825–1864) began to go about telling the workmen that the only chance of improving their condition lay in organizing themselves. His appeal was so effective that he was able the next year to form a new political party at Leipzig called the Universal German Workmen's Association. While he was founding his association in northern Germany, Workmen's Educational Associations were being formed in southern Germany. Somewhat more conservative at first than the northern Association, they gradually moved in the direction of Marxian socialism and formed a political party in 1869. Thus there were two socialist parties in Germany. Together they polled 124,655 votes in the elections of 1871 and won two seats. During the succeeding years their membership increased rapidly. In 1874 they polled 351,952 votes and won ten seats in the Reichstag. Their position became even stronger in the next year through the fusion of the two into the Socialist

Workmen's Party, which in 1890 officially adopted the title "Social Democratic Party." Before long it threatened to become the strongest party in the larger industrial centers.

The increase in the number of socialists thoroughly alarmed Bismarck as well as most other conservatives. The Iron Chancellor had long regarded with disfavor socialist ideas on religion, marriage, private property, and monarchy, but his struggle with the Catholics had prevented him from taking any action. Now he would apply his two sovereign remedies, force and bribery. First he would destroy the socialist organization by repression and then he would wean the workmen from socialist ideas by legislation designed to make them dependent on the state. When in March, 1878, an attempt was made on the emperor's life by an individual in whose lodgings radical literature was found, Bismarck at once introduced a severe bill for the suppression of the socialists. But the bill, so comprehensive that it threatened all political organizations, was rejected by the Reichstag. A second attempt to assassinate the emperor in June of the same year caused Bismarck to dissolve the Reichstag and to appeal to the country for support. This time his hopes were not disappointed. In the elections the liberal and radical forces lost seventy seats to the conservatives, and the new Reichstag soon passed the antisocialist bill in a modified form.

The law which came into force in October, 1878, gave the government the right to prohibit public meetings, dissolve political associations, suppress newspapers and books, and decide who was and who was not a socialist. In short, it enabled the government to break up the public organization of the Social Democrats. Bismarck's efforts had a temporary success, for in the next elections the voting power of the party sank to 311,961. But rigorous as the law was, it failed to check permanently the growth of socialism. The party continued to exist in secret and soon overcame its setback. The lack of a party organ was supplied by the founding of the *Socialdemocrat* at Zurich (1879), and each week thousands of copies of this paper were smuggled into Germany. In spite of everything the government could do, the socialists grew in strength and in numbers. This they demonstrated in the election of 1884 by winning twenty-four seats in the Reichstag.

Meanwhile Bismarck had embarked on a policy of state socialism. In 1883 a series of laws had been passed which were designed, as he himself put it, "to bribe" the working classes to be content. His plan was stated in the words: "Give the workman the right to work as long as he is healthy, assure him care when he is sick, assure him maintenance when he is old. If you do that . . . then I believe the gentlemen of the Social Democratic program will sound their bird calls in vain." The Sickness Insurance Law of 1883 compelled all salary or wage earners receiving less than 2000 marks annually, with but few exceptions, to join a sickness fund. Two thirds of the contributions to the fund were to be paid by the worker, one third by the employer. In case of sickness the worker was to receive half of his average wage and also medical care, for a period of thirteen weeks. Closely linked with this law was the Accident Insurance Law, passed in 1884, which required employers to form associations for the care of those injured in industrial accidents. The entire cost of this insurance was borne by the employer. During the first thirteen weeks of disablement caused by an accident the worker was treated as an ordinary case of sickness; thereafter he came under the provisions of the Accident Law. Compensations from the fourteenth week onward consisted of two thirds of the former wages for complete disability and a proportional sum in other instances. In case of a fatal accident the surviving relatives received a pension in addition to a sum amounting to twenty days' wages for funeral expenses.

Five years later, in 1889, the Old Age Insurance Law which was to protect the worker against a penniless old age was passed. Its scope was somewhat wider than that of the earlier acts. Practically every worker between seventeen and seventy, male or female, whose wages did not exceed 2000 marks a year came under its provisions. Only the government servants, who were already insured, were exempted. The costs were shared by the government, the employers, and the workers, each paying one third. Each worker beginning at the age of sixteen had to pay his contributions for thirty years in order to be entitled to a pension which he could draw when he reached the age of seventy-one. Since employment had to be sufficiently regular to permit the worker to make the necessary payments, the very poor were excluded from the benefits of this bill.

At the end of ten years it was evident that Bismarck's efforts to exorcise the "insanities of Social Democracy" were no more successful than his struggle with the Roman Catholic Church had been. Neither repression nor state socialism was effective in weakening the movement. The social legislation did confer great benefits on the workers, but it did not cause the Social Democrats to cease their agitation. Far from satisfying them, it seems to have stimulated their ambitions to achieve their own aims. By 1890 their party boasted a vote three times as large as it was when the first of the antisocialist laws was passed. Its popular vote in the elections of that year was nearly a million and a half, and its representation in the Reichstag increased to thirty-five. Yet Bismarck appears to have learned nothing from his failure. Force having proved ineffective in the first place, his only remedy was more force. When the Reichstag refused to renew the antisocialist law early in

1890, he demanded its dissolution. This stubborn insistence upon the renewal of the repressive law was one of the immediate causes of the break between him and Emperor William II in 1890.

DROPPING THE PILOT

In 1888 Emperor William I had died at the patriarchal age of ninety-one and had been succeeded by his son, who took the title of Frederick III. The Liberals, who had long looked forward to his accession, hoped that he would inaugurate a new policy, but at his accession he was already in the grip of a mortal illness. His reign covered only ninety-nine days and left no mark on German politics. However, a new era opened when his son, William II, ascended the imperial throne on June 15, 1888. Twenty-nine at the time of his accession, William was a man of strong constitution and almost tempestuous energy. Despite the fact that his left arm was withered, he excelled as a rider, fencer, swimmer, and hunter. His intellectual gifts were also above the average. No occupant of the Prussian throne since Frederick the Great had possessed intelligence of such high order. His active mind, which neglected no sphere of national life, was characterized by the faculty of quickly grasping the essence of things. This faculty explains in large part the kaiser's supreme self-confidence. He did not harbor the least doubt regarding his own ability to deal with any problems he might be called on to solve. Actually, however, this faculty proved to be a weakness since it misled him into believing that he could understand a complex problem by merely superficial study. Hence his many insufficiently considered or ill-considered actions, particularly in the domain of international politics.

It was the obsession of his own importance that probably caused him to take the divine-right theory of the Hohenzollern more seriously than any ancestor since Frederick William I (1688–1740). At his accession he promised to preserve and protect the constitution and concluded by stating that he would always bear in mind the words of Frederick the Great that in Prussia "the king is the first servant of the state." But during the reign that followed he never missed an opportunity to indulge his autocratic tendency within the limits of his power both as German emperor and as king of Prussia; in fact, he was able in practice to disregard the constitution in certain important respects. In his speeches he repeatedly asserted the anticonstitutional theory of divine right. Thus, for example, he said at Königsberg in 1890, "It was on this spot that his Majesty the late Emperor William I again proclaimed before the whole world . . . that we Hohenzollern accept our crown only from Heaven and that we are responsible to Heaven for the performance of all duties attached to the crown. I, too, am animated by this conception and am resolved to act and govern on this principle." In Munich, where he was asked to write something in the Golden Book as a souvenir of his visit, he inscribed the words, *Suprema lex, regis voluntas* (the will of the king is the supreme law). Since the German people, with the exception of the socialists, were intensely monarchic, they were ready to overlook the absolutist tendencies of their kaiser.

Because William II believed so firmly in divine-right rule, it was inevitable that a conflict should break out between him and Bismarck. Their conceptions of the place and function of the monarch in the state were too divergent for harmonious cooperation. Bismarck, on the one hand, while doing lip service to the doctrine of divine right, had for a generation exercised powers akin to dictatorship. He had, it is true, never wielded completely unrestrained power. He often had to wring decisions on trivial as well as on important matters from William I. But the old emperor had always yielded in the end. All Germans realized that under the first emperor it was Bismarck who had really governed. The exercise of authority had, in fact, become such a passion with him that he hoped "to die in harness." He felt that he alone could command the situation; in other words, that he was indispensable. William II, on the other hand, was not satisfied to stand as the empty symbol of authority. Believing that the chancellor had too long overshadowed the wearer of the crown, he was firmly minded to assume the actual direction of affairs. As the humorists put it, William the Second was determined to be second to no one. Thus it was basically a struggle for power between a dictatorial chancellor and a self-assertive monarch, both of whom were greedy of popular applause and passionately fond of ruling. Besides being a contest for power, it was also a story of crabbed age and impetuous youth. As Bismarck stated it, "An old carthorse and a young courser go ill in harness together."

Gradually a number of tangible differences arose. One immediate point of discord was disagreement over the continuance of the antisocialist law. While the Iron Chancellor insisted on continuing the policy of stern repression, the kaiser advocated milder measures. Although he denounced the socialists as "vermin which gnaw at the roots of the imperial oak" and as "a horde of men unworthy to bear the name Germans," he was certain that milder measures would prove more successful than repressive legislation had been. The idea of winning over the socialists by "kindness" Bismarck, with his belief in force as a remedy for social disaffection, regarded as a foolhardy utopian scheme, and when he had to support this policy his pride was deeply wounded. Other differences widened the rift. When Bismarck discovered that some of his ministers, unknown to him, had conferred directly with the monarch, he demanded that, in accord with the Prussian Cabinet Order of 1852, all negotiations between the throne and the several ministers be carried on through him. Instead of complying, William, who wished the ministers to be his servants and not the chancellor's, demanded that the order be abrogated.

Had Bismarck been a little less inflexible, the open breach might have been postponed. During the reign of the first emperor he had always managed to get his way by threatening to resign. But the device which had invariably caused William I to yield had lost its magic. William II did not believe the old chancellor was indispensable. Nevertheless he did hold Bismarck in high regard and repeatedly tried to conciliate him, knowing that because of his advanced age he must retire before many years. But as the differences gradually became more acute, William finally decided that he must go. When Bismarck again offered to resign, the offer, much to his amazement, was accepted. However, in the letter in which the kaiser accepted the resignation and which was published in the newspapers, William sought to give the impression that the chancellor had resigned in spite of the repeated efforts of the sad-hearted sovereign to keep him in office. "The reasons adduced by you for your decision," he wrote, "have convinced me that further attempts to persuade you to withdraw your request would be futile." So on March 21, 1890, William calmly "sent the veteran pilot over the side." With the dismissal of Bismarck the emperor's personal rule may be said to have begun. Future chancellors accepted office on the tacit understanding that there was "only one will in the empire" and that was the will of William II.

When Bismarck became minister-president of Prussia in 1862, he had found Germany a medley of miscellaneous states, but by working resolutely with an unvarying purpose he managed in less than nine years to make the "discordant Germanies a single Germany" which was the strongest power on the Continent. In doing so he compelled the German people to sacrifice liberalism for the sake of nationality. As Georg von Bunsen put it, "Bismarck has made Germany great and the Germans small." Moreover, he displayed but few scruples in his choice of means. The man who in private life bowed his knees to the Christian God was in his public career an apt disciple of Machiavelli. In other words, he was an unblushing opportunist, ready to use any principles or methods to achieve his ends. Gladstone said of him, "A very big man, no doubt, but very unscrupulous." Probably the best one could say of his methods is that they were no worse than those of Napoleon III or Cavour. In general he had little consideration for the opinions of others, always insisting that his views prevail even when they were opposed by the emperor's. A staunch upholder of the divine right of

A painting of Emperor William I and his suite. Reading left to right: Bismarck, the crown prince, the emperor, and von Moltke

marck holding down the Socialists, artoon from *Punch*, 1878

SOCIALIST JACK IN THE BOX.

William II posing as Frederick the Great

The Queen and her Hindu secretary. One of the
last portraits of Victoria

Disraeli receiving Queen Victoria in 1877, from
a contemporary print

W. E. Gladstone, from a drawing by Phil May
(National Portrait Gallery)

kings in public, he often ridiculed kings and courts in private conversation. For example, he said to a group of friends on the anniversary of his retirement, "I have seen three kings naked and there was nothing striking about any of them."

Bismarck had few interests outside of politics and his estates. This became increasingly true with the passing of time. He himself wrote in retrospect, "Politics was the biggest trout in my pond; it has devoured all other passions, as the fattest trout eats up its fellows." Toward the end of his life he began to wonder whether the game of politics as he had played it was worth the candle. Busch reported him as saying, "But for me three great wars would not have taken place, and eighty thousand men would not have been killed and would not now be mourned by parents, brothers, sisters, and widows." Having achieved the unification of the German states except Austria, he became a staunch advocate of peace, but he left as a heritage to the German people the idea of "blood and iron."

GERMANY UNDER WILLIAM II

The reign of William II was for Germany a period of development along many lines. Among the various details to which the government gave much thought and care was the army; in fact, the army was one of the major interests of William II. During his early training, which was largely of a military nature, he had developed a fondness for soldiers and soldiering that remained with him throughout life. He had an absorbing passion for military reviews, and he delighted in fraternizing with the officers of the army at luncheons and banquets. It is reported that he knew more than a thousand officers by name. He believed that the army was the strongest support of his throne, a conviction which he frequently stated in public. In 1891 he said, "The soldier and the army, not parliamentary majorities or parliamentary resolutions, have welded together the German Empire. My trust is in the army." Not that he was bellicose. "I have no intention of using this force for offensive war," he stated before the Reichstag. "Germany stands in need neither of further glory nor of conquests." He believed that if Germany had a strong army, other nations, and particularly France, would be less eager to attack it. Accordingly he sought to strengthen the military forces in every possible way. Troops in all branches of the service were carefully trained and supplied with the most modern weapons. In 1890 the standing army was increased by 20,000 to 486,983 men. Thereafter it was further augmented at various times so that it numbered over 800,000 men in 1913. On the basis of compulsory service every young man of military age, if called, had to serve two or three years and was then put in the reserves. When the war broke out in 1914, Germany was able to muster seven million men, of whom four million were the best trained soldiers in the world.

The most striking development of the reign of William II, however, was in the field of industry and commerce. In this area Germany was surpassed by no other nation. What had generally been regarded as a nation of poets, thinkers, and peasants became a nation of businessmen. Although the economic forces responsible for the growth of industry and commerce had been at work long before the reign of William, they gathered considerable momentum during this period. German industry and commerce, as if determined to make up for lost time, strode forward in seven-league boots. Between 1882 and 1913 the number of strictly industrial workers rose from six to thirteen millions. Especially notable was the growth in the heavy industries. The production of pig iron, for example, more than trebled between 1888 and 1910, by which year German iron production was far ahead of all other European countries, including Great Britain. The output of coal increased from 73 million tons in 1891 to 160 million tons in 1913. Even more phenomenal was the development of the electrical and chemical industries. The former, which was practically nonexistent in 1882, manufactured products in 1900 valued at 368 million marks. In the manufacture of chemicals Germany held an undisputed supremacy in 1914, its exports of dye-stuffs amounting to about 80 per cent of the world's supply. In brief, by 1914 Germany had taken rank as a leading industrial nation. Among European nations it yielded precedence only to Great Britain in the gross value of its manufactures.

During the same period German commerce was organized on a hitherto undreamed-of scale. Not only did the government foster trade by paying export bounties and by reducing freight charges; it also built a huge merchant fleet and extended its network of railways to transport cargoes to and fro in Germany. So much mileage was added to the railways that by 1907 the railway system was by far the most important in continental Europe. In 1911 Germany had 61,936 kilometers of railways in operation as compared with 37,649 kilometers in England, an increase of 42.6 per cent since 1890. The net tonnage of the merchant marine increased two and a half times, and the value of the export trade more than trebled between 1888 and 1913. More and more articles with the inscription "Made in Germany" found their way into every quarter of the globe. In 1912 German salesmen found a market in Australia for products valued at $90 million. Whereas fifty years earlier German exports had consisted largely of foodstuffs and raw materials, coal was the only raw material exported in quantities after 1900. Among the more important manufactured products that Germany exported were hardware, chemicals, electrical supplies, and cotton goods. By 1914 Germany had outstripped both France and the United States in the value of its foreign commerce and was second only to Great Britain.

The rapid development of industry and commerce wrought other impressive changes in German life. One of these was a shift of the population from country to town. Attracted by the larger opportunities and the greater returns of industrial employment, more and more Germans left the soil and migrated to the industrial centers. Some idea of the shift may be gained from the fact that in 1885 only 18.4 per cent of the population lived in cities over 20,000, but by 1910 the number had increased to 34.5 per cent. Thus Germany had become a country of large cities while developing into an industrial nation. Furthermore, the expansion of commerce and industry greatly increased the wealth of Germany, raised the standard of living, and brought increased contentment. The result was that emigration, which during the previous decades had reached enormous proportions,[5] dwindled almost to insignificance. In the early eighties emigrants were still leaving Germany at the annual rate of 221,000, but by 1900 the number dropped to 22,000 per year and by 1912 to 18,500. By the beginning of the twentieth century, in fact, the emigration was more than balanced by immigration from Poland and other Slavic countries.

As trade and capital increased, certain individuals and groups loudly demanded the acquisition of colonies; in fact, since the early part of the century publicists had been urging Germany to acquire colonies while there was still unclaimed territory. They argued that emigration must be a national loss unless the emigrants settled in German colonies, and that if Germany had tropical possessions, it would not have to depend on other countries for such products as cotton, jute, coffee, tea, and cocoa. Prominent among the zealots of the colonial cause was the economist Wilhelm Roscher (1817–1894). "Germany," he wrote, "must lose no time if the last suitable territories are not to be seized by other and more resolute nations." However, until it was unified politically Germany was in no position to participate in the scramble for colonies. As soon as the Franco-Prussian War welded the German states into a coherent whole, the colonial enthusiasts began to present their various schemes; but Bismarck resolutely set his face against such adventures. Colonies he regarded as a luxury which Germany could not afford. "I want no colonies," he stated in 1871; "they are only good for providing offices. For us to acquire colonies would be like a poverty-stricken Polish nobleman providing himself with silks and sables when he needs

---

[5] It is estimated that between 1815 and 1879 four million Germans emigrated, of whom 3.6 million went to the United States.

shirts." Nevertheless, when the demands of the growing colonial party became insistent, Bismarck finally relented. The result was that between 1884 and Bismarck's retirement in 1890 Germany acquired South-West Africa, the Cameroons, Togoland, and German East Africa on the African continent and a large part of New Guinea, the Bismarck archipelago, and the Marshall Islands in the Pacific.

With the accession of William II the acquisition of colonies became an integral part of national policy. The new kaiser began at once to scan the map of the world for unallotted regions. When the Sino-Japanese War of 1894–1895 demonstrated the defenselessness of China, he eagerly awaited an opportunity for laying claim to a share of the spoils in that country. Upon receiving the report that two German missionaries had been murdered in Chinese territory, he used the incident as an excuse for sending a naval force to the Far East and in 1898 succeeded in obtaining from China a ninety-nine-year lease of Kiaochow on the Shantung Peninsula. The next year he purchased the Caroline, Palau, and Mariana Islands (except Guam) in the Pacific from Spain and in 1900 acquired two of the Samoa islands (Upolu and Savaii). Finally, in 1911 he obtained part of French Equatorial Africa (the New Cameroons) in return for recognizing France's predominant interest in Morocco. Thus by 1914 Germany possessed a colonial empire covering 1,484,944 square miles, with a native population of about fourteen millions. But the venture was not profitable. Having launched their colonial policy so late, the Germans had been able to get only such regions as the other imperialist nations regarded as too poor to occupy. Only Togoland and the two Samoa islands were self-supporting. It has been estimated that the colonies cost Germany more than a billion marks up to 1914.

William II was not only fired by the colonial idea; he was also ambitious to make Germany a great naval power. Before his reign Germany, relying chiefly on military power, had cut but a small figure at sea. It did of course possess a few ships, but they were of no importance as a fighting force. Such a navy did not satisfy the kaiser. He felt that Germany needed a strong fleet in order to protect its colonies and its trade interests. During the decade of the nineties the idea of building a great navy was never far from his thoughts. Even before 1890 he acquired Helgoland in exchange for the recognition of England's suzerainty in Zanzibar, and then transformed the island into a great naval base. In his public speeches he missed no opportunity to expound the doctrine of a big fleet.

William II did not stand alone in his desire for a large navy. His enthusiasm was vigorously supported by many others, including some of the most prominent men in Germany. Nevertheless it was only with the maximum effort that the proponents of the idea succeeded in getting the Reichstag to pass the first important navy bill (1898), which provided for the addition of nineteen battleships and forty-two cruisers to the navy. Supporters of the program realized that if the kaiser's plan was to be carried out, some means would have to be found to overcome the Reichstag's opposition to the expenditure of huge sums. They decided to form a large organization to put irresistible pressure on the Reichstag. The German Navy League (*Deutscher Flottenverein*), organized in 1898, had a quarter million members within two years. After it had carefully prepared the ground by distributing pamphlets, by countrywide rallies, and by agitation of every sort, the second navy bill, providing for the further construction of thirty-eight battleships and fourteen cruisers, was successfully introduced in 1900. Other measures followed, so that by the beginning of the First World War Germany had a navy second only to that of Great Britain. Although William II insisted that his aims were peaceful, his program inevitably alarmed the British, who saw their naval supremacy threatened.

A further development during the period after 1890 was the growth of the Social Democratic Party. William II had hoped to detach the workers from socialism by measures that would improve their conditions, but he soon discovered that the working classes refused to turn their backs on the movement. When he did not renew the antisocialist law, the exiled leaders swarmed back to Germany and redoubled their efforts to strengthen their cause. The result was that the party gained nearly three million votes between 1890 and 1912. In the elections of 1912 it polled 4.25 million votes, sending more representatives to the Reichstag than any other party (110 of the 397 members were Social Democrats). As it grew in strength, its aims did become more moderate, but its attitude toward the Hohenzollern state remained one of mild hostility, especially in the case of the various army bills. Just before the outbreak of the war the party issued an appeal which stated, "The ruling classes, who in peacetime oppress you, despise you, exploit you, want to use you as cannon fodder. Everywhere the cry must ring in the despot's ears: 'We want no war! Down with war! Long live international brotherhood!' " However, when the German government declared war, it did so with the almost unanimous support of the Social Democrats. The trade unions at once terminated all existing strikes and lockouts, and the Social Democrats in the Reichstag proved that they were Germans first and socialists second by voting the funds the government requested.

GERMAN LITERATURE AND MUSIC

With the long-expected dream of national unity realized in a measure, many Germans hoped that a great national literature, one that would dwarf the literary achievements of the past, would be forthcoming. But the hope was not fulfilled. The tone of the literature of the new empire was prevailingly pessimistic, materialistic, naturalistic, or socialistic; from the standpoint of art it was largely mediocre. The period produced no figure even remotely comparable to Goethe. While a number of writers may be classed as second rate, the rest were of lesser or of no importance whatsoever. Particularly conspicuous was the paucity of humorous works and of works which are definitely national in their reflections. While national unity was an aspiration, it realized itself in literature, but no sooner was political unity attained than the national spirit evaporated from literature. In the popular mind the novel and the short story doubtless outweighed all other forms. Each year German writers produced hundreds of novels and thousands of short stories, but there was not one writer whose stature approached that of Dickens or Balzac.

The best works were undoubtedly in the drama; yet even in this form the first fifteen years of the new empire produced little that is worth remembering. The foremost German dramatist of the last years of the century was Gerhart Hauptmann (1862–1946). Although he learned much from Zola, Ibsen, and Tolstoi, his work as a whole does not merit comparison with that of these three masters. A great proportion of his work is superficial and imitative, but it does include moments of imagination and poetry. His dramas are a protest against the exploitation of the poor; however, he offers no solution for the social problems he raises. *The Weavers* (1892), which is generally regarded as his best play, reproduces in a realistic manner the hopeless misery existing among the Silesian weavers in the early decades of the nineteenth century. The scenes of exploitation, hunger, and despair were so grim that the Social Democrats at once claimed the play as their own, although the author disavowed any socialistic aims.

The literary figure of the period who undoubtedly excited the most violent controversy was Friedrich Nietzsche (1844–1900), philosopher and moralist. In his writings, of which *Thus Spake Zarathustra* (1883) and *Beyond Good and Evil* (1886) are probably the best known, he revolted against the ideas of his time. The old moral system, he argued, must be discarded in favor of a new set of principles, the most fundamental of which is the "Will to Power." The Will to Power, he stated, is the root of all life and action, and everything is good or bad only in relation to it. The ultimate purpose is to produce the Superman. Sometimes Nietzsche's ideal is the creation of great individuals; at other times he appears to mean by Superman a new type of man, a higher, grander, nobler race in the Darwinian sense. "Man," he wrote, "is something that shall be surpassed." In the struggle for a higher life the so-called virtues of pity, humility, and the like are symptoms of weakness and degeneracy. The marks of a true man are pride, ruthlessness toward himself and others, courage, and love of battle. "The weak and the helpless must go to the wall." In his revolt against tradition his most elaborate and sustained attacks were directed against the social ideal of democracy and the moral ideal of Christianity, because he saw in them a standing refutation of his philosophy. Unfortunately his philosophy attracted a group of unripe worshippers. In Germany it was used as an apology for militarism and imperialism, although this was far from Nietzsche's intent.

In the sphere of art the German mind found its highest expression in music. Undoubtedly the most striking figure among the German musicians of the period was Richard Wagner (1813–1883), creator of the modern music drama. As a boy he played the piano so badly that his teacher often chided him. On one occasion young Wagner disarmed the teacher by saying, "But I play a great deal better than Berlioz." The point is that Berlioz could not play at all. The great ambition of his life was to unite in himself the powers of both Shakespeare and Beethoven. His first operas were hardly successful. Either they were not performed at all or they failed to please the audience. Even *Tannhäuser* was no striking success when it was first produced in 1845, and when he finished *Lohengrin* (1848) he was unable to find a producer for it. Nevertheless he refused to be discouraged. During the succeeding years he wrote the libretto of his greatest work, *Der Ring des Nibelungen*. The composition of the *Ring* was probably the most colossal task ever attempted by a musician, one which occupied him intermittently over a period of twenty-six years. Taking his material from Teutonic myth and legend, he completed the libretto in 1852 and the next year wrote the music for *Das Rheingold,* the first opera of the *Ring*. He completed the second, *Die Walküre,* in 1856, and then started the third, *Siegfried;* but in 1857 laid it aside to spend the next two years writing *Tristan und Isolde,* generally considered his most perfect work.

In 1864 King Ludwig II of Bavaria invited him to live in Munich. Several of his operas were staged there and he also finished his *Meistersinger* there. His enemies, however, made life so unpleasant for him that he withdrew to Switzerland, where he finished *Siegfried* (1871) and started writing the score of *Götterdämmerung,* the last opera of the *Ring*. In 1872 he settled in Bayreuth to build a mammoth theater for the presentation of the *Ring* on a site granted to him by the city administration. Although the performances were an artistic triumph, the financial deficit was so large that they had to be discontinued for the time being. After Wagner's death the *Bayreuth Festivals* became enormously profitable. Wagner's last opera was *Parsifal* (1882), based on the legend of the Holy Grail. In the summer of that year Wagner directed the performance of this opera sixteen times. The exertion was too great a strain on his heart. He died early in 1883.

Wagner was not merely a great musician; he was also a dramatist of high rank. Instead of a mere mosaic of unconnected arias, choruses, and orchestral interludes he set himself to produce a drama in which all parts are intimately connected by means of leading motives or characteristic musical phrases. This music drama he regarded as the ultimate goal of all previous music development. He exhorted men everywhere to turn from the French and Italian operas to the new gospel of musical drama. His theories were world-embracing, his dramas were colossal, the theater he built at Bayreuth was of mammoth size, and even the orchestra for which he scored was immense. Some critics have summed it all up in the word "megalomania."

CHAPTER ELEVEN

The Growth of Democracy in Britain

THE EARLY YEARS OF
VICTORIA'S REIGN KING William IV died in 1837 and was
succeeded by his niece Victoria, then eighteen years old. According to
a contemporary the new ruler was "a laughing, pretty girl with large
blue eyes, sunny hair, and a sweet smile, and one of her many charms
was a singularly beautiful voice." On many sides there were fears that
the task of ruling Great Britain would be too onerous for one so young.
Carlyle said, "Poor little Queen! She is at an age at which a girl can
hardly be trusted to choose a bonnet for herself; yet a task is laid upon
her from which an archangel might shrink."

But she soon demonstrated that all such fears were unfounded. Although she had seen little court life, she was well educated and had
thoroughly assimilated the teaching of her uncle, King Leopold of Holland and Belgium. The quiet dignity and composure with which she assumed her tasks at once won the praise and admiration of experienced
statesmen. She carefully studied the problems demanding solution and
would not sign a document until she felt that she completely understood it. Her stern sense of duty was manifest in an entry in her
diary on the day of her accession: "Since it has pleased Providence to
place me in this station, I shall do my utmost to fulfill my duty toward
my country." Her persistent and punctual attention to affairs lasted
until several days before her death. It was Victoria's highest ambition
to represent and personify her people and to serve their highest interests. "It will be my care," said the young queen, "to strengthen our
institutions, civil and ecclesiastical, by discreet improvement wherever
improvement is required, and to do all in my power to compose and
allay animosity and discord." Throughout her reign she tried to persuade statesmen to sink their minor differences in a common and hearty

support of the national interest. She was successful in stimulating love and respect for the monarchy. When she came to the throne, kingship in England was not rated highly. As the real achievements of the queen's life became evident, the lukewarm feeling which prevailed at the beginning of the reign gradually gave way to intense devotion and loyalty.

The very important question of her marriage the queen decided by herself. She did so by summoning her cousin, Prince Albert of Saxe-Coburg, into her presence and offering him her hand. Her defense of this action was that "he would never have presumed to take such a liberty" as to ask for the hand of the queen of England. The marriage was an unusually happy one. "She is as full of love as Juliet," Sir Robert Peel reported.

Although as a foreigner Albert never became popular with the English people, he was a man of considerable ability. Disraeli said, "He has great abilities and wonderful knowledge — I think the best-educated man I ever met; most completely trained, and not overeducated for his intellect, which is energetic and lively." The Prince Consort was Victoria's constant adviser. The harmony between the two was so complete that he was practically as much the ruler of the country as she. When Albert died in 1861 after twenty-one years of married life, the queen was inconsolable. For a time she withdrew so completely from the sight of the people that she was criticized for "permitting herself an undue indulgence in the luxury of grief."

During Victoria's reign revolution did not visit Britain as it did France, Germany, and Italy, and yet a considerable advance was made in political democracy. Whereas Britain at the time of her accession was a predominantly aristocratic nation, it had become predominantly democratic by the time of her death in 1901. Progress was slow and gradual. The Reform Act of 1832 had adjusted the apportionment of parliamentary seats more equitably, but the lower middle class and the laborers still had no vote, and the number of voters barely exceeded 800,000 out of the six million males over twenty-one. Having achieved its triumph with the help of the working classes, the upper section of the middle class was ready to regard the act as a final measure. The well-to-do were, in the words of Lord John Russell, spokesman of the Whig Party, "determined to go no farther, but to use their best endeavors to preserve the renovated constitution entire and unimpaired."

But the working classes had other ideas. They resolved to fight on until they too were accorded the right to vote. This determination gave rise to the Chartist movement, which was essentially a struggle inspired by the consciousness of class interests. The six points of the charter which gave the movement its name were: (1) universal suffrage; (2) vote by ballot instead of by voice; (3) annual parliaments;

(4) abolition of property qualification for membership in parliament; (5) payment of salaries to members of parliament; (6) equal electoral districts. Of the six the first was the most important. It was the prerequisite to the achievement of the others. The Chartists, according to their writings, wanted to "send their own representatives from the ranks of those who live by labour into the Commons House, to deliberate and determine, along with all other interests, that the interests of the laboring classes — of those who are the foundation of the social edifice — shall not be sacrificed."

Chartist agitation maintained a constant ferment from 1838 to 1848. From its very inception the movement was sharply divided over the means to be employed to achieve its aims. Those who favored constitutional action finally carried the day against a small but vigorous minority who advocated the use of force. Meetings were held throughout the country to discuss the demands, but parliament remained undisturbed. In 1848 the news of attempted revolutions in other countries stimulated a last attempt to invigorate the movement. A monster petition was prepared, supposedly bearing six million signatures, and a great demonstration in support of it was planned. To guard against possible disorder the government enrolled 170,000 special constables, among them such future notables as William Ewart Gladstone and Louis Napoleon. But rain dampened the ardor of the mass meeting. The petition was bundled off in three cabs to Westminster, where it was found that the total number of signatures was less than two million and that many were fraudulent. They included such names as "Victoria rex, April 1st," Prince Albert, and Sir Robert Peel. The duke of Wellington was represented as having recorded his signature no less than seventeen times.

The ridicule aroused by this discovery dealt the final blow to Chartism. But the demands were not forgotten. A little more than half a century later they were, with the exception of annual parliaments, universally accepted as indispensable conditions of British political life.

Shortly after the middle of the century a group of men imbued with the ideas of the new age appeared on the political scene, men who from conviction or the need of votes for their parties were disposed to fulfill some demands for political reform. The two great political leaders who dominated this era were William Ewart Gladstone (1809–1898) and Benjamin Disraeli (1804–1881). Although the fame of most British prime ministers is notoriously short-lived, these two have not been forgotten. Both gave their lives to politics and became leaders of their respective parties. Disraeli, having begun as a Liberal, made his way to leadership in the Conservative (Tory) Party, while Gladstone, starting as a Tory, managed to become the leader of the Liberal Party (for-

merly the Whigs).[1] Regarding the differences between the two parties
one historian wrote, "In the affairs of Great Britain it is difficult to distinguish the Conservative program from the Liberal program except by
the details of execution. The former wishes, like the latter, to finish the
transformation begun in 1832."[2] Gladstone himself stated, "The great
English parties differ no more in their general outlines than by a somewhat different distribution of the same elements in each."

But in the two men the differences were far greater than the resem-
blances. Both were great orators and parliamentarians, but while Disraeli was a master of phrase, believing with Goethe's Mephistopheles
that "with words you can do anything," Gladstone was wholly insensi-
tive to the demands of style. Disraeli's power over the English language
was so extraordinary that it has been compared with that of Byron.
"Perhaps no great orator ever lived," wrote Sir Spencer Walpole,
"whose sarcasms and whose epigrams carried a greater sting." Gladstone's eloquence was that of the evangelist. It seldom touched the
reasoning faculty of his hearers; it was more frequently an appeal to
passion or emotion. The differences in the two men engendered a strong
feeling of mutual dislike and distrust. Neither showed any hesitation in
expressing his feelings toward the other. Lord Granville wrote to Queen
Victoria that Lord Beaconsfield (Disraeli) and Mr. Gladstone "are men
of extraordinary ability; they dislike each other more than is usual
among public men. . . . [Disraeli] has a power of saying in two words
that which drives a person of Mr. Gladstone's peculiar temperament
into a great state of excitement." Disraeli, on the other hand, complained of Gladstone's "vindictiveness," which he termed a great fault
in the leader of a party. Nevertheless, after Disraeli's death Gladstone
proposed that a monument be erected in Westminster Abbey to the
memory of his rival.

Gladstone's career spanned nearly the whole length of the nineteenth
century. Of Scottish descent, he was born in 1809, at a time when Napoleon was still at the height of his fame. The same year also saw the birth
of Abraham Lincoln, Edgar Allan Poe, Mendelssohn, Tennyson, and
Darwin. Gladstone outlived all of them. He died in 1898, having retired
from public life only four years earlier. For more than sixty years he
sat in parliament, and he was four times prime minister. As a young
man he considered seriously the idea of entering the church but deferred
to his father's wish that he choose a political career. Nevertheless, service to the church remained one of the prime motives of his life. In 1843
he wrote, "I contemplate secular affairs chiefly as a means of being useful in church affairs." His curiosity was insatiable. Throughout his life

[1] From this time on the Tories and the Whigs became known respectively as the Conservatives and the Liberals.
[2] *Histoire Générale*, Lavisse and Rambaud, editors, XII (1904), 52.

he read incessantly, the fields of his special interest being history, poetry, and economics, in addition to theology.

Like all human beings Gladstone had his faults, but his great qualities were sufficient to overshadow them. During the early part of his career he was opposed to reform. In 1831 he denounced the Reform Bill as calculated "to break up the whole frame of society." But later he moved into the Liberal camp and became the champion of democracy and liberty. The liberty he championed was a "liberty for all without distinction of class, creed, or country." His love of liberty made him a great admirer of the first President of the United States. "Washington," he said, "loved freedom and believed in it and lived up to his belief. He is one of the characters most to be admired in all history." The intensity of passion he threw into every question evoked a corresponding passion of reverence for him among his followers. On the other hand, he also excited much antagonism and was the object of much criticism.

Although his Jewish origin hampered him greatly in his ambitions, Benjamin Disraeli succeeded in lifting himself by sheer force of intellect and determination to the highest position in England attainable by man's effort. A career in politics attracted him very early. "My musing even as a boy," he later said, "was the elements of our political parties." As a young man he carefully mapped out his future, adhering to the plan for the rest of his life. He would further his career in politics by writing. Since fiction afforded the best opportunity of winning the public ear, he decided to write novels. At the age of twenty-two he published his first book, *Vivian Grey* (1826), which depicts the efforts of the ambitious hero to get into political life. The very methods Vivian Grey adopted to gain political influence were those which Disraeli successfully employed. The following excerpt from the novel might be applied to Disraeli himself, "He became habituated to the idea that everything could be achieved by dexterity, that there was no test of conduct except success; to be ready to advance any opinion, to possess none; to look upon every man as a tool, and never to do anything which has not a definite though circuitous purpose."

During the succeeding years he dabbled in journalism, joined the Conservative Party, and painstakingly prepared himself for leadership. Meanwhile he was careful to keep himself before the public by his eccentricities in dress, his affectations, and his audacity in society as well as by his writings. After four attempts he finally succeeded in being elected to the House of Commons in 1837 at the age of thirty-two. An important milestone in his progress was his marriage two years later to Mrs. Wyndham Lewis, who was wealthy, twelve years his senior, and the widow of a colleague in parliament. Her means freed him from financial worries, and her good sense was a great aid in his career. She said humorously in her later years, "Dizzy married me for my money, but if he had the chance again he would marry me for love." After his marriage Disraeli made some powerful speeches in parliament and in spare time wrote *Coningsby* (1844) and *Sybil* (1845), both of which had a large circulation. Both novels are valuable for the picture they present of the political world and social life of the day. *Sybil* was undoubtedly one of the influences which led to the elimination of many evils in the factory system.

DEMOCRATIC REFORM

Disraeli's unflagging resolve for democratic reform enabled him, after a considerable struggle, to become in 1852 Chancellor of the Exchequer and leader of the House of Commons. His first budget speech deeply impressed Queen Victoria, with whom he became a prime favorite. Throughout his political career he steadfastly adhered to what he regarded as the cardinal principles of the Conservative Party: the maintenance of the Established Church and the aristocracy, the development of the empire, and the elevation of the masses.

One of his signal triumphs came in 1867, when he carried through a new Reform Bill, the second great measure by which political democracy was advanced in England during the nineteenth century. In 1866 Gladstone, leader of the House of Commons under the Earl Russell ministry, proposed a broadening of the suffrage, but the extension was so moderate that the bill evoked little enthusiasm and much indignation. Seeing that there was a real demand for reform, Disraeli decided that his party might as well get credit for granting it. Besides providing for the redistribution of a number of seats, the bill so widened the franchise as to add about 500,000 voters to the lists. As finally passed in 1867 it gave votes to all householders, whatever the value of their houses, and to all lodgers who for a year had occupied lodgings of the value of £10 unfurnished (about a dollar a week). Thus the working classes in the towns were at last granted some share in political life. It was a long step toward making England a democracy. Only two large groups of the population, the agricultural laborers and the miners, still remained outside the pale of political influence.

Although the measure which became the Reform Bill of 1867 was introduced by Disraeli as the leading member of Lord Derby's cabinet and passed with the support of the Conservatives, it was the Liberals who derived immediate benefit from it. In the elections of 1868 the new electors returned a majority of Liberals to parliament, and Gladstone became prime minister. During the six years he remained in office, a period known as the Great Ministry, reforms followed one another in bewildering succession They included Civil Service Reform (1870), which provided that candidates for the civil service be subjected to competitive examinations; Army Reform (1871), which opened officers' positions to merit and no longer to purchase; and the Ballot Act (1872), whereby secret voting was introduced in place of the oral and public voting that had given rise to intimidation and bribery. Outstanding was the Education Bill of 1870, which laid the foundation for a national system of education. Previously the work of educating the young had been largely under church control, with the result that there were not enough schools, many of the existing ones were of inferior grade, and only about half of the children of school age were receiving instruction. By the provisions of the Education Act of 1870 church schools that maintained certain standards were to be subsidized, and new schools, supported by local taxation, were to be opened in districts where there were not enough schools. As a result the number more than doubled during the next two decades. In 1880 attendance was made compulsory.

In 1874 the constituencies returned a decided majority for the Conservatives, and Disraeli again became prime minister.[3] He too was eager to improve the condition of the people. During the six years in which he held office a number of acts for the welfare of the working classes were passed, among them the Artisans' Dwelling Act to improve housing, an act to prevent shipowners from sending sailors on voyages in unseaworthy ships, a group of acts which increased the powers of the trade unions, and a Factory Act which set up a $56\frac{1}{2}$-hour week for cotton workers. But Disraeli put the greatest emphasis on imperial and colonial affairs. It was he, in fact, who again turned Britain into imperialist paths after a period during which the ideas of the Little Englanders prevailed.

"In my judgment," Disraeli had said in 1872, "no minister in this country will do his duty who neglects any opportunity of reconstructing as much as possible our colonial empire and of responding to those distant sympathies which may become the source of incalculable strength and happiness to this land." Upon this principle he acted during the rest of his career. His first conspicuous achievement was the purchase in 1875 from the khedive of Egypt of a large block of shares in the Suez Canal. These shares together with those independently owned gave Britain control of the highroad to India and the Orient.[4] Since the shorter route to the East increased the importance of India to the British, Disraeli proposed for the queen the title of "Empress

[3] He had been prime minister from February to November, 1868, after the death of Lord Derby.
[4] See p. 258.

of India." This title Queen Victoria officially assumed on January 1, 1877.[5]

Various factors, including his expensive imperialist policy, the decline of prosperity in the later seventies, and Gladstone's vigorous denunciation of his policies, deprived Disraeli of the nation's confidence, with the result that the Liberals won a good majority in the elections of 1880 and returned Gladstone to power. The most notable achievement of Gladstone's second ministry (1880–1885) was the Reform Bill of 1884, which he had promised as a campaign pledge. This Reform Bill, in giving votes to the agricultural laborers who had been overlooked in preceding bills, established a substantially uniform franchise throughout the United Kingdom. The only males still unable to vote were domestic servants, bachelors living with their parents, and those having no fixed abode. The measure increased the electorate by some two million to a total of more than five million. The next year both parties joined in passing the Redistribution of Seats Act, which for the first time attempted to distribute the seats in accordance with the population.

As the years went by, one after another of the statesmen passed from the scene. In 1881 Disraeli died, and in 1894 Gladstone finally retired from politics. Gradually the composition of both houses of parliament changed entirely, new faces replacing the old. In this ever-changing world of politics only Queen Victoria seemed to remain the same. Her life bridged so broad a period of time that she gradually acquired something of the permanence of an institution. Finally in 1901, when she was eighty-two, her hour struck, bringing to an end the longest reign in English history. In the midst of her work, with only the briefest warning, her sympathetic heart and alert brain sank to rest. The death of few monarchs ever evoked such profound sorrow.

THE IRISH QUESTION

The Irish question was one of long standing. The connection of England with Ireland began as far back as the twelfth century, when Anglo-Norman invaders set foot on Irish soil. Although English settlements were established only in the northeastern area, the chiefs of the Celtic tribes in the rest of the island were dispossessed and the land was converted from tribal to feudal or quasi-feudal ownership, the new owners being Englishmen who were largely absentee landlords. The attempts of the Irish to free themselves were ruthlessly punished. The subjection of this proud people became more burdensome and galling as the years passed, creating a deep-rooted bitterness in their hearts.

[5] Disraeli himself had received the title of Lord Beaconsfield from the queen in 1876.

The years from 1845 to 1849 were a particularly unhappy period for Ireland. Famine and pestilence stalked the land. During the preceding decades Ireland had experienced a rapid growth of population, from 2.5 millions at the time of George III's accession in 1760 to eight millions at the accession of Queen Victoria. The great bulk of this population was engaged in agriculture and subsisted mainly on potatoes. Starvation, which was to some extent a recurring phenomenon, reached colossal proportions during years of potato blight. Such a blight ruined the crop in 1845. It was evident at once that the peasants would suffer severely if the British government did not bring food into the island. But it was the era of the Corn Laws, which had been passed in 1815 by a parliament of English landlords for the purpose of excluding foreign wheat from the British Isles until the domestic grain sold at high prices. Hence the Irish were unable to buy food at prices they could afford. Actually Ireland produced enough food to sustain its population, and at the very time when many Irishmen were dying of starvation, much food was being sold to foreign purchasers by the landed gentry. The value of foodstuffs exported during the years 1845 to 1849 has been set at £50 million. Included were sheep, cattle, pigs, oats, oatmeal, and wheat.

In 1846 parliament did repeal the Corn Laws in order to facilitate the supplying of foreign grain to the starving Irish. But in the meantime conditions had become much graver. The potato crop of 1846 was again a total failure. In this year the government did bring in large quantities of Indian corn, but the move came too late to save the starving multitude. The following year again saw blight destroy the potato crop, while pestilence in the form of "road fever" claimed many lives. It has been calculated that starvation and the plague caused no less than 729,033 deaths. Nor did the depopulation stop there: large numbers decided to emigrate to other countries, many of them going to America, and as a result the population declined almost to the figure of 1800.

Starvation and plague had rendered the Irish incapable of agitation for some years. But many of the emigrants soon acquired wealth and achieved positions of importance in America. The hatred they carried in their hearts for England caused them to organize secret societies to liberate Ireland from British rule. Such movements before long stirred the Irish themselves to action. Although they did not at once demand independence, they did have a number of grievances for which they demanded redress. Outstanding among them were (1) the land question, (2) the religious question, and (3) the political question.

(1) The land question. Although the Irish regarded themselves as the real owners of the land, most of them were mere tenants of absen-

tee English landlords who had little interest in their welfare. Many landlords rented land to middlemen who ground the tenant without mercy in order to derive the greatest possible income. Rents were so high that tenants had to devote the largest part of the year accumulating enough to pay them. Consequently most peasants lived in abject poverty, subsisting on potatoes. In renting a farm the peasant rented the soil alone. He then had to supply the dwelling house, roads, drainage, and fencing. But after improving the property he had no claim to it. He could be evicted at the caprice of the landlord or middleman without receiving compensation for his improvements. In other words, the peasant lacked the fixity of tenure which even the medieval serf enjoyed. What he desired in addition was fair rents and the right to sell his improvements.

(2) The religious question. There had been religious unity in Ireland until the Reformation. At that time the Anglican Church became the Established Church of Ireland and took over all endowments as well as the right to levy tithes on all inhabitants. Thus despite their hopeless poverty most Irishmen [6] contributed to two churches — the Catholic, to which they were devoted, and the Anglican, which they detested.

(3) The political question. The Irish deeply resented the fact that they did not make the laws that governed them. In 1782, when an independent Irish parliament was established, many believed that an era of self-government would follow. But the parliament was abolished in 1800 as a result of the rebellion of 1798, and the Act of Union which went into operation on January 1, 1801, required the Irish representatives to sit in the British parliament in London. Although the act was intended to admit the Irish to membership in the United Kingdom and the British Empire on terms of equality with Englishmen and Scotsmen, the Irish did not like the arrangement. Their members were of course in a minority and could therefore pass legislation regarding the island only with the support of other members. Consequently agitation for the repeal of the Act of Union began almost at once.

For some decades nothing was done to right the wrongs of the Irish. It was not until Gladstone rose to power that any definite steps were taken to conciliate them. When asked to form a cabinet in 1868, he expressed his attitude toward the Irish question in the words, "My mission is to pacify Ireland." In 1869 he laid the ax to the root of one grievance by introducing a bill which provided that the Irish church should cease to be a legal establishment after January 1, 1871. The passage of this bill was followed the next year by a land-reform measure which marked the first serious effort to adjust the grievances between

[6] In 1861 the Irish Protestants numbered only about 690,000.

landlords and tenants. It provided that a tenant evicted for any reason but nonpayment of rent could claim compensation for his improvements. Gladstone hoped that these two measures would settle the question once and for all, but his hopes were not fulfilled. The landlords found ways of circumventing the land act, and evictions were more numerous than in the previous period. Moreover, provisions for fair rents and fixity of tenure were still lacking. Finally in 1881 Gladstone managed to secure the passage of a further act which provided the "three F's" demanded by the peasants — fair rents, fixity of tenure, and free sale of improvements.

Even this neither satisfied the Irish nor solved the land problem. An increasing number were becoming convinced that the ills of the country were in large part due to the absence of a native and sympathetic legislature. Consequently there arose a movement which had as its object the establishment of an Irish parliament with full control over domestic affairs, leaving purely imperial affairs to the imperial parliament. The goal was summarized in the two words "Home Rule." Organized in 1870, the new movement was formally launched in 1873. Secret societies formed to agitate for Home Rule committed outrages, even murders, and caused general unrest. Again Gladstone supported the Irish cause. Having condemned the idea of Home Rule during much of his life, he was now won over to the idea that greater concessions would allay Irish discontent. Soon after his return to power in 1886 he therefore introduced an Irish Home Rule bill based on the principle that Irishmen should be allowed to manage Irish affairs. But both this bill and another introduced in 1893 were rejected by parliament; and after Gladstone's retirement in 1894 the Irish cause lost its position on the Liberal program. The Irish, however, did not cease their agitation.

THE FIRST YEARS OF THE NEW CENTURY

Edward VII succeeded his mother on the British throne in 1901 when he was in his sixtieth year. Excluded from all state affairs until a short time before her death, Edward had given most of his time to sport, travel, and pleasure. His periodic visits to Paris, where he explored the various facets of life, had caused much eyebrow-lifting; but his travels in general had given him a first-hand knowledge both of foreign countries and of the British Empire. Many, particularly in the more austere circles, viewed the accession of the erstwhile playboy with misgiving and even apprehension. But their fears were quickly dissipated. At the time of his accession he promised his people that he would strive to follow his mother in her devotion to duty, a promise which he carried out faithfully to the last day of his life. His tact, his kindly disposition, and the fact that he was intensely human endeared him to his subjects. His love of pageantry and the trappings of royalty also ushered in a certain gaiety after the austerity of Victoria's reign.

One of the important achievements of Edward's reign is the series of diplomatic alliances which were concluded with his help. Having obtained an intimate knowledge of the personnel and main lines of European diplomacy during the years before he became king, Edward was well equipped for his task. When he came to the throne in 1901, Britain's popularity in Europe was at a lower ebb than ever before. The policy of "splendid isolation" which the British had long pursued had left them with hardly a friend. Bismarck had bound up Germany, Austria, and Italy, and, on the other hand, France and Russia joined in the entente of 1893. Thus the British stood alone. There was a time in 1898 when they seemed to be faced with the hostility of Russia, Germany, and France as well as of Japan. A decade later the situation was much different. The British then had friends and allies. The policy of concluding a system of alliances was not proposed by Edward VII, but he helped to create a favorable atmosphere for the diplomatists. "Trustworthy evidence makes it clear," Sir Sidney Lee stated, "that King Edward was in a large measure personally responsible for this wide and welcome change in England's international relations."

How effective this attitude was is demonstrated by his dealings with France. At his accession the relations between the two countries were strained as a result of the Dreyfus case and other incidents. Edward was so positive he could create a more favorable atmosphere that he insisted on going to Paris in 1903. His genial demeanor and personal tact soon won the hearts of the French. The next year the Anglo-French entente was concluded. André Maurois said of the visit, "Strange as it may seem that the journey of one single man should have the power to transmute in less than a week the sentiments of a people, it is nevertheless true that the decline of Anglophobia in France dates from this visit." This sudden drawing together of France and Britain was matched by a similar understanding between Britain and Russia in 1907. Edward captured good will in many countries, so that British statesmen soon realized that his visits were an excellent way of developing friendship between nations. Only between Edward and his nephew, William II of Germany, was there considerable friction, the kaiser often being unwarrantedly rude and arrogant. Edward was, however, eager to cultivate friendly relations with Germany; he once wrote to his nephew, "I have but one desire, my dear William, and that is that our two countries should 'pull well' together."

The last years of Edward's reign were a period of intense political activity and of many-sided reforms. In the General Elections of 1906 the Liberal party won 366 seats in the House of Commons, while the number held by the Conservatives was reduced to 157. Another significant feature was the return of 51 members by the new Labor party. The Liberals with a clear majority in Commons began at once to introduce bills to effect many changes. Among the first measures were a number for the protection of children. One of these was the Provision of Meals Act (1906), which enabled education authorities to feed children who came to school hungry and to recover the cost from any parents whose means were sufficient. Another measure, the Medical Inspection Act (1907), put all school children under medical supervision. A step in the direction of better housing was taken in the Housing and Town-Planning Act (1909), which greatly enlarged the powers and duties of municipalities in regard to the demolition of dilapidated and unhealthy houses and the construction of better ones. This act made possible the elimination of some of the worst slums and the gradual reconstruction of British towns.

Important progress was also made in labor legislation. In 1906 the Workmen's Compensation Act extended to all trades the right to compensation for injuries received during working hours which had been applied to a few trades in 1897. Another important achievement of this period was the passage in 1908 of the Old Age Pensions Act, which provided, with certain restrictions, that persons seventy years of age whose annual income did not exceed a set minimum (25 guineas) receive a small weekly pension (5 shillings). Those with larger incomes were granted proportionately smaller amounts if their annual income did not exceed 30 guineas and 10 shillings. In 1908 the hours of labor in the coal mines were limited to eight per day and in 1910 the hours and conditions of work in factories were defined by law. In certain industries in which wages were exceptionally low and which had no adequate trade union organizations the government assumed the function of determining a legal minimum wage (Sweated Industries Act of 1909). Trade Boards composed of an equal number of employers and employees were appointed for each industry and the wage-rates they set were enforced by the courts of law.

Edward VII was succeeded by his son, who ascended the throne as George V in 1910 at the age of forty-five. Although he was in many ways unlike his father, he also possessed qualities which won the hearts of his people. He was sober, temperate, abstemious, and unaffectedly pious. Not only was it his custom to read in his Bible every day; he also held family prayers regularly and never omitted the saying of grace at meals. In his wife, Queen Mary, he had an able and intelligent helpmeet. Both as a youth in the royal navy and during the years before he became king, George had traveled widely and had acquired a first-hand knowledge of the British dominions. He had visited Canada six times, India and Ceylon three times, and South Africa and Australia twice. Unlike his father he did not care for fuss and ceremonial and court life. In his relationship with others he was inclined to be somewhat blunt. He lacked intellectual subtlety and a sense of humor but had an acute consciousness of duty. Throughout his reign he spent long hours carefully perusing countless official reports and documents. His conduct toward his ministers was always friendly and proper.

The burning issue at the beginning of his reign, one which he inherited from his father, was that of abolishing the veto power of the House of Lords. This had been discussed repeatedly over a longer period, but with the return of the Liberals to office in 1906 it became a major question. The grievance of the Liberals was that the House of Lords, which was permanently controlled by the Conservatives, effectively blocked their efforts to enact progressive legislation. Gladstone had found the position of the Liberal government intolerable on this account. If they had played their trump cards with more restraint, the Lords might have continued their authority for another generation; but they made the crucial mistake of demonstrating how effectively the veto power could be employed. During the years after 1906 they either rejected or mutilated so badly that they had to be rejected, four bills dealing with education, land valuation, plural voting, and licensing reform. Finally in 1909 they crowned their work of obstruction by rejecting Mr. Lloyd George's budget. Many believed that the hereditary and indissoluble House of Lords was forcing the popularly elected House of Commons into a position of subordination.

The rejection of the budget by the Lords moved the Liberals to resolve on immediate action. A general election returned them to power, with a diminished majority, it is true, but a majority that was determined to abolish or at least curtail the veto power. Just when it seemed as if something decisive was about to be achieved, Edward VII died. Respect for the king's memory moved both sides to suspend the open contest, and an effort was made to settle the issue by discussion. This having failed, the question was again presented to the people in a general election, with a result much like that of the former election. When parliament met in February, 1911, the bill dealing with the veto was at once re-introduced. This time it was passed by the Commons and sent for their approval to the Lords, who in turn proposed so many amendments that the whole procedure was equivalent to rejection. But the Liberals were prepared to go to extremes in order to achieve their purpose. They informed the Lords that if necessary the government would request the king to create a sufficient number of peers to ensure the passing of the bill. The Lords finally yielded and passed the bill by a narrow majority of seventeen, with only 245 of a total membership of 618 voting.

The passing of the Parliament Act of 1911 was another step in the advance toward democratic government. Any bill of a financial nature passed by the House of Commons becomes law if the Lords do not assent within one month after receiving it. On other legislation they can still exercise a temporary check, but a measure passed by the Commons in three consecutive sessions becomes law despite the Lords' veto, provided that two years have elapsed between its introduction and its third and final passage by the Commons. In brief, the change made in the British constitution by the Act of 1911 was to give the final decision in all matters of legislation to the elected representatives of the people.

THE INDIAN SUMMER OF BRITISH ECONOMIC LEADERSHIP

Meanwhile widespread changes had taken place in British trade and industry. Because Britain was far ahead of other nations in her industrial development, the government concluded that protectionism was unnecessary. Consequently the complicated regulations, including the Navigation Acts which governed overseas trade, and also the Corn Laws which imposed a tariff on the importation of grain, had been discarded in the decade of the forties. Indeed, the government had demolished its tariff walls. At the time the British, it is true, could afford to dispense with protectionism. Their industrial predominance was unprecedented in history. They produced more cotton goods, more coal, and more iron than the rest of the world combined. With their superior industrial system they could manufacture great quantities of goods at such low prices that other countries were unable to compete with them. British machinery, British cutlery and hardware, British cottons, British pottery, and other British manufactures of many kinds found their way into all civilized countries. During the third quarter of the century Britain remained so far ahead of other countries that few fears of serious rivalry were entertained. Many merchants and industrialists even believed that Providence had destined their country to be the abiding workshop of the world.

During the last decades of the nineteenth century, however, they gradually lost some of their industrial supremacy. In embracing the policy of free trade the government hoped that other nations would follow suit. The hopes were soon blasted. A wave of economic nationalism swept most of the other countries into the protectionist camp. Behind the tariff barriers various nations began to build industries of their own as a means of overtaking the British and garnering some of the world's riches. The United States during and after the Civil War inaugurated protectionism, and other countries did not wait long before adopting similar policies. Moreover, their industries began to develop at an accelerated pace.

Although British industry continued to expand, the expansion was much slower than that of the United States, Germany, and even France. The following table showing the development of the pig-iron industry illustrates the difference:

	Britain	U.S.A.	Germany	France
1870–1874 (million tons)	6.4	2.2	1.8	1.2
1900–1904 " "	8.6	16.4	8.9	2.6

Thus, although she produced more pig iron in the first period than the combined output of the other three countries, Britain had dropped to third place by the end of the second period. The British also lost the lead in the production of coal:

	Britain	U.S.A.	Germany	France
1870 (million tons)	110	30	26	13
1900 " "	225	241	108	32

The table shows that while Britain was responsible for nearly two thirds of the estimated world production in 1870, her output in 1900 comprised only about one third and in volume she was exceeded by the United States. During the same period her leadership was also challenged in textiles and steel.

Though Britain was unable to keep pace with the industrial development of her rivals, her export trade remained high and even increased. Whereas most of the iron, steel, coal, and cotton goods output of the other countries was being consumed at home, increased production in Britain resulted in increased export. While she had in 1870–1874 exported only 13.22 per cent of her coal, the percentage had increased to 34 in 1913. Her coal exports in the latter year amounted to 98 million tons as compared with 47 million exported by Germany and 24 million by the United States. The export of cotton goods to the countries which were developing their own industries gradually decreased, it is true, but markets in China, India, and the Near East were expanding more rapidly than the markets in the western countries were contracting.

As a result of increasing exports the national income continued to rise during the early years of the present century. This and other factors combined to give Britain an atmosphere of bustling prosperity. Not only did the flow of bullion from South Africa continue, but the discovery of gold in Canada and Australia also augmented the wealth that was flowing into Britain. London still remained the Mecca for those who wished to borrow money. Nevertheless, the fact that Britain was being outstripped in her industrial development by other nations augured ill for her future prosperity. Despite the high export volume profit-making was becoming more difficult because of foreign competition. Even more discouraging was the state of the domestic market. Since there were no tariff fences to keep them out, foreign goods, and particularly those of Germany, were invading Britain. As early as 1897 one observer tried to show his compatriots, with some exaggeration, the extent of the invasion when he wrote:

The industrial supremacy of Great Britain has been long an axiomatic commonplace; and it is fast turning into a myth. . . . The industrial glory of England is departing, and England does not know it. . . . Take observations, Gentle Reader, in your own surroundings. . . . You will find that the material of some of your clothes was probably woven in Germany. Still more probable is it that some of your wife's garments are German importations. . . . The toys, and the dolls, and the fairy books which your children maltreat in the nursery are made in Germany. Roam the house over and the fateful mark will greet you at every turn, from the piano in your drawing-room to the mug on your kitchen dresser. . . . As you rise from your hearthrug you knock over an ornament on your mantelpiece; picking up the pieces you read, on the bit that formed the base, "Manufactured in Germany." And you jot your dismal reflections down with a pencil that was made in Germany.[7]

From the point of view of the working classes the period was not a happy one. The two great evils were low wages and unemployment. While prices rose rapidly after the turn of the century, wages did not increase commensurately. Low wages made for human inefficiency and industrial stagnation. Periodically there was also widespread unemployment. Although it was low at the beginning of the present century, it rose to 6.4 per cent in 1904 and to 8.7 per cent in 1907. The number of those forced to seek poor-law relief in 1910 reached a fifty-year high.

During the same period British agriculture declined greatly. For three decades after the close of the Napoleonic wars Britain had produced an increasing supply of grain and at the end of the period was nearly self-supporting. The price of bread was high because the Corn Laws, passed in 1815 by a landlord parliament, forbade the importation of foreign grain until the price in the home market reached 80 shillings per quarter. The repeal of the Corn Laws in 1846 ushered in a period of gradual decline in British agriculture. With the restrictions on the import of foreign grain removed, it was easy for other countries to flood the British market with cheaper grain. Raised on the virgin lands of overseas countries, it was quickly transported by steamship to the only country from which it was not excluded by tariffs. As a result the price

[7] Ernest E. Williams, *Made in Germany* (1897), pp. 10 f.

of wheat and barley fell 50 per cent in Britain during the next twenty years.

This decline dealt the tillage districts a severe blow. Grain prices fell so low that only those who had modern agricultural machinery could cultivate their land with profit. In some districts farms could not be rented or sold. Many small owners were compelled to give up their holdings and drift to the already overcrowded towns, where they swelled the ranks of unskilled workers. At the same time great numbers of agricultural laborers whom power machinery had deprived of their jobs also left the countryside. Lord Randolph Churchill said in 1884, "In former times and not so long ago, the moment that a man made a fortune in trade he invested that money in a landed estate; the possession of a landed estate gave him social status, political influence, sporting rights, and possessed many other amenities and attractions. . . . But now all that is gone; the investment is no longer safe, and the bloom has been altogether rubbed off the peach." Thirty years later another observer wrote that British agriculture "looks like an industry which has had the heart taken out of it and in which everybody has lost faith — landlords, farmers, and laborers." Meanwhile depopulation of the countryside had progressed to such an extent that in 1900 only about 25 per cent of the population lived on the land, and by 1911 the percentage had dropped to 20. In comparison, Germany — the most urbanized of the larger Continental states — still had 48 per cent of her population living on the land in 1900.

Not only did the agricultural districts lose much of their population; the area under cultivation became smaller despite the introduction of power machinery. Whereas in 1827 there were on an average two acres of cultivated land for every man, woman, and child in the United Kingdom, by 1903 the average had shrunk to about nine-tenths of an acre per head. As early as the middle of the nineteenth century it had been patent to some that Britain could not for long expect to grow the major part of the food supply needed for her population. During the second half of the century, while countries like Russia and the United States exported large quantities of foodstuffs, Britain was importing them in ever-increasing volume. The total value of agricultural products imported increased from £61 million in 1865 to £170 million in 1898. Many of the foreign foods, such as tea, sugar, coffee, and semitropical fruits, cannot of course be grown in Britain; but even when these are excluded from calculation, the increase in the import of the principal necessaries is striking. During the years 1901 to 1913 the British imported no less than 78 per cent of the wheat and 40 per cent of the meat they consumed. To put it in another way, in 1914 food imports per head were three times as large as they had been in 1850. This dependence upon foreign countries for her food supply is a key to the understanding of British history since that time.

VICTORIAN CULTURE

The outstanding characteristics of some periods of culture can be easily and briefly stated because the writers, artists, and musicians were animated by one spirit. But the Victorian age was an age of many trends, particularly in literature. Victorians in every line of artistic and literary endeavor certainly owed much to the great romanticists, but it is equally true that they struck out along many new paths of their own, each one in his or her own characteristic manner. Consequently the Victorian age, combining as it did trends of romanticism with those of realism or naturalism, was rich in variety and in complexity.

Alfred Tennyson (1809–1892) probably had a wider appeal than any contemporary poet. He kindled the imagination and stirred the blood of both highborn and lowly. Although he does not rank as a poet with Shakespeare and Milton, he is in the minds of many Englishmen the peer of Byron, Shelley, Keats, and Wordsworth. The year 1850 is memorable in his life for his appointment as poet laureate to succeed Wordsworth. The same year saw the publication of *In Memoriam,* a collection of short poems in which he gave expression to his spiritual struggles over the meaning of life and death. *The Idylls of the King* (1859–1885) represents his greatest effort and remains the most ample of his realizations. Few English poets have surpassed him in the exquisite music of his verse, the representative character of his thought, skill in the use of words, and simplicity.

Two other notable figures who helped to make the nineteenth century a period of great literature were Robert Browning (1812–1889) and Elizabeth Barrett Browning (1806–1861). In 1845 when Robert began to correspond with Elizabeth Barrett she had written two volumes of poetry and was the more famous of the two. Because of her delicate health Elizabeth spent most of her time in seclusion, but this did not prevent Browning from declaring his love. In the next year he married her without the knowledge and consent of her father and took her to Italy. There, under his loving care, her health improved and she was able to devote much time to writing. *Sonnets from the Portuguese* composed at that time is undoubtedly her one work of permanent worth. Contemporaries were so moved by the poems that they deemed her the greatest of English poetesses, but posterity has not given her rank beside her more talented husband. When his wife died in 1861 Robert Browning was forty-nine. Although he had written much poetry, he had received little recognition. This came to him only with the publication of *Dramatis Personae* in 1864; then in 1869 came his great masterpiece, *The Ring and the Book*. Whereas Tennyson's poetry is so simple that no effort is necessary for its enjoyment, Browning's demands special study. Many of the intellectually acute have found his poetry virile and stimulating.

Great as Tennyson and Browning undoubtedly were, the novel was nevertheless far ahead of poetry in general favor. The once despised novel not only left the deepest imprint on the popular imagination, but with the drama largely in a state of decline it could claim to be the principal interpreter of the mind of the age. In technique, it is true, it offered little that was new. In simple prose it did not match Swift or Defoe; in eloquence it did not attain the heights of Milton or Burke. It was, nevertheless, a tremendous influence in the life of the time, and many of the Victorian novels are still widely read.

If literary standing can be measured by popularity, Charles Dickens (1812–1870) is the outstanding figure of the era. Although his schooling was irregular he did supplement it by much reading and at nineteen became a roving reporter. The experiences of these years are incorporated in his novels. His first important work, *Sketches by Boz,* published in book form in 1836, was so successful that a publishing firm asked him to write a series of humorous articles. The result was *Pickwick Papers* (1837). The book was such a phenomenal success that it relieved him of financial worries and permitted him to devote himself entirely to writing. During the next thirty-three years book after book flowed from his pen. Only a few can be listed here. His next outstanding success was *Oliver Twist* (1837–1839); then came *Nicholas Nickleby* (1838–1839), *The Old Curiosity Shop* (1840–1841), *Barnaby Rudge* (1841), *A Christmas Carol* (1843), *Martin Chuzzlewit* (1843–1844), *David Copperfield* (1849–1850), *A Tale of Two Cities* (1859), and *Great Expectations* (1860–1861).

The great theme of Dickens' novels was always the downtrodden and oppressed. In this respect he was not typical of his period. Nearly everyone from Tennyson down was tainted with the worship of caste. Emphasis was put on money, property, and position. Dickens, however, showed that the poor and lowly had hopes, aspirations, brotherly kindness, and unselfishness, and that they could be happier than their superiors. Each of his characters is a quality personified. The heroes and heroines are exaggerations of the virtues, and the scoundrels of the vices. Such figures as Mr. Micawber, Pickwick, Uriah Heep, and Mr. Pecksniff have no real existence outside his books. They are caricatures. But Dickens did not write merely to amuse his readers; he made his novels vehicles for social reform. His purpose in writing *Oliver Twist* was to improve the working conditions of the poor; in *Little Dorritt* and *David Copperfield* he aimed at reform of the prison system; and in *Nicholas Nickleby* he called for a change in the system of education.

Two other outstanding novelists of the period were William Makepeace Thackeray (1811–1863) and George Eliot (1819–1880). While Dickens portrayed the masses, Thackeray depicted the classes. His style was well-nigh faultless and his figures have a reality and a vitality which have seldom if ever been excelled in prose fiction. It was the appearance of *Vanity Fair* in 1847 that established his reputation. Many critics regard this novel as one of the great works of fiction of all time. In 1852 he published *Henry Esmond,* the great historical novel which has its setting in the age of Queen Anne. Two other important works are *Pendennis* (1848–1850) and *The Newcomes* (1853–1855). George Eliot, whose real name was Mary Ann Evans, made her first attempt at writing fiction when she was thirty-seven. Her *Scenes of Clerical Life* (1858) was so successful that she devoted the rest of her life to writing. The best of her novels are *Adam Bede* (1859), *The Mill on the Floss* (1860), and *Silas Marner* (1861). Critics have given lesser rank to her later novels because they lack spontaneity and their style is often labored.

The outstanding musical figure of the Victorian era was Sir Arthur Sullivan (1842–1900). He is probably most widely known as the music creator of the Gilbert and Sullivan comic operas. In meeting W. S. Gilbert, Sullivan found a man whose abilities complemented his own. The collaboration began with the musical novelties *Thespis* and *Trial by Jury,* which gave evidence of the originality of Gilbert's lines and of the appeal of Sullivan's music. The success of these compositions encouraged them to produce a full evening's entertainment in *The Sorcerer* (1877). This was followed by *H.M.S. Pinafore, Pirates of Penzance, Patience, Iolanthe,* and *Princess.* In 1885 *The Mikado,* the most widely popular of the whole series, was staged. Next in the series came *Ruddigore;* then *The Yeoman of the Guard,* which is perferred by many over all others. To a public which was accustomed to associating coarse suggestions and vulgar expressions with comic opera the Gilbert and Sullivan operas with their wholesome and humorous atmosphere came like a breath of spring. But if Sullivan had never written comic operas he would still hold a high place in the history of music. He also wrote the incidental music to *The Tempest, Macbeth, Henry VIII, The Merry Wives of Windsor, The Foresters,* and *King Arthur.* In devotional music he wrote two cantatas and many hymn tunes, including "Onward, Christian Soldiers" and "Lead Kindly Light."

CHAPTER TWELVE

Difficulties in Italy and Spain

PROBLEMS OF THE
NEW ITALIAN STATE ITALIAN political unity, which appeared a
hopeless dream in 1849, became a reality in 1870. Innumerable had
been the difficulties that had to be overcome, but the end had been the
fulfillment of the prophecy of Napoleon Bonaparte, "Sooner or later
the Italian peoples will be united under a single government." Victor
Emmanuel II now presided over the whole nation as constitutional sovereign. It was he who had said after the battle of Novara, March 23,
1849, "I must firmly hold aloft the tricolored flag, symbol of Italian nationality, which has today been vanquished but which will triumph one
day. That triumph shall henceforth be the object of my efforts." There
had been a strong demand for a republic; it had to give way, however,
to the idea of a constitutional monarchy for reasons of national expediency. When a group of Italian workmen presented a demand for a republic, Garibaldi said (1860), "My children, you know that I am as
good a republican as any of yourselves. But as I sacrifice my republican
feelings, I ask you to do likewise because the unity of Italy requires it."
On July 2, 1871, Victor Emmanuel II made his public entry into Rome
to take up his residence in the Palace of the Quirinal. He was welcomed
by the Romans with an enthusiasm worthy of the occasion. In November of the same year he opened the first Italian parliament ever to meet
in Rome.

The final achievement of geographical unity did not mean, however,
that all problems had been solved. In his speech from the throne the
king, after acknowledging that "the work to which we have consecrated our lives is accomplished," wisely reminded the deputies that
they must now give their attention to the many difficult problems ur-

gently in need of solution. Achievement of the political and social ideal cherished by Italian patriots was still in the future.

It was necessary, first of all, to unify the different systems of administration, to put uniform laws into operation, and to establish a uniform fiscal administration. This was not an easy matter, for each of the states had lived under different systems of law, trade, coinage, weights and measures, agriculture, and education. There was also the task of establishing modern industries. In 1870 Italy had almost no organized machine industry, no equipment for it, and little knowledge of it. Only in the northern part had some beginnings been made. What was far worse, Italy had little coal and iron, which are the *sine qua non* of modern industry. In 1870 Italy also had but few miles of railways, few good roads, and no well-equipped harbors. The old quarreling states which had been swept away by the *risorgimento* had opposed intercommunication lest it lead to the importation of revolutionary ideas.

Equally urgent was the task of making the citizens of the new state conscious of a common nationality — in other words, of building a spiritual unity. The idea was expressed in the famous saying of d'Azeglio, "We have made Italy; now we must make Italians." In Germany a customs union had prepared the way for national unity, but this was not the case in Italy. Swayed by an intensely local patriotism, most Italians regarded themselves primarily as Sicilians, Neapolitans, Romagnoles, Florentines, Venetians, or Piedmontese. The cities still cherished the ancient rivalries which had previously caused them to enter into alliances with foreign powers against other Italian states. Moreover, there was a great spiritual cleavage between the north and the south. The two halves of Italy represented two distinct stages of civilization. While many of the citizens of the north looked with contempt on the backward south, many people of the south regarded the northerners as foreigners. The local and sectional sympathies, it is true, were to some extent offset by the illustrious Roman past, by a great literature boasting Dante, Petrarch, and Boccaccio, and by a common cultural inheritance which included the achievements of such men as Michelangelo, Leonardo da Vinci, and Raphael. But the consciousness of a great past was the possession of only a small minority.

Another problem which challenged the ingenuity of the new government was the lot of the poverty-stricken masses. The nation was divided into a number of social classes. There were the great nobles and the wealthy bourgeoisie who together controlled the large landed estates, banks, and commercial enterprises; and there was the lower middle class in whose ranks were to be found most of the officials of the new state, the merchants and traders, and the moderately wealthy landowners. But more than three quarters of the population was comprised of peasants, small tenants, and agricultural laborers, ranging from the prosperous cultivator of the soil who owned a fair-sized farm to the agricultural laborer of the south living in semiserfdom a life bordering on starvation. The perpetual state of undernourishment coupled with the filthy surroundings made the latter an easy prey to the ravages of malaria, tuberculosis, and pellagra. The largest class was probably that of the small tenant farmer, who was often little better off than the agricultural laborer. He usually had to give the major portion of his crops to the landlord and in addition do many unpaid chores. It was only by many hours of back-breaking labor that he could maintain any degree of productivity, for outside a few fertile regions much of Italy was barren rock, swampland, or parched soil in need of irrigation.

A further condition which called for remedy was the widespread illiteracy. It is estimated that in 1870 about 70 per cent of the Italian people were illiterate. In no other country of western Europe was the average so high. Conditions were particularly bad in Naples and Sicily, where a despotic government discouraged all education as likely to promote the circulation of revolutionary ideas. There, 835 of each thousand male inhabitants and 938 of each thousand females could neither read nor write. The situation was not much better in the former states of the church. The report of a government survey made soon after the unification notes that "of a system of popular instruction, adapted to the wants of all, good as a preparation for further studies, but good also in itself as serving to awaken intelligence, . . . there was not even an idea. When asked about well-known facts of Italian history there were, with but rare exceptions, none who could state anything. One said Brutus was a despot; another that Dante was a French poet, Petrarch an illustrious poetess. Of Columbus I was told by one that he was an apostle, and by another that he was the Holy Spirit." Even in the comparatively enlightened regions of the north the number of those who could read and write was only between 40 and 50 per cent. This illiteracy not only made the people unfit for self-government but also engendered much superstition.

Another problem awaiting solution was that of church and state. When the troops of Victor Emmanuel II marched into Rome on September 20, 1870, and deprived the pope of his temporal power, they gave rise to the so-called Roman Question, which poisoned the relations between the Catholic church and the Italian state for more than half a century. Soon after the government established its capital in Rome, the parliament (May 13, 1871) passed the Law of Guarantees to regulate the relations between church and state. This law, after stating that "the person of the Sovereign Pontiff is sacred and inviolable," pledged the Italian government to render the pope the honors due a king. The

Vatican and certain other places in or near Rome were to enjoy the right of extraterritoriality and could not be entered by Italian officials without the pope's consent. The pope was permitted to have his own armed guards in the Vatican and also his own telegraph and post office. Furthermore, the crown surrendered its right to approve the appointment of bishops; thereafter the pope could appoint anyone he wished without consulting the state. It was greater liberty than was accorded the Roman church in Spain, France, or Austria. In general, the law embodied Cavour's principle of "a free church in a free state." Finally, the Vatican was granted an annual sum of 3,225,000 lire (about $622,-425) as an income "perpetual, inalienable, and exempt from every species of taxation."

By some the change was regarded as a liberation of the Holy See from the duties of civil administration. Thus Antonio Fogazzaro, a Catholic writer, said, "September 20 is today a civil fête; but who knows that one day it may not count as a religious festival." But this opinion was not shared by the pope. Bereft of a sovereignty it had exercised for centuries, the Holy See refused to pardon the "usurpation" or "despoliation." Cardinal Antonelli stated the issue in the following words: "The Holy Father will never commit himself to any act which might prejudice the imprescriptible rights of the Holy See, whose duty it is to preserve these intact." Two days after the Law of Guarantees was passed, Pius IX rejected it, retired into the Vatican as a voluntary "prisoner," and announced that neither he nor his successors would leave it until the wrong which Italy had committed was repaired. He rejected the law because it was a law and not a treaty between Italy and a co-equal sovereign, and he also refused to accept the money granted him. As a means of forcing the hand of the Italian state he issued the famous bull *Non Expedit* which forbade all Catholics to vote or hold office under the royal government. Thus the relations between church and state became an open quarrel.

THE NATURE OF THE ITALIAN GOVERNMENT

The constitution on which the new government was based was an expanded version of the Statuto which Charles Albert of Piedmont had given his people in 1848. The king as the executive head exercised his authority through ministers who were responsible to a parliament of two houses — the Senate and the Chamber of Deputies. The Senate was composed of the royal family and of members appointed by the king for life; the Chamber of Deputies consisted of some five hundred elected members. Suffrage was at first limited to adult male citizens who could read and write and who possessed certain additional educational or property qualifications. Since so large a part of the population was illiterate, less than 2.5 per cent were entitled to vote. This was felt to be too small a proportion, and in 1882 the restrictions were eased so that practically every Italian who could read and write might have a voice at the polls. It was not, however, until 1912 that universal manhood suffrage was adopted, thus increasing the number of voters from three to eight million.

The problems demanding solution would have challenged the ingenuity of the most efficient government. But the Italian government was hardly efficient. Such leadership as existed came largely from the middle classes. The nobles, divided as they were by regional differences, appeared to have little taste for politics. Nor did the masses show much interest in political matters, a fact which is not surprising when one remembers that they were largely excluded from the franchise and had no political experience or parliamentary training. They had not taken active part in the struggle for unification, for the *risorgimento* had been carried through by a vigorous minority. The spirit of patriotism, which was the motive force, emanated from the towns. There were, of course, some peasants and workers in the armies of Garibaldi and Victor Emmanuel, but the majority had stayed at home. All had looked forward to the golden age which they were certain would be ushered in by the political unification; but when years of struggle and economic distress followed, the masses largely lost faith in the new government. The earlier enthusiasm gradually gave way to indifference and apprehension. The result was that the government, both national and local, was controlled by the bureaucracy and a small section of the wealthier classes, with the actual control exercised by political bosses.

In the Chamber of Deputies there were no strong parties with definite principles like those of Britain or the United States. The units in the political struggle were crude political factions which were little more than cliques formed about some more or less important individual. The political shadings of the various groups were usually so delicate as to be unintelligible to the man in the street. Only by a combination of groups was it possible to obtain a majority. Such coalitions were based not on broad national policies but on mutual concessions. Their life-span was short. Hence the long series of coalition ministries that followed each other in rapid succession. During the two decades after 1870 only Premier Depretis (1881–1887) succeeded in retaining his post for more than four consecutive years. Control of the government, rather than national betterment, became the primary concern. There is much truth in the statement of Giovanni Papini, "Our political parties remain in the aerial sphere of words, in the limbo of vocabulary. They sputter many phrases but they show little feeling. They become enthused over symbols but they remain immune to deeds."

On January 9, 1878, Italy lost Victor Emmanuel II, the leader who had succeeded in effecting the political unification of the peninsula. "But for him," an observer wrote, "Italy would never have existed, however great Cavour's genius, Garibaldi's heroism, the people's patriotism." His successor was his son Humbert I, a bluff, good-natured, and easygoing king. Endowed with considerable physical courage, he had fought for Italian unity and was the only monarch of Europe who could show a scar received on the field of battle. But Humbert the Good, as even his enemies called him, did not display the same intrepidity in political matters. Here his action or inaction dangerously bordered on weakness. He saw parliament becoming less effective year by year; yet he remained passive and apparently unconcerned. In the words of a contemporary, "The only initiative he ever displayed in affairs of state was the initiative of negation." Another wrote at the time of his death, "It seemed as though Humbert aimed less at being an umpire between the contending parties than at being merely the faithful recording scribe of his parliament, charged with announcing the name of the winning party and investing it with power." Two attempts made on his life by would-be assassins caused him to make the oft-quoted statement that assassination was among the inevitable risks of his profession. The third attempt cost him his life. In July, 1900, as he was seating himself in his carriage, an anarchist mounted the steps and fired three shots with fatal effect. He was succeeded by his only son, Victor Emmanuel III.

The new ruler was determined not to be a do-nothing king. At the time of his accession he told the people, "Unabashed and steadfast, I ascend the throne, conscious of my rights and of my duties as a king. Let Italy have faith in me, as I have faith in the destinies of my country, and no human force shall destroy that which our fathers built with such self-sacrifice." Such strong vibrant tones had not been heard since the time of Victor Emmanuel II. But the high hopes gradually collapsed. Victor Emmanuel III failed to prove his ability to cope with a chaotic situation. The bitter strife of parties continued with little concern for the welfare of the people. The outstanding political boss of the period from 1900 to World War I was Giovanni Giolitti (1842–1928). His method, like that of Depretis and Crispi, was to attract a body of devoted followers sufficiently large to enable him to gain a majority in temporary alliance with whatever party suited his purpose. After winning an election he would appoint a figurehead and then recede into the background until the next election.

What made the government particularly unpopular was the heavy taxation it was obliged to impose in order to meet its financial commitments. "Italy," Francesco Nitti wrote, "is naturally a poor country, so that even if it be well-governed it will still be poor." But the government was not inclined to be economical. Instead of spending the national revenues in improving internal conditions, it sought by colonial ventures and by the maintenance of an army and navy out of all proportion to the wealth of the country to raise the nation in the esteem of foreigners. To quote Minghetti, "No country has ever laid such heavy burdens on itself in order to meet its engagements. The owners of real estate often pay to the tax collector one third or even half of their income." The major burden of these taxes did not fall on the rich but on the poor.

ITALIAN PROGRESS

Notwithstanding the weakness of the government and other obstacles, considerable progress was achieved. In the establishment of modern industry the advance was steady despite the lack of coal and iron, which it was necessary to import. The number of industrial concerns grew from a few hundred in 1870 to about 244,000 in 1914. Although Italy herself produced but a small amount of cotton, a cotton industry was established which numbered 769 mills in 1903. Production of both raw materials and manufactured goods increased by leaps and bounds. The output of salt doubled during the period from 1871 to 1906; the production of sulphur increased tenfold. Moreover, commerce with other countries more than doubled between 1870 and 1914. Exports increased from about one billion lire to more than two billions. Internal trade also increased tremendously after the construction of additional railroads and the removal of the customs barriers which had separated the states of Italy.

The mileage of the railways increased from 3830 in 1870 to 11,165 in 1914. This total was still far behind that of the major European countries. France and Britain, for example, had 25,471 and 23,718 miles respectively, while Germany's mileage was near 40,000. One of the great obstacles to railroad building was the hills and mountains, particularly the Apennines, which form the backbone of the peninsula. It has been calculated that almost 25 per cent of the mileage of Italian railways runs through tunnels or over bridges and viaducts. This increased the cost far above what it was in Great Britain, France, or Germany. Since the railroads were expensive and the volume of traffic was small, financial returns were never satisfactory and operation was poor. Consequently the government assumed the operation of the major roads in 1905. Service improved under state management, but it was still far from good.

Great strides were also made in improving agricultural methods and the condition of the poor peasant and farm worker, but the improvement was not as far-reaching as might have been expected. Better methods, including the use of machinery, were introduced by means of articles in the press and by increasing the number of agricultural schools from five in 1861 to 260 in 1910. Large tracts of swampland were drained, and irrigation and afforestation projects were started to reclaim wastelands. Steps were also taken to curb malaria, which claimed 20,000 lives each year and prevented the cultivation of large tracts of fertile land. Stagnant pools which served as breeding places for the germ-carrying anopheles mosquito were drained, and means for destroying the larvae in other places were developed. The peasants themselves did much to improve their own lot. Among other things, they organized cooperatives for the purpose of buying seed, implements, and fertilizers at lowest cost. By the beginning of the twentieth century there were also between four and five hundred cooperative dairies.

Some idea of the progress made in agriculture may be gained from the fact that the annual importation of agricultural machinery increased from $20,000 in 1861 to about $3.7 million in 1910. The production of wheat more than doubled between 1870 and 1914; that of rice increased sevenfold between 1884 and 1910. Furthermore, the sugar beet industry, which was practically nonexistent in 1881, produced 200,000 tons of sugar in 1914. The export of cheese rose from 1600 tons in 1861 to 33,000 tons in 1913, and in the export of fruit Italy was second only to the United States in 1914. Finally, total exports of silk, in its raw and in its manufactured state, amounted to more than $500 million in 1913.

In one respect Italy was exceedingly productive. Her birthrate was the highest in Europe with the exception of that of Russia and of Hungary. The growing density of the population, which contributed no little to the existing poverty and unemployment, induced many Italians to migrate to countries where higher wages were offered. So many left that workers were often humorously referred to as one of Italy's principal exports. The Italian worker was welcome in all parts of the globe. He made his appearance wherever arduous labor was to be done, whether it was building the Trans-Siberian Railway, digging the Panama Canal, deepening the harbor of Marseilles, or working in the paper mills of France, in the coal mines of Pennsylvania, or on the fruit farms of California. The need for agricultural labor in both North and South America attracted large numbers to this part of the world. In 1876 there were only 96,000 emigrants, but the total gradually increased until it reached 787,977 in one year. The average from 1900 to World War I was about 600,000 a year. Most of the early emigrants came from northern Italy, but growing prosperity soon shifted the source to the south. About one half later returned home with the money they had saved. Those who did return were more or less prosperous and usually brought with them a taste for orderliness. But even those who did not return were a source of revenue to Italy. The annual receipts of money from emigrants ran as high as a billion gold lire a year. Arriving as it did year after year, this kin money was a significant addition to the national wealth. It helped to buy railroads and machines and other means of industrial life. Yet notwithstanding all this deep pruning of the native tree by emigration, the population continued to increase.

One reason why so many emigrants left Italian soil was that Italy had no suitable outlets for population in her colonies. Not that the government was uninterested in acquiring such colonies. The difficulty was that the flags of other nations were already flying over all the more desirable territories. In Italy expansionist ideas were already held by Giuseppe Mazzini, who envisaged a state which included much of North Africa. Other leaders also had dreams of Italy playing a great role in a rejuvenated Mediterranean. Soon after the unification the argument was advanced that colonies were necessary as a source of supply for raw materials and an outlet for excessive population. A beginning was made when a private company in 1870 purchased a settlement in Africa which became the colony of Eritrea. What the Italians would have liked was Tunisia, on the African coast just south of Italy, but this choice territory was occupied by the French in 1881, an act which caused Italy to join with Germany and Austria-Hungary in forming the Triple Alliance in 1882. The Italians fared even worse in their attempts to include Abyssinia (Ethiopia) and its adjoining coastlands in their empire. When they sought to enforce their claim by arms, a native army under Menelik, the Abyssinian emperor, decisively defeated two small Italian armies at Aduwa (March 1, 1896), capturing more than two thousand and killing or wounding more than six thousand. But the failure of the Abyssinian venture did not dampen the ardor of the Italians for colonization. In 1912 troops occupied Tripolitania and Cyrenaica and gave it the old Roman name of Libya.

The first determined effort to wipe out the reproach of illiteracy was the Orlando Law of 1904, which made primary education obligatory up to the age of twelve and provided for the opening of evening and Sunday schools in the districts where the percentage of illiterates was highest. It also set a certain standard of education for those desiring employment in the government. Two years later the law was supplemented by additional provisions for the south. Finally in 1909 the parliament took away such control as the communes had previously exercised and made education largely a concern of the national state. By 1911 the percentage of illiteracy decreased to 46.7, but it was still appalling in certain districts. While the city of Rome showed an illiteracy of about 15 per cent, 456 communes in southern Italy still had a percentage as high as

75. During the years immediately prior to World War I considerable progress was made in opening spacious, well-ventilated, and properly equipped schools. But in 1915 the total number of illiterates over six years of age in Italy was 11,050,454 or 37.8 per cent of the total population.

Meanwhile the relations between the state and the Vatican remained lukewarm. Although Pius IX always remained on excellent personal terms with Victor Emmanuel III, public relations were certainly not improved by such incidents as the dedication in 1889 of a monument in Rome to Giordano Bruno, the apostate monk who was burned at the stake in 1600. The prohibition of the *Non Expedit* was not particularly successful; many Catholics did vote and even hold government office, and only in the ultra-Catholic province of Bergamo was there general observance of the papal injunction. In 1905, however, Pius X at last permitted Catholics to vote in elections sanctioned by the bishops, but he still remained firm in the declared intention to excommunicate any head of a Catholic state who visited the king of Italy in Rome and he maintained the demand for the restoration of the pope's temporal power.

Socialism made its appearance somewhat late in Italy, although the ideas of Karl Marx had begun to penetrate as early as 1844. The absorbing interest of the *risorgimento*, Mazzini's influence, and above all, the absence of great industries made Italy before 1870 unfertile soil for socialism, so that it was not until 1892 that a strong Marxian party (*Partito Socialista Italiano*) was organized. Although the government fought it with every possible weapon, the party grew in strength. In 1895 it polled 60,000 votes and returned twelve deputies. In its famous "minimum program" it demanded, among other things, universal suffrage for adults of both sexes; freedom of press, of speech, of meeting, and of combination; neutrality of the government in disputes between capital and labor; a more humane penal code; improved factory legislation; insurance and old-age pension laws; improvement of the condition of the agricultural classes; compulsory primary education; and nationalization of the railways and mines. These reforms were to be achieved by peaceful means, not by revolution. In other words, Italian socialism abandoned the idea of class warfare as a means of overcoming middle-class society. The influence of the party was salutary so far as it encouraged the cooperative movement and spurred the government on to pass social legislation for the protection of the working classes. On the eve of World War I, after the imperialist venture in Libya, the Marxist revolutionary idea was revived. In 1913 the socialists numbered almost half a million and had forty seats in the Chamber of Deputies.

DYNASTIC STRUGGLES AND CONFUSION IN SPAIN

Spanish history for almost half a century after 1833 is a story of dynastic quarrels, chronic disorders, and instability. In 1833 Ferdinand VII, who had ruled Spain despotically since the fall of the Napoleonic monarchy, finally died. His first three marriages having produced no heir, he had taken a fourth wife, who bore him a daughter. Shortly before his death he had annulled the old Salic law which restricted the succession to the male line and had summoned the great officers of state, the grandees of Spain, and the members of the Cortes to take a solemn oath of allegiance to his daughter as the future sovereign. Upon her father's death she was proclaimed queen as Isabella II, with her mother, Maria Christina, as regent. This act was bitterly resented by Ferdinand's younger brother, Don Carlos. The fact that the first three marriages had failed to bring his brother an heir was regarded by Don Carlos as a special intervention of Providence in his favor. Hence he decided to fight for what he regarded as his right to the throne. His claim was, generally speaking, supported by the church and by the great nobles, while Isabella's claim was upheld by a large part of the army, by the Cortes, and by most of the middle class. The civil war raged for seven years and was conducted with great ferocity. Neither side demonstrated much military or political capacity but in the end the Carlist cause collapsed. During the next century, however, it was to rear its head again and again. The identification of the church with Carlism was one of the causes of the anticlericalism of the liberals during the subsequent period.

In 1843 Isabella, being thirteen, was declared of age. She continued to occupy the throne for the next quarter century. As a queen she was foolish and frivolous, impulsive, and impatient of restraint. At sixteen she was married to a cousin, Don Francisco; but when the marriage proved unhappy she threw all restraint aside and moving from one affair to another shocked Europe with the scandals of her private life. During her reign the practice of caciquismo,[8] or the manipulation of elections by political bosses (caciques), appears to have been established. Increasing financial difficulties and endless erratic changes of ministries caused the Spaniards to revolt against Isabella in 1868 and to drive her into exile.

In 1869 a constitution based on popular sovereignty was promulgated and it was determined to offer the crown to some prince other than Alfonso, the twelve-year-old son in whose favor Isabella had abdicated. But it was easier to jettison Isabella from the ship of state than to find

[8] "Cacique" was the title of the Mexican chieftains at the time of the conquest. The term "caciquism" was applied to all wire-pulling and political bossism.

a new navigator. In the words of Prim, the Minister of War, "Finding a democratic king on earth is like looking for an atheistic king in Heaven." The crown was offered to and refused by a number of candidates including Prince Leopold of Hohenzollern, whose candidature, it will be remembered, was the immediate cause of the Franco-Prussian War. Finally Amadeo, second son of Victor Emmanuel II, accepted the crown and was proclaimed king in 1871. He soon realized, however, that the throne was no bed of roses. He sought to placate all factions but soon found himself cordially disliked, largely because he was a foreigner. Realizing the hopelessness of his position he resigned in 1873 and made his departure. The first Spanish Republic followed, but the people were not ready for it. In less than two years after its establishment it made way for the restoration of the Bourbons in the person of Alfonso XII, the son of Isabella.

Under Alfonso XII (1874–1885), after a decade of unsettlement bordering much of the time upon anarchy, Spain attained some degree of stability. A constitution drawn up by the Cortes in 1876 sharply limited the powers of the sovereign, provided for a ministry responsible to the lower house of the Cortes, and guaranteed individual liberty. This constitution remained in force until after World War I. While the Senate was partly appointive and partly elective, the members of the House of Representatives were elected for a period of five years, the ratio being one deputy for every 50,000 inhabitants. Notwithstanding the new constitution, disorders persisted in the administration and caciquism flourished. In other words, the primary purpose of politics was the advancement of the interests of certain individuals, not the public well-being. Nevertheless, the country did make some recovery after nearly three quarters of a century of intermittent warfare. Alfonso XII, after a reign of eleven uneventful years, died in 1885 at the age of twenty-eight.

Some months after his death a son was born to his wife, Maria Christina of Austria. Until the child grew up, the mother acted as regent. The most conspicuous event of the regency was the loss of the kingdom's remaining colonies. Spain, it will be remembered, had lost her South American colonies during the time of Charles IV and Ferdinand VII. The most important of those that remained were Cuba, Puerto Rico, and the Philippines. Cuba, which for decades had been a hotbed of misrule and shameless corruption, had risen in revolt in 1868. Although the fighting ceased after a decade, the Cubans were far from satisfied. Finally a group of Spaniards who knew the situation suggested a form of home rule, but the Cortes rejected it in 1894. The next year rebellion broke out on a large scale. When the government resorted to savage repression, the Americans grew indignant over the treatment of the Cubans. At length the government decided to inaugurate real reforms, but before anything could be done the American battleship *Maine* was blown up in Havana harbor. Although responsibility for the disaster was never fixed, public opinion in the United States demanded the evacuation of the Spaniards from Cuba. War was declared in 1898.

The heart of the Spanish people was not in the war, nor was the government prepared for it. Consequently Spain was promptly and easily beaten. During the early days of the war Spanish newspapers often referred to the "Yankee Hogs," an allusion to the widespread belief that Americans had become wealthy through pork packing. But when the hopelessness of the war effort became evident, a leading Madrid newspaper stated in an editorial, "It is about time to stop calling the Americans 'pigs', for when we are beaten, as we shall be within a week, it will not be a pleasant reflection to remember that we have been defeated by pigs." The blows launched by the United States navy were devastating. After an immensely superior force under Admiral Dewey won the battle of Manila Bay and Admiral Sampson destroyed the Spanish fleet as it came out of Santiago harbor, the Spaniards gave up the fight. Peace was signed in December of the same year at Paris. By the provisions of the treaty Spain relinquished her sovereignty not only over Cuba but also over Puerto Rico and the Philippines. A little later she sold most of the scattered remnants she still held, thereby ending the vast cycle of Spanish colonialism which had started with the voyages of Columbus.

In 1902 the regency came to an end and the young prince, having reached the age of sixteen, took his place among the monarchs of Europe as Alfonso XIII. Since he was sickly as a child, his mother had encouraged him to develop his body through outdoor sports. Consequently as a young man he excelled in polo, tennis, yachting, and hunting. It was generally believed that this young sportsman would take little interest in affairs of state, but much to the astonishment of his ministers he insisted upon taking a vigorous role in the solution of his country's problems. In the words of one observer, he was a "gay, hard-playing, out-of-doors, extrovert king." But he did find time for serious work.

Alfonso's physical courage was tried on numerous occasions by efforts to assassinate him. It was a time in which the hazards of being a ruler were running higher than usual. A wave of anarchist assassinations, beginning in 1894 with that of the French president, Sadi Carnot, claimed the lives of many rulers and statesmen. Two years before the coronation of Alfonso the victims had been President McKinley of the United States and King Humbert of Italy, and after 1902 came the grisly slaughter of King Alexander and Queen Draga at Belgrade. During Alfonso's early years as a monarch no fewer than ten attempts were made on his life, the first on the day of his coronation. The outstanding incident took place on the day of his marriage to Princess Ena (Victoria Eugenie) of Battenburg, the beautiful granddaughter of Queen Victoria of England. As the bridal couple was returning to the palace from the wedding ceremony, an anarchist threw a bomb which killed more than a score of persons and wounded more than a hundred. Although one of the horses that were drawing the carriage was killed, the royal couple was unhurt.

Alfonso was successful in effecting a workable truce which for a time brought relative peace to a country which for many decades had been torn by dynastic, religious, personal, economic, and regional hatreds. During this period Spain made steady progress in the development of her industries, in the expansion of her foreign trade, in wiping out illiteracy, and in other respects. But the old hatreds were there. Like a volcano they were seething beneath the surface, preparing for a great eruption.

SPAIN ON THE EVE OF WORLD WAR I

After the Spanish-American War the opinion was widely expressed that foreign and colonial foes had done Spain a favor in depriving her of the colonies which for generations had been a drain upon her material resources, her military strength, and her productive human labor. A Spanish historian said, "They brought us little good, for their rich incomes remained in the hands of the administrators, only a small remnant reaching the public treasury; on the other hand, they were responsible for a lengthy chapter in the volume of the public debt." It was hoped that the loss of her colonies would mark the beginning of Spain's regeneration, that it would release energies for national development. Much capital found its way back to Spain from the former colonies, and as a result the material prosperity of the country did advance during the two decades after 1898. There was an increase in enterprises of every kind — banks, financial establishments, industries, and mines. Despite the rugged and mountainous character of the land, 15,000 kilometers of railroads stretched across Spain in 1920. Spanish trade increased considerably and credit recovered as a result of a vigorous reorganization of finance and budgets. But the advance was trifling when compared with the possibilities of development.

The condition of the masses, on the whole, left much to be desired. The ill-paid agricultural laborers lived in squalid huts on a diet that was little above the subsistence level. About 1900, agricultural laborers received fifteen cents a day plus coarse food, or thirty to forty cents without board, if we allow the high rate of twenty cents for each peso. At Jerez, from which name the word "sherry" derives, laborers worked fifteen to sixteen hours a day for twenty cents. Small as the wages were, they were not steady, for there was work only about half of the year. Hence many were reduced to beggary. Wages rose during the succeeding period but not enough to improve the condition of the agricultural laborer to any great extent. Agriculture suffered from the systems of land tenure. The proprietors of the large estates were mostly absentee landlords who left the cultivation of the soil to men who lacked both the knowledge and the funds to make a success of it. Consequently the total production was very low, the wheat crop, for example, averaging about eleven bushels to the acre.

The condition of the industrial worker was but little better. Although the cost of living had risen 216 per cent between 1827 and 1902, wages had increased only by some 18 per cent. Nor was there any proportionate increase in wages during the succeeding decade despite a further rise in food and rents. It was therefore inevitable that discontent should be rife. The government did little to improve the lot of the industrial proletariat. During the first years of the twentieth century laws were passed to protect workers against accidents, old-age pensions were established, and the hours of labor in the mines were limited. But employers were able to evade the application of these laws. Although some did endeavor to help their workmen, these well-meant efforts often had small effect.

This gave socialism its opportunity. As a movement it was late in coming to Spain. Before World War I the proletariat was small in numbers. As late as 1919 only 3.5 per cent of the working population was engaged in manufacture, while agriculture occupied 70 per cent. Actually, anarchism had a greater following in the second half of the nineteenth century than did socialism. But Marxian socialism grew apace with the founding of such producing centers as the ironworks of Biscay, the textile and engineering industries at Barcelona, the coal districts of the Asturias and Cordova. Many of the recruits of socialism were workmen who had received their political education under the banner of one of the Republican parties. In 1910 the Socialist Labor Party had one member elected to the Cortes. The program of the party was much the same as that of the Marxian parties in other countries.

Progress in wiping out illiteracy was also slow. The number of schools was insufficient, the teachers lacked proper training, most instruction was superficial, and the disgracefully small salaries were often left unpaid for long periods. Statistics show that illiterates constituted 75 per cent of the population in 1860, 70 per cent in 1877, 68 per cent in 1887, and 63 per cent in 1900. As late as 1910 nearly twelve million people, or almost 60 per cent of the population, were unable to read or write.

Spanish leaders do not appear to have realized the seriousness of the menace; hence little that was constructive was attempted. In the decade preceding 1916 only 250 new schools were built. In Barcelona only 16,000 of an estimated school population of 82,000 were enrolled in any kind of school in 1916. One reason for the situation was the opposition of the church to liberal reforms. According to the concordat of 1851 all education whether public or private had to conform to the doctrines of the church, and the leaders of the church were determined to keep education under ecclesiastical influence. While the Jesuits were the principal teachers of the upper classes, instruction among the poor was largely under the direction of the Order of the Escolapios. Both orders were vigorously opposed by the liberal parties and by many workmen in the towns.

In general there was considerable friction between church and state in Spain. "The history of the nineteenth century in Spain," a Spanish historian wrote,[9] "would have been much quieter and much richer in results had the evolution of the Spanish people taken place in the absence of clericalism and militarism." The power of the Roman Catholic Church in Spain was very great. According to the first article of the concordat of 1851, "the Catholic, Apostolic, Roman religion continues to be the only religion of the Spanish nation, to the exclusion of all other forms of worship." In 1869 this exclusiveness was modified, but public ceremonies or public manifestations of dissenting cults were forbidden. Although the English ambassador, for instance, was permitted to hold service according to the Anglican Church in the chapel of the English embassy, this could not be announced by a sign in the street. It was not until early in the twentieth century that the government, over the objections of the Vatican, permitted non-Catholics to display their emblems of worship in public. The concordat of 1851 also put education and the censorship of the press under clerical control. Although the state permitted civil marriages, the church would not permit those who contracted only civil marriages to be buried in consecrated cemeteries.

Feelings in some quarters were especially strong against the monastic orders. After most of the religious orders had been suppressed during preceding decades, the concordat of 1851 legalized the existence of certain orders of nuns and limited the orders of monks to those of "St. Vincent de Paul, St. Philip de Neri, and another from those approved by the Holy See." Inasmuch as the third order was never determined, all the principal missionary orders established their houses in Spain and made that country the headquarters of their labors in the colonies

[9] Madariaga, *Spain* (1930), p. 220.

and abroad. In 1913 there were about 3800 religious orders in Spain with some 55,000 members, almost three quarters of them being women. This number does not seem disproportionately large, however, when it is considered that a majority of the orders were devoted to such beneficent and charitable purposes as teaching, nursing, and the care of the poor.

The causes of the friction between clericals and anticlericals were many and complex. It appears to have been generated, above all, by the fact that the clerical party had supported Don Carlos. From that time onward the relations between the church and the government became steadily more strained. Some of the liberals, in fact, became frankly anticlerical. Much resentment was engendered by the fact that the religious orders were permitted to engage in trade without being taxed and were thus able to undersell their competitors. The reactionary attitude of the orders in matters of education also stimulated much opposition. In general, many Spaniards, particularly of the working classes, were enemies of the monastic orders, while quite ready to profess sympathy for the underpaid parish clergy. Finally in 1910 the government passed the Congregations Bill, which provided that no new congregations could establish houses without authorization from the government and also that orders engaged in trade or manufacture of whatever description must pay taxes and submit to inspection like any private individual. Moreover, all orders were forbidden to own any property which was not absolutely indispensable for the purpose to which the association was devoted.

ITALIAN AND SPANISH CULTURE

At the time of the Renaissance most of the leading thinkers, poets, painters, and engineers of Europe were Italians. But the intellectual vigor together with the material glory of Italy began to decline in the sixteenth century with the shifting of the center of commercial activity from the Mediterranean to the Atlantic and the English Channel. Thereafter Italians had to live largely on the memories of past greatness. The decline was particularly evident in literature, which became more and more a soulless imitation of foreign literatures. It was not until they were moved by the common hope of the *risorgimento* that Italian writers again became eloquent. The predominant figure of this period was Alessandro Manzoni (1785–1873), whose *I Promessi Sposi* (The Betrothed) is regarded by many critics as the one great Italian novel. Both Goethe and Sir Walter Scott considered it one of the great novels of all time. Its central theme is the struggle of a nation against tyranny and obscurantism.

After the political unification, literature again fell into a somewhat torpid state. "In the literary life of the nation," an Italian critic wrote, "there are signs of the same languor that paralyzes its economic life. I see no sign of improvement. I should be very glad if there were a way out of so great a lethargy; but I do not find it. I think that the chief cause is the lack of any strong moral movement; there is nothing that agitates the public mind." Conditions were not conducive to the development of belles lettres. What is known to the literary world as the Italian language was not the language of the Italian people in the same sense as English and French are to the people of England and France respectively. It was restricted largely to literature and science. Nowhere was it spoken as a living tongue, as the language of everyday life. Most Italians used a dialect for the expression of the intimate realities of life. Literary Italian, therefore, lacked contact with the feelings and the life of the people, a contact which is essential to the development of a great literature. To most Italians it appeared formal and academic. Moreover, because of the widespread illiteracy few writers, if any, whose books were sold only in Italy were able to earn a livelihood with the pen.

The greatest, and certainly the most conspicuous, literary figure of modern Italy was Gabriele D'Annunzio (1863–1938). His versatility was stupendous. He was, among other things, poet, novelist, dramatist, journalist, politician, propagandist, popular orator, temporary dictator, and an adventurer who sought to rival the amorous exploits of Byron and Casanova. As a man he was eccentric and egotistical, bombastic and blustering, ostentatious and pompous. Theatrical effects were of the very essence of his life. There was something distinctly childish about the man who wanted everything that pleased him but soon grew tired of it; who spent borrowed money with reckless abandon, making no effort to pay his debts; and who doused himself with perfumes.

His adventurous life notwithstanding, D'Annunzio was a great artist in an age that boasted Tolstoi, Ibsen, Zola, Maupassant, and Anatole France. First of all, he was undoubtedly the greatest master of Italian prose in modern times. Pope Leo XIII, who was a humanist of the first rank, stated that D'Annunzio was the only man living who could write Italian. The least that can be said for him is that he enormously enriched and refined the language. Second, he is one of the consummate lyric poets of Italian history. *Primo Vere,* his first volume of poetry, published when he was only sixteen, won for him immediate recognition. His mature work is contained in four volumes, entitled *Laudi del Cielo, del Mare, della Terra, a degli Eroi,* but usually referred to simply as *Laudi.* His poetry is distinguished by an unbelievable richness in words and an unerring taste in rhythm. Third, he was the most popular Italian novelist of his time. In an enchanting style he combined beauty, color, rhythm, and picturesque imagery. His novel *Virgins of the Rocks* has been called a prose poem. Finally, he did much for Italian drama. In 1895 he wrote *La Città Morta* (The Dead City) for Sarah Bernhardt and in 1898 *La Gioconda* for Eleonora Duse. His *Francesca da Rimini* (1902) was presented throughout Europe and the United States with Mme. Duse in the principal role. One critic has summed up his importance to Italian literature in the following words: "By the long series of his novels and tragedies and more particularly by the consummate art of his poetical masterpieces, the *Laudi,* he raised Italian literature, set it free from insularity and ignorance of the main streams of modern thought, and gave it universality and a modern consciousness."

When the new Italian state was established in 1870 Italy already had a rich tradition of music, particularly in opera. The best known Italian composer is undoubtedly Rossini (1792–1868), who composed thirty-eight operas. Of these only one, *The Barber of Seville,* first produced in 1816, remains in the current repertory. Many of his overtures, however, are still played frequently, above all his *William Tell* overture (1829).

The man who represents in his own development the flowering of nineteenth-century Italian opera is Giuseppe Verdi (1813–1901). Some of his early operas were successes and others were failures, but his career was one of artistic progress from the first opera to the last. During the second period of his development which began in 1851 he wrote *Rigoletto, Il Trovatore, La Traviata,* and *La Forza del Destino (The Face of Destiny).* But it is the works of his last years which gave him rank among the great composers of all time. The first of these is *Aïda* (1871) in which he turned away from the old conventions, the boisterous instrumentation, the cheap dance tunes, and the old operatic claptrap. In this opera Verdi for the first time demonstrates the proper balance between the singers and the orchestra. When his *Otello,* based on Shakespeare's tragedy and written in collaboration with the poet-composer Arrigo Boito, was produced in 1887, critics at once hailed it as one of the most powerful operas of all time. His last opera, *Falstaff,* which was also written in collaboration with Boito and is based on Shakespeare, is by many regarded as the best of Verdi's operas. At the time of Verdi's death Edvard Grieg, the great Norwegian composer, stated: "I would go so far, even, as to say that side by side with Wagner he was, on the whole, the greatest dramatist of the century." Verdi's *Requiem* and his *Swan Song,* sacred pieces for choir and orchestra, represent Roman Catholic culture at its highest.

The composer whom Verdi named as his probable successor was Giacomo Puccini (1858–1924) whose success was established with the production in 1893 of the opera, *Manon Lescaut.* But it was the production of *La Bohème* in 1896 that made him famous. *La Tosca* followed in 1900 and in 1904 came the charming *Madame Butterfly* which curiously enough was hissed by an Italian audience at its first performance. In 1910 Puccini produced his operatic setting of the American play, *The Girl of the Golden West*. Although it is not to be classed with Puccini's four great operas it is still performed occasionally. As a composer Puccini does not rank with Verdi, but he did possess skill in technique, a rare gift of melody, and an unusual sense of orchestral color. Since his death the four great operas on which his fame rests — *Manon Lescaut, La Bohème, La Tosca,* and *Madame Butterfly* — have continued to be a constant feature of the world opera houses.

The most popular Spanish writer of this period was Vicente Blasco-Ibáñez (1867–1928). As a man he ranks with D'Annunzio, Zola, and Victor Hugo in picturesqueness, popular appeal, and capacity for making enemies. "Your greatest work is the romance of your own life," Anatole France told him. Ibáñez himself said, "I am a man of action and my life has been spent in work that is far removed from the manufacture of books." Throughout his whole career he was devoted to republicanism. In his own words he was "preparing with all his might a revolution," one which should "free Spain from the rule of a despotic king." For his activities he was exiled and imprisoned at various times. "I have been a political agitator," he wrote, "and I have spent a part of my youth in prison; I have been there at least thirty times." In 1891, after a period of exile he founded *El Pueblo* (*The People*), a liberal newspaper in which he exposed government corruption. At various periods of his career he was a businessman, a founder of Spanish-American colonies, leader of the republican party in Spain, and deputy from his native city of Valencia to the Cortes.

In addition to his other activities Ibáñez was a prolific writer. Besides his many newspaper articles and voluminous translations, he produced sixteen novels, three volumes of short stories, and three books of travel. The steady succession of novels achieved not only fame but also fortune for him, enabling him to devote much time and energy to politics. As a writer he carried on the tradition of the naturalist school of Émile Zola; in fact, he has frequently been called the Spanish Zola. The secret of the success of his novels lies in the burning passion and the powerful earnestness he instilled in them. He overwhelms his readers with the crushing reality of the conditions he depicts. His glaring weakness is his discoursiveness, displayed in long harangues that often do violence to the general theme. His approach was that of the eighteenth-century rationalist, for he was, in his own words, a spiritual son of Voltaire and the philosophes. This accounts for his sharp attacks on the Roman Catholic Church and particularly on the Jesuits.

Like Cervantes, Ibáñez wrote novels which he hoped would cure Spain of many of her ills. His *La Barraca* (*The Cabin*) (1898) presents a picture of the life of the poor peasants around Valencia and is so vividly written that the reader lives with the peasants in their hardship and toil. After he was elected to the Cortes he began to write propaganda novels which deal with contemporary problems. Thus in *The Shadow of the Cathedral* (1903) he attacked in relentless fashion the Roman Catholic Church, the monarchy, and Spanish society in general. *La Bodega* (*The Wine Vault*) (1905) is a novel of protest against alcoholism among poor workmen. *Sangre y Arena* (*Blood and Sand*) (1908) is an arraignment of bullfighting which shows the demoralizing influence of the bloody bullring combats on the various classes of Spanish society.

CHAPTER THIRTEEN

Imperialism in the Nineteenth Century

THE NATURE OF
NINETEENTH-CENTURY IMPERIALISM
T HE nineteenth century was a period not only of nation building but also of empire building on a colossal scale. The word "imperialism," which is used to designate this movement, is not easy to define. In its broadest meaning it is a national policy of establishing control over new areas. It also carries the suggestion that force is employed both in establishing domination and in maintaining it. For the present study imperialism refers to the subjection and control which European states established over industrially undeveloped regions of Asia and Africa. The peoples involved were not necessarily backward, for some of them, such as those of China and India, possessed fully as rich a cultural heritage as the conquering countries. What they lacked, besides machine industry, was the military power and iron discipline which new instruments of destruction gave the western nations. The control established varied greatly, ranging from control of the commerce of a given area to complete political domination.

While acquisition of territory was not difficult, profitable exploitation posed many problems. The large staffs required to administer the colonies and the large navies needed to protect them imposed heavy financial burdens on the colonizing powers. Colonial interests often involved them in wars which further drained the national exchequer. Moreover, after footing the bill over a long period of time some of the countries lost their colonies. Thus a series of wars, ending in 1815, deprived France of most of her possessions in America and in the east. The British Empire, to which the French colonies were added, had previously suffered the loss of its thirteen American colonies. During the

253

years immediately after 1810 the Spanish colonies of South America severed the ties which bound them to the mother country. In 1822 Portugal lost Brazil. These events certainly substantiated the well-known epigram of Turgot, "Colonies are like fruits that drop off when they are ripe."

These developments throughout the world corresponded with a change of economic doctrine. In France, during the second half of the eighteenth century the Physiocrats preached freedom from restriction (*laissez faire*), making the old French colonial system with its monopoly regulations their special target. In England, Adam Smith in *The Wealth of Nations* (1776) asserted that the burdens of the British colonial system were undeniable but the benefits purely imaginary. Jeremy Bentham wrote a letter entitled "Emancipate Your Colonies," which was published in both France and England. The fact that trade between Great Britain and her former American colonies increased after the latter became independent seemed proof that the trouble and expense of administering colonial empires outweighed any possible benefits. All this gave rise to an aggressive and very vocal anti-imperialism in England. One group, known as the "Little Englanders," of which Gladstone was a member, even believed that the time was not far distant when the British Empire would dissolve completely. Even Disraeli, who later became the champion of a strong British Empire, wrote to the British foreign secretary in 1852, "These wretched colonies will all be independent in a few years and are millstones around our necks." For a time anti-imperialism was a prevailing note in British foreign policy.

Nor was such sentiment restricted to Britain. To most of the French statesmen of the period colonies were an unjustifiable luxury which their country could ill afford. During the period from 1815 to 1870 France did, it is true, more than double her possessions outside Europe by securing footholds in Algeria, Senegal, and Indo-China. But these ventures were launched by a small group and were not part of a wider policy. In 1861 the government expressed its idea of empire by throwing open the trade of her colonies to all nations. In Germany, too, neither the government nor public opinion evinced much interest in colonies before the decade of the eighties. "All the advantages claimed for the mother country," Bismarck stated in 1868, "are for the most part illusory. England is abandoning her colonial policy; she finds it too costly."

But during the last decades of the nineteenth century the pendulum swung in the other direction. Not only did the existing empires fail to dissolve; new empires were staked out by various powers. Books and pamphlets were written to prove that colonies are a necessity instead of a burden; colonial societies were organized to stimulate an interest in imperialism; and, except in Britain, protective tariffs soon put an end to free-trade policies. In England the movement received considerable impetus from the fact that Disraeli announced his conversion to imperialism in 1872. Thereafter the "Little England" influence waned. In France a number of prominent statesmen, including Gambetta and Jules Ferry, led the revival movement. Ferry, the archchampion of the French imperialist renaissance, stated that "every fragment of our colonial domain, every tiny morsel should be sacred to us. . . . It is not a question of tomorrow's future, but the future of fifty or a hundred years from now." In 1882 the economist Leroy-Beaulieu asserted that "colonial expansion must occupy the first place in our national consciousness" because it "is for France a question of life or death; either France will become a great African state or she will be in a century or two but a second-rate power." In Germany, too, imperialist sentiment became fashionable in the early eighties. A colonial society, organized in 1882, enrolled more than ten thousand members within three years.

The revival of imperialism cannot be explained by a single or simple cause. Among the factors which contributed to it were political ambition, military adventure, and missionary enterprise. An argument often given was overpopulation; but it has been overstressed. Actual overpopulation did not exist in any serious degree until near the end of the century. A further factor was national prestige, i.e. the belief that the acquisition of new areas reflects glory on the mother country. Some defenders of imperialism have tried to attribute altruism to its advocates. Since imperialism, they argued, bestows on "backward" nations the blessings of civilization, law, and order, Europeans must be ready to sacrifice their own ease and comfort in order to bring these blessings to the benighted natives. This theory has been designated as "The White Man's Burden." Rudyard Kipling was one of those who glorified it:

> Take up the White Man's Burden,
> Send forth the best ye breed,
> Go bind your sons to exile,
> To serve your captive's need.

All the aforementioned factors were behind the rise of the new imperialism, but it would be a mistake to assert that they were the fundamental causes of the imperialist ventures. Regarding the "White Man's Burden" Lord Olivier said bluntly, "No nation has ever colonized, annexed, or established a sphere of influence from motives of disinterested philanthropy towards a native people." The assertion of high principle by statesmen and imperialists was a pretext for acquiring colonies rather than a statement of the basic motives. In other words, sentimental, moral, and altruistic considerations were convenient justifications of imperialism. Of themselves they would not have set imperialism in motion. Bernard Shaw stated the point in words that apply to imperialists of every country:

When an Englishman wants a thing, he never tells himself that he wants it. He waits patiently until there comes to his mind, no one knows how, a burning conviction that it is his moral and religious duty to conquer those who have the thing he wants. . . . He is never at a loss for an effective moral attitude. As a great champion of freedom and national independence he conquers and annexes half the world, and calls it Colonisation.

The actual motives of the imperialists were economic and were rooted in the new industry carried on by mechanical processes under the factory system. Bismarck, for example, frankly stated that his actions were governed by economic reasons. What he wanted outside Europe, he said, was "not provinces, but commercial enterprises." The primary motives may be conveniently summed up under three headings: (1) the increased demand for raw materials, (2) the search for new markets, (3) the existence of surplus capital seeking outlet in foreign investment.

1. *The increased demand for raw materials.* If steady employment was to be given to the ever-increasing millions who were flocking to the new industrial towns, the wheels of industry had to keep turning. For this, large quantities of raw materials were necessary. Many of these staples were not produced in Europe and had to be imported from abroad. There was, of course, nothing essentially new in this. During the eighteenth and nineteenth centuries the English had imported raw cotton from the United States, but when the Civil War broke out, this supply was cut off and many British cotton mills were forced to close down. To prevent a recurrence British industrialists began to look in other directions for a possible supply. Other raw materials needed for European industries included silk, rubber, petroleum, vegetable oils, coal, iron, copper, zinc, nickel, mercury, and precious metals. In many of the undeveloped countries these materials, as well as foodstuffs, were available in great quantities. It was, above all, over such regions that the new industrial nations sought to establish control. The goal, particularly after the policy of free trade began to give way to protectionism, was to form a self-sufficient empire within which all the needed raw materials and foodstuffs could be produced.

2. *The search for new markets.* The application of power machinery to manufacturing processes had for a time given Britain a definite lead over other European nations in the manufacture of textiles, hardware, and machinery. As long as their superiority continued, the British found a market in the other countries of Europe. Overseas colonies were, therefore, of secondary importance. But by 1870 other nations, including

France, Germany, and Belgium, had developed their industrial facilities to a point where they were beginning to close their markets to British manufactures by means of tariffs; in fact, industrial expansion was so rapid in a number of countries that the home markets were soon unable to absorb the output of the factories. Instead of increasing the buying power of the masses or of shutting down inferior mills and rigidly restricting the output to accord with the demands of the domestic markets, manufacturers and traders looked abroad for new outlets. Groups of industrialists and merchants used their respective governments to secure undeveloped territories for exploitation. Often no attempt was made to conceal the real purpose. For example, in a speech before the Rouen Chamber of Commerce, the French governor of Indo-China declared in 1899 that the colony's *raison d'être* was to furnish a market for the manufactured products of France.

3. *The existence of surplus capital seeking outlet in foreign investment.* The new industry was so profitable that industrialists and merchants soon accumulated large fortunes which could not be used to extend industry endlessly. Consequently a number of European countries were suffering from what has been called "a glut of capital." As the rate of interest fell in Great Britain, France, Germany, Holland, and Belgium, the surplus capital was invested in undeveloped countries where capital was scarce and where higher returns could be secured. Jules Ferry said: "For wealthy countries colonies are most advantageous investments. It is in the interest of France, which is glutted with capital, to consider this aspect of the question." The movement for overseas investment, which began in 1880, soon developed amazing proportions. The annual foreign investments of Great Britain alone were as high as one billion dollars in some years, with the result that in 1913 the total overseas investments of that country amounted to $20 billion. France's total in 1913 was estimated at $8 billion. Even Germany, which entered the colonial field somewhat later, managed to invest about $5 billion in imperialist ventures.

All these causes combined to produce a sudden outbreak of imperialism during the last quarter of the century. It was a mad scramble for colonies, protectorates, concessions, and spheres of interest such as the world had not previously seen. Even the conquests of Caesar and Alexander were trivial in comparison. Great Britain increased her empire by some 4 billion square miles and added 57 million people to her population. France's small empire of 1880 had by 1914 grown to an empire of three and a half million square miles and a subject population of 37 millions. During the same period Germany expanded by a million square miles, while Belgium and Portugal made additions of about the same size. Russia, too, extended her rule over vast territories, and even Italy and Japan gained a quarter of a million square miles. Asia Minor fell largely under the domination of England, France, and Germany, but most of the territory acquired by the European powers was in Africa or in Greater Asia. Largely an unexplored wilderness in 1875, Africa was carved up almost entirely before the end of the century. In an area of more than 5 million square miles, only Abyssinia and the small republic of Liberia retained their independence. In Asia only Japan remained completely free of European control. Even the islands of the Pacific became either possessions or colonies of European states.

PARTITIONING AFRICA

The vast continent of Africa, nearly four times the size of the United States, was largely an unknown continent at the middle of the nineteenth century. Such interest as Europeans had was centered in the Mediterranean area. In 1830 the French had conquered Algeria, not because they saw any intrinsic worth in the territory but because King Charles X hoped that the conquest would stimulate patriotic pride in France. Not until 1881 did the French take over the neighboring region, called Tunisia. After the first quarter of the century Britain had become more and more interested in Egypt because of its position on the Red Sea route to India. Its importance was greatly augmented through the construction in the third quarter of the century of the Suez Canal by a French company organized by Ferdinand de Lesseps (1805–1894). In 1875 Disraeli succeeded in purchasing a large block of stock in the company and in 1882 a British force moved into Egypt to establish political control.

During the earlier centuries the interior of central and south Africa had been the hunting ground for slave traders, but with the decline of the slave trade European possessions shrank to fortified trading stations along the coast. Only Portugal still held considerable stretches of land in both West and East Africa (Angola and Mozambique), but they were held weakly. The unsuitable climate, the decaying trade, and conflicts with the natives had discouraged colonization even of the coastlands. Only in Cape Colony situated in the temperate zone at the southernmost point of Africa did European immigrants settle in any large numbers. The interior of Africa was so completely unknown that on early nineteenth-century maps it was almost completely blank.

After 1850 interest in the interior gradually increased. Missionaries who traversed the continent in various directions opened a new chapter of geographical discovery. The individual whose work drew the attention of a wider public to the great unexplored continent was David Livingstone (1813–1873), a medical missionary working under the di-

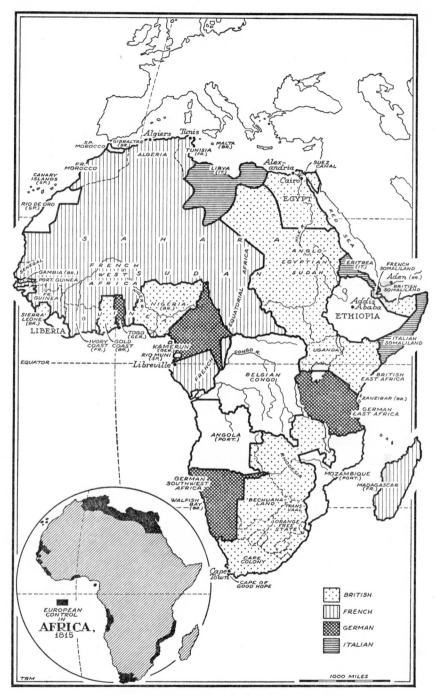

THE PARTITIONING OF AFRICA TO 1914

Map labels:

S. P. MOROCCO
GIBRALTAR (BR.)
Algiers
Tunis
MALTA (BR.)
TUNISIA (FR.)
FR. MOROCCO
ALGERIA
CANARY ISLANDS (SP.)
LIBYA (T.)
Alexandria
Cairo
SUEZ CANAL
EGYPT
RIO DE ORO (SP.)
S A H A R A
RED SEA
SENEGAL
GAMBIA (BR.)
PORT. GUINEA
FR. GUINEA
FRENCH WEST AFRICA
SUDAN
ANGLO-EGYPTIAN SUDAN
ERITREA (IT.)
FRENCH SOMALILAND
Aden (BR.)
BRITISH SOMALILAND
SIERRA LEONE (BR.)
LIBERIA
NIGERIA (BR.)
Addis Ababa
ETHIOPIA
IVORY COAST (FR.)
GOLD COAST (BR.)
TOGO (GER.)
KAMERUN (GER.)
RIO MUNI (SP.)
Libreville
FRENCH EQUATORIAL AFRICA
CONGO R.
UGANDA
ITALIAN SOMALILAND
EQUATOR
BELGIAN CONGO
BRITISH EAST AFRICA
ZANZIBAR (BR.)
GERMAN EAST AFRICA
ANGOLA (PORT.)
MOZAMBIQUE (PORT.)
MADAGASCAR (FR.)
GERMAN SOUTHWEST AFRICA
RHODESIA
WALFISH BAY (BR.)
BECHUANA LAND
TRANS VAAL
ORANGE FREE STATE
CAPE COLONY
Cape Town
CAPE OF GOOD HOPE

EUROPEAN CONTROL IN AFRICA, 1815

TRM

1000 MILES

Legend:
BRITISH
FRENCH
GERMAN
ITALIAN

rection of the London Missionary Society. On his travels he suffered more than fifty attacks of African fever and endured great hardships, but he doggedly pushed on, contacting many tribes, exploring unknown regions, and making a new map of the interior. Gradually his missionary activities became secondary and those of explorer paramount. In 1857 during his year at home he said: "I go back to Africa to open a path for commerce and Christianity." This time he returned under the auspices of the British government. Among his achievements was his exploration of the Zambesi River. He astonished the world with his description of Victoria Falls, the greatest of all cataracts. The last seven years of his life were spent searching for the source of the Nile and accounts of his travels published in European and American newspapers excited a deep interest. When no word was received from him for some years James G. Bennett of the *New York Herald* commissioned the intrepid Henry M. Stanley to find Dr. Livingstone. After many months of incredible hardships Stanley found him in 1872 on the shores of Lake Tanganyika. His efforts to induce the explorer to leave the jungle were in vain. Livingstone died the next year.

Stanley's story of how he found Livingstone excited a widespread interest in Africa. After the latter's death the cloak of primacy in central African exploration fell on Stanley's shoulders. It was he who gathered the threads of his predecessor's discoveries into a coherent and connected whole. Moreover, his reports of the great riches to be found there precipitated a scramble for African territory. After his discovery of the source of the Congo River in 1875 he wrote to the *London Daily Telegraph* "that the power possessing the Congo would absorb to itself the trade of the whole enormous basin behind." He told the English of the immeasurable riches in ivory, copper, cotton, copal, and other things that were waiting in the Congo region, but they paid little attention. Finally the explorer turned to Leopold II, king of the Belgians, who as a private venture formed the Association Internationale Africaine which sent Stanley to explore the Congo and to acquire trading rights from the native chiefs.

As the territorial claims of the association based on Stanley's explorations clashed with those of the French, British, Portuguese, and Germans a conference of the interested powers was held in Berlin near the end of 1884. The United States and all the European states, except Switzerland, were represented. It was the first big colonial conference in modern times. At this conference Leopold succeeded in obtaining recognition of the claims of the Association Internationale to the Congo territory and a new state embracing an area of 900,000 square miles was organized. It was called Independent State of the Congo, but was also known as the Congo Free State. Before long the venture, originally conceived as an international undertaking, was transformed into a strictly Belgian affair. In 1887 Leopold paid back all the contributions the association had received from non-Belgians and by 1890 all the important officials of the new state were Belgians. Although the promoters had promised at Berlin "to protect the natives in their moral and material well-being," those natives who failed to bring a specified quota of rubber, gum copal, or foodstuffs to the trading posts were flogged and in some instances mutilated by having a finger or even a hand cut off. Reports of the cruel oppression created such widespread indignation that an International Commission launched an investigation after which conditions improved somewhat. The new state was put under full Belgian sovereignty in 1908.

After the Congo Free State had been established the partitioning continued until the continent was virtually dominated by France, Great Britain, and Germany. A glance at the map of Africa on the eve of World War I will show that France held most of the territory in the northwest, including French Guinea, the Ivory Coast, Dahomey, and the French Congo. The British holdings on the West Coast were small in comparison, the two most important being the British Gold Coast and British Nigeria. In 1884 the Germans established a protectorate over a large slice of territory in the southwestern part, just below Portuguese West Africa (Angola), and called it German South-West Africa. During the same period the territories on the East Coast of Africa were also partitioned. While Britain occupied Somaliland, which faces the entrance to the Red Sea at its southern end, Italy took the far larger Italian Somaliland to the southward. In 1884 three members of the newly founded Society for German Colonization concluded enough treaties with African chiefs to establish German control in the territories opposite Zanzibar. The next year this territory, later known as German East Africa, was placed under German protection. For the time being this German colony prevented the British from realizing Cecil Rhodes' dream of an unbroken stretch of empire from Cairo to Cape Town.

Near the end of the century there were still two large regions that were not under European rule, the Egyptian Sudan and Ethiopia (Abyssinia). The former, originally ruled by the khedive of Egypt, was lost in 1885 to a religious fanatic called Mahdi, but was reconquered by Anglo-Egyptian forces during the years 1896 to 1898 and thereafter ruled as a joint Anglo-Egyptian dependency. As for Ethiopia, Italy, which had not fared too well in the scramble for colonies, was eager to annex this vast country. But an Italian army sent to conquer it in 1896 was so completely routed in the battle of Aduwa that further attempts to establish European rule in Ethiopia were abandoned. In 1904 France reached an agreement with Britain regarding her claims to Morocco and in 1911 Italy occupied Tripoli. Thus practically the entire continent, except Ethiopia and Liberia, was under European rule.

PENETRATION OF ASIA

Asiatic imperialism differed from African imperialism in the degree of control the European nations were able to establish. The peoples of Asia with their old and highly developed civilizations offered greater resistance to conquest and domination. Japan, in fact, completely repelled all attempts at control and soon became a full-fledged imperialist nation in its own right.

The outstanding characteristics of nineteenth-century imperialism in the Orient are illustrated in the history of China. A vast empire covering a territory as large as the whole of Europe, China was ruled by the Manchu dynasty. The domination of the Manchu emperors was, however, somewhat shadowy. For all purposes of administration the heads of the eighteen provinces into which the country was divided were largely independent. Thus China was disunited. In addition it was militarily weak. The Chinese did not want foreigners in their country. They believed that their civilization was infinitely superior to that of the Occident and wished to preserve it against outside influences. To keep foreigners out of the country the government had restricted foreign trade to the port of Canton. But the Chinese lacked the military force to resist foreign encroachments. Consequently they were compelled to open more and more ports to foreign trade. The first ports were opened as a result of the Opium War (1840–1842). In addition to cotton, which was the principal article of trade with China, the British East India Company was selling in Canton considerable quantities of opium, a product of India which yielded large profits. For some years the Chinese took no action, but when the opium trade grew to such proportions that it caused widespread demoralization Chinese officials tried to stop the importation of the drug. After various other measures had failed, the Chinese Imperial Commissioner in 1839 confiscated the opium held by some British merchants who at once called on the British government to avenge the insult to the British flag. The British fleet responded by smashing the forts at the entrance to the Canton River and British troops took possession of Canton and other maritime cities. The Opium War was concluded by the treaty of Nanking (1842) in which the Chinese government agreed to pay the British a large indemnity, cede the island of Hongkong to them, and open four additional ports (Amoy, Fuchow, Ningpo, and Shanghai) to foreign trade. France, Spain, Belgium, the Netherlands, and also the United States quickly signed treaties giving them the same commercial rights.

These concessions did not satisfy the European nations and the United States very long. In 1843 the British signed a commercial treaty which extended their privileges by setting land aside for their residence. A short time later both the United States and France, by a small display of force, secured similar advantages. These treaties mark the beginning of "the right of extraterritoriality," i.e. the right which gave foreigners immunity from Chinese jurisdiction. Thereafter the provision was incorporated in the treaties which all the western nations signed with China. Consequently no foreigner residing in China was subject to Chinese law as regards either his person or his property. Any charge or claim against him had to be presented before the consul of his own country and was judged according to the laws of his nation.

Much to the surprise of the Chinese government the treaty of Nanking which ended the Opium War had not settled the opium question and during the succeeding period its sale was extended to other ports. When Chinese authorities in 1857 seized a small Chinese boat engaged in opium smuggling which was flying the British flag, the Second Opium War broke out. By the treaty of Tientsin (1858) the Chinese government agreed to open fourteen additional ports to British trade, to open the Yangtse River to British ships, to allow British subjects to travel freely in China, and to permit the trade in opium. Other nations quickly followed suit in extorting the same privileges.

Up to this time the efforts had been restricted to obtaining commercial and extraterritorial rights; during the succeeding decades various western powers proceeded to establish their domination over large sections of Chinese territory. Through the conquest of Cochin China, Cambodia, Tonkin, and Annam the French virtually laid claim to southern China. The British also extended their sway by compelling China to recognize British sovereignty over Burma in 1886. Even the Japanese, encouraged by the example of the western nations, forced China in the treaty which ended the Sino-Japanese War (1894) to turn over to her the Liaotung Peninsula together with Port Arthur, acknowledge the independence of Korea, and surrender to Japan the island of Formosa. But the Russians, seeing in the presence of the Japanese on the Asiatic mainland an obstacle to their plans, compelled them by a threat of force and with the support of France and England to relinquish their claims. The Russians then proceeded "to lease" from China the same Port Arthur which they had forced the Japanese to restore to China. The Russians also received permission to run a branch line of the Trans-Siberian railway through Manchuria. Not to be outdone by the Russians the British obtained a lease on the harbor of Weihaiwei; the French pulled another plum out of the Chinese pie by getting several railroad concessions as well as control of the Bay of Kwang-chow-wan; and the

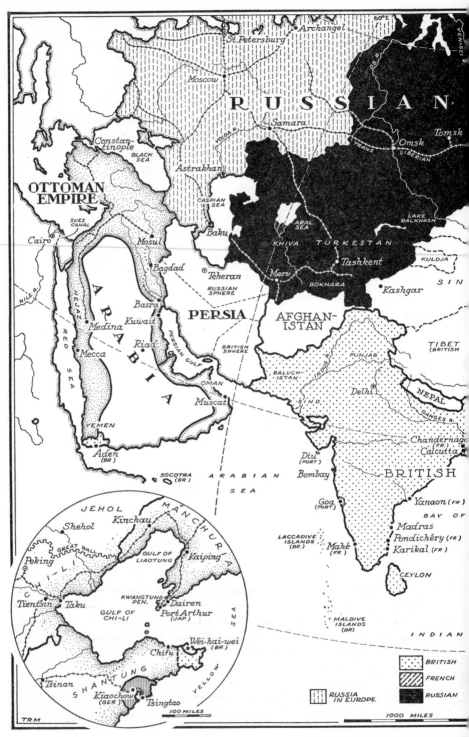

IMPERIALISM IN ASIA I

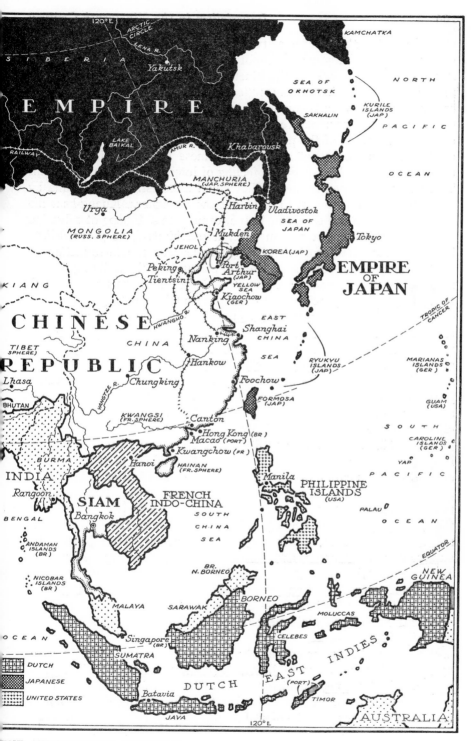

THE NINETEENTH CENTURY

Germans, using the murder of two German missionaries as an excuse, obtained a ninety-nine-year lease of Kiaochow Bay.

Thus before the end of the nineteenth century the Chinese found themselves with their best ports "leased" to foreign nations and their coastal and inland trade controlled by foreigners. Almost two thirds of their country had been marked out in "spheres of influence" by the powers and in fourteen of the principal ports foreign settlements had been established that were not subject to Chinese law. All this excited in the hearts of the Chinese a deep feeling of humiliation and resentment. Two paths were open to them. They could either strengthen China by westernizing it or attempt to drive out the foreigners. Kuang-hsu, the reigning Manchu emperor, saw in the former the sole hope of salvation for China. Gathering a reform party about himself, he proceeded to issue a series of reform edicts which called for the introduction of western methods of education. He also encouraged the building of railroads, the establishment of a bureau of mines, and the translation of foreign technical and scientific literature into Chinese.

But the widespread enthusiasm for reform caused alarm among the reactionaries. The Dowager-Empress Tzu-hsi emerged from her semi-retirement and with the help of a group of reactionaries seized the reins of government, dismissed the members of the reform cabinet, revoked most of the reform edicts, suppressed the reform newspapers, and subjected all progressives to petty persecutions. Moreover, she encouraged the formation of societies whose basic platform was opposition to foreigners and everything foreign. Most important of these societies was the Iho-ch'üan, translated as "Righteous Harmony Fists," but popularly known as "Boxers." Its aim was the extermination of all foreigners and the eradication of all traces of western civilization. The special hatred of the Boxers was reserved for the missionaries. They believed that by denouncing ancestor worship the missionaries were destroying the very wellsprings of Chinese spiritual life. Hence the churches and mission stations became primary targets of attack. After isolated instances of looting, arson, and murder in the spring of 1899, bands of Boxers made widespread raids in which foreigners were murdered and their homes were looted and burned. Scores of missionaries and thousands of Chinese Christians were slain in cold blood. In Peking and other cities the Boxers laid siege to the foreign legations after the foreigners refused to leave.

When the powers recognized the seriousness of the situation a relief expedition consisting of British, French, German, Russian, Japanese, and U.S. troops was dispatched to China. This mixed force managed to rescue the besieged foreign legations just as their supplies were exhausted after two months of severe suffering (June 13 to August 14).

In the British legation at Peking it rescued 873 foreigners and 3100 Chinese Christians. The Boxer movement was then stamped out with unnecessary cruelty. By the terms of the treaty concluded between the powers and China (1901) the latter agreed to pay an indemnity of $325 million, to punish the leaders of the uprising, and to grant further commercial advantages to the powers.[1]

JAPAN TURNS IMPERIALIST

In their search for lucrative trade connections the western powers did not overlook Japan. But when they sought entry into that country they found the door tightly locked. As far back as 1647 after expelling all missionaries the Japanese government had hermetically sealed the country against all foreign influences. The situation did not change until 1853 when a squadron of U.S. ships under Commodore Matthew Perry sailed into Yeddo Bay. Commodore Perry presented to the Japanese government a friendly letter from President Fillmore together with certain demands, among others that the country be opened to foreign trade. Realizing that refusal would mean hostilities, the Japanese authorities finally complied and a treaty was signed (March 31, 1854) which terminated the Japanese policy of exclusion. Treaties with Great Britain, Russia, the Netherlands, and France followed in rapid succession.

A small but informed Japanese minority realized their country, if it wished to escape domination by the western powers, must adopt the political, military, and economic systems of the west. This progressive element soon became influential enough to inaugurate a program of westernization. The first major step was toward centralization of authority. Although the emperor was ruler in name, the real power had long been exercised by a great feudal lord called the shogun. The feudal principalities into which the country was divided were ruled in an autocratic manner by daimios who paid homage to the shogun. Sentiment to restore the emperor's power gradually increased until the pressure forced the shogun to resign in 1867. Thereafter the daimios gradually surrendered their feudal rights, so that the emperor could announce the end of feudalism in 1871. The throne was once more the real seat of authority. In 1889 the emperor promulgated a constitution providing for a parliament or Imperial Diet of two houses, a House of Peers and a House of Representatives. This constitution was a gift from the emperor to his people and in no way limited his full sovereignty. Cabinet ministers were responsible only to him. Despite such forms as the Diet

[1] In 1908 the indemnity assigned to the United States was set up as a fund for the education of Chinese students in American schools.

and male suffrage, the essential spirit of the constitution was not democratic.

During the period after 1868 changes were introduced into many phases of Japanese life. The laws of the land were revised on the basis of the Code Napoleon and a new educational system was established for all levels from elementary school to university. Railroad construction was started in 1870 and by 1900 there were more than four thousand miles of railroad in operation. By 1901 Japan also had more than five thousand vessels built on the European pattern. Equally remarkable was the military reform. As early as 1866 French officers were called in and after the Franco-Prussian war were replaced by German officers. Thus the Japanese developed an army based on a combination of French and German tactics. At the same time the Japanese also built a navy, and British experts were invited to organize it. In order to build up armaments it was necessary to create heavy industries, for Japan was up to 1870 an almost completely agricultural nation. A characteristic feature of Japanese industrialization was the concentration of control over finances, commerce, and industry in the hands of a few great capitalist families.

Unfortunately the Japanese also imitated the western nations in becoming aggressively imperialist. Seeing the western powers bent on establishing their dominion over as much territory as possible, they decided to join in "the game of grab." The part of China which stretched invitingly toward Japan was the Korean peninsula with an area of 80,000 square miles. It was not difficult to pick a quarrel with China. When the Sino-Japanese War broke out in 1894, it was generally believed outside of Japan that China would find little difficulty in crushing her smaller antagonist. But the Chinese forces were no match for the new Japanese army and navy. A quick and decisive victory permitted the Japanese to dictate the treaty of Shimonoseki (April 17, 1895) which required China to acknowledge the independence of Korea, to cede Formosa to Japan, and to transfer to Japanese control the Liaotung Peninsula (which is the southern tip of Manchuria), together with Port Arthur.

The fact that the Russians forced them to relinquish the Liaotung Peninsula rankled deep in the hearts of the Japanese. Before long they were making preparations for war against Russia. To keep Russia from getting help in the war the Japanese government concluded an agreement with Britain (1902) in which the latter promised that the armed forces of the British Empire would come to the assistance of Japan if any other nation joined with Russia. After some diplomatic maneuvering the Japanese employed the same technique they were to use again at Pearl Harbor in 1941. Without making a declaration of war they launched a surprise attack on the Russian fleet at Port Arthur (February 8, 1904) and inflicted much damage.

This time the world took the Japanese more seriously, but the general opinion was that an Asiatic people would stand little chance of victory in the fight against the tsar's military forces. However, the unprepared Russians were anything but a match for the Japanese. After bottling the Russian fleet up in the ports of Port Arthur and Vladivostok, they destroyed it bit by bit whenever ships ventured out into the open. On land the Japanese were equally successful against the ill-equipped Russian troops. While one army quickly drove the Russians out of Korea, another landed behind Port Arthur to keep supplies from reaching the main Russian army in Manchuria. The last of the great battles lasted from February 23 to March 16, 1905, and ended in a Russian defeat. Still the Russians did not make overtures for peace.

Finally President Theodore Roosevelt, to prevent further bloodshed, requested the belligerent nations to send plenipotentiaries to a peace conference at Portsmouth, New Hampshire. In the treaty signed September 5, 1905, Russia agreed to transfer to Japan the lease on the Liaotung Peninsula and Port Arthur and to cede to Japan the southern half of Sakhalin Island. No indemnity was paid by either side.

During the succeeding years the Japanese strengthened their hold on the Asiatic continent. Despite earlier promises they annexed Korea in 1910, making it an integral part of the Japanese empire. In southern Manchuria they acquired control of railways which gave them a firm hold on the trade and industry of that part of China.

THE RISE OF SELF-GOVERNMENT IN THE BRITISH EMPIRE

For the British Empire the nineteenth century was not only one of great expansion but also one of inner development. The idea of an empire in which the rights of every colony depended upon enactments of the parliament in London gradually gave way in some of the leading colonies to the idea of responsible self-government. After the American War for Independence the English had settled into acceptance of the idea that the course taken by the American colonies would be followed by others as the occasion arose. As Lord Blachford, Permanent Under-Secretary for the Colonies put it, "The destiny of our colonies is independence." From this point of view it was regarded as a wise policy not to put any barriers in the way of their development toward self-government. The British did not want the achievement of independence to be accompanied by bitterness; after the parting the mother country would have all the advantages of trade without the expense of administration and protection.

The first colony to advance along the road to self-government was Canada. In 1791 Canada had been divided into two provinces, Lower Canada and Upper Canada. Each province was given an elective legislature, but the executive authority was vested in the governor appointed by the crown. The Canadians, French and English alike, resented the lack of a ministry responsible to the legislature. Constant friction between the elected assembly and the appointed governor led to an armed outbreak in both colonies in 1837. Although the uprisings were easily suppressed, the home government, alarmed at the prospect of losing another colony, sent Lord Durham to investigate. In his classic report, which is rightly regarded as the Magna Carta of colonial self-government, he recommended that the executive be made responsible to the legislature. Accepting the report, parliament in 1846 granted the two provinces responsible government. The next step in the constitutional evolution of Canada was federation. In 1867 the British parliament passed the British North America Act which joined Upper and Lower Canada, Nova Scotia, and New Brunswick in a federation called the Dominion of Canada. Provisions were made for a federal parliament consisting of a Senate and a House of Commons, to sit at Ottawa. The Governor-General, appointed by the crown, nominated the members of the Senate for life and bestowed honors in the name of the crown, but the real ruler was the prime minister who had to have the support of the leading party in the House of Commons. During the succeeding decades Canada spread westward until by 1905 it embraced all of British North America from ocean to ocean.

Other British colonies soon followed in Canada's footsteps. The second British colony to become a self-governing state was Australia. For many decades after Captain Cook discovered the new continent (1770) it was used mainly as an outlet for convicts and undesirables. Not until 1839 was the transportation of convicts suspended. During the succeeding years the rapid development of sheep breeding and corn growing, followed in 1851 by the discovery of gold, attracted many settlers. By 1859 there were six states on the new continent and each state had a government modeled after that of Britain. The advancement to a federal Australia came more slowly, the great obstacle being clashing economic interests. Over a period of several decades so little progress was made toward federation that in 1881 the project was temporarily laid aside. But negotiations were soon resumed and in 1897 agreement was reached on a plan which the British parliament embodied in the Australian Commonwealth Act (1900). In the division of powers Australia followed the model of the United States rather than that of Canada. While certain definite powers were entrusted to the federal government, the right to legislate on all other matters was retained by the states.

When the Australian federation was formed New Zealand was asked to join, but it preferred to shape its own destiny. After its discovery by Captain Cook in 1770 this island had been left to sealers, whalers, and traders of various kinds. Rumors of French designs finally moved the British government to sign an agreement with the Maoris (1840) which put New Zealand under British protection. British settlers began to migrate to the new country and in 1867 self-government was voted by the British parliament. The inevitable rush of fortune hunters followed the discovery of gold in 1861 with the result that the country soon had a white population of almost half a million. In 1907 it achieved dominion status and became a separate nation of the British Empire.

Greater difficulties were encountered by the British in South Africa. When Cape Colony, at the southernmost point of the African continent, was ceded to Britain in the settlement of 1814, its white population consisted largely of Boers (peasants) who were of Dutch stock. Friction was generated immediately when the Boers questioned the right of the British to rule them. But the act which stirred the Boers to the depths was the abolition of slavery by Great Britain in 1834. The compensation paid them by the British government for the some 30,000 slaves they had owned failed to satisfy them. They claimed that a great wrong had been inflicted on them because slavery is sanctioned by the Old Testament. In 1835 they began the Great Trek. About 10,000 Boers transported their families and possessions in oxcarts to regions across the Vaal River where they hoped to be free of the British authorities. There they crowded the natives off their pastures and founded two independent republics, the Orange Free State and the Transvaal.

During the succeeding decades the relations between the two republics and the British were somewhat uneven. After forcing both states to acknowledge British sovereignty, the British recognized their independence shortly after the middle of the century. But the revival of the imperialist spirit later in the century caused the British to take a new interest in the republics. In 1867, after two children on an Orange River farm were found playing marbles with diamonds, great numbers of fortune hunters crowded into the country. Among these was Cecil Rhodes (1853–1902), who started as a digger and in time gained virtual control of the diamond market. He was the great apostle of British imperialism, convinced that in building the British Empire he was fulfilling the Divine Will. His plan was gradually to move the British sphere of influence northward from Cape Colony. This soon resulted in a new clash with the Boers.

The discovery of rich gold deposits in the Transvaal in 1885 attracted a large number of adventurers to that state. Although the newcomers whom the Boers called Uitlanders (outlanders or foreigners) paid so much in taxes that Transvaal had a larger revenue than before, the

Boers put obstacles in the way of their becoming citizens of the republic because they feared that they themselves would become a minority in their own country. President Kruger, known as Oom Paul, explained the attitude of the government by saying that if he granted the franchise he might as well pull down the national flag. In 1894 he increased the time of residence necessary for naturalization from five to fourteen years. This policy caused Cecil Rhodes to enter into a conspiracy with the Uitlanders to overthrow the government. He was convinced that he could not realize his dream of a united South Africa so long as the Kruger regime continued. But the plan miscarried. Dr. Jameson, the leader of the expedition and personal friend of Rhodes, grew impatient because the men who were to participate in the *coup d'état* did not assemble quickly enough. He decided on his own initiative to make a dash for Johannesburg, the capital, with a force of less than five hundred. This small group was quickly surrounded and forced to surrender.

The Rhodes conspiracy led directly to the Boer War. In the negotiations that followed, the British continued to urge that the Uitlanders be admitted to citizenship. In 1899 President Kruger abruptly terminated negotiations by issuing an ultimatum which demanded that Britain withdraw her troops from the frontiers of Transvaal within forty-eight hours. The British answer was a declaration of war. The Boer War, in which the Orange Free State joined on the side of Transvaal, proved to be far longer and costlier than expected. Although the British succeeded in defeating the Boer armies and in occupying the capitals of both republics, the Boers persisted in carrying on a stubborn guerrilla warfare. Peace was not concluded until May, 1902. By its terms the Boers accepted British sovereignty, but were promised self-government in the future. This promise was carried out in 1906.

In the meantime a movement for federal union in South Africa had been launched. After 1906 even the support of the Boer leaders was enlisted for this cause. The plans reached fruition in 1908 in a convention of delegates from the Transvaal, Orange River Colony, Natal, and Cape Colony. The next year the plan of union which the convention had formulated was accepted by the parliaments of the four provinces and was then sent to the British parliament which obliged by passing the Union of South Africa Act and thus gave the new federation dominion status. The new federal constitution went into effect in 1910.

TROUBLE IN INDIA

One of the gravest problems which beset the British in the nineteenth century was the demand of India for self-government. India was ruled not directly by the British government, but by the English East India

Company, which during the early decades of the nineteenth century had established its dominion over the entire country. This company tried to win the support of the native population by various reforms, two particularly noteworthy ones being the establishment of equality of British and Indian subjects before the law and the suppression of the inhuman custom of burying alive or burning Hindu widows. The company also introduced the telegraph and began the construction of railways.

The masses of India did not always welcome such reforms and the introduction of western inventions. Chained down as they were by ingrained prejudices, many natives regarded the railway as an attempt to abolish caste by forcing the higher castes into polluting physical contact with the "untouchables." The telegraph, which was incomprehensible to them, savored of deviltry. Other factors also contributed to the development of hostility. One cause of friction was the introduction of breech-loading rifles in which cartridges were used that were rumored to be lubricated with the fat of cows and pigs. Since to the Hindu the cow is a sacred animal and the pig is regarded as unclean, and the Mohammedans are forbidden to eat the flesh of swine, the greased cartridges gave offense to the native soldiers of both religions. The British sought to quiet the fears of the sepoys or native soldiers by assuring them that the grease employed was a compound of mutton fat and wax. It was all to no avail. When the members of a cavalry regiment which refused to accept the cartridges were sentenced to imprisonment, comrades staged an open revolt at Meerut in Bengal (May 10, 1857). It was the beginning of the Sepoy Mutiny of 1857. After murdering their officers, the sepoys marched on Delhi, the ancient capital of the Moguls, where they proclaimed the restoration of the Mogul empire and proceeded to massacre all the English within reach. Sepoys in other parts of India also rose in revolt. The mutiny occurred at a time when there was only a small British force in India, many troops having been withdrawn for service in the Crimean War. Fighting against great odds the British troops managed to hold their own until reinforcements arrived almost six months later. Even then the mutiny was stamped out only after months of fighting during which terrible atrocities were committed by both sides.

One of the important results of the mutiny was that parliament terminated the control of the East India Company in 1858 and transferred the administration of India to the crown. In her proclamation of 1858 Queen Victoria stated that it was her government's "earnest desire to stimulate the peaceful industry of India, to promote works of public utility and improvement, and to administer its government for the benefit of all our subjects resident therein." Some attempts were made to

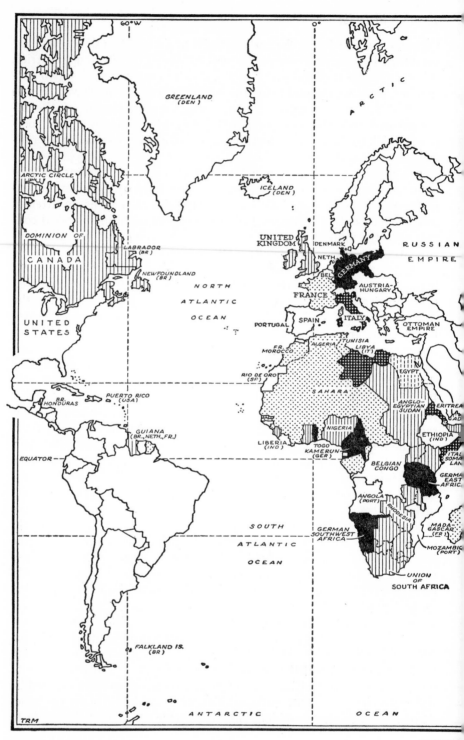

TRM

carry out this policy. The British covered the country with a network of railways which in half a century increased to more than 30,000 miles. They also spun a gigantic spider's web of macadamized roads totaling more than 50,000 miles. Postal service was established, telegraph lines were extended to the larger cities, and bridges were built. The government devoted special attention to the construction of irrigation canals as a means of converting wastelands into fruitful fields and of permitting a wider distribution of the population. By 1907 it had constructed or repaired 55,928 miles of such canals.

Accomplishments in the field of education are equally noteworthy. Widespread ignorance and ingrained superstition had often frustrated the best efforts of the government for the welfare of the people. For example, sanitary and quarantine regulations, introduced to stamp out the plague which repeatedly took a terrible toll in native lives, were largely ignored. Realizing the urgent need of eradicating ignorance and barbarism, the British opened primary and secondary schools in many parts of the country. Schools were first established in the larger cities, but the villages were not completely overlooked. By 1905 there was a grammar school in one village out of five. Agricultural schools were also established or students were sent abroad to study new farming methods at government expense. Experimental farms were maintained which demonstrated scientific methods and modern agricultural machinery. The crowning achievement in the realm of higher education was five universities (Calcutta, Bombay, Allahabad, Madras, and Lahore) which prescribed courses of study and conferred degrees.

All the concrete and tangible blessings the British brought to India did not spell contentment for the people. In so far as the bulk of the population accepted British dominion it was with mute acquiescence. There was no one special grievance to which the anti-British feeling can be ascribed. While the peasant complained of high taxes and exorbitant rents, artisans charged that British imports were ruining native industries. Other grievances were the impoliteness of the Englishman toward the native and the fact that natives were not permitted to carry firearms. A more general source of discontent was the curse of recurring famine which hung over India. In a country half the size of the United States with a population of about three hundred million the problem of raising enough food would have been a serious one under the best conditions; in India the task was aggravated by such factors as antiquated agricultural methods and periodic droughts. A crop failure meant famine and such a famine in the years 1899–1900 claimed the lives of about four million people. Undoubtedly the basic cause of the opposition to British rule was the fact that foreign domination is contrary to human nature. All the accomplishments of the British were overshadowed by their presence in India. To the natives of India they were men of another blood, of different habits, manners, and ideals.

The disaffection first became evident in the upper strata of Indian society, particularly among the members of the educated class. All educated Indians of whatever religion, caste, or race had one desire in common: they wanted a self-governing India. It was but natural that instruction in western philosophy should awaken in them such a desire, for during their university careers they read the writings of Rousseau and of Mazzini, and John Stuart Mill's *On Liberty*. They learned that the American colonies in 1776 took their stand on the principle that "just government must be based on the consent of the governed." They read the history of the French Revolution and the story of the rise of self-government in Britain. Viscount Morley, Secretary of State for India, said, "It would be idle to deny that there is a living movement among the people for objects which we ourselves have taught them to think desirable." During the period before World War I the demands were amazingly moderate. Although some demanded that the British get out of the country, the majority of educated Indians looked to the attainment of dominion status in the empire.

Among the particular grievances of the educated classes was the failure of the government to provide more places for them in the civil service, particularly in the higher administrative posts. Their aim was to destroy the monopoly of high office enjoyed by the British. Many of those who could not find government employment upon the completion of their academic career turned their ability to the organization of anti-British groups and the publication of seditious journals.

Gradually the spirit of revolt against British rule infected the masses. The first evidence of its widespread existence came during the Boer War, when news of British reverses was hailed with great delight. During the next decade it penetrated to every part of the country. An American observer wrote in 1907, "Everywhere there is ferment and a murmur of discontent. The cry 'Bande mataram!' (Hail to the mother country!) is heard throughout the land, and 'swaraj' (home rule) and 'swadeshi' (home country) have become words of magic to conjure with."

The tones in which the Indian leaders demanded self-government were so menacing that the British decided to permit a greater degree of native representation in the government. The Indian Councils Act of 1909 gave the natives representation on both the provincial and central legislative councils. Native members could now introduce resolutions leading to legislation. But the changes fell far short of the demands of the Indian people.

CHAPTER FOURTEEN

Tsarist Russia

RUSSIA IN THE EARLY NINETEENTH CENTURY WITH the Grand Duchy of Moscow as a nucleus the Russian state had since the fifteenth century gradually expanded in every direction, until at the opening of the nineteenth century it was by far the largest state in Europe. It reached from the Baltic Sea and the Arctic Ocean in the north to the Black Sea and the Caspian in the south; from the borders of Prussia and Austria in the west to the Pacific in the east. Additions during the first half of the century, including Finland and the central portions of Poland, further increased its area so that it finally embraced more than eight million square miles, or about one sixth of the land surface of the earth. This vast territory was inhabited by a congeries of peoples and tribes, differing widely in languages and customs. Among the more than sixty ethnic groups were Germans, Estonians, Latvians, Lithuanians, Poles, Jews, Czechs, Finns, Serbs, Rumanians, Lapps, Tartars, Kalmuks, Armenians, and Georgians. The predominant ethnic group was the Great Russians, who together with the White Russians and Little Russians (Ukrainians) formed about two thirds of the population.

Perhaps the most striking feature of the Russian Empire was the autocracy of the tsar. In the earlier centuries, when Russia was continually subject to foreign invasion by countless Asiatic hosts, there had been a paramount need for a strong government, and the people had been quite willing to commit absolute power into the hands of their rulers in return for protection. The tsars had gradually riveted the idea of autocracy upon the nation so firmly that even the period of the French Revolution and Napoleon left its power unshaken. At the beginning of the nineteenth century the tsar's will was still the sole source of law, of taxation, of justice. No legal limitations restricted his control over the lives and property of his subjects. His large empire he governed through a bureaucracy chosen from among the landed gentry. All the imperial officials, of whatever dignity, were responsible to him. His shadow hovered over every act or meeting. As an old proverb has it, "In Russia two are everywhere, God and the tsar."

Nor were there any classes or institutions that might impose a check on autocracy. In most of the other countries of Europe the nobility, the clergy, or the middle class had already restricted the power of the ruler or at least had served as a potential check. But in Russia such balancing forces were entirely lacking. Even the highest nobles were merely the servants of the tsar, without any security against arbitrary confiscation of property or exile to Siberia. The church, which in western Europe stood as a strong independent power, was completely subordinated to the tsar. As for the middle class, it was so small and ill developed as to be practically nonexistent; the free citizens of the towns, exclusive of the parish clergy, constituted less than 3.5 per cent of the total population. In the earlier centuries a national assembly (*Zemsky Sobor*), consisting of representatives of the nobility, the clergy, and, in some instances, the peasants, had been convoked on rare occasions to advise the tsar; but even this modest form of popular representation had disappeared since 1698.

Perhaps the greatest force in preserving the principles of autocracy was the Holy Orthodox Eastern Church. Since Peter the Great the church had been part of the political apparatus with which the tsar ruled his people. It was the official concern of the church to invest the tsar with a sacred character and to inculcate in the people an unquestioning obedience to his autocratic rule. Unreasoning acceptance of the teachings of the church and devotion to its forms became the primary test of loyalty to the government. How the church developed submissiveness of character in the masses can be seen in the following extracts from the New Imperial Catechism published in 1833:

QUESTION: "In what light is the authority of the tsar to be considered?" ANSWER: "As proceeding immediately from God." Q. "What duties does religion teach us, the humble subjects of his Majesty, to practise toward him?" A. "Worship, obedience, fidelity, the payment of taxes, service, love, and prayer." Q. "Wherein does this worship consist? And how should it be manifested?" A. "By the most unqualified reverence in words, gestures, demeanor, thoughts, and actions." Q. "What kind of obedience do we owe him?" A. "An entire, passive, and unbounded obedience." Q. "In what does the fidelity we owe to the tsar consist?" A. "In executing his commands most rigorously and without questioning; in performing the duties he requires of us; and in doing everything willingly and without murmuring."

Next to autocracy the central feature of Russian life was serfdom. At the beginning of the nineteenth century the peasants constituted 94.5 per cent of the population, and the great majority of the peasants were serfs. Serfdom in Russia was of more recent origin than that of western Europe; in fact, while serfdom was declining in most other countries, it was just being established in Russia. Toward the end of the sixteenth century the government, in order to facilitate the collection of taxes and the enrollment of recruits for the army, began to restrict the right of the peasants to migrate from one estate to another. Thereafter the process of enserfment continued until most of them were bound to the soil. Russian serfdom reached its zenith during the reign of Catherine II, who in her desire to unify the social and political structure of her empire extended it to the Ukraine, thereby creating millions of new serfs. She also gave the landlords almost unlimited power, even permitting them to sentence "refractory" serfs to hard labor in Siberia. Although the law put some restrictions on the power of the landlord, the serfs could in practice be ill used at the will of the owner, for the expense of judicial procedure made it impossible for a serf to seek justice in the courts. The result was the arbitrary rule of innumerable petty tyrants who if necessary flogged or tortured their serfs into obedience. These practices put a stamp of brutality upon Russian society as a whole.

There were, of course, many degrees of serfdom and different kinds of owners, some benevolent and others cruel. But even the best regarded their serfs as "baptized property." The wealth of a nobleman was not estimated according to the number of acres in his estate but according to the number of "souls" he owned. One owner might have a hundred serfs, another thousands, while some few had as many as a hundred thousand. They were bought and sold in open markets like so much merchandise. As serf labor was for most landlords the principal source of income, they exacted all they possibly could. In 1797 the government limited the labor an owner could demand from his serfs to three days a week, but many landlords managed to circumvent this restriction and others ignored it with impunity. Bound to the soil, weighed down by illiteracy, and exploited by his owner, the Russian serf was indeed in a sad plight. So long as these conditions remained, there was little hope for progress.

It appeared as if an age of liberal reform was to be ushered in by Alexander I, who became tsar in 1801. When he announced his plans for a complete reconstruction of the social and political system, Russia overflowed with joy and enthusiasm. Among the points included in his program were the liberation of the serfs, the limitation of autocracy by the establishment of elected assemblies, and the spread of popular education. He even took some slight steps toward carrying out his plans. Besides appointing a Ministry of Public Instruction to foster education, he deprived landlords of the right to exile their serfs and prohibited the sale of serfs in the open markets. But Alexander's early enthusiasm for reform gradually evaporated. At the end of his reign there still remained autocracy above and serfdom below, and the last hope of achieving reform in a peaceful way had disappeared.

December, 1825, saw the first of a series of uprisings that were ultimately to put an end to the autocracy of the Romanovs. The occasion was the accession of Nicholas I upon the death of Alexander I. The leaders were chiefly army officers. Russian officers and troops had come into contact with currents of liberal thought, with new social conditions, and with new political institutions in western Europe during the struggle against Napoleon. Upon their return home they saw that the idea of the rights of man was regarded with contempt by their rulers, that their country lay trodden under the heel of an autocracy which made all progress impossible. As they had no legitimate means of making their desires known, they organized secret societies which agitated for reforms, including the establishment of a constitution. These societies, afterwards called the Decembrists, were planning a widespread uprising but, when Alexander suddenly died, resolved to take advantage of the uncertainty that existed regarding the succession to attempt a *coup d'état*. Alexander's younger brother, Constantine, who was next in line, had no desire to assume the troublesome burden of ruling an unsettled and disturbed empire, so he renounced his right of succession in favor of his brother Nicholas. When the time came for the army to take the oath of allegiance to the new sovereign, several regiments, at the instigation of their officers, appeared in Senate Square in St. Petersburg on December 14 and began to shout for Constantine and a constitution. In their ignorance the common soldiers believed that Nicholas was a usurper, that Constantine was being held a prisoner, and that the "Constitutia" for which they were shouting was Constantine's wife.

Although Nicholas addressed the troops in person, they still refused to take the oath of loyalty to him. Finally the new tsar decided to put down the uprising by force. A regiment of artillery which had remained faithful to him was ordered to open fire upon the misguided troops. It strewed the vast square with dead and wounded. After a few rounds of grapeshot the rioters dispersed and Nicholas settled down to the task of eradicating the revolutionary movement. The leaders were apprehended, a number of them were hanged, and the rest were exiled to Siberia. Thus the Decembrist Revolution, as it is called, came to an end and a regime of the darkest autocracy began

Nicholas I, a narrow-minded man with strong convictions, never forgot the rebellion. It is reported that for the rest of his life he "trembled at the spectre of revolution." To forestall any further attempts to change the *status quo* he fought liberal ideas relentlessly, seeking to stamp them out by every means at his command. He harbored no doubts about the correctness of his principles. Some years before he ascended the throne he had already written, "A sovereign has no right to pardon enemies of the state. Louis XVI faced a real conspiracy, disguised by the false name of liberty; he would have spared much misery to his people by not sparing the conspirators." Upon a state document which contained the word "progress" he is said to have written, "This word must be deleted from official terminology." To prevent the spread of liberal ideas a strict censorship was imposed upon the press, and a firm control was established over the bureaucracy. Even education was carefully supervised. Only a limited number of students were permitted to attend the universities because the government needed only a limited number of educated servants. Education for others was a "pernicious luxury" in the eyes of Nicholas. He particularly opposed the education of the poor because, as he put it, they "become accustomed to a way of life, to a way of thinking, and to ideas which are not compatible with their position." He was truly, as Frederick William IV of Prussia called him, "supreme lord of the narrow world."

By relentlessly suppressing all revolutionary ideas and by mercilessly crushing all revolutionary movements Nicholas was able to prevent any widespread domestic uprisings, but in his foreign policy he was not so successful. In trying to liquidate the Turkish Empire for the benefit of Russia he became involved in war not only with Turkey but also with Great Britain and France. The Crimean War showed, in the words of a contemporary, "the rottenness of the [Russian] system of government and its suffocating principles." Under the strain of the war the military system broke down and the administrative machinery almost collapsed. The humiliation of a defeat which blighted his hopes of making Russia the dominant power in Near Eastern affairs was too much for "the Quixote of Autocracy." At the beginning of March, 1855, he suddenly died and was succeeded by his son, Alexander II.

REFORM AND REACTION

The accession of Alexander II opened a new era in Russian history, known as the Era of Reform. Russia's humiliating defeat in the Crimean War had not only exposed the weakness and rottenness of the governmental system but had also revealed the extent to which Russia was lagging behind the other states of Europe. In technical matters this backwardness had proved catastrophic. In the days of Napoleon the

Russian army had been able to meet the armies of western Europe on comparatively equal terms, but in the Crimean War it was another story. Not that the Russian soldiers were wanting in courage. What they lacked was up-to-date weapons. Their artillery and small arms were obsolete. While the rifles of the enemy, for example, had a range of 1200 paces, those of the Russians had a range of only 300 to 450 paces. Russia simply had to manufacture better weapons. A further result of technical backwardness was lack of means of rapid communication and transportation. Because there were at the time practically no railways in the country, it was impossible to move troops quickly to desired points. Far-reaching reforms were imperative if these weaknesses were to be remedied.

Alexander II was well aware of these facts and immediately after his accession began to prepare reforms in many departments of the state. His first reform was the abolition of serfdom. It was clear to his conservative as well as to his progressive advisers that this was the great obstacle to industrial progress, that the illiterate serf was no match for the free, skilled labor of the west. Just at this time, moreover, many owners feared that their serfs might rise in revolt. Russia had not forgotten the great uprisings of the seventeenth and eighteenth centuries; and now there were signs of growing restiveness. During the reign of Nicholas I there had been more than five hundred agrarian riots. Particularly serious disturbances had taken place while the levies of recruits were being raised for the Crimean War. Some of the rebellions were so serious that the government found it necessary to send whole regiments with artillery to quell them. The tsar himself told the nobles as early as March, 1856, that "the existing manner of possessing serfs cannot remain unchanged. It is better to abolish serfdom from above than to wait until it abolishes itself from below."

The tsar had hoped that the landlords would take the initiative and request the abolition of serfdom; but when they showed no inclination to do so, he formed a committee early in 1857 to discuss the complex problem. What made it so complex was that he wished to free the serfs without damaging the interests of the nobility. After a number of committees had discussed the question for years, the tsar finally signed the ukase abolishing serfdom on February 19, 1861. The fundamental principles of the reform were, first, that the person of the serf was to be freed without compensation to the owner; second, that the serfs were to be freed not as landless proletarians but as peasant proprietors.[1] They were to receive land allotments sufficient to provide for their

[1] Serfs who worked as domestic servants were obliged to continue their service for two years, after which they were free but without land. The male serfs numbered about twenty-three million in 1860.

needs and to meet their tax obligations to the state. However, they were not to receive the land as a gift. Ultimately each was to pay for his allotment. In order that they might obtain land at once, the government paid the former landlord and then collected the money from the peasants, distributing the payments over a period of forty-nine years. Actually the full rights of ownership were conferred not on the individual peasant who had been freed but on the mir or village community, and the village community as such was responsible for the annual redemption dues. In making the mir responsible, the government achieved its aim of keeping the peasants on the land.[2] Thus the peasant, although no longer a serf, was tied to the village.

Alexander did not stop at liberating the serfs; in 1864 he also established a limited home-rule system in thirty-three provinces of European Russia. This was to be exercised by local assemblies called *Zemstvos*, composed of elected representatives of the nobles, the peasants, and the townsmen. The district Zemstvo had charge of such matters as the maintenance of roads, bridges, schools, hospitals, and charitable institutions. It also concerned itself with problems of public health, with the prevention of local famines, and with the introduction of new methods of agriculture. Once each year it sent deputies to a provincial Zemstvo for the discussion of problems affecting the province as a whole. In both the district and the provincial Zemstvo the nobles retained their dominant position; nevertheless, the establishment of these assemblies marked an advance in that they admitted the peasants and the townspeople to a share in local government. In 1870 "the Tsar Liberator" also created new forms of self-government for the municipalities by issuing a ukase which provided for a municipal council composed of representatives elected by all those who paid municipal taxes. The municipal councils exercised the same functions in the cities as the Zemstvos did in the country.

Further changes included curtailment of the power of the secret police, relaxation of the censorship of the press, reform of the judicial system, and extension of education. Among the more notable changes in the judicial system were the introduction of jury trial in criminal cases and the appointment of judges for life so that they would be independent of outside control. How great the need was for more schools can be seen from a report of the British consul at St. Petersburg in 1870 that only about 8 or 9 per cent of the population could read and write. Although Alexander increased the number of primary schools, his measures in this respect were only half measures. By the end of his

---

[2] At intervals the land was redistributed among the members of the community according to the size of each family. There was never collectivization in the actual working of the land.

reign only 13.8 per cent of the boys and 3.3 per cent of the girls of school age were attending school. More important were his measures in behalf of higher education. He increased the number of the universities to eight and granted all of them administrative autonomy and comparative freedom of teaching. Furthermore, he repealed the law which limited the number of students, and he also provided fellowships which enabled poor students to attend the universities. The result was that the number of university students more than doubled during his reign.

The reforms of Alexander pleased some of the people but fell far short of the demands of the progressive and radical groups. The ideas of the latter ranged from the relatively mild sentiments of those who demanded a constitution to the radical theories of Michael Bakunin, the founder of European anarchism. His followers, who were known as nihilists, aimed at nothing less than complete annihilation of all institutions and all forms of authority. The state, the family, law, property, religion, and morality, all must be utterly destroyed. "Nothing" must remain as it exists; hence the name "nihilists" (from Latin *nihil*, nothing). "Our first work," Bakunin stated, "must be destruction and annihilation of everything as it now exists. You must accustom yourself to destroying everything; the good with the bad; for if but an atom of this old world remains, the new will never be created." What the new world was to be like he never stated, but his doctrine of destruction was enough to inflame the minds of many young Russians who determined to strike at tsarism by assassinating key officials and, if possible, the tsar himself. The first of many attempts on Alexander's life took place in 1866. The discovery of a widespread secret society pledged to overthrow the government dampened Alexander's ardor for reform and even caused him to reverse some of his policies. But this only spurred the nihilists to further attempts on his life. After a number of narrow escapes the tsar finally decided in 1881 to establish a national parliament which would give the people a voice in the government. Before he could publish the measure, however, he was killed in March of the same year by a bomb hurled by a young nihilist.

If the revolutionaries believed they could destroy tsarism by assassinating Alexander II, they erred sadly. The autocratic machinery continued to function as before; in fact, reform was postponed for almost a generation. The new tsar, Alexander III, at once announced his determination to maintain the old system in its strictest form. In an imperial manifesto he proclaimed to the people that "the voice of God hath commanded us to take up vigorously the reins of government, inspiring us with the belief in the strength and truth of autocratic power which we are called upon to establish and safeguard." Not even a dream of a constitution was to be tolerated. A reaction, he declared, was necessary because the government, in granting too much freedom, had opened the way for the pest of liberalism, generated in western Europe, to penetrate into Russia. Only the good fortune of their illiteracy had saved many Russians from being contaminated by this pest. The great problem of the government, as he saw it, was to wipe out liberalism in all its manifestations. Accordingly he not only ordered the police to launch a rigorous crusade against nihilism but he also greatly reduced the power of the Zemstvos, gagged the press, and abolished the autonomous administration of the universities. The gymnasia (secondary schools) were carefully supervised, the teachers being ordered to send the government detailed reports on the character of each student. If a graduate manifested any opposition to the government or to the church, he was refused admission to the universities. In short, Alexander instituted a reactionary regime which was much like that of his grandfather Nicholas.

Alexander was not satisfied with introducing reactionary measures and hunting down revolutionaries; he was also determined to weld the heterogeneous nationalities of the empire into one homogeneous nation. The basic purpose, of course, was to strengthen his autocratic rule. His motto was the half-forgotten triad of the reign of Nicholas I, "autocracy, orthodoxy, and nationality," which is the Russian version of the old principle "one king, one law, one faith." Everyone who questioned the absolute power of the tsar, spoke a language other than Russian, or worshipped outside the Orthodox Church was in his eyes not a true Russian. As a means of bringing the minorities into the national fold the government subjected them to a policy of Russification. The Finns, for example, were deprived of most of the separate rights they had enjoyed since Finland had been annexed in 1809. Autonomy in regard to customs duties was abolished, Russian postage stamps replaced Finnish stamps, a new Russian archiepiscopal see was founded in Finland, and the Russian language was made the medium of instruction in Finnish colleges. A similar policy was adopted toward the Poles and other national minorities. The results of these attempts were more apparent than real. Although Alexander managed to impose a considerable degree of outward conformity, he actually succeeded only in stirring an unspeakable hatred for the government in the hearts of his non-Russian subjects.

The treatment meted out to the other national minorities was mild in comparison with that accorded the Jews. During the last decade of the eighteenth century a series of ukases had deprived the Jews of their freedom of movement by forbidding them to settle outside the so-called Pale, which comprised fifteen provinces in the southwestern part of the empire. There they lived quite apart from their Christian neighbors, retaining their national consciousness and cultivating Jewish customs and manners much as they had during the Middle Ages. Their lot was improved considerably during the early decades of the nineteenth century, although they were not accorded equal rights with other citizens. They were given free access to all schools, including the universities and technical schools, and during the reign of Alexander II numbers of them were allowed to settle outside the Pale. The result was that many entered the liberal professions, especially law, medicine, and journalism.

But after the accession of Alexander III the rights of the Jews were sharply curtailed. As a youth his teachers had already instilled prejudices against the Jews in his mind by telling him, among other things, that they made bad soldiers and that they shirked manual and agricultural labor. Later his dislike deepened because the Jews refused to amalgamate with the Russians and because he believed that they were the brain power of all revolutionary movements in the country. Not many months after his accession he issued a number of ukases which not only forced thousands of Jews to return to the Pale but also forbade them, with certain exceptions, to live in rural districts. These laws encouraged anti-Semites to give vent to their feelings. Influential newspapers at once took up the cry, and before many weeks passed pogroms broke out in many parts of Russia. Jewish homes and stores were attacked and demolished, and the goods were carted away by the mobs. A pogrom in the town of Balta in 1882 resulted in the destruction of 976 houses, the death of eight persons, and the wounding of 211. As the police received no instructions to stop the despoilers, the opinion soon spread that the government approved the excesses.

Meanwhile the complaints of the peasants over their condition grew louder and louder. During the years the emancipation act was in preparation it had been keenly awaited by almost all the serfs, but when the day of emancipation arrived many were bitterly disappointed at once, while others gradually discovered that freedom from serfdom did not realize for them the hopes they had held. Discontent became so widespread that during the two years subsequent to the publication of the emancipation act the government had to quell no less than 1100 agrarian riots and uprisings, some of them with considerable bloodshed. The emancipation, it is true, had given the serfs a certain legal freedom, but economically many were worse off than before. In the first place, the redemption payments were so excessive that in years of bad harvests many had to borrow money at exorbitant rates. Second, most of the allotments were too small for adequate maintenance even in ordinary years. Third, as the population of the mirs increased,[3] the individual holdings of the male peasants were reduced proportionately. Whereas the average holding had been 4.8 dessiatines (a dessiatine = 2.7 acres) in 1861, it was only 3.5 dessiatines in 1880, and by 1900 it was to drop to 2.6 dessiatines. Besides being small, these holdings probably yielded less per acre than land in any other country of Europe. Agricultural methods and implements were most primitive. Only the large landowners used machinery and fertilizers, and even on their estates the level of production was below that of the farmers of France or England. In 1872 the wheat area had the greatest crop grown in Russia up to that time; yet the yield was less than nine bushels per acre. Many peasants were compelled by the burden of redemption dues, high taxes, and threat of starvation to lease additional land from the nobles at exorbitant rents or to work on the lord's land at the lowest wage. As a result an intense land hunger developed which vented itself in demands for more land, in continued riots, and in attacks on the landlords.

RUSSIA UNDER THE LAST TSAR

When Alexander III died suddenly in 1894 and was succeeded by his son Nicholas II, all Russia heaved a sigh of relief. The new tsar, having won the reputation of being a liberal by his simple mode of life as heir apparent, was confidently expected to inaugurate an era of reform. The masses firmly believed that he would lighten their economic burdens; the liberals were certain that he would grant some sort of constitution, if only a conservative one. But the hopes of both the credulous masses and the optimistic liberals were dashed again. The new tsar was a man of great personal charm, great kindness of heart, and impeccable manners. He was also sincere in his desire to rule his country justly. "I have only one object in view," he wrote to Stolypin, "the welfare of my country; all petty feelings against individuals disappear when I think of this." However, he was sadly lacking in understanding. Of his country and its needs he seems to have known very little. Moreover, like his father, he was a firm believer in divine right. It was his sincere conviction that God had called him to rule the Russian people just as He had in biblical times summoned Saul and David to rule the children of Israel. Nicholas took his imaginary mission so seriously that he even believed that God was directing his will and thoughts for the good of Russia. As God's lieutenant he regarded it as his duty above all to preserve the *status quo*. Hence when a number of Zemstvos openly voiced the demand for a constitution soon after his accession, he told them to

[3] Between 1860 and 1897 the peasant population of European Russia increased from fifty to seventy-nine millions.

dismiss "such foolish dreams," and during the subsequent years repeatedly declared the hope that he could transmit to his successor the autocratic power he had inherited.

When it became clear that the new tsar was opposed to reform, a more revolutionary mood began to appear among the masses. Not only was there an increase of peasant risings, accompanied by arson, robbery, and pillage, but opposition to the government was fostered by organized groups. The strongest of the moderate groups was the Constitutional Democratic Party or Cadets (from the initial letters of the party's Russian name), composed of merchants, manufacturers, liberal gentry, and the professional class of the bourgeoisie. This party aspired to a constitutional monarchy on the English model. The extreme group was the Social Revolutionary Party, which devoted its attention mainly to the peasants and their problems. Its basic tenet was seizure of the land of the nobility.

But a new force, the force that ultimately was to grind the autocracy of the Romanovs to powder, was beginning to make its influence felt. It was the industrial proletariat, which was increasing with the growth of large-scale machine industry. Conditions had on the whole not been favorable to the development of skilled industries because the factory owners had to depend for labor largely on illiterate serfs. However, after 1861 a number of things favored the progress of industry. First, large masses of the landless proletariat drifted to the cities and thus provided an ample supply of cheap labor. How considerable the migration was can be seen from the fact that between 1861 and 1870 the town population increased by approximately 45 per cent. Second, the cheapness of labor and the wealth of natural resources attracted much foreign capital into the country for purposes of industrial expansion, particularly after 1880. Great railway developments took place, coal and iron mines were opened, and many large factories were built. By 1898 the railway system open for transportation amounted to 28,446 miles, and 6973 miles were in process of construction. The output of coal was five times as great in 1896 as the average annual output had been during the decade of the seventies. Even in the textile industries development was rapid. Cotton spinning, for example, more than doubled between 1885 and 1896.

One consequence of this rapid growth was that a real working class came into existence. It is estimated that by 1896 the large-scale industries employed no less than 1,742,000 workers. In the factories and in the mines large numbers of men, women, and children worked under conditions reminiscent of the early factories in Great Britain. There were, it is true, some model factories and some good housing, but in general the conditions were bad. A twelve-hour day was the exception.

Lighting and ventilation were poor. As late as 1880 there were in many
factories no sanitary arrangements whatsoever. The worker received
but a fraction of the wage paid in western countries.[4] Many families
were lodged in damp, dirty, prisonlike barracks. A family was fortunate
if it had any privacy; frequently one room housed several families
crowded into bunks. The government made various attempts to limit
the working hours, but most of the laws proved useless because no
proper means were devised to carry them out. The hours for children,
for example, were not effectually limited until 1882; then provisions
were made for inspectors who were to enforce the law forbidding the
employment of children under twelve and limiting to eight hours daily
the working hours of young persons aged twelve to fifteen. These regulations, however, limited only the time of minors. Not until 1897 was
an act passed which restricted the day for men to eleven and a half
hours. This reduction was accompanied by a rise in the rate of pay,
but many flagrant evils remained.

The feeling that they were being exploited kindled in the minds of
the workers a hatred for the regime and made them tools in the hands
of revolutionary propagandists. The existing conditions might have
been tolerable to peasants just emerging from serfdom, but to the second
and third generation, who could read and write and had a fragmentary
knowledge of industrial conditions in other countries, the state of affairs
was inexcusable. And the Marxist preachers were not slow to make the
most of their opportunities. In almost every industrial city they won
converts who met clandestinely to organize local societies. Finally in
1898 the Marxists combined to form the Social Democratic Labor
Party. Before many years passed, differences of opinion began to manifest themselves within the party, and in 1903 a split occurred. The right
wing believed that Russia was ripe only for a "bourgeois" or liberal
democratic revolution which would establish freedom of speech and
assembly and thus open the way for the ultimate realization of a socialist order. This was too moderate for the left wing led by Vladimir
Ilyich Ulyanov, better known as Lenin. He would establish a new social
order at once and by force. "Give us an organization of revolutionaries,"
he stated, "and we shall turn Russia upside down." The members of the
left wing, because they secured a small majority, became known as the
Bolsheviks or "majority men." The name stuck despite the fact that
the Mensheviks (minority men) gained a majority at the next congress.
Not until 1911 did the two groups become separate parties. Meanwhile
both were active in fomenting opposition to the government.

In these circumstances of general unrest the government was so

---

[4] Despite the low wages the cost of labor was higher in Russia than in western Europe,
for the Russian worker was less efficient than the western worker.

shortsighted as to become involved in war with Japan,[5] a war which was to reveal inner weaknesses as mercilessly as the Crimean War had half a century earlier. Before many months passed, Russia was staggering under the blows of a foe it had despised. The blackness of defeat was not relieved by a single victory. Even the fleet was wiped out. As the prestige of the government sank lower and lower, the revolutionists mustered courage to speak out. Newspapers, long compelled to conceal all real opinions, spoke with a freedom hardly more restrained than in western Europe. Labor unions and revolutionary societies in all parts of the empire issued proclamations in which they denounced the government as weak in war and strong only in the ability to oppress. Late in December, 1904, the workingmen of St. Petersburg declared a general strike as a protest against what they regarded as the intolerable conditions of their daily life. On all sides there were unmistakable signs that the political storm that had long been brewing would soon break. Still the government did nothing to avert it.

THE REVOLUTION OF 1905

The so-called Russian Revolution of 1905 which grew out of the St. Petersburg strike began with the tragedy of "Bloody Sunday." After negotiations had failed to adjust the differences between the workers and the industrialists, Father Gapon, a priest of the Orthodox Church, proposed that the workers lay their grievances directly before the tsar. Accordingly on Sunday, January 22, a mass of unarmed men, bearing ikons and portraits of Nicholas as proof of their peaceful intentions and of their loyalty to him, formed themselves into eleven processions and marched toward Palace Square from various directions. Father Gapon himself, dressed in ecclesiastical robes and carrying a crucifix, led the largest of the processions, which was made up of about fifty thousand men and women. The atmosphere was not one of revolution but of pious exaltation which vented itself in the singing of hymns and patriotic songs. However, the processions did not reach their destination. Troops stationed in all parts of the city dispersed them with rifle fire, killing hundreds and wounding more than a thousand. This unprovoked massacre of workers who believed in the benevolence of the tsar caused intense popular excitement all over Russia. Industrial strikes and street demonstrations took place in many cities. In Riga, for example, sixty thousand workmen declared a strike, and enormous crowds gathered in the streets shouting, "Down with the government" and "We want a republic." In the central part of Russia many agrarian riots broke out and in some sections the spirit of revolution was rife even in the army

[5] See p. 268.

and the navy. The spring of the same year saw the organization of the first soviets or councils of workers' deputies. The most important was that at St. Petersburg, in which Leon Trotsky was the leading spirit.

When political strikes, street demonstrations, armed conflicts, and agrarian discontent became more and more prevalent, the tsar promulgated a law which provided for the election of a national Duma that was to be an advisory council rather than a legislative assembly. This half-hearted measure, instead of appeasing public sentiment, only fanned the flame of revolt. The struggle culminated in October with a nationwide strike. It began with the employees of one railroad, who were quickly joined by the employees of other railroads until the entire empire was without means of transportation. Suddenly, without any preconcerted plan, the workers seemed to realize that they could bring irresistible pressure on the government by a general strike. One observer reported: "Telegraph and telephone lines ceased to work; electric lights went out; street cars stopped running; newspapers suspended publication; the postal service came to an end; and even such classes of men as lawyers, druggists, bank clerks, and clerks of the circuit courts stopped work as a means of showing their sympathy with the revolutionary movement." The common slogan was, "Don't accept the tsar's Duma! Demand a constitutional convention!" The tremendous pressure of events finally compelled the tsar to yield. He issued the Freedom Manifesto or, as it is also called, the October Manifesto, which promised the Russian people "inviolability of person, with freedom of conscience, speech, assembly, and association." It further declared that no law should be enforced without the consent of the Duma.

The Freedom Manifesto marks the peak of the Revolution of 1905. With its publication, concerted opposition to the government began to melt away. On the one hand, the middle class, which felt that the changes had gone far enough, hastened to make peace. On the other, the continuance of agrarian disorders drove most of the landed proprietors, who had supported the struggle for freedom, into the ranks of the reactionaries. Even among the Social Democrats the less radical were alienated by the insistence of the left wing upon radical economic and social changes. The Petrograd soviet, for example, called upon the whole population to refrain from paying taxes, to withdraw all deposits from the banks in gold, and to demand payment of salaries and wages in gold. Widespread disorder and confusion which followed caused the government to adopt a policy of stern and pitiless repression. When a series of strikes and disorders in Moscow culminated in an armed insurrection of workers, the government forces drowned the uprising in blood.

No sooner had the last revolt been quelled than it became clear that the tsar had no intention of keeping the promises he had made. Whatever good intentions he previously may have had, evaporated under the relentless pressure put on him by his advisers. As General Kropotkin put it in his diary, "His counselors persuaded him that any shadow of freedom was a misfortune." With such advisers wielding the upper hand, reaction became the order of the day. In many parts of Russia the so-called Black Companies were formed for the purpose of restoring the old order by terrorizing the population until no one would dare mention the promised "freedoms." The weapon they employed was the pogrom. In hundreds of cities, towns, and villages they pillaged and often burned the homes of those suspected of revolutionary sympathies. On a number of occasions buildings in which revolutionists were holding meetings were surrounded and set on fire. Those who remained in the building were burned to death, and those who tried to escape were clubbed to death. In some places the pogroms were directed particularly against the Jews, who were regarded as the prime instigators of the revolutionary movement. The mob would go to the Jewish quarter, pick a quarrel on some pretext, and then begin an orgy of plundering and murder. It is estimated that no less than 3500 people were massacred in these pogroms. All this took place without a word of remonstrance or objection from the tsar. A government investigator reported that in Kiev a pogrom "lasted for three days, and stopped only when all Jewish shops and many Jewish houses had been ransacked. The police were almost entirely absent. The troops walked slowly down the middle of the street while robbery was proceeding on both sides of them. When private persons or officials asked for help from the troops, the answer was always, 'We have no orders.' "

On April 10, 1906, the First Duma met. Although the socialists had boycotted the election, an overwhelming majority of the members of this assembly were liberal or radical. If Nicholas II had resolutely pursued the policy he had outlined in the Freedom Manifesto, the meeting might have marked the beginning of a great transformation. Unfortunately he was as shortsighted as he was insincere. No sooner had the Duma met than he issued a series of decrees which limited its rights by declaring certain matters outside its legislative competency and also by establishing a State Council with an overwhelmingly conservative membership as an upper chamber, coequal in power with the Duma. Furthermore, the government assumed the right to promulgate laws while the Duma was not in session. When the Duma, determined to make a fight on the question of its rights, appealed to the nation for support, it was promptly dissolved by imperial decree. About half its members went to Viborg in Finland, where they were not likely to be molested by the police, and issued a manifesto which called on the Russian people to come to their support by refusing to pay taxes or render military

EMPIRE OF TH[

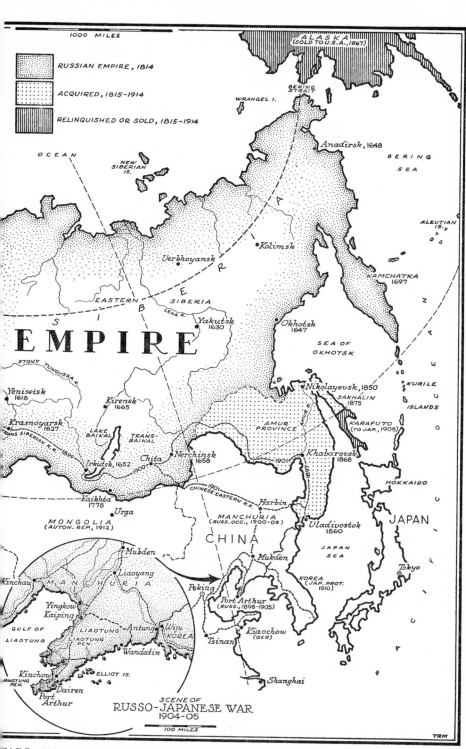

SCALE

1000 MILES

☐ RUSSIAN EMPIRE, 1814

⋮ ACQUIRED, 1815–1914

▦ RELINQUISHED OR SOLD, 1815–1914

ALASKA
(SOLD TO U.S.A., 1867)

WRANGEL I.

BERING
STRAIT

BERING
SEA

OCEAN

NEW
SIBERIAN
IS.

Anadirsk, 1648

ALEUTIAN
IS.

Verkhoyansk

Kolimsk

KAMCHATKA
1697

EASTERN   SIBERIA

LENA R.

EMPIRE

Yakutsk
1630

Okhotsk
1647

SEA OF
OKHOTSK

KURILE

ISLANDS

STONY TUNGUSKA R.

Yeniseisk
1618

Nikolayeusk, 1850

SAKHALIN
1875

Kirensk
1665

Krasnoyarsk
1627

AMUR
PROVINCE

KARAFUTO
(TO JAP., 1905)

TRANS SIBERIAN R.R. 1900

LAKE
BAIKAL

TRANS-
BAIKAL

Khabarousk
1868

HOKKAIDO

Irkutsk, 1652

Chita

Nerchinsk
1658

1901

1900

CHINESE EASTERN R.R.

1901

Harbin

JAPAN

Kaikhta
1778

Urga

MONGOLIA
(AUTON. REP., 1912)

MANCHURIA
(RUSS. OCC., 1900–05)

Uladivostok
1860

JAPAN
SEA

CHINA

Mukden

Tokyo

Mukden

KOREA
(JAP. PROT.
1910)

Liaoyang

Peking

Port Arthur
(RUSS., 1898–1905)

Kinchau

MANCHURIA

Yingkow
Kaiping

Antung

Wiju
KOREA

Kiaochow
(GER.)

GULF OF
LIAOTUNG

LIAOTUNG

LIAOTUNG
PEN.

Wandatin

Tsinan

Kinchow

ELLIOT IS.

ANGTUNG
PEN.

Dairen

Port
Arthur

SCENE OF
RUSSO-JAPANESE WAR
1904–05

Shanghai

100 MILES

TRM

SARS, 1815–1914

service. But the response was very feeble. Most of the people had been so thoroughly cowed by the pogroms and the bloody reprisals of the government that they decided to make themselves, as a Russian proverb has it, "stiller than water and lower than grass." When the Second Duma met in March, 1907, it was found to be even more hostile to the government than the first had been. No less than four hundred of a membership of about five hundred belonged to opposition parties. Such a Duma could not, of course, be permitted to remain in session long, and it was accordingly dissolved in June.

If the tsar had permitted the election of a third Duma on the basis of the existing laws, he probably would have gotten one quite as intractable as the first two had been. But he arbitrarily changed the election laws in such a way as to disfranchise most of the voters in the liberal classes, thereby ensuring the election of a Duma that would pass the government's bills without clamoring for rights or otherwise making trouble Although the Third Duma was not wholly subservient, it did in some measure meet the expectations of the tsar and his ministers; but it did not fairly represent the people and it exercised no real power. Not one of the reforms the tsar promised was carried out in full. Men were still arrested, imprisoned, and exiled without judicial process; nor was there any real freedom of conscience, speech, assembly, or association. On the other hand, although the counterrevolution had triumphed, all that had been gained was not lost. Theoretically Russia had become a constitutional monarchy, even though the constitution was the least liberal of all those in Europe.

The period from 1905 to 1914 saw Russia make considerable progress along many lines. Industries developed at a rapid rate; trade increased in volume; and the wages and living standard of the worker improved greatly, although they still remained far below those in the industrial nations of western Europe. One indication of the improvement in economic conditions was the large increase in the deposits in the state savings banks. Notable progress was also made in the spread of education. During the decade from 1906 to 1916, for example, the number of elementary schools was doubled. Steps were also taken to solve the peasant problem. In 1906 premier Stolypin caused a law to be passed which permitted the head of a peasant family to detach his holding from the communal land and thus make it private property. The government even went so far as to grant such peasants easy credit for the purchase of implements and for the improvement of their livestock. All this, however, was not enough to satisfy an awakening nation. It is estimated that on the eve of World War I about ten million Russian farms were too small to support their occupants. Having given up hope that the government would alleviate their condition, the masses were supporting the revolutionary parties in ever-increasing numbers.

RASPUTIN AND THE EMPRESS

Meanwhile Nicholas II, blind to the forces that were operating on the minds of his subjects, continued his autocratic rule. The Duma was to him nothing but an attempt to encroach on his God-given prerogatives. From the Revolution of 1905 he had drawn no warning whatsoever. He did not realize that the workers had learned the art of organizing, that they had tasted freedom of action, and that the peasants no less than the workers had lost faith in him. While insisting upon his right to rule autocratically he was more and more out of touch with the people. As his reign wore on, he manifested a tendency to retire from society and to lead the secluded life of a private individual. At Tsarskoe Selo, his favorite residence, he even refused to read the newspapers. In time, nothing seemed real to him except what happened in his presence. Curiously enough, while the gulf between the government and the people was broadening, the tsar's conviction that Russia could be happy only under an autocrat was growing stronger and stronger.

An even more firm believer in divine right than Nicholas himself was the Tsarina Alexandra. A woman of a singularly narrow and obstinate nature, she was convinced that without an autocratic rule Russia would fall to pieces. This conviction she repeatedly communicated to the tsar, who literally adored her and whose affection she returned in equal measure. This love, together with their common interest in the heir to the throne, permitted the tsarina to wield an ever-increasing influence over her husband. From the tenor of the letters she wrote to him it becomes clear that she was the dominating personality. She was indefatigable in exhorting him to show his authority with an iron hand. One may read in her letters to him such statements as, "We are placed on the throne by God and must keep it strong"; "You are Lord and Master in Russia, remember that"; "Be a Peter the Great, an Ivan the Terrible, an Emperor Paul; destroy them all"; "Be more autocratic, my very own Sweetheart, show your mind"; and "Ah, my Love, when at last will you thump upon the table with your hand?" Her unhappy influence over her husband was prompted not only by her interest in him but also by her desire to conserve the whole fabric of autocracy complete and unimpaired for their son and heir, who was born in 1904. Again and again she pleaded with Nicholas to "keep the rule strong" for the sake of their son. Thus she wrote: "We must hand to our baby a strong country. We dare not be weak for his sake, otherwise he will find it more difficult to rule. He will have to repair our errors and tighten the reins you are loosening."

It was her devotion to her son, coupled with a religious mysticism, that made her an easy subject for the disastrous influence of Grigori Efimovich, better known as Rasputin. When the long-expected heir to the throne finally came after the successive birth of four daughters, the joy of the imperial couple was clouded by the discovery that the tsarevitch was afflicted with the dread disease of haemophilia.[6] As medical science could offer no hope of a cure, the tsarina turned to religion and superstition for help and found it, as she believed, in the person of a half-illiterate peasant to whom his fellow peasants had given the name "Rasputin," meaning "dissolute." About the age of thirty he had become a strannik or roving "man of God" and thereafter spent several years traveling from shrine to shrine. Although he continued to live as dissolutely as in earlier years, this did not prevent him from acquiring the reputation of being a saint. So extraordinary was his influence that he convinced many he had divine dispensation for indulging his vices. In 1903 he arrived in St. Petersburg, where he was soon introduced at court. After the birth of the heir he succeeded in persuading the weak-minded empress that he had a mysterious power to protect her son from harm. Whenever the tsarevitch became ill, the intriguing "holy man" would mumble prayers over him and the child would improve. By skillfully playing on the superstitions of the tsarina Rasputin gained an ascendancy over her which neither reasoning nor advice nor warning could undermine.

Rasputin's activities were by no means confined to the private life of the imperial family. He was able to exercise a profound influence on the destiny of Russia as a whole. This he did, not by the direction of policy, for he knew little of political science, but by obtaining for his sycophants many high positions in the government. His personal authority with the empress sufficed to throw open the doors of almost every important position to his nominees. He made and unmade ministers of state almost at pleasure, removing men of ability and filling the vacated positions with corrupt intriguers. So great was his influence that during the last years of the reign he was virtually uncrowned ruler of Russia. Every attempt was made by the tsarina and her supporters to conceal his activities, even to forbidding the press to mention his name or to allude to him. But his political machinations could not be kept secret and soon powerful enemies were plotting his downfall. However, nothing could shake the tsarina's faith in "the Man of God," as she was wont to call him. Consequently his evil influence continued to undermine whatever faith the people still had in the tsar. Rasputin's historic role consisted in uniting all Russia in a general hatred of the Romanov dynasty. The tsar himself, it is true, was never completely under the sway of this dissolute charlatan, but he lacked the courage to refuse his demands when they were communicated to him by the tsarina.

[6] A hereditary disease which appears only in males. Its effect is that the slightest accident might set up internal bleeding which there was no way of arresting.

Members of Commodore Perry's expedition delivering American presents to the Japanese, 1853

In a Tight Place, a cartoon from *Punch* which shows Korea attempting to preserve neutrality in the Russo-Japanese conflict

A part of the Russian fleet sunk by the Japanese at Port Arthur in the Russo-Japanese War

Rasputin surrounded by admiring women

Nicholas II at a military review in 1901

Burial of the dead after the revolt of 1905
in St. Petersburg

Revolution was becoming not only inevitable but imminent. The signs of its approach were written large throughout the country. Almost every class was estranged from the dynasty. Discontent was particularly rife among the peasants and the workers. The peasants were dissatisfied because the government after abolishing serfdom had not completed the emancipation. Even Count Witte, the tsarist statesman, was moved to declare that "the peasants are free from the slave owners, but they are now slaves to arbitrary power, legal disabilities, and ignorance." Among the workers the failure of the government to keep the promises of 1905 had given new vigor to the revolutionary movement. As Lenin put it, the Revolution of 1905 had been but a dress rehearsal; the real revolution would come at the first opportunity. Nicholas himself provided this opportunity when he signed the order for the general mobilization of the army in 1914. He might as well have signed the death warrant of himself and his dynasty.

RUSSIAN CULTURE

The nineteenth century was a golden age for Russian literature. During the preceding century it had been dominated by foreign, particularly by French, influences. But during the Napoleonic invasion a wave of national enthusiasm swept over the country, and authors now began to choose their themes from Russian life and to give expression to the Russian spirit. The first important literary figure of the new age was Alexander Pushkin (1799–1837), foremost of Russian poets and one of the great poets of all time. Soviet Russia, no less than did tsarist Russia, regards him as the greatest poet of the nation. He is to Russian what Shakespeare is to English, Goethe to German, and Dante to Italian literature. Working in many fields, he was in all of them primarily and thoroughly Russian. It was he who "placed Russian literature firmly on Russian soil." In his poetic works he made ample use of the folklore and the folk stories in which Russia is peculiarly rich. More than this, like Dante, he created the smoothly flowing poetic language with all its beauty and richness. Two of his best works are *Boris Godunov*, a play, and *Evgeni Onegin*, a novel in verse. Both are known outside Russia chiefly through the operatic settings they inspired, *Boris Godunov* having furnished the libretto for an opera by Moussorgsky and *Evgeni Onegin* for one by Tchaikovsky.

To most non-Russians the words "Russian literature" mean primarily the novel and, to a lesser extent, the drama. In Russia the novel was a more serious form of expression than poetry; it was, in the words of a Russian writer, "the tragic utterance of one hundred million people aching to be born into humanity." It gave voice to a Russia suppressed and tyrannized, blind with ignorance, and scarred with suffering and oppression. The government, stupidly bent on preserving its autocracy, sought to prevent all discussion of public questions. Only one avenue, that of literature, was left open. Through it, and particularly through the novel, the best minds made known their aspirations, ideals, and conceptions of life. This explains the peculiar nature of the Russian novel, its seriousness, its realism, its social character. It was not a literature for entertainment; it had a social message to convey.

Hence it is that some of the great names in the struggle for freedom are not those of revolutionists but of men of letters. They subtly exposed the prevalent despotism and corruption; they wrote satires so true in their aim and so bitter in their hidden wrath that they could not fail to stir sentiment for reform. Not all the writers, however, were social reformers. Some had no revolutionary sympathies, while others were firm upholders of the *status quo*. But even the writings of such reactionaries became a force for reform so far as they depicted existing conditions.

The first of the great masters who made realism a tradition in Russia was Nikolai Gogol (1809–1852). It was he who first put the vague longings and the patient endurance of vast millions into words. He also has the distinction of being the only humorist in the period of realist literature. In *The Inspector General* (1836), regarded by many as the greatest Russian comedy, he satirized the corruption, the ignorance, and the inefficiency of the officials. As he himself put it, "I tried to expose every crime that is committed in those offices where the strictest uprightness should be required and expected." The authorities at once recognized their own portraits in the play and would have prevented its presentation, but Nicholas heard of it, read it, and laughing heartily ordered it produced. Gogol's most important work is *Dead Souls* (1842), a novel without a plot and without a love element. It has been called the "Divine Comedy" of Russia because it is a mirror of Russian life much as Dante's work was of medieval life. Although he was a staunch upholder of serfdom, his accurate delineation of the system in *Dead Souls* called its evils to the attention of many.

The realism of Gogol was further developed by the next generation of writers, which included such outstanding figures as Turgenev, Dostoevski, and Tolstoi. Ivan Turgenev (1818–1883), consummate master of Russian prose, wrote many novels which for artistic construction and beauty of style give him a high rank among nineteenth-century novelists. The three principal ones, *A Nest of Gentlefolk, Fathers and Sons,* and *Virgin Soil,* have permanent value because they reflect the life of his time, particularly of the cultured and wealthy classes. They were the first means of bringing the literary public of other European countries in touch with Russian life. But the work that probably brought him the greatest fame was *A Sportman's Sketches* (1852), which presents, on the one hand, a series of portraits of serfs patiently enduring their yoke and, on the other, pictures of the serf owners in their shallowness and meanness. It is said that Turgenev's sketches had a direct bearing upon Alexander II's decision to liberate the serfs.

The second great pillar of nineteenth-century Russian prose literature is Feodor Dostoevski (1821–1881) to whom Russia owes much as a novelist but little as a reformer. As a young man he became associated with a socialist literary circle, was arrested, and sentenced to death, but the sentence was at the last minute changed to hard labor in Siberia. There in a prison camp he gained an intimate knowledge of, and a deep sympathy for, the unfortunates of Russian society. Upon being pardoned in 1856 he wrote the series of novels which made him famous. His great characters are criminals, idiots, degenerates, mystics, and madmen. He would have us see the image of God in every individual, no matter how low he may have fallen. His masterpiece is *Crime and Punishment* (1866), one of the most powerful novels in Russian or any other language. Other great novels are *The Idiot* (1869), *The Possessed* (1871), and *The Brothers Karamazov* (1880). Despite his sympathy for the outcast and oppressed, Dostoevski was paradoxically an ardent supporter of the autocracy which kept the people in bondage.

The greatest pillar in the temple of Russian prose literature of the nineteenth century is Leo Tolstoi (1828–1910), whose best works are known wherever books are a part of daily life. Tolstoi's work was on a much more normal plane than that of Dostoevski. The writings which showed him to be of the first rank were the *Sevastopol Sketches* (1851–1856), in which he set down the horrors of war as he saw them while engaged in the defense of the beleaguered town. Turgenev, upon reading the sketches, was moved to say, "When this young wine has done fermenting, the result will be a liquor worthy of the gods." In 1869 he completed his *War and Peace,* a long historical novel which depicts the epoch ending with Napoleon's invasion of Russia, the burning of Moscow, and the disastrous retreat of the French. Almost at once the whole of educated Russia, and before long all of Europe and America, acknowledged its author to be a great master. *Anna Karenina,* published in 1877, is also to be ranked as one of the great novels of all time. In later life Tolstoi adopted a form of ascetic life without entering a monastery, abandoned literature as he had formerly understood it, and turned to the writing of religious, ethical, and sociological tracts. He who had earlier possessed an ardent faith in autocracy now became a Christian anarchist who eloquently denounced all government. Three novels which he wrote during this period are *The Death of Ivan Ilyich* (1886), *The Kreutzer Sonata* (1889), and *Resurrection* (1899–1900).

Important for their criticism of the more recent scene were Anton Chekov (1860–1904) and Aleksei Peshkov (1868–1936), better known as Maxim Gorky. As a physician Chekov gained an intimate knowledge of all sorts of people and conditions which he incorporated in his stories. After the publication of his *Humorous Folk* in 1887 one or more volumes of his stories appeared almost every year. He also wrote eleven plays for the theater, the best known being *The Cherry Orchard* (1904). In his plays no less than in his stories he expressed the disillusionment, sadness, and despair of the intellectuals who aspiring to political freedom suddenly found their aspirations to be futile when Alexander III inaugurated a period of political reaction. In the decade of the nineties a new literary force arose in Gorky, meaning "the bitter one." It is a fitting pseudonym, for a sardonic bitterness against social injustice characterizes most of his writings. No one has revealed the ailments and shortcomings of Russia more frankly than he. His first long novel, *Foma Gordeev* (1900), depicts a tragedy of wealth allied with unbridled sensuality. *The Spy* (1908) deals with events immediately preceding and succeeding the Revolution of 1905. His most important contribution to the theater during this period was *The Lower Depths* (1903). In 1914 Gorky returned home from Capri where he had been living and became active in the movement for the overthrow of the tsarist regime.

While the Russian writers of the realist school were producing their masterpieces, a group of musicians known as the nationalist school (because they aimed at writing thoroughly Russian music) were giving expression to the Russian spirit in music. The most distinguished members of this group were Borodin (1834–1887), Moussorgsky (1835–1881), and Rimski-Korsakov (1844–1908). It is a notable fact that no one of the three was a professional musician. Borodin was professor of chemistry in the St. Petersburg academy of medicine, Moussorgsky an army officer and then a government clerk, and Rimski-Korsakov an officer in the navy. Borodin's life was so crowded that he found time to compose only in scanty leisure or when he was unwell; nevertheless, he managed to produce many compositions, among them some superb songs, the famous *B Minor Symphony,* the symphonic sketch *In the Steppes,* and the magnificent opera *Prince Igor,* which was completed after his death by Rimski-Korsakov and Glazunov. Probably the best known of Moussorgsky's works are the operas *Boris Godunov* and *Khovanshchina.* The former is based on Pushkin's work of the same name and the latter on an episode in the religious history of Holy Russia. Rimski-Korsakov, though less original, was probably a better all-round composer than Borodin or Moussorgsky. His compositions include three symphonies, the symphonic suite *Scheherezade,* a number of songs, choral music, and fifteen operas. His operas contain a wealth of historical, legendary, and spiritual material from Russian life and history.

The greatest Russian musician of the nineteenth century, all things considered, was Peter Ilyich Tchaikovsky (1840–1893). He was a master of all the resources of the art. Although he made less use of folk songs than the members of the nationalist school, his work bears a definite Russian stamp. It is regarded as being particularly Russian in that it strongly expresses the melancholy which is characteristic of the Russian spirit. His first operas were not very successful, but when he was thirty-four he wrote *The Oprichniki,* an opera which was a pronounced success. It is interesting as developing a distinctly national theme taken from the time of Ivan the Terrible.[7] Having become a success, Tchaikovsky worked so hard that in 1877 he suffered a nervous breakdown which caused him to state, "I think I am *homme fini.*" But he pulled himself together and in the next year wrote his masterly *Fourth Symphony* and his best opera, *Evgeni Onegin,* based upon Pushkin's work of the same name. Besides eleven operas, he wrote many songs which rank high for melody and harmony, originality and fervor. He also wrote six symphonies, among them the *Symphonie Pathétique.* Probably the most popular of his works are his *Fifth Symphony* and the overture *Romeo and Juliet.*

Although nineteenth-century Russian writers and musicians are widely known outside Russia, painting in Russia did not reach the heights it attained in western Europe. The painter who achieved the greatest popularity in foreign countries is Vereshchagin (1842–1904). Even his popularity was due more to the message of his paintings than to their purely artistic merit; in fact, critics have declared the technique in his larger pictures to be somewhat uncouth. He was, above all, an evangelist of peace. Moved by an intense hatred of war, he used his brush to depict its horrors and realities in the hope that he might thereby promote the cause of peace. His *Apotheosis of War,* for example, shows a pyramid of human skulls with a flock of carrion crows flying about it. He also painted a series of fifteen pictures entitled *Napoleon in Russia,* probably inspired by Tolstoi's *War and Peace;* but this series lacks the emotional appeal of his other pictures.

Vereshchagin was by no means the best painter Russia produced; there were others of superior talent. The decade of the sixties saw the appearance of the first of a group of talented artists who pictured on canvas the same actualities of Russian life that the realist writers ex-

[7] The oprichniki were a new gentry of nonaristocratic origin created by Ivan. They served as his bodyguards and upholders of his autocracy.

pressed in words. The paintings, like the novels of the period, were scathing indictments of existing conditions. The outstanding member of this group was Repin (1844–1930), whose work, technically considered, does not compare unfavorably with that of the schools of western Europe. Most of his pictures express the sad note of oppression. At the age of twenty-six he painted the *Bargemen of the Volga,* which is generally acknowledged to be the first masterpiece of the Russian realist school. It depicts a group of shaggy creatures wearily towing a heavy vessel along sandy flats under a pitiless sun. Two scenes from Russia's past, *Ivan the Terrible and His Son* and *The Cossack's Reply to the Sultan,* reveal Repin as an historical painter of incontestable mastery. The first pictures the unspeakable remorse and horror of Ivan, who clasps in his arms the son he murdered in a fit of anger; the second is a masterful portrayal of an incident from Cossack life. Besides these larger pictures, Repin also painted many portraits which some critics regard as his best work. Most of the prominent Russians of the late nineteenth century sat for him. Of particular interest are his portraits of his close friend, Tolstoi, whom he painted many times and in many different poses.

CHAPTER FIFTEEN

The Decline of the Austrian and Ottoman Empires

TWO RAMSHACKLE EMPIRES STATESMEN still assumed at the time of the Crimean War, after the general struggle for national independence had been suppressed, that land could be parceled out without regard to the wishes of the inhabitants. Government, it was held, was the business of the great powers with their hereditary rulers and their elaborately organized bureaucracies. People were so much material to be governed. But the statesmen failed to take into account the passionate nationalism which was growing into vigorous life especially in eastern Europe. As a matter of fact, the development of nationalism is the most striking phenomenon in eastern Europe during the second half of the nineteenth century. The movement was spasmodic, it is true, rather than uniform or on one front. Often dikes were built to stop its flow, and it then sought underground channels.

The two states in which, above all others, this spirit was working like a mighty leaven were the Ottoman Empire and the Austrian Empire, which largely encompassed those regions of eastern Europe not ruled by Russia. The two empires had many points of resemblance. Both were collections of nationalities; hence both were devoid of that unity which a common nationality effects. Each of the national groups comprising the two empires had a separate and distinct language of its own, and each had its own history and traditions. What is more, the nationalities were not only distinct but mutually antagonistic. Consequently both empires were permanently in a state of unrest. In the Austrian as well as in the Turkish Empire the ruling element was in the minority.

The Ottoman Empire, also known as the Turkish Empire or Turkey, was not mainly inhabited by Turks as Italy is inhabited by Italians and Spain by Spaniards. Asiatic Turkey was populated in large part, and European Turkey in even greater degree, by peoples who whatever they may have been were not Turks. They were not related to the Turks in blood or in language. As the word "Austria" was used to connote a congeries of non-Austrian peoples, so Turkey or the Ottoman Empire stood for a number of non-Turkish peoples held together by the militarist and theocratic dynastic system of the Ottoman sultanate. In the main, the European provinces were populated by five national elements; these were — in addition to the Turks — the Serbs, the Albanians, the Greeks, the Bulgarians, and the Rumanians. Each group predominated in a certain part of the Balkan Peninsula: the majority of the Greeks lived in what had been ancient Hellas, and the Serbs were most numerous in the central regions of the peninsula. In some regions, however, members of all these groups intermingled in an inextricable tangle.

This ethnographic crazy quilt was ruled by the Turks. The founders of the empire had been a mere fraction of a Turkish tribe that had left central Asia on account of the Mongol invasions. Upon conquering Asia Minor the Ottomans (Osmanli, or followers of Osman) had crossed over into Europe. Although their army was the most efficient and most progressive force of the time and their leaders were undoubtedly men of genius, they were never an overwhelming horde. Their success was in large measure the result of existing conditions. When they marched into Europe, the Byzantine Empire, a fabric of shreds and patches pieced together out of many diverse elements, was in a state of advanced decay. Some of the more progressive citizens even welcomed the Turkish overlordship as the beginning of a new life. Entire Christian cities voluntarily opened their gates to the Osmanli. Many also became "Turks" — that is, they embraced Mohammedanism and learned the Turkish language — and as a result the word "Turk" soon lost its ethnological meaning. The standing army of the sultan (the Janissaries) was largely made up of converts to Mohammedanism.

After the sixteenth century the efficiency of both the Turkish government and the Turkish army declined. The empire they had built up with the sword they continued to maintain with the sword. They did nothing to weave into an enduring fabric the shreds and patches of which their empire was composed. Consequently there was no closer bond between the Turks and the peoples over whom they ruled than that of masters and subjects. This relationship might have continued for a much longer time if the Turks had remained progressive; but they remained medieval in their organization and military methods while the nations of the west were leaving the Middle Ages behind. Besides the restricting influences of the Koran, the main sources of the weakness of their empire were twofold — the degeneration of the sultans and the ambitions of the pashas or provincial governors. Most of the sultans from the seventeenth century onward were degenerate weaklings who seldom left the enclosure of the royal borough, known as the Yildiz Kiosk. Palace cliques (camarillas), whose rule was both corrupt and inefficient, took control of the government. The actual rulers of the provinces, however, were the pashas, who either antagonized the subject peoples by their ambitions or did nothing whatsoever. In short, the Ottoman Empire, which in the sixteenth century had functioned efficiently, had by the nineteenth become ramshackle and was beginning to fall to pieces. By this time the Turks had lost much of their former warlike vigor as well as their ability to govern and, as a consequence, much of their power and prestige.

The Austrian Empire was a medley of heterogeneous elements collected in various ways and in different centuries by the acquisitive descendants of Rudolf of Habsburg. Whereas the various subdivisions of the Ottoman Empire had been added by conquest, the Habsburgs had made many additions by propitious marriages. As a result of marriages, inheritance, and artificial political arrangements, German counties, Italian principalities, countries like Bohemia and Hungary, and also portions of Poland had been joined with other lands. Some idea of the hodgepodge that was bound together by dynastic ties may be gained from the emperor's title, which read in part: Emperor of Austria; Apostolic King of Hungary; King of Bohemia, Dalmatia, Croatia, Slavonia, Galicia, Lodomeria, and Ilyria; Archduke of Austria; Grand Duke of Tuscany, Cracow, Lorraine, etc. This patchwork was inhabited by an equally assorted mixture of nationalities, including Germans, Czechs, Poles, Ruthenians, Slovenes, Magyars, Croats, Serbs, Rumanians, and Italians. Among them there was none that carried the name Austrian. Nor was there any common patriotism: when the German spoke of Austria he thought of Vienna, the Czech of Prague, and the Pole of Cracow.

No single nationality had a clear majority. The two dominating groups, the Germans and the Magyars, together formed only a minority. In one sense there was a larger racial group, the Slavs, but there was little feeling of unity among them despite Russia's efforts to cultivate the idea of pan-Slavism. The Czechs of Bohemia appear to have felt little kinship with the Poles, or Serbs, or Croats. Certainly in the case of the Poles and Ruthenians the feelings were openly antagonistic. Moreover, each of the Slavic nationalities spoke a different language, possessed a different culture, had peculiar historical traditions, and held its own political aspirations. These various nationalities were also geographically scattered. If the members of each group had been massed together in one district, the problem would have been considerably simplified. But this was far from being the case; the territory of each was dotted with ethnographic islands formed by rival groups. The result was constant agitation and friction, and this not only between the subject national groups but between the ruling nationalities.

At various times during the nineteenth century statesmen and publicists raised the question whether the Austrian Empire was serving any good purpose. The answer of its apologists was that it held some of the most unruly elements in the political life of southeastern Europe in wholesome restraint; that if it did not exist, it would have to be created. They asserted that the conglomeration of nationalities it ruled — any one of which was too weak and too scattered to form a powerful nation by itself — would have waged perpetual civil war and would also have tempted the cupidity of the neighboring great powers. Even the celebrated historian Palacký, who led the Czechs in demanding home rule for Bohemia, said, "If it were not already in existence, an Austrian empire would have to be established, not only to insure the welfare of the numerous nationalities involved, but also to secure the peace of Europe."

In both the Austrian and the Ottoman empires the claims of nationalism asserted themselves ever more forcibly as the century progressed. Subject nationalities became more and more vocal in demanding the right to govern themselves and to decide their own futures. The result was a howling chaos of conflicting demands, a furious and persistent clash of opinions, an incessant tumult of hostilities that shook the two states to their very foundations and threatened to break them up into their component parts. This destructive tendency was shared to a greater or lesser degree by all the national groups which composed the two states. The central governments tried desperately to stop the forces of disintegration. Here and there they were able to check them temporarily, but they could not restrain the surge permanently. Neighboring states which hoped to profit from the dissolution of the two empires freely heaped fuel on the fires of nationalist agitation. Among these were Russia, Rumania, and Serbia. The latter two, for example, hoped practically to double their territory and their population by the acquisition of those parts of Austria-Hungary which were principally inhabited by Rumanians and Serbians. In short, the governments of the two empires were, so to speak, sitting on the top of a volcano.

THE GREAT COMPROMISE

Under the strain of the revolutions of 1848 it appeared for a time as if the breakup of the Austrian Empire was inevitable. After the Hungarians defeated the Austrian armies, the emperor was able to subdue his rebellious subjects only with the help of the troops of Tsar Nicholas, who felt himself called upon to intervene "for the sake of the principle of divine rulership." Reaction followed suppression. Because they had risen against their Habsburg ruler the Hungarians were deprived of their constitution and their kingdom, divided into five provinces, was made an integral part of the Austrian domain, with the same political, financial, and administrative system then in force in the Austrian provinces. Not only were all Hungarian laws abolished but the Hungarian language was also proscribed. In other words, everything possible was done to eradicate those things that might remind the population of its former laws, customs, or institutions. But this reactionary rule served only to consolidate national sentiment among the Hungarians and to draw all parties closer together. Their attitude was one of sullen passive resistance. For the next decade and a half they had to be ruled in every department of state without their cooperation.

After the suppression a wise and far-reaching policy might still have enlisted many elements on the side of the emperor and preserved the cohesion of his state. But the task required statesmanship of a kind that Francis Joseph neither possessed himself nor had the judgment to discern in others. The monarch whose personal reign (1848–1916) is the longest in modern history — longer by four years than Queen Victoria's — was only eighteen when he assumed the heavy burden of ruling the Austrian Empire.[1] He brought to his tasks an extraordinary seriousness and a stern sense of duty. Day after day he spent twelve to sixteen hours perusing dull official documents, never permitting them to accumulate on his desk. His grasp of administrative detail was such that he often astounded his ministers. Bismarck after meeting him said, "If he were not an emperor I should say that he is rather too serious for his age." The long hours of work left him no time for intellectual pursuits, and so literature, art, and music were sealed books to him.

In general, Francis Joseph's views were routine and his ideas out-and-out conservative. His mind was without a shred of imagination. As the years passed, he acquired much administrative experience but few ideas. He was a hard-working, routine-ridden bureaucrat. His conservatism was such that he refused to the end to enter an elevator or use a telephone or a typewriter. When he did use an automobile, it was with great reluctance. His ruling idea was to preserve intact the heritage of his forefathers and to weld his heterogeneous peoples into a compact state. Just how he would achieve the latter he did not seem to know. Nor was he able to tolerate men of first-class ability, men who had the judgment

[1] Louis XIV was king of France for seventy-two years (1643–1715), but he did not assume personal control until 1661.

and foresight demanded by the tasks. He disliked the proximity of men of initiative and energy, was envious of men of achievement, and distrusted the ideas of progressive men because he could not understand them. In all fairness to Francis Joseph, however, it must be stated that few rulers have been confronted with more difficult tasks. At the time of his accession there was war and nationalist agitation in every corner of the empire. Even though the war ended, the unrest continued. It was already too late for any attempt to put an end to it by Germanizing the Slavs and Magyars. The sentiment of nationality was already strong among the Magyars, it had never been extinguished among the Poles, and it was growing stronger in the breasts of the Czechs and the members of other nationalities. Consequently Francis Joseph employed a show of force to keep his empire together.

The dream of maintaining the empire by reliance on the sword was, however, soon dispelled. In 1859 Austria became involved in war with Piedmont and France. In two great battles (Magenta and Solferino) the Austrian armies suffered disastrous defeats, defeats which revealed the impotence of both the Austrian armies and Austrian diplomacy. One reason for the defeats was the attitude of the Hungarians. Their discontent was such that the government was afraid to withdraw its troops from Hungary for use in the battles; many Hungarians even enlisted with the enemy to fight against the Austrians. When he realized the import of the defeats, even Francis Joseph saw that he could no longer maintain his rule by military strength alone. The necessity of conciliating public opinion by constitutional concessions was patent, but in his vacillating way he still resisted the move.

Finally in October, 1860, he issued a decree (October Diploma) which announced the establishment of constitutional government; and four months later (February, 1861) he promulgated the constitution. By its provisions the crown lands were divided into seventeen provinces, each with its own legislative body and each with representatives in a central imperial parliament at Vienna. Although the new government was more liberal than any the empire had theretofore known, it left much to be desired. None of the legislative bodies was truly representative. For example, the bishops and archbishops of the Roman Catholic and Greek Orthodox churches were ex officio members, together with the rectors of the universities. The gilds and the small landowners did, it is true, send representatives, but the delegates of the wealthy urban classes and the great landowners predominated. Article 19 of the constitution stated that "all nationalities enjoy equal rights, and each of them has the inviolable right to the maintenance and cultivation of its nationality and language. Equality of rights for all local languages in schools, administration, and public life is guaranteed by the state."

Theoretically this abolished the privileged position of the German language, but in practice many of the local administrators managed to circumvent the provisions of the constitution. The general result was that these concessions, which at an earlier time might have been effective in winning much support from the various nationalities, now failed to satisfy their demands.

During this time the Magyars refused to accept any concessions that would not grant full recognition of the historic rights they claimed. They asserted that Hungary had always been a separate nation. What they wanted was not a new constitution but the constitution which had been abolished in 1849. Ever since that time they had nursed rage in their hearts, waiting for an opportunity to compel the Habsburgs to give them their due. From 1861 to 1865 neither side yielded; then in 1866 came the decisive defeat of Austria by the Prussian armies at Sadowa (Königgrätz), which deprived the Austrians of the leadership of the German states and, so to speak, expelled them from Germany. Thus the Habsburgs became dependent on the good will of the non-Germans under their rule.

The defeat from without and the unrest within convinced the government that it would be wise to make friends with the Magyars. Francis Joseph sent for Ferencz Deák, the Hungarian leader, and asked him what the Hungarians wanted. When Deák answered that they wanted "their rights," the emperor replied, "I suppose it must be as you insist." After prolonged negotiations a compromise (Ausgleich) was reached which provided for the restoration of Hungary's constitutional independence. It was given a separate Diet on the model of the Austrian Reichsrat, with a separate responsible ministry. In short, Hungary obtained control of the administration of her internal affairs. Beyond the fact that the emperor of Austria was also the king of Hungary the bonds of union between the two consisted of a joint interest in three matters: foreign policy, common defense, and imperial finance. For these there was a common ministry comprising ministers of foreign affairs, war, and finance. The imperial chancellor, whose office was combined with that of minister of foreign affairs, presided. The element of popular control over the common interests was supplied by a system of delegations or committees. Sixty members were elected by the Hungarian Diet and sixty by the Austrian Reichsrat. Each delegation met separately and communicated with the other in writing. The delegations could meet only after three exchanges in writing had proved unavailing, and then only to vote, not to debate. This was done to prevent the two delegations from ever developing into a central federal body.

Thus the new state was a dual monarchy. The Slavs had advocated federalism instead of dualism. They demanded autonomy for all nationalities that could lay claim to historic rights. Bohemia, in particular, deemed herself as entitled to autonomy. The refusal on the part of the Magyars to accord to the other nationalities the same rights they had demanded for themselves created a great deal of friction in the new state.

Count Apponyi, the president of the Hungarian House of Deputies, vigorously rejected the term "Austro-Hungarian Empire," stating that Hungary was not a constituent part of the empire, but an independent kingdom. He insisted on the term "Austro-Hungarian monarchy." "The imperial title," he stated, "has nothing whatever to do with Hungary; it has legal existence only with respect to those other domains which . . . can be properly called 'Austria,' to the exclusion of the kingdom of Hungary. As a ruler of those other domains, His Majesty may call himself whatever he pleases, but in Hungary he is merely king." The Hungarians agreed to the compromise not because they loved the Austrians but because it seemed the only way to preserve their national existence. They knew that if there should be war they could not single-handedly resist the Russian colossus. In short, the two states were held together by pressure from without. With respect to territory and population the division was fairly even: the population of the Austrian Empire numbered nearly 24 millions, that of Hungary about 17.5 millions, in the year 1890; the total area of Austria was 115,903 square miles, against an area of 125,039 square miles included in Hungary. Thus the Austrian Empire was a little larger than the state of Arizona, and Hungary was a little larger than the state of New Mexico. It was in these comparatively small areas that eight nationalities battled for recognition. The subjoined table shows in some detail the division of the population.

	Austria	Hungary
Germans	8,461,580	2,107,577
Magyars	8,139	7,426,730
Czechs and Slovaks	5,472,871	1,910,279
Poles	3,719,232	
Ruthenians	3,105,221	383,392
Croats and Serbs	644,926	2,604,240
Slovenians	1,176,672	94,679
Rumanians	209,110	2,591,905
Italians and Latins	675,305	21,861
Gipsies		96,497
Other minorities	422,357	226,631
	23,895,413	17,463,791

NATIONALIST STRIVINGS

In Hungary the Magyars assumed absolute rule. After giving Croatia a system of restricted home rule, they proceeded with their efforts to assimilate the other nationalities in the kingdom. Ferencz Deák, the Hungarian leader, said in a speech in parliament (1872), "If we wish to win over the nationalities, we must seek at all costs to Magyarize them; this can only happen if we create in them love and attachment for Hungarian conditions. Two things are clear to me: to exterminate them would be a godless act of barbarism, even if they were not in any case too numerous for this to be possible. And to make them our enemies is not in our interest." Some years before this statement was made, the first steps in the program had already been taken. Whereas the Austrian government made many concessions in regard to language, the Hungarian government unequivocally stated its position in a law of 1868: "The official language of the government in all government services is and will remain Magyar." It was also made the language of instruction at the universities and the language of local assemblies. If one fifth of the members of a county assembly demanded it, however, a second language could be used. The Magyars largely monopolized the administrative offices and also the seats in parliament.

The aggressive and unscrupulous means by which the Magyars endeavored to impose their way of life on the national groups of the country evoked strong opposition in some districts but met with considerable success in others. To encourage non-Magyars to become Magyars the fee for Magyarizing a name was set very low. For a few pennies men called Rosenberg, Meier, Schmidt, or Blitzstein could acquire such sonorous and aristocratic Magyar names as Hunyadi, Petofi, or Fejérváry. Probably the most effective instrument of conversion was the public school system. In 1898 a Hungarian statistician asserted that in Budapest sixty-two out of every one hundred Slovak children and thirty-six out of every one hundred German children left school as Magyars. Large numbers of Jews were also absorbed. For a time it seemed as if the nationality question might well be solved by absorption, but toward the end of the century the various groups began to offer more resistance. Pressure and persecution seems to have stimulated the obstinacy of the Slavs and the pride of the Rumanians.

Although there was much friction in Hungary, the iron methods of the government prevented it from developing into open conflict. In the Austrian Empire, however, the national question manifested itself in a series of problems and controversies, chief of which was the contest with the Slavs of Bohemia. When the demands of the Magyars were met in 1867, the Slavs of Bohemia, and particularly the Czechs, confidently expected that they would receive the same treatment and that a virtu-ally autonomous government would be set up in Bohemia.[2] They were not satisfied with the local parliament that had been established in 1861; they wanted the same status that the Hungarians enjoyed. After years of agitation and bickering the emperor was ready to recognize the rights of the kingdom of Bohemia, and an appropriate bill was drafted. But the bill did not pass (1871). There was, first of all, the opposition of the Germans in Bohemia to Slav predominance. Second, many members of the Austrian government circle disliked the idea of splitting the em-pire any further. Finally, the Magyars who had won a privileged posi-tion for themselves were not ready to share it with the Czechs. Re-buffed in their efforts to achieve their goal by legal procedure, the Czechs turned to such means as systematic parliamentary obstruction. The result was that the sessions of the Imperial Parliament were thence-forth in a continuous uproar.

During the last decades of his reign it was Francis Joseph's honor-able and unswerving endeavor to reconcile the claims of the national groups who were struggling to free themselves from the Austrian or Magyar yoke. He was untiring in his efforts to do justice to their na-tional grievances and to make them contented. His good intentions, however, reaped little more than ingratitude. He was never able to please more than one group at a time, and then not for long. No sooner did he make a concession to one nationality than the others accused him of favoritism. As one writer put it, "Even a Bismarck would not have been able to achieve much in Austria by constitutional means, and Francis Joseph was no Bismarck and the same was true of his minis-ters." On a number of occasions during crises his ministers suggested that he employ force to restore order and outward peace, but the em-peror peremptorily rejected the suggestions. Having taken the oath to the constitution he was determined to adhere to constitutional methods. Hence the strife continued. The ministers in the midst of this witches' Sabbath, unable to find a solution, resorted to a see-saw policy as a means of keeping some kind of order and cohesion. They played one group off against another in accordance with the old maxim, *Divide et impera* (divide and rule).

Thus the Austrian Empire presented a distressing picture of dissen-sion and strife. The nationalist parties paralyzed one another's activi-ties to such an extent that the Imperial Parliament reached a virtual deadlock. There was little hope of reconciling the diverse opinions. The acrimonious wranglings caused many publicists to prophesy the col-lapse of the empire in the immediate future. But there was still one

[2] In 1898 the population of Bohemia was about 5.8 million, of which almost two thirds were Czechs and most of the rest Germans.

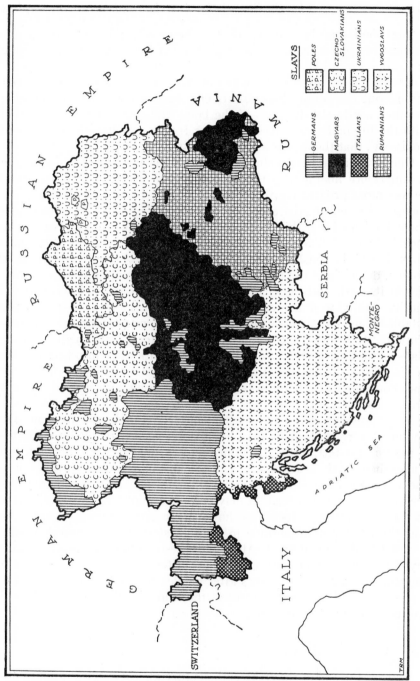

THE NATIONALITIES OF AUSTRIA–HUNGARY, 1914

GERMANS

MAGYARS

ITALIANS

RUMANIANS

SLAVS

POLES

CZECHO-
SLOVAKIANS

UKRAINIANS

YUGOSLAVS

strong bond that held it together — the affection of its citizens for Francis Joseph. As a contemporary observer put it, "There is nothing in Europe quite like this homely, familiar affection for the monarch." Not only did the people of Vienna idolize him as "unser Kaiser," but throughout the empire his subjects cherished a real affection for him. In other words, the destinies of the Dual Monarchy seemed bound up with the life of Francis Joseph. It was freely stated, with apologies to Louis XV, that the deluge would come after his death.

One of the amazing developments in Francis Joseph's life was that he became more liberal with the passing of the years. At seventy-seven he was more progressive than he had been at twenty-five. In 1907 he sponsored a reform, the essence of which was universal manhood suffrage. He hoped that this would enable a vast number of voters to make their influence felt in favor of social reform and that nationality questions would be pushed into the background. Certain conservative groups, determined to prevent the passage of the bill, put many obstacles in its path, but the emperor's determination and his personal authority finally won the day.[3] To many contemporary observers the establishment of universal manhood suffrage was tantamount to revolution. "It is one of the paradoxes of history," an English writer stated, "that he should accomplish this revolution by an unsparing use of his personal authority at a time when the young emperor of Russia, once considered so liberal in tendency, is fighting with his full force to preserve autocracy."[4]

At the opening of the first parliament elected under the new suffrage on June 19, 1907, Francis Joseph made a speech that was by many regarded as his testament. "It is my most ardent desire," he said, "to leave when the time shall come, as a precious inheritance to my peoples, the assured existence of their national possessions and thereby guarantee to all a national peace that may become a joint treasure of all lovers of the Fatherland." His hopes, however, that the empire of which he was the head would continue to grow in strength and cohesion were doomed to disappointment. Although the strife and bickering was allayed to some extent during the years after 1907, the prophecy that the empire would fall to pieces after his death was fulfilled. Under the stress of World War I the seams of the ship of state opened wide and caused it to sink in the storm.

THE SICK MAN OF EUROPE

Toward the end of the eighteenth century almost every European observer who wrote on the Turkish Empire felt constrained to state that

---

[3] The allotment of representatives for each national group was still unequal.
[4] *Living Age*, vol. 255 (1907), p. 707.

since the process of decay and destruction was so far advanced, the end of the Turk in Europe was a matter of only a few months. Among the more prominent figures who expressed this opinion one might mention Napoleon, who wrote to the Directory, "It is of no use to try to maintain the Turkish Empire; we shall witness its fall in our time." During the War of Greek Independence the Duke of Wellington believed that the end was at hand. Many others before and after this time expressed similar opinions. But the classic statement was that of Nicholas I of Russia. In 1853 he told Sir Hamilton Seymour, the English ambassador, "We have a sick man on our hands and must prepare for his demise. As long as Russia and England are in accord I do not fear the rest of Europe. I have not inherited the policy of Catherine II, for my empire is sufficiently vast; but there are many millions of Christian subjects whose interests I must preserve. I will therefore occupy Constantinople as a gauge for the future, and England may take Egypt and Crete." The patient, it is true, was weak in body and suffering from an incurable disease, but Nicholas erred if he believed that the Ottoman Empire was in its last agonies. What he was really trying to do was to persuade the British to help him strangle his sick friend so that both could divide his possessions, with the Russians getting the long-coveted Constantinople.

Where the prophets for the most part failed was not so much in their diagnosis of the illness as in not allowing sufficient time for the disease to kill the patient. A more accurate summary of the situation is that of an observer who wrote in 1866 regarding the empire: "Whether the time has now arrived for its fall must depend on the course which events will take and which it is at present impossible to foresee." Despite a series of amputations and excisions without anesthetic or antiseptic, operations which would have killed almost any other patient, the sick man continued to live.

Among the things that extended the life span was the fact that the national groups under its rule were unable to sink their differences and act together against it. Any effective union of these peoples would have spelled sudden death for the empire, but such a union did not come about. For one thing, the Turks, who were accomplished opportunists in politics, sedulously fostered the mutual suspicions. In other words, they played one group off against another in much the same manner that the Habsburgs used to foment antagonism among their nationalities.

Another factor in extending the life of the sick man was the rivalry of the great powers. Had these states, and particularly Austria and Russia, acted together, they could have divided European Turkey much as they had divided Poland in the eighteenth century. But each nation feared that in the division another would get the lion's share or gain special advantages. Thus England did not accept Nicholas's offer because a Russia ensconced in Constantinople would have been a threat to British maritime interests in the Mediterranean. Austria, for her part, feared that Russian ascendancy in the Balkans would lead to the formation of a great Slav empire which would eventually absorb the Slavs of the Dual Monarchy. Hence Austria abandoned her historic role as the bulwark of Europe against the Turk in order to become the bulwark of the Turk against Russia. Russian propagandists said much about freeing their brethren of the Greek Orthodox Church from the yoke of the infidel, but their primary object was to realize the ambition of reaching the open Mediterranean. Toward the end of the century Germany, too, entered the contest for the purpose of gaining commercial advantages in the Near East. In short, like vultures the great powers longed to sink their talons into the carcass of the sick man in order to tear out a rich morsel, but none dared to do so lest the others pounce upon him. And so the sick man lived on.

Yet while the great powers to some extent protected Turkey against division from without, they could not stop the inner disruption. The basic cause of the unrest was not oppression or intolerance on the part of the Turkish government. In times of panic, it is true, representatives of the government often punished acts of hostility with a brutal and horrible revenge, but in general the Turk was not so fiercely intolerant as his enemies painted him. If anything, his rule was marked by excessive leniency. From the very beginning he made no attempt to interfere with the religion and the customs of the peoples he had conquered. Only in Albania was there a general acceptance of the Moslem creed by the masses of the population. The great landowners of Bosnia and in a lesser degree of Bulgaria became converts to gain the favor of the Turks, but in most places Christianity survived as before. Those who differed from the Mohammedan faith had to pay a poll tax; otherwise they enjoyed full religious liberty.

In one respect, however, the freedom of the Christians was restricted: they were not permitted to serve in the army. War to the Moslem meant fighting for his faith; hence the faithful believer resented the idea of having the Christian fight by his side as his equal. Moreover, many Turks felt that it would be dangerous to have a large number of armed Christians in the empire. The Christians themselves did not regard their exclusion from military service as an unmixed evil. When shortly after the middle of the century an attempt was made to extend conscription to them, they vigorously opposed the measure and even enlisted the foreign legations at Constantinople in support of their opposition. The measure was abandoned, and in lieu of military service the Christians agreed to pay a small exemption tax. Many could well afford this because of the prosperity they had achieved. In many towns the dilapidated houses were those of the Turks. "Is it not strange," a Turk is reported to have said to a Greek, "that you giaours live in palaces, while we Moslems live in hovels? You walk in the streets richly dressed, and we wear patched-up caftans. You are princes, we are beggars." [5]

The force that was slowly tearing the Ottoman Empire apart was nationalism; the various national groups were determined to be satisfied with nothing short of complete independence. Even if the Turkish government had been the best on earth they would not have been satsified, for they regarded any subjection whatever to the rule of another nationality as humiliating. When military defeat demonstrated the weakness of the government, the subject peoples readily entertained thoughts of rebellion. The beginning of the process of disruption was made in Serbia, where a rising took place in 1804 under the peasant leader George Petrovic, later known as Karageorge (Black George). With the indirect aid of the Russians they repeatedly defeated the armies which the sultan sent against them. But in 1812 the Russians after coming to terms with the Ottoman government (treaty of Bucharest) left the Serbs to the mercy of the sultan who at once proceeded to crush the uprising. In 1815 Milosh Obrenovich led a second rising and this time the Serbs were more successful. In 1821 after the insurrection of the Greeks shook the empire to its foundations the sultan finally conceded Serbian autonomy. Later he tried to forget his promise, but pressure from the Russians during the period from 1830 to 1834 forced the Ottoman government to recognize Serbia as an autonomous state with Milosh as hereditary prince.

Nor did the disintegration of the empire stop with the loss of Serbia. In 1829 the independence of the Greeks was finally recognized. The Rumanians, too, whose national awakening dates from the early years of the century, were demanding independence. After the Crimean War Moldavia and Wallachia (the two provinces which later became Rumania) were given autonomy under the suzerainty of the Turkish government, but this did not satisfy the inhabitants. In 1859 they elected Alexander Cuza as governor (hospodar) of a joint administration of both provinces. Three years later the Ottoman government recognized the union and the name Rumania. Cuza launched a program of reform which gradually undermined his popularity. His efforts to dissolve the remaining feudal relations alienated the nobles (boyars), confiscation of the monastic estates lost him support of the clergy, and the introduction of a tobacco monopoly and his failure to complete the agrarian reforms deprived him of the support of the masses. As a result he was

[5] Ubicini, *Les Serbes de la Turquie* (Paris, 1865), p. 3. *Giaours* is a term applied to Christians by Turkish Moslems.

compelled to abdicate in 1866. Prince Carol of the House of Hohenzollern-Sigmaringen was imported as his successor. Early in the Russo-Turkish war of 1877–1878 the principality proclaimed its independence, which was recognized by the treaty of Berlin (1878). In 1881 Prince Carol became King Carol I.

The most important provision of the treaty of 1856 purposed to bolster up Turkey against further inroads on the part of Russia. Article 7 read: "Their Majesties engage, each on his own part, to respect the independence and territorial integrity of the Ottoman Empire. They guarantee in common the strict observance of this engagement, and will consequently consider every act of a nature to infringe upon it as a question of general interest." It was, in other words, an attempt to make Turkey strong and to keep Russia weak. The Turk, who had previously been regarded as a barbarian, was also admitted into the European family of states. What he lacked to raise him to a level with the Europeans was to be supplied by a series of reforms. But the sultan's promise to inaugurate these reforms was an empty one. Conditions, if anything, became worse. In 1875 the Slavic peasants of Herzegovina, a Turkish province to the west of Serbia, rose in revolt. The insurgents were tired of Turkish promises, embittered by the taxes imposed on them by Turkish officials, and infuriated by the demands of their Mohammedanized nobles for forced labor. Despite the sultan's further promises to improve the lot of his subjects, the revolt gradually spread. When insurgents in Bulgaria killed a number of Turkish soldiers, the sultan's government sent hordes of irregular soldiers, called bashi-bazouks, who proceeded to destroy dozens of villages and to massacre thousands of unarmed and inoffensive men, women, and children in cold blood.

The massacre shocked the civilized world. Both in Russia and in England there was a widespread demand for military action. Gladstone became so indignant that he urged the expulsion of the Turk from Europe "bag and baggage." When the British government did not join Russia, the tsarist government decided to act alone. It was another opportunity to push closer to Constantinople, to unite the Slavic nationalities into one group under Russian leadership. As early as 1867 the Russian government had already prepared its people for the move. Early in that year the Moscow *Gazette* exclaimed (February 17):

Beneath the rotten covering of Ottoman tyranny three groups of strong and energetic nationalities are awakening, the Hellenic, the Slavonic, and the Rumanian. Closely united to each other by a common faith and by historic traditions, those three groups are equally united to Russia by all the ties of religion and national life. When once these three national groups are reconstructed, Russia will stand forth in a new light. She will no longer be alone in the world; instead of a somber Asiatic power she will become a moral force indispensable to Europe. She must assume toward the Slavonic races the attitude which France has assumed toward the Latin nationalities, and Prussia toward the German groups, and she must employ all her forces to realize it.

Although the tsar gave the British solemn assurance that he had no intention of occupying the Turkish capital, he told his military staff that the object of the campaign was Constantinople.[6] After breaking the back of the Turkish resistance, the Russian armies pushed on until they were within a day's march of Constantinople. Their rapid and triumphant progress, which caused consternation in certain European circles, produced threats of interference which acted as a deterrent upon the tsar. Instead of ordering his troops to press on, he concluded with the sultan the treaty of San Stefano (March 3, 1878). Its principal feature was Russia's attempt to erect a large self-governing Bulgaria that would be under Russian control. This Bulgaria was so large that Turkey would have retained only a small strip of territory in Europe.

But the treaty of San Stefano did not satisfy the European powers. Great Britain and Austria informed the Russian government that the treaty was unsatisfactory and must be submitted to a European congress for revision. A Russian mission succeeded in overcoming the objections of Austria-Hungary, but the British persisted in demanding a complete review of the treaty. For a time war between the two powers appeared inevitable. In the end, however, the Russians gave way and a congress, composed of representatives of all interested nations, met in Berlin on June 13, 1878, with chancellor Bismarck presiding over the deliberations. In revising the treaty the conference gave a marked, though a somewhat hesitant, recognition to the principle of nationality. Montenegro, Serbia, and Rumania were recognized as completely independent states, on condition that there be no discrimination in the granting of civil and political rights and that full religious liberty be accorded to all subjects. The Bulgaria which Russia had designed was divided into three parts: the autonomous principality of Bulgaria, under the suzerainty of the sultan but having a Christian governor; the province of Eastern Rumelia, which was "to remain under the direct political and military authority" of the sultan; Macedonia, which was returned to the Turkish government.

While curbing the ambitions of tsarist Russia the powers did not hesitate to extend their control of various Turkish possessions. England was given the right to "occupy" the island of Cyprus. Austria-Hungary was given the right to administer the provinces of Bosnia and Herze-

[6] Gabriel Hantoaux, *La France Contemporaine*, vol. IV (1900), p. 21.

THE PARTITIONING OF EUROPEAN TURKEY, 1878

govina, although they remained nominally a part of the Turkish Empire. The purpose of this peculiar arrangement was to prevent the consolidation of a strong Slavic state on the borders of Hungary. The general result of the treaty was that it left a badly mutilated European Turkey about as much land as is included in the state of Missouri.

THE YOUNG TURK AND AFTER

After three decades characterized by agitation and unrest the so-called Eastern Question entered upon a new phase in 1908, when the Young Turk Committee of Order and Progress staged a revolution. The object of this revolution was to overthrow the corrupt, despotic, and inefficient government of the sultan and to set up a parliamentary system on a western model. The directing heads of the party were largely young men who had been exiled for their liberal ideas. In spite of the network of secret police, the members of the party had worked quietly and adroitly to suborn the soldiers of the army upon which the sultan's power rested. In July, 1908, the Young Turks raised the revolutionary banner with the slogan, "Liberty, Fraternity, Equality, Justice," and peremptorily demanded the restoration of the constitution of 1876.[7] Abdul-Hamid II would have liked to suppress the revolutionary party; but when he realized that he had lost control of the army, he promptly restored the constitution and blamed his advisers for the misrule of the past. Elections were ordered for a parliament, which convened in December, 1908, amidst general rejoicing. Early in 1909 reactionaries made a determined effort to turn back the clock but were defeated with very little bloodshed. Abdul-Hamid was sent into exile.

During the early months of the new government the general enthusiasm knew no bounds. There was a widespread conviction that the evils of misrule had vanished or were about to vanish. The words "liberty" and "fraternity" were on everyone's lips. Turk, Greek, Bulgar, Albanian, and Jew fraternized as they had not in a century. The legions of spies that had dogged the footsteps of residents and visitors disappeared. Article 10 of the constitution as revised in 1909 read: "The liberty of the individual is absolutely inviolable. No one can under any pretext be arrested or made to suffer any penalty except according to the forms and in the cases prescribed by the religious and civil laws." There was greater freedom of action than formerly. One evidence of this is the multitude of newspapers in various languages which sprang up after the proclamation of the constitution. The abolition of local passports gave the people the opportunity to travel from place to place.

[7] In 1876 Abdul-Hamid II had granted a constitution as a means of weathering a crisis and had then suspended it almost immediately.

The removal of restrictions on trade promised a general improvement of economic conditions. In short, to many it appeared as if the millennium was about to be ushered in.

So successful did the revolution appear that many believed the Ottoman Empire would again become a power to be reckoned with. Consequently neighboring states decided to move quickly before the Young Turk movement gathered enough strength to thwart their purposes. On October 5, 1908, Prince Ferdinand of Bulgaria, after he was assured that Austria would raise no objections, proclaimed the complete independence of his country from Turkish suzerainty and took the title of Tsar Ferdinand I. The next day Francis Joseph announced the annexation of Bosnia and Herzegovina in a proclamation which stated: "We deem that the moment has come to give the inhabitants of the two lands new proof of our trust in their political maturity in order to raise Bosnia and Herzegovina to a higher level of political life." [8] On October 12 the Cretan Assembly severed its connection with the Ottoman government and declared for union with Greece. Thus the area of the Ottoman Empire was reduced still more.

The Young Turks, after a promising beginning, failed to live up to expectations. The cleansing of the Augean stables of Abdul-Hamid's misrule was a gigantic task, one which would have taxed the ingenuity of experienced statesmen. And experience was not the forte of the Young Turks. Many of those who were brought to the front by the revolution had no experience in the management of government affairs. Their enthusiasm was such that they deluded themselves into believing that the old Asiatic world of Turkey could be transformed by a wave of the hand. Month after month passed and the grandiose program of the Young Turks remained a program. Such schemes of public utility as the construction of roads and bridges and the production of electricity for the towns did not get past the discussion stage. The law courts continued to be what they had been, i.e., nurseries of corruption in which a litigant's prospects of success were commensurate with the size of his purse. Brigands continued to roam the country, and the police committed the same excesses and cruelties as they had under Abdul-Hamid. Nor was anything done for agriculture, which languished as before. With the passing of the months the exaggerated hopes gradually died down and optimism gave way to pessimism. Many began to ask: "What has the revolution really done for us? The cost of living is increasing rather than declining, and the government is going to raise taxes." Laudable as it was, the attempt to give equal rights to all subjects also encountered difficulties. Long-standing enmities between the

---

[8] For the reaction of the annexation see p. 363. The annexation was scheduled for October 7, but when the news leaked out Francis Joseph proclaimed it the day before.

various groups flared up anew. To many, liberty meant that they could do what they pleased; the result was chaos and anarchy in some parts of the empire.

At the beginning a number of Young Turk traders advocated conciliation of the various national groups through the fulfillment of their aspirations so far as this was compatible with the solidarity of the empire. Unfortunately the chauvinistic spirits of the party soon jettisoned this part of the program. In their blind enthusiasm they believed that the nationalities which had resisted absorption for centuries could be forcibly assimilated. In other words, they looked forward to a time when there would be a Turkish nation as homogeneous as the German or the French. What actually came about, as they might well have foreseen, was a great surge of nationalist sentiment. All the nationalist associations, which at the time of the revolution had become constitutional clubs, reverted to the old nationalist programs, and all the old discontents again came to the fore. Since they could not register their complaints in the open, they resorted to secret conspiracy. The upshot was a general revival of revolutionary agitation.

In 1911 Italy began again the process of dismembering the Turkish Empire. Ever since the unification the Italian government had been looking at Africa with a covetous eye. Many Italians felt that the territories of North Africa which touch the Mediterranean rightfully belonged to Italy since they had been part of the old Roman Empire. The other European powers had, however, taken all the North African territories except Tripoli. For some years there had been a gradual occupation of Tripoli by Italians; and in 1911, when the chaos in Turkey appeared to be approaching its climax, the Italian government decided that the time had come to occupy the province. Italian troops did occupy the coastal towns, but their hold on the interior was precarious because of native opposition instigated by Turkish agents. Finally as a means of compelling the Turkish government to release its hold on the province, the Italian forces seized the Dodecanese in the Aegean. The Turkish government, harassed by internal troubles, was forced to open peace negotiations with Italy. On October 15, 1912, the two nations signed the Treaty of Lausanne, whereby Turkey ceded to Italy its last African province.

Meanwhile a group of Balkan states, all of which had at one time been provinces of the Ottoman Empire, saw in the weakness and internal dissensions of Turkey an opportunity to liberate the members of their respective nationalities who were still living under Turkish rule. They decided to lay aside their mutual animosities, which had been bitter in the extreme, in order to form an alliance against the Turks. The first step of the so-called Balkan League — composed of Bulgaria,

Greece, Montenegro, and Serbia — was to make military preparations. The great powers of the west, seeing that war clouds were gathering fast, sought to prevent the outbreak of hostilities by promising to see that reforms were carried out at once. The Turkish government, too, declared its willingness to introduce reforms immediately, but the Balkan League stated that it had no faith in the sincerity of the declaration. Having mobilized their troops as early as September 30, 1912, the allies started hostilities on October 15, the same day on which the treaty of Lausanne was signed between Italy and Turkey.

The war was brief and ended as an overwhelming success for the Balkan states. The old Turkish army had been broken up by the Young Turks, and a new one which was being organized under German officers was not yet ready for battle. The Turkish government kept its best troops, numbering about 70,000, on the eastern frontier of Asia Minor to meet a possible attack by the Russians. The troops which were rushed up to stem the allied invasion of Macedonia were largely untrained recruits without able officers. They were hopelessly outnumbered, and the absence of field telephones and telegraphs, the disruption of the railway service, and the collapse of the food and ammunition supply system put them at a further disadvantage. Consequently the allied troops went from victory to victory. By the middle of November they had penetrated to within twenty-five miles of Constantinople, and the complete collapse of the Turkish government in Europe was imminent. Peace negotiations were started in London but were unsuccessful because the Turks refused to relinquish Adrianople, which Bulgaria demanded. In March, fighting was resumed. Within a few weeks the Turks lost much of their remaining territory and were compelled to accept the proffered terms. The treaty of London, signed on May 30, left the Turks little more than Constantinople and just enough territory around it to defend the city.

The settlement, however, proved to be very short-lived, for the Balkan states soon started fighting over the division of the spoils. Before they started the war, the Serbs and Bulgarians had by a secret treaty (March 13, 1912) arranged for the distribution of territory in case of victory. Eastern Macedonia was to go to Bulgaria. Serbia was to get the western part, together with the much-desired Adriatic coast. When the war was over, both Austria and Italy opposed the transfer of the seacoast territory to Serbia. The Austrian government feared a powerful Serbia, and Italy had little desire to share the Adriatic with a new rival. Both countries therefore insisted upon creating an autonomous Albania that would include the section of the coast which the Serbs wanted. Indignant because their country had to remain landlocked, the Serbs demanded compensation in Macedonia from the Bulgarians. There was also a contest between the Greeks and the Bulgarians for the control of Salonika. But the Bulgarians, having played a major role in annihilating the Turk, refused to give up any part of their acquisitions. They were, in fact, so elated over their victories at Kirk-Kilissa (October 25, 1912) and Lüleburgaz (October 28–30, 1912) that they were contemptuous of the Greek and Serbian military prowess.

After bitter recriminations the Bulgarian government attacked the military forces of both Serbia and Greece in June, 1913. Once the fighting had started, Montenegro also entered the fray on the side of Serbia and Greece. This trio was soon reinforced by Rumania, which had been a spectator in the first Balkan war. The Rumanians joined the fighting because they saw an opportunity to get a strip of Bulgarian territory which they felt should be a part of their country. For the Turks also the opportunity was too good to miss. They joined the group fighting Bulgaria because they hoped to regain some of the territory they had recently lost. Opposed by this formidable array of states, the Bulgarians soon realized that their situation was hopeless and consented to a redistribution of the spoils. By the treaty of Bucharest, signed August 10, 1913, Rumania received the strip of territory she wanted, while both Serbia and Greece obtained more territory than they had anticipated. All the changes were made at the expense of Bulgaria, which had foolishly started the war. Although the Turks regained Adrianople, the conclusion of the Balkan wars found Turkey shorn of the bulk of her European possessions. All that remained, in addition to Constantinople and the Gallipoli Peninsula, was the single province of Adrianople, or eastern Thrace. The force of nationalism had literally dismembered the European Turkey of 1815.

From the very day the first Balkan war started, many western diplomats feared that the spark kindled in southeastern Europe might set the whole continent ablaze. When peace was concluded, they breathed a sigh of relief. But the period of peace was a brief one. Those who predicted that a general European war would start in the Balkan Peninsula soon found their prophecies fulfilled. There in 1914 the event took place which started the conflagration that was to envelop most of the globe before it was put out.

CHAPTER SIXTEEN

The Progress of Science

SCIENCE is admittedly the dominating intellectual force of the modern age. The period since Waterloo has been one of unparalleled advance in man's knowledge and command of the physical forces of nature. The advance has been so tremendous, so varied, and so striking that it would require at least a large volume to present any appreciation of it. Consequently only the barest mention can be made of some of the great discoveries and of some of the important developments in scientific thought.

DARWIN AND DARWINISM

The idea of evolution, i.e., that the complex existing species might have originated by descent from very simple forms of life, is not modern. It is to be found as far back as the Greeks. Aristotle sketched the theory and through him it was handed down to the schoolmen of the Middle Ages. During the Renaissance it appeared in the writings of Giordano Bruno and in the seventeenth century Descartes (1596–1650) and Leibnitz (1646–1716) stated it in their works. In the eighteenth century a number of men opposed the conception that the various species of animals and plants were created once for all. In France the naturalist Buffon (1707–1788) put forward the idea of transmutation of species shortly after the middle of the century and reiterated it from time to time until his death in 1788. In Germany Johann Gottfried Herder (1744–1803) based his philosophy of history on the idea of evolution. It was through his influence that Goethe (1749–1832) became an evolutionist. Frau von Stein wrote in 1777 after the appearance of Herder's *Another Philosophy of History,* "Herder's new book makes it seem likely that we were once plants and animals. Into what else nature may fashion us remains, however, unknown. Goethe is now busy speculating on these subjects." Although the idea of evolution was basic in Goethe's thought, there is, however, no evidence to show that Goethe was in any way the herald of Darwinism. For him as well as for Herder it remained largely the conception of a poet's imagination.

At the end of the eighteenth century and in the early years of the nineteenth the idea of evolution exercised a strange fascination on many naturalists. In 1796 Erasmus Darwin, grandfather of Charles, published his *Zoonomia* in which he defined the law of descent. Early in the nineteenth century the Frenchman Lamarck (1744–1829) stated the theory of evolution in greater detail than had any predecessor. After spending a number of years studying the lower forms of animal life he conceived the idea that all forms are modified descendants of an original organism. He published his conclusions in his *Philosophie Zoologique* (1809), but his idea of the mutability of species did not carry conviction. In his epoch-making *Principles of Geology* (1830–1832) Charles Lyell delicately and timidly touched on the evolutionary hypothesis. He gave vivid pictures of the struggle for existence between various species and of the causes which led to their extinction. This work had a great influence on Darwin.

Where his predecessors had failed, Charles Darwin (1809–1882) succeeded because of his outstanding ability to observe and reason. First, he advanced an adequate working hypothesis. Second, he marshaled a most imposing array of facts to support it. Third, he offered in "natural selection" a simple explanation of the process of evolution. Fourth, he demonstrated that the theory of evolution made thousands of facts in nature comprehensible which would be meaningless without them.

One might well believe that young Charles, as the grandson of Erasmus Darwin, was born into a family in which evolution was an intellectual tradition. This was not the case. He was brought up on the idea of special creation and as a youth regarded his grandfather's notions as fanciful. His father, a well-to-do physician, sent Charles to Edinburgh to study medicine, but he found the lectures insufferably dull. Transferring to Cambridge to study theology, he still complained of dullness. He did, however, manage to pass his examinations and was graduated with the degree of Bachelor of Arts. His career might have been a purely conventional one if he had not come under the influence of John Stevens Henslow, a botanist, who discussed science with him and was also instrumental in getting for him in 1831 the post of naturalist on the *Beagle,* a naval vessel which was being sent around the world by the British government for the purpose of making nautical observations.

The voyage of the *Beagle* was in Darwin's own words "the most important event in my whole life, and has determined my whole career." In putting upon him the necessity of being geologist, botanist, zoologist, and general man of science, it gave him a training such as few naturalists have received. He took with him a well-chosen library which included the first edition of the first volume of Lyell's *Principles of Geology,* and he also used his opportunities for observation to the full. The journal he kept is filled with a wealth of observations about plants and animals as well as about man. Upon his arrival in South America he wrote: "The day has passed delightfully. Delight itself, however, is a weak term to express the feelings of a naturalist who, for the first time, has wandered by himself in a Brazilian forest. . . . To a person fond of natural history such a day as this brings with it a deeper pleasure than he can ever hope to experience again."

Darwin's studies and observations raised doubts in his mind regarding the fixity of species and upon his return to England in 1836 after an absence of five years, he decided to devote himself to further study of the question. Independent means permitted him to do so. He persistently followed every clue, coming step by step under the sway of evolutionary ideas. His observations of the infinite variety of life finally convinced him that the organic world had not been created immutably but had slowly evolved. He could see that the evolution had taken place, but the "how" still escaped him. Then one day he happened to read Malthus' *Essay on Population* which advances the thesis that most animals tend to increase at a faster rate than the means of subsistence and as a result there is a constant "struggle for existence." "It at once struck me," Darwin stated, "that under these circumstances favorable variations would tend to be preserved, and unfavorable variations be destroyed. The result of this would be the formation of new species. Here, then, I had at last got a theory by which to work." Thus he discovered the principle of "natural selection," in which he saw the master key to the problem of the development of the species.[1] Although by 1844 Darwin had committed a sketch of his theory to paper and had also confided it to a few friends, he kept on with his observations for many years, collecting a prodigious amount of data and answering a multitude of objections which arose in his mind. Finally he decided in 1856 to make a draft for publication. Before he was able to complete the work, a strange thing happened. He received an essay from a young naturalist, Alfred Russel Wallace (1823–1913), who for some time had

[1] The idea of natural selection occurred to others before Darwin. He, however, discovered it independently and his conception of it was clear and his statement of it positive.

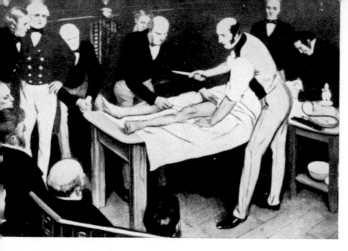

The first amputation performed under ether in England, from an old print (from Thomas Nelson and Sons)

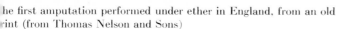

An operation being televised for the Congress of the American College of Surgeons meeting at Los Angeles in 1948 (from Wide World)

Charles Darwin, a caricature from *Vanity Fair*, 1871

One of the last photos of Madame Curie in her laboratory

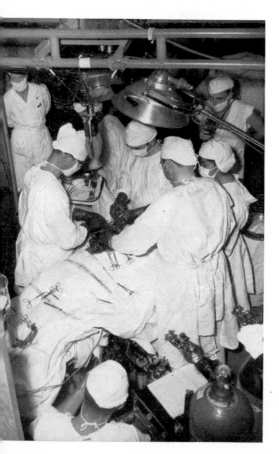

Dr. Enrico Fermi, a leader in the experiments that produced nuclear fission (from Wide World)

Dr. Niels Bohr, the Danish atom scientist (from Press Association, Inc.)

Dr. Albert Einstein on his 74th birthday (from Wide World)

An atomic furnace at Brookhaven National Laboratory, Upton, N.Y. (from Wide World)

Sir Alexander Fleming, discoverer of penicillin, his laboratory (from W World)

been making observations in the Malay Archipelago. This essay contained an outline of the theory of natural selection upon which Darwin had worked for twenty years. "Were Wallace's paper an abstract of my unpublished manuscript of 1844," Darwin said, "it could not better express my ideas." Young Wallace, too, had chanced to read Malthus' *Essay on Population* and as a result had reached the elder naturalist's conclusions.[2] Having no intention of permitting Wallace to claim priority in the statement of the theory, Darwin deposited Wallace's paper and a section of his own 1844 sketch with the Linnaean Society of London, before which both were read July 1, 1859. During the succeeding months Darwin applied himself diligently to the completion of his manuscript, which was finally published in November, 1859, under the title, *The Origin of Species by Means of Natural Selection*.

The private presentation of the two papers before the Linnaean Society did not create a sensation, but the publication of the *Origin of Species* did. The first edition of 1250 copies was sold out on the day of publication and a second and larger edition within a short time. The fundamental doctrine of the book is that "the innumerable species, genera and families of organic beings with which the world is peopled have all descended, each within its own class or group, from common parents, and have all been modified in the course of descent." Actually it suggested more problems than it solved. Darwin himself made no great claims for it. "No one," he wrote, "ought to feel surprised at much remaining as yet unexplained in regard to the origin of species and varieties. . . . Much remains obscure and will long remain obscure." Even today many of the problems posed by the Darwinian theory await a solution.[3]

THE INFLUENCE OF DARWINISM

Despite the fact that it did leave many problems unsolved, the *Origin of Species* gave the first reasonable answer to the question as to how evolution might have come about. Natural selection made it a plausible hypothesis.[4] "The *Origin*," Thomas Henry Huxley wrote, "provided us with the working hypothesis we sought. . . . It is doubtful if any

[2] Wallace believed, however, that man had "escaped natural selection." "I differ grievously from you," Darwin wrote to him, "and I am very sorry for it." He always gave the greatest possible credit and encouragement to young Wallace.
[3] Other important works of Darwin are *Variations of Animals and Plants under Domestication* (2 vols., 1868), *The Descent of Man and Selection in Relation to Sex* (1871), *Expression of the Emotions in Man and Animals* (1872). In all he published thirty-three books, if we count the various editions, and eighty-two articles.
[4] Darwin did not attempt to account for the whole of evolution by natural selection. In a later edition he wrote, "I am convinced that natural selection has been the most important, but not the exclusive means of modification." The fact that many scientists have of late rejected Darwin's selection theory as a workable hypothesis does not indicate a rejection of the idea of evolution.

single book, except the *Principia* (of Sir Isaac Newton) ever worked so great and so rapid a revolution in science, or made so deep an impression on the modern mind." In 1901 a London daily paper requested its readers to send in lists of the ten books, English or foreign, which in their opinion had been the most influential during the preceding century. The lists varied widely, with one exception. All of them included Darwin's *Origin of Species*.

This is not to say that Darwin's theory met with immediate general acceptance. In orthodox religious circles it aroused a storm of opposition and denunciation. So long as the theory included only plants and the lower animals there was relative unconcern but when Darwin applied it to "the lords of creation" the church militant gave battle, contending that such teachings contradicted the Bible. Clergy of all denominations scored the theory; many who had not read a line of the *Origin of Species* denounced it; and people generally condemned it as the "monkey damnification of mankind." Many attributed views to Darwin which he did not hold. Darwin himself foresaw the rumble and roar the publication of his theory would cause when he stated that the conclusion "that man is descended from some lowly-organized form will, I regret to think, be highly distasteful to many persons."

But his theory of evolution was well defended. A number of the keenest intellects of the time rallied to his standard and took up the defense with enthusiasm. While Herbert Spencer (1820–1903) became its leading exponent in philosophy, Thomas Henry Huxley (1825–1895) stood as its champion in public controversy. Time and again he stated that if the doctrine of evolution did not exist it would have to be invented to explain the varied forms of life. Other scientists soon followed him over to Darwin's side. Some continued to disagree with him regarding certain phases or details, but by the end of the century few informed scientists doubted the fact of evolution any more than physicists doubted the law of motion. Few would approach any scientific problem without considering how much light the theory of evolution could shed on it. The application of the idea to biology, anthropology, geology, and the other sciences became part of the scientific method. In general, the theory of evolution transformed the concept of nature from that of a fixed and static system established at creation to that of a dynamic, developing process. This transformation constitutes one of the great changes in the thought of the nineteenth century.

In geology the idea of the progressive development of the earth by the action of forces residing within it preceded the acceptance in biology of the idea of evolution of organic forms. Such geologists, though they were inclined to adopt the idea of the development of the earth, still shared the universal belief in the supernatural origin of organic forms a few thousand years before their time. But the appearance of Darwin's *Origin of Species* in 1859 threw a new light on the vast body of largely unconnected facts regarding fossils which geologists had collected during the preceding decades. Confirmatory evidence gradually pushed the history of the earth back until its beginnings were lost in the dim recesses of time. Evidence was also presented to show that in the history of the earth there have been periods of comparative quiet during which evolutionary changes were slow and periods during which changes were much more rapid, resulting in widespread modifications of physical geography.

Gradually the theory of evolution was even reconciled with religious faith. The novel doctrine which had at first called forth the grave censure of churchmen was gradually accepted by many. Man's ascent from the lower forms of life was regarded as adding to his worth and dignity rather than as detracting therefrom. Some claimed that the religious attitude was greatly strengthened by the enlarged vision which evolution opened. One writer went so far as to state, "It is surprising that the theologians have failed to recognize that Darwin, more than any one man, is responsible for stemming the advance of nineteenth century materialism." [5] Many churchmen began to regard the first chapters of Genesis as a symbolic and metaphysical rather than as a literal account. Christian evolutionists seem to agree that "the body of the first man was not created in the ordinary sense of the word, but evolved naturally from the slime of the earth through the various stages of vegetable perfection in which it received from God the created soul, and became Adam."

ASTRONOMY, PHYSICS, AND CHEMISTRY

Great advances were also made in astronomy, the oldest of the sciences. Here the record of progress is so rich and varied as to make the selection of a few great landmarks hazardous. During the nineteenth century the problem of celestial mechanics occupied the attention of a large number of distinguished men with the result that new planets, comets, and stellar systems were discovered. Progress was greatly facilitated by the development of the telescope and the use of photography. When Pierre Guinard, a Swiss artisan, after many years of patient labor succeeded in producing pure disks of flint glass as large as six inches in diameter he made the modern refracting telescope possible. By the end of the century the size of the refractor reached forty inches. Toward the middle of the century photography became an invaluable aid to astronomy. In 1842 Becquerel photographed the whole solar spectrum, and

[5] *Christian Century*, vol. 65 (September 8, 1948), p. 916.

photographic plates showed a portion of the spectrum which had not been visible to the unaided eye. As longer exposures were employed, revelation followed revelation.

At the end of the eighteenth century the known major planets numbered seven. On the first day of January, 1801, Piazzi at the University of Palermo discovered Ceres, one of the minor planets or asteroids. The discovery of three more asteroids followed soon after and then the application of photography to the study of the heavens made possible the wholesale discovery of such heavenly bodies. A plate taken October 22, 1900, showed no less than five unknown till then. Of satellites, or secondary planets, seven were added to the list during the century. At the beginning of the century one comet was known to be a member of our system, but before the end about a score had been observed. Another subject which was more carefully investigated was that of meteors. Whereas at the opening of the century many astronomers ridiculed the idea that meteors enter the earth's atmosphere from outer space, the fact that they do so was firmly established during the succeeding decades. Painstaking and fruitful studies were also made of eclipses. Some general idea of the progress made in astronomy during the nineteenth century may be gained from the fact that the star catalogues of 1801 listed about three thousand stars scattered all over the heavens, but a catalogue published at Bonn in 1857 and 1863 listed 324,198 stars in the northern hemisphere alone.

One of the outstanding discoveries of the nineteenth century in physics was the doctrine of the conservation of energy, which states that energy can neither be created nor destroyed, although it may appear in different forms which are interconvertible. This doctrine was not the discovery of one man. A considerable number of scientists contributed by study and experimentation to its final discovery. Another great discovery was spectrum analysis, the key to which was found about 1860 by the German physicists Kirchhoff and Bunsen, after a number of observers had prepared the way. By means of the spectroscope, an optical instrument, the spectra emitted by bodies or substances could be analyzed. Its use permitted the study of gases or vapors surrounding the sun, one of which is helium. As a result of these studies it was found that the sun is surrounded by an atmosphere of metallic vapors and hydrogen. If the nineteenth century had revealed nothing but this, it would have marked the beginning of a new era.

The greatest development in any one field of physics took place in electricity. It was not until Volta invented his pile or battery in 1799 that electricity could take its place as an agent of practical value. Even then the volume was limited and the cost high. Only two years after its appearance Sir Humphry Davy observed that if an electric current is made to flow through two pieces of carbon whose ends are slightly separated, it produces an arc light. In 1831 Faraday discovered how to make electricity continuously and in great quantities by means of a dynamo or generator. This opened the way for better lighting. For decades scientists worked on the incandescent lamp, but the lack of a satisfactory filament and the difficulty of creating a vacuum prevented a solution of the problem. Thomas A. Edison finally succeeded in 1879 in constructing a lamp in which a carbon filament was sealed in a vacuum. The lamp was soon improved with better filaments. By the end of the century electric lighting was beginning to be common in every civilized country.

In the meantime electricity had also been converted into mechanical energy. The first direct-current motor was built in 1860 by the Italian physicist, Antonio Pacinotti. During the succeeding period motors of various types were invented and the possibility of using electricity as a means of propulsion was developed. As a result, electricity was soon furnishing the driving power for machinery, trolley cars, boats, trains, and elevators. Great electric furnaces were also constructed for smelting, and electric cranes and hoists were developed that could have built the pyramids with ease and dispatch. In short, all modern life and industry became either directly or indirectly dependent upon electric power.

Fully as important as the great strides in physics were the advances in chemistry. By establishing the constancy of matter and by recognizing the fundamental distinction between elements and compounds Lavoisier (1743–1794) had earned for himself the title of "the founder of modern chemistry." Beyond this, however, chemists knew very little. Chemistry consisted almost entirely of descriptive matter. The first step forward was taken in 1801 when Louis Joseph Proust (1755–1826) announced that every chemical compound has a fixed definite composition and that when substances unite they do so in definite ratios by weight. Since that time the law of proportions, which he stated in the words "The composition of a compound never varies," has been demonstrated by countless investigators. The next great advance was made only a few years later when John Dalton (1766–1844) from his study of gases came to the conclusion that elements are made up of smaller particles called atoms and that chemical compounds of the elements are formed by the union of these atoms in simple numerical proportion. He gave the theory to the public in his *New System of Chemical Philosophy*, published in 1808.

The research of the succeeding period centered about the verification of known laws, the development of methods of analysis, and the discovery of new elements rather than in the development of generalizations. As such it was exceedingly fruitful. Whereas at the end of the eighteenth century only a small number of substances had been identified as elements, and it was even doubtful if some of these were actually elements, no less than seventy-eight were known at the end of the nineteenth century. Notable events of the last decade of the century were the discoveries of new gases in the atmosphere. One of these was helium, the spectral lines of which had previously been noted in the spectrum of the sun; others were argon, krypton, xenon, and neon. Furthermore, by the end of the century nearly 70,000 chemical compounds were known, most of which had been discovered after 1830.

THE BIRTH OF MODERN MEDICINE

Despite its long history, medicine was still in its infancy when the nineteenth century opened. Harvey's discovery was nearly two hundred years old, but no great advance had been made in the interval. Almost all parts of the human body, it is true, had been named, but few were understood, and diagnosis was largely sheer guesswork. As one writer put it, "Anatomists were like postmen; they knew all the streets and houses, but nothing at all of what went on in the houses." Disease was widely regarded as being due to influences beyond human control. The commonest therapeutic practices of the eighteenth century were copious bleeding and the giving of mercury. Operative surgery was in advance of medicine so far as skill and speed were concerned. Since anesthetics were unknown, the great surgeon was one who could amputate a limb in a few seconds.

Modern medicine may be said to date from the discovery in 1796 by Edward Jenner, an English physician, of the method of producing immunity to smallpox, a discovery which introduced the whole vast question of immunity. Throughout the Middle Ages and right through the early centuries of the modern period smallpox was one of a dreadful group of scourges which included also influenza, cholera, typhus fever, and bubonic plague. The inhabitants of Europe were never free from it for any length of time and in many parts it was practically endemic. That it was regarded as something more or less inevitable was indicated by the saying, "Few escape love or smallpox." In the eighteenth century so many faces were pitted from smallpox that an unmarked woman was almost the exception. Some attempts were made to inoculate human beings with the virus of the disease so that they would have a mild attack and become immune to a much more serious attack during an epidemic, but the inoculated form was often virulent and it was also as infectious as the natural variety.

It was Jenner who finally delivered humanity from the great pestilence by discovering that cowpox gave protection against smallpox. This fact, it is true, was not unknown to scientists. As early as the days of Charles II of England the court beauties envied the dairy maids who having had cowpox were immune to smallpox. Convinced that here was a possible line of investigation, Jenner began to make experiments. When in 1796 a dairy maid contracted cowpox, he took some fluid from a sore on her hand and inoculated it by a slight scratching into the arm of an eight-year-old boy, who suffered only a slight illness. Six weeks later Jenner took the momentous step of inoculating the same boy with smallpox lymph, but the boy did not contract the disease. The next year he inoculated thirty persons with cowpox. When they developed an immunity to smallpox, he announced his conclusions to the Royal Society, the highest scientific tribunal in England. This body, however, returned his report with the remark that the investigations had not been extensive enough. Jenner spent several more years inoculating persons and in 1800 went to London to vindicate his position.

Like anything that is new, Jenner's ideas were ridiculed by some, including physicians. The majority, however, soon adopted his methods. One physician enthusiastically wrote to him, "I think the substitution of cowpox for smallpox one of the greatest improvements that have ever been made in medicine." In England the royal family helped to overcome whatever prejudice the laity harbored against it by openly supporting Jenner's methods of inoculation, which became known as vaccination. On the Continent its acceptance was almost immediate. In Paris a Vaccine Institute was established, and Napoleon ordered the vaccination of all his soldiers who had not had smallpox. The Empress Catherine II of Russia also accepted vaccination at once. Within a short time it was compulsory in a number of countries. Statues were erected to Jenner in both France and Germany, and in the latter country his birthday was for a time a holiday. Even a group of American Indians forwarded to him a note of thanks in which they stated, "We shall not fail to teach our children to speak the name of Jenner and to thank the Great Spirit for bestowing on him so much wisdom and so much benevolence."

Another great advance was in the field of anesthetics. For many centuries various means had been used to deaden pain. We read in the Bible that the crucified Christ was given "wine mingled with myrrh" as a means of lessening his suffering. During the succeeding centuries carbonic acid gas and the juice of mandragora, poppy, and Indian hemp were used for this purpose. In the year 1800 Sir Humphry Davy (1778–1829) announced the discovery of the anesthetizing properties of nitrous oxide gas, suggesting that "it may probably be used with advantage in surgical operations." But no one appears to have paid attention to his suggestions, and surgeons continued to perform operations while strong men held the shrieking patient down by force.

A new era dawned for surgery when in the fifth decade of the century the anesthetic quality of ether was discovered independently by a number of individuals. The first to use it for a surgical operation appears to have been Crawford W. Long, a surgeon in Jefferson, Georgia. In 1842 Long attended an "ether frolic" at which ether was inhaled for its intoxicating effects. Upon considering these effects he used the drug to perform a painless operation upon a patient. During the next four years he performed seven other operations in which he used it but, hidden away in an American village, he had no means of making public his discovery. The man who introduced the use of ether to the world was W. T. G. Morton, a dentist in Boston, Massachusetts. Dr. Morton started his experiments by inhaling the ether fumes himself. "Taking the tube and flask," he wrote, "I shut myself up in my room, seated myself in the operating chair, and commenced inhaling. I found the ether so strong that it partially suffocated me but produced no decided effect. I then saturated my handkerchief and inhaled it from that. I looked at my watch and soon lost consciousness. . . . Gradually I regained power over my limbs, and full consciousness. I immediately looked at my watch, and found that I had been insensible between seven and eight minutes." Morton next used ether in connection with the extraction of a badly infected tooth. In October, 1846, he administered it to a patient for an operation performed at the Massachusetts General Hospital in Boston by Dr. John C. Warren.

When the news reached Britain, Sir James Simpson, a professor of medicine at Edinburgh, began to experiment with a number of chemically related compounds; he finally pronounced in favor of chloroform after using it in about fifty cases to relieve the pains of childbirth. Not all physicians and surgeons accepted anesthetics as readily as he; some even argued that pain was beneficial to a patient. But all doubts vanished in view of the results. The hue and cry from many pulpits that pain was God-given were stilled when it was pointed out that the Lord Jehovah had put Adam into a deep sleep before removing a rib. Before long the new anesthetics were in use throughout the civilized world. They not only robbed the surgeon's knife of its terrors but also greatly widened the sphere of operative surgery. Furthermore, they made possible medical research on living animals as a means of studying the functions of various organs and the effects of different drugs. Finally, they contributed much to the improvement of nursing. As long as surgery was torture, only women with extraordinary courage would volunteer to attend a patient during an operation.

THE BEGINNINGS OF BACTERIOLOGY

The next great advance was the development of bacteriology, or the study of germs. By establishing the fact that bacteria are responsible for infectious diseases this science effected a radical alteration of medical conceptions as a whole. The germ theory soon gave rise to antitoxin treatments as the first step toward preventive medicine.

These advances were largely due to the initiative of Louis Pasteur (1822–1898), a French chemist, whose influence on medicine was as great as that exerted by Darwin in general biology. The rapid sequence of his brilliant discoveries has few if any parallels in the history of science. Bacteria had first been seen in 1673 by Leeuwenhoek, a Dutch lens maker. This was long before the day of the compound microscope, but his short-focus single lenses were so good that he detected a number of microorganisms. Further progress was made during the early part of the nineteenth century after the appearance of the compound microscope. Bacteria were then classified as cocci (spherical forms) and bacilli (rodlike forms). As early as 1850 bacteria had been found in diseased animals and plants, but no general relation was established between bacteria and disease in man.

Then came Pasteur. As the result of a series of experiments he showed that fermentation is due to the presence and growth of microbes which may multiply indefinitely if they find a suitable environment. This discovery again raised the question, "Whence comes the microscopic life?" Although Spallanzani in the eighteenth century had disproved the occurrence of spontaneous generation, the idea was advanced in the nineteenth as an explanation for the presence of germs. The dispute was ended only by Pasteur's proving that when sterile solutions are not exposed to the air no fermentation or decomposition occurs. His studies of fermentation suggested a similar study of infectious diseases. After an audience with Napoleon III in 1863 he wrote to his father, "I assured the emperor that all my ambition was to arrive at the knowledge of the causes of putrid and contagious diseases." Before he could take up the study of diseases of the human body, he was asked to suggest a remedy for the mysterious disease which was decimating the silkworms in the district of Alais. Again relying on the experimental method and his microscope, he found that moths and eggs were infected by a microbe. As a remedy he prescribed the rejection of the eggs of those moths that had the characteristic marks of the disease. In the meantime he had also conducted investigations of the "diseases of wines" to discover why some wines were sour, bitter, or muddy. This time he developed the process, known as "pasteurization," of heating the wine in order to free it from all "germs of wine disease." Pasteurization was soon applied to milk.

In 1868 Pasteur's work was interrupted by a cerebral hemorrhage, but the summer of 1871 saw him take up new studies. He now made a careful microscopic examination of yeast for the English brewers and formulated the following maxim: "Every marked alteration in the quality of the beer coincides with the development of microorganisms foreign to the nature of true beer yeast." Next he devoted his attention to anthrax, an infectious disease which was ravaging the herds of cattle and sheep in France. Although he was not the discoverer of the anthrax bacillus, he did demonstrate how a pure culture of it might be made in sterile broth. By keeping this culture at a temperature of about 42 degrees centigrade for several days he found that the bacilli lost much of their virulence and that when the culture was injected into healthy animals, it gave them a mild case of the disease which immunized them against the more virulent forms. Having solved this problem, he attacked chicken cholera, isolated its bacillus, prepared a vaccine, and showed how easy it was to render chickens immune.

Finally in 1880 Pasteur began to investigate rabies. It was not a simple matter, for he had to find where the offending germ was localized; but he finally determined that the virus had its seat in the nervous system, and particularly in the brain. He also found that the disease in man, though communicated through the bite of a mad dog or other animal, exhibited symptoms that were somewhat different from those exhibited by the diseased animal. The great problem was how to prepare the vaccine and how to attenuate its virulence. After many failures he found the solution which, when injected into a dog, rendered it immune to rabies. It was not until the summer of 1885 that he succeeded in immunizing a human being against hydrophobia. Interest by this time was so widespread that there was a demand for a central bureau where treatment could be given. For this purpose the Pasteur Institute was founded in Paris. Pasteur himself saw it in operation but because of poor health could not take as active a part in it as he desired. He did, however, derive much pleasure from seeing the continuation of the work which he had started. On the occasion of Pasteur's seventieth birthday Joseph Lister, the famous English surgeon, paid him the following tribute: "You have raised the veil that for centuries cloaked the infectious diseases."

While Pasteur was making his epochal discoveries, Joseph Lister (1827–1912) established a landmark in the history of medicine by discovering the principles of antiseptic surgery. Successful surgery holds three fundamental problems: the control of hemorrhage, the prevention of pain, and the care of the wound. Ambroise Paré, a sixteenth-century military surgeon, had introduced the ligature to control hemorrhage. Long and Morton had done much to eliminate pain by introducing the use of anesthetics. But the problem of preventing infection of wounds was still unsolved; there was no security that a simple operation would not end in fatal septicemia (blood poisoning). The hospital diseases — gangrene, tetanus, erysipelas, pyemia, and septicemia — were simply accepted as inevitable. Sterilization of instruments was unknown, and surgeons often wore their operating coats for years without having them washed. Since no attempt was made to isolate cases, the mortality was particularly high in the larger hospitals, nurses and dressers carrying the infection from patient to patient. In the large Paris hospitals 62 in 100 and in the large English hospitals 60 in 100 died after amputations in 1861. Sir James Simpson, the discoverer of chloroform anesthesia, stated that "the man laid on the operating table in one of our surgical hospitals is exposed to more chances of death than the English soldier on the field at Waterloo."

Lister's introduction to antiseptic surgery came soon after the discovery of anesthetics. He himself told the story in the following words:

When it had been shown by the researches of Pasteur that the septic property of the atmosphere depended not on the oxygen or gaseous constituent, but on the minute organisms suspended in it, which owed their energy to their vitality, it occurred to me that decomposition in the injured part might be avoided without excluding the air by applying as a dressing some material capable of destroying the life of the floating particles.

While he was searching for a chemical antiseptic, his attention was attracted to an experiment by the city authorities at Carlisle in destroying the odor of sewage with carbolic acid. He at once seized upon the idea and began his experiments by applying lint soaked in carbolic acid to the wounds. The first solutions were so strong that they burned the surrounding tissues and skin surfaces; but when he reduced the strength of the solution by diluting it with oil, he was more successful. Soon he was also using mild solutions to wash the skin in preparation for the operation. He further found that catgut sterilized in carbolic acid was by far the best ligature to use. The result of these new methods was that in his wards, erysipelas, hospital gangrene, pyemia, and septicemia were almost completely eliminated. His epoch-making discoveries, published in 1867, were received with incredulity by some, apathy by others, and ridicule by those who disliked change. Its gradual acceptance, however, greatly reduced surgical diseases. One writer declared that the antiseptic method saved more lives in the nineteenth century than were lost in all the wars of the century. During the celebration of her Diamond Jubilee in 1897 Queen Victoria raised Lister to the peerage with the general approval of the peoples of all civilized countries.

But the advance did not stop with the rise of antiseptic surgery. Besides Pasteur and Lister there was a host of other investigators, among whom none occupies a more illustrious and honored place than Robert Koch (1843–1910), a German physician. While Pasteur was establishing the germ theory of disease, Koch made of this theory the science of bacteriology. As a physician in private practice he succeeded in isolating pure cultures of bacilli by preparing a mixture containing gelatin which, when poured over a glass plate sterilized by heat, became a solid mass and fixed the organisms in it. When each organism gave rise to a colony, this colony was isolated and could be studied separately. To this method of cultivating bacteria in solidifying media we owe many of the most important advances in bacteriology. As early as 1876 he isolated the bacillus of anthrax and by inoculation proved it to be the cause of the disease. Soon thereafter he invented the staining methods by which different bacteria can be identified.

In recognition of his work Koch was appointed to the Imperial Health Department and thereafter devoted himself entirely to research. In 1882 he demonstrated the presence of the tubercle bacillus in the diseased tissues of tuberculous animals and in the sputum and tissues of human beings suffering from tuberculosis. Unfortunately the various tuberculins he prepared proved disappointing; nevertheless they became the basis for the effective antitoxins of diphtheria, meningitis, pneumonia, tetanus, and other diseases. In 1883 Koch went to Egypt on a quest for the cause of cholera and in the following year announced that the disease is due to the comma bacillus. During the late years of his life he found, among other things, that the bacillus of the bubonic plague was conveyed by rats. In 1905 he was awarded the Nobel Prize for his service to medicine.

THE MARCH OF MODERN MEDICINE

Koch's solid culture media and staining methods of identification opened a new chapter in the book of pathology. An amazing series of discoveries followed, including the bacillus of leprosy, the gonococcus (of gonorrhea), the typhoid bacillus, the bacilli of diphtheria and tetanus, the pneumococcus (of croupous pneumonia), and the meningococcus (of meningitis). The early years of the twentieth century saw the discovery of the organism which causes syphilis (spirochaeta pallida) and the discovery by August von Wassermann of the diagnostic test for this disease. In addition to finding disease-producing bacteria scientists also discovered the parasites which cause malaria and sleep-ing-sickness and the manner in which they are transmitted to human beings. Further research added much to the knowledge of vaccines, serums, and antitoxins. Thus gradually were laid the foundations of preventive medicine, which is the crowning glory of the nineteenth century.

As the century progressed new methods of diagnosis made for greater precision in the treatment of disease. When Napoleon chose Jean Corvi-sart as his personal physician he chose a man who used the novel pro-cedure of tapping the chest of a patient to elicit sounds indicative of diseased tissues within. He was not the first to use percussion, as the chest tapping method is called; nor was it accepted by other physicians at once. But it did become one of the cornerstones of modern diagnosis. Percussion told only part of the story. More could be learned by apply-ing the ear to the chest (auscultation). In 1815 another Paris physician, René Laënnec, discovered that the sound of the heartbeat could be heard clearly through a cylinder of paper held to the ear and against the patient's chest. This was the first step in the development of the instrument which Laënnec himself named the stethoscope and which in its modern form embodies the principle of the telephone.

Other inventions further aided diagnosis. Among these are the clini-cal thermometer, microscopes which can magnify infinitesimal bits of matter up to 100,000 times, and a host of instruments to examine the various organs of the body, including the ophthalmoscope to examine the interior of the eye, the otoscope to examine the ear, and the rhino-scope to examine the nose. An outstanding discovery which became at once of practical value to medicine was that of the X rays in 1895. In this year Wilhelm Conrad Röntgen (1845–1923), a German professor, discovered that when an electric current passed through a vacuum tube, the tube emitted rays which could penetrate bodies opaque to ordinary light. More particularly, they could pass through the flesh of the human body and throw a shadow of the bones on a suitable screen. Because of their unknown nature, the rays were called X rays. The X-ray machine soon became an invaluable aid in diagnosing broken bones, in locat-ing a bullet or other foreign objects, and in setting fractures.

In the realm of medical chemistry many new agents which can be used therapeutically were discovered. One of the most important of these is insulin, which robbed diabetes of much of its terror. In 1920 Frederick Banting, a physician in London, Ontario, conceived the idea that an extract from the pancreas might relieve the high sugar content in the blood of diabetics. This extract, called insulin, proved so suc-cessful that within a short time all the countries of the civilized world were enjoying its blessings. A further important discovery was the liver treatment for pernicious anemia, which began with a liver diet but soon progressed to the injection of liver extract.

This period also saw the discovery of vitamins and the study of their physiological action. For many centuries mankind had been plagued by deficiency diseases. Scurvy hampered the crusaders on the pilgrimages to the Holy Land, struck down soldiers who were away from home for a long period of time, and ravaged seamen on long voyages to such an extent that it became known as "the plague of the sea and the spoil of the mariners." The British found a remedy for it by giving their sailors fresh citrus fruits, particularly lime juice; hence the name "limey" which was often applied to British seamen. Both the Spaniards and the Italians associated pellagra with the eating of unsuitable food. In conducting experiments to eliminate beriberi in their East Indian possessions, the Dutch found that the disease resulted from a diet of polished rice. Such "cures" forced upon scientists the conviction that there are special substances in foods which even in very small quantities are of paramount importance in nutrition.

In 1911 Casimir Funk, a Polish biochemist attached to the Lister Institute in London, suggested that these substances be called "vitamines," later spelled "vitamins." During the first years vitamins were so mysterious that they were designated merely by letters of the alphabet. Further research, however, gradually revealed the chemical formulas of many of them. Great strides have been made through experiments in determining the mode of action of many vitamins. Thus scientists learned that the absence of vitamin A causes night blindness; that thiamin is necessary for the heart and that a pig develops shortness of breath in its absence; that animals lacking vitamin B6 become anemic, suffer convulsions, and develop a peculiar gait; that the hair of a rat turns gray in the absence of vitamin E; and that the absence of vitamin C causes serious hemorrhages in the tissue of guinea pigs. In regard to man great advances have also been made, although much remains to be learned.

A new era in medicine began with the discovery of antibiotic medication for the treatment of bacterial infections. Ever since the days of Pasteur scientists had cherished the conviction that a substance detrimental to germs but harmless to human beings would be found, and many tried to find it. Paul Ehrlich, the German scientist, for example, persistently searched for such an antibacterial chemical compound which he called a "magic bullet." The first definite step was the discovery in 1932 of the therapeutic qualities of sulfanilamide, which had been known to chemists as early as 1908. Experiments with the drug resulted in the discovery of other sulfonamides or sulfa drugs. These compounds do not kill germs; rather, they arrest their growth by interfering with their metabolism, and thus weaken them so that the body can overcome them. Early use of the sulfa drugs showed that they could be successfully used in combating a number of diseases and for a time many chemotherapists believed that the long-sought "magic bullet" had been found. But wider use led to the discovery that they are inactive against many germs and that they may produce a variety of toxic reactions which are seriously debilitating and at times even fatal.

Sulfa drugs were soon overshadowed by the discovery of penicillin, which was found to be superior in many respects. In 1928 while preparing a culture of staphylococci (bacteria which cause blood poisoning) Sir Alexander Fleming, bacteriologist at St. Mary's hospital, London, observed that after a few days a mold settled on the agar plate of the culture and that an area all around the mold was completely free of bacteria. He devised a series of tests to observe the effect of the mold on various bacteria and in each case obtained satisfactory results. Although Dr. Fleming published his findings in 1929, more than ten years passed before they produced definite results. It was then that Dr. H. W. Florey at Oxford took up the culture of the mold, extracted the chemical (penicillin) that killed bacteria, used it experimentally on countless animals, and finally tried it on human beings suffering from various bacterial infections. The publication of the results in 1940 soon made penicillin a household word. The new drug was found to be effective in a large number of cases in which sulfa drugs had proved useless. Among the diseases that have been successfully treated with it are bone infections (osteomyelitis), meningitis, syphilis, gonorrhea, certain types of heart infection, and some forms of pneumonia. On the other hand, it is ineffective against malaria, tuberculosis, typhoid fever, and the virus diseases.

The year 1943 saw the discovery of another important antibiotic. Whereas penicillin was discovered by accident, streptomycin was discovered by design. Impressed by the fact that bacteriologists could find no pathogenic bacteria in the soil, Dr. Selman A. Waksman, microbiologist of the New Jersey Agricultural Experiment Station at Rutgers University, deliberately set out to find a nontoxic antibiotic among the soil-inhabiting microorganisms. After making hundreds of cultures he finally discovered streptomycin, which is neither a bacterium nor a mold but occupies an intermediate position. Streptomycin did not prove to be the miracle cure many had hoped, but its discovery did considerably broaden the field of infectious diseases which can be treated successfully.

The conquest of virulent bacteria by the known antibiotics has inspired research workers to continue their search. As a result antibiotics are being developed at a bewildering rate, two of the more promising being aureomycin and chloromycetin. As the years passed physicians and bacteriologists uncovered more and more evidence to show that many strains of disease-producing germs develop resistance to antibiotics. This did not, however, destroy the hope of a final complete victory.

Besides the advances mentioned, new surgical techniques and new anesthetics have been developed, glandular disorders have yielded some of their secrets, and better knowledge of nervous and mental disorders has been gained. The use of blood plasma has been found to be important in the management of shock. Research workers have also discovered new information about heart disease, high blood pressure, hardening of the arteries, anemias, ulcers, and cancer. Educational standards in medical schools have been raised and international exchange of health information has been sedulously fostered. With the passing of each decade more and more attention has been given to the preventive aspects of disease. All this has added up to better health and a substantial lengthening of the life span. In some countries the increase has been as much as 50 per cent. This accomplishment is one of the major attainments of modern science.

FROM THE X RAY TO ATOM AND HYDROGEN BOMBS

Hundreds of scientists from many countries played a part in the development that eventually led to the release of the energy in the atom's nucleus. Only a few of these, and then only toward the end of the drama, were aware that an atomic bomb would emerge. The one man who stands pre-eminent in this development, so much so that he has been styled "the godfather of the atomic age," is Albert Einstein (born 1879). At the opening of the seventeenth century Kepler showed that the orbits of the planets round the sun are elliptical in shape, and not circular, but he did not put forward a theory to explain this observation. It remained for the genius of Sir Isaac Newton (1642–1727) to show that Kepler's laws were all capable of being explained if there existed a force of attraction between any two bodies which was directly proportional to the product of the masses of these two bodies and inversely proportional to the square of the distance between them. During the succeeding centuries Newton's law of gravitation was accepted as one of the basic principles of science. Its validity was not called in question, despite the fact that there was at least one unreconciled discrepancy between calculation and observation in the case of the planet Mercury. It was believed that subsequent observations would eliminate the discrepancy.

The solution of the problem which presented itself was not the one scientists expected. Instead of better observation Dr. Einstein suggested a better law of gravitation. In 1905, when he was only twenty-six and serving as a clerk in the patent office in Bern, Switzerland, Einstein put forth the theory of relativity which challenged man's existing concepts of time and space, of matter and energy. Einstein claimed that his theory, in addition to explaining Newton's law, would also show that the calculation for Mercury actually agrees with the observed results.[6] He also predicted that if astronomers would carefully observe light rays from distant stars they would find that the rays as they pass near the edge of the eclipsed sun bend by an amount just double that predicted by Newton's law. It was not until 1919 that the theory could be put to its most exacting test. On May 29 of that year a total eclipse of the sun was visible both in Brazil and in West Africa. Two British expeditions sent to these places to gather, among other things, evidence for or against Einstein's theory returned with proof that light rays as they passed the sun were bent to the exact amount Einstein had predicted. Other verifications of his theory followed.

Besides profoundly affecting science and philosophy, Einstein's theory contained a concept expressed in the form of an equation which opened the way to the development of the atomic bomb. It is the concept that matter is nothing but energy. In other words, Einstein found that all matter can be described in terms of energy. He even worked out the exact amount of energy to which a quantity of matter is equivalent. Without Einstein's equation for the conversion of mass into energy ($E=mc^2$) experimenters might still have stumbled on the fission of uranium, but it is doubtful if they would have realized its significance in terms of energy.

The complacency which characterized physics toward the end of the nineteenth century had already been upset experimentally before Dr. Einstein upset it philosophically. A new age of physics may be said to have begun with the discovery of X rays by Professor Röntgen in 1895. Upon hearing of the discovery, Professor Henri Becquerel of the University of Paris undertook a systematic investigation to ascertain whether fluorescent substances emitted visible rays similar to Röntgen rays. The results were negative until he placed uranium salts on a photographic plate and obtained photographic effects. No sooner had Becquerel reported his discovery than a number of physicists began to study the new phenomenon of radioactivity. Two of this number were Pierre and Marie Curie. In measuring the new form of radiation by means of an electrometer designed by her husband, Marie Curie found that the radioactivity of a sample of pitchblende from an Austrian

[6] The theory of relativity effected a modification rather than a rejection of Newton's work.

mine was particularly marked. Devoting themselves wholeheartedly to further investigation the Curies tracked down and isolated a new element which they called polonium (in honor of Marie Curie's native country, Poland) and soon thereafter found another new element which they named radium.

Two years of arduous labor was necessary to isolate a small amount of radium, for a ton of pitchblende contains less than 1/70 of an ounce of radium and they could extract only about half this amount. The Curies found that radium has the properties of an element, but that it differs from previously known elements in that it is spontaneously going to pieces. It continuously gives off light, heat, and electricity. Moreover, the rays it emits are more powerful than X rays. These discoveries demolished the idea of the indestructibility of the atom. It was evident that elements were not indestructible, for here were elements that were spontaneously going to pieces. A special professorship was created to permit Pierre Curie to continue his work, but in 1906 he was tragically crushed to death under the wheels of a carriage. Madame Curie continued the work alone until her death in 1934 from anemia which undoubtedly resulted from the action of the rays with which she worked.

The discovery that the heaviest metals — uranium, radium, polonium, and actinium — emit particles which are much smaller than atoms effected a revolution in physics, making it necessary to abandon the conception of the atom as the smallest material particle that could combine with another. Instead of the old indivisible atom physicists now saw a complex structure. It was as a result of the further study of this atom and of radioactivity that the atomic bomb became a reality. The release of atomic energy really began with many discoveries and experiments in nuclear physics during the decade of the 1930's. The first important step was the discovery in 1932 by Sir James Chadwick, an Englishman, of the existence of a new atomic particle which is neither positive nor negative, but neutral and was therefore named "neutron." Of the many scientists who studied the atomic problem during the succeeding years Dr. Enrico Fermi, a young Italian physicist, made the greatest single contribution. As a result of experiments in which he bombarded atoms of practically all the known elements with Chadwick's neutron, he found that the neutron was the key to the splitting or fission of the uranium atom. On August 2, 1939, just a month before Hitler sent his legions into Poland, Dr. Einstein wrote a letter to President Roosevelt in which he stated:

Some recent work by E. Fermi and L. Szilard, which has been communicated to me in manuscript, leads me to expect that the element uranium may be turned into a new and important source of energy in the immediate future. . . . This new phenomenon would also lead to the construction of bombs . . . extremely powerful bombs. A single bomb of this type, carried by boat and exploded in a port, might very well destroy the whole port, together with some of the surrounding territory.

German and French scientists repeated Fermi's experiments, and the fact of atomic fission became generally known. But no one knew a practical method of releasing atomic energy. The next important advance was made in 1939, when Dr. Niels Bohr, the great Danish physicist, who was in the United States at the time, propounded the theory that the most easily split nuclei are those of a rare type of uranium, called uranium-235. Thereafter both theory and experiments progressed at a staggering tempo. A group of American scientists with the assistance of Fermi, who was now also in the United States, succeeded before the end of 1939 in producing miniature charges with uranium-235. During the succeeding months the important discovery was made that neutrons are emitted in addition to the highly energetic heavy fragments thrown off in fission. It was therefore reasoned that if one neutron produces others, a chain reaction can be established, causing the whole mass of uranium to explode like a barrel of firecrackers. In 1940 experiments also confirmed that uranium-235 is more readily fissionable by slow neutrons than by fast. Consequently methods were developed to slow down the neutrons by having them pass through a material like paraffin, heavy water, or graphite. It has been calculated that in a chain reaction one such neutron can release six billion times as much energy as it possesses itself. Hence the frightful results.

Meanwhile atomic experiments were also being conducted in other countries, particularly in Germany. By 1942 we knew definitely that the Germans were working feverishly to add atomic energy to the other engines of war, but no one knew how far their experiments had gone. Government leaders realized that if the Germans succeeded in producing an atomic bomb, all attempts to stop their advance would be futile. Haste was essential. Thus the race began. Just before the Japanese attack on Pearl Harbor the National Defense Research Committee of the United States government had already set in motion the research which eventually produced the atom bomb. In the following year British and American scientists pooled their knowledge and joined forces in the battle of the laboratories. On December 2, 1942, the scientists succeeded in initiating a self-maintaining nuclear chain reaction in a uranium-graphite pile at Stagg Field Stadium, Chicago. This success induced government authorities to go into large-scale production of uranium-235 and to construct plants to make atomic bombs.

More than thirty years earlier H. G. Wells had created an imaginary atomic bomb and put it to work in *The World Set Free* (1914). In this book he has an airplane propelled by a noiseless atomic engine flying over Germany toward Berlin carrying a "long coffin-shaped box which contained the three atomic bombs, the new bombs that would continue to explode indefinitely and which no one so far had ever seen in action. Hitherto carolinum, their essential substance, had been tested only in almost infinitesimal quantities within steel chambers imbedded in lead." In 1945 this atomic bomb became a reality. Its production in so brief a period of time has been styled "the greatest technological triumph of our time." On July 16, 1945, the first great atomic explosion created by man blasted the desert of New Mexico. The atomic bomb was ready for military use.[7]

The Hiroshima-type bomb was only the beginning in atomic weapons. During the years immediately after World War II the destructiveness of the atom bomb was greatly increased. In the United States a Super A-bomb was developed which was reported to be approximately six times as powerful as the weapon used at the end of World War II. Experiments were also being conducted with a view to the production of atomic missiles, atomic artillery shells, and other atomic weapons. For some years the atom bomb was by many believed to be the exclusive secret of the British and United States governments. President Truman said in 1945: "The atomic bomb is too dangerous to be loose in a lawless world. That is why Great Britain and the United States, who have the secret of its production, do not intend to reveal the secret until means have been found to control the bomb so as to protect ourselves and the rest of the world from the danger of total destruction." But in 1949 it was learned that the Russians had exploded an atomic bomb.

This knowledge and the threat of war caused President Truman, in 1950, to authorize the construction of an even more powerful bomb, the hydrogen or H-bomb. Whereas the older type bomb gets its energy from the splitting or fission of the large atoms of such heavy elements as uranium and plutonium, the newer bomb derives its greater energy from the fusion of the small atoms of such light elements as hydrogen. Although it was generally believed that the Russians, too, were working on an H-bomb, the announcement by the Soviet government in August, 1953, that it had tested "one of a variety of hydrogen bombs," and that the experiment had produced an explosion of "great strength," came as a shock.[8] Subsequently, the United States government announced that

---

[7] For the use of the atom bomb in World War II see Chapter 30.
[8] Most experts were of the opinion that it was a device rather than a bomb. A device becomes a bomb when it is put into a casing that can be dropped from an airplane. Since more elements than hydrogen are employed in a fusion device, the name "hydrogen bomb" is a misnomer. Scientists use the term "thermonuclear" to cover all varieties of fusion devices.

in the summer of 1951 a test amount of hydrogen material had been exploded at Eniwetok through the use of a fission bomb as trigger; furthermore, that in November, 1952, a fusion device was carried by boat to a Pacific island that was $\frac{1}{2}$ mile by three miles. This device, rated at 200 to 400 times the power of the Hiroshima bomb, obliterated the island. Scientists have calculated that a fair-sized H-bomb can blast to death every living creature in an area of three hundred square miles and burn everything in an area of twelve hundred square miles.

Unfortunately, during the early period of experimentation the major effort in the study of the atom was concentrated on its possibilities for destruction. Progress toward putting nuclear energy usefully to work has been extremely slow. In the field of medicine radioactive isotopes have been used for helpful treatments, notably against cancer. Radioactive phosphorus has proved to be an aid in surgery for brain tumors. The phosphorus when injected into the blood is absorbed by the tumor about a hundred times as fast as by the normal brain tissue. Thus the surgeon with the help of a small radioactive detector can tell exactly when he has removed all the malignant cells. The atom also has great possibilities as a source of power for peacetime activities, more particularly power for turning the wheels of industry and agriculture. Nuclear scientists have calculated that a single pound of fissionable uranium or plutonium measuring slightly more than a cubic inch contains ten million kilowatt hours or thirteen million horsepower hours of available energy. In terms of horsepower the single pound would produce as much as a 13,000-horsepower engine working twenty-four hours a day for forty-two days or as a 100-horsepower automobile engine working continuously for fifteen years. A piece of uranium or plutonium the size of a grapefruit could supply electric light for New York City for an entire week.

CHAPTER SEVENTEEN

The Origins of the First World War

THROUGHOUT the seventeenth and eighteenth centuries Europe had been racked by long and bloody wars, but the nineteenth century was comparatively an era of peace. After the defeat of Napoleon in 1815 there was no widespread war until 1914. The most natural question is: why, after a long period of peace, did World War I break out in 1914? The answer is not a simple one. Many factors contributed toward bringing about the event. In describing the causes that produced the disaster it is necessary to distinguish between the immediate causes, that is, the series of events which precipitated the war, and the fundamental causes which go back indefinitely into European history. Among the deeper causes of the war one must include (1) the system of European alliances which took form during the decades preceding 1914; (2) the armament race; (3) nationalism; (4) imperialism and economic rivalry.

ALLIANCES DIVIDE EUROPE INTO TWO HOSTILE CAMPS

The system of European alliances which took form during the decades preceding 1914 was started by Bismarck. After achieving a political unity of the German states through victory in a series of wars, the Iron Chancellor desired peace and the assurance that the *status quo* would not be disturbed. Germany needed time to assimilate Alsace-Lorraine, to develop her industrial facilities, and generally to consolidate the new state. But Bismarck had created a formidable enemy. Much as he tried to turn their interests in other directions, the French refused to forget Alsace-Lorraine; in fact, certain French circles were active in keeping the idea of regaining the lost provinces in the fore-ground.

Bismarck, who keenly realized that the French would embrace the first possible opportunity to regain the provinces, at once took steps to prevent such a move. He was fairly certain that France alone would not attack Germany. What he feared was a coalition against Germany. Consequently he bent his efforts toward the isolation of France and toward binding to Germany the powers he thought might join France. The British were not included in this category, for he felt that colonial rivalry would stand in the way of any rapprochement between France and Britain. In 1872 he was instrumental in forming the Dreikaiser-bund (League of Three Emperors), a kind of Holy Alliance composed of the emperors of Germany, Russia, and Austria to preserve peace and maintain the *status quo*.

For three years the Emperor's League was kept alive by annual meetings of the august rulers, but after 1875 relations between Russia and Austria-Hungary became more and more strained. The latter's efforts to regain the prestige she had lost in the Austro-Prussian war (1866) by extending her sway over the Balkans conflicted with Russian ambitions in the same region. When this League was not renewed in 1878, Bismarck was compelled to choose between Russia and Austria. He chose Austria. In 1879 he concluded with Austria-Hungary a secret treaty which is known as the Dual Alliance. Its basic provisions were that if "one of the two empires be attacked by Russia, the High Con-tracting Parties are bound to come to the assistance of the other with the whole war-strength of their empires, and accordingly only to con-clude peace together and upon mutual agreement." If either power were attacked by a power other than Russia the other signatory was pledged to benevolent neutrality. This alliance remained the cornerstone of both German and Austro-Hungarian foreign policy for almost forty years.

But Bismarck did not stop with the Dual Alliance. Despite the fact that he had entered into a protective alliance against Russia, he wished to keep that country from moving into the French camp. In 1881 he managed to revive the Dreikaiserbund; and when it again shattered on the rocks of Austro-Russian rivalry, he concluded a secret treaty with Russia in 1887, known as the Reinsurance Treaty. By this treaty Bis-marck in return for a promise to support Russian interests in the Bal-kans reinsured himself against any danger on his eastern frontier in case France should attack. In other words, Russia promised not to join France if the latter were to make war on Germany. But the treaty in no way conflicted with his obligation to protect Austria in case of a Russian attack. Bismarck was also careful to keep his relations with

Britain on a friendly basis by repeated offers of an alliance. "I see in England," he said, "an old and traditional ally. . . . No differences exist between England and Germany. . . . It would be the height of folly to make an enemy of England."

In the meantime Bismarck had further strengthened Germany's position by concluding the Triple Alliance (1882) with Austria and Italy. He did not hold Italy in high regard as a military power but still thought it best to tie her to the German chariot. He could always use another ally to make French *revanche* more remote. Neither were the Austrians enthusiastic about an Italian alliance, but they needed additional help, for Germany would probably be occupied with France in case of war. The Italians, for their part, cherished little love for the Germans and less for the Austro-Hungarians. Not only had the latter been an obstacle in the path toward Italian unification but most of the territory which the Italians regarded as Italia irredenta was part of the Habsburg empire. But Italy standing alone needed allies. Thus it was clearly a marriage of interest, not affection.

What caused the Italians to agree to it was the French seizure in 1881 of Tunis, which Italy had marked as her own. In Rome the feeling against France ran high, and Bismarck quickly made the most of the opportunity. The treaty, signed at Vienna on May 20, 1882, was defensive in character. It neither supplanted nor modified the Austro-German treaty of 1879; in fact, the existence of this treaty was unknown to the Italians. In case Italy should without provocation be attacked by France, the other two parties would come to her aid. Italy, in turn, would aid Germany in case of a French attack. If one of the parties were attacked by two or more great powers the other signatories were to come to its aid. At Italy's request each of the parties signed an additional declaration stating that the treaty could in no case be regarded as directed against Great Britain. Although the existence of the treaty soon became general knowledge, its terms were not divulged until the collapse of the Central Powers in World War I. In 1883 Rumania attached herself to the powers forming the Triple Alliance, and later Turkey was drawn into the same orbit. In 1903 Germany gained from the sultan's government the concession to build a railway line connecting Constantinople with Bagdad.

So long as Bismarck remained chancellor, France was successfully isolated; but after his retirement it did not take the young kaiser long to undo much of Bismarck's work and to create fear and suspicion. When the question of the renewal of the Reinsurance Treaty came up, General Caprivi, the new chancellor, together with other members of the Foreign Office, prevailed upon William II to let the treaty lapse. And this despite the loud protests of Bismarck from his retirement.

It is questionable whether even so skilled a diplomatist as he could have held Russia if he had remained in power, for the relations of the tsar's government with France had been growing friendlier and French gold had been flowing into Russia. On the other hand, it is obvious that the German government's refusal to renew the treaty compelled the Russians to change their foreign policy.

The result of this change was that France and Russia gradually drew closer together. When the French made overtures to the Russians they did not at once respond. They had no desire to become involved in a war for the recovery of Alsace-Lorraine, and besides, the tsar was suspicious of French republicanism. In the end the Russian need of French gold overcame the scruples. In 1891 through a series of letters between French and Russian ministers an entente, a sort of vague friendship without a specific agreement, was created. This was followed on December 31, 1893, by the signing of a military convention. Article One stated that if France were attacked by Germany, or by Italy supported by Germany, Russia would employ all her forces to attack Germany; if Russia were attacked by Germany, or by Austria supported by Germany, France would employ all her forces to combat Germany. Although the fact that a treaty existed between the two countries was announced as early as 1895, the terms were not revealed until 1918. In justice to William II it must be stated that he suggested a fusion of the two alliances into a Continental League for the preservation of peace; but as the French refused to entertain the idea of permanently losing Alsace-Lorraine, nothing came of the suggestion.

The conclusion of an alliance between France and Russia left the British diplomatically isolated. They now had to decide which alliance they would join. Although British imperialism clashed with both French and Russian ambitions in a number of regions, Germany's industrial development loomed as a greater threat. At first France and Russia failed to respond to British suggestions for an alliance. Both still saw Britain as their hereditary foe. Consequently Britain concluded an alliance with Japan. The alliance was directed against Russia. While Britain believed Russia to be threatening India, the Japanese were bitter over their expulsion from the Chinese mainland by the Russians. On January 30, 1902, the two powers signed a defensive alliance which was a startling innovation. For the first time a great European power had concluded an agreement with an Asiatic power on terms of equality.

Two years later the British and French composed their differences and created the Anglo-French Entente Cordiale. On April 8, 1904, they signed a series of conventions which settled a number of long-standing disputes regarding colonial questions such as Newfoundland fisheries, Siam, Madagascar and other subjects. The most important convention was that which recognized Britain's position in Egypt in return for granting France a free hand in Morocco. After Russia's defeat in the Russo-Japanese War (1904–1905) convinced the British that they had nothing to fear from the tsarist empire, relations between the two gradually improved, culminating in the agreement of 1907 which transformed the Dual Entente into the Triple Entente. In 1910 Japan definitely ranged herself on the side of the Triple Entente by coming to an understanding with Russia.

THE ARMAMENT RACE

After the formation of the Triple Entente Europe found herself divided into two hostile alliances. The purpose of the alliances had been security, but they had actually heightened the insecurity instead of dissipating it. Each group began to fear that the other would overwhelm it. While France viewed the Triple Alliance as a means of preventing her rightful recovery of Alsace-Lorraine, the Germans saw in the Triple Entente an attempt to keep them from achieving their "place in the sun." All this engendered fears, distrust, and suspicions which in turn gave rise to an armament race. The European states vied with one another in strengthening their armies and navies. All the large states except Great Britain remodeled their armies along Prussian lines and spent huge sums on military equipment; so much, in fact, that many of the governments lacked the necessary funds to deal with domestic problems. Nevertheless, no nation dared withdraw from the race for fear of being annihilated by the others.

A special phase of the race was the naval contest between Great Britain and Germany. Bismarck had during the first years after German unification built a modest navy without causing Anglo-German friction, but William II had more ambitious plans. He was not satisfied with having the strongest army in Europe; he also wanted a large navy. During the first years his program of naval expansion did not excite much apprehension in Britain; but as the general alienation between the two countries developed, special attention was focused on naval matters. The unfolding of the successive naval programs convinced many Englishmen that the Germans were intent upon wrenching from them the dominion of the sea. To the British this supremacy was necessary because Great Britain was an Asiatic, African, Australian, and North American as well as European power. What was more, naval supremacy was essential to an island power dependent upon imported food and sea-borne trade. Thus the British saw themselves compelled by the German competition to spend large sums in maintaining their naval supremacy.

William II took great pains to deny that he had any aggressive designs. He was, it is true, at heart a peaceful and timid man, even to the extent that certain Frenchmen referred to him as Guillaume le Timide. But he frequently pretended to be other than he truly was. In this respect he was his own worst enemy. Winston Churchill later said that the kaiser wanted only to "strut about and pose and rattle the undrawn sword. All he wished was to feel like Napoleon and be like him without having had to fight his battles." Carried away by his liking for histrionics, William not only staged military and naval parades but in his flamboyant speeches made statements which nourished British misgivings. He made such provocative declarations as "We Germans fear God, and nothing else in the world"; "The trident must be in our fist"; and "Our future lies upon the water." "The Ocean," he said, "is indispensable for Germany's greatness, but the ocean also reminds us that neither on it nor across it in the distance can any great decision be again consummated without Germany and the German emperor."

A number of European leaders who saw that the race would end in war proposed plans for curbing the growth of armaments. Notable among these was the plan of Nicholas II, who in 1898 instructed his foreign minister to invite all powers to meet in a conference to discuss reduction. Although the invitation was received coldly, he sent out a second letter in January, 1899. This time twenty-six powers accepted the invitation to meet at The Hague. For more than ten weeks the First Hague Conference discussed the question but achieved little beyond general agreement that "the limitation of the military charges which at present oppress the world is greatly to be desired." The only concrete achievements were the establishment of a permanent court of international justice, the formulation of certain laws for the conduct of war, and the founding of a permanent court of arbitration at The Hague to which nations could refer their grievances. The Second Hague Conference, which met in 1907, was no more successful.

Meanwhile the frenzied competition continued. In 1912 Austria-Hungary called more recruits to the colors, and Russia increased both the length of enlistment and the size of her army. The next year France added to the size of her army by extending the period of military service from two to three years. The increase of the armed strength of both France and Russia seriously alarmed the German government and caused it to raise its standing army to almost 800,000 men. Thus the greater states of Europe, organized in two groups, faced each other in full panoply. Even the small nations began arming because they felt that a European war was impending. All this moved Count Witte, the Russian statesman, to say, "When and how will it all end? . . . war is the only issue I can perceive."

THE DIVISIVE FORCE OF NATIONALISM

Much friction was also generated by the growth of nationalism, particularly of that phase which is known as self-determination. While this spirit had been instrumental in the formation of a number of new states, including Germany and Italy, its effect in some of the states was a disintegrating one. It excited in submerged national groups the desire to create national states of their own or to join their fellow nationals in a state beyond the borders of the one in which they were living. Many states regarded certain areas in other states as "irredentas," i.e., as areas which should rightfully be a part of their respective states because they were inhabited by fellow nationals. These states kept up a more or less intensive propaganda, with the result that a whole swarm of different irredentisms were working to undermine the binational or multinational states.

The divisive effect of the nationalist spirit was particularly evident in the Balkans. During the nineteenth century it had pretty well disrupted the Ottoman Empire and was now undermining the Austro-Hungarian state. Russia and Rumania were able to bridle their greed for the Habsburg possessions, but Serbia made no secret of her impatience to annex the five million Serbs in the Austrian Empire. Serbia had the support of Russia, which had previously helped to weaken the Ottoman Empire and was endeavoring to hasten the disruption of Austria-Hungary. On the other hand, the nationalist activities and ambitions in Austria-Hungary were frowned on by the German government, which sought to keep Austria strong and also endeavored to prevent the expulsion of the Turk from Europe. But the nationalist strivings continued to demand fulfillment.

IMPERIALISM AND ECONOMIC RIVALRIES

The most prolific source of international discord was imperialism and economic rivalry. Almost every alliance and alignment of European powers was more or less directly the result of imperialist policies and ambitions. The desire of Germany, for instance, to dominate the Near East and of Austria to extend its influence in the Balkans was a major factor in Germany's foreign policy. Again, a far-reaching imperialist bargain was the basis of the entente between France and England in 1904, and the same may be said of the agreement between Great Britain and Russia. Except for imperialism there would have been little armed conflict from the close of the Franco-Prussian War to 1914. The many local wars of this period were due almost entirely to imperialism. Among others one might list the British wars in the Sudan, in Burma,

Afghanistan, and South Africa; the French wars in Africa, Madagascar, and Cochin China; the Italian campaigns in Abyssinia and Tripolitania; and the Japanese war with China. Moreover, the great powers were not only fighting the natives of backward regions but they were constantly bickering among themselves over partitions of territory, spheres of influence, and trade facilities in Asia and Africa. On many occasions before 1914 it appeared as if the ruthless competition for raw materials and markets would precipitate a major war.

In 1901 a Chinese living in Britain wrote:

Competition for markets bids fair to be a more fruitful cause of war than was ever in the past the ambition of princes or the bigotry of priests. The people of Europe fling themselves, like hungry beasts of prey, on every yet unexploited quarter of the globe. Hitherto they have confined their acts of spoliation to those whom they regard as outside their own pale. But always, while they divide the spoil, they watch one another with a jealous eye; and sooner or later, when there is nothing left to divide, they will fall upon one another. That is the real meaning of your armaments; you must devour or be devoured. And it is precisely those trade relations which it was thought would knit you in the bonds of peace, which, by making every one of you cut-throat rivals of the others, have brought you within reasonable distance of a general war of extermination.[1]

Economic rivalry was particularly bitter between Great Britain and Germany. For some years after 1870 the Germans offered Great Britain little competition because their manufactures were generally regarded as *billig und schlecht* (cheap and bad). But after a slow start Germany developed at an unprecedented rate into an industrial and commercial power. By the early years of the twentieth century the German Empire had left France far behind as an industrial nation and was beginning to outstrip England in the race for economic leadership in Europe. German commerce reached every nook and corner of the globe, and German merchant ships floated on every sea. The tremendous progress of Germany called forth the envy of her neighbors. In England particularly the challenge caused fear, dissatisfaction, and jealousy. In a book which appeared just a few weeks before the outbreak of the war H. G. Wells stated:

We in Great Britain are now intensely jealous of Germany not only because the Germans outnumber us and have a much larger and more diversified country than ours, and lie in the very heart and body of Europe, but because in the last hundred years, while we have fed on platitudes and vanity, they have had the energy and humility to develop a splendid system of national educa-

[1] *Saturday Review*, vol. 91 (1901), p. 78.

tion, to toil at science and art and literature, to develop social organization, to master and better our methods of business and industry, and to clamber above us in the scale of civilization.[2]

The rivalry was equally bitter in the field of colonial activity. After the unification of Germany Bismarck had for a time discouraged the acquisition of colonies; but as the industry and commerce of Germany developed, the demand for colonies grew more insistent in many German circles. Even Bismarck made concessions to these demands in the latter years of his chancellorship by permitting the acquisition of some islands in the Pacific and some unprofitable colonies in Central Africa. After the accession of William II in 1888 the government took up in earnest the search for undeveloped territories. They soon discovered, however, that most of the desirable portions of the earth had been claimed by other nations. Consequently every attempt to acquire even a coaling station resulted in a clash with another imperialist power and most frequently with the British, who felt that their interests were menaced by any nation which attempted to take over lands or islands adjacent to theirs. In 1912 an Australian wrote regarding Anglo-German relations:

The attitude of England towards Germany in such a position is not altogether creditable. England has treated herself well in the matter of territory, yet if it is announced that Germany has acquired territory in the South Pacific or in the South of Africa or the West Coast of Africa, a howl arises from the jingo party that Germany is acquiring a strategic point which will command a British colony or trade route. It is idle for such arguments to be used against the progress of an expanding nation.[3]

The Germans, for their part, were most untactful in their efforts to acquire colonies. At the least opposition they would complain, though not always unjustly, that the other nations were keeping them from achieving their rightful "place in the sun." They would state that other countries were envious of their rapid progress and some Germans even threatened to employ force to achieve their goal. Thus the German Crown Prince wrote in 1913, "It is only by relying on our good German sword that we can hope to conquer that place in the sun which rightly belongs to us and which no one will yield to us voluntarily." A manifesto of the German Navy League read in part, "We need a fleet strong enough not only to protect the colonies we now have, but to bring about the acquisition of others." The result was that Germany created much ill will among the European nations but reaped only a meager harvest of colonies.

[2] *An Englishman Looks at the World* (1914), pp. 36–37.
[3] *Round Table*, vol. 2 (1912), pp. 730–731.

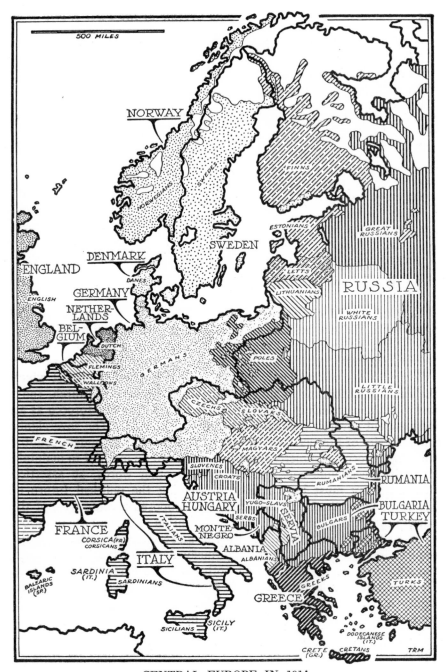

CENTRAL EUROPE IN 1914

CRISES PRECEDING WORLD WAR I

Besides the deeper forces that were inevitably working for war, a series of crises hastened its coming and finally caused its outbreak. Two developed over French attempts to establish a protectorate over Morocco, which had strategic as well as economic importance since it flanks the southern shore of the Mediterranean and extends down the western coast of Africa. When France and Great Britain arrived at an understanding regarding their possessions and spheres of influence in North Africa (1904), the French agreed that the British were to have a free hand in Egypt, and in return were given freedom of action in Morocco. The French foreign minister then proceeded to obtain the consent of both Italy and Spain to France's control of Morocco. But Germany, which like the other nations had signed the Madrid Convention of 1881 relating to Morocco, was not consulted. The French Foreign Office did not even inform the Germans that agreements had been concluded.

German official circles, when they realized the full import of the agreements, did not hesitate to express their dissatisfaction. They regarded the action of the French both as a slight and as a threat to German interests. As the German diplomatic agent in Morocco put it, "We are being systematically set aside." The method of protest which the kaiser adopted was to land at Tangier in Morocco in March, 1905, and to make a speech in which he greeted the sultan of Morocco as an independent sovereign. Among other things he said, "The sovereignty and integrity of Morocco will be maintained. In an independent country such as Morocco, commerce must be free. I will do my best to maintain its politico-economic equality." It was, in other words, an assertion that Germany must have a part in shaping the political future of Morocco. Later the German government proposed a conference of the powers that had signed the Madrid Convention to discuss the question.

In Britain as well as in France the kaiser's speech, and even the request for a conference, were vigorously denounced; however, when the situation became threatening both countries agreed to a meeting. Held at Algeciras in June, 1906, it theoretically recognized the sovereignty and independence of the sultan. In reality France and Spain were given a large measure of control over Morocco in that they received permission to police the coast towns and to establish a state bank. Thus France emerged from the conference with its hold on Morocco strengthened.

Hardly had this crisis passed when a new one strained the relations between Russia and Austria-Hungary. In October, 1908, the Austrian government proclaimed the annexation of Bosnia-Herzegovina without consulting the other signatories of the treaty of Berlin (1878) which had put the provinces under Austrian administration although they nominally remained a part of the Turkish Empire. The reason the Austro-Hungarian government annexed them was that the Young Turk movement was trying to breathe new life into the old Ottoman Empire. The Habsburgs feared that if the Turkish government became stronger it would contest Austrian administration of the provinces. Nor were the Austrians and the Turks the only ones who wanted these provinces. The Serbs hoped by annexing them to double the population of their state and also to acquire an outlet to the sea. Hence the annexation was a severe blow to the Serbs who supported the Greater Serbia movement. When the news was published great crowds gathered in the streets of Belgrade, the Serb capital, smashed the windows of the Austrian embassy, burned the Austrian flag, and shouted, "Down with Austria."

If the Serbs had stood alone, the danger would not have been so great. As it was they had the support of Russia for their plans. The Russians protested that since the annexation violated the treaty of Berlin (1878) the question should be laid before a European congress. Both France and Britain also protested. The Austrian government was willing that a congress should be held, but insisted that the annexation of the provinces must first be considered an acknowledged fact. In Germany the kaiser was deeply hurt because the Austrian government had not informed him of the proposed annexation in advance, but his ministers soon persuaded him to give his ally unqualified support. For a time the situation was tense, but calmer counsel gradually prevailed. The Russian leaders realized that their country had not recovered sufficiently from the disastrous defeat of the Russo-Japanese War (1904–1905) to wage war alone and the French and British were unwilling to bear the brunt of the fighting for fulfillment of Serbian and Russian plans. The upshot was that Russia retreated and the crisis passed. The powers that had signed the treaty of Berlin recognized the annexation, Serbian protests were ignored, and Turkey was satisfied with a money payment.

The question "Will there be war?" was asked again in 1911 when a second crisis developed over Morocco. The settlement at Algeciras in 1906 had pleased neither side. Nor had there been any improvement in the internal condition of Morocco. The police force established by France and Spain failed to restore order, and the sultan's finances remained chaotic. In the summer of 1911 the French marched an army into the interior to occupy Fez, the capital, on the ground that the sultan was unable adequately to protect the lives of foreigners. The German government, interpreting the move as a step toward complete control of Morocco, countered by sending the gunboat *Panther* to the port of Agadir "to help and protect German subjects and clients in those regions." Like the kaiser's speech in 1905, the gunboat incident precipitated a crisis. This time the French, supported by the British, resolved not to yield. Just when it seemed that war was inevitable, the Germans gave way. Later a Franco-German agreement provided for German consent to the occupation of Morocco by France and Spain in return for a section of the French Congo.

THE OUTBREAK OF WAR

By the year 1913 the situation was critical. Passions were rising, nerves were tense, and the alliances were tightening. The eminent author Georg Brandes wrote in this year, "A great European war would be an overwhelming tragedy for all concerned. Yet in recent years many people have come to look upon such a war as inevitable, and some even seem naively confident that it would usher in a reign of justice. . . . Statistics showing war's absurdity are of little use. They convince only those who know how to think." [4] Near the end of the year the French envoy to Austria wrote home, "The feeling that the nations are moving towards a conflict urged by an irresistible force grows from day to day." Early in 1914 a St. Petersburg newspaper published an article entitled "Russia is ready; France must be ready too." Colonel House, who was sent to Europe by President Wilson in May, 1914, to observe conditions, was greatly disturbed by what he saw. "The situation is extraordinary," he reported; "it is militarism run stark mad. . . . It only needs a spark to set the whole thing off."

The "incident" that precipitated the outbreak of war was the murder on June 28, 1914, of the Archduke Francis Ferdinand and his wife in the streets of Sarajevo, the capital of Bosnia. The instigators of the crime were members of the Serbian Black Hand, a Pan-Serbian society whose motto was "Union or Death." Its leading spirit was Colonel Dimitrievich who held the position of chief of the intelligence section of the Serbian general staff. When it was announced that the archduke would visit Sarajevo the society decided to assassinate him. Three Bosnian youths were provided with revolvers and bombs by assistants of Dimitrievich in Belgrade and were then smuggled across the frontier into Bosnia. Several members of the Serbian cabinet, including the prime minister, were aware of the plot and had they wished to do so they could easily have prevented the crime.

The Black Hand's reason for removing Francis Ferdinand from the scene was his desire to keep Bosnia-Herzegovina in the Habsburg em-

---

[4] Brandes, *The World at War* (1917), p. 34.

pire. He aimed to end the quarrels which were weakening the monarchy, to convince the discontented national groups that each one could find salvation in its own way within the empire. One part of his plan called for the conversion of the Dual Monarchy into a triple monarchy through the creation of a Slavonic state which would embrace about 7 million people. He had already gained the support of a large number of Serbs for his plan. Its success, the Pan-Serbs feared, would put an end to the dream of a Greater Serbia.

On the morning of June 28 the archduke and his consort arrived in Sarajevo and were driven along the narrow and crooked streets of the older section. Although large crowds had gathered and there were several army corps in the vicinity, nothing was done to provide the protection customary for royal visits. As the archduke's automobile proceeded toward the city hall for a welcome by the mayor one of the would-be assassins hurled a bomb which missed its mark, but wounded several persons. Even after this incident nothing was done to give the archduke adequate protection. As the party was returning from the city hall two shots were fired which mortally wounded both the archduke and the archduchess. How the Pan-Serbs felt about the assassination is illustrated by Cettinje, the Serb minister, who exclaimed upon receiving the news, "This cartridge will bring liberty to the whole Serb race."

While Europe mourned the death of the archduke, the Austro-Hungarian government was faced with the problem not only of punishing the murderers but also of retaining control of its people. Not many hours after the assassination the chief of the military staff stated that the Dual Monarchy must "choose between allowing itself to be strangled and making a last effort to prevent its destruction." It did not take the Austrian officials long to arrive at a decision. On June 29 Count Berchtold, the foreign minister, told the chief of staff that the time had come for settling the Serbian question once for all. Soon thereafter the Austrian emperor himself in explaining the situation to William II of Germany said, "Serbia is to be eliminated as a political factor in the Balkans."

What the Austrian government wanted in order to crush the Serbs was a local war, but it could not embark on one without German support. Bismarck had refused to become involved in the conflict over the Near East, declaring that "the whole Balkan question is not worth the bones of a single Pomeranian grenadier." But for the kaiser it was another matter. That his Austrian ally should remain strong was essential to his plans. If the progress of Serb nationalism was not stopped, there was great danger that the Austrian Empire would be divided bit by bit and cease to be a great power. Hence he could not afford to refuse his support. He felt that the struggle would be localized because

Russia was not prepared for war and would back down as it had on previous occasions.

Having received a promise of "wholehearted support," the Austrian Crown Council decided to make the most of it. It drew up an ultimatum couched in terms which were believed to be unacceptable to the Serbs. What it demanded, among other things, was the suppression of anti-Austrian publications, anti-Austrian societies, and anti-Austrian propaganda. Finally, it stipulated that Austrian officials be permitted to participate in the suppression of anti-Austrian propaganda in Serbia and in the proceedings against the authors of the Sarajevo crime. This ultimatum was not submitted to the German Government for approval or modification; it was sent at once to Serbia with a forty-eight hour limit for acceptance. When the terms became known in other countries, it was generally believed that the ultimatum meant war. But to the general amazement of the Austrians and Germans the Serbs accepted all the demands but two and even offered to enter into discussions regarding these. When William II heard of the abject Serbian submission he exclaimed, "A brilliant diplomatic triumph; no excuse for war; no need to mobilize."

The kaiser's optimism was short lived. Acceptance of most of the points in the ultimatum by the Serbian government did not satisfy the ministers of the Dual Monarchy. They were still determined to put an end to Serbia's intrigues once for all. After declaring the Serbian reply to be unsatisfactory, the Austrian government declared war on July 28. But the Russian government was no less resolved to honor its promises to Serbia. To the military party the war loomed as an opportunity to gain the long-coveted prize, Constantinople. Hence when Austria's declaration of war became known in Petrograd mobilization in the south was ordered at once.

Then came the final stage of the crisis. The succeeding days saw both the German and the British representatives make feverish attempts to prevent the war from spreading. "We are ready, to be sure," the German chancellor wired the Austrian government, "to fulfill our obligations as an ally but must refuse to allow ourselves to be drawn by Vienna into world conflagration frivolously and in disregard of our advice." At the same time Sir Edward Grey, the British foreign secretary, was trying his utmost to prevent a general mobilization in Russia, a move which he knew would cause Germany to declare war. Both he and the kaiser hoped that Nicholas II would be firm in his opposition to general mobilization. But the tsar lacked the moral courage. He did, it is true, hold out against his ministers for several hours, but finally gave his consent (July 29). Nicholas took the fatal step without consulting the French, although French and Russian experts understood that mobilization was equivalent to a declaration of war. When he received a conciliatory telegram from the kaiser several hours later, he tried to countermand the order but it was too late.

The news of the Russian mobilization caused the German government to act immediately. Determined not to sacrifice the advantage of being able to strike rapidly, it demanded a cessation of Russian mobilization within twelve hours under threat of war. The Russian government did not even take the trouble to answer the ultimatum. Before the expiration of the time limit Russian troops crossed the frontier into East Prussia. Germany at once declared war (August 1). On the previous day Germany had also dispatched an ultimatum to France asking whether that country would remain neutral in case of war between Russia and Germany. When the French government replied that it would consult its own interest, Germany declared war on France (August 3). Thus four of the six great powers were at war, with only Britain and Italy as nonbelligerents.

The event that caused the British to enter the fray was the German invasion of Belgium. Although Grey had promised France naval aid, he could do nothing until the British had declared war. But he did not have to wait long for the event which inflamed public opinion. On August 2 the German government requested permission from the Belgian government to march through Belgium, promising to make full reparation for all damages. The Belgian government replied that the king of Prussia had guaranteed the independence of Belgium in 1870 and that the Belgian army would offer the most determined resistance to any attempt to violate this agreement. This did not deter the Germans. During the early hours of August 4 their troops crossed the border. On the same day the British parliament declared war on Germany. Italy did not, however, join Germany and Austria-Hungary. The Italian government decided to remain neutral, claiming that its obligations to the Triple Alliance did not include support in a war of aggression. Thus the war began with Germany and Austria-Hungary (known as the Central Powers) on the one side and Britain, France, Russia, Belgium, Serbia, and Montenegro (the Allies) on the other. Within a few weeks Japan threw in her lot with the Allies, and Turkey joined the Central Powers.

The storm clouds which had hovered over Europe for some time had finally burst. Each side at once vigorously denounced the other as being responsible for the war. For a time there was a tendency in neutral and Allied countries to saddle the Central Powers with all the blame. Thus one historian wrote, "It is now fairly evident that the present war is but a violent phase in the unfolding of a grandiose idea — the subjugation of Europe by the Teuton — which was being steadily realized ever since the close of the Franco-German campaign of 1870." A "war-guilt clause" which compelled the Germans to accept the responsibility for the war was even included in the treaty at the end of the war. But when calmer minds carefully sifted the evidence after the war's end, the idea that the Central Powers were solely responsible was revised. Historians reached the conclusion that all countries were more or less to blame. "It was not the kaiser or any other 'war criminal' who caused the war," a British historian wrote as early as 1920, "but the millions of men and women who read the German, English, and French papers, believed what those papers told them to believe, and desired what those papers told them to desire." [5] No nation wanted a general European war. It was, in the words of Lloyd George, "something into which they glided, or rather staggered and stumbled." The power which was perhaps most responsible for the immediate origin of the war was Austria. Its plan to crush Serbia in a localized war was both short-sighted and dangerous. The Russian government was also responsible to a greater degree than the other powers. While British and German representatives were making a desperate last effort to prevent the war from becoming a general European conflict, the Russian mobilization precipitated it.

[5] Leonard Woolf, *Economic Imperialism* (1920), p. 10.

CHAPTER EIGHTEEN

The First World War

THE DRIVE THROUGH BELGIUM AT the outbreak of the war each side enjoyed certain advantages. For the Allies the most potent weapon was the British navy. During the years before 1914 the British, spurred on by the German naval program, had strengthened their navy and raised it to a point of efficiency unprecedented in history. When the strength of the French and Russian navies was added to it, the combination was so formidable as to overshadow the German navy, although the latter was the second largest in the world.

On land the advantage was with the Germans. They had not only the most efficient striking force in the world but also a large reserve of young male citizens. Their reservoir of man power was larger than any other excepting that of Russia. Moreover, much of the best brains of Germany had long been devoted to military science. The Austrian army, though it was outstanding for its siege artillery, did not approach the caliber of the German military machine. Since it was composed of many nationalities, it suffered from a lack of homogeneity and a consequent danger of defection and mutiny. The army which ranked second to the German was the French, but it was weak in reserves because the population was about twenty-five millions less than Germany's. France did, however, have a large colonial population from which it could recruit men. Russia had the largest number of trained men. The Russian army was almost twice as large as that of Germany, but its effectiveness was much lower. As for the British army, it was well equipped and well trained but small. Together with its reserves it numbered less than half a million, of which about one third were ready for immediate service.

Inferiority in numbers made the German general staff all the more determined to utilize its striking power to the fullest extent and hence to drive through Belgium with Paris as the goal. This plan was not a new one. It is ascribed to Count Alfred von Schlieffen, who was chief of the German general staff from 1891 to 1905. Von Schlieffen, seeing that the alliance between France and Russia made a war on two fronts a certainty for Germany, planned for a quick decisive victory over France before the slow-moving Russian army could get under way. But the heavily fortified frontier between France and Germany presented a formidable, if not insuperable, obstacle, and von Schlieffen consequently advocated a march through Belgium, hoping to achieve a rapid break-through there. The plan was to be carried out in a few weeks. Having reached Paris the Germans would dictate peace terms to France before Britain could make her power felt. Next the German might would be turned toward the east, where meanwhile delaying strategy aided by Austrian arms would suffice. The French had known of this plan for almost a decade and in 1913 a British writer had stated, "The violation of Belgium by Germany may be regarded as a practical certainty in the event of war." [1]

It was the German military timetable that frustrated the last-minute efforts of Allied statesmen to prevent the war. The general staff had made careful preparations, down to the last shoelace, to demolish the French with one quick blow. They now determined not to lose the initiative. To draw as many French troops as possible to the south, German cavalry crossed the frontier between Luxembourg and Switzerland on the night of August 1–2. The main attack, however, was directed through Luxembourg and Belgium. Early on the 4th the advance guard began the invasion of Belgium. The Belgian army, with a maximum strength of about 210,000, gallantly met the first shock, but the German forces advanced as far as Liége on that day. There the Belgians had built a ring of twelve forts constructed of steel and concrete, which they hoped would stop the Germans. But siege howitzers of a new type soon demonstrated that the best forts cannot withstand a bombardment of armor-piercing explosive shells. The first day one and the next day three of the forts were reduced to masses of wreckage. By August 15 all the forts had been pounded into submission. Five days later the Germans entered Brussels and on the same day began bombarding the ring of fortresses at Namur. With previous experience as a guide, the great 42-centimeter howitzers needed even less time to demolish these. The fall of this ring of fortresses marked the end of Belgian resistance.

Although the delay secured by the brave Belgian army was only a matter of days, it did give the Allies some time to bring their armies

[1] *Round Table*, vol. 3 (1913), p. 418.

into position. While the French were moving five armies in line, the British transported all available troops across the Channel. On August 17 the British government officially announced that the army was on the Continent. The first engagement between the Germans and the French took place near Charleroi on August 22, and the next day the British engaged the Germans at Mons. Although both the French and the British fought bravely, they were unable to stop the advance. The heavy losses convinced General Joffre, the Allied commander, that further resistance in so advanced a position would be useless. He therefore ordered a general retreat. The long Allied line fell back until the Germans were within twenty-five miles of Paris and the fall of that city seemed certain. The government left Paris to set up headquarters at Bordeaux.

The time for an offensive had come if Paris was to be saved. During the days of retreat Joffre had actually strengthened his forces by bringing up new units. On the other hand, the Germans had moved farther and farther from their bases of supply. On September 5 Joffre ordered his soldiers to stand firm and to "die in their tracks rather than retreat." Early next day they took the offensive in what is known as the battle of the Marne. In this battle more than two million men were engaged over a period of seven days (September 6–12). The French, fighting with the courage of desperation, drove the Germans back across the river and continued to force them back until they reached the Aisne, where they had previously prepared positions. Students of military tactics have styled the battle as one of the most significant of the war. The German General Falkenhayn asserted that the war was really lost in the battle of the Marne. Its importance lies in the fact that it stopped the German drive on Paris and thereby wrecked the hope for a quick victory over France.

The force of the German drive having spent itself, the war settled down to an indecisive struggle. Trench warfare — the war of positions — replaced the war of movement. In the battle of the Marne both sides had constructed lines of trenches from the Aisne to the Swiss border, and later the length was extended to a distance of some six hundred miles. This was done to seek protection against the machine gun and the quick-firing field gun. In 1915 the multiple-trench system appeared. Second and third line trenches were prepared so that the troops could retreat to them in case they failed to hold the first line. In some places veritable underground towns were built, with first-aid stations, kitchens, and storage rooms, besides sleeping quarters for officers and men. Fighting in trenches was, of course, nothing new; entrenched lines had been a feature of many previous wars. But never before had so many troops held such lines month after month. It was, in the words of one historian, a mode of warfare which doomed millions of men "to watch each other from burrows in the earth a few yards apart, striking to kill now and again as opportunity offered." In between the opposing lines of trenches was the cheerless waste of barbed wire called "no man's land."

THE EASTERN FRONT

In the east the German plan failed as signally as in the west because the Russians moved faster than the Germans had assumed they could. By the middle of August a number of Russian armies were ready to move against the enemy. When the high command realized that the Germans were striking the main blow against France, it decided to invade East Prussia. On August 17 two Russian armies entered that province, one from the east and the other from the south, and pushed the small German force back on Königsberg. Soon much of the province was in Russian hands. At the same time strong Russian forces had also unexpectedly invaded Galicia, had driven back the Austrian armies, and were threatening Lemberg, the provincial capital. Thus the Russians achieved a number of successes, much to the surprise and consternation of the German leaders. Even the French and British hoped that the Russian gains might counterbalance the territorial losses in the west.

But these hopes were soon dispelled. The Germans, smarting under the infamy of having the Russians occupy the province which was the cradle of the Prussian monarchy, decided that East Prussia must be cleared at once. The man chosen as leader for the task was General Paul von Hindenburg, a retired general of sixty-seven who had been in the Prussian army which besieged Paris in 1870 and had been present in the Hall of Mirrors at Versailles when the German Empire was proclaimed. Having for years planned and rehearsed every tactical move in defending that part of the country against invasion, he knew the terrain in which the Russians were operating "as if it were his own garden." It was said that he knew "every road, lane, and cowpath, every lake, pond, and puddle, every forest and field in the district." He was so pre-eminently the right man for the emergency that the kaiser called him out of retirement to take command of the armies in the east. Together with General Ludendorff, his chief of staff, he laid plans for the campaign.

The two advancing Russian armies, one commanded by Rennenkampf and the other by Samsonov, obligingly walked into the trap prepared for them. Eager to capture Königsberg and contemptuous of the opposition the Germans had offered, they threw caution to the winds.

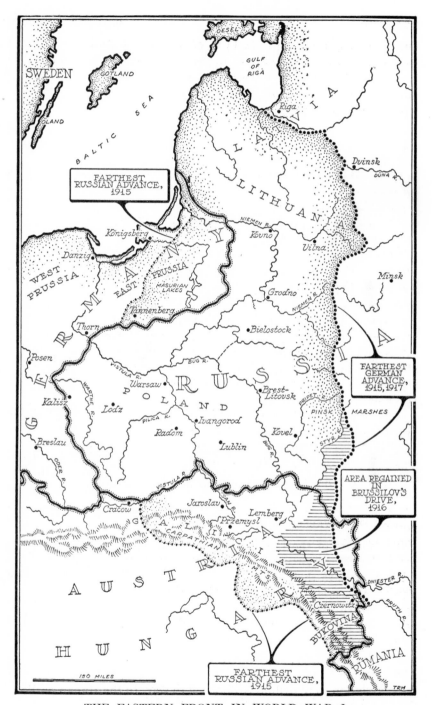

THE EASTERN FRONT IN WORLD WAR I

When Samsonov's army reached the line Hindenburg had prepared, the German center yielded. As the Russians drove ahead, the German forces on both sides closed in until Samsonov's army was practically surrounded. Only a few remnants escaped the encirclement. This victory at Tannenberg (August 26–31) offers one of the few examples in history of the complete destruction of an army in battle. By the end of a month after Tannenberg, Rennenkampf's army had also been driven out of East Prussia with heavy losses in men and materials. The victory at Tannenberg made Hindenburg the popular hero of Germany. His portrait was in every home; he was hailed as invincible; the Hindenburg legend grew to the proportions of an epic. Continued successes on the eastern front won him such fame that his nomination as the chief of the general staff became inevitable.

The Austrians were no less surprised than were the Germans. Convinced that the Russian armies would be unable to take the offensive, the Austro-Hungarian general staff divided its armies, holding one in the region of Lemberg and sending the other into Poland. Two Russian armies administered a crushing defeat to the Austrians at Lemberg in a battle that lasted for some days (August 26 to September 1). Losses in men and materials were so heavy that the Austrian army was obliged to evacuate the town. To relieve the situation the Germans transported large numbers of troops to the east from the western front. Hindenburg organized an expedition for the purpose of driving the Russians out of Poland, but the tsar's troops made an effective stand in prepared positions along the line of the Vistula. On the eastern front as in the west the situation gradually settled down to trench warfare. The end of 1914 saw both sides facing each other from long lines of trenches both on the eastern and on the western front.

A YEAR OF REVERSES FOR THE ALLIES

The failure of the Central Powers to achieve a quick victory gave the Allies the opportunity to strengthen their forces and to draw two other nations to their side. One of these was Italy. In 1915 the Allies signed the secret Treaty of London (April 26), which promised Italy certain territories, including the much-desired Trentino and part of Istria but not Fiume. The same treaty stated that "in the event of France and Britain increasing their colonial territory in Africa at the expense of Germany, Italy might claim some equitable compensation." This agreement satisfied the Italian government, but large sections of the population were definitely opposed to war. In the Italian parliament there was a strong party which favored neutrality. Moreover, the Germans were working frantically to gain Italian support. The man who was largely instrumental in convincing the Italian people to intervene on the Allied side was Gabriel D'Annunzio. Sharing the passionate belief of Mazzini that Italy had an indisputable right to all territory within the upper circle of the Alps down to Fiume, he communicated this conviction to the Italian people through his fiery addresses at Genoa and Rome. As a result public opinion rose to fever height. Another Italian who played an important part in stimulating the war fever was Benito Mussolini, whose instrument was the newspaper *Il Popolo d'Italia*. On May 23, 1915, Italy formally declared war. Rumania, too, joined the Allies upon receiving pledges of compensation similar to those given to Italy (August 27, 1916).

The addition of Italy and Rumania did not give the Allies as much strength as they had hoped. Italy was ill prepared for playing a leading role in a great war. Her army was of good size but lacked sufficient munitions as well as equipment and stores of every kind. What was worse, the country was not united in a wholehearted prosecution of the war. With factions of many kinds hampering the war efforts, the Italian troops made little progress in wresting the Trentino from Austria. About all they achieved during the early years was to divert Austrian troops from the eastern front.

The year 1915 was a bad year for the Allied powers in a number of ways. It saw, for instance, the failure of the Allied attempt to gain possession of the Dardanelles and Constantinople.[2] The plan for an expedition was projected in part by Winston Churchill, who was at the time First Lord of the Admiralty. Success would have given the Allies a channel through which they could have sent supplies and munitions to Russia and would also have relieved Turkish pressure on Russia's army in the Caucasus. A powerful fleet of British and French ships was gathered in the Mediterranean, but the assault failed of its purpose (March 6–7; again on March 18). More than a month later a landing was made on the Gallipoli Peninsula, but Turkish resistance was so effective that the troops were unable to advance beyond the beaches. Finally the project was abandoned, a tragic failure that was costly in prestige as well as in men and materials.

The Allies also suffered reverses on other fronts. The Russians, after holding the line for some time, were steadily forced back. The German howitzers leveled every fort that resisted and literally blasted the Russians out of their trenches. The Russian position gradually deteriorated and in August, 1915, they evacuated Warsaw. Thereafter the Germans

---

[2] In the secret treaty of London, signed March 20, 1915, and published by the Bolsheviks in 1918, Britain consented to "the annexation by Russia of the Straits and Constantinople, in return for a similar benevolent attitude on Russia's part towards the political aspirations of Britain in other parts." Thus the tsars would have fulfilled at least temporarily an ambition of centuries if the Allies had been able to take the Straits.

continued to force them back until almost all of Poland was in German hands. In the fall of 1915 the Serbian army, which had twice driven back the invading Austrians, was forced to give way before a strong force of Germans and Austro-Hungarians and to retreat into the mouл.- tains of Albania.

At the end of 1915 the Central Powers were in a strong position. While holding the Allied lines in the west they had won a number of successes in the east. They had frustrated the Allied attempt to take the Dardanelles, wrested most of Poland from the Russian armies, and driven the Serbian army out of Serbia. In the words of one historian, the year "ended with the spectacle of military success on a scale such as Europe had not even seen in Napoleon's time." On all fronts the Allied forces had either been checked or driven back.

A YEAR OF INDECISION

Although the outlook for the Allies was anything but cheerful, they were determined that the tide must turn in 1916. The Germans, who were equally determined to force a decision before the end of that year, had already during the last months of 1915 made preparations for a great concentrated offensive to be launched early in the new year before the Allies could get a spring offensive under way. While the Austrians were attacking the Italians, the Germans would attempt a break- through at Verdun through the use of masses of artillery and infantry. In order to meet the attack it would be necessary for the French to throw every possible man into the fray, and the nation would conse- quently "bleed to death." Verdun was not one fortress but a ring of forts built in commanding locations and protected by a system of trenches. So thorough were the preparations for the attack that the German generals were convinced that it would bring victory on the western front. The French, who were aware of some of the prepara- tions, believed that the Germans were merely trying to draw the French reserves to Verdun and that the main blow would be delivered else- where. Their preparations were therefore anything but adequate.

The attack was launched on February 21 with a terrific artillery bom- bardment which destroyed the advance defenses. For several days thereafter progress continued until it seemed that a German victory was assured. But the Germans had underestimated the courage and tenacity of the French. Although losses were heavy and their entrenchments were destroyed, the troops, taking "They shall not pass" as their slogan, made a determined stand which slowed the German advance and inflicted heavy losses. Gradually the impetus of the advance was broken. During the succeeding weeks the Germans repeatedly tried to force the French positions without avail. On June 20 they even employed a new gas (diphosgene) in their efforts to dislodge the French. The resulting casualties were large, but the Germans lacked the strength to achieve a final victory.

If the Germans were unsuccessful in the west, they did achieve considerable success in the east. Early in June, 1916, the Russian armies attacked the Austrians along the whole front from the Pripet marshes to Rumania and routed them so completely that a collapse seemed certain. For a time Allied hopes of victory ran high. But when the situation became serious, Hindenburg quickly rushed troops to support the Austrians. These reinforcements under the expert command of General Ludendorff quickly stopped the Russian advance.

Furthermore, before the end of 1916 the Central Powers also dealt a decisive blow to Rumania. After watching the progress of affairs for a favorable moment to join the Allies, Rumania was encouraged to take the step by the apparent success of the Russian drive. But the move proved to be a great mistake. Actually the force of the drive was spent when Rumania declared war on August 27, 1916. A short time later Hindenburg was made chief of staff of all the armies of the Central Powers and together with General Ludendorff at once proceeded to demonstrate his control of the military situation in the east by roundly defeating the Rumanian army. Before the end of the month the entire province of Wallachia with its rich oil deposits and fertile grain lands was in the possession of the Central Powers and Rumania's role as a factor in the war was ended.

Meanwhile on July 1 the British forces, assisted by the French, made the first assault on the German lines in the area of the Somme. At various intervals during the succeeding weeks the British and French attacked along a wide front. The attacks became heavier in September and continued on into October; in fact, the battle of the Somme continued until the rain and mud of the fall discouraged any further attempts. The Germans managed to withstand the attacks but they paid a high price in men, a price they could ill afford. The British also suffered heavy losses. One of the features of this long battle was that on September 15 tanks were used in action for the first time. They were introduced by the British. Many bogged down in the mud or were stranded in shell holes, and it was not until late in 1917 that they were used with any degree of success.

In general, the Central Powers won important military successes in 1916, but in doing so they exhausted their resources and man power. "The strain of the year 1916," Ludendorff later wrote, "had proved too great; the endurance of the army had weakened; we were completely exhausted on the western front." The German government, which was not unaware of the weakness of its forces, hoped the Allies would accept a peace on the basis of its territorial holdings. On December 12, 1916, it suggested the possibility of peace discussions, but the Allies vigorously rejected the offer. On December 18 President Wilson independently asked all the belligerents to state their peace terms. The Germans expressed "great satisfaction" with the President's "wise and high-minded action"; they did not, however, state their terms. When the Allies stated their terms on January 10, 1917, it became clear that no agreement was possible at the time. Consequently a decision had to be forced on the field of battle.

NAVAL WARFARE, 1914–1916

Although the advantage on land rested with the Central Powers, this was not true on the oceans and seas, with the exception of the Baltic. From the very beginning the British navy was the controlling force on the sea. After holding a test mobilization in the summer of 1914, the British naval command had decided to hold the Grand Fleet together because of the threatening European situation. Consequently it was ready for action when the war started. William II decided not to contest the British supremacy but to keep his fleet intact in order to ward off any attempted invasion by sea. The fleet, ordered to engage the enemy only if "circumstances are exceptionally favorable," sought the protection of the island of Helgoland. Meanwhile the British were speedily able to banish German commerce from most of the waterways and to deprive Germany of all its colonies.

The Allies employed their naval superiority in an effort to stop the Central Powers from importing foodstuffs and raw materials. From the United States, for example, Germany had previously purchased all the raw cotton, three fifths of the copper, and three fourths of the mineral oils used in her industries. Large-scale imports from other countries included wool and hides, rubber, manganese, and tin. Even the home production of food was largely dependent on imported fertilizers and fodders. The Allies were convinced that if they could establish a blockade that would exclude food and raw materials from Germany, the country would be compelled to surrender. At first only "war materials" were placed on the list of contraband goods, but more and more articles were added until finally on March 11, 1915, it was announced that the British government was determined "to prevent commodities of any kind from reaching or leaving Germany." All this was in violation of the rules of international law, which accorded to neutrals the right to trade with Germany. The British, for their part, sought to justify the blockade on the ground of sheer necessity.

Meanwhile the Central Powers were not idle. Besides commanding the Dardanelles and the Baltic, which enabled them to limit Russia's trade with the western Allies, they sent out individual German ships to harry, capture, or destroy Allied merchant ships. When the British captured some of the raiders, others were sent out to replace them. Mines were also used with good results. But Germany's chief offensive weapon at sea was the submarine. At first both sides regarded the submarine as of value only for purposes of observation, but as early as September 22, 1914, a German U-boat (U for Untersee) proved its importance as an instrument of destruction by sinking three armored British cruisers off the coast of Holland. Thereafter the idea of using the submarine to attack Allied shipping took shape.

The thinking of the German naval leaders soon progressed from the attack on specific ships to unrestricted submarine warfare. "The waters around Great Britain and Ireland, including the whole of the English Channel," the announcement of February 4, 1915, stated, "are herewith declared to be in the War Zone. From February 18 onward every merchant ship met with in this War Zone will be destroyed, nor will it always be possible to obviate the danger with which the crews and passengers are hereby threatened." Such a policy was, of course, no less contrary to international law than the English blockade. During the succeeding months ships were sunk with abandon. March saw twenty-seven torpedoed, and in April eighteen more went to the bottom.

As a result of this policy the relations between Germany and the United States became more and more strained until the breaking point was reached with the sinking on May 7, 1915, of the giant Cunard liner *Lusitania*. A single torpedo discharged by a German U-boat struck the ship within sight of the coast of Ireland and exploded with terrific force. The ship sank twenty minutes after the first alarm was sounded, carrying to the bottom 1198 men, women, and children, of whom 124 were Americans. This tremendous loss of life and the complete surprise of the attack outraged public opinion in the United States. The Germans stated in defense of the deed that they had warned travelers two days before the *Lusitania* sailed from New York that "the zone of war includes the waters adjacent to the British Isles" and that "vessels flying the flag of Great Britain or any of her allies do so at their own risk." They also claimed that the *Lusitania* carried contraband of war in the form of munitions,[3] but this defense did not satisfy public opinion. Many Americans clamored for a declaration of war. After President Wilson sent a strong protest to Germany, the latter finally promised

[3] It was later verified that there were 4200 cases of Springfield cartridges listed among the small arms on the *Lusitania's* manifest.

that henceforth "liners will not be sunk without warning and without safety of the noncombatants."

Having promised to curtail the program of unrestricted submarine warfare, the German admiralty became more aggressive in the use of its fleet. This resulted in the only great naval battle of the war, known as the battle of Jutland (May 31, 1916). On the previous morning the German fleet left the Jade and sailed northward in the hope of enticing a part of the British fleet out into the open. The strategy was successful. No sooner did the British intercept a radio message divulging the move than a strong force set out in pursuit. During the afternoon of May 31 both sides opened fire (150 British and 99 German vessels). When the battle ended the next day, it was found that the British had lost three battle cruisers, eight light cruisers, and eight destroyers, while the Germans had lost one battleship, one battle cruiser, three light cruisers, and five destroyers. British casualties numbered 6274 and those of the Germans 2545. The German admiralty at once claimed a decisive victory but did not risk another engagement. Thus the battle really confirmed British rule of the seas.

THE UNITED STATES JOINS THE ALLIES

After more than two years of fighting the struggle was still far from a decision. The advantage was on the side of Germany. There seemed little likelihood that the Allied armies by themselves could evict her from the territories she had conquered. If therefore she could collect enough food from the conquered territories, she could endure the blockade and wait until the Allies were ready to make peace on her terms. But the year 1917 saw two events take place which changed the picture completely. One was the entry of the United States on the side of the Allies; the other was the collapse of Russia.

When the war broke out in 1914, the old policy that Europe's concerns were her own was dominant in the United States. Public opinion in general still adhered to the platform laid down by the American delegation to the Hague Conference of 1899: "Nothing contained in this convention shall be so construed as to require the United States of America to depart from its traditional policy of not intruding upon, interfering with, or entangling itself in the political questions or policy or internal administration of any foreign state." In other words, the American people regarded the dispute as something entirely European. "We felt ourselves aloof," one observer stated,[4] "and above all we wanted no war. We were busy developing our internal resources; we

---

[4] Ray S. Baker in *Current History*, vol. 19 (1923), p. 547.

still had plenty of room for expansion; and unlike the nations of Europe we had no fear for our safety and little or no interest in those vital problems of elbow-room, and food and shelter for rapidly expanding populations, which were beginning to plague all of the other populations of the earth." Any man who had proposed in August or September, 1914, that the United States enter the conflict would have been regarded as mentally unbalanced.

President Wilson supported the determination to keep out of the war by issuing the famous proclamation of neutrality, which asked the American people to be neutral in thought as well as in action. Later he again appealed to them in these words: "Every man who really loves America will act and speak in the true spirit of neutrality, which is the spirit of impartiality and fairness and friendliness to all concerned. . . . It will be easy to excite passion and difficult to allay it." For his country and for himself President Wilson conceived the mission of ending the war by mediation and establishing a peace based on moral principles. "May we not look forward," he said in January, 1915, "to the time when we shall be called blessed among the nations, because we succored the nations of the world in their time of distress and of dismay?" A short time later he said, "The test of friendship is not now sympathy with the one side or the other, but getting ready to help both sides when the struggle is over." The theme was restated in August, 1915, when he said, "It would be a great calamity to the world at large if we should be drawn actively into the conflict and so be deprived of all disinterested influence over the settlement."

Although the American people had no desire to become entangled in the war, sentiment was by no means neutral. From the beginning, the sympathies of a large number of citizens were drawn to the Allied side by the German violation of Belgian neutrality. Nor were the Allies slow in making the most of this violation to influence public opinion in the United States. The phrase "scrap of paper," referring to the treaty with Belgium, was widely circulated as a means of arousing indignation. Before the war was many hours old, the British navy cut the one cable connection the Central Powers had with the United States and thereafter all news via the cables was obliged to pass through England, where the censors naturally deleted anything unfavorable to their cause. Thus the people of the United States saw the war largely through British eyes. Later the Allies manufactured horror propaganda to sway American sentiment; among the many atrocity myths were those which pictured the German soldiers as chopping off the hands of Belgian babies. The resulting sentiment was anti-German rather than pro-Allied. The Germans were also, of course, endeavoring to win American public opinion for their cause, but their propaganda was poorly managed and therefore less effective. Much of it was centered on German newspapers in this country which had a limited circulation.

But propaganda was not a direct cause of the war. If it had been the sole impetus, the United States would probably have remained a non-belligerent to the end. It was the German policy of unrestricted submarine warfare which finally forced a declaration of war. Little by little it drew the United States irresistibly into the conflict. As a result of sharp protests over the sinking of the *Lusitania* the Germans decided to abandon unrestricted submarine warfare. Many believed that the issue had been settled permanently and that the United States would succeed in staying out of the war. President Wilson himself sounded a warning when he said in February, 1916: "I know that you are depending upon me to keep this nation out of the war. So far I have done so and I pledge you my word that, God helping me, I will — if it is possible. But you have laid another duty upon me. You have bidden me to see that nothing stains or impairs the honor of the United States, and that is a matter not within my control; that depends upon what others do, not upon what the government of the United States does."

After the *Lusitania* controversy had died down and the feelings against the Germans had subsided, British interference with American rights excited much comment. Repeated protests were ignored. Colonel House recorded in his *Papers* that President Wilson became so angry as to suggest on one occasion, "Let us build a navy larger than theirs and do what we please." House himself stated in his diary, "I will confess that the Allies are irritating almost beyond endurance." British seizure of United States mails even caused Wilson to ask the Congress to grant him the power to levy an embargo as a means of retaliation. The Congress complied with his request (September 8, 1916). Count von Bernstorff was not slow to see the swing of the pendulum in the other direction, as he noted in his *Memoirs*.

But the Germans soon dissipated whatever feeling of good will existed. Hardly had President Wilson been re-elected in November, 1916, because "he kept us out of war," when they announced the resumption of unrestricted submarine warfare. Since the man power reservoir of the Central Powers was nearing depletion and the blockade of Germany was becoming more effective, a quick victory was necessary if the Germans were to win at all. Both Hindenburg and Ludendorff, convinced that land forces could not achieve a speedy victory, urged the immediate resumption of unrestricted submarine warfare. Inside Germany the food situation was critical. With fats, meats, and milk scarce, the Germans had depended largely on potatoes and turnips as a staple diet. But in the summer of 1916 the potato crop failed, limiting the fare largely to turnips. The succeeding winter, known as the "turnip winter,"

SUBMARINE WARFARE, 1917-1918

saw the population suffer from shortage of fuel as well as from the pangs of hunger. Consequently civilian leaders added their voices to the demand for the resumption of unrestricted submarine warfare. The "unrestricted" was necessary because it had previously been demonstrated that the U-boats could not be used successfully so long as they did not sink all ships without regard for passengers and crews.

On January 31, 1917, the German government announced that it would resume unrestricted submarine warfare the next day — that every ship, whether Allied or neutral, in certain areas, including the waters round the British Isles, was liable to be sunk without notice. In doing so Germany quite frankly ran the risk of adding the United States to the list of enemy nations ranged against her. The German leaders, it appears, were confident that even if the Americans did join the Allies, the submarine would force a decision before the United States could send any sizable force to Europe. Upon hearing the news, the President acted promptly. On the afternoon of February 3 he announced to the Congress that diplomatic relations between Imperial Germany and the United States had been severed. He also sounded the warning that "if American ships and American lives should in fact be sacrificed by their commanders in heedless contravention of the just and reasonable understandings of international law and the obvious dictates of humanity, I shall take the liberty of coming again before the Congress, to ask that authority be given me to use any means that may be necessary for the protection of human right, of which we are only a single champion."

The Germans paid little heed to the President's warning. Before many months had passed, revelations of German intrigue followed by the sinking of American ships pushed this country completely over the precipice. First of all, widespread resentment was excited by the disclosure that on January 19 the German foreign minister had instructed the German minister to Mexico to propose a military alliance to the Mexican government for war against the United States. As its share of loot at the conclusion of the war Mexico was to receive accessions of territory which roughly included the states of Texas, New Mexico, and Arizona. Although nothing came of the proposal, American indignation ran high. Next came the reports of the sinkings of American ships. On March 12 the steamer *Algonquin* was torpedoed and sunk without warning off the English coast. But the news that really outraged public opinion was the report on March 16 that three American ships had been sunk by German torpedoes. From all sides came the demand for a declaration of war.

President Wilson, feeling that he could no longer refuse the demand,

appeared before a joint meeting of both Houses of Congress on April 2
to read his war message which stated in part:

Neutrality is no longer feasible or desirable where the peace of the world
is involved and the freedom of its peoples, and the menace to that peace and
freedom lies in the existence of autocratic governments backed by organized
force which is controlled wholly by their will, not by the will of their people. . . . We enter this war only where we are clearly forced into it because
there are no other means of defending our rights. . . . It is a fearful thing
to lead this great, peaceful people into war, into the most terrible and disastrous of all wars, civilization itself seeming to be in the balance. But the
right is more precious than peace.

At three o'clock on the morning of April 6 the Congress officially voted
for war, and the President signed the resolution the same day.

RUSSIA DROPS OUT

Hardly had the United States entered the war when the military
power of Russia collapsed and that country was forced to sue for peace.
The military successes of the first weeks of the war had engendered an
unfounded optimism and concealed certain fatal weaknesses, such as
lack of equipment. Although the government reported at the opening
of the war that it had a large supply of guns and ammunition, the army
actually had only sixty batteries of artillery against Germany's 381
and only about 12 per cent of the machine guns it needed. As early as
October, 1914, a circular order called for the greatest possible economy
in the use of artillery stores; and within a few weeks the shortage of
other kinds of munitions also became critical. Unfortunately, it was
difficult to obtain supplies from the other Allied powers because all
the Russian ports except Archangel, Murmansk, and Vladivostok were
blockaded.

Inadequate equipment and shortage of materials gradually undermined the morale of the army and caused many soldiers to desert. The
general confusion also roused discouragement and discontent among
the civilian population. Bitter criticism was leveled at the government
and particularly at the tsar and the tsarina. In June, 1915, an excited
mob in Red Square even insulted the royal portraits and demanded the
removal of Rasputin. In September of the same year the military situation became so desperate that the tsar decided to take command in
person, leaving the tsarina and her reactionary group in control of the
administration. She was determined to show her husband that she could
rule with firmness. Of the Duma she said, "I have no patience with

these meddlesome chatterboxes." The result was that Rasputin, as her adviser, exerted a greater influence than ever and the confusion in the government increased. Ministers succeeded one another in rapid succession. Finally in December, 1916, three nobles, two of them close kinsmen of the tsar, took it upon themselves to deliver Russia from the evil genius. They plied him with wine heavily charged with cyanide of potassium, but hours later there was no sign that the poison had taken effect. After a long and anxious time of waiting Prince Yussupov shot him, and a physician pronounced him "in his last agony." But a little later they were amazed to see him crawl across the room in an effort to escape to the street. Two more shots were fired into his body, which was then put under the ice of the River Neva to make certain he would not revive again.

The assassination of Rasputin was widely hailed by the Russian people, but by that time the estrangement between the autocracy and the masses was so complete that reconciliation was no longer possible. The atmosphere was so tense that any cause would have been sufficient to start a revolt. There was no dearth of causes, but the one that excited the greatest dissatisfaction was the shortage of foodstuffs in the larger cities. Those who wished to purchase food found it necessary to wait for hours in long queues. Discontent vented itself on March 8, 1917, in a strike of the Petrograd workers, who were joined by crowds of women in staging street demonstrations. On each of the following days the riots were repeated on a larger scale. When the commander of the garrison informed the tsar of the growing seriousness of the situation, he replied, "Stop the disorder in the capital at once." Even at this time revolution might have been averted if the commander had been able to carry out the order. But the soldiers, too, were in a revolutionary mood. They refused to fire on the crowds and gradually joined in the demonstrations against the government. Thus the city was completely in the hands of the revolutionaries. By March 12 the tsarist rule had disintegrated so completely that the Duma appointed a provisional government to take charge of affairs. On the same day the workers of Petrograd organized a Soviet of Workers' Deputies modeled after the Petrograd soviet of 1905.

Nicholas II stood quite alone without anyone to protect him or to uphold the monarchy. On the day before, the tsarina had written: "I think everything will be all right. The sun is shining so brightly and I feel so calm and at peace at his (Rasputin's) grave. He died to save us." The next day the regime which had resisted revolution for centuries collapsed. Nicholas himself did not realize what had happened. He still hoped to save his throne, but after hearing that even his own bodyguard had deserted him finally followed the advice of his generals and resigned

(March 15). If Russia had not entered the war, Romanov rule might have continued for some time. Defeat had caused all the smoldering discontent to burst into flame. As one writer put it, "The Russian Empire was like an old, rotten, badly constructed ship, which might have navigated some time longer so long as there was no storm. As soon as the storm broke out, the ship was unable to face it and sank."

In the Allied countries the news of the revolution was received with rejoicing. President Wilson, for example, wrote, "No people must be forced under sovereignty under which it does not wish to live." The fact that autocratic Russia was fighting for the Allied cause had been embarrassing to those who believed theirs was the side of freedom and justice. After the overthrow of the tsarist government they could say that they were fighting to "make the world safe for democracy." They were also convinced that the elimination of autocracy would increase Russia's capacity and strengthen her determination to prosecute the war successfully.

But their hopes were soon dispelled. The Romanov rule collapsed so quickly that no party or group was ready to dominate the situation. The new government, organized under the presidency of Prince Lvov, a landowner, was controlled by the Constitutional Democrats, but it included one Social Revolutionary, Alexander Kerenski, a young lawyer who was vice-president of the Petrograd soviet. This government at once proclaimed freedom of religion and of the press, liberated all who had been imprisoned for political reasons, and permitted all political exiles to return to Russia. It also made provisions for the election of a national assembly which was to draw up a constitution. Beyond these changes it planned no innovations, allowing itself to be "carried along on the momentum of the old tsarist government, with the same officials and the same police control." It also continued to stress the necessity of prosecuting the war to a successful close, so that Russia might fulfill its historic mission of annexing Constantinople and the Straits.

The provisional government failed to realize that the policy of continuing in the war was completely out of harmony with the desires of the people. Hence it struck the wrong chord when it called upon all classes to help win the war. The masses, drunk with the wine of liberty, believed that the revolution meant they could do what they pleased. The peasants wished to seize the estates of the landlords; the workers were impatient to take control of the factories; and the soldiers wanted above everything else to go home. "Dominant in his being," an observer wrote, "was the irresistible desire to return home and to take part in the organization of his future economic life." Encouraged to desert by agitators, they did so in large numbers.

What the situation needed was a determined leader. Any group with real leadership would have been able to preserve order and introduce reforms in a systematic manner. But the provisional government did not include such a man. Nor did its members, who were typical liberals, exercise the ruthlessness needed to win the respect of the masses. In an effort to gain the support of the disaffected parties, the government was reorganized (May, 1917) with Alexander Kerenski as its head. It was hoped that since he was a Social Revolutionary, both the workers and the peasants would accept his leadership and that the soldiers would submit to discipline at his behest. The experiment failed. The more radical groups were determined to be satisfied with nothing less than a thoroughgoing social revolution.

The lack of determined leadership gave the Bolsheviks their opportunity. When the government permitted the political exiles to return, the thousands who flocked back into Russia included many Bolshevik leaders who were the real enemies of the new regime. Before long the British ambassador, whose sympathies were with the provisional government, was compelled to admit, "The Bolsheviks, who form a compact minority, have alone a definite political program." The acknowledged leader of this group was Lenin. When the March Revolution took place, Lenin was in Switzerland. The German government, believing that his doctrines would hasten the demoralization of the Russian army, gave him passage through Germany in the famous "sealed train." In his farewell message to the Swiss workers Lenin told them that the Russian revolt was the prologue to world revolution. No sooner did he arrive in Russia than he called for the overthrow of the provisional government. He even went so far as to denounce the Bolshevik leaders for having supported it during his absence in Switzerland.

Lenin knew exactly what he wanted. His goal was the establishment of a soviet republic — in other words, of a commonwealth in which the central power would belong to a committee of all the soviets (councils) in the country and the local government would be carried on by the local soviets composed of delegates from the working classes. For his task he had funds supplied by the German government and he also had a compact organization of picked men united by strict discipline. He quickly discovered that the two elements upon which he could place the greatest reliance were the soldiers and the peasants. He knew that the soldiers were tired of war — that, in the words of the British ambassador, "the Russian soldier of today does not understand for what or for whom he is fighting." Accordingly he won their support by promising them peace. He further knew that the peasants longed for land and he therefore promised them the lands they coveted. Soon Russia was ringing with the slogans "End the war" and "All power to the soviets." Actually the slogan "All power to the soviets" was a mask for his real objective, the dictatorship of the Bolshevik Party.

During the next months the Bolshevik agitators worked feverishly among the soldiers and sailors, the garrisons in the cities, the workers, and the peasants. Trotsky, for example, created the Military Revolutionary Committee of the Petrograd soviet and obtained complete control of the garrison and the military supplies of Petrograd. Early in November Lenin and Trotsky insisted against the advice of other Bolshevik leaders that the proper time had arrived for the seizure of power on behalf of the soviets. On the night of November 6–7 [5] a picked group of Bolsheviks quietly seized the railway stations, the fortresses and military staff quarters, the central postal, telegraph, and telephone offices, and the state bank. A cruiser was stationed on the Neva ready, if necessary, to bombard the Winter Palace, which was the headquarters of the provisional government. This was unnecessary, for the members meekly submitted to arrest the next day. Thus the provisional government was overthrown as easily as the tsarist government had been some months earlier.

Russia was proclaimed a "soviet republic" and on the evening of November 7 Lenin appeared before the All-Russian Congress of the soviets which had opened its sessions in Petrograd that day and announced, "We shall now proceed to construct the Socialist Order." The congress then adopted three decrees submitted by Lenin. First, it offered to conclude immediate peace with all nations on the basis of "no indemnities, no annexations." Second, private property was abolished and the use of the land was transferred to the peasants. Third, control of production was to be vested in soviets or working-class committees.

Lenin's first act as head of the new government was to declare a cessation of hostilities. In December, 1917, he opened peace negotiations with the Central Powers at Brest Litovsk. In January the conference broke up for a time because Lenin felt that the German terms were too severe. But the Germans were determined, and orders were given for the army to march toward Petrograd. Since the Russian troops were in no condition to stop the advance, there was no course open to Lenin but to accept. On March 3, 1918, the treaty of Brest Litovsk was signed. It required Russia to renounce sovereignty in favor of the Central Powers over Russian Poland, Kurland, Livonia, and Estonia. In addition she had to cede Ardahan, Kars, and Batum to Turkey; recognize the independence of Finland, the Ukraine, and Georgia; and agree to reparation payments in the amount of six billion marks. In short, European Russia was completely dismembered for the benefit of the Central Powers. The withdrawal of Russia had discouraged the Rumanians from continuing in the war. On December 9, 1917, they concluded an armistice followed by the signing of the treaty of Bu-

---

[5] According to the Russian calendar it was still October; hence this movement is often referred to as the October Revolution.

charest on May 7, 1918. Thus Germany had eliminated its opponents on the eastern front. Winning the war on the western front was another problem.

THE FINAL GERMAN DRIVE

Meanwhile the German submarine campaign had gotten under way with high promise of success. The first week no less than twenty-two ships were sunk, and during the succeeding weeks the sinkings continued despite everything the Allies were able to do in the way of protection. For a time one out of every four ships leaving British ports was sunk. The month of April, 1917, saw 881,027 tons of shipping disappear beneath the waves. Some U-boats were, of course, destroyed by Allied pursuit ships, but the Germans were building them faster than they could be destroyed. If the Germans had been able to sustain the rate of sinkings it would have spelled victory for them, but the Allies did finally devise a method of guarding their shipping. In May, 1917, they introduced the "convoy system." Under this system merchant ships went out in large fleets protected by warships. The result was a great reduction in losses. By midsummer of 1917 the German leaders realized that their attempt to win a quick victory with the submarine had failed.

The Germans were now confronted with the necessity of forcing a decision on the western front. By this time they were war weary and hungry. Since the submarine had not succeeded in breaking the blockade, they were being slowly starved into submission. Austria's fighting strength, undermined by hunger and dissension, was largely spent. Nevertheless Ludendorff, who at the beginning of 1917 had said that Germany could not bring the war to an end by military action of the armies alone, now assured the nation that it could win a victory with its land forces. He told the Germans that the French were too exhausted to withstand another attack and that with Russia and Rumania out of the war they could by a supreme attempt drive through to victory before the United States could transport any considerable body of troops to Europe. To the kaiser he said that the offensive on the western front "will be an immense struggle, but it will be victorious." Nor can it be said that the plan was based entirely on hope. The Germans did have the advantage of deciding where the attempt to crack the Allied line was to be made, while the Allies, not knowing at which point to expect the attack, had to be ready to defend at all points.

It was essential to launch the attack before the Americans could send reinforcements into battle. During the last weeks of 1917 and the early ones of 1018 the Germans transferred their troops from the eastern front to the west, and by the third week in March everything was ready. The attack began at dawn on March 21. Week after week the Germans made gains, until at one point they were again on the Marne. On the way they had taken 225,000 prisoners and inflicted almost a million casualties. A large gun popularly known as "Big Bertha" even dropped shells into Paris from a distance of seventy-five miles. The damage resulting from this bombardment was not very great, but it did cause much alarm. Again victory appeared to be within the grasp of the Germans.

But the situation was not so hopeless as it appeared to many. The drive to the Marne had cost the Germans much in man power and matériel. They had, in fact, spent both so freely that they lacked the strength to achieve the final break-through. This fact together with the hope of vast reinforcements from the United States strengthened the morale of the Allies. Up to January 1, 1918, only a few American contingents had arrived in Europe and only one division had taken up a position on the firing line, but in the succeeding months United States troops began to arrive in ever-increasing numbers. After the declaration of war many had insisted that the United States send only volunteers. When a suggestion was offered in the Senate regarding the financing of an American Expeditionary Force, the head of the Appropriations Committee is reported to have said, "My God, you don't intend to send men over, do you?" But President Wilson was determined to send a great national army to Europe. In May Congress voted the conscription which was to result in a large military force. On June 14, 1917, General John J. Pershing, who was chosen to lead the AEF (American Expeditionary Force), arrived in Paris to make arrangements for the arrival and further drilling of large numbers of American soldiers.

The six months after the Germans launched their drive in the spring of 1918 saw no less than one and a half million United States soldiers arrive in France. Most of them had received only the rudiments of military training, but they were confident that they were more than a match for the Germans. Both the British and the French military leaders had a low opinion of the raw American troops. The chief of the British general staff declared that the American troops were "unfit to fight." Marshal Foch, the Allied commander in chief, hesitated to use the insufficiently trained troops for purposes of attack because he feared that their organization would disintegrate under the strain of battle. The need for troops, however, was so desperate that he finally decided to use the "Yanks." Their attack was so determined that the German positions in the Château Thierry salient soon became untenable. Nor was this all. The unexpected strength displayed by the Americans also helped to shatter the German morale, causing the Germans

THE WESTERN FRONT IN WORLD WAR I

to withdraw all along the Marne salient. Consequently the Marne, which had been the farthest point reached by the Germans in 1914, was also destined to be the farthest point reached in their last drive.

As the Allies pressed on, it became evident that the Germans lacked the strength to repair their lines. This caused Foch to seek victory that autumn instead of postponing the attempt until 1919. All the Allied troops from Verdun to the sea were to combine in a simultaneous offensive. The assault by the combined American, British, French, and Belgian forces was launched on September 26 and the battle continued relentlessly. Each day the Allied forces pressed forward, with the result that by September 30 they had pierced the Hindenburg line to a depth of seven miles. In the meantime the first nation dropped out of the ranks of the Central Powers. Bulgaria, her armies defeated, capitulated on September 29, 1918, and an armistice was concluded the next day. The German high command, which had always been optimistic, suddenly insisted that a request for an armistice be sent to the Allies at once. "Today," said Ludendorff, "the troops are holding their own . . . but the line might be broken at any moment and our proposal would come at the most unfavorable time." He saw that a suspension of hostilities at that time would enable the Germans to save their army and to use it, as the German Colonel Hey put it on October 9, "as a means of pressure during the peace negotiations."

THE FOURTEEN POINTS

When the United States declared war, Wilson the peacemaker was seemingly transformed into a war lord. This was more true in appearance than in reality. Even after this country was committed to war, his primary concern was still peace. The settlement at the end of hostilities was the central theme of all his speeches. The peace, he repeated over and over again, must be a truly just and permanent one. From the start he made a sharp distinction between the German people and the German government. "We have no quarrel," he said, "with the German people. We have no feeling toward them but one of sympathy and friendship." He believed that the war had been forced on them by an autocratic government. Against the masters of Germany the Allies must fight until a final and complete victory had been achieved. He was convinced that after Germany's defeat the people would thrust the kaiser and the military clique aside, thereby opening the way for a just and lasting peace. Thenceforth to the end of the war he unceasingly proclaimed "war on the German government, peace to the German people."

President Wilson did not stop at stating with whom he would make peace; he also formulated the principles on which it must be based. They were embodied in the so-called Fourteen Points, which were duly announced in the historic utterance of January 8, 1918. Some of these points were concerned with the adjustment of the affairs of such particular nations as Russia, France, Italy, Rumania, Serbia, Turkey, Poland, and the peoples of Austria-Hungary. In the other points he laid down more general principles. In Point One the program called for "open covenants of peace, openly arrived at, after which there shall be no private international understandings of any kind, but diplomacy shall proceed always frankly and in the public view."

Point Two: "Absolute freedom of navigation upon the sea, outside territorial waters, alike in peace and in war, except as the seas may be closed in whole or in part by international action for the enforcement of international covenants."

Point Three: "The removal so far as possible of all economic barriers and the establishment of an equality of trade conditions among all the nations consenting to the peace and associating themselves for its maintenance."

Point Four: "Adequate guarantees given and taken that national armaments will be reduced to the lowest point consistent with domestic safety."

Point Five: "A free, open-minded, and absolutely impartial adjustment of all colonial claims, based upon a strict observance of the principle that in determining all such questions of sovereignty the interests of the populations concerned must have equal weight with the equitable claims of the Government whose title is to be determined."

The last of the Fourteen Points was the most important in President Wilson's mind. It called for "a general association of nations . . . formed under specific covenants for the purpose of affording mutual guarantees of political independence and territorial integrity to great and small states alike." Throughout the war the two forces, nationalism and internationalism, were struggling for mastery. In Wilson's solution the first was expressed in the principle of self-determination, which was in essence an attempt to satisfy the nationalist longings of subject peoples. The idea of internationalism was to be perpetuated in the League of Nations. This League was the foundation stone of the Wilsonian peace. It would not only prevent future conflicts but also guarantee the enforcement of the terms and principles outlined in the Fourteen Points. The emphasis was placed on the international aspects. Whereas the nineteenth century had seen the triumph of the principle of nationalism, the twentieth would witness the triumph of internationalism. The President's ultimate ideal was a World State in which all peoples would participate as equals and in which nationalism would

King Ferdinand of Bulgaria and Kaiser Wilhelm II
before World War I

Dropping bombs during World War I, from
Sphere, 1914

German troops with a heavy artillery gun

A British tank in World War I

Desolation in northern France in World War I

A front-line trench showing use of land periscope in World War I

In a front-line trench in World War I. Notice precautions against gas attack

be no more than a principle allowing the development of diverse cultures.

The Fourteen Points reverberated round the globe. There was, to be sure, no lack of adverse criticism. A prominent lawyer, for example, declared that the President had spoken "like God Almighty." Nor were some of the Allied leaders, who had concluded a series of secret treaties, happy over the pronouncement. Nevertheless the Fourteen Points must be listed among the greatest pronouncements ever made by the responsible head of a great government. To the war-weary masses of the world who had for years suffered from the rigors of war the pronouncement was an expression of their deep-rooted aspirations and the gospel of better things to come.

The Fourteen Points found a ready and eager echo. Allied statesmen, recognizing the power of Wilson's idealism, seized upon it as a means of stimulating the war effort. But no nations greeted the Fourteen Points more enthusiastically than did the Germans and the Austrians. They believed that President Wilson, as leader of the Allies, could persuade the other belligerent nations to accept his principles as the basis of peace. That is why the Germans addressed their appeal for an armistice to him. Prince Maximilian of Baden, who became imperial chancellor on October 3, proceeded at once in conjunction with Austria-Hungary and Turkey to launch the movement for peace negotiations. On October 5 the President received a request for an immediate armistice, with the added comment that the German government "accepts the program set forth by the President of the United States in his message to Congress on January 8, and in his later pronouncements, especially his speech of September 27, as a basis for peace negotiations." Instead of answering the specific request, Wilson asked further clarification. He asked particularly "whether the imperial chancellor is speaking merely for the constituted authorities of the empire who so far have conducted the war." When the chancellor replied that he was speaking "in the name of the German government and of the German people," the peoples of the Central Powers generally believed that their offer would be accepted. Throughout Germany the people shouted "Peace at last!" But further sinkings by German submarines caused the President to demand a change of government as "a condition precedent to peace."

The confidence of the German nation now collapsed altogether, and the "will to victory" gave way to a demand for peace. There were some among the conservatives who hoped to save the Hohenzollern rule, but the majority, and particularly the parties of the left, openly demanded the kaiser's abdication when this became a preliminary condition of peace negotiations. At the beginning of November ominous signs of an insurrectionary temper appeared. On November 3 a mutiny in the fleet at Kiel excited a spirit of revolution throughout the country. Four days later Bavaria deposed its state rulers and proclaimed a republic, an example which was followed by most of the other states. On November 8 the revolutionists even gained control of Berlin. As a last resort the kaiser sought refuge with the army, but was informed by the generals that they would not be responsible for his safety because the soldiers were sympathizing with the revolutionists. It was indeed a bitter blow to William II, who had taken such pride in his army. There was nothing for him to do but to submit. On November 9 he abdicated and hastily left the country to take up his residence in Holland at the Château of Amerongen, which had once upon a time housed the exiled King Charles II of England.

When the Allies realized that German surrender was imminent, representatives of the major countries met in Paris to formulate the terms for an armistice. A number of the Allied leaders, among them General Pershing, wished to carry the war into Germany, but Marshal Foch could see no sense in further slaughter and was supported in his stand by Haig and Pétain. Wilson, too, was opposed to the further shedding of blood. He was eager to build on his Fourteen Points a peace which would eliminate future wars. He therefore pressed for an armistice, one which he thought would make it impossible for Germany to renew the struggle. It was later stated that by failing to carry the war into Germany and to march into Berlin the Allies missed the opportunity to make the defeat evident to the German people. Later the Nazis persuaded the Germans that their army was not beaten in the field but "stabbed in the back." This myth not only contributed to the acceptance of Hitlerism but also prepared the ground for World War II.

On the morning of November 8 Marshal Foch received the German Armistice Commission in a railroad car stationed in the forest at Compiègne. In a loud voice he read the terms which had been formulated by the Allies. They included, among other things, cessation of operations six hours after the signing of the armistice; immediate evacuation of the invaded countries; surrender in good condition of specified war matériel, including 5000 heavy guns and field guns, 25,000 machine guns, and 1700 airplanes; evacuation of the territories on the left bank of the Rhine; occupation by Allied troops of the principal crossings of the Rhine (Mainz, Coblenz, Cologne); immediate repatriation, without reciprocity, of all Allied prisoners of war being held by the Central Powers; renunciation of the treaties of Bucharest and Brest Litovsk; surrender of all submarines with their complete armor and equipment; internment of German warships in neutral or Allied ports; and immobilization of all aircraft.

In giving the armistice terms to the Germans Foch stipulated that they must be accepted or rejected in seventy-two hours. The German Commission discussed the terms from November 7 until November 11 and finally signed them at 5 a.m. on the morning of the latter day. Marshal Foch at once issued orders that firing was to cease at 11 a.m. When the appointed hour arrived, the big guns became silent all along the western front. After fifty-one nightmare months the fires of Mars had finally been extinguished. Everywhere the peoples of the Allied world, released from the tension of conflict, gave unrestrained expression to their joy. In the streets of Paris, London, Rome, and New York jubilant crowds shouted themselves hoarse; in fact, celebrations were held in all cities, towns, and hamlets of the Allied world. Even the peoples of the Central Powers were happy that the war had ended, in spite of the fact that their armies had suffered defeat.

After the firing ceased, the nations that had participated in the fighting began to count the dead, wounded, and missing. Statistics as to casualties vary considerably. The one thing certain is that the number was tremendous. It has been calculated that all the wars of the nineteenth century from the Napoleonic wars down to the Balkan wars of 1912–1913 claimed 4,449,300 lives, while the known dead of World War I reached 9,998,771.[6] The wounded have been estimated as numbering 21,219,452. The total cost in money has been put at something over $330 billion. These figures do not, however, take into account the human suffering caused by the war, the devastation of a large part of Europe, and the effect on the economic well-being, ethics, morality, and other phases of human life and activity.

[6] See Ernst L. Bogart's *Direct and Indirect Costs of the Great World War* (1919), p. 299. John I. Knudson and Waldo E. Stephens' *Disarmament* (1921), p. 4, estimated the number of killed at 10,873,500. Another estimate puts the number at 8,544,315.

CHAPTER NINETEEN

Peacemaking at Paris

ALLIED IDEALISM EVAPORATES O N Armistice Day in 1918 Woodrow Wilson seemed to hold the trump cards. Not only had American troops played a decisive part in shattering the Hindenburg lines, but Wilson's own promise of a magnanimous peace and a general disarmament had helped break the German will to fight. The Allied leaders had accepted as a basis of peace the principles he had laid down in the Fourteen Points. They had solemnly agreed that impartial justice was to be meted out without discrimination and that such things as territorial aggrandizement, transfer of populations against their will, and the old idea of the balance of power were outlawed. In an address to the United States troops in France (1918) Lloyd George had summed up the Allied attitude in these words: "We are fighting for the great principles laid down by the President." Thus it appeared as if a new system of international relationships had been adopted, one in which discredited diplomatic traditions were to have no place. All that remained, it seemed, was to apply the Fourteen Points to specific problems. At that time the President appeared to be uttering anything but a hollow boast when he said, "Everything for which America fought has been accomplished. It will now be our fortunate duty to assist by example, by sober friendly counsel, and by material aid in the establishment of just democracy throughout the world."

But the idealism which had raised the Allies to the heights just before the armistice, quickly evaporated once it was signed. It soon became clear that despite the earlier appearance of unity of purpose each of the leaders had specific ambitions, aims, and purposes. The secret treaties again came to the fore, the idea of national aggrandizement resumed control, and in both Britain and France the Germans were declared to be solely responsible for the war and were expected to pay its entire cost. As early as December 12 Lloyd George stated in an election speech that the loser must pay. This gave Clemenceau courage to voice his objections to the Wilsonian idealism. Other leaders soon followed suit with demands of various kinds.

President Wilson did not fail to perceive the change. He did not, however, permit it to daunt him. He was determined to fight for the principles he had so eloquently proclaimed. He felt that if the leaders did not support him, the masses in the Allied countries would. There was little doubt in his mind that the masses shared his hatred of war, his determination to establish international justice and to outlaw the old diplomacy, and his opposition to bartering away peoples like chattels. He was convinced that with the masses on his side nothing in the world could prevent the establishment of the new order. Buoyed up by this conviction, he boarded the steamship *George Washington* in New York harbor on December 4, 1918, in order to make certain that his ideas would prevail at the Peace Conference. The journey to Paris was to him a sort of divine mission that would result in the establishment of an era of universal peace.

Whatever doubts he may still have had regarding the support of the masses vanished upon his arrival in Europe. In London, Paris, Rome, and all the smaller cities and towns they welcomed him with an enthusiasm that outstripped all known precedents. Secretary of State Lansing, who accompanied him, wrote, "His name was on every lip; throngs of admirers applauded him as he entered the special train for Paris and at the stations en route; and multitudes, delirious with enthusiasm, cheered him a welcome as he drove through the beflagged streets of the French capital in company with President Poincaré." Subsequent visits to England and Italy evoked even more enthusiasm. In Rome his picture was in every window. In some parts of Italy the homage took on the character of worship, the peasants burning candles before his portrait. All this convinced him that the peoples of Europe would support him even against their own governments.

But Wilson's conviction was self-deception. The people did, it is true, look to him to improve their lot, to save them from a recurrence of war, but they were not ready to forgive and forget. Theirs was a desire for vengeance. During the unrelenting struggle they had made great sacrifices and suffered terrible hardships. For four years their feelings had been kindled to a white heat by propagandists. They had been told that the Germans had inflicted the war upon them, purposefully and wantonly. It was too much to expect them to discard their feelings and prejudices overnight. As they licked their wounds and buried their dead, they demanded that the Germans not only make reparation for the damages they had caused but also pay the complete costs of the war. Lloyd George quickly discovered this in his campaign for re-election. His talk of a just peace left his audiences cold. It was only when he talked of squeezing the Germans "till the pips squeak" that he got enthusiastic roars from the crowds.

For the people of the United States it was somewhat easier to be idealistic. Devastation had not stalked the American countryside nor had death descended on the American cities from the skies. The American soldiers upon their return did not find their home towns heaps of rubble with charred rafters and gaunt chimneys dotting the devastated areas. No blockade had jeopardized the American food supply; the people of the United States were well nourished and had made money as no others had. They had known the war only at a distance for about a year and a half; whereas in the Allied countries of Europe the masses had struggled in the very midst of the terror for more than four years. Enemy hosts had invaded their towns and villages and carted off their property. While the total American casualties were about 126,000 dead and some 200,000 wounded, more than a million Frenchmen had lost their lives and more than four millions had suffered wounds. The number of dead from the British Empire was nearly a million, with another two million wounded. These facts go far in explaining the desire for vengeance.

THE STRUGGLE OVER THE PEACE

The Paris Conference was not a peace conference in the sense that the victors and the vanquished sat down together to draw up the terms of peace. It was a meeting of the victors, and the peace was made without negotiating with the Germans. They were not consulted until the terms of the treaty were completed; then the treaty was imposed on them by threat of force.

The opening meeting took place on the afternoon of January 18, 1919, with representatives of most of the fifty-three allied and associated powers present. Since it was evident that progress would be slow if all the representatives were to debate each issue in public, the heads of the great powers agreed that the work of drawing up the terms was to be entrusted to the Council of Ten, composed of two representatives each from Great Britain, France, Italy, Japan, and the United States. This Council was supplemented by a series of committees constituted to deal with such specific problems as war responsibility, reparations, the League of Nations, and others. Plenary sessions which all the delegates were permitted to attend were convoked only a few times, and even then not to give the delegates an opportunity for a frank exchange of views, but to inform them of decisions that had been made. They did not receive the entire treaty until the day before it was handed to the German delegation. Thus Wilson's First Point, that the covenants of peace should be "openly arrived at," was thrown overboard.

Eventually during President Wilson's absence [1] it was found that an even smaller group could work more effectively than the Council of Ten, and upon his return the business of framing the conditions of peace was assumed by the so-called Big Four, a council composed of President Wilson, M. Clemenceau, Mr. Lloyd George, and Signor Orlando of Italy. These four met day after day to settle the fate of the world, most of the meetings taking place in President Wilson's study in the Place des États Unis. The meetings were quite informal, without any written rules of procedure. All the men were far from young, and all were tired from their strenuous activities during the war years. Nevertheless they had to work under a terrifying pressure of haste. As Lloyd George put it, "We had to . . . work crowded hours, long and late, because, while we were trying to build, we saw in many lands the foundations of society crumbling."

The most dynamic figure of the Big Four was Clemenceau. Witty, determined, and wise with old cynicism, he represented the fears, hatreds, and ambitions of the French people. His whole life had been one of burning passion for France. For decades he had fought so relentlessly in the political arena that he had earned the nickname "the Tiger." During the war when all had seemed lost he had shouted defiance at the enemy. His was a will to victory that no reverse could shake. "I wage war," he said. "Before Paris I wage war. Behind Paris I wage war. If we retreat to the Pyrenees, I shall continue to wage war." Now that the war was won, he was determined that France must not lose the peace. Wilson's idealism was to him a luxury he could ill afford. "Lloyd George," he said, "thinks he is Napoleon, but President Wilson believes himself to be Jesus Christ." He had witnessed the German invasion of 1870 and in 1914 had seen France escape defeat by a seeming miracle. What he wanted, above all else, was security against another German invasion. To obtain this security he was ready to cripple Germany permanently.

Lloyd George, the British prime minister, stood, as it were, between President Wilson and M. Clemenceau. At times he would side with Clemenceau and then again he would support Wilson. The reason was that he represented the policy known as "the balance of power." He wished to prevent the domination of Europe by any one power. This

---

[1] On February 14, 1919, the President left Paris for four weeks to return to the United States.

had been the policy of the British for centuries. They did not want to see their ally too strong or their conquered foe too weak. Hence he often sided with Wilson to keep the French from dominating Europe. In December, 1918, he had in an election speech urged impossible reparations, declaring that "we have an absolute right to demand the whole cost of the war from Germany," but he relented when he realized that they could not be collected and that such a demand would generate bitter feelings. He therefore proposed reparations that would "disappear with the generation which made the war." A further policy represented by Lloyd George was that of acquiring for the British Empire as much as possible of the spoils, which included the German colonies and Turkish possessions.

Signor Orlando, the fourth member of the Big Four, played a role that was irritating rather than important. He and the other Italian delegates came to the conference with the single-minded purpose of claiming the territories Italy had been promised in the secret treaties. They appeared completely untroubled by the fact that their claims were contrary to the Fourteen Points. Italy's sacrifices, Signor Orlando urged, entitled her to colonial compensation.

Against the ideas of these three men President Wilson pitted his dream of a just and enduring peace. No soldier ever went into battle with more enthusiasm and greater devotion to a cause. He was "the inspired prophet of an ideological venture." But he was working under a number of handicaps. First, the general atmosphere of Paris was not favorable to idealism. A neutral city such as Geneva would have been infinitely preferable as a center for dispassionate discussion. Paris, which had been menaced by the German forces and bombarded by Big Berthas, was still vibrating with fierce and vindictive hatreds. When the President realized this, it was too late to make a change. Second, great idealist that he was, President Wilson lacked both the experience and the physical stamina to compete with such experts in the game of diplomacy as he had to face. His health was, in fact, so delicate that he often carried on the work of drawing up the terms while he was confined to his bed. It all added up to the fact that in the game of give and take he was frequently induced to give way on an essential matter in return for some vague promise.

Third, the President lacked a definite program. M. Clemenceau knew exactly what he wanted, but Mr. Wilson had only the principles he had laid down in the Fourteen Points. The war had ended so suddenly and unexpectedly that he was unable to work out detailed plans. When he arrived in Paris, he had only a rough draft of a Covenant for a League of Nations. The situation would have been much more promising if he had definitely nailed down the Allies to his peace terms before he took the United States into the war in 1917, a time when the Allied position was desperate. At that time he could have smoothed his path, but he failed to do so.

The result was that the sessions of the Big Four were a prolonged struggle between the old and the new. Since the President had no specific plan, a French or British draft usually formed the basis of discussion. In order to bring the draft nearer to his ideas he had to adopt a persistent attitude of obstruction, criticism, and negation. Compromise was, therefore, inevitable. Gradually one after another of the principles laid down in the Fourteen Points went by the board. It did not take his colleagues long to realize that he was willing to make concessions in return for support of the League Covenant. He himself knew that he was giving ground, but he clung to the hope, as he told Colonel House, that once the League of Nations was "a *fait accompli* nearly all the serious difficulties would disappear." He was certain that the League would right any unjust terms that might be included in the treaty. On a number of occasions he said to friends: "I would never have done what I did if I had not been sure that the League of Nations would revise that decision."

Even though he did make compromises again and again, he stood firm on a number of questions. Thus he was adamant in his insistence that the Covenant of the League become a part of the treaty with Germany. Both Clemenceau and Lloyd George wished to divorce the League from the peace treaty, but Wilson refused to acquiesce. He further resisted French efforts to deprive Germany of the territory on the left bank of the Rhine and to set it up as a buffer state between Germany and France. In this stand he was supported by Lloyd George, who felt that the separation of the Rhineland from Germany would strike a wound that would never heal. For a time Clemenceau stubbornly held to his demands but was finally prevailed upon to accept as a compromise the demilitarization of the Rhineland and its occupation by Allied troops for a period of fifteen years.

More difficult of solution was the problem of Fiume. According to the secret treaty of London (1915) Italy was to receive the whole of the Dalmatian coast of the Adriatic; she now also laid claim to the port of Fiume. This greediness irritated Wilson, who felt Italy did not need the port. He wished to include it in Yugoslavia as the principal outlet to the sea for the new state. Italian feeling gradually grew so bitter that the Italian representatives threatened to quit the conference and for a time actually did return to Italy.[2]

---

[2] Encouraged by the temporary withdrawal of the Italian delegates, a band of freebooters led by Gabriele D'Annunzio, the poet and novelist, seized Fiume and declared that they would hold it no matter what the Peace Conference decided. Thereafter the conference made no further efforts to solve the question. By the Treaty of Rapallo concluded between Italy and Yugoslavia in 1920 (revised in 1924), Fiume was annexed to Italy, but the Yugoslavs were given free commercial use of the port.

The general result of the struggle between Wilsonian idealism and reactionary nationalism was that the treaty was a compromise between the two. If Wilson did not succeed in holding his colleagues to their pledge, neither did Clemenceau manage to make his ideas prevail. Thus the Covenant of the League was a Wilsonian feature of the treaty, while the reparations settlement shows the influence of Clemenceau. The latter paid Wilson this tribute: "The chief merit of his attempt at making a lasting peace is the fact that, for the first time in history, a search was made for firm ground on which to build a system of justice between nations who up to this time had lived by violence alone." Left to themselves the Allied statesmen would probably have resorted to the old diplomacy of secret bargaining, but Wilson refused to be reconciled to such methods and thereby exerted a beneficent influence.

None of the members of the Big Four was satisfied with the treaty, least of all President Wilson. Although he hoped that the people of the United States would sanction it, he confessed to the members of the American delegation that "we did not keep them [the French and British] from putting irrational things in the treaty." Colonel House, the man who next to Wilson was the most influential member of the United States delegation, confided to his diary on the day he left Paris: "Looking at the conference in retrospect there is much to approve and much to regret. It is easy to say what should have been done, but more difficult to have found a way of doing it. . . . While I should have preferred a different peace, I doubt whether it could have been made, for the ingredients of such a peace as I would have had were lacking at Paris." The saving feature of the treaty in President Wilson's opinion was the League of Nations. It would rectify everything.

THE TREATY OF VERSAILLES

After working untiringly for some months the Big Four finished drawing up the treaty so that it was ready to be submitted to the Germans early in May. On May 7, 1919, the terms were handed by Clemenceau to the Germans, not for oral discussion but for written comment. This was a great disappointment to the delegation, which had brought a large staff of experts for purposes of negotiation. But the great shock came when the German people, who had expected a peace settlement on Wilson's Fourteen Points, found in the treaty the huge reparation demands, the losses of German territory, the disarmament of the Reich, the loss of the Saar mines, and other unexpected terms. The opinion was widespread among the German people that they had been tricked. The new government stated its comments and objections in a document of 443 pages. The Allies allowed the German objections on a number of points, but did not appreciably narrow the gulf which separated the principles of the treaty from those of the Fourteen Points. On June 16 the modified treaty was returned to the Germans for final acceptance or rejection.

Many Germans of high rank favored rejection. President Ebert, after styling the peace terms "the product of the enemy's revengeful hysteria," sought to resign but was persuaded to reconsider. Premier Scheidemann and his cabinet did resign in protest. Refusal on the part of the German government to sign would have meant a renewal of the war. Marshal Foch had his forces ready to cross the Rhine and was authorized to begin the advance on the evening of June 23 if the Germans had not sent their acceptance of the terms by that time. Germany's only possible course was to form a cabinet pledged to ratification. Gustav Bauer, the premier of the new cabinet, appeared before the National Assembly at Weimar on June 22 to declare the intention of his cabinet to sign the treaty. In his address he stated:

At this hour of life and death, under the menace of invasion, for the last time I raise in free Germany a protest against this treaty of violence and destruction. I protest against this mockery of self-determination, this enslavement of the German people, this menace to the peace of the world under the mask of a treaty of peace.

In conclusion he said, "Our power of resistance is broken and there is no means of averting this treaty." Dr. Herman Müller, the foreign minister, then advocated ratification so that the Allied blockade would be lifted. "We are about to enter a forty-years march through a desert," he said. "I can find no other term for the suffering which fulfillment of the treaty prescribes for us." The Assembly voted 227 to 138 to sign the treaty.

The next day the German delegation signed the treaty after being refused a further extension of time by Clemenceau. In a written statement the head of the delegation pointed out that the terms did not conform with the pre-armistice pledges the Allies had made. "Yielding to overwhelming force," he said, "but without on that account abandoning its view in regard to the unheard-of injustice of the conditions of peace, the Government of the German Republic declares that it is ready to accept and sign the conditions of peace imposed by the Allied and Associated Governments." Before the treaty was signed, riots and demonstrations had been staged in various cities by crowds who knew that the Allied armies would resume the war if the Germans did not sign. In Berlin excited crowds marched along Unter den Linden and other streets shouting, "Sign the peace terms." Socialists gathered in front of the government offices crying, "Let us have peace! We want bread, not bullets!" Later, however, after the peace had been signed, demonstrations against the treaty were staged at various places. What rankled most during the early days was the loss of so much German territory. A foreign correspondent reported in June, 1919, that the people of eastern Germany were deeply enraged over the loss of the Polish Corridor. "It is not yet war," he wrote, "but it is something very like it. Here, unless something is done, will be the next war, and you may as well know it." This was, indeed, a prophetic utterance.

The first part of the treaty consisted of the Covenant of the League of Nations. The idea of a League was not original with Woodrow Wilson. It goes back many centuries. The philosophers of classical Greece wrote of a Golden Age when the world would not be controlled by force. During the many centuries that followed, the idea was expressed in more or less vague form by many writers. Thus Tennyson, for example, spoke of "the Parliament of Man, the Federation of the World." The decades preceding World War I saw peace groups in many lands working for an international order that would abolish war and substitute international cooperation for international competition. As the casualties mounted, many people hoped fervently for a league of nations that would put an end to human slaughter for all time.

But it was President Wilson who gave the plan worldwide prominence. As early as 1915 he stated that the war must not end without the organization of a league to outlaw war. In a speech on July 4, 1918, at Mount Vernon, he called for "the establishment of an organization of peace which shall make it certain that the combined power of free nations will check every invasion of right and serve to make peace and justice the more secure by affording a definite tribunal of opinion to which all must submit." It was, above all, to insure the establishment of such a league that he went to Europe. Both Lloyd George and Clemenceau had misgivings as to the practicability of the idea. Clemenceau particularly doubted the efficacy of a moral deterrent, feeling that it would not give France the protection she desired. He wanted the League to have a strong military force at its disposal. In the end, however, Wilson's views prevailed.

The primary purpose of the League, according to the Covenant, was to be "the promotion of international cooperation and the achievement of international peace and security." Thus it was to be more than a mere device for preventing wars. It was confidently expected by its sponsors to be the agency of common action for all affairs of common concern. Although the signatories of the Covenant were to be regarded as the original members of the League, "any fully self-governing state, dominion, or colony" could become a member if its admission was agreed to by a two-thirds vote of the Assembly. In this Assembly, which met at Geneva as occasion required, each state of the League had one vote, although permitted three representatives. The second important organ of the League was the Council, in which the executive functions of the League were vested. It was originally specified that five of the nine members, representing Great Britain, the United States, France, Italy, and Japan, were to have permanent seats, while the four others were to be elected annually, but this plan fell through when the United States repudiated the League.[3] All decisions in both the Assembly and the Council, except on questions of procedure, were required to be unanimous.

Another noteworthy organ of the League was the Permanent Court of Justice, which had its headquarters in the Peace Palace at The Hague. This court was formally opened in 1922 with fifteen judges chosen by the Council and the Assembly. These judges, selected for their ability, in no way represented the countries from which they came. At different times two eminent American jurists were members of this court. Its purpose was to settle disputes referred to it by various governments and the formulation of advisory opinions on questions submitted to it by the League Council.

A question of more immediate interest to the Germans was, "How much territory will the Allies take from us?" They soon discovered that changes had been made on every frontier. Thus they lost Alsace-Lorraine, which they had taken from France as recently as 1871. The rich Saar basin, which is geographically connected with Alsace-Lorraine, was to be put under the administration of the League of Nations for a period of fifteen years; at the end of the period the inhabitants of the district were to decide by plebiscite under which sovereignty they desired to be placed. To the north the small districts of Eupen and Malmédy were assigned to Belgium, while still farther north a plebiscite prescribed by the treaty gave a portion of Schleswig (annexed by Prussia in 1864) to Denmark. Along their eastern frontier the Germans lost to the new state of Poland the province of Posen, the greater part of West Prussia, and much of Upper Silesia. This strengthening of Poland can be ascribed in part to the efforts of the French to set up a strong Poland as a means of keeping the Germans in check. Germany also had to give Poland the so-called "corridor" to the sea, thus severing East Prussia from the rest of Germany. In all, Germany lost about one seventh of her territory and one tenth of her population.

Nor was this all. Soon after the war started, most of the German colonies had been occupied by Allied forces. Before the end of the war the division of these colonies had been largely arranged by secret

[3] In 1926 Germany took the vacant permanent seat and in the same year the number of nonpermanent seats was increased to nine.

treaties. The first step toward carrying out these treaties was taken when Germany was required to renounce "all rights, titles, and privileges" in all territories outside her European frontiers and "to recognize any arrangements which the Allied and Associated Powers may make" regarding them. The road to the prearranged division among the Allies was still barred by a formidable obstacle in the form of the fifth of President Wilson's Fourteen Points. The President had stated the gist of Point Five quite succinctly in one of his speeches. "Every territorial settlement," he said, "must be made in the interests and for the benefit of the people concerned." But the Allies managed to circumvent this obstacle by setting up the so-called mandate system under which the colonies, instead of being annexed outright, were declared to be the common property of the League of Nations; then they proceeded to distribute them in accordance with the secret treaties.

Point Four of the Fourteen Points, which prescribed the reduction of national armaments "to the lowest point consistent with domestic safety," was applied only to Germany. Fully convinced that the Germans had been responsible for the war, the Allies sought to make sure that they would not go to war again. Accordingly their army was reduced to 100,000 men, including officers. To prevent the building up of a large reserve, the treaty decreed that enlistment in the *Reichswehr,* as the new army was called, must be voluntary and for a period of twelve years. Furthermore, the number of guns, machine guns, trench mortars, and rifles and the amount of ammunition and equipment which Germany was allowed to maintain were strictly limited, and the manufacture or importation of tanks, armored cars, and similar vehicles was prohibited. The German navy, too, was pared to a minimum. "The German naval forces," the treaty stated, "must not exceed six battleships, six light cruisers, twelve destroyers, and twelve torpedo boats." The navy personnel was limited to 15,000, and submarines were prohibited. Thus Germany was practically disarmed. As a further measure in the interest of French security the right bank of the Rhine was demilitarized to a distance of fifty kilometers; all fortified works or fortresses in this area were to be razed. The left bank, together with the bridgeheads, was to be occupied by Allied troops for fifteen years.

The question of reparations absorbed much of the attention of the peacemakers and was in some respects the storm center of the conference. The peoples of the Allied countries believed almost without exception that Germany was solely responsible for the war. This belief was endorsed as unanimously by the American people as by the European associates. Had not the German people, among other things, invaded Belgium, devastated northern France, and sunk the *Lusitania?* This conviction caused the peacemakers to include in the treaty the so-called "war-guilt clause." According to it (Article 231): "Germany accepts the responsibility of Germany and her Allies for causing all the loss and damage to which the Allied and Associated Governments and their nationals have been subjected, as a consequence of the war imposed upon them by the aggression of Germany and her Allies." Since Germany was the guilty author of the war, it followed logically that she, together with her allies, should pay the entire cost of the war. Even this did not satisfy the French press, which went so far as to demand in addition the repayment with interest of the indemnity Germany had collected from France in 1871.

After much debate, however, the peacemakers decided that they could not claim compensation for the entire costs of World War I, but only for "damage done to the civilian population," since the Allies had in the pre-armistice note of November 5, 1918, renounced all claims to total reimbursement. Only Belgium was to be compensated for the entire loss that resulted from the invasion. On the question of the amount Germany was to pay there were sharp differences. The suggestion of the experts from the United States that the maximum figure be set at $15 billion was not acceptable to the French, who demanded an amount almost three times as large. Finally it was decided to submit the entire question of reparations to a special commission which was to determine by May 1, 1921, both the amount and the manner of payment. As a first payment Germany was required to pay at once the sum of $5 billion in the form of gold, merchant ships, reconstruction material, coal, dyestuffs, and other commodities.

Even before President Wilson's return the treaty had become an issue in domestic politics in the United States. The President had been so occupied with the task of drawing up the treaty that he had done nothing to insure its passage by the Senate. A group of Republicans which included former President Taft and former Secretary of State Elihu Root had offered to do all in their power to secure ratification if the President would include two prominent Republicans in his peace delegation. But Mr. Wilson refused the offer. Even before he left for Paris the voters had returned a Republican majority in both the Senate and the House of Representatives. Near the end of his stay in Paris the President was informed that the outlook for ratification was bad. Yet he hoped to turn the tide in his favor upon his return. Colonel House steadfastly insisted that "everything will come out all right once the 'Governor' [President Wilson] returns and gets in touch with the people."

But the hopes of President Wilson and Colonel House soon collapsed. When the treaty came before the Senate in November, 1919, the hostile Republican majority voted it down by a vote of 55 to 39. A number of other votes were taken, but in the end the treaty remained unratified. Although the opposition may have been motivated in part by personal feeling toward the President, the primary reason for the vote seems to have been the conviction that further participation in European affairs was not in the interest of the people of the United States.[4] The repudiation was a severe blow to the entire Versailles settlement.

FURTHER TREATIES

The Paris Peace Conference produced not one treaty, but five. In addition to the treaty of Versailles it drew up the treaty of Saint Germain with Austria, the treaty of Sèvres with Turkey,[5] the treaty of Trianon with Hungary, and the treaty of Neuilly with Bulgaria. Like that of Versailles, each of the others took its name from one of the suburbs of Paris. The treaty of Versailles was the model for the rest, and many of its sections, as for example the Covenant of the League, were incorporated in all. Reparations were demanded from Austria, Hungary, and Bulgaria in the same terms as from Germany.

In the fall of 1918 the Austrian humpty-dumpty which had so long been maintained by the Habsburgs had fallen to earth. Its frail shell had been shattered so completely it was obvious that all the emperor's horses and the emperor's men could not put the Austrian Empire together again. Before the Peace Conference opened in January, 1919, each of the nationalities had set up a state of its own and laid claim to certain boundaries. In many cases rival nationalities were claiming the same territory. Thus the conference was confronted with a difficult task in adjusting boundaries. The guiding principle was to be self-determination, which was to be applied alike to victors and vanquished in accordance with President Wilson's statement, "It must be a justice that plays no favorites and knows no standard but the equal rights of the several peoples concerned." Actually, however, the conference appeared to be guided to a large extent by the desire to reward faithful friends and to punish the conquered foe. Although Wilson had said that "peoples and provinces are not to be bartered about from sovereignty to sovereignty as if they were mere chattels and pawns in a game, even the great game, now forever discredited, of the balance of power," the Peace Conference was more concerned with the establishment of a new balance of power than in "a peace of justice" or "a peace of healing." In justice to the peacemakers it must be stated, however, that in some regions the nationalities were so hopelessly mixed that it was utterly impossible to disentangle them politically.

The treaty of Saint Germain put the Allied stamp of approval on the disruption of the Habsburg Empire into small bits. It confirmed the

[4] On July 2, 1921, the United States signed a separate treaty with Germany.
[5] This treaty was superseded by the treaty of Lausanne in 1923.

annexation of Galicia by Poland, and the seizure of territory by Czecho-slovakia in Bohemia and Moravia, by Italy in South Tyrol, and by Yugoslavia in the Slav districts of the south. The small remnant that was left, outside of Hungary, was labeled Austria. Austria thus became one of the smallest states of Europe. It embraced only about 32,000 square miles with a population of less than 6.5 millions according to the census of 1920. Of this population about two millions, or nearly one third of the total, lived in Vienna. Thus Vienna, which before the war had been the capital of the third largest empire of Europe, became the center of a few counties whose resources were at best sufficient to sup-port a moderate-sized provincial town. The relationship of Vienna to the small republic has often been likened to that of a huge unwieldy head to a tiny body. Moreover, this small state was saddled with re-sponsibility for reparations which it was not in a position to bear.

The terms of the treaty were handed to the Austrian delegation at St. Germain on June 2. When they became known in Vienna, feeling among the masses ran high. Although there were no demonstrations, the Austrian newspapers vied with one another in denouncing the treaty. *Der Neue Tag* stated, "We can be forced to sign the treaty, but it can-not be said to represent our consent. No one in German Austria would hesitate to tear up such a treaty. It is a crime against mankind and all high and noble ideas." Among the government officials the terms caused consternation. Dr. Karl Renner, head of the peace delegation and chan-cellor of Austria, said, "The Austrian people must suffer for the mis-deeds of their rulers. We never wanted the war and were not guilty of bringing it about." President Seitz said the treaty was completely de-void of "sympathetic understanding." "It must be taken into considera-tion," he said, "that a majority of the Austrians did not want the war. They were forced to fight, just as the Czechs were. . . . We are ready for a peace that will let us live." The only gleam of hope lay in the Austrian counterproposal that plebiscites be held in all the transferred territories. The proposal was, however, turned down, and the Austrians had no course but to accept the treaty, since they were in no position to resist. As Dr. Renner put it, "We have the option of shooting our-selves or being shot." Staggering under the burden of old debts and freshly imposed indemnities, hemmed in by hostile tariff walls, and faced by hunger and financial collapse, little Austria was left to strug-gle on alone.

Hungary was dealt with no less severely in the treaty of Trianon. She lost Transylvania to Rumania, Slovakia to Czechoslovakia, Croatia to Yugoslavia, and Fiume to Italy. All transfers were made without plebiscites, the Allies having rejected Hungary's request for them. The total loss amounted to two thirds of the Hungarian territory and population. Hungary herself was left an area of about 35,000 square miles with a population of about eight millions. Her army was limited to 35,000 and she had to shoulder her share of the reparations. The Hungarians were naturally very bitter about the treaty. Most objectionable to them was the transfer to Rumania of Transylvania with three million Hungarians. This, according to one Hungarian, was "a monstrous deed." The loss of so much territory gave Hungary a series of grievances against Rumania, Czechoslovakia, and Yugoslavia.

The Peace Conference completed its work, so to speak, by drawing up the treaty of Neuilly. In the hope of rectifying territorial grievances resulting from the Balkan wars of 1912–1913, the Bulgarian government had, contrary to the wishes of the Bulgarian people, cast its lot with the Central Powers in 1915. As a loser Bulgaria was asked to help pay the bill. Furthermore, in flagrant violation of the principles laid down by President Wilson, a strategic strip of Bulgarian territory was given to Yugoslavia. She was also required to cede eastern Thrace to Greece, a loss which cut her off completely from the Aegean Sea. Thereafter it was necessary for the Bulgarians to cross alien and unfriendly territory in order to reach the Aegean. The amputations of territory put no fewer than 1.7 million Bulgarians under foreign rule. The settlement came as a distinct shock to the people, for they had naively believed that the peace would be based on the principles laid down by President Wilson.

It can be said in favor of the treaties that there were fewer discontented minorities in Europe after the war than before. But the settlement certainly failed to solve the vexing problem of subject peoples. In removing old grievances it created new Irredentas. Thus Rumania was given a generous slice of Transylvania inhabited by Magyars; many Germans, Rumanians, and Magyars were included in Yugoslavia; a quarter of a million German-speaking people were ceded to Italy; and more than three million Germans were transferred to the new state of Czechoslovakia. All this was hardly in accord with the statement made by Lloyd George on March 25, 1919: "I cannot conceive any greater cause of future war than that the German people . . . should be surrounded by a number of small states, many of them consisting of people who have never previously set up a stable government for themselves, but each of them containing large masses of Germans clamoring for reunion with their native land." It was indeed a prophetic utterance that the Austrian Assembly made in 1919: "The 4 million Germans forced under foreign rule will for all times insist on self-determination as the only possible basis on which the modern state may be founded." In short, the treaties established not peace, but an uneasy armistice.

CHAPTER TWENTY

Europe after World War I

THE QUEST FOR
COLLECTIVE SECURITY $\quad$ **A**FTER more than four years and three
months of bloody war, in which most of Europe and much of the rest
of the world participated, hostilities ended abruptly. Besides exacting
a vast toll in human lives the war brought much of prewar society
down in ruins, for its end saw the collapse of the Turkish, Austrian, and
Russian empires. Out of the ruins rose new states with new governments and new economic systems. Even those states which retained the
same governments emerged from the war greatly changed. In all the
European states that had been active in the war, wide disorganization
prevailed soon after the armistice. When the war broke out industry
was, by and large, converted to the production of war matériel and
about a third of the workers were withdrawn for military service. Demobilization of the armies flooded the labor market, and the reconversion of industry to the production of the necessaries of human life produced much confusion, since the war ended before reconversion plans
were ready. What the economic systems in the various countries needed
was to recover balance.

Although the nations that had participated in the long struggle
emerged from it exhausted, having sacrificed the flower of their youth,
dissipated their national wealth, and suffered social and moral injuries,
they had one consolation. The belief was widespread that the "war to
end war" had really ended war, that never again would there be another such bloody contest as the one that had just been concluded.
When the treaty-makers left Paris, most of them were confident that
their labors had assured for the world a long period of peace. They
were convinced that since Germany and Austria, whom they regarded

as the authors of war, were disarmed, the task of keeping the peace would be an easy one. They reasoned that the League would include most, if not all, of the nations and that any aggressor would therefore stand alone. In any case, aggressors could always be brought to their senses by means of economic sanctions imposed by the League. They were certain that in general the League would be able to mete out stern justice to wrongdoers. The possibility that one nation or a group of nations could successfully challenge the authority of the League never entered their thoughts.

But no sooner had the new order been set up than it began to disintegrate. One historian has gone so far as to state that the history of the period between World War I and World War II "is essentially the history of the breakdown of the peace" settlement of Paris. The process began in the repudiation of the entire settlement by the United States, which now embraced an isolationist policy concerned almost exclusively with American affairs. The British refused to assume the responsibility of protecting the French against another German attack, an obligation which an Anglo-French treaty would have imposed on them. As they saw the situation, security had been attained and the next war lay in too remote a future to be of any immediate concern. Feeling somewhat secure in their insular position, they did not wish to see one power dominate the Continent; hence they were not opposed to a restoration of a considerable part of German power as a counterbalance to French hegemony. Thus the interests and policies of Britain and France began to diverge.

Although the French still hoped to collect huge reparations from the Germans, they were bitter over the fact that they had not obtained the security they desired against another German invasion. They had hoped by an agreement with Britain and the United States to establish so great a superiority of force that it would be impossible for the defeated powers to challenge the settlement. When both the United States and Britain refused to conclude such an agreement, France was left to face alone a Germany with a much larger population and much greater industrial strength. This filled the French with new fears. To secure some measure of protection they turned to the countries that were interested in keeping Germany disarmed and in upholding the Paris settlement. Among these were Belgium, Poland, Czechoslovakia, Rumania, and Yugoslavia. Gradually this group of nations drew closer together. On the other hand there was a group which included Germany, Austria, Hungary, and Bulgaria who regarded the treaties as unjust. Although for the time being they had to accept the decisions of the Paris peacemakers, they hoped that the settlement would soon be revised. Thus soon after the end of "the war to end war" Europe was again divided into two camps, the upholders of the *status quo* and the revisionists.

The League of Nations, too, made an inauspicious start. It came into operation on January 10, 1920, and six days later the Council met for the first time to inaugurate a new order of international peace and justice. Participation in the League was woefully incomplete. Public opinion in the United States was not in favor of participation. The ex-enemy nations, in a deliberate separation of the sheep from the goats, were not invited to join. Soviet Russia, which had not as yet been accorded recognition by the other states, did not become a member until 1934. Thus seven nations were not represented at the first meeting. Repudiation of the League by the United States was a serious blow to the new organization. The absence of the one strong power which could have spoken freely in the Council shattered the hope of a universal League. On the other hand, the League did embrace a majority of the self-governing nations. As early as December, 1920, both Austria and Bulgaria were admitted, thereby raising the membership to forty-four states.

During the next few years the League was largely occupied in setting up its machinery of administration. It also did much in the field of reconstruction and relief work. Such other problems as were brought before it dealt largely with the delimitation of frontiers, and most of these were settled to the satisfaction of the parties involved. The League also undertook with excellent results the administration of Danzig and the Saar. During this early period the delegates watched one another with doubt and distrust, but by 1924 the spirit of the League was changed. The question of offering Germany a seat was discussed, and in the next year Germany was actually admitted with a permanent seat on the Council. The next three years were the most flourishing period in the League's history. The assemblies, which had previously been poorly attended, now attracted the prime ministers and foreign ministers of the whole continent. In 1927 membership numbered no less than fifty-six nations and the future looked promising. For a time it appeared as if the world might succeed in creating a world community.

The year 1925 saw also the conclusion of the Locarno treaties, which did much to clear the atmosphere of distrust and suspicion. By this time a number of German leaders had come to realize that the controlling factor in the French mind was fear of a new German aggression, of another war to recover Alsace-Lorraine and to take vengeance for the defeat of World War I. They saw that a stable peace could be achieved only by improving the relations between Germany and France. On the other hand, the Allies recognized that the return of Germany into the family of great powers as a respectable member would contribute much toward the establishment of a more peaceful order. The result of this change of attitude was that in the summer of 1925 representatives of a number of nations met at the little Swiss town of Locarno in the shadow of the Alps. Besides such leading statesmen as M. Briand of France, Sir Austen Chamberlain of England, and Dr. Gustav Stresemann of Germany, Premier Mussolini appeared to solemnize the event by his presence.

After some days of discussion the "Locarno agreement" was reached, of which the Treaty of Mutual Guarantee is the cornerstone. In Article One the five powers (France, Great Britain, Germany, Italy, and Belgium) guaranteed "collectively and severally" the inviolability of the western frontiers set up by the Versailles Treaty. Article Two contains the fundamental clause outlawing war. "Germany and Belgium, also Germany and France, mutually undertake that they will in no case attack or invade each other or resort to war against each other." Questions of every kind were, according to Article Three, to be settled by peaceful means. Thus it appeared as if France had finally gained the security she had sought so long. Though Germany renounced her claims to Alsace-Lorraine, she made no renunciation of territory in the east. This left the way open for a revision by peaceful means of the frontier between Germany and Poland. To many "the spirit of Locarno" was even more important than the treaties. It seemed to augur an era of peace and international cooperation. As such it was hailed by the press of many countries.

A further gesture in favor of peace was made three years later in the Briand-Kellogg Pact for the Renunciation of War. In 1928 a group of American officials led by Frank B. Kellogg, then United States Secretary of State, joined with M. Briand in initiating the treaty. The sixty-one signatory nations, including Japan, Italy, and Germany, promised that thenceforth they would settle all disputes or conflicts of whatever nature by pacific means. War was permanently outlawed except in self-defense. Article I of the treaty states: "The High Contracting Parties solemnly declare in the names of their respective peoples that they condemn recourse to war for the solution of international controversies and renounce it as an instrument of national policy in their relations with one another." There was even talk of carrying out the disarmament program to which the powers had pledged themselves at the Paris Conference.

The Locarno treaties together with the Kellogg Pact promised for a time to lead to a general appeasement. But the promise was illusory. If things looked better on the surface, underneath the same old hostilities persisted. The Locarno treaties had produced no real reconciliation, because they had not removed the basic causes of friction. They had not led to a reconsideration of those features of the Versailles treaty to which the Germans objected, nor had they dispelled French fear of Germany. On the one hand, France still continued to pursue her policy of military alliances; on the other, the Germans cherished their hope for revision of the Versailles settlement.

Before long some rapid changes took place in the international kaleidoscope. The attitude of certain states became menacing. This deterioration in the relations between the European states was due to a number of causes. As is always the case in such changes, some of the factors were in part cause and in part effect of the move away from internationalism toward war. Among them were such factors as fear, national grievances, prestige, and national jealousies. But the cause which undoubtedly contributed most was the economic depression. The prosperity bubble burst with a crash in Wall Street in October, 1929, only a little more than a year after the ratification of the Briand-Kellogg Pact. The effect of this economic collapse, which was more catastrophic than any other in history, was soon felt in other parts of the globe. The following year economic crises descended on the European continent, which had not as yet recovered from the ravages of the war. The effects in France and Great Britain were considerable, but they were most sinister in Germany. Gradually the number of unemployed increased in Europe until it reached an estimated thirty millions and distress was widespread.

The economic distress again brought national self-interest to the fore, at the expense of international cooperation and good will. In other words, it undermined the system of collective security. Gradually the old nationalist ideas and policies which had produced the prewar system of Triple Alliance and Triple Entente became more and more prominent. Nations began to build up their armed forces and to prepare for what they regarded as the inevitable conflict. At the same time the influence and appeal of the League steadily declined. The European nations were again drifting toward war. In 1933 an Englishman wrote:

The whole European continent seems to be writhing in the various distressing symptoms of some terrible disease. Fear and suspicion obsess the people of nations great and small. National ambitions and short-sighted self-interests show themselves on the one hand, with a spirit of discontent and zeal for re-gain prominent on the other. Armaments, comprising the most ingenious and diabolical devices of mechanical science for the destruction of mankind and the handiwork of the human race, are being piled up by some nations, sought after by others, and at the same time condemned with horror by the men and women of whom these nations are composed.[1]

[1] *Nineteenth Century and After*, vol. 113 (1933), p. 12.

THE DEMOCRATIC EXPERIMENT IN GERMANY

The establishment of the Weimar Republic was not due to the victory of a German republican party over the monarchists. At no time had the Germans been fighting for liberty and democracy. There had been, in fact, little demand for a change of government. Only when President Wilson insisted that he would not deal with the government that had brought on the war did the demand arise for the resignation of William II. The Germans were ready to sacrifice the kaiser only because they believed that they could obtain better peace terms by doing so. Thus the Weimar Republic was, in a sense, imposed on the people. There was little real enthusiasm for it. To the people who were not in favor of it, it was the result of defeat in the war and of foreign intrusion into German affairs. As such it became to many the symbol of humiliation.

What actually took place can hardly be called a revolution. The change did not go much beyond the change of government. After the kaiser's departure for Holland, the twenty-five sovereigns of the individual states resigned and Germany was proclaimed a republic, but the entire social and economic organization remained much the same as it had been before. Practically all the imperial officials remained at their posts and continued to administer the routine of their bureaus. Inspired by the success of the Bolshevik Revolution, a small group of Independent Socialists, called Spartacists, did try to establish a communist government; its leaders, Karl Liebknecht and Rosa Luxemburg, addressing gatherings in Berlin and other industrial centers, urged the proletariat to rise up and establish "a free Socialist republic," and on November 9, 1918, a group of Spartacists even went so far as to seize the royal palace and police headquarters in Berlin. But the group lacked real support. On the afternoon of the same day a committee of Majority Socialists (Social Democrats) took over the task of ruling Germany from the cabinet of Prince Max, the last chancellor of the kaiser's government. Friedrich Ebert, the head of this provisional government, simply announced that the government would be conducted on constitutional lines and then proceeded to create a trustworthy republican force capable of keeping order. A further attempt of the Spartacists (January, 1919) to set up a communist government also failed.

The election of deputies to the National Assembly which was to draw up the constitution for the new republic took place on January 19, 1919, both men and women over twenty being permitted to vote. When the votes were counted, it was found that, although the Majority Socialists had polled more votes than all the other parties combined, they had elected only 163 of a total of 399 deputies (one deputy for

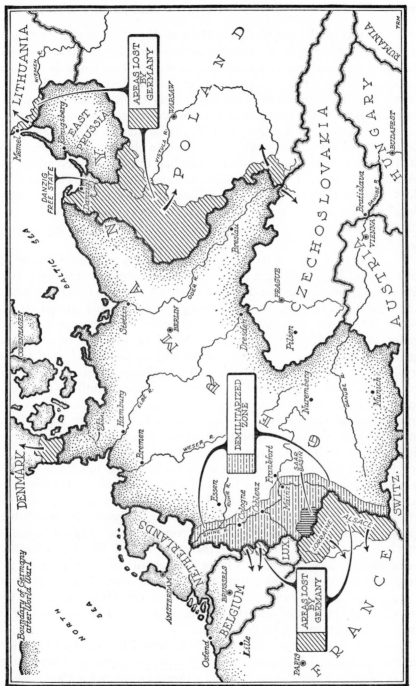

GERMANY DURING THE PERIOD OF THE WEIMAR REPUBLIC

each 150,000 of the population). Most of the old political parties of prewar Germany had been revived and had elected their quota of deputies. The old Conservatives appeared under the new name of German National People's Party; the Catholic Center Party retained its old name. The only important new party was the German Democratic Party, formed by the bourgeoisie for the avowed purpose of supporting the establishment of a republic. This predominance of the bourgeois element ruled out a purely socialist regime. In choosing a meeting place Ebert, remembering how the Paris mobs had threatened the various assemblies during the French Revolution, ruled out Berlin. The place he chose was Weimar, which is famous because Goethe, Schiller, Herder, Bach, and Liszt wrote many of their great works there. From the fact that the constitution was drawn up at Weimar, the new government took the name of the Weimar Republic.

The Assembly opened its sessions on February 6. Before taking up the major task of drafting a permanent constitution, it drew up a provisional republican constitution and elected Friedrich Ebert president. Ebert said in assuming the presidency, "I desire and intend to act as the authorized representative of the entire German people, not as leader of a single party." He did remind his hearers that he had "grown up in the world of ideas according to socialism," but as the president of the republic he was quite moderate in his outlook. Although not a man of extraordinary gifts, he stood until his death in 1925 as an unflinching supporter of parliamentary democracy. In drawing up the constitution, the Assembly did not borrow freely from any one country but incorporated features of many governments, including those of Britain, France, Switzerland, and the United States. It provided for a one-chamber legislative body, called the Reichstag, to be elected by equal franchise for men and women above twenty. The executive power was vested in a president elected by popular vote for a term of seven years. He was given the power to dissolve the Reichstag, appoint ambassadors, conclude treaties, command the army, and appoint the chancellor and the ministers of the cabinet. Both the chancellor and the ministers, however, had to have the support of a majority in the Reichstag. In other words, the president was elected for a term of seven years, as in France, and had powers resembling those of the president of the United States, but his ministers were responsible to the Reichstag in truly British fashion.

Even before the constitution was promulgated in August, 1919, German sentiment had begun to turn away from the republic. This change was in large measure due to dissatisfaction with the peace treaty which the republic was compelled to accept. The conservative trend of German sentiment convinced a group of reactionaries under the leadership of a Prussian official named Kapp that they could overthrow the re-public. The attempt, known as the Kapp Putsch, was made in March, 1920, and succeeded so well that President Ebert and his cabinet had to leave Berlin. But the rebellion collapsed when the trade unions, whose members were largely socialists, practically paralyzed the city by cutting off the water, gas, electric, and transportation services. Although the republic was saved, its support was anything but secure. This was clearly demonstrated by the fact that in the first Reichstag election under the new constitution (June, 1920) the vote of the parties who had openly accepted the republican government was much smaller (the socialist vote alone decreased by almost three millions), while the parties with monarchist tendencies gained three million votes. Nor was monarchist sympathy confined to the older generation. Education in the German high schools and universities was still almost completely in the hands of reactionaries who instilled monarchist ideas in the minds of the young. Thus the republic led a precarious existence from the very beginning.

REPARATIONS AND INFLATION

The most serious problem of the new republic, next to keeping the reactionaries from overthrowing it, was economic. The economic chaos which reigned in all belligerent countries at the end of the war was aggravated in Germany not only by the loss of territories rich in raw materials but also by the fact that the Germans were required to turn over to the Allies large quantities of materials. The transfer to France of Alsace-Lorraine with its iron ore and potash deposits, the temporary loss of the highly industrialized Saar district, and the ceding to Poland of Upper Silesia with its coal mines, dealt a severe blow to German industry. It has been calculated that in 1913 the ceded areas produced 48.2 per cent of Germany's iron ore output, 59 per cent of her zinc, 24 per cent of her lead, and 15.7 per cent of her coal. The German government was also required by the terms of the armistice to surrender to the Allies all merchant ships exceeding 1600 gross tons, half of the merchant ships between 1000 and 1600 gross tons, one quarter of the fishing fleet, 5000 locomotives, and 150,000 motor trucks. Furthermore, all German investments in the Allied countries had been seized or sur-rendered, and German credit in the world's capital markets had been seriously undermined. Thus Germany was hardly ready for the vast burden of reparations that was about to be imposed on her.

Early in May, 1921, the Reparations Commission announced that Germany's total indemnity bill would be 132 billion marks, an amount which, according to a number of Allied economists, exceeded Germany's ability to pay. The reparations demands were given the Germans in the form of an ultimatum which they were to accept in six days or suffer an Allied invasion of the Ruhr. In 1921 the government did pay a billion marks and there were additional payments early in 1922, but in June of the same year it was forced to request a moratorium on reparation payments for two years because the economic situation had deteriorated so greatly. Since the announcement of the reparation debt the mark had declined steadily. Inflation had already set in during the war, but had been checked temporarily in 1920. In May, 1921, the mark was worth 62 to the United States dollar (4.2 to the dollar was par). After the announcement of the Reparations Commission it declined to 105 in September and to 270 by the end of November.

When the British and French representatives met to discuss the request, the former, fearing a general economic collapse in Germany, were ready to agree to a moratorium. The French took the opposite view. They believed that the German request was a trick to evade payment. Instead of granting the moratorium the French dispatched a force into the Ruhr (January, 1923) to make sure that the Germans would make reparation deliveries of coal and coke. This move, which was a frank appeal to force, caused the mark to drop to 40,000 for a dollar by the end of January. In the Ruhr the Germans, eschewing violence, resorted to "passive resistance." The workers refused to mine coal and produce coke, with the result that all deliveries were discontinued. But the population of the Ruhr, numbering about five millions, had to be fed and supported. To do this the government had to issue more and more marks. As the astronomer Copernicus put it in a letter to King Sigismund of Poland in 1596, "Money loses its value when it has become too much multiplied." German presses worked at top speed day and night to supply the demand. The effect on the value of the mark was catastrophic. By the middle of June, 1923, it fell to 100,000 for a dollar; by August 8 to 5,000,000; by the middle of September to 100,000,000; by October 9 to more than 1,000,000,000,000; and by November 15 to 4,200,000,000,000.

The inflation crisis was unprecedented in severity in the history of modern industrial states. Among the less serious effects was the complication of all business affairs. Rates at first had to be increased every week, then each day, and finally workmen were paid several times a day so as to enable them to change the marks into anything that had inherent value before they became worthless. Shopkeepers, in order to ward off bankruptcy, were compelled to increase the selling price of their commodities from hour to hour. In the rural districts peasants most frequently refused marks and would exchange goods only for other goods.[2] More serious was the fact that the inflation reduced to poverty many families of established wealth and position. Fortunes that had been built up over a period of centuries disappeared overnight. Hardest hit was the lower middle class. At one fell swoop inflation wiped out pensions, savings, and insurance. This class never recovered from the blow, and many of its members became embittered toward the republic. It was from the ranks of these impoverished Germans, most of whom had normally voted the ticket of the moderate party, that Hitler later gained many of his most fanatical followers.

During the time inflation was running wild, Germany fortunately saw one of her great modern leaders appear on the scene. He was Gustav Stresemann. During his early life he had been a liberal monarchist, and at the time he became the leading figure in the government he was only a half-hearted republican. But he did realize that the Ruhr question must be settled before the German economy could be rehabilitated. Conciliation was the means by which he hoped to achieve this. With feeling in Germany running high against France he had the courage boldly to proclaim a policy of reconciliation and cooperation. The fruit of this policy was an agreement in November, 1923, whereby the Ruhr industrialists promised to deliver commodities to the Allies, an agreement which eventually led to the withdrawal of the French forces from the Ruhr in the summer of 1925. November, 1923, also saw Stresemann's government stabilize the mark through the issuance of the Rentenmark, which had little intrinsic value and was supported by public confidence.[3] The public was happy to accept it at the rate of one Rentenmark for a trillion old paper marks. As the old marks gradually disappeared from circulation, economic activities became more normal.

The policy of reconciliation together with the stabilization of the mark opened the way for a reconsideration of the reparation problem. It resulted in the appointment by the Reparations Commission of two committees to study economic conditions in Germany and to estimate her ability to pay. The committee of which Charles G. Dawes, later Vice-President of the United States, was chairman drew up the so-called Dawes Plan, the principal feature of which was that it reduced the indemnity to a sum Germany could pay. Payments were set up in an ascending series beginning with a billion marks in 1924–1925 and increasing to 2.5 billions in the year 1928–1929. Soon further progress was also made in the field of international relations. In 1925

[2] To many peasants the inflation was a boon in that it enabled them to pay off their mortgages in almost worthless money.
[3] In November, 1924, it was supplanted by the standard Reichsmark, which was put on a gold basis.

Dr. Stresemann started negotiations which resulted in the signing of
the Locarno treaties before the end of that year.

Meanwhile Germany's economic recovery was progressing by leaps
and bounds. An important factor in this recovery was the foreign loans
which infused new blood into Germany's anemic economic arteries.
During the entire period up to the depression of 1930 vast sums of
foreign capital continued to flow into Germany, particularly from
the United States, where the postwar boom had created surplus capital. According to figures prepared by the German government in 1931,
the influx of capital amounted to no less than $7.8 billion, during the
period from 1924 to 1931. By the end of 1928 the stock of gold of
the Reichsbank was twice as large as it had been at the outbreak of
the war. These funds enabled Germany to reconstruct her industries
along the most modern lines, so that by the end of the period Germany
had the most modern industrial equipment in Europe and was consequently able to regain the leadership which she had held before the
war in the optical, chemical, and electrical industries. By 1929 the
volume of industrial production was well above the prewar level. At
the same time German trade also expanded rapidly. The fact that
the Germans had been required to deliver cargo ships and railway
rolling stock to the Allies turned out to be a boon, for they were all
replaced by the most modern ships, locomotives, and railway cars.
Export figures rose until Germany was again among the leaders of
world trade.

While economic conditions were improving, Germany suffered a
great loss in the death of President Ebert early in 1925. Whatever his
limitations, he had stood firmly for the preservation of the republic.
His death seemed to leave a vacuum. Many candidates were put
forward, but in the election none was able to secure an absolute
majority of the votes, and a second election became necessary. In the
search for a candidate with a wide appeal the idea was hit upon of
bringing Field Marshal von Hindenburg, "the hero of Tannenberg,"
out of retirement. He was in truth poorly fitted for the post. A life
member of the Junker caste, he had little understanding of or sympathy
for democratic government. Nor was his mental equipment adequate
to the task: politics, economics, and finance were a closed book to
him; such knowledge as he possessed was limited to the science of
warfare. At the age of seventy-eight he had little desire to shoulder
the burden of public office, but finally surrendered to the urging of
his friends. The election was hotly contested. When the votes were
counted it was found that he had won by some 800,000 votes. The
report of his victory caused consternation among ardent supporters
of the republic and jubilation in the ranks of the reactionaries. But

despite his conservative past Hindenburg was determined to keep his oath to the constitution. In later years he came more and more under the influence of the reactionaries and finally yielded to Hitler.

Payments under the Dawes Plan were made promptly, but it was only "provisional"; what the Germans wanted was a final plan. Such a plan, setting forth for the first time the total amount Germany was expected to pay, was drawn up by a committee of experts, of which Owen D. Young of the United States was chairman. Under this so-called Young Plan the payments were to begin in 1930 with the sum of $400 million, gradually increase to a maximum of $570 million in 1965–1966, then gradually decrease and finally cease in 1988. By the time the first payments were due, however, the great depression had set in.

THE TWILIGHT OF GERMAN DEMOCRACY

At the beginning of 1929 the German people had reached a stage of contentment which augured well for the long life of the republic. As a result of Stresemann's efforts foreign relations, especially those with France, had improved greatly. Internally Germany was enjoying a prosperity that promised better things for the masses. The republic appeared to be in a most healthy condition. But before many months had passed the situation began to change rapidly. Two events were responsible for the change. The first was the death of Stresemann in October, 1929, at the age of fifty-one. This is not to say that he would have been able to save the republic if he had lived longer. But when his hand was taken from the tiller, the ship of state began to founder. Reactionaries whom he had held in line now openly turned against the republic. There was also a change for the worse in Germany's foreign relations. After the death of the man who had worked so hard to establish a permanent friendship between Germany and France, the two nations began to drift apart.

It was, however, from the economic depression that the Weimar Republic received its mortal blow. The economic blizzard which started with the stock market collapse in Wall Street in October, 1929, hit Germany, which was particularly vulnerable because its economy was based on borrowed money, with devastating force in 1930. Foreign creditors at once began to withdraw the funds they had sent into Germany, thereby depleting the German gold reserves to such an extent that there was a serious shortage of capital. Many Germans, fearing the loss of their bank deposits, withdrew them either to hoard them or to transfer them abroad for safekeeping. Unable to meet the withdrawals, a number of the larger banks were forced to close their doors. Before long the lack of working capital also forced industry to curtail its output. The number of unemployed rose from two millions in 1929 to more than three millions in 1930, and by the early months of 1932 the number had increased to six millions. These figures do not include the many whose working hours were reduced. In addition, wages were reduced by 17 per cent in 1931 and still further the next year. As the purchasing power of the working class declined, the home markets collapsed, tax receipts fell off sharply, and bankruptcies mounted steadily. The year 1931 saw more than 17,000 bankruptcies, the next year a still larger number.

Opposition to the republic grew apace as the economic conditions deteriorated. In the minds of some Germans the Weimar constitution had always been associated with the defeat in World War I. The acceptance of the treaty of Versailles, necessary though it was, also discredited the republic in the eyes of many. Furthermore, the lower middle class which had been impoverished by the inflation of 1923 cherished little love for the republic. To all these a large number of workingmen were now added. As unemployment increased and poverty became widespread, many among the working classes blamed the republican system for the existing conditions. This attitude, in turn, engendered a revolutionary spirit, inclining the masses to give ear to the preachments of the parties who were endeavoring to overthrow the republic. Many joined the Communist Party and others associated themselves with the National Socialist movement, the leader of which was Adolf Hitler. The trend toward extremism in Germany was definitely revealed by the general elections of September, 1930. The Communist vote increased from 3.25 to 4.5 millions; the Nazis at a single bound became the second largest party in the state. In 1928 only twelve Nazis were elected to a chamber of nearly 600, but in 1930 no fewer than 107 were returned, much to the astonishment of the Hitlerites themselves. Only the more moderate socialists continued to support the Weimar constitution.

Long before the Weimar Republic itself gave way to a dictatorship, democracy had gone by the board. The constitution carried within itself from the very beginning the seeds of its own death in the famous Article 48 giving the Reichspraesident the right to issue emergency legislation. This power enabled him to suspend many articles of the constitution itself. It does not appear to have been the intention of the framers of the constitution that the emergency decrees should supersede normal legislation. In other words, Article 48 was to apply only to cases of real emergency such as armed revolt. Antidemocratic tendencies, however, caused the new chancellor, Dr. Brüning, to use it as a regular instrument of government. After the

Hitler, von Hindenburg, and Goering. The old and the new sit together after Hitler's achievement of power (from Kemsley Photo).

...orthless German marks being ...ed as waste paper after the ...bilization in 1924

...yalist volunteers fighting the ...tionalists in the Spanish Civil ...r, 1936

...izens of Moscow return from ...vesting, 1931.

Chamberlain, Daladier, Hitler, Mussolini, and Count Ciano at the Munich Conference (October 6, 1938)

A Modern Moloch, a caricature of Hitler by Derso and Kelen (from *Pour la Victoire*)

Franco flanked by two lieutenants during the Spanish Civil War (from Black Star)

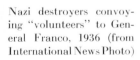

Nazi destroyers convoying "volunteers" to General Franco, 1936 (from International News Photo)

elections of 1930 the National Socialists and the Nationalists had about 150 deputies in the Reichstag, the Marxists 220, but the government of Chancellor Brüning (Centrists) only about 200. His government was thus a minority government, one without a majority in the Reichstag. His only hope of staying in office was that the Social Democrats would tolerate his government rather than force him into a coalition with Hitler. This the Social Democrats did. Having no majority in the Reichstag, Brüning was forced to rule by means of decrees. Thus the Reichstag ceased to function in a positive sense. Brüning's government was no longer dependent on the Reichstag, but on the president. It was a definite step away from democratic procedure toward dictatorship.

The year 1932 saw another presidential election in Germany. This time Hitler, encouraged by the growing strength of his party, entered the lists against von Hindenburg, who was eighty-four. Hitler referred to his opponent as a doddering old man and boasted that he was forty years younger. But these tactics did not win the election for him. Although the Social Democrats and the Catholic Center knew Hindenburg to be a reactionary, they believed that he would stand by his oath to uphold the constitution. When the votes were counted it was found that Hindenburg had received some 19 million votes against 13 million for Hitler. Hindenburg kept his oath to the constitution, but with the passage of time he did become increasingly susceptible to reactionary influences. When Chancellor Brüning in May, 1932, attempted to settle the crucial problem of landed property, a measure which would have encroached on the power of the Junkers (great landlords), he was dismissed by the Hindenburg government. Ironically enough the same power of emergency decrees which Brüning had used to keep himself in office was employed by the president to put an end to Brüning's liberal-minded dictatorship.

The end of the Weimar Republic was gradually drawing near. After Brüning's dismissal, Hindenburg summoned Franz von Papen, a confirmed reactionary, to organize a government. Von Papen, however, had little support in the Reichstag. Even the dissolution of the Reichstag and a new election failed to gain more support for him. Hindenburg next sought to gain support for the von Papen regime by offering Hitler a post in the cabinet, but the future Führer demanded nothing less than complete power, as complete as that wielded by Mussolini in Italy. For several months General von Schleicher sought as chancellor to hold off the Nazis but failed to do so. Hitler, seeing an opportunity to get control of the government, now entered into a coalition with von Papen. The latter, hoping that he might hold a high place in the Nazi order, convinced Hindenburg that the appointment of Hitler as chancellor was the only solution to the political crisis. Hindenburg, who was certain that Hitler's cabinet "would inevitably develop into a party dictatorship," held off for several months but finally yielded and on January 30, 1933, gave Hitler the chancellorship.

It has often been asked why Hindenburg signed the decree which gave Hitler the chancellorship. The act is quite irreconcilable with Hindenburg's record up to that point. Moreover, it was common knowledge that Hindenburg disliked and distrusted Hitler. Some writers have stated in his defense that the senile president's mind was so clouded that he did not know the import of the decree he signed. One of the jokes of contemporary Germany relates that Hindenburg's secretary had to discard promptly miscellaneous scraps of paper, including sandwich wrappers, lest the venerable gentleman put his signature on them. Others advanced the theory that Hindenburg was tricked into signing the decree. Be that as it may, the decree made Hitler chancellor and definitely marked the end of the Weimar Republic. The constitution, though not officially abrogated, became just another scrap of paper.

THE DECLINE OF DEMOCRACY IN EUROPE

The one thing that seemed to be inevitable on the eve of World War I was the triumph of democratic government. The belief that it was the most natural and the best form of government for a civilized nation had during the nineteenth century found ever-widening acceptance. Representative institutions in one form or another had taken root in nearly all the countries of Europe. In the decade preceding the war the only nonparliamentary states had fallen into line by the establishment of parliamentary institutions. Even in tsarist Russia a Duma was convened, and 1909 saw a parliament open in Turkey. Thus by the eve of 1914 parliamentary institutions had become almost universal either as the controlling factor of government or at least as an important element in government. Monarchies remained, to be sure, but they were limited monarchies. The old doctrine of divine right was accorded scant recognition. Kings now exercised their authority *populi gratia* (by the will of the people) and not *dei gratia*. Complete democracy appeared to be only a question of time.

The conviction that democratic government must ultimately prevail was further strengthened during World War I; in fact, the war exalted the ideals of democracy as no earlier event had done. Not only was it regarded on the Allied side as a struggle of democratic freedom against autocratic militarism; the universal establishment of democracy was made the avowed political aim of the Allied effort. This was boldly proclaimed in the slogan, "Make the world safe for democracy." As the war progressed, the way for the final triumph of democracy was cleared, it seemed, by the collapse of the three dynasties of emperors — the Romanovs, the Habsburgs, and the Hohenzollern — which were widely regarded as the bulwarks of reactionary absolutism. At the end of the war it was widely believed that the succeeding years would see the completion of the process of establishing democracy. This view was encouraged by the orgy of constitution-making which followed. During the four years after 1918 democratic constitutions were adopted in many countries, including Germany, Austria, Poland, Czechoslovakia, Finland, Latvia, Estonia, and the Irish Free State.

It soon became apparent, however, that those who regarded democratic government as inevitable were misreading the signs of the times. Just when it appeared certain that the democratic idea would triumph in all the countries of Europe, a widespread reaction set in. This reaction was the outstanding political phenomenon of the period between the two great wars. Dictatorship again made its appearance and was adopted by an increasing number of nations as the form of government best suited to their needs. As early as 1926 a European observer wrote, "The star of democratic government is everywhere on the wane." Before many years had passed the world was sharply divided into nations ruled by dictators and those which still clung to the ideals of democracy. The first dictatorship was established in Russia as a result of the Bolshevik Revolution in 1917. Theoretically it was "the dictatorship of the proletariat," but in practice it was exercised by one man. In 1922 Mussolini became the dictator of Italy, and three years later Kemal Atatürk started his benevolent dictatorship. Finally, in 1933 the German people accepted Hitler as their Führer. In short, the reaction against democratic government was so widespread that the champions of democracy lost most of the ground they had gained during the earlier years of the century.

It is a noteworthy fact that the new dictatorships were established in countries which had little experience in democratic government, as, for example, Russia, Italy, Germany, and Spain. In such countries as Norway, Sweden, Denmark, Holland, Belgium, and Great Britain, where there was a longer tradition of liberal or democratic government, the idea found only limited acceptance. In the former countries the masses were largely unprepared for the task of conducting their political affairs. They had not learned how to exercise their sovereignty. Moreover, in most of them illiteracy was so widespread that the masses lacked sufficient education to participate efficiently in a democracy. Consequently the new democracies were handicapped from the start. Moreover, the new democracies inherited problems of almost unexampled complexity, problems that would have taxed the most experienced statesmen. Among these were stabilization of the currency, reconversion of industries to peace-time purposes, repair of material damages, liquidation of huge war debts, regaining old markets and opening new ones, and providing employment for demobilized soldiers. The solution of these problems was made even more difficult by tariff barriers, exchange restrictions, tension between capital and labor, and machinations of the reactionaries.

Most of the new states had adopted the system of proportional representation, with the result that a large number of small party groups were returned to the popular chamber. In order to form a cabinet with a majority support it was necessary to organize a bloc or coalition. Such coalitions were short-lived; in fact, they seldom lasted long enough to achieve anything in the way of constructive legislation. Month after month was consumed by the bickering groups while the general confusion was increasing. In short, the existing parliamentary system of many of the new states failed to provide a remedy for the evils of the postwar period.

While the factional strife was increasing in intensity the forces of revolution and reaction were working tirelessly to discredit the existing governments. Thus the parties of the extreme Left, encouraged by the success of the Bolshevik Revolution, were trying in every possible way to bring about the collapse of the existing states in order to erect upon their ruins a communist order. At the same time the extremists of the Right were working with equal determination "to turn back the clock." The collapse of the Habsburg and Hohenzollern empires had come so suddenly that the masses were not ready to assume the official positions in the new governments. Consequently the old antidemocratic forces had preserved much of their power. In Germany, Poland, Austria, and Hungary, for example, the old bureaucracy, the nobility, the great landowners, and the military cliques remained to a large extent untouched because the revolutions had not been thoroughgoing enough. After the first few months they became bolder and asserted themselves more and more.

The enthusiasm of the masses for democratic government waned as the confusion increased and economic conditions deteriorated. Many who had earlier demanded liberty now felt they had not chosen wisely. They wanted remedial action at all costs and when it was not forthcoming concluded that democratic government had failed them. What they now asked for was security. This the prospective dictators were ready to promise; in fact, to achieve their objective they did not hesitate to promise anything and everything. In each state they appealed to the patriotism of the masses by promising to raise the country to its proper place in the world's esteem. This was a favorite device of the Italian Fascists and the German Nazis. Another means employed by the parties of the Right to make converts was to preach the menace of communism. Many of those who were not converted permitted a dictatorship to be imposed upon them. "Democracy," said President Roosevelt, "has disappeared in several great nations, and not because people of those nations dislike democracy, but because they had grown tired of unemployment and insecurity, of seeing their children hungry while they sat helpless in the face of Government confusion and Government weakness. . . . Finally, in desperation, they chose to sacrifice liberty in the hope of getting something to eat."

In organization the new dictatorships might be monarchical (Yugoslavia), presidential (Turkey), or military (Poland and Spain). Others, such as the Fascists and Nazis, had or purported to have special philosophies upon which the dictatorship was founded. Nevertheless, all showed a striking similarity in governmental technique. Their central doctrine was the supremacy of the state. They asserted the Hegelian doctrine that the state is an end in itself and man is but the means. In other words, they taught that the individual exists for the state, as opposed to the democratic idea that the state exists for the individual. In a democracy the freedom of the individual is limited only at the point where it encroaches on the rights of others; under a dictatorship the ordinary citizen not only has nothing to say about the government or the laws under which he lives, but he also has no protection against acts of force perpetrated by agents of the all-powerful state. Those who wield the power comprise only a minority, usually only a small minority organized as a party. Thus the state is actually not a state of the people. It is little more than the apparatus of one party which absorbs the functions of the state and uses them to achieve party ends. In the words of a contemporary writer: "It may be communistic in its stated philosophy, as in Russia, or Nazi as in Germany, or Fascist as in Italy, or something else as in many dictator countries in Europe. But in whatever guise it may cloak itself, its outstanding feature is that the ordinary citizen comes to have nothing to say about the government or laws under which he lives."

Another outstanding characteristic of the new dictatorships is the fact that they are totalitarian. It is this which differentiates them from the dictatorships of preceding periods. Earlier dictators from the time of the Romans to World War I had attempted to regulate only the broader aspects of life, but the new dictators made their rule an all-absorbing one. The instrument employed by them to achieve this was the party, a hand-picked and highly disciplined group upon which the dictatorship could rely. The members of the party supervise every phase of life, direct all activities of individuals and groups, and pry into everything. Consequently there is no longer anything like "a private life." The life of every individual is regulated down to the minutest detail.

CHAPTER TWENTY-ONE

The Soviet Experiment

THE NEW ORDER　　 EARLY in November, 1917 (October according to the Russian calendar), the Bolsheviks overthrew the wavering provisional government and set up the Union of Soviet Socialist Republics. This so-called October Revolution was not something that developed suddenly. For more than a decade the Bolsheviks had been perfecting their plan and waiting for an opportunity to put it into action. The master mind behind the plan was Nikolai Lenin, who had been a revolutionist during his entire adult life. When he was seventeen his brother was hanged as a member of a band of terrorists which had tried to assassinate Tsar Alexander III. The death of his brother convinced Nikolai that attempts on individual autocrats as a means of achieving a revolution were utterly futile. He would reach his goal by organizing the proletariat as a class. After studying law he turned his back on the practice of law in order to become an organizer of revolution. Although his efforts made him a marked man and subjected him to prison and exile, he did not desist. In his work he had few scruples about means or methods. Anything that might contribute to the desired end was acceptable. "Party members should not be measured by the narrow standards of bourgeois morality," he stated; "sometimes a scoundrel is useful to our party precisely because he is a scoundrel."

The party which under Lenin led the revolution in 1917 numbered only a few thousand members, but they were picked Bolsheviks who had been steeled in the furnace of political underground activity and tsarist persecution. At the time of the revolution against the tsar's government in March, 1917, most of the Bolshevik leaders had been either in foreign countries or in Siberian exile. Trotsky was in New York editing an émigré newspaper, Stalin was in Siberia, and Lenin in Switzerland. No sooner did the provisional government permit the return of the exiles than the roads to Petrograd were crowded with returning expatriates. *Pravda,* the organ of the Bolshevik party, whose publication had been suspended while its editor Stalin was in Siberia, was quickly revived and proceeded at once to attack the provisional government. The radicals felt that a great opportunity was at hand. None had more positive ideas on this point than Lenin. As he put it, "Politically things are quite ripe for a change of power." Upon reaching Petrograd from Switzerland through the "courtesy" of the Germans who supplied the transportation, he was greeted by a large crowd at the railway station. He answered the cheers of the crowd by climbing to the top of a car at the entrance to the station and shouting to the mob, "Long live the Social Revolution! All power to the Soviets!" A few days later he stated in an article in *Pravda* that the revolution against the tsar's government had been only preliminary to the real revolution which would establish the rule of the proletariat. How the Bolsheviks under Lenin's leadership succeeded in overthrowing the provisional government has been related in an earlier chapter. The brief existence of the provisional government came to an end when Trotsky as the leader of the Petrograd Soviet issued the brief proclamation after the fall of the Winter Palace: "In the name of the Militant Revolutionary Committee I declare that the Provisional Government has ceased to exist."

Having succeeded in overthrowing the provisional government, the Bolsheviks were confronted with the problem of establishing a new order. Lenin told Trotsky, "Within six months we shall establish socialism in Russia." Events soon proved that he was unduly optimistic. The task was gigantic. Not only had the framework of the old society collapsed under the strain of war and revolution, but the men of knowledge and ability belonged to the opposition. As members of the proletariat the Bolsheviks largely lacked the theoretical and practical knowledge necessary for the task. But Lenin, though fully aware of the limitations of his followers, pressed on. Under his leadership the Russian Congress of Soviets at once abolished private property in land and nationalized the banks. For the time being, small landholders were not molested and bank depositors were permitted to withdraw up to 1500 rubles from their accounts each month. All larger landholdings, including church and monastery lands, were confiscated at once without indemnity to the former owners and placed under the administration of soviets, or committees of peasant deputies. These agencies were to divide the land among the peasants according to the size of each family and its capacity to cultivate land. Holdings were allotted to those who cultivated the land, the hiring of labor being expressly forbidden. This was not Lenin's final goal. It was a policy of "incomplete communism" which he hoped would win the support of the peasants for the new order.

The question of nationalizing trade and industry was also taken up during the succeeding months. In March, 1918, both foreign and domestic trade were put under state control. This action was motivated in part by the fact that peasants demanded manufactured goods for their grain in place of worthless paper money. Consequently a system of barter was set up. In every town having a population over ten thousand, committees were formed which then proceeded to confiscate the merchandise of all shops and to use it for purposes of barter. To obtain food the workers had to have workbooks which they received in return for their services.[1] In the nationalization of industry Lenin proceeded with caution. Although workers' committees were given a share in running the industries, more particularly in fixing the output program and in determining prices, they were not permitted to interfere in the executive work of running the enterprise. During the months after the October Revolution a number of industrial enterprises did pass into state ownership, but the first industry as such to be nationalized was the sugar industry (May, 1918). This was followed by a more general nationalization. A decree of June 28, 1918, declared all industries and commercial enterprises having a capital of a million rubles or more to be the property of the state. Included in this decree were mining, insurance companies, and the privately operated railroads as well as the large manufacturing industries.

A further problem of the Bolshevik government was to give the Russian people the peace they desired. How Lenin finally agreed to the terms of the treaty of Brest Litovsk (March 3, 1918) has been related. But when peace had been made with the Germans, there was still no peace in Russia. After the October Revolution civil war had broken out between the Reds and the Whites or anti-Soviet forces. A motley collection of men, including former imperial officers, members of the outlawed nobility, former landowners, supporters of the church, professional men, and even peasants, gathered at a number of points to organize armies for the purpose of opposing the Bolsheviks. The first center of armed opposition was the country near the Don where the Don Cossacks, who had enjoyed special privileges under the tsars, raised the standard of revolt. In the north Admiral Kolchak organized an army which in addition to the Russians included about 45,000 Czechs who had deserted from the Austrian army. All the Allied countries, including the United States, sent supplies and money as well as

[1] The wealthy could purchase them.

troops to aid the White armies. The Allies believed that if the Bolshevik rule were overthrown the Russians would re-enter the war against Germany.

For a time the White armies were successful on all fronts. While the forces of Admiral Kolchak extended their sway over most of Siberia, the southern White army advanced to within 250 miles of Moscow and a third army was threatening Petrograd. Meanwhile Leon Trotsky, as Commissar of War, was busy organizing a Red army and inculcating in it a strong hatred for the Whites. It was a fight to the death by hungry and ragged soldiers, with neither side asking or giving quarter and both sides committing the most terrible brutalities. But the White armies were finally forced to give way. On the one hand, the Allied support of the anti-Bolshevist forces had been half-hearted from the beginning; on the other, the White armies came to be more and more regarded by the peasants as representative of the old order. The peasants feared that if the Whites triumphed they would lose the land they had seized during the Revolution. The opinion also gained ground that the White armies were merely Allied tools. Consequently many Russians began to throw in their lot with the Reds, who were associating their cause with that of Russian nationalism. This tooting of the nationalist horn was an important factor in the triumph of the Red forces. By the spring of 1920 all the White armies, except the one in the south, had either been driven out of Russia or forced to surrender. Before the end of 1920 the southern White army, too, was forced to evacuate Russian soil.

Even the end of the civil war did not bring peace to Russia. Since the Bolsheviks were only a minority, they were compelled to resort to force in order to retain their power and to establish their social system. Their particular enemies were the classes which had been the principal upholders of the old order. At the head of this list stood the old nobility and the bourgeoisie. After the success of the October Revolution Lenin had declared, "Yes, we will destroy everything and on the ruins we will build our temple! It will be a temple for the happiness of all. But we will destroy the bourgeoisie, grind it to a powder." The "liquidation" or elimination of both the nobility and the bourgeoisie was carried out with thoroughness and much cruelty. But the suppression did not stop there. All who were either actively or passively opposed to the Bolshevik plans, even if they were workers or peasants, were crushed as counterrevolutionists and enemies of the people. All political parties were gradually broken up and outlawed, so that no organized opposition could develop. Such freedom of the press as had existed under the tsars was terminated by a decree suppressing all opposition newspapers. Thereafter the communist-controlled press published only such news as was specifically authorized by communist censors.

The special instrument set up to eradicate all opposition to the rule of the Bolsheviks was the All-Russian Commission for Combating Counterrevolution, Speculation, and Sabotage, more familiarly known as the Cheka. Organized in December, 1917, the Cheka was during the first months of its existence quite mild in its operations, limiting itself to the arrest of outstanding opponents of the communist regime. But after an attempt by a member of the Social-Revolutionary Party to assassinate Lenin nearly succeeded (August, 1918), the so-called Red Terror was proclaimed. The purpose was to destroy some of the opposition and to terrorize the rest into accepting the communist dictatorship. Wholesale arrests were made of large numbers suspected of opposition. The time of arrest was usually late at night or in the first hours after midnight. Often the families of the arrested heard nothing of the fate of their loved ones. The Communists, being in no mood to spare the blood of the opposition, repeated the worst excesses of the French Revolution. Many of those arrested were shot at once in large batches. Since the Cheka recognized no sex distinctions, many women were included among the victims. At first the names of the victims were published, but the unfavorable reaction abroad to the cold-blooded executions caused the government to cover the activities of the Cheka with a veil of secrecy. How many persons were executed during the first three years of the Cheka's existence is a matter of controversy. While most estimates run into the hundreds of thousands, on-the-spot observers have set fifty thousand as the maximum.

By 1922 the Cheka had acquired such a bad reputation that it was reorganized and given the name of Government Political Office, better known as GPU (Gay-Pay-Oo). A foreign resident of Moscow observed, "It's like changing the name of a dog with a bad reputation for biting people in the hope that people will forget it's the same animal." A decree of January 19, 1920, had abolished the death penalty in Russia, but the GPU does not appear to have observed the decree. Although it did not equal the Cheka in the number of its executions, it remained an agency of terror which carried on the program of stamping out some of the opposition and frightening the rest into outward submission to the communist dictatorship. In 1933 the GPU was replaced by the NKVD, which during World War II gave way to the MVD.

Among those who became the victims of the communist zeal were ex-Tsar Nicholas II, his wife, and his children. After the fall of his regime the tsar and his family had been taken to Ekaterinburg, in the foothills of the Urals, where they lived quietly under guard. But the advance of the White army under Admiral Kolchak toward Ekaterinburg excited the fear in the minds of many Communists that the Whites might liberate the former imperial family and use it to attract supporters to the cause of counterrevolution. To prevent this the local Soviet shot the entire family, together with a number of attendants (July 18, 1918), and threw the bodies into an abandoned mine shaft. Later it was decided to burn the remains so that if the advancing army should reach Ekaterinburg it would find not a vestige of the family.

In their attempts to uproot established institutions the Communists did not overlook the Orthodox Church of Russia. This was in harmony with Lenin's dictum, "We must fight against religion, the opium of the people." The church in itself was a special target since its function had in large part been to preach obedience to the rule of the tsar. Moreover, during the revolution it had been a rallying center of the counterrevolutionary forces. After the revolution Lenin himself announced that not only the church but also the worship of God must be extirpated. The first step in this direction was a decree of February 5, 1918, establishing the separation of church and state. Although congregations could, by special permission, continue to use church buildings, the Communists did all they could to discourage both the belief in and the practice of religion, whether it was Judaism, Mohammedanism, or Christianity. In an effort, for example, to break down the faith of the peasant masses holy water was sprinkled on one cabbage patch and chemical fertilizer on another and the peasants were shown the poor results obtained from the one and the good results from the other. When the peasants became enraged by the violent assault on religion, Lenin counseled moderation.

After his death, however, the League of Militant Atheists was founded and by 1932 claimed 5.5 million active members. The League circulated such slogans as "Religion is a weapon of reaction" and "Religion is a deception." Churches were turned into antireligious museums, and Christmas and Easter were transformed into pagan festivals. In the Communist Party itself the complete renunciation of religion was made a condition for membership. Communism became the new orthodoxy which was supposed to replace the old religious faiths. Icons were replaced with the pictures of Marx, Lenin, and later Stalin. But despite the antireligious crusade of the Militant Atheists the interest in religion did not die out. Persecution even deepened and broadened the spiritual life of some Russians.

THE RETREAT FROM COMMUNISM

While the communist government was putting down the civil war and terrorizing the opposition, the economic situation had deteriorated to the verge of collapse. The system of workers' control broke down in most industries because the workers lacked experience in management. The output of factories, mills, and mines declined until at the beginning of 1921 it was only 17 per cent of the 1913 figure. Manufactured articles became so scarce that prices rose inordinately. Large numbers of workers deserted the towns to return to the villages, where they hoped to find food. Collection of taxes was so chaotic that receipts covered only 10 per cent of the government expenditures. A great decline also took place in agricultural production. By 1921 the area under cultivation had shrunk to a little more than 60 per cent of the prewar area, and the annual grain yield was only 47 per cent of the prewar period. The government requisitioned from the peasants most of the produce they raised, permitting them to keep only enough for food and for the next year's sowing. The peasants received for their produce commodity cards which were theoretically exchangeable for manufactured goods, but no manufactured goods were available for the peasants because most of the industries were producing very little. Consequently many peasants decided to raise only enough food for their own immediate needs. In some parts of Russia there were even peasant revolts to prevent confiscation of produce.

In 1920 the situation had become critical. Widespread famine claimed the lives of hundreds of thousands. Undernourishment also weakened many, making them easy victims of epidemics. Finally revolt began to brew even in the communist ranks. All this moved Lenin to reconsider, with the result that he deliberately retreated from communism in 1921. He adopted a policy known as the New Economic Policy or NEP. This policy permitted the existence of small private industries and also private trading side by side with state retailing. To facilitate private trading, a regular currency system was revived. Lenin was careful, however, to maintain state ownership and control over the large industries, transportation, and foreign trade. For the peasants relief came in the form of a fixed grain tax which replaced the system of requisitions. The result was a gradual improvement of economic conditions. In agriculture the tilled area rapidly increased until it reached the prewar level, while industry and commerce revived until in 1927 they surpassed the levels of 1913.

From the time Lenin returned to Russia in 1917 until May, 1922, he worked with an energy that amazed those about him. For weeks at a time he would work most of the day and night. These relentless labors gradually undermined his constitution. Late in 1921 his health began to decline, and in May, 1922, he suffered a paralytic stroke which for a time robbed him of his speech and the ability to move his right leg and hand. Forced to withdraw from participation in the government, he tried desperately to recover his health. July saw him back on his feet and before long he was again active in the government, but he was soon forced to delegate most of the work to others. He died on January

21, 1924. The man who had denounced religion as the opiate of the people assumed the stature of a saint after his death and was accorded the veneration usually reserved for supernatural beings. His body, instead of being buried or cremated like the remains of other communist leaders, was carefully embalmed and put on display in a mausoleum built for this purpose in Red Square. This mausoleum soon became a shrine to which hundreds of thousands annually made pilgrimages.

No sooner was the news of Lenin's illness published in 1922 than a series of intrigues began among his possible successors. Before long it was evident that the two leading candidates were Trotsky and Stalin. The most popular figure in Russia next to Lenin was undoubtedly Trotsky. He appears, too, to have been the final choice of Lenin. For a time Lenin entertained the idea of having Trotsky and Stalin share the leadership, but in his *Political Testament,* written early in 1923, he turned against Stalin. While styling Trotsky "the most able man in the present Central Committee," he characterized Stalin as "rude" and expressed doubts that he would know "how to manage power with sufficient caution." Lenin even went so far as to call upon his fellow Communists "to find a way to remove Stalin" from the position of General Secretary of the Communist Party. Both Trotsky and Stalin were ardent Communists and fanatical revolutionists. They differed, however, on the question of tactics. Trotsky stood for uncompromising effort toward world revolution; Stalin felt that the new order must prove itself successful at home before it could be established elsewhere.

While the brilliant Trotsky strutted, the plodding Stalin worked quietly behind the scenes. Patient and crafty, he laid his plans carefully during the years of Lenin's illness, and gradually managed to maneuver himself into the position of General Secretary of the Communist Party. As such he gradually planted his henchmen in key positions, so that by the time of Lenin's death he largely controlled the party machine. When Lenin died, Trotsky made the big mistake of remaining in the Caucasus, where he had gone to recuperate from an illness, instead of hurrying to Moscow to attend the funeral. No explanation was made to the hundreds of thousands who expected to see Trotsky in the funeral cortege. Soon Stalin opened a press campaign against Trotsky in every town and village of the Soviet Union and also attacked him before the All-Russian Central Committee. Trotsky tried to defend himself, but in vain. He had missed his big opportunity. The "uncouth Asiatic," whom Trotsky despised, had succeeded in appropriating Lenin's mantle. In January, 1925, Trotsky's political career virtually came to an end when he was relieved of his post as War Commissar. All his subsequent efforts to regain lost ground achieved nothing. In 1927 the Fifteenth All-Russian Congress of the Communist

Party expelled him and his supporters, and the next year he was forced into exile.[2]

THE NEW DICTATOR AND THE FIRST FIVE-YEAR PLAN

Just before the Fifteenth Congress adjourned, Stalin was handed a steel broom symbolical of his efforts to sweep the opposition out of the party. He was now the all-powerful dictator. Stalin was born Joseph Djugashvilli at Gori in Georgia in 1879. Thus he was by birth essentially an Asiatic. Intended for the priesthood, he was sent to the ecclesiastical seminary at Tiflis but was expelled at the age of nineteen for advocating Marxian socialism. In the same year he became a member of the Social Democratic Party, which split up into Bolshevists and Menshevists. Later he joined the compact group of "professional revolutionaries" which Lenin was organizing. The succeeding period was one of arrests and escapes. Escaping from Siberia in 1904, he appears to have organized raids against banks and post offices as a means of replenishing the coffers of the Bolshevik party. A bomb outrage at Tiflis, of which he was the planner, netted the party a large sum of money. During the next years he slowly forged his way into the higher ranks of the party and in 1912 became managing editor of *Pravda,* the official paper of the Bolsheviks. It was in this paper that he signed an article with the pseudonym "Stalin" (of steel), the name by which he has been known ever since.

His rise from obscurity to supreme power has been ascribed to two factors, his extraordinary skill at political intrigue and his ruthlessness in suppressing opposition. In short, he was a past master in the game of Machiavellian politics. According to a number of writers who knew him at this time, Stalin lacked general education and a cultural background. One ex-Communist described him as an "uncultured Georgian despotically rude to his subordinates."

The major task Stalin and his associates set for themselves was the establishment of a socialist order. Many foreign observers had hoped that since the NEP promised so much it would expand into full-fledged capitalism. But the communist leaders had other ideas. They soon laid plans to eliminate the "capitalist elements" from agriculture, industry, and trade. In agriculture the particular targets of the government attack were the kulaks or well-to-do peasants, many of whom had farm machinery and employed hired labor. In industry and trade more and more restrictions were imposed on the so-called Nepmen, with the result that by the spring of 1924 more than 300,000 had gone bankrupt.

[2] After spending some time in Turkey, Trotsky finally settled in Mexico, where he was assassinated in 1940.

Against those private enterprises which continued to thrive despite the government restrictions, a policy of direct repression was adopted.

In 1928 the various efforts of the government were fused into a great plan called the Piatiletka or Five-Year Plan (1928–1932). In projecting this plan the communist leaders aimed, first of all, to create a modern industrial system which would free their country from dependence on a hostile capitalist world for machinery and weapons of defense. Second, they were determined to demonstrate the superiority of their system by surpassing the capitalist countries in industrial production. In order to do this it was necessary to transform the country in the speediest possible manner from an agricultural into an industrial nation. At the same time agriculture was not to be neglected. If Russian agriculture was to furnish enough food for the workers in the new industrial state, its productivity had to be greatly increased. This was to be achieved by collectivization, or the merging of many small holdings into a comparatively few large collective farms (kolkhozi), and by mechanization (the introduction of modern farm machinery). The basic aim in both agriculture and industry, according to Stalin, was "to eliminate completely all capitalist elements, to widen the front of socialist forms of economy, and to create the economic foundation for the abolition of classes in the U.S.S.R. for the creation of a socialist society."

The Five-Year Plan did not stop at generalities; it set specific quotas for each industry. Industrial production, on the whole, was to be increased from 18.3 billion rubles in 1927–1928 to 43.2 billion rubles in 1932–1933. Special emphasis was put on the building of factories, the output of machinery, and the development of transportation — in other words, on the development of heavy industry. The manufacture of agricultural machinery, for example, was to increase by four times during the five years. Less emphasis was placed on the production of shoes, clothing, and household goods. Thus the Russians had to forgo necessaries as well as comforts. The slogan was, "Build despite everything and no matter at what cost." Because the government needed all the gold it could collect to purchase machinery and tools for the big steel and electrical plants it was constructing, it could not import the cotton it needed to manufacture clothing. Consequently there was a dearth of textiles in Russia. The government, in fact, found it necessary to export large quantities of grain and sugar in order to get the necessary exchange values for the purchase of the indispensable needs of heavy industry. This, in turn, made it necessary to ration both bread and sugar, the sugar allotment being a mere crumb. How meager the rations were is expressed by the conundrum, "Who are the greatest eaters in the world?" Answer: "The Russians, because they can easily eat up a week's rations in a day." As compensation for their short rations the workers had the promise of the government that more coal, oil, machinery, and factories would ultimately mean more food and clothing.

Stalin himself announced in January, 1933, that 93.7 per cent of the program had been realized. Many foreign observers wondered by what method of calculation he reached this figure. In some phases of industry, it is true, the goal was either attained or nearly reached; in a few, such as the construction of railroad cars, it was even exceeded. But it is equally true that in many phases the achievement fell far short of the goal. In some cases in which the goals were achieved, quality had been sacrificed to quantity. The following table will give some general idea of both goals and achievements:

	Planned	Fulfilled
Steel (million tons)	10.4	5.9
Cast iron (million tons)	10.0	6.1
Rolled metal (million tons)	8.0	4.2
Coal (million tons)	75.0	65.4
Petroleum (million tons)	21.7	21.3
Electric power (milliard kw)	55,000	50,640
Cotton textiles (million metres)	4,700	2,417
Woolen textiles (million metres)	270.0	88.7
Footwear (million pairs)	145.0	84.7

Even though the goal was not reached in some respects, the over-all achievement was tremendous. It is particularly impressive when one keeps in mind the shortage of raw materials, the lack of skilled technicians, the difficulty of obtaining the necessary exchange values, and the general backwardness of Russia. During the four years the Russians, besides improving many old factories, succeeded in building more than 1500 new ones. Included in this number were many giant projects such as the great tractor plants at Kharkov and Stalingrad, the huge automobile factories at Moscow and Nizhni Novgorod, the mammoth steel plants at Magnitogorsk and Kuznetsk, and the Dneprostroi hydroelectric project. The construction of so many giant enterprises in so brief a period is unique in history.

A further goal of the Five-Year Plan was to increase agricultural production from 16.6 billion to 25.8 billion rubles. The great obstacle here was the existence of some 26 million peasant holdings which were so small that modern agricultural machinery could not be used profitably on them. Moreover, the peasants who owned them had little desire to adopt improved methods. The remedy, as the Soviet government saw it, was agricultural collectivization, that is, the merging of many small holdings into a large collective farm (kolkhoz) which would be run by an elective management committee. But the peasants were not psychologically prepared for this. They were not interested in the establishment of a socialist order; they wished to retain as private property the land they had seized at the time of the revolution, to manage their own plot as they wished. Many believed they were being pushed into a new kind of serfdom. It is significant that up to 1928, when it was a matter of choice for them to enter a collective farm, only 2 per cent did so. Lenin himself said in March, 1919, "Up to the present they are prejudiced against large-scale farms. The peasant thinks 'if it is a big farm, I shall again become a laborer.' Of course, he is mistaken. But in the peasant mind the idea of large-scale farms is closely bound up with hatred, with his recollections how the landed estate owners oppressed the peasantry." Lenin, it appears, conveniently overlooked the idea that the peasant preferred private ownership, something that Stalin was later forced to recognize.

Many of the peasants, and particularly the kulaks or wealthy peasants, resisted collectivization in every way they could. Rather than surrender their cattle, sheep, and pigs to the common ownership of a collective farm many slaughtered them. It has been estimated that in the winter of 1929–1930 a quarter of the cows, a third of the sheep, and half of the pigs were slaughtered. The result was a serious shortage of meat, fats, and dairy products. Peasants also began to leave much of their grain unharvested because they felt it would be taken from them anyway. For a time the government sought to coerce the kulaks. As a means of frightening other peasants, many kulaks were driven from their land and left to shift for themselves, or they were consigned to forced labor in Siberian lumber camps, where they suffered great hardships. Even this did not convince the other peasants. The situation became so critical that Stalin ordered forcible collectivization to cease.

THE SECOND AND THIRD FIVE-YEAR PLANS

The Soviet government did not rest content with the results of the First Five-Year Plan. No sooner was its completion announced than the Second Five-Year Plan (1933–1937) was launched. Like the first it was largely devoted to laying the foundations of the Soviet industrial structure. Although the emphasis was again put on heavy industry, more attention was given in this plan to the production of shoes, clothing, and household goods. But the plan was soon revised. The rise to power of Hitler and the Nazis in January, 1933, posing a threat to Bolshevism, caused the Soviet government to make more provisions for the manufacture of war materials. The Second Five-Year Plan was, therefore, even less successful in the production of consumers' goods than the first had been. Such goods as were produced were largely of poor quality. Of particular importance in the Second Five-Year Plan was the decision to build factories near the source of raw materials rather than to transport these materials long distances. Much attention was also given to improving the means of transportation, particularly to the rehabilitation of old railway lines and the construction of new ones. Again the major part of the plan was fulfilled:

	Planned	Fulfilled
Steel (million tons)	17.0	17.7
Cast iron (million tons)	16.0	14.5
Rolled metal (million tons)	13.0	13.0
Coal (million tons)	152.5	127.9
Petroleum (million tons)	46.8	30.5
Electric power (milliard kw)	38.0	36.4
Cotton textiles (million metres)	5100.0	3447.0
Woolen textiles (million metres)	220.0	108.3

On the agricultural side the principal aim of the Second Five-Year Plan was the completion of rural collectivization, an aim which made it necessary to overcome peasant opposition. To make the collectives more attractive to the peasants, the grain procurement system was changed. Instead of taking all that was left after the needs of the peasants were satisfied and enough had been put aside for the next season's planting, the government set a quota for each kolkhoz. Whatever was left over after the quota had been delivered, the tractor tax paid,[3] and a seed and fodder fund set up, the collectives were permitted to divide among their members in proportion to the quantity and quality of the work each had done. Such produce as the peasant did not need for himself and his family he could sell in the open market. The government also made further concessions to the peasants' instinct for private enterprise. In 1935 it decreed that each peasant family could hold as private property "living quarters, family cattle and fowls, and the buildings necessary for their use." In addition each family was permitted to have its own kitchen garden and fruit orchard.

The government measures made collective farming so attractive to the peasants that large numbers voluntarily asked to become members. During a period of three months in 1935, according to Soviet statistics, more than half a million peasants joined the collectives. Side by side with the collective farms the government created several thousand state farms with managers appointed by the state and with hired labor

---

[3] The individual collectives had no tractors of their own, but rented them from tractor stations set up by the government.

paid at fixed rates on the same principle as in the state factories. By
1937 more than 90 per cent of the peasants were included in the collective farms. The use of scientific methods of fertilization and crop
rotation, as well as of modern farm machinery, greatly increased the
yield. By 1935 sufficient food was being produced to permit the termination of the rationing system. The year 1937 saw the Russians harvest
a grain crop of unprecedented size, 29 per cent above the best previous
harvest. The following are the official figures for grain production:

1934	894.0	million hundredweights	
1935	901.0	”	”
1936	827.0	”	”
1937	1,202.0	”	”
1938	949.9	”	”

An important factor in this increased production was the introduction of power machinery. In 1930 there were only 34,900 tractors in the
whole Soviet Union, and almost half of them were unfit for service.
By 1938 the Soviet Union led all of Europe in the number of its tractors, with 470,000 individual units. Furthermore, in 1929 there were
only 45 harvesting and threshing combines in the Soviet Union. By
1938 the number had reached the impressive figure of 137,000. This
machinery was rented to the collectives by machine and tractor stations established by the government. In 1930 there were only 145 such
stations; by the end of 1938 there were no less than 6356 scattered over
the country.

After declaring the fulfillment of the Second Five-Year Plan, Stalin
at once announced a Third Plan which began in January, 1938, and
was, in general, a continuation of the preceding plans. Soon after its
inauguration the European situation became more menacing, with the
result that the Russians concentrated more and more on the production
of armaments and munitions.

In the Third Plan special emphasis was put upon increasing the productivity of labor; in fact, the government hoped to increase the output
of the individual workman as much as 65 per cent. One writer estimated
that the average level of productivity of Russian industry in 1913 was
25 per cent of that of the United States and 35 per cent of that of
Germany; [4] and after the revolution it had declined to a still lower
point. Although it had risen during the period of the First and Second
Five-Year Plans, the average output of the individual worker in 1938
was still far below that of the worker in the capitalist countries.

As a spur to greater production the government introduced a comprehensive system of wage differentiation. Originally the Communists had

[4] Yugov, *Russia's Economic Front* (1942), p. 183.

made an attempt to secure that economic equality which had always been one of the professed aims of socialism. But the Soviet leaders soon discovered that economic equality robbed the worker of all incentive and kept able men from accepting positions which involved responsibility. Economic inequality was, therefore, deliberately introduced and before long became greater in Russia than in many other countries. Among the favored were factory managers, engineers, scientists, actors, authors, and artists. While the average income of the urban worker in 1937 was approximately 250 rubles a month, members of the newly privileged classes earned from one thousand to ten thousand rubles. Even among the workers those who produced more than their fellow workers received higher wages, were rewarded with special vacation trips, and were granted permission to own automobiles. After Stakhanov, a Donets miner, set a new coal mining record in 1935, Stakhanovites, as they were called, set new production records in many industries under the incentive of special rewards. The speed-up however often resulted in a lowering of the standards of quality.

Although the lot of the average worker improved considerably during the period of the Five-Year Plans, it still left much to be desired. His standard of living was still far below that of workers in most other countries. In 1937 the cheapest pair of shoes cost the low-paid factory worker nearly a month's salary, while the purchase of a suit required the equivalent of four months' wages. On the other hand, bread was reasonable in price and vegetables were inexpensive. Rents in the Soviet Union were exceedingly low, but there was much overcrowding, since the urban population had increased faster than housing accommodations. Frequently an entire family had only one room. For the factory worker the high cost of living was offset by the substantial and inexpensive meals that were served at noon in the special dining room for workers. Medical care was free to the worker, and social insurance was broader than in many capitalist countries. Luxuries, however, were few and far between.

Before the Third Five-Year Plan could be completed, the Nazi armies invaded western Russia (June, 1941), which was still the great manufacturing center of the Soviet Union. Enough industries had, however, been established in central and eastern Russia to stave off industrial paralysis. Some idea of the progress Russia made during the period of the Five-Year Plans may be gained from the fact that the industrial production at the time of the Nazi invasion was more than nine times the output of 1913 and the number of workers employed in industry was more than three times the number employed in 1913. In short, Russia had developed from an economically backward country that was primarily agricultural into a strong industrial nation.

THE GOVERNMENT OF THE SOVIET UNION

Communism has been defined as socialism from which the taint of capitalism has been removed. In other words, it is a perfected socialism. As Lenin put it in his book, *The State and Revolution,* "That which is generally called socialism is termed by Marx the first or lower phase of communist society." While socialism would abolish private property in land and capital only, communism aims to abolish private property altogether. The important political difference between socialism and communism is that the aim of Socialists is the complete control of life by the state, while Communists theoretically detest the state. According to Lenin the state will wither away completely when full communism has been established. This is, of course, a restatement of an original dogma of Marx and Engels which reads: "With the disappearance of classes, the state, too, will inevitably disappear." In short, the state gradually commits a form of suicide. "The interference of the state in social relationships," Engels wrote, "will become superfluous and will be discontinued in one domain after another." After the disappearance of the state, society will be "one gigantic cooperative running itself without supervision of officials, soldiers, police, or industrial managers." In practice the exact opposite has taken place in Russia. Instead of disappearing, the state has become more and more the all-controlling factor in the life of the people. It has developed into one of the most powerful and most arbitrary state machines in history.

What is the nature of this Russian state? The Soviet state is not a state of one nationality in the sense that France is. Its population is composed of many racial stocks. No less than two hundred vernacular languages are spoken in the U.S.S.R. (Union of Soviet Socialist Republics) or Soviet Union. This state was not at once called the U.S.S.R. after the revolution in 1917. At first the country was known as the Russian Socialist Federated Soviet Republic. The first Soviet Congress, representing four republics (R.S.F.S.R., Ukraine, White Russia, Azerbaijan), met in December, 1922, and adopted the Treaty of Union. It was not until June 6, 1923, that the U.S.S.R. was formally proclaimed and its first constitution inaugurated. In 1925 the number of the republics in the federation rose to six through the admission of the Uzbek and Turkmen republics, and in 1929 the Tadzhikistan republic was added. Subsequently the U.S.S.R. was enlarged by the admission of other republics.[5]

The Soviet state may be regarded as a pyramid with the village, town, and factory soviets or councils forming the base. Above these in

[5] Georgian, Armenian, Tadzhik, Kazakh, and Kirgiz republics (1936), Karelo-Finnish, Moldavian, Estonian, Latvian, and Lithuanian republics (1940).

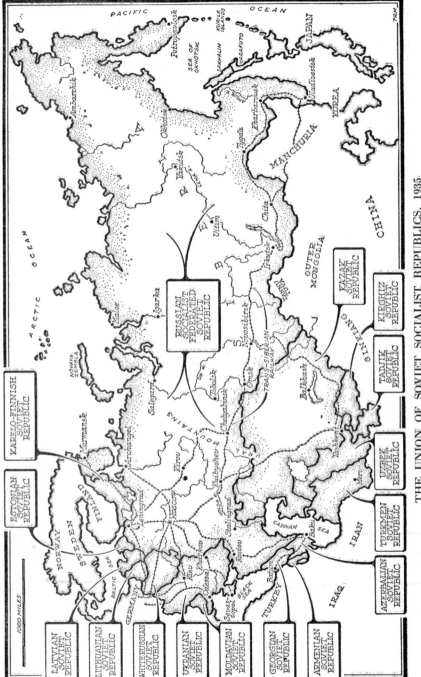

THE UNION OF SOVIET SOCIALIST REPUBLICS. 1935.

the political structure are the district and provincial soviets. The next layer is composed of the supreme soviets of the individual republics. At the apex of the pyramid we find the Supreme Soviet, which alone exercises legislative power and theoretically represents the highest authority in the U.S.S.R. The Supreme Soviet consists of two chambers, the Soviet of the Union and the Soviet of Nationalities, the members of both being elected by the people. Together the two chambers form a kind of legislative assembly which is often referred to as the "Soviet Parliament." Without the approval of a majority of both chambers no bill can become law. In the interim between the sessions of the Supreme Soviet the Central Executive Committee, elected by the Supreme Soviet and consisting of about two hundred members, is the "supreme legislative, executive, and controlling organ."

Such is the organization of the government, but the ruling body which actually directs the government and dominates the life of the country is the Communist Party. It is the only legal political party in Russia. The theory of the one-party state is that the Communist Party alone represents "the interests of the workers" and is alone capable of leading them toward communism. The Communist Party considers itself "the conscious will of the proletariat." The members of this party form only a small proportion of the population of the Soviet Union. Although the membership had increased to two million in 1932, the ratio was still one Communist for each eighty-five persons of the population. The nucleus of the party was the cell. A cell could be formed in a factory, office, or village with a minimum of three members. The cells elected delegates to the provincial and regional party congresses which, in turn, elected delegates to the All-Union Party Congress, the organ of supreme authority in the party. During the period preceding World War II the All-Union Congress was usually convoked every two years.

In the intervals between meetings the All-Union Congress was represented by an Executive Committee composed of three sections: (1) a secretariat; (2) an organization bureau (Orgbureau), which was entrusted with the administrative functions; (3) a political bureau (Politbureau) of thirteen members who formulated the party policies. The Politbureau was the real source of power in the Soviet Union.[6] In the words of one writer, "All other governmental bodies are mere window dressing. All decisions rest with these men." Although the members of the Politbureau are theoretically chosen by secret ballot, they are actually selected by the Secretary-General of the party, who is himself a member of the Politbureau. In him all power is centered. He controls every wheel and screw in the party machine. Thus he is the dictator

[6] In 1952 the functions of the Politbureau and the Orgbureau were transferred to the Presidium of the Supreme Soviet.

both of the party and of the state which it controls. The Soviet state has, therefore, been described as a dictatorship over the proletariat rather than a dictatorship of the proletariat.

Admission to the Communist Party is not open to everyone. It is reserved for the few and is obtained only after a difficult probationary period. Only those who measure up to the standards set by the party for zeal and devotion are admitted. Applicants under twenty years of age are admitted solely through membership in the Komsomol or Union of Communist Youth; other applicants must be sponsored by from three to five members. Once within the party the members are subjected to a rigorous discipline. Lenin himself stated that the Communist Party "can accomplish its task only on condition that it is highly centralized, that it is dominated by an iron discipline which is quasi-military in its severity." Especially stressed is strict adherence to the party line. Once a decision is reached by the head of the party, discipline demands that all discussion and questioning cease. The basic formula is "theirs not to reason why."

Periodical purges banished the less reliable members into outer darkness. Not only infractions of discipline but also lukewarmness or insufficient activity was sufficient to bring about expulsion. Some idea of the thoroughness of the purging process may be gained from the fact that in the years 1933 and 1934 purges reduced the membership of the party from two million to 1,655,000. A more specific example is the expulsion in June, 1935, of about a quarter of the membership in the Uzbek republic. Expulsion of higher officials was not rare. How great the "mortality" was is illustrated by the fact that of seventy-one members selected for the Executive Committee early in 1934, only twenty-one were active in political life four years later. Of the original number nine had been sentenced to be shot and thirty-one had been removed from their positions with varying degrees of disgrace.

In 1936 and succeeding years the Soviet Union witnessed what even the Bolsheviks have called "the great cleansing." A series of purges and public trials swept the party clean of all opposition to Stalin. Among those executed after trial were a number of "Old Bolsheviks," men who had been members of the inner circle which carried through the Revolution of 1917. Included in the list were such names as Zinoviev, Kamenev, and Bukharin; also the military leaders whom Stalin suspected of being opponents or potential rivals, including Marshal Tukhachevski. The cleansings reached their peak in October and November, 1937, when every party leader whose past was tainted with "Trotskyism" or "bourgeois nationalism" was removed from office.

In 1935 Stalin promised the peoples of the U.S.S.R. a new and liberal constitution. The next year the All-Union Party Congress adopted the new constitution. The communist propaganda machine styled the constitution "the most democratic in the world," and communist sympathizers throughout the world hailed it as a step along the path of true democracy. Many of the provisions of the "Stalin constitution" did appear to support such claims. Article 127 stated that "citizens of the U.S.S.R. are guaranteed inviolability of their person. No one may be subject to arrest except by an order of the court or with the sanction of the state attorney." It further stated that "freedom of religious worship and freedom of antireligious propaganda is recognized for all citizens"; also "freedom of speech; freedom of the press; freedom of assembly and meetings; freedom of street processions and demonstrations." Article 135 guaranteed to all persons of sane mind, without criminal records, and at least eighteen years of age "the right to take part in the elections of deputies and to be elected."

First impressions, however, were deceiving. Stalin and the communist leaders did not interpret the constitution in the same spirit as the students of western democracy. According to the communist interpretation the freedoms must be exercised in "the interests of the working people." The Communists alone decide what the interests of the working classes are. Hence it follows that anyone who does not accept the teachings of the Communist Party is not fit to exercise the freedoms — he is abnormal and criminal. In like manner the Communist Party made a farce of the right to vote and of free elections. The government did not permit the nomination of various candidates who would compete for an office, nor did it allow meetings at which the views of various candidates were aired. The local committees of the Communist Party simply chose a single candidate for each office, and the voter had the option of voting for or against the candidate. To vote against a candidate was not particularly healthful.

THE THIRD INTERNATIONAL

When the Communists gained control of Russia they did not achieve their ultimate aim. They regarded the Russian Revolution as but the first act in the drama of world revolution, firmly accepting the Marxian dogma that world revolution and the triumph of the proletariat are inevitable. Lenin himself was confident that communism was destined to conquer the world. "It is not a question of only Russia," Lenin said; "I spit on Russia. . . . This is merely one phase through which we must pass on the way to a world revolution." He regarded the world revolution not only as inevitable but also as imminent. Thus he stated in November, 1918, "The international world revolution is near. . . . Imperialism cannot delay the world revolution." He feared that the

Soviet system could not continue to exist as an island in a capitalist sea. "We are doomed to destruction," he declared soon after his accession to power, "unless revolution breaks out without delay in other countries." Consequently the Bolsheviks took steps to hasten this revolution. In 1919 they founded the Third Communist International, known more briefly as the Comintern,[7] with headquarters in Moscow. Although the Comintern's connection with the Russian Communist Party was not direct, it was controlled by the latter. No fewer than fifty-eight communist parties from as many states or colonies were represented in it. Its avowed object was "the overthrow of the international bourgeoisie and the establishment of an international Soviet republic, as a transitional stage toward complete annihilation of the state." This was to be achieved by any and all means at its disposal, including violence. The program of action drawn up by a later congress declared that the aims of the Third International "can be accomplished only through an overthrow by force of the whole existing social order."

But the world revolution failed to materialize. Such communist experiments as had been inaugurated in Hungary and Bavaria collapsed, and Soviet Russia stood alone as a pariah among nations. At the end of 1920 only Estonia, Lithuania, Latvia, and Finland had established diplomatic relations with the Soviets. With the country in a state of economic collapse and communism giving way to the NEP, the government decided on a measure of cooperation with the capitalist states. A number of countries, convinced that Russia was reverting to capitalism, were quick in responding to the friendly overtures. Before the end of 1921 the Soviet Union had concluded trade treaties with a group of countries that included Poland, Turkey, and Great Britain. By 1924 most of the powers had recognized the Soviet Union, but the United States did not accord the U.S.S.R. formal recognition until 1933, sixteen years after the revolution. Entry into the League did not come until September, 1934.

Up to 1928 cooperation between Soviet Russia and the outside world remained restricted. The inauguration of the First Five-Year Plan, however, made Soviet cooperation with the capitalist world imperative, for the Russians needed machines, equipment, and technical experts if the plan was to be a success. To promote friendly relations with other states the communist leaders began to stress the idea of cooperation rather than of world revolution. In harmony with the new policy Stalin pushed the revolutionary activities of the Comintern into the background. At its Sixth Congress in 1928 he declared that since "the victory of socialism is possible only in a few countries" the Soviet government would concentrate on the task of strengthening communism at

[7] The First International lasted from 1864 to 1872; the Second from 1889 to 1914.

home. Many were comforted by the thought that the Comintern was
losing its dangerous aspect and that the Soviet Union would thenceforth work in harmony with the democracies. But the hopes cherished
by the outside world had little effect on Stalin. He did not renounce the
ultimate revolutionary aims of the Communists. His plan was to
strengthen the Soviet Union so that it would be ready for the decisive
struggle to inaugurate world revolution. In 1932 on the fifteenth anniversary of the Bolshevik Revolution he predicted the imminent overthrow of the noncommunist states. "Be not impatient," he said, "and
do not chafe at delays; universal war has now become inevitable and is
not far distant."

SOVIET EDUCATION AND CULTURE

One of the outstanding achievements of the Soviet government during the period between the two great wars was its progress in the field
of education. As stated earlier, Russia on the eve of World War I had
the highest percentage of illiteracy among the great powers. At the
time of the Bolshevik Revolution about 60 per cent of the population
could neither read nor write. The percentage of illiterates was particularly high in the Asiatic provinces, the literates numbering less than
1 per cent in some districts. Illiteracy was a great obstacle to communist indoctrination. How could the masses be converted to "communism" if they could not read the voluminous sheafs of propaganda
which the Communist Party was publishing. As Lenin put it, "You
cannot build a communist state with illiterate people." The Bolshevik
leaders also realized, and this particularly after the inauguration of
the First Five-Year Plan, that education is necessary for the development of skilled workers.

The chief obstacles in the path toward a better educational system
were a serious lack of schools and equipment and an even more serious
shortage of teachers. The new educational program made phenomenal
progress against these obstacles. The construction of schools advanced
so rapidly that by the school year of 1931–1932 there were enough
to allow education to be made compulsory for all children between
eight and eleven. In that year more than 67 per cent of all children of
school age were attending school. Nor did the efforts of the government
stop with the children. Schools were also opened to wipe out illiteracy
among adults as well as to provide vocational and professional training. In 1933 Stalin announced that 90 per cent of the adult population
had achieved literacy. Although his figure was somewhat too high,
the progress had certainly been considerable. Some idea of the success
of the program among children may be gained from the fact that the

number attending school rose from eight million in 1914 to thirty million in 1939.

During the period immediately after the revolution there was a tendency to ignore the cultural heritage of Russia and to despise culture as something bourgeois. But a change of attitude gradually took place. The growing interest in culture and in the Russian classics was in part due to the fact that the number of literates increased rapidly. Furthermore, in the decade of the thirties the government encouraged the revival of the Russian classics by publishing anniversary editions, staging exhibitions, and presenting lectures. The result was a tremendous demand for books. It is estimated, for example, that during the centennial celebration of Pushkin's death in 1937 no less than thirteen million copies of his books were sold. Former Ambassador Joseph E. Davies relates in *Mission to Moscow* (1941) that the number of people he found reading under the lights in the parks and on the street corners amazed him. Whereas in 1913 the published titles numbered 26,174 and the total copies about 86 million, the titles published in 1936 numbered 43,348 and the total copies about 571 million. Certain foreign authors whose books were approved by the government were also widely read in Russia. Among these were Shakespeare, Dickens, H. G. Wells, Robert Louis Stevenson, O. Henry, and Jack London. Shakespeare's works not only became a prescribed subject for study in the schools; his plays were also acted more frequently in one year during the decade of the thirties than in England and America combined.

Literature and art, like everything else in the Soviet Union, were carefully controlled. There was little freedom of cultural or artistic expression except within the boundaries of communist thought. Writers and artists were expected to serve the interests of the workers and of the Soviet social order. "Art belongs to the people," Lenin said; "it must have its deepest roots in the broad masses of the workers. It must be understood and loved by them. It must be rooted in and grow with their feelings, thoughts, and desires." The prose of the early years of the Bolshevist rule was more propaganda than literature. The only outstanding writer of the old generation who succeeded in ingratiating himself with the Bolsheviks was Maxim Gorki; the rest were either silent or in exile. Gradually, however, a new group of writers appeared on the scene, writers who were moved by the Soviet spirit. The literature they produced was designed to promote such movements as rural collectivization and the construction of heavy industries. Most of these writings were dull and low in artistic value, but as the years passed the literary quality of the literature improved greatly.

The outstanding prose writer of the period was Mikhail Sholokhov, whose novels are the closest approach to enduring literature that Soviet

Russia produced during the period between the two wars. Born in 1905 in a Don Cossack village, he used the milieu of his youth as the setting for all his important works. His characters are all Don fishermen or Cossack peasants. His most famous work, *The Silent Don,* published in four parts (1928–1940), portrays the life of a group of Cossack families under the last tsar, through World War I, the Russian Revolution, and the period of civil war. For this work Sholokhov received one of Stalin's 100,000-ruble literary awards. Not only were millions of copies sold in Russia; it was also made into a film, and Ivan Dzerzhinski, the Soviet composer, used it as the libretto for an opera which became a great favorite in the Soviet musical world. It was also translated into most of the civilized tongues of the globe. In the United States it appeared in two parts, *And Quiet Flows the Don* (1934) and *The Don Flows Home to the Sea* (1941). While he was writing *The Silent Don,* Sholokhov interrupted his work on it to write *Seeds of Tomorrow* (1933), which deals with the life of the new collective-farm Cossacks. This novel was dramatized as a successful four-act play and in 1935 was published in English as *Virgin Soil Upturned*. Critics have ranked Sholokhov with a number of giants of Russian literature. To many the realism and epic sweep of his works are reminiscent of Tolstoi.

Although many facts regarding the Russian culture of the period are still wrapped in mystery, particularly as regards painting, sculpture, and the theater, we do know that it was a great age of Russian music. The Bolshevik Revolution largely put an end to the music of the old school of Russian musicians. Sergei Rachmaninoff left Russia never to return. Stravinsky left Russia to live in France and the United States. Only a few of the lesser musicians came to terms with the new Soviet regime. Gradually a new school of Russian music took form under the sponsorship of the government. Supervision of musical production was vested in the Soviet bureau called Glavmus, which commissioned various musicians to write operas and symphonies. During this period Russian musicians produced a larger crop of compositions than any other nation. Much of this music is shallow, noisy, pretentious, and without emotional appeal. It lacks the heart-warming human quality so characteristic of the music of Mozart and Schubert. On the other hand, the Russian school of this period wrote many of the better symphonies and operas of the twentieth century. The purpose of Soviet music as well as of Soviet literature, as prescribed by the government, was to glorify the social aims of the government and to advertise the Soviet Union and Soviet culture to the rest of the world. How well some composers achieved this purpose is illustrated by the careers of Shostakovich and Prokofiev.

The most important Russian composer of the period was probably

Dimitri Shostakovich (born 1906). His musical biography starts with the *First Symphony,* composed before he reached his twentieth birthday. In it he displays a perfect mastery of musical technique and the ability to portray emotions. In the compositions that followed, the technique remained but the tenderness disappeared. This is particularly true of the *Second Symphony,* the *Age of Gold* ballet, and the opera *Lady Macbeth of Mtsensk.* The last became a sensation in New York, but was withdrawn from Soviet theaters after Moscow critics publicly flayed it as "bourgeois formalism." Subsequently his ballet *The Limpid Stream* was also withdrawn for the same reason and his *Fourth Symphony* was suppressed without a performance. For two years Shostakovich was *persona non grata* with the Soviet authorities, but the official attitude underwent a change during this time. The main feature of the new musical party line was the development of a great respect for such romantic composers of the nineteenth century as Tchaikovsky and Rimski-Korsakov. In 1937 Shostakovich won the favor of the new romantic-minded order with his *Fifth Symphony* and was restored to grace. The *Sixth Symphony,* first performed in 1939, was greeted with the same approbation as the *Fifth.* During the war years Shostakovich became the musical voice of Russia.

Another important musical figure of the period was Sergei Prokofiev (1891–1953). He began composing at the age of five and thereafter continued to compose prolifically. For a time he studied under Rimski-Korsakov. When World War I broke out he was exempted from military service as the only son of a widow and soon after the establishment of the Bolshevik regime received official permission to leave Russia (1918), spending the next years in France, Britain, and America. December, 1921, saw the premier of his opera *The Love of Three Oranges* at the Chicago Opera House. Next he wrote the music for the ballet *The Age of Steel,* which glorifies life in a Soviet village. After being received in a friendly manner on a visit to Russia in 1927, Prokofiev struggled with the idea of settling in Russia permanently. In 1932 he again returned to Russia and in 1938 finally settled in Moscow. The music he wrote after 1932 was, with few exceptions, propaganda music built on Russian themes and designed to glorify Russia. Thus for Stalin's sixtieth birthday he wrote a piece called *Homage to Stalin* based on the works of Marx, Lenin, and Stalin. In 1936 he did take time out to write the fairy tale *Peter and the Wolf* in music. In the United States this is probably his most widely known composition. His symphonies have had a varied reception in this country. His music, though hard and unsentimental, is nevertheless brilliant. Many non-Russian critics are agreed that among the twentieth-century composers he is unmatched as regards technical adroitness.

CHAPTER TWENTY-TWO

Britain and the British Empire

THE AFTERMATH OF THE WAR W"AR," Edmund Burke said, "never leaves a nation where it found it." Although the British government as such changed little during the war, the economic life of the country suffered a severe dislocation. To achieve success in the war it was necessary to concentrate on vital manufactures and hence to give up many of the products previously exported to foreign markets. The consequent shortages led many countries to seek to produce substitutes within their own confines, and other countries turned to new markets in which the products they desired were available. This gave the manufacturers of the United States an opportunity to strengthen their international position, with the result that, before the war ended, supremacy in foreign trade passed to America. The war was not, of course, wholly responsible for this development: it was but an acceleration and intensification of a movement which had started in the nineteenth century against Britain's supremacy.

Most Englishmen were convinced that the old customers would eventually return, and a trade boom at the end of the war appeared to support this belief. Not only did the British people purchase things they had postponed buying, but the continental countries whose industries had been damaged or wrecked also bought large quantities of British goods. Business prospered to such an extent that the four million demobilized soldiers were able to find jobs without displacing the many thousands of women who had kept the wheels of industry turning during the war. It appeared for a time as if the politicians had really told the truth when they promised to build "a land fit for heroes to live in."

The man who originally made the promise was David Lloyd George, who had become prime minister in December, 1916. His coalition government, composed of Conservatives and Liberals,[1] won by a landslide in the elections of 1918 and he immediately began to spend money in an effort to make the promised land a reality. As long as the boom lasted and everybody was enjoying prosperity, there were few objections to his program of spending. But in the fall of 1920 the purchases by other European states for the purpose of covering their shortages suddenly ceased, and in 1921 a wave of economic depression struck the country, particularly in textiles, iron, steel, hardware, coal, and ships. Some idea of the sharpness of the decline may be gained from the fact that British exports were 46 per cent less in 1921 than they had been in 1920. Unemployment, which previously had been very low, quickly assumed huge proportions. In December, 1921, the number of unemployed reached 1,934,000, or 16.5 per cent of the members of the trade unions. The Unemployment Insurance Act of 1920, which extended unemployment benefits to practically all industries, had been passed just in time to meet the emergency. The cost of supporting the unemployed, however, drained the national treasury and necessitated higher taxes which in turn dried up purchasing power.

The fact that exports declined was particularly detrimental, for Britain depended on international trade to a larger extent than any other great nation. She needed the income from the sale of exports to purchase food for her population and raw materials for her industries. In 1913 foreign countries supplied no less than 73.9 per cent of Britain's food and 67.6 per cent of her raw materials. The quantity of food imported increased with the increase in population. Thus in 1925 the imports of food were 16.7 per cent above 1913. Imports of manufactured goods also increased until their value was almost twice that of exports. The situation was a critical one. Sir Alfred Mond offered the following solution:

If the people in other countries who grow food are no longer prepared to buy our manufactured goods and so enable us to obtain the food we want in order to feed the people who make those goods, obviously there are only two things left for us to do. One is to grow more food in this country, and the second is to send our people to countries where they can grow food for themselves and, at any rate, manage to live, because people live on wheat and not on coal.

During the first years of the depression there were general hopes of early recovery. It was thought that the dislocation was due to political unsettlement in Europe and that as soon as certain adjustments took place Britain would regain her supremacy. But there were deeper causes

---

[1] The Labor members of the cabinet withdrew at the end of the war.

at work. After the conclusion of the Napoleonic wars in 1815 Britain
had experienced an economic depression, but at that time the country
possessed an advantage she did not have in 1919: then she had no
rivals for industrial supremacy, but in 1919 she was competing for
world markets with rivals who were in some respects better equipped
than she.

First, British plant equipment and methods of production now tended
to be out of date. While Belgian, French, German, and American industrialists were installing the latest machinery and adopting the newest
techniques, the British were lagging behind. British captains of industry
and finance seemed to have lost some of the initiative and enterprise
which had characterized them in the nineteenth century. Not that they
did not install any of the new machinery or that they refused to adopt
any of the improved techniques. What they failed to do was to keep
step with their competitors. They were not as alert to the needs of the
market as their rivals. Some could not afford to purchase new machinery, but among those who could there were many who, accustomed to
the old way of doing things, seemed unaware that change was imperative, that the market demanded methods of mass production. Noteworthy also is the fact that in some instances the unions opposed labor-
saving machinery because they feared an increase in unemployment.
Hence the British industrial machine was more or less out of tune with
the new era.

Second, British industry was handicapped by a low standard of individual production. In the words of one British writer, "If our output
per man were as great as that of the United States, our public expenditure, excessive though it may be, would be a burden we could bear
without difficulty." [2] For example, the output of coal per man in Britain
in the first quarter of 1921 was 3¾ tons against 20 tons in the United
States. Low output per man in all industries helped to keep prices high
and made it difficult for Britain to compete with other countries. Before the war Britain sent more than half of her cotton exports to Asia,
but after the war the cheaper goods from the factories of Japan, China,
and India tended to crowd British textiles out of these markets. The
decline of exports to India was particularly serious since it was the
largest of Britain's overseas markets. In numerous instances British
firms lost contracts because production costs abroad were lower. The
most conspicuous example was the shipbuilding industry. In September, 1924, for instance, British shipbuilders lost a contract to build six
oil tankers because their price was £150,000 higher than that of the
Dutch shipbuilders. [3]

[2] J. W. Lea, *Britain's Decline* (1922), p. 66.
[3] London *Times*, September 17, 1924.

Third, new sources of power curtailed the demand for British products, particularly for coal. During the war, industry in many countries had been passing from the era of steam and coal into the era of electricity and oil. In Norway, Sweden, and Italy hydroelectric power had been developed on a large scale. As a result there was less demand for coal, which had played a major part in the economic development of the nineteenth century and up to the outbreak of World War I. The increasing use of fuel oil in some countries, combined with the fact that more coal fields were being opened in other countries, was also reflected in the decline of the British coal industry. Britain found herself with large coal piles for which there were no buyers.

Thus the depression persisted. There was, it is true, some improvement in the general situation during the later twenties, but British foreign trade did not achieve its prewar levels. Even in 1928, which was one of the better years, exports were 15.6 per cent under those of 1913. Although 1929 was the best year in shipbuilding since World War I, the total output reached only 2,793,000 tons as compared with 3,333,000 tons in 1913. Unemployment decreased somewhat during the same period but still remained high, the general average being over a million.

POLITICAL CHANGES

The economic depression spelled the downfall of Lloyd George in the autumn of 1922. If he had been as skillful in dealing with postwar problems as in directing British energies during the war, his coalition might have continued over a long period; but his supporters quickly lost faith in him when they discovered that the treasury was empty. When the Conservatives withdrew from the coalition, he had no alternative but to resign. A noteworthy political change under his government was embodied in the Representation of the People Act (1918) which nearly doubled the number who could vote in parliamentary elections. It gave the vote to every man at the age of twenty-one and, with certain exceptions, to every woman over thirty who was either a local government elector or the wife of one. Qualification for the local franchise was six months' ownership or tenancy of land or premises. At the same time women also became eligible for seats in Parliament.[4]

In the elections of 1922 the Conservatives won 344 out of 615 seats. But their tenure was short-lived. Prime Minister Baldwin was convinced that he could not restore prosperity unless he was allowed to impose tariffs on foreign manufactures imported into Britain. This

[4] The extension of the franchise to the adult population was completed in 1928, when all women of twenty-one or over were granted the right to vote.

caused him to dissolve Parliament and to "go to the country" with a program of protection. The people were not ready yet to give up the idea of free trade, and although the Conservatives retained 257 seats, the control of Parliament passed to a coalition of the Labor Party (192) and the Liberal Party (157).

Since the Labor Party occupied a larger number of seats in the House than the Liberal Party, King George V asked Mr. Ramsay MacDonald, the leader of the former party, to form a cabinet. It was Britain's first labor government. The Labor Party was a socialistic working-class party and as such was committed to the inauguration of vast changes. This roused many hopes and also many fears, but the regime did not remain in office long enough to realize either. The Labor Party could do nothing without the support of the Liberal Party, and the Liberals were not inclined to let it go far in the direction of socialism. In an effort to revive the lagging export trade, MacDonald proposed to lend money to the Soviets so that they could buy British goods. Since both Liberals and Conservatives regarded such a plan as unwise, he lost much of his support. His appeal to the electorate (1924) won only 151 seats, while the Conservatives returned 413 members to the House.

A noteworthy change of this period was the progressive decline of the Liberal Party. The fading of its power, already under way before the war, went on much more rapidly after 1918. The primary reason undoubtedly was that it had exhausted its mission. The major political freedoms it sponsored had been won, and the social reforms it advocated were largely those supported also by the Conservatives. On the other hand, the Labor Party was committed to a social policy far in advance of anything the Liberals were prepared to accept. In 1924 the Liberals, by this time hopelessly split into factions, polled only a small percentage of their former vote. Thenceforth the Conservative Party and the Labor Party were the two major contestants in the British political arena.

During the four and a half years which followed the election of 1924 the Conservatives dominated the scene. They gradually lost their majority, however, because they failed to reduce public expenditures sufficiently to balance the budget and were also unable to find a remedy for the trade depression. Mr. Stanley Baldwin, the prime minister, hoped to revive foreign trade by putting the currency back on the gold standard, in the belief that if foreign traders knew the exact value of the pound in francs or marks, they would be encouraged to buy British goods. But the results were very disappointing. The new currency raised the price of British goods at a time when the currencies of Germany, France, and Italy were badly depreciated. In some instances prices rose so high that foreign merchants could not afford to buy.

Consequently British manufacturers lost more ground in foreign markets. Many mineowners and industrialists tried to reduce prices by reducing wages. This caused strikes and labor unrest but did not solve any economic difficulties. In the elections of 1929 the electorate expressed its disapproval of the conservative program by returning only 260 Conservatives to the House. As a result the Labor Party, with 287 seats, again came into office with Ramsay MacDonald as prime minister.

THE GREAT DEPRESSION

A few months after the Labor government took office, the great depression spread over the world. Great Britain had experienced depression to a greater or lesser extent since 1921, but other countries had enjoyed years of prosperity. This was particularly true of the United States, where industry and trade had flourished to such an extent that the Americans seemed to have found the secret of eternal prosperity. Then in the fall of 1929 the prosperity bubble suddenly burst. Before many months had passed, the repercussions were felt in Britain. In 1930 unemployment increased sharply and the value of exports declined by 22 per cent from the figures of 1929. But it was in 1931 that the economic storm hit Britain with real fury. The volume of international trade gradually shrank until it was barely one third of what it had been in 1929. Meanwhile unemployment increased to 2,825,772 by September, 1931, and to 2,859,828 by August, 1932. In the coal fields it reached such proportions that there were villages in which not a single wage earner enjoyed the security of continuous employment. The drain on the unemployment fund was so heavy that it went bankrupt and had to borrow heavily from the general fund raised by taxation. Financiers and foreign merchants who had deposits in British banks began to ask for them in gold, thus causing a run on the Bank of England which nearly exhausted its gold supply.

That is the situation which confronted the Laborites, and they were completely at loss for a remedy. The principal feature of their program appears to have been a public-works scheme financed by borrowed funds. Even this did not get past the discussion stage. The inability of the government to cope with the situation forced Ramsay MacDonald's resignation in August, 1931. He did, however, continue to hold the premiership because after his resignation the king requested him to form a "National government" containing members of all three parties. The new National cabinet, composed of four Laborites, four Conservatives, and two Liberals, at once devoted itself earnestly to the tasks of balancing the budget and lifting the depression. The first was achieved by decreasing government expenditures and increasing taxes.

To reduce expenses, cuts in all government salaries and in the allowances of the unemployed were voted.

Much more difficult of solution was the problem of restoring prosperity. One of the first steps was abandonment of the gold standard. An act was rushed through Parliament (September, 1931) which freed the Bank of England of the responsibility of giving gold in exchange for notes. By removing the handicap of an overvalued currency this act gave Britain the advantage of reduced prices in foreign trade. Furthermore, the government promoted the establishment of new industries and encouraged the modernization of the old ones so that they could compete better with the industries of other countries. But the most striking departure was the adoption of a general protective tariff. Not that there had previously been no duties whatsoever on imports. Although the British had adhered by and large to a policy of free trade, there had been some exceptions. In 1915, for example, Parliament had voted the imposition of duties on various luxuries in order to relieve pressure on foreign exchange and to conserve ship space for war materials and food. These so-called McKenna duties levied a duty of $33\frac{1}{3}$ per cent on motor cars, motion-picture films, musical instruments, watches, and clocks. In 1920 protection was also given to British-made dyes. During the next years Parliament also imposed tariffs designed to protect against German competition industries that had been established during the war.

British sentiment had nevertheless remained strongly in favor of free trade, while other countries were entrenching themselves behind tariff walls. Sentiment gradually changed, however, until the nation came to the conclusion that it could not afford the luxury of free trade in a world of rigid customs barriers. The change-over to protection was carried out swiftly and smoothly. Early in 1932 Parliament passed the Import Duties Act which imposed a minimum tariff of 10 per cent on all imports except raw cotton, wool, meat, fish, and wheat. The act also provided for the creation of a tariff commission, which was empowered to raise any duty as much as 100 per cent. Successive modifications of the Import Duties Act during the remainder of the year raised duties considerably on most imports. These tariffs gave British manufacturers most of the home markets which had formerly been supplied from abroad.

The Ottawa agreements signed in the same year gave Britain a larger share of the markets of the British Empire. At the opening of the Imperial Conference at Ottawa in August, 1932, a message from King George V was read which stated in part, "The British Empire is based on the principle of cooperation, and it is now your common purpose to give the fullest possible effect to that principle in the economic sphere." Of chief importance among the agreements reached at this conference were seven concluded between Britain and her dominions [5] giving the raw materials and food products of the dominions a tariff preference of about 10 per cent. The dominions, for their part, granted new and increased margins of preference to certain classes of British goods. On Britain's side these agreements amounted to the imposition of tariff restrictions on foreign foodstuffs, while the foodstuffs and raw materials from the dominions were admitted free. For the dominions it meant the purchase of a larger share of their manufactured imports from Britain and the sale of a larger share of food exports to Britain.

Under the stimulus of the tariff, the Ottawa agreements, the abandonment of the gold standard, and the partial modernization of industry a gradual revival took place. In 1933 a slow but continuous decline in the unemployment figures began. This was in large part due to the development of new industries such as the manufacture of automobiles, but even in coal mining, shipbuilding, and textiles, where the depression had been deepest, there were some signs of improvement. In steel there was a spectacular revival which soon saw the British steel plants working at 90 per cent of capacity. This general improvement gave a fillip to the confidence of the nation, but the basic questions had still not been solved. A former member of the House of Commons stated the problem this way:

The salvation of Great Britain depends on her ability to differentiate between courage and complacence, and abandoning the latter, to organize her industries drastically on a basis that eliminates waste, applies work to actual production, and advances distribution by supplying to the world that of which the world stands in actual need. England is not going to the dogs. But she has to make a fresh start.

In the summer of 1935 Prime Minister MacDonald retired because of ill health, and his place was taken by Stanley Baldwin, a Conservative. An election held in the same year gave Mr. Baldwin enough support to continue in office. It was the last general election before World War II. In 1937, however, he retired for reasons of health and was succeeded by Neville Chamberlain, "the man with the umbrella," who later met with Hitler a number of times in an effort to prevent World War II.

LONG LIVE THE KING

The year 1936 is notable for the fact that it saw three successive kings occupy the British throne. In the previous year George V, who

[5] Ireland was the exception.

had succeeded his father, Edward VII, on May 6, 1910, had amid scenes of splendor celebrated the Silver Jubilee of his coronation. A few months later, on January 20, 1936, he died after a short illness. Although he never achieved the popularity his father enjoyed, George V did endear himself by his uprightness, simplicity of character, and unwavering devotion to duty. His passing was deeply mourned by his people. Although many thrones of Europe had toppled during his reign, the British throne stood more firmly at his death than it had at his accession.

George V was succeeded by his eldest son, who was proclaimed king as Edward VIII on January 20. The new king's reign proved to be one of the shortest in English history. As Prince of Wales he had been highly popular throughout the empire. He had disappointed the people in only one respect. He had not married. When asked about it he had always answered, "I shall never marry until I am in love." His accession to the throne gave no hint of the storm that was soon to break. The crisis came some months later over his determination to marry an American, Mrs. Wallis Warfield Simpson, who had already divorced one husband and was about to divorce another. After rumors of the king's intentions began to circulate, Prime Minister Baldwin pointed out to Edward that such a marriage would endanger the prestige of the throne and the ties of empire. This view was shared by the Church of England, the members of the royal family, most of the members of Parliament, and many newspapers. Fortified with this knowledge the prime minister told the king at a second interview (November 16) that the country did not approve the contemplated marriage.

But Edward remained adamant. Some days later in a third interview with the prime minister he proposed a morganatic marriage. Mrs. Simpson was to be the king's wife, with the title Duchess of Cornwall, but was not to hold the position of queen. Mr. Baldwin, however, pointed out that English law did not recognize such a marriage and that he was certain Parliament would not pass such an act. Edward then decided he would rather give up the throne than the marriage. On December 9 the cabinet requested him to reconsider, but the next day the king announced his "final and irrevocable decision" to renounce the throne. On December 11 Parliament rushed a bill of abdication through both houses and Edward immediately signed it. In his farewell over the radio to the people of the empire he said: "You must believe me when I tell you that I have found it impossible to carry the heavy burden of responsibility and to discharge my duties as king as I would wish to do without the help and support of the woman I love." Having abdicated, he left the country as the Duke of Windsor.

Edward's successor was the Duke of York, the oldest of his brothers, who was crowned as George VI on the day originally set for Edward's coronation. Outside England many felt the affair had permanently undermined the prestige of the monarchy, but in this they were wrong. The storm subsided as quickly as it had arisen. George VI soon gained both the respect and love of his people. In a few months everything was as if he had directly succeeded his father.

PROBLEMS OF EMPIRE

During the nineteenth century the question was frequently asked whether the British Empire could be prevented from disintegrating. When World War I broke out, many were convinced that the great upheaval must rend the fabric of empire. The Germans particularly, motivated in part by wishful thinking, prophesied the disruption. Although a rebellion did break out in Ireland and there were uprisings and disturbances in other quarters, the general revolt did not take place. Not only was the empire kept intact; it was even extended by 800,000 square miles in the peace settlement. With six votes in the League of Nations, Britain appeared to be at the very zenith of her power.

But before long British sovereignty itself was rudely questioned by the dominions. During the war a strong local national feeling had developed, with the result that they insisted more and more on independence. Each was, it is true, practically independent in the regulation of its internal affairs, but this was not enough. The dominions also wanted a share in the formation of international policies, the policies which might generate war. In general, the inferior legal status of their institutions proved galling.

Although no legal changes were made immediately after the war, the dominions did make rapid strides in the direction of complete nationhood. Two milestones in this progress were the separate representation they were accorded at the Peace Conference and the separate signatures they appended to the treaty of Versailles. Moreover, their independence received signal recognition when they were given individual memberships in the League of Nations. The trend continued during the next years. When Canada in 1922 concluded an independent treaty with the United States regarding the halibut fisheries, she established, as it were, the right of the dominions to make their own treaties. In 1926 the Imperial Conference attempted a formal definition and description of dominion status in the following terms: "They [the dominions] are autonomous communities within the British Empire, equal in status, in no way subordinate one to another, in any respect of their domestic or external affairs, though united by a common allegiance to the Crown and freely associated as members of the British Common-

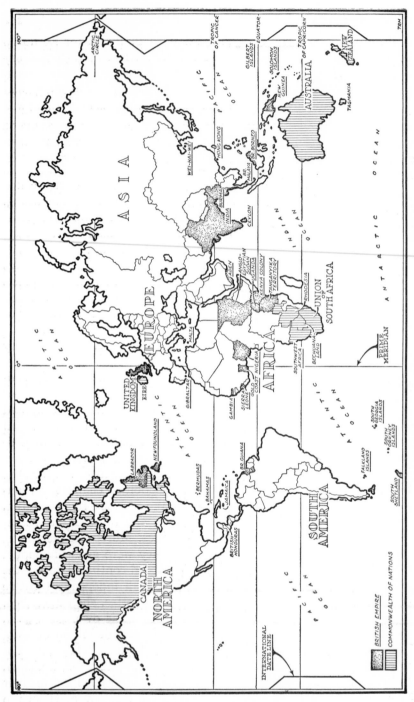

THE BRITISH COMMONWEALTH OF NATIONS

wealth of Nations." This idea was restated at the Imperial Conference in 1929. These statements did not, however, alter the law of the constitution in any respect.

The legal restraints were removed by the Statute of Westminster, passed by Parliament in 1931. The Statute affirmed that "no law hereafter made by the Parliament of the United Kingdom shall extend to any of the said Dominions as part of the law of that Dominion otherwise than at the request and with the consent of that Dominion." [6] In other words, the Statute of Westminster removed the last vestiges of British control over the dominions. The Parliament of the United Kingdom was no longer "imperial," but only British. Thus the old British Empire ceased to exist and its place was taken by the British Commonwealth of Nations, an empire resting solely on voluntary cooperation. The binding link of the new Commonwealth was a common allegiance to the British sovereign. Whereas Parliament had been the pivot of the old empire, the king was the pivot of the new Commonwealth. Many feared that the Statute of Westminster had removed the cement of empire and that the nations of the Commonwealth would soon drift apart. Events soon proved that the fear was unfounded. In dissolving the legal bonds the Statute greatly strengthened the moral ties. In the words of a Dominion minister, "So long as any form of control remained, cooperation had to be tinged with compulsion. That made it less wholehearted and less effective."

This does not mean, however, that Britain had no imperial problems during the two decades which separated World War I from World War II. Not all the peoples of the empire were satisfied to remain in it. The ferment of nationalism was particularly active throughout the period, causing many peoples of the empire to demand changes. One such center of disaffection was Ireland. The Irish Home Rule Bill which Gladstone had demanded was for decades at the point of being passed, only to elude final action. Not until 1914 did Parliament finally pass it, and even then it was not immediately put into operation. Using the war as an excuse, the British suspended the operation of the act for the duration. The people of southern Ireland were not happy over this and on Easter Monday, 1916, a group of insurgents, encouraged by the promise of German aid, proclaimed Ireland a republic. But before the Germans could send help, the British put the uprising down with a strong hand. This did not, however, solve the problem. The Sinn Fein Party,[7] which became the dominant political factor in Ireland, continued to preach rebellion. Under Sinn Fein leadership the members

---

[6] The dominions as named in the act were Canada, Australia, New Zealand, the Union of South Africa, the Irish Free State, and Newfoundland.
[7] Sinn Fein = "we ourselves alone."

who had been elected to the House of Commons constituted themselves a sort of National Assembly instead of entering the Parliament. This assembly called itself the Dail Eireann, Gaelic words meaning "Irish Parliament."

Regarding this move as open revolt, the government took steps to suppress the republic. A special constabulary force recruited from demobilized British units carried on a bitter warfare against the Irish, who reciprocated with equal bitterness. From the fact that the British units wore khaki uniforms with black caps they were known as Black and Tans. Finally after a period of bloody fighting the government set up two parliaments, one for the six counties of Northern Ireland (Ulster) inhabited by a population composed largely of Protestants, and the other for Southern Ireland where the majority of the inhabitants are Catholic. Both were subordinate to the British Parliament. Although the Sinn Fein would have no part of this plan, those who represented the more constructive forces did in 1921 sign a treaty with the British which constituted Southern Ireland the Irish Free State, with a dominion status like that of Australia, New Zealand, Canada, and South Africa. The vexatious question of allegiance was settled by merely requiring members of the Free State Parliament "to be faithful to His Majesty King George V." When the Dail or Irish Parliament accepted the treaty, it seemed as if the period of strife and contention was over.

But the extreme Sinn Feiners were far from satisfied. Under the leadership of Eamon de Valera, an American by birth, they objected. As he put it, "Ireland will accept no settlement except independence." This time the extremists were arrayed against the rest of the Sinn Feiners. After a period of civil war the followers of de Valera decided in 1923 to participate in the elections for the Dail. With the establishment of the Irish Free State the Gaelic language was dug out of the musty past and made the official tongue. Before the end of 1923 the Free State entered the League and in the next year sent representatives to the Imperial Conference in London.

Cooperation with the Irish Free State did not, however, terminate the demands of de Valera and his followers. They were determined to be satisfied with nothing less than complete independence and a united Ireland embracing both Northern and Southern Ireland. During the years after 1932 while de Valera's party (Fianna Fail) was in power, it introduced various policies aimed at severing the last ties with Britain. The crowning effort was a new constitution (1937) designed for the whole of Ireland. Abolishing the office of governor general, the constitution established the complete independence of the Irish Free State, the name of which was changed to Eire. Thus the southern Irish achieved independence, but Irish unity did not follow. Protestant

Northern Ireland firmly refused to join with Southern Ireland. Even the election of Dr. Douglas Hyde, a Protestant, to the Irish presidency in 1938 failed to entice the people of Northern Ireland into a union with Eire. During World War II Eire adhered to a policy of neutrality, while Northern Ireland joined forces with Britain against Germany.

A further problem was that of Palestine, regarded as the Holy Land by Christian, Jew, and Moslem. Here the difficulties arose from a clash of Arab and of Jewish nationalist aspirations. Although Jewish independence in Palestine had been destroyed by the Romans in A.D. 68, the Jews kept alive through the centuries the hope of re-establishing it. In 1897 at an international congress they organized a movement for this purpose. Zionism, as the movement was called, derives from the word "Zion," the name of a hill in Jerusalem on which the royal palace of David stood. Zionist aims were regarded with anything but enthusiasm by the Turkish government which ruled Palestine at the time. Nevertheless, the Zionists encouraged Jews to migrate to Palestine, with the result that there were approximately 50,000 in that country when World War I opened. During the course of the war the British, as a means of exciting rebellion, made vague promises of independence to the Arab provinces of Turkey, promises which the Arabs interpreted as including Palestine. On the other hand, in 1917 the British government issued the Balfour Declaration (named after the British foreign minister, Sir Arthur James Balfour), which supported the plan to establish a Jewish national home in Palestine on condition "that nothing shall be done which may prejudice the civil and religious rights of existing non-Jewish communities in Palestine."

In 1922 the League of Nations approved a British mandate over Palestine, but nothing was done to advance the cause of a Jewish national state. Meanwhile more Jewish immigrants were entering the country, some of them settling in Tel Aviv and others founding agricultural colonies. The Hebrew language was also revived as a living tongue and in 1925 the Hebrew University in Palestine was opened. At the same time modern agricultural machinery and improved methods were being introduced by the immigrants. All this excited a wave of opposition among the Arabs, who not only resented the continuing immigration but also feared that Palestine would be transformed into an occidental state. Consequently they demanded that the immigration cease. When it did not, they resorted to terrorism and the Jews retaliated in kind. Soon waves of mutual hatred engulfed both Arabs and Jews although both are Semitic and claim descent from Abraham. The bitterness increased with the passing years, particularly after 1933 when Jews began to arrive in larger numbers to escape Nazi persecutions. So many came that by 1936 their number had grown to 350,000, or almost one third of the population. In 1936 a British Commission proposed a plan for settling the question; the country was to be divided into three parts: one for the Jews, a second for the Arabs, and the third for the British. Both Jews and Arabs denounced the plan with equal vehemence.

LITERATURE AND MUSIC

The three names that stand out above the rest in the English literature of this period are Arnold Bennett (1867–1931), H. G. Wells, (1866–1946), and George Bernard Shaw (1856–1950). There were many other distinguished authors, including Rudyard Kipling, Joseph Conrad, John Galsworthy, and Oscar Wilde; but Bennett, Wells, and Shaw are the men whose writings did most to mold the minds of the first generation of the twentieth century. An English writer who was a young man at the time wrote, "These men, as I say, we drank in like thirsty plants. We grew by their vigor. We throve by their warmth. They are part of whatever bone and tissue we have."

Two of the three figures, Arnold Bennett and H. G. Wells, were primarily fiction writers. By its very nature the novel is closer to contemporary life and thought than other forms of literature, and in England it has reflected with particular clarity the social structure in which it originated. Thus Fielding, Stern, and Smollett in the eighteenth century, Dickens and Thackeray in the nineteenth, depicted the society of their time. Bennett, too, was a chronicler of certain phases of contemporary life. The industrial midlands of England is the scene of his most enduring novels. As a young journalist he wrote a number of novels, but he did not demonstrate his mastery until the appearance in 1902 of *Anna of the Five Towns,* Five Towns being the name he gave to the pottery district of North Staffordshire. Further volumes in this series were *Leonora* (1903), *The Grim Smile of the Five Towns* (1907), *The Old Wives' Tale* (1908), and *Clayhanger* (1910). Of these *The Old Wives' Tale* is by far the best. Although the subject matter of his novels is often ugly and depressing, Bennett always managed to find some beauty and nobility in the lives he depicted. He endowed his characters wtih abounding life in a degree reminiscent of Dickens.

Herbert George Wells, better known as H. G. Wells, was, according to Anatole France, the greatest intellectual force in the English-speaking world during the early decades of the present century, and at the time of his death in 1946 an editorial writer of the New York *Times* called him the greatest public teacher in the world. Wells attained the foremost rank among contemporary novelists by focusing his gifts of keen analysis upon the tremendous problems of the individual set in the midst of the infinite complexities of industrial civilization. He was a self-appointed crusader whose mission it was to convince man that he must form his own future. He assured his fellow men that the universe was infinitely plastic and amenable to man's will, that with science and purpose all things are possible. His writings are an outstanding example of the impact of science and technology on literature.

In his early novels, which include *The Time Machine* (1895), *The Island of Dr. Moreau* (1896), *The Invisible Man* (1897), and *The War of the Worlds* (1898), he combined farseeing scientific vision with an awakening passion for social reform. Among the things he conceived in these early writings were a drug that made men float like balloons, another drug that enabled men to live a thousand hours in one, a man who could stop the sun like Joshua, a gigantic bird hatched from a prehistoric egg, a crystal egg through which one could watch the life on Mars, a machine that could travel through time, a man who could pass outside space, and another who found a way to be invisible.

During the second stage of his development he was predominantly the eager propagandist for a new and better social order. Important novels of this period include *Mankind in the Making* (1903), *A Modern Utopia* (1905), and *New Worlds for Old* (1908). But the storyteller in H. G. Wells was not dead, as was demonstrated by the publication of *Kipps* (1905), *Tono-Bungay* (1909), and *Ann Veronica* (1909). In the third period his materials are the commonplaces of everyday life. The novel is now an "essay in fiction form." The mission is still the betterment of human life. Important books of this period are *The History of Mr. Polly* (1910), *The New Machiavelli* (1911), *Marriage* (1912), *The Passionate Friends* (1913), *The Wife of Sir Isaac Harmon* (1914), and *The Research Magnificent* (1915).

During his last years Wells, who had been an optimist during most of his life, suffered disillusionment. After 1925 his optimism evaporated with that of the postwar generation. He lived to see the invention of the atom bomb and its use at Hiroshima and Nagasaki. Having spent his life exhorting mankind to rise to greater heights, he became convinced that human beings were bent on self-murder. In his last published work, *Mind at the End of Its Tether* (1945), he prophesied the imminent death of mankind.

In the early twentieth century the most resounding name among the dramatists, which also included Wilde and Galsworthy, was that of George Bernard Shaw. His personality impressed his age almost as Voltaire's did the mid-eighteenth century. Some critics have gone so far as to label him "the greatest dramatist writing in the English language since Shakespeare." His first attempts were not commercial successes, but he gradually became master of his craft and during the succeeding decades produced a series of witty, unconventional plays which delighted audiences the world over. Among his better known plays are *Man and Superman* (1903), *Major Barbara* (1905), *The Doctor's Dilemma* (1906), *Getting Married* (1908), *Fanny's First Play* (1911), *Androcles and the Lion* (1912), *Pygmalion* (1912), *Back to Methuselah* (1921), *Saint Joan* (1923), and *The Apple Cart* (1929).

The society of the post-Victorian period was in Shaw's opinion a sick society and he set about the task of curing it. In play after play, like a surgeon, he laid bare the diseased tissues of the social organism. He shattered social idols, bitterly assailed prejudice, and roundly denounced the conventions of an age in which a wide gulf separated profession and practice. His mission is stated in the words he makes Jack Tanner say in *Man and Superman,* "I no longer break cucumber frames, I shatter creeds and demolish idols." As a disciple of Ibsen he used the stage as a vantage point for his attacks, which were at once serious, brilliant, and infinitely entertaining. The apparent callousness was due to his belief that the naked and sincere truth is the best remedy for social ills.

Only a few of his many themes can be mentioned here. In *Getting Married* he deals with the absurdity of marriage laws and the legal difficulties of divorce. Militarism is attacked in *Man of Destiny, The Devil's Disciple,* and *Major Barbara.* In *The Philanderer* and *The Doctor's Dilemma* he objects to certain phases of modern medical practice. As the champion of youth he demands in a number of plays that the young be given the right to choose for themselves without being forced to accept the ideas of their parents. Religious problems are treated in *The Devil's Disciple, The Shewing Up of Blanco Posnet,* and *Androcles and the Lion.* He believed that too many people who professed to be religious were spiritually dead. But the greatest evil of society, in Shaw's opinion, is poverty. It "blights whole cities, spreads horrible pestilences, strikes dead the very souls of all who come within sight, sound, or smell of it."

Shaw wrote so much during the first fifteen years of the century that one critic, thinking that the dramatist had used himself up, wrote a book with the title, *An Epitaph.* Thirty-five years later the book was dead, but G.B.S. was still very much alive. At sixty-five he wrote *Back to Methuselah,* in which he advocated that man should by biological processes develop a long-lived race, because at present men die just as they begin to attain to wisdom. Two years later he finished *Saint Joan,* which some regard as his greatest play. Although the plays of his last years were not as popular as his old ones, he went right on writing until his death in 1950 at the age of ninety-four. Whatever may be said about

Shaw, it cannot be denied that he was the most vigorous controversialist of his age.

In the world of music Britain found its voice in Sir Edward Elgar (1857–1934), one of the great musicians of the twentieth century. His first outstanding work was his *Enigmatic Variations,* depicting the personalities of his friends. In 1900 he wrote the greatest of his choral works, *The Dream of Gerontius.* In 1901 he composed *Pomp and Circumstance,* a set of six military marches, for the coronation of Edward VII. These marches have stirred many people since that time. His *First Symphony* (1908) proved that he was a composer of world importance, worthy to be ranked with the great continental masters. His *Second Symphony* (1911) was also accorded an enthusiastic reception. This was followed in 1913 by *Falstaff,* which put the seal on his fame as orchestral composer. His compositions possess qualities which have moved critics to regard them as typically English. One critic wrote, "When Elgar is not praising God, he is praising England." Some have compared him with Richard Strauss and Sibelius.

CHAPTER TWENTY-THREE

France in Travail

REPAIRING THE DAMAGES $\quad$ **D**URING the war it had appeared at times as if the French would be overwhelmed, but after a long struggle they finally emerged as victors. When the smoke of battle cleared and they surveyed the extent of the damage, they found they had paid a terrible price. The invasion and occupation differed greatly in both character and results from the previous invasion during the Franco-Prussian War. In 1870–1871 the Germans encountered no serious resistance on their drive to Paris, except at Metz. The fighting was of such short duration that little injury was done to either public or private property. In 1914–1918 the situation was entirely different. For more than fifty months the battle lines, traversing practically the entire breadth of northern France from the Channel to the Swiss border, advanced and receded as both sides fought to hold or to take strategic positions. In addition to the damage wrought by artillery and machine-gun fire, thrusts and counterthrusts, there was much deliberate destruction on the part of both invaders and defenders.

No other country in modern times had suffered such widespread havoc. Even the roving armies of the Thirty Years' War had not denuded districts so completely. According to one estimate 2600 towns were damaged, 300,000 houses were demolished, and 360,000 were partially destroyed. In more than a hundred towns not a single building was standing; only dismal heaps of brick and debris were left. When the first refugees returned to the sites of their former homes, they found the countryside comparable to the surface of the moon. Vast stretches were dotted with the remains of forts and artillery emplacements, shell holes, mine craters, and trenches. It has been said that the peasant had to reconquer his soil from trench to trench and from shell

476

hole to shell hole, in the last battle of the war. The eminent French historian, Gabriel Hanotaux, wrote regarding his return to the village in which he had been living when the war broke out, "I walked over the pile of ruins to a heap of stones which had been my own house, and from it looked over the tragic landscape. As far as I could see there was nothing but a desert of debris, which looked like a ragpicker's dump. The scene had the appearance of a cemetery with piled mounds of graves, over which nature had thrown a red carpet of poppies."

The actual warfare, it is true, had laid waste only ten departments, but they comprised the richest and most active industrial regions of France. Here were located most of the coal mines, two thirds of the steel industry, half of the textile looms, and some of the richest vineyards and farmlands. Almost every factory was either damaged or entirely destroyed. It has been estimated that 90 per cent of the sugar mills and 80 per cent of the iron foundries were damaged and more than 60 per cent of the textile mills were destroyed. In short, the entire industrial capacity of the region was reduced to a shadow of its normal production. Knowing that much of France's economic vitality came from her coal mines, the Germans made these the particular objects of destruction. They flooded them, dynamited them, filled them with waste materials, or set them on fire.

Most appalling was the loss of human life. Of the 7,935,000 men mobilized, nearly a million and a half were killed or reported missing. No other nation had suffered such high proportionate losses. The more seriously wounded numbered nearly a million and a half, of whom about a third were permanently crippled. The war reduced the entire population indirectly as well. In the departments that had not been invaded there were 1,389,916 more civilian deaths than births during the years from 1914 to 1919. As a general result the population, which had been thirty-nine millions before the war, dropped to thirty-six millions. In order to fill the gaps in the ranks of agricultural and industrial laborers it became necessary to enlist the service of workers from neighboring countries.

The least the French expected was that the Germans would pay for civilian damages. At the close of the Franco-Prussian War the French had paid. Now the roles were reversed. This time the Germans had lost; hence it was their turn to pay. That an exhausted country could pay such vast amounts as the French expected was a preposterous assumption. Nevertheless successive governments were founded on that assumption.

The Germans did make some payments in 1921 but in June, 1922, requested a moratorium on the ground that their economy could not stand the strain. They warned that a financial collapse was inevitable if the moratorium were not granted. In France many were convinced that this move was merely a ruse to evade payment. When the Germans defaulted on coal and iron deliveries, Poincaré decided to exert pressure by occupying the Ruhr (January, 1923). He believed that the Germans might make an effort to pay reparations rather than lose this highly industrialized area. Although they agreed after some months to resume deliveries of coal and iron, Poincaré obtained no money. Even partial money payments on the debt were delayed until the Dawes Plan went into effect.

But rehabilitation of the devastated areas could not wait. No sooner had the fighting ceased than the French at once attacked the gigantic task. It proceeded with amazing rapidity. Roads and railways, homes and factories were rebuilt and the land was cleared of the debris of war, leveled, and returned to use. In 1921 M. Briand, then premier, was able to announce that 80 per cent of the land which had been farmed before the war was again under cultivation. By 1921, too, the destroyed railways had been rebuilt mile for mile. The industrial restoration was almost as rapid. At the beginning of 1922 the Minister for the Liberated Regions announced that of the 4084 factories destroyed, 3986 had been rebuilt. It was also reported that of the 280,147 buildings destroyed and of the 422,736 damaged, 335,479 had been rebuilt or repaired. The rehabilitation of the mines proceeded somewhat more slowly. The water was pumped out of flooded mines, the shafts and passageways were cleared in those which had been dynamited, and the fires were extinguished in those which had been set on fire. Soon they too were producing as they had before 1914. In one respect the destruction of factories and machinery was not an unmixed evil, for the new installations of the latest and best machinery contributed toward raising the technical level of industry.

POLITICAL INSTABILITY

The outstanding characteristic of French governments under the Third Republic was their instability. It has been calculated that the average life of a cabinet was less than nine months. It is remarkable that the conduct of affairs achieved even the degree of prudence and consistency which actually obtained. In certain periods the changes were so frequent that they became the butt of humorous remarks. Will Rogers in narrating his European experiences stated that after witnessing the change of the guard at Buckingham Palace he had flown to Paris to see the cabinet change. It is true that a new cabinet frequently contained a considerable number of ministers from the preceding one, and that in some instances the change in personnel did not extend much beyond the selection of a new premier. But since even such a change usually meant an alteration or deflection of policy, the instability was great enough to be disturbing. The kaleidoscope of politics not only discouraged statesmanship and lowered the tone of political life; it also gave rise to frequent political crises.

There were two major causes of the frequent changes of cabinet: first, the group system, and second, the inability of the government to dissolve the Chamber of Deputies. French citizens did not organize themselves into two major parties, like the Republicans and Democrats of the United States. The outstanding feature of political life was a multiplicity of parties and groups both within and outside the chamber. In 1936, for example, there were no fewer than nineteen groups in the chamber, most of which did not correspond to organized parties on the outside. Some groups, such as those espousing clericalism or royalism, had a more constant existence, but others were organized about a personality or were drawn together by some issue of the moment. Hence they coalesced or disintegrated as personalities or issues rose and fell. Such stability as a cabinet had was maintained by adroit interparty bargaining.

The fact that the cabinet could not dissolve the Chamber of Deputies was also a source of political weakness. The constitution of the Third Republic originally included a law which permitted the president to dissolve the Chamber of Deputies with the assent of the Senate. But the supporters of the republic did not like this presidential right. It savored too much of monarchy and circumscribed the sovereignty of the people. After being used only once, it was revoked in 1878. Thereafter the deputies were secure in their four-year mandate, regardless of any change in popular sentiment. The premier could not, like the British prime minister, exert discipline by threatening dissolution or an appeal to the voters. His only recourse was to resign if he could not command sufficient support.

Behind the confusion of French politics two general tendencies are clearly distinguishable, those of the right and those of the left. Originally the right was composed of the parties opposed to the republic; but as the years passed, a steady growth of republican sentiment took place. On the extreme right there were, however, still clerical and royalist reactionaries. The right was composed of small groups. The left included three fairly large ones, the Radical Socialists, the Socialists, and the Communists. The name of the first group is very misleading. The Radical Socialists, with a membership composed mainly of the lower bourgeoisie and peasants, were hardly radical in the generally accepted sense. They firmly supported private property, law, and order. The party which sponsored a Marxian program was the Socialist Party, but it, too, wished to achieve its aims through peaceful parliamentary methods and not through revolution. In the two decades after 1919 it drew much of its support from the trade union organization called the General Confederation of Labor. The Communist Party, like others of its kind in Europe, was affiliated with the Third International and in close contact with communist Russia.

In general the parties were not organized on the model of those in Britain or the United States. Only those of the left were able to exert discipline over their members. A candidate for the chamber could present himself to the electorate under the aegis of a certain party and if elected join one of the many groups into which the some six hundred deputies were divided, or he might even form a new group. Again, he could stand for election without associating himself with any political party. M. Tardieu, who was prominent in politics during the decade of the twenties, was elected as a "Républicain de Gauche," which was the designation of a group in the chamber and not of a political party. Even the parties of the left were not all able to control their deputies. Although the Socialists formed a fairly compact party organization, they were not successful in getting their deputies to vote *en bloc*. Only the Communists were able to exercise party restraint on their deputies.

FINANCIAL DIFFICULTIES

The most difficult problem with which French statesmen were compelled to grapple during the two decades after World War I was financial. Such issues as clericalism, Bonapartism, and royalism had lost some of their urgency, but the financial difficulties became more pressing. At the close of the war there was a large debt, and the budget was badly out of balance. As a result of increased government expenditures during the succeeding years it became more and more unbalanced. An important item in the growing debt was the money borrowed to rebuild the devastated areas. The government hoped eventually to recover the vast sums this work necessitated, but the "dreams of Rhinegold" failed to materialize. As the months passed, the hopes grew dimmer. Poincaré's Ruhr venture, launched as a means of assuaging public feeling, only aggravated the financial plight by draining the treasury of billions of francs. A decline of the franc resulted. The prospect of even further depreciation caused owners of capital to change their francs into the currency of other countries. This so-called "flight from the franc" brought about a still further decline. Despite the efforts of six successive cabinets the decline continued until the franc dropped to a level of two cents in gold (July, 1926).

Finally the chaotic state of business and the fear of runaway inflation such as had wrought financial havoc in Germany brought about the recall of Poincaré from his retirement. He at once took vigorous measures to set the finances in order. Confidence in the franc gradually returned, depreciation ceased, and in the winter of 1926–1927 capital that had taken refuge abroad began to flow back. Business boomed, giving France her only years of prosperity. The favorable exchange rate caused foreign buyers to make large purchases of French goods and also attracted large numbers of tourists. The government was now able to accumulate a stock of gold and in June, 1928, the franc was officially stabilized on a four-cent gold exchange basis. Since this was only one fifth of its prewar value, many people with fixed incomes and small savings were hit hard, and in some cases tragically. Industrial workers, peasants, and businessmen, however, soon adjusted themselves to the new currency.

When the world depression was ushered in by the Wall Street crash of 1929, it did not at first affect France. The country still coasted along under the impetus of the Poincaré boom; in fact, after the crash industrial activity continued on the upgrade for more than another half year, reaching its maximum index figure of 144 as late as June, 1930. Many were quick to contend that since industry had not overexpanded as much as in other countries, and the economy was so well balanced between industry and agriculture, the depression was not likely to prove very severe in France. Events did not, however, support this opinion. Although the crisis came comparatively late, it was nevertheless severe. The situation took a decided turn for the worse in 1931 and during the next two years business conditions grew progressively worse. Some idea of the general decline may be gained from the fact that returns from the sales tax were 34 per cent less in February, 1934, than they had been in the same month in 1929. During this period the tourist and export trades also suffered greatly and budgetary deficits again became a major problem, one that was magnified by the cessation of reparations payments in 1932.

THE POPULAR FRONT

The economic depression was accompanied by a widespread political deterioration which undermined popular confidence in the whole parliamentary democratic system. Many Frenchmen had previously harbored resentment against the Chamber because of the frequent changes of government, the flouting by the politicians of the will of the majority, and the continual increase of the public debt. Now the dissatisfaction expressed itself in the demand for the modification and, among extremist groups, for the abolition of the existing political system. Most of the latter groups had either a fascist or monarchist complexion. The political ferment reached the boiling point through the exposure of a series of financial scandals involving government leaders. The leading figure in the scandals was Serge Alexander Stavisky, an international adventurer, who with the apparent connivance of high officials was swindling the public out of large sums of money through the sale of worthless bonds. His suicide under suspicious circumstances revealed to a wider public his malodorous schemes and the fact that high officials were implicated. From many sides there were cries of "thieves in the government." Riots and demonstrations were instigated by reactionary groups. On February 6, 1934, mobs staged some of the severest rioting in the history of the Third Republic. A surging crowd appeared before the Palais Bourbon, where the deputies were in session, and tried to force its way into the building. It required military force to disperse the mob. The toll was 218 killed and more than two thousand wounded.

One result of the disclosures and the rioting was a great increase in the membership of the fascist and semi-fascist organizations. The most prominent was the Croix de Feu, originally a group of veterans who had been decorated for gallantry under fire. Under the leadership of Colonel François de la Rocque this organization built an army of 300,000 men by the middle of 1935. At numerous secret mass meetings of the organization he urged the members to continue their efforts to overthrow the government. It appeared as if the French stage were being set for the entrance of a fascist dictator.

If the fascist groups were attracting many members, so were the socialist and communist organizations. As a means of combating the rising fascism all the important groups of the left from the Communist Party to the bourgeois Radical Socialist Party formed a coalition called the Popular Front (1934). In the elections of that year neither the fascists nor socialist-communist group made marked gains, but in 1936 the Popular Front carried the elections. The Popular Front won 381 seats of the 618 in the Chamber or 62 per cent of the total. Since the parties of the right obtained only 38 per cent of the seats the possibility of a fascist coup became remote.

When the cabinet was formed the premiership fell to Léon Blum, well-to-do member of the bourgeoisie, who was head of the Socialist Party, the largest in the Chamber. Since the communists refused to supply a minister, the new cabinet was composed largely of Socialists and Radical Socialists. The difficulties confronting the government were tremendous. In 1935 economic conditions had become progressively worse. The production index dropped considerably and the value of exports declined more than two and a quarter billion francs below the 1934 level. At the end of the year only about half of the French workmen had been employed full time. Only the efforts of the government to bolster weak businesses with credit and loans had prevented wholesale bankruptcies. General economic conditions were mirrored by the decline of more than five billion francs in tax receipts. During 1935 the unbalanced budget and the general economic decline had caused a substantial drain on the gold reserves of the Bank of France.

Further difficulties developed during the three weeks between the election and the first meeting of the new Chamber. On May 26 a series of "stay-in" or sit-down strikes started and by the end of a week involved a million workers. They occupied factories, shops, and even farms to enforce their demands for higher wages, shorter hours, and paid vacations. Although Premier Blum admitted that the strikes were illegal, he refused to evacuate the workers by force, fearing that it might precipitate disorders and even revolution. He called together representatives of the employers and the strikers and secured from the former promises that they would grant immediate wage increases of 7 to 15 per cent and improve sanitation facilities and other working conditions. Then Blum pushed through the chamber measures providing for collective bargaining, vacations with pay, and a forty-hour week. Thereafter the sit-down strike rapidly waned. Nor were the peasants overlooked. A Wheat Board was organized for the purpose of limiting speculation, limiting the profits of middlemen, and fixing the price of wheat so as to insure farmers a remunerative price for their crops. The flood of bills rushed through the Chamber was often called the French New Deal. In a wider sense, the legislation marked the end of the period in which an employer could hire labor on his own terms.

Other legislation also changed the economic structure of France in important respects. Noteworthy is the nationalization of the Bank of France which, since it was founded by Napoleon in 1801, had enjoyed the exclusive privilege of issuing currency and in other ways influenced the course of French financial and economic life. Under the bank's old statutes the two hundred largest of its 40,000 stockholders elected a majority of the board of regents, although the government appointed the governor and the two vice-governors. The reform left the stockholders their dividends but altered the statutes so that twelve of the twenty-three were appointees or representatives of the government. A further change was a plan for the gradual nationalization of the armament industry. As a beginning only about a dozen armament factories were converted into state enterprises, while the rest were put under government supervision.

The reforms of the Blum cabinet were not the sovereign remedy for France's financial difficulties many had hoped they would be. Most of the small firms could not absorb the greatly augmented cost of production resulting from the rise in wages and the forty-hour week. Hence they raised the prices of their products, thereby nullifying any increased purchasing power. Food also went up as a result of the higher prices set by the Wheat Board. While the increase in prices curtailed trade on the one hand, it brought, on the other, demands for still further wage increases. The higher cost of living put an added strain on the government finances in that it necessitated raising the incomes of government employees and pensioners. This extra expense magnified an already colossal deficit, which was further aggravated by large expenditures for armaments in the face of the Nazi threat. Then, too, the economic depression persisted and unemployment remained high, a devaluation of the franc bringing only temporary relief. The inevitable consequence was that the Blum cabinet lost much of its popular support. The very classes it had tried to help turned against it. By midsummer of 1937 the financial situation compelled M. Blum to request those full powers to legislate by decree which he had hitherto always opposed. When the Senate refused, he had no recourse but to resign.

The first Blum cabinet was followed by other Popular Front cabinets, and in 1938 M. Blum headed a second cabinet for a brief period. Little headway was made, however, in settling the financial difficulties. The second Blum cabinet was succeeded by one under Édouard Daladier composed largely of representatives of the Radical Socialist Party. The financial situation was so critical by this time that parliament voted Daladier the right to legislate by decree in the hope that he could induce financial and economic recovery. He, too, was unable to master the situation. In general, the years immediately preceding the outbreak of World War II were marked by currency depreciation, agitation for wage increases, and widespread strikes. Conspiracies by royalists hopelessly divided the country. The budget remained unbalanced, and rearmament was not proceeding according to schedule. As the workers insisted on having Saturday and Sunday off, the plants and factories were closed for two days each week at a time when equipment was vitally needed for rearmament. Finally in November, 1938, an emergency decree was issued which retained the forty-hour week but permitted overtime at a slight pay increase and a shifting of the hours so that the armament plants could be kept open six days a week. The resulting increase in armaments, the French hoped, would enable them successfully to meet any Nazi attack.

THE GREAT FEAR

World War I restored to France her traditional supremacy. Germany lay prostrate at her feet, exhausted by the strain of the gigantic struggle. Furthermore, Germany's loss of her colonies, her merchant fleet, the mills and factories of the Saar and of Upper Silesia, and the mineral deposits of Alsace-Lorraine, and the derangement of her entire economic life by the imposition of reparations payments seemed to relegate her to the status of a second-rate power. Moreover, she was disarmed, while France was heavily armed. It seemed as if the French had "security" to spare. Actually, however, they could not forget the four bitter years during which they had more than once stood on the brink of defeat. They realized that without foreign aid they would have gone down as they had in 1870. They were aware that the Teutonic giant had been laid low only with the aid of Great Britain, the United States, and other nations. Would this help be forthcoming in the future?

The fear of facing Germany alone continued to haunt millions of Frenchmen. Germany was prostrate but would rise again. Having been forcibly disarmed, she would rearm at the first opportunity; then the war of revenge. The fear was nourished by the fact that France had a much smaller population than Germany — about forty-two millions as compared to about seventy-five — and her birth rate was dropping more rapidly than that of Germany. In France the number of births had declined from a million in 1870 to 682,000 in 1933. Although the number of births was also decreasing in Germany, the year 1933 saw the birth of about 300,000 more German than French babies. In other words, France lacked the reservoir of man power which would enable her to contend with Germany on an equal basis.

The French had hoped to obtain security against renewed German aggression at Versailles. Although Clemenceau, according to foreign observers, lived up to his nickname of "the Tiger" in his treatment of the enemy, he was censored by many of his compatriots for his leniency. They wanted Germany crushed so completely that she could never recover strength to invade the holy soil of France again.[1] When this was not done, they felt that security had not been achieved. For a time they hoped to enjoy some degree of security as a result of the pacts signed by President Wilson and Lloyd George guaranteeing them the aid of the United States and Great Britain in case of an attack. But disillusionment followed when the United States Senate and the British government refused to ratify the pacts, leaving France alone against a potentially stronger Germany.

Having failed to receive a guarantee from Britain and the United States, the French were obliged to seek security in other directions. First, they maintained a strong standing army, increasing its efficiency

[1] Paradoxically the French wanted Germany to be militarily weak but industrially strong enough to pay large reparations.

by mechanization, scientific research, and application of the lessons learned in World War I; as a result they enjoyed the greatest preponderance of military might on the Continent since the days of Napoleon Bonaparte. At the same time they continued to insist that the provisions of the treaty of Versailles regarding disarmament be enforced. Second, since France had no natural geographical protection against a German invasion, they began in 1927 the construction of a powerful line of fortifications called the Maginot Line. Third, they worked to strengthen the League as a convenient instrument to uphold the *status quo* prescribed by the treaty.

But the course which appealed to the French most in their search for security was the re-establishment of the so-called balance of power in Europe. Determined to build up an unquestioned preponderance of power, they contracted a series of alliances with Belgium, Poland, and the Little Entente (Czechoslovakia, Rumania, and Yugoslavia). The system of alliances, however, was to the Germans a revival of the old policy of encirclement, reminiscent of the alliances with which they were confronted in 1914.

Despite their fear of Germany, the French made no real attempt to cultivate German friendship; the German remained "the Boche" or "modern Hun." Many French acts caused resentment in Germany, among others the demand that she pay the full costs of the war and the insistence on disarmament and the demilitarization of the Rhineland. It was, however, the invasion of the Ruhr which aroused the greatest bitterness. The lesser bourgeoisie, which was ruined by the collapse of the German monetary system, did not forget that the Ruhr invasion had speeded the process of inflation. This episode, it is true, was followed by a period during which relations between the French and Germans ostensibly improved as a result of the work of two farseeing statesmen, Aristide Briand and Gustav Stresemann. Both, however, faced unpopularity at home because of their attempts to bring about a lasting improvement in the relations between the two nations.

Hitler's accession to power in January, 1933, greatly magnified the French fear of war. His foreign policy, as he had sketched it in *Mein Kampf*, called for the crushing of France as the necessary preliminary to eastward expansion. This threat caused the French to extend and strengthen their system of alliances. M. Barthou, the French foreign minister, visited the capitals of Poland and the Little Entente to remove any doubts regarding French policy and to tighten the strings which bound these countries to France. The most sensational development, however, was the conclusion of the Franco-Soviet alliance. Since Soviet Russia, too, faced the German armed might, rapprochement was not difficult. The first step was a nonaggression pact and commercial treaty

(January, 1934). This was followed by a treaty of mutual assistance (May, 1935), which stated that if either of the two countries "should be the object of unprovoked aggression on the part of a European state, the U.S.S.R. and France would immediately come to each other's assistance."

All this made it appear for a time as if France would adhere to a policy of defiance, but the forces of defeatism and appeasement soon gained the upper hand. The crucial test came in March, 1936, when Hitler openly tore up the treaty of Versailles by sending troops into the demilitarized Rhineland. We now know that Hitler's military and diplomatic advisers tried to dissuade him from taking the step, pointing out to him the possible consequences. It was therefore with considerable uneasiness that he made the move. Goebbels revealed that the Führer did not sleep well during the days prior to the one chosen to execute the plan. He even ordered a retreat in case of French military opposition. It was an opportunity to thwart Hitler's plans at a time when the French forces appeared to be more than a match for those of Germany. But the French failed to act. When the news of Germany's action reached Britain the foreign secretary advised the French to remain calm and not take any "irreparable" step. Hence the French contented themselves with an appeal to the League of Nations and let slip the last possible chance to stem German aggression without another world war. France lacked both the unity and the vigor to meet the challenge unflinchingly and effectively. She was a nation torn by internal troubles, harassed by economic and financial problems, and paralyzed by the passionate hostility between the right and the left.

In general, the French were in the grip of an apathy which made them reluctant to face difficulties of any kind. As early as 1935 an American observer wrote, "France asks to be left alone. It is a tired and sated country. It is neither economically enterprising nor politically ambitious." [2] France also had a great aversion to war. Successive governments did, it is true, make liberal appropriations for national defense, but few Frenchmen thought in terms of aggressive warfare. The Maginot Line, completed in 1938, appears to have fostered a purely defensive outlook.

LITERATURE AND MUSIC

In France, as in the other countries that had participated in the war, the postwar period was one of disillusionment and unrest. The sacred idols and traditions of the past had been discredited. Not one of the great writers of the prewar decades continued to exercise a profound

[2] Louis Fischer in *The Nation*, vol. 141 (December 25, 1935), p. 733

influence upon the younger writers. Thus Anatole France, whose skepticism had been so entertaining before 1914, was now denounced as supplying unsubstantial food. The unanimous longing of the people was for new values, for life along new lines. There was a great impatience to open the new era in civilization which they were certain was in the offing. Since they found their environment unattractive, writers struck out in many directions according to their individual leanings or temperaments. The result was that fiction by and large became something apart from the time in which it was written or something above and beyond it. Some turned to the realms of pure fancy; others busied themselves in writing about love; others, again, devoted themselves to psychological analysis. The last became one of the major trends in French literature during the period between the two wars.

The great psychological novelist of his time, and the most significant literary figure in France during the period after World War I, was Marcel Proust (1871–1922). A keen observer and masterly interpreter of men's thoughts, emotions, and conduct, he was to normal what Dostoievski was to abnormal psychology. In French literature he ranks with Balzac as one of the great figures of all time; if his creative ability was inferior to Balzac's, his interpretative power was far greater. His interest in psychological analysis was profound and absorbing; description, setting, and morals are secondary in his novels.

Born into the upper middle class, he had as a young man frequented the best society. Everything that he saw he noted and recorded with unprecedented minuteness. Because of ill health, he withdrew about 1910 almost completely from the world to his workroom, which was lined with cork to keep the sounds of the city from interrupting his labors and his slumbers. There like a scientist who spends his days and nights examining with a powerful microscope the creatures that live in a stagnant pool, he turned his acute perception to the task of analyzing the minds and motives of the people he had known. He continued his work even when he was confined to his bed.

The great work of his life was a cycle of novels called *À la Recherche du Temps Perdu* (*Remembrance of Things Past*), which in its final form included eleven volumes. The first part, entitled *Du Côté de chez Swann* (two volumes, 1913, translated into English in 1922 as *Swann's Way*), excited but little interest, appearing as it did just before the outbreak of the war. The next part was not given to the public until 1918. Entitled *À l'Ombre des Jeunes Filles en Fleurs* (two volumes, translated in 1924 as *Within a Budding Grove*), this part won for him the Prix Goncourt [3] and gave him stature as a writer. In 1920 he published

---

[3] A prize intended for the encouragement of young writers. There was much criticism because Proust was forty-eight at the time.

Le Côté Guermantes II, Sodome et Gomorrhe I, both of which were published in English in 1925 under the title *The Guermantes Way.* In 1922 the next part, *Sodome and Gomorrhe II,* was published in three volumes which were translated into English in 1927 as *Cities of the Plain.*

Proust continued to write almost to the last day of his life, despite great suffering. It is characteristic of him that just a few hours before his death in 1922 he asked a servant to bring to his bed a certain page of his manuscript on which he had described the last sufferings of one of his characters. "I have several retouchings to make here," he said, "now that I find myself in the same predicament." Two years after his death two more volumes of the series were published under the title *La Prisonnière,* which appeared in an English translation as *The Captive* a few years later. In 1926 appeared two further volumes, entitled *Albertine Disparue* (*The Sweet Cheat Gone,* 1930), and the following year the last two volumes were given to the public as *Le Temps Retrouvé* (*The Past Recaptured,* 1932). The style of the series is very uneven, but at its best its musical power has seldom been matched.

The most noted French composer of the first decades of the twentieth century was Maurice Ravel (1875–1937). Opinion is still divided as to his final rank in the history of French music: many include him in the list of the greatest French musicians, but others regard him merely as a great musical craftsman. He was born in the Basque country of the French Pyrenees and throughout life retained an affection for Spanish folk music. The Spanish inspiration is evident in many of his compositions. The first were published in 1895, and for the next two decades he wrote many compositions which were greatly esteemed in the musical world, but he himself remained unknown to the general public. In 1928, however, a new era opened for him when he was commissioned to write a ballet, the now famous *Boléro.* After it was performed in Paris, the distinguished conductor Arturo Toscanini introduced it in the United States at a concert in New York, where a staid audience stamped, clapped, and howled its approval. The best known of his other compositions are his choreographic poem *La Valse,* the one-act comic opera *L'Heure Espagnole,* the orchestral suite *Rhapsodie Espagnole* in four parts (*Prélude à la Nuit, Malaguena, Habanera,* and *Feria*), the piano composition *Jeux d'Eau,* and the ballet *Daphnis et Chloé.* Many critics regard the last as his masterpiece. At the time of his death in 1937 one critic wrote, "As an orchestrator his gifts and his craftsmanship were truly extraordinary. He will remain unexcelled as a poet of luscious and shimmering instrumental hues."

Eastern Europe

THE NEW STATES OF
AUSTRIA AND HUNGARY   THE collapse of the Dual Monarchy in the fall of 1918 did not come as a surprise to those who had knowledge of existing conditions. Revolt against the Habsburgs had, in fact, been a prominent characteristic of the empire since the days of William Tell, and the development of a militant nationalism during the nineteenth century had made the threat of dissolution very real. In 1914 the government, in the hope of preventing dismemberment of its empire, had declared war against Serbia, but the move only accelerated the dissolution. The determination of each of the nationalities to set up its own state or to be united to an outside neighboring state of the same nationality became stronger as the war progressed. Their cause found a champion in President Wilson. Encouraged by his proclamation of the right of self-determination, a number of the peoples of the Dual Monarchy proclaimed their independence early in October, 1918, and began to set up their own administrations. President Wilson then sounded the death knell of the empire by recognizing the independence of the Czechs and the Yugoslavs on October 18. Thus the breakup of the Austro-Hungarian state was an accomplished fact before the war ended.

One by one the various national groups fell away until only German Austria, the original nucleus, remained. Charles I, who had succeeded Francis Joseph in 1917, still hoped to remain as the ruler of Austria. The situation in Vienna, however, became so ominous that the socialist leaders informed him on November 10 they could not promise him protection if he did not abdicate immediately. Early the next morning he renounced all part in the government and left to seek asylum in Switzerland. On the following day the Provisional National Assembly adopted a resolution with Article I stating that "Austria is a democratic republic; all public powers reside in the people." The republic was to embrace all the territory of the former Austrian empire that was inhabited by German Austrians. In accordance with the principle of self-determination, the Assembly declared that "German Austria is an integral part of the German Republic." The Austrian undersecretary telegraphed to Berlin: "German Austria has given expression to its will to be united again with the other parts of the German nation from which it was forcibly separated fifty-two years ago."

The Paris Peace Conference, however, gave little if any consideration to the desires of the Austrian people. First of all, when it fixed the boundaries in the treaty of St. Germain it left the new republic much less territory than the Provisional Assembly had claimed. Besides allotting to Italy and Yugoslavia extensive territories inhabited largely by German Austrians, it deliberately included three million German Austrians (Sudeten Germans) in the new state of Czechoslovakia. Regarding this transfer President Seitz of Austria said: "There are three million German Bohemians who are made foreigners in their own country under the rule of a people not sympathetic to Germany. The same may be said of the Tyrol, where commercial and racial questions are subordinated to the strategic, although President Wilson's point said the opposite."

Second, the Allies flatly forbade the union (*Anschluss*) of German Austria with the German Republic, except with the consent of the League of Nations. Having defeated the Germans the Allies could hardly be expected to reward them with Austria. To the Austrians, however, it was a great disappointment. "I wish to say in the most solemn manner," the president of Austria said, "that Austria is doomed to die if she is not permitted to join Germany. We cannot live alone. We have a great city with a small territory composed of mountains and plains." It appeared as if the Allies were ready to apply the principle of self-determination only when it was in their interest to do so. The Austrian sentiments were expressed by the German foreign minister, who said when he heard that France would not tolerate the union with Germany: "It is incompatible that the Slav nations should receive the unrestricted right of self-determination while it is refused to German Austria."

In paring Austria down to the core the treaty deprived her of a large part of her former markets and sources of raw materials. Austria now faced hostile states which had surrounded themselves with high tariff barriers and were artificially fostering their own industries. Moreover, although the republic had large deposits of magnesite (which is of special importance in the manufacture of lighter metals) and of iron ore, her coal was of such inferior quality that she had to import more than half of her fuel.

Nor was the state self-sufficient in regard to food. Of the land surface allotted to her by the treaty, only 34.5 per cent was arable and meadow land, while another 16 per cent could be used as a pasture in the summertime. Thus about half of her total area was of no value for food production. The government therefore found it necessary to import food, which was then sold at a loss. The continuing drain caused an ever-increasing budget deficiency. Reparations and inflation added to the woes of the new state so that by the beginning of 1922 it was on the verge of economic collapse. In that year, however, a loan was raised for the republic by the League of Nations, the currency was stabilized, and reparations payments were suspended for twenty years. All this gave the country a new start, and during the next years she made a remarkable recovery.

In 1930, however, new economic woes developed. Austrian economic conditions proved to be particularly susceptible to the world depression. Markets quickly disappeared for the luxury goods in which Austria specialized. A sharp fall in customs receipts threw the budget badly out of balance. Unemployment increased rapidly. Some idea of the decline may be gained from the fact that the index of industrial production dropped from 103 in 1929 to 76 in 1931 and to 67 in 1933. During the succeeding years there was again some improvement.

The political setup was equally unhappy. Most of the political woes sprang from the contention between the two principal parties, the Social Democrats and the Christian Socialists. The former, whose strength was in the trade unions of Vienna where they controlled the municipal government, advocated certain Marxist reforms while adhering to democratic principles. The strength of the Christian Socialists, on the other hand, was in the provinces, most of its members being peasants. Founded under the leadership of a Catholic priest, the Christian Socialists combined religion with politics. There was little about the party that was socialist in the generally accepted sense, its program being directed largely against Marxian socialism. Thus there was a fundamental opposition between a "red" Vienna and a "black" countryside. The tragedy of the situation was that the parties could not put their antagonisms aside long enough to pass constructive legislation. For a time the bitterness was so great that the provincials forbade the sending of foodstuffs to Vienna.

At the beginning of the decade of the thirties a vigorous fascist movement, inspired and abetted by Hitler's Nazis, added further complications to the troubled scene. The aim was union with Germany, but it was opposed by the Social Democrats, who were appalled by the terrorist methods employed by the Nazis. The Christian Socialists were also opposed. Dr. Engelbert Dollfuss, a Christian Socialist who became chancellor in 1932, responded to the terrorism and intimidation by proscribing the Nazi Party. So that he could better curb their activities, he himself set up a dictatorship. The Nazis retaliated in July, 1934, by assassinating him. His successor, Dr. Kurt von Schuschnigg, continued his dictatorial methods, but the illegal Nazi movement continued to work for the *Anschluss* which Hitler was to achieve in 1938.

While the empire was collapsing, the Hungarians had on November 16, 1918, proclaimed their country a republic. At the time chaos reigned supreme. The utter defeat of the Hungarian armies had broken down all discipline, and the end of the empire had dislocated economic life. As the neighboring nations claimed various parts of the country, a shortage of salt, coal, wood, and grain developed in the cities. The lack of coal particularly menaced Hungary with the gravest consequences. Houses were unheated during severe winter weather, factories were shut down, and streets were dark. Successive governments were able to do little in the way of restoring order and supplying the needs of the people. In general, Hungary was a hotbed of political factions, all at odds with one another. Only in one respect was there agreement: all Hungarians of all classes were at one in their desire to keep prewar Hungary intact.

During the confusion Béla Kun, a friend of Lenin, succeeded in setting up a communist regime in Budapest. At no time, however, did it have universal support. One factor which attracted many to his banner was the belief that Soviet Russia would help Hungary retain her prewar boundaries; a second was his promise to supply the masses with food and fuel. But the experiment was short lived. Since coins were scarce in Budapest, Kun issued a huge amount of paper money for paying wages. The peasants, however, refused to accept it as payment for food, and consequently food became scarce in the cities and prices rose inordinately. Beef cost $12 a pound and fat or butter $15, in terms of American money. High prices, expropriation of all personal property above a small amount, the arbitrary penalties of the Revolutionary Tribunal, the muzzling of the press, and a program of terrorism soon lost him much of his earlier support. The final collapse of the regime was brought about by Kun's military ventures. Gathering an army of 150,000 men he decided on an invasion of Rumania for the purpose of spreading Bolshevism. When his purpose became evident, many soldiers who had joined to preserve prewar Hungary, deserted. The weakened army was quickly driven back by the Rumanians. Whatever support Béla Kun still had in Budapest vanished and he resigned after stating that "Hungarian democracy is obviously not ripe for communism."

After a number of attempts to set up a stable government had failed,

Hungary was again formally proclaimed a monarchy. It was, however, a monarchy without a king, for King Charles was not permitted to return. The country was ruled by Admiral Miklós Horthy under the title of regent. Theoretically there was an elected parliament of two houses, but it was only a mask to hide his dictatorship. Every opposition was summarily suppressed. Soon after his establishment in power he inaugurated the "White Terror," the purpose of which was to wipe out all radicals and liberals. Reaction became the order of the day. In other words, the government sought to restore so far as possible the old social and political regime. Whereas Czechoslovakia, Rumania, and Yugoslavia carried out various agrarian reforms, Hungary, where the agrarian situation was most desperate, not only stopped the breaking up of the old estates but actually restored some which had been divided into small farms. Consequently the great landowners, comprising only 1.3 per cent of the population, continued to own 50 per cent of the land, while 75 per cent of the peasants were landless. Their growing discontent and their demand for land provoked one crisis after another during the period between World War I and World War II.

Hungary paid a heavy penalty for having fought on the wrong side. The reduction of its area from 109,000 to 35,800 square miles (a little larger than the state of Maine) by the treaty of Trianon continued to rankle in the hearts of all classes. The worst feature of the treaty was the transfer of more than three million Hungarians to Czechoslovakia, Rumania, and Yugoslavia. Hungarian writers labeled this an international injustice comparable with the eighteenth-century division of Poland. Few if any Hungarians accepted the division as permanent. The union of *Hungaria Irredenta* with the fatherland was a goal to be achieved by force if necessary, and foreign policy was steadfastly shaped with a view to clearing the way for the return of these provinces. To the neighboring states the determination to regain the lost territories did not remain a secret very long, and they anxiously watched every move of the jingoists. Finally Czechoslovakia, Rumania, and Yugoslavia formed the Little Entente to oppose Hungarian ambitions. Thus held in check on all sides, the Hungarians continued to stew in their discontent. In the early thirties the government became openly fascist.

POLAND AND CZECHOSLOVAKIA

It will be remembered that in the partitions of Poland which took place in the eighteenth century Prussia grabbed territory inhabited by three million Poles and Austria took a somewhat larger slice, but the lion's share went to Russia. Throughout the nineteenth century the

Russians sought in every possible way to assimilate the Poles. They tried to suppress their language and their poetry and songs. They even made it a criminal act to possess books containing Polish literature. But they did not succeed in stifling the national spirit. The Poles not only kept alive in their hearts the legends of their heroes; they also made secret vows to recover their national independence, although the penalty for conspiracy was either death or exile in Siberia. The very fact that they were under foreign rule seemed to draw them closer together. During World War I both Russia and the Central Powers in a bid for their support promised to set up a Polish kingdom after the war. As early as 1917 the Allied states recognized the Polish National Committee, and President Wilson later made the erection of an independent Poland one of his Fourteen Points. The collapse of Russia in 1917 and of the Central Powers the next year gave the Poles the opportunity to fulfill their long-cherished dream.

At the Peace Conference the cause of Poland was championed by the French, who looked upon it both as a buffer against Soviet Russia and as an ally against Germany. There was, however, a wide division of opinion on the question of how much territory was to be included in the new Poland. The one point upon which all were agreed was that the new state must have an outlet to the sea. Accordingly it was given a strip of land which cut straight through German territory and separated East Prussia from the rest of Germany. The Germans did have access to East Prussia by rail through the so-called Corridor or by sea above the Corridor, but this strip of land was a source of friction between the two countries. Danzig, at the upper end of the Corridor, was made a free republic and the Poles were accorded certain rights of access to the quays and of establishing storehouses. This arrangement was resented not only by the Germans but also by the citizens of Danzig. After much discussion the final delimitation of the Polish boundaries was postponed. In a brief war against Soviet Russia in 1920 the Poles under Marshal Pilsudski advanced as far as Minsk and forced the Russians to sign the treaty of Riga, which gave the Poles a free hand in eastern Galicia. They also took Vilna, the capital of Lithuania, and converted it into a Polish city. By decision of the League of Nations Poland also received a considerable part of Upper Silesia. Consequently when the Allies got around to settling the question of the boundaries, it remained for them only to sanction those that had already been established.

The tasks which faced the new state were staggering. First of all, there was the welding of the Poles into a unified national group. For more than a century they had been living under three different governments, each of which had its peculiar administration and system of education. When the fragments were reunited, each found itself unlike the others. Second, there were such problems as repairing the ravages of war, setting up an effective administration, unifying the currency, and rebuilding the industries that had existed in the prewar period. Third, the pronounced discontent among the peasants, together with the possible communist influence on them, made sweeping land reforms imperative. Fourth and most serious was the problem of the disaffected minorities. In making Poland the fifth largest state of the Continent as regards population, the Allied powers sanctioned the inclusion of many minority groups in the new state. Minority groups, in fact, comprised no less than one third of the total population. The largest were the Ukrainians, Jews, Lithuanians, and Germans.

Unfortunately the men who were called upon to offer a solution for Poland's problems had little experience in government. Nevertheless, although the succeeding period saw the collapse of many of the democratic experiments which were inaugurated in 1918, the efforts of the republican government were not entirely without success. One of its early achievements was agrarian reform. In 1920 a law was enacted which restricted the amount of land a person could own, the limit being sixty to one hundred hectares [1] according to the district in which the owner lived. During the next years some 5000 estates had to surrender a million acres, from which 24,000 new properties were created. The division continued throughout the period between the two wars, with the result that in 1939 Poland was no longer a country of great landlords but one in which more than 80 per cent of the land was owned by small farmers.

On the other hand the government failed to find a solution for the minorities problem. The lesson of the many years the Poles had spent under foreign rule seems to have been lost on them. Instead of giving consideration to the feelings of the minority groups, they treated them as they themselves had been treated by the tsar's government. They inaugurated a systematic policy of Polonization and imposed disadvantages on those who opposed assimilation. Such treatment made the minorities restive and resentful. In general, the problem was a threat to both internal and external peace.

In 1921 the Polish Constituent Assembly completed a constitution which provided for a parliament of two houses elected by popular vote and for a president to be elected for a term of seven years by the members of the two houses in joint session. But a parliament whose members represented some thirty parties could not provide a stable government. In five years sixteen cabinets rose and fell. In these circumstances many looked to Marshal Pilsudski, the George Washington of Poland,

[1] One hectare equals about 2.5 acres.

to set up a strong government. Refusing the presidency, he took the post of Minister of War. While his friend Dr. Ignacy Mościcki was president, the marshal was the unofficial dictator, his power resting on the support of the army. Pilsudski did not abrogate the constitution or rule without parliament, but he had a group in parliament which was strong enough to carry out his will. In 1935 a new constitution was drawn up which increased the power of the president by giving him the right to issue decrees when the Sejm or lower house of parliament was not in session. No sooner was the new constitution inaugurated than Pilsudski died. Just before his death he appointed his friend, General Śmigly-Rydz, his successor. The latter did not wield as much power as Pilsudski had. President Mościcki, whose hand was strengthened by the new constitution, now exercised a larger share of power.

The Czechs, who had been under Habsburg rule for centuries, developed during the nineteenth century a vigorous nationalism which was accompanied by a desire for complete independence. World War I gave them the opportunity to achieve this desire. During the war two Czech college professors, Dr. Thomas Masaryk and Dr. Eduard Beneš, who had escaped from Bohemia, succeeded by patient pleading in gaining Allied support for their cause, while the underground at home was working ceaselessly to free the Czechs from Austrian rule. After the Slovaks decided to make common cause with the Czechs, both Great Britain and the United States formally recognized the nation, and on October 18, 1918, a provisional government was set up in Paris. Not many days later the Czechs established their rule in Prague, and on November 14 a National Assembly declared Czechoslovakia an independent democratic republic. The legislative power was vested in a National Assembly of two houses elected by universal suffrage, and the two houses in joint session elected the president. Dr. Masaryk was chosen as first president and served until 1932, when he was succeeded by Dr. Beneš.

Czechoslovakia was undoubtedly the most successful and the most prosperous of the succession states of the Dual Monarchy. This new state had the great advantage, first of all, of inheriting from the old empire rich coal and iron deposits and so much fertile agricultural land that it was in the enviable position of being almost self-sufficient in regard to food. In addition it was the foremost sugar-exporting country in Europe. Second, much of the industrial strength of the old Habsburg empire was concentrated in Czechoslovakia, which produced textiles, beer, spirits, paper and leather goods, china, machinery, hardware, and furniture. Czech industries which had previously found their principal markets within the empire were now successful in creating a demand for their goods in other countries. Third, while confusion reigned in the other new states, there was a considerable degree of order and economic stability in Czechoslovakia. Without foreign aid the government managed to consolidate its finances, stabilize its currency, and establish budgetary equilibrium. During the years between 1920 and 1924 the currency stood beside the Swiss franc as the only stable money of central and eastern Europe. Czechoslovakia was not able, however, to escape the effects of the world depression; the index of industrial production dropped from 104 in 1929 to 58 in 1933 but gradually recovered in the years that followed.

The government also carried out land reforms according to a carefully projected plan. After the Habsburg domains were confiscated by the state, provisions were made for the expropriation of the remaining large holdings. A land office was created as the agency for determining the compensation landlords were to receive and for working out the details of subdividing the land. In certain districts it was distributed on the basis of temporary leases. Although the execution was not as radical as the plan, the breaking up of the large estates did go far toward solving the land problem and toward maintaining social peace.

One of the most serious problems was that of minorities. In a population of fourteen millions there were more than three million Germans and nearly a million Magyars, as well as smaller groups. In general these minorities were accorded better treatment than those of the other new European states. Their rights, as assured in the peace treaties, were further elaborated by a law (February, 1920) which stipulated that a language must be accepted in the courts and by the administration officials in the districts in which it was spoken by 20 per cent of the inhabitants. Furthermore, the state pledged itself to support schools to instruct children in the language of their parents. It was also decreed that minorities were to have proportional representation in parliament and in the administration. At first, it is true, most of the administrative posts were held by Czechs who had been trained as officials in the old Habsburg empire, but members of other nationalities were gradually substituted in many positions. All this, however, failed to satisfy the minority groups. The Slovaks adopted either a hostile or a negative attitude because they were not granted the autonomy which, they claimed, had been promised them in 1918. In Ruthenia, too, there was much discontent, fomented in large part by Hungarians who regarded the province as *Hungaria Irredenta.*

By far the most serious minority problem was that of the Sudeten Germans. When Czechoslovakia was declared a republic this group organized a separatist movement in the hope that the Peace Conference would grant their wish to be united with German Austria. When their desires were ignored, they showed little inclination to cooperate with the Czechs, whose masters they had previously been. The relationship improved somewhat after two Germans were appointed members of the cabinet in 1926, but the coming of the world depression again reversed the trend. Since the area inhabited by the Germans was the most highly industrialized district, it bore the brunt of the depression. One complaint by the Germans stated that the machinery of their textile factories was not moving because the government had given most of its textile contracts to Czech firms. During the next years the relations between the Czechs and Germans grew progressively worse, the opposition being sedulously fostered by Hitler and his Nazis, who hoped eventually to annex the Sudeten territories. In 1935 the Sudetens, with the backing of the Nazis, organized a Sudeten party which by 1937 became the second strongest in the country, with forty-four members in parliament. Not many months later it aided and abetted Hitler in terminating the existence of the Czechoslovakian state.

THE BALKANS

For many decades prior to World War I the Balkan Peninsula [2] had been in such a state of turmoil that someone named it the Peninsula of Unrest. Prominent among the factors in this situation was the desire of some of the national groups who were a part either of the Habsburg or of the Ottoman empire to be independent or to be united with another state of the same nationality. The Peace Conference sought to satisfy this desire on the basis of the principle of self-determination, but unfortunately the final arrangement left much to be desired. While Rumania and Greece nearly doubled their population and Serbia nearly quadrupled hers, the Bulgarians had their territory pared down very considerably.

What stirred all the old unrests anew was, on the one hand, the policy adopted by various governments of forcing assimilation on the newly acquired populations and, on the other, the refusal of the minorities to transfer their allegiance to a state of another nationality. They were encouraged in their stand by the "mother country" of the same nationality. In general those states which had received acquisitions of territory were determined to retain them and those that had lost territory were no less determined to recoup their losses at the first opportunity. As previously mentioned, Czechoslovakia, Rumania, and Yugoslavia went so far as to form the Little Entente as a means of preventing Bulgaria and Hungary from forcibly overturning the territorial arrangements.

But these were not the only problems that plagued the Balkan states.

[2] For the purposes of this chapter the Balkans are regarded as the area covered by the states of Rumania, Yugoslavia, Greece, Bulgaria, and Albania.

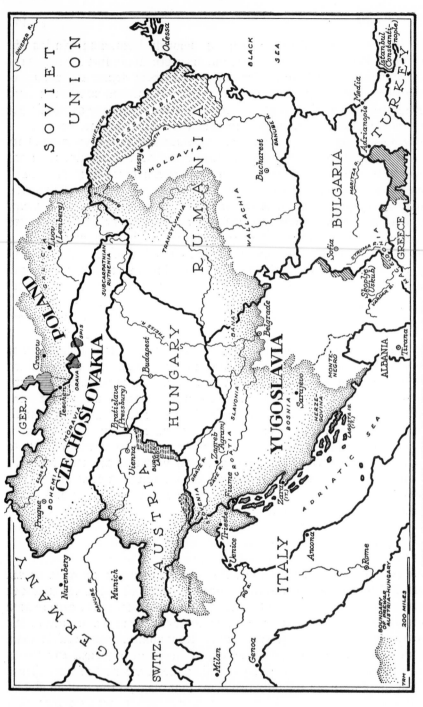

THE DANUBIAN AND BALKAN SETTLEMENT AFTER WORLD WAR I

One of the basic reasons for serious domestic discontent during the period between the two wars was the agricultural problem. All Balkan states were predominantly agricultural in their social structure. In Rumania no less than 81 per cent of the population was engaged in agriculture, in Bulgaria 82 per cent, in Yugoslavia 76 per cent, in Greece 61 per cent, and in Albania approximately 90 per cent. In most of the states the division of the large holdings into small farms was regarded as a measure of social justice, and during the years after the war much was done in this direction. Although there were still many large estates at the opening of the decade of the thirties, the vast majority of all properties were below five hectares each. It was hoped that ownership of land would make many small proprietors contented citizens, but this was not the case. Although the ownership of land heightened the political importance of the peasants, it did not solve their economic problems. Intensive cultivation was necessary if small farms were to be cultivated profitably. Most peasants were without proper equipment and lacked the credit to purchase it. Those venturing to borrow money for improvements became victims of usurious money-lenders and banks, who charged as much as 36 per cent interest. A further handicap was the progressive subdivision of the land. Families were large in most parts of the area and at the death of the head of the family the land would be divided among all the sons. Gradually the parcels became too small to support a family adequately. When agricultural prices broke during the world depression, the results were catastrophic. In Bulgaria, for example, prices fell from 100 in 1929 to 55 in 1934. Agricultural wages declined until they were barely enough to keep the workers from starving. In Rumania the most wretched part of the peasant population lived on *mamaliga,* a kind of corn-meal mush. Because of the widespread undernourishment, mortality from disease was high.

RUMANIA AND YUGOSLAVIA

Rumania was both the largest and economically the most important state of the Balkan group. Her wealth in mineral resources included iron, copper, manganese, petroleum, coal, and some of the richest gold mines in Europe. In 1929 she ranked seventh among the nations of the world in petroleum production. Her large industries were still in their infancy, but on the eve of World War II they expanded rapidly to carry out the rearmament program. Her fields, among the most fertile in Europe, produced vast harvests of corn and wheat. Before World War I most of the arable land was included in large estates owned by a small group, peasant owners being few in number, and even after the war the great landlords showed little inclination to share the land with the peasants. But the Bolshevik Revolution excited in King Ferdinand and his ministers the fear that the peasants might take matters into their own hands if the government refused to act. Consequently they promised the peasants that the great estates would gradually be split up. During the succeeding years 13,500 estates were actually expropriated and allotted to peasants, who were required to pay 65 per cent of the expropriation price, the government paying the remainder.

Theoretically Rumania was a constitutional monarchy with King Ferdinand as the ruler. The real ruler, however, was Ion Bratianu, whose ancestors had played an important role in the struggle for independence. By the wholesale manipulation of elections his National Liberal Party managed to gain a majority of seats in parliament; hence he was able to act as virtual dictator from 1922 to his death in 1927. During the last years of his rule his power had been increasingly contested by the most important party of the left, the National Peasant Party, whose basic plank was peasant ownership of the land. Soon after his death this party came into power. King Ferdinand himself had died about four months before Bratianu and had been succeeded not by his son Carol but by his grandson Michael. Because of the scandals of his personal life and his frequent clashes with Bratianu, Carol had been prevailed upon to renounce his rights to the throne. A regency was established with Michael as king and Iuliu Maniu, the leader of the National Peasant Party, as the real ruler.

But the rule of Maniu and his party did not achieve what the masses expected of it. The new government did abolish or liberalize many of the restrictions imposed by Bratianu, but the obstacles were too great for an inexperienced statesman. He managed to carry on for several years, but when the world-wide depression made itself felt in Rumania he became helpless. In their determination to hold on to the reins of government the leaders of the party decided to invite Carol to return as king. Carol accepted and after parliament revoked the act which excluded him from the throne he was proclaimed king (June 8, 1930). He at once formed a national government in which all parties were represented. His rule was in many ways a beneficent one: he gave special care to the welfare of the peasants, fostered the spread of education, tried to curb antisemitism, and sought to placate the minorities by permitting them to organize themselves into communities for the defense of their cultural, economic, and social interests. His most formidable opposition centered in the Iron Guard, a fascist group which had developed indigenously in Rumania but which borrowed the swastika, antisemitism, and other things from Hitler's Nazis and received support and encouragement from them. When Carol adopted a vigorous policy of repression toward the movement, Hitler threatened to support Hungary and Bulgaria in their claims to Rumanian territory.

The most persistent problem of Rumania was that of the minorities. This was not a new one, for it had existed in prewar Rumania, but the nation as a whole had then been more homogeneous. When the population was more than doubled as a result of the peace treaties, the country acquired millions of Hungarians, Germans, Jews, Bulgarians, Ukrainians, and members of other national groups. No less than 25 per cent of her population of seventeen millions was made up of such groups. Toward these the government pursued a relentless policy of denationalization. The members of the various national groups were, however, by no means predisposed to permit themselves to be assimilated; and even if they had been, the "mother countries" would not have regarded the change with complacency. Bulgaria hoped that a turn of the wheel of fate would enable her to regain the Dobruja, a province which she had lost in the Balkan wars (1913); Soviet Russia had never recognized the annexation of Bessarabia; and Hungary vowed to grasp the first opportunity to recover Transylvania. The plots and plans of these states and others kept the minority groups in Rumania in a state of constant agitation.

Yugoslavia, with a population of some twelve millions, was the second largest of the Balkan states. It was formed through the addition of Montenegro and a group of provinces of the old Habsburg empire (Croatia, Slovenia, Dalmatia, and Bosnia-Herzegovina) to Serbia, the original nucleus. The new state came into existence in December, 1918, as the "Kingdom of the Serbs, Croats, and Slovenes" and officially adopted the name Yugoslavia only in 1929. It also was anything but a homogeneous state. Even the three major national groups (Serbs, Croats, and Slovenes), which formed about 80 per cent of the population, had little in common beyond the fact that their languages were similar. The other 20 per cent was composed of various minorities, including Germans and Magyars. Besides national and linguistic differences there were deep religious cleavages, 47 per cent of the population being members of the Orthodox Church, 39 per cent Roman Catholics, and 11 per cent Moslems.

In form the new government was a constitutional monarchy with Alexander, the heir to the Serbian throne, as king. From the first the constitutional government was handicapped by the fact that more than half the population was illiterate, that there was no tradition of democratic participation in the government, that particularist feelings were strong, and that the various provinces represented different stages of civilization. The adoption of a constitution that supplanted the provincial diets by one central legislative body in Belgrade satisfied no one but the Serbs; the other national groups, and particularly the Croats, demanded some form of decentralization or federation. The question caused so much agitation that in January, 1929, King Alexander suspended the constitution. Thereafter, with the support of the army and a new bureaucracy, he carried on the government along autocratic lines. In 1931 he did endeavor to allay internal resentment and placate foreign opinion by promulgating a new constitution which, however, restored constitutional monarchy more in appearance than in reality. Under thinly veiled forms it maintained all the old features of dictatorship.

King Alexander's dictatorship failed to solve the basic problems of unity. In his efforts to weld the three ethnic groups into one nationality, he abolished the old territorial divisions together with their historical names (Croatia, Slovenia, etc.) and also decreed the dissolution of all associations and agencies which might help to preserve group differences. He definitely broke with the past by renaming the country Yugoslavia and then arbitrarily divided it into new provinces possessing no historical or ethnic significance. These measures created only grievances. The national groups became more determined than ever to preserve and cultivate their traditions and differences. A change came in 1934 as the result of Alexander's death at the hands of an assassin who believed the king was oppressing his kinsmen. Although Alexander's young son became king as Peter II, the government was carried on by a regency in which Alexander's cousin, Prince Paul, played the leading role. Prince Paul adopted a more conciliatory attitude toward the various national groups, but he did not modify the constitution in the interests of greater local autonomy. Nazi designs on Czechoslovakia did, however, cause him to grant a large degree of autonomy to Croatia (1939) lest the internal dissension serve as an invitation to Hitler to repeat the Czechoslovakian episode in Yugoslavia. This measure removed the animosity which the Croats had nursed against the Serbs, but discontent was still rife among the Slovenes, who also desired autonomy.

GREECE, BULGARIA, AND ALBANIA

Although Greece had entered the war on the Allied side only in June, 1917, Premier Venizelos managed by adroit diplomacy at the Peace Conference to gain enough territories to double the size of his country. One of these, Smyrna, was soon seized by the Turks; but even without it, the gain, which included the greater part of Thrace, was still considerable. It gave the new Greece an area of about 50,000 square miles and a population of about 6.5 millions. Although agriculture was the mainstay of the country, the Greeks were also noted as traders and fishermen. Moreover, Greece was in its industrial development less backward than some of the other Balkan countries. In 1930 there were almost 4000 factories in addition to many thousands of smaller establishments. The country was handicapped, however, by its poor transportation facilities. The principal exports were wine, olive oil, and tobacco.

The political life of Greece during the period from 1919 to 1939 was characterized by violent strife. Many changes of government took place, most of which were manipulated by politicians without bloodshed. Between 1919 and 1924 three kings occupied the throne. In 1920 King Alexander died from blood poisoning resulting from the bite of his pet monkey. He had ascended the throne in 1917 when King Constantine, a relative by marriage of Emperor William II of Germany, resigned rather than fight against Germany. Constantine was now recalled, but opposition to him soon became so widespread that after a few months he resigned to avoid civil war. His son, who succeeded him as George II, had hardly been crowned when the republicans staged a *coup d'état* and proclaimed a republic which was ratified by a plebiscite. Cabinets now rose and fell in rapid succession. Even the return of Venizelos from his retirement brought no political peace. Finally in 1935 a group of army officers engineered the return of George II. Political rivalry was so intense that he was unable to form a stable ministry despite his announcement that he wished to be "king of all the Greeks." In 1936 General Joannes Metaxas with the support of the army set up a dictatorship. By military rule and by muzzling the press he established some outward semblance of law and order, and he also redressed some of the wrongs from which the poorer classes were suffering.

Of all the conquered states Bulgaria was treated most severely at Paris. Although the great majority of the people wished to remain neutral, King Ferdinand decided in 1915 that the Central Powers were sure to win and so he joined them in the war. The Allies made the Bulgarians pay heavily for his bad choice, leaving them only an area of some 30,000 square miles with a population of less than five millions. A reparations burden of 2.25 billion gold francs was also forced on the weary shoulders of a country which had been almost continuously at war since 1912. As early as 1923 the indemnity was reduced to about one fourth of the original sum, but the load was still too heavy for a war-weakened land. Resentment against the king was so great that he fled the country in 1918 and was succeeded by his son, King Boris III.

The rule of the new king was less autocratic than that of the old king had been, but class strife and hatreds continued. Although the peasants [3] comprised more than four fifths of the population, the administration had been in the hands of the townspeople before World War I. This was greatly resented by the peasants. The cleavage between town and country was wide. While the townspeople enjoyed many modern conveniences, peasants struggled to obtain the barest necessities. The average size of the peasant's holding was smaller than that in the other Balkan states, his methods and implements were more primitive, and his crop yields much lower. In 1936 there were still twice as many wooden plows as iron ones. Early in the century the peasants had organized the Agrarian League, which by 1919 had grown into the strongest party. This gave Alexander Stamboliski, the leader of the League, an opportunity to rule the country as virtual dictator for some years. During this time he inaugurated many agrarian reforms, including the division of large private and government estates. He was, however, assassinated during a *coup d'état* staged by the army and the townspeople in 1923.

After various coalitions had tried in vain to solve the social and economic problems of Bulgaria, a dictatorship by a fascist group was set up in 1934. The next year King Boris himself by guileful methods discredited this group and set up his own dictatorship. But he was no more successful than the preceding governments had been in solving the country's problems. During the months before the outbreak of World War II Bulgaria was gradually drawn into the Axis orbit. Many Bulgarians hoped with the help of the German army to regain the territories they had lost in 1919.

The smallest and most backward of the Balkan states was Albania with an area of about 10,000 square miles and a population of less than a million. There was little or no industry in the country. Most of the people raised only enough food and grew enough wool to feed and clothe themselves. Since instruction in the Albanian language was prohibited as long as the country was under Turkish rule, the vast majority of the population remained grossly ignorant. At the Paris Conference there was considerable discussion as to what was to be done with this small country. The Italians, for whom possession of Albania would have meant control of the gateway to the Adriatic, were eager to extend their sway over it. But the Albanians decided to settle the question in their own way. They drove the Italian forces into Valona and besieged them until the Italian government agreed to withdraw them (1920). The League of Nations then recognized Albanian independence by admitting the country to membership.

After a period of confusion a Constituent Assembly finally declared Albania a republic in 1925 and elected Ahmed Bey Zogu as the first

[3] The word Bulgar derives from "Bol-Alagar" meaning plowman or peasant.

president. In 1928 the government was changed to a monarchy and he became King Zog I. Considerable progress was made under his rule. By a law of 1928 he made primary education obligatory for children of both sexes; he improved the means of communication and travel; and he took steps to develop the natural resources. To finance his program he found it necessary to borrow a large sum from Italy and to pledge the customs receipts as a guarantee. On a number of occasions he endeavored to restrict the gradual Italian penetration of Albania but was repeatedly forced to give way by threats of force. Finally in April of 1939 Mussolini sent a considerable army to occupy the country, forcing King Zog to flee to Greece.

THE WESTERNIZATION OF TURKEY

The armistice of October, 1918, saw the forces of the Ottoman Empire beaten and the empire itself dismembered. The "sick man" of Europe had finally passed away. The treaty of Sèvres, which the sultan's government signed on August 10, 1920, deprived Turkey of Arabia, Syria, Mesopotamia, and Palestine as well as of all former Ottoman territory in Europe except Constantinople. It also stipulated the creation of an independent Armenian state and an autonomous Kurdish state, and the cession to Greece of Smyrna with a considerable hinterland. If the Turks had accepted the treaty, it would have left their country an insignificant little state in the interior of Anatolia. But many of the Turks were far from ready to do this. Their pride was deeply touched and they began to organize committees for local resistance when the Greeks sent troops to occupy Smyrna.

In the moment of need a leader also made his appearance. He was Mustafa Kemal, a general who had emerged from the war as a great military figure. Despite the opposition of the government he proceeded to organize an army for the defense of Turkish soil against the Greeks. He also had the Turks elect deputies to the Grand National Assembly which met at Ankara in April, 1920. After the members of this body had declared themselves to be the sole lawful representatives of the nation, they elected Kemal as the first president of the assembly.

The difficulties in the way of a successful war were tremendous, but Kemal was tireless in his efforts to excite in the war-weary Turks the desire to resist, to find arms for his nondescript collection of troops, and to mold them into an effective fighting force. His success was demonstrated when this army under the command of his friend Ismet Pasha defeated the Greeks at Inönü (1921). The next year the army under the personal command of Kemal drove the Greeks completely out of Smyrna.

As the Greeks were still in possession of eastern Thrace in European Turkey, Kemal started to move his troops toward the Straits, but the Allies (Britain and France), who had set up neutral zones on both sides of the Bosporus and the Dardanelles, refused him permission to cross these zones. For a time it appeared as if there might be a clash between the Allied troops and the Turks, but more peaceful counsels prevailed. In October, 1922, the two sides negotiated an agreement which provided for the return of eastern Thrace to Turkey and blasted the Allied plans of confining Turkey to Asia Minor. Next Kemal and his followers settled the question as to who had the real authority in the Turkish state, the sultan or the Grand National Assembly. In November, 1922, the Assembly reaffirmed its sovereignty in no uncertain terms. Upon hearing of the decision the sultan decided that the climate of Turkey was no longer healthful for him and left the country. The caliphate, which had been combined with the sultanate, however, still remained as a distinct office, the caliph being the spiritual head of the Moslem religion.

The next problem that Kemal and his government solved was that of making a peace to replace the treaty of Sèvres. In November, 1922, representatives of Great Britain, France, Italy, Turkey, Greece, Rumania, and Yugoslavia met at Lausanne in Switzerland and after long and stormy negotiations signed the treaty of Lausanne (July 24, 1923). It was a remarkable diplomatic triumph for the Turks. Besides being permitted to retain eastern Thrace as far west as the Maritsa River, they were accorded the boundaries they claimed in Anatolia. Furthermore Armenia, which according to the treaty of Sèvres was to have been an independent state, was apportioned between Turkey and Soviet Russia. The treaty also terminated capitulations, i.e., the special privileges which had been granted by the Ottoman government to foreign communities under which foreigners could be tried only according to the laws of their home country. The sole restriction imposed on the Turks by the treaty was in the provision which forbade them to fortify the Straits without the consent of the powers.

In October, 1923, the new Turkish state was officially proclaimed. The first article of the constitution said that "the Turkish state is a republic," and Kemal was chosen as the first president. But forms are often deceptive. Behind the republican façade stood Kemal the dictator. He ruled as head of the People's Party, the one party recognized in Turkey. The general aim of his rule was to transform Turkey into a modern westernized nation. There was nothing new in this idea, for Western customs had infiltrated throughout the nineteenth century, but now Kemal was determined to speed up the process. He wanted to raise the Turks quickly to the level of the Western nations. "They shall know," he said, "that we are as good as they are." The first thing he did was to tear up by the roots the old institutions that were opposed to westernization. The greatest obstacle, he believed, was the religion of Islam. He therefore carried through the abolition of the caliphate in 1924, thus leaving Islam without a spiritual head. Next he repealed many of the laws based on the Koran, and later even the official oath in the name of Allah was abolished.

The religious changes were only a prelude to others. In 1925 the "Hat Law" forbade the wearing of the fez, the headdress which had been the tangible distinction between Moslem and Christian in Turkey. Henceforth the Turks were to wear Western hats and caps. Much more far-reaching were the changes in the status of women, who under the Mohammedan law had always been subject to men. Brought up without education, they were veiled at fourteen, married a year or two later, and then shut away in the harem. Any woman could be divorced by her husband at will. Kemal gave women equal rights with men, including the right to vote and the right to hold office. He also provided for the education of girls on the same basis with boys. Then, too, he succeeded in getting at least the urban women to wear Western clothes. Whereas Turkish women had previously been covered completely from head to foot excepting one or both eyes when they ventured into public places, under Kemal's regime many dressed in the latest European fashion and gradually became active in business and the professions.

Still other changes followed. The Gregorian calendar was substituted for the old Islamic calendar which dated from A.D. 622; the metric system was introduced; and the international clock was adopted in place of the day which began at sunrise. Noteworthy, too, is the law which required all Turks to adopt family names, the use of which had disappeared. Certain given names were so common that teachers in the schools found it necessary to designate the pupils by numbers. The National Assembly set the example by bestowing on Kemal the surname Atatürk, which means "Father of the Turks." For Ismet, his prime minister, Kemal himself chose the name Inönü in memory of the victories Ismet had won at that place over the Greeks. The most important changes, however, took place in the field of education. One of the reasons so many Turks were illiterate was that the Arabic script was so difficult to learn. To facilitate the task of learning to read and write, Kemal had a commission prepare a new Latin-type alphabet in 1928. He was so enthusiastic about this reform that he himself set up a blackboard on street corners to teach his people the new alphabet. Other educational developments included compulsory education for all children over seven, night schools for adults, and the opening of a number of vocational and professional schools. It has been estimated that as a result of these educational reforms the number of literates in Turkey tripled in five years.

Much attention was also given to the economic development of the country. During the period before World War I, Turkey had been largely a seller of raw materials and a purchaser of manufactured products. Its industries were limited to a few textile mills and foreign-owned cigarette factories. The government now offered free land for the construction of factories. Banks were also established to lend money to those who wished to build factories. Following the example of Soviet Russia, Kemal in 1934 embarked on an ambitious Five-Year Plan which was so successful that by 1939 Turkish factories were supplying almost all of the country's requirements of woolen cloth and about 80 per cent of its needs for cotton cloth. Other production facilities turned out iron, steel, chemicals, and pottery. The government also took pains to improve agricultural techniques. Although Turkey was primarily an agricultural country, its yields were so low during the years after World War I that much food had to be imported. The government greatly improved the yields by giving special training to farm youths, setting up model farms, and fostering irrigation schemes. The result was that by 1930 Turkey raised sufficient food for her population and had a surplus for export.

In 1938 Kemal Atatürk's strong physique finally crumbled under the strain of hard work and loose living. His remains were laid to rest on a hill overlooking the city of Ankara which he had built as the capital of the new Turkey. During his years as dictator he had accomplished much. The changes he introduced in a short time were far-reaching. As his successor the Grand National Assembly chose Ismet Inönü by unanimous vote. The new ruler, who had been Kemal's right-hand man for two decades, shared the latter's determination to westernize Turkey and make it as self-sufficient as possible.

CHAPTER TWENTY-FIVE

Fascism in Italy and Spain

POSTWAR DISILLUSIONMENT

FASCISM,[1] unlike communism, was not the outcome of a deliberately thought-out creed. It arose spontaneously from the pressure of postwar events. Whereas the opportunity for Bolshevism came as a result of defeat, Italian fascism was the offspring of disappointment in victory. The founders of fascism gained control of the government first; then they proceeded to develop a philosophy to fit their needs. What gave them their opportunity was the dissatisfaction of the Italian people with existing conditions and with the territorial gains Italy had made. The entry of the Italians into the war was not motivated by a desire to establish liberty or justice; in fact, the masses of Italy had no desire to become involved in the war. Italy's participation was brought about by a turbulent minority which saw in the war an opportunity to achieve Italy's expansionist aims. The fulfillment of Italy's "national aspirations" was "guaranteed" by the Secret Treaty of London (May, 1915), in which the Allies promised the Italians lavish territorial rewards for agreeing to fight against the Central Powers. The promises raised such expectations as to cause the poet D'Annunzio to exclaim: "The dawn of a new era has come at last."

But the expectations were not fulfilled. During the war the country had seen its exchequer drained and a large debt accumulate. What was worse, about 600,000 Italian soldiers lost their lives. In the fighting Italy did not fare well; her final triumph was largely overshadowed by previous defeats. Her sole consolation was the hope of territorial rewards and better times, but at the end of the war even this hope was

---

[1] The word *fascism* originated in Italy, but was soon applied to similar dictatorships in other parts of Europe. It derives from *fascio,* meaning a bundle or group.

blasted. The ardent enthusiasm of the war years was followed, as D'Annunzio put it, by "a twilight of the heroes." Whereas the French share of territory was 253,000 square miles and the British share 989,000, Italy obtained only 23,726 square miles — far less than she had been promised in the secret treaty. The Italians felt that their contribution to the Allied victory had been belittled; some went so far as to declare that Italy had been robbed by her allies.

The promise of better times also remained a dream. Economic life suffered a more severe dislocation in Italy than in any other country that had participated in the war, with the exception of Russia. When the war ended, both trade and industry were in a grave condition, and conditions grew progressively worse. Servicemen upon their return to civil life had great difficulty in finding employment. The value of the lira declined sharply and prices rose to almost fantastic heights. In November, 1920, the cost of living was eight times what it had been in 1914. Such bread as the masses could buy was not only of the poorest quality but also hard to get. The price of coal was so high that the poorer people were forced to collect sticks and vines for fuel. Lodgings were high and scarce and in many towns practically unobtainable. Everyone except war profiteers and some munitions workers was worse off than before. Those who had been opposed to war began to ask, "What has the war brought us?" They asked without receiving an answer. The true answer was "disillusionment."

In this situation the people looked to the government for relief, but the government was woefully weak. Many people were excluded by illiteracy from participation in the government, and others boycotted it at the request of the Roman Catholic Church.[2] The actual control was exercised by political bosses. The Chamber of Deputies was made up of many cliques whose shifting opinions were unintelligible to the masses and whose endless bickering left them no time to pass constructive legislation. A strong monarch might have made a difference, but Victor Emmanuel III was no leader. An English writer had written very early in the century: "We look upon the monarchy in Italy as a house of cards; the first hostile breath of wind will blow it down." The clouds were gathering for a storm which the little king was powerless to prevent.

During the period immediately after the war various parties made a bid for power. For a time the Catholic Popularists (People's Party), who offered a program of reform, gained considerable support, but inner disagreement and other causes soon sapped their strength. A stronger try was made by the Socialists, whose support came largely

[2] In 1904 Pope Pius X decreed that Roman Catholics could vote at such elections as the bishop of the diocese considered desirable.

from factory workers, railway, postal, and telegraph employees, and the agricultural laborers of the Po valley. Reinforced after the war by many disillusioned servicemen, the party returned 156 deputies to the Chamber in 1919. It is estimated that in the early months of 1920 about a third of the Italians were "reds." The general situation offered the Socialists a great opportunity, but they lacked a determined leader who could make the most of it. In the summer of 1920 they decided that the time for action had come. More than half a million workers "occupied" the factories of northern Italy and attempted to run them. They appointed managers, made arrangements for the exchange of raw materials, and began to produce. The factory owners, however, refused to cooperate. In a few days production fell off to practically nothing, and after a fortnight arrangements were made to turn the factories back to the proprietors. But although the experiment ended as a complete fiasco, it had wide repercussions. The seizures roused the bourgeoisie to a sense of danger which caused its members to open their ears and pockets to the Fascist Party organized by Benito Mussolini. They also frightened the government into giving the Fascists arms and permitting members of the army and police to join them.

THE GENESIS OF FASCISM

Benito Mussolini, the man who now stepped forward to offer himself as the savior of Italy, was born in 1883, the son of a blacksmith who had previously been imprisoned for his political opinions. Young Benito, named after the revolutionist Benito Juarez, was fed politics with his porridge. His mother, who for some years had been the village schoolteacher, wanted her son to follow the same profession, but he had other ideas. After a brief try at teaching, which he found monotonous, Benito, now nineteen, went to Switzerland, where he lived in poverty, doing odd jobs to keep from starving. He found time to read cursorily in the writings of Nietzsche, Schopenhauer, Machiavelli, and Georges Sorel, and to engage in many love affairs. His radical opinions caused him to be banished from one canton after another, and in 1904 he was expelled from Switzerland. The next year saw him serve the period of military training which he had sought to evade by going to Switzerland. At its end he again became a socialist agitator. In 1908 he journeyed to Trent, then under Austrian rule, and there worked on the staff of several socialist newspapers until his radical opinions caused his expulsion.

In Italy Mussolini continued his work as a journalist, eventually becoming editor of *Avanti (Forward)*, the principal organ of the Italian Socialist Party. In this periodical he denounced nationalism, imperialism, militarism, war, and religion. Curiously enough the man who was later to become a symbol of militarism was arrested for his anti-militarist activities and imprisoned for five months. When the war broke out, Mussolini, consummate opportunist that he was, advocated active participation on the side of the Allies and even founded a newspaper of his own, *Il Popolo d'Italia*,[3] to promote intervention. "Neutrals," he said in 1914, "have never dominated events. . . . It is blood that moves the wheels of history." For his stand in favor of war he was expelled from the Socialist Party — an action for which he took vengeance at a later time. Toward the end of the war he entered the Italian army and upon his discharge immediately proceeded to organize a party. In answer to his summons a spirited group [4] of Fascists met at Milan on March 23, 1919, to form the first of the *Fasci di Combattimento*, a term which literally means "combat groups." As Mussolini explained it later, "For us Fascists life is a continuous and incessant combat." The movement was made more "colorful" by the adoption of black shirts as a distinctive uniform and by the resurrection of the old Roman salute. Discipline was on a strict military basis, and the highest virtue was fanatical devotion to Italy and Mussolini. The basic rule was: "He who is not ready to sacrifice body and soul to Italy and to serve Mussolini without question is unworthy to wear the black shirt, symbol of fascism."

During the first years of its existence the Fascist Party had, beyond an unquestioning devotion to Italy and Mussolini, no detailed program or consistent body of principles. As one writer put it, the movement came in "like a naked savage and gradually accumulated a suit of armor." Only after they were ensconced in power did the Fascists begin to develop a body of doctrines. In the words of Mussolini, "Fascism was not suckled on a doctrine in advance around a table. It was born of a need for action, and it was action. It was not a party, but in the first two years it was anti-party and anti-movement." As anti-movement it was particularly opposed to communism. For a time after their accession to power the Fascists advanced the claim that they had saved Italy from communism. This myth served its purpose, but there was little support for it in fact. In 1932 Mussolini himself admitted that the "left revolutionary" brand of socialism "never got further than talk in Italy."

At the beginning the Fascists formulated only one goal: to become strong enough to achieve the rule of Italy. Mussolini himself stated this quite frankly in a speech on September 25, 1922:

[3] This paper later became the principal organ of the Fascist Party.
[4] The number was variously set by Mussolini as "perhaps 100," "a few handfuls," and "a few dozens."

Our program is simple: we wish to govern Italy. They ask us for programs, but there are already too many. It is not programs that are wanting for the salvation of Italy, but men and will-power. . . . We want Italy to become Fascista. That is simple and clear. We want Italy to become Fascista, because we are tired of seeing her governed by men whose principles are continually wavering between indifference and cowardice.[5]

The means of achieving power, Mussolini told the Fascists, must be either "the legal method of elections or the extralegal one of insurrection." Dino Grandi, one of the leading Fascists, stated the issue bluntly when he said: "Fascism intends to govern the country. . . . Either the door is opened or we will be constrained to break it down."

The Fascists first tried ballots, but succeeded only in obtaining thirty-one seats in the election of 1921, one of which Mussolini himself occupied. The legal means to power having failed, Mussolini determined to try force. The rapid growth of the Fascist Party had put him in a position to do so. It is estimated that by the end of September, 1922, two and a half years after the organization of the first *Fasci di Combattimento,* the Fascisti numbered about 300,000. On October 3, Mussolini openly demanded control of the state, but the government refused to yield. In his answer Prime Minister Facta declared that "the government will remain at its post. . . . Only the Chamber has a right to tell me that the relinquishment of my position is necessary." In a fiery declamation on October 26 Mussolini ridiculed the prime minister's answer and advocated seizing the government by force. "At turning points in history," he said, "force always decides when it is a question of opposing interests and ideas. . . . The moment has arrived, in fact, when the arrow must leave the bow, or the cord, too far stretched, will break." The next day the cry was raised, "To Rome! To Rome!"

On the morning of September 28 about ten thousand Fascists armed with revolvers and clubs arrived in Rome. Fascist historians later made much of the "march on Rome," but they failed to state that the march was not led by Mussolini. He remained in safety in Milan until he was assured by telephone that all was well; then he traveled to Rome by rail. When the first Fascists arrived, Premier Facta wished to invoke martial law. If he had done so, the army could have driven the Fascists out with ease, but Victor Emmanuel III lacked the will to use force. As news of his refusal spread, more Fascists flocked into Rome from the surrounding towns and Fascist squads began circulating in the streets. Seeing no other way out of the difficulty, Facta resigned. The king then asked Mussolini to form a government.

[5] *Mussolini as Revealed in His Political Speeches,* selected and translated by B. Q. di San Severino (1923), pp. 150 f.

CRUSHING THE OPPOSITION

The first battle had been won. Mussolini was premier, he also kept in his own hands the portfolios of the home and foreign offices. But his support was anything but secure. Of a total of about 365 seats in the Chamber of Deputies, the Fascists held only 35; and in the cabinet which he formed only four of the fourteen members were Fascists. It was only because the Nationalist, "Democratic," and Catholic People's parties supported him that he was able to stay in office. He asked the Chamber to grant his cabinet full powers for one year, threatening dissolution and new elections under Fascist supervision if his demands were not met. The deputies replied by surrendering their authority 275 to 90. Thenceforth it became the goal of Mussolini and the Fascists to maintain themselves in office at any cost. One of his first acts was to increase the peacetime strength of the army from 175,000 to 275,000 and to make certain that the key positions were held by Fascists. In the national and local administration, too, non-Fascists were whenever possible replaced with Fascists, particular care being taken to restaff the police departments.

Meanwhile the Fascist militia was endeavoring to compel respect for fascism by force. Its primary targets were the socialists, who dared oppose the Fascist rule. Hundreds of Fascists would break up socialist meetings and beat up all the socialists they could catch. Socialist printing plants were wrecked and socialist headquarters turned into shambles. Nor were other groups spared. A favorite stunt of the Fascists was to force the milder anti-Fascists to drink a toast with quantities of castor oil. If this did not purge an anti-Fascist of his erroneous ideas, he would be beaten in the streets; or his home would be wrecked, as were those of Benedetto Croce, Italy's most distinguished philosopher, and Francesco Nitti, ex-premier of Italy. Even the dagger was used in some instances.

The Fascist attacks did not, however, intimidate everyone. Toward the end of the year for which he had been voted dictatorial powers, Mussolini found it necessary to hold elections of deputies. Everything possible was done to hamper and discourage the opposition, but it showed considerable strength, though the Fascists did manage to gain a majority of the seats. One of Mussolini's most courageous opponents in the Chamber of Deputies was Matteotti, a young socialist. Having previously written a pointed indictment of Fascist rule, Matteotti in May, 1924, questioned in the Chamber the validity of the Fascist majority. Soon thereafter he was seized in the streets of Rome, taken into the country, and murdered. The murder caused a sensation in Italy, and anti-Fascist papers and pamphlets boldly stated that Mussolini was the instigator of the crime. The murderers were not brought to trial, however, for nearly two years, and then were only sentenced to six years of penal servitude; two months later they were released.

The accusations hurled at Mussolini after the Matteotti murder caused him to speed up the process of concentrating all power in his hands. All opposition newspapers were suppressed either peacefully or otherwise, opposing political parties were dissolved, and the activities of all groups outside the Fascist organizations were sharply circumscribed as a preliminary step toward their dissolution. Whatever freedom of the press still remained was completely abrogated; thenceforth nothing could be published that was not favorable to fascism. Finally in May, 1926, all possibility of opposition from organized groups was removed by a law which in effect outlawed all non-Fascist organizations. Thus Italy became a one-party state, with the Fascist Party controlling the state in much the same way as the Communist Party in Russia. The members of the Fascist Party were, like those of the Communist Party, hand-picked. After 1921 membership was largely closed to all but those who had been indoctrinated while members of the Fascist youth organizations.[6]

In the government, too, changes were made in the direction of eliminating every possible check on Mussolini's rule. The Italian state remained a monarchy in form with a nominated Senate and a parliamentary Chamber of Deputies. All real power, however, was gradually vested in Mussolini as premier and as chairman of the Grand Council of the Fascist Party. To this end a law of 1925 stipulated that "no question can be included in the agenda of the Senate or Chamber without the consent of the Premier." It also made the premier responsible solely to the king, thus assuring Mussolini the premiership even against an adverse vote of the Chamber. His power was even extended to include municipal offices. In 1925 the election of municipal officials was terminated by a law which entrusted their appointment to the national government. The officials of the national government were little more than a group of men to carry out the will of the leader or "Duce," as Mussolini was called. Thus Mussolini was the absolute ruler of Italy. The sole function of the masses, as prescribed by the Fascist slogan, was to "believe, obey, fight."

The Fascists did not stop at complete domination of the political life of Italy. Rigid controls were imposed on every phase of Italian life in accordance with Mussolini's motto: "Everything in the State, nothing against the State, nothing outside the State." Domination of the

---

[6] The two Fascist organizations for boys were "Balilla" and "Avanguardia." The former, for boys under fourteen, was a military adaptation of the Boy Scout movement. "Avanguardia" was for older boys. There were also youth organizations for girls.

nation's economic life was achieved through the dissolution of the old labor unions and the organization of a series of great company unions called "syndicates." The officials of these new unions were appointed by the Fascist Party, i.e. by Mussolini. The employers, too, were organized in "associations" corresponding to the syndicates of the workers but having some freedom in choosing their own representatives. The syndicates and associations settled all ordinary disputes between capital and labor. While membership in the new unions was not required, the possession of a membership card was virtually a prerequisite to securing a job. Moreover, whatever agreements were reached between the government-sponsored associations of employers and employees were binding on all employers and employees. Under this arrangement the workers lost the right to strike, both strikes and lockouts being declared illegal. Mussolini and the Fascists tried to justify the absolute dictatorship with the theory that the masses are unable to govern themselves. The peculiar gift of governing, the official apologists stated, had been bestowed on only "a chosen few."

THE FRUITS OF FASCISM

After the confusion, even chaos, that characterized the preceding regime, the Fascist rule was one of order and discipline. Foreign observers who visited Italy pointed out that the streets were free from disorders, that the trains ran on time, and that beggary had disappeared. Mussolini's government also devoted considerable attention to the development of water power for the production of electricity, to a scientific survey of the resources of the country, and to the development of foreign markets. Land reclamation projects converted disease-breeding swamps into fertile farmland. Much was done to wipe out the widespread illiteracy by opening more schools and training more teachers, so that by 1930 more than 90 per cent of the children of school age were able to attend school. But the Fascist educational program was formative rather than informative, more interested in making good Fascists than in developing intelligent citizens. It was Mussolini himself who said, "The textbook and the musket make a perfect Fascist."

Another achievement to which Fascist historians pointed with great pride was the settlement of the sixty-year feud between the Vatican and the Italian state. Earlier in his career Mussolini had styled religion as something "curtailing and pauperizing the individual." Not long before his accession to power he said: "Give me a pagan people who will fight for life and progress, who will not accept a creed blindly nor a miracle without question." Even in his first Fascist program he had still advocated the nationalization of church property. Moreover, the majority of the original Fascists were anticlerical. But, like Napoleon, Mussolini soon realized the importance of enlisting the support of the church for his regime. Consequently he began to feign a devotion to Catholicism. He had the crucifix restored to the schoolrooms of Italy, introduced compulsory religious education under church supervision, and pledged that divorce would never find a place in Italian legislation. Negotiations were opened with the Vatican in 1926 for settlement of the so-called Roman Question, but it was not until February, 1929, that the Lateran Treaty was signed. By its terms the Roman Catholic Church accorded recognition to the Italian state; the latter, for its part, recognized Vatican City as a sovereign state under the exclusive jurisdiction of the pope. The Holy See accepted as full payment for its claims against the state for the confiscation of church territory the sum of 750,000,000 lire (about $40 million) in cash plus a billion lire in 5 per cent government bonds. Finally, the relations between church and state were regulated by a special concordat or agreement which made Roman Catholicism the official religion of Italy and religious instruction compulsory in both elementary and secondary schools, except by express wish of the parents; provided that the religious ceremony of marriage should be binding in the eyes of the law; and recognized the legal existence of monastic orders, together with their right to own property.

For a time it appeared as if the Lateran treaty had removed all misunderstandings between the Vatican and the Italian government. In July of the same year the self-imposed imprisonment of the papacy was terminated when Pope Pius XI emerged into the Square of St. Peter's. But the cordial relations which many had hoped would follow did not materialize. Mussolini and the pope soon found themselves at wide variance in the interpretation of certain clauses. Thus while the pope insisted that the "marriage clause" required anyone born a Catholic to be married by the church, Mussolini insisted that the individual had the right to choose between a religious and a civil ceremony. The most serious disagreement was over the question of the education of the young. In presenting the Lateran treaty to the Chamber Mussolini emphatically stated that the clause in the treaty regarding education did not imply the surrender of the right to educate the young. "In this field I am intractable," he said. "Education must be ours." The pope in an open letter denounced Mussolini's statement as "heretical and worse than heretical," insisting that the education of the young was exclusively the business of the church. On a number of subsequent occasions the pope scored as "unchristian" some of the tenets of the Fascist educational program. On the Fascist side there were frequent objections to alleged political activities by Catholic organizations. In

May, 1931, Mussolini signed a decree dissolving all Catholic societies not connected directly with the Fascist Party.

Although the Fascist regime did have some achievements on the credit side of the ledger, it failed to fulfill most of the hopes it had raised. Above all, it failed to provide the economic progress and material security in exchange for which the Italian people had yielded such liberties as freedom of speech, of the press, of association, of assembly, and of education. Actually under fascism the standard of living declined until it was among the lowest in Europe. The first four years of the Fascist dictatorship were a period of prosperity in a large part of the world and Italy shared to some extent in this prosperity. A declining lira enabled foreign merchants to buy cheaply in the Italian market, and the demand for Italian products created employment. But the cost of living went up faster than the wage index. Whereas the cost of living index rose from 498 in 1922 to 653 in the first half of 1926 the wage index went up only from 505 to 559. Mussolini's efforts to improve the situation by stabilizing the lira at a high rate in 1926 was followed by a severe economic crisis. Export trade slumped and the tourist trade fell off sharply, while unemployment increased and wages declined. During 1928, however, there was some improvement, which caused Mussolini to announce: "We are out of the dangerous waters. We are in full convalescence."

Mussolini had been too hopeful. Instead of prosperity, world depression was just around the corner. The world economic crisis which followed the Wall Street crash in the fall of 1929, caused a decline in both exports and wages and an increase in unemployment. In October, 1930, Mussolini himself acknowledged that the depression had "become considerably worse all over the world, and hence in Italy." By 1934 no recovery had taken place, but Mussolini was still asserting that "we reached the bottom some time ago." According to one estimate wages declined nearly 40 per cent from 1926 to 1934. Hardest hit were the agricultural workers, who suffered reductions of from 50 to 70 per cent. Since prices had not declined to any corresponding degree, the purchasing power of the masses was sharply curtailed; it has been estimated as about one-third less in 1934 than in 1926. Furthermore, there was probably a higher percentage of unemployment in Italy at the beginning of 1935 than in most European countries.

MUSSOLINI'S COLONIAL AMBITIONS

It had long been Mussolini's ambition to build up a great Italian empire, one that would rival the empire of the ancient Caesars. He was convinced that destiny had chosen him to make the Mediterranean an

Italian sea. Moreover, he realized that a campaign for colonial empire would be an excellent means of distracting the Italian people from their sad plight at home. If he could not give his subjects bread, he could at least win military glory for them. During the time he professed to be a socialist, he had denounced imperialism, but he soon changed his views. At the very first Fascist meeting on March 23, 1919, he said, "Imperialism is the foundation of life for every people that aims to expand economically and spiritually. . . . We want our place in the world because we have a right to it." On another occasion he said: "The tendency to empire is a manifestation of vitality; its contrary, or the stay-at-home mentality, is a sign of decadence." He had no desire, however, to become involved in war with one of the great powers. He therefore promised that any Italian expansion would be "a peaceful expansion."

What Mussolini wanted above all was territories that were rich in raw materials and that would attract Italians desiring to emigrate. The colonies that Italy then held lacked both qualifications. When he looked about for lands to conquer, Mussolini found that the only worthwhile territory which had not already been claimed by some European power was Ethiopia (Abyssinia), a primitive country of volcanic mountains, deserts and jungles, embracing an area of about 350,000 square miles and inhabited by a chaotic jumble of tribes. Its chief products were coffee, sugar cane, and cattle, but Mussolini hoped to discover mineral wealth. The conquest of Ethiopia also offered the Italians the opportunity to take revenge for the humiliating defeat an Italian army had suffered at the hands of native tribesmen in the battle of Adowa (1896).

When preparations for the campaign had been completed, the Italians found a pretext for picking a quarrel with Ethiopia and then invaded it in October, 1935. The poorly equipped and poorly organized Ethiopians managed to slow down the Italian advance but could not stop it. An appeal to the League of Nations by Haile Selassie, the emperor, resulted in the denunciation of Italy as the aggressor and in the application of limited sanctions by certain nations. But this did not stop Mussolini. After an arduous campaign Italian troops entered Addis Ababa, the capital, in the spring of 1936. At their approach Haile Selassie fled to England on a British destroyer and Victor Emmanuel was proclaimed Emperor of Ethiopia. But Italian rule brought no real peace. The Italians controlled only those districts in which Italian soldiers were actually stationed. While waiting for the day of reckoning the natives did everything they could to make the occupation difficult for the Italians. It has been estimated that more Italians were killed during the two years following the campaign than in the war itself.

If Italy was to be successful in building and populating a large empire something had to be done to stop the decline of the birth rate.

"With a declining population," Mussolini said, "a country does not create an empire but becomes a colony." "Without a growing population," the Fascist Grand Council stated, "there is neither youth, nor military power, nor economic expansion, nor a secure future for the fatherland." The decline was not peculiar to Italy; in fact, it was less drastic in Italy than in most of the other countries of Europe. Even so, the birth rate in Italy had fallen from 39.3 per thousand in 1876 to 25.6 per thousand in 1929. To encourage marriage a special tax was imposed on all bachelors between twenty-five and sixty-five. Income tax for the heads of small families was increased, and stringent measures were adopted to curb the dissemination of birth control propaganda. Conversely, parents of large families were rewarded with tax exemptions, special awards, and preference in public employment. The general result was that the birth rate rose in 1927 but declined again in the next year.

In his foreign policy Mussolini had during the early years of the thirties considered an agreement with England and France. But France proved to be a hard bargainer. Furthermore, when Mussolini marched his armies into Ethiopia, the whole force of public opinion in Britain, which for a century had been friendly to Italy, turned against the Duce and the kingdom of which he was premier. Britain, in fact, became the champion of coercive measures against Italy to terminate the Ethiopian adventure. The French lack of benevolence and the British attempts to thwart his plans caused Mussolini to turn toward Germany, despite a clash of interests, especially in Austria and the Danubian basin. After considerable negotiation he attached himself to Hitler, forming the so-called Rome-Berlin Axis in opposition to the British-French alliance. The existence of the Rome-Berlin Axis was made known in November, 1936.

MONARCHY, DICTATORSHIP, AND REPUBLIC IN SPAIN

For Spain, which did not become involved in World War I, the war years were a period of considerable prosperity. When the belligerent countries turned to the production of war materials an opportunity was created which resulted in the establishment of many new Spanish industries. The products of the new industries not only supplied the home markets but were also in demand in France, Britain, Italy, and other countries. Much wealth flowed into the country, and Spain, which had previously been a debtor nation, began to make loans to other countries. But the wealth largely passed into the hands of profiteers. The prosperity was not shared by the industrial and agricultural workers. The agricultural laborers earned barely enough to maintain a miserable undernourished existence. The industrial workers were not much better off; they did receive wage increases, a shorter work-week, and old-age pensions subsidized by the state, but their standard of living remained low, for the cost of living increased more rapidly than wages.

With the return of peace the foreign demand for Spanish goods declined sharply and foreign manufactures began again to invade the home markets. The demand for Spanish manufactures was so low that manufacturers and merchants could not sell the stocks on hand even at prices less than cost. As in Britain during the same period, a general depression followed. Thousands of workers were thrown out of employment, and the wages of those who kept their jobs were reduced despite the gradual increase in living costs. All this gave rise to violent unrest accompanied by constant strikes. Some idea of the low wage scale which prevailed may be gained from the following report:

In 1918 printers in Salamanca were receiving daily wages ranging from $0.29 to $1.06, the majority of workers in the various trades receiving less than a dollar a day, and in only a few instances did the wages exceed $2. In Vigo in 1919 maximum wages ranged from $0.58 for miners and farm laborers to $2.32 for ship carpenters, workers in the majority of the trades receiving between $1 and $1.50, while in Barcelona in August, 1920, the lowest wage per day for skilled labor was $1.35 and the average was a little less than $2. In Bilbao in January, 1921, wages ranged from a minimum of $1.06 to $1.26 up to a maximum of $1.54 to $1.93 in different trades, farm laborers receiving from $0.72 to $1.16. Women's wages varied from $0.29 to $0.77 per day.[7]

Conditions among the agricultural workers were particularly bad. Although Spain was an agricultural country with 70 per cent of its population deriving a living from agriculture, the country did not raise sufficient cereals or leguminous vegetables to supply the national needs. The yield of wine per cultivated acre of grapes was about half that of an acre in France, while the average grain yield was about eleven bushels per acre. The low production may be ascribed largely to the medieval methods of cultivation, the illiteracy and ignorance of the cultivators, and the unequal distribution of the land. It has been calculated that about one five-hundredth of the population owned more than half of the land. The actual cultivation of the land was done either by tenants who leased land or by hired laborers, both of whom were ruthlessly exploited. Socialist, communist, and syndicalist agitators were not slow to point out the vast inequalities that existed between landowners and cultivators. The example of the "nationalization" of land in Russia made a vivid impression on the simple soul of the Spanish peasant. Discontented industrial workers also readily accepted the ideas presented

[7] United States Labor Statistics Bureau: Monthly Review, vol. 12 (1921), p 163.

to them by anarcho-syndicalist and revolutionary socialist agitators. Of the two groups the anarchists were much the stronger, particularly in Barcelona, which was an important center of Spanish industry.

Dissatisfaction was not limited to economic and social conditions; it also extended to the government. In theory the Spanish monarchy was of the approved constitutional type, with the king (Alfonso XIII) governing in name only, and governmental powers resting in a cabinet responsible to the Cortes, which was elected by a universal suffrage of men over twenty-five. But in actual practice the real power was still wielded by the caciques or political bosses. Each cacique ruled his district as supreme master, owing allegiance only to a higher cacique whom he served. It was, in short, the rule of a political machine. As employers of labor or money lenders the caciques were able to get a firm hold on their constituencies and thus control elections. Even the judiciary was largely under their control. In addition to the unrest generated by this arrangement, entire regions within the Spanish state demanded the right to set up autonomous, even independent, states. The Basques and the Catalonians by virtue of their non-Spanish language and literature appealed to the principle of self-determination. Thus the Spanish state seemed to be coming apart at the seams.

In 1921 the defeat inflicted on the Spanish army in Morocco by the Riffs opened the way for the establishment of a dictatorship in Spain. Sporadic warfare between Spain and the Riff tribesmen had been going on since 1909, but in 1921 hordes of wild tribesmen suddenly attacked a Spanish army of about 20,000 and wiped out the major part of it. It was a defeat comparable to that suffered by the Italians at Adowa. The disaster stirred all Spain to the depths. Across the length and breadth of the country the demand was voiced for a probe to establish the responsibility for the unspeakable disgrace to Spanish arms. The Cortes acknowledged the demand by appointing a Committee of Inquiry. The thorough investigation that followed revealed widespread disobedience, disorder, and corruption. Among those implicated were many high-ranking officials.

Before the report could be made public a group of military men under General Primo de Rivera staged without bloodshed a successful *coup d'état* (September 13, 1923) which forced the resignation of the cabinet. In its place Rivera set up a military directory with himself as president or chairman. He then dissolved the Cortes and proceeded to rule as dictator. If the king did not give his advance consent to these changes, he did endorse them after they were made. In the European press Rivera was hailed as the Spanish Mussolini, but his dictatorship lacked the dramatic elements that characterized the rule of the Italian dictator. Rivera did not indulge in the sort of theatrical pomp which the Duce employed to impress his subjects. He was one of the quiet dictators. Among his achievements were the restoration of law and order, the uprooting of the caciques and the termination of the Moroccan campaign by the final defeat of the Riffs. He endeavored to promote the well-being of the masses by subsidizing new industries and imposing tariffs on foreign goods imported into Spain. He also brought comparative peace to industry through his efforts to create a system of arbitration between labor and management by means of mixed committees of workers and employers.

Nevertheless, the fact that his rule was one of martial law with all freedoms suspended antagonized all those who believed in republican government. To escape imprisonment many critics of the government became refugees in foreign lands. Among these was the novelist Blasco Ibáñez, who, in his own words, had "been a republican ever since my childhood." From his home on the French Riviera he discharged blast after blast against the dictatorship of Rivera, denouncing him as the oppressor and remover of all liberty. "There has never been," he wrote, "such wholesale corruption in the administration of affairs. Nothing like it has ever been known. Since there is neither Parliament nor press to protest, thieving continues unchecked." Nor did he spare Alfonso XIII. Declaring that the king was personally responsible for the conditions of disorder and disaster in Spain, he demanded the immediate overthrow of the monarchy. "I am determined to overthrow the king of Spain," he said, "and I will remain in exile until I shall have succeeded. I am ready to spend all my wealth to make my once great country a republic." In 1924 Ibáñez published a book under the title "Alfonso XIII Unmasked" through which ran the refrain, "King Alfonso must go." His attacks were reminiscent of the unrelenting warfare Victor Hugo waged from his exile against "Napoleon the Little."

When he assumed the dictatorship in 1923 General Rivera had announced that the move was only a temporary expedient. As the months and years passed, however, he showed no disposition to relinquish the power he had seized. In 1925, it is true, the military directory was replaced by a directory composed of civilians, but Rivera remained as dictator. Finally in 1930 the king, grown tired of the dictator, asked him to go. The dictator himself was tired and consented to resign. But the aftermath was not favorable to Alfonso XIII. During the period of dictatorship a strong popular feeling for a republic had developed, extending to many thousands who had previously been devoted to the monarchy. When municipal elections were held for the first time in eight years (April 12, 1931), the vote was overwhelmingly republican. The cabinet took the hint and resigned, leaving the king to choose between resigning and trying to rule by force. Alfonso, realizing that the latter course would mean civil war, resigned. Before leaving Madrid he signed a statement which read in part: "The elections which took place on Sunday have told me clearly that I have now lost the love of my people. . . . I deliberately suspend the exercise of the royal power, and depart from Spain, thus recognizing that she alone is mistress of her destiny."

Spain was now a democratic republic in name. A Cortes elected in July, 1931, promptly drew up a constitution in which all Spaniards were declared equal before the law with guaranteed rights of freedom of speech, press, and assemblage. The framework of the new government was simple. The legislative power was vested in a one-chamber Cortes elected by all citizens of both sexes who had attained the age of twenty-three. The Cortes together with an equal number of popularly elected delegates elected the president for a term of six years. Although the president had the right to choose the members of his cabinet, he was required to select men who had the confidence of the Cortes. Regarding religion the constitution stated that "the Spanish state has no official religion." Thus all religions and religious sects were put on the same level. Many religious orders, including the Jesuits, were declared dissolved and the remaining orders were put under rigid government control. Furthermore, education was secularized and divorce was permitted upon presentation of due cause.

The constitution was proclaimed on December 10, 1931, with Alcalá Zamora as president. Besides inaugurating the changes stipulated in the constitution, the Cortes gave the industrial worker social insurance benefits and guaranteed the right of collective bargaining. Other changes included a far-reaching reorganization of the army, particular stress being put on the modernization of military equipment and the establishment of rigid examinations for promotion to the rank of commissioned officer. Some progress was also made toward settling the Catalan question by the grant of a substantial measure of autonomy to Catalonia. Noteworthy, too, is the fact that measures were passed to build more schools as a means of wiping out the blight of illiteracy. Although the republican regime did succeed in opening more than nine thousand new schools, the number was still far from sufficient to enable all Spanish children to receive some kind of elementary education. Finally, efforts were made to improve the economic status of the peasants and agricultural laborers. In September, 1932, the Cortes passed the Land Reform Bill, which accorded to the government the right to expropriate large estates by paying the owners the values declared for taxation. Such lands were then distributed to landless agricultural workers, ownership being vested in the state. This program was, however, carried out so slowly that many of the land-hungry became converts to extreme philosophies.

All the aforementioned changes encountered the bitter opposition of both the left and the right. On the one hand, the anarcho-syndicalists and the communists denounced the reforms as only scratching the surface. Workers of the leftist persuasion staged strikes, riots, and disorders to force more radical changes. On the other hand, the groups of the right objected that the reforms had gone too far. Merchants, manufacturers, and landlords were antagonized by the government's prolabor policies, and many army officers disliked the military reforms. But it was the Roman Catholics who offered the most determined opposition. Even many republicans who were Roman Catholic were antagonized by the anticlerical laws. Pope Pius XI himself in an encyclical denounced the law which excluded the religious orders from all except religious education. In the general elections near the end of 1933 the parties of the right and right center won a sweeping victory, capturing 373 seats of a total of 472. Early in 1934 the new rightist government announced a program which called for modification of some of the new laws. To the parties of the left the conservative government seemed intent upon nullifying the economic and social gains. After much bickering the socialists, communists, anarcho-syndicalists, and left republicans finally succeeded by the beginning of 1936 in forming the so-called Popular Front as a means of preventing the conservative government from "turning back the clock."

CIVIL WAR AND FASCISM

The elections of 1936 were fiercely contested by the two sides, but when the ballots were counted it was found that the Popular Front had succeeded in electing a majority of its candidates to the Cortes. The Popular Front held 266 seats; the right and the center, 217. Although the new government at once began to inaugurate the program drafted by the Popular Front, many extremists of the left were too impatient to wait for orderly changes. They burned convents and churches, destroyed fascist and monarchist newspaper offices and political headquarters, and in the country districts seized large estates. Soon groups of the right retaliated by attacking leftist headquarters. The general result was a turmoil in the face of which the government seemed helpless. A group of army officers finally informed the government that it would take matters into its own hands if order were not restored. In answer the government dismissed some of the high-ranking officers and transformed others to more distant posts.

Among those who were transferred was General Francisco Franco, who had at one time been Chief of Staff. The new post assigned to him was in the Canary Islands, but he crossed over to Spanish Morocco and there raised the standard of revolt in July, 1936. After quickly making himself master of Spanish Morocco he moved his army into southern Spain, where he was joined by about 90 per cent of the officers and about two-thirds of the troops of the Spanish army. Most of the air force and the navy, however, remained loyal to the government. By November the insurgents, who were later called the Nationalists, had advanced to the suburbs of Madrid forcing the republican government to move its headquarters to Valencia. In other countries the Spanish Civil War was by many regarded as a struggle of fascism against communism. Actually the adherents of the two ideologies were in a minority on both sides. On the Nationalist side there were, in addition to fascists, many monarchists, large landowners, and supporters of the Roman Catholic Church. The Loyalists, on the other hand, included not only socialists, syndicalists and communists but also liberals of all shades. The groups on each side were drawn together not so much by a common ideal as by a common fear.

It was outside intervention that made the war appear to be a fight between communism and fascism. No sooner had the war started than Mussolini sprang to General Franco's aid with remarkable alacrity, sending arms and munitions, pilots and technicians to Spain. Nor was Hitler slow in sending Nazis to fight in the Nationalist ranks. In the meantime the Loyalist side was receiving support from the Russian communists. Lenin had earlier regarded Spain as a promising field for Bolshevism, and Trotsky's opinion after residing in Spain for a time was that "the Spaniards are ripe in town and country" for communism. Hence the Soviet government dispatched elements of its air force as well as munitions to Spain. It also encouraged volunteers to enlist in the International Brigade which was fighting on the Loyalist side. "It is evident," said President Manuel Azaña (October 16, 1936), "that this is not merely an internal conflict; its scope is international." France and Britain, both desiring to remain neutral, imposed a ban on arms shipments to Spain; but the Germans and Italians kept pouring more men and materials into the Spanish war.

In starting the uprising the Nationalists had planned for a quick victory, but they were soon disillusioned. Month after month the Loyalist defenders of Madrid fought back fiercely. Many who did not have guns fought with knives, paving stones, or clubs until more arms arrived from Russia. By the beginning of 1937 both Italy and Germany were sending both men and supplies to Spain more or less openly. Early in 1937 the Loyalist government protested that four regular divisions of the Italian army were fighting on the Nationalist side. Gradually the heavy shipments of men and arms to General Franco began to turn the scale in favor of the Nationalists. In the spring of 1938 a powerful Nationalist army equipped with German and Italian artillery, tanks, and planes invaded Catalonia and gradually closed in on Barcelona, which surrendered in January, 1939. This left the Loyalists only central Spain with the two important cities of Madrid and Valencia. The epic siege of Madrid ended on March 29 and the same evening Nationalist troops entered Valencia unopposed. The civil war which had cost untold damage and destruction was over.

Long before the fighting ended, General Franco had begun to lay the foundation for a totalitarian fascist state for which the German and Italian states served as models. As early as April, 1937, he merged all the groups of the right into one political party, the Falange Española Tradicionalista (Spanish Traditionalist Phalanx), which had been a small but enthusiastic fascist party before the war. This party, the only legal party in Spain, became the basis of the new government. As chief of the party Franco was the keystone of the entire political structure. His official title was Caudillo, meaning leader or chief, like Mussolini's "Duce" and Hitler's "Führer." In addition to being leader of the party and head of the government, Franco was also the Generalissimo of the army. Certain powers, it is true, were exercised by the National Falangist Council, analogous to the Fascist Council in Italy, but even this council was directly responsible to the Caudillo. His authority was so absolute that he declared himself to be "responsible only to God and to history."

Soon after the cessation of hostilities the government repealed much of the legislation that had been passed under the republic. One of the first changes involved the restoration to the Roman Catholic Church of many privileges it had enjoyed before the period of the republic. Roman Catholicism was again made the official state religion, instruction in the Roman Catholic religion was reintroduced into primary, secondary, and higher education, and both divorce and civil marriage were prohibited. The fascist government also restored the property which had been taken from the religious orders, rebuilt the churches and religious monuments that had been destroyed, and resumed payment of an annual stipend to the clergy according to the provisions of the Concordat of 1851. Dictator Franco claimed the right as ruler of Spain to appoint and control the bishops of the Spanish church, and he decreed that all religious disputes be settled by a Spanish court of the Rota rather than by the Vatican. Both claims immediately elicited objections from the Vatican. A further noteworthy change was the termination of such autonomy as Catalonia and the Basque provinces had been accorded under the republic. Both the Catalonians and the Basques were forbidden to speak their regional languages.

When the war ended, Spain was in a pitiable condition, with ruins and destruction, hunger and famine dominating the scene. The government gradually repaired most of the war damage. Roads were repaired, towns rebuilt, harbors re-equipped, and railroads rehabilitated. Progress was also made in re-establishing prewar industries and in increasing the output of mines and of the iron, steel, and certain other industries. But little was done toward improving Spanish economy as a whole. Not only was there a lack of machinery and raw materials; there was also a shortage of skilled workers, due primarily to the fact that a large percentage of Spain's technicians and trained workers had been Loyalists. At the conclusion of hostilities the Franco government inaugurated a thoroughgoing purge of all who had been associated with the Loyalist cause or sympathetic toward it. Some who had participated in or abetted executions of Nationalists or had attacked churches and the clergy were executed, while hundreds of thousands of others were given long prison terms or sent to concentration camps. Consequently skilled workers were not available to man the factories.

The Franco government also failed to improve the condition of agriculture and the agricultural worker. During the years after the civil war harvests were small. In 1940, for example, the wheat crop was about half the average annual yield of the period 1931–1935. Scarcity of food products meant high prices, but wages had not risen commensurately. The decline in the purchasing power of the income of both agricultural and industrial workers was responsible for widespread undernourishment in many parts of Spain.

ITALIAN AND SPANISH LITERATURE

The story of postwar literature in Italy is much the same as in France and Germany. A critic who surveyed the situation reported in 1924:

> One cannot escape the impression that . . . a throng of immature artists — uneasy, nervous, shattered — have sprung up, among whom scarcely one emerges as a great leader and master. A tumult of voices, loud and many-toned, often impure, has arisen, in which it is hard to distinguish any common note. That it should be so is comprehensible when one considers how this country has been affected by the rivalries of political, social, economic and religious interests. In every field of human activity the inheritance of earlier generations is shaken.

As in France the literary figures that had been pre-eminent in prewar days lost much of their popularity and influence. This was true of D'Annunzio as well as others. His speeches and pronunciamentos, his heroics in occupying Fiume, appealed to the national feeling of the Italian people and astounded those who had regarded him as a mere man of letters; nevertheless his literary influence gradually dwindled.

The Italian of this period whose writings had a wide circulation outside Italy was the playwright Luigi Pirandello (1867–1936). Between 1915 and 1934 more than thirty of his plays were performed in various countries. The most popular one, *Six Characters in Search of an Author* (1921), was translated into fifteen languages and produced on the stage in most of the countries of the western hemisphere. In 1934 he received the Nobel Prize for Literature for "his bold and brilliant renovation of the drama and the stage."

When fascism rose to power in Italy it regimented and fostered literature like any other branch of production, forcing the intellectual classes into line with Fascist teachings. Fascist leaders promised a great spiritual awakening and a great literature that would be characteristic of fascism. As the years passed, the inability of fascism to get the literature it wanted became more and more patent, to say nothing about the spiritual awakening, which did not take place. Not that the Italian men of letters were anti-fascist. In Germany after Hitler assumed the reins of government in 1933 most of the outstanding writers either left the country or were driven into exile. This was not the case in Italy. There the majority of the authors embraced the new regime with enthusiasm and lived in harmony with its ruling ideas. Still the great literature did not materialize. Many books, of course, were written to glorify fascism, but they were outpourings of propaganda almost entirely without literary merit and can hardly be called belles-lettres. Other writers, disdaining all heroic pose, described the life of the peasants and the townspeople, but even their works were characterized by apathy, disillusionment, and slovenliness of style. In short, during the period of Fascist rule Italian literature was stagnant.

Conditions in Spain after World War I did not favor the development of belles-lettres. For almost all Spanish writers the period was a lean time. The fact that more than 50 per cent of the population was illiterate sharply restricted the sale of books. Books that had a sale of more than a thousand copies were unusual, and most writers were obliged to seek government jobs or devote themselves to journalism in order to make a living. The great exception was Blasco Ibáñez. During the war he wrote two novels, *The Four Horsemen of the Apocalypse* and *Mare Nostrum,* in which he pictured modern warfare in all its horrors both on land and on the sea. Both novels were indictments of German methods of warfare. Although the literary value of the two books is not high, their propaganda value was great. Both quickly became best sellers in many parts of the world, particularly in the United States, where their popularity stimulated translation and publication of his earlier works.

Nazi Germany

THE ROAD TO DICTATORSHIP IT is often asked how the National Socialists (Nazis) were able to take absolute control of Germany. The simple answer is that the state of mind of the German people was propitious for the acceptance of nazism. Many factors helped to prepare the Nazi victory. First among these was the defeat of Germany in World War I, which bitterly hurt the pride of the strongest Continental power. Since the Weimar system was associated with the defeat, there was never much zeal for the republic. Second, the inflation of 1922–1923 was a contributing factor. In impoverishing the lower middle class or petty bourgeoisie it caused the members of this class to seize on the extravagant promises of Hitler and the Nazis. Third, the resentment against the treaty of Versailles must not be overlooked. Most Germans regarded this treaty as a humiliation and were willing to listen when Hitler and the Nazis promised to free Germany from its shackles. Fourth, the economic blizzard which hit Germany in 1930, leaving widespread unemployment and bankruptcies in its wake, prepared millions of Germans to follow anyone who promised them jobs and bread. Fifth, Hitler with the power of his oratory convinced the German people that he was their man of destiny.

The future Führer was born on April 20, 1889, not in Germany but in the little provincial town of Branau in Austria. His father, Alois Schicklgruber, who changed his name to Hitler, was a minor official in the Austrian civil service. Thus Hitler came from that lower middle class which later formed the bulk of his support. His mother, of whom there is little mention in Hitler's later writings, regarded her son as a dreamer — a view which his later life confirmed. In school he was indifferent to all of his studies except history, particularly German history, which he read avidly and which aroused in him a rabid admiration for all things German. He had little love for the Habsburgs because they lacked a sense of German patriotism. At an early age he appears to have tried out the Führerprinzip (leader-principle) by bossing his schoolmates; as he himself put it, "I became a little ringleader at school."

Hitler's father wished Adolf to follow in his footsteps, but the son manifested little ambition for anything. His father's death in 1903 effected little change in young Hitler; it was only after the death of his mother in 1908 when he was nineteen, that he had to make a decision, for, as he later put it, "I stood alone in the world." He decided to become an artist. Packing his few clothes in a suitcase, he set out for Vienna to enter an art school, but he was refused admission because he lacked the necessary ability to draw. Had he been accepted he might have spent the rest of his life as a mediocre artist. As it was, he rapidly sank into the ranks of the unskilled and unemployed class. During the next five years he eked out a miserable existence selling postcards, working as a bricklayer's assistant, and doing other odd jobs. Much of the time he lived in the humblest lodging houses. His experiences in Vienna, however, were decisive as regards his future thinking. His association with the masses generated in him a feeling of contempt. He regarded them merely as raw material to be used by superior intelligence in the interest of racial greatness. The experiences of this period also deepened his Pan-German feeling, excited in him a hatred of Marxian philosophy, and made him a confirmed anti-Semite. The few Jews he had previously known were like other Europeans in external appearance — so like "other human beings," as he put it later in *Mein Kampf,* that he had regarded them as unjustly penalized for their faith. In Vienna he saw a Galician Jew for the first time. He himself described the experience in these words: "One day when I was walking through the inner city, I suddenly came upon a being clad in a long caftan, with black flowing hair. Is this also a Jew? was my first thought. . . . But the longer I stared at this strange face and scrutinized one feature after the other, the more my mind reshaped the first question into another form. Is this also a German?" This experience, together with others, served as the basis of a ferocious race hatred which was later expressed in the anti-Semitism of the Nazis.

In 1913 Hitler moved to Munich, where he continued to live a slum existence until the outbreak of the war in the next year. Being eligible for military service he joined a Bavarian regiment instead of returning to Austria to fight with the troops of the Dual Monarchy. He was twice wounded in action and before the end of the war was promoted to the rank of corporal and decorated with the Iron Cross. Hitler's first step upward out of complete obscurity was taken in postwar Munich. It was a time when all sorts of persons, including down-at-the-heel journalists, frustrated poets, and other ne'er-do-wells were making speeches and organizing political movements. This gave him an idea. Failing to find employment, he decided to become a politician. He too could drum up an audience and make political speeches. In the summer of 1919 he joined with a small group of malcontents like himself in forming the German Workers' Party, later reorganized as the National Socialist German Workers' Party. The program of the party, drawn up by one Gottfried Feder in 1920, included among other things a demand for the union of all Germans by the right of self-determination, the abrogation of the treaties of Versailles and St. Germain, the expulsion of all non-Germans from the Reich, the abolition of unearned incomes, the nationalization of all trusts, and widespread agrarian reform.

During the early years of the party's existence Hitler gathered around himself one by one the members of the group who were later to form the inner circle of the Nazis. One of the first of these was Rudolf Hess; after him came Hermann Goering, Alfred Rosenberg, and Dr. Joseph Goebbels. Before 1923 the party was known only in Bavaria, but in that year it became more widely known when Hitler together with General Ludendorff attempted to seize the Bavarian government as a means of liberating Bavaria from the Berlin government. This attempted *coup d'état*, more generally known as the Beer Hall Putsch because the plans were laid in the back room of a Munich café, failed. When the followers of Hitler and Ludendorff gathered in the Odeonplatz, the Bavarian police quickly scattered them with a few shots. Hitler and Ludendorff were both arrested for treason. The latter was acquitted because of his war record; Hitler was sentenced to five years' imprisonment but was released before he had served a year.

The months Hitler spent in the fortress of Landsberg were important ones for the history of National Socialism. It was during this time, with Rudolf Hess as his "secretary," that he wrote the first volume of *Mein Kampf*, which became the bible of the movement. The second volume was written after his release. As the Bolsheviks had the Marxian writings to guide them, the Nazis had *Mein Kampf*. The book is not a systematic exposition. Hitler's mind lacked the ability to organize his ideas in a logical sequence. The contents are a jumble of this and that. It has been styled "10 per cent autobiography, 90 per cent dogma, and 100 per cent propaganda." Every word in this tome of 782 printed pages was included for the sake of propagandist effect. The immature style and the repetition of ideas often make the book uninteresting reading, but *Mein Kampf* was a tremendously influential book, for in it Hitler expounded the ideas, beliefs, and plans that would

guide him after his accession to power. It was, in short, a blueprint
of revolution. Seldom has a plotter set forth his plans and purposes in
more explicit detail. Many intellectuals laughed at the plans and set
Hitler down as a crackpot, but the ex-corporal took himself very seriously. In its first edition of two volumes *Mein Kampf* did not enjoy a
wide circulation, but when it appeared in a one-volume edition at about
one third the original price it became a best seller. The proceeds from
this book financed Hitler and his followers until they were able to
command the support of the big industrialists.

The central idea of *Mein Kampf* is that of race. Hitler did not define
the word "race," nor did he distinguish between "race" and "nation."
The one thing he was definite about was that all races are not equal in
regard to creative ability. He divided them into three categories: the
culture creators, the culture bearers, and the culture destroyers. Only
the Aryan or Nordic race was classed as a culture creator. The outstanding people of this race, according to Hitler, were the Germans.
While he was somewhat vague about the culture bearers, he definitely
classified the Jews and the Negroes as culture destroyers. He believed
that the Aryans or Nordics had degenerated through intermarriage
with other races. Such race pollution, as he called it, must be stopped;
Nordics must be permitted to marry only Nordics. This pseudo philosophy later formed the basis of much of the Nazi legislation regarding internal affairs. As to the external aims of his party he stated that
Germany must acquire more territory if she was to become a world
power. He did not, however, want overseas colonies; the new territories
must be closely connected with the fatherland. He even went so far
as to indicate which territory the Germans were to acquire as *Lebensraum* (room to live). The Bolshevik regime, he thought, was about
ready to collapse, and the Germans could win new territory through
"the might of a victorious sword." The attack on Russia must, however,
be preceded by the defeat of France. He was certain that the French
would not stand idly by while Germany was increasing her strength at
the expense of Russia. Here was the plan for World War II.

During the years after his release from the fortress of Landsberg
Hitler continued to address crowds at every opportunity and to sway
them with his demoniac oratory. His power lay not so much in what
he said as in the way he said it. He was a spellbinder. Even Bismarck
had not possessed Hitler's ability to move the masses. Much of his
appeal was in his intense emotionalism, which convinced many of his
listeners that he was inspired. His primary hatred was directed against
communists and Jews. Another target was the treaty of Versailles;
he missed no opportunity to denounce it, and particularly the "war-
guilt lie," as he called it. With a voice shaking with emotion he would

demand that the restrictive clauses of the treaty be abolished at once. He also soundly flayed the existing republican regime, asserting that it was responsible for the lowered prestige of Germany. All democratic institutions, in fact, were to him anathema. "These institutions," he wrote in *Mein Kampf,* "can only be dear to the greatest liars and rogues, such as avoid the light of the sun. They will always be hated by every honest, straightforward fellow willing to take responsibilities." In a more positive way he offered the people a line of propaganda based on ideals of patriotism, empire building, and race mastery.

Besides being a powerful orator Hitler was also a consummate opportunist. He and the Nazis put something in their program for each class of the German population. In other words, Hitler told the German people what they wanted to hear. To the industrialists and financiers he offered escape from the threat of a communist revolution. The great magnates were not averse to joining their fortunes with his, particularly since they believed they would be able to control him. It did not occur to them that this lackey might one day become their master. To the small businessmen Hitler promised protection against the trusts and chain stores which were endangering their livelihood. The peasants he sought to attract to the Nazi standards by promise of sweeping agrarian reforms. As bait for the working class he stressed the "socialist" part of the Nazi program, but the "socialism" was mere demagogy. His later promise of jobs was much more effective. The strongest support came from the lower middle class which had been ruined by the inflation of 1922–1923. To this class Hitler promised financial security and a firm leadership. Thus the Nazi success was really based on the "little man" of Germany, with the benevolent support of the elements of the right.

With his phenomenal capacity for self-deception Hitler was able to convince himself that it was his mission to build a new heaven and a new earth. "I know I can save my country," he declared, "and I know that no one else can." He had much the same fanaticism that characterized the Jacobins of the French Revolution and the more recent Bolsheviks. But with it all his record was marked by a series of falsifications and deceptions. In his public speeches he would make such statements as: "The first and best point of the program is that we won't lie and we won't swindle." But in *Mein Kampf* we read the following: "The great masses of a people . . . with the primitive simplicity of their minds will more easily fall victims to a great lie than to a small one." And again, "The German has not the faintest idea of how a nation must be swindled if one wants to have masses of supporters." His sole criterion was that of expediency. "Success," he wrote, "is the only earthly judge of right or wrong."

The victory of the Nazis was not, however, achieved by Hitler alone. It was the result of a cooperative effort. Behind Hitler, and giving him its full support, stood the Nazi Party, organized along military lines. The Nazis, in imitation of Mussolini's blackshirts, also had a party militia of brownshirts called SA (Sturm Abteilung) or Storm Troopers. In 1929 a second unit was organized, the SS (Schutz Staffel) or Elite Guard, whose special duty it was to protect the person of the Führer. Besides the idea of a party militia Hitler borrowed from Mussolini the ancient Roman salute. In imitation of Mussolini's fascio, Hitler imported the swastika from India as a symbol for the National Socialist Party. Mussolini's title of "Duce" was translated into "Führer" for Hitler; the Fascist anthem was imitated in a similar rhythm; and the National Socialist battle slogan, "Germany awake!" was borrowed from Richard Wagner, Hitler's favorite composer.

The Nazi Party overlooked nothing that might win converts. In Dr. Goebbels it had a master propagandist who evolved a technique of mass propaganda and mass emotionalism which made the efforts of the other parties appear feeble and amateurish. The Nazi success was indebted to propaganda in a greater measure than any similar movement preceding it. Nothing that might appeal to the emotions was overlooked. Parades, uniforms, banners, music, and meetings like those held by religious revivalists brought excitement into the drab lives of the Germans. In every mass meeting uniformed Nazi storm troopers were scattered throughout the audience to applaud certain phrases, to shout "Heil Hitler," and to lead in singing the Nazi songs. One such song, written to attract the peasant and proletarian, read:

> We soldiers of the swastika
> Hold now the red flags high
> To blaze the German worker's way
> "To freedom" is our cry.

This stagecraft was supplemented by the distribution of Nazi pamphlets from door to door or by dropping them from airplanes. The party also published a hundred newspapers and periodicals for propaganda purposes.

Despite their high-pressure propaganda the Nazis made little progress from 1924 to 1929. The party won followers when times were bad, but lost them when economic conditions improved. In 1924, when economic chaos still reigned as a result of the inflation, the Nazis increased the number of their seats in the Reichstag from three to thirty-two; but a second election held later in the same year after the restoration of the mark saw the Nazi vote reduced over a million and their representation in the Reichstag fall to fourteen. In 1928 they won only twelve seats. Their big opportunity came when the economic depression hit Germany with extraordinary fury. As unemployment and poverty became widespread the Germans were only too eager to clutch at any hope of relief and to follow anyone who promised them bread. Since the Nazis were very free with their promises they won many followers. Their vote increased from 800,000 in 1928 to nearly 6.5 millions in 1930 and the number of their deputies in the Reichstag from 12 to 107, making the National Socialist Party the second largest in Germany. When the number of deputies increased to 230 in July, 1932, Hitler was so certain of victory that he refused to join a coalition. His answer to the invitation was a demand for the same power Mussolini exercised in Italy. When, however, the Nazis lost nearly two million votes in the election of November, 1932, Hitler consented to head a coalition cabinet as chancellor. His appointment by President Hindenburg on January 30, 1933, marks the beginning of the Third Reich. During the succeeding months Hitler eliminated all competition and made himself absolute ruler of Germany.

THE NAZI REGIME

Although Hitler was now chancellor he and the Nazis still did not control the state. In addition to Hitler there were only two other Nazis in the cabinet, Dr. Frick as Minister of the Interior and Hermann Goering as Minister of Aviation and Prussian Minister of the Interior. All posts were held by virtue of a coalition between the Nazis and the Nationalist Party. Such a coalition did not satisfy Hitler. He was determined to gain an absolute majority for the Nazis alone. Soon after he became chancellor, Hitler demanded a new election which was set for March 5, 1933. As the first step toward gaining a majority of deputies in the Reichstag the Nazis put their entire strength behind their own electioneering efforts and did everything possible to curb those of the other parties. The latter task was made easier by the fact that Goering, who had charge of the Prussian police, made use of the slightest pretexts to suspend opposition newspapers and to break up opposition election meetings. But as the time for voting drew near, the Nazis were still not certain that they would obtain the desired majority. Consequently on February 24 the police raided the Karl Liebknechthaus, Berlin headquarters of the communists, and then announced that they had found plans for a general uprising in Germany. Three days later a fire broke out in the Reichstag building, and the communists were at once accused of having started it, although not one vestige of proof was ever presented. The government used the incident as a pretext for suspending the fundamental liberties guaranteed by the constitution.

This enabled Goering to suppress the election propaganda, forbid election meetings, and suppress the newspapers of the opposition, particularly of the communists and socialists.

Even intimidation did not stampede the Germans into voting the Nazi ticket. A tabulation of the votes showed that the Nazis had received only 43.9 per cent of the total vote. Thus they were still a minority party, with 288 seats out of a total of 647. Only with the support of the Nationalists, who elected 52 deputies, did the government have a slender majority. Since it was by no means certain that the Nationalists would not withdraw their support, the inner circle of the Nazis decided to achieve a clear majority by eliminating the eighty-one communist deputies from the Reichstag. This was achieved by simply not "inviting" them to attend the sessions of the Reichstag. Actually most of them would have been unable to do so because they were under arrest. Two days after the Reichstag convened, the Nazis, with the support of the Catholic Center Party, passed the Authorization or Enabling Act which empowered the cabinet to legislate without the Reichstag and thus gave the Nazi dictatorship a legal basis. Thenceforth even President Hindenburg's consent to legislation was not needed. In short, the Weimar constitution was dead, even though it had not been legally abolished.

Hitler proceeded at once to achieve "totality of power." One of his first acts was to evict all the non-Nazis from the state governments and to replace them with Nazi officials. In April, 1933, he promulgated a law which gave him the power to name the governors (Statthalter) of the seventeen individual states. These governors received full control over the appointment and control of officials. Thus a centralized dictatorship of the Nazi Party replaced Bismarck's old federal empire. Next Hitler and the Nazis took steps to suppress and dissolve all other political parties. The process began with the outlawing by the Reichstag of the Communist and Social Democratic parties and the confiscation of their property. This was followed by the "voluntary" dissolution of the Catholic Center and Nationalist parties. Under pressure the rest of the parties took similar action and on July 14, 1933, the National Socialist Party was declared to be the only legally constituted party. Germany had become a one-party state. Meanwhile the Nazis were also establishing their control over the economic life of Germany. Gradually the trade unions which had been the backbone of German economic life during the Weimar Republic were dissolved; some were "liquidated" by storm troopers and others decreed their dissolution under orders from the government. Their place was taken by the Labor Front, an organ of the Nazi Party. No other labor organization was permitted.

The goal of the Nazis was a totalitarian regime, with every phase of German life submissive to their yoke. Consequently they were not slow to hoist the swastika in the domain of education and culture. Their purpose in the field of education was, above all, to mold the minds of the young, for Hitler firmly believed that "whoever has the youth has the future." The schools were converted into propaganda mills to turn out good Nazis. Besides reorganizing the curriculum to include race study, genetics, and race hygiene, the Nazi regime also introduced textbooks which properly glorified the National Socialist movement. Outside the school other agencies were organized to inculcate Nazi doctrines in German youth. The various Hitler youth organizations enrolled both boys and girls from ten to eighteen. After 1936 membership was made obligatory for all boys and girls of Aryan stock.

The press, too, was subjected to rigid control. Any newspaper or magazine which dared to publish anything unfavorable to the Nazis was immediately taken over by Nazi agents. To escape such a fate most of the independent newspapers and periodicals were careful not to stray from the party line. The press, Goebbels said, must be like "a piano on which the government can play." The same criterion was applied to the theater and the cinema. All were required to adjust themselves to the new purpose of promoting Nazism.

The Nazis excluded from the administration, the press, the educational system, and the agencies of German cultural life most Jews and persons of Jewish descent. "It suffices," a statute issued by Hitler in April, 1933, stated, "if one parent or grandparent is a non-Aryan." Many professors of Jewish descent were dismissed from the universities, many books written by non-Aryans were removed from the libraries, and non-Aryan musicians and artists were not permitted to give concerts or stage art exhibitions. By a law of July, 1933, a Jew or a person married to a Jew was prohibited from holding government office. At first exceptions were made in the cases of Jewish war veterans, but later even they were retired. With some exceptions Jews were forced out of the legal profession, medicine, dentistry, and the universities. Teachers colleges were closed to Jewish students, and in the universities their number was limited to 1.5 per cent of the total enrollment. Jews were forbidden to own land, were barred from the army, and could not join the Labor Front. In 1935 the so-called "Nuremberg Laws" deprived all full-blooded Jews, even those of the Christian faith, of the rights of German citizenship, but they did permit persons whose ancestry was 25 or 50 per cent Jewish, formerly called "non-Aryans," to become citizens.

In August, 1934, Hitler took a further step toward absolute power. On August 2 President Hindenburg died at the age of eighty-six. On all sides the question was asked, "Who will be Hindenburg's successor?" Hitler answered the question without delay by merging the offices of president and chancellor. He did not assume the title of president, contenting himself with that of "Führer," but the merging of the titles gave him supreme command of the army and the navy. Soon thereafter he required all members of the armed forces to take an oath of allegiance to "the Leader of the German Reich and People, Adolf Hitler." Several months earlier in the bloody purge of June 30 he had eliminated not only those who opposed his control of the armed forces but also scores of others within the party who opposed his absolute rule. The former insignificant bricklayer's helper was now the absolute head of the German nation. The loud-speakers all over Germany roared forth again and again the words, "One people, one party, one leader." On August 14 Hitler asked the German people to vote their approval of him as Führer and chancellor; this they did with more than thirty-eight million votes. His closest associates, in addition to Rudolf Hess, who had helped him write *Mein Kampf*, were the fat Hermann Goering, who liked to strut in a Nazi uniform covered with a plethora of medals and decorations; Heinrich Himmler, the notorious Jew-baiter; and Dr. Goebbels, the master of propaganda.

Students are often eager to know how the former inmate of flophouses lived after he became the dictator of Germany. In his private life he remained the petty bourgeois with simple tastes. Dr. Theodor Morell, his personal physician for eight years, has stated that Hitler was a vegetarian, a teetotaler, and a nonsmoker. The simplicity of his life, which has become almost legendary, was one of the sheet anchors of his hold on the people. His working hours were very irregular, usually from noon until the early hours of the next day. Nothing delighted him more than to get away from Berlin for a picnic in the hills. He never became accustomed to the life of Berlin; whenever possible he withdrew to Berchtesgaden, near the Austrian border, where amidst superb scenery he laid many of his nefarious plans. Almost to the end of his life he remained the romantic who dreamed colossal dreams. Unfortunately he lacked the education to give balance to his romanticism. After he became dictator contradiction was insupportable to him; anyone who attempted it was summarily dismissed. As a result the men of independent judgment gradually dropped from his circle and were replaced by "yes-men." He did not forgive easily and could make life intensely disagreeable for anyone under his authority. In general, Hitler's life is devoid of great deeds. His vindictiveness characterized him as a man with a small soul.

One of the first endeavors of the Nazis after they were effectively entrenched in power was to create jobs as a means of allaying the general discontent. Their methods were not all novel, some of them having been initiated during the preceding period. Vast sums were spent on the construction of auto roads (Autobahnen), harbors, and housing. Home owners were granted subsidies for the repair and modernization of their homes, and farm owners received money for improvements on the promise to employ more farm hands. Families hiring new servant girls were permitted for tax purposes to regard them as dependents. To encourage the purchase of automobiles and new machinery, buyers were permitted to deduct their cost from taxable income. To make more jobs available for men, the Nazis proclaimed that the primary interest of women must be *Kinder, Kirche und Küche* (children, church, and kitchen). Women were also given marriage loans on condition that they would give up their jobs after marriage. These measures reduced the number of unemployed but by no means solved the problem of unemployment. It was only when rearmament was started on a vast scale in 1935 that the number of the unemployed was reduced to a minimum.

Peace within the ranks of labor was assured by the creation of the Labor Front, a kind of superunion which included employers as well as employees. It was not a government department but rather an organ of the Nazi Party and as such its supervising head was appointed by Hitler. Membership was in theory not compulsory; in practice, however, few employers or employees could afford to remain outside. Through the Labor Front the Nazis decided where each workman was to be employed and what he was to do. Strikes were, of course, out of the question. The supervision of the Labor Front was not limited to industrial relations; it also organized the leisure of its members. This phase of the Labor Front's activities was known as *Kraft durch Freude* (strength through joy) and was copied from the Italian Dopolavoro. Among other things it provided the German masses with low-cost sports and sport festivals, musical and theatrical entertainments, and vacations at special summer resorts.

The emphasis on pastimes and amusements for the masses was designed to obscure the fact that the Nazis failed to provide a higher standard of living. As a result of the industrial revival which took place in Germany after 1933 the index of industrial production rose from 54 in 1932 to 126 in 1937 (1928 = 100), and the gross income of wage earners showed an increase of 15 per cent. But the increase resulted from longer working hours. The actual hourly wages of both skilled and unskilled workers declined under the Nazi regime. And the increased income was more than offset by a rise in the cost of living. Despite the determined efforts of the government to hold prices down, they continued to rise. Then, too, the Nazi Party imposed various levies for the

Labor Front, "Winter Aid," [1] and other purposes, which took from 4 to 5 per cent of the workers' income. According to conservative estimates the living standard of the wage earner fell at least 10 per cent during the period of Nazi rule.

PREPARING FOR WAR

Although the treaty of Versailles limited the Reichswehr to 100,000 men and outlawed heavy artillery, aircraft, and tank units, German military tradition was preserved in a number of ways. Instruction in the "science of defense" was introduced in the higher schools, the German military triumphs were glorified in school readers, and old soldiers were encouraged to hold regimental reunions. Various forms of military drill were featured in rifle, riding, and hunting clubs. Numerous athletic associations also stressed sports and drills that were semimilitary. Civil aviation was developed in such a way that the transformation to military aviation could be carried out quickly. Thus much of the ground was ready for the Nazi rearmament program. Lest the other states of Europe become alarmed over too bold a progress in rearmament, Hitler at first secretly enrolled recruits in excess of the 100,000 permitted by the Versailles settlement. Military airfields were constructed ostensibly for civil aviation, and commercial planes were used to train bombing and fighting crews. Such steps did not remain secret long. In the neighboring states they caused great alarm, but the other states could not agree on a course of action. Meanwhile Hitler took special pains to assure other states that his designs were peaceful and that a rearmed Germany would be a force for continued peace.

When the powers did nothing to stop him Hitler gradually accelerated the rearmament pace. In March, 1935, General Goering announced that Germany had created an air force in defiance of the treaty of Versailles and a few days later Hitler declared that Germany would reintroduce conscription. Again the powers did nothing beyond issuing a few protests. The conscription law promulgated in May of the same year prescribed a year of active military training for all able-bodied Aryan Germans between the ages of eighteen and forty-five. When the powers once more offered only protests, the Nazis quickened their pace. Military pilots were trained as fast as planes could be constructed for their use. Shipyards were busy twenty-four hours a day building warships of all types. In 1936 the size of the standing army was doubled by an order which increased the training period to two years. Moreover, the civilian population in all parts of Germany was drilled against air raids and gas attacks.

[1] Akin to the American Community Chest.

Nor did the Nazis stop at producing armaments and drilling soldiers. One of the basic causes of the German collapse in 1918 had been a breakdown of food supplies and a shortage of essential war materials. To avoid a repetition of such shortages in another war the Nazis aimed at "autarchy" or self-sufficiency. First of all, they endeavored to make Germany independent of other countries, at least for indispensable products. Germany produced only enough wheat, rye, potatoes, and sugar for peacetime needs, and only about 80 per cent of the meat, cheese, and eggs and less than half of the fats and oils consumed by her population. Imports of other foodstuffs were also considerable. To make Germany independent of foreign supplies, the Nazis limited the acreage used to grow rye and potatoes, added much to the tillable area by draining marshes and diking the lowlands along the coast, and improved the yield by a wider use of fertilizers and agricultural machinery. The yield of dairy products was augmented by the importation of high-capacity cows to replace those of low capacity. To induce more Germans to engage in agriculture, prices of farm products were raised and wages of farm hands were increased.

For a time the new policy brought good results. The yields of such products as vegetables, oil-yielding plants, and fodder proteins were increased and more livestock was raised. But after 1934 the trend began to reverse itself. The rearmament program claimed more and more land for military camps, airfields, and other military purposes. Some farm laborers were drafted for military service, while others were attracted by the opportunities for employment in the armament industries. In 1937 the shortage of farm hands became so acute that foreign laborers were imported for the harvest and even storm troopers were sent into some districts. Actually fewer hogs were raised in 1938 than in 1932; hence there was still a shortage of fats. In general, at the end of the so-called first Four-Year Plan there was no substantial increase in agricultural production. Above all, the Nazis had failed to achieve self-sufficiency in food production. Food rationing began even before World War II. As early as February, 1939, lard, butter, margarine, fish, and meat were rationed, and a few months later other necessaries, including clothing, were added to the list.

The second Four-Year Plan aimed at achieving self-sufficiency in raw materials needed for industrial purposes. The Nazis needed cotton, rubber, nickel, tin, iron, coal, oil, copper, lead, nitrates, sulphurs, manganese, zinc, wool, chromite, aluminum, mica, mercury, potash, tungsten, antimony, and phosphates. Only four of these — coal, potash, nitrates, and zinc — were produced in sufficient quantities within the country. All the rubber, for example, and nearly 80 per cent of the minerals used in Germany were imported; so were practically all the cotton and silk, and nearly 90 per cent of the wool. During World War I Germany had suffered from a lack of essential industrial supplies even before the Allied blockade became effective. Finding means to prevent the recurrence of such a breakdown was an ambitious undertaking. Among other things the government mined low-grade ores which private enterprise had found unprofitable; it promoted sheep-raising to increase the production of wool and meat; it advised greater economy in the use of metals; and it laid plans for producing substitutes wherever possible.

Another factor which did not augur well for future strength was the declining birth rate of Germany. This alarmed the Nazis, whose plans called for a population large enough to provide large armies in the future and settlers for the lands they hoped to conquer in eastern Europe. The number of births in Germany had declined from 34.3 per thousand in 1901 to 15.1 per thousand in 1932, or, in terms of the totals, from more than two million in 1901 to 993,000 in 1932. The decline was sharpest after World War I because approximately 1.75 million German young men had lost their lives in the war. The population policy of the Nazis included heavy taxation for bachelors, the construction of many small homesteads which could be paid for by small monthly rentals, and marriage loans. The last measure appears to have been the most effective. No interest was charged on the loans, which had a set maximum of 1000 marks and were repaid at the rate of 1 per cent a month. For each child born during the period of the loan one fourth of the loan was canceled. At first the results were promising. The number of marriages rose more than 23 per cent in 1933 and more than 43 per cent in the following year. The number of births increased from 971,000 in 1933 to 1,279,000 in 1936. The rise was, however, merely temporary.

LITERATURE AND MUSIC

German literature during World War I was largely reflection of the fortunes of war. In the poetry, for example, the feats of German arms are lauded at first, but when the movement of the German battalions was stopped poets began to question the price the Germans had paid for their advances. During the last months of the war the tone was one of desperation and resignation. It is natural that the great disillusionment which followed the war should be reflected in literature. The German soldiers who marched off to war in 1914 with victory on their minds and Nietzsche's *Thus Spake Zarathustra* in their pockets, returned, if at all, to find that the Nietzschean "will to power" had lodged in the minds of the Allied armies. The state of the German mind was

much like that of the French after the war of 1870 as described by
Romain Rolland in *Jean-Christophe:*

A nation that has lost a war is like a man who has lost his God. A dull
weariness suddenly takes the place of fantastic exaltation. Gray ashes simmer
to the ground where flames had burned in millions of human hearts. All values
become valueless. Deeds which but yesterday seemed heroic now appear trite.
Faith itself takes on the guise of madness.

Lion Feuchtwanger in his novel *Success* has given the most readable
account of the postwar confusion, but the most notable event in the
field of fiction was undoubtedly the publication in 1924 of *Der Zau-
berberg (The Magic Mountain)*, Thomas Mann's second great novel
which pictures life in a tuberculosis sanatorium. His first great novel,
Buddenbrooks (1901) which has been styled the "German Forsyte
Saga," had been the prewar masterpiece of German fiction. In both
novels Mann achieved a lucidity and precision of style which is rare in
German writing. Both were translated into many languages.

The Germans were slow in writing about their war experiences. During the years immediately after the close of hostilities their chief desire
was to forget the past and resume normal life. It was only after some
years had passed that war novels began to appear. The masterpieces
in this class are Arnold Zweig's *Der Streit um den Sergeanten Grischa*
(The Case of Sergeant Grischa, 1928) and Ludwig Renn's *Krieg (War,*
1928), both of which were widely read outside Germany. But the book
that enjoyed the widest circulation was Erich Remarque's *Im Westen
Nichts Neues (All Quiet on the Western Front,* 1929). Within a year
an estimated three million copies were sold in Germany and translations were published in twenty-three languages. Opinions of its merit
differed widely. Some praised the book as presenting a faithful picture
of life and death on the western front; others labeled it misleading and
obscene.

When the Nazis rose to power they lost no time in establishing control over both writing and reading. As early as May, 1933, they publicly burned all books which good Nazis were not supposed to read.
Authors who were in any sense liberals or who were classed as non-
Aryans were blacklisted and left with no choice but to stop writing or
emigrate. As a result German literature in exile soon comprised the
major German talents.[2] Those authors who remained in Germany and
were permitted to publish their writings had to glorify nazism or write
harmless dream novels and fantasies. What the Nazis wanted was
patriotic lyrics and martial songs. Typical statements of Nazi writers

[2] Among the exiles were Thomas Mann, Arnold Zweig, Emil Ludwig and Franz Werfel.

are those of the poet Lersch: "I believe in Germany as I believe in God" and "Germany must live even if we must lay down our lives."

The control of literature by the Nazis spelled the death of all creativeness. The Nazi period did not produce a single poet who can be compared with the greater poets of the Weimar period, to say nothing of the classical period of Goethe and Schiller. The same is true of fiction and drama. In 1938 the *Deutsche Allgemeine Zeitung,* one of the few better journals that had managed to survive, stated, "Precious little in the way of good literature has been produced up to now." Both Hitler and Goebbels realized that the quality of the Nazi writers was not high. The former confessed at the Nuremberg Cultural Conference in 1937 that "the new singers and poets of the new Germany are still lacking."

The outstanding German composer of the first half of the present century was Richard Strauss (1864–1949). While still in his twenties he won a world reputation, the outstanding work of this period being the tone poem *Don Juan.* Soon after he reached thirty he wrote *Till Eulenspiegel, Thus Spake Zarathustra,* and *Don Quixote,* which are among the best known of his symphonic poems. In 1903 he finished an operatic version of *Salome* which was regarded as objectionable at first, but later became popular, in America as well as in Europe. The opera *Elektra* (1909) had the same kind of history. The best known and most popular of the Strauss operas is *Der Rosenkavalier (The Bearer of the Rose,* 1911), with a libretto of eighteenth-century Viennese intrigue. His later works do not quite match the luster of the great early ones, but are nevertheless outstanding compositions. Even in his debatable works he displayed a consummate craftsmanship which established him as one of the great masters of orchestral technique. He must also be given high rank among the succession of great composers of Lieder that began with Franz Schubert.

The Revolt of Asia

THE EMERGENCE OF NATIONALISM IN ASIA DURING much of the nineteenth century the peoples of Asia were so passive that their role in modern world history seemed likely to be a subordinate one. Most westerners regarded them as almost entirely lacking in national feeling and national pride. Lord Curzon, the British minister, wrote that in Asia the dominant note was "the mute acquiescence of the governed." But if acquiescence was the temper of the nineteenth century, disaffection and revolt were the prevailing notes of the first half of the twentieth. The sleeping giant was awakening. The spirit of revolt embraced not one or two countries but the entire Orient, populated by more than half of the human race. Nations whose very names had been synonymous with submissive obedience were moved by the spirit of nationalism. All gave notice that the day had passed when they would passively submit to western domination. Although the revolts took various forms in the different countries, the underlying cause was everywhere the same. The Asiatic peoples wished to free themselves of the centuries-old bondage imposed by the occidentals. All efforts pointed in the direction of self-government. Each nationality wished to be master of its own house. All were convinced that a bad native government would be better than the best foreign rule.

Among the factors which nourished the longing for political independence were resentment against economic exploitation, desire for social equality, and, above all, opposition to the imposition of western culture. Though the eastern peoples were ready to accept the western technological progress, they scorned western values. One Asiatic expressed the general feeling in the following words:

Hatred universal reigns from the Siberian tundras to the burned south of India. We hate the European because we consider him an intolerable barbarian, who bullies where his wheedling is unsuccessful. We hate him because . . . he is tortuous and cannot speak the truth; because he prates about his new-found hygiene, but is personally unclean compared to the majority of Asians. We despise him as a hypocrite who ships whisky, rifles, disease, and missionaries in the same mixed cargoes. We despise him because he is a recent parvenu. We are convinced that in spite of his present leadership in mundane affairs, he is inferior physically, morally, and mentally.[1]

The inspiration for the nationalist movement came largely from western sources, for many of the leaders had been educated in the West or in schools at home based on western models, where they studied the life and thought of the West. From accounts of the American and French revolutions and the works of the western political theorists they drew principles of self-government which they wished to put into immediate operation. Most of the university graduates had received an education which was exclusively philosophical and literary, one which did not prepare them for industrial life; in fact, many felt that an industrial career was beneath them. Their only hope was to become teachers or government officials. But the supply of such candidates exceeded the available positions. Hence they coveted many of the positions held by foreigners. A contributor to the *Indian Spectator* stated bluntly: "Whether the Government likes the truth or not, they must know that the educated native of India has learnt to look upon himself as heir presumptive to the collectorships or any of the numerous paid offices which have hitherto been so ably administered by foreign workers."[2]

The native independence movements which had been developing during the last decades of the nineteenth century received a special impetus from events during the early years of the twentieth century. The first of these events was Japan's victory in the Russo-Japanese War. Previously European armies had suffered reverses at the hands of Asiatics, but never before had an occidental power been defeated so decisively by an oriental state. The naval victories of Japan were unprecedented in the annals of warfare between the East and West. At the news of the victories the entire oriental press went into ecstasies. *New India*, published in Calcutta, stated that the Japanese people had achieved a moral victory which "seems already to be absolutely complete, and it is impossible to estimate the value of it. . . . Japan has already rendered a service to modern humanity, the full value and significance of which history and human valuation in the centuries

[1] *Open court*, vol. 36 (1922), p. 557.
[2] B. T. McCully, *English Education and the Origins of Indian Nationalism* (1940), p. 199.

alone can reveal." On all sides journalists lavishly praised the development of Japan which had enabled her to defeat the occidental with his own weapons and thus to demonstrate that the Asiatic is not inferior to the European. In short, the Japanese victory had the effect of awakening the national self-consciousness of "nations crowding to be born."

The movement was further stimulated by the propaganda stressing national rights which the Allies circulated during World War I. Particularly effective was President Wilson's enunciation of the right of self-determination, which created among many Asiatic peoples the belief that they — in fact, all subject races — were to be freed from foreign control. The disappointment of this hope gave rise to a widespread unrest which was gradually organized into movements with definite programs. The Russian communists, too, were an important factor in stimulating the spirit of revolt. When they appeared on the scene the fires of Asiatic nationalism were already burning, but the communists poured oil on them. They missed no opportunity to encourage the revolt against western imperialism. Without propaganda and money from the Soviet Union the revolt would not have shown the same vitality.

In 1927 an oriental journalist wrote: "All Asia is athrob with new life. Its people are discontented with their existing status and are striving for freedom — for race equality." In some countries there were only mass demonstrations against European rule, but in others the nationalists did not hesitate to use force.

INDIA DEMANDS INDEPENDENCE

During World War I British India and the Indian States were ungrudging in their contributions to the Allied cause. In addition to providing 1.5 million men for military service, they furnished large sums toward paying for the war. This contribution together with the Allied preachments of democracy and self-determination engendered in the people of India the hope of obtaining home rule (swaraj). As early as 1916 the demand for home rule was voiced in a combined meeting of the Indian National Congress and the All-India Moslem League. In the following year Mr. Montagu, the Secretary of State for India, sought to allay the rising nationalist feelings by declaring that the basic aim of British policy in India was the development of self-government. No sooner had the war ended than the people of India demanded the fulfillment of the British promises, and nationalist uprisings began to multiply rapidly. Finally in 1919 the British sought to placate Indian sentiment with the so-called Government of India Act, which put such matters as

agriculture, education, public health, and public works under the jurisdiction of Indian Provincial Councils, but left in British hands the
control of finances, the police, and the final power of legislation. The act
applied only to British India; the Indian States still remained under
the despotic rule of the Indian princes.

Far from satisfying the demands of the Indian nationalists, the
Government of India Act only evoked widespread condemnation. A
minority in the Indian National Congress, it is true, advised acceptance
of the reforms, but the majority refused to be satisfied with anything
short of home rule. In some parts of India the disappointment over the
Act vented itself in minor uprisings. The British responded with the
so-called Rowlatt Acts, which empowered the police to imprison without
formal trial anyone suspected of antigovernment activities. This moved
the Indian National Congress to proclaim a day on which all were to
cease work as a peaceful protest against the Rowlatt Acts. In general
the protest was peaceful, but in a few localities rioting took place. One
result was the tragedy at Amritsar in the Punjab. When a large crowd
in the public square attacked a number of Englishmen, the civil authorities called in the military to restore order. General Dyer, the
British brigade commander, in an effort to disperse the mob, ordered his
men to fire, with the result that four hundred Indians were killed and
one thousand two hundred wounded. Furthermore, he issued the
"crawling order," which required all Indians to pass the scene of the
shooting on their hands and knees.

The humiliation of the "crawling law" was widely felt in India and
did much to strengthen the determination of the Indian nationalists to
achieve home rule. Moreover, it caused Mohandas K. Gandhi (1869–
1948), who had previously been a loyal British subject, to become a
staunch Indian nationalist and to assume the leadership of the home
rule movement. Born in 1869 of Hindu parents of the Jain sect,[3] he
went at the age of nineteen to England to study law. Soon after his
return to India he went to South Africa (1893) to defend a law suit.
He remained there and for more than twenty years worked untiringly
to improve the conditions under which the indentured Indian coolie
laborers lived and worked. Although he was a confirmed pacifist, Gandhi
did participate in the recruiting campaigns when World War I broke
out and he also advocated loyalty to the British. "The British Empire,"
he said in 1915, "has certain ideals with which I have fallen in love."

But the disappointing course of British postwar policy in India
caused him to affiliate himself with the nationalist cause, and before
long he was its most ardent champion. His deep sincerity, his utter

[3] Jainism, an ascetic religion which advocates nonviolence and prohibits the killing of any
living creature, deeply influenced Gandhi.

simplicity, and his profound understanding of the problems and emotions of the masses soon earned for him the reputation of a saint. Popular sentiment bestowed on him the title "Mahatma" or "Great Soul," and multitudes worshipped him as a demigod. As a member of the Jain sect he eschewed the eating of meat and the use of alcohol or drugs. His staple diet was goat's milk. The most unpretentious of men, he usually wore only a white loincloth of coarse homespun material.

After the Amritsar affair Gandhi decided to launch a stupendous crusade designed to paralyze the British administration in India. He was convinced that if his countrymen would see to it that British rule in India was not a paying proposition they would quickly obtain swaraj or home rule. He would achieve this by noncooperation, or passive resistance. The people of India must not, he told them, work for British employers, enter British courts, attend British schools, buy British goods, pay taxes to the British government, or obey British laws. In other words, he proposed a general strike on the vastest scale yet conceived. To enable the people of India to dispense with British textiles, Gandhi revived the art of home spinning and weaving. Soon khaddar or homespun was widely proclaimed as the only proper attire for patriots. Gandhi himself wore nothing else. In calling for noncooperation he was careful to denounce all violence. He told his compatriots over and over again that the plan could be successful only if carried out absolutely without violence.

At first the movement was confined largely to the immediate followers of Gandhi, but before many weeks had passed it gained widespread support. As early as September, 1920, the Indian National Congress officially adopted noncooperation as the national program. Next the Mahatma himself won the support of the lower castes by advocating the removal of "untouchability." For a time he even had the support of the Moslems for his noncooperation movement. Thus it became an affair of the masses. The support of the movement was so tremendous that the British feared it would break the back of British power in India. But Gandhi's crusade unleashed forces which he soon found himself powerless to control. As the weeks passed the movement began to lose its peaceful character. Many of the more fanatical nationalists committed acts of violence. In November, 1921, riots in Bombay took the lives of fifty-three persons and injured about four hundred. Riots and attacks also occurred in numerous other places. Gandhi continued to implore his followers to eschew violence and also sought to expiate the bloodshed by fasting and prayer; but eventually the attacks grew so serious that the Mahatma, as the recognized leader of Indian nationalism, was arrested on a charge of sedition (1922) and sentenced to six years imprisonment.[4] With the leader in prison the movement gradually declined.

Meanwhile the Indian nationalists continued their struggle for self-government. In 1927 the British sought to allay the increasing resentment against them by appointing a commission (called the Simon Commission after its chairman, Sir John Simon) to study the question of revising the Indian constitution. But they made the mistake of failing to include one or more Indians in the membership. Hence the appointment of the commission tended only to aggravate the discontent. In 1928 the National Congress meeting at Calcutta issued a demand for full dominion status. When the British did nothing toward fulfilling the demand, Gandhi, who had not taken an active part in politics since his release from prison, again assumed the leadership of the nationalist cause. At the meeting of the National Congress in December, 1929, he introduced a resolution which declared that the people of India would be satisfied with nothing less than complete independence. Early in 1930 Gandhi launched a fresh civil disobedience campaign, calling on the people of India to boycott British goods, particularly cotton cloth, and to manufacture salt in violation of the British monopoly. He himself defied the British government by taking salt water from the sea to his bungalow. Thousands of members of the National Congress joined him in manufacturing salt and in boycotting British textiles, with the results that British imports of textiles dropped sharply.

Again Gandhi proclaimed his doctrine of love and nonviolence. "I personally would wait, if need be, for ages," he said, "rather than seek to obtain the freedom of my country through bloody means." Nevertheless, riots and outbreaks occurred at many places, soaking the soil of India with blood and causing heavy destruction of property. When the Moslems did not support the movement, Hindu mobs attacked them in a number of localities. The British government responded with widespread arrests, so that the prisons of India were soon bulging. Most of the nationalist leaders were arrested, including Gandhi's sons and Pandit Jawaharlal Nehru, the president of the Indian National Congress; finally Gandhi himself, after ignoring repeated warnings, was imprisoned. Left leaderless, the civil disobedience movement gradually ebbed. Gandhi himself lost his enthusiasm when the National Congress did not support his campaign for home spinning which required party members to spin 8000 feet of cotton yarn a month.

After much delay parliament finally passed the Government of India Act (1935), which gave the eleven provinces of British India a considerable measure of self-government. Provision was made for an elected legislature in each province, with jurisdiction over such matters as

[4] In February, 1924, the frail Mahatma was released because of ill health.

agriculture, education, and public health; and for a federal or national legislature consisting of two houses in which both the provinces of British India and the native states were represented. But the new constitution did not satisfy the Indian nationalists. They claimed that whatever grants of self-government had been made were more than offset by the dictatorial powers accorded the governors and viceroy. They were not slow to point out that police and civil service, currency and exchange, railroads and defense, banking, tariffs, and foreign affairs were still under British control. When the constitution was put into effect in 1938 the National Congress at first declared that it would have no part of it, but finally, at the insistence of Mahatma Gandhi, it agreed to accept the measures regarding provincial self-government.

ANTI-IMPERIALISM AND CIVIL WAR IN CHINA

At the opening of the twentieth century China was still, as Pushkin had described it much earlier, "in dotage buried." The Manchu rulers were weak and reactionary, and the people were largely indifferent to everything we associate with the state. The peasants attended to their own affairs with little concern for the emperor and his government. The attitude is expressed in the Chinese proverb, "Heaven is high and the emperor far away." As for the government, weakness was its outstanding characteristic both in internal and in foreign affairs. China's best ports were "leased" to or controlled by foreigners, her coastal and inland trade was controlled by foreigners, and her customs duties and other revenues were pledged to foreigners. Almost two-thirds of China had been marked out in "spheres of influence" by the powers, and in fourteen of the principal ports foreign settlements had been established that were not subject to Chinese law. Thus foreigners under the right of extraterritoriality were free to flout Chinese laws. As the civil governor of Shantung put it:

Of all the obstacles to friendly intercourse with other nations there is none greater than extraterritoriality. Foreigners at treaty ports are governed each by the laws of his own nation, and no matter what crimes they commit our courts have no jurisdiction. When a Chinese has dealings with a foreigner and suffers damage he must apply to the Consular court for redress. This may well result in justice being done, but the prospect fills the Chinese with fear and suspicion. He regards it as a very improbable chance that a just judgment will be rendered.

Reform was imperative if China was to occupy a respected place among the nations. The reactionary empress dowager Tsu-hsi herself bowed before the demand for reform and in 1905–1906 issued edicts reintroducing some of the reforms she had frustrated in 1898; but after her death in 1908 the conservatives again controlled the throne, dimming any hope of reform so long as the Manchu dynasty continued to rule. Meanwhile, however, the Manchu dynasty found itself exposed to increasing pressure from a new generation of reformers. The outstanding figure of the new revolutionary movement was Dr. Sun Yat-sen (1866–1925), who had turned his back on a promising medical career to become a revolutionist. "The term 'the Chinese government' is a term without meaning," he wrote in 1904, calling for the overthrow of the Manchu dynasty as the first step toward reform. His teachings and activities finally caused antidynastic riots to break out in 1911, and before the end of that year the Manchus were swept from the throne.

While preaching revolution Sun Yat-sen had organized a party which in 1912 adopted the name of Kuomintang or National People's Party. After the fall of the Manchus this party became the central organ of a new government which had its headquarters at Canton. A provisional constitution provided for a republic, and on New Year's Day, 1912, Sun Yat-sen was inaugurated as provisional president. It was, as he wrote in his *Autobiography,* "the successful accomplishment of the great ambition for which I had struggled during thirty years." But he soon realized that the Chinese were not ready for so radical a change. What China needed to put some order into the existing chaos was a "strong man." Sun Yat-sen therefore resigned the presidency in favor of General Yüan Shih-k'ai, who had a strong military force at his disposal. Yüan proceeded to rule as dictator. When many disappointed republicans called him "the Napoleon of China," he replied, "Why should I want to be a Napoleon when I might become another George Washington?" Although he failed to achieve his ambition, he did establish some semblance of order. After his death in 1916 China again lapsed into chaos and the political and economic domination of China by foreign powers remained unchallenged for the time being.

China was not concerned with the complicated issues which plunged Europe into war in 1914. Even if she had been, her chaotic internal conditions would not have permitted her to participate. Officially, therefore, the government remained neutral during the first two and a half years of the conflict. During this time the official sympathy tended to favor Germany, since Japan was on the other side. In 1917, however, after the United States severed diplomatic relations with Germany, China declared war against the Central Powers. Her contribution to the war effort was the dispatching of a work force of 175,000 to the war zone. Finding themselves among the victors at the conclusion of the war, the Chinese leaders hoped that the reward would be a status of equality with the other nations. As a Chinese spokesman stated the issue, "All the countries of Europe, great and small, reap the benefit and the glory of this great victory. China does not ask for a full measure of reward as her portion. She only makes one modest request, namely, that the Powers treat us as an equal. It is surely not unreasonable or extravagant to hope that the Powers will condescend to grant our request."

Two Chinese delegations journeyed to Paris to claim the rewards of victory. They requested complete postal and tariff autonomy for China, cancellation of "spheres of influence," restoration of "leased" territories, and termination of extraterritoriality. But their requests were completely ignored. Without consulting their wishes the Peace Conference handed over to the Japanese the province of Shantung together with the "rights, titles, and privileges" acquired by Germany under the infamous treaty of 1898. The embittered Chinese refused to sign the treaty of Versailles.

China did, however, make some gains as a result of the war. The extraterritorial rights of the Habsburg empire and those of Germany were terminated, the former automatically when the empire collapsed, the latter by a special treaty. As a result the Germans and the nationals of the old Habsburg empire in China became subject to Chinese laws and the jurisdiction of Chinese courts. In addition, German and Austrian residential concessions reverted to Chinese control. During the succeeding years China made further progress toward freedom from foreign domination. At the Washington Arms Conference (1921) Japan was induced to restore Shantung to China and it was agreed that on January 1, 1923, foreign postal agencies in China were to be abolished. Furthermore, nine powers signed a treaty pledging themselves to respect the political, economic, and territorial sovereignty of China.

Meanwhile Sun Yat-sen, far from discouraged over the fact that the treaties failed to end western imperialism in China, continued his efforts to achieve this goal and to further the cause of reform. He patiently rebuilt the Kuomintang or National People's Party as the basis for a government which he hoped would unify and democratize China. Convinced that both Britain and the United States were sympathetic to his plans, he sought help from them, but his requests met with refusal. Next he turned to the Soviet Union, which heartily welcomed the opportunity to cooperate in reorganizing the Kuomintang, training a Chinese army, and putting an end to western imperialism. Sun Yat-sen accepted the proffered aid with the proviso that "the Communist order or even the Soviet system cannot actually be introduced into China." Soon both political advisers and generals from the Soviet Union arrived in China, so that Sun Yat-sen could say: "China no longer looks to the West for assistance. We now look to the Soviet Union." The Nationalist government then gave diplomatic recognition to the Soviet Union, which, in turn, relinquished Russian extraterritorial rights in China.

On March 12, 1925, Sun Yat-sen died at the age of fifty-eight. Realizing that his work was still unfinished, he had urged the members of the Kuomintang to complete it. The message read in part:

For forty years I have been engaged in the democratic reconstruction of China. It has been my cherished aim to elevate China to a state of freedom and independence. . . . The fight for the completion of the revolution must be continued. . . . I call upon the Party to concentrate all efforts upon the speediest realization of its aims.

After his death he became the symbol of the unfinished revolution and was accorded a reverence usually reserved for a deity. His remains, like those of Lenin, were carefully embalmed and were then put on display in an imposing mausoleum built on Purple Mountain overlooking Nanking. Posthumously he was accorded the title "Father of the Chinese Republic." In the decades that followed, each of the contending parties insisted that it alone was faithful to the principles of Sun Yat-sen.

One of his disciples, General Chiang Kai-shek, became the leader of the Nationalist movement. Under his command formidable Kuomintang armies in 1926 launched a military campaign to extend Nationalist rule over the whole of China. In their advance the armies overwhelmed city after city, until by the end of March, 1927, most of China acknowledged the rule of the Nationalist government. It seemed as if Sun Yat-sen's dream of a united China was about to come true. But as the armies approached the Great Wall, dissension broke out in the ranks of the Kuomintang over the question of communism. The right flank of the party, and particularly the bankers who were financing the military expedition, became apprehensive of the increasing communist influence in the party. Personal choice as well as the necessity of pleasing the bankers caused Chiang to halt the northern advance and to purge the Kuomintang of communists. The Russian advisers returned to Moscow together with some of the Chinese communist leaders, many of whom remained in Russia until 1945. Other Chinese communists fled into Kiangsi province in the center of China. Among the latter was Mao Tse-tung, who was later to become the communist leader in China. After the purge General Chiang set up a conservative middle-class government at Nanking.

Thus China was again split into two main factions, the communists and the nationalists. The former found the most fertile ground for their ideas among the peasants, most of whom were in virtual bondage to their landlords. In some parts of China communist teachings impelled peasant mobs to rise against the landlords and to commit arson and even murder. In the towns communist ideas found acceptance among the underpaid industrial workers. In general, communism's hold on the masses increased until by 1934 it extended over about one sixth of China, including some of the richest parts of Central China. Meanwhile Generalissimo Chiang Kai-shek, as he was now called, had launched a series of campaigns against the communist forces, but he was unable to crush them. Communist guerrilla groups, often supported by the peasants of the districts in which they operated, proved to be elusive foes. After each raid or battle they would retreat into the hills. In 1934 the communists moved en masse from central and southern China to the northwest. One of the marchers was Mao Tse-tung, whose shrewdness and diplomacy soon made him the dominant leader among the communists in the northwest province of Shensi. When the Japanese invaded China in 1937 Mao called for a united front against them, and a conference between Chiang and the communist leaders resulted in an entente between the Kuomintang and Mao Tse-tung's guerrilla fighters.

Although the Nationalist government was waging constant warfare against the communists it did not miss an opportunity to attack the control of China's ports by foreigners, the domination of large areas of Chinese territory by foreigners, the special privileges of foreigners — every inequality which made China, as the Generalissimo put it, "a subcolony of imperialism." Representatives of the Nationalist government made bold at various international congresses to demand the abolition of special privileges and grants in China. And their demands were not without results. In 1929 the British returned their Chinkiang concession to China and the Belgian government canceled its Tientsin concession. The next year the British also surrendered their Amoy concession. As a further step toward independence the Nationalist government issued its own schedule of duties in 1929, thereby establishing tariff autonomy. Finally the Nationalist government set January 1, 1930, as the date for the termination of all extraterritorial rights, stating that thereafter all foreigners residing in China "shall abide by the laws, ordinances and regulations duly promulgated by the central and local governments in China." For a time a serious crisis seemed imminent, but the British saved the day by accepting the decree. Actually, however, no immediate change occurred. The extraterritorial courts continued to function during a period of study and experimentation to find a proper substitute for them.

During the period between World War I and World War II the Nationalist government did make considerable progress in modernizing

China. Existing highways were improved and new hard-surfaced roads were constructed to promote motor transportation; and the railway systems, which had previously been limited largely to the coastal areas, were extended into the hinterland. Industrial expansion was encouraged, with the result that in the larger cities industrial production of textiles, iron, and steel began to replace hand industry. Measures to promote sanitation and hygiene were introduced into the larger cities. New primary and secondary schools were opened. Some idea of the progress made in education may be gained from the fact that the number of children attending school increased from three million in 1921 to eleven million in 1934. The one matter which the government neglected — and this was to prove fatal in the end — was the agrarian question. The widespread demand for the distribution of land was ignored and nothing was done to improve the lot of the peasants who were living on the brink of starvation in virtual slavery to the landowners.

As the disciple of Sun Yat-sen, Chiang was theoretically committed to democratic principles of government. Actually, however, his government became increasingly autocratic. Communist opposition and dissension within the ranks of the Kuomintang caused him to rely more and more on the army as the chief support of his rule.

JAPANESE IMPERIALISM

World War I offered the Japanese an unusual opportunity to strengthen their position in the Far East. It was an opportunity which they refused to miss. Not only was Germany's Kiaochow in Shantung province on the Chinese mainland to be had for the taking but there were also the German possessions in the Pacific which included the Marshall and Caroline islands. Determined to gain control of these possessions, the Japanese government declared war against Germany on August 23, 1914, and proceeded at once to occupy the German Shantung colony, taking over Germany's railroads, mines, and other developments. When the Chinese demanded the return to them of the conquered territory, the Japanese countered with the Twenty-one Demands, which would virtually have converted China and Inner Mongolia into a Japanese protectorate. Since China was in no position to resist and the western powers were too busy waging war to support her, she was compelled to accept all but the most objectionable of the demands. Protests of the United States and British governments, however, did much to invalidate many of the concessions China had been compelled to make.

At the end of the war the Japanese representation occupied a place at the peace table among the Big Five who drew up the peace treaties

Since the peace negotiators were harassed with European troubles and were not particularly interested in the Far East, Japan managed to do well for herself. She not only retained her hold on the German Shantung territories but also secured from the new-born League of Nations a mandate over all former German islands in the Pacific north of the equator. The peacemakers seemed to take no particular notice of the fact that Japan's new island possessions (the Marianas, Caroline, and Marshall islands) extended very near to Australia and to two islands of the United States, Guam on the west and Midway Island on the east. Japan did not long hold the former German properties on the mainland of China. At the Washington Naval Conference of 1921–1922 they were returned to China.

For some years after World War I Japan made no overt imperialist moves, but she continued to spend a large part of the national budget for armaments and strengthened her hold on Manchuria by building railways, opening industrial plants, and encouraging Japanese colonists to settle there, at the same time insisting that her interests in Manchuria were purely economic. The Wall Street crash of 1929 dealt Japan's economic life a severe blow. Particularly serious was the decline of her foreign trade. The demand for raw silk in the United States dropped so sharply that in 1930 the export of raw silk from Japan decreased 47 per cent in value. The smaller demand for and lower prices of raw silk brought acute distress to the peasants of Japan. Nor was this all. The export of cotton textiles declined by 34 per cent in value in 1930. The general decline of all exports was 27 per cent, a far greater drop than that experienced by world trade as a whole. For a country whose population depended on exports for livelihood this was a serious situation. The next year the budgetary deficit was so large that the Japanese government had to borrow large sums to meet expenses.

What Japan needed was food for her teeming population, raw materials for her industries, and an outlet for her surplus population.[5] During the decades since she had emerged from her self-imposed isolation, her population had increased rapidly. From 1875 to 1914 it had nearly doubled and the increase continued during the period that followed. Birth control and emigration were tried as solutions of the population pressure, but without satisfactory results. By 1930 the density of the population per square kilometer of cultivated ground was twice that of China, and the country was unable to produce sufficient food to sustain it. Furthermore, Japan lacked most of the raw materials needed to keep the wheels of her industries turning. Practically 70 per cent of her imports consisted of raw materials. Her iron-ore reserves are limited and her coal deposits are small and of poor quality. Consequently more

[5] Japan had Korea, but more Chinese migrated there than Japanese.

than half of her iron and steel supplies came from overseas. Oil, too, was in such short supply that more than 60 per cent of her needs were imported. In addition Japan imported nearly all her cotton, rubber, lead, zinc, and dyes. The country's real economic necessities could have been met without political penetration, for none of the western countries could compete with Japan successfully in her region of the globe. But the Japanese chose to turn to imperialism.

It was ostensibly in search of food supplies and raw materials that the Japanese leaders turned in the direction of Manchuria on the mainland of China. This province had great coal and iron deposits and vast reserves of timber; it also produced large quantities of oil, aluminum, and agricultural fertilizers. Moreover, it held out the promise of supplying the teeming population of Japan with food. Particularly noteworthy is the fact that Manchuria produced nearly 70 per cent of the world's supply of soy beans. Other important agricultural products included oats and millet. Manchuria also offered an outlet for the overflow of Japan's population. It was expected that such comparatively unpopulated and undeveloped regions as Manchuria would attract a large number of Japanese immigrants. Finally the Japanese hoped to find new markets for their manufactures in Manchuria and, in a wider sense, in all of China.

If Japan was to occupy Manchuria without stiff opposition, haste was necessary, for the Nationalist government of China was also interested in gaining control of it. The Japanese had ready a large force and superior military equipment. All they needed was an occasion, and this was soon found. On September 18, 1931, a mysterious bomb exploded on the tracks of the Japanese-owned South Manchurian Railway near Mukden. Although the damage was so small that a train passed over the spot a few hours later, the Japanese claimed that the incident, which they attributed to Chinese bandits, made it necessary to send an army to restore law and order. It took the army just a few days to overrun Manchuria and to bring under Japanese control an area about three times as large as Japan proper. On February 18, 1932, the Japanese announced the independence of Manchuria and Inner Mongolia and the next month proceeded to set up a puppet Japanese state which they called Manchukuo. Although the Japanese had originally promised to withdraw as soon as order was restored, they made no move to do so.

The next move was formally announced in 1934, when a spokesman of the foreign office declared (Amau Declaration) that it was the special mission of Japan to keep order in the Far East and that his country would no longer brook the interference of western nations in Chinese affairs. China, he continued, was to accept no more foreign loans, nor were western nations to send munitions or military goods to China. In

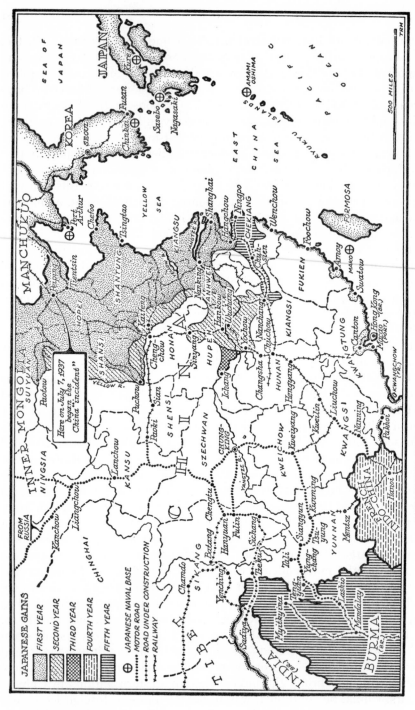

JAPANESE EXPANSION ON THE CONTINENT OF ASIA

short, Japan declared to the world that China was hers and hers alone. The Japanese statesmen seemed to have forgotten that Japan was one of the powers which in the Nine Power Pact (1922) had agreed "to respect the sovereignty, the independence and the territorial and administrative integrity of China."

In 1937 the Japanese leaders believed that China was ripe for plucking, and large-scale military operations were launched without an official declaration of war. It was confidently believed in Japanese military circles that China would be forced to her knees in three months. But they grossly underestimated the Chinese power of resistance. The Japanese armies, with their tanks, mechanized units, and planes, did make rapid advances. In a short time they had in their possession many of the most important cities of China, including Peiping, Nanking, Shanghai, Hankow, and Canton. Airplanes swept over the country machine-gunning the population and bombing and burning cities. But to the great astonishment of the Japanese the Chinese refused to be defeated. They continued to resist with furious energy. While the organized troops supplied by Generalissimo Chiang Kai-shek resorted to skillful retreats to save themselves from annihilation, guerrilla bands sprang up behind the Japanese lines to harass the enemy ceaselessly. Thus month after month passed without a conclusive Japanese victory. Even the Japanese efforts to set up puppet civil governments in the conquered territories were a signal failure. The Chinese masses withdrew into a sullen noncooperation. By the spring of 1939 it was evident that the attempt to reduce China had failed.

By 1940 American aid to China had increased so substantially that the Japanese were forced to face the possibility of eventual defeat. The government began to consider ways of concluding the Chinese venture without losing face. Withdrawal was ruled out because it would have meant loss of prestige abroad and repercussions at home. Any peace terms acceptable to the Japanese people would have been rejected by the Chinese. Chiang Kai-shek had repeatedly stated: "There can be no peace while a Japanese soldier remains on Chinese soil." Some of the Japanese leaders began to consider war against the United States as a solution of the Chinese puzzle. The fact that American aid to China had been an important factor in upsetting the Japanese schedule of conquest helped to win support for the idea. The Japanese were so certain the Axis Powers (Germany and Italy) would win the European war that they entered into a tripartite pact with Germany and Italy in September, 1940. During the months that followed, Hitler's agents continued to urge them to enter the fray by attacking the United States. On December 7, 1941, the Japanese attacked Pearl Harbor without a declaration of war.

The Road to World War II

WORLD War I reduced large sections of Europe to ashes, but out of these ashes there arose the hope for permanent peace, democracy and social justice. For a time it seemed as if that hope, or at least a large part of it, might be realized. After 1929, however, the international situation gradually deteriorated and before long it was evident that the nations were again drifting toward war. In 1939 the catastrophe which had been hanging over Europe and the world for more than five years fell with the invasion of Poland. What were the causes that produced the war? In answer many would say, "Hitler and the Nazi leaders precipitated the catastrophe by ordering the German armies to attack Poland." This is undoubtedly true, but it is not the whole story. War is not an isolated occurrence, something that breaks out suddenly because of a single act on the part of one man or government. It is the result of a series of factors and events whose roots lie deep in the past. Although the war did not break out until 1939, nations had been talking of war, preparing for war, and drifting toward war for almost a decade. Hitler, Mussolini, and the "war lords" of Japan would not have embarked on a mad career of conquest and destruction if the underlying conditions had not been favorable for such developments. They were the puppets or symbols of deep social and economic forces. Their strength and their weakness in action came to them from these forces. It is, therefore, in these conditions that the true causes of the war are to be found. In considering them one must remember that the failure of peace and the triumph of war are one and the same thing.

The deeper causes of World War II are as complex as were those which produced World War I; in fact, many were the same ones that had helped generate the earlier war. Among the factors that frustrated the efforts to establish collective security and helped to carry the nations toward the abyss of war one might include: (1) the struggle for markets, raw materials, and colonies; (2) the impotence of the League of Nations; (3) the disarmament fiasco; (4) the problem of national minorities; (5) the resentment caused by the Versailles settlement; (6) the resurgence of a selfish nationalist spirit. The last played an essential part in all the preceding five. As is the case in all complex movements some factors were in part cause and in part effect of the breakdown of collective security and the drift toward war. Some were more productive of friction than others, but all contributed to a greater or lesser extent to the inevitable end.

THE STRUGGLE FOR MARKETS, RAW MATERIALS, AND COLONIES

Of all the factors making for war the struggle for markets, raw materials, and colonies was certainly one of the most important. It had also been one of the major causes of World War I. The Industrial Revolution and the development of transport in the nineteenth century had destroyed the self-sufficiency of the European nations and made them dependent on one another and the outside world for both raw materials and markets. During the early part of the century the nations who were politically unified and whose industrial systems were more highly developed expanded their colonial empires until they controlled most of the sources of raw materials outside Europe. Thus Great Britain extended her sway over nearly a quarter of the world's territory and population. France, Belgium, and the Netherlands also acquired vast empires. But two countries, Germany and Italy, had been so busy creating political unity that they could not participate in the scramble for colonies. When they did take up the hunt, most of the desirable portions of the earth had been claimed. Nevertheless, their efforts to acquire colonies were a prolific source of friction. Neither country was less dissatisfied when World War I ended. The Italians felt that they should have received a larger share of the spoils; the Germans were resentful because the Allies took from them the few colonies they had managed to acquire. These two countries, together with Japan, formed the so-called "have-not" group; that is, they were poorest in natural resources in relation to the extent of their industries and their population.

The situation would not have been so critical if there had been internal free trade in Europe. But this was not the case. Europe was literally bristling with tariff barriers and every conceivable impediment to a free exchange of goods. One of the Fourteen Points had provided for "the removal, so far as possible, of all economic barriers" and the establishment of "an equality of trade conditions." Nothing, however, was achieved in this direction; in fact, as a result of the Paris settlement the number of tariff frontiers increased greatly. Each of the new nations, seeking to cultivate its own preserves, erected tariff barriers to keep out imports. The purpose of the governments in excluding imports was to compel their nationals to purchase goods manufactured within the boundaries of the state in which they were living. They feared that free international commerce would undermine their national well-being.

During the era of prosperity the nations found ready markets for their manufactured goods. Even the "have-nots" were thus able to purchase the raw materials they needed. But with the coming of the economic depression in 1930 the situation changed. As economic conditions deteriorated, methods were adopted which made the situation worse. Nations established the closed-door policy in their colonial as well as in their home territories. Higher tariffs were erected against imported goods, and colonies were persuaded to discriminate in favor of the mother country. Even tariffs were not the final weapons. Various other devices to keep out imports, such as quotas and embargoes, were adopted. Meanwhile campaigns were launched at home to convince the people that they must buy only products that were manufactured in their own country. The British opened the "buy-at-home" campaign with the slogan "Buy British." Before long most of the countries of the world coined similar slogans — "invest in France," "Buy American," "Buy Japanese," and "Buy German goods and give work and bread to your fellow citizens."

The western democracies were the leading exponents of this economic nationalism. However much they believed in political liberty, they did not sponsor international freedom of trade. In the year following the Wall Street crash the Congress of the United States adopted the Hawley-Smoot tariff. The other democracies soon followed suit, with the result that the movement of goods was obstructed in every direction. In 1931 France inaugurated the quota system, which drastically reduced her imports. In the same year Britain not only abandoned the gold standard but subsequently raised a tariff wall against imports. Nor did she stop there. The following year saw the Ottawa Agreement establish the policy of the closed door in the entire British Commonwealth of Nations. The inability of some nations to sell their manufactured articles and to purchase raw materials produced a sense of economic suffocation. They began to demand a fair share of the earth's natural wealth or, at least, access to the materials needed for their industries. When nothing was done to effect a more equitable distribution, the three "have-not" countries decided to get their share by force. The Japanese invaded Manchuria, the Italians overran Ethiopia and Albania, and Hitler annexed Austria and the Sudetenland. Such military expeditions were part of the undeclared war that preceded the major struggle.

IMPOTENCE OF THE LEAGUE

So long as prosperity continued, the League had managed to settle with some degree of success the questions presented to it; but when the economic depression brought self-interest to the fore and the nations became less tractable, it was unable to cope with the situation. The League was weak because its members lacked the will to make it succeed. Actually there never was any real internationalism based upon friendly cooperation and the promotion of common interests. The various states were eager to use the League up to a point, but there was a general reluctance to pay the price necessary to achieve a stable peace. The general motto of the nations was not "Each for all" but "Each for self." They were not ready for the surrender of sovereignty, as were the American states in 1787, to achieve a real federation. All insisted on the retention of full national sovereignty. What they wanted was to get rather than give.

The League of Nations was merely what the countries who sent delegates to it wanted it to be, a sort of debating society where the other countries' shortcomings were discussed. "The history of the League of Nations between World War I and World War II," Gaetano Salvemini wrote, "was the history of the devices, ruses, deceptions, frauds, tricks, and trappings by means of which the very diplomats who were pledged to operate the Covenant of the League managed to circumvent it. They were its most effective foes, since they were undermining it from within, while the nationalists, militarists, and fascists were attacking it openly from without in all lands."[1]

When the drift toward war started, the League was unable to arrest it. Being merely a debating society, it had neither arms nor moral authority with which it could discipline any constituent state or make any common front binding on all its members. It did have one weapon, that of economic sanctions. In Article 16 of the Covenant the constituent states agreed to impose sanctions against any nation embarking on an aggressive war. But the small nations were unable to make the larger ones, more particularly France and England, apply sanctions when they would have been effective. When the United States turned its back on the League, Great Britain refused to undertake the responsibility of enforcing sanctions and the system broke down. As early as 1923 Lord Curzon, who was at that time foreign minister, regarded

[1] *Atlantic Monthly,* vol. 178 (August, 1946), p. 56.

the League as nothing but "a good joke." To the Frenchman Berthelot it was "a grotesque hoax." Later the Nazis ridiculed it as "a joint stock company for the preservation of the booty won in the war." When the League sought to curb their imperialist ambitions, Japan, Germany, and Italy quit Geneva with impunity. The first of the three to challenge the authority of the League was Japan in invading Manchuria in 1931. Although this was a definite breach of the League Covenant, no serious effort was made to check Japanese aggression, the Japanese being let off with a scolding.

When Mussolini embarked on the Ethiopian venture in 1935 the League had its last opportunity for making the system of collective security effective. Western public opinion was definitely in favor of such a step. In Britain, and overseas in Australia, Canada, and South Africa, public opinion demanded that Article 16 be invoked against the Italian aggressors as a means of saving the throne of Haile Selassie and of stopping the general drift toward war. The occasion was certainly a favorable one for a test. Italy was badly in need of oil for its operations. Moreover, since Mussolini was embarking on an expedition on the other side of the Suez Canal, the British and French could have checked him by closing the canal to shipping. The Italian General De Bono later stated in his *Memoirs* that Italy might have abandoned the expedition if Great Britain had interposed serious objections. Mussolini put up a big bluff in threatening to fight if the League and the United States were to impose an oil embargo. Since no one was prepared to fight, Mussolini had his way. The incident clearly demonstrated that an international organization without spirit is of little avail. It further demonstrated that the League was dead for purposes of preventing aggression. About all that remained of it was the new white palace at Geneva, a tombstone of frustrated hopes.

THE DISARMAMENT FIASCO

As an essential step toward the prevention of war, disarmament was a cherished goal of the founders of the League. The treaty of Versailles specifically stated (Part V, Article 159-213) that the disarmament of Germany and her associates was merely a beginning and that the maintenance of peace required a general reduction. The idea was further developed in a memorandum to the German government: "The Allied and Associated Powers wish to make it clear that their requirements in regard to German armaments were not made solely with the object of rendering it impossible for Germany to resume her policy of military aggression. They are also the first steps toward that general reduction and limitation of armaments which they seek to bring about as one of the most fruitful preventives of war, and which it will be one of the first duties of the League to promote." Not only did the Allies promise a general disarmament, but the Germans expressly accepted the provisions on the understanding that the other countries would disarm in equal measure. "The German government," the German peace delegation stated, "is willing to consent to the abolition of compulsory military service on the condition that this will be the initiation of a general limitation of armaments of all nations." In reply Clemenceau said that it was the intention of the Allied and Associated Powers "to open negotiations immediately with a view to the adoption eventually of a scheme of general reduction." Lloyd George also said at the Peace Conference: "To my mind it is idle to endeavor to impose a permanent limitation of armaments on Germany unless we are prepared to impose similar limitations on ourselves."

Despite the pledges, promises, and good intentions little was achieved in the way of disarmament. During the next twelve years there was much talk, and even a number of conferences. The most successful of the latter was the Washington Disarmament Conference of 1921, which met at the invitation of the United States. Its outstanding achievement was the outlawing of poison gas and the conclusion of an agreement between the United States, Great Britain, and Japan for the construction of capital ships on a ratio of 5:5:3, the last being the ratio of Japan. Beyond this there was no progress toward disarmament. France, still gripped by fear of a Germany with a larger population and a greater industrial potential, showed no inclination to reduce its land forces; nor were the British ready to scrap any part of their navy. The German government reminded the Allies again and again of the promises they had made to disarm, but the reminders fell on deaf ears. Even in France and Britain there were some who continued to urge disarmament. Thus a French historian wrote in 1925: "The treaties of Versailles, St. Germain, Neuilly, and Trianon disarmed Germany and her Allies in effect on land and sea, but they did not restrict the armies of the Entente countries in any way. Not only was this a new flagrant violation of promises made, but the most serious of them all. For what imaginable act could be more serious and more unjust than to leave any country whatsoever unarmed amongst a world of armed enemies?" In 1927 Lloyd George lamented the fact that the pledges to disarm had not impelled the nations to reduce their armaments "by a single division, flight of airplanes or battery of guns."

If the Allies had carried out in some degree their pledges to disarm or if, failing to do so, they had granted Germany equality in armaments, they might have saved the German republic; at any rate, they would have taken much of the wind out of Hitler's sails. When a disarmament conference convoked by the League finally met at Geneva, the Allies were in no mood to disarm. Chancellor Bruening in pleading with the powers stated explicitly that Germany would be happy to remain on the armament level prescribed by the treaty if the other states were willing to reduce their armaments to a comparable level. Finally in January, 1933, Germany received a conditional promise of arms equality, but Hitler's accession to power in the same month caused the French and British to postpone taking any practical steps to carry out the promise. The Allied refusal became grist for the Nazi propaganda mill and greatly facilitated the task of convincing the German people that rearmament was the royal road to national power and self-respect. While Hitler was rearming Germany, Italy and Japan were also busy building up their armaments. Soon they were all to join forces in order to bathe the world in blood.

THE PROBLEM OF NATIONAL MINORITIES

President Wilson's wartime slogan of "self-determination" created the hope that the peace would settle the minorities problem once and for all. This hope was, however, realized only in part. After the Paris treaties of 1919 there were certainly fewer discontented minorities than there had been before, but the settlement not only failed to correct some of the existing grievances but created some new ones. Although the principle of self-determination was the theoretical basis for the settlement of the minorities question, it was applied only when it coincided with the social, political, and economic interests of France and her allies (Poland, Czechoslovakia, Rumania, and Yugoslavia). The factors which conditioned the decisions of the Allies and the application of the principle were economic necessity, military defense, religious and political traditions, and punishment of the defeated nations. Even if the peacemakers had tried to apply the principle in a strict sense they would have been unable to do so. Innumerable migrations had mixed the diverse nationalities so thoroughly in certain districts that Solomon with all his wisdom would have found it impossible to assign proper frontiers to the various states.

Thus some national groups were forced to remain in states in which the majority of citizens were of another nationality, while others were transferred by boundary revisions to the jurisdiction of states controlled by other nationalities. It has been estimated that the total number of people in such minority groups approximated thirty millions. There were groups in foreign lands composed of Poles, Germans, Hungarians, Italians, Bulgars, Ruthenians, Macedonians, Albanians, and Russians. In Rumania there were no less than 1.5 million Hungarians, and other Hungarian minorities were living in Czechoslovakia and Yugoslavia. In Bessarabia, which Rumania had wrested from Soviet Russia in 1918 and had been permitted to keep in the settlement, there were large numbers of Russians. The largest minority group was the 3.5 million Sudeten Germans who had been included in Czechoslovakia. Practically all of these minority groups made irreconcilable citizens of other states, each group remaining conscious of its peculiar characteristics, language, and culture, and retaining its ties with the mother country.

The peacemakers were by no means ignorant of the grievances they had caused. Most of them hoped, however, that the League of Nations would later rectify the mistakes. Furthermore, the Allied and Associated Powers induced seven states (Austria, Hungary, Poland, Rumania, Greece, Czechoslovakia, and Yugoslavia) to sign treaties guaranteeing the rights of minorities. But the League of Nations, as stated earlier, achieved nothing in the way of rectifying the frontiers, and the treaties guaranteeing the rights of minorities were honored only when it served the purposes of the states involved to invoke them. For a time the minority groups clung to the hope of eventual reunion with their respective mother countries. When the League did nothing and the states in which they lived endeavored to absorb them into the dominating nationality, the minority groups became restive and intractable. In 1934 one Balkan observer wrote:

The spirit of Sarajevo is not dead. Indeed it refuses to be laid. It stalks uneasily through the gloomy ways of the Balkans and Central Europe, as restless as in the summer of 1914, lighting the petty blazes of international strife and fanning to flame the sparks of intra-national friction. And one of these local conflagrations could provide the spark that would fire the Balkan powder magazine with the explosion that would be the opening shot of another world war. . . . The problem of the ethnic minorities is possibly the most inflammable of the many factors interwoven in the complex discord of Central Europe.[2]

The so-called mother states were not slow to encourage their nationals who formed minority groups in other states to agitate for reunion. It was the Nazis who made the fullest use of the possibilities offered by the principle of self-determination. Long before they rose to power they repeatedly asked such questions as: If World War I was fought for the self-determination of nationalities, why was Austria forbidden to unite with Germany? Why were a large number of Germans included in other states? "The unity of all Germans in a Greater Germany" became one of their party slogans. After they had gained control

[2] *American Scholar*, vol. 3 (1934), p. 437.

of the government they invoked the principle of self-determination as their justification for annexing Austria and the country of the Sudeten. In 1939 this same principle was used as a pretext for the invasion of Poland, the event which kindled the fires of World War II.

In 1814 Castlereagh declared, "I go to Vienna, not to bring home trophies of victory, but to restore Europe to the paths of peace." This, too, was President Wilson's aim when he went to Paris. The Congress of Vienna was, however, more successful in restoring peace than the Conference of Paris. Whereas the treaties signed at Vienna resulted in a fairly durable peace, the treaty of Versailles established not peace but an uneasy armistice. Moreover, it contained the seeds of another conflict. Thus it became "the peace to end peace." Not that the treaty was wholly bad, as some writers have stated; nor were its provisions unbearable. It was undoubtedly severe in some respects, but not crushing. As a whole it was much softer than the peace which the Germans imposed on the Russians at Brest-Litovsk in 1918. Such a drastic step as the confiscation of all the German colonies was a blow rather to German prestige than to German economy. Germany's trade with her colonies was so small as to be negligible. As for reparations, after the invasion of the Ruhr the German payments were more than offset by Anglo-American loans.

The great weakness of the treaty of Versailles was that it was an unfair peace. It was a betrayal of the promise to make the Fourteen Points the basis of a peace. In most respects it did apply the principles of the Fourteen Points; in some few it did not. Included in the latter category was the creation of the Polish Corridor, the cutting of Danzig away from Germany, the confiscation of the German colonies without plebiscites, and the reparations settlement. The most indefensible clause of the Versailles Treaty was the so-called "war-guilt" clause (Article 231) whereby Germany accepted full responsibility for the war. This imputation that Germany and her allies were exclusively responsible for the world catastrophe was productive of much ill feeling. The Germans themselves felt that they had been tricked. They were resentful both of the charges brought against them and of the penalties exacted. Particularly the former aroused a burning sense of injustice. During the succeeding period they did not cease protesting against this accusation of guilt. Chancellor Wilhelm Marx said at the time of the adoption of the Dawes Plan by the German Reichstag: "The admission in the treaty of Versailles that Germany, by her aggression, caused the World War was wrung from us by superior force. Such a statement is contrary to historical fact and is consequently repudiated by the German government. The German people have a right to claim release from this false charge."

In his statement Chancellor Marx also pointed out the second great weakness of the Versailles settlement, namely that it was a dictated, not a negotiated, peace. No real attempt was made to understand the psychology or enter into the feelings of the vanquished. The Germans were simply instructed to sign on the dotted line without any oral negotiation. In 1922 Signor Nitti, who was at the time prime minister of Italy, said: "It will remain forever a terrible precedent in modern history that against all pledges, all precedents and all traditions the representatives of Germany were never even heard." The Germans felt that they had been treated as inferiors. As early as June 29, 1919, a Berlin newspaper said in an editorial: "The German people will again strive to attain that place among the nations of the world to which they are entitled. Then, vengeance for 1919!" Not many years later Hitler began to refer to the treaty, not as the treaty of Versailles, but as the "Versailles Diktat (Dictation)."

Time and again the Germans asked for a revision of the treaty, but without results. Article 19 of the League Covenant made provisions for the reconsideration of treaties which had become unfair, but the League members made no use of this article. France, convinced that European peace and French security were assured so long as the treaty enforced inequality for Germany, staunchly opposed any change whatsoever in the treaty. Her associates, Poland and the Little Entente, joined her in upholding the *status quo*. Thus the treaty divided Europe into two camps. On the one hand there were France and her associates, who insisted that not one iota of the settlement be changed; on the other, the revisionist states, which included Germany, Austria, Hungary, and Bulgaria. The conflict between these two groups was one of the main causes of European unrest. Ironically enough, the mistakes of the treaty of Versailles and the refusal of the Allies to revise it placed in Hitler's hands one of the most powerful of his ideological weapons for the destruction of German democracy.

While Germany was enjoying economic prosperity during the period from 1925 to 1929 there was a growing tendency on the part of the German people to accept the treaty, at least for the time being. Although the hysterical voices of Adolf Hitler and Joseph Goebbels continued during this period to blame the treaty of Versailles for all the evils of Europe, they made little headway; indeed as late as 1929 the Nazis were losing seats in the Reichstag. But the economic suffering of the succeeding years again made the Germans conscious of their position of inferiority and ready to listen to anyone who promised to raise

them from it. It was Hitler's great opportunity, and he exploited it to
the full. The Allies might still have spiked his oratorical guns by revising the treaty during the years from 1930 to 1933. In 1931 Chancellor
Bruening did explore the possibility of getting some support in Paris,
London, and Rome for a projected revision, but his reception in all
three capitals was a cold one. Hitler did not share Bruening's hope
for revision by international negotiation. No sooner did he rise to power
than he started on the road toward demolishing the treaty, a road
which finally led to Armageddon.

RESURGENCE OF THE NATIONALIST SPIRIT

It was this spirit which frustrated all attempts to cultivate an abiding
international attitude. During the period before World War I the nationalist spirit had dominated every department of human life, and it
had been one of the basic causes of the war. When many people realized
during the war that unrestrained nationalism was in large part responsible for the bloodshed, they became lukewarm converts to internationalism. As a background for the international spirit there was the
vast system of international cooperation in such fields as commerce,
industry, finance, the post, the telegraph, and the railroad. The new
attitude was also nourished by the speeches and proclamations of President Wilson. Many shared the hope that the League would become the
focus of a dynamic internationalism. And the first period was not disappointing. During the decade that succeeded World War I further important progress was made in fostering the international spirit, and
many came to believe that it would gradually prevail.

But the psychology which regards the common interests of nations
as infinitely more important than the interest of one nation did not
strike its roots deep enough to survive. The wave of internationalism
which had predominated since the end of World War I was replaced
after 1929 by a wave of nationalism. The major cause of the change
was the economic depression. So long as prosperity continued, the international spirit flourished in certain circles, but the coming of the depression led to a resurgence of the spirit of economic nationalism and
this in turn stimulated nationalism in other forms. As in the period
before World War I it again pervaded all phases of human life.

This nationalism manifested itself in its most intolerant form in the
totalitarian states. There it allied itself with the institution of dictatorship. Citizens were taught to worship the state as an end in itself, as
man's highest good. From this followed the doctrine that the state has
the right to satisfy "a need of expansion" even at the expense of another state. The dictators even resorted to aggressive measures as a

means of impressing their subjects, for dictators have never flourished on the defensive. In Germany, above all, the nationalist spirit was converted into a juggernaut of destruction.

HITLER UNDERMINES THE PEACE

The fact that the treaty of Versailles limited the German army or Reichswehr to 100,000 men serving twelve-year enlistments did not stop the Germans from secretly planning a full-size army that would raise the nation to its former military rank. "All the lessons of the war were thoroughly and systematically studied," Winston Churchill stated in *The Gathering Storm;* [3] "new principles of training and instructional courses of all kinds were introduced. All the existing manuals were rewritten." The German military leaders noted the mistakes that had been made in World War I and prescribed ways of avoiding them in the next war. In general, the Reichswehr of 100,000 men was made the training school for officers of the huge army they planned to build. In the training forbidden weapons were either imagined or represented by dummies. Similar evasions were also practised in the sphere of naval activity. Everything possible was done to keep the German navy and its spirit alive against the day when it could again take its place beside the other navies of the world. Meanwhile the Germans openly built pocket battleships and secretly constructed U-boats for which officers and men were trained in other countries.

In the last years of the Weimar Republic the question of rearming in defiance of the treaty of Versailles was openly discussed. General von Seeckt, head of the Reichswehr, in a public speech at Magdeburg in 1931 proposed an increase of the standing army to 200,000 effectives and the reduction of the period of enlistment to six years. During the next two years tanks and antitank units made their appearance in the Reichswehr. Thus rearmament was already under way when the Nazis took control. Hitler himself lost no time in promoting the rearmament program. At first he moved secretly so as not to excite the fears of the other European states. Only two months after he became chancellor, recruits in excess of 100,000 were enrolled in the Reichswehr. Early in 1934 the Reichswehr began to accept volunteers for a training period of one year. Military airfields were constructed in various parts of Germany and military planes disguised as commercial planes were used to train aviation personnel. By 1935 Hitler felt strong enough to announce his rearmament program publicly and to declare that since the other powers had not fulfilled their pledge to disarm, Germany must reintroduce conscription. He and the Nazi leaders then waited uneasily

[3] (1948), p. 45.

to see what would happen. When the other powers did nothing beyond making a few protests, the Nazis proceeded with their rearmament and troop-training program at a rate that was probably unparalleled up to that time. Before the end of 1936 Hitler could announce that Germany was "already in a state of war, only the guns have not gone off."

The fact that Hitler was rearming did not spur the other European powers into action. Both French and British politics were dominated by "peace-at-any-price" blocs. The governments of both countries were so preoccupied with internal developments that they were unwilling to spend money on armaments. When the French received information regarding the extent of German rearmament they did lengthen the term of universal military service from one to two years (March, 1935), but there was no plan of common action with other powers at a time when a resolute plan might have avoided disaster. The British, for their part, did little or nothing to bolster their land, sea, and air forces. Financial London was opposed to rearmament; in fact, not one of the British parties was advocating rearmament. The British mind, in general, was so completely blanketed with a psychological revulsion against war that it was not sensitive to danger. There were some Britons, however, who saw the danger, among them Winston Churchill. He kept sounding the alarm again and again, but only a few listened. Others ridiculed his statements regarding the extent of German rearmament. It was not until November, 1935, that many of the doubters realized the truth of his statements. By that time the Germans had an air force three or four times as strong as that of Great Britain. The British now began to arm feverishly, putting special emphasis on the land and air forces. Because she began to rearm two years too late, Britain was to reach the brink of disaster.

While he was rearming, Hitler repeatedly tried with honeyed words of peace to calm the misgivings his rearmament program was arousing in other countries. In a broadcast speech in October, 1933, he said, "The history of the last one hundred years should in its changing course have taught France and Germany that essential and enduring changes are no longer to be gained by sacrifice of blood. . . . No one could demand that millions of men in the flower of youth should be annihilated for the sake of a readjustment of indefinite scope of our present frontier." Several weeks later he said, "I am not crazy enough to want a war. . . . The German people have but one wish — to be happy in their own way and to be left in peace." In January of the next year he stated, "I can give the assurance that this sovereign nation has no other wish than to apply joyfully the strength and weight of her political, moral and economic resources, not only for the healing of wounds which the past has inflicted on the human kind, but towards the cooperation

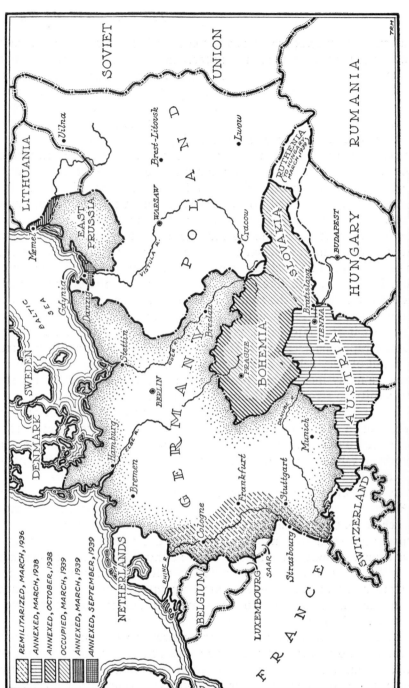

THE EXPANSION OF GERMANY BEFORE WORLD WAR II

REMILITARIZED, MARCH, 1936
ANNEXED, MARCH, 1938
ANNEXED, OCTOBER, 1938
OCCUPIED, MARCH, 1939
ANNEXED, MARCH, 1939
ANNEXED, SEPTEMBER, 1939

SOVIET UNION
RUMANIA
LITHUANIA
Vilna
Brest-Litovsk
Lwow
POLAND
EAST PRUSSIA
WARSAW
Cracow
RUTHENIA (TO HUNGARY MARCH, 1939)
HUNGARY
BUDAPEST
Memel
Gdynia
Danzig
VISTULA R.
SLOVAKIA
Bratislava
Stettin
Breslau
BALTIC SEA
ODER R.
BOHEMIA
PRAGUE
VIENNA
AUSTRIA
SWEDEN
DENMARK
Hamburg
BERLIN
ELBE R.
Danube R.
Munich
Bremen
GERMANY
Frankfurt
Stuttgart
Cologne
RHINE R.
SAAR
Strasbourg
SWITZERLAND
NETHERLANDS
BELGIUM
LUXEMBOURG
FRANCE

of all cultured and civilized nations." His actions and secret statements, however, belied his public utterances. As early as September, 1934, Hjalmar Schacht, Hitler's finance minister, stated in a report that "the Reich Ministry of Economy has been charged with the economic preparation for war." When Hitler was asked in 1934 by one of his confidants, "Do you seriously intend to fight the West?" he retorted, "What else do you think we are arming for?" [4]

In March, 1936, Hitler made the next move. He sent 30,000 troops to occupy the Rhineland in order to reassert German sovereignty there and to proclaim Germany's right to refortify it. Many of the German military leaders expected armed opposition to this move. Accordingly Hitler, whose preparations for war were not as yet complete, gave his generals orders to evacuate the Rhineland if the French should mobilize and cross the frontier. Much to the surprise of the Germans, nothing happened. Next Hitler strengthened his position by drawing closer to Italy. Mussolini, who like Hitler had been "a lone wolf" up to this time, was angered by the sanctions invoked against him in the Ethiopian conflict. Both felt that they had much to gain by cooperation. As Hitler put it at a later time, "For us National Socialists . . . the attempted rapprochement with Italy is not a matter of sentiment, but the result of very selfish considerations."

Before many months had passed, both Hitler and Mussolini saw an opportunity to strengthen the cause of fascism in Europe by intervening in the Spanish civil war on the side of General Franco. They believed that a strong dictatorship in Spain, one that would cooperate with Germany and Italy, was well worth the sacrifice of some men and materials. Furthermore, intervention offered them an opportunity to test their military equipment and strategy in preparation for a greater struggle. Another consideration was the fact that a Franco victory would hem France in between two hostile fascist powers. For a time France and Britain sought to discourage intervention by sponsoring a neutral policy; in 1936 a Nonintervention Committee was even set up by a group of powers which included Germany and Italy. But the whole thing was a farce from the beginning. Neither Germany nor Italy respected the agreement. As the civil war continued they sent more and more men and material into Spain until a victory for Franco was achieved.

The failure of the other European powers to do anything beyond voicing mild protests seems to have convinced Hitler that he could do much as he pleased. On January 30, 1937, in a speech before the Reichstag to commemorate four years of Nazi rule, Hitler openly announced to the world that he would no longer be bound by the treaty

[4] Rauschning, *The Voice of Destruction* (1940), p. 119.

of Versailles. When the other powers again did nothing the Führer decided that the time was propitious for the first of a series of territorial aggrandizements. His immediate goal was the annexation of Austria, which, he had stated in *Mein Kampf*, was "a life task to be achieved by any and every means." On February 13, 1938, Hitler summoned Chancellor Schuschnigg of Austria to Berchtesgaden and there tried to browbeat him into coordinating his government with that of the Nazis. Schuschnigg conceded nothing, but on 'his return to Austria he did elevate five pro-Nazis to ministerial posts. Failing to find any foreign support for his government, he announced, in a last desperate attempt to save Austria, that a plebiscite would be held on the question of Anschluss. This Hitler could not permit. It might have upset his applecart. Consequently he demanded that the plebiscite be called off on threat of immediate invasion. Unable to cope with the situation any longer, Schuschnigg resigned, and Dr. Seyss-Inquart, the Austrian Nazi leader, invited German troops in to "restore order." The Nazi forces marched in at once and on March 13 the union of Germany and Austria was proclaimed.

HITLER DEVOURS CZECHOSLOVAKIA

Having achieved the Anschluss without opposition from the other European states beyond the usual protests, Hitler waited only two months before he moved into position for an onslaught on Czechoslovakia — this despite the fact that on March 11, the day the Nazi forces entered Austria, Goering had assured the Czech minister in Berlin that Germany had no designs on Czechoslovakia and had later repeated the assurance on Hitler's behalf. Because of the German position in Austria, only an unfortified frontier separated Czechoslovakia from the Nazi forces. In May, 1938, the Nazi radio volubly denounced the "oppression" of the Sudeten Germans in Czechoslovakia, and German troops were massed along the Czechoslovak frontiers. Though the Nazi government declared the troop movements to be "routine," the Czechoslovak government at once strengthened its border defenses and also petitioned France and Britain for assurances of help in case the Germans moved into Czechoslovakia. When both powers responded by pledging help, Hitler saw that annexation of the Sudeten districts was fraught with the threat of war. For the time being he did nothing.

At this point the British prime minister, Neville Chamberlain (the man with the umbrella), boldly stepped into the picture in an effort to find an honorable alternative to the catastrophe of war. Chamberlain had assumed the premiership in 1937. His government had made no adequate preparations for war; if war could not be averted, Britain would need time to prepare for it. Consequently he sent Hitler a telegram (September 14, 1938) suggesting a meeting "with a view to trying to find a peaceful solution." The mistake Chamberlain made was in his judgment of Hitler. As a diplomatist of the honorable school, he was naive enough to believe that no European leader would break his promise. Chamberlain had never met a man who was as cunning a wolf as Hitler. The sheep's clothing completely misled him until he paid a visit to the wolf's lair and saw the ugly fangs.

Hitler replied to the telegram that he could see the British prime minister the following afternoon at his Berchtesgaden retreat. Accordingly Chamberlain and his umbrella boarded a plane the next day (September 15) with the best wishes of the British cabinet. At Berchtesgaden he learned in a three-hour conversation with Hitler that the latter was determined to give the Sudeten Germans the right to join the Reich. "He declared categorically," Chamberlain told the House of Commons on September 28, "that rather than wait he would be prepared to risk a world war." [5] At the time Hitler's statement was regarded by many as a gigantic bluff, but confidential papers captured by the United States Army at the end of World War II show that he and the German high command were ready to risk a world war to achieve their objective. The revelation of Hitler's plans shocked the British prime minister, but he refused to sanction the incorporation of the Sudeten districts in the German Reich even though Hitler promised peace in return. Chamberlain told Hitler that he must consult his colleagues before giving an answer.

Back in London, Chamberlain discussed Hitler's demands with the cabinet, and on Sunday, September 18, Premier Daladier and Foreign Minister Bonnet of France traveled to London for a consultation with British leaders. The representatives of both governments agreed that the principle of self-determination was to be applied to the Sudetens; in other words, that Hitler could transfer to Germany all districts in which 50 per cent or more of the inhabitants were Germans. To this both the French and the British added a guarantee of the new Czechoslovak frontiers. The news caused dismay in Prague. The Czech cabinet termed it "the basest betrayal in history," but they had no recourse but to yield. On September 22 Chamberlain again boarded a plane to meet Hitler at Godesberg. There, much to his amazement, he discovered that Hitler had made his demands considerably more drastic. The Führer was determined to occupy the Sudeten territory with the German army no later than October 1, and stated that he would brook no delay. Chamberlain refused to

[5] Chamberlain, *In Search of Peace* (1939), p. 187.

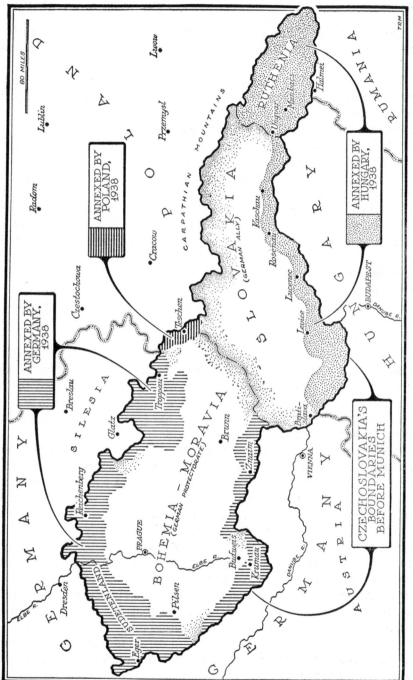

THE DISMEMBERMENT OF CZECHOSLOVAKIA

accept the terms. When Hitler sought to continue the conversations the following day, the British prime minister said that he must again consult his cabinet.

Upon Chamberlain's return to London both the French and British governments informed the Czech cabinet that they were no longer opposed to Czech mobilization. While the Czech army was being mobilized, the French called more men to the colors and the British put their fleet in readiness. From all quarters frantic last-hour efforts for peace were being made. Instead of sending his forces into the Sudeten district, Hitler decided to try once more to achieve his aims by diplomacy. Mussolini, who was not ready for war, appears to have influenced the decision to some extent. The Führer accepted Chamberlain's suggestion of a four-power conference. On September 29, 1938, Chamberlain, Daladier, Hitler, and Mussolini met at Munich. Russia was not invited; nor was Czechoslovakia represented. After long discussions the four men set their signatures to the agreement dismembering Czechoslovakia. Both the French and the British had yielded. Ostensibly Hitler made slight concessions in consenting to the delimitation of the new frontiers by an international commission and in agreeing that German troops would occupy the Sudeten districts by stages over a period of ten days rather than completely on October 1; but in almost every other respect the agreement conformed to the Godesberg terms. The text of the agreement was at once dispatched to the Czech government, whose only alternative to destruction was to accept.

In London Neville Chamberlain was the hero of the hour. On his return he announced that he had brought "peace with honor." "I believe," he said, "it is peace for our time." The cheers of the populace and the votes of the House of Commons, which approved the settlement by a vote of 366 to 144, expressed agreement with his conviction. The London *Times* stated that "no conqueror returning from a victory on the battlefield has come home adorned with nobler laurels than Mr. Chamberlain from Munich yesterday"; the *Daily Telegraph* declared, "No one can deny the honours of a noble battle nobly won"; the *Daily Express* said confidently, "There will be no European war involving Britain this year, or next year either." Among the dissenting voices was that of Winston Churchill, who rightly said that there was little honor about the settlement and that far from representing peace it would inevitably lead to war. Before many months had passed, Munich was styled "the great diplomatic defeat of the century. It was the culmination of a series of shameful submissions that began in 1936 when German troops entered the demilitarized Rhineland."

Promptly on October 1 the German army crossed the Czech frontier. The clause providing for international supervision proved to be a farce. Hitler took exactly what he had said he would take. The rest of Czechoslovakia became a satellite of Germany.

THE DARKENING SKY

Just before he occupied the Sudeten districts Hitler assured the world that "the Sudetenland is the last territorial claim I have to make in Europe." At the time of the Munich settlement he was ready to guarantee the new frontiers of Czechoslovakia. In a speech in Berlin on September 26 he stated emphatically that he had no wish to include other races than Germans in the population of his realm. More specifically he said, "We do not want any Czechs." But Hitler's appetite for territory was insatiable. He now turned away from the idea of self-determination to that of *Lebensraum* (living space) and in flagrant disregard of all his pledges made ready to swallow the rest of Czechoslovakia. In March, 1939, he summoned President Hacha of Czechoslovakia to Berchtesgaden and there announced the decision. "I give you one hour to sign the capitulation of your country," Hitler said. Old Hacha replied with tears, "I cannot — I cannot sign." "Very well," Hitler retorted, "tomorrow our planes will reduce Prague to ashes; millions of women and children will die. And you will have killed them." Hacha yielded. The next morning at nine o'clock Nazi troops entered Prague. Bohemia and Moravia were annexed outright to Germany, while Slovakia was set up as an independent state under German protection. Ruthenia, the last province of the former Czechoslovakian state, was occupied by Hungarian troops, undoubtedly with Hitler's sanction.

Nor did Hitler stop with the destruction of Czechoslovakia. A week later he demanded that Lithuania cede to Germany its chief city and only seaport, Memel, which had been a part of Germany before World War I. The Lithuanians could hardly refuse, and on March 23 Hitler added an area of more than a thousand square miles to Germany. Meanwhile Mussolini, who shared the Führer's opinion that the French and British leaders were nonentities, had decided to join in "the game of grab." While Hitler was annexing vast territories Mussolini had succeeded only in acquiring Ethiopia, a possession of doubtful value. In emulation of his German ally he sent the Italian legions to occupy Albania on Good Friday (April 7), 1939. Within a few days the country was overrun and put under Italian control. Having incorporated Albania into the Italian state Mussolini shouted from the Palazzo Venezia: "We regard peace as a catastrophe for civilization and mankind." It did appear as if the dictators could do much as they pleased with impunity.

The blows of Hitler and Mussolini at the foundations of world peace finally aroused the French and British governments to a full sense of danger. Even Neville Chamberlain was now convinced that Britain must rearm as quickly as possible. Feverish activity followed also in diplomacy. Britain pledged assistance to Poland, Greece, and Rumania in the event that their independence was threatened, and France immediately made similar declarations. Steps were also taken toward establishing a common front among France, Britain, and Russia against further aggression.

All this did not, however, induce Hitler to mend his ways. Convinced that France and Britain would fight only if they were actually attacked, he made no attempt to disguise his next moves. In a speech before the Reichstag (April 28, 1939) he demanded that Poland return the port of Danzig to German control and that she also grant Germany a road and railroad route with extraterritorial rights through the Corridor. In 1934 he had signed a nonaggression treaty with Poland and as late as January, 1939, both he and Ribbentrop, his foreign minister, had declared that the former enmity between the two countries had been replaced by a true friendship. Less than three months later, however, the Führer used the Anglo-Polish mutual assistance agreement as a pretext for denouncing his nonaggression pact with Poland. A few weeks later he also moved closer to Italy by concluding (May 22) a military alliance with Mussolini which provided for consultation of the two parties if the interests of either were threatened. Arrangements were also made for cooperation in case of war. Thus the so-called Rome-Berlin Axis was firmly established.

Meanwhile the French and British were making little progress in their negotiations with Soviet Russia. The Russians could not forget that they had previously been ignored by the French and British; and the British, particularly the upper classes, still put little faith in any agreement with Russia. This distrust of the Bolsheviks was carefully nurtured by Hitler, who posed as the defender of private property and Christian civilization. But at the beginning of August, 1939, the situation seemed favorable for concluding a defensive alliance against Germany. Military missions from France and Britain were received in Moscow and began their work on August 11. The expected announcement was not, however, forthcoming. The talks were protracted, with the Soviets repeatedly introducing objections, complications, and delays. Both French and British representatives were blithely unaware that crucial talks were taking place behind their backs.

Suddenly on August 24 there came, like a bolt out of the blue, the announcement that a ten-year nonaggression pact had been concluded between the Soviets and the Nazis. The negotiations had been conducted with such secrecy that the announcement was almost as great a surprise to the inner-circle Nazis as it was to the average Frenchman, Briton, or American. The shock was particularly severe because of the open enmity between the Communists and the Nazis. Not only had Hitler expressed a glowing hatred for "die Bolsheviken" in *Mein Kampf*, but "Down with the Communists" had been one of the chief slogans in his rise to power. "Never forget," he had written, "that the rulers of present-day Russia are common bloodstained criminals; that they are the scum of humanity." Having set a tentative date for the invasion of Poland, he was ready temporarily to submerge his antipathy in order to achieve his aims. What he and the German generals feared above all was a two-front war, and an alliance with Russia would eliminate that threat. On the day before the pact was signed Hitler told his top generals, "I have decided to go with Stalin! For the first time in history we have to fight on only one front." Thus the way was open from the Nazi side for a rapprochement between the two most powerful continental nations.

Stalin, too, the supreme opportunist, was not averse to burying the hatchet. A number of reasons inclined him to do so. First, there was war in the air, and a nonaggression pact with Germany would enable him to remain neutral. He may even have had dreams of an exhausted Europe which he could dominate. Second, a pact with Germany offered the "anti-imperialist" Bolsheviks an opportunity to engage in imperialist ventures. Third, he was angry at the French and British because they had largely ignored Soviet Russia up to that time. Moscow made the first of the overtures leading to the diplomatic reversal when the Soviet ambassador in Berlin expressed the hope in the spring of 1939 that Russo-German relations "might become better and better." Soon thereafter the two countries opened discussions on trade matters, which before long expanded into cautious political parleys. While the conferences continued, Hitler, ever distrustful of the Russians, was on tenterhooks fearing that Stalin would outwit him. The Nazi ambassador to Russia mirrored the Führer's fears when he wrote: "We must be extremely cautious in this field as long as it is not certain that possible proposals from our side will not be used by the Kremlin only to exert pressure on England and France." As the time set for the invasion of Poland approached, Hitler became increasingly anxious. His fears were not stilled until the treaty was signed in Moscow on August 23, in the presence of Stalin, by Ribbentrop for Germany and Molotov for Russia.

The pact pledged the contracting parties to refrain from acts of aggression against one another for a period of ten years. Equally significant but unannounced was a secret protocol signed at the same time. This protocol divided eastern Europe into Russian and German spheres. All territory east of a line drawn from the Baltic to the Black Sea was to be in the Russian sphere and everything west of the line was to be left to the Germans. Thus "anti-imperialist" Russia was given a free hand in Estonia, Latvia, and Finland. In the south she was to regain Bessarabia, which she had lost after World War I. As for Poland, the line split her territory into halves, the eastern one assigned to Russia, the western to Germany. In his scheme of things Hitler regarded the concessions to Russia as being worth while. "Let us think of the pact," he said confidentially, "as securing our rear." He would first crush Poland, then overwhelm the West, and finally settle accounts with Russia. That was the itinerary of conquest which he charted and to which he adhered. But the outcome was not what he expected.

Hitler, seeing his aims accomplished by the pact with Russia, became bolder in his demands. At the same time the Nazi press and radio poured an avalanche of abuse on the Poles, accusing them of perpetrating every possible atrocity on the German minority. All this, following upon the Russo-German pact, was highly disquieting, but the British and French did not retreat. Mr. Chamberlain stated emphatically, "Whatever may prove to be the nature of the German-Soviet agreement, it cannot alter Great Britain's obligations," and France stood equally firm. When the French called up fresh reserves, the British reiterated their determination to support Poland. Meanwhile President Roosevelt sent a series of appeals against war to Hitler and Mussolini, and others sent Hitler pleas for peace — the Pope, the queen of Holland, and the king of Belgium, the last speaking in the name of the ruling heads of Norway, Sweden, Denmark, Holland, Belgium, Luxembourg, and Finland.

All this had little effect on Hitler. Drunk with power, he adhered to his determination to overwhelm Poland. As early as August 22 he had summoned his top generals and had briefed them for the invasion. "I have Poland where I want her," he told them. In informing them about the plans he said: "No one will ask the victor whether or not he told the truth. In starting the war it is not right that matters, but victory." Nevertheless, in the succeeding days he made one more attempt to keep Britain and France neutral. On August 25 he summoned Sir Nevile Henderson, the British ambassador to Germany, and requested him to fly to London for the purpose of assuring his government of German friendship after the Polish question had been solved. He had tried this trick once too often. The British ambassador answered at once that the Polish question could be settled only by peaceful negotiation. On the same day Chamberlain announced the conclusion of a five-year mutual assistance agreement with Poland, and on August 28 he suggested to Hitler that direct negotiation with Poland was the best means of settling the question. The Führer appeared to accept the proposal, telling the British ambassador that he was ready to receive a Polish plenipotentiary the next day. On August 31 the Polish ambassador sought to obtain an interview with Ribbentrop, but was not received until evening and was then informed that the time for negotiation had expired.

At dawn the next morning (September 1, 1939) the Nazi armies struck. While the infantry and mechanized forces were crossing the frontier, the German Luftwaffe dropped bombs on strategic targets. If Hitler thought the democracies would stand idly by, he was certainly disillusioned. They had, it is true, only begun to arm and were therefore not prepared to fight; but they were determined to carry out their obligations. On the evening of the same day the British and French ambassadors handed Foreign Minister Ribbentrop statements proclaiming their intention of adhering to their promises to aid Poland unless the German government suspended all aggressive action at once. When Hitler did not reply, the British sent an ultimatum on September 3. This time he answered, but in an evasive, unsatisfactory manner. Britain at once declared war and France followed suit on the same day.

World War II: the Period of Axis Predominance

THE CONQUEST OF POLAND $\quad$ AT the outset of World War II, as in World War I, the power of the offensive was on the side of the Germans. Hitler and his general staff had hoped that the British and French would not keep their pledges to Poland, but they stood firm, and the prospect of a two-front war again loomed before the German high command. This Hitler wished to avoid at all costs; he was determined that the German legions should not bog down as they had in 1914. Hence he sent into Poland a force strong enough to overwhelm the Poles completely before the British and French could launch a major offensive in the West. The German armies that moved into Poland on the morning of September 1 were probably the best-equipped force on the face of the globe at the time. It was a motorized force which could move at a pace that dwarfed all previous speed records, and it was equipped with the latest inventions of military science, including tanks of various sizes, antitank guns, reconnaissance and fighter planes, dive bombers, and antiaircraft artillery.

The plans for the invasion had been carefully laid. Two main bodies of troops were to enter Poland, one to the north and the other to the south. Once on Polish territory they were gradually to converge on Warsaw. To meet the attack by the German mechanized forces the Poles had an army with fighting spirit but without modern weapons.[1] It was the Polish horse against the German motor. Having foreseen the German plan of campaign, the Polish military leaders sought to

[1] The Poles had one armored brigade and 12 cavalry brigades.

prevent their armies from being caught in a pincers movement. Their plan called for a gradual retreat to the line formed roughly by the rivers Narew, Bug, Vistula, and San. There the main Polish forces hoped to make a stand until the British and French could send help. But the Polish general staff had underestimated the speed of the German advance, a mode of warfare designated by the word *Blitzkrieg* (lightning war). At dawn on September 1 the German Luftwaffe (air force) struck. Swarms of planes dropped bombs on more than thirty key cities and on the stations of the Polish air force, which was eliminated before it could do much to defend Poland. The bombing of the principal railway and communication centers was an important factor in delaying troop mobilizations and troop movements. By September 5 Poland was at the mercy of the German war machine.

Although western Poland had been overrun by the Germans, Polish patriots still cherished the hope that effective resistance could be organized in the east. Even this hope was soon blasted. On September 17 the Russians suddenly invaded eastern Poland in what they styled "armed intervention to protect their own frontiers." In the secret protocol to the nonaggression pact between Germany and Russia (August 23, 1939), by which eastern Europe was divided into German and Russian spheres of influence, it had been agreed that Finland, Estonia, Latvia, and Bessarabia were to be in the Soviet sphere and Lithuania in the German sphere. But the question whether an independent rump Polish state was to be permitted to exist was to be determined by the course of events. When it became obvious that Poland could not resist long, Stalin feared that the Germans would not stop on the line formed by the Narew, Vistula, and San rivers. After sending Russian troops into eastern Poland, Stalin on September 20 proposed a territorial revision which would do away with Poland entirely. In the new agreement Germany received a larger share of Poland in return for renouncing her claim to all but a small strip of Lithuania. With the Russians occupying eastern Poland, Polish resistance was over except in Warsaw and a few other pockets. Even Warsaw after a heroic resistance capitulated on the 27th, and two days later the German foreign office announced the division of Poland between Russia and Germany. In the central part of southern Poland a Polish state was set up under German protection, but it was small and hopelessly landlocked. The former Polish government fled the country and finally set up headquarters in London. In Poland a vigorous underground movement developed against the Nazis, a movement which the Nazis were unable to crush by torture and mass executions.

THE RUSSO-FINNISH STRUGGLE

Having annexed the eastern part of Poland, the Russian government took steps toward establishing its rule in the other states allotted to the Russian sphere in the Russo-German treaty. Under pressure the Estonian government signed a treaty on September 29 which gave Soviet Russia the rights of military garrison and of establishing naval and air bases in Estonia. Similar treaties were signed with Latvia and Lithuania. Next the Soviet government approached the Finns with a demand to lease a section of Finnish territory for military purposes. When the Finns, believing that such a lease would jeopardize their independence, refused the communist press launched a campaign of denunciation against them, even going to the ridiculous length of stating that the Finns were preparing to attack Russia. It was all reminiscent of Nazi technique before the invasion of Poland; in fact, the communist press even hinted that Finland might meet the fate of Poland.

After the campaign of abuse the Soviet government on November 28 denounced its nonaggression treaty with Finland, and two days later Russian troops marched into Finland at a number of points. The general opinion was that the Finns could not stand up long before the Russian attack, but they surprised the world. From behind the Mannerheim Line they fought back so fiercely that not one of the Russian spearheads was able to reach its objectives by the end of the year. Two months later the Finns had to give way before tremendous numbers and superior equipment. On March 6, 1940, the Finnish government sent a delegation to negotiate peace. The terms which the delegation finally accepted were more severe than those offered earlier by the Soviet government. They required the cession of the entire Karelian Isthmus with Viborg (Viipuri), the second largest city of Finland, in addition to other pieces of territory including islands in the Gulf of Finland. The Russians also received the right to construct a railroad across Finland to Sweden. With Russian bases scattered over her territory, Finland was placed militarily at the mercy of Russia. The extension of its domination over Estonia, Latvia, and Lithuania and in part over Finland marked the first phase in the imperialist program of the Soviet government.

While the Russians were establishing their control over the border states there was little activity on the western front. Neither the British nor the French were ready to attack Germany. The French, after a series of skirmishes in the direction of the German Siegfried Line, fell back to the extensive fortifications called the Maginot Line, where they were joined by a British expeditionary force. The Germans, for their part, manned the newly completed Siegfried Line. Both sides pursued a policy of watchful waiting. In short, the Blitzkrieg turned into a Sitzkrieg (sitting war) or, as it was labelled by some, a "phony war." On the Allied side many began to wonder if Hitler had not missed his great opportunity in not overwhelming France and Britain before they had strengthened their forces.

If all was quiet on the western front, this was not true on the seas. When the war broke out, the British navy at once proceeded to drive the German merchant ships off the sea as it had done in 1914. Nor were the Nazis inactive. Hitler's navy was not, of course, strong enough to challenge the British fleet in combat, to say nothing of the combined fleets of Britain and France. The Nazis did, however, use what naval strength they had in an attempt to "starve out" the British. It was a repetition of the strategy they had used in World War I. Because of the lack of strength in surface ships, the campaign was again launched with U-boats or submarines. U-boats, stationed at various points along the routes usually used by British merchantmen, went into action immediately after war was declared and in a week sank eleven British merchant ships. British losses during the first two months totaled fifty-four ships. Two outstanding feats of the early German submarine campaign were the sinking of the 22,500-ton battleship *H.M.S. Courageous* and that of the *H.M.S. Royal Oak,* a 29,150-ton battleship. In the latter sinking more than 800 lives were lost. After the adoption of the convoy system the number of sinkings by German submarines decreased sharply as it had in World War I. To support the submarine campaign the German Admiralty sent out raiders to prey on British commerce. Particularly effective in this respect were the pocket battleships, but the protection of British ships by convoys limited even their activity. Further heavy toll of British shipping was taken by the magnetic mines which the Germans laid by means of submarines and seaplanes in the narrow channels of the Thames estuary. But the result of the German effort was far from "starving out" the British. By March, 1940, only 3 per cent of the British merchant fleet had been sunk.

THE NAZIS OVERWHELM FIVE NATIONS

Victory in Poland and the treaty with Soviet Russia permitted the Germans to turn their attention elsewhere without any great concern about the eastern frontier. In many circles it was believed that the western front would become the theatre of active operations, and the Nazis encouraged this belief by concentrating troops along the western front and making a few feints in the direction of the Maginot Line.

Their actual aim was in an entirely different direction. Hitler purposed to extend the Nazi control over Denmark and Norway. The strategical aims of this move were: (1) to establish air bases in Norway from which Britain and British shipping could be attacked; (2) to acquire harbors on the west coast of Norway from which submarines and naval units could operate in the North Atlantic; (3) to gain an additional food supply from Denmark and Norway and also to stop the British from getting it. Early on the morning of April 9, 1940, a Nazi force crossed the border into Denmark and proceeded with such speed that it soon appeared before the royal palace at Copenhagen. King Christian, seeing that resistance was hopeless, asked his people to accept the situation. Thus in a few hours the Nazis established their control over Denmark.

Simultaneously the Nazis also moved against Norway. Hitler had no intention of attacking the Norwegian army, which numbered only 114,500 men. For months the Nazi propaganda machine had been working on susceptible elements in Norway and had created a considerable body of sympathizers under Major Vidkun Quisling, whose name has become an international synonym for traitor. He was the leader of the so-called "Fifth Column" which was waiting to aid the invaders. The Fifth Columnists held both airfields and ports pending the arrival of Nazi troops. Airborne troops were flown into Norway in considerable numbers, while seaborne troops, under a powerful naval escort, approached the coast of Norway. Only at Kristiansand, where a fort battery sank the cruiser Karlsruhe, did the Nazis meet serious resistance. Before the Allies were ready to act, the Nazis had a firm grip on the country. Several small Franco-British expeditionary forces did, it is true, land in central Norway on April 15 and the succeeding days; but they were able to do little, since they had no airfield from which they could launch fighter planes to protect them against German bombers. When the Nazis threatened to envelop the expeditionary forces with their mechanized detachments, all expeditionary troops, except those stationed at Narvik in the far north of Norway, were withdrawn (May 2).

The conquest of Denmark and Norway had political repercussions in both France and Britain. In France the failure of the government to deliver a counterstroke to the invasion of the Scandinavian countries caused the overthrow of Daladier as premier. His successor was Paul Reynaud. In Britain the subjugation of Denmark and Norway brought the increasing dissatisfaction with the government and its foreign policy into the open. Chamberlain's record as an appeaser of dictators, his lack of vigor in the prosecution of the war, and his Micawberish optimism caused a revolt against him even in the Conservative Party itself. When he sought to defend himself before the House of Commons there were boos, catcalls, and cries of "You missed the bus." [2] The demand became insistent for a truly national government with representatives of all the major parties. Chamberlain's request for the cooperation of all parties under his leadership drew only a resounding "No." On May 10, 1940, he resigned. King George then asked Winston Churchill, who had been a member of Chamberlain's cabinet, to form a national government. After forming a three-party coalition government Churchill immediately took steps to increase the output of aircraft and to strengthen the country in every possible way. In a speech before the House of Commons (May 13) he told the British people that he could offer them no quick road to victory but only "blood, toil, sweat and tears." "Our only aim is victory," he said, "for without victory there is no survival."

There was considerable speculation as to where the Nazis would strike next. On January 30, 1937, Hitler had said, "The German government has assured Belgium and Holland of its readiness to recognize and guarantee those states as untouchable and neutral regions for all time." But by 1940 he seemed to have forgotten that he ever made such a statement. It was now expedient for him to include Belgium, Luxembourg, and the Netherlands in the ring of states controlled by the Nazis. Possession of these countries would give the Germans bases for an attack on both France and England, increase their industrial resources, and afford them further sources of food supply. Moreover, it would enable them to outflank the Maginot Line and to invade France across the unfortified Belgian frontier. At dawn on May 10 the Nazi legions moved into the three countries. Luxembourg, which had no army, was occupied without a contest, but the other two countries resisted with every resource at their command.

Again the Nazis adjusted their Blitzkrieg methods to fit a particular situation. Especially noteworthy in this campaign was the use of parachute troops on an unexampled scale to capture airfields and disrupt mobilization facilities. The first blow fell on the Netherlands. Soon after midnight on May 9 numerous parachutists were dropped on the Dutch airfields; others came down at various places to occupy strategic bridges and to join with groups of the Dutch Fifth Column. At the same time a powerful German armored force entered the Netherlands. To impede the progress of the invaders until help arrived from France and England, the Dutch had flooded wide areas, constructed pillboxes at strategic points, and mined important bridges. But the Nazis moved so quickly that they captured the bridges before

[2] A reference to Chamberlain's earlier statement that Hitler had "missed the bus" in not overwhelming France and Britain immediately after the fall of Poland.

they could be blown up; and they used shallow-draft rubber boats to cross the flooded areas. On May 13 Queen Wilhelmina and some of her ministers crossed over to England, and on the next day, after Nazi planes had bombed the heart of Rotterdam into a heap of rubble, the Dutch laid down their arms. By their Blitzkrieg methods the Germans had overwhelmed the Dutch in five days.

Two weeks later the Belgians also surrendered. In 1914 Belgium had been able to muster only 120,000 men for her field army. This time the Belgian regulars numbered 170,000. Another 480,000 men with some training were mobilized, but there was not sufficient modern equipment for all of them. The German air force disrupted communications so completely that the Belgians were unable to organize a defense with the equipment they had. Meanwhile mechanized forces moved in rapidly and within a few days occupied Brussels, Louvain, Malines, and Antwerp. At this juncture the cabinet urged King Leopold to follow the example of Queen Wilhelmina of the Netherlands and leave the country, but he refused to do so. By May 28 the military situation had become so hopeless that King Leopold, to prevent further bloodshed, ordered his men to surrender. Leopold was then interned in his castle on the outskirts of Brussels.

While Belgium was being overrun detachments of German mechanized divisions drove clear across northern France to the channel coast at Abbeville. This surprise move isolated large Allied forces leaving them only the port of Dunkirk as an avenue of escape. According to ordinary reckoning these forces were doomed, for they were greatly outnumbered by the forces which surrounded them on all sides but the sea. The Germans were so certain they had the Allied forces securely trapped that they made an announcement to this effect. To make escape as difficult as possible hundreds of German planes literally bombed Dunkirk into a shambles. But all this did not convince the Allies that their forces could not be saved. For a time British and French destroyers were able to evacuate troops from the Dunkirk docks. When the docks were destroyed by German bombers a motley flotilla of small shallow-draft ships, including merchantmen, passenger steamers, private yachts, fishing smacks, and even tug-drawn barges, were pressed into service under the protection of French and British battleships. For six days (May 30–June 4) the evacuation continued, while German bombers, despite the heavy antiaircraft fire, took a toll of thirteen British and French destroyers and some smaller ships. The operation did, however, succeed in evacuating more than 330,000 British, French, and Belgian troops, thereby making the military disaster appear almost like a victory. Winston Churchill called it "a miracle of deliverance."

THE FALL OF FRANCE

After twenty-six consecutive days of fighting, the Germans, it was generally believed, would need some time to reorganize their striking forces. Actually the Germans still had motorized divisions which had not seen service and these were now used for another lightning campaign which resulted in the fall of France. The drive, launched on June 5, had as its first aim the capture of the French ports. A second phase, inaugurated on June 9, aimed to take the Maginot Line from the rear. For several days the French held, but then the superiority of the German mechanized forces prevailed. Bombers and tanks with more than a million men behind them began to smash all opposition and on June 13 it was evident that General Weygand, the French commander, had lost control of the military situation. On the French side there appears to have been a total lack of understanding of the character of the war. The French general staff, in spite of what had happened in Poland, refused to consider the tank and the airplane as anything but auxiliary arms. Their reliance on defensive tactics shows that they grossly underestimated the offensive power of the new weapons. Moreover, there was an effective lack of leadership to stimulate a spirit of resistance at the critical moment. There was no Gambetta to raise the feelings of the people to heroic heights. The result was ignominious defeat.

During the drive into France the Nazis had gained an ally. Mussolini, who had been waiting for a propitious moment, decided on June 10 that the moment had arrived. He was certain that the Germans would overcome French resistance and that after the fall of France he could share in the division of the spoils. On that day he announced to a cheering crowd assembled before the Palazzo Venezia that he had "done all that was humanly possible to halt the war" and that since the nations were determined to continue the fight it was time for Italy to enter the war "to safeguard her honor, interests and the future." Italian forces attacked France at once, but the attack contributed little to the final defeat. Moreover, the territorial gains which the Nazis permitted the Italians were so small that some observers regarded them as almost an insult.

Although the military situation appeared hopeless, Premier Reynaud announced on June 13 from Tours, to which the government had withdrawn, that the French would go on fighting "even if it were in one province only; even if it were in North Africa only." By this time Paris was doomed. In the hope of saving it from destruction, the Allied command decided not to defend it and withdrew the troops to the south. The next day the Nazi legions moved into the city which had last capitulated to Germans seventy years earlier. On that day, too, the German forces occupied Versailles where the German Empire had been proclaimed in January, 1871. Two days later, on June 16, Reynaud was forced out of office and President Lebrun called on the octogenarian Marshal Pétain to form a government. The aged marshal, acting as the tool of the defeatists, broadcast on the same day the fatal words, "We must cease to fight." The next day French negotiators met Hitler and his staff in the same railway car on the same spot in the forest of Compiègne where the Germans had signed the armistice in 1918.

Marshal Pétain had surrendered before he knew the armistice terms. He believed that Hitler would talk to him as one soldier to another and that the Nazis might take away Alsace-Lorraine but would do little more. But the terms were much more stringent than expected. Among other things, the whole of the French coastline and a considerable belt of territory inland were placed under German occupation, with the costs of the occupation to be paid by the French. Furthermore, the French army was to be demobilized and all its equipment and materiel surrendered at German discretion. Finally, the French navy, excepting such part of it as was needed for the protection of the French colonies, was to be turned over to Germany and Italy for demobilization and internment. The Germans did, however, promise not to use the French ships for their own war purposes. This promise was not enough for the British, who had not forgotten that Hitler was always ready to make promises he did not keep. With the French fleet added to the German and Italian fleets the Axis could have challenged the British control of the sea. Consequently the British took charge of the French ships that happened to be in British ports and through recourse to force demilitarized the French ships in the North African ports, thereby gaining control of most of the French navy.

FROM THE BATTLE OF BRITAIN TO THE INVASION OF RUSSIA

The conquest of Holland, Belgium, and France in less than six weeks is one of the great triumphs in the history of war. After such achievements it appeared as if nothing could prevent the Nazis from dominating Europe. Britain stood alone as the last of Germany's declared enemies. As a Cockney put it, Britain "had reached the final round, and was playing for the championship on the home grounds." The Germans were not only in possession of the North Sea and Channel coasts, which were of great strategic value; they had also strengthened themselves economically by plundering the conquered countries. But France had collapsed so quickly that the Nazis had no time to project a plan for the invasion of Britain; nor were they prepared for the amphibious campaign an invasion of Britain would have entailed. The German troops were not trained in landing operations and had no landing craft for the purpose. Hitler, in fact, seemed to think that an invasion of Britain would not be necessary. He believed that the British would agree to accept the favorable terms he was ready to offer them. So sure was he of having his terms accepted that many troops were granted leaves of absence after the fall of France and others were shifted to other parts of Europe.

He was therefore greatly surprised when Churchill announced his determination to continue the war. At first he believed that Churchill was bluffing, but when he finally grasped the situation he began to give serious consideration to the problem of invading Britain. The Nazi generals and admirals were not sanguine about the success of an invasion. They were particularly worried about what would happen if the British navy appeared on the scene. For propaganda purposes, however, it was announced that the Nazi forces would quickly overwhelm Britain. Goebbels told the German soldiers that after one more battle "the bells of peace will ring." Hitler himself went so far as to set August 15 as the date on which he would dictate peace in London. The time seemed propitious: at Dunkirk the British troops had abandoned their heavy equipment, in some cases even their rifles, and the British had but one fully equipped division available for defense. But the Nazi leaders underestimated the British capacity for resistance. They failed to take into account the indomitable spirit of the British leader, Winston Churchill, who after Dunkirk electrified the British with such fighting phrases as: "We shall defend our island whatever the cost. We shall fight on beaches, in fields, in cities and on the hills. We shall never surrender."

The campaign, as the Germans had planned it, called for the Luftwaffe to soften Britain up for the invasion. Nazi propaganda broadcasts sought to intimidate the British by declaring that London would suffer the same fate as Warsaw. The Battle of Britain began on August 8, 1940. At first German bombers came to Britain in mass formations of from fifty to a hundred. These raids were made in the daytime because the Nazis believed that daylight bombing was more efficient. The objective of the raids varied from time to time. The first efforts were directed against British naval bases, warships, and convoys, next the British airfields became the targets, and later British docks and industries. Although the Germans had more planes than the British, the latter's planes and pilots were better. The antiaircraft gunners, too, soon displayed superior marksmanship. At the approach of enemy planes the Royal Air Force would fiercely attack the Nazis, while the antiaircraft guns sent up showers of lead. Day after day the Luftwaffe suffered heavy losses. On August 15 the Nazis sent an armada of about 1000 planes; of these the British shot down 180. In one week the Germans lost no less than 492 planes, while the British loss was only 115. The success of the R.A.F. evoked from Winston Churchill the glowing tribute, "Never in the field of human conflict was so much owed by so many to so few."

The heavy losses caused the Nazis to shift both their tactics and objectives. Instead of sending planes in large groups, they dispatched them in small flights of from three to twelve. The new targets were the docks, industrial plants, power plants, and railroad stations of London and other British cities. Although these raids wrought considerable destruction, they failed to break British morale; in fact, the British became angry rather than frightened. Meanwhile the Germans continued to pay dearly for their attacks. By the end of October their losses in planes totaled 2375. In an effort to reduce their losses the Germans now turned to night bombing; this was less accurate, but the Nazis were aided by radio beams which guided the bombers to their destination. Besides continuing their attacks on London, the German bombers also raided the shipbuilding centers of western Britain, the textile centers of the Midlands, and the principal ports. For a time incendiary bombs caused considerable destruction, but the British soon organized groups of civilian fire fighters who learned to extinguish the bombs quickly. The attacks continued month after month until May, 1941. Although there was much destruction, the R.A.F., growing stronger with the passing of time, continued to punish the Germans severely. Whatever loss in production the bombings caused was more than offset by imports from Canada and the United States.

During these months the British were not content with defensive action. In August small groups of British bombers began to make raids on Germany. On August 25, 1940, the R.A.F. bombed Berlin for the first time. The damage done by this raid was not as important as the effect on German morale. Marshal Goering, the commander in chief of the Luftwaffe, had repeatedly told the Germans that not one bomb would drop on German soil. This illusion was quickly dispelled. The principal objectives of the British were the mines, factories, foundries, steel mills, and railway lines of the Ruhr, which was the heart of industrial Germany. These bombings brought war directly to the German civilians for the first time since Napoleon's day. German airfields in Belgium, the Netherlands, and France were also bombed.

In March, 1941, aid came to the British in the form of the Lend-Lease Bill passed by the Congress of the United States. This bill was, in effect, a pledge that the United States would supply Britain with sufficient war materials to match the growing output of Germany. Thus Britain had in reality gained an ally in the war. But the supplies were worthless to the British unless they could be delivered. The navy had for a time given the merchant ships better protection through the use of the convoy system, but after the signing of the Lend-Lease Bill, the Battle of the Atlantic began raging with increased fury, with the result that the loss of British and Allied merchant ships increased sharply. The fundamental reason for the increase was that after June, 1940, the German submarines had easy access to the Atlantic trade lanes from the northern French ports. In one week of March, 1941, twenty-nine British and Allied ships were sunk. The Nazis were sinking ships faster than the British could build them, so that the menace of a Nazi blockade became for the British the most critical aspect of the war. President Roosevelt at once attacked the problem by transferring to Britain a million tons of shipping, including the vessels of Axis or Axis-controlled nations which had been tied up in United States harbors. The Congress also permitted President Roosevelt to turn over to Britain fifty over-age destroyers which enabled the British to give their convoys better protection.

THE STRUGGLE FOR THE MEDITERRANEAN AREA

Italy's entrance into the war changed the picture in at least one respect. Whereas the Mediterranean area had previously seen no major struggle, it now became one of the principal arenas of the war. Mussolini had ambitions to build himself a great Mediterranean empire at the expense of Britain. He felt that the moment was auspicious for such an enterprise because the Battle of Britain would necessitate the recall of the bulk of the British fleet. According to the Italian plans one army was to move northward from Italian East Africa and a second one was to enter Egypt from Libya. The two armies would gradually move toward each other and would thus force the British out of North Africa. For a time it appeared as if the plan might be successful. An army of 70,000, composed largely of native troops under Italian command, overran British Somaliland, which was defended by a garrison numbering only 7,000. In September a second Italian army of about 250,000 Italians and native troops moved into Egypt from Libya, aiming to move across northern Egypt to the Suez Canal. This army managed to take Salûm and Sidi Barrâni, but halted at the latter place to await mechanical equipment and to gather supplies for a drive on Alexandria. This gave General Wavell, the British commander, an opportunity to train and strengthen his forces for a counterattack.

While Mussolini was trying to drive the British out of North Africa,

Hitler was attempting to establish his "new European order" in the Balkans. Among other things Hitler wanted the foodstuffs of the Balkan states so that the Germans could withstand the British blockade. He wished to achieve this through pressure, threats, and cajolery without the use of force. As the first step in adjusting the affairs of the Balkan states the Axis powers prevailed on Rumania to cede the southern Dobrudja to Bulgaria and the northern half of Transylvania to Hungary. Opposition to King Carol for having yielded to the Axis demands became so strong that he abdicated (September, 1941) and went into exile. Pressure was then put on General Antonescu, who ruled as the "strong man" of Rumania during Prince Michael's minority, to join the circle of states supporting the new Nazi order, after which Nazi troops occupied certain areas of that country. Three days before General Antonescu signed with the Axis powers, Count Csacky, Hungarian Foreign Minister, formally made his country a member of the Axis alliances. Efforts were also being made to force Bulgaria and Yugoslavia into the Axis-dominated group. Only Greece remained staunchly on the side of the British.

When all efforts failed to entice Greece into the Axis circle, the Italian government decided to subjugate the Greeks by force. On October 28 Mussolini's government sent the Greeks a three-hour ultimatum over an alleged border incident, and before the government of Premier Metaxas could reply an Italian army of about 200,000 moved into Greece from Albania. It appeared as if the Greeks would be quickly overwhelmed, for they had no mechanized equipment, very little heavy artillery, and only about two hundred obsolete planes. But the Greeks were accustomed to mountain warfare, while the Italians were not. During the first days the Greeks permitted the Italians to advance unopposed and when the Italian lines were extended in the valleys they went into action with their mountain artillery. Unable to return the attack with their mechanized forces, the Italians became completely disorganized. By a series of attacks the Greeks forced the Italian columns to retreat toward Albania. Following in hot pursuit they expelled the enemy from their country, and then went on into Albania, where they took Koritsa (Corizza), the principal Italian base in that country, together with many prisoners and much equipment. This defeat by the Greeks was a bitter pill for the Italians.

Still other defeats were in the offing for the Italians. General Wavell, encouraged by the defeats in Albania and the British naval superiority in the Mediterranean, started an offensive against the Italian army which had invaded Egypt. The British force, composed largely of troops from the dominions plus Polish and Free French contingents, was a small but well-equipped force. In quick succession it retook Sidi Barrâni, Salûm, and Fort Capuzzo and drove the Italians out of Egypt. Thereafter Wavell's army moved westward to take Bengasi on February 7 and El Agheila two days later. In the drive the British captured large quantities of military booty and took about 140,000 prisoners. The British success caused the Germans to send General Rommel, their great expert in mechanized warfare, to take charge of the Axis troops in North Africa. The situation was favorable for a counter-attack, for the British had transferred some of their troops to the Balkans. Quickly moving to the attack, Rommel's forces took one place after another. Within ten days they had pushed into Egypt and taken Salûm. Thus the Suez Canal was again threatened.

Elsewhere the Italians continued to fare badly. With an army of 60,000 men collected during the campaign in Libya, the British first drove the Italian forces out of Italian and British Somaliland and then invaded Eritrea and Ethiopia. In Ethiopia the British were aided by native warriors who harried the Italians at every turn. As the British forces approached Addis Ababa, the capital of Ethiopia, the Italians withdrew and on April 6, 1941, the British marched in. Thus Italy lost her East African empire. Earlier, on March 27, the Italians had also suffered a naval defeat in the battle of Cape Matapan. Upon discovering a force of Italian ships out in the open, a British squadron supported by planes attacked it, sinking three heavy cruisers and two destroyers besides inflicting damage on other ships. The series of defeats was a severe blow to Italian morale. In a number of Italian cities crowds urged withdrawal from the war. To forestall any such move the Germans quickly increased the number of their army and air-force units stationed in Italy.

Meanwhile the Germans were continuing their "diplomatic offensive" in the Balkans. On March 1, 1941, Bulgaria agreed to enter the Axis orbit, and German troops at once entered the country. Pressure was also put on Yugoslavia to become a part of the "new Nazi order." In response to this pressure the prime minister signed an agreement (March 25), but the masses refused to concur. A *coup d'état* forced Prince Paul, the regent, and his cabinet into exile. The new government with Prince Peter as king at once repudiated the agreement with the Nazis, although professing friendship with the Axis. But Hitler refused to be satisfied with anything less than complete domination. He again turned to Blitzkrieg tactics. The Luftwaffe went into action and in a short time disrupted communication and transportation services in Yugoslavia. Airfields were also bombed and bridges demolished. Hope persisted that the Nazi ground forces would meet their match in the mountainous terrain, but before the Yugoslavs could reach their battle stations the Nazi mechanized divisions had moved into southeastern Yugoslavia through four passes. While one spearhead turned south into Greece, the others moved across Yugoslavia toward Albania. At the same time two other spearheads moved into Yugoslavia from Rumania. On April 13, Belgrade, the capital, fell, and two days later the Yugoslavs opened negotiations for surrender.

Greece was next on the list of victims. The spearhead which had entered Greece moved on with but little opposition. Still another German column moved into the Vardar valley. Even the Metaxas Line, which was the Greek equivalent of the Maginot Line, failed to stop the Nazi advance very long. In the south of Greece a British force, fearing another Dunkirk, evacuated Greek soil while a small force fought a rearguard action at Thermopylae. On April 26 a Nazi spearhead entered Athens unopposed. By the end of the month all of Greece had been overrun. Blitzkrieg methods had achieved another speedy triumph. The British, however, still held the island of Crete. On May 19 the Nazis dropped about three thousand troopers on the island. At first the British shot or captured many of them, but German planes continued to drop more. The paratroopers worked so efficiently that by the end of the third day they had captured most of the key points of the island, and a few days later all the British troops on the island were overwhelmed. The Nazis had hoped to capture the Greek king, George II, who had taken refuge in Crete, but he managed to escape on a British warship.

THE NAZIS INVADE RUSSIA

As the months passed, Hitler realized that if he continued the Battle of Britain he would risk the destruction of the Luftwaffe. This would leave Germany exposed to an attack from Russia. The Soviet-German alliance had not proved satisfactory to either party. During the early months of the war the Russians did materially aid the Germans to evade the full force of Britain's blockade by shipments of food and supplies. The Russians, for example, transported rubber from the Far East all the way across Siberia, together with copper and nickel, for Hitler's war machine; they also sent thousands of tons of grain to Germany. But the Nazi successes in Poland, Scandinavia, the Lowlands, and France produced a cleavage in the partnership. Frightened by the apparent strength of the German forces, the Russians began to curtail shipments to Germany. This naturally displeased Hitler greatly. When the Soviet government demanded control of the Dardanelles as the price of participation in the Italian-German-Japanese Axis, Hitler did not even answer the proposals. On December

18, 1940, he ordered his general staff to prepare for an attack on the Soviet Union.

During the succeeding winter careful plans were laid for the invasion. The campaign had to be a short one if the Nazis were to overwhelm Russia before the United States could send large quantities of war materiel to Britain. A powerful German army began to march into Russia at 4 A.M. on Sunday, June 22, 1941. An hour and a half later the German ambassador in Moscow informed Foreign Minister Molotov that German troops had crossed the Russian border, giving the concentration of Red army units near the German frontier as the reason for the move. Some time later Hitler stated in a speech that he had remained silent while Soviet Russia was overpowering Finland and the Baltic States. "I took decision," he said, "only when I saw that Russia had reached the hour to advance against us. . . . We gradually received proof that on our frontiers one airfield after another was set up and one division after another from the gigantic Soviet army was being assembled there."

The growing strength of Russian arms undoubtedly influenced the decision. Russia's rearmament was at the time proceeding at a rapid pace. According to reports presented to Hitler the Russian armament program was to be largely completed by August, 1941. So Hitler decided to strike before Russia was ready. Other motives also played a part in the decision. Among these one might list Hitler's desire to punish the Russians for their failure to deliver the grain and oil they had promised, Germany's need of foodstuffs and raw materials from the Russian territories Hitler planned to conquer, and the general hatred Hitler cherished for communism. Ever since the founding of the Nazi Party the Russian communists had been Enemy No. 1. All this was not unknown to the Soviet leaders. They knew that the Nazis would strike at the first good opportunity. Nor were the preparations for the invasion of Russia a well-kept secret. In April, 1941, about two months before the invasion date, Stalin concluded a pact of neutrality with Japan as a means of protecting Russia's eastern flank in case of a German attack.

The invasion of Russia was, in a sense, a challenge to the record of Napoleon. Hitler sent his mechanized forces into Russia on the anniversary of the day on which the Little Corporal had attacked Russia in 1812. It was, so to speak, a declaration to the world that he would do what Napoleon had failed to achieve. His Blitzkrieg methods would force the Russians to their knees in a few weeks. Many military experts in all parts of the world shared his belief, and the initial progress of the German forces appeared to bear it out. Advancing along a front which extended more or less compactly from the Baltic to the Black Sea, a distance of a thousand miles, the Germans quickly forced the Russians to abandon Poland and the Baltic states, with the exception of the coast line of Latvia and Estonia. The Russians hoped to retire behind the Stalin Line, a series of fortified posts, but before they could do so the Germans caught and annihilated two of their armies. Even the Stalin Line did not stop the German advance long. After piercing it at a number of points the Nazis reached Smolensk on July 17. Several days earlier the official German News Agency had announced that "the route to Moscow is open."

But the announcement was unduly optimistic. At Smolensk, on the central front, the Russian resistance stiffened, holding the Nazi forces more or less stationary. In the north and south, however, the German advance continued. On September 9 the Nazis took Shlisselburg, the great railway center. They were now within artillery range of Leningrad. To save this city the entire civilian and military population devoted itself to the raising of defenses. Meanwhile the Nazis made spectacular advances in the south, reaching Kiev on August 8 and Odessa on August 13, but even there Russian resistance became so effective that the Nazis required some weeks to take the two cities. In November the Germans started another drive on the central front. The advance continued as far as Klin, only thirty-one miles from Moscow, but was then stopped by the Russians. At the end of the first week in December Corporal Hitler, who was determined to dwarf the achievements of the "Little Corporal," realized that his efforts to overwhelm the Russians by Blitzkrieg methods had failed. On December 8 he announced, "The German army does not expect to take Moscow this winter." In five months of fighting the Germans had occupied about 614,000 square miles of territory, an area about three times the size of Germany before the Hitler annexations, but the casualties in killed, wounded, and missing up to December 1 numbered 673,415, to say nothing of the tremendous losses in equipment.

Before many more weeks passed it became clear that the invasion of Russia was the gravest error of Hitler's career. Not only were Russian armaments stronger than he had supposed, but the Russian spirit of resistance was firmer. No sooner had the German spearheads passed a given point than the guerrilla units went into action against German lines of communication and smaller German groups. Hitler had also misjudged the quantity of booty that would be forthcoming. He had firmly believed that if he could control the Ukraine with its vast resources, he could laugh at the Allied blockade of Germany. But the Russians adopted the "scorched-earth" policy, destroying everything in the path of the German advance. Machinery was removed from the factories, railroads were torn up, and bridges were burned. Hitler's plan to paralyze the Russian war effort by conquering the western industrial centers also failed. Some of the destroyed factories and captured mines were replaced through the construction of new factories and the opening of new mines in eastern Russia. Moreover, aid from Britain and the United States arrived soon to supplement Russian production. Since the Leningrad-Murmansk railway had been cut by enemy action, it became necessary for British and Russian troops to occupy northern Iran (Persia) in order to open a route into southern Russia for the arms and supplies from the United States.

The Nazis had been so confident of overwhelming Russia within a short time that they had not bothered to prepare for the rigors of winter. Most of the troops had very little heavy clothing; nor were there adequate supplies of other essential materials. Furthermore, only a few divisions were trained in the special requirements of winter warfare. In short, many of the advantages which the Germans had enjoyed were canceled by the sub-zero temperatures. The Russians, who realized this, launched a counteroffensive along the entire front with troops that had been systematically trained for winter warfare. In the south the Russian advance continued until the Germans were driven back beyond Taganrog; in the north the Russians recovered Shlisselburg; and on the central front they drove the Nazis out of Klin. Although they regained only a small part of the territory they had lost, they did achieve something no other nation had been able to do — they stopped the advance of the Nazi forces.

PRELIMINARIES TO PEARL HARBOR

When World War II broke out in 1939 the isolationist tradition was still deeply entrenched in the United States. Although opinion, by and large, was partial to France and Great Britain because they were fighting to maintain the principles of democracy, the determination to remain aloof from the conflict was strong. On September 5, 1939, President Roosevelt proclaimed the neutrality of the United States and in accordance with the Neutrality Act of 1935 placed an embargo on the sale of arms to belligerent nations. Unlike Woodrow Wilson in 1914, however, he did not call for neutrality in thought as well as in deed. He stated that though the nation would remain neutral, a citizen of a neutral country could not be asked "to close his mind or his conscience." Even the neutrality in deed was of brief duration. Only a short time later on September 21, the President summoned the Congress to convene in special session for the purpose of considering a revision of that part of the embargo act which prohibited the sale of arms to belligerents. Although isolationists denounced the requested

EUROPE IN 1942 AT THE

HEIGHT OF THE NAZI EMPIRE

revision, sympathy for France and Britain carried the day. After several weeks of debate the Congress enacted on November 4 the revised Neutrality Act which permitted Britain and France to purchase munitions from the United States on a "cash and carry" basis. United States vessels were still forbidden to carry arms or to enter ports of nations at war.

During the succeeding months further changes of opinion occurred. The German conquest of Denmark and Norway caused the American attitude to swing in the direction of stronger support of the Allies. The attack on Belgium and Holland, particularly the wanton destruction of Rotterdam, aroused great indignation, even horror, in the United States. But it was the fall of France which undermined the last props of isolationism and convinced even those who had ardently supported a policy of "the war is not our business" that it was time to take stock of the military strength of the United States. Moreover, with Britain standing alone against Germany it became clear that only the United States could supply the British with the necessary arms. While a minority demanded immediate entry into the war, the majority urged the sending of all possible materials and supplies to the British. Even before the final defeat of France, after the Germans had broken through the French lines at Sedan, some aircraft, field artillery, machine guns, and more than a million rifles together with hundreds of millions of rounds of ammunition were sent to Britain at the behest of President Roosevelt. Steps were also taken to arm the United States. In September, 1940, the Congress passed the first peacetime military draft in the history of the United States. Just two days before the end of 1940 the President urged the people of the United States to make this nation "the great arsenal of democracy" by producing more planes, ships, and guns.

During 1941 the United States gradually became a more active participant in the war. In March the Congress passed the Lend-Lease Act, which empowered the President to send arms and other war necessaries to the countries fighting the Axis. The budget which he submitted for this purpose involved $7 billion. Thus the aims and purposes of Britain and the United States were becoming more and more closely identified. Early in April the United States government negotiated an agreement with the Danish minister to the United States which placed Greenland under American protection. This made it possible for the United States to establish naval and air bases on the island and to give merchant ships protection to within 1800 miles of Britain. When a German submarine attacked a United States destroyer that was en route to Greenland with mail President Roosevelt ordered the navy to shoot if necessary. The sinking of a number of United

States ships during the succeeding months impelled the Congress on November 14 to repeal the remaining provisions of the Neutrality Act, thereby permitting the arming of United States merchant ships and their entry into the war zones. Thus the last remnants of neutrality had disappeared.

The long debate on the question of whether the United States should join in the "shooting war" was decided by the Japanese. In September, 1931, the Japanese had opened a decade of aggression in the Far East by invading Manchuria. But instead of conquering the Chinese, the Japanese army had bogged down so badly that the Japanese government began to seek an "honorable" way out of the dilemma. In looking about the Far East the Japanese militarists decided that there were other fish to fry. With the British occupied at home in fending off the Nazi attacks, the Dutch and French under the Nazi heel, the United States busy aiding Britain, and the Russians engaged by the Germans, the Japanese saw an opportunity to establish their "new order" in southern Asia. In September, 1940, the Japanese had moved completely into the Axis camp by signing a tripartite treaty with Germany and Italy. Now that the Axis was threatening the United States with a two-ocean war, the Japanese hoped the American people would adopt a policy of laissez faire toward any move the Japanese might make in the Far East.

In July, 1941, Japan took the last step on the road to the "new order" that she could take without war. The Japanese government sent an ultimatum to the French authorities at Hanoi, the capital of Indo-China, and Japanese troops moved into the country. The United States did not, as the Japanese had hoped, ignore the move. For two years the United States, in order to gain time for rearmament, had shipped large quantities of scrap iron and much oil to Japan. Realizing that it was time to stop the Japanese expansion, President Roosevelt on July 26 froze all Japanese assets in the United States. A few days later he also put drastic limitations on the shipment of scrap iron and subjected all oil shipments to licensing. When the Dutch East Indies and the nations of the British Commonwealth also sharply restricted exports to Japan, the imports into Japan dropped 75 per cent. This curtailment not only caused widespread economic distress in Japan but also threatened to frustrate the plans of the Japanese militarists. Action of some kind was necessary if the militarists were to regain their power and prestige. The action for which the Germans were pressing the Japanese was war against the United States. Hitler hoped that such a war would stop the flow of materials to Russia and Britain.

Before taking this step the Japanese decided to make a final effort to reach an agreement with the United States, one which would permit them to establish their "new order" in Asia without interference by the United States. Early in November Saburo Kurusu was rushed to Washington to effect such an agreement. The talks with Secretary of State Hull, in which Japanese ambassador Nomura also participated, soon demonstrated how far apart the two countries were. What the Japanese demands amounted to was a free hand in Asia. For some days President Roosevelt and Secretary Hull studied the demands, and on November 26 the answer was handed to the Japanese representatives. Both verbally rejected it at once before sending it to their government. To meet the United States position the Japanese would have had to withdraw their forces from China and Indo-China, relinquish the idea of a "new order" in Asia, and renounce their association with the Axis powers. In short, it meant a complete reversal of Japanese policy. This the Japanese were not ready to accept. They preferred war to an about-face.

THE ATTACK ON PEARL HARBOR

Meanwhile preparations had already been started for an attack on Pearl Harbor, the United States base in the Hawaiian Islands. On November 5 Admiral Nagano, chief of the Japanese naval general staff, informed Admiral Yamamoto, commander in chief of the combined imperial fleets: "War with Netherlands, America, England inevitable; general operational preparations to be completed by early December." Two days later Yamamoto sent out the following message: "Task force will gather at Hitokappu Bay (in the southern Kurile Islands)." On November 9 he received a second message from Admiral Nagano which read: "Fleet to prepare, watch carefully against attack. At opening of hostilities task force will attack United States Navy in Hawaiian area and cripple it. First attack at dawn of day. At conclusion of the attack force will regroup and withdraw to Japan." On November 25 the fleet of forty-six ships was ordered "to stand out to sea and wait" at a point about 1500 miles northwest of Pearl Harbor.

The attack caught the United States forces completely by surprise. When the first wave of Japanese planes struck Pearl Harbor on Sunday, December 7, 1941, at 7:55 A.M., the air-warning system (radar) was not operating. It had been in operation from 4 A.M. to 7 A.M., but was then turned off. The radar station at Opana, which continued to operate the radar screen fifteen minutes longer while the operator was awaiting the arrival of a truck to take him to breakfast, picked up the approaching planes when they were 136 miles away. Upon reporting his findings to a superior officer he was told to "forget it," that they were friendly planes. For some reason neither the army nor the navy maintained a long-range patrol. The Hawaii-based planes were on the ground. The guns of many of them had been removed for cleaning, the gas tanks of most of them were empty, and many pilots were on leave for the week-end. Moreover, antiaircraft batteries were not manned; in fact, no ammunition had been issued for them or for ground machine guns. As for the United States warships, they were tied up in the harbor like a flock of decoy ducks.

During the years immediately after the attack there were many investigations for the purpose of ascertaining who was responsible for the fact that the United States forces were completely off guard at the time of the attack. The fact that the Japanese planned to attack Pearl Harbor was certainly no secret. As one writer put it, "The officers in charge had only to read the newspapers to discover that war was imminent." Warnings had been sounded nearly a year in advance. As early as January 24, 1941, Secretary of the Navy Knox wrote Secretary of War Stimson: "If war eventuates with Japan, it is believed easily possible that hostilities would be initiated by a surprise attack on the fleet or the naval base at Pearl Harbor. In my opinion the inherent possibility of a major disaster to the fleet or naval base warrants taking every step as rapidly as can be done." Just three days later Ambassador Grew in Tokyo informed the State Department in Washington that a member of his staff had heard "that a surprise mass attack on Pearl Harbor was planned by the Japanese military forces in case of 'trouble' between the Japanese military forces and the United States." On February 7 General Marshall as chief of staff warned the commanding general in Hawaii that "the risk of sabotage and the risk involved in a surprise raid by air and submarine constitute the real perils of the situation." Further alarms were sounded in subsequent months by General Marshall, Admiral Stark, Ambassador Grew, Secretary of State Hull, and others. On November 27, for instance, Admiral Stark sent to the commanding naval officer in Hawaii, who in turn communicated it to the commanding general, the following message: "Japan is expected to make an aggressive move within the next few days." The next day he cabled that hostile action was possible at any moment. Despite all this the United States forces were not alerted; no precautions whatever were taken.

The first attack was made by torpedo planes, the pilots of which had been carefully briefed so that they knew where each ship was. Because the United States naval authorities did not believe that torpedoes could be used in the shallow waters of Pearl Harbor, the ships were not protected by torpedo baffles. But the Japanese planes dropped torpedoes especially designed for shallow water. It was these torpedoes which did most of the damage to the ships. Eight ships were sunk and eighteen others damaged. By dropping bombs on nearby airfields the Japanese also destroyed 240 army and navy planes. The death toll suffered by the United States forces was 2343 officers and enlisted men, with 960 reported missing. Soon after the attack on Pearl Harbor the Japanese also struck at other United States bases, including Wake Island, Midway, Guam, and bases in the Philippines. Not until December 8, many hours after the Pearl Harbor attack, did Tojo call at the imperial palace with a declaration of war. Squinting through his glasses Hirohito signed the declaration at 11:30 A.M. When he was asked by General MacArthur in the fall of 1945 why he had permitted the war, Hirohito replied: "If I had not, they would have had a new emperor. It was the will of the Japanese people."

The attack on Pearl Harbor was, in a sense, a blunder. First of all, it did not achieve what the Japanese hoped it would. Although the United States Pacific fleet was temporarily crippled, it was not destroyed. A Japanese lieutenant who was captured on December 7 in a two-man submarine said the next day that the attack was much less successful than had been anticipated. Two carriers and ten cruisers which happened to be at sea escaped damage, as did two other cruisers, two light cruisers, and twenty-seven destroyers that were stationed in Pearl Harbor. Second, it united the people of the United States in a resolve to fight to a victorious conclusion. If the Japanese had attacked Dutch and British possessions instead of Pearl Harbor and the Philippines, the United States would probably have become involved, but public opinion would have been divided. As it was, the news of the attack on Pearl Harbor dissipated whatever dissension may have existed. The next day the two houses of the Congress met in a joint session and, after hearing the President's message, passed a formal declaration of war. Britain, too, declared war against Japan, an example which was soon followed by the other nations of the British Commonwealth and by the Dutch West Indies. Those who were interested in the question of the future relations of the United States with Germany and Italy did not have to wait long for an answer. On December 11 both countries announced that they were joining Japan in the war against the United States. Thus the lines were drawn for the fight both in Europe and in the Pacific.

THE JAPANESE MARCH OF CONQUEST

The Japanese did not make the most of the opportunity to take the Hawaiian Islands or even to threaten invasion of the United States.

They struck in another direction. Their first aim was to conquer the territories which could supply them with vital war materials. The march of conquest was an amazingly swift one, one that surprised the Japanese themselves. In about six months they came into possession of some of the world's great storehouses of basic raw materials including oil, rubber, tin, copper, lumber, and foodstuffs as well as the basic minerals and ingredients for explosives needed by a great war nation. First they overwhelmed the United States garrisons on Guam and Wake, because they believed that these islands would be used as stepping stones in moving American forces to the East. At the same time Japanese forces were dispatched to take the British possession of Hong Kong, which surrendered on Christmas Day after a spirited defense. Equally successful was the attack on Singapore, which was generally regarded as the key to the defense of both British and Dutch possessions in the Far East. Although the garrison fought back desperately it was compelled to surrender to superior force on February 15, 1942.

When Singapore surrendered, Premier Tojo announced that the possession of this base would enable the Japanese to conquer all the British and Dutch possessions in the Far East. For a time it appeared as if Japan might translate the boast into reality. During the attack on Singapore the Japanese had started a campaign to conquer the Dutch East Indies, and after the release of the forces which had overwhelmed Singapore they hoped to use these troops for an all-out attack on the Dutch colonies. Although the Allied Far Eastern fleet succeeded in inflicting considerable damage on the convoy carrying these troops, a large Japanese fleet subsequently crippled the Allied fleet in a series of engagements (February 27–March 1), thereby spelling the doom of the Dutch East Indies. After a short but fiercely fought campaign the Dutch army surrendered on March 9, and the Dutch East Indies passed into Japanese hands as the third month of the war in the Pacific ended.

Simultaneously with the conquest of the Dutch East Indies the Japanese were also fighting in other parts of the East. In Burma an inadequate British force was gradually pushed back to the capital city of Rangoon, which fell on March 8. With the Japanese in possession of Burma, the situation of the Chinese became critical for lack of supplies which had formerly been transported into China over the famous Burma Road. Some supplies were, however, carried to the Chinese through the use of air transport and alternate land routes. In the meantime bitter fighting was also taking place in the Philippines, where a force of about 55,000 Americans and Filipinos under the command of General Douglas MacArthur tried to stop large Japanese forces. The Japanese, with their superior air and naval forces, succeeded in making a number of landings on Luzon, the main island of the Philippines, during the month of December, 1941. On January 2 they took Manila and the United States naval station at Cavite, compelling MacArthur's troops to retreat to the Bataan Peninsula and the island of Corregidor. The American-Filipino troops made a valiant defense, but fresh Japanese troops gradually wore them down. At President Roosevelt's order General MacArthur left to accept the supreme command of the Allied forces in the Southwest Pacific and Major-General Jonathan Wainwright took command. But after months of valiant fighting against insuperable odds, 35,000 Filipino-American troops surrendered. For almost a month longer General Wainwright and the 3500 troops in the fortress of Corregidor refused to capitulate. Hunger, disease, and shortage of ammunition finally forced General Wainwright to accede to the surrender not only of the Corregidor troops but of all the scattered American and Filipino forces operating in various parts of the Philippines. The fall of Corregidor marked the end of an epic fight that was acclaimed by Allied leaders in many parts of the world.

For about five months the Japanese had things very much their own way. At the end of this period the Japanese were established in Burma, Malaya, the Dutch East Indies, the Philippines, and many Pacific islands. It appeared as if they had been successful in their efforts to establish the "new order" in the Far East. But their successes had been achieved largely because the United States was unprepared, the British were fighting off the Germans, and the Netherlands were under Hitler's heel.

As early as May, 1942, the Japanese met their first setback in the Battle of the Coral Sea. This naval engagement was unique in that it was a battle in which surface ships did not exchange a single shot. It was the first great duel of aircraft carriers in the history of naval warfare. The fighting was done by planes, not by the ships. The battle started on May 7, 1942, just five months after the attack on Pearl Harbor, when United States planes from the aircraft carriers Yorktown and Lexington sighted a Japanese carrier, attacked it, and sank it. The next morning a considerable Japanese naval force was sighted. In the subsequent attack the Japanese lost one carrier, three heavy cruisers, one light cruiser, two destroyers, and several transports. During the counterattack the Lexington was lost and the Yorktown was badly damaged. About a month later (June 3) a Japanese armada of fifty-three ships was sighted on its way to attack Midway Island. In the attack by United States torpedo planes and dive bombers the Japanese lost four carriers, two heavy cruisers, and three destroyers besides having many ships damaged. The United States forces lost one carrier and one destroyer. Upon being attacked the Japanese force turned tail and ran for home. This defeat of the Japanese restored the balance of naval power which had been lost at Pearl Harbor.

Having spent the first months after the declaration of war building up their naval and military strength, the Allies struck the first blow of their counteroffensive in August, 1942. The blow was directed at Japanese positions in the Solomons, a string of volcanic islands across the northern end of the Coral Sea. These positions were a threat both to Australia and to the United States supply lines to Australia. A particular threat was an airfield which the Japanese were building on Guadalcanal. To prevent them from using this field a force of United States and Australian troops was collected for an attack. After the Japanese air bases at Rabaul, Lae, and Salamaua had been bombed to prevent Japanese planes from attacking the Allied convoy, General MacArthur's troops (August 6–7) landed at Tulagi Harbor on Florida Island and on the island of Guadalcanal. The Japanese, though taken by surprise, offered vigorous and stubborn resistance, particularly on Guadalcanal, but MacArthur's troops succeeded in occupying the airfield, which was renamed Henderson Field. During the succeeding months the Japanese did everything possible to dislodge the Allied forces. Among other operations, six naval battles were fought. After the arrival of reinforcements from the United States the Japanese were gradually driven from Guadalcanal. The conquest of the Solomons gave the Allies a base for attacks on other Japanese positions.

CHAPTER THIRTY

World War II: the Defeat of the Axis

THE GERMANS LOSE THE
INITIATIVE IN RUSSIA ALTHOUGH the Germans lost some
ground in Russia during the winter of 1941–1942, there was little
doubt that they would launch another offensive in the spring. Throughout the winter both sides were busy with preparations. The Germans,
for their part, developed a new strategy. Having discovered that they
could not annihilate the Russian forces in a short time, as they had
hoped, they decided to mass troops and equipment for a major drive
at one point. The locale of the first great effort was to be the Ukraine.
The Germans reasoned that a successful drive to the Volga and into the
Caucasus would deprive the Russians of territory in which many of
their industrial establishments were situated and from which they
derived such essential military supplies as oil, iron, and manganese in
addition to food supplies and reinforcements. One task remained to
be completed before the drive could start. Sevastopol, which had resisted so staunchly in the Crimean War of 1855, had been holding out
against a Nazi attack since October, 1941. Determined to force the
surrender, the Germans reduced the town to a mass of ruins with dive
bombers and large mortars. Even then the defenders did not evacuate
Sevastopol until the beginning of July, 1942.

On June 28, a few days before the surrender of Sevastopol, the German drive was launched with a force which included at least ten
armored divisions, two thousand tanks, and three thousand planes.
The first objective was the city of Voronezh, about 125 miles from
Kursk, where the drive began. After a terrific bombardment by the
air force the German spearheads managed to penetrate the Russian defenses and by July 7 to reach the suburbs of Voronezh, which is east
of the Don River. But the battle for the city raged fiercely for many

days with the result that by July 20 the Germans were driven back across the Don at one or two places. The determined resistance of the Russians at Voronezh caused the Germans to shift the direction of their drive southward toward the city of Voroshilovgrad, which they took on July 20. Rostov, their next objective, fell on July 28. The Germans then divided their offensive. While one part of their forces moved toward the Caucasus and the Black Sea coast, the other part pointed toward the Volga at Stalingrad. One of their chief objectives in the Caucasus campaign was to gain possession of the Baku oil fields. For a time they advanced rapidly, reaching a point 275 miles southeast of Rostov, but they failed to reach the Baku oil fields. The other part of the offensive forces reached Stalingrad, where the communists had built large tractor and armament plants. In anticipation of the German drive the Russians had thrown up such fortifications as they could and were determined to hold the city at all costs. Although the Germans did penetrate into the city, the Russians contested every building with their lives. Casualties on both sides were high. While the fighting continued, the Russians projected a plan for encircling the attacking force. It was carried out so successfully that fourteen German divisions were caught in the trap. A desperate German attempt on Christmas Day to relieve the encircled troops proved unsuccessful. Thus the Germans not only failed to take Stalingrad; the end of the year 1942 saw the German army before Stalingrad hopelessly surrounded by the Russians.

The year 1943 opened with the most serious blow the Germans had received in the war. The Russians began to liquidate the encircled German army before Stalingrad. At the end of the first week of January less than 200,000 Germans remained of the original force of 330,-000. On January 8 the Russians sent an ultimatum to the German army; receiving no reply, they launched a determined attack to annihilate the enemy. By January 17 only about 80,000 Germans remained, and ten days later the number had been reduced to 12,000. Finally on January 31 the remnant of the German army, together with sixteen German generals, surrendered. The news of the destruction of this army was a bitter blow to German morale.

The epic of Stalingrad marked a turning point in the Russian campaign. While the Germans were using up much of their available man power, the Russians had achieved their success without the use of reserves. During the fall and early winter of 1942–1943 the Russians replaced the losses in military man power they had suffered in 1942. By this time the new production centers they had set up in the Urals were beginning to turn out great quantities of planes, tanks, mortars, and artillery. Thus strengthened and equipped, the Russian forces early in February struck at the tired Germans on a front extending from

Moscow to the Caucasus. On February 8 they took the strongly fortified city of Kursk in the Ukraine and on February 16 recaptured
Kharkov, which the Germans had held for fifteen months. On the same
day Russian forces also entered Rostov, the key to the entire German
front. At the beginning of March the Germans were forced to evacuate Rzhev, situated on the central front some 130 miles from Moscow,
and on March 12 Vyazma also fell to the Russians. But the Russians
·in moving too quickly had overextended their supply lines and the
Nazis made the most of the opportunity to retake Kharkov. Despite
this loss, the Red army had managed to reconquer almost 200,000
square miles of territory in its winter drive.

The coming of spring in 1943 posed a problem for Hitler. His only
hope of victory lay in an all-out attack, but to launch such an attack
meant throwing all the German reserves into battle at a time when the
shortage of man power was becoming a pressing problem. To add to
his problems, the Russians had gained control of the air. Consequently
he decided on a limited attack in a 160-mile sector running from Orel
through Kursk to Belgorod. The offensive, which started on July 5, at
once encountered superior Russian forces which inflicted heavy losses
on the Germans. At the end of the first week the offensive had been
stopped, and not many days later the Russians launched a counteroffensive aimed at the German fortified base at Orel (July 12). After
being defeated in an important tank battle the Germans were forced
to evacuate both Orel and Belgorod on August 5, thereby losing the last
two important bases which they could have used for an attack on Moscow. On the southern front, too, the Russians forced the Germans back
and on August 24 regained Kharkov. In other sectors of the line the
Russians also pushed forward beating the inventors of the Blitzkrieg
at their own game.

The forlorn offensive of July, 1943, was the swan song of German
military power. During the weeks that followed, the Russians did not
ease the pressure on the German line. In the mid-sections of the great
Dnieper River Russian forces took Kiev on November 6, then pressed
on to take the town of Zhitomir, only 67 miles from the old Polish border. Although the Russians again lost the town to the Germans, they
did recover and hold no less than 135,000 square miles of territory.
The losses in dead and wounded were tremendous. According to figures
released by the Russian government, the Russian casualties numbered
4.2 millions to June, 1943. German casualties were estimated at almost
6.5 millions. It was clear that the Germans were scraping the bottom
of the man-power barrel. They saw the handwriting on the wall, but
there was little they could do about it. The Finns, who had sided with
the Germans in the hope of regaining some of the territory they had

A phase of the Dunkirk evacuation (June 12, 1940)
(from Acme)

U.S. convoy with supplies for Russia halts in Irania
during World War II (from Acme)

The Burma Road, a vital link between China and
India, being rebuilt by Chinese laborers, 1945 (from
Acme)

A scene from the battle for Stalingrad — the Russians
tighten the ring around the Germans (from Sovfoto).

An infantry assault on South Pacific island (from Armstrong Roberts)

Ruins of Cologne — spires of the cathedral in the background (from Armstrong Roberts)

Obstacles erected by the Germans to prevent the landing of Allied troops along the French Channel coast (from Acme)

lost to the Russians, saw a German defeat in the offing and through the mediation of Sweden began to put out feelers for a separate peace. Hitler's Balkan satellites were also becoming extremely nervous.

THE WAR IN THE MEDITERRANEAN

In 1942 the war in North Africa continued to swing back and forth. During the spring General Rommel strengthened his forces through the acquisition of tanks, aircraft, and artillery in preparation for a big push. After some preliminary skirmishes Hitler's "master of desert warfare" struck hard at the British in June, forcing them to retreat into Egypt. During an earlier drive Tobruk had fended off Axis attacks for a period of eight months, but this time it was overwhelmed by Rommel's forces in a few hours and capitulated on June 21. General Rommel did not stop at Tobruk. He pursued the British into Egypt and quickly took Mersa Matrûh. But the British retreated only to El Alamein. Since the desert narrows there to a passage of thirty miles, they decided that Rommel could not at that place employ his favorite strategy of using his tanks to threaten the British with encirclement. On July 1 Rommel hurled his entire force at the British in an effort to smash through to Cairo and the Suez Canal, but the British line refused to give way and the Axis drive was stopped.

During the succeeding weeks General Rommel fortified the German positions until he confidently believed they could withstand any assault. General Montgomery, who assumed the command of the British North African army in August, 1942, accepted the challenge. After making careful preparations he launched an offensive on October 23. The attack continued for more than a week until the British succeeded in driving two armored wedges through the Axis defenses. The British armored divisions which pressed through these gaps forced Rommel to order a rapid retreat which the pursuing British soon turned into a rout. Within a few days the British retook Mersa Matrûh, Bardia, and Tobruk. Besides much military booty, the British took large numbers of prisoners. Six Italian divisions which had been outdistanced by the retreating Germans surrendered en masse. After regaining Tobruk, the British in quick succession took Derna, Bengazi and El Agheila. At the end of the year Rommel's forces were still in full retreat.

General Montgomery's drive had wrested so much territory from the Axis forces that it was feared the Axis leaders might decide to occupy the French colonies in North Africa as compensation for their losses. To forestall such a move, President Roosevelt and Prime Minister Churchill laid plans for a tremendous Anglo-American armada, to consist of more than 500 troop and supply ships and more than 350 warships. Preparations were made with great secrecy and on November 7 the armada left Gibraltar to land troops at a dozen points in French Morocco. President Roosevelt himself told the people of the United States about the expedition when he announced on the night of November 7 that a powerful amphibious force under the command of Lieutenant-General Dwight D. Eisenhower was landing on the Mediterranean and Atlantic coasts of French North Africa. The landings came as such a surprise that there was little time to organize resistance. Algiers was taken on the first day and Oran fell on November 10. At Casablanca the resistance was more determined. The landing craft met fire both from French coastal batteries and from a squadron of French destroyers. Finally all major resistance was overcome and on November 11 Admiral Darlan, the commander in chief of the French forces, ordered all fighting in French North Africa to cease.

Thus in four days French North Africa with its 1500 miles of coastline was occupied with the loss of some 800 killed and about a thousand wounded. General Rommel's forces were now in danger of attack from both the east and the west. Hitler's answer to the Anglo-American occupation of French North Africa was to overrun unoccupied Corsica and Nice. A protest on the part of Marshal Pétain, head of the French government with headquarters at Vichy, that the Nazis were violating the terms of the armistice was ignored.

BOMBERS AND ROBOT BOMBS

Besides the occupation of French North Africa the year 1942 also saw the Allies increase the tempo of the air attacks against Germany. Until the Allies were ready to open a second front, an assault on Germany remained the most effective way of weakening that country. The scattered attacks by small numbers of planes were replaced during the early months of 1942 by large-scale bombing of increasing intensity. Mass formations of British bombers devastated large parts of the cities of Lübeck and Rostock. On May 30 more than a thousand planes dropped two thousand tons of explosives on Cologne in ninety minutes, and three days later a similiar number raided Essen, the home of the Krupp armament works. German fighter planes, however, took such a large toll of British bombers that only smaller detachments were sent out during the last months of the year.

The air raids over Germany in 1943 dwarfed those of 1942. Not only were larger bombers used, bombers that could carry a bomb load four times as large as that carried by earlier bombers; but the bombs they carried were also more destructive, as is indicated by the name "blockbuster." Moreover, the British air force was supplemented by units of the United States air force. The addition of the United States flying fortresses with their precision bomb sights made high-altitude bombing possible in the daytime. Thus Germany was subjected to "around-the-clock" bombings. The occupation of North Africa made possible what is known as "shuttle bombing." Instead of turning back after dropping their bombs, the bombers would continue southward to North Africa, and after resting a few days the crew would drop another load of bombs on the trip back to England. The Luftwaffe fought fiercely but could not stop the raids. The Germans did strike back occasionally by bombing London or some other English city; yet they were hardly able to return one ton of bombs for each two hundred dropped on Germany. The Allies, however, often paid dearly for these mass raids; a daylight raid on the ball-bearing works at Schweinfurt, for instance, cost sixty heavy bombers. On the other hand, the raids did greatly reduce German production and lower German morale.

During the year 1943 Allied planes dropped their loads on objectives from Norway to Italy. During a thirty-day period in May and June no less than ten thousand tons of bombs rained down on the industrial towns of the Ruhr valley, where the largest single concentration of heavy industry and coal mines were located. Cologne, which was the target of 119 raids, was destroyed so completely as to be eliminated as an industrial city. Other favorite targets were the principal ports and U-boat shipyards, including Bremen, Emden, Wilhelmshaven, Kiel, and Flensburg; the giant Krupp munitions works in Essen; the locomotive and aircraft plants at Kassel; and the Zeiss instrument factories at Jena. As a climax to the summer raids the Allied bombers dropped eight thousand tons of bombs on Hamburg in six days, reducing it to heaps of rubble. Among the objectives outside Germany were the Skoda armament plants in Czechoslovakia, the great Renault tank factories near Paris, and the Ploesti oil refineries in Rumania. Up to August, 1943, Berlin had experienced a number of small raids with small bombs, but in that month Allied bombers dropped 1800 tons of bombs on the city in forty-two minutes, leveling four square miles of the city at a cost of fifty-eight heavy bombers.

The bomb damage was almost beyond description. Millions of homes were blown to fragments by block-busters or burned to ashes by incendiary bombs. It has been calculated that twenty out of every hundred residential buildings in Germany were destroyed. Utility and transportation facilities were severely damaged, often so badly that they could no longer be operated. The principal targets were, of course, the war industries. Soon bombed-out factories dotted the entire map of Germany. Later one of the officials of the Krupp industrial empire said, "It is beyond a shadow of doubt that your bombing shortened the war by at least two years." The managing director of the German steel syndicate stated after the war that the bombing had reduced German steel production from twenty million tons in 1941 to practically nothing in 1945.

If Hitler was unable to strike back vigorously with his air force, he did have a weapon which he hoped would bring the British to their knees. This was the flying robot bomb, called the V-1 — a pilotless plane capable of traveling at a speed of 400 miles per hour, and carrying in its nose an explosive charge equivalent to a one-ton bomb. About the middle of June, 1944, the Nazis began launching these robot bombs in the direction of southern England, and during the next eighty days launched about 8000 of which about 29 per cent came down on British soil, mostly in the London area. Up to the end of August the bombs killed more than 5000 persons and destroyed 25,000 houses. In September, 1944, the Nazis turned to a new weapon — the rocket bomb, known as the V-2. Traveling at a speed of about 3000 miles per hour, the rocket bomb rose to a height of sixty or seventy miles, from which it descended with such speed that it buried itself deep in the earth before exploding. Actually its blast effect was less than that of the V-1 and it was more erratic. But from September to December, 1944, it took a toll of almost 1500 lives.

The war on and under the sea was no less active than the war in the air. During the early months of 1942 losses in United States and British ships were extraordinarily heavy. The toll exacted by German U-boats during one week in March was twenty-two ships. Axis submarines became so bold as to sink ships within sight of spectators on the United States shore. The total number of Allied ships sunk during the first six months of 1942 was 327. But the Axis powers also suffered their share of ship losses. About the middle of June, 1942, the Royal Air Force announced that it had sunk or damaged 750,000 tons of Axis shipping since the beginning of the year. In the succeeding year the loss of Anglo-American merchant shipping declined sharply — according to one estimate, to 40 per cent of the 1942 total. Factors which contributed to this decrease were the use of aircraft carriers to protect convoys, the development of improved detection devices, including radar, and, finally, the reduced output of submarines resulting from bombings of the U-boat factories and bases.

FROM NORTH AFRICA TO ITALY IN 1943

In 1943 the Germans also suffered a serious defeat in North Africa. Continuing its drive from the east, General Montgomery's British army took Tripoli and by the end of January forced Rommel's Afrika

Korps to withdraw to Tunisia. A United States army which moved eastward against Rommel's army met defeat at Faïd Pass and was forced to retreat a considerable distance. The British, too, tasted defeat at the hands of a strengthened German force. But both the British and the Americans resumed the offensive for the purpose of closing the vise on the Germans. When it became clear that the Germans could not extricate themselves from this trap, Hitler recalled Rommel in March, 1943, to save the reputation of his foremost general. General von Arnim, Rommel's successor, continued the struggle for some weeks, but failed to stop the Allied advance. On May 7 British-American forces captured Tunis and Bizerta. During the next few days swarms of planes harried the retreating Germans with the result that on May 12 von Arnim surrendered with his remaining troops. Coming as it did after the Stalingrad surrender, von Arnim's capitulation was a serious blow to German morale.

After the conclusion of the battle of Tunisia the Allied command decided upon an invasion of Italy. First the little Italian island of Pantelleria, midway between Tunisia and Sicily, was bombed into submission; then on July 10, 1943, Allied forces under the command of General Eisenhower invaded Sicily. Although the Italian troops surrendered in droves, German troops who were waiting in anticipation of the Allied landings offered stiff resistance, particularly in the sectors in which United States troops had landed. But the Germans were gradually beaten back until the entire island was won by August 17.

The invasion of Sicily spelled the doom of the Fascist regime in Italy. The masses had not wanted the war and they came increasingly to feel that it had been foisted on them by Mussolini and his regime. The military defeats had exposed the emptiness of the Duce's promises; instead of reviving the glories of the Roman Empire, he had lost the colonies Italy had possessed before the war began. After the invasion of Sicily the outstanding Italian military leaders pressed upon King Victor Emmanuel III the necessity for a change of leadership, but the king, though he too was tired of the war and of the Fascist regime, was too timorous and indecisive to act. It remained for the Fascist high officials to take the initiative. They hoped by sacrificing Mussolini and repudiating the Germans to gain enough popular support to remain in office. On July 24 a majority of the Fascist Council demanded Mussolini's resignation. When he refused, the king summoned him to the palace, personally informed him of his dismissal, and had him taken into custody. The news of Mussolini's dismissal caused an explosion of joy all over the country. In many cities happy crowds tore down the Fascist banners, trampled on Mussolini's portrait, and danced in the streets. His dismissal marked the end of

Fascism and the imminent end of the war. The Fascist Party melted away, and the other parties which had been working underground came into the open again. Temporarily General Badoglio became the head of the new government.

On August 19 the Allies opened the next phase of their attack against Italy. For the next two weeks large numbers of planes bombed the principal airfields and the transportation and communication centers of Italy in preparation for an invasion of the mainland. The invasion began on September 3, and within a few days Canadian and British troops had established firm beachheads at several points. The Italians, eager to withdraw from the war, had negotiated an armistice with General Eisenhower while the first landings were taking place. Hitler, however, was determined to prevent the Allied forces from taking Italy. Collecting as many divisions as could be spared from other fronts, he sent them into Italy to oppose the invaders. Consequently bitter fighting took place, particularly at Salerno, where the United States troops had established a beachhead. For a time it seemed as if the beachhead could not be held, but British and United States troops finally forced the Germans back.

Progress during the succeeding months was slow. The Germans employed every possible means to retard the Allied advance, including ground mines, booby traps, and surprise attacks, with the result that the Allied forces were still nearer to Naples than to Rome at the end of 1943. The Germans made the most of the natural barriers to set up a defense line eighty miles south of Rome. Seeing the hopelessness of trying to break through this line, the Allies made a landing to the north of it, at Anzio. The Germans immediately brought up 98,000 men to stop the advance of the 92,000 Allied troops that had landed at Anzio. After some very bloody fighting the Allies broke through the German line at Cassino and advanced on Rome. Rome had been proclaimed an open city, and the Germans fought only restraining actions to permit the evacuation of all their troops; hence the Eternal City suffered but little damage. Curiously, it was the first time in its long history that the city had been taken from the south. On June 5, the day after the Allied forces marched into Rome, Victor Emmanuel III turned his royal powers over to his son, Crown Prince Humbert, although retaining for himself the title of king of Italy. The capture of Rome by no means ended the Italian campaign. The Allied troops immediately launched a drive northward. During the succeeding months they gradually moved northward through Tuscany, despite the difficult terrain, the adverse weather conditions, and the determined enemy resistance. On January 6, 1945, President Roosevelt announced that the Allied force had reached the "heights overlooking the valley of the Po."

STRATEGIC ADVANCE TOWARD JAPAN

Because of limited resources in men and materials Allied operations in the South Pacific during 1942 had been confined to the Solomons. Even in 1943, after the campaign to drive the Japanese out of Guadalcanal was successfully concluded (February 10), there was little fighting for some months. The lull was broken only by the Battle of Bismarck Sea (March 3–4), in which a Japanese convoy of ten warships and fifteen transports carrying 15,000 troops was annihilated by an Allied air attack. Many began to fear that the absorption of the United States in the European phase of the war would permit the Japanese to entrench themselves securely in their newly acquired territories. The Allies were, however, not idle. They were laying plans and accumulating supplies and men for an offensive to be aimed at penetrating the outer defenses of the Japanese Empire and then slowly moving toward the Japanese homeland.

The first step in this larger plan was to eliminate all the Japanese forces from the Solomons and New Guinea. The advance started from Guadalcanal toward the end of June. An Allied force under Admiral Halsey occupied Rendova Island and early in July attacked Munda airbase on near-by New Georgia Island. Every foot of ground was bitterly contested by the Japanese, but by August 7 the entire island was finally overrun. After another bitter struggle Bougainville Island, the last Japanese stronghold in the Solomons, was taken. Meanwhile American, Australian, and New Zealand troops under the command of General Douglas MacArthur were engaged in the conquest of New Guinea. Progress there was slower than in the Solomons because the areas involved were larger and the terrain was more rugged; but the Allied force gradually succeeded in taking the important Japanese bases of Salamaua, Lae, and Finschhafen. Thus the first goal of the larger plan was achieved.

As the next step a force under Admiral Nimitz launched a powerful offensive against the British Gilbert Islands, a group of atolls (low coral islands) which the Japanese had seized in December, 1941. The force, composed largely of United States marines, quickly overwhelmed Makin atoll, but Tarawa was a different story. The capture of this atoll proved to be one of the most difficult and bloody tasks an Allied force had attempted. Never before had a tropical island been converted into such a mighty fortress. The Japanese had constructed pillboxes and blockhouses of concrete, steel rails, and stone-hard cocoanut logs. The blockhouses had outer walls ten feet thick and roofs covered with three or four feet of sand so as to make the defenses impervious to bombs and shells. Although 700 tons of bombs and 2900 tons of shells were dropped on Betio Island, which was hardly a square mile in size, most of the garrison of Japanese marines managed to survive, so that when the Allied troops landed on the island they encountered a devastating fire from the pillboxes and blockhouses. Only after three days of the bloodiest fighting did they reduce the enemy fortifications with TNT charges, torpedoes, and flame throwers.

The Allies were still far from Japan, but they had succeeded in breaching the outer defenses of the Japanese fortress and in building up their armed forces for further attacks. The first great operation of 1944 aimed at the occupation of the Marshall Islands, which the Japanese had held for a quarter of a century. On February 1 a force under Admiral Nimitz, composed largely of United States troops, landed on Kwajalein, the world's largest atoll of almost 1200 square miles. Only after a week of bloody fighting against 8000 Japanese was the atoll occupied. About the middle of February the forces of Admiral Nimitz landed on Eniwetok atoll, situated midway between the Marshalls and the Marianas. More than 2500 Japanese were killed before the Allied control of Eniwetok was complete. These conquests aroused grave concern in Japan. The Greater Asia Co-Prosperity Sphere was shrinking.

Again the Allied forces moved nearer Japan. This time Admiral Nimitz' goal was the Marianas, some parts of which were only 1400 miles from Tokyo. The first landings were made June 14 on Saipan. Saipan is only seventeen miles long, but the mountain range in its center gave excellent cover to the Japanese. Retreating to the caves with which the mountains are honeycombed, they fought with such determination that it required almost a month of hard fighting to subdue them. The conquest of Saipan was followed by the occupation of Guam and Tinian in the Marianas group. Tinian was taken after nine days of fighting, but stiffer resistance was encountered on Guam, a United States possession which had been seized by the Japanese after Pearl Harbor. Only after twenty days of fighting did organized resistance end. Another month was required for the conquest of the strongly defended Palau Islands. Admiral Nimitz reported that from the invasion of the Gilberts to the conquest of Guam the dead on the Japanese side numbered 52,323, on the Allied side 5903. From airfields on Saipan and Guam bombers ranged far and wide against the Japanese, even attacking the main Japanese island of Honshu.

Meanwhile preparations were also being made for the reconquest of the Philippines. The time had come for General MacArthur to fulfill his promise of delivering the islands. On October 19, 1944, two great assault forces closed upon the eastern coast of the island of Leyte, and after a heavy bombardment landings were made the next day.

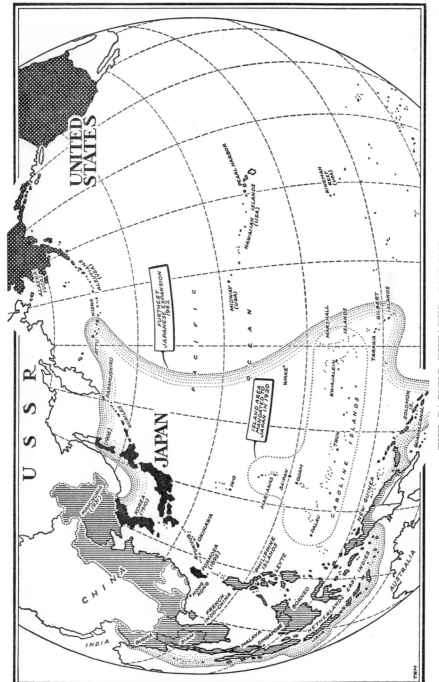

THE PACIFIC THEATER, 1941–1945

Later in the day MacArthur himself, accompanied by President Osmeña of the Philippines, went ashore. After his barge grounded he waded to the beach to make his liberation speech. "People of the Philippines," he said, "I have returned. By the grace of Almighty God our forces stand again on Philippine soil. . . . Let the indomitable spirit of Bataan and Corregidor lead on." At first the ground troops met with little opposition and pushed on rapidly. But after three days they were halted to await the outcome of an impending sea battle which threatened to isolate them. The Japanese, on hearing of the landings on Leyte, had collected all available warships to overwhelm the fleet that was protecting the landing forces, but in three engagements, known as the Battle of Leyte Gulf (October 24–26), the Japanese navy suffered a decisive defeat. With their safety assured, the land forces were ordered to continue their advance. The Japanese nevertheless managed at great cost to reinforce their troops, so that MacArthur's men were unable to overcome the organized resistance on Leyte until near the end of December.

Other landings followed those on Leyte. On December 15 amphibious forces landed on Mindoro, where they established an airfield only 155 miles from Manila. The invasion of Luzon, on which Manila is located, took place on January 9, 1945, when a force of 68,000 United States troops landed at the head of Lingayen Gulf. During the succeeding weeks the United States forces moved steadily southward on Luzon. At the beginning of February the forces converged on Manila, and on February 6 the capital was attacked from all sides. To dislodge the Japanese it was necessary to drive them back from house to house. Not until February 23 were they finally eliminated from the city. While this battle was in progress, landings were also made by parachutists and landing forces on Bataan, which was retaken after a battle of two weeks. During the succeeding months the reconquest of the Philippines proceeded against bitter Japanese resistance. It is estimated that 317,000 Japanese were killed, with the United States casualties numbering 60,600 killed, wounded and missing.

THE ALLIED INVASION OF FRANCE

For many months the Russians had been asking British and United States leaders to speed the establishment of a second front as a means of relieving the pressure on the eastern front. This second front was to be established by an invasion of western Europe for the purpose of liberating France, Belgium, and Holland and ultimately crushing the Nazis in Germany. Such an invasion necessitated careful planning and long preparation, for it was probably the most dangerous military operation of the war. The Nazis believed that their defenses along the Atlantic coast were impregnable. Hitler himself boasted, "Our enemies will discover that it is one thing to land against the Italians in Sicily and a very different thing against the Germans on the Channel." One thing was against the Germans. During the first months of 1944 the Allies had broken the back of the Luftwaffe. Thus the Allied commander was able to say truthfully to the invading forces, "Don't worry about planes overhead. They will be ours."

The task of collecting men and materials, welding the diverse elements into a powerful fighting machine, and carrying the invasion to a successful conclusion was delegated to General Dwight D. Eisenhower, who had distinguished himself in the North African campaign. Two million troops from the British Empire and the United States were massed in Britain together with mountains of supplies and equipment. Although Hitler and his Nazis were expecting an attack, the exact time and place were the secrets of the Allied high command. To mislead the Germans, feints were made in various directions.

The invasion began at 5 A.M. on June 6, 1944, just two days after the Allies had entered Rome. First, more than a thousand heavy bombers attacked the beach defenses along the Normandy coast; then another thousand planes dropped parachutists in Normandy behind the enemy lines. This parachute force was to sever communications and seize key defense posts. While the parachutists were being dropped, the Allied warships bombarded the German shore batteries and defense installations. Meanwhile the Allied fleet of about four thousand vessels, protected by a great canopy of aircraft, had left embarkation ports along the British coast and was proceeding toward France. Between 6:30 and 7:30 on June 6, which has become known as D Day, the first waves of Allied troops landed on the Normandy shores between Cherbourg and Le Havre. The element of surprise enabled the invasion forces to establish a beachhead sixty miles wide and to protect their positions successfully. They also succeeded by July 2 in gaining complete control of Cherbourg and the peninsula on which it is situated.

But the attempt to penetrate into France was another problem. For some weeks the Germans, who had moved in large numbers of men and much materiel, managed to restrict the Allies to the beachhead; but on July 26 a United States armored column succeeded in breaking through the German lines at Saint-Lô. Other columns quickly passed through the gap and fanned out in a wild dash through France. On August 15 another army of United States and French troops landed on the Mediterranean coast of France and quickly took Toulon, Marseilles, Nice, and Lyons. Meanwhile a large mixed force of Allied troops was forcing the Germans eastward. This force at first by-passed

Paris, but several days later the Germans in Paris surrendered. There was great joy in the Allied countries over the liberation of the French city.

Having gained momentum the Allied force under General Patton which had broken through at Saint-Lô continued to drive back the Germans in Blitzkrieg fashion, while a second force, composed largely of British and Canadians, went about the task of driving the Germans out of Belgium. The armies under General Eisenhower advanced so rapidly that by the middle of September six of them were near the western border of Germany. Barring their way, however, was the Westwall or Siegfried Line. Satisfactory if somewhat slow progress was being made in penetrating it when suddenly on December 16 the German Marshal von Rundstedt launched a counteroffensive in the Ardennes. United States troops holding this sector were pushed back about fifty miles toward the Meuse. From the great bulge thus created the battle took its name. After some bitter and tenacious fighting the United States troops managed to stop the German advance and then proceeded to regain the territory they had lost. The Battle of the Bulge was the last great German offensive.

While the Allied forces under General Eisenhower were driving the Germans out of France and Belgium, the Russians were moving rapidly toward the German border from the east. On the northern front the Red Army reached the 1940 Finnish-Soviet frontier by the beginning of July, 1944. By the middle of July the Russian armies on the central front had advanced far enough to take Vilna in Lithuania and those on the southern front moved into Poland. This rapid advance caused Finland to leave the Axis camp (September 4) and Rumania to sign an armistice with Russia (September 13). On October 28 Bulgaria also withdrew, leaving Hungary as the only German satellite. In Hungary, too, Admiral Horthy, the ruler of the country, requested an armistice, but he was overthrown by fascist elements who continued the fight against Russia.

THE DEFEAT OF THE NAZIS

During the early weeks of 1945 the Russians opened their last great offensive, with Berlin as the goal. While some divisions were moving through East Prussia and others were taking the capital of Hungary, the main Russian forces were driving through Poland toward Berlin. Progress was rapid. Early in February the Russians reached the Oder, which in places is only about thirty miles from Berlin. Had the German command recalled all its troops from the various countries in which they were stationed, the Russians might have been held off for a time. As it was, the Red armies took Vienna on April 13 and a few days later launched the final drive on Berlin.

Meanwhile in western Europe eight Allied armies had battered their way through the Siegfried Line and were advancing toward the Rhine. At Remagen the First United States Army was so close on the heels of the enemy that a considerable force managed to cross the Rhine bridge before the Germans could destroy it. Crossings were also made at other places which resulted in cutting Holland off from Germany and also in segregating the Ruhr industrial area from the rest of the Reich. Thereafter the weakened and demoralized German forces were able to offer but little resistance. The road to Berlin was open to the Allied armies under General Eisenhower; in fact, the Nazis were ready to surrender the German capital to him as a means of keeping the Russians out, but President Truman refused to accept anything but unconditional surrender on all fronts. General Eisenhower's men were eager "to keep going" until they reached Berlin, but the Russian deputy chief of staff objected, with the result that the British-American advance was halted on the west bank of the Elbe. President Roosevelt had agreed in a secret treaty with Stalin at Yalta (February, 1945) that the Russians should occupy Berlin. Churchill nevertheless urged General Eisenhower to proceed to the capture of Berlin before the Russians took it; but the agreement was kept. In the light of later events President Roosevelt's deal was denounced as a fateful mistake.

The terms for the German surrender had been set long before this time. At a press conference in Casablanca in January, 1943, President Roosevelt stated that the Allies would accept nothing less than unconditional surrender from the Axis countries. The idea derives from General Grant's answer to General Buckner, the Confederate commander of Fort Donelson, when the later asked for surrender terms (February, 1862): "No terms except an unconditional and immediate surrender can be accepted." The President subsequently explained that the idea had come to him on the spur of the moment. "The next thing I knew," he stated, "I had said it." Only later did he clear the term with Prime Minister Churchill. Neither appears at the time to have weighed the implications of the policy. The Nazi leaders, and particularly Goebbels, at once seized upon the idea and exploited it to the full. Goebbels told the Germans that defeat would mean slavery and forced labor for them. Thus the words "unconditional surrender" stiffened German morale instead of breaking it. In Italy they had the same effect. Before long the Allied leaders themselves began to question the wisdom of the policy. In February, 1944, Mr. Churchill tried to clarify it by stating:

Here I may point out that the term "Unconditional Surrender" does not mean that the German people will be enslaved or destroyed. It means, however, that the Allies will not be bound to them at the moment of surrender by any pact or obligation. . . . No such arguments will be admitted by us as were used by Germany after the last war, saying that they surrendered in consequence of President Wilson's Fourteen Points. Unconditional Surrender means that the victors have a free hand. It does not mean that they are entitled to behave in a barbarous manner, nor that they wish to blot out Germany from among the nations of Europe.

If the policy of unconditional surrender did prolong the struggle, as some have said, it also promised the Axis countries nothing. Consequently when the Germans laid down their arms in 1945 it was an open confession of defeat.[1]

During the final days of the war death removed both Mussolini and Hitler from the scene. Mussolini was the first to go. After his release from arrest by German troops in September, 1943, Mussolini was set up by the Nazis as a puppet ruler in northern Italy. But when in the spring of 1945 the German power in Italy collapsed, the Nazis abandoned Mussolini and he was captured at Como by a group of anti-Fascists while attempting to escape from the country. The next day (April 28) they executed the former Duce together with his mistress (Claretta Petacci) and sixteen of his Black Shirt followers. The reputed executioner, known to the Italian underground as "Colonel Valerio," declared that "Mussolini died a coward." Shaking with terror, he offered his captors "an empire" if they would spare his life. It was all in vain. After he was shot, Mussolini's body was exposed to the populace in the Piazza Loreto, a public square of Milan. An eyewitness reported that citizens of Milan kicked the body, spat upon it, and vented their feelings in other ways against the man who had brought the horrors of war down upon them and their country.

Hitler followed Mussolini to the grave. Soon after the middle of April the German Führer had lost all hope. "There is no question of fighting now," he said; "there is nothing left to fight with." On April 20, the day before the first Russian troops entered Berlin, he and Eva Braun, whom he reportedly married before his death, took refuge in the specially built bunker under the Chancellery. Only three days after

[1] Later Foreign Secretary Bevin blamed the policy of "unconditional surrender" for Germany's troubles. He said in the House of Commons (July 21, 1949): "I must go back for a moment to the declaration of unconditional surrender made at Casablanca, on which neither the British Cabinet nor any other cabinet had a chance to say a word. It was in the middle of a war and it was just made. But it left us with a Germany without law, without a constitution, without a single person with whom we could deal, without a single institution to grapple with the situation, and we have had to build from the bottom with nothing at all."

the former Duce's execution the German radio broadcast the news of Hitler's death. Various versions have been given of Hitler's passing. Some of his followers maintained that he was killed in the Berlin Chancellery by artillery fire; another and more generally accepted version has it that he and Eva Braun committed suicide. It is generally believed that Hitler's remains were buried in the rubble of the Chancellery.

Within a few days after the death of the two dictators German resistance collapsed completely. On April 29, the day after Mussolini's execution, the Allied forces in Italy compelled the Germans there to accept the terms of unconditional surrender, and on May 2 the Russians captured Berlin. It was generally believed that fanatical Nazis would continue to put up a stubborn resistance even after the main German armies had surrendered. During the preceding winter the cry "We shall never capitulate" had been sounded with great frequency. But it was only an attempt of the Nazis to bolster their waning courage. Hitler's death seems to have snapped the thread of German morale. On May 7 Admiral Doenitz, who temporarily succeeded Hitler as Führer, signed the articles of surrender, and hostilities ceased at 12:01 on May 9. The war in Europe was over.

THE SURRENDER OF JAPAN

By the time of the German collapse the Japanese had been driven from many strategic positions in the islands of the central and southwest Pacific, their naval power had been largely shattered, and their air power outmatched. But they still held the Dutch East Indies, a large part of China, and a number of strategic islands. Furthermore, Japan still had strong armies at home and in the conquered territories she held. On the other hand, she had since the conquest of the Marianas lost the immunity from air raids which she had enjoyed since the Doolittle raid in 1942.[2] Even before the conquest of Saipan was completed, the construction of an airbase on Saipan was begun; other bases were built on Guam and Tinian. Superfortresses from these bases subjected Japan to an increasing bombardment. Because of their inflammable nature Japanese cities were more vulnerable than the cities of Europe. But the Allies as yet held no base near enough to the Japanese home islands to permit the dispatch of fighter planes, which alone could give an invasion force proper air support. It was necessary, therefore, to gain command of a base within easy striking distance of Japan.

The choice fell upon the island of Okinawa in the Ryukyus group.

[2] On April 18, 1942, Lt. Col. Doolittle led an air raid on the Tokyo area by 16 medium bombers launched from the aircraft carrier *Hornet*.

Okinawa, sixty miles long and from two to twenty miles wide, is situated about 370 miles from the southern tip of Japan. It was garrisoned by a force of 70,000 Japanese with some 500 artillery guns. For the conquest of Okinawa a force of 100,000 soldiers and marines was collected. They were transported in 1400 ships, a larger number than had been employed in the invasion of North Africa. After a terrific bombardment by the fleet, against which the Japanese defenses stood up well, United States marines and soldiers began the landing operations on Easter Sunday morning (April 1, 1945). Occupation of the northern end of the island was rapid, but in the southern part, where the Japanese commander chose to make a stand, every inch had to be purchased with blood. It took almost three months of bloody fighting to overcome organized Japanese resistance. United States casualties numbered 7283 killed and 31,398 wounded; the Japanese dead totaled 101,853.

One noteworthy feature of this operation was the use by the Japanese of suicide (Kamikaze) planes and boats. A Kamikaze plane would be loaded with explosives, and the aviator would then try to crash land on the deck of a ship. At a cost of more than four thousand planes and pilots the Japanese sank thirty vessels, the largest of which were destroyers, and damaged some of the larger warships. In a further attempt to cripple the United States naval force engaged in the operation, a task force which included the last big Japanese battleship started in the direction of Okinawa, but it was sighted and attacked by four hundred United States carrier planes, which sank some of the Japanese ships and forced the others to turn back.

When the capture of Okinawa was completed the United States forces had the bases required for the final great assault on Japan. After the surrender of Germany on May 8 Allied troops were deployed as quickly as possible to the Pacific theatre. The invasion as planned was to take place in two stages. Secretary of War Stimson outlined the plans in these words:

> We were planning an intensified sea and air blockade, and greatly intensified strategic air bombing, through the summer and early fall, to be followed on November 1 by an invasion of the southern island of Kyushu. This would be followed in turn by an invasion of the main island of Honshu (on which Tokyo is situated) in the spring of 1946.[3]

Early in August, however, the dropping of two atomic bombs quickly brought the war to an end. When the atom bomb was ready for military use the United States, Great Britain, and China warned the Japa-

[3] H. L. Stimson and M. Bundy, *On Active Service in Peace and War* (1948), pp. 618–619.

nese government (July 26) in an ultimatum that if it did not accept at once the terms of unconditional surrender "the alternative for Japan is prompt and utter destruction." Three days later the Japanese government rejected the ultimatum. President Truman [4] then decided to unleash the new weapon. On August 6 a United States Army B-29 bomber dropped the first bomb on the Japanese city of Hiroshima, which was at the time the headquarters of the Japanese army defending southern Japan and a major military storage and assembly point. The effects were devastating. Of a population of 245,000 about 80,000 were killed and an equal number were seriously injured. More than 60 per cent of the buildings were destroyed including the main administrative, commercial, and residential sections. In announcing the dropping of the bomb President Truman said: "We are now prepared to obliterate more rapidly and completely every productive enterprise the Japanese have above ground in any city. . . . Let there be no mistake. We shall completely destroy Japan's power to make war."

Events moved rapidly in the days that followed. Before the Japanese recovered from the shock of the first atomic bomb, Russia declared war against Japan (August 8) and on the following day invaded Manchuria. This was in accordance with the promise Stalin had made at the Yalta Conference (February, 1945) that Soviet Russia would join in the war against Japan within ninety days after the surrender of the Germans. By this time Russia's help was no longer needed. On August 9 the second atomic bomb was dropped. This time the target was Nagasaki, a major seaport containing several large industrial plants of great wartime importance. Casualties of the second bomb were between 35,000 and 40,000 killed and about the same number injured. This bomb convinced the Japanese government of the folly of further resistance and on August 10 it sued for peace, offering to surrender under the terms of the ultimatum of July 26 on condition that the emperor's sovereignty remain unimpaired. The Allied governments replied on August 11: "From the moment of surrender the authority of the Emperor and the Japanese government to rule the state shall be subject to the Supreme Commander of the Allied Powers. The ultimate form of government of Japan shall be established by the freely expressed will of the Japanese people." Finally, after deliberating for several days, the Japanese government accepted the provision of "unconditional surrender."

Secretary of War Stimson said regarding the decision to drop the atomic bomb that after the New Mexico test "it was immediately clear that the power of the bomb measured up to our highest estimates. We had developed a weapon of such revolutionary character that its use

[4] President Roosevelt had died suddenly on April 12, 1945.

against the enemy might well be expected to produce exactly the kind
of shock on the Japanese ruling oligarchy which we desired, strengthening the desire of those who wished peace, and weakening that of
the military party." President Truman, in telling why the atomic bomb
was dropped, said: "The Japanese were given fair warning, and were
offered the terms which they finally accepted, well in advance of the
dropping of the bomb. I imagine the bomb caused them to accept the
terms." On September 5 Prince Higashi-Kuni, Japan's premier,
acknowledged that the bomb had been the immediate inducement to
surrender. "This terrific weapon," he said, "was likely to result in the
obliteration of the Japanese people." World War II formally ended
at 9:08 on Sunday morning, September 2, 1945, when in the presence
of United States, British, Chinese, Dutch, French, and Russian officers and officials the last signature was affixed to the document of
Japan's unconditional surrender on the deck of the U.S.S. Missouri in
Tokyo Bay.

After six years of bloody fighting the war had finally come to an
end. Hardly a nation of the earth had succeeded in remaining aloof.
Even the few countries which did not participate in the actual fighting did not escape certain consequences of the war, particularly the
economic dislocations it caused. In the belligerent states approximately
a hundred million men and women had been mobilized in the armed
forces, while the larger part of the civilian population was engaged in
war production. After the shooting ceased, men were able to stand
back and survey the costs of the war and the destruction it had wrought.
The costs can be briefly surveyed under two headings: the material
costs and the cost in human lives. Figures naturally do not tell the
whole story. They are only approximates from which we get some idea
of the magnitude of the disaster rather than an accurate account of its
costs.

The cost of training men, providing them with weapons, and keeping
them supplied with food and ammunition can be expressed only in
astronomical figures. It is estimated that Germany spent $272 billion
on matériel alone, while the expenditures of the United States were
over $300 billion. Italy, one of the poorest of the great powers, spent
$94 billion. According to one estimate, the cost of the military material
reached the staggering total of $1,154 billion. To this must be added
the cost of destruction, which was unparalleled in history. Even World
War I was only one-seventh as destructive. With the losses by destruction figured in, the total cost of the war has been estimated at four
trillion dollars.

The cost in human lives was appalling. General George C. Marshall
estimated the loss of life in battle to be fifteen millions. But the civilian

deaths were even more numerous than those of men in uniform, giving point to the sardonic joke that the front line is the safest place in wartime. Deaths from bombings were three hundred times more numerous than in World War I. To these must be added deaths resulting from deliberate attempts at extermination, losses in underground movements, and refugee deaths. When all these losses are taken into consideration the cost of the war in human lives reaches a total of almost forty millions.

CHAPTER THIRTY-ONE

The Elusive Peace

PEACEMAKING after World War II differed in a number of respects from peacemaking after World War I. First, the peacemaking after World War II was characterized by the absence of such idealism as heralded the Paris conference of 1919. No Woodrow Wilson appeared with a program of Fourteen Points. Certain principles were laid down in the so-called Atlantic Charter resulting from a conference between Prime Minister Churchill and President Roosevelt (August 9–12, 1941), but by the end of the war they were largely forgotten. Second, the victors were in no hurry to make peace after World War II. After World War I the Allies took up the work of making peace soon after the guns were silenced. Within three months after the armistice representatives of the victorious powers met in Paris and three months later the treaties were practically ready for signing. After World War II there was a considerable cooling-off period during which it was hoped the emotional feelings aroused by the war would subside. More than eighteen months passed before even the lesser treaties were ready for signing. After that the negotiations dragged on month after month. In March, 1948, Winston Churchill wrote: "The human tragedy reaches its climax in the fact that after all the exertions and sacrifices of hundreds of millions of people and of the victories of the Righteous Cause, we have still not found Peace and Security, and that we lie in the grip of even worse perils than those we have surmounted."

THE CONFERENCE AT YALTA

A number of conferences which were held during the war may be regarded as the first stages in the peacemaking. Of these the conference held at Yalta in the Crimea was probably the most important. It was also by all odds the most controversial. Thus one author states, "Yalta has been blamed for many of the ills with which the world was afflicted in the years following the total defeat of Nazi Germany and Japan." [1] More recently a man who was secretary of commerce under President Roosevelt wrote that at Yalta Roosevelt "made commitments from which our country and the rest of the non-Communist world may never recover." [2] Yalta was the most comprehensive conference of World War II. Present were Prime Minister Churchill, President Roosevelt, and Marshal Stalin; also British Foreign Secretary Eden, Soviet Foreign Minister Molotov, and U.S. Secretary of State Stettinius. In addition the delegation from each of the three countries included a considerable number of distinguished advisers and specialists. Finally, all the Chiefs of Staff of the three countries, with one exception, were there.[3] All in all, it was a notable array of political and military talent.

When this group of notables converged on Yalta in February of 1945, early victory over the Germans seemed assured. In the east the Russians had pounded their way through Poland to the German frontiers and were ready to launch the final drive on Berlin. On the western front more than a million troops were opposing the Germans. Most of France had been liberated and the Allied armies had penetrated some distance into Germany. The Battle of the Bulge, it is true, had stopped their progress for a time, but before the conference opened at Yalta the German counteroffensive had been smashed. It was ostensibly to complete the plans for the final defeat of Germany and to discuss the broad outlines of a German settlement that this conference was called.

While the military experts were formulating the military plans, Churchill, Roosevelt, and Stalin discussed other questions regarding Germany. One of these was the division of Germany into zones. According to the first plan there were to be three, one each for Britain, the Soviet Union, and the United States. Unity of administration was to be secured as far as possible by a Central Control Commission. Later Churchill and Roosevelt proposed that a zone be given to France. Stalin did not think France had any right to a zone, but he agreed when it was specified that the French zone was to be carved out of the British and American zones. "I am in favor of France being given a zone," Stalin declared, "but I cannot forget that in this war France opened the gates to the enemy." [4] Subsequently President Roosevelt also succeeded in convincing Stalin to give France representation on the Allied Control Council for Germany. A further question regarding Germany

---

[1] Robert Sherwood in *Roosevelt and Hopkins* (1948), p. 853.
[2] Jesse Jones in *Fifty Billion Dollars* (1951), p. 287.
[3] U.S. General H. H. Arnold was absent because of illness.
[4] James F. Byrnes, *Speaking Frankly* (1947), p. 25.

was that of reparations. Churchill and Roosevelt did agree with Stalin that Germany must repay in kind the losses suffered by the Allied nations. When the Soviet delegation sought, however, to fix the total reparations at $20 billion, of which the U.S.S.R. was to receive $10 billion, Churchill flatly refused such valuation. Finally President Roosevelt suggested that a Reparations Commission take the Soviet figure "as a basis for discussion."

When the Polish boundary question came up for discussion Stalin demanded that it be settled to his liking. He insisted that the Curzon Line be made the western boundary of the Soviet Union. This meant the inclusion of about 47 per cent of Poland or almost half of Poland's pre-war territory in the U.S.S.R. Both Churchill and Roosevelt finally approved the Curzon Line, but expressed the hope that the Soviet Union would make some concessions, such as Lwow, to the Poles. Stalin also suggested that Poland be extended into Germany as far as the Neisse River. Both Churchill and Roosevelt objected, the former saying that "it would be a pity to stuff the Polish goose so full of German food that he will die of indigestion." The question was left open and the statement issued by the Big Three at the close of the conference merely announced that "Poland must receive substantial accessions of territory in the North and West." In the military occupation of Germany, however, Stalin arbitrarily made the Neisse River the Polish-German frontier.

Both Churchill and Roosevelt, fearing a Soviet plan to dominate eastern Europe, insisted that once the war was won the Poles be permitted to choose the kind of government they want without interference from beyond the borders. Roosevelt told Stalin that he favored a government "which would represent all the political parties." The latter in a long speech accepted the suggestion of Churchill and Roosevelt that Poland should be "free and sovereign," but added that for security reasons the government must be friendly to the Soviet Union. Stalin also accepted the pledge of "free and unfettered elections as soon as possible on the basis of universal suffrage and secret ballot." At the time of the Yalta conference the Soviets had already set up their own Polish provisional government without any consideration for the Polish government-in-exile in London. Soon the western states were to learn that Stalin's concept of a friendly government is one completely under the domination of the U.S.S.R.

The Big Three also declared in the Yalta communiqué that whatever changes were to be made in Europe should be carried out in accordance with the principles laid down in the Atlantic Charter. The communiqué promised that the three nations would jointly assist "the peoples liberated from the domination of Nazi Germany and the peoples of the former Axis satellite states of Europe to solve by demo-cratic means their pressing political and economic problems." The Big Three further pledged themselves "to form interim governmental au-thorities broadly representative of all democratic elements in the popu-lation" and to hold free elections at the earliest possible moment. Finally the signatories agreed to consult together regarding conditions in any European liberated state "on the measures necessary to dis-charge the joint responsibilities set forth in this declaration."

The decisions on Germany, Poland, and the liberated countries of Europe did not conclude the discussions. President Roosevelt had two other objectives. The first of these was to secure the Soviet Union's aid in the war against Japan. Actually the western allies did not need Russia's help. When the Big Three met at Yalta in February, 1945, Japan's offensive strength had been largely destroyed. The Japanese navy had lost its striking force and could do little more than harry an invasion fleet. American naval craft were already cruising at will in Japanese home waters. As for the Japanese airforce, it was reduced "mainly to reliance on Kamikaze or suicide attacks." But the Japa-nese land forces were still believed to be intact and ready to fight to the finish. As late as July of 1945 the intelligence section of the U.S. War Department General Staff estimated the strength of the Japanese army at about five million men. Mr. Henry L. Stimson who was Secre-tary of War at the time wrote in his memoirs:

> As we understood it in July, there was a very strong possibility that the Japanese Government might determine upon resistance to the end, in all the areas of the Far East under its control. In such an event the Allies would be faced with the enormous task of destroying an armed force of five million men and five thousand suicide aircraft, belonging to a race which had already demonstrated its ability to fight literally to the death.[5]

The strategic plans which the U.S. Joint Chiefs of Staff had pro-jected called for the invasion of the Japanese home island of Kyushu about November 1 of that year. This was to be followed by an inva-sion of the main island of Honshu in the spring of 1946. In U.S. mili-tary circles it was believed that the war would not end before the latter part of 1946. Churchill was of the opinion that it might be prolonged into 1947. The fighting was expected to be bloody and to cost up to a million American lives. Thus there appeared to be impelling reasons why Russia's entrance in the war should be assured. Having been told in an intelligence report that the Japanese force in Manchuria was "the cream of the Japanese army," the Joint Chiefs of Staff wanted to get Russia into the war to contain the Japanese forces in Manchuria and

[5] H. L. Stimson and M. Bundy, *On Active Service in Peace and War* (1948), p. 618.

prevent their transfer to the Japanese home islands. Neither they nor President Roosevelt appeared to know that the report of the intelligence section exaggerated Japanese potentialities. No one expected the Russians to defeat the Japanese force in Manchuria with the ease with which this was later accomplished. Hence President Roosevelt was urged to make certain of Russian participation in the war, even if the price demanded by the Russians was heavy.

In informed circles Russia's entry into the war was regarded as certain. The basis for this belief was that the Kremlin could share in the division of the spoils only by participating in the war. Stalin had, in fact, pledged the entry of the Soviet Union many months before the Yalta conference. In October, 1943, he had assured U.S. Secretary of State Hull that his country would enter the war against Japan after the defeat of Germany. Two months later at Teheran Stalin reiterated this promise to Churchill and Roosevelt. But when the question was broached at Yalta, Stalin told President Roosevelt that certain concessions in the Far East would have to be made if the Soviet Union was to join in the war against Japan. "I only want to have returned to Russia," Stalin said, "what the Japanese have taken from my country." [6] Eager to obtain the support of the Soviet Union, Roosevelt paid the price. A secret treaty was negotiated by the Big Three without the participation of either the U.S. State Department or the British Foreign Office and was kept secret for months.

The agreement stated that the Soviet Union would enter the war against Japan "in two or three months" on the following conditions:

(1) That Russia's *status quo* in Outer Mongolia be preserved.

(2) That the sovereignty of the Kuriles be transferred to the Soviet Union.

(3) That the rights Russia lost in the Russo-Japanese War be restored. This included the return of the southern half of Sakhalin Island to Russia, the restoration of the lease of Port Arthur as a naval base, port rights at Darien, and joint Russo-Chinese operation of the Chinese Eastern and Southern Manchurian railroads. The agreement, however, stated expressly "that China shall retain full sovereignty in Manchuria."

Another of President Roosevelt's objectives was to win the cooperation of the Soviet Union in the work of building a United Nations Organization to establish security and preserve the peace. When the discussion of such an organization was opened the Soviet delegation proposed that not only the U.S.S.R., but also two of its component states, White Russia (Byelorussia) and the Ukraine be given seats in the U.N. General Assembly. There is little doubt that the President

6 Leahy, *I Was There* (1950), p. 318.

was against such a concession. Before going to Yalta he had told Congressional leaders that he would oppose the Soviet request and if necessary demand forty-eight votes for the United States. But at Yalta he found that Churchill favored giving the Soviet Union two extra votes. As Churchill was unwilling to join him in opposing the Soviet request, President Roosevelt agreed that the United States would support the Russian proposal at the United Nations conference in San Francisco the following April. Later, upon considering the possible effect of his promise on the Congress, the President asked from both Marshal Stalin and Prime Minister Churchill a definite commitment that the British and Russians would support a demand for two additional votes for the United States in case such a request were to be made. Both promptly agreed. At San Francisco, however, the United States did not ask more than one vote, but the Russians got their extra votes.

At the conclusion of the conference the Big Three appeared to be in a happy mood and toasted the others at the final banquet. President Roosevelt upon his return to the United States told the Congress: "I come from the Crimean Conference with a firm belief that we have made a good start on the road to a world of peace. . . . I think the Crimean Conference was a successful effort by the three leading nations to find a common ground for peace." Churchill in his address to the House of Commons expressed similar sentiments. "I trust," he said, "the House will feel that hope has been powerfully strengthened by our meeting in the Crimea. The ties that bind the three great powers together, and their mutual comprehension of each other, have grown."

But the Yalta agreement soon gave rise to suspicion and distrust. The men in the Kremlin had the choice of either accepting the good-neighbor principles of Yalta and building a sincere peace on the basis of them or of ignoring the agreement. They chose the latter. Stalin never made any pretense of carrying out the Yalta agreement. The ink was hardly dry before the Kremlin flagrantly violated its terms. Even before President Roosevelt reported to the Congress, Soviet Deputy Foreign Minister Vishinsky had intervened in Rumanian affairs to compel King Michael to replace a coalition of moderates with a Soviet puppet regime. The agreement to establish interim governments "broadly representative of all democratic elements in the population and pledged to the earliest possible establishment through free elections of governments responsible to the will of the people" was also violated in Poland. The Kremlin recognized the Lublin government which it had arbitrarily established as the legitimate government of Poland and transferred it to Warsaw, demonstrating clearly that the agreements of Yalta were not intended by the Kremlin to lead to any genuine coalition of democratic parties. The pledge of free elections at the earliest possible time was ignored. Elections were not held for almost two years and then were anything but "free and unfettered."

The result was that many who had rejoiced over Yalta soon became seriously disturbed. Among these was President Roosevelt himself. He told Mr. Byrnes that in view of the Kremlin's conduct since Yalta he had grave misgivings about the future. Shortly before the President's death Marshal Stalin greatly offended him by charging that Britain and the United States were offering to ease German peace terms if the German army in Italy would surrender. In his reply the President objected to the "vile misrepresentations" and a conciliatory exchange of messages followed. On the day before his death Mr. Roosevelt wrote to Stalin: "There must not, in any event, be mutual distrust, and minor misunderstandings of this character should not arise in the future." But the discord deepened and in May President Truman sent Harry Hopkins to Moscow in an effort to improve relations. The latter was successful in smoothing over some of the differences so that for a time better relations prevailed.

THE POTSDAM CONFERENCE

After Germany had been defeated and the occupation zones had been set up, representatives of Great Britain, the Soviet Union, and the United States met at Potsdam, near Berlin (July 17, 1945). Of the Big Three that had made the decisions at Yalta only Stalin remained. Winston Churchill was there when the conference opened, but was replaced by Clement R. Attlee, the new British prime minister as a result of the British parliamentary election of July 23. President Truman represented the United States. At this conference the victors' terms were drawn up for Germany. The representatives of the three victor nations stated that "it is not the intention of the Allies to destroy or enslave the German people," that the German people by amending their ways will be able "in due course to take their place among the free and peaceful peoples of the world." But "to assure that Germany never again will threaten her neighbors or the peace of the world" they deprived her of the power to make war by abolishing all the armed forces of that country and by forbidding the manufacture of all armaments. "The production of arms, ammunition and implements of war, as well as all types of aircraft and seagoing ships," the decision read, "shall be prohibited and be prevented. Production of metals, chemicals, machinery and other items that are directly necessary to a war economy shall be rigidly controlled and restricted to Germany's approved postwar peacetime needs." Other decisions regarding Germany included the abolition of nazism and its institutions, the trial and punishment of war criminals, and the control of German education as a means of inculcating democratic ideas.

When the question of reparations was settled Stalin again obtained pretty much what he wanted. The fact that the Russians had borne the brunt of battle against the Nazis and had suffered the greatest economic losses caused the representatives of the western democracies to vote the major part of German reparations to the Soviet Union. First, the Soviet Union was permitted to satisfy its reparations claims by the removal of industrial equipment from its own zone and by the appropriation of German assets in that zone. The total amount of the reparations the Soviet Union was to receive was not determined at the Potsdam conference. It was specified, however, that the payment of reparations by Germany "should leave enough resources to enable the German people to subsist without external assistance." In addition to reparations from its own zone the Soviet Union was permitted to take from the western zones 25 per cent of such industrial equipment as was not needed for the new German peace economy. Ten per cent of the equipment the Soviet Union was to receive without any return payment; for the remaining 15 per cent it was to pay an equivalent amount in food and raw materials. Furthermore, the Soviet Union was given complete control over German external assets in Finland, Bulgaria, Hungary, Rumania, and Eastern Austria plus an unannounced portion of those elsewhere. Out of its share of reparations the Soviet Union promised to settle Poland's claims for reparations. As for the western Allies, they were to collect their reparations from the remaining industrial wealth in their own zones of occupation.

Two further decisions were made which favored the Soviet Union. The city of Koenigsberg and the eastern part of East Prussia were provisionally handed over to the U.S.S.R. What remained of East Prussia including the free city of Danzig and an additional slice of German territory extending westward to the Oder and Neisse Rivers were turned over to Poland, pending the fixing of the boundaries in the final peace settlement. The reason for this was, of course, to compensate the Poles for the eastern half of Poland which Stalin had annexed in 1939.

DRAFTING THE FIRST TREATIES

At Potsdam Prime Minister Attlee, Generalissimo Stalin, and President Truman also decided that, instead of calling a peace conference to draft the treaties of peace, this task was to be carried out by a Council of Foreign Ministers composed of the foreign ministers of Britain, France, the Soviet Union, China, and the United States. The

Potsdam declaration stated that "as its immediate important task the Council shall be authorized to draw up, with a view to their submission to the United Nations, treaties of peace with Italy, Rumania, Bulgaria, Hungary, and Finland."

The basic prerequisite for drawing up fair and lasting treaties was harmony and cooperation between the victor nations. But this prerequisite was completely lacking. During the war the necessity of keeping the coalition together had moved Allied propagandists to do their best to create the illusion that harmony and mutual love reigned supreme among the Allies. They were so successful that the people of Britain and the United States were misled into believing that the Soviet government was eager to cooperate in translating the idea of "one world" into reality. Actually there had never been a real friendship between Soviet Russia and the western powers. Behind the scenes there was much distrust and suspicion.[7] Churchill himself stated in a speech of October 9, 1948: "The gulf which was opening between Asiatic Communist Russia and the western democracies, large and small, was already brutally obvious to the War Cabinet of the national coalition even before Hitler was destroyed and the Germans laid down their arms." There was little cooperation even in military matters. While Britain and the United States pooled their war efforts, Soviet Russia largely played a lone hand. During most of the war British and United States military observers were barred from all Russian fronts. Only late in 1944, when General Eisenhower's armies were already inside Germany, did the Russians deign to divulge to the western military leaders information about their campaign plans.

As soon as the war ended even the semblance of unity disappeared and the distrust and suspicion came out into the open. The Soviet government was now ready to sacrifice the good-will of the non-Communist nations in order to consolidate its power and achieve its imperialist aims. The western powers, on the other hand, were no longer inclined to make the concessions the Russians demanded. The quick surrender of the Japanese and the possession of the atomic bomb caused them to adopt a firmer attitude toward Soviet demands.

Thus the meetings of the Council of Foreign Ministers became, in a sense, an open struggle for power and there was endless wrangling over strategic areas, colonial possessions, and spheres of political influence. Agreement on the smallest matters became more and more difficult. At the first meeting of the Council of Foreign Ministers which opened in London on September 10, 1945, there was little agreement on any question. When discussion of a peace plan for Italy was opened,

---

[7] See John R. Deane's *The Strange Alliance* (1946) and W. T. R. Fox's *The Superpowers* (1944).

disagreement arose at once over the question of the Italian colonies. Britain and the United States vigorously opposed Mr. Molotov's proposition that Italian Libya be assigned to the Soviet Union. They did not wish Russia to establish her influence in the Mediterranean. A further point of disagreement was the question of reparations. Mr. Molotov's demand that Italy pay the Soviet Union $300 million in reparations was also opposed by the representatives of Britain and the United States. There was further disagreement over the question of Trieste. Whereas the Soviet representative insisted that Trieste and adjacent territory should go to Yugoslavia, the British, French, and United States representatives urged that Trieste remain with Italy, but be transformed into a free port. The western democracies feared that if Trieste were put under the exclusive control of Yugoslavia it could be used as an entering wedge for Soviet expansion to the Adriatic Sea. Britain, France, and the United States also objected to Russian domination of totalitarian governments in Bulgaria, Hungary, and Rumania, asserting that treaties could not be signed with these countries unless free and unfettered elections were assured. At the conclusion of the conference the foreign ministers found themselves so far apart that they did not even issue a communiqué. Former Secretary of State Byrnes shows this very clearly in his *Speaking Frankly:*

Now at London, Mr. Molotov saw no chance of taking home any packages. He could not understand why we would not accept his interpretation that friendship between our governments required that we let the Soviets establish complete suzerainty over the Balkan states. As far as I was concerned Christmas was over — it was now January 1, and we had many bills to pay. Instead of issuing more I.O.U.'s, I wanted to collect some we held. One of these I felt was the Yalta pledge on the treatment of the liberated.

The failure of the conference to reach any agreement was so signal that it was feared in western circles the split might be carried to the United Nations General Assembly scheduled to convene in London on January 10, 1946. Secretary of State Byrnes, therefore, urged that another attempt be made to reach some kind of agreement before that time. The result was a meeting of the foreign ministers in Moscow on December 16, 1945. At the close of the meeting (December 26) the Big Three issued a communiqué which incorporated the decisions that had been reached. One decision specified that only those members of the Big Five who had signed the surrender terms with the Axis satellites were to participate in the actual drafting of the treaties. Thus the peace treaty with Italy was to be drafted by Britain, the Soviet Union, the United States, and France, the last being regarded as a signer of the armistice for this purpose. The treaties with Rumania, Bulgaria, and Hungary were to be drafted by Britain, the Soviet Union, and the United States. Since the United States had not declared war on Finland, the Finnish treaty was to be drafted only by Britain and the Soviet Union.

Decisions were also reached on a number of other subjects. Soviet Russia was given representation on the Far Eastern Commission, but it was definitely stated that General MacArthur was to remain "the sole executive authority for the Allied powers in Japan." The foreign ministers further decided that the Soviet Union and the United States set up a joint commission to unify Korea and assist in the establishment of a provisional Korean government under the control of democratic leaders. After a trusteeship under the Big Four (U.S., Britain, China, and the U.S.S.R.) for a period "up to five years" Korea was to be granted its independence. Mr. Byrnes and Mr. Molotov also agreed on the desirability of withdrawing Soviet and United States troops from China "at the earliest moment." Both saw "the need for a unified and democratic China under the National Government" of Chiang Kai-shek and reaffirmed the policy of "non-intervention in the internal affairs of China." The decision that was regarded as the most significant at the time was that the Big Three agreed jointly to propose, together with Canada, China, and France, to the first meeting of the United Nations General Assembly a resolution urging the creation of a commission "to consider problems arising from the discovery of atomic energy and related matters."

The Moscow agreements were hailed widely in the press of Europe and the United States as a hopeful step toward peace with such statements as "the stalemate has been broken" and "the achievements of the Moscow Conference provide substantial reason for a rebirth of hope in the world." An editorial in the New York *Herald Tribune* stated: "The Christmas Eve communiqué from the Big Three Foreign Ministers, issuing from the star-jeweled cold of Moscow's northern skies as the bells were pealing and the carols were being sung around the world, was a happy gift and a happy augury." But before long many people realized that the agreements were reached largely as a result of concessions by the western powers. On January 7 *Newsweek* displayed the following headline: "Moscow results clear the air at the cost of concessions to Russia," and the New York *Herald Tribune* stated: "Washington officials acknowledged privately that the decisions contained sweeping concessions by the Anglo-American powers to the views of Soviet Russia. It was assumed that the American delegation agreed to many of the provisions only as a means of obtaining extensive participation in the United Nations Organization to keep peace."

The next meeting of the Council of Foreign Ministers opened in

Paris on April 15, 1946, with the foreign ministers of Britain, France, the Soviet Union, and the United States present. As the Russians were temporarily cooperative things went well for a time. The ministers unanimously agreed to limit the future naval strength of Italy and to appoint a committee of naval experts to apportion surplus Italian craft among their countries and also Greece and Yugoslavia. Transylvania was awarded to Rumania, the southern Dobruja was accorded to Bulgaria, and the Soviet Union was permitted to retain Bessarabia and northern Bucovina. But thereafter disagreements again became the order of the day, with each side trying to consolidate its own sphere of influence. As U.S. Secretary of State Byrnes put it, "The Russians' well-publicized amiability at the start of the sessions has progressively diminished as the discussions have moved into the crucial areas. . . . Evidently it is Mr. Molotov's tactic to surrender on minor points while remaining adamant on the greater issues." Finally the foreign ministers, realizing that the sessions were "getting nowhere," decided on May 16 to recess them lest a continuation result in open rupture.

After the Council reconvened on June 15 the foreign ministers of Britain, France, and the United States reluctantly agreed that the Soviet Union could over a period of seven years receive reparations up to $100 million from Italy. No final decision was reached, however, on the Italian colonies. It was finally agreed that the ultimate disposition of the colonies should be made at a later time by the four principal allied powers in the light of the wishes and welfare of the inhabitants. Although it had reached no agreement on Trieste and other questions, the Council decided to submit the drafts of the treaties with Italy, Rumania, Bulgaria, Hungary, and Finland to the other allied nations for discussion. For this purpose a conference of delegates of the twenty-one victor nations was summoned to meet in Paris.

THE PARIS CONFERENCE

The delegates of the Big Four (Britain, France, the U.S.S.R., and the U.S.A.) and the "Little Seventeen" to the first peace conference after World War II assembled in Paris on July 29, 1946. It was not, however, a peace conference in the sense that the Conference of Paris had been in 1919. The Peace Conference of 1946 was not called for the actual purpose of drawing up peace treaties; nor was it empowered to make decisions on the contents of the treaties to be signed with the Axis satellites. The sole function of the peace conference was to make recommendations which the Council of Foreign Ministers could subsequently, as it saw fit, either incorporate in the treaties or discard. In other words, the Little Seventeen could only submit their views on the treaties which had been drawn up by the Big Four. This peace conference, like that of 1919, was dominated by the Great Powers. The conference of 1946, however, differed from the conference of 1919 in that the five nations whose treaties were discussed were given opportunity to state their case and plead their cause. Thus, for example, Premier de Gasperi of Italy was permitted to protest before a plenary session against the "punitive character" of the Italian treaty, and the Foreign Minister of Finland asked for a reduction of the reparations payments required of his country.

When the conference opened, the hopes of international cooperation and good will were high. Premier Bidault of France in his speech of welcome to the delegates expressed the confident hope "that the representatives of all our countries will work in common accord and in a spirit of friendly cooperation on the important task set before them." Other speakers also sounded the note of friendly cooperation. But their hopes were quickly dissipated. Soon one correspondent wrote: "This conference would have been better understood if it had been frankly labeled 'The Battle of Paris' and had been accepted as an integral part of World War II." The conference got off to an explosive start when Dr. Herbert V. Evatt, Australia's representative, insisted that the smaller nations were "entitled not merely to the right of consultation but to equal rights of actual participation in the peace-making process." "Each of the twenty-one nations," he said, "has equal rank and voice in this conference." He, therefore, demanded that all recommendations be accepted by a simple majority vote of the delegates rather than by a two-thirds majority. A week of acrimonious debate followed in which the Big Four argued in favor of the two-thirds procedure, with Soviet Russia as its particular champion. This procedure held special advantages for the Soviet Union which with its bloc of six votes (Yugoslavia, Byelorussia, the Ukraine, Poland, and Czechoslovakia, in addition to the U.S.S.R.) could hamper any action it disliked. Finally on August 9 a compromise proposal was approved according to which the recommendations of the conference were to be of two kinds, those adopted by a two-thirds majority and those adopted by a simple majority.

The real issue of the conference, however, was the contest for power between the eastern communist nations and the western democracies. This contest was a basic factor in almost every dispute. Whereas the Russians sought to expand their power and influence, the representatives of the western democracies endeavored to confine Russian expansion and limit Russian power. The Soviet delegates missed no opportunity to make claims either for Russia or her satellites. Whenever a Soviet satellite requested treaty changes the Soviet delegates supported

A round table discussion at the Yalta Conference in the Crimea, February, 1945 (from Sovfoto)

enry Cabot Lodge, Jr., chief of the U.S. delegation of the nited Nations, replies to an attack by Soviet Foreign Minister shinsky (from United Press).

nloading a "flying boxcar" during the Russian blockade of erlin in 1948 (from Acme)

ne of the first group of UN returnees, dismounting from a orth Korean truck at Panmunjom (August 8, 1953)

Premier Joseph Laniel of France, Prime Minister Sir Winston Churchill, and President Eisenhower at the Bermuda Conference, December 4, 1953 (from United Press)

Georgi Maximilianovich Malenkov

Alcide de Gasperi of Ita

Marshal Tito of Yugoslavia (from United Press)

West German Chancellor Konrad Adena

the request. By the same token they opposed the requests of nations that were not Soviet satellites. The result was tiresome, endless debates, punctuated with angry words and bitter wrangling. Often the representatives of the western democracies did not even bother to reply to the tirades which were in large part reiteration of stock communist epithets. So much time was consumed by the delegates of the Soviet Union and its satellites that Senator Tom Connally of the United States was moved to exclaim (August 15): "They sit all day and go ya-ya-ya."

Finally after more than six weeks of debate the delegates approved the drafts of treaties with Finland, Bulgaria, Rumania, Hungary, and Italy and then disbanded (October 15). The Conference of Paris was a success in the sense that many of its recommendations were later incorporated in the satellite treaties by the Council of Foreign Ministers. On the other hand, it provided no solution for the split between the Soviet and Western blocs on a number of major issues.

When the Council of Foreign Ministers met in New York City on November 4, 1946, to consider the recommendations of the Paris conference the gloomy atmosphere in which the Paris meeting had broken up was not improved. On Trieste, the Danube, reparations, the Italian fleet, and a number of other issues the U.S.S.R. and the western powers were still at odds. But in the fourth week the attitude of the Soviet representatives led by Foreign Minister Molotov suddenly softened. They capitulated on such issues as the internationalization of Trieste under the rule of the United Nations and freedom of navigation on the Danube against which the U.S.S.R. had previously taken an inflexible stand. The settlement reached in regard to Trieste called for its establishment as a free territory under a governor to be appointed by the UN Security Council. As for the Danube, provisions for free navigation and trade on it were included in all the Balkan treaties. After further agreements it was decided that the treaties were ready to be signed. On December 12 the Council closed its session with the announcement that the treaties would be signed in Paris on February 10, 1947.

SIGNING THE SATELLITE TREATIES

The ceremony of signing the treaties with Italy, Bulgaria, Finland, Hungary, and Rumania took place in the historic Salle de l'Horloge (Clock Room) of the French Foreign Ministry, the gold and crimson hall in which the Briand-Kellogg Pact outlawing war had been signed in 1928 and in which Clemenceau, Wilson, and Lloyd George planned the treaty of Versailles. The actual signing took place on a seventeenth-century table once owned by Louis XV and Louis XVI. It was the table on which the wounded Robespierre had lain before he was carted to the guillotine. Twenty Allied nations participated in the signing as well as the five former enemy nations. For a time it was feared that Yugoslavia might not sign because it had not been awarded Trieste. But the fears were dispelled when the Yugoslav Foreign Minister signed under protest. All five of the treaties included definite provisions designed to limit armaments, prevent the revival of nazism or fascism, and to guarantee the civil rights of every citizen.

The first treaty to be signed was that with Italy which had been the chief satellite of Nazi Germany. First, various frontier rectifications were specified with regard to France and Yugoslavia. Five small boundary areas were given to France and about two-thirds of the north-Adriatic province of Venezia Giulia was transferred to Yugoslavia. Second, Italy, by the terms of the treaty, also surrendered Trieste, renounced her special rights in China, and recognized the sovereignty and independence of Albania. Third, the treaty definitely dispelled the imperial dreams of Italy by depriving her of her African empire which had included Libya, Eritrea, Italian Somaliland, and Ethiopia. The Dodecanese Islands, whose importance was largely strategic, were turned over to the Greeks. Fourth, Italy was required to pay a total of $360 million in reparations. Of this sum the Soviet Union was accorded $100 million, Yugoslavia $125 million, Greece $105 million, Ethiopia $25 million, and Albania $5 million. Finally, Italy's military forces were reduced to a minimum. Her army was limited to 250,000 men, her airforce to 25,000 men (with bombers outlawed), her navy to 115,000 tons.

The treaties with the other Axis satellites included similar terms. In their efforts to impose armament limitations the Allies sharply reduced the armies, navies, and air forces of the defeated nations. Thus, for example, the Rumanian army was restricted to 125,000 men, the airforce to 8000 men (with bombers outlawed), and the navy to 15,000 tons. Similar armament reductions were also decreed for Bulgaria, Hungary, and Finland. The five former enemy nations were also forbidden to experiment with or possess atomic weapons, to manufacture or possess self-propelled or guided missiles, to have as military equipment guns having a range of over thirty kilometers, and to experiment with or possess torpedoes capable of being manned. All four satellites, like Italy were required to pay reparations. Hungary was required to pay $200 million to the Soviet Union and $50 million each to Czechoslovakia and Yugoslavia. Finland, for its part, was to pay $300 million to Russia, while Bulgaria was ordered to pay $45 million to Greece and $25 million to Yugoslavia.

Various territorial shifts were also made. Hungary lost territory in southern Slovakia to Czechoslovakia and was compelled to cede to Rumania northern Transylvania which she had acquired during World War II. In other words, Hungary was, by and large, pared down to the dimensions established by the treaty of Trianon after World War I, leaving approximately three million Magyars in neighboring countries. Bulgaria was required to return to Yugoslavia the Serbian territory it had gained with Nazi support. For Rumania it meant the loss of Bessarabia and part of Bucovina to Russia. In addition Finland transferred to Soviet Russia the arctic province of Petsamo, thereby giving the U.S.S.R. a common frontier with Norway.

In signing the instruments of ratification President Truman stated that the terms of the treaties were "not in full accord with our desires" and expressed the hope of a later revision by the United Nations. But most of the former enemy states were not content to wait. Only Finland accepted the treaties without protest. The other four nations filed official requests for revision on the day the treaties were signed. Greece and Yugoslavia also issued protests. The former objected that her northern border was not rectified to give her better strategic protection, while the latter assailed the Allies for not giving her Trieste. It was, however, the Italians who were most bitter. What they particularly resented was the loss of their colonies. One government leader said that the treaty was squeezing forty-five million people into an area "which cannot possibly nourish them." Newspapers appeared with black borders, black crepe was hung on houses and public buildings, and flags were flown at halfmast. In some Italian cities demonstrations were staged, with crowds marching through the streets waving Italian flags and singing patriotic airs.

THE TREATY WITH JAPAN

Although five treaties had been signed with former enemy nations, drafts of treaties with Japan, Austria, and Germany were still lacking. Differences between the Soviet Union and the western democracies regarding the settlement for these countries were pronounced. On March 10, 1947, the Council of Foreign Ministers convened in Moscow for the purpose of drawing up treaties for Germany and Austria. The discussions continued week after week without producing any agreement on the basic issues. Finally, after the longest session in the series, the meeting disbanded on April 24 without having reconciled the clashing interests. The foreign ministers had failed to agree on the total sum of reparations the Soviet Union was to receive from Germany, on Russia's demand for the German assets in Austria, on the scope and form of Germany's provisional and permanent governments, on the future of the Ruhr and Saar, and other matters. In short, every major German and Austrian issue remained unsolved.

The Council reconvened in London on November 25, 1947, in the hope that some agreement would be reached on the basic issues. But the meeting turned out to be much like the one in Moscow had been. Foreign Minister Bevin blamed Molotov for the "long speeches, unjustified and false accusations" and "hostile propaganda" that "made it really impossible for us to get to grips with the fundamental principles involved." Secretary Marshall, too, expressed his disappointment at the "dreary repetition" of the previous session. The deepest dissension was over the question of reparations. Molotov firmly insisted that Germany must pay Soviet Russia $100 billion with current production as well as with transfers of capital goods. The British and United States position was that the Soviet Union must not take goods out of Germany so long as Britain and the United States continued to supply goods to support the Germans. Although the discussions continued week after week no compromise was reached. Finally on December 15 Secretary Marshall proposed adjournment when, in his own words, "it finally became clear that we could make no progress." The Council adjourned without making arrangements for another meeting.

When the succeeding years brought no improvement in the relations between the Soviet Union and the western powers, and no agreements regarding Germany and Austria, President Truman turned to the task of preparing a treaty for Japan. In September, 1950, he sent John Foster Dulles, Republican adviser to the State Department, to collect the opinions of other governments regarding the principles upon which the treaty was to be based. The principles to which the governments agreed were then incorporated into the treaty for which General MacArthur had previously constructed the framework. Meanwhile the British government had also produced its own draft; hence the next step was to reconcile the two drafts. After this was done the text was circulated among the other Allied powers for suggestions and changes.

On September 4, 1951, almost six years after the Japanese gave up the bloody struggle, delegates from fifty-two nations assembled in the San Francisco War Memorial Opera House, the scene of the signing of the U.N. Charter in 1945. President Truman said in his address to the conference: "We meet to restore our former enemy to the community of peaceful nations." A number of nations were not represented. While China — Nationalist and Communist — was not invited, India, Burma, and Yugoslavia did not attend. Soviet Deputy Foreign Minister Gromyko laid before the conference a number of amendments which would have changed the character of the treaty essentially, but found little support. Only Poland and Czechoslovakia followed the Soviet lead; hence the amendments were voted down 46 to 3. At the final session on September 8 the delegates of forty-nine nations walked to the rostrum and affixed their signatures to the treaty, Japan being the last. The representatives of Soviet Russia, Poland, and Czechoslovakia did not appear for the signing. When Japan had signed the bulky parchment it contained more signatures than any other peace treaty.

The Japanese treaty is one of the shortest and simplest signed at the conclusion of a major war in modern times. In its territorial aspects the treaty deprived Japan of her overseas empire, amounting to 45 per cent of all territory she held on Pearl Harbor Day. Japan renounced all right to southern Sakhalin Island and to the Kurile Islands, both having been under Russian occupation since the end of World War II in accordance with the Yalta agreement. Japan also concurred in a trusteeship administered by the United States of the Bonins and Ryukyus, including Okinawa. Furthermore, Japan renounced all right to Formosa, but the treaty makes no provision for the future disposition of the island. Japanese sovereignty, in accordance with the surrender terms, was limited to the four main islands of Honshu, Kokkaido, Kyushu, and Shikoko, and some minor islands. Thus Japan was returned to the territorial status of 1854 before she began her imperialist campaign to dominate the Far East.

No restrictions on Japanese rearmament were written into the treaty. The only pledge it requires of Japan is to accept immediately the basic obligations of the U.N. Charter, i.e. to refrain from aggression, to settle disputes peacefully, and to support U.N. peace efforts. The treaty further states that "nothing . . . shall . . . prevent the stationing or retention of foreign armed forces in Japanese territory." In accordance with this provision Japan immediately signed a mutual security pact with the United States which makes possible the keeping of United States forces and bases in Japan until the Japanese are able to rebuild their military forces.

As for reparations, the treaty recognizes Japan's responsibility, but states that the Japanese economy cannot stand the strain of immediate large payments. Japan is, therefore, required to negotiate a system of reparations with individual countries. The treaty suggests indirect reparations by which Asian countries would send raw materials to Japan and get manufactured goods in return.

The treaty was not entirely satisfactory to any nation. The fact that it did not impose armament limitations on Japan caused Australia and New Zealand to fear future Japanese aggression. The Philippine Foreign Minister Carlos P. Romulo, said with some bitterness: "Surely it is straining human credulity to believe that Japan . . . has been permanently transformed from the aggressive, feudal, militarist policy state . . . into a practicing and thorough-going democracy." But the chief criticism of the treaty by the Asiatic states was that it did not specify large sums of cash reparations. It was for this reason that Burma did not send delegates to the convention. The Philippines Foreign Minister, in particular, denounced the failure of the treaty to provide large reparations for his country.

Despite the criticism the treaty was widely hailed as "a treaty of reconciliation" and the settlement as "a peace without revenge." President Truman described it thus: "It is a treaty that will work. It does not contain the seeds of another war. It is a treaty of reconciliation, which looks to the future, and not to the past." Some of the most eloquent comments on the treaty came from Asiatics. The Finance Minister of Ceylon said that the treaty was in line with the message of Buddha that "hatred ceases not by hatred but by love." The Foreign Minister of Pakistan said: "If this is a treaty of benevolence, it is benevolent both to Japan and to ourselves. If this is a treaty of magnanimity, we are being magnanimous to posterity." Japan's Premier, Shigeru Yoshida, told the conference that the great loss of territory caused much disappointment in Japan, then added: "We will not fail your expectations of us as a new nation, dedicated to peace, democracy, and freedom."

The treaty went into effect April 28, 1952, after it had been ratified by the nations whose representatives had previously signed it. When Premier Yoshida officially announced to the Japanese Parliament that the treaty had been ratified, the national flag (a red ball — the Rising Sun — on a white ground) was raised on all public buildings for the first time since the unconditional surrender in 1945. It also marked the end of foreign occupation. The way was now open for the resumption of diplomatic relations between Japan and other countries. India which had not signed the San Francisco treaty formally announced the end of her state of war by reopening diplomatic relations with Tokyo, but this was not the case with Russia, Poland, and Czechoslovakia.

The United Nations

ORGANIZING THE UNITED NATIONS THE League of Nations, after raising high hopes in the twenties, had gradually expired in the decade of the thirties. By the time World War II broke out it no longer exerted any influence as a peace-making agency. It stopped performing its "peace" functions after the special meeting of the Assembly in December, 1939.[1] But the concept of an international organization for the establishment and preservation of peace and security did not die with the League. The first stones in the foundation of a new world organization were laid in August, 1941, when President Roosevelt and Prime Minister Churchill met aboard the U.S.S. Augusta in the Atlantic and outlined the principles which were soon called the Atlantic Charter. In the Atlantic Charter there is a reference to the possible future "establishment of a wider and more permanent system of general security." Not many months later the words "United Nations" made their official appearance. On January 1, 1942, representatives of twenty-six Allied countries signed a pledge subscribing to a common declaration of the purposes and principles contained in the Atlantic Charter. This declaration was released as a "joint declaration by the United Nations." During the succeeding period to March 1, 1945, twenty-one other nations joined this wartime alliance.

Although the primary purpose of the alliance was victory in the war, the idea of establishing a permanent security organization was not shelved. At the meeting in Moscow of the foreign ministers of China, Britain, the U.S.S.R., and the U.S.A. (October, 1943) a declaration was prepared which stated in its Fourth Article that "the four Powers recognize the necessity of establishing at the earliest practi-

---

[1] The League of Nations was officially dissolved on April 18, 1946.

cable date a general international organization, based on the principle of the sovereign equality of all peace-loving states, large and small, for the maintenance of international peace and security." In August of the next year representatives of the same four powers assembled at the Dumbarton Oaks estate near Washington for the purpose of elaborating a plan which might serve as a basis for discussion. The conference at Dumbarton Oaks, however, failed to reach agreement on one point, the procedure of voting within the Security Council. But a working formula to cover the point was reached by the Big Three at Yalta (February, 1945). It was also agreed at Yalta that representatives of the United Nations be summoned to meet at San Francisco in April, 1945, to prepare the charter for the new international organization.

The San Francisco conference opened on April 25 and closed on June 25, 1945. The opening date preceded the termination of the fighting in Europe by almost two weeks and the conference finished its work a considerable time before the surrender of Japan on August 15. Thus the Charter of the United Nations was prepared by the Allied powers while they were still engaged in the war. The sponsoring powers invited to San Francisco all nations that were at war with one or more of the Axis powers. At the opening session forty-six national delegations were present and four were admitted later.[2] Besides having the Dumbarton Oaks proposals as a basis for discussion, the delegates also had a mass of suggestions and proposed amendments sent in by other nations. The work was completed on June 25 and the next day the Charter was signed in a solemn ceremony. It went into force on October 24, 1945.[3]

In an effort to close all possible loopholes the framers of the Charter went into considerable detail on many points. This makes the Charter somewhat heavy reading. The purposes of the United Nations are stated in the preamble: "We, the people of the United Nations, determined to save succeeding generations from the scourge of war, which twice in our lifetime has brought untold sorrow to mankind . . . do hereby establish an international organization to be known as the United Nations." But, if the primary purpose of the United Nations is to make war impossible or, at least, unlikely, it is also a welfare organization. Its further purpose is to promote the general well-being. The nations which participated in preparing the Charter are styled "original members," but membership in the United Nations, according to the Charter, "is open to all other peace-loving States which accept the

[2] The Ukraine, Byelorussia, Denmark, and Argentina. Space was also left on the Charter for the signatures of Poland which because of the disorganization prevailing in that country did not send a delegation.
[3] October 24 was later officially designated United Nations' Day by the General Assembly.

obligations contained in the present Charter and, in the judgment of the organization, are able and willing to carry out these obligations."

There was a tendency in some circles to dismiss the old League of Nations as a failure and to regard the new international organization as a radical departure. Those who shared this tendency failed to see the essential continuity between the two organizations. Winston Churchill, above all, realized the evolutionary development of the United Nations. In telling the House of Commons about the projected international organization after his return from Yalta he said: "It will embody much of the structure and characteristics of its predecessor. All the work that was done in the past, all the experience that has been gathered by the workings of the League of Nations will not be cast away." More recently an historian who has been active in United Nations affairs wrote: "The student of international organization must recognize the United Nations for what it quite properly is, a revised League, no doubt improved in some respects, possibly weaker in others, but nevertheless a League, a voluntary association of nations, carrying on largely in the League tradition and by the League methods." [4]

But the architects of the UN departed from League precedent in a number of respects. A special uniqueness that has been claimed for the Charter is its complete separation from the peace treaties. One of the grounds on which the Covenant of the League had been criticised was the fact that it was made a part of the treaties of peace at the end of World War I. Some went so far as to regard the close connection of the Covenant with the treaties as one of the great weaknesses of the League. Consequently the Charter of the UN was made an independent instrument.

In its greatest advance over the Covenant of the League the Charter provides that when the Security Council is unable to preserve peace and stop aggression by peaceful means it may invoke military force. Before World War I the waging of war had been one of the normal rights of any sovereign nation, but during this struggle aggressive war came to be regarded as an international crime. Such crimes were thenceforth to be prevented by common action of the "peace-loving majority" in the League. But the plan did not succeed. A half-hearted and hesitating multitude was no match for a determined minority, as the Japanese, the Fascists, and the Nazis successively proved. The Charter includes provisions for an "international police force" strong enough to curb aggression. The troops for this military force are to be provided by all members of the United Nations according to special agreements and are to be under the command of the Military Staff

[4] Leland M. Goodrich in *International Organization,* vol. 1 (1947), p. 20.

Committee. "The new body," Winston Churchill said, "will differ from it (the League) in the essential point that it will not shrink from establishing its will against the evil-doer, or evil-planner, in good time and by force of arms."

The Charter provides for the establishment of six principal organs: a General Assembly, a Security Council, an Economic and Social Council, a Trusteeship Council, an International Court of Justice, and a Secretariat. The political basis of the UN is the General Assembly consisting of representatives of all the member states. This body meets annually, and in special sessions when summoned either by the Security Council or by a majority of the member states. It may discuss any matter within the scope of the Charter. This includes recommending measures relating to the cooperation of the United Nations in maintaining international peace and security, and "assisting in the realization of human rights and fundamental freedoms for all." Each member may send up to five representatives to the General Assembly, but has only one vote. Article 18 of the Charter states: "Decisions of the General Assembly on important questions shall be made by a two-thirds majority of the members present and voting. . . . Decisions on other questions . . . shall be made by a majority of the members present and voting."

Although the General Assembly occupies a central position in the UN it is not the supreme authority. The organ which has the primary responsibility for the maintenance of international peace and security is the Security Council. It functions continuously and is composed of eleven members, five of which — Britain, France, China, the U.S.S.R., and the U.S.A. — have permanent seats. The others are elected for a two-year term by the General Assembly. The elections are arranged in such a way that three members retire annually and cannot be reelected immediately. Each nonpermanent as well as each permanent member of the Security Council has one vote. On procedural matters decisions can be made by an affirmative vote of seven of the eleven members, but on all other matters the seven votes must include the concurring votes of the five permanent members. If one of the five permanent members is a party to a dispute he is to abstain from voting in decisions concerning the dispute. Thus the concentration of authority for purposes of international peace and security is largely in the hands of the five great powers and the negative vote of one permanent member is sufficient to defeat a resolution.

The activities of the other organs may be summarized briefly. The Economic and Social Council, consisting of eighteen members elected by the Assembly for a period of three years, was organized for the purpose of advancing social progress and human rights. Among its many endeavors are the promotion of higher standards of living, the cultivation of educational cooperation, and the solution of economic problems. The Trusteeship Council exercises authority over the territories held under League of Nations mandates, territories taken from enemy states in World War II, and territories voluntarily placed under its administration. The International Court of Justice was set up to replace the World Court of the League, which had been established to settle disputes of an international nature. Finally, the Charter provided for a Secretariat consisting of a secretary-general, appointed by the Assembly on the recommendation of the Security Council, and a staff of assistants who draft reports, prepare material for meetings and conferences, and do general clerical work.

One of the first questions to come up before the General Assembly was the question of where the permanent home of the UN was to be located. At the first session of the UN in London (February, 1946) it was decided that it was to be in the United States. The permanent site was chosen during the second part of the first session which opened in New York City on October 23, 1946. After various sites had been considered the Assembly accepted the offer of John D. Rockefeller, Jr. to spend $8.5 million for a site extending from 42nd to 48th streets along the East River in the heart of New York City. While the buildings on the site were being demolished an international board of architects and engineers drew up the plans for a group of skyscrapers including a Secretariat office building, a hall for the General Assembly, a conference area for Council chambers and committee rooms, and underground garages. The construction of the $65 million project proceeded rapidly. The work of erecting the 39-story Secretariat building was started in April of 1949 and completed to permit the Secretariat to move in toward the end of 1950. The General Assembly building on which construction was started in 1950 was ready for the 1952 session of the General Assembly.

THE UNITED NATIONS IN ACTION

During the years since it was organized the United Nations has scored some signal successes. In a substantial number of cases it has helped to avert dangerous situations and to promote peaceful settlements. It has even been instrumental in restoring peace after fighting had started. Through the mediation of the United Nations, for example, a settlement was reached in Palestine and the new State of Israel was admitted as the 59th member; under United Nations auspices a cease-fire agreement was reached between India and Pakistan thus preventing 400 million people from engaging in bloody warfare; and in Indonesia the United Nations aided in working out a peaceful solution between the Dutch and the Indonesians.

Although public attention is almost entirely concentrated on its efforts to establish peace, this is by no means the only important activity in which the United Nations is engaged. On the social and economic side the United Nations and its specialized agencies have also scored many unspectacular victories. So many peacetime activities and enterprises are being conducted under United Nations auspices that only the barest sampling of what is being done is possible here. President Truman mentioned some of these activities in his address before the General Assembly at Flushing Meadows on the fifth anniversary of the United Nations Organization (October 24, 1950):

> To millions of people, the United Nations is a source of direct help in their everyday lives. To them it is a case of food or a box of schoolbooks; it is a doctor who vaccinates their children; it is an expert who shows them how to raise more rice, or more wheat on their land; it is the flag which marks a safe haven to the refugee, or an extra meal a day to a nursing mother.

More than 95 per cent of the three thousand members of the UN staff are engaged in work that aims to raise the standards of living, to promote the progress and welfare of all mankind, and to protect fundamental rights and individual liberties. In terms of the limitless job that remains to be done the achievements are fragmentary, but nevertheless significant.

The great directing and policy-formulating organ which supervises the economic and social work is the Economic and Social Council. Its field is so broad that it covers all phases of international government except those directly related to international peace and security. To assist it in coping with the economic problems of the world three Regional Commissions were set up, one for Europe, another for Asia and the Far East, and a third one for Latin America. The Economic Commission for Europe, in which all the nations of Europe except Spain have participated, has some conspicuous accomplishments to its credit. Among other things, it has done excellent work allocating natural resources such as coal, timber, and ore among the member nations. Its economists also found that the annual production of timber in Europe could be increased fourfold merely by spending $15 million for such basic equipment as sawmills and tractors. The Commission for Asia and the Far East has been concerned principally with such problems as increased food production for an increasing population and the development of industry in the Far East. One of its special problems is to find ways and means of controlling the floods which annually destroy millions of acres of food. The Economic Commission for Latin

America has devoted itself to economic rehabilitation and advancement in an unevenly developed continent. At its conference in 1949 it adopted plans for cooperation in such fields as the control of animal and plant diseases, soil and forest conservation, and the development of fisheries.

Much of the work of achieving the UN aim of improved economic and social conditions is carried on by specialized agencies. Some of these such as the Universal Postal Union and the International Labor Organization were in existence before the UN was founded, but others were organized for specific purposes. The International Refugee Organization (IRO) was a temporary organization created to give care and assistance to refugees and displaced persons. As a result of its efforts more than a million persons were either repatriated or resettled in other countries. Other agencies include the Committee on Freedom of Information which is trying to offset the world-wide movement toward censorship, the Central Opium Board which is trying to curb illicit traffic in drugs, and the Food and Agriculture Organization (FAO) which was created to raise standards of nutrition throughout the world and to improve the production and distribution of food and agricultural products. A further notable specialized agency is the United Nations Educational, Scientific, and Cultural Organization (UNESCO) organized to promote "collaboration among nations through education, science and culture in order to further universal respect for justice, for the rule of law and for the human rights and fundamental freedoms." A program adopted in 1946 included, first, rehabilitation and reconstruction in the field of education and, second, a campaign to wipe out illiteracy and raise the standards of education.

A specialized agency of the UN which has outstanding achievements to its credit is the World Health Organization (WHO). Its objective, in brief, is "the attainment by all peoples of the highest possible level of health." Its main efforts have been directed toward the elimination of some of the world's major diseases — malaria, tuberculosis, and venereal diseases — toward environmental sanitation, and toward maternal and child health. It has also launched a drive to standardize vaccines, vitamins, and various medicines throughout the world. In Ethiopia, for example, where it found only one native physician for twelve million people WHO has taken steps to curb malaria and venereal disease which afflicted 90 per cent of the population in some parts of the country, to train hospital orderlies and sanitary workers, and to set up delousing stations. Probably WHO's most spectacular achievement was in the Egyptian cholera epidemic of 1947. When the epidemic broke out WHO quickly collected six million units of cholera vaccine from nineteen countries and sent them to Egypt, together with other medical supplies, including blood plasma. As a result of the prompt action of WHO it was possible to curb the epidemic which at its height was spreading to more than a thousand people each day. Within a comparatively few weeks the epidemic was over.

A further important achievement for the United Nations was the preparation of a Universal Declaration of the Rights of Man. The Declaration was the first effective step on the part of the UN to implement its obligation, contained in its Charter, to promote universal respect for fundamental human rights, regardless of race, sex, language, or religion. More than this, it is the first attempt in history to proclaim in a precise form the minimum rights each individual should enjoy regardless of where he may live. To draw up this Declaration was not an easy task. It took many meetings and hard work on the part of the Committee on Human Rights before the Declaration was ready for presentation to the General Assembly. The work came to fruition on December 10, 1948, when the General Assembly adopted the Universal Declaration of Human Rights without a dissenting vote, proclaiming it "a common standard of achievement for all peoples and nations." [5] In doing so the members of the United Nations agreed that they would strive for the attainment of these standards. The declaration contains thirty articles, of which the first ten read as follows:

Article 1. All human beings are born free and equal in dignity and rights. They are endowed with reason and conscience and should act towards one another in a spirit of brotherhood.

Article 2, part 1. Everyone is entitled to all rights and freedoms set forth in this Declaration, without distinction of any kind, such as race, color, sex, language, religion, political or other opinion, national or social origin, property, birth or other status.

Part 2. Furthermore, no distinction shall be made on the basis of the political, jurisdictional or international status of the country or territory to which a person belongs, whether this territory be an independent, Trust, Non-Self-Governing territory, or under any other limitation of sovereignty.

Article 3. Everyone has the right to life, liberty and the security of person.

Article 4. No one shall be held in slavery or servitude; slavery and the slave trade shall be prohibited in all their forms.

Article 5. No one shall be subjected to torture or to cruel, inhuman, or degrading treatment or punishment.

Article 6. Everyone has the right of recognition everywhere as a person before the law.

Article 7. All are equal before the law and are entitled without any discrimination to equal protection of the law. All are entitled to equal protection

---

[5] Forty-eight nations voted in the affirmative with eight abstaining. Representatives of two nations were absent.

against any discrimination in violation of this Declaration and against any incitement to such discrimination.

Article 8. Everyone has the right to an effective remedy by the competent national tribunals for acts violating the fundamental rights granted him by the constitution or by law.

Article 9. No one shall be subjected to arbitrary arrest, detention or exile.

Article 10. Everyone is entitled in full equality to a fair and public hearing by an independent and impartial tribunal in the determination of his rights and obligations and of any criminal charge against him.

On the other hand, it would be unrealistic to assert that the UN has fulfilled the hopes it engendered at the time of its organization. There was a widespread hope at the end of World War II that the strength and moral authority of the United Nations would be sufficient to prevent further bloodshed and destruction. Many were convinced that the new world organization would be able to speak effectively for the world community, that it would, like a giant policeman with a big club, immediately go into action against an aggressor nation. The spirit of optimism which prevailed in 1945 blinded many to the obstacles that would have to be surmounted before the United Nations' ideal of peace and security can be achieved. They did not realize that the United Nations would be afflicted with the same diseases that had gradually sapped the vitality of the League of Nations and that a remedy for these diseases must be found. The fact that fifty nations had subscribed to the United Nations Charter was no guarantee that they would put aside their selfish interests and work together harmoniously for the good of all. Actually the victors of World War II were more divided from the outset than the victors of World War I had been. There was no common front against aggression. The plan for maintaining peace was adequate, but there was no will to apply it. The statesmen were not prepared to carry out a plan which would limit the sovereignty of the national state. Hence the vast possibilities inherent in the UN have not been realized and the UN has been unable to achieve peace and security.

Other hopes centered in the UN have also not been realized. The United Nations has been no more successful in carrying out its disarmament program than the League of Nations had previously been. Although some countries promptly disbanded their wartime armies, others continued to maintain forces so large that they posed a constant threat of aggression, causing the former to rebuild their forces and armaments. As in the League of Nations each member of the United Nations is ready to disarm other nations, but keeps on producing armaments frantically itself. The result has been that the world has spent more on armaments since the organization of the United Nations than ever before in peacetime history. The United Nations has further failed to reach agreement on the control of atomic energy; the use of rockets and germ warfare has not even been discussed. Despite all this, however, the United Nations remains the most powerful influence for peace in the world.

CIRCUMVENTING THE VETO

The great obstacle that repeatedly thwarted the will of the majority in the Security Council was the voting procedure which demands an affirmative vote by the five permanent members of that body on all except procedural questions. Hence any one of the five great powers can block or veto any majority decision of the Security Council. At San Francisco many of the small and medium-sized nations objected strongly to the inclusion of the veto in the Charter, but the great powers said, in effect, "either we have the veto or we have no United Nations." This insistence on the veto by the great powers was in essence a desire to avoid any commitments that would limit their freedom of action. The veto, it appears, was originally intended to keep differences from arising. "It cannot be repeated too often," Secretary-General Trygve Lie said, "that the United Nations was founded on the assumption that the major powers would be in substantial agreement with one another."

In practice, however, the veto certainly did not promote unanimity. Time and again its use prevented the Security Council from fulfilling its functions. Through its use inquiry and investigation into disputes has been blocked and applicants have been refused membership in the UN. At times the use of the veto has effectively barred any action. Thus the New York *Times* reported (May 26, 1946):

> After two months of deliberations in New York, delegates to the United Nations Security Council are discouraged because the organization is not making satisfactory progress. . . . In their New York meetings the Council members have not been able to settle a single major issue in the cases formally brought before them.

Dr. Hafez Afifi of Egypt, upon concluding his month as president of the Council, stated that the great mass of humanity is disappointed because it believes "the great powers are not working as a united family of nations in the interest of all the people, but are trying to further their own interests without regard or consideration for others." The nation which repeatedly paralyzed the Security Council by means of the veto is Soviet Russia. The frequent use of the veto by the Soviet delegates moved U.S. Deputy Under-Secretary Rusk to state:

To the extent that the loyal participation of the Soviet Union is not required, the United Nations, by and large, is getting on with its job. To the extent that the help and assistance of the Soviet Union is essential, the United Nations is frustrated, faltering and disappointing. It is a serious charge, but it is based on sober fact.[6]

At a number of annual meetings of the General Assembly the question of eliminating the veto was raised, but the great powers were unanimous against any change. But the invasion of South Korea (June 25, 1950) clearly demonstrated that certain structural defects would have to be remedied if aggression was to be deterred by fear of the UN. Only the chance circumstance that the Soviet Union was boycotting the Security Council at the time of the invasion permitted this body to rally collective aid for the Republic of South Korea. The frightening consciousness that the veto might in the future paralyze any action of the UN moved several powers to take steps toward setting up a method of procedure which will permit the UN to act in future cases of aggression. U.S. Secretary of State Acheson drafted a set of resolutions entitled "United Action for Peace" containing a proposal for by-passing the veto-bound Security Council. The resolutions proposed, first, that when aggression impends and the Security Council fails to act, an emergency session of the Assembly may be called on 24-hour notice at the request of any seven members of the Security Council or by a majority of the members of the Assembly. Second, they called for the formation of a fourteen-nation Peace Observation Commission or Peace Patrol which, as the eyes and ears of the UN, is to observe and report on any situation likely to endanger world peace, so that the UN will not be caught unawares. Third, they recommended that each member maintain elements within its national armed forces for prompt availability as United Nations units. Fourth, they advocated the creation of a fourteen-nation Collective Measures Committee to report to the Assembly on methods of peace enforcement.

The proposals were presented to the Fifth General Assembly which met at Flushing Meadows in the fall of 1950 and were approved (October 18 and 19) by an overwhelming majority. Fifty-two members voted for the adoption, with only the U.S.S.R. and its satellites opposing. Thus the machinery of the UN for preserving the peace was greatly strengthened.

THE KOREAN CHALLENGE

The armed attack by North Korean forces on the Republic of South Korea on June 25, 1950, posed the most severe test that has confronted the United Nations. Korea had since 1910 been a part of the Japanese

[6] *U.S. State Department Bulletin,* October 31, 1949, p. 656.

Empire, but in the Cairo Declaration (December, 1943) President Roosevelt, Prime Minister Churchill, and Generalissimo Chiang Kai-shek pledged their determination that Korea would become free and independent. This pledge was reaffirmed in the Potsdam Declaration (July 26, 1945) which stated that "the terms of the Cairo Declaration shall be carried out." Soviet Russia, it will be remembered, was one of the signers of this declaration. Thus the Koreans had every reason to believe that their desire for independence would be fulfilled at the end of the war.

Unfortunately the country was soon divided into two parts by the Soviet Union and the United States. The division along the Thirty-Eighth Parallel was not to be a permanent division. It was only a temporary expedient suggested by the United States to facilitate the surrender of Japanese forces. But the line which the U.S. regarded as a temporary expedient became a more or less permanent division when the Soviet Union and the United States failed to agree on a provisional government for Korea. The issue which caused the deadlock was the Soviet Union's insistence that only leaders who were friendly to the Soviet government should be included in the provisional government. When it became apparent that no agreement was possible the United States government set up a provisional government in its zone and the Soviet Union did likewise.

Finding itself blocked by Soviet intransigeance the United States laid the case in the lap of the United Nations. In November, 1947, the UN General Assembly called for an election in the whole of Korea under the supervision of the UN Temporary Commission on Korea, but the Communist authorities refused to permit the Commission to enter North Korea. In the south, however, the elections were held in May of 1948 and in August the government of the Republic of Korea was established with Seoul as capital and Dr. Syngman Rhee as president. Accepted by the General Assembly in December of the same year as the lawful government of Korea, the new government was quickly recognized by the U.S.A. and thirty-one other nations. But the Soviet Union and its satellites did not recognize it. The former also blocked membership of the new government in the UN through the use of the veto in the Security Council. Meanwhile in open defiance of the UN the Soviet Union had established a communist regime north of the Thirty-Eighth Parallel calling it the "Democratic People's Republic of Korea" (September 9, 1948). Both governments now claimed sovereignty over the entire peninsula. In accordance with the recommendation contained in the General Assembly resolution of December 12, 1948, the U.S. withdrew its occupation forces (June, 1949). The Soviet Union then announced that it had completed the withdrawal of its troops in December, 1948, but refused to permit the UN Commission to verify the claim.

In May, 1950, the Republic of South Korea held elections which brought into power many of the so-called "middle-of-the-roaders," men who advocated Korean unity through rapprochement with totalitarian North Korea. This caused North Korean officials to believe that the South Koreans would offer little resistance to an invasion of North Korean forces. On June 25, 1950, the world was startled by the announcement that at 4 A.M. (Korean time) the forces of the puppet communist regime of North Korea, equipped with Soviet-made tanks and planes had crossed the Thirty-Eighth Parallel. The size of the attack and the equipment involved indicated clearly that the invasion had been carefully planned a long time in advance. The South Korean army which was taken by surprise was no match for the well-equipped North Korean forces. Its morale was excellent, but it did not have a single plane or tank and such artillery as it had was not heavy enough to stop opposing tanks. Consequently it was forced to retreat. In the meantime the United States as sponsor of the Republic of South Korea brought the act of aggression to the attention of the UN and at 2 P.M. on June 25th the Security Council met to consider the matter. By a vote of 9 to 0 (the Soviet Union being absent and Yugoslavia abstaining) the Security Council adopted a resolution declaring the attack to be a breach of the peace and called an immediate cessation of the fighting and the withdrawal of the North Korean forces above the Thirty-Eighth Parallel. When the North Korean invaders ignored the cease-fire call the United Nations took the unprecedented step on June 27 of recommending direct military action by its members to restore peace in Korea. Up to this time only moral force had been used by the UN.

WAR IN KOREA

United Nations forces soon went into action in Korea. Even before the vote was taken in the Security Council on the evening of June 27 President Truman had ordered United States air and sea forces to give South Korean troops cover and support, in accordance with the Council's call to all member states for aid. During the succeeding months other nations contributed contingents, but U.S. land, sea, and air forces bore the main burden of the fighting. For some weeks the UN forces were on the defensive and had to make long gruelling withdrawals. But by early September they were ready to launch a counteroffensive. For a time things went well for the UN forces. On September 25 they entered Seoul and during the next days the North Koreans were driven across the Thirty-Eighth Parallel. The UN forces halted at the parallel while General MacArthur, the joint commander, broadcast a surrender ultimatum. When it remained unanswered he ordered his troops to cross into North Korea early in October. Against Red resistance his troops swept northward until it appeared as if the military adventure in Korea was about to be terminated. Late in October, however, the capture of a number of Chinese soldiers was clear evidence that the Chinese were entering the fighting. Toward the end of November as the UN forces were approaching the Yalu River four Chinese armies, estimated at 200,000, launched an overwhelming attack which tore wide gaps in the UN lines and forced a swift retreat. The end of 1950 saw the Chinese and North Koreans facing the UN forces and the South Koreans across the Thirty-Eighth Parallel.

In an effort to end the war the UN, on a number of occasions, declared its readiness to negotiate a cease-fire, but the Communist government of China made no response. Hence the fighting continued. On New Year's Day of 1951, the Red forces launched an offensive along the Thirty-Eighth Parallel with the result that the South Koreans lost their capital for the second time in the war. UN forces pulled out of Seoul on January 4 and continued to retreat southward for some weeks while taking a heavy toll of the advancing enemy. In February, however, the UN forces started a counteroffensive which carried them northward and on March 14 they reoccupied Seoul. During the succeeding days the Reds retreated across the Thirty-Eighth Parallel with the UN forces on their heels. But again the tide turned in the opposite direction. In late April a drive by an estimated Communist force of 400,000 pushed most of the UN troops back to the south of the Thirty-Eighth Parallel. But this time the UN forces did not abandon Seoul and on May 1st the Chinese Reds gave up the attempt to take the South Korean capital. All further attempts by the Communists to launch major offensives foundered.

On June 23, 1951, the Soviet Union excited the hope of a quick termination of hostilities by proposing a cease-fire. Finally on July 5 the opposing parties agreed to begin truce talks at Kaesong on July 8. No sooner had the talks started than they hit various snags. Disagreement arose over the cease-fire lines, the refusal of the Chinese Communists to permit UN newsmen to be present, and over other questions. Week after week the talks continued without appreciable progress until they reached a complete deadlock. Having reached an impasse the talks were at first broken off temporarily several times and then discontinued (August 23), but on October 25 after a sixty-three day lapse they were resumed at Panmunjom. Meanwhile the fighting had continued with the UN forces making small gains and pushing slowly northward from the Thirty-Eighth Parallel.

During the weeks of November agreement was reached on three of the four principal items on the truce agenda: (1) the battle line of November 26, 1951, would be the cease-fire line if an armistice were signed in thirty days, otherwise it would be redrawn along the existing line of battle; (2) Poland, Czechoslovakia, Sweden, and Switzerland were chosen as truce supervisors; (3) a high level political conference was to be held within ninety days after an armistice. The item on which agreement could not be reached was the one on prisoner exchange. While the communists insisted on the repatriation of all prisoners, regardless of whether they wanted to return, the United Nations held that every prisoner must have a free choice as to whether he was to be repatriated. In October, 1952, truce talks were suspended because the negotiations seemed hopelessly deadlocked. At the beginning of April, 1953, China's premier Chou En-lai upon returning from Moscow reopened the issue by suggesting the exchange of seriously ill and wounded prisoners of war. The agreement, signed on April 10, set April 21 as the date on which the exchange was to begin. During the succeeding week the UN returned nearly six thousand prisoners and the Communists about six hundred.

On April 25, 1953, full-blown armistice talks were resumed, but the return of the war prisoners after a cease-fire remained the main stumbling block in the path of an armistice. Finally on June 8 the two delegations signed a 26-point agreement on prisoner repatriation. The UN plan for General Assembly arbitration was dropped in favor of a five-nation neutral commission headed by India. The agreement stated that all prisoners of war wishing to return should be sent home at once after the signing of the armistice; the rest to be held. The fate of those who at the expiration of a period of three months still opposed repatriation was to be discussed by the political conference to be called under armistice terms. If their fate was not decided within 30 days, they were to be reclassified as civilians and permitted to go to a neutral country.

The armistice went into effect on July 27 as scheduled. After three years and 32 days of fighting the front was silenced. To prevent incidents a "demilitarized zone" $2\frac{1}{2}$ miles wide was established between the former combatants. The prisoners of war who wished to return home were quickly repatriated and those who refused repatriation were put under neutral custody. On January 20, 1954, the Indian custodial force turned back to the UN about 21,500 prisoners who had refused repatriation. Two days later they were proclaimed free civilians.

CHAPTER THIRTY-THREE

Western Europe since World War II:
Germany, Austria, and France

WESTERN EUROPE AFTER THE WAR — THE blood, sacrifices, and sufferings of the war had not eliminated the basic causes. Nationalism was still aggressive, militarism was still the order of the day, and the problem of access to raw materials and markets had not been solved. In addition there were many new problems generated by the war. Among these was the gigantic task of rebuilding the bombed and devastated areas. The scale of destruction in World War II was far greater than it had been in World War I. In Britain the destruction wrought by air raids was tremendous, but it was much greater in Germany. It has been estimated that 22 per cent of the buildings in Germany or about one out of four were destroyed. Piles of rubble still lined the streets of many communities years after the cessation of hostilities.

There was also widespread disruption of economic life. The bombings caused considerable damage to production facilities, though the loss has often been exaggerated. The greatest damage was done to harbors, shipping, and transportation facilities. It is estimated that 40 per cent of the two million freight cars were damaged, nearly half beyond the possibility of use. Overseas trade had been reduced to a trickle both for Continental Europe and for Britain. Even the intra-European trade had been badly dislocated. In all the European countries, neutral as well as belligerent, the stockpiles of raw materials were largely used up and in some there was a serious shortage. "In 1945 Europe was perhaps more denuded of resources than at any time in modern history," the report of the Committee of European Co-operation states; "there was a shortage of basic materials, of fertilizers to renovate the soil, of raw materials and equipment to quicken production." There were also acute shortages of food and other consumer goods which acted as deterrents to the reorganization of production.

For a time the work of putting Europe back on its economic feet proceeded well. As early as 1943 the United Nations Relief and Rehabilitation Administration (UNRRA) was created by forty-four nations to aid in the recovery and rehabilitation of the liberated areas. But western Europe derived little benefit from the relief distributed by UNRRA. At the conclusion of the war the United States government did, however, grant loans and extend considerable credit to most of the western European countries to permit them to purchase abroad much-needed materials and commodities. The imports obtained enabled them to achieve a considerable degree of recovery. By the end of 1946 industrial production in Belgium, France, and the Netherlands had reached at least 85 per cent, and in Italy about 60 per cent of the prewar level. In Great Britain the prewar level of production was fully restored. In agricultural production, too, recovery was evident in all countries in 1946. But the picture changed in the winter of 1946–1947. The convalescing economy suffered a setback. In purchasing abroad the necessary food and raw materials many countries had almost depleted their gold reserves in addition to exhausting the credit they had obtained in the early postwar period. By June, 1947, the European deficit in the trade balance with the United States had increased to $1 billion a month. Further purchases could be made only at the cost of a total depletion of the financial reserves and this would have caused a growing unbalance of the European economy. In short, there was a shortage of dollars needed to make further purchases abroad.

The dollar deficit had existed before World War II; the war had only accelerated it. In the nineteenth century vast wealth had flowed into Europe from the colonial empires and from countries in a pre-industrial or semi-industrial stage. More than a billion consumers in Russia, Asia, and Africa had purchased the goods Europeans produced. But with the decline of imperialism and the growth of industrialism in these regions these markets were gradually closed to the manufactures of western Europe. Whereas Europe's share in world production was 46.6 per cent in 1913, it was only 39.5 per cent in 1937. Steel production alone fell from 50 to 40 per cent. By the end of World War II western Europe's industrial position had deteriorated still more. It had not kept pace with the expansion in other parts of the globe, more particularly in the United States and in Russia.

The result was that at the end of the war the countries of western Europe were spending more for imports than they were receiving for exports. Hence the dollar deficit. On the eve of the war they had been able to pay for a considerable part of their foreign purchases with income from foreign investments, the tourist trade, and the shipping trade. But during the war most foreign investments were liquidated and the income from the other sources ceased. Meanwhile import requirements had increased greatly. Thus the problem of paying for the imports was a serious one. If the import of vitally needed materials was to continue fresh dollar resources had to be found.

In the United States it was generally recognized that European prosperity was closely related to the prosperity and security of this country. Moreover, support of the countries of western Europe was regarded as essential to prevent them from becoming an easy prey to Soviet imperialism. On June 5, 1947, in a commencement address at Harvard University, U.S. Secretary of State Marshall outlined a plan for the economic rehabilitation of Europe which soon became known as the Marshall Plan. He said:

> Europe's requirements for the next three or four years of foreign food and other essential products — principally from America — are so much greater than her present ability to pay that she must have substantial additional help or face economic, social and political deterioration of a very grave character. . . . It is logical that the United States do whatever it is able to assist in the return of normal economic health in the world, without which there can be no political stability and no assured peace.

General Marshall accentuated the fact, however, that the efforts to place Europe on its feet economically must not be one-sided. The states of Europe must take the initiative by working out a program for recovery.

The reaction in both Britain and France was enthusiastic. Leaders in both countries welcomed it as offering at least a temporary solution. In recalling the announcement of the plan Mr. Bevin said: "I remember that morning, with a little wireless set alongside the bed, just turning on the news, and there came this report of the Harvard speech. I assure you, gentlemen, it was like a lifeline to sinking men. It seemed to bring hope where there was none." Foreign Secretary Bevin and Foreign Minister Bidault immediately invited the Soviet Union to a three-power conference regarding the plan. Hopes ran high when the Kremlin accepted, but they were soon dispelled when Molotov stated at the conference that his government had rejected the plan as unsatisfactory. The Soviet Union was opposed to any plan which would revive Europe's economy and increase the prestige and influence of the United States. Molotov charged that the United States was extending credit merely as a means of stretching capitalist tentacles into foreign markets. But the foreign ministers of France and Britain nevertheless went ahead with arrangements for a meeting of representatives in Paris. All the states of Europe were invited except the Soviet Union, Germany, and Spain. Whereas the Russians had rejected the plan in advance, the Germans had no government to represent them, and the Spanish government was not in good standing with Britain and France.

On July 12, 1947, representatives of sixteen European countries met in Paris to discuss plans for economic rehabilitation. Absent were the representatives of the Soviet satellite states. The invitation to participate in the Marshall Plan had been tempting to them, particularly to Poland and Czechoslovakia, but the Soviet government put pressure on them to turn it down. As a result the Marshall Plan was confined to the countries which were not controlled by Russia. Thus even the last semblance of outward harmony between the victorious powers disappeared. The Soviet newspaper *Pravda* announced that Europe was now split into eastern and western blocs.

At Paris the representatives of the sixteen countries [1] during a four-day session set in motion the machinery for surveying the resources of the particular states and of determining how much each country could contribute and how much more was needed. The fundamental idea of the Marshall Plan was to make Europe more economically self-supporting through economic cooperation between all the countries sharing in the Plan. Among the objectives to be realized were: (1) a general increase in production, including both industrial and agricultural production; (2) internal economic, financial, and monetary stability; (3) mutual assistance between all the participating countries. The task of carrying out the recovery plan in Europe was entrusted to the Organization of European Economic Cooperation (OEEC) composed of representatives of the sixteen participating countries and the three western zones of Germany. The work of the OEEC was implemented by the Economic Cooperation Administration (ECA) with headquarters in Washington.

In the United States the Congress passed the Interim-Aid Bill in December, 1947, which allotted $597 million to alleviate the difficulties of some of the countries until the Marshall Plan could be organized. This was followed by the Foreign Assistance Act of 1948, passed in April of that year, which appropriated $5.3 billion to the Marshall Plan for the purchase of commodities, raw materials, machinery, and equipment. Further appropriations were made in the succeeding years.[2] Re-

---

[1] Austria, Belgium, Denmark, France, Greece, Iceland, Eire, Italy, Luxembourg, Netherlands, Norway, Portugal, Sweden, Switzerland, Turkey, and Britain.
[2] In 1951 the Congress passed the Mutual Security Act based on the policy of "defense support," i.e. that the funds be devoted to the build-up of defense industries. A mutual Security Administration replaced the Economic Cooperation Administration and the Marshall Plan ended in January, 1952.

sults achieved during the first three years are impressive. The total output of goods and services in the Marshall Plan countries rose to new high levels, unemployment decreased, and intra-European trade increased. In the last quarter of 1948 the aggregate production rose above the level of 1938. The production increase continued in 1949 and in the first three quarters of 1950 the output was 24 per cent above the prewar level. Substantial progress was also achieved in agricultural production. In 1949 the prewar level was exceeded in every country except Germany and Greece. The next year the general average rose above prewar levels.

Just when it appeared as if western Europe would soon be able to stand on its own financial feet, hostilities broke out in Korea and a new program of rearmament was launched. The raw materials needed for armament production not only increased the volume of imports but also caused the prices of these materials to rise sharply. Since exports did not increase commensurately a new dollar shortage resulted, except in West Germany which did not adopt the rearmament program. The two countries hardest hit were Britain and France. Both countries at once made a plea to the United States for further financial aid and the Congress responded by granting it.

THE TREND TOWARD EUROPEAN UNITY

One of the major developments since World War II has been the trend toward European unity. The idea of a supranational European community had been entertained by statesmen and philosophers, but it was the communist threat that gave it forceful impetus. What alarmed the European states was the striking power of the Soviet Union, its efforts to consolidate its hold on the peoples under its domination, and its persistent pressure to extend its sway. While other nations had demobilized most of their armed forces after the conclusion of hostilities in 1945, the Soviet Union continued to build up its army, navy, and air force. Military experts have estimated that by 1950 there were east of the iron curtain 175 battle-ready divisions. This threat of overwhelming force caused the leaders of western Europe to realize that a divided Europe is a weak Europe. The Soviet threat necessitated large expenditures for arms, and a compartmented Europe was experiencing increasing difficulty in drawing from individual national economies a satisfactory level of material existence for the restive millions and also military security under the menace from the Soviet East. The obvious solution was closer economic, political, and military cooperation. Paul Reynaud, former premier of France, wrote in his *Unite or Perish* (1951):

A magnificent future lies ahead of us if we will unite. We can be the second and in some fields the first, of the world's three giants. This Europe would produce more coal, steel, and electrical power than Russia. It would have three or four times more freight cars on its railroads, and fifteen times more ships on the seas. When this third giant stands up to full stature, its size will astonish everyone. Europe could then make the giant in the East tremble.

The cornerstone in the structure ultimately intended to become a United States of Europe is the European Coal and Steel Community, based on the Schuman Plan. This plan, sponsored by Robert Schuman, then foreign minister of France, provided for the pooling of the coal, iron, and steel industries in six western nations: France, Italy, West Germany, and the Benelux countries (Belgium, the Netherlands, and Luxembourg). More specifically the plan contained provisions to set up a tariff-free market of 150 million Europeans for coal, iron, and steel; to make the coal, iron, and steel industries of the Ruhr a part of a European system; and to establish mutual confidence between the states of western Europe. Britain did not join in the plan, but promised to cooperate closely. After many months of negotiation representatives of the six nations initialed the plan in March, 1951, but it was still necessary for the parliaments of the participating nations to ratify it. The important question was whether France and Germany would do so, for the adherence of both countries was essential to its success. All misgivings were dispelled when the parliaments of both countries voted approval.

The first organ of the European Coal and Steel Community was set up on August 10, 1952. It was the High Authority, an executive cabinet of nine members charged with the day to day direction of the community, particularly as regards prices, production, and allocation of coal and steel. The High Authority must answer to the Assembly in the same way in which cabinets are responsible to national assemblies. This Assembly is composed of seventy-eight parliamentarians from six countries (France, West Germany, and Italy eighteen members each, Belgium and the Netherlands ten, and Luxembourg four). It came into being on September 10, 1952, and meets annually to review the work of the High Authority. Two days earlier the Council of Ministers, composed of one cabinet member from each of the participating nations, had held its organizational meeting. It acts as a link between the individual governments and the High Authority and may veto the decisions of the latter body. The last organ is the High Court of Justice which hears appeals from the decisions of the High Authority and, in general, settles disputes. It offers both the governments and the industrialists the opportunity to attack any decision of the High Authority which they believe to be contrary to the purpose or principles of the Coal and Steel Community. The entire machinery is organized in such a way that it can eventually be the basis for a political federation.

The Coal and Steel Community which began to function on February 10, 1953, may be regarded as a bold step toward breaking away from national practices in economic affairs. The tariffless market it established was for the moment limited to coal, iron ore, and scrap iron. On April 10 it was extended to steel. Thus there is a common market in an area where each country had previously protected these industries behind tariff walls and restrictive quotas. There is also the possibility of extending it to other products until a complete European customs union has been established. Much will depend on the success with which the Coal and Steel Community meets the many concrete problems facing it.

The Council of Ministers made an attempt to speed up the timetable of European unity by suggesting that the Assembly take upon itself the task of drafting a constitution for a European political federation. On March 10, 1953, the Assembly, meeting at Strasbourg, approved the draft by a vote of 50 to 0. The constitution provides for neither a federation nor a confederation but for a union that is in between — a political community of a supranational character. It does not call for any fresh surrender of national sovereignty, but rather bases itself on the powers already delegated to the authorities of the Coal and Steel Community. Its further fate is now in the hands of the individual governments who must ratify it.

A further step toward closer cooperation in western Europe was the signing of the North Atlantic Treaty in Washington on April 4, 1949, by representatives of twelve nations: Denmark, Portugal, Iceland, Britain, France, Italy, the Netherlands, Norway, Belgium, Luxembourg, Canada, and the United States.[3] The purpose of the treaty, made to fit into the framework of the United Nations Charter, was to create a solid defense structure that would deter further Soviet aggression against the West. "Under the ominous threat of communistic dictatorship," General Eisenhower said, "the nations of the North Atlantic area have looked at the situation and said: 'We may defend ourselves collectively, but individually we are badly exposed.'" The preamble of the treaty states that the signatories "are determined to safeguard the freedom, common heritage and civilization of their peoples, founded on the principles of democracy, individual liberty, and the rule of law. They seek to promote stability and well-being in the North Atlantic area. They are resolved to unite their efforts for collective defense and for the preservation of peace and security."

[3] Turkey and Greece were added in 1951.

After the treaty was signed the North Atlantic Treaty Organization, better known as NATO, gradually took form. The beginning was made in the establishment of a joint military command to coordinate the rearmament efforts and pool the forces of the member nations. Supreme Headquarters of the Atlantic Powers in Europe (SHAPE) were established in Paris and General Eisenhower was chosen to fill the post of Supreme Commander.[4] Other administrative organs came into existence and at the Lisbon meeting of the representatives of the North Atlantic nations (February, 1952) the decision was made to incorporate the various organs into a permanent organization with headquarters in Paris. Provisions were also made for a NATO secretariat modeled after that of the United Nations and for a "Permanent Council" of fourteen men with authority to speak for the governments of the treaty nations.

Spurred by the threat of a Soviet attack the fourteen nations set the military goal of NATO for 1952 at twenty-five ready divisions and twenty-five more in reserve. By the end of 1953 the NATO forces were to consist of seventy-five divisions. But accomplishments fell short of the aim. One reason for this was the shaky economies of several NATO countries, particularly of France which was staggering under a budget so heavy as to imperil political stability. Britain, too, was beset with grave economic difficulties. Another reason was a lessening of fear that Russia would strike into Europe. After Stalin's death early in 1953, Georgi Malenkov, his successor, further dissipated the fear of invasion by launching a "peace drive." At its meeting in Paris (April 23–25, 1953) the Council of the North Atlantic Treaty Organization was warned by a number of ministers against the danger of a letdown in the defense effort. After considering the situation the Council concluded "that there had not yet been any change in the fundamental threat to the security of free peoples." It did, however, revise its rearmament program. The new defense philosophy stresses the "long pull" rather than immediate urgency.

The Lisbon meeting of February, 1952, also decided to establish a European Defense Community with a supranational army composed of troops from six nations (France, Italy, Belgium, the Netherlands, Luxembourg, and West Germany). On May 27, 1952, the foreign ministers of eight western countries and representatives of seven others met in the famous Clock Room of the French Foreign Office to sign a series of documents to create this unified European defense force and to bind West Germany with the Atlantic defense system. The indispensable core of the European Defense Community is to be an alliance between France and West Germany, the two major continental nations of west-

---

[4] His successors were General Matthew Ridgeway (May, 1952) and General Alfred Gruenther (May, 1953).

ern Europe that have so long been bitter foes. Germany is to contribute twelve divisions to the new European army (four infantry, four tank, and four mechanized) and France's share is to be fourteen. All are to wear a common uniform and use the same arms and equipment.

Two other documents were also signed at the same time. The first was a treaty between the six nations and Britain in which the latter agreed to give military and other aid to any member of the European Defense Community or its forces if attacked, and the members of the E.D.C. gave the same guarantee to Britain. Finally, to allay French fears the United States and Britain undertook in a special protocol not only to keep troops on the continent as long as necessary but also to regard any action from "whatever quarter" which puts the integrity or unity of the Defense Community in peril as a threat to their own security, and to take such action as is necessary.

Ratification by the parliaments of the participating countries has been a slower process than expected. In Germany and France, the two key treaty nations, ratification stalled for a time in the face of strong pressures. This removed the incentive to press for ratification in the four other E.D.C. countries. In Germany the most determined opposition came from the Social Democrats, the second largest political party. But in March, 1953, the first ratification was voted. The West German Bundestag (lower house of parliament) approved the European army treaty by a vote of 224 to 165. On May 15 the Bundesrat (upper house) decided that no vote was necessary by it on either the Bonn peace contract with the western Allies or the European Defense Community Treaty and that the pacts therefore could be considered to have passed through the upper house. This put the final fate of the treaties up to the Federal Constitutional Court which must decide whether or not the treaties are compatible with the constitution of West Germany.

Opinion in the countries which the Germans invaded during the war is not yet fully reconciled to the idea of rearming Germany. This is particularly true in France. Although the creation of a European Defense Community was originally proposed by the French National Assembly, enthusiasm for it has not grown with the passage of time. Opposition is strongest among the Gaullists and in the Communist Party, but misgivings run through practically all parties. Regardless of guarantees and safeguards the fear persists that Germany, having rearmed, will pull out of the combine and go on military adventures of her own. In January, 1953, the trend toward European unity suffered a setback when Robert Schuman, leading French proponent of European unity, lost his post as foreign minister in the new government of René Mayer who became premier on the strength of his pledge to revise the treaty which provides for the rearmament of West Germany.

Even among those who favor the treaty there is a marked tendency to attach various conditions to ratification. They believe that if they do agree to the European Defense Community they should receive the highest possible price in exchange. Among the things they want are more aid for the war in Indo-China, firm support in the UN in their conflict with the nationalist groups of the North African protectorates, and a favorable agreement on the Saar. The last is probably the biggest obstacle to a French-German agreement. The Saar, a 900-square-mile highly industrialized valley between France and Germany, is ethnically German, economically linked with France, and politically autonomous. Possession would give the French approximate equality with West Germany in steel production, an equality that so many Frenchmen contend is indispensable to the success of the Schuman Plan. To the Germans it represents territory that was lost at the end of World War II and that they long to get back; hence they are not ready to surrender their claim to it. It is improbable that any further steps toward European unity will be taken until this question has been settled to the mutual satisfaction of both countries.

DIVIDED GERMANY

When the Allied occupation began Germany lay prostrate. Six years of war effort had drained the moral as well as the physical reserves of the German people. This was, of course, also true of the Allied countries. Until the last year of the war the Germans had not been as fully mobilized or as closely rationed as the British. But the Germans did not have the tonic of victory. Neither did they have prospects for a better life. It is, therefore, not surprising that the German mood at the end of the war was one of hopelessness and apathy. After the defeat in 1918 a new German government was set up at once and continued to function despite the many difficulties it encountered. The situation was quite different in 1945. President Roosevelt's insistence upon unconditional surrender caused the collapse of the entire framework of government in Germany, making it necessary for the Allied armies to assume supreme authority on all levels of administration.

The second mistake the Allies made was to divide the country into four zones of occupation rather than to organize joint occupation of Germany as a whole. Although an Allied Control Council, consisting of the commanders in chief of the occupation forces, ruled Germany as a whole, each commander in chief exercised supreme authority in his own zone. It was still not too late to set up a central administration for the whole of Germany, but the French were adamant against any such move. The old specter of a new German invasion still haunted them.

They felt that their security required that Germany be kept permanently weaker than France. Consequently the French blocked every effort to start a centralized administration. They vetoed national trade unions and national political parties and even refused to agree to postage stamps for the whole of Germany. General de Gaulle stated the issue bluntly when he said: "We do not want any more Reich."

One of the first moves of the military governments was to purge Germany of Nazis and nazism. At Yalta Roosevelt, Churchill, and Stalin had declared that it was their "inflexible purpose to destroy German militarism and nazism" and to "bring all war criminals to justice and swift punishment." At Potsdam President Truman, Prime Minister Churchill, and Premier Stalin reiterated the determination to uproot the Nazi party and all its institutions and to supervise education as a means of eliminating "Nazis and militarist doctrines and to make possible the successful development of democratic ideas." Neither the Russians nor the British and Americans carried out the drastic measures they proclaimed. In the words of one observer, the British and Americans wooed the Germans for the future rather than whipping them for the past. Only a few of the "bigger" Nazis were purged. The Russians, for their part, were not troubled long by the problem of denazification. They quickly decided that punitive measures were a poor way to win German favor. After excusing the "little" Nazis they proceeded to propagandize them into joining one of the People's Front parties in their zone.

If the military governments were lax in purging the masses, they were not remiss in punishing the Nazi leaders. With the arrest of foreign minister von Ribbentrop in June all former Nazi bigwigs were in custody except Heinrich Himmler, Hitler, and Goebbels. Himmler had committed suicide, and Hitler and Goebbels were presumably dead. On October 18, 1945, an indictment was handed by the four powers to the International Military Tribunal in Berlin charging twenty-four war leaders with participation in Hitler's plot against peace and humanity. This indictment set a precedent in calling before a tribunal of justice men of a defeated nation who were responsible for war crimes, atrocities, and acts of aggression on a vast scale. "If there is no law under which to try these people," Justice Robert H. Jackson said in his opening address to the court on November 20, 1945, "it is about time the human race made some." All the defendants responded to the accusations with the words "not guilty." To prove the guilt of the accused vast quantities of evidence were presented to the court, including captured films and documents of many kinds, some of them containing secret orders from Adolf Hitler.

The trials continued for many months. Finally on October 1, 1946, the court brought in a decision condemning twelve of the surviving leaders to death by hanging, three to life imprisonment, and four to prison terms ranging from ten to twenty years, while three were acquitted. Prominent among those who were condemned to death were Hermann Goering, commander in chief of the Luftwaffe and next to Hitler the most prominent figure in the Nazi regime; Joachim von Ribbentrop, Nazi foreign minister; Alfred Rosenberg, official philosopher of the Nazi Party; Julius Streicher, militant anti-Semite and one of the earliest members of the party; General Wilhelm Keitel, chief of the high command; and Arthur Seyss-Inquart, governor of Austria after the Anschluss. Hermann Goering cheated the gallows by taking poison a few hours before his scheduled execution. Dr. Robert Ley, former head of the Labor Front, had committed suicide during the previous October. Rudolf Hess, Hitler's closest personal confidant and the man who made the sensational flight to Britain during the war, was sentenced to imprisonment for life. Dr. Hjalmar Schacht, financial expert of the Nazi regime and Franz von Papen were acquitted over the dissent of the Russians.

At Yalta, at Potsdam, and in the meetings of the Council of Foreign Ministers the Russians had sought as much as possible in reparations to help them pay for the war damage, but the representatives of Britain and the United States hoped to avoid the mistake made after World War I when an impossible indemnity was demanded from Germany. This time they decided that reparations were to be paid in capital goods instead of money. The Russians had already started paying themselves by removing machinery from the plants in the western zones before they turned these zones over to the western powers. In their own zone they dismantled many industries piece by piece and removed them to Russia, but a drop in production caused them to slow the dismantling process. Many of the industries that remained were reorganized into Russian limited companies which produced for export to Russia; others were turned over to communist-dominated state governments and reparations were exacted from current production.

In the other zones the western Allies planned to dismantle about four hundred war plants to prevent the production of armaments and about 1600 others to curb excess production of civilian goods. Most of the armament plants were dismantled, but the Allies soon realized that a Germany held down to a low level of industry would become a liability. They therefore decided not to dismantle all the plants earmarked for this purpose and also to raise the permitted level of steel production.

During the months after the cessation of hostilities the breach between the Soviet government and the western democracies over Germany had grown wider. When it became clear that no agreement was possible, the three western powers reconciled their views and combined their zones in an economic unit. Next discussions were held by the three powers on the question of establishing an elected government in western Germany. The Soviet reply took the form of a blockade of the British-French-American sectors of Berlin in an attempt to drive the western powers from the city. The Russians blocked the single railway and the single auto road and the barge canals which connected the sectors of the western powers with the outside world leaving only the air corridor to Berlin open (June 18, 1948). The blockaded zones faced starvation, cessation of industry, and exhaustion of water, power, gas, and fuel stocks. Fortunately there was an airport in the American sector through which food and supplies could be brought in. The Americans and British organized an airlift and assigned more and more planes to it until they numbered hundreds. Day and night, month after month these planes carried in the food and supplies necessary to sustain the Berlin population and to keep essential industries operating. It took almost a year before the successful operation of the airlift convinced the Russians that their attempt to force the western powers out of Berlin had failed. A Russian order to lift the blockade became effective at midnight, May 11, 1949.

Meanwhile Germany had been split into two federal states, the "Federal Republic of Germany" (commonly called West Germany) and the "German Democratic Republic" (Soviet Germany). During the blockade of western Berlin the foreign ministers of Britain, France, and the United States had met in Washington for the purpose of discussing the German question. On April 8, 1949, they released a communiqué announcing that agreement had been reached on all questions. The western Allies had agreed on the establishment of a German Federal Republic. After a constitutional convention finished the work of drawing up a temporary constitution (Basic Law) modeled on the Weimar constitution it was approved by the representatives of the three western democracies and was promulgated on May 8. The new constitution provided for a legislature of two chambers, a lower house or Bundestag elected by universal suffrage and an upper house or Bundesrat appointed by and representing the governments of the states. The city of Bonn was chosen as the capital of the new state; hence the popular designation "Bonn government."

Elections for the Bundestag were held August 12, 1949. When the votes were counted it was found that of the four hundred seats the Christian Democratic Union sponsoring a liberal economy had won 139 and the Social Democrats 131. The communists succeeded in winning only fifteen. The two houses of the West German parliament convened at Bonn on September 7. Five days later the Federal Convention of 804 (402 Bundestag deputies and 402 special delegates from the state legislatures) met and elected Theodor Heuss, a noted scholar, the first president of the republic. On September 15 the Bundestag chose Dr. Konrad Adenauer, the leader of the Christian Democratic Union, federal chancellor by the margin of one vote. The chancellor formed a right-wing coalition government. This government at once opened negotiations with the Allied representatives for the purpose of inducing them to relax the existing restrictions on German shipping and to remove from the reparations list nineteen plants that were marked for dismantling. The new chancellor was successful in achieving both aims. Plants that were spared included steel, synthetic oil, and rubber works.

For a time recovery in the economic field was slow, but the introduction of a new mark in West Germany in June, 1948, stimulated a substantial revival. Further impetus resulted from the inclusion of Germany in the Marshall Plan. The production of steel ingots, for example, increased from about three million tons in 1947 to more than eleven million in 1950. After Chancellor Adenauer succeeded in removing the restrictions on the size, speed, and number of commercial cargo ships that the West German shipyards could build, the shipbuilding industry flourished almost immediately. In general, in 1950 the index of industrial production reached 125 per cent of the 1936 level. The food situation also improved greatly. Better than average harvests in 1949 and 1950 erased many shortages. At the end of 1950 the standard of living was much higher, with only housing and fuel remaining on the list of scarce items.

In eastern Germany the establishment of a state ran somewhat the same course, with the exception that there were no free and democratic elections. The Russians were determined to establish a satellite government and anyone who offered opposition was styled a "fascist." On March 18–19, 1949, the "People's Council" approved the constitution which had been drafted by a committee and on May 15–16 all eligible voters were summoned to the polls to endorse or reject the single slate of candidates for the People's Congress. More than four million cast a negative vote, while eight million voted in the affirmative. At its first meeting the People's Congress transformed itself into the People's Chamber and then proclaimed the establishment of the "German Democratic Republic," with the capital at Berlin. Thus two separate states were established in Germany. Neither state, however, could claim independence. The eastern state was supervised by the Soviet Control Commission, while western Germany was under the supervision of the three-power High Commission for Germany.

PEACE COMPACT WITH WEST GERMANY

During the years since World War II the Soviet propaganda machine has repeatedly broadcast that Russia desires to see German unity restored. At the same time Britain and the United States were denounced as wishing to dismember Germany. The purpose was nothing more than an attempt to win the support of the German people. Actually the Russians had no desire to see Germany unified except on their terms, namely that a communist government be established in Germany. The propaganda device of advocating German unity was employed by the Soviet government again and again in an effort to stop West Germany from allying itself more closely with the west European states. Thus in March, 1952, after the Lisbon conference had decided to rearm West Germany the Soviet authorities delivered a note to the United States, Britain, and France containing a proposal for German unity. The Russian note proposed all-German elections for the establishment of an all-German government, the frontiers of the German state to be determined in accordance with the Potsdam agreements of 1945. In return the all-German government would have to promise "not to enter any kind of coalition or military alliances directed against any power which has taken part with armed forces in the war against Germany."

U.S. Secretary of State Acheson termed the issuance of the note the "golden apple tactic," in other words, an attempt to create dissension between West Germany and the western democracies. Nevertheless, efforts to reach an agreement were made. Notes were exchanged but did not result in agreements. Chancellor Adenauer who had not been swayed by the Russian proposal continued with the plans to align West Germany with the North Atlantic alliance. On May 26, 1952, the foreign ministers of the United States, Britain, France, and West Germany signed a virtual peace treaty with West Germany in the form of a contractual agreement giving that country a new and almost sovereign status on condition that it enter the European Defense Community. The opening sentence of the "peace contract" read: "The effect of the contractual arrangements is to include the (West German) Federal Republic in the community of free nations as an equal partner." Section Two of the "contract" reads:

The granting of freedom to the Federal Republic is achieved in the following way: the Occupation Statute is repealed; the Allied High Commission and the Land Commissions are abolished; henceforth the three powers will conduct their relations with the Federal Republic through ambassadors; the foreign armed forces stationed in the Federal territory are no longer occupation forces, their sole mission now being to secure the defense of the free world; the Federal Republic, released from all control, will thus be able on its own responsibility, to develop its democratic and Federal institutions within the framework of its basic law.

Although the "contract" states that "these agreements have been freely negotiated on the basis of complete equality," the necessity of maintaining troops in West Germany to defend the freedom of the new state caused the western Allies to reserve certain powers for themselves. Secretary Acheson together with the representatives of Britain and France promised, however, that these powers will be surrendered when the necessity of defending German freedom no longer exists. A noteworthy feature of the "contract" is that it renounced the repressive measures of Versailles and Potsdam, replacing them with a new order based on mutual service and cooperation.

Since 1952 the new republic has enjoyed a spectacular economic boom. If we regard the year 1936 as the base year at 100, the index of industrial production reached 159 in October, 1952, and 167 by the end of that year. Unemployment was at a record low with virtually full employment in some districts, and the production of coal and iron, the basic factors of the West Germany economy, set new records. A daily record was set in October, 1952, with the production of 412,000 metric tons of coal. While the cost of living had risen only 8 per cent over 1950, wages increased 13 per cent. A socialist newspaper which had usually been critical declared late in 1952, "A genuine rise in the standard of living must be reported."

A notable feature of the boom was the emergence of West Germany as a strong competitor for world markets. German trade missions and industrial technicians are again busy rebuilding the trade positions Germany had enjoyed before the war, in Europe, in the Middle East, and in South America. The industries are not only producing goods in greater quantity for export; the West Germans also offer more attractive credit terms and earlier delivery dates than most of their competitors. In September, 1952, German exports exceeded imports by $36.5 million. This is to be ascribed in part to the fact that West Germany as yet has no rearmament program and can therefore concentrate its efforts on civilian goods. After the absence of German competition since 1945, the revival of German trade has caused considerable concern among other European powers.

AUSTRIA AND THE POWERS

The collapse of the Third Reich in 1945 freed Austria from Nazi rule after a subjugation of seven years, but did not give the country full independence. Nazi rule was followed by Allied control. One of the first things the Russians had done after they occupied Vienna was to set up a provisional government (April 29, 1945) composed of members of the three principal anti-fascist parties: Social Democrats, People's Party (Volkspartei: the old Christian Socialists who were closely allied with the Roman Catholic Church), and Communist Party, with Dr. Karl Renner who had been the first chancellor of the Austrian republic in 1918 as chancellor. On June 25 four occupation zones were established and Vienna, like Berlin, was divided into four districts. The Russians imposed such severe restrictions upon movement between the Russian and other zones that there was little intercourse. In their zone the Russians requisitioned not only plants and factories but also clothing and cattle alleging them to be German assets to which they were entitled. Denazification was carried on much as in Germany.

On November 25, 1945, elections were held to choose delegates to a National Assembly. The People's Party and the Social Democrats won nearly all the seats, the former gaining eighty-five and the Social Democrats seventy-six. The Communist Party succeeded in winning only four.[5] Dr. Renner who had resigned was succeeded as chancellor by Leopold Figl of the People's Party. On December 20 the National Assembly unanimously elected Dr. Renner president of the republic for a six year term.[6] Early in 1946 the Allied Council decided that the government could exchange diplomatic representatives with all countries that would recognize it, excepting Germany and Japan. The Allies also asked the National Assembly to have a draft of the constitution ready by July 1. The answer came on April 13 when the chancellor announced that the National Assembly had decided to reestablish the constitution of 1927.

The economic conditions in Austria have, on the whole, been poor. The rise of prices after the war coupled with a fall of wages created a critical situation for the workers. Many found it necessary to deplete their savings to purchase food in the black market in order to supplement their meager rations. Help came first from UNRRA and later through the Marshall Plan.[7] The great need is increased productivity to pay for imports which greatly exceed exports. In October and November, 1951, there was a total trade deficit of about $10 million even though the production index had reached 171 (1937 = 100). The $120 million in United States aid during the fiscal year of 1951–1952 failed to dissipate the economic gloom. At the end of 1952 the outlook was still dismal. If we take April, 1945, as 100, the cost-of-living index

[5] In the elections of 1949 the Independents, a new party widely regarded as neo-Nazi, won 16 seats, but the Volkspartei and Social Democrats remained the two major parties.
[6] He died on December 31, 1950. On May 27, 1951, Theodor Koerner was elected his successor.
[7] Total United States aid to January 1, 1953, amounted to $909 million.

was about 700 in 1951 and about 819 in 1952, while the index of wages was 80.7 in 1951 and 78 in 1952. Prices were at so high a level as to make the necessary increase of exports difficult.

When the war ended in 1945 the Austrians hoped that the powers would soon agree on a peace treaty and that the occupation troops would be withdrawn. Hopes ran high when the announcement was made that the Council of Foreign Ministers would meet in Moscow on March 10, 1947, to discuss peace treaties with Austria and Germany. The foreign ministers did reach accord on the size of the Austrian army and on a number of minor questions, but they did not agree on a peace treaty. At Moscow and during the years that followed Britain, France, and the United States were unsuccessful in their attempts to induce the Soviet Union to sign a treaty for Austria. The points of difference were narrowed down, but the final gap was not bridged. Austria remained a political pawn in the rivalry between the East and the West. How the Austrians felt about it we can learn from a speech made by Minister Ferdinand Graf in 1947: "Go back to the Volga," he said, "go back to the Mississippi, and leave us on the Danube. Austria is no football field for the game between the East and the West." Despite all this Austria was still under four-power occupation nine years after the end of the war.

DISPIRITED FRANCE

When France collapsed under the Nazi onslaught in 1940 Premier Paul Reynaud handed the reins of government (June 16) to Marshal Pétain, a soldier of eighty-five. The regime sponsored by Pétain was a strange mixture of Fascist and royalist ideas. It became known as the Vichy regime because its headquarters were established in the city of Vichy. As the exploitation of France by the Nazis increased the French people became more restive. Fearing an uprising against the Nazis which he believed could only end in disaster for the French people, Pétain proclaimed a series of restrictive measures which abolished freedom of speech, the press, and association in that part of France which was not occupied by the Germans. After Pétain had gagged the French the Nazis bound them. Gradually the Nazis and their collaborators gained control of the industrial and financial life of France and in November, 1942, German troops occupied the whole country.

At the time of the French surrender General Charles de Gaulle had organized the "Free French" movement which later became known as "Fighting France." The basic purpose of this movement was to free France from the clutches of the Nazis. While some Free Frenchmen joined the Allied forces, others entered occupied France to become a part of the underground movement. In 1943 de Gaulle's movement was merged with the French resistance movement in North Africa and a Committee of National Liberation was organized. Gradually de Gaulle became the sole leader of all the political and military forces of the Committee. In June of 1944 the Committee adopted the title of "Provisional Government of the French Republic" and was accorded recognition by a number of European states.

After the Allied invasion of Italy the Vichy ringleaders sought to escape the consequences of their treasonable acts by trying to surrender their power to a national assembly so that it could select a government favorable to the Allies. When this move failed Marshal Pétain called upon the people to be neutral in the announced invasion of France. The actual invasion on June 6, 1944, caused Pétain, his right-hand man Pierre Laval, and the rest of the cabinet to flee to Belfort after the cabinet voted itself out of existence. Later Pétain and his quisling associates were removed to Germany, while Laval fled to Spain. The widespread demand by the French people that the Vichy leaders be punished caused Pétain to surrender to the French authorities (April, 1945). Several months later he was tried for "intelligence with the enemy" and sentenced to death. General de Gaulle, however, because of Pétain's age and distinguished service to his country, commuted the sentence to life imprisonment.[8] Laval, too, was sentenced to death, but without a recommendation of clemency. After a futile attempt to end his life by poison, he was executed by a firing squad (October 14, 1945).

After the reconquest of France General de Gaulle as the head of the provisional government exercised general supervision over the country. In October, 1945, an election was held to choose delegates for a National Constituent Assembly (522 for France; 64 for overseas territories). The voters in addition to choosing their delegates were asked to decide whether the new body was to function as a legislative chamber as well as a constituent assembly and whether the power of the assembly over the president should be restricted. Both questions were answered with resounding affirmatives. The election was unique in that women voted in a national election for the first time. Although thirty parties presented candidates, about three quarters of the votes went to three groups. Of the 522 deputies chosen to represent France proper the Socialist Party won 133 seats and the MRP (Movement Républicain Populaire) whose support came from the Catholic trade unions and young Catholic Leftists 140. The Communists with 142 seats returned the largest number of deputies. It was the first time they gained this distinction.

[8] Marshal Pétain died July 23, 1951.

When the Constituent Assembly met on November 6 President de Gaulle surrendered his powers, but was reelected provisional president by unanimous vote. He had difficulty, however, in forming a cabinet because of his refusal to give the Communists one of three major positions — foreign affairs, war, or interior. After trying several times he reached an impasse which caused him to resign with finality on January 22, 1946. During the succeeding weeks the Constituent Assembly finished the work of drawing up a new constitution, but the voters of France rejected it because it gave the legislature too much power. A second constitution differing but little from the first was ratified by the voters in September, 1946, by a small majority. It provided for a parliament of two houses, a National Assembly elected by equal, direct, and secret universal suffrage, and a Council of the Republic chosen by means of indirect elections. The former is the dominant chamber. The Council can delay measures for a time, but cannot prevent them from becoming law. The constitution also made provisions for the election of a president for a term of seven years by the two houses in joint session.

The old fear of a strong executive which dates back to the French Revolution and Napoleon persisted. Consequently the presidency in the Fourth Republic is much the same as it was in the Third Republic, an office with routine functions but without powers. The new constitution went into force on December 24, 1946. Vincent Auriol was elected first president of the Fourth Republic. During the years that followed France, as in the interwar period, suffered from the malady of short-lived cabinets. Coalition governments have followed each other in rapid succession. The average life of a cabinet since World War II has been somewhat under six months. From the Liberation in 1945 to May, 1953, the Assembly has voted out seventeen governments. Since six divergent parties — the Communists and Socialists on the left, the Radicals and Popular Republicans in the center, the Independents and Gaullists [9] on the right — hold almost equal blocs of votes in the French Assembly, it has proved almost impossible to put together a strong government.

At the end of the war the economic life of France was badly disorganized. Although hostilities had consisted only of one month of invasion in 1940 and two months of counterinvasion in 1944 destruction of buildings was greater than in World War I — according to some estimates twice as great. Thousands of homes and factories were completely demolished, but it was the transportation facilities which suf-

[9] Early in May, 1953, General de Gaulle announced that his party, the R.P.F. (Reunion of the French People), would no longer function as an organized party, leaving his followers free to vote as they please.

fered the heaviest damage. During the last year of the war the Allies had thoroughly bombed the railway systems destroying engines and cars, bridges and trestles, stations, junction points, and marshaling yards. In addition Allied bombers had also destroyed harbor facilities. Loss of merchant ships during the war reached 70 per cent of the total tonnage. Consequently there was not only a shortage of food, clothing, fuel, and building materials; but the breakdown of transportation greatly impeded the distribution of such vital materials as were imported.

During the period of occupation the Germans had drained more wealth out of France than the French had received in reparations after World War I. Moreover, the French tourist trade had practically disappeared during the war. The luxury industries, including fashions, cosmetics, and perfumes, were experiencing greater competition from new industries in the various countries in which French luxuries had found ready markets before the war. Consequently the dollar shortage was even greater than in Britain. There were no funds to meet the requirements for reconstruction, modernization, and expansion of her productive apparatus. During the years that followed the burden of a heavy financial deficit, postwar inflation, and an industry that was slow to return to peacetime production repeatedly brought the country to the verge of economic bankruptcy.

The postwar economic difficulties of France must not, however, be ascribed wholly to the war. The French industrial system had gradually fallen behind during the interwar period, particularly in regard to machine renewals. During the years between the two wars the British had invested very little new capital in industry, but the French had invested less — in fact, only about one quarter as much. Immediately after World War I the French had used available funds to rebuild the devastated regions and later to prepare for World War II. Machines and machine tools were not replaced. During World War II few replacements were made because France was cut off from her foreign source of supply of machinery and machine tools. At the end of the war it was calculated that while the average age of machine tools in Britain was seven years, it was twenty-five years in France. French industry had not kept pace with a rapidly changing world. Poor equipment and antiquated techniques spelled low productivity. Even before World War II the average productivity of the French industrial workman was about one third that of a workman in the United States. Agricultural production, too, was low because the system of small farms (averaging about thirty acres) made for inefficiency. Whereas the U.S. farmer raised enough food for twenty people, the French peasant produced enough only for five.

The flood of dollars which the Marshall Plan poured into France acted as a stimulant in a number of ways. Above all, it permitted France to import much-needed products, particularly machinery and machine tools. Industrial production increased about 14 per cent in 1948, and in 1949 attained the prewar levels of output. Agricultural production also increased slowly during the years after 1945. The manpower shortage was temporarily alleviated through the use on French farms of about 400,000 German prisoners of war. Many immigrant farm workers, particularly Italians and displaced persons from Germany, were also admitted into the country. Furthermore, large quantities of equipment including farm machinery were imported from Britain and the United States. Increased food production enabled the government to curtail imports while exports were increasing. By 1949 the French coal mines had been largely restored and supplied with new machinery with the result that in this year France produced more coal than in any previous year except 1929. The recovery continued into 1950. There was every indication that the French government would be able to balance the budget by 1952–1953.

But after the middle of 1950 an economic decline set in. Two of the principal causes of the economic reversal were the necessity for rearming under the threat of Russian aggression and the heavy drain of continuing the war in Indo-China.[10] The index of industrial production which had stood at 133 in May, 1951, dropped to 106 by August, 1951. The prospects of a favorable balance of trade were sharply reversed in 1951 by the declining prices of exports and the rising prices of imports; in 1951 the budget deficit also increased sharply, the difference being made up in part by the United States funds. During 1952 France made a serious effort to clear up her economic and financial situation, but without much success. M. Pinay who became premier in March embarked on what was called the "triple gamble." He sought to build up purchasing power by holding down prices, to balance the budget without new taxation, and to avoid devaluation of the franc. Within three months he had put through a balanced budget and cut wholesale prices by 10 per cent. Although Frenchmen hailed him as a financial wizard, the actual situation was not promising. The halt in the rise of prices and government expenditures affected business adversely. Tradesmen complained of a drop in sales because consumers were postponing purchases in expectation of further price cuts. Manufacturers, unable or unwilling to make the cuts, were reducing output and laying off workers. At the year's end M. Pinay's cabinet fell after the Gaullists withdrew their support. Thus the French were still seeking the road to stability.

In January, 1953, the government of René Mayer came to power. In

10 See page 711.

his speech when he obtained endorsement by the Assembly as premier M. Mayer promised a revision of the constitution to give the government greater stability. A bill was introduced to strengthen the executive department over the Assembly and to provide a less cumbersome system of selecting and endorsing new premiers. But the Mayer cabinet fell (May, 1953) before it could be passed. The fall came on a minor budgetary question despite the premier's plea that an unfavorable vote would advertise "that governmental instability that has done so much to discredit France throughout the world."

After a crisis of $5\frac{1}{2}$ weeks, Joseph Laniel, a conservative Independent, finally succeeded in forming a cabinet that won the approval of the National Assembly (June 30). In a brief policy statement the new premier pledged continued allegiance to NATO. On December 23 René Coty, a moderate conservative, was elected president on the 13th ballot. It was the first time since 1875 that more than two ballots were required for a French presidential election. M. Coty took office January 17, 1954, as successor to Vincent Auriol.

CHAPTER THIRTY–FOUR

Western Europe since World War II: Britain, Spain, and Italy

SOCIALIST BRITAIN
W HEN Big Ben lighted up again at dusk above the houses of parliament it indicated that peace had returned to Britain, but the troubles of the British were far from over. Besides suffering heavy losses in manpower, the British also saw German bombers devastate wide areas in many cities. Factories, railways, and docks were wholly or partially destroyed. More than four million houses or one out of every three in the entire United Kingdom were either demolished or damaged. As a result almost a quarter of the population was in need of housing. Food was so short that the government offered free cartridges to anyone wanting to shoot grey squirrels. Furthermore, the British economic system was badly dislocated. Not only was it necessary to convert Britain's entire industrial system to peacetime production but Britain's world trade was also in need of restoration. Moreover, there was a great shortage of industrial raw materials.

To understand Britain's plight one must remember her basic dilemma which, put briefly, is "export or die." More than half of the country's food and most of the industrial raw materials, except coal, were obtained from abroad. There was no possibility of providing food for the 48 million people out of Britain's agricultural resources and without imported raw materials the major industries would soon collapse. Before the war the British had paid for these imports in three ways: first, with income from extensive foreign investments; second, with income derived from their merchant marine which carried goods for other nations; third, with income gained from the sale of exports abroad. But the war in accelerating developments that had started earlier greatly reduced all these sources of income. To pay for essential war materials and food the government had liquidated more than $5 billion of overseas investments and in addition had incurred large overseas debts. At the end of the war Britain was for the first time in modern history a debtor country. Of her carrying trade only a fraction remained. Not only had half the shipping fleet been sunk during the war but much of the British carrying trade had been absorbed by the merchant marines of the United States and other countries. In summary, the liquidation of foreign investments and the decline of the carrying trade had wiped out most of the "invisible income" which had financed the excess of imports over exports.

This left only exports as a means of purchasing abroad the food for a swollen population and the raw materials for her manufacturing industries. To secure enough overseas income to pay for essential food and raw materials it was necessary to raise exports to three and a half times the level to which they had dropped during the war. But the British industries were not equal to the task. Much of the British machinery and equipment was obsolete. With most of the energies of the nation concentrated on winning the war, little was done in the way of renewing plants and replacing worn-out machinery in the civilian industries. Even during the interwar period only a limited amount had been spent for new machinery. Transportation machinery, too, was being used long beyond the time when it should have been discarded. Poor machinery and inefficient production methods raised the price of British manufactures thereby handicapping them in the competition for world markets.

An example in point was the production of coal. Before the war Britain had still produced much coal for export. But at the end of World War II her mines were old, the shafts were deep, and many of the remaining coal seams were thin. The Bituminous Coal Institute reported in 1952 that the average depth of coal mine shafts is 190 feet in the United States and 1,170 feet in British coal mines. The available labor force was also insufficient to achieve production equal to pre-war. The British mining population had been ground down by hard labor and recurring depressions. Such labor force as existed was aged and tired from the heavy effort of sustaining war production. The poor working conditions and the obsolete equipment caused the sons of the old miners to seek employment in other branches of industry. Production per man, which before the war had been only about one-quarter of the production of a United States miner, declined further after the war. Although the U.S. miner in the period immediately after World War II received double the wages of British miners, the cost of producing a ton of coal was much higher in Britain. The high price of coal, in turn, raised the production costs of all British manufactures.

The general result was an acute dollar shortage. Britain could no longer pay her way in the world. She could no longer earn enough to keep her population on Western living standards or to rebuild the factories that could ultimately support her. It appeared as if the country was headed for disaster. In 1946 Britain's imports cost her $1,800 million more than the value of the goods exported to pay for them.

The task of raising export quotas sufficiently to pay for the necessary imports fell to the Labor government which rose to power in July, 1945. The electorate, it appears, was convinced that the task of reconstruction needed different men and new points of view. Mr. Churchill himself had written in an autobiographical volume entitled *My Early Years:* "Those who can win a war well can rarely make a good peace, and those who could make a good peace would never have won the war." When he proposed that his coalition government remain in office until the end of the Pacific war, the proposal was rejected by the Labor Party. The Prime Minister at once drove to Buckingham Palace to tender his resignation and early in July, 1945, elections were held. When the results were announced on July 26 it was found that the Labor Party had won a victory far more sweeping than its leaders had expected. The Labor representation in the House of Commons increased from 164 to 393, while that of the Conservatives dropped from 358 to 198. Thus Britain replaced Winston Churchill's coalition government with a Labor government headed by Clement R. Attlee as Prime Minister. Ernest Bevin was chosen Foreign Secretary. Mr. Churchill himself later wrote: "I wielded (the chief power in the state) in ever-growing measure for five years and three months of world war, at the end of which time, all our enemies having surrendered or being about to do so, I was immediately dismissed by the British electorate from all further conduct of their affairs."

The new government at once took steps to meet the situation. Many controls and restrictions were imposed as a means of reducing imports. For the British population this meant austerity rations. There was, of course, nothing new in this, since it was but the continuation or resumption of war-time controls. In addition to the temporary regulations a whole body of permanent controls were also put into operation. The innovations included: (1) a central planning commission to study and assess the possible sources of national income and to allocate the distribution of capital; (2) a long-term plan for the nationalization of the basic industries; (3) a further plan for the industries (about 80 per cent) which were to be left in private hands; (4) a long-term program for agricultural development to make Britain less dependent on imported foods.

The long-term nationalization plan was definitely socialistic, but not

Moscow-inspired. The Labor Party did not advocate national owner-ship of all the means of production and distribution. The projected plan called for the nationalization of only about 20 per cent of the British industrial assets. A beginning was made in the nationalization of the Bank of England. Public ownership of this bank had long been a pri-mary aim of the Labor Party. The reason the Labor Party regarded the nationalization of the Bank of England as particularly necessary was because it could not carry out the other planned reforms unless it had control of the credit facilities. The bill, introduced in October, 1945, provided for the issuance of government stock to replace that held by the shareholders, each shareholder being guaranteed the same income for twenty years that he had received during the preceding twenty-two years. The bill became law on February 14, 1946.

Further nationalizations followed. Before the end of 1945 a bill to nationalize the coal industry was introduced. Since all political parties had long considered the nationalization of the coal industry as inev-itable, there was little opposition to the bill which became law on July 12, 1946. It provided for a nine-member National Coal Board with full power to carry out all operations involved in production and distribu-tion. Other utilities including gas, electricity, and telephone services were also nationalized. Next on the schedule was inland transportation by road, rail, and canal. The final item in the program was the national-ization of the iron and steel industry. After stormy debates in 1948 the Iron and Steel Act was finally passed in 1949. The plan specified that the ninety-two companies affected by the Act would not be dis-solved as were the electric, gas and transport companies. They were to continue to exist as separate units, but the transfer of all securities to an Iron and Steel Corporation was made compulsory.

In the meantime the government also opened negotiations for a loan from the United States. As early as September, 1945, talks began in Washington and finally on December 6, 1945, an agreement was signed which provided for a loan to Britain of $3.75 billion to be repaid by the year 2001. In 1946 the British military forces were reduced in order to provide more manpower for industry. But the dollar shortage still continued. On August 6, 1947, Prime Minister Attlee stated that longer working hours and a reduced standard of living would be the lot of the British for an indefinite period. Such sacrifices, he said, are essential if the rapidly diminishing dollar reserves are to be conserved and the country's foreign trade brought into balance. "First" said Sir Stafford Cripps,[1] popularly known as Mr. Austerity and Minister of Perspira-tion, "we must produce more goods to sell abroad. Then we must build new factories. The needs, comforts and amenities of the family must come last."

[1] Minister of Economic Affairs and then Chancellor of the Exchequer.

When the Marshall Plan began to operate Britain became the largest single recipient of funds. Money was poured into new factories, equipment, and electric power stations. Everywhere great stress was put on more efficient production. As a result progress was rapid. By the end of 1948 industrial production was 18 per cent above 1938 and the exports 38 per cent above 1938, while imports were down 20 per cent. Agricultural production in 1948 was 25 per cent above 1938 despite a bad harvest. With these achievements the British halved their yearly trade deficits. Although the country was well on its way toward a balanced economy, the situation was still not stable. In 1949 a temporary decline set in. In the second quarter of 1949 U.S. purchases of British goods dropped sharply and other purchasers motivated by rumors of a coming devaluation of the pound postponed their purchases. On August 31 the British government decided to devalue the pound from $4.03 to $2.80 in the hope that lower prices would stimulate purchases of British goods abroad, particularly in the dollar countries. Within a period of a little more than a month twenty-eight countries, including all the dominions except Pakistan, followed suit.

Marked improvement followed. The situation regarding foreign exchange became so favorable as to permit the Chancellor of the Exchequer to announce on December 13, 1950, that "the economic recovery of Britain and the sterling area as a whole has made such good progress that the dollar deficit has in recent months disappeared." On the same day the announcement was made in Washington that at the end of 1950 Marshall aid to the United Kingdom would cease. The announcement that Britain was becoming financially independent nineteen months before the scheduled end of the Marshall Plan was received with pride in Britain. But the rearmament program launched after the outbreak of the Korean war undid much of the progress. The demand for raw materials needed by the armament industries caused the prices to rise sharply. The gap between imports and exports widened considerably, despite all efforts to increase production for export.

The margin of seats which the Labor Party had gained in 1945 had gradually been whittled down until the Laborites had only half a dozen votes more in the House of Commons than Churchill's Conservatives. The Labor Party's hold became so precarious that Prime Minister Attlee decided to ask for a new mandate. The elections were held on October 25, 1951, with more than 80 per cent of the electorate voting. The results showed a victory for the Conservatives. The score was 321 seats for the Conservatives and 295 for the Laborites. The margin of victory was so small that the membership of the House was again divided almost equally. Thus the task of trying to solve Britain's financial difficulties was lifted from the shoulders of Attlee and placed upon those of Churchill and his associates. Winston Churchill, nearing 77, was asked by King George to form a new government. The new cabinet with Anthony Eden as foreign secretary and Richard Austen Butler as chancellor of the exchequer immediately attacked the problem. It proposed no radical changes in the welfare state the Laborites had established. Churchill did, however, state that the steel industry and long-distance trucking would be returned to private ownership.

During the first year and a half of Conservative rule economic conditions improved in a number of respects. This despite the fact that one-third of the national budget and about 12 per cent of gross national production were devoted to national defense. By the end of September, 1952, the huge deficits in the balance of trade that were draining away the gold reserves had begun to turn into small but reassuring surpluses. This was achieved by sharply reduced imports, by a favorable swing in the terms of trade that made imports cheaper and exports dearer, and by a revival of confidence brought about by anti-inflationary monetary policies.[2] In April, 1952, Chancellor of the Exchequer Butler in making the annual budget speech asked for no new taxes for the first time since World War II. Instead, he announced an income tax cut of sixpence (7 cents) on each pound ($2.80) earned, a 25 per cent reduction in the purchase tax on consumer goods, and the end of the excess profits tax on January 1, 1954. The sugar ration was increased to 12 ounces a week and a prompt end to sugar rationing was promised. In summing up the chancellor of the exchequer said: "We step out from the confines of restriction to the almost forgotten but beckoning prospects of freer endeavor and greater reward for effort."

On February 6, 1952, Britain and the world were stunned by the announcement that King George VI had died in his sleep that morning. Four months earlier he had undergone a surgical operation for the removal of a cancerous lung and the British people thought he was gradually regaining his strength, but his other lung was also infected. On his last day he bagged nine rabbits and a pigeon and at dusk told one of his shooting companions, "I've had a thoroughly enjoyable day." At the news of his death Britain and the Commonwealth at once went into deep mourning. Seldom has the passing of a monarch been mourned more genuinely.

George VI's successor is his daughter Elizabeth who was acclaimed queen at the age of twenty-five. At the time of her father's death she was in East Africa on the first leg of a good-will tour which her father had originally planned for himself. She returned at once to Britain to take the royal oath.[3] When Mr. Churchill in his role as prime minister met the new queen on her return to Britain he said: "I, whose youth

[2] The one disturbing portent was that industrial exports were 3 per cent lower in the first ten months of 1952 than in the preceding year.
[3] The coronation took place on June 2, 1953.

was cast in the august, unchallenged and tranquil glories of the Victorian era, may well feel a thrill in evoking once more the prayer and the anthem, 'God Save the Queen.' " Painters went to work replacing the signs reading "King's Bench" with signs reading "Queen's Bench." In answer to the challenge, "Who goes there?" the sentries in a traditional nightly ritual at the Tower of London now say, "The Queen's Keys." As in Gilbert and Sullivan the British navy is now "the Queen's Navee."

The new queen took up her duties as well prepared for her responsibilities and as well versed in the problems of her people as any sovereign of modern times. She stepped into her triple role as queen, wife, and mother with a calm confidence that amazed her ministers, her court, and the British people generally. Since her accession she has shown a determination to learn the reasons behind the government decisions made in her name. In general, she has given every indication of being a successful sovereign according to the modern British concept of sovereignty.

FASCIST SPAIN

Spain, as in World War I, did not become an active participant in World War II. During the early years of the war Nationalist Spain wavered between outright participation on the Axis side and a position of pro-Axis nonbelligerency. Pressure was exerted from both sides. While the Axis powers not only demanded that Generalissimo Franco repay the assistance he had received during the civil war but also sought to entice him with promises of Gibraltar and a part of North Africa, Britain threatened to establish a complete blockade of hungry Spain. The Nazi success in France appears to have convinced Franco that Germany would win. Instead of entering the war, however, he presented to the Nazi ambassador in Madrid his terms for becoming an active participant. Franco's price was Gibraltar, French Morocco, and the Oran section of Algeria; also economic assistance plus military supplies. But Hitler regarded the price as being too high. During the months that followed each tried to convince the other to give in. When the Germans invaded Russia in 1941 a new wave of pro-Axis feeling welled up in Spain. Volunteers were recruited for service against the Russians and in Madrid Falangist demonstrators stoned the British embassy. It appeared as if Spain was about to cast its lot on the side of the Axis. But Franco still did not move.

Events in the fall of 1941 appear to have instilled doubts in Franco's mind. After the Nazis failed to reach Moscow in the fall of 1941 Franco said no more about joining the Axis in the war. The Japanese attack on Pearl Harbor and the entrance of the United States into the conflict exercised a powerful effect on the Spanish mind. Convinced that the pendulum of victory was swinging toward the Allied side he issued a decree which declared that Spain would maintain her status of nonbelligerency. As it became evident that the Allies were increasing their strength, the government officially retreated from its policy of "all aid to the Axis short of war" to one of more definite neutrality. But Franco continued to give secret aid in various ways. After the success of the Allied offensives in Russia and North Africa convinced him that the Axis cause was doomed, he sought to ingratiate himself with Britain and the United States by offering Spain's offices in the cause of "a speedy and just peace." His offer of mediation was, however, spurned by the Allies.

It was widely believed that the fall of Mussolini and Hitler would spell the doom of Franco. The Allied victory, it is true, did cause many parties in Spain to stiffen their opposition to the Franco regime. Private business grew more bitter in its opposition, the monarchists more insistent regarding the restoration of monarchy, and the republicans more determined to overthrow the Nationalist government. This did not, however, cause Franco to drop the reins of government and leave the country. What saved his regime was the fact that the opposition was not united. He was thus able to continue his "divide and rule" policy. But he did seek to allay internal dissension and to improve his international position by making a gesture at liberalizing his regime. He promised less harsh treatment for political prisoners and the restoration of civil liberties and freedom of the press. On May 7, 1945, he proclaimed a bill of rights permitting freedom of speech, of assembly, and of religion. Closer examination, however, revealed that the "freedoms" forbade criticism of the fundamental principles of the Franco state, permitted assemblies only for "lawful purposes," and barred non-Catholics from holding public office

Franco's efforts did not convince anyone and his government was regarded as a sort of outlaw by other nations. At Potsdam (August, 1945) the Big Three condemned the Spanish regime and excluded it from the UN. A joint note issued by Britain, France, and the United States stated that "it is hoped the leading patriotic and liberal-minded Spaniards may soon find means to bring about a peaceful withdrawal of Franco." In December, 1946, after the Spanish question had been studied and discussed by various UN organs, the General Assembly passed a resolution which recommended that all UN members recall their ambassadors from Madrid. Spain was also barred from membership in the UN so long as the government remained unchanged.

The cold relations with the Franco government continued until friction developed between the Soviet Union and the western democracies. When military considerations became primary, the Pyrenees came to be regarded as a secondary defense line in Europe. During the succeeding years various attempts were made to gloss over the arbitrariness of Franco's rule and to groom Spain for association in the Atlantic Pact. Unanimous approval of all members, however, is necessary to bring a new participant into the alliance. An effort was also made to include Spain in the list of countries eligible for Marshall Plan aid. But opposition to the Franco regime was still too strong.

Beginning in 1947 Franco himself sought to pave the way for better relations with the other nations by announcing a plan for the eventual restoration of the monarchy. A Regency Council was organized to take charge of the government if the chief of state should die or be incapacitated. "In case of death or incapacity of the chief of state," the decree stated, "there will be called to succeed him that person of royal blood with the best right to the position." The decree also provided that Franco might at any time suggest to the Cortes that it summon "the person of royal blood" best qualified to assume the Spanish crown. At the same time the Spanish government also tried to have the UN resolution revoked. For a time in 1949 it appeared as if these efforts would meet with success, but the General Assembly voted down the proposal. In July, 1951, the U.S. government began exploring the possibilities of a treaty with Spain which would permit the establishment of U.S. air and naval bases on Spanish soil in return for economic and military assistance. Franco who was badly in need of economic aid to alleviate suffering and calm the unrest among his people remodeled his cabinet replacing several of the extreme fascists with members of the monarchist and Catholic groups in the hope of making it more palatable to the West.[4]

One of the outstanding weaknesses of the Franco regime has been its inability to solve Spain's economic problems. Emerging from the civil war in a state of economic prostration, Spain was able to recuperate during World War II. There was a ready market for all the industrial surpluses Spain produced. But the income from this foreign trade was not used to buy new equipment and machinery for industry, transportation, and agriculture. The end of the war, therefore, found Spain in a worse condition than it had been in 1939. Worn-out machinery hampered industry, aged equipment slowed transportation, and a lack of farm machinery and fertilizer drastically curtailed food production. Inflation, unemployment, and a dollar shortage followed. While wages rose only about 300 per cent food prices increased by 570 per cent.

---

[4] In September, 1953, pacts were signed in Madrid which provided for the use of Spanish air and naval bases by the United States in return for economic aid.

Hardest hit was the workingman. Unemployment and low wages forced many members of the working classes to sell their sugar and coffee rations in the black market in order to get money to purchase bread.

In general, the gap between the rich and poor of Spain is a wide one. While some men in high places possess considerable wealth the masses as such are poverty-stricken. This is true both of the urban and agricultural population. In agricultural production there has been a general decline under the Franco regime. During the years before the civil war Spain was not only self-sufficient in regard to food but exported large quantities of fruit, vegetables, and wine. The income from these exports was used to pay for industrial imports. The only crops that have maintained their prewar levels during recent years are olive oil and lentils. On the other hand, the production of fruits and cereals has declined more than 30 per cent. The necessity of buying food for a growing population has helped to cause the dollar shortage.

THE ITALIAN REPUBLIC

After Mussolini's fall (July 25, 1943) Victor Emmanuel III, who had been king since 1900, because he was subjected to blistering criticism for his pro-Axis policies, issued a statement announcing his retirement from public life. On June 4, 1944, the day the Allies entered Rome, Crown Prince Umberto became regent and a coalition government of anti-fascist parties was formed. After two short-lived cabinets tried to cope with the problems of Italy Alcide de Gasperi, leader of the Christian Democrats, formed the first of his many cabinets (November 24, 1945). The state was a constitutional monarchy, but there was widespread agitation for the establishment of a republic. Finally a referendum was set for June 2, 1946. In an effort to strengthen the cause of monarchy Victor Emmanuel III abdicated in favor of his son. Umberto II was king of Italy for only a short time. When it was announced on June 10 that a majority of the voters had declared for a republic Umberto went into exile.

The first cabinet of the Italian Republic, officially proclaimed on June 10, 1946, was a coalition cabinet representing communists, socialists, and Christian Democrats, with de Gasperi as prime minister. The problems confronting this government were the speedy conclusion of a treaty with the Allies, the rehabilitation of industry, the alleviation of unemployment, better housing, and agrarian reform. The Italian government was successful in signing a treaty (February 10, 1947), but its terms made few Italians happy. The provisions which excited the deepest resentment were those which deprived Italy of her colonies and Trieste. Many Italians felt that their efforts to aid the

Allies during the last period of the war had not been appreciated. Consequently the demands for a revision of the treaty were loud and insistent. The Constituent Assembly did, however, ratify the treaty and the Allied occupation troops were withdrawn before the end of 1947.

Meanwhile the Constituent Assembly had been busy drafting a constitution for the new republic. Much of the debate centered about Article Seven which recognizes Roman Catholicism as the sole state religion and incorporates the Concordat of 1929 in the constitution. Although the Republicans and old-line socialists offered vigorous opposition, the Communists as a move to convince the Italian people that they were not the enemies of religion joined the Christian Democrats in approving the inclusion of the Lateran Pacts in the constitution. As a result the article was approved by a vote of 350 to 149. The completed draft, accepted by the Assembly December 22, 1947, provides for a bicameral legislative body consisting of a Chamber of Deputies and a Senate. Meeting in joint session as the National Assembly the two bodies by a two-thirds majority elect the president for a term of seven years. All presidential acts must be countersigned by the ministers of the cabinet. The president may name a prime minister, but the cabinet the latter forms must have the support of a majority in both legislative chambers. Women are by the constitution granted equal rights in all matters.

The first elections under the new constitution were held in April, 1948. Of the 574 seats in the Chamber of Deputies 307 were won by the Christian Democrats, the old reorganized Catholic party of the prewar period. The Popular Front, a coalition of communists and left-wing socialists, gained only 182 seats. In the Senate the proportion of seats won by the Christian Democrats was about the same. Thus one party had secured a parliamentary majority for the first time since the unification of Italy. De Gasperi could have formed a cabinet of only Christian Democrats, but he invited the Republicans, Liberals, and the moderate Socialists to participate in it. The cabinet was, however, militantly anticommunist. The communists, for their part, sought to hamper and disrupt the government in every possible way. They fomented strikes and unrest among the agricultural as well as the urban population. In the larger industries they staged slow-down and sit-down strikes. They even went so far as to try to prevent the unloading of military equipment and weapons that were sent to Italy from the United States as part of the program to rearm the European members of the North Atlantic Treaty Organization.

Under the republican government Italy made a rapid economic recovery. Industrial plants were reopened, transportation facilities were restored, and the Italian merchant marine was rebuilt. The stock of raw materials for industrial purposes which had been depleted during the war were gradually replenished by purchases from abroad. Attempts were also made to relieve the food shortage which has been chronic in Italy for many years. The frugal diet of bread and spaghetti has never been far above the starvation level. At the end of the war the situation was particularly critical. The disruption and confusion caused by the war, the disappearance of cattle, the shortage of farm machinery and equipment resulted in an acute food shortage. To relieve the shortage steps were taken to break up some of the larger estates into small farms and to educate the peasants in crop rotation and better agricultural methods. When the immensity of the needs are considered the accomplishments, though notable, are very limited.

The deterrent in speeding the rehabilitation and improvement of agriculture and industry was the shortage of gold or foreign exchange credit. Even during the prewar years the value of the imports had exceeded that of exports. The resulting drain on the gold reserves had reduced them to $181 million in 1939 and by 1945 they had fallen to $24 million. Moreover, since 1922 the national debt had increased more than fourfold. The situation was such that the Italian government had no money with which it could buy food for its population. In 1947 Premier de Gasperi secured 50,000 tons of wheat from the United States and a loan from the Import-Export Bank. The next year Italy obtained large sums from the Marshall Plan. The sum allocated to Italy from April, 1948, to February, 1951, was one and a quarter billion dollars. As a result both industrial and agricultural production gradually increased. By October, 1951, production, according to Premier de Gasperi, had surpassed the prewar level by 30 per cent. Even this was not sufficient to provide sustenance for an increasing population.[5] Imports still exceed exports, the excess in 1951–1952 being about $450 million. The problem of producing more remained vital.

In the elections of June, 1953, Premier de Gasperi's coalition (Christian Democrats, right-wing Socialists, Liberals, and Republicans) lost some of its support, winning only 303 seats against 218 for the left opposition, and 69 for the neo-fascist and monarchist groups. When the new cabinet lost a vote of confidence in the Chamber of Deputies after an existence of thirteen days de Gasperi resigned (July 28). He was succeeded by Giuseppe Pella, who resigned January 5, 1954. Amintore Fanfani, a left-of-center Christian Democrat who had been former Premier de Gasperi's land reform expert, was the next choice but he lost a vote of confidence and resigned January 31.

[5] The annual increase is approximately 400,000.

CHAPTER THIRTY-FIVE

The Passing of the Old Imperialism

THE DEMANDS FOR INDEPENDENCE $\quad$ NO sooner had the fighting ceased in World War II than a mighty surge of nationalism welled up in the countries of the Middle and Far East. The subject peoples, rising, as it were, from long simmering to a boil, demanded the right to cut loose from European moorings and to fashion their own destiny. After World War I layer after layer of subject peoples in Asia had demanded independence, but the demands were either suppressed or the peoples were led up blind alleys by the imperialist nations. This time they would not be denied. They were determined to submit no longer to foreign rule. As one oriental writer put it: "Asia is today generating its own motive force which cannot be harnessed to meet the exclusive convenience of imperial interests. Asia has left the road of serfdom to take an equal place on the world's stage." [1] The oft-repeated statement that they were not ready for self-government carried no persuasion for the subject peoples. They felt that the European nations were not only ruling the colonies badly but that they could not even rule themselves well. What the colonial peoples wanted was the chance to face their own problems, to make their own mistakes. One Asiatic said pointedly: "We are fighting for the right to make our mess for ourselves." Most of the nationalist leaders were confident, however, that emancipation would bring in its wake the high standards of living the western countries had achieved.

Although conditions and backgrounds varied among the subject peoples, the impulse was everywhere the same. The areas involved in this tidal wave of revolution were vast. In the Far East alone the territories affected embraced an area more than four times the combined

[1] S. Raja Ratnam in *Asia*, vol. 45 (1945), p. 378.

707

size of Great Britain, France, and the Netherlands; the populations of the area revolting against western imperialism were more than six times the total populations of these countries. At the Asian Relations Conference, Pandit Jawaharlal Nehru said: "For too long we of Asia have been petitioners in the western courts and chancelleries. That story must now belong to the past. We propose to stand on our own feet and cooperate with all others who are prepared to cooperate with us. We do not intend to be the playthings of others."

The factors which stimulated the revolt against western domination were many and varied. No one single factor is sufficient to explain the widespread revolt. One reason for discontent with western rule was the poverty of the masses. In almost all of the colonies the bulk of the population was living at a bare level of subsistence. In Java, for example, the average annual income for a peasant family before World War II was estimated at less than $30. The situation after the war was even worse. Living in stark poverty, these masses became increasingly conscious of the wealth, luxury, and high living standards of the western peoples. While a minority who were educated in the west or traveled there saw them at first hand, many saw in the movies how the western peoples lived — or were supposed to live. They also saw evidence of the wealth of the west in the equipment of the armies that were sent to Asia. In short, the colonial peoples saw that those who ruled them lived far better than they did. It was not difficult for the communists and others to convince many inhabitants of the colonies that the western nations had gained much of their wealth by exploiting the colonies.

The Japanese were in no small degree responsible for the upsurge of nationalism at the end of World War II. First, the initial Japanese victories dealt a severe blow to the prestige of the white man in Asia. To many these early successes were a demonstration of the superiority of the Asiatics. Even though the Japanese were eventually defeated, the earlier respect for the white man was not restored. Second, the Japanese stimulated nationalist feelings through propaganda. They excited resentment against the French, Dutch, and British with such slogans as "Asia for Asiatics." Third, the Japanese appealed to the Asiatics to support them in the war, promising them independence and freedom. The colonial peoples' failure to receive the promised independence and freedom from the Japanese only stimulated their desire for it. When the Japanese hold was broken the colonial peoples became determined not to return to their former status as European dependents.

The western countries, too, were instrumental in stimulating the desire for independence. The words "liberty," "democracy," and "independence" were used so insistently by western propagandists during the war that they could not fail to create a desire in the minds of the colonial peoples. So much was promised that they looked forward to a new life based on the Four Freedoms of President Roosevelt and the promise of the Atlantic Charter. In the Atlantic Charter President Roosevelt and Prime Minister Churchill proclaimed that "they respect the right of all peoples to choose the form of government under which they will live; and they wish to see sovereign rights and self-government restored to those who have been forcibly deprived of them." Influential, too, in kindling the hope of independence was the statement in the United Nations Charter which proclaimed that it was one of the purposes of that organization to promote "friendly relations among nations based on respect for the principle of equal rights and self-determination of peoples."

Two other factors — the weakness of the imperialist nations at the end of World War II and the influence of communism — exerted considerable influence in stimulating revolt. The French and Dutch, and even the victorious British, emerged from the war militarily and financially weak and could no longer maintain a tight hold on the colonies. This was quickly realized by the colonies and the demands for independence followed. Also common to all countries which demanded independence has been the presence of an aggressive communist minority which has sought to turn the nationalist agitation into hostility to the West. The communists did not start the revolt; in fact, there was little communist influence in the early stages of the revolt. But later the communists capitalized on the discontent of the colonial peoples wherever they could. In Indo-China the leadership fell into communist hands because the communists identified themselves with the nationalist struggle. But in the Philippines, India, Pakistan, and Ceylon the nationalist movements developed into democratic states along lines of the western tradition. Even Indonesia was successful in mustering enough strength to curb communist influence. The communists won their greatest victory in China where they were able to make the most of the weaknesses of Chiang Kai-shek's government and the general economic dislocation.

REVOLT IN THE FRENCH EMPIRE

At the end of World War II France, with the second largest colonial empire, faced seething nationalism among her colonial peoples. During the period of the war the Free French had granted independence to the two mandates, Syria and Lebanon, after the Vichy forces had been ejected. In 1945 the demand for freedom became insistent in most of the other colonies. The French who emerged from the war economically and militarily weak realized that they did not have the strength to suppress the nationalist risings. They proposed, as a means of cultivating better relations with their colonies, to organize a "union" in which the colonial peoples would no longer be subjects, but French citizens. In this union France herself would be a sort of senior partner. According to the provisions of the plan, as outlined in the new constitution of 1946, the French Union is composed of two component parts, the French Republic and the Associated Territories and States. The President of France serves as the president of the union which also has its own High Council and Assembly. The Assembly does not, however, have legislative powers. It can only examine and consider legislative proposals submitted to it by the government of the French Republic or by the governments of the Associated States.

While the French were developing the plans for a French Union the nationalist agitations had not only continued but revolt had actually broken out in Indo-China, which, as the name indicates, is the bridge between India and China. Besides being rich in raw materials it also has fertile agricultural lands which in normal times produce vast quantities of rice. In size it is more than a third larger than France with a population of about 25 millions. Before the war it was divided into five states: Annam, Cambodia, Cochin China, Tongking, and Laos. When France fell in 1940 the Japanese had moved into Indo-China, but they did not at first make radical changes in the French colonial administration they found there. The French in Indo-China were cooperative until they realized that the Japanese were doomed to defeat; then they organized resistance movements. This caused the Japanese early in 1945 to set up their own colonial administration in Indo-China and to encourage the Indo-Chinese nationalists in their demands for independence.

Indo-Chinese nationalism was not, however, a product of the war period; long before World War II there were demands for independence and even small uprisings. During the war years the nationalist movement had grown strong, its growth being accelerated by the fall of France and the arrival of the Japanese. In 1941 the nationalists organized the League for the Independence of Indo-China, which became known as Viet Minh. When it became clear that Japanese defeat was inevitable and that the French would seek to reimpose their rule, the Viet Minh went into action. Ten days after the surrender of the Japanese (August 25, 1945) the nationalists proclaimed the independent Republic of Viet Nam [2] consisting of northern Annam and Tong-

---

[2] Viet Nam means "Southland" and is the old name for the country which includes Annam, Tongking, and Cochin-China.

king. Ho Chi-minh, a Russian-trained communist, became the premier of the new republic and the leader of its military forces. In 1946 the French made an attempt to reach a settlement by recognizing the Viet Nam republic as a free state within the French Union, but a dispute soon broke out over the extent of territory that was to be included in the new republic. While the French hoped to limit the territory, the Indochinese nationalists wanted to include all of Indo-China in it.

Before the end of 1946 fighting broke out when Ho Chi-minh, after accusing the French of betraying their promises, launched an attack against the city of Hanoi. It was the beginning of a full scale colonial war. Although the French were successful in retaining control over the principal cities of southern Indo-China, they could make little real progress against the guerrilla tactics of the Viet Minh forces which had the support of the population. The Indo-Chinese supported Ho Chi-minh not because he was a communist, but because he promised them freedom from French rule. Month after month the fighting continued without either side winning a decisive victory. As the years passed it became increasingly evident that the French forces alone could not win a decisive victory. Public pressure to put an end to the six-year war, and its drain on the manpower and finances of France, was mounting. In October, 1953, France gave full independence to Laos and then signed a treaty which made the newly sovereign state a member of the French Union. Subsequently the French government invited the state of Viet Nam to conclude a similar treaty, but it was doubtful if the invitation would be accepted.

Meanwhile there have been uneasy nationalist stirrings in other parts of the French empire. Although the administrations in Algeria, Morocco, and Tunis are all different the demand for independence is strong in each colony. In Algeria, which is a part of Metropolitan France and is administered by the Ministry of the Interior, there were riots and demonstrations in behalf of independence after V-E Day. Although there is no open revolt, the demand for complete independence is strong. In Morocco and Tunisia, which are governed through their native ruler, the nationalists are also impatient for self-rule. The fact that both have been brought closer to France in the French Union has not satisfied the nationalist demands.

THE UNITED STATES OF INDONESIA

The Dutch East Indies, about fifty-seven times the area of the European Netherlands, during the years prior to the war had produced nearly all the world's quinine, 83 per cent of its pepper, 77 per cent of its kapok, 37 per cent of its rubber, and a large share of other important materials. Although the Dutch had gained a reputation for administrative efficiency during more than three centuries of colonial rule, this did not stop the natives of the East Indies from demanding their independence. After the cessation of hostilities in World War II the question of independence became a burning issue; actually, however, nationalist groups had been active since 1905. During the war, and particularly when they saw that defeat was inevitable, the Japanese had encouraged the nationalist movement in every way, even to supplying its members with weapons. Only two days after the Japanese surrender a group of nationalists led by Achmed Soekarno declared their determination not to revert to a colonial or semicolonial status. Insurgents in Java, Sumatra, and other islands of the Dutch East Indies organized a union, proclaimed the Republic of Indonesia, and adopted a national flag. They also drew up a provisional constitution modeled after that of the U.S.A.

After three years of intermittent fighting between the Dutch and the Indonesians a conference was held in 1949 at The Hague. During the ten weeks of the conference it appeared many times as if the negotiations would end in failure. While the Dutch wanted to retain as much sovereignty as possible, the Indonesians wanted as much independence as possible. Gradually, however, mutual trust was established. The Dutch Minister for Overseas Territories described the situation in these words: "The only way to gain confidence is to treat people as normal equals. The fortunate thing is that our interests run parallel. They can't do without us, nor can we do without them." The final agreement, reached late in 1949, set up the United States of Indonesia, a federal union of sixteen states with a constitution much like that of the United States. The new federation, in turn, joined the Netherlands in the Netherlands-Indonesian Union. In this union Indonesia and the Netherlands have "equal status with equal rights." Queen Juliana, as head of the Union, embodies "the concept of voluntary and lasting cooperation between the partners." In the framework of the union Indonesia controls its own army and navy, but the Dutch were accorded the right to use the Surabaya naval base under Indonesian supervision. Indonesia also took control of its own economy, but agreed to pay for any Dutch property that had been seized and to consult with the Dutch before making trade arrangements with foreign nations.

The transfer of sovereignty from the Netherlands to the United States of Indonesia was made effective on December 27, 1949. In Jakarta (formerly called Batavia) which had been chosen as the new capital the new red and white Indonesian flag was raised. Other red and white banners, many of them made by tearing the blue stripe from the Dutch flag, draped the buildings and cheering crowds milled in the streets crying "merdeka" (freedom). But not all the Indonesians were happy. Some of the nationalist leaders denounced the Hague agreement as conceding too much to the Dutch. A spokesman for Masjumi, the largest political party of Indonesia, said: "We are not very contented. Yet we will make the best of it."

THE EMPIRE SHRINKS, THE COMMONWEALTH EXPANDS

The most widespread disturbances and changes took place in the British Empire. Those colonies and dominions which had attained some degree of independence demanded more, while other colonies demanded at least partial independence. Everywhere the bonds of empire were loosening perceptibly. Not that the British had any intention of giving up their empire. Winston Churchill had stated his position when he said in 1942: "I haven't become the King's First Minister to preside over the liquidation of the British Empire." Nor did the Labor Party have different ideas. The general attitude of the Labor Party was expressed by Foreign Secretary Bevin when he said: "I'm not prepared to sacrifice the British Empire, because I know if it fell a great collection of free nations would go into the limbo of the past and would create disaster." To meet the situation the Labor Party developed new forms and new techniques. It proclaimed, for example, that it would "open a new epoch in Commonwealth history by establishing a great partnership in planned enterprise." "If we link the Commonwealth and the overseas territories which are jointly responsible for the skill, the ability and the productive capacity of the West," Mr. Bevin said, "then we can solve our balance of payments problem and they can have a continuing rise in the standard of living for generations to come. That is British foreign policy." In 1948 parliament passed the British Nationality Act which created Commonwealth citizenship. Any person who is a citizen of the United Kingdom or its colonies or of the countries of Canada, Newfoundland, Australia, New Zealand, South Africa, India, Pakistan, Ceylon, or Southern Rhodesia shall, "by virtue of that citizenship, have the status of a British subject."

Meanwhile many changes had taken place in the British Empire and Commonwealth. Independence movements in Burma, Ceylon, Palestine, and India were carried to successful conclusion. While Palestine and Burma seceded completely, Ceylon, India, and the new state of Pakistan remained in the Commonwealth. About the same time that India decided on continued association with the Commonwealth, Eire (Ireland) decided to withdraw. According to the External Relations

Act of 1936 Eire was a republic as regards internal affairs, but used the name of the British king in its external relations. But in 1948 the government of Eire cut the last official tie by repealing the External Relations Act. However, the Irish were granted the same trading and citizenship rights they had previously had as members of the Commonwealth.

Among the first to gain independence were the Ceylonese and Burmese. The inhabitants of the island of Ceylon which lies off the southern tip of India were promised a constitution as early as 1943. Although this promise was carried out in 1946, the Ceylonese were disappointed because they were not given dominion status. But in February, 1948, their hopes were fulfilled. Burma, which until 1937 had been a part of India, was the scene of bitter fighting between the Allies and the Japanese during World War II. In 1943 the Japanese set up a puppet government in Burma and proclaimed it an independent state. After the surrender of the Japanese, the British tried to reestablish their rule, but the independence movement continued to assert itself. Anglo-Burmese discussions finally resulted in British recognition of "a free and independent Burma, whether within or without the British Empire." For a year Burma was to remain a member of the Commonwealth and at the end of this period was free to withdraw if it so desired. The Burmese decided to become an independent country outside the British Commonwealth. The new order took effect January 4, 1948.

In Palestine the end of the war saw no improvement in the relations between the Jews and Arabs. The same irreconcilability existed as before the war; in fact, the unremitting conflict was intensified by further Jewish immigration. For the British it was the old story of being unable to satisfy either party. In seeking to win Arab support on the eve of World War II the British had stated in a White Paper: "Jewish immigration during the next five years will be at a rate which, if the economic absorptive capacity permits, will bring the Jewish population up to approximately one third of the total population of the country. . . . After the period of five years no further Jewish immigration will be permitted unless the Arabs of Palestine are prepared to acquiesce in it." But after 1944 the British did agree to permit 1500 Jewish immigrants to enter Palestine each month. This antagonized the Arabs, while failing to satisfy the Zionists, who wanted to open Palestine as a haven for the Jewish victims of Nazi persecution.

Unable to offer a satisfactory solution of the problem, the British Labor government proposed, and the United States accepted the proposal, that an Anglo-American Committee of Inquiry be named to determine the facts of the situation and to make recommendations. The committee recommended in its report of April 30, 1946, that 100,000 displaced persons be admitted to Palestine immediately. When the Arab leaders threatened outright war if the recommendation were carried out, the British did not proceed with the plan. Instead they sought to placate the Zionists by increasing the monthly immigration quota from 1500 to 2000. This was not enough to satisfy the Zionists, particularly the Jewish underground groups of Palestine. These groups inaugurated a series of terrorist outbreaks which wrecked or damaged bridges, railway lines, shops, and police stations. In further efforts to solve the dilemma the British advocated a partition of Palestine into semi-autonomous Arab and Jewish states. Both Arabs and Jews opposed this suggestion. Finally the British, in desperation, handed the problem to the United Nations and declared its intention of giving up the mandate. The UN, after studying the problem, supported the idea of partitioning Palestine. In May, 1948, the British surrendered their mandate and the Zionists at once proclaimed the State of Israel, with Tel Aviv as capital (Jerusalem in 1950). Hostilities broke out with the neighboring Arab states, but through the offices of the United Nations the fighting was finally stopped. To protect the Holy Places within its environs Jerusalem was placed under an international regime. The rest of Palestine was officially divided between the State of Israel and the Kingdom of Jordan.

Manifestations of the world-wide revolt against the old colonialism are evident even in Africa which had previously slumbered through many centuries of history. The natives, the vast majority of them illiterate, some of them savage and uncivilized, are becoming increasingly conscious of race, nationality, and the possibilities of economic and social advance. The leaders are a small minority who have been abroad and have learned the techniques of achieving power through political agitation. These leaders are busy inciting rebellion against European rule. The surge of nationalism has forced Britain to withdraw her troops from Egypt proper. The British have continued to guard the Suez Canal Zone, but the Egyptian government is threatening to drive the British forces out. In the Anglo-Egyptian Sudan the British found it necessary to promise the natives local self-government under a new constitution that envisages eventual self-determination.

In Central and Southern Africa the natives are also astir. The granting of local self-government to the Gold Coast, one of Britain's West African colonies, has stirred the hope of self-government in the hearts of many Negro-natives. This hope has, however, made the whites apprehensive. Every outburst of native nationalism and every concession to it creates concern in the white communities because they envision themselves eventually engulfed by Negro-native rule. In the Union of South Africa where the black majority is kept in submission by draconic legislation the Negro-natives who outnumber the ruling white population six to one are demanding political and economic equality. Various tactics have been adopted to achieve this goal, among other things the waging of a civil disobedience campaign. In Central and Eastern Africa the Negro-natives fear the spread of white domination and anti-native discrimination northward from the Union of South Africa. In Kenya, one of Britain's East-African colonies where a few thousand white settlers exercise far more influence and power than millions of native Africans, the Mau Mau, a secret terrorist society is endeavoring to assert the supremacy of the natives. Members of this society are slaying many whites, and also Negroes who are friendly to white rule, in an effort to drive out the white settlers.

INDIA ACHIEVES INDEPENDENCE

When World War II broke out the Indian National Congress, the largest political party in India, refused to join the British in the war, claiming that only an independent India could give effective support. In 1942 Sir Stafford Cripps was sent to India for the purpose of gaining the wholehearted cooperation of India. But the people of India put no faith in his promise of independence after the war in return for active Indian participation in the war. The Indian leaders countered by asking why the British, if they were sincere in their intentions, did not grant the independence at once. Even after the war had ended the executive committee of the National Congress stated that "British policy toward India . . . seems to be based on delaying every advance and attempting to create new problems and fresh complications."

After the war the situation in India deteriorated rapidly. Whereas both the Hindus and Moslems opposed the British, they were also antagonistic toward each other. The Moslems, believing that they were being slighted in the political arrangements by the Hindus who controlled the National Congress Party, demanded that in those parts of India where they were in the majority they should have the right to set up a separate state to be called Pakistan. The demands were voiced in the slogan, "Pakistan or death." The National Congress Party, on the other hand, wanted India to remain as one country under one government. Severe riots broke out in many parts of the country. The British, after trying vainly to settle the differences, decided that whatever happened they would transfer power to Indian hands. The announcement aggravated the bitterness between the Hindus and Moslems, causing the riots to increase in intensity. It is estimated that in Calcutta alone ten to fifteen thousand people were killed. Riots and massacres in other parts also took a high toll of lives.

Meanwhile the British worked out a plan for the transfer of power. It was of necessity a compromise which fell short of the desires of all parties concerned, but it was the best that could be arranged at the time. It provided for the division of India into a Moslem-ruled Pakistan with a population of about 90 million and a Hindu-ruled Union of India with a population exceeding 220 million, both states being accorded Dominion status. In addition the more than five hundred states with some 95 million inhabitants ruled by native princes were given the choice of setting up a third independent state or joining the Union of India or Pakistan.[3] On August 15, 1947, the British flag was hauled down all over India after two hundred years of British rule to make room for the flags of the two new nations. Thus the new India was born without violence between the British subjects. But there was violence between the Moslems and Hindus. Rioting continued in parts of India pending the final settlement of the boundaries between the two states.

From the British standpoint Indian independence spelled the end of the grandeur of empire. It meant the loss of "the brightest jewel in the royal crown." The British ruler lost the title, Emperor of India. In the words of one writer: "The whole world of Kipling's imagery sinks into oblivion, the captains and the kings that strutted across the scenes of India's history depart."

The terms of the independence of Pakistan and India which became effective in August, 1947, provided that both should remain members of the Commonwealth for one year, after which they were free to remain or to withdraw as Burma had done. While Pakistan chose to remain as a dominion, India decided to become a republic. But strategic needs and economic factors increased the Indian desire for continued association with the Commonwealth. In the spring of 1949 a conference of prime ministers met in London for the express purpose of reaching a decision on India's membership in the Commonwealth. It is another evidence of the elasticity of the Commonwealth bonds that the conference found a formula for keeping India in it. Even though India renounced her allegiance to the Crown, she was prepared to continue to recognize the Crown as the symbol of the free association of the independent member nations. It was regarded as sufficient for membership. The Indian Constituent Assembly approved this settlement with only two dissenting votes. Prime Minister Nehru said to the Assembly: "We join the Commonwealth obviously because we think it is beneficial to us and to other causes in the world that we wish to advance."

If the foregoing events marked the passing of colonialism, they were

[3] By 1948 all of these states had joined either the Indian Union or Pakistan.

not signs of the demise of the British Commonwealth. The loss of India, for example, was more apparent than real. While a discontented India would have been a liability, a republican India was an asset to the Commonwealth. While the achievement of independence by a number of colonies had caused the British Empire to shrink, it had, on the other hand, greatly expanded the Commonwealth. True, Eire, Palestine, and Burma were lost in the shuffle, but the new members of the Commonwealth were Ceylon, Pakistan, and India. Their addition included nearly a quarter of the world population in the Commonwealth. Moreover, as a result of the accession of these nations the character of the Commonwealth underwent a radical change. It was no longer an association in which Europeans were preeminent. Of the 500 million people in the Commonwealth 420 million are Asians. Thus the Commonwealth is international rather than British; in fact, since 1949 the word "British" has for most purposes been dropped from the title of the association.

THE END OF THE ITALIAN EMPIRE

In 1940 when Mussolini joined his Axis partner in the war against the Allies Italy had an overseas empire of a million and a quarter square miles with a population of more than 14 millions. In 1941 British and Allied forces overran Eritrea, Ethiopia, and Italian Somaliland and during the next two years also occupied Libya. This left Albania and the Italian Aegean Islands, both of which were occupied by either Allied or German troops. Consequently the end of the war saw Italy without an empire. Many Italians hoped that in the peace settlement their country would regain the colonies that had been acquired during the period before Mussolini's rise to power. They wanted these colonies partly to salve their national pride and partly as an outlet for the surplus population of Italy. The communists and many socialists opposed the restoration of any colonies. The newspaper *Italia Socialista* protested that since Italy is largely "backward, illiterate, bandit-infested, and poor," the colonies had always been a serious drain on the Italian economy and that ruinous consequences would follow the reimposition of this burden.

By the terms of the peace treaty signed in 1947 Italy was obliged to renounce her sovereignty over her former colonies. Independence had earlier been restored to Ethiopia and the ties that bound Albania to Italy had been cut. According to the provisions of Article 23 of the treaty Great Britain, France, the U.S.A., and the U.S.S.R. were to reach a joint decision regarding the former Italian colonies in Africa.

If no agreement was reached by September 15, 1948, the question was to be referred to the General Assembly of the United Nations. The Council of Foreign Ministers found the problem too difficult of solution. After vain debates and discussions the question of the former Italian colonies in Africa was laid on the doorstep of the United Nations. After investigations and reports by committees were presented to the General Assembly it finally reached a decision in November, 1949, regarding Libya and Italian Somaliland. The former, comprising Cyrenaica, Tripolitania, and the Fezzan, was granted its independence, effective not later than January 1, 1952. Regarding Italian Somaliland, the Assembly recommended it be given its independence at the end of ten years. These years were designated as a period of preparation for self-government, with Italy as the administering authority. Provisions also included a UN advisory board to assist and advise the Italian government in the administration.

After sending a commission to study the problem, the UN General Assembly decided in December, 1950, that Eritrea, after an interim period, be federated with Ethiopia. This solution provided Ethiopia with an outlet to the sea and satisfied the aspirations of the popular movement in Eritrea which demanded "reunion with the homeland."

THE COMMUNISTS CONQUER CHINA

A rebellion against the West of vast and incalculable consequence also took place in China. The final result was the conquest of all of China by the communists. When the Japanese invaded China in 1937 the Communist and Kuomintang parties, after many years of intermittent warfare, managed to establish a united front against the enemy. Chiang Kai-shek even went so far as to give money and arms to the communists. The communists, for their part, did yeoman service both in fighting the Japanese and in organizing popular resistance. They were particularly successful in winning the support of the peasants and in gaining many peasant recruits. This they achieved through kind treatment. Instructions from central headquarters specifically ordered the guerrilla fighters not to steal from the peasants or to abuse them in any way. Wherever the communists succeeded in driving out the Japanese, they set up their governments and recruited men for their armies. This caused the Nationalist government to become suspicious and later to stop sending money and arms to the communists.

Soon civil war flared up again at a number of places between the communists and the government of Chiang Kai-shek. In December, 1945, General George Mashall was sent to China as President Tru-

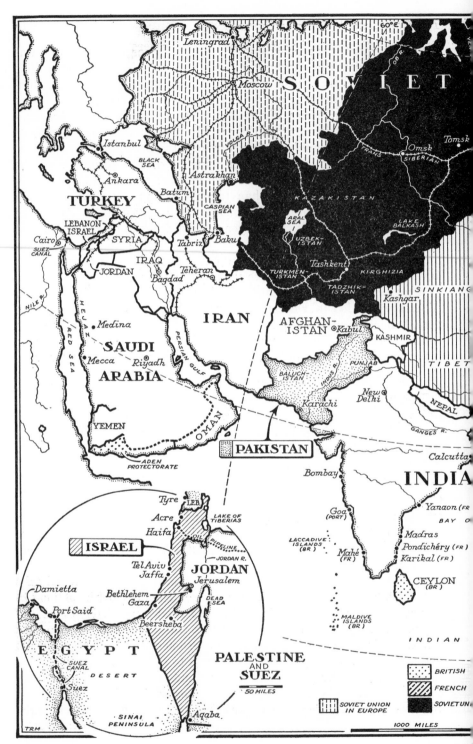

1954

man's personal representative for the purpose of bringing the civil war in China to an end by effecting a reconciliation between the Nationalist government and the Chinese communists. He finally persuaded Generalissimo Chiang to sign an armistice with the communists on January 10, 1946. Chiang consented to do this only because pressure was brought to bear on him. He saw more clearly than any other Allied leader the threat of communism in China. In 1941 he had said: "You think it is important that I have kept the Japanese from expanding during these years . . . I tell you that it is more important that I have kept the communists from spreading. The Japanese are a disease of the skin; the communists are a disease of the heart." But he needed arms from the United States. During the eight years China fought against Japan nearly all her arsenals had been destroyed. Thus General Marshall had powerful means of persuasion.

The accord was of short duration, for the communists had no intention of abandoning their attempt to conquer China. During the early months of 1946 Chinese communists had been congregating in Manchuria where the Russians supplied them with equipment the Red army had taken from the Japanese. In April of the same year the well-armed communists broke the armistice by an attack on Changchun. Truce teams composed of Kuomintang and communist representatives and members of General Marshall's staff tried repeatedly to negotiate a truce. They succeeded in arranging temporary cease-fire arrangements but failed to compose the differences of the opposing groups. The diplomatic stalemate coupled with the increasing intensity of hostilities caused General Marshall to admit on August 10, 1946 that "it appears impossible for the two sides to reach a settlement." Upon his return to the United States General Marshall reported to the Senate (January 7, 1947):

In the first place, the greatest obstacle to peace has been the complete, almost overwhelming suspicion with which the Chinese Communist Party and the Kuomintang regard each other. On the one hand, the leaders of the government are strongly opposed to a communistic form of government. On the other hand, the communists frankly state that they are Marxists and intend to work toward establishing a communistic form of government in China, though first advancing through the medium of a democratic form of government of the American and British type. The leaders of the government are convinced that the communists expressed desire to participate in a government of this type had for its purpose only a destructive intention. . . . The course which the Communist Party has pursued in recent months indicated an unwillingness to make a fair compromise. It has been impossible even to get them to sit down at a conference table with government representatives to discuss given issues.

Generalissimo Chiang Kai-shek did order his troops to cease fire on November 11, 1946, "except as may be necessary to defend their present positions" in preparation for the scheduled opening of the National Constituent Assembly on November 12. The purpose of this order was to induce the communists and other minority groups to participate in the Assembly. But no communist representatives appeared. The excuse offered by the communists was that the delegates from the communist areas were hand picked by the Kuomintang. Chiang himself presented to the Assembly the draft of a constitution which was accepted on December 25, 1946, to go into effect a year from that date. In theory the constitution provided for the equality of all persons, racial groups, sexes, and individuals regardless of party, and for secret ballot and universal suffrage for all over twenty. "It is unfortunate," General Marshall reported, "that the communists did not see fit to participate in the Assembly since the constitution that has been adopted seems to include every major point that they wanted."

Meanwhile democratic writers were urging Chiang to eliminate the totalitarian features from his government and to wipe out the prevailing corruption. Writers scored Chiang's government as a "corrupt, reactionary, and quasi-fascist regime" and "one of the most corrupt governments of modern times," while Chiang himself was styled "the greatest obstructionist to true democracy in China." An American observer wrote after visiting China in 1946:

After the surrender the locusts swarmed over the Chinese cities, too. Kuomintang machine politicians and carpetbaggers seized what the Japanese had left and sometimes what the Chinese had, too. Administrative inefficiency and the spoils system the Chinese may be accustomed to; but the corruption, worse now than ever before in modern times and hard to bear in a time of inflation and impoverishment, has produced a sullen resentment. . . . Equally effective as a means of repression are the secret police and the espionage service of the Kuomintang. The pretense that censorship has been abolished deceives no one. No university professor dares openly to express an opinion, in or out of the classroom, unless it is favorable to the regime. Newspapers take a little more latitude, but not often on serious questions or in such a way as to reflect unfavorably on those at the top. It would not be accurate to call contemporary China fascist, since the system is not closely enough organized, but fascistic it certainly is.[4]

Chiang Kai-shek himself said in his message of December 31, 1946:

The national morale is also low. Honesty is regarded as pedantic and self-respect as backward. The practice of speculation and trickery has spread from business circles to the community as a whole. Officials and gentry, in seeking

[4] Nathaniel Peffer in the New York *Times,* May 4, 1947.

gratification of their selfish purposes, resort to manipulation and other ill
practices in total disregard of the country as well as of the people.

Gradually the civil war became more intense and widespread. At
first the communist forces carried on guerrilla warfare against the
forces and government of Chiang. Gradually, however, larger armies
were trained and equipped with arms the Russians had taken from the
Japanese. These soldiers, described as "tattered rabble," were anything but formidable, but they gradually pushed back Chiang's weary
and dispirited troops. Whatever chances Chiang had of defeating
communism were weakened by the fact that he linked his political
fortunes to a group committed to the maintenance of the old land-
owning system. His position was further weakened by his reliance on
aid from the United States. While this dependence exposed him to the
accusation of being the "running dog" of foreign imperialism, he actually received very little aid. Not only was a proposed loan withheld,
but from the summer of 1946 to February, 1948, there was a virtual
embargo on the shipment of military supplies from U.S.A. to China.
Not a single combat or bombing plane was sent to China. Even the
flow of small-arms ammunition was reduced to a trickle. With the
halting of ammunition shipments the fire power of divisions equipped
with American guns withered away. Meanwhile the Russians were
supplying the Chinese communists with vast quantities of military
supplies.

The man who laid the groundwork for the communist victory in
China was Mao Tse-tung. Born in 1893 of peasant stock, Mao early
resented the injustice of the treatment accorded the peasants. At the
age of eighteen he started his revolutionary career by becoming a
leader of minor revolts. While attending various schools, including
teacher-training colleges, he read omnivorously. Observers who knew
both Mao and Stalin have stated that the former "possesses intellectual
gifts of which Stalin must always be unaware." Mao did not become a
convert to Marxism until 1921, in which year he and eleven others
founded the Chinese Communist Party in a secret meeting at Shanghai. For several years after 1924 he was, together with other communists, a member of the Kuomintang party, but when Chiang Kai-shek's
army did not introduce agrarian reforms in the territories it conquered
Mao started peasant rebellions throughout Hunan in the spring of 1927.
When these rebellions were crushed he fled to the mountains where
he became the organizer of Red guerrilla bands. From this time on he
was also the intellectual leader of the party. Beginning in 1931 he
served as the chairman of the Communist Party, although the official
title was only bestowed on him in 1944.

Gradually Mao's leadership and strategy emerged as the unique dynamic force in Chinese communism. The Maoist strategy was not the result of masterful planning by the Kremlin, but was developed independently. Before Mao's rise the successive communist leaders had actually retarded the rise of communist influence by insisting that power must be won in the cities since the peasantry, according to Marxian doctrine, could not play a decisive independent revolutionary role. But after a period during which the communists failed to win the urban proletariat, Mao developed a strategy based on his deep conviction that the peasantry could by itself provide the driving force to effect a complete revolution. Thus his strategy consisted of building a political party organized in accordance with Marxist-Leninist principles on a purely peasant mass base. The peasant masses were to be won by a program of land reform designed to satisfy their basic grievances. For acting on his conviction of the peasantry's key role, Mao was for a time dismissed from the Central Committee, but he was willing to carry on in the very face of the Committee's disapproval. Only after the bankruptcy of the communist policies based on the revolutionary leadership of the proletariat had been demonstrated did the Sixth Congress of the Comintern legitimize Mao's strategy and give it a place in the total communist program. Hence Mao regards himself as one who made a contribution to the theoretical development of Marxism-Leninism.

But Mao was not only a fervent communist because he believed it would bring much-needed relief to the oppressed peasantry; he was also a fervent Chinese. By combining agrarian reform with Chinese nationalism he arrived at the formula which attracted many to his banners. When the Japanese armies invaded North China and devastated vast areas the farming populace gave its support to Mao and his communists because they alone held out the promise of relief. They supported the cause by supplying both manpower and food for Mao's guerrilla armies. Mao's fighters harried Chiang's armies in every possible way after the civil war was resumed. In the meantime he prepared the "Peoples' Liberation Army" for the conquest of China. After it started moving southward its progress was steady. It gradually forced back the Kuomintang armies. On January 15, 1949, Tientsin surrendered to the "Peoples' Army" and five days later Chiang's forces evacuated Peiping. In April the communist armies crossed the Yangtze at six points and before the end of May Shanghai was in their possession. The fall of the year saw the communists take Canton and Chungking. Thus by the end of the year the communist armies were in control of most of the mainland.

Meanwhile both the Nationalists and communists had established new capitals. Chiang Kai-shek and his government had withdrawn to the island of Formosa off the southeast coast of China. Mao Tse-tung, for his part, proclaimed the "Chinese Peoples' Republic" with Peiping as the capital (September 22, 1949). The new government was quickly recognized by the U.S.S.R. (October 2, 1949). Britain, too, accorded it recognition, but the U.S. government did not follow suit.

The Soviet Union and the New Imperialism

THE SOVIET UNION
AFTER WORLD WAR II
O N September 4, 1945, the State Committee for Defense which had exercised complete governmental authority since the German invasion of 1941 was dissolved and its political functions were restored to the agencies of the Supreme Soviet and the Communist Party. During the war many able noncommunists had been given key posts in the government and had contributed much toward the war effort. Some of the ablest generals of the Red Army were noncommunists. All these were now unostentatiously retired with pensions and other rewards. The Communist Party became again the sole directing force in Soviet life. During the war years there had been no elections of deputies to the Supreme Soviet of the U.S.S.R. The deputies elected in 1937 had been held over from year to year after their four-year term had expired. Finally, however, the government decided to hold an election in February, 1946. Electoral procedures remained the same as they had been before the war. Despite the provisions in the electoral rules for multiple candidates, the voters were given the choice of only one name. The one candidate for each position was named by the Communist Party. Thus the voter could either accept or reject the candidate. An observer who spent many years in Russia has described the voting as follows:

Voting for the ticket merely requires folding the ballot and dropping it into the urn. Voting against the ticket, however, means crossing out the name or names on the printed form. To do that the voters would have to use one of the curtained booths provided at every polling place. It is easy to see why practically everybody shuns the booths and prefers to stick to the simpler procedure of dropping the ballot unaltered and in full view of the election officials.[1]

According to the official report 101,717,686 registered electors or more than 99 per cent of the registered electors turned out for the election. Of this total less than 1 per cent crossed out the name of the candidate presented by the Communist Party.

The primary task of the government was reconstruction and rehabilitation. The Russians suffered greater losses of both life and property than all the other Allied nations combined. According to Stalin's statement of March 13, 1946, more than seven million lives were lost in battle or as a result of the occupation. The Nazi armies were particularly ruthless in Russia. During the German retreat demolition squads destroyed factories, bridges, and transportation facilities. It is reported that in the districts occupied by the Nazis most of the machinery in the power plants was either removed or burned out. About 40,000 miles of railroad tracks were destroyed and the loss in freight cars was about 428,000, or nearly half the prewar rolling stock. The chairman of the state planning commission reported that in the occupied towns about half the dwelling houses had been destroyed or badly damaged. At the end of the war many Russians were living in abandoned army dugouts, in caves, and in storm cellars. The report submitted to the Allied Reparations Commission on September 13, 1945, listed the number of buildings destroyed as six millions, including 84,000 schools.

Of all the devastated regions the Donbas, a small region in the Ukraine which has been called the Russian Ruhr, probably suffered most. This area had been a dominant factor in prewar production. From it came between 50 and 60 per cent of the coal, iron ore, steel, and aluminum produced in the U.S.S.R. Power stations in this area produced nearly a quarter of the electrical energy generated in Russia. After the Germans had taken what they wanted, their demolition squads made certain that none of the machinery they left behind was usable. More than 80 per cent of the productive capacity of this region was destroyed.

But the foregoing account of the losses does not complete the picture. The Russians did not wait until the end of the war before they began the task of rebuilding their factories. First, they managed to dismantle many shops and plants and transport the machinery to the eastern districts of Russia. Second, the destruction in the west was balanced to a large extent by plant expansion in the east, thanks sub-

[1] Edmund Stevens: *This is Russia-Uncensored* (1950), p. 24.

stantially to lend-lease materials and technological help from the United States. Some idea of the importance of this expansion may be gained from the fact that production in the eastern areas was twice as great during the first half of 1945 as it had been in the corresponding period of 1941. By 1945 the industrial development had to a large extent offset the war losses. In 1945 the gross industrial output of Soviet Russia was only 8 per cent below the prewar level. In the heavy industries the output even exceeded to a small extent that of the prewar period.

THE FOURTH FIVE-YEAR PLAN

At the end of the war there was no period of rest for the weary Russians. In February, 1946, Stalin, in formally announcing the fourth Five-Year Plan, called the Russians to great new tasks. The plan had a twofold goal. First, it aimed at the complete rehabilitation of the devastated areas by 1950. Second, it purposed to increase industrial production and potential military strength to match the might of any power in the world. Other aims of the new plan were the expansion of internal and external communications, the building of a large fleet of merchant vessels, and the construction of highways and canals. It further projected a substantial railway building program and increased production of railway cars and equipment. It called also for the building of twice as many tractors by 1950 as there were on the collective farms when the Nazis invaded Russia. Another noteworthy project was the creation of a new building industry to make prefabricated factories and houses. An interesting point is that the new houses were not to be owned by government agencies as in the period before the war, but were to be sold to the workers on generous terms.

The principal emphasis, as in the earlier plans, was on the expansion of the capital goods industries. Russia's standard of living was to rise somewhat and the output of consumer goods was to increase. But the promise of abundance which served to sustain morale during years of incredible hardships was again not to be fulfilled by the new plan. Consumer demands — the chief clothing materials, leather footwear, and so forth — were again subordinated to heavy industry. In his speech of February 9, 1946, Premier Stalin called for an industrial output of 50 million tons of pig iron a year, 60 million tons of steel, 500 million tons of coal, and 60 million tons of oil. Only when these goals are reached, he said, "only then can we consider our country guaranteed against any eventuality." He believed that "perhaps three new Five-Year Plans will be required" to achieve the goals he set. "But it can be done and we must do it," he said in conclusion.

All efforts were at once turned toward the fulfillment of the new Five-Year Plan. Mines were pumped dry or the water was drained into subterranean sand pits with the aid of drilling equipment. A beginning was also made in repairing or rebuilding the wrecked dams, pumping stations, reservoirs, and power plants to provide power for the coal mines and steel mills. The opening of more than one hundred major mines and hundreds of small pits, for example, restored a major part of the coal output in the Donbas. The necessary manpower for the proposed industrial development was quickly marshalled. The process of demobilization which had been started in 1945 was continued in the following year with the result that by the end of 1946 the armed forces had been reduced to less than six million. This did not mean, however, that the Soviet Union had embarked on a course of demilitarization. On February 23, 1946, the twenty-eighth anniversary of the founding of the Red Army (officially renamed Soviet Army on September 20, 1946), Stalin enjoined it "not only to keep up with progress in the art of war, but to advance it."

Tremendous progress was made during the succeeding years. The devastated industry of the west was gradually rebuilt and Russia's railroad system was reconstructed and extended. While industry was being restored, the process of decentralization which had started during the war was continued. Instead of being grouped in the west as before the war, industrial plants were scattered over both the eastern and western parts of Russia. To escape the Nazi armies the government had moved a number of industries eastward. Not only did they remain in their new localities, but others were established there. By the spring of 1951 pig iron production in the Urals was reported to have risen 160 per cent over 1940. In Siberia, too, there was a considerable increase in iron and steel production. Probably about one-half of the Soviet steel production now comes from the Urals and beyond.

In April, 1951, the Moscow radio broadcast the announcement that the fourth Five-Year Plan had been completed in four years and three months and that production under the plan had been increased by 73 per cent over 1940. Three categories — pig iron production, smelting of steel, and production of rolled metal — were listed as having exceeded production estimates. The total production of iron and steel was reported as having increased by 45 per cent instead of the planned 35 per cent. Electric production was reported as being 87 per cent above the 1940 figure and almost 10 per cent higher than the goal set by the plan. Oil production rose to 22 per cent above prewar production which was higher than the goal set. Coal production, too, exceeded the five-year goal slightly. In addition to the overall growth of production, the industries were at the end of the fourth Five-Year Plan more evenly distributed over the country and hence less vulnerable to air attack. Farm output, with the exception of cotton production, fell below expectations. This was particularly true with respect to livestock and their products.

The production of consumer goods lagged as had been the case in the previous Five-Year Plan. At the completion of the fourth Five-Year Plan the ordinary Russian was little better off than he was before the war. His condition had improved in comparison with the wartime privations, but he was still incredibly poor by western standards. In 1945 shoe production was almost entirely for the army and only 60 million pairs of shoes were manufactured for a country of virtually 200 million inhabitants. In 1950 the shoe output had increased to about 192 million pairs which was still less than one pair for each person and substantially below the 230 million pairs turned out in 1940 and the 1950 goal of 240 million pairs. In one respect, however, there was considerable improvement. The program for building and housing was somewhat overfulfilled, easing but far from ending Russia's perennial housing shortage. Because resources originally allocated to consumer goods and related production were diverted to heavy industry and transport, the U.S.S.R. was stronger from the military-economic point of view at the end of the fourth Five-Year Plan. To achieve the progress made in the fourth Five-Year Plan the Soviet people had to work forty-eight hours a week rather than the prewar forty hours. They also had to work many millions of additional hours on their rest days.

After the announcement of the fulfillment of the fourth Five-Year Plan the Soviet government continued to drive its people hard toward the achievement of further goals. In August, 1952, after nearly twenty months of the new plan had passed, the Soviet government made public the goals of the fifth Five-Year Plan to be achieved by 1955. As in the past plans, the program puts emphasis on increasing the output of the Soviet Union's steel mills, smelting furnaces, coal mines, oil fields, power plants, heavy machine and tool factories. The chief interest is centered in the Soviet steel industry. The projected increase is 62 per cent over 1950's output. Production in 1951 was 31.7 million tons and the goal by 1955 is an annual output of 44.7 million tons. Comparable increases are also planned in other industries. Aluminum production is scheduled to rise 176 per cent above the output of 1950. The output of copper is to rise 90 per cent, lead 170 per cent, zinc 150, nickel 53, and tin 80. Automobile production is to go up 20 per cent over 1950 and that of tractors 19 per cent. Particularly noteworthy is the projected increase in oil production of 85 per cent over 1950's 37.6 million tons. Equally important is the plan for power expansion which will raise electric production 85 per cent above 1950's 90 billion kilowatts.

In terms of rubles the general industrial production is to rise 70 per cent by 1955 as compared with 1950. The increase is dedicated primarily to an "all-round strengthening of the active defense of the Soviet country."

Other features of the new plan include continued dispersal of industry throughout the country so that plants will be closer to the sources of raw material and not so vulnerable to attack by invading armies. To facilitate distribution a vast new railroad building program is projected calling for 150 per cent more construction and a 60 per cent increase in double-track mileage. The plan also provides for increases in river and ocean transport and in truck haulage. Another goal of the plan is an increase of 100 per cent in the construction of living quarters. In addition to the rise in industrial production railroad building, and the construction of living quarters, the plan projects an agricultural program calling for a 40 to 50 per cent increase in grain production over that of 1950. Other agricultural goals, compared with the production of 1950, call for 65 to 70 per cent more sugar beets by 1955, 55 to 65 per cent more cotton, 18 to 20 per cent more cattle, 45 to 50 per cent more hogs, and 60 to 62 per cent more sheep and goats.

If the Soviet Union attains the goals set forth in the fifth Five-Year Plan the per capita production of industrial goods will be about one-third as great as in the United States. While the Soviet output of certain commodities may be almost two-thirds as large as that of the United States, production in other lines may be less than 10 per cent. The closest approach to the United States in the production of a major commodity is that of coal. The Soviet goal of 375.5 million metric tons [2] by 1955 is more than two-thirds of the U.S. production for 1951. As regards steel and pig iron, the *sine qua non* of modern industry and warfare, the projected Soviet goal is about half that produced in the United States in 1951. The 1955 petroleum goal is less than a quarter of the 1951 production in the United States.

CHANGES AND DEVELOPMENTS

Among the important changes which took place during and after the war the official reestablishment of the Russian Orthodox Church is particularly noteworthy. The sustained antireligious policy of the Soviet government was not successful in stamping out religious faith and attendance at public worship. Despite the threat of the loss of their ration tickets and their jobs or exile to Siberia many continued to attend public worship in the churches the government did not close. Even the large congregations which gathered for worship were not an accu-

[2] A metric ton is equal to 1.1 short tons.

rate index to the survival of religion. There was a larger number of citizens who retained their religious faith but who rarely if ever attended public services.

As early as 1939 the Soviet government had inaugurated a new policy toward organized religion, particularly toward the Orthodox Church, by abolishing all "direct action" against religion and by moderating its antireligious propaganda. A further change came after the Nazi invasion. The Nazis helped to bring about this change by opening the churches as they advanced into Russia. This and the fact that under the stress of war many Russians were turning to God and the Orthodox Church forced the Soviet government to revise its attitude. Stalin's attitude toward the leaders of the Orthodox Church became more cordial. Not that the men of the Kremlin experienced a change of heart toward religion. The fact is that, like Napoleon, they wished to gain wider support among the Russian masses. They saw that religion and the Orthodox Church could be used both to control the masses in Russia and to serve the Soviet expansionist policy in the Balkans where the Orthodox Church had many members. The task of enlisting the Church in the service of the state was facilitated by the fact that the Church was no longer the center of organized opposition to the Soviet regime. Leaders of the Church had displayed a growing disposition to cooperate with the state.

In September, 1943, Stalin officially received Acting Patriarch Sergei and other officials of the Orthodox Church and granted them permission to summon a congress for the election of a patriarch. Sergei was chosen patriarch and was enthroned in his packed cathedral with great pomp. Thus the existence of the Orthodox Church in Russia was legalized. Since that time it has been for all practical purposes the "spiritual" mouthpiece of the state. The Church which for centuries enabled the tsars to broaden and strengthen their influence in Eastern Europe became a powerful political instrument of the Kremlin. During the months after the enthronement of the patriarch the government also permitted the opening of a theological school and the printing of the Bible which had been forbidden since the revolution. In 1945 one half of the Church property which had been confiscated was returned and permission was also granted to restore certain ancient religious shrines.

During the war the government also took steps to abolish the easy procurement of divorces. During the years after the Revolution of 1917 the marriage ties could be cut quickly and easily. A couple could get a divorce simply by registering at the proper bureau and paying a small fee. But the marriage instability that followed finally caused the Soviet government to outlaw easy divorces. A law of 1944 required that a couple desiring divorce go before a judge and present valid reasons for dissolving the marriage bonds. Judges were ordered to effect reconciliations whenever possible. In 1949 the Soviet Supreme Court further tightened the marriage ties by ordering the lower courts to refuse divorces for "temporary divergences of opinion or unwillingness of one side to continue the marriage." The new attitude toward marriage was also reflected in Soviet literature. Heroes and heroines have since that time, with rare exceptions, been depicted as loyal and pure in marriage. Any act, however, which jeopardizes "the principles of communist morality" constitutes "serious and well-founded" grounds for divorce.

The Soviet government did not stop at enlisting the support of religion and the Orthodox Church for the *status quo,* it also endeavored to use education, literature, and the fine arts to strengthen and perpetuate the communist regime. This is in accordance with the communist philosophy which regards all institutions — political, cultural, and economic — as weapons for perpetuating the rule of the Communist Party. During the war the communists, as a means of gaining a wider support among the masses, had permitted digressions from the Party line. Outstanding figures in the field of the arts and sciences took advantage of the situation to express ideas that were not in harmony with the tenets of the Party. Even composers departed from prescribed paths to compose the kind of music they thought best. This raised hopes in the hearts of many that the unprecedented intellectual liberty, according to communist standards, would continue after the war.

But the hopes were soon dispelled. After the cessation of hostilities the Communist Party put increasing emphasis on the enforcement of unflinching orthodoxy. A beginning was made within the Party itself. During the war the membership had increased from 2.5 million in 1941 to a total of 5.7 million in 1945, including candidates for admission. This increase had resulted from a liberalization of admission requirements. In the latter year, however, the weeding-out process was started. Many communists who were found wanting either in zeal or in "political knowledge" were summarily expelled from the Party. But the purge was mild in comparison with the mass arrests, expulsions, and liquidations of the years 1936–1938.

The purge was soon extended to other phases of Russian life. Unflinching orthodoxy became the order of the day. The result was a system of thought control which ruled out all divergences of opinion. The communists were determined that all phases of Russian life must promote the aims and interests of the Party. Thus the *Literary Gazette* stated regarding the purpose of education: "It is in the school, at the desk, in the first class, that the foundations of a communist outlook are laid in future Soviet citizens." The Party demanded that the children be taught that the Soviet way of life is superior to all others. In general, the Soviet propaganda machine used the full facilities of the press, radio, and motion pictures in its efforts to enforce unflinching orthodoxy and to convince the Russian masses that Russian life is superior. "As Stalin teaches us, our press is in daily and hourly contact with the working masses," *Pravda* stated, "it is truly a people's press — active propagandist, organizer, and agitator."

Artists and composers were also told that their work must be the expression of Marxist-Leninist convictions. To compel adherence to the Party program a strict control of content and form was established. Under this control the range of permissible subjects and techniques was sharply narrowed. Those who deviated were purged. The purge inaugurated in the arts was more thorough than any previous cultural purification. It began in earnest in August, 1946, when the Central Committee warned those writers who had strayed from the Party line to return from the paths "where interests of the party were made victims of personal interest and general self-praise." Two writers, the poetess Anna Akhmatova and the satirist Zoshchenko, were expelled from the Union of Soviet Writers and forbidden to publish further works. The union itself was reorganized, a new head was appointed, and membership was limited to those who "stand on a platform of Soviet power and participate in socialist construction." Andrei Zhdanov, Secretary of the Central Committee, said emphatically: "Our literature is not a private enterprise. . . . We demand that our comrades, both those who give leadership in the literary field and those who write, be guided by that without which the Soviet order cannot live, i.e., politics." Literature, he said, "must help the Party and the people educate the youth in the spirit of unreserved devotion to the Soviet social order."

Zhdanov also attacked many of the leading composers of Soviet music, including Prokofieff, Shostakovich, and Khachaturian, accusing them of writing music "alien to the Soviet people." "What a step away from the highroad of our musical development our formalists take," he said, "when, undermining the bases of real music, they compose false, ugly music, filled with idealistic emotions alien to the broad masses of the people. . . . Two extremely important tasks now face Soviet composers. The chief task is to develop and perfect Soviet music. The second is to protect Soviet music from the infiltration of elements of bourgeois decadence." The composers denounced by the Central Committee quickly did penance and then proceeded to write compositions which they hoped would meet with the approval of the Communist Party. Shostakovich, for example, wrote an oratorio dedicated to the Soviet reforestation program for which he received a Stalin prize in 1950.

Prominent in the program of reeducation was the denunciation of western values as "bourgeois." This was in part made necessary by the fact that many soldiers of the Red Army who had come into contact with western life found it attractive. To offset this the Soviet propaganda machine sought to sell the Russians the idea that in the West democracy and liberty are only pretenses, that they are realised to a higher degree in the Soviet Union than anywhere else. Soviet literature was ordered to protect itself against pollution by western bourgeois forms. "Is it becoming to our advanced literature, the most revolutionary literature of the world," Zhdanov asked, "to kowtow to the narrow, petty bourgeois literature of the West?" Even humor was enlisted in the campaign of denunciation. *Krokodil,* the Soviet humor magazine, was ordered by the Central Committee to "subject the bourgeois culture of the West to criticism, revealing its ideological insignificance and degeneracy."

To keep the Russian people from being "polluted by the bourgeois culture" of the West, more particularly, to keep them from hearing about the freedom and higher living standards of the western democracies, the Kremlin sought to erect an impenetrable barrier against western ideas. A sharp line, named the "iron curtain," was drawn to separate the peoples under Soviet domination from those of western Europe. To penetrate the iron curtain is no easy matter. An American who visited Russia in 1950 wrote:

The extent to which the regime has gone in isolating the Russians from any foreign contacts and in keeping from them any news from abroad is beyond the imagination of any American who has not actually witnessed the situation with his own eyes. No Soviet citizen is permitted to travel abroad. No Soviet citizen is allowed to marry a foreigner. Few foreigners are permitted to enter the country: those who are permitted to enter are either foreign officials or communist stooges. The foreign officials are restricted in their movements and constantly spied upon. Even the foreign communists are kept well in hand. It is against the law for Russians to have any dealings with foreigners. A Russian practically never sees a foreign publication.[3]

For a time the one means of sending messages to Soviet Russia was the airwaves, but even this has been largely cut off by a colossal jamming effort on the part of the Soviet regime.

SOVIET IMPERIALISM

One of the most far-reaching changes resulting from World War II was the spread of Russia into Europe. World War I gave the Bolsheviks the opportunity to establish Bolshevism in Russia itself, but outside of Russia the attempts to establish Bolshevism enjoyed only a few brief

[3] F. D. Kohler, Chief of the Division of International Broadcasting, in U.S. Department of State Bulletin, vol. 22 (March 20, 1950), p. 430.

successes. In 1917 the Soviet government had found it necessary to retreat in eastern Europe to a frontier that was farther to the east than any Russia had known since the eighteenth century. Such loss of territory appeared to be in harmony with communist denunciation of imperialism and imperialist exploitation. Shut off from the rest of the world and weak militarily, the Soviet government sought to protect its western flank by entering into a series of nonaggression pacts. But as the regime grew stronger at home the idea of extending Soviet domination over the smaller countries on its western borders took on greater importance.

Security against future aggression, however, is only the minimum object. The maximum goal is world revolution. Morbid fear of attack from the outside was so closely identified with the dogma of the inevitability of communism that a theoretically defensive attitude was transformed into a practically aggressive one. "It is inconceivable," Lenin stated, "that the Soviet Republic should continue for a long period side by side with imperialist states. Ultimately one or the other must conquer." Marxist-Leninist doctrine is positive about the outcome. Communism would conquer the world no matter what happened. But when a number of decades passed without communism making any appreciable progress toward world domination, the Soviet government entered an acute imperialist stage. The program of expansion is so vast that it dwarfs the imperialist expansion of the tsars. While continuing the pretense of being anti-imperialist, the Kremlin extended its sway over 100 million people.

The initial step toward greater security and toward world revolution was the establishment of Soviet domination over eastern Europe. After Hitler's rise to power these states became particularly important as buffers against an invasion of Russia. When the opportunity presented itself in 1939 the Soviet Union annexed Estonia, Livonia, and Lithuania, and parts of Finland, Poland, and Rumania. This was only a beginning. When the defeat of Hitler and his Nazis left Soviet power unchallenged in eastern Europe, Stalin, a thoroughgoing opportunist, decided to make the most of the situation. His methods of establishing control over the nations of eastern Europe differed from those employed by the tsars. For the tsars force was all important. In the Soviet technique it is also important, but not the primary factor. In 1939 the Soviet Union did use force to acquire the Isthmus of Karelia, Latvia, Lithuania, Estonia, and half of Poland, but after World War II the Russians used different tactics. Although the presence of Soviet troops in all the countries of Europe exercised a powerful influence, the Kremlin leaders did not use the Russian army directly to establish communist rule.

SOVIET RUSSIA IN EUROPE

By far the most important factor in sovietizing eastern Europe were the communist parties in the various states. After the war various coalition governments were formed in the eastern European countries. These governments were known under various names in the different countries (National Liberation Front, Fatherland Front, National Independence Front, etc.), but their general organization was much the same as that of the Popular Fronts of an earlier period. When the coalition governments were organized the communist parties joined with the other parties in forming United Fronts. The parties which attempted to collaborate with the communists in the United Front governments believed that their own political organizations could continue to exist, that it was possible to cooperate on a friendly basis with the communists. But their calculations were incorrect. Once the communists were in the government, they made the most of every opportunity to strengthen their position and as they grew stronger they gradually neutralized and finally liquidated the other political groups which shared the government.

The communist tactics varied in the different countries, but the general plan was the same. The first goal was to gain control of the police, the press, and the radio, a technique the Nazis had employed so successfully in 1933. To achieve this goal they frequently made deals with discontented factions of other parties. The communists then were in a position to not only propagandize the masses but also to attack the opposition. Frequently false charges were made against opposition leaders to discredit them. In some cases opposition leaders were even imprisoned on trumped-up charges. After the influence of the democratic opposition had been undermined and the noncommunist leaders had been discredited or imprisoned, the communists would go through the farce of holding elections in which fraud and terror were employed to insure a communist victory. Thus the communists succeeded in setting up minority regimes. These governments, supported by a ruthless secret police trained in Moscow, thereafter exercised dictatorial powers.

In carrying out their program of sovietization the Russians placed considerable reliance on a twofold appeal, the appeal to nationalism and the appeal to the land-hunger of the peasants. The Kremlin boldly proclaimed the fiction that it had no intention of exploiting the eastern countries in a financial way, that its purpose was merely to insure the independence of these states against "the growing pressure" of western imperialism. Stalin himself said that "the growing pressure of American imperialism and its European myrmidons is encountering the growing resistance of the peoples in the countries of the new democracy." He called the puppet governments which the Soviet minions established "democracies of a special nature." They wooed the peasants by promising to divide large estates among them. In this they followed the model of the Russian revolution. According to the model the next step after giving the peasants land would be to collectivize it. This step met great opposition in Russia and will meet equal resistance in the satellite states.

One after another the coalition governments in Poland, Rumania, Bulgaria, Hungary, Yugoslavia, and Czechoslovakia were transformed into governments under exclusive communist control. As soon as the communist parties achieved control they purged all government bureaus of anticommunists. Unquestioning subservience to the policy dictated by the Soviet Union was required. Politicians of all parties who refused to accept absorption into the communist groups were quickly liquidated. Clubs, lodges, and sports groups were merged into communist-led movements. Newspapermen, authors, and radio writers who did not adhere strictly to the Moscow line were summarily dismissed. Judges were replaced by communists and lawyers who wished to appear before a court had to pass communist "bar examinations." In the schools all teachers who did not teach according to Moscow dictates were carefully purged. Businesses employing more than fifty persons (in some instances one hundred) were taken over by the government. A license to conduct any kind of business could be obtained only by producing a police certificate of political reliability. Farmers who owned more than 125 acres lost their farms and pressure was put on those owning less to join communist cooperatives. Church property, too, was seized by the government, priests and ministers becoming state employees. All opposition to communist rule was ruthlessly suppressed. Those who did not cooperate voluntarily were either forced or frightened into accepting communist government. Thus Stalin and the Central Committee became the omnipotent masters of a great Soviet empire in eastern Europe. The government in these states has been euphoniously called "Popular Democracy." George Dimitrov, a Moscow-trained communist who was premier of Bulgaria, 1946–1949, said in 1948:

> The Soviet regime and the Popular Democratic regime are two forms of one and the same system of government, based on the union between the town and agricultural workers. Both are based on the dictatorship of the proletariat. Soviet experience is the only and the best pattern for the building of socialism in our country as well as in other countries of popular democracy.[4]

As a means of exercising control over the communist parties in the puppet states the Kremlin founded the Communist Information Bureau or Cominform. It was organized in September, 1947, by representatives

[4] Cited in H. Seton-Watson, *The East European Revolution* (1951), p. 167.

of the communist parties in the direct sphere of Russian control. The name gave no indication of the nature of the bureau, but in 1948 the Cominform revealed itself as a supreme governing body charged with the duty of keeping the communist parties in the satellite states strictly obedient to Moscow. In a wider sense its purpose was to spread Soviet domination over the entire globe. Curiously enough, Belgrade was chosen as the headquarters of the new bureau and the Yugoslav communist party was entrusted with the task of editing the Cominform Journal.

POLAND AND HUNGARY BECOME SATELLITES

When Poland was invaded by the Nazis in 1939, and Moscow sent the Red Army into Poland from the East, the Polish government, caught between two giants, fled to London. Later, after Hitler threw his armies against Russia in 1941, the U.S.S.R. recognized the Polish government in London and Stalin even went so far as to declare that he wished to see a "strong and independent" Poland emerge from the war. No sooner, however, did the tide of battle turn at Stalingrad than the Soviet view changed. It was announced at Moscow that any Poles remaining in the Soviet Union would be regarded as citizens since they came from territory belonging to the Soviet Union. Upon entering Poland in the drive toward Berlin the Red Army quickly created a provisional government called the Polish Committee of National Liberation (Lublin government), despite the fact that the Soviet government had previously recognized the Polish government in London. Thus by the time the Big Three met at Yalta (February, 1945) the Soviet government was in full control of Poland. Roosevelt and Churchill finally worked out a compromise with Stalin which called for the inclusion of a number of officials from the London government and the Lublin government in a provisional government. This government as required by the Yalta Agreement was actually created, but it was controlled by the communists and their sympathizers drawn largely from the Lublin government. Realizing that a popular vote would not support them the pro-Soviet elements in the government postponed the "free and unfettered" elections.

Meanwhile the communists, a small minority, were destroying the opposition. One of the first moves was the creation of a Polish secret police, known among the people as UB (Urzad Bezpieczenstwa). Organized by agents of the Soviet secret police and supervised by Moscow-trained Poles, the UB had no less than 100,000 agents by 1947. This organization directed its efforts in general against all noncommunists, and in particular against members of the opposition parties. Soon the Polish prisons were jammed with political prisoners. When the elections were finally held the count showed a vote of more than 80 per cent against the communists, but the provisional government announced that 68 per cent of the voters had allegedly voted in favor of the provisional government. Protests of the British and United States governments against the referendum frauds availed nothing.

Having learned from the elections the identity of those who voted against communist rule, the communists launched a new campaign to eliminate the opposition. For this purpose the Polish secret police was enlarged to 230,000. A special drive was directed against the Peasant Party which was offering determined opposition to the communist program. Before the election more than 100,000 members of the Peasant Party had been arrested to keep them from voting, and after the election the efforts to crush this party were continued. Many large estates were confiscated and converted into state farms. Strong pressure was put on the peasants who owned smaller farms to compel them to join collective farms. One measure employed was to increase the taxes of individual farmers by 300 per cent. Industry was also largely sovietized. The larger factories were confiscated by the government, strikes were forbidden, and workers were frozen in their jobs. Thus the power of the labor unions was practically abolished through the elimination of their essential functions. Religious education was sharply limited, religious periodicals were put under strict censorship, and all youth movements were merged in the Communist Union of Polish Youth. Steps were also taken to limit the power and influence of the Roman Catholic Church, the government claiming that the hierarchy and clergy were meddling in politics. Attacks against the Church were launched over the radio and in the press. The Vatican was even denounced as "a capitalist state" and the Pope was accused of being pro-Nazi.

As an ex-enemy country Hungary was to be ruled by an Allied Control Commission of which the Soviet member was made chairman. From the beginning the chairman acted without consulting the other members. The Soviet Union had a particular advantage in that the armistice agreement gave the Soviet high command a firm hold on Hungary's economy by compelling the Hungarians to provision the Red Army and to place factories, transport, and communications at the disposal of the Soviets. The Soviet authorities made the most of the opportunity by assuming censorship of the telegraph system and by seizing control of most of the newsprint which was then doled out to the newspapers that were friendly to the communists. At first the communists were a small minority, but they were soon reinforced by Moscow-trained Hungarian communists who included followers of Bela Kun and Hungarian prisoners of war who had been indoctrinated in Russia.

These communists were aided by the advice of members of the Soviet N.K.V.D.

Although the communists polled but few votes in the first elections they nevertheless succeeded in gaining in the provisional government the post of ministry of the interior which controls the police and security agencies. Thereafter, with the protection of the police they proceeded to instigate civil and political disorders as a means of embarrassing the opposition. During the weeks before elections were held to establish a Popular Front government the communists did everything possible to hamper the opposition. Among other things, they made it extremely difficult for opposition newspapers to reach the public and they disfranchised many opposition voters. On election day (August 31, 1947) truckloads of communists were rushed from one voting place to another to cast votes. Despite all this the communists received only 22 per cent of the vote. But when the new cabinet was formed by the three leftist parties the Communist Party received one-third of the cabinet posts. This, as it turned out, was enough for the communists to achieve complete control. They gradually terminated all effective opposition by eliminating some parties and absorbing others. The army and civil service was purged of all opposition; the trade unions were reorganized along communist lines, and a strict censorship was clamped on press and radio. By the fall of 1948 the communists were the masters of Hungary.

RUMANIA, BULGARIA, AND ALBANIA

When the British liberated Greece in 1944 they found the country under the domination of the communists. In the months that followed the British were instrumental in breaking the power of the communists and in establishing a rightist government. After seeing this happen the Soviet leaders in Moscow became apprehensive that the same thing might take place in Rumania and Bulgaria. Hence the Soviet government intervened directly in Rumania. It sent Andrei Vishinsky, the deputy foreign minister, to Bucharest where he forced the noncommunist government to resign and ordered King Michael to appoint the so-called "National Democratic Front" government, a bloc led by the Communist Party and including the left wing of the Social Democratic Party. Both the British and U.S. officials objected to the manner in which the new government was put into power, but received little satisfaction.

In November, 1946, elections were held in an atmosphere of intimidation. As in Poland and Hungary the communists did everything possible to discredit and weaken the opposition. Many opposition voters were disfranchised, communist gangs broke up political rallies of the opposition parties, and opposition leaders were threatened or beaten. The official results were announced as 348 seats for the government bloc and 64 for the opposition parties. Then followed the various steps in the elimination of the noncommunists from the government. As the various opposition groups were gradually liquidated, it became clear that the days of the monarchy were numbered. Upon his return from London (November, 1947) where he had attended the wedding of Princess Elizabeth, Michael was asked by the communists to resign. Resistance was impossible as the power was largely in communist hands. Michael resigned and went into exile. After his departure the political sovietization of Rumania was completed. Thereafter all other phases of Rumanian life were gradually brought under communist control.

In Bulgaria a Popular Front government (Fatherland Front) was organized as early as September, 1944. One of the first acts of this government was to punish those who had voted for the adherence of Bulgaria to the Axis, collaborated with the Germans, or were guilty of brutality to the population. The repressive organs which carried out the punishments were largely under communist control, for the communists had succeeded in getting control of the ministry of the interior. Having secured control of the police, the communists made use of it to take over other key positions. When the Bulgarian government announced its intention to hold elections in the summer of 1945, the communists at once resorted to the old tactics of threatening opposition leaders and even opposition candidates. When the British and U.S. governments protested against such tactics the elections were postponed. They were finally held in November in an atmosphere of terror. The result was that the new parliament contained no representatives of the opposition parties. In the summer of 1946 a campaign was launched against the monarchy. A plebiscite held in early September was overwhelmingly in favor of a republic. Simeon, the boy king, and his mother left the country.

In the fall (October 27, 1946) new elections were held for a Grand National Assembly which was to draw up a constitution. Although opposition candidates were selected they had little opportunity to do any electioneering. Before any votes were cast most of them were in prisons or in concentration camps. The "official" returns gave 78 per cent of the votes to the Fatherland Front. In the new parliament the communists had 277 seats, the other Front parties 87 and the opposition 101. The premier of the new government was George Dimitrov who had formerly been general-secretary of the Comintern and had spent much time in Moscow. He proceeded at once with the task of exterminating the opposition. In this he was so successful that before the end of 1947 the Popular Front was completely controlled by the communists.[5] In December, 1947, the Bulgarian parliament ratified a constitution modeled on that of the Soviet Union.

In the meantime Nikola Petkov, leader of the Agrarian Party, who had dared to oppose communist control had been executed and his party dissolved. During the summer of 1948 all other noncommunist parties were gradually strangled, so that by the beginning of 1949 the Bulgarian government virtually became a one-party system. Steps were also taken to collectivize agriculture. The five-year plan adopted in 1949 called for the collectivization of no less than 75 per cent of the holdings. It provided that 5 per cent revert to the state and the rest be divided into small farms. Before long, however, pressure was put on the individual owners to join collectives. Bulgarian youth was carefully indoctrinated. Non-Marxist students were expelled from the universities. Religious instruction was banned in the schools and many priests of the Orthodox Church were arrested because they disapproved of the communist regime. In general, during the years 1949 and 1950 trials of anti-Marxists and non-Marxists followed each other in rapid succession. Many were sentenced to prison terms and more to the twenty known penal labor camps.

In Albania, as in Yugoslavia, communism had established itself during the war. Enver Hoxha (pronounced Hodja), an ex-schoolteacher, organized the communists into the National Liberation Front which was successful in driving out the Axis troops, so that by 1944 all of Albania was free. In 1945 the National Liberation Front was renamed Democratic Front and elections were held in December of that year. According to the official results 93 per cent of the votes were cast for the candidates of the Communist Party. When the Constituent Assembly met in January, 1946, it proclaimed Albania a republic, Hoxha becoming premier and minister of foreign affairs. The constitution which the Assembly accepted was modeled on that of Soviet Russia. Up to this point relations between Albania and the western powers had been friendly, but they deteriorated during the succeeding period. Although Albania was not accepted as a member of the Cominform, its government has been no less loyal to the Soviet Union. When the Cominform-Tito break occurred, Premier Hoxha's government joined in the denunciation of the Yugoslav communists. In November, 1949, Yugoslavia abrogated its treaty of friendship with Albania giving as the reason that her neighbor had been selected by the Soviet government to play the role of provocateur.

[5] Dimitrov died in July, 1949.

YUGOSLAVIA AND TITOISM

Yugoslavia had been neither an ex-enemy nation like Rumania, Bulgaria, or Hungary, nor a subdued and then "liberated" nation like Poland or Czechoslovakia. Consequently communism in Yugoslavia was not imposed by Moscow on a reluctant nation. The Yugoslav Communist Party, more than any other communist party, was the creation of one man. This man was Josip Broz, better known as Tito. After working as an organizer in the Yugoslav communist underground movement, Tito organized the communists into a resistance movement against the Axis and against General Mihailovich's Chetnik force of Yugoslavs. The latter was also a resistance movement against the Axis, but was dedicated to the preservation of the old order, while Tito was determined to set up a communist order. With the help of agents from the Soviet Union, Tito organized a provisional government with himself as president and commander-in-chief of the army. The national assembly abolished King Peter's right to the throne and under Tito's leadership set up a strict totalitarian regime. Tito was so successful as a military leader that by the summer of 1944 his forces held a large part of Yugoslavia. The war continued until the spring of 1946 when Tito's forces captured General Mihailovich. Found guilty of collaborating with the Axis, the latter was shot.

Previously Tito's National Liberation Front had been renamed People's Front and in January, 1946, a constitution, modeled on that of U.S.S.R., was formally adopted. All key positions in the People's Front were held by the Communist Party. Its methods were those of the other communist parties of eastern Europe. The various organizations were purged of noncommunists and the Yugoslav secret police compelled dissidents to adhere to the Marxist line. In 1949 the government intensified its drive to collectivize agriculture. As a result the number of collectives increased from 1300 at the end of 1948 to more than 4250 a year later.

The big difference between the situation in Yugoslavia and the other communist states was that a rift developed between Tito and the Kremlin. The high-spirited Tito was not ready to limit his own independence and that of the country in the interests of the Kremlin or Cominform. As early as 1945 differences had arisen between Tito and Stalin over the question of Trieste. The former felt that Stalin was supporting Italy's claim to Trieste rather than that of Yugoslavia. In a speech of May, 1946, he stated bluntly that Yugoslav interests must not be used by the Soviet Union for bargaining purposes. "We demand," he said, "that everyone shall be master in his own house." The Kremlin, aghast over this heresy, at once informed Tito through the

Soviet ambassador at Belgrade that such statements "cannot be tolerated." "Tell Comrade Tito," the ambassador said, "that if he should once again permit such an attack on the Soviet Union we shall be forced to reply with open criticism in the press and disavow him." But Tito refused to be intimidated and was supported in his stand by his colleagues in the Yugoslav government. Further disagreements followed with Tito refusing to give way. He was determined that Yugoslavia was not to become just a link in the Soviet chain. He repudiated the right of the Kremlin to think for all Reds everywhere.

When Tito refused to change his attitude he was roundly denounced. One Russian writer said "the puppy is feeling so big that he's barking at an elephant." Propaganda broadcasts over the Moscow radio called Tito such names as "bandit, traitor, greedy ape, chattering parrot, deserter, coward, comedian, and insolent dwarf." The Central Committee of the Russian Communist Party also reproved Tito and his communists. "We are disturbed," the reproof read in part, "by the present condition of the Yugoslav Communist Party." Even this did not cause Tito to repent. He reacted to the Soviet attacks by open criticism of the Politburo tactics and asked such questions as, "Who is deporting millions of various nationalities to Siberia?" To a group of visitors from the United States he said, as reported in the American press: "Stalin regards me as small fry and wants me to knuckle under."

Finally the Kremlin and the Cominform decided that Tito's rebellious mood could no longer be tolerated. In 1948 the Cominform expelled both Tito and the Yugoslav Communist Party. Tito could still have been restored to good standing by confessing his sins and asking for forgiveness. However, he was confident that the Yugoslav Communist Party would continue to support him. The Yugoslav Communist Party, in fact, retaliated by denouncing the Cominform charges as "slanders and fabrications" and by accusing the Cominform of trying to undermine its prestige. The rift between Tito and Stalin did not mean, however, that the former would turn away from the Marxist-Leninist path. Tito's government remained totalitarian and continued to carry out the Russian program of industrialization and agricultural collectivization.

The rift did, however, cause Tito to change his foreign policy. Previously a friendly front had been maintained between Yugoslavia and the Soviet Union against the capitalist states in foreign affairs. But in 1949 this changed. Yugoslavia began to cooperate with the western democracies. The Soviet Union retaliated by denouncing its treaty of friendship and collaboration with Yugoslavia, and the satellite states soon did the same. Thereafter many border incidents occurred on the common boundaries of Yugoslavia and the communist states that are dominated by the Kremlin. On the other hand, Yugoslavia's friendly attitude to the non-Cominform countries resulted in the conclusion of a number of trade treaties, including those with Italy and Great Britain. Thus Yugoslavia, the first communist state to raise the banner of revolt against Soviet Russia, stood firm in its determination not to become a puppet of the Kremlin.

Among other things Tito's rebellion excited a fear in the Kremlin that leaders in other east European countries might follow suit. Therefore it issued orders for a general purge of the communist parties in the satellite states. Leaders who had manifested any separatist leanings were replaced with Moscow-trained communists. The armed forces which could be used to suppress an uprising against the Soviet Union were also strengthened by replacing the generals of some of the satellite armies with Russian generals.

THE SOVIETIZATION OF CZECHOSLOVAKIA

The process of sovietization in eastern Europe culminated in the destruction of the democratic regime in Czechoslovakia. On the eve of World War II Czechoslovakia had been the only democratic country in eastern central Europe. At the end of the war President Eduard Beneš and Foreign Minister Jan Masaryk returned to their country determined to maintain its democratic liberties and its national independence. As Stalin had pledged not to interfere in the affairs of Czechoslovakia the noncommunist parties believed there could be equal cooperation of all parties in a Popular Front. The elections of 1946, which were still fairly free, resulted in a noncommunist majority, but the communists succeeded in gaining key positions in the cabinet. They held the ministry of the interior which controlled the police, the ministry of agriculture which had charge of the redistribution of the lands from which the Sudeten Germans had been expelled, and the ministry of information which controlled radio broadcasting. Many soldiers in the army had been considerably indoctrinated while being trained in Soviet Russia, and in the general staff, too, the communists had strong representation. Moreover, the prime minister, Klement Gottwald, was a communist. It was about President Beneš and Foreign Minister Masaryk that the hopes of the democrats were centered.

For several years the collaboration worked well, with the communists observing the rules of parliamentary procedures. The turning point came in the summer of 1947 when Czechoslovakia was invited to join the Marshall Plan. After the cabinet dared to accept the invitation to send representatives to the conference in Paris, it was forced to reverse itself under pressure from the Soviet government. Then the Cominform posed for the communists the problem of gaining complete control of the Czechoslovak government. While still continuing to profess the old principles of parliamentary government, the communists worked single-mindedly to achieve full power. Considerable attention was given to the organization of action committees or subversive secret cells within every business, factory, and important organization. Action committees, as it later turned out, were even organized in opposition political parties. At the same time the communists were busy reinforcing their grip on the police, starting strikes in various unions, and smashing the opposition by force. They even resorted to the old Nazi ruse of discovering a plot to overthrow the government. Some opposition leaders fled and others were arrested. Finally on the night of February 20, 1948, the action committees went into action. They dismissed chairmen, directors, and others who did not support their cause. The move was so unexpected that scarcely a finger was raised. In a few hours the life of Czechoslovakia on every level had passed into communist hands.

Only President Beneš still held out in old Hradcany Castle high upon the rocks overlooking the city. He could have tried to keep his country from becoming a Soviet satellite by an appeal to the people. He knew, however, that the communists controlled both the radio and the police. He also knew that the communist workers' militia was ready for action and the Red Army was ready to support it in case of civil war. Moreover, his health — he had suffered two strokes — did not permit vigorous action. On February 25, 1948, he yielded, accepting a cabinet composed largely of communists and communist puppets. Jan Masaryk remained foreign minister in the desperate hope of being able to continue the collaboration. But he soon realized that the game was up. On March 10 his body was found in the courtyard of the foreign ministry. It is believed that he committed suicide as a dramatic protest against the suppression of democracy. On September 6 Beneš died. His passing symbolized the passing of Czechoslovak democracy.

After the communists achieved political control a series of purges eliminated all open opposition from the civil service, universities, press, and even from the sports clubs. In Prague alone no less than 3500 persons were arrested. Communist leaders announced that the arrests were made to break up an underground network seeking to destroy the Communist Party. Czech libraries were purged of all books that were not pro-Marxist. Teachers were told that "everybody in that field must be clear about his role in the fight for socialism. . . . From the conception of Masaryk education must go forward to the conception of Marx, Engels, Lenin, and Stalin." All known anticommunists were expelled from the universities and the rest were subjected to re-education. Ownership of land was limited to 123 acres. All farmers who owned more than 125 acres had to turn their farms over to the government. Pressure was put on the peasants who owned land to have them join cooperatives. Meanwhile the nationalization of industrial enterprises proceeded rapidly. Not only heavy industries but also export and import firms, wholesale and distributing agencies, department stores, spas, and hotels were nationalized. It has been estimated that by the end of 1949 nearly 95 per cent of the nation's industrial enterprises had been brought under state control.

Nor did the Church escape sovietization. The drive against organized religion was opened with the announcement that the religious life of the nation was a matter of primary concern to the government. During the succeeding months the Catholic press was gradually silenced, many Catholic schools were closed, and the youth of the nation was regimented under communist leadership. On May 28, 1949, the clergy were notified that the entire educational system would thenceforth be administered in the spirit of communist teachings. A law enacted in mid-September reduced all Catholic priests and Protestant pastors to the status of civil servants. Their appointment, and supervision over them, was vested in the ministry of education. Every clergyman of whatever rank was required to take an oath of loyalty to the government.

Meanwhile a new election had been held at the end of May, 1949. A single list, without opposition candidates, was presented to the voters. According to the official report 90 per cent of the Czechs voted for the list and 86 per cent in Slovakia. On May 8 a new constitution modeled on that of the U.S.S.R. had been proclaimed. Like its model it is liberal in appearance, but illiberal in reality. All the provisions regarding individual freedom or independence of the judiciary are hedged with restrictions which dilute or eliminate these rights.

EXIT STALIN; ENTER MALENKOV

On March 4, 1953, the world was startled by the announcement that Premier Stalin had suffered a brain hemorrhage during the night of March 2. Periodically thereafter medical bulletins reported that the Soviet leader was fighting a losing battle. On March 6 the following statement was broadcast: "The heart of the comrade and inspired continuer of Lenin's will, the wise leader and teacher of the Communist Party and the Soviet people has stopped beating." He had died on the preceding day at the age of 73 after being in power 29 years. A non-Russian, he became one of the great figures in Slavic history. To what degree he was the prime mover in the vast changes which took place during the period of his rule, and to what extent he was merely an instrument, only the final appraisal of time will establish. That his achievements were notable in any case can hardly be contradicted. Under his rule a backward agrarian nation developed into the second greatest industrial power on earth. During World War II he built mighty armies and air fleets which threw back the Germans. Under his sponsorship communism spread over a large part of the globe and presented the greatest challenge ever faced by western civilization. At his death he left an empire far larger, more centralized and cohesive, infinitely more powerful than the empire of the tsars.

Stalin's methods were reminiscent of Ivan the Terrible and Peter the Great, of Genghis Khan and Hitler. Like the ruler described by Machiavelli, he was governed throughout his career by the philosophy that the end justifies the means. In international politics he was a better poker player than anyone since Talleyrand. Wendell Willkie said: "Stalin is a hard man, perhaps even a cruel man, but a very able one. He has few illusions." He must be held responsible for the millions of victims claimed by forced collectivization and the famine which accompanied it. His policies sent other millions to enslavement in labor camps. In concluding the nefarious pact with Germany in 1939 he encouraged Hitler to start World War II and thus shares responsibility for the widespread destruction and the tremendous losses of life. His ruthless and aggressive policies created an atmosphere of international tension and distrust that has seldom been paralleled. Few, if any, men have had such a potential for good or evil. If he had so willed the years since World War II could have been a period of international peace and friendship. What he has left the world is a legacy of fear and hate, deceit and intolerance, duplicity and atheism.

There was much speculation as to who would succeed Stalin. But the world did not have to wait long for the answer. Only twenty-six hours after Stalin's death the Soviet radio announced that in order "to insure the uninterrupted and correct leadership of the whole life of the country" Georgi Maximilianovich Malenkov had been appointed prime minister. Officially his title is Chairman of the Council of Ministers, a group of about fifty which corresponds roughly to our cabinet. The speed with which Malenkov occupied the seat of the "Great Stalin" contrasted dramatically with the slow and difficult transition of power after Lenin died in 1924. It showed that the oligarchy was determined not to have any quarrels — at least in public — that would risk disintegration of the vast empire ruled from the Kremlin. The new premier was 51 at the time of his appointment. His build is short and stocky. His weight of 250 pounds attests to his fondness for rich food and good drink. Observers have characterized him as "wily, competent, ruthless, and humorless."

In the case of Stalin the statement "Caesar has no heir" was not

true. His mantle fell on the shoulders of a man who had long been regarded as the "crown prince," one who was thoroughly trained in the
school of dictatorship by the master himself. Bourgeois-born Malenkov
joined the Red Army during the civil war and became a member of the
Communist Party in 1920. During the succeeding years he gradually
worked his way up in communist ranks. He became secretary of the
Komsomol youth organization in 1924 and the next year was made a
member of Stalin's personal secretarial staff. When the Nazis invaded
Russia Malenkov was put in charge of plane and tank production and
made a spectacularly good record. He became an alternate on the Politburo in 1941 and in this year first appeared with Stalin in the reviewing
stand on Lenin's tomb. After he was made a full member of the Politburo in 1946 he took over much of Stalin's former work of running the
communist political machinery. Thus he was able, like Stalin before
him, to place his henchmen in key posts both in the government and in
the party.

In his inaugural address to the Supreme Soviet on March 15 Malenkov made a statement which suggested a completely new direction for
Soviet foreign policy. "At the present time," he said, "there is not one
disputed or undecided question that cannot be decided by peaceful
means on the basis of the mutual understanding of interested countries.
This is our attitude toward all states, among them the United States
of America." When other Soviet leaders made similar statements hopes
ran high that the cold war might give way to an era of international
friendship and cooperation.

Whatever the motive the opportunity could not be ignored. On April
16 President Eisenhower in a major foreign policy speech made a chal-
lenging response to the Soviet "peace offensive." After referring to the
western world's "hunger for peace" he called on the Kremlin leaders
to support their words with deeds. He even went so far as to blueprint
a peace program which besides a Korean settlement included "an end
to direct and indirect attacks on Malaya and Indo-China," "a free and
united Germany with a government based on free and secret ballot,"
"conclusion of a treaty with Austria," and "full independence of the
East European nations." On April 25 the Soviet Union made its reply
in an editorial on the front page of *Pravda:* "The Soviet government
will welcome any step of the American government or any other government if it is directed at the friendly settlement of difficult questions.
This is evidence of the readiness of the Soviet side for serious business-
like discussions of outstanding problems."

But the fact that the Kremlin stopped growling like a bear and began
cooing like a dove did not disarm all non-Russians. Many western observers questioned the sincerity of the Russian "peace drive." While

some ascribed it to internal difficulties; others were of the opinion that it was merely a shrewd attempt to achieve by soft talk what the Communists had been unable to gain by warlike gestures. All hoped, however, that it was a step in the direction of international peace and goodwill.

Encouraged by the Russian "words of peace," Sir Winston Churchill (May, 1953) proposed a top-level meeting of western leaders with Soviet Premier Malenkov. He found little support for the plan he hoped would bring peace to the world; however, during the succeeding months a lengthy exchange of diplomatic notes regarding a lower-level meeting took place. Each reply from Moscow was indefinite — neither acceptance nor outright rejection. When the Western Allies were about convinced that the Kremlin did not want to confer, the latter suddenly agreed to a conference of the Big Four Council of Foreign Ministers. January, 1954, was chosen as the time for the meeting and Berlin as the site.

As these words are being written (January 25, 1954) the foreign ministers are opening their conference in Berlin, the seventh of the series since World War II. Present at the meeting are U.S. Secretary of State John Foster Dulles, British Foreign Secretary Anthony Eden, French Foreign Minister Georges Bidault, and Soviet Foreign Minister V. M. Molotov. As the conference has no fixed agenda, the talks will probably range over the whole complex of East-West differences. The reunification of Germany, however, is the basic issue. On this the prospect of agreement is faint to the vanishing point. There is no indication that the diametrically-opposed ideas held by the two sides can be reconciled. While the Western Allies continue to insist that free elections must precede unity, the Kremlin demands that the first united German government must be formed from among the members of the present East and West regimes. This would permit the Russians to intrench communists in key positions in any future German government. If Malenkov really desires to end the "cold war," any attempt to reach a *modus vivendi* on Germany will reveal the fact. As Mr. Dulles put it, the time has now come to back up the "words of peace" with "deeds of peace."

Regarding the world situation at the moment it may be said that the death of Stalin and the shift of the fighting in Korea "from the trenches to the table" appear to have relaxed the tension in some degree. Churchill said of the present state of the world: "I think it would be true to say that it is less formidable and more baffling." A factor which is certain to have a tremendous influence on the future is "the rapid and ceaseless" development of atomic weapons. In the words of Sir Winston, "When the advance of this destructive weapon enables everyone to kill everybody else nobody will want to kill anyone at all."

Select Bibliography

Series, surveys, and readings. One of the important series which has a number of volumes covering the period since 1815 is *The rise of modern Europe*, edited by W. L. Langer (1936 seq.). Another useful series is *Berkshire studies in modern history* (1927 seq.). A somewhat older but still important series is the *Cambridge modern history* (13 vols., 1902–1911). The general trends of the period are discussed in H. Kohn's meaty short survey, *The twentieth century* (1949). On nineteenth-century thought in England, France, and Germany there is T. Merz, *History of European thought in the nineteenth century* (4 vols., 4th ed., 1923–1924). Among the better surveys of European economic history are S. B. Clough and C. W. Cole, *Economic history of Europe* (3rd ed., 1953); C. Day, *Economic development in Europe* (new ed., 1949); and W. Bowden, M. Karpovich, and A. P. Usher, *Economic history of Europe since 1750* (1937). A more recent useful volume is E. Friedlaender and J. Oser, *Economic history of modern Europe* (1953). E. Friedell, *Cultural history of the modern age* (3 vols., 1930), is often stimulating, at times erratic. For nineteenth century literature G. Brandes, *Main currents in nineteenth-century literature* (6 vols., 1901–1905), is still useful. There are well-written chapters on nineteenth-century literature, philosophy, and science in C. Brinton, *Ideas and men: the story of western thought* (1950). A competent appraisal of the constitutions from 1787 to 1938 may be found in J. A. Hawgood, *Modern constitutions since 1787* (1939). The student will find very helpful such collections of readings and source materials as *Main currents of western thought: readings in western European intellectual history*, edited by F. L. Van Baumer (1952); *Readings in western civilization*, edited by G. H. Knoles and R. K. Snyder (1951); *Pageant of Europe: sources and selections from the Renaissance to the present day*, edited by R. P. Stearns (1947); *The quest for a principle of authority in Europe, 1715–present: select problems in historical interpretation*, edited by T. C. Mendenhall and others (1948); *Readings in European history since 1814*, edited by J. F. Scott and A. Baltzly (1934); *Readings in modern and contemporary history*, edited by A. N. Cook (1937). There is also a broad selection of political documents in *Source book on European governments*, edited by W. E. Rappard and others (1937).

755

CHAPTER I   *The French Revolution and Napoleon*

Eve of the Revolution. An excellent survey of the period preceding the outbreak of the French Revolution is to be found in Leo Gershoy's *From despotism to revolution, 1763–1789* (1944). G. Le Febvre, *The coming of the French Revolution,* translated by R. R. Palmer (1948) presents an interesting picture of France at the end of the Old Regime. *The spirit of revolution in 1789* by C. B. Rogers (1949) carefully analyzes the spirit of revolution as revealed in political songs and other popular literature. Paul H. Beik's *A judgment of the Old Regime* (1944) is an important contribution to the study of the Old Regime. Frances Acomb's *Anglophobia in France, 1763–1789; an essay in the history of constitutionalism and nationalism* (1950) is a brief scholarly study on a neglected phase in the genesis of the French Revolution. S. K. Padover, *The life and death of Louis XVI* (1939), is a readable biographical study of the ill-fated monarch. See also the bibliography of R. Ergang, *Europe from the Renaissance to Waterloo* (new ed., 1954).

French Revolution. For an excellent discussion of more recent books on the French Revolution see Beatrice F. Hyslop's "Historical publications since 1939 on the French revolution," *Journal of modern history,* vol. 20 (1948), pp. 232–250. Crane Brinton's *A decade of revolution, 1789–1799* (1934) is a sound, readable survey of the period. The same author's *Anatomy of revolution* (rev. ed., 1952) contains a penetrating discussion of the French Revolution. *The French Revolution* by J. M. Thompson (1945) is an engrossing volume based on sound scholarship. A revealing brief discussion of a phase of French constitutional history is to be found in H. B. Hill's "French constitutionalism: Old regime and revolutionary," *Journal of modern history,* vol. 21 (1949), pp. 222–227. R. R. Palmer's *Twelve who ruled: the committee of public safety during the terror* (1941) is an important contribution to the study of the Reign of Terror. Equally important is John B. Sirich's *The revolutionary committees in the departments of France, 1793–1794* (1943). J. L. Godfrey's *Revolutionary justice: a study of the organization, personnel, and procedure of the Paris tribunal, 1793–1795* (1951) is a compact scholarly monograph on the Revolutionary Tribunal. *Pageant-master of the republic: Jacques-Louis David and the French revolution* by David L. Dowd (1948) is a comprehensive and readable volume. *The debate on the French revolution, 1789–1800,* edited by A. Cobban (1950), deals with contemporary problems in Britain. Still useful despite its age is G. P. Gooch's *Germany and the French revolution* (1920). H. T. Parker, *The cult of antiquity and the French revolutionaries* (1937), is an important study. A. A. Lobanov-Rostovsky's *Russia and Europe, 1789–1825* (1947) is a readable and informative summary. *A documentary survey of the French revolution* by J. H. Stewart (1951) offers the student an opportunity to read many of the important documents.

Napoleon. Pieter Geyl's *Napoleon: for and against,* translated by Olive Renier (1949), offers an extensive review by a Dutch historian of Napoleonic literature since Waterloo by French historians. The first revaluation of Napoleon in many years is to be found in J. M. Thompson's *Napoleon Bonaparte; his rise and fall* (1952); the first biography to make use of Napoleon's voluminous correspondence. G. G. Andrew's *Napoleon in review* (1939) is a readable, sound survey of Napoleon's life. Raoul Brice, *The riddle of*

Napoleon, translated from the French by B. Creighton (1937), is a character analysis rather than a biography. Among the less recent biographies of Napoleon, those by J. Bainville (1932), F. M. Kircheisen (1931), A. Fournier (1903), and J. H. Rose (11th ed., 1934) are outstanding. Eugene Tarlé, *Bonaparte,* translated by J. Cournos (1937), is a study by a Russian Marxist historian. Tarlé, *Napoleon's invasion of Russia* (1942), is useful because it is based on Russian sources. A. L. Guerard's *Reflections on the Napoleonic legend* (1923) strips the Little Corporal of much of the glamor with which earlier writers surrounded him. R. M. Johnston, *The Corsican* (1910), and F. M. Kircheisen, *Napoleon's autobiography,* translated by F. Collins (1931), tell the story of his life as told in his diaries and letters. A more recent volume, *Napoleon's memoirs,* edited by S. de Chair (1950), pictures Napoleon as he saw himself and wished posterity to see him. Octave Aubry's *Private life of Napoleon,* translated by E. Abbott (1947), depicts the man, the lover, the husband, skilfully, but not always critically. A. H. Carr, *Napoleon speaks,* translated by J. Van Huele (1941), contains selections from Napoleon's letters so arranged as to tell their own story.

Surveys and special studies. Geoffrey Bruun's *Europe and the French imperium, 1799-1814* (1938) is a well-written survey of the period. R. B. Holtman in a study of real merit entitled *Napoleonic propaganda* (1950) presents a detailed analysis of Napoleon's propaganda system. C. Deutsch's *Genesis of Napoleonic imperialism* (1938) is a readable scholarly study. *Three Napoleonic battles* by H. T. Parker (1944) is a penetrating analysis of the battles of Friedland, Aspern, and Waterloo. All the military campaigns are ably discussed in J. H. Rose's biography of Napoleon. Carola Oman's *Napoleon at the channel* (1942) contains a wealth of behind-the-scenes information. V. J. Puryear, *Napoleon and the Dardanelles* (1951), is a lucid scholarly monograph on the place of the Near East in Napoleonic foreign relations. Hans Kohn's "Napoleon and the age of nationalism," *Journal of modern history,* vol. 22 (1950), pp. 21-37, is an important brief discussion. On the concordat of 1801 there is the scholarly monograph of H. H. Walsh, *The concordat of 1801: a study of the problems of nationalism in the relations of church and state* (1933).

CHAPTER 2 *The Congress of Vienna and After*

Congress of Vienna. A. J. May has written a readable brief survey, *The age of Metternich, 1814-1848* (1933), for the Berkshire series. C. K. Webster's *The congress of Vienna, 1814-1815* (3rd ed., 1920) still remains one of the best accounts of the congress. A more recent useful volume is H. Nicolson, *The congress of Vienna; a study in allied unity, 1812-1822* (1946). A third important book on how Europe made peace in 1815 is Guglielmo Ferrero, *The reconstruction of Europe,* translated by T. R. Jaeckel (1941). J. G. Lockhart, *The peacemakers, 1814-1815* (1932), presents the leading figures of the congress. Hannah A. Straus, *The attitude of the congress of Vienna toward nationalism in Germany, Italy, and Poland* (1949) is a short informative study. For the peace treaties see R. B. Mowat's *Great European treaties in the nineteenth century* (1918).

Metternich. The most important biography of Metternich is that by H. von Srbik (1925), two volumes in German. All English biographies that have appeared since 1925 are more or less indebted to von Srbik. The best of these is Helene du Coudray's *Metternich* (1935). Another useful biography is A. Cecil's *Metternich, 1773–1859* (1933), but it is pro-Metternich. A competent biography which owes much to Srbik is A. Herman's *Metternich* (1932). To get the ideas of Metternich at first hand the student should turn to the *Memoirs of Prince Metternich* (5 vols., 1880–1882). P. R. E. Viereck, *Conservatism revisited: the revolt against revolt* (1950), offers a revaluation of the policies and political philosophy of Metternich. C. S. B. Buckland, *Metternich and the British government from 1809 to 1813* (1932), is a scholarly monograph based on British manuscript sources. J. B. Stearns, *The role of Metternich in undermining Napoleon* (1948), is a valuable monograph which shows how Metternich prepared Napoleon's undoing.

Other personalities. The perennial fascination about Talleyrand has produced a number of good biographies. C. Brinton, *The lives of Talleyrand* (1936), is a stimulating interpretative study. A. D. Cooper, *Talleyrand* (1937), is a well-written short biography. The French historian Madelin wrote a biography which is characterized by a strong bias against Talleyrand; translated by R. Feltenstein (1948). Émile Dard, *Napoleon and Talleyrand,* translated by C. R. Turner (1937), is a competent study of the relationship between the two. On Tsar Alexander there is the sound and readable volume by L. I. Strakhovsky, *Alexander I of Russia, the man who defeated Napoleon* (1947). Ernest Knapton, *The lady of the Holy Alliance; the life of Julie de Krüdener* (1939), is a careful, impartial, and well-written biography. This is also true of Paul R. Sweet, *Friedrich von Gentz, defender of the old order* (1941). Golo Mann has summarized the diplomacy of the period as it centered about Gentz in *Secretary of Europe: the life of Friedrich Gentz, enemy of Napoleon,* translated by W. H. Woglom (1946). P. Guedalla's *Wellington* (1930) is both informative and entertaining. F. H. Cramer has written a series of short studies on the chief figures at the Congress of Vienna in *Current history,* n.s. 14 (1948).

Period of the post-Vienna congresses. F. B. Artz, *Reaction and revolution, 1814–1832* (1934), ably sketches the huge panorama of the years after Napoleon. H. G. Schenk, *The aftermath of the Napoleonic war; the concert of Europe, an experiment* (1947), is a competent scholarly survey. There is also a clear account of the congress and the succeeding period in W. A. Phillips, *The confederation of Europe: a study of the European alliance, 1813–1823, as an experiment of peace* (2nd ed., 1919). C. K. Webster, *The European alliance, 1815–1825* (1929), contains much sound and useful information. On British foreign policy there is the well-balanced scholarly work of C. K. Webster, *The foreign policy of Castlereagh, 1815–1822; Britain and the European alliance* (2nd ed., 1934). The narrative is carried forward in an equally valuable volume, *The foreign policy of Canning: England, the Neo-Holy Alliance, and the New World,* by H. Temperley (1925). On Russia's foreign relations there is the conscientious scholarly study of A. Lobanov-Rostovsky, *Russia and Europe, 1789–1825* (1947). W. P. Cresson, *The Holy Alliance, the European background of the Monroe Doctrine* (1922), sees the Holy Alliance as a real attempt at international organization.

The rise of German nationalism. Louis L. Snyder's *German nationalism: the tragedy of a people* (1952) is an interesting study by an able historian. Hans Kohn, *The idea of nationalism* (1944), contains some excellent chapters on the origins and background of German nationalism. Valuable chapters on early German nationalism can also be found in C. J. H. Hayes, *The historical evolution of modern nationalism* (2nd ed., 1948). W. C. Langsam, *The Napoleonic wars and German nationalism in Austria* (1930), is a well-done scholarly study. For the Napoleonic period in Prussia there is the competent scholarly book by Eugene N. Anderson, *Nationalism and the cultural crisis in Prussia, 1806–1815* (1939). H. C. Engelbrecht, *Johann Gottlieb Fichte: a study of his political writings* (1933), discusses Fichte's role in stimulating nationalism. Arndt's role is competently discussed in A. G. Pundt, *Arndt and the nationalist awakening in Germany* (1935). For the preceding period see K. S. Pinson, *Pietism as a factor in the rise of German nationalism* (1934), and R. Ergang, *Herder and the foundations of German nationalism* (1931).

National uprisings. There is a good survey of the reign of Ferdinand VII in R. E. Sencourt, *The Spanish crown, 1808–1931* (1932). J. A. Brandt, *Toward the new Spain* (1933), offers a survey of Spanish political history from 1810 through 1931. The period of Spanish history from 1815 to 1845 is ably treated by R. Altamira in *The Cambridge modern history*, vol. 10 (1907), pp. 205–243. H. B. Clarke, *Modern Spain, 1815–1898* (1906), is sound, but somewhat overcrowded with facts. George T. Romani, *The Neapolitan revolution of 1820–1821* (1950) is a solid scholarly study. A. P. Whitaker, *The United States and the independence of Latin America, 1800–1830* (1941), is an intelligent survey of U.S. policy toward Latin American independence. The classic account of the Greek struggle is W. A. Phillips, *War of Greek independence, 1821–1833* (1897). A shorter and more recent account is to be found in E. S. Forster, *Short history of modern Greece, 1821–1940* (1941). Still useful is W. Miller, *History of the Greek people, 1821–1921* (1922), but it is rather factual and short on interpretation. C. W. Crawley, *The question of Greek independence* (1930), is an informative study of British policy in the Near East, 1821–1833. For the attitude of the United States see H. J. Booras, *Hellenic independence and America's contribution to the cause* (1934). *Belgium*, edited by J. A. Goris, contains a good brief survey of Dutch rule in Belgium. Readable and informative chapters on Belgium in the early nineteenth century are also to be found in H. Vander Linden, *Belgium, the making of a nation* (1920). There are two readable volumes on Belgium by E. Cammaerts, *Belgium from the Roman invasion to the present day* (1921) and *The keystone of Europe; history of the Belgian dynasty, 1830–1939* (1939). There are two good short accounts of the Polish revolution of 1830, S. Askenazy, "Poland and the Polish revolution," *Cambridge modern history*, vol. 10 (1907), pp. 445–474, and A. Lewak, "The Polish rising of 1830," *Slavonic review* (1930).

CHAPTER 3 *The Struggle for Democratic Principles*

Revolutions of 1848. The most recent and best general survey of the revolutions of 1848 is Priscilla Robertson, *Revolutions of 1848* (1952), which contains a wealth of material from contemporary sources and devotes much attention to social history. There are also some fine chapters in *The opening of an era, 1848*, edited by F. Fejto (1948), a collection of short studies on various phases. Useful also is *A hundred years of revolution: 1848 and after*, edited by G. Woodcock (1948). There are a number of excellent short discussions of 1848 as seen from the vantage point of a century, among them: F. E. Hirsch's "The intellectuals revolution, 1848," *Current history*, n.s. vol. 14 (1948), pp. 209–213, 283–288; H. Rothfels' "1848–One hundred years after," *Journal of modern history*, vol. 20 (1948), pp. 291–319; P. Farmer's "Some Frenchmen review 1848," *ibid.*, pp. 320–325; and H. Kohn's "Mid-century: the turning-point," in his *The twentieth century* (1949), pp. 3–18. There are some interesting documents pertaining to the revolutions in R. W. Postgate. *Revolutions from 1789 to 1906* (1920). Arnold Whitridge, *Men in crisis: the revolutions of 1848* (1949), tells the story of 1848 in the form of biographical sketches of its leading characters. L. B. Namier, *1848: the revolution of the intellectuals* (1944), offers a brief critical discussion of the forces behind the revolutions; not always convincing. A. J. May, *Contemporary American opinion of the mid-century revolutions in Central Europe* (1927), is an able portrayal of the reactions on this side of the Atlantic.

Germany and Italy. Veit Valentin, *1848: chapters of German history*, translated by E. T. Scheffauer (1949), is readable, but not always satisfactory. For this period in German history A. W. Ward's *Germany, 1815–1890* (1908) remains unsurpassed as a storehouse of facts. J. G. Legge, *Rhyme and revolution in Germany* (1918), contains many interesting extracts from contemporary papers and literature. U. S. Allers, *The concept of empire in German romanticism and its influence on the national assembly at Frankfort, 1848–1849* (1948), is a competent scholarly study. On the Habsburgs there is a readable survey by A. J. P. Taylor, *The Habsburg monarchy, 1809–1918* (new ed., 1948). Jerome Blum, *Noble landowners and agriculture in Austria, 1815–1848: a study in the origins of the peasant emancipation of 1848* (1948), is a careful and significant study of the social and economic conditions in the Habsburg monarchy. For Italy there is Kent R. Greenfield's solid study, *Economics and liberalism in the risorgimento; a study of nationalism in Lombardy, 1814–1848* (1934). G. M. Trevelyan, *Manin and the Venetian revolution of 1848* (1923), is the standard account of the heroic defense of Venice against the Austrian attack. The period from 1815 to 1848 in Italian history is presented in almost minute detail in G. F. H. and J. Berkeley, *Italy in the making, 1815–1846* (1932); *Italy in the making, June, 1846, to January, 1848* (1936); *Italy in the making, January, 1848, to November, 1848* (1940); viewpoint is Roman Catholic. A. J. P. Taylor, *The Italian problem in European diplomacy, 1847–1849* (1934), shows the extent of the interest of other nations in Italy. For further references see the bibliography for Chapter Eight.

France, 1815–1848. *History of modern France, 1815–1913*, by Émile Bourgeois (2 vols., 1919), is a careful study by a distinguished French historian. J. P. Plamenatz, *The revolutionary movement in France between 1815 and 1871* (1952), traces the development of the republican and socialist groups which destroyed the French monarchy. G. L. Dickinson, *Revolution and reaction in modern France* (1892), is an illuminating little book covering the period, 1789–1871. G. Elton, *The revolutionary idea in France, 1789–1871* (1923), contains much useful material. F. B. Artz presents a vivid portrayal of the early part of the period in his *France under the Bourbon restoration, 1814–1830* (1931); emphasis is on the social and intellectual development. John B. Wolfe's *France, 1815 to the present* (1940) is a good readable survey. S. B. Clough, *History of national economics, 1789–1939* (1939), is lucid and well-written. In J. M. S. Allison, *Thiers and the French monarchy, 1797–1848* (1926), one of the foremost leaders of the period is portrayed against the background of his time. J. Lucas-Dubreton, *The restoration and the July monarchy*, translated by E. F. Buckley (1929), is a useful account which covers the intellectual and social as well as the political history of the period. An older but still useful volume is J. R. Hall, *The Bourbon restoration* (1909). C. I. Gavin's brief biography, *Louis Philippe, king of the French* (1933) is devoted largely to diplomatic affairs. Donald C. McKay, *The national workshops: a study in the French revolution of 1848* (1933) is a sound scholarly study. Louis Blanc's *History of ten years, 1830–1840* (2 vols., 1844–1845) is an account by the man who sponsored the national workshop movement. J. A. R. Marriott, *The right to work; an essay introductory to the French revolution of 1848* (1919), is an enlightening short study originally written as an introduction to an edition of Blanc's *Organisation du travail* and Émile Thomas' *Histoire des ateliers nationaux* (2 vols., 1913).

Britain, 1815–1837. Volumes One and Two of Élie Halévy's monumental *History of the English people,* translated from the French by E. I. Watkin (1924–1927), cover the period from 1815 to 1830. A shorter account is to be found in G. M. Trevelyan, *British history in the nineteenth century and after, 1782–1919* (new ed., 1937), a well-written survey. The same author's *Lord Grey and the Reform Bill* (1920) relates the movement of parliamentary reform from the French Revolution to 1832. There is a good short account of the period by H. Temperley in *The Cambridge modern history,* vol. 10 (1907), pp. 573–619. E. L. Woodward, *Age of reform, 1815–1870* (1938), is a learned and impartial survey. For further references see the bibliography for Chapter Eleven.

CHAPTER 4 *The Coming of the Machine*

Britain. Judith B. Williams, *A guide to the printed materials for English social and economic history, 1750–1850* (2 vols., 1926), is invaluable. Two other useful bibliographies are H. L. Beales and G. D. H. Cole, *A select list of books on economic and social history, 1700–1850* (1927), and E. Power, *The industrial revolution, 1750–1850: a select bibliography* (1927). P. Mantoux, *The industrial revolution in the eighteenth century* (1938), sketches the background of nineteenth-century developments. T. S. Ashton, *The industrial revolution, 1760–1830* (1948), is a short, skillfully-written survey. An older, well-balanced discussion is to be found in L. C. A. Knowles, *The industrial and commercial revolutions in Great Britain during the nineteenth century* (4th rev. ed., 1926). For Britain there is also the valuable work of J. H. Clapham, *Economic history of modern Britain* (vol. 1, 2nd ed., 1931). Much eighteenth-century background is presented in Ivor B. Hart, *James Watt and the history of steam power* (1949). Early factory legislation is ably discussed in M. W. Thomas, *The early factory legislation: a study in legislative and administrative evolution* (1948). L. S. Marshall, *The development of public opinion in Manchester, 1780–1820* (1946), offers a detailed study of one of the early industrial centers. Still valuable is M. C. Buer, *Health, wealth, and population in the early days of the industrial revolution* (1926). G. D. H. Cole, *A short history of the British working class movement* (vol. 1, 1925), is a standard work by a British economist. The condition of the English working classes is described in dark colors in the three volumes of J. L. and Barbara Hammond: *The village labourer, 1760–1832* (2nd ed., 1920); *The skilled labourer, 1760–1823* (1919); and *The town labourer, 1760–1832: the* *new civilization* (new ed., 1950). The entire story of man's technological accomplishments is surveyed in R. J. Forbes, *Man the maker: a history of technology and engineering* (1950). For the eighteenth-century background in France there is an able study by S. T. McCloy, *French inventions of the eighteenth century* (1952).

Agriculture. The student will find much sound information on English agriculture in R. E. Prothero, *English farming past and present* (4th ed., 1932), and W. Hasbach, *History of the English agricultural labourer* (1908). Henry C. Taylor, *Decline of land-owning farmers in England* (1904), tells the story of the growth of tenant farming in the nineteenth century. For a more general survey there is Lord Ernle, *English farming, past and present* (1912).

France and Germany. A. L. Dunham, "The economic history of France, 1815–1870," *Journal of modern history*, vol. 21 (1949), pp. 121–139, is a valuable critical discussion of important works on the period. One of the best single works is J. H. Clapham, *The economic development of France and Germany, 1815–1914* (3rd ed., 1928).

CHAPTER 5 *The Birth of Modern Socialism*

Pre-Marxian socialism. J. O. Hertzler, *History of utopian thought* (1926), offers good accounts of the various utopian systems and movements. A. Shadwell, *The socialist movement, 1824–1924* (1925), is a clear, succinct account of the origin, meaning, and progress of socialism. Sally Graves, *A history of socialism* (1939), gives a fairly detailed account of the movement in the various European countries. There is a good account of French utopian Socialism in T. Kirkup, *History of socialism* (rev. ed., 1913). S. F. Markham, *History of socialism* (1930), is a useful survey. N. Mackenzie, *Socialism* (1950), surveys the entire movement in less than 200 pages. C. E. Raven, *Christian socialism, 1848–1854* (1920), is a masterly account of the movement associated with the names of Maurice and Kingsley. Donald O. Wagner, *Social reformers* (1934), contains excerpts from the works of the utopian socialists. *Backwoods utopias: the sectarian and Owenite phases of communitarian socialism in America, 1663–1829*, by A. E. Bestor, Jr. (1950), contains an interesting account of the Owenite movement. E. M. Butler, *The Saint-Simonian religion in Germany* (1926), is a worthwhile study of the Young Germany movement. There are a number of good biographies of Owen. The oldest and still one of the best is that by F. Podmore (new ed., 1923). G. D. H. Cole, *Robert Owen* (1925), is a valuable and well-informed biography. R. W. Leopold, *Robert Dale Owen* (1940), is scholarly, objective, well-written and intelligent. *The life of Robert Owen* by himself (1920) is a brief worthwhile autobiography.

Marx and marxism. The literature on Marx and marxism is so voluminous that only a very few titles can be listed here. Franz Mehring's *Karl Marx, the story of his life*, translated from the German (1936), is by many marxists regarded as the standard life in English; to be used with caution. More impartial is *Karl Marx, man and fighter* by B. Nicolaievsky and O. Maenchen-Helfen, translated from the German (1936). L. Schwarzschild's *The red Prussian: the life and legend of Karl Marx* (1947) is a highly critical account of the public life and character of Marx, written with gusto. Jacques Barzun in his *Darwin, Marx, Wagner: critique of a heritage* (1941) discusses the three as the fashioners of much of the "mechanical materialism" that has characterized western thought. E. H. Carr's *Karl Marx: a study in fanaticism* (1934) is a good, not unsympathetic short life. There is a good brief biography of Marx in the Home University Library by Isaiah Berlin (1939), and an even shorter one in *Some makers of the modern spirit,* edited by J. Macmurray (1933). In *What Marx really meant,* by G. D. H. Cole (1934), a British historian puts down his interpretation of various controversial statements in the writings of Marx. Sidney Hook's *Toward the understanding of Karl Marx* (1933) is enlightening, but at times abstruse. H. W. Laidler, *A history of socialist thought* (1933), contains several chapters on Marxian theory, but is somewhat pro-Marxist. *A handbook of Marxism,* edited by E. Burns (1935), is a collection of extracts from the writings of Marx, Engels, and other communist writers; a comprehensive and representative selection. Max Eastman, *Marxism, is it science?* (1940), tells what Marxism is and what is the matter with it. *Karl Marx's interpretation of history,* by M. M. Bober (2nd rev. ed., 1948), is one of the best guides to Marx in English. S. F. Bloom, *The world of nations: a study of the national implications in the work of Karl Marx* (1941), contains a wealth of reflection and research in a small compass; the conclusion is that Marx was not a nationalist. G. M. Stekloff, *History of the First International,* translated by E. and C. Paul (1928), is the most comprehensive history of the subject in English; sympathetic to communism. *The economic interpretation of history* by Henri E. See, translated by M. M. Knight (1929), is an able discussion by an outstanding historian. K. Federn, *The materialist conception of history* (1940), subjects this conception to a critical examination. H. W. B. Joseph, *The labor theory of value in Karl Marx* (1923), is an enlightening volume.

Socialism in individual countries. M. Beer, *History of British socialism* (2 vols., 1929), is the most complete account and one of the best. A. B. Ulam's *Philosophical foundations of English socialism* (1951) is an able performance of a difficult task. *The history of the Fabian society,* by E. R. Pease (1925), is the most complete history of the Fabians. George Bernard Shaw as one of the leading members of the society wrote a tract in 1892 entitled *The Fabian society: its early history* (1892). S. Bernstein, *The beginnings of Marxian socialism in France* (1933), is based on a careful study of the sources. H. R. Weinstein, *Jean Jaurès: a study of patriotism in the French socialist movement* (1936), is a well-documented study of the career and political beliefs of the socialist leader. Henri de Lubac, *The un-Marxian socialist: a study of Proudhon,* translated by R. E. Scantlebury (1948), is a revaluation of the social and political ideas of Proudhon. The student will find W. H. Dawson's *German socialism and Ferdinand Lassalle* (1888) useful despite its age. David Footman, *Ferdinand Lassalle: romantic revolutionary* (1947), lays particular stress on Lassalle's relationship with Marx. E. H. Carr's *Michael Bakunin* (1937) is a first-rate biography.

CHAPTER 6 *The Age of Romanticism*

Romanticism. A good introduction to the period is to be found in R. B. Mowat, *The romantic age: Europe in the early nineteenth century* (1937). H. N. Fairchild, *The noble savage: a study in romantic naturalism* (1928), is the fullest and most useful account of the subject in English. *The romantic quest* (1931) by the same author contains discussions of naturalism, medievalism, and transcendentalism. I Babbitt's *Rousseau and romanticism* (1919) traces the rise and growth of the idea of romanticism; is anti-Rousseau and often undiscerning in its criticisms. As an antidote there is J. Barzun, *Romanticism and the modern ego* (1943), which regards romanticism as being essentially realistic rather than escapist. E. Bernbaum, *Guide through the romantic movement* (2nd rev. ed., 1949), deals principally with England, but contains discussions on the meaning and scope of romanticism. *Random studies in the romatic chaos,* by F. A. Waterhouse (1923), contains some interesting analyses of the romantic mind. J. G. Robertson, *Studies in the genesis of romantic theory in the eighteenth century* (1923), discusses the influence of Italy on the rise of romanticism.

Literary romanticism. The literature on this phase of romanticism is so voluminous that only a very small part of it can be listed. There are useful studies on the early phase of romanticism in the various countries, as for example: *The origins of French romanticism* by M. B. Finch and E. A. Peers (1920); *Early German romanticism; its founders and Heinrich von Kleist* by Walter Silz (1929); and *The origins of the romantic movement in Spain* by Ivy L. McClelland (1937). Malcolm Elwin's *The first romantics* (1948) is a solid and lively account of the early phases of the literary movement in Britain. Two important volumes on English romanticism are H. A. Beers, *A history of English romanticism in the eighteenth century* (1932) and *A history of English romanticism in the nineteenth century* (1929). Rich discussions of the last phases of English romanticism are to be found in G. G. Hough, *The last romantics* (1950), and F. L. Lucas, *The decline and fall of the romantic ideal* (1936). C. Brinton, *The political ideas of the English romanticists* (1926), is a spirited and provocative study. *French romantic plays,* edited by W. W. Comfort (1933), and *The French romanticists, an anthology of verse and prose,* edited by H. F. Stewart and A. Tilley (1931), present actual examples of romantic literature. N. H. Clement, *Romanticism in France* (1939), is a good general survey. Of the many books on Victor Hugo the student will find E. M. Grant, *The career of Victor Hugo* (1945), and Matthew Josephson, *Victor Hugo* (1942), useful and authoritative. E. A. Peers, *A history of the romantic movement in Spain* (2 vols., 1940), is the definitive work on the subject in English. A. Cippico, *The romantic age in Italian literature* (1918), is a brief informative survey. Brief surveys of German romanticism are to be found in L. A. Willoughby, *The romantic movement in Germany* (1930); K. H. Breul, *The romantic movement in German literature* (1927); and A. W. Porterfield, *An outline of German romanticism, 1766–1866* (1914). Selections from German romantic authors may be read in *Fiction and fantasy of German romance, 1790–1830,* edited by F. E. Pierce and C. Schreiber (1927). The treatment in O. F. Walzel, *German romanticism,* translated by A. E. Lussky (1932), is philosophical rather than factual and presupposes some acquaintance with the subject.

Music. A. Einstein, *Music in the romantic era* (1947), is the best survey. Another good survey is D. G. Mason, *The romantic composers* (1926). A. W. Locke, *Music and the romantic movement in France* (1921), contains a series of suggestive essays. G. Grove, *Beethoven, Schubert, Mendelssohn* (1952), offers three essays by a well-known musical authority. Among the best biographies of Schumann are those by H. Bedford (1925), J. Chissell (1948), and R. H. Schauffler (1945). A. Einstein, *Schubert* (1951), is a parallel volume to the same author's excellent life of Beethoven. *The music of Schubert,* edited by G. Abraham (1947), is a symposium by a group of music critics. H. Weinstock, *Chopin: the man and his music* (1949), is an exhaustive study. An appreciation of Mendelssohn's contribution to music is to be found in J. Erskine, *Song without words: the story of Felix Mendelssohn* (1941). Two informative short biographies of Berlioz are those by W. J. Turner (1934) and T. S. Wotton (1935). J. Barzun, *Berlioz and the romantic century* (2 vols., 1950), is a monumental attempt to place Berlioz in a just relationship to the society with which he was so often in collision. E. Newman's *The man Liszt* (1934) is a study by a distinguished music critic. R. Hill, *Liszt* (1936), is a good brief biography. Short biographies of many of the romantic composers are to be found in *The men behind the music,* edited by C. H. Warren (1931).

Architecture and painting. In *Romanticism and the Gothic revival* (1938) Agnes E. Anderson surveys the Gothic revival in England, France, Germany, and the United States. Kenneth Clark, *The Gothic revival* (1928), is a charming book which traces the origins of the movement and its relations with literary romanticism. There is also an account of the Gothic revival in T. F. Hamlin, *Architecture through the ages* (1940), which is probably the best one-volume history of architecture in English. In *Modern painting, a study of tendencies* (1927) F. J. Mather presents entertaining and instructive summaries of schools and tendencies. Probably the best short volume of its kind is E. Newton, *Introduction to European painting* (rev. ed., 1949). An excellent treatment of art in England is to be found in T. E. Welby, *The Victorian romantics, 1850–1870* (1929). A. Comfort, *Art and social responsibility* (1946), is a series of lectures on the ideology of romanticsm.

CHAPTER 7 *The Second Empire in France*

Napoleon III. For an excellent review of the literature on Napoleon III which had appeared up to that time see R. Schnerb, "Napoleon III and the second French empire," *Journal of modern history,* vol. VIII (1936), pp. 338–355. The story of the Napoleonic legend has been ably told by A. Guerard in *The Napoleonic legend* (1924). The same author has also written *Napoleon III: an interpretation* (1943), one of the most interesting interpretations of the man and his rule. F. A. Simpson, *The rise of Louis Napoleon* (3rd ed., 1950), is a well-written account. *Louis Napoleon and the recovery of France, 1848–1856* (new ed. 1952) by the same author, is based on a careful study of much unpublished material. Probably the best account of the period is to be found in Octave Aubry's *Second empire,* translated by A. Livingston (1940). In a somewhat lighter vein there is P. Guedalla's witty and incisive account, *The second empire: Bonapartism, the prince, the president, the emperor* (1922). *The secret of the coup d'état,* edited by Earl of Kerry and P. Guedalla (1924), gives some interesting sidelights on Napoleon III. F. C. Palm, *England and Napoleon III: a study of the rise of a utopian dictator* (1948) is a revealing brief study dealing in the main with the attitude of the British government toward the establishment of the second empire. Rita Wellmann's *Eugénie* (1948) is distinguished by perspicacity, wit, and good organization. E. Corti, *Maximilian and Charlotte of Mexico* (2 vols., 1929), tells the story of the ill-fated Mexican venture.

Crimean War. V. J. Puryear, "New light on the origins of the Crimean War," *Journal of modern history,* vol. 3 (1931), pp. 219–234, has a self-explanatory title. Much

valuable information is to be found in a longer study by the same author, *England,
Russia, and the Straits question, 1844–1856* (1931). C. E. Vulliamy, *Crimea: the campaign of 1854–1856* (1939), is a useful study by a British historian. Another useful volume
is G. F. MacMunn, *The Crimea in perspective* (1935). B. K. Martin, *Triumph of Lord
Palmerston: a study of public opinion in England before the Crimean War* (1924) shows
how Britain became involved in the war. C. Woodham-Smith, *Florence Nightingale*
(1951), is a biography of the first order, based on much new material. H. Temperley,
"The treaty of Paris of 1856 and its execution," *Journal of modern history,* vol. 4 (1932),
pp. 387–414, 523–543, is an enlightening discussion.

Literature and art. There is a good short discussion of Balzac in Y. Lavrin, *Studies
in European literature* (1929). A longer critical discussion is to be found in E. P. Dargan,
Honoré de Balzac (1932). R. P. Bowen, *The dramatic construction of Balzac's novel*
(1940), is an enlightening study. Émile Faguet, *Balzac,* translated by W. Thorley (1914),
is an acutely critical study of the man and his work. S. Zweig, *Balzac,* translated by
William and Dorothy Rose (1946), is an enthusiastic biography, largely on the personal
side. F. Steegmuller, *Flaubert and Madame Bovary* (2nd rev. ed., 1951), presents an
absorbing account of Flaubert's development working up to a climax in the story of the
inception and completion of his masterpiece. Émile Faguet, *Flaubert,* translated by Mrs.
R. L. Devonshire (1914), describes Flaubert and his work in superlatives. There is an informing essay on Flaubert in G. Brandes, *Creative spirits of the nineteenth century*
(1923). Corot and Millet are ably discussed in F. Gibson, *Six French artists of the nineteenth century* (1925). A. Hoeber, *The Barbizon painters* (1915), discusses the entire
school at greater length. C. S. Smith, *Barbizon days* (1902), is an interesting account of
the period. Julia M. Ady, *Jean François Millet* (1896), is a careful comprehensive study
of the man and his work. *Courbet and the naturalistic movement,* edited by George Boas
(1938), is a series of essays by a group of art critics. There is a full-length biography
of Courbet by G. Mack (1951).

CHAPTER 8 *The Triumph of Nationalism in Italy
and Germany*

Background of the Risorgimento. The best of the more recent surveys of Italian
history is R. Albrecht-Carrie, *Italy from Napoleon to Mussolini* (1949). A. J. Whyte's
Evolution of modern Italy, 1715–1920 (1950) is a well-done survey that is particularly
good on the Risorgimento period. The preparatory period of Italian nationalism is ably
surveyed in E. P. Noether, *Seeds of Italian nationalism, 1700–1815* (1951). Gaudens
Megaro's *Vittorio Alfieri, forerunner of Italian nationalism* (1930) is a competent scholarly study. Another scholarly study of one phase of the rising nationalism is Kent R.
Greenfield's *Economics and liberalism in the Risorgimento; a study of nationalism in
Lombardy, 1815–1848* (1934).

Risorgimento. G. F. H. Berkeley has written a monumental work on the Risorgimento
in his *Italy in the making* (3 vols., 1932–1940). Still useful among the older books are
A. Solmi, *The making of modern Italy* (1925), and Bolton King, *History of Italian unity*

(2 vols., 2nd ed., 1912). Well-written but in some respects superseded are the three volumes by G. M. Trevelyan: *Garibaldi's defence of the Roman republic* (1907), *Garibaldi and the thousand* (1909), and *Garibaldi and the making of Italy* (1911). Older but still useful is W. R. Thayer's *Dawn of Italian independence* (2 vols., 1892). The same author's *Life and times of Cavour* (2 vols., 1911) is a work of solid scholarship. There is a stimulating essay on Mazzini in H. Kohn, *Prophets and peoples* (1946). Probably the two best biographies of Mazzini in English are those by G. Salvemini (1925) and S. Barr (1935). Bolton King's *Life of Mazzini* (1911) can still be read with profit. G. O. Griffith's *Mazzini, prophet of modern Europe* (1932) is a successful attempt to portray the inner life of the Italian patriot. The writings of Mazzini have appeared in a number of English editions. Particularly noteworthy is *The living thoughts of Mazzini*, edited by I. Silone (1939). P. Frischauer's *Garibaldi, the man and the nation* (1935) is an entertaining but somewhat romanticized biography. Not to be overlooked are *The memoirs of Garibaldi*, translated by R. S. Garnett (1931). D. R. Larg's *Garibaldi* (1934) is a good popular biography. *The last days of Papal Rome, 1850–1870*, by R. de Cesare (1909), is an informative volume. The history of the papacy has been ably written by F. K. Nielsen, a Danish Protestant, in *The history of the papacy in the nineteenth century* (2 vols., 1906).

Germany. J. A. R. Marriott and C. G. Robertson, *Evolution of Prussia: the making of an empire* (1915), is still the best survey of Prussian history. There are two good monographs on the Zollverein in English: W. O. Henderson, *The zollverein* (1939), and A. H. Price, *The evolution of the zollverein; a study of the ideas and institutions leading to German economic unification between 1815 and 1833* (1949). The monumental work on German unification is Heinrich von Sybel, *The founding of the German empire by William I*, translated by M. L. Perrin (7 vols., 1890–1898); readable, but has a strong Prussian bias. The story of the contest between Prussia and Austria is ably told in H. Friedjung's *The struggle for supremacy in Germany, 1859–1866*, translated by A. J. P. Taylor and W. L. McElwee (1935). C. W. Clark, *Franz Joseph and Bismarck: the diplomacy of Austria before the war of 1866* (1934), is an important contribution. An older short but informative volume is Munroe Smith, *Bismarck and German unity* (3rd rev. ed., 1923). P. Wiegler, *William the First*, translated by C. Vesey (1929), is a detailed scholarly work. R. H. Lord, *The origins of the war of 1870* (1924), is still the best treatment of the subject in English. For a good critical discussion of books that appeared before 1934 see C. W. Clark, "The foreign policy of Prussia, 1858–1871," *Journal of modern history*, vol. 6 (1934), pp. 444–450. See also the bibliography for Chapter Ten.

CHAPTER 9 *The Third Republic in France*

Third republic. R. A. Winnacker, "The third French republic, 1870–1914," *Journal of modern history*, vol. 10 (1938), pp. 372–409, is an excellent critical discussion of pertinent literature. *The beginning of the third republic* by F. H. Brabant (1940) is an urbanely-written history of a few momentous months (Feb.–Sept., 1871). H. M. Stannard, *Gambetta and the founding of the third republic* (1921), contains a useful account of political and military affairs. The political system of the Third Republic is ably described in H. G. Daniels, *The framework of France* (1937), and W. L. Middleton, *The*

French political system (1932). *The French parliamentary committee system* by R. K. Gooch (1935) is a valuable monograph based on a careful study of official documents. W. Hale, *The third republic from Sedan to Vichy* (1941), is a successful attempt to "show the average American what France was like." P. Farmer, *France reviews its revolutionary origins: social politics and historical opinion in the third republic* (1944), is an important contribution toward a better understanding of the period. D. W. Brogan, *France under the republic; the development of modern France, 1870–1939* (1940), is a stimulating volume written with clarity and insight. J. Bainville, *The French republic, 1870–1935,* translated by H. Miles (1936), is a readable survey by a noted French historian. John B. Wolfe, *France: 1815 to the present* (1940), is a successful survey of political and cultural history. *The story of modern France, 1610–1914* by J. G. Coulter (1939) is an unassuming but lucid narrative. R. H. Soltau, *French political thought in the nineteenth century* (1931) is impartial and thoroughly documented. J. P. Mayer, *Political thought in France: from the revolution to the fourth republic* (1949), is a readable and informing survey.

The economic history of the period is ably surveyed in S. B. Clough, *France, a history of national economics, 1789–1939* (1939). For social history there is A. D. Vandam's *Men and manners of the third republic* (1904). *The civilisation of France* by E. R. Curtius, translated by O. Wyon (1932), is a highly informative as well as sympathetic account of French civilization. R. Recouly, *The third republic* (1928), is a readable survey which devotes special attention to foreign and colonial policy. The machinery of foreign policy is subjected to a careful analysis in F. L. Schuman, *War and diplomacy in the French republic* (1931). E. M. Carroll, *French public opinion and foreign affairs, 1870–1914* (1931), is a careful and logical analysis of the relationship between public opinion and foreign policy; comprehensive and readable. *Religious thought in France in the nineteenth century* by W. J. Simpson (1935) is an able survey by a leading British clergyman. C. S. Phillips, *The church in France, 1848–1907* (1936), is a judicious and authoritative volume. C. J. H. Hayes, *France, a nation of patriots* (1930), is a revealing study of patriotic propaganda.

Special studies. M. Kranzberg, *Siege of Paris, 1870–1871* (1950), is a valuable scholarly study of the political and social history of the Paris Commune. Two other important volumes are: E. S. Mason's *Paris commune* (1930) and F. Jellinek's *Paris commune of 1871* (1937). J. P. T. Bury, *Gambetta and the national defence* (1936), is a careful and impartial study of Gambetta's career. There is a good biography of Gambetta by Paul Deschanel, translated into English (1920). J. Kayser, *The Dreyfus affair* (1931), is an informative volume but not always impartial. B. Schwertfeger, *The truth about Dreyfus* (1931) tells much of the truth, but not all of it. *The Dreyfus case* by Alfred Dreyfus and his son Pierre, translated and edited by D. C. McKay (1937), tells the story in a simple, concise way. L. M. Friedman, *Zola and the Dreyfus case* (1937), is a brief presentation of the facts regarding Zola's connection with the case. R. F. Byrnes, *Antisemitism in modern France,* vol. 1: *Prologue to the Dreyfus affair* (1951), is a well-written volume based on a careful study of the sources. On Clemenceau there is the well-written biography by Geoffrey Bruun (1943). J. H. Jackson's *Clemenceau and the third republic* (1948) is a brief, readable and interpretative biography in the Teach Yourself History Library. W. Williams, *Tiger of France* (1949), is a vivid biography by an American newspaper man who knew Clemenceau personally.

French literature. There are a number of good histories of French literature, among them W. A. Nitze, *A history of French literature from the earliest times to the present* (rev. ed., 1927), and G. E. B. Saintsbury, *A short history of French literature* (7th ed., 1937). Denis Saurat, *French literature, 1870–1940* (1946), is a stimulating up-to-date survey. There are lucid and well-written essays on Zola, Maupassant, and Anatole France in P. D. Bâcourt and J. W. Cunliffe, *French literature during the last half-century* (1923). E. A. Boyd's *Maupassant* (1926) is a straightforward study of the twisted personality of the brilliant story-teller. *Maupassant: a lion in the path,* by Francis Steegmuller (1949), is an acute and sympathetic biography which proves that many stories generally accepted as Maupassant's are really fakes. M. Josephson's *Zola and his time* (1928) is a vigorous and absorbing biography, but is oversympathetic. In *Émile Zola: an introductory study of his novels* (1952) A. Wilson endeavors to accord to Zola his rightful place in literary history. Still a valuable treatment of Zola's life and work is E. A. Vizetelly's *Émile Zola* (1904). J Axelrad, *Anatole France, a life without illusions* (1944), is a competent and comprehensive chronicle of the man and his work.

Painting and sculpture. R. H. Wilenski, *French painting* (1931), is a stimulating survey. *Masters of modern art,* by Walter Pach (1924), discusses the masters who gave a new direction to the evolution of painting — in the nineteenth century they were all French. There is a brilliant summary of French painting in G. Mourey's *French art in the nineteenth century* (1928). C. L. Borgmeyer, *The master impressionists* (1913), is a lucid account with a plethora of illustrations. Roger E. Fry, *Characteristics of French art* (1932), is a lucid discussion by a noted art historian. There are also a number of good biographies on each of the artists and sculptors.

Music. In his *Five great French composers* (1946) Donald Brook portrays the lives and discusses the works of César Franck, Saint-Saëns, Debussy, and others. Franck and Debussy are also discussed in Neville Cardus, *Ten composers* (1945). The composers Franck and Saint-Saëns and their art are ably treated in D. G. Mason's *From Grieg to Brahms* (1927). An older but still useful survey is A. Hervey, *Masters of French music* (1894). Rollo H. Myers, *Debussy* (1948), is a good brief biography. Two good fuller biographies are: O. Thompson, *Debussy, man and artist* (1937), and L. Vallas, *Claude Debussy; his life and works,* translated from the French (1933). There is a good short life of Saint-Saëns by A. Hervey (1921). W. Lyle, *Camille Saint-Saëns; his life and art* (1923), is a fuller treatment — judicious and interesting. For Bizet there is a good brief biography by Martin Cooper (1938) and a fuller one by Winton Dean (1948). N. Demuth, *César Franck* (1949), is a vivid account of Franck, his music, and his contemporaries.

CHAPTER 10 *Hohenzollern Germany*

Bismarck. The best and most up-to-date biography of the Iron Chancellor is Erich Eyck's *Bismarck and the German empire* (1950), a skillful summary of the author's three-volume work published in German. Although it was published many years ago C. G. Robertson's *Bismarck* (1918) is still useful; written from a British viewpoint. The same is true of J. W. Headlam-Morley's *Bismarck* (3rd edition, 1922). Emil Ludwig's *Bismarck;*

the story of a fighter, translated by Eden and Cedar Paul (1927), is a readable popular biography. Bismarck's memoirs translated under the title of *Bismarck, the man and the statesman* (2 vols., 1898) are valuable for an understanding of both the man and the statesman. P. B. Mitchell, *The Bismarckian policy of conciliation with France, 1875–1885* (1935), is a scholarly study based on official documents; shows how Bismarck tried to win the good will of France. Bismarckian diplomacy is ably discussed in W. L. Langer, *European alliances and alignments, 1871–1890* (1931). *Bismarck's diplomacy at its zenith* by J. V. Fuller (1922) carefully points out the weak spots in Bismarck's diplomacy. W. O. Aydelotte, *Bismarck and British colonial policy; the problem of Southwest Africa, 1883–1885* (1937), and A. J. P. Taylor, *Germany's first bid for colonies* (1938), are two worthwhile volumes.

William II. E. Ludwig, *Wilhelm Hohenzollern, the last of the kaisers* (1927), is a diatribe rather than a balanced study of a complex personality. One of the best brief sketches of William II is to be found in S. C. Hammer, *William the Second* (1917); based on contemporary documents and the kaiser's speeches. *The German emperor as shown in his public utterances,* edited by C. Gauss (1915), is a skillful compilation of selections from the kaiser's speeches. The memoirs of William II are available in English in a translation by T. R. Ybarra under the title *Wilhelm II, my memoirs, 1878–1918* (1922).

Germany, 1870–1914. For the political history of the period there are many surveys. Among the older ones that are still useful there is H. Lichtenberger, *Germany and its evolution in modern times,* translated from the French by A. M. Ludovici (1913); also valuable for German culture. G. P. Gooch, *Germany, 1848–1918* (1925), is a readable survey by a distinguished British historian. More recently a number of surveys have been published, the best being that by A. J. P. Taylor, *The course of German history: a survey of the development of Germany since 1815* (1946). Other useful surveys are: G. N. Schuster and A. Bergstraesser, *Germany* (1944); V. Valentin, *The German people* (1936); K. F. Reinhardt, *Germany* (1950); and S. H. Steinberg, *A short history of Germany* (1945). H. von Loewenstein, *The Germans in history* (1945), traces the development of the German people to Hitler. Lysbeth W. Muncy, *The Junker in the Prussian administration under William II, 1888–1914* (1944), is sound, readable and enlightening. R. Emerson, *State and sovereignty in modern Germany, 1871–1928* (1929), is a readable and thoroughgoing analysis.

Two of the older surveys of the economic development are J. H. Clapham, *The economic development of France and Germany, 1815–1914* (1921), and W. H. Dawson, *The German empire, 1867–1914* (2 vols., 1919). The latter author has also published other important scholarly works including *The evolution of modern Germany* (2nd ed., 1918), *Industrial Germany* (1912), *Bismarck and state socialism* (2nd ed., 1891), and *Social insurance in Germany 1883–1911* (1911). A more recent valuable survey is G. Stolper, *German economy, 1870–1940* (1940). The development of German economic life is ably surveyed in W. F. Bruck's *Social and economic history of Germany from William II to Hitler, 1888–1938* (1938). In *German agrarian politics after Bismarck's fall* (1952) Sarah R. Tirrell presents an illuminating exposition of the German agricultural problem in the reign of William II. R. H. Lowie, *The German people: a social portrait to 1914* (1945), is a worthwhile little volume.

Culture. Jethro Bithell's *Modern German literature, 1880–1938* (1940) is indispensable for information about German writers in the period it covers. J. Lavrin, *Nietzsche* (1948), is a good short biography. *Nietzsche* by H. A. Reyburn, in collaboration with H. E. Hinderks and J. G. Taylor (1948), is a first-rate full biography. W. A. Kaufmann's *Nietzsche: philosopher, psychologist, antichrist* (1951) is a masterly reappraisal of the weird genius. So many works have appeared on Richard Wagner during the last two decades that only a few can be listed. Sir Wm. H. Hadow's *Richard Wagner* (1934) is a good brief biography in the Home University series. Two important longer biographies are those of E. Newman (2 vols., 1937) and G. A. Hight (2 vols., 1925). M. Boucher's *Political concepts of Richard Wagner,* translated from the French by M. Honoré (1952), shows how the Nazis used and distorted Wagner's ideas. *The racial thinking of Richard Wagner* by Leon Stein (1950) discusses Wagner's ideas on Volk, Kultur, language, and music — and their influence.

CHAPTER 11 *The Growth of Democracy in Great Britain*

Britain in the nineteenth century. R. A. Evans, *The Victorian age, 1815–1914* (1950), is an excellent example of historical condensation and evaluation, despite some oversimplification. G. Smith, *A history of England* (1949), is a clear and readable survey with a particularly good account of the nineteenth century. G. M. Trevelyan's well-written *British history in the nineteenth century* (1922) is still valuable. An older but still useful volume is J. A. R. Marriott, *England since Waterloo* (1913). Volume 3 (1950) of E. Halévy's monumental *History of the English people* has the title *The triumph of reform* and is invaluable. R. H. Gretton's *Modern history of the English people, 1880–1922* (3 vols., 1930; one vol. ed., 1932) is a mine of facts about the period. An illuminating account of the earlier period is to be found in G. M. Young, *Early Victorian England, 1830–1865* (2 vols., 1935). J. W. Dodds, *The age of paradox: a biography of England, 1841–1851* (1952), is an uninhibited, entertaining story of a decade of English life. R. H. Gretton's *Victorian sunset* (1932) dispels many myths regarding the period. A. L. Lowell, *The government of England* (new ed., 2 vols., 1912), is still useful for the nineteenth century. G. B. Adams, *Constitutional history of England* (1921), is a penetrating survey which assumes some knowledge of political history. I. Jennings, *The British constitution* (3rd ed., 1950), is an illuminating volume. G. L. Haskins, *The growth of English representative government* (1948), is a series of clear, well-organized lectures. British foreign policy is presented by a group of specialists in *Cambridge modern history of foreign policy, 1783–1919* (3 vols., 1922–1923). Crane Brinton's *English political thought in the nineteenth century* (2nd ed., 1949) is a well-written and intelligent summary of English political philosophy during the period. H. D. Traill and J. S. Mann, *Social England* (6 vols. in 12, 1901–1904), is a storehouse of information; also published under the title, *Building of Britain and the empire* (1909). M. and C. H. B. Quennell, *History of everyday things in England* (4 vols., 1930–1934), tells the all-around story of the changes which took place in the period. Helen M. Lynd, *England in the eighteen-eighties: toward a social basis for freedom* (1945), is a meaty, skillfully done, and authoritative volume. C. J. H. Hayes, *British social politics* (1913), contains extracts from parliamentary debates regarding social legislation. *The British people, 1746–1946* by G. D. H. Cole and R. Postgate (1947) is a history of the British working classes written with a socialistic slant.

Economic and social history. F. C. Dietz, *An economic history of England* (1942), is a sound and readable survey. Two older but still valuable surveys are: A. P. Usher, *Introduction to the industrial history of England* (rev. ed., 1920), and W. Cunningham, *Growth of English industry and commerce* (6th rev. ed., 2 vols. in 3, 1915–1921). J. H. Clapham, *An economic history of modern Britain* (3 vols., 1932–1938), is a masterpiece of research which carries the story to 1914. L. H. Jenks, *The migration of capital to 1875* (1927), is a solid study of British financial expansion. A. L. Bowley, *Wages and income in the United Kingdom since 1860* (1937), is indispensable to an understanding of working-class history. P. Blanchard, *Outline of the British labor movement* (1923), is a good account of the beginnings of the origins of the Labor movement. G. D. H. Cole, *Short history of the British working class movement* (3 vols., 1927), is a useful account colored by the author's advocacy of guild socialism. R. Wearmouth, *Some working-class movements of the nineteenth century* (1948), contains an interesting discussion of Chartism. S. Maccoby, *English radicalism, 1853–1886* (1938), is a painstaking scholarly study.

Biographical studies. L. Strachey's *Queen Victoria* (1921) is a vivid readable biography. H. Bolitho, *The reign of Queen Victoria* (1948), is largely a personal biography engagingly written. The same author had also written *Albert the good and the Victorian reign* (1928). P. Crabites, *Victoria's guardian angel: a study of Baron Stockmar* (1938), is an interesting biography of the man who exercised a profound influence on the queen. The period of the queen's life up to her marriage is covered in D. Creston, *The youthful Queen Victoria* (1952), a book of scrupulous scholarship. W. F. Monypenny and G. E. Buckle, *Life of Benjamin Disraeli* (6 vols., 1910–1920), is a classic to which all more recent biographies are deeply indebted. Among the better short lives of Disraeli one must include H. Pearson's *Dizzy* (1951) and A. Maurois, *D'Israeli, a picture of the Victorian age* (1928). J. Morley, *The life of William Evart Gladstone* (3 vols., 1903), is a monumental authoritative work. W. P. Hall's *Mr. Gladstone* (1931) is a well-informed biography. *The queen and Mr. Gladstone* by P. Guedalla (1934) is a sparkling study by a noted British historian. P. Knaplund, *Gladstone and Britain's imperial policy* (1927), and F. W. Hirst, *Gladstone as a financier and an economist* (1931), are important studies of certain aspects of Gladstone's life. R. W. Seton-Watson, *Disraeli, Gladstone and the eastern question* (1935), and J. L. Hammond, *Gladstone and the Irish nation* (1938), are comprehensive, scholarly studies. *British prime ministers of the nineteenth century: policies and speeches* by J. H. Park (1951) contains valuable selections from important speeches with enlightening brief comments. Sir Sidney Lee, *King Edward VII* (2 vols., 1925–1927), is the official life based on a careful study of the records.

Ireland. E. Barker, *Ireland in the last fifty years, 1866–1916* (rev. ed., 1919), contains much useful information. There is a fair and full presentation of the Irish problem in E. R. Turner, *England and Ireland in the past* (1919). S. L. Gwynn, *History of Ireland* (1923), is written from the Irish nationalist standpoint. Sir James O'Connor, *History of Ireland, 1798–1924* (2 vols., 1925), is valuable despite its nationalist sympathies. *A history of Ireland under the union, 1801–1922* by P. S. O'Hegarty (1952) is an authoritative, swiftly moving narrative with voluminous quotations from the sources. N. D.

Palmer, *The Irish land league crisis* (1940), is a scholarly treatise dealing with the movement against landlordism, 1879–1881. W. H. McNeill, "The introduction of the potato into Ireland," *Journal of modern history,* vol. 21 (1949), pp. 218–222, is an interesting short discussion.

Victorian culture. M. J. Quinlan, *Victorian prelude: a history of English manners, 1700–1830* (1941), is an important study of the intellectual antecedents of Victorianism. *The nineteenth century and after* by S. C. Chew (1950) offers a fresh account of English literary history. *The reinterpretation of Victorian literature,* edited by J. E. Barker (1950), refutes many of the standard views. There are a number of good biographies of Elizabeth and Robert Browning, among the more recent ones D. Hewlett, *Elizabeth Barrett Browning* (1952), and B. Miller, *Robert Browning* (1953). There is much new material on Tennyson in the biography by his grandson, *Sir Charles Tennyson* (1949). Another informative volume is P. F. Baum, *Tennyson sixty years after* (1948). R. J. Cruikshank, *Charles Dickens and early Victorian England* (1950), is a vivid study of Victorian life and customs. *Dickens* by H. Pearson (1949) is a sympathetic well-written biography. E. Johnson, *Charles Dickens: his tragedy and triumph* (2 vols., 1953), recaptures Dickens' zest for life in a penetrating study. *Marian Evans and George Eliot* by L. and E. Hanson (1952) is a new biography which enlarges our previous knowledge. W. A. Darlington, *The world of Gilbert and Sullivan* (1950), is largely an analysis of Gilbert's scripts by a dramatic critic.

CHAPTER I 2 *Difficulties in Italy and Spain*

Italy. R. Albrecht-Carrié, *Italy from Napoleon to Mussolini* (1950), is a readable volume, sound in scholarship with many illuminating interpretations. E. Wiskemann, *Italy* (1947), is a brief but lively survey. In B. Croce's *History of Italy, 1871–1915,* translated by C. M. Ady (1929), a mind of the first order views not single occurrences, but the whole sweep of events. L. Salvatorelli, *A concise history of Italy from prehistoric times to our own day,* translated by B. Miall (1940), is a well-written synthesis of political, economic, and cultural history. Two older but still useful volumes are J. P. Trevelyan's *Short history of the Italian people* (1929) and H. D. Sedgwick's *Short history of Italy* (1905). Another informative volume is B. King and T. Okey, *Italy today* (rev. ed., 1909). A. W. Salomone, *Italian democracy in the making: the political scene in the Giolittian era, 1900–1914* (1945), is a readable, scholarly account of Italian political currents in a neglected period. C. J. S. Sprigge, *The development of modern Italy* (1944), is a conscientious study of the rise and fall of democracy in Italy (1870 to 1922). On the question of church and state there are two sound scholarly studies by S. W. Halperin, *The separation of church and state in Italian thought from Cavour to Mussolini* (1937) and *Italy and the Vatican at war, a study in their relations from the outbreak of the Franco-Prussian war to the death of Pius IX* (1939). W. C. Askew, *Europe and Italy's acquisition of Libya, 1911–1912* (1942), is a competent scholarly account.

Spain. The choice of books on nineteenth-century Spain is somewhat limited. One of the best available histories of Spain is R. Altamira's *History of Spain from the beginning to the present day,* translated from the Spanish by M. Lee (1949) R. E. Sencourt (R. E. George), *The Spanish crown, 1808–1931* (1932), is readable and interesting, written with a clear sense of the issues involved. J. B. Trend, *The origins of modern Spain* (1934), is a careful study of the revolutionary movement from 1868 to 1933. One of the best surveys of the nineteenth century is to be found in A. R. Oliveira, *Politics, economics and men of modern Spain, 1808–1946* (1946). J. A. Brandt, *Toward the new Spain* (1933), surveys the political history from 1810 through 1931. The most useful of the older histories of Spain is E. W. Latimer's *Spain in the nineteenth century* (5th ed., 1903). H. B. Clarke's *Modern Spain, 1815–1898* (1906) is accurate but rather over-crowded with detail. M. A. S. Hume, *Modern Spain, 1788–1898* (2nd ed., 1906), is super-ficial. For a summary of the Spanish constitution see W. F. Dodd, *Modern constitutions* (vol. II, 1909). S. de Madariaga, *The fall of the Spanish American empire* (1948), is a competent account by a Spanish historian. The origins of the Monroe Doctrine are ably discussed in Dexter Perkins, *The Monroe doctrine, 1823–1826* (1927). W. A. Smith, "The background of the Spanish revolution of 1868," *American historical review*, vol. 55 (1950), pp. 787–810, is an illuminating study. W. Millis, *Martial spirit; a study of our war with Spain* (1931), is lively and caustic; characterized by scholarly accuracy.

Spanish civilization and culture. J. B. Trend, *The civilization of Spain* (1944), is a good brief survey in the Home University series. R. Altamira, *History of Spanish civilization,* translated by P. Volkov (1930), is somewhat sketchy. J. P. Oliveira Martins, *History of Iberian civilization,* translated by A. F. G. Bell (1930), is a competent, and in some respects brilliant, achievement. *Spain: a companion to Spanish studies,* edited by E. A. Peers (1929), is an attempt by a group of scholars to present a general idea of Spain and its culture. M. A. Dieulafoy, *Art in Spain and Portugal* (1913), is a useful introductory survey. G. Brenan, *The literature of the Spanish people from Roman times to the present day* (1951), is a comprehensive, informative summary. *Spain, a short history of its politics, literature, and art* by H. D. Sedgwick (1925) is a readable survey.

Italian civilization and culture. L. Olschki, *The genius of Italy* (1949), is a readable discussion of Italian culture and intellectual life. *Readings in modern Italian literature from Alfieri to D'Annunzio,* edited by J. F. de Simone (1952), is a very useful volume. In *The legacy of Italy* (1948) G. Prezzolini attempts to set forth the unique quality of Italian civilization. F. Nardelli and A. A. Livingston, *Gabriel the archangel* (1931), is a readable biography of d'Annunzio. Two other substantial biographies are: T. Antongini, *D'Annunzio* (1938), and G. Griffin, *Gabriele d'Annunzio, the warrior bard* (1935). On Puccini there are two careful and comprehensive biographies, one by R. Specht, translated from the German by C. A. Phillips (1933), and the other by G. R. Marek (1951). On Verdi there is a succinct biography together with a discussion of his works by D. Hussey (1940) and a longer exhaustive biography by F. Toye (1931); both are written by noted musicographers. The Italian contributions to the development of modern opera are discussed in *The opera, a history of its creation and performance, 1600–1941* by W. Brockway and H. Weinstock (1941) and in D. J. Grout's *Short history of opera* (1947).

CHAPTER 13 *Modern Imperialism*

Imperialism. Still useful among the older interpretations of the nature of imperialism is J. A. Hobson's *Imperialism* (3rd rev. ed., 1938). E. M. Winslow, *The pattern of imperialism, a study in the theories of power* (1948), is based on the theory that imperialism is the product of political thinking rather than of economic necessity. Eric A. Walter, *Colonies* (1944), is an intelligent brief discussion of colonialism. P. T. Moon, *Imperialism and world politics* (first printed in 1926; reprinted in 1936), is still the best general survey. Another good, though less vigorous, survey is Mary E. Townsend, *European colonial expansion since 1871* (1941), with the collaboration of C. H. Peake. There is also a brief survey by S. J. B. Whybrow, *Europe overseas; a survey of modern empires* (1939). L. J. Ragatz, *The march of empire: the European overseas possessions on the eve of the first world war* (1948) is a brief revealing survey covering the period from 1898 to 1914. A very useful little volume is J. F. Horrabin's *An atlas of empire* (1937). In *A place in the sun* (1936) Grover Clark has attempted to answer the question, "Do colonies pay?" The statistical tables and documentary materials upon which his conclusions are based were published separately in *The balance sheet of imperialism; facts and figures on colonies* (1936). Periodical literature published in this country is listed in L. J. Ragatz, *A bibliography of articles, descriptive, historical, and scientific, on colonies and other dependent territories, appearing in American geographical and kindred journals through 1934* (2 vols., 1935).

Africa. One of the classic accounts of imperialism in Africa is Sir H. H. Johnston's *A history of the colonization of Africa by alien races* (new rev. ed., 1930). Another useful older account is Elizabeth Latimer, *Europe in Africa in the nineteenth century* (3rd ed., 1898). Sir Charles P. Lucas, *The partition and colonization of Africa* (1922), is a series of interesting lectures. L. Middleton, *The rape of Africa* (1936), is broad in scope, but marred by bitterness against the old system. C. E. Nowell, "Portugal and the partition of Africa," *Journal of modern history,* vol. 19 (1947), pp. 1–17, is an enlightening brief discussion. H. A. Wieschoff, *Colonial policies in Africa* (1944), is a valuable study. R. I. Lovell, *The struggle for Africa, 1875–1899* (1934), is a useful study which includes an account of the Boer war. M. V. Jackson, *European powers and south-east Africa; a study of international relations on the south-east coast of Africa, 1796–1856* (1942), is based on the thesis that geography and history are inseparable and should be studied together. L. S. Woolf, *Empire and commerce in Africa* (1920), is a discussion by a British economist. W. W. Claridge, *History of the Gold Coast and Ashanti* (1915), is still a standard work. C. H. Huberich, *The political and legislative history of Liberia* (2 vols., 1947), is a definitive study. D. C. Somervell has written a good brief biography of Livingstone in the Great Lives series (1936). Two competent longer biographies are those by R. J. Campbell (1929) and J. I. Macnair (1940). J. Wassermann tells the story of Stanley with enthusiasm in *Bula Matari: Stanley, conqueror of a nation,* translated by E. and C. Paul (1933). Then there is Stanley's *How I found Livingstone* (1872 and other editions).

French and German imperialism. T. F. Power, *Jules Ferry and the renaissance of French imperialism* (1944), is a careful, balanced appraisal of Ferry's role. Agnes Murphy, *The ideology of French imperialism, 1871–1881* (1948), is a well-documented account of the reawakening of interest in imperialism. J. F. Cady, "The Beginnings of French Imperialism in the Pacific Orient," *Journal of modern history,* vol. 14 (1942), pp. 71–87, is an excellent critical discussion of pertinent books. H. J. Priestley has written two sound, detailed volumes: *France overseas; a study of modern imperialism* (1938) and *France overseas through the old régime; a study of European expansion* (1939). Valuable also is S. R. Roberts, *History of French colonial policy, 1870–1925* (2 vols., 1929).

Jacques Stern, *The French colonies, past and future* (1944), is a brief sketch of French colonial activity by a former French minister of colonies. On German colonization there is Mary E. Townsend, *Origins of modern German colonialism, 1871–1885* (1921); scholarly and readable. The earlier period is ably discussed in M. L. Hansen, *German schemes of colonization before 1860* (1924). A. J. P. Taylor, *Germany's first bid for colonies, 1884–1885* (1938), attempts to show that Bismarck wanted colonies only to provoke a quarrel with England; overstates the case. H. Schnee's small volume, *German colonization, past and future* (1926), is a defense of Germany as a colonizing power; part of the organized propaganda for the return of the German colonies.

China. E. R. Hughes, *The invasion of China by the western world* (1938), is a competent survey. Good shorter accounts may be found in H. M. Vinacke, *A history of the Far East in modern times* (rev. ed., 1933), and K. S. Latourette, *The Chinese: their history and culture* (2 vols., 1934). The struggle for concessions is ably recounted in T. W. Overlach, *Foreign financial control in China* (1919). Invaluable is C. F. Renner, *Foreign investments in China* (1933). The legal aspects are competently discussed in W. W. Willoughby's monumental *Foreign rights and interests in China* (2 vols., 1927). M. Collis, *Foreign mud* (1946), is a luminous account of the opium imbroglio at Canton in the 1830's and the war of 1840–1842. E. V. G. Kiernan, *British diplomacy in China, 1880 to 1885* (1939), critically examines British diplomacy during an important period. D. Varè, *The last empress* (1938), and H. Hussey, *Venerable ancestor: the life and times of Tz'u Hsi, 1835–1908* (1949), tell the story of the passing of the dynasty. Foster R. Dulles, *China and America: the story of their relations since 1784* (1946), is a lucid and intelligent account of Sino-American relations. An interesting survey of the reform movement during the first decade of the twentieth century may be found in M. E. Cameron, *The reform movement in China, 1898–1912* (1931). P. H. Clements, *The Boxer rebellion; a political and diplomatic review* (1915), is a good account. A more picturesque account is J. G. Andersson, *The dragon and the foreign devils,* translated from the Swedish by C. W. Stork (1928).

Japan. E. H. Norman, *Japan's emergence as a modern state; political and economic problems of the Meiji period* (1940), is a competent, comprehensive account, with chapters on industrialism and agrarianism. *Japan since Perry* by C. Yanaga (1949) is a frank and simple account, based on Japanese sources, of the rise of Japan from feudalism to a world power. M. M. Dilts, *The pageant of Japanese history* (rev. ed., 1947), is a good introduction to Japanese history. G. C. Allen, *Short economic history of modern Japan, 1867–1937* (1947), is an informative brief survey. Mary A. Nourse, *Kodo, the way of the emperor; a short history of the Japanese* (1940), shows how the dream of grandeur developed in the Japanese mind. E. O. Reischauer, *Japan, past and present* (1946), is a brief survey written with scholarly objectivity. K. S. Latourette, *The history of Japan* (1947), is a crisply-written history covering Japan from the mythical age to 1947. G. B. Sansom, *The western world and Japan: a study in the interaction of European and Asiatic cultures* (1950), is a thoughtful treatment of the nature and extent of European cultural influences in Japan. The same author has also written *Japan: a short cultural history* (1943), a stimulating survey.

British Empire. There is an excellent discussion of articles and books on the British Empire by W. F. Craven in *The journal of modern history,* vol. VI (1934), pp. 40–69.

Among the larger works on the British Empire the two most useful are: *The Cambridge history of the British empire,* edited by J. H. Rose, A. P. Newton, E. A. Benians, and H. H. Dodwell (vols. 1–2, 4–8, 1929–1940); *The British empire, a survey* (12 vols., 1924), edited by H. Gunn with contributions from noted historians. For a one-volume lucid and logical survey the student may turn to Paul Knaplund, *The British empire, 1815–1939* (1941); a sound scholarly work by an American historian. S. B. Leacock, *The British empire; its structure, its unity, its strength* (1940), is a description of the British empire and its component parts for the general reader by a Canadian. Lord Elton, a British historian, has surveyed primarily for American readers the development of the empire from 1845 to 1939 in *Imperial commonwealth* (1946). One of the most successful books on the British empire is J. A. Williamson, *A short history of British expansion* (2 vols., 2nd ed., 1930). G. W. Southgate, *The British empire* (1936), is a useful survey. W. L. Strauss, *Joseph Chamberlain and the theory of imperialism* (1942), is an interesting and enlightening monograph. C. E. Carrington, *The British overseas: exploits of a nation of shopkeepers* (1950), is a comprehensive account covering the entire field of British migrations and colonization. W. B. Willcox, *Star of empire: a study of Britain as a world power, 1485–1945* (1950), offers a well-written interpretation of British imperial history. Another very useful book is C. B. Fawcett, *A political geography of the British empire* (1933). L. C. A. Knowles, *Economic development of the British overseas empire* (2 vols., 1924–1936), is a mine of information.

Canada, Australia, and New Zealand. For a sound short summary of Canadian history the student may consult A. R. M. Lower, *Colony to nation: a history of Canada* (1947), E. McInnis, *Canada: a political and social history* (1947), or Carl Wittke, *A history of Canada* (3rd ed., 1941). For the constitutional and legal development W. P. M. Kennedy, *The constitution of Canada, 1534–1937* (2nd ed., 1938), is a good introduction. The same author has collected and edited *Documents of the Canadian constitution, 1759–1915* (1918). R. G. Trotter, *Canadian history, a syllabus and guide to reading* (rev. ed., 1934), is invaluable for those interested in further references on Canadian history. *Australia,* edited by C. H. Grattan (1947), is a readable and concise symposium written for the general reader. J. A. Williamson, *Cook and the opening of the Pacific* (1948), is an interesting brief survey (Teach Yourself series). A longer informative account is A. S. Kenyon, *The story of Australia, its discoverers and founders* (1940). One of the more successful histories of Australia is Sir Ernest Scott's *Short history of Australia* (7th rev. ed., 1947). Two other able surveys are W. K. Hancock, *Australia* (1931), and B. Fitzpatrick, *The Australian people, 1788–1945* (1947). The latter has also written an economic history of Australia under the title *The British empire in Australia* (1941). D. C. Gordon, *The Australian frontier in New Guinea, 1870–1885* (1951), is a mature scholarly volume. H. Miller, *New Zealand* (1950), is a well-informed, objective short survey. Another interesting volume is A. H. Clarke's *The invasion of New Zealand by people, plants, and animals; the south island* (1949). The story of the first governor is ably told in J. C. Beaglehole, *Captain Hobson and the New Zealand company* (1928). A. J. Harrop, *England and New Zealand* (1926), is a readable account by a New Zealand historian.

India. *The Cambridge shorter history of India,* edited by H. H. Dodwell (1934), is composed of chapters of unequal merit and interest; good for reference. Two useful shorter surveys of Indian history are: V. Chirol, *India* (1926), and H. G. Rawlinson, *A* *concise history of the Indian people* (1938). Sir George Dunbar, *A history of India from the earliest times to 1939* (2 vols., 4th ed., 1950), is a good longer account. Emma Hawkridge, *Indian gods and kings, the story of a living past* (1935), deals with many aspects of India and Indian life; stimulating and well-written. T. W. Wallbank, *India: a survey of the heritage and growth of Indian nationalism* (1948), is a well-organized and well-written brief survey. K. M. Panikkar, *Indian nationalism; its origin, history and ideas* (1920), is written from the Indian viewpoint. Bruce T. McCully, *English education and the origins of Indian nationalism* (1940), is a worthwhile study. The story of the Sepoy rebellion is ably told in G. Dangerfield, *Bengal mutiny* (1933), and H. Gilbert, *The story of the Indian mutiny* (1916).

British in Africa. Lois A. Raphael, *The Cape-to-Cairo dream, a study in British imperialism in the nineteenth century* (1936), is a readable survey of British influence in Africa. A more recent informative volume is Josephine Kamm, *African challenge; the story of the British in tropical Africa* (1946). More limited in its scope is E. W. P. Newman, *Britain and northeast Africa* (1940). Arthur N. Cook, *British enterprise in Nigeria* (1943), is a straightforward and intelligent account of the political development of the largest British colony in West Africa. There is an excellent critical survey of books on South Africa by F. J. Klingberg in *The journal of modern history,* vol. 10 (1938), pp. 77–93. E. A. Walker, *A history of South Africa* (1928), is an objective record of events by a South-African historian. *The great trek* by the same author (1934) is a vivid narrative. A. Keppel-Jones, *South Africa* (1950), is a clear and balanced short account. C. W. DeKiewiet in his *History of South Africa* (1941) surveys the social and economic history of South Africa; presupposes a knowledge of political history. Two other valuable contributions by the same author are: *British colonial policy and the South African republics, 1848–1872* (1929) and *The imperial factor in South Africa: a study in politics and economics* (1937). M. S. Green, *The making of the union of South Africa, 1487–1939* (1947), is a brief volume of closely packed facts; commendably impartial. B. Williams, *Botha, Smuts, and South Africa* (1948), is a brief account by a noted British historian. The same author has also written a sound and readable biography of Cecil Rhodes (1921). A more recent biography is Sarah G. Millin, *Cecil Rhodes* (1933), based on a painstaking study of the documents. A. F. Hattersley, *The British settlement in Natal: a study in imperial migration* (1950), is an important study.

CHAPTER 14 *Tsarist Russia*

Tsarist Russia. M. M. Karpovich, *Imperial Russia, 1801–1917* (1932), is a good brief survey of the period (Berkshire series). W. Kirchner's *Outline history of Russia* (1950) is an able condensation of the course of Russian history from the earliest times to 1948. A good cross-section of source and secondary materials is to be found in *Readings in Russian history,* edited by W. B. Walsh (1948). A. A. Kornilov, *Modern Russian history,* translated by A. G. Kaun (2 vols., rev. ed., 1924), is scholarly and objective, but deals mainly with political history. The main currents of Russian history are competently traced in I. Spector, *Introduction to Russian history and culture* (1950). S. S. Harcave, *Russia: a history* (1952), is one of the best surveys of Russian history in English; lucid and well-organized. S. R. Tompkins, *Russia through the ages* (1940), is a political history with special emphasis on wars, dynastic changes, and territorial expansion. M. M. Kovalevski, *Russian political institutions* (1902), offers a general sketch of the constitutional evolution of tsarist Russia. Volume 5 of V. O. Kliuchevsky's monumental *History of Russia* covers the period 1762–1907; contains much material on social history. F. H. Skrine, *Expansion of Russia, 1815–1900* (3rd ed., 1915), is a competent scholarly work. D. S. Mirsky, *Russia, a social history*, translated by C. G. Seligman (1931), contains a mass of information not easily accessible to the English reader. Still the best general survey of Russian economic life in the nineteenth century is J. Mavor's *Economic history of Russia* (2nd rev. ed., 2 vols., 1926). P. I. Lyashchenko, *History of the national economy of Russia to the 1917 revolution*, translated by L. M. Herman (1949), is a dry and factual pro-Soviet account. H. Seton-Watson, *The decline of imperial Russia, 1855–1914* (1953), is a lucid scholarly volume which contains little that is new. S. P. Turin, *From Peter the Great to Lenin* (1935), is a history of the Russian labor movement.

Specialized works. A. G. Mazour, *The first Russian revolution, 1825* (1937), is a conscientious and illuminating study based on a mass of archival material. A. Levin, *The second duma, a study of the social-democratic party and the Russian constitutional experiment* (1940), is a valuable study of one phase of the constitutional experiment. G. T. Robinson, *Rural Russia under the old régime* (1932), is a work of precise scholarship, an invaluable storehouse of facts. Two other illuminating volumes on agricultural life under the tsars are G. Pavlovsky, *Agricultural Russia on the eve of the revolution* (1930), and L. A. Owen, *The Russian peasant movement, 1906–1917* (1937). Valuable for the light they throw on Russian affairs of the early nineteenth century are *The memoirs of Count Witte*, edited by A. Yarmolinsky (1921). J. S. Curtiss, *Church and state in Russia: the last years of the empire, 1900–1917* (1940), is a lively, impartial, illuminating study. I. Levitats, *The Jewish community in Russia, 1772–1844* (1943), is a work of painstaking research. The definitive work on the Jews in the Romanov empire is S. M. Dubnov, *History of the Jews in Russia and Poland* (3 vols., 1916–1920). T. A. Bailey, *America faces Russia; Russian-American relations from early times to our day* (1950), is devoted mainly to American reactions to Russia, while M. M. Laserson, *The American impact on Russia: diplomatic and ideological, 1784–1917* (1950), gives particular attention to the impact of American political and social ideas and institutions on Russian thinking; both are worthwhile illuminating studies. W. H. E. Johnson, *Russia's educational heritage* (1950), surveys the major educational policies of tsarist Russia. A. G. Mazour, *An outline of modern Russian historiography* (1939), is an indispensable guide for students of Russian history; reliable and impartial.

Romanovs. W. Gerhardi, *The Romanovs* (1940), covers the period from Rurik to Nicholas II; marred by errors. *Tsar of freedom, the life and reign of Alexander II,* by S. Graham (1935), is despite some inaccuracies a readable and competent biography. C. Lowe, *Alexander III of Russia* (1895), is still useful. *The emperor Nicholas II as I knew him* (1922) by Sir J. Hanbury-Williams is a volume of reminiscences. M. Essadbey, *Nicholas II, prisoner of the purple* (1936), is a historical novel rather than a sound biography. *The real Romanovs* by Gleb Botkin (1931) was written by the son of the personal physician of Nicholas II; interesting, but not always convincing. *The letters of the tsar to the tsaritsa, 1914–1917,* translated by A. L. Hynes (1929), throw much light on the fall of the Romanovs. R. Fülöp-Miller, *Rasputin, the holy devil,* translated from the

German by F. S. Flint and D. F. Tait (1928), is a sensational account of the uncouth, sinister figure. Rasputin's daughter, M. G. Rasputina, tried to correct the impression made by Fülöp-Miller's volume by writing two books: *The real Rasputin* (1929) and *My father* (1934). Elizabeth Judas, *Rasputin, neither devil nor saint* (1942), was written by one who knew him.

Russian culture. P. Miliukov, *Outlines of Russian culture,* edited by M. Karpovich, translated by V. Ughet and E. Davis (3 vols., 1942), is the fruit of a lifetime of study by a distinguished Russian historian in exile. T. G. Masaryk, *Spirit of Russia; studies in history, literature, and philosophy,* translated by E. and C. Paul (2 vols., 1919), is a first-rate synthesis of religious, philosophical, social, and political thought. *The golden age of Russian literature* by I. Spector (1943) is a readable survey which gives a brief biography of the leading Russian authors, a short excerpt from the outstanding work of each author, and a list of major works. H. Muchnic, *An introduction to Russian literature* (1947), discusses the work of the six great nineteenth-century Russian writers. D. S. Mirsky, *A history of Russian literature,* edited and abridged by F. J. Whitfield (1949), is a new edition of a useful work first published in 1927. E. J. Simmons, *English literature and culture in Russia* (1935), has a self-explanatory title. Marc Slonim, *The epic of Russian literature; from its origin through Tolstoy* (1950), is a rich, illuminating volume, the result of many years of scholarly effort. *Slavic studies,* edited by A. Kaun and E. J. Simmons (1943), is a series of informative essays on Russian literature. J. Lavrin, *An introduction to the Russian novel* (1947), was first presented as a series of lectures. *Russian poetry, an anthology,* edited by B. Deutsch and A. Yarmolinsky (1927), will give the student a real taste of Russian poetry. *The Russian arts,* by R. H. Newmarch (1916), is a survey written after twenty years of first-hand study. A. N. Benois, *The Russian school of painting,* translated by A. Yarmolinsky (1916), is an authoritative discussion of tendencies and traits by a painter. On Russian music there are two informative surveys in English: M. Montagu-Nathan, *History of Russian music* (1914), and A. Pougin, *A short history of Russian music,* translated by L. Haward (1915). G. E. H. Abraham, *Studies in Russian music* (1935), offers a series of critical essays on important Russian composers. D. Brook, *Six great Russian composers* (1946), includes the great masters of the nineteenth century.

Literary figures. Probably the best biography of Pushkin in English is that by E. J. Simmons (1937) and of Turgenev that by A. Yarmolinsky (1926). The best biographies of Dostoevski are those by A. Yarmolinsky (1934) and E. J. Simmons (1940). W. H. Bruford, *Chekov and his Russia* (1948), presents a picture of the old Russia as mirrored in Chekov's art. There is an informative short biography of Tolstoi by J. Lavrin (1944).

CHAPTER 15 *Decline of the Austrian and Ottoman Empires*

Austria-Hungary. A. J. May, *The Hapsburg monarchy, 1867–1914* (1951), is a readable survey of the political, social, and cultural history of the Dual Monarchy. R. A. Kann, *The multinational empire: nationalism and national reform in the Habsburg monarchy, 1848–1918* (2 vols., 1950), is a comprehensive and well-documented work on a complex subject. A. J. P. Taylor, *The Habsburg monarchy, 1809–1918: a history of the Austrian empire and Austria-Hungary* (rev. ed., 1949), is a complete revision of a work published under the same title in 1941; readable, but sometimes hostile. E. H. Buschbeck, *Austria* (1950), is an impartial survey. An older but still useful survey is H. W. Steed, *The Hapsburg monarchy* (2nd ed., 1919); somewhat antipathetic. E. E. Kraehe, "Austria and the problem of reform in the German confederation, 1851–1863," *American historical review*, vol. 56 (1951), pp. 276–294, is an illuminating study. Another important short study is A. G. Kogan, "The social democrats and the conflict of nationalities in the Habsburg monarchy," *Journal of modern history*, vol. 21 (1949), pp. 204–217. W. A. Jenks, *Austrian electoral reform of 1907* (1950), is a lucid scholarly presentation. G. H. Rupp, *A wavering friendship: Russia and Austria, 1876–1878* (1941), is a careful study of the sources. C. M. Knatchbull-Hugesson, *The political evolution of the Hungarian nation* (1908), is marred by a strong nationalist bias. There are a number of enlightening chapters on the nineteenth century in O. Zarek, *History of Hungary*, translated by P. Wolkonsky (1934), and in D. G. Kosáry, *History of Hungary* (1941). R. W. Seton-Watson has written three important books on various phases of Hungarian or Austro-Hungarian history: *Racial problems in Hungary* (1908), *Corruption and reform in Hungary* (1911), and *The southern Slav question and the Hapsburg monarchy* (1911). J. Redlich, *Emperor Francis Joseph of Austria* (1929), is one of the best biographies of the Austrian emperor. Much valuable information can also be found in O. Ernest, *Franz Joseph as revealed by his letters* (1927).

Ottoman empire. W. Miller, *The Ottoman empire* (3rd rev. ed., 1927), tells the story of the empire and of Rumania, Bulgaria, and Serbia. The same author's *Ottoman empire and its successors, 1801–1927* (4th ed., 1926), is a revised and enlarged edition of the former work. F. Schevill, *The history of the Balkan peninsula*, revised by W. M. Gewehr (1933), is a competent survey. B. H. Sumner, *Russia and the Balkans, 1870–1881* (1937), is an important scholarly work. M. D. Stojanovic, *The great powers and the Balkans, 1875–1878* (1939), is a careful study based on multilingual documents. From the point at which Stojanovic left off the narrative is carried on by W. N. Medlicott in *The congress of Berlin and after: a diplomatic history of the near-Eastern settlement, 1878–1880* (1938), an equally important volume. D. Harris, *A diplomatic history of the Balkan crisis of 1875–1878* (1936), is a carefully organized, scholarly, and exhaustive study. *Modern Turkey, a politico-economic interpretation, 1908–1923* by E. G. Mears and others (1924) is a fair-minded and authoritative volume. The Young Turk movement is treated in E. F. Knight, *Turkey: the awakening of Turkey, the Turkish revolution of 1908* (1910). There are two useful biographies of Abdul Hamid: E. Pears, *Life of Abdul Hamid* (1917), and A. S. Wittlin, *Abdul Hamid, the shadow of God*, translated from the German by N. Denny (1940). E. C. Helmreich, *The diplomacy of the Balkan wars, 1912–1913* (1938), is a thoroughgoing study, an important contribution to the history of the period. The story of the Balkan wars is told in W. H. C. Price, *The Balkan cockpit; the political and military story of the Balkan wars* (1914). J. G. Schurmann, *The Balkan wars, 1912–1913* (1914), is a series of lectures by the American ambassador to the sultan's court. A further useful volume is G. Young, *Nationalism and war in the Near East* (1915).

Individual states. Probably the best history of Serbia in English is that by H. Temperley (1917), definitely pro-Serb. There is a useful shorter account in the Home University series by L. F. Waring (1917). C. Sforza, *Fifty years of war and diplomacy in the Balkans; Pashich and the union of the Yugoslavs* (1940), is a lively study of the career of a Serbian statesman. There are two substantial scholarly works on the formation of Rumania: W. G. East, *The union of Moldavia and Wallachia* (1929), and T. W. Riker, *The making of Rumania: a study of an international problem, 1856–1866* (1931), the latter being devoted largely to the diplomacy of the period. There is a brief survey of Rumanian history by C. Kormos (1944) and a longer one by C. U. Clark (1932). The best account of the earlier period is R. W. Seton-Watson, *A history of the Roumanians from Roman times to the completion of unity* (1934). There are two substantial accounts of Bulgarian history in English: W. S. Monroe, *Bulgaria and her people,* with an account of the Balkan wars (1914) and G. C. Logio, *Bulgaria, past and present* (1936). A. M. Hyde, *A diplomatic history of Bulgaria from 1870 to 1886* (1927), is an important contribution to the history of the period.

CHAPTER 16 *The Progress of Science*

General Science. J. A. Thomson, *Modern science* (1930), is a short, well-balanced account. One of the better manuals is J. D. Dampier-Whetham, *History of science* (2nd ed., 1932). H. Butterfield, *Origins of modern science* (1950), offers a fresh approach. F. S. Taylor, *A short history of science and scientific thought* (1949), sketches the highlights in the development of modern science. Another survey which contains a great deal of information is W. B. Shepherd, *New survey of science* (1950). P. Lenard, *Great men of science* (reprint, 1950), offers a series of essays on individual scientists. A. N. Whitehead, *Science and the modern world* (1926), is a stimulating philosophical survey. In *The impact of science on society* Bertrand Russell (1953) suggests the humane and prosperous society science can make possible. J. Stokley, *Science remakes our world* (1946), is a survey of recent achievements in various fields. W. Kaempffert, *Science today and tomorrow* (1945), surveys the spectacular progress of recent decades. J. D. Bernal, *The social function of science* (1939), discusses the role of science in the first third of the present century. J. B. Conant, *Modern science and modern man* (1953), is a modest but informative small volume. E. Farber, *The evolution of chemistry* (1952), tells the absorbing story of the origin and progress of chemistry. The progress of chemistry from 1830 to the present is ably discussed in A. Findlay, *Hundred years of chemistry* (2nd ed., 1949). B. Jaffe, *Crucibles* (1948), tells the story of chemistry from ancient alchemy to nuclear fission.

Darwin and Darwinism. C. Singer, *A history of biology; a general introduction to the study of living things* (rev. ed., 1950), is a stimulating and well-written survey. J. Huxley, *Evolution in action* (1953), looks back at millions of years of biological evolution. P. A. Moody, *Introduction to evolution* (1953), is an up-to-date discussion. G. G. Simpson, *The meaning of evolution* (1949), is a nontechnical analysis; one of the best recent books. R. E. D. Clark, *Darwin: before and after* (1948), is a useful little book. G. West has written a good short biography of Darwin (1938). P. B. Sears, *Charles Darwin: the naturalist as a cultural force* (1950), is a survey of Darwin's influence on the contemporary world.

Medicine and bacteriology. R. H. Shryock, *The development of modern medicine* (2nd rev. ed., 1947), traces the interrelations of medicine and social movements. D. Guthrie, *A history of medicine* (1948), is a skillfully done survey. Another competent survey is J. Garland, *Story of medicine* (1949). W. H. Woglom, *Discoverers for medicine* (1949), gives a clear account of the evolution of medical knowledge. M. S. Clark, *Medicine on the march* (1949), is a readable survey of the progress made during and after World War II. *The conquest of bacteria,* by F. S. Taylor (1942), is a short history of chemical agents which have conquered disease. B. Sokoloff, *The miracle drugs* (1949), tells the dramatic story of the discovery and use of antibiotics. The same author has also written *The story of penicillin* (1950). P. R. Hawley, *New discoveries in medicine* (1950), offers a series of lectures in nontechnical language. A rather full account of the history of anesthetics is to be found in V. Robinson, *Victory over pain* (1946). The story of surgery through the centuries is engagingly told in R. A. Leonardo, *History of surgery* (1943). Among the more recent biographies of individuals one must include: D. Guthrie's *Lord Lister* (1949), R. J. Dubos' *Louis Pasteur* (1950), and M. Marquardt's *Paul Ehrlich* (1951).

Modern physics and the atom. H. Semat, *Physics in the modern world* (1949), offers a broad survey of the subject. P. Frank, *Einstein: his life and times,* translated from the German by G. Rosen (1947), is a charmingly written revealing volume. L. Infeld, *Albert Einstein* (1950), is a small volume on Einstein's work and influence. In *The world as I see it* (1949) Albert Einstein briefly states his views. The new vision of universe as seen by Einstein is set down with clarity and grace in L. Barnett, *The universe and Dr. Einstein* (1949). J. Sacks, *The atom at work* (1951), is a good introduction. J. W. Feinberg, *The atom story* (1953), presents a history of atomic research from ancient times to the present. B. W. Leyson, *Atomic energy in war and peace* (1951), is a pleasantly written comprehensive discussion. *Atomic energy and the hydrogen bomb* by G. Wendt (1951) discusses the potentialities of nuclear energy. *The atomic era,* edited by F. Kirchwey (1951), is a symposium on the problem of atomic energy. *Economic aspects of atomic power* by S. H. Schurr and others (1950) explores the future possibilities of the atom for the coming age. The use of atomic energy in industry and medicine is discussed in *Constructive uses of atomic energy,* edited by S. C. Rothmann (1949). The hydrogen bomb is discussed in W. L. Laurence, *The hell bomb* (1951). *The H bomb,* with an introduction by A. Einstein and commentary by G. F. Eliot (1950), is a collection of 13 articles on the subject.

CHAPTER 17 *Origins of the First World War*

Causes. S. B. Fay, *The origins of the world war* (2 vols. in one, rev. ed., 1930), still remains the best account of the causes of the war. B. E. Schmitt, *The coming of the war, 1914* (2 vols., 1930), is a notable work slightly pro-Entente in tone. N. Mansergh, *The coming of the first world war: a study in the European balance, 1878–1914* (1949), contains little that cannot be found in the two aforementioned volumes. A more recent work by L. Albertini, *The origins of the war of 1914* (vol. 1, 1952), is detailed and objective; agrees in general with the conclusions of Professors Fay and Schmitt. Not to be overlooked is G. L. Dickinson, *International anarchy* (1926), which covers the period from

1904 to 1914 and is painstakingly objective. S. Adler, "The war-guilt question and American disillusionment, 1918–1928," *Journal of modern history*, vol. 23 (1951), pp. 1–28, is a penetrating discussion of books and attitudes. H. E. Barnes, *The genesis of the world war* (1928), lays the blame at the door of France and Russia. J. S. Ewart, *The roots and causes of the war* (2 vols., 1925), is a readable, scholarly work. The best defense of Germany and Austria-Hungary is Count M. Montgelas, *The case for the central powers* (1925). C. Bloch, *The causes of the world war* (1935), is an anti-German book by a Frenchman. On the economic causes of the war there is R. J. Hoffman, *Great Britain and the German trade rivalry, 1875–1914* (1933). R. W. Seton-Watson, *Sarajevo: a study in the origins of the great war* (1928), is a worthwhile volume though not wholly free from partisanship. On the Bagdad railway and the Near East there are three notable studies: E. M. Earle, *Turkey, the great powers, and the Bagdad railway* (1923), M. K. Chapman, *Great Britain and the Bagdad railway* (1948), and J. B. Wolf, *The diplomatic history of the Bagdad railroad* (1936). T. Wolff, *The eve of 1914* (1936), translated by E. W. Dickes, is a careful study by a German historian. There are a number of excellent critical surveys of published source and secondary materials in the *Journal of modern history*. B. Schmitt discusses works on the origins of the war in vol. 6 (1934), pp. 160–174; vol. 13 (1941), pp. 225–236; and vol. 16 (1944), pp. 169–204. O. H. Wedel discusses Austro-Hungarian documents in vol. 3 (1931), pp. 84–107. R. J. Sontag's review article on "British policy in 1913–1914" is in vol. 10 (1938), pp. 542–553. In vol. 12 (1940), pp. 69–86, there is P. E. Mosely's excellent critical discussion of printed documents and secondary works on Russian foreign policy on the eve of the war.

Diplomacy. W. L. Langer, *European alliances and alignments, 1871–1890* (1931), and the same author's *The diplomacy of imperialism, 1890–1902* (2 vols., 1935), are standard works on the subject. R. B. Mowat, *A history of European diplomacy, 1815–1914* (1927), is a good survey. G. P. Gooch, *Studies in statecraft and diplomacy* (1936 and 1942), throw much light on the background of the war. E. Brandenburg, *From Bismarck to the World War* (1927), is an account of German foreign policy from 1870 to 1914 by a German. Disclosures at Vienna have been embodied in A. F. Pribram, *The secret treaties of Austria-Hungary, 1879–1914* (2 vols., 1920–1921). The British side is represented in *British documents on the origins of the war, 1898–1914* (11 vols., 1926–1938), edited by G. P. Gooch and H. Temperley. R. W. Seton-Watson, *Britain in Europe, 1789–1914* (1937), is a carefully-done detailed survey. R. J. Sontag, *European diplomatic history, 1871–1932* (1933), contains an excellent summary of prewar diplomacy. O. J. Hale, *Germany and the diplomatic revolution: a study in diplomacy and the press, 1904–1906* (1931) and *Publicity and diplomacy, with special reference to England and Germany, 1890–1914* (1940), are well-written worthwhile studies. There are two important books by E. M. Carroll, *French public opinion and foreign affairs, 1870–1914* (1931) and *Germany and the great powers, 1866–1914* (1938). A. F. Pribram has written two valuable books on Austrian foreign policy, *Austrian foreign policy, 1908–1918* (1923) and *Austria-Hungary and Great Britain, 1908–1914*, translated by I. F. D. Morrow (1951). The steps that led to the formation of the Triple Alliance are traced in A. C. Coolidge, *The origins of the triple alliance* (1926). R. P. Churchill, *The Anglo-Russian convention of 1907* (1939), is a valuable treatise. On the crises that preceded the war there are a number of scholarly studies including E. N. Anderson, *The first Moroccan crisis, 1904–1906* (1930), and I. C. Barlow, *The Agadir crisis* (1940). The naval competition between Britain and Germany is ably described in E. L. Woodward, *Great Britain and the German navy* (1935). B. Schmitt, *The annexation of Bosnia, 1908–1909* (1937), is a meticulous study. Equally important is the same author's *Triple alliance and triple entente* (1934). W. C. Askew, *Europe and Italy's acquisition of Libya, 1911–1912* (1942), is an important study. Pauline R. Anderson's *Background of anti-English feeling in Germany, 1890–1902* (1939) is a book of high merit.

CHAPTER 18 *The First World War*

General surveys. C. R. M. Cruttwell, *A history of the great war, 1914–1918* (1935), is one of the best short histories of the war written in nontechnical language. L. Hart, *A history of the world war, 1914–1918* (1934), deals largely with the strategical and tactical side. Other good military histories of the war are G. L. McEntee, *Military history of the world war* (1937); A. F. Pollard, *Short history of the great war* (1928); and *Short history of world war I,* compiled by J. E. Edmonds (1951). Good longer accounts include J. Buchan, *A history of the great war* (4 vols., 1922), and F. H. Simonds, *A history of the world war* (5 vols., 1917–1920). There is an excellent critical discussion of military histories by A. L. P. Johnson in *Journal of modern history,* vol. 3 (1931), pp. 266–286. *The first world war: a photographic history,* edited by L. Stallings (1933), tells the story of the war in pictures. W. S. Woods, *Colossal blunders of the war* (1930), is an interesting volume.

Special studies. The opening drive of the war is ably described in S. Tyng, *The campaign of the Marne, 1914* (1935), and in *The march on Paris, 1914* by A. von Kluck (1920), a German general. H. W. Gatzke, *Germany's drive to the west: a study of Germany's western war aims* (1950), is an important contribution. The fighting on the eastern front is brilliantly described in Winston Churchill's *The unknown war* (1931). N. N. Golovine, *The Russian campaign of 1914* (1933), and Sir E. Ironside, *Tannenberg: the first thirty days in East Prussia* (1925), are good accounts of the fighting in East Prussia. Italy's part in the war is related in L. Villari, *The war on the Italian front* (1932); G. L. McEntee, *Italy's part in winning the world war* (1934); and T. N. Page, *Italy and the world war* (1920). H. Kannengisser, *The campaign in Gallipoli* (1928), is an account by a general who fought on the side of the Central Powers. The same campaign is authoritatively discussed in E. Ashmead-Bartlett, *The uncensored Dardanelles* (1928). On the Arabian venture there are a number of good books including R. Graves, *Lawrence and the Arabian adventure* (1928), and L. Thomas, *With Lawrence in Arabia* (1924). The operations in Palestine are graphically described in A. P. Wavell, *The Palestine campaigns* (1928), and in two books by W. T. Massey, *How Jerusalem was won* (1920) and *Allenby's final triumph* (1920). *Makers of modern strategy: military thought from Machiavelli to Hitler,* edited by E. M. Earle (1943), contains illuminating essays on World War I.

Naval warfare. Sir J. Corbett, *History of the great war: naval operations* (5 vols., 1920–1931), is a monumental work. British operations are ably surveyed in Sir H. Newbolt, *A naval history of the war, 1914–1918* (1920). The German side is presented in Admiral R. Scheer, *Germany's high seas fleet in the world war* (1920). J. E. T. Harper, *The truth about Jutland* (1927), and *The riddle of Jutland,* by the same author in collaboration with L. Gibson, are authoritative accounts. Submarine warfare is carefully treated in D. Masters, *The submarine war* (1935), and R. H. Gibson and M. Prendergast, *The German submarine war, 1914–1918* (1931). Two graphic popular accounts are W. G. Carr, *By guess and by God* (1930), and L. Thomas, *Raiders of the deep* (1928). British policy is set down in J. R. Jellicoe, *The submarine peril* (1934). L. Guichard, *The naval blockade* (1930), is a valuable contribution.

Entry of the United States. A critical discussion of works on the subject is to be found in B. E. Schmitt, "American neutrality, 1914–1917," in *Journal of modern history,* vol. 8 (1936), pp. 200–211. C. Seymour, *American neutrality, 1914–1917* (1935), is a series of enlightening essays. H. C. Peterson, *Propaganda for war: the campaign against American neutrality, 1914–1917* (1939), traces British influence in the United States. C. C. Tansill, *America goes to war* (1938), is a readable detailed account. W. Millis, *Road to war: America, 1914–1917* (1935), is an effort in interpretation rather than research. The most comprehensive account of the war effort of the United States is F. L. Paxson, *American democracy and the world war* (2 vols., 1939). Other informative volumes are S. T. Moore, *America and the world war* (1937), H. J. Reilly, *America's part* (1928), and F. Palmer, *Our gallant madness* (1937). T. A. Bailey, "German documents relating to the 'Lusitania,'" *Journal of modern history,* vol. 8 (1936), pp. 320–337, contains valuable information on the Lusitania controversy. There is much important information on the entry of the United States in the memoirs of contemporary leaders including those of the American ambassador to Germany, J. W. Gerard; J. von Bernstorff, the German ambassador to the United States; and United States secretary of state Robert Lansing. T. G. Frothingham, *The American reinforcement in the world war* (1927), discusses the problem of recruiting the A.E.F. On the military participation the student should consult General J. G. Harbord, *America in the world war* (1933) and *The American army in France* (1936). Other useful volumes are S. Thomas, *History of the A.E.F.* (1920), H. Liggett, *A.E.F.* (1928), and D. Van Every, *The A.E.F. in battle* (1928). W. S. Sims, *The American navy in the war* (1920), is an authoritative account by the admiral who commanded the U.S. Fleet.

The Russian revolution. See the bibliography for Chapter Twenty-one.

End of the war. A detailed scholarly account of the events leading to the armistice is to be found in H. R. Rudin, *Armistice, 1918* (1944). Another well-documented study is Sir F. Maurice, *The armistices of 1918* (1943). The same author has also described the last military campaign in *The last four months* (1919). The documents regarding the armistice are reprinted in *Preliminary history of the armistice,* edited by J. B. Scott (1924). Documents on the German situation are to be found in *The causes of the German collapse in 1918* (1934) and *Fall of the German empire, 1914–1918* (2 vols., 1932), both edited by R. H. Lutz. The same author has also written a careful monograph with the title *German revolution, 1918–1919* (1922). K. F. Nowak, *The collapse of Central Europe* (1924), is packed with information. M. Baumont, *The fall of the kaiser* (1931), is a mature work. The cost of the war is discussed in H. Folks, *The human costs of the war* (1920); E. L. Bogart, *Direct and indirect costs of the great world war* (1919); J. M. Clark, *The costs of the world war to the American people* (1931); and L. Grebler and W. Winkler, *The cost of the world war to Germany and to Austria-Hungary* (1940).

Miscellaneous. K. Forster, *The failures of peace: the search for a negotiated peace during the first world war* (1942), is a revealing study. S. J. Hurwitz, *State intervention in Britain: a study of economic control and social response, 1914–1919* (1948), takes up a phase of history that had been greatly neglected. *Unknown Germany: an inner chronicle of the first world war* by H. Hafkesbrink (1948) throws new light on the German war experience.

CHAPTER 19 *Peace-making at Paris*

General studies. *History of the peace conference at Paris,* edited by H. W. V. Temperley (6 vols., 1920–1924), is the standard work for all time. E. M. House and C. Seymour, *What really happened at Paris* (1921), is a series of lectures by members of the U.S. delegation. H. W. Harris, *The peace in the making* (1919), S. Huddleston, *Peacemaking at Paris* (1919), and E. J. Dillon, *The inside story of the peace conference* (1920), are three brief accounts by journalists. *Peacemaking, 1919* by H. Nicolson (1933) offers excerpts from the diary of an Englishman who was at Paris. D. H. Miller, *The drafting of the covenant* (2 vols., 1928), is an authoritative account by an American jurist. F. S. Marston, *The peace conference of 1919: organization and procedure* (1944), shows how the conference began without a plan and never fully repaired the omission. There are excellent discussions of pertinent books in R. E. Binkley, "Ten years of peace conference history," *Journal of modern history,* vol. 1 (1929), pp. 607–629; P. Birdsall, "The second decade of peace conference history," *ibid.,* vol. 11 (1939), pp. 362–378; B. E. Schmitt, "The peace conference of 1919," *ibid.,* vol. 16 (1944), pp. 49–59. S. Bonsal, *Suitors and suppliants: the little nations at Versailles* (1946), tells the story of the maneuvers of the small nations. R. Albrecht-Carrié, *Italy at the Paris peace conference* (1938), is a well-done volume. P. M. Burnett, *Reparation at the Paris peace conference from the standpoint of the American delegation* (2 vols., 1940), contains documents and valuable discussion.

Miscellaneous. A. P. Scott, *Introduction to the peace treaties* (1920), is a serviceable summary. The text of the treaties is to be found in *The treaties of peace, 1919–1923* (2 vols., 1924), issued by the Carnegie Endowment for International Peace. P. Birdsall, *Versailles twenty years after* (1941), reviews the peace settlement from the vantage point of twenty years. The struggle over the treaties is vividly depicted in T. A. Bailey, *Woodrow Wilson and the lost peace* (1944). Another important study by the same author is *Woodrow Wilson and the great betrayal* (1945). R. S. Baker, *What Wilson did at Paris* (1919), is a defense of the President. The same author has also written a longer defense under the title *Woodrow Wilson and world settlement* (3 vols., 1923). G. Cox, *The road to Trieste* (1947), sketches the historical background of the Trieste problem. F. Déak, *Hungary at the Paris peace conference* (1942), is one-sided. A. M. Luckau, *The German delegation at the Paris peace conference* (1941), is a good detailed account. *The treaty of St. Germain,* edited by N. Almond and R. H. Lutz (1934), is valuable both for its documents and its interpretation. W. O. Molony, *Nationality and the peace treaties* (1934), is an enlightening discussion. R. B. McCallum, *Public opinion and the last peace* (1945), refutes some popular misconceptions about the Versailles treaty. J. B. Mason, *The Danzig dilemma: a study of peacemaking by compromise* (1946), is an informed comprehensive study. T. Jones, *Lloyd George* (1951), is an objective biography. Clemenceau's attitude toward the treaties is to be found in his *Grandeur and misery of victory* (1930).

The League. F. P. Walters, *A History of the league of nations* (2 vols., 1952), is a careful, comprehensive and well-written account. Another detailed volume is T. Marburg, *Development of the league of nations idea* (2 vols., 1932). The World Court is adequately treated in E. Lindsey, *The international court* (1931), M. O. Hudson, *the permanent court of international justice* (1934), and D. F. Fleming, *The United States and the world court* (1945). H. M. Winkler, "The development of the league of nations idea in Great Britain," in *Journal of modern history*, vol. 20 (1948), pp. 95–112, is a careful and revealing short study.

CHAPTER 20 *Europe after World War I*

Miscellaneous. E. M. Kulischer, *Europe on the move: war and population changes, 1917–1947* (1948), is a painstaking exposition of population shifts. A. Sturmthal, *The tragedy of European labor, 1918–1939* (1943), is a thought-provoking analysis of labor in Germany, Austria, England, France, Italy, and Spain. L. Schwarzschild, *World in trance: from Versailles to Pearl Harbor* (1942), is a survey by a German journalist who migrated to America. The story of Locarno is lucidly told in A. Fabre-Luce, *Locarno, the reality,* translated from the French by C. Vesey (1928). R. H. Ferrell, *Peace in their time: the origins of the Kellogg-Briand pact* (1952), presents the behind-the-scenes story of the famous treaty renouncing war. F. A. Hermens, *Europe between democracy and anarchy* (1951), shows the tragic effects of proportional representation between 1918 and 1950.

Weimar republic. A. Rosenberg, *The birth of the German republic* (1931), tells the story of the origins of the republican government. S. W. Halperin, *Germany tried democracy: a political history of the Reich from 1918 to 1933* (1946), is a solid, fair-minded survey. Two good surveys of conditions in Germany at the end of the war are G. Young, *The new Germany* (1920), and H. Stroebel, *The German revolution and after* (1923). A. J. Berlau, *The German social democratic party, 1914–1921* (1949), is a useful scholarly study. The Weimar constitution is carefully analyzed in I. R. Brunet, *The new German constitution* (1922), and H. Oppenheimer, *The constitution of the German republic* (1923). One of the best accounts of the early years of the republic is E. Luehr, *The new German republic* (1929). Economic conditions during the early years of the republic are surveyed in J. W. Angell, *The recovery of Germany* (rev. ed., 1932). H. Quigley and R. Clark, *Republican Germany* (1928), is a well-written survey. R. Emerson, *State and sovereignty in modern Germany, 1871–1928* (1928), is a penetrating discussion of political theory. C. Landauer, "The Bavarian problem in the Weimar republic, 1918–1923," in *Journal of modern history*, vol. 16 (1944), pp. 93–115, 205–223, presents valuable information on the subject. K. Bergmann, *History of reparations* (1927), is a detailed account by a German expert. J. W. Wheeler-Bennett, *Wreck of reparations* (1933), tells the story of the failure to extract reparations from Germany. F. D. Graham, *Exchange, prices, and production in hyperinflation: Germany, 1920–1923* (1930), is an informative volume. The most intimate biography of Stresemann is that by A. Vallentin

(1931). R. Olden has written one that is more balanced (1930). The best biography of Hindenburg in English is that by J. W. Wheeler-Bennett (1936). R. W. Logan, *The African mandates in war politics* (1948), is a study of Germany's demands for the return of her African colonies. Ruth Fischer, *Stalin and German communism: a study in the origins of the state party* (1948), is an imposing contribution to an understanding of communism.

Democracy vs. totalitarianism. A. F. Hattersley, *Short history of democracy* (1930), is a good brief survey. J. F. Coar, *Democracy and the war* (1922), discusses the influence of the war on the development of democracy. *The clash of political ideals: a source book on democracy, communism, and the totalitarian state*, edited by A. R. Chandler (rev. ed., 1949), contains much useful material. Another useful book is *Man and the state: modern political ideas*, edited by W. Ebenstein (1947). J. A. Leighton, *Social philosophies in conflict: fascism and nazism, communism, liberal democracy* (1937), is an interesting carefully-done volume. Three other illuminating discussions are A. Zimmern, *Modern political doctrines* (1939), F. W. Coker, *Recent political thought* (1934), and M. Oakeshott, *The social and political doctrines of contemporary Europe* (1939). A. Carr, *Juggernaut: the path to dictatorship* (1938), is a good exposition. For the roots of fascism see the scholarly and interesting volume, *Liberalism and the challenge of fascism: social forces in England and France, 1815–1870*, by J. S. Schapiro (1949). W. M. McGovern, *From Luther to Hitler: a history of fascist-nazi political theory* (1941), sketches the development of fascist thought since the sixteenth century. H. Arendt, *The origins of totalitarianism* (1951), is a lucid analysis of the factors making for the growth of totalitarianism. J. H. Hallowell, *Main currents of modern political thought* (1950), contains skillful, brief discussions of socialism, fascism, and communism. In *European ideologies*, edited by F. Gross (1948), a group of scholars discuss the forces that are stirring and changing the modern age.

CHAPTER 21 *The Soviet Experiment*

Revolution of 1917. Good short accounts of the revolution are to be found in L. P. Kirby, *The Russian revolution* (1940), L. Lawton, *The Russian revolution, 1917–1926* (1927), G. Vernadsky, *The Russian revolution, 1917–1931* (1932), and J. Mavor, *The Russian revolution* (1928). A good longer work is W. H. Chamberlain, *History of the Russian revolution* (2 vols., 1935). The most recent study is E. H. Carr, *The Bolshevik revolution, 1917–1923* (Volume III in *A history of Soviet Russia*, 1953), a penetrating and objective volume. B. Pares, *The fall of the Russian monarchy: a study of the evidence* (1939), is distinguished by its scholarship and literary craftsmanship. O. H. Radkey, *The election to the Russian constituent assembly of 1917* (1950), is a valuable analysis. J. S. Reshetar, Jr., *The Ukrainian revolution, 1917–1920* (1952), is readable and scholarly. Documentary materials are to be found in *Documents on Russian history, 1914–1917*, edited by F. A. Golder (1927); *The Bolshevik revolution, 1917–1918*, edited by J. Bunyan and H. H. Fisher (1934); and *The red archives*, edited by C. E. Vulliamy (1929). The revolution in rural Russia is vividly depicted in M. G. Hindus, *The Russian peasant and the revolution* (1920). J. A. White, *The Siberian intervention* (1950), is a well-done volume. C. A. Manning, *The Siberian fiasco* (1952), is scholarly, but somewhat heavy reading. L. I. Strakhovsky, *The origins of American intervention in north Russia, 1918* (1937), is a revealing study. B. D. Wolfe, *Three who made a revolution* (1948), is a carefully documented account of the lives and works of Lenin, Trotsky, and Stalin. The best biography of Lenin in English is that by D. Shub (1948). C. Hill, *Lenin and the Russian revolution* (1949), is a brief survey in the Teach Yourself History series. I. Deutscher's *Stalin* (1949) is lucid and interesting. N. Basseches, *Stalin* (1953), is a defense of Stalinism, though advertised as being "objective." B. Souvarine, *Stalin* (1939), is a long scholarly study. R. D. Warth, "Leon Trotsky: writer and historian," *Journal of modern history,* vol. 20 (1948), pp. 27–41, is an illuminating essay. Lenin's, Stalin's, and Trotsky's writings are available in many translations. There is a selected bibliography by W. B. Walsh with the title *Russia under tsars and commissars* (1946).

Communism and the Soviet state. M. Salvadori, *The rise of modern communism* (1952), is an excellent brief introduction to world communism. W. Gurian, *Bolshevism: an introduction to Soviet communism* (1951), lays bare the aims and methods of the Soviet communist party. M. T. Florinsky, *Toward an understanding of the U.S.S.R.* (new ed., 1951), is reliable and informative. Other good introductions are E. T. Colton, *The xyz of communism* (1931), A. R. Williams, *The Soviets* (1937), A. Feiler, *The Russian experiment* (1930), and R. Fülöp-Miller, *The mind and face of Bolshevism* (1928). *U.S.S.R.: a concise handbook,* edited by E. J. Simmons (1947), is a collection of twenty-seven articles originally prepared for the *Encyclopedia Americana.* The general structure of the Soviet government is ably discussed in *Government of the Soviet Union,* by S. N. Harper and R. Thompson (2nd ed., 1950). *The Soviet Union: background, ideology, reality,* edited by W. Gurian (1951), is a symposium by a group of scholars with the accent on the constriction of the spirit in Soviet Russia. J. Fischer, *Why they behave like Russians* (1947), develops the thesis that fear is the dominant factor in Russia. H. Kohn, *Nationalism in the Soviet Union* (1933), is a well-written, scholarly volume. N. de Basily, *Russia under Soviet rule* (1938), and V. Serge, *Russia: twenty years after* (1937), are careful appraisals of twenty years of Bolshevik rule. H. Kelsen, *The political theory of Bolshevism* (1949), shows in a brief study the contradictions that exist within Bolshevism. R. N. C. Hunt, *Theory and practice of communism* (1950), is a temperate appraisement. W. Walsh and R. Price, *Russia: a handbook* (1947), is a useful brief survey for students. F. L. Schuman, *Soviet politics at home and abroad* (1946), is a well-written and well-documented treatise. J. Towster, *Political power in the U.S.S.R., 1917-1947* (1948), contains an extensive body of information not previously available; indispensable for every serious student of Russian history. B. Moore, Jr., *Soviet politics, the dilemma of power* (1950), is a valuable contribution to the understanding of communism at work. D. J. Dallin, *The real Soviet Russia,* translated by J. Shaplen (1944) sets down some of the essential facts regarding the Soviet regime. N. S. Timasheff, *The great retreat* (1946), is a competent analysis of the movements toward communism and the retreat from it. For an excellent discussion of recent works on the Soviet experiment see R. D. Warth, "The Russian 'enigma': Some recent studies by western writers," *Journal of modern history,* vol. 22 (1950), pp. 346–357.

Economic history. M. H. Dobb, *Soviet economic development since 1917* (1949), is a smoothly written, painstaking analysis. A fuller account of the early years is to be found in L. Lawton, *An economic history of Soviet Russia* (2 vols., 1932). A. Yugow,

Russia's economic front for war and peace (1942), and L. E. Hubbard, *Soviet labor and industry* (1942), are two good accounts. There are also two useful books by W. H. Chamberlin, *Soviet planned economic order* (1931) and *Russia's iron age* (1935). H. Schwartz, *Soviet economy: a selected bibliography of materials in English* (1950), offers many helpful comments. The first two five-year plans are treated in M. Farbman, *Piatiletka: Russia's five-year plan* (1931), and W. P. and Zelda Coates, *The second five-year plan of development of the U.S.S.R.* (1934). J. Beauchamp, *Agriculture in Soviet Russia* (1931), discusses the state farms. The abolition of private ownership is graphically depicted in M. G. Hindus, *Humanity uprooted* (rev. ed., 1930). L. E. Hubbard, *The economics of Soviet agriculture* (1939), is a good survey. N. Jasny, *Socialized agriculture in the U.S.S.R.* (1950), is a careful analysis. An interesting comparison of conditions under the tsars with those under communism is to be found in M. Gordon, *Workers before and after Lenin* (1941). J. F. Normano, *The Spirit of Russian economics* (1944), is a penetrating brief analysis of Russian economic thought. Life in the slave labor camps is vividly described in D. J. Dallin and B. I. Nicolaevsky, *Forced labor in Soviet Russia* (1947); V. Petrov, *Soviet gold: my life as a slave laborer in the Siberian mines* (1949); and J. Gliksman, *Tell the west* (1948).

Religion and education. G. P. Fedotov, *The Russian religious mind* (1946), is a scholarly and well-written study. J. S. Curtiss, *Church and state in Russia* (1940), deals mainly with the period from 1900 to 1917. R. P. Casey, *Religion in Russia* (1946), is a well-written book by a well-informed author. N. S. Timasheff, *Religion in Soviet Russia, 1917–1942* (1943), is a competent study. M. Spinka, *The church and the Russian revolution* (1927), discusses the effect of the revolution on the Orthodox Church. M. J. Shore, *Soviet education: its psychology and philosophy* (1947), is a worthwhile work. *Making bolsheviks* by S. N. Harper (1931) is an interesting study. B. King, *Changing man: the education system in the U.S.S.R.* (1936), discusses the educational changes under Soviet rule.

Miscellaneous. A. Inkeles, *Public opinion in Soviet Russia: a study in mass persuasion* (1950) is a competent analysis of the propaganda machinery in the Soviet Union. Keen insight into the propaganda techniques of the Soviet government is also offered in G. Counts and N. Lodge, *The country of the blind* (1950). F. Beck and W. Godin, *Russian purge and the extraction of confession,* translated from the German by E. Mosbacher and D. Porter (1951), is a concrete account of the Soviet purge methods. G. K. Popov, *The Tcheka: the red inquisition* (1925), S. Melgunov, *The red terror in Russia* (1925), and G. Agabekov, *Ogpu* (1931), tell the story of the dreaded secret police. W. G. Krivitsky, *In Stalin's secret service* (1939), recounts the experiences of the former chief of the Soviet intelligence.

Foreign policy. Two comprehensive and authoritative accounts of Soviet foreign policy are L. Fischer, *The Soviet Union in world affairs, 1917–1929* (2 vols., 2nd ed., 1951), and M. Beloff, *The foreign policy of Soviet Russia, 1929–1941* (2 vols., 1947–1949). *The development of Soviet foreign policy in Europe, 1917–1942,* edited by M. M. Laserson (1943), is a useful symposium. *Soviet documents on foreign policy* (vol. 1, 1917–1924), edited by Jane Degras (1951), is a chronological collection of important documents. S. N. Harper, *The Soviet Union and world problems* (1935), is an informed volume. E H. Carr, *German-Soviet relations between the two world wars, 1919–1939* (1951), is a lucid, well-organized brief survey. M. M. Laserson, *Russia and the western world* (1945), discusses the role of the Soviet Union in world affairs; written in the "optimistic period." H. L. Moore, *Soviet far eastern policy, 1931-1945* (1945), is a very good survey of Soviet Far Eastern policy after 1931. Pauline Tompkins, *American Russian relations in the far east* (1949), is a fair-minded survey of relations between the two countries from 1800 to 1932. F. Borkenau, *The communist international* (1938), is a good account of the evolution and activities of the Comintern.

Culture. I. Spector, *Introduction to Russian history and culture* (1949), is a readable survey. *The seven Soviet arts* by K. London (1937) is an enlightening volume. M. Eastman, *Artists in uniform: a study of literature and bureaucratism* (1934), discusses the Soviet view of art and culture. G. Struve, *Soviet Russian literature* (1935) is a good account of the new literature to 1935. J. Freeman, J. Kunitz, and L. Lozowick, *Voices of October: art and literature in Soviet Russia* (1930), surveys the early years of the Soviet rule. *Soviet poets and poetry* by A. S. Kaun (1944) shows the theories and trends of individual writers and groups. H. Borland, *Soviet literary theory and practice during the first five-year plan, 1928-1932* (1950), is an important study. Among the useful anthologies there are *Soviet literature,* edited by G. Reavey and M. L. Slonim (1934), and *Treasury of Russian life and humor,* edited by J. Cournos (1944). P. Miliukov, *Outlines of Russian culture* (3 vols., 1942), has a section on Soviet culture. Important biographies of leading musicians include V. I. Seroff, *Dmitri Shostakovich* (1943); I. Martynov, *Dmitri Shostakovich,* translated from the Russian by T. Guralsky (1947); A. Tansman, *Igor Stravinsky,* translated by T. and C. Bleefield (1950); and F. Onnen, *Stravinsky,* (1950).

CHAPTER 22 *Britain and the British Empire*

Economic history. The economic consequences of the war are surveyed in F. W. Hirst, *The consequences of the war to Great Britain* (1934), A. L. Bowley, *Some economic consequences of the great war* (1930), C. F. G. Masterman, *England after war* (1922), and F. Plachy, *Britain's economic plight* (1926). K. Hutchinson, *The decline and fall of British capitalism* (1950), is a good survey. The economic catastrophe of 1929-1931 is carefully analyzed in F. Benham, *Great Britain under protection* (1941), and P. G. Donald, *The paralysis of trade* (1939). A. E. Kahn, *Great Britain in the world economy* (1946), is an able survey of the change in Britain's economic position. R. K. Snyder, *The tariff problem in Great Britain, 1918-1923* (1944), is a thoughtful analysis. A. Hutt, *The post-war history of the British working class* (1938), is an important volume. The problem of coal production is discussed in J. P. Dickie, *The coal problem, 1910-1936* (1936); I. Lubin and H. Everett, *The British coal dilemma* (1927); and G. D. H. Cole, *Labour in the coal mining industry, 1914-1921* (1923).

Politics and foreign policy. Ramsay Muir, *How Britain is governed* (3rd ed., 1933), is an excellent introduction to the study of British history. D. C. Somervell, *British politics since 1900* (1950), is a clear and readable survey. C. F. Brand, *British labour's rise to power* (1941), deals with the British labor movement during and after the war. There is a brief sympathetic biography of Lloyd George by T. Jones (1951). C. F. Mallet, *Mr. Lloyd George* (1930), is critical. P. Guedalla, *A gallery* (1924), contains brief incisive studies of British political leaders. There are good biographies of George V by J. Gore (1941) and H. Nicolson (1953). J. L. White, *The abdication of Edward VIII* (1937), tells the factual story. For contemporary opinion see M. M. Knappen, "The Abdication of Edward VIII," *Journal of modern history,* vol. 10 (1938), pp. 242–250. W. N. Medlicott, *British foreign policy since Versailles, 1919–1939* (1940), is a comprehensive survey. In *King's story: the memoirs of the duke of Windsor* (1951) the former Edward VIII tells his own story. E. H. Carr, *Britain: a study of foreign policy from the Versailles treaty to the outbreak of war* (1940), is a series of short essays on various facets of foreign policy.

The empire. P. Knaplund, *The British empire, 1815–1919* (1942), is an excellent objective survey. There is a readable brief survey in the Berkshire series by R. G. Trotter with the title, *The British empire-commonwealth.* R. Muir, *The British commonwealth: how it grew and how it works* (1941), is a good introductory treatise. Another good discussion is E. Barker, *The ideas and ideals of the British empire* (1941). W. Y. Elliott, *The new British empire* (1932), is a series of interesting lectures. G. M. Carter, *The British commonwealth and international security: the role of the dominions, 1919–1939* (1947), is a standard work. R. Briffault, *The decline and fall of the British empire* (1938), is a vitriolic indictment of the British by an Englishman. W. P. Hall, *Empire to commonwealth* (1928), is a readable survey. W. A. Phillips, *Revolution in Ireland, 1906–1923* (1923), is an impartial study. Other informative volumes are B. O. Brian, *The Irish constitution* (1929); W. Moss, *Political parties in the Irish Free State* (1925); and J. G. MacNeill, *Studies in the constitution of the Irish Free State* (1925). L. P. Dubois and T. P. Gill, *The Irish struggle and its results* (1934), gives special attention to the period after 1914. G. P. de T. Glazebrook, *History of Canadian external relations* (1951), is a survey of Canada's growing influence in foreign affairs. J. C. Hurewitz, *The struggle for Palestine* (1950), achieves a high degree of objectivity. J. M. N. Jeffries, *Palestine: the reality* (1939), is unsympathetic. Books with moderate viewpoints include N. Bentwich, *England in Palestine* (1932) and *Fulfillment in the promised land* (1938); and F. F. Andrews, *The Holy Land under mandate* (2 vols., 1931).

Culture. One of the most recent and also one of the best biographies of Arnold Bennett is that by R. Pound (1953). A. Vallentin, *H. G. Wells: prophet of our day* (1951), and V. Brome, *H. G. Wells* (1951), are readable but not definitive biographies. H. Pearson's *G. B. S.* (1942) is on the whole the best full-length biography that has appeared. In 1951 the same author published his *G. B. S.: a postscript* as a footnote to the longer biography. B. E. Patch, *Thirty years with G. B. S.* (1951), is an interesting account by a woman who was his secretary for 30 years.

CHAPTER 23 *France in Travail*

Politics and foreign policy. E. J. Knapton, *France since Versailles* (1952), is an admirable brief survey. R. K. Gooch, *The French parliamentary system* (1935), and W. R. Sharp, *The government of the French republic* (1938) are excellent introductory volumes. P. Vaucher, *Postwar France* (1934), is a brief survey in the Home University Library series. H. G. Daniels, *The framework of France* (1937), is a good discussion of political forces and national characteristics. Another useful volume is R. K. Gooch,

Regionalism in France (1931). W. L. Middleton, *The French political system* (1933), is an informative volume. R. H. Soltau, *French parties and politics* (1930), gives a good brief account of the political confusion. G. Wright, *Raymond Poincaré and the French presidency* (1942), is based on painstaking research. R. W. Hale, *Democratic France: the third republic from Sedan to Vichy* (1941), and D. W. Brogan, *The development of modern France, 1870–1939* (1940), are good surveys of a wider period of French history. *Modern France; problems of the third and fourth republics,* edited by E. M. Earle (1951), is a penetrating analysis by a group of "experts." C. A. Micaud, *The French right and Nazi Germany, 1933–1939* (1943), is an invaluable study of public opinion. W. de Ormesson, *France* (1939), is a good survey of foreign policy after World War I.

Economic conditions. W. F. Ogburn and W. Jaffé, *The economic development of postwar France* (1929), W. MacDonald, *Reconstruction in France* (1922), and J. H. Rogers, *The process of inflation in France, 1914–1927* (1929), contain enlightening discussions of economic conditions during the years following the war. S. B. Clough, *France: a history of national economics, 1789–1939* (1939), has a number of penetrating chapters on the period between the two wars. There are also two good volumes by G. Peel: *The financial crisis of France* (1925) and *The economic policy of France* (1937). R. M. Haig, *The public finances of postwar France* (1929), is a clear discussion of a complex subject. M. Wolfe, *The French franc between the wars, 1919–1939* (1951), contributes much to an understanding of the period. D. J. Saposs, *The labor movement in postwar France* (1931), surveys the early postwar years. The labor movement from 1934 to 1944 is ably discussed in H. W. Ehrmann, *French labor: from popular front to liberation* (1947). F. A. Haight, *A history of French commercial policies* (1941), surveys the changes of tariff policy.

Culture. M. Turnell, *The novel in France* (1951), is a readable survey. A. Maurois, *Proust: portrait of a genius* (1950), is the best single volume on the subject. F. Mauriac, *Proust's way,* translated from the French by E. Pell (1950), is a series of essays. *The mind of Proust* by F. C. Green (1950) is a painstaking study. *Musical trends in the twentieth century* by N. Demuth (1952) contains brilliant essays on Ravel and other modern Frenchmen. There is also an informative essay on Ravel in D. Brook, *Five great French composers* (1945). V. I. Seroff, *Maurice Ravel* (1953), is a well-documented biography. An older good biography is that by M. Gross (1940).

CHAPTER 24 *Eastern Europe*

General accounts. *Central-eastern Europe: crucible of world war* by J. S. Rouček and associates (1946) aims to dispel many popular misconceptions. O. Halecki, *Borderlands of western civilization: a history of east central Europe* (1952), is an excellent introductory survey. Another good survey is H. Seton-Watson, *Eastern Europe between the wars, 1918–1941* (1945). J. S. Rouček, *Balkan politics: international relations in no man's land* (1948) provides a considerable amount of information. *Slavonic encyclopedia,* edited by J. S. Rouček (1949), is a valuable aid to the history student. F. Schevill and W. M. Gewehr, *History of the Balkan peninsula* (1933), is one of the best surveys. There are two solid scholarly books on the minorities question by O. I. Janowsky:

People at bay, the Jewish problem in east-central Europe (1938) and *Nationalities and national minorities* (1945). H. Kohn, *Nationalism and imperialism in the hither East* (1932), has pertinent chapters.

Austria and Hungary. O. Jaszi, *The dissolution of the Habsburg monarchy* (1929), is an authoritative analysis of the causes of the dissolution. *The tragedy of Austria,* by J. Braunthal with an appendix by J. R. Sweet (1948), is a penetrating survey from World War I to the Anschluss. C. A. Gulick, *Austria from Habsburg to Hitler* (2 vols., 1948), covers the various facets of Austrian life during the period; a monumental achievement. M. Macdonald, *The republic of Austria, 1918–1934: a study in the failure of democratic government* (1946), is a brief account. C. A. Macartney, *The social revolution in Austria* (1926), is an informative study. For the economic side there is K. W. Rothschild, *Austria's economic development between two wars* (1947). P. R. Sweet, "Democracy and counterrevolution in Austria," *Journal of modern history,* vol. 22 (1950), pp. 52–58, offers an excellent bibliographical discussion. S. W. Gould, "Austrian attitudes toward anschluss, October, 1918–September, 1919," *Journal of modern history,* vol. 22 (1950), pp. 220–231, is an informative short study. C. A. Macartney, *Hungary and her successors* (1937), is intelligent and readable. D. G. Kosáry, *A history of Hungary* (1941), is one of the best general histories of Hungary in English.

Poland and Czechoslovakia. *Poland,* edited by B. E. Schmitt (1945), is a symposium by outstanding historians. O. Halecki, *A history of Poland* (1943), is a sympathetic but lively survey. R. Machray, *The Poland of Pilsudski* (1936), is a careful narrative by an admirer of Poland. There are also valuable materials on the period in R. Dyboski, *Poland in world civilization,* edited by R. Krzyzanowski (1950). A detailed factual account of the period is to be found in *The Cambridge history of Poland,* edited by W. F. Reddaway and others (2 vols., 1941–50). *Czechoslovakia: twenty years of independence,* edited by R. J. Kerner (1940), is a comprehensive and authoritative manual. S. H. Thomson, *Czechoslovakia in European history* (rev. ed., 1953), is a comprehensive well-informed study. There is a good brief survey by R. W. Seton-Watson under the title *Twenty-five years of Czechoslovakia* (1945). E. Wiskemann, *Czechs and Germans* (1938), is a competent illuminating study. F. J. Vondracek, *The foreign policy of Czechoslovakia, 1918–1935* (1937), is a careful survey.

Rumania and Yugoslavia. C. Kormos, *Rumania* (1945), is a readable brief survey. J. S. Rouček, *Contemporary Rumania and her problems* (1932), is a penetrating study. R. W. Seton-Watson, *History of the Rumanian people* (1930), is a good survey. The problem of the peasant is ably discussed in D. Mitrany, *The land and peasant in Rumania* (1930). An earlier but still useful volume is I. L. Evans, *The agrarian revolution in Rumania* (1924). G. Gay, *King Carol of Rumania* (1940), is a careful study of Carol's government. R. D. Hogg, *Yugoslavia* (1944), is a good survey of the period between the great wars. Two other good surveys are E. J. Patterson, *Yugoslavia* (1936), and R. G. D. Laffan, *Yugoslavia since 1918* (1929). On the government and administration of Yugoslavia the student may consult C. Beard and G. Radin, *The Balkan pivot: Yugoslavia* (1929).

Greece, Bulgaria, and Albania. E. G. Mears, *Greece today: the aftermath of the refugee impact* (1929), is a good survey which does not neglect economic factors.

Greece, compiled by K. Gibberd (1945), offers brief accounts of crucial periods. N. Kaltchas, *Introduction to the constitutional history of modern Greece* (1940), is a valuable treatise on a neglected phase of Greek history. D. Caclamanos, *Greece: a panorama* (1944), is an interesting account by a Greek journalist. *Bulgaria: past and present* by G. C. Logio (1936) is a judicious study. C. E. Black, *The establishment of constitutional government in Bulgaria* (1944), is a well-done treatise. The economic life of Bulgaria is ably analyzed in L. Pasvolsky, *Bulgaria's economic position* (1930). C. Anastasoff, *The tragic peninsula* (1938), includes an account of the Macedonian separatist movement. The best account in English on Albania after World War I is J. Swire, *Albania: the rise of a kingdom* (1929).

Turkey. W. Miller, *The Ottoman empire and its successors* (3rd ed., 1927), is a standard survey. H. N. Howard, *The partition of Turkey, a diplomatic history, 1913–1923* (1931), is a careful study based on a vast amount of research. E. Jackh, *The rising crescent: Turkey yesterday, today, and tomorrow* (1944), is a mine of information. The social and religious changes are competently surveyed in H. E. Allen, *The Turkish transformation* (1935). E. Bisbee, *The new Turks, pioneers of the republic, 1920–1950* (1951), is fluent and informative but highly apologetic. H. Kohn, *Western civilization in the near east* (1936), is an interesting scholarly study of the process of Europeanization. Two other good studies of the transformation are D. E. Webster, *The Turkey of Atatürk* (1939), and B. Ward, *Turkey* (1942). The changes as they affected women are vividly portrayed in R. F. Woodsmall, *Moslem women enter a new world* (1936), and Selma Ekrem, *Unveiled: the autobiography of a Turkish girl* (1930). The economic deficiencies of Turkey are appraised in M. W. Thornburg, *Turkey: an economic appraisal* (1949). One of the best biographies of Kemal Atatürk is H. C. Armstrong, *Gray wolf* (1933).

CHAPTER 25 *Fascism in Italy and Spain*

Italy. For the period before the advent of fascism M. Hentze, *Prefascist Italy* (1939), is a good survey. A. Rossi, *The rise of fascism: Italy from 1918 to 1922* (1938), is one of the best accounts. H. W. Schneider, *Making the fascist state* (1929), is a searching analysis of the origins of fascism. The same author has also written two other scholarly volumes: *The fascist government of Italy* (1936) and *Making fascists* (1929), the latter in collaboration with S. B. Clough. R. Albrecht-Carrié, "Italian foreign policy, 1914–1922," *Journal of modern history,* vol. 20 (1948), pp. 326–339, is an excellent bibliographical article. G. Megaro, *Mussolini in the making* (1938), graphically reconstructs the early years of Mussolini's life. J. A. R. Marriott, *Makers of modern Italy* (1937), contains a good brief life of Mussolini. The definitive life of Mussolini has not appeared. Three of the best scholarly accounts of fascism are W. Ebenstein, *Fascist Italy* (1939); H. Finer, *Mussolini's Italy* (1935); and S. Rauschenbush, *The march of fascism* (1939). M. T. Florinsky, *Fascism and national socialism* (1936), offers a comparison of the two "isms." G. A. Borgese, *Goliath: the march of fascism* (1937), is a well-written account but omits certain phases. The plight of the Italian peasant is vividly portrayed in C. T. Schmidt, *The plough and the sword: labor, land, and property in fascist Italy* (1938). M. H. H. Macartney and P. Cremona, *Italy's foreign and colonial policy, 1914–*

1937 (1938), is a valuable series of essays on select aspects of Italy's foreign policy. F. A. Ridley, *Mussolini over Africa* (1935), is a good brief discussion. Fascist education is ably treated in H. R. Marraro, *The new education in Italy* (1936). Efforts to increase the population are discussed in D. V. Glass, *The struggle for population* (1936). W. S. Halperin, *Italy and the Vatican at war* (1939), is a careful study of the relations between the Vatican and the Italian state. The story of the Lateran agreements is told in B. Williamson, *The treaty of the Lateran* (1929), and T. E. Moore, *Peter's city* (1930). C. T. Schmidt, *The corporate state in action* (1939), and H. L. Matthews, *The fruits of fascism* (1943), attempt to evaluate the achievements and weaknesses of fascism.

Spain. The early postwar years are interestingly portrayed in G. Young, *The new Spain* (1933), and F. B. Deakin, *Spain today* (1924). J. A. Brandt, *Toward the new Spain* (1932), traces the development of republicanism to 1931. F. E. Manuel, *The politics of modern Spain* (1938), is a well-documented study. E. A. Peers has written two scholarly books which cover the period: *The Spanish tragedy, 1930–1936* (1936) and *The Church in Spain, 1737–1937* (1938). The constitution of 1931 is discussed in R. M. Smith, *The day of the liberals in Spain* (1939). The causes of the civil war are carefully analysed in G. Brenan, *The Spanish labyrinth* (1943), and T. J. Hamilton, *Appeasement's child* (1942). *Report from Spain* by E. J. Hughes (1947) paints the Spanish situation in dark colors. Sir Samuel Hoare, who was British ambassador to Spain, deals sharply with Franco in *Complacent dictator* (1947). F. E. Manuel, *The politics of modern Spain* (1938), is an informative volume. There is no definitive history of the Spanish civil war. Among the more readable volumes one must include H. W. Buckley, *Life and death of the Spanish republic* (1940); H. Gannes and T. Repard, *Spain in revolt* (1936); W. Foss, *The Spanish arena* (1938); E. White, *War in Spain* (1937); A. L. Strong, *Spain in arms* (1937); and F. Borkenau, *The Spanish cockpit: an eyewitness account of the Spanish civil war* (1937). A. R. Oliveira, *Politics, economics, and men of modern Spain, 1808–1946,* translated by T. Hall (1948), is a serious, well-documented volume. C. Salter, *Try-out in Spain* (1943), develops the thesis that World War II started in Spain in 1936. E. A. Peers, *Catalonia infelix* (1938), is a keen analysis of the Catalonian question.

CHAPTER 26 *Nazi Germany*

Rise of Nazism. R. G. L. Waite, *Vanguard of nazism: the free corps movement in postwar Germany, 1918–1923* (1952), is an interesting well-documented study of a neglected phase. L. L. Snyder, *Hitlerism: the iron fist in Germany* (1932), is one of the best of the early accounts on the rise of nazism. The same author has also written two good scholarly analyses of German nationalism: *From Bismarck to Hitler: the background of modern German nationalism* (1935) and *German nationalism: the tragedy of a people* (1952). Probably the fullest account of the origins of nazism is C. Heiden, *History of national socialism* (1934). R. D. Butler, *The roots of national socialism* (1942), is a penetrating study of the mental climate in which Hitlerism was nurtured. *The struggle for democracy in Germany,* edited by G. A. Almond (1948), is a worthwhile symposium by a group of specialists in German history. R. Heberle, *From democracy to nazism* (1945), is a competent investigation of Germany's turn from democracy to National Socialism. A. Brecht, *Prelude to silence: the end of the German republic* (1944), is a thoughtful, suggestive study. O. J. Hammen, "German historians and the advent of the national socialist state," *Journal of modern history,* vol. 13 (1941), pp. 161–188, is an illuminating article. Peter Viereck, *Metapolitics: from the romantics to Hitler* (1941), is excellent for background. The question of race is ably treated in L. L. Snyder, *Race: a history of modern ethnic theories* (1939), and J. Barzun, *Race: a study in modern superstition* (1938). T. Taylor, *Sword and swastika: generals and nazis in the Third Reich* (1952), tells the sombre story of the rise of nazism and the horrors that followed its rise to power.

Nazism in action. F. L. Neumann, *Behemoth: the structure and practice of national socialism* (1942), is a lucid account of the complex social, political, and economic setup of Hitler's Reich. F. Schuman, *Hitler and the Nazi dictatorship* (1936), is a sprightly critical analysis. H. Lichtenberger, *The third reich: Germany under national socialism,* translated from the French by K. Pinson (1937), is one of the best accounts. S. Roberts, *The house that Hitler built* (1938), is a good analysis of both the Führer and his system. In *The revolution of nihilism* (1939) H. Rauschning, a former Nazi, exposes Nazi techniques. R. A. Brady, *The spirit and structure of German fascism* (1937), is based on a careful study of the sources. On the Nazi state there are three careful studies: W. Ebenstein, *The Nazi state* (1943); F. M. Marx, *Government in the third Reich* (1936); and F. Ermarth, *The new Germany: national socialist state in theory and practice* (1936). Nazi economics are discussed in C. W. Guillebaud, *The economic recovery of Germany, 1933–1938* (1939); A. Gerschonkron, *Bread and democracy in Germany* (1944); and V. Trivanovitch, *Economic development of Germany under national socialism* (1937). Nazi preparations for war are described in E. Banse, *Germany prepares for war* (new ed., 1941), and O. Nathan and M. Fried, *The Nazi economic system: Germany's mobilization for war* (1944). E. Y. Hartshorne, *The German universities and national socialism* (1937); G. A. Ziemer, *Education for death: the making of the Nazi* (1941); E. Mann, *School for barbarians* (1938); and G. F. Kneller, *The educational philosophy of national socialism* (1941), are interesting accounts of Nazi educational and propaganda techniques. Among the better accounts of the German-Jewish question there are M. Lowenthal, *The Jews of Germany* (1936); S. Liptzin, *Germany's stepchildren* (1944); *Nazi Germany's war against the Jews,* compiled by S. Krieger (1947); and M. Weinreich, *Hitler's professors: the part of scholarship in Germany's crimes against the Jewish people* (1946). H. Rothfels, *The German opposition to Hitler* (1948) is an intelligent analysis of the resistance movement. J. Bithell, *Modern German literature, 1880–1938* (1947), is a survey by a noted student of German culture. C. W. Guillebaud, *The social policy of Nazi Germany* (1941), is a valuable contribution.

Biographical. Hitler's own story is of course recorded in *Mein Kampf,* of which there are a number of translations. The most complete collection of Hitler's speeches is to be found in *The speeches of Adolf Hitler, April, 1922–August, 1939,* edited by N. H. Baynes (2 vols., 1943). The best biography of Hitler in English is A. Bullock, *Hitler: a study in tyranny* (1953); comprehensive, well-written, and accurate. Two other good biographies though not as up-to-date are K. Heiden, *Der fuehrer, 1884–1934,* translated by R. Manheim (1944), and L. Wagner, *Hitler: man of strife* (1942). C. Riess, *Joseph Goebbels: the devil's advocate* (1948), is a lively biography of the cynical, contemptible master of Nazi propaganda. Some of the daily effusions of this propagandist may be read in *The Goebbels diaries, 1942–1943,* translated and edited by L P. Lochner (1948). W.

Frischauer, *The rise and fall of Hermann Goering* (1951), is a balanced study of an unbalanced Nazi. T. Koeves, *Satan in top hat: the biography of Franz von Papen* (1941), is a psychological analysis of the evil genius who opened the way for Hitler's accession to power.

CHAPTER 27 *The Revolt of Asia*

General. Among the earliest books which discuss the awakening of Asia are G. M. Dutcher, *Political awakening of the East* (1925); Upton Close (J. W. Hall), *Revolt of Asia* (1927); N. Peffer, *The white man's dilemma* (1927); and J. A. Spender, *The changing East* (1926). More recent studies are M. M. Hyndman, *Awakening of Asia* (1939), and M. J. Bonn, *The crumbling of empire* (1938). M. A. Nourse, *Ferment in the Far East* (1949), is a popular survey which omits some of the basic trends. O. Hardy and G. S. Dumke, *A history of the Pacific in modern times* (1949); H. M. Vinacke, *A history of the Far East in modern times* (5th ed., 1950); P. H. Clyde, *The Far East since 1500* (1947); and H. S. Quigley and G. H. Blakeslee, *The Far East* (1938), are clear, informative and readable surveys. C. A. Buss, *War and diplomacy in eastern Asia* (1941), is an enlightening study. The history of the impact of the occident on the orient is carefully and interestingly discussed in P. H. Clyde, *The Far East* (new ed., 1952), and H. Kohn, *Orient and occident* (1934). *Government and nationalism in southeast Asia* by R. Emerson and others (1942) is a mine of information. *Northeastern Asia, a select bibliography,* collected and edited by R. J. Kerner (2 vols., 1939), is a monumental work.

India. An excellent birdseye view of the awakening of India is to be found in T. W. Wallbank, *India: a survey of the heritage and growth of Indian nationalism* (1948). B. T. McCully, "The origins of Indian nationalism according to native writers," *Journal of modern history,* vol. 7 (1935), pp. 295–314, is a first-rate discussion. G. D. Sanderson, *India and British imperialism* (1951), is a monumental work of research. E. Thompson and G. T. Garratt, *Rise and fulfillment of British rule in India* (1934), is a fair-minded survey. R. P. Dutt, *The problem of India* (1943), forcefully argues for India's freedom. L. Fischer, *The life of Mahatma Gandhi* (1950), is the first full biography of the "little man in a loin cloth" — as objective as personal admiration permits. V. Sheean, *Lead, kindly light* (1949), is a discussion of Gandhi and his principles by an American who came under his spell. Gandhi himself tells the story of the emergence of a timid man into a world leader in his *Autobiography: the story of my experiments with truth* (1949).

China. The story of China during World War I is told in T. E. LaFargue, *China and the world war* (1937). A. N. Holcombe, *The Chinese revolution: a phase in the regeneration of a world power* (1930), contains a good account of the first decade after World War I. Two other good studies are H. F. MacNair, *China in revolution* (1931), and H. F. Misselwitz, *The dragon stirs: an intimate sketch-book of China's Kuomintang revolution, 1927–1929* (1941). H. R. Ekins and T. Wright, *China fights for her life* (1938), tells the story of the Japanese invasion. *China,* edited by H. F. MacNair (1946), has some excellent essays on the period. W. R. Fishel, *The end of extraterritoriality in China* (1952), is a conscientious and well-documented study covering the period from 1917 to

1943. P. M. A. Linebarger, *The China of Chiang Kai-shek: a political study* (1941), is a competent study. The same author's *Political doctrines of Sun Yat-sen* (1937) is the fullest treatment of the subject available in English. S. A. Hedin, *Chiang Kai-shek: marshal of China* (1940), is an informative biography. There are several editions in English of Chiang Kai-shek's *China's Destiny* in which he states his political creed. The best available biography of Sun Yat-sen is that by L. Sharman (1934). R. T. Pollard, *China's foreign relations, 1917–1931* (1933), is a useful account of China's efforts to free itself from the unequal treaties. K. S. Latourette, *The Chinese: their history and culture* (2 vols., 1934), is a standard text.

Japan. A. M. Young, *Imperial Japan, 1926–1938* (1938), is a good survey. M. M. Dilts, *The pageant of Japanese history* (2nd ed., 1947), is a good introduction to Japanese history. D. H. James, *The rise and fall of the Japanese empire* (1951), contains informative chapters on the period. On the government of Japan there are a number of good discussions including R. K. Reischauer, *Japanese government and politics* (1932), and C. B. Fahs, *Government in Japan* (1940). H. Borton, *Japan since 1931* (1940), is a competent survey. F. C. Jones, *Manchuria since 1931* (1949), is the best all-around study in English. Sara R. Smith, *The Manchurian crisis, 1931–1932: a tragedy in international relations* (1948), is a well-done account. T. A. Bisson, *Japan in China* (1938), is a well-balanced account of the invasion. H. F. MacNair, *The real conflict between China and Japan* (1938), is a provocative discussion. H. S. Quigley, *Far Eastern war, 1937–1941* (1942), is a well-balanced analysis. G. C. Allen, *Japanese industry* (1940), is an interesting brief discussion of the efficiency of Japanese industry. C. Lowe, *Japan's economic offensive in China* (1939), is a good discussion of one phase of Japanese imperialism. H. M. Vinacke, "Japanese Imperialism," *Journal of modern history*, vol. 5 (1935), pp. 366–380, is an excellent critical discussion of books which appeared up to 1934. F. R. Dulles, *Forty years of American-Japanese relations* (1937), is an interesting survey.

CHAPTER 28 *The Road to World War II*

General accounts. D. E. Lee, *Ten years: the world on its way to war, 1930–1940* (1942), is a first-rate survey. *The origins and consequences of world war II,* by F. A. Cave and associates (1948), is a successful attempt to deal with an intricate subject — objective and readable. C. J. Haines and R. J. S. Hoffman, *The origins and background of the second world war* (1943), is written with insight and a good sense of proportion. F. L. Schumann, *Europe on the eve: the crises of diplomacy 1933–1939* (1939), is a lively detailed survey. *The diplomats, 1919–1939,* edited by G. A. Craig and F. Gilbert (1953), is an impressive achievement by a group of highly competent scholars. F. T. Birchall, *The storm breaks* (1940), is a clear discussion of the origins and issues of the conflict. *Documentary background of world war II, 1931–1941,* edited by J. W. Gantenbein (1948), is a valuable collection of documents. E. H. Carr, *The twenty years' crisis, 1919– 1939* (1940), is a stimulating survey. In W. Millis, *Why Europe fights* (1940), an American writer lists the broader issues that made for war.

Efforts to outlaw war. In R. Dell, *The rise and fall of the league of nations* (1943), an acute observer records his impressions. J. T. Shotwell and M. Salvin, *Lessons on* *security and disarmament from the history of the league of nations* (1949), argues that the efforts of the League were not futile. *Guide to league of nations publications* by H. Aufricht (1951) is a comprehensive bibliographical survey. R. H. Ferrell, *Peace in their time* (1952), is an excellent study of the Kellogg-Briand pact. J. W. Wheeler-Bennett wrote two good books on the failure of the disarmament efforts: *The disarmament deadlock* (1934) and *The pipe dream of peace* (1935). J. H. Morgan, *Assize of arms: the disarmament of Germany and her rearmament, 1919-1939* (1946), develops the thesis that the Reichswehr officers defeated all attempts to disarm Germany. W. E. Rappard, *The quest for peace* (1940), is a thoroughgoing survey of the peace efforts. Margaret S. Gordon, *Barriers to world trade* (1941), discusses the question of tariffs. Another careful study is H. Liepmann, *Tariff levels and the economic unity of Europe* (1938).

Nazi Germany. K. Loewenstein, *Hitler's Germany: the Nazi background to war* (rev. ed., 1944), shows that the Nazi government was a war government from its inception. O. D. Fraser, *Germany between two wars: a study of propaganda and war-guilt* (1945), contains the story of how Germany sabotaged the peace of Versailles and prepared for war. E. Wiskemann, *Czechs and Germans: a study of the struggle in the historic provinces of Bohemia and Moravia* (1938), is a competent, detailed study. E. H. Carr, *German-Soviet relations between the two world wars, 1919-1939* (1951), is written with insight and literary skill. M. M. Ball, *Post-war German-Austrian relations, 1918-1936* (1937), is a careful account of the Anschluss movement. The absorption of Austria by the Nazis is detailed in O. Dutch, *Thus died Austria* (1938), G. E. R. Gedye, *Betrayal in Central Europe* (1939), and M. Fuchs, *Showdown in Vienna* (1938). K. von Schuschnigg, *Austrian requiem* (1946), is an account by the ex-Chancellor of Austria. E. Wiskemann, *The Rome-Berlin axis: a history of the relations between Hitler and Mussolini* (1949), tells the story of a sinister relationship.

Britain. One of the best accounts of British appeasement is P. Einzig, *Appeasement before, during and after the war* (1942). Winston Churchill vigorously attacked the policy of appeasement in *While England slept* (1938) and *Step by step, 1936-1939* (1939). E. H. Carr, *Great Britain: a study of foreign policy from the Versailles treaty to the outbreak of war* (1939), and W. M. Medlicott, *British foreign policy since Versailles* (1940), are two accounts by distinguished historians. J. F. Kennedy, *Why England slept* (1940), shows how and why Britain permitted Germany to outdistance her. A. Wolfers, *Britain and France between two wars: conflicting strategies of peace since Versailles* (1940), is a readable and carefully-done work.

Munich and after. J. W. Wheeler-Bennett, *Munich: prologue to tragedy* (1948), is a readable scholarly treatise. Another good account is R. W. Seton-Watson, *Munich and the dictators* (1939). A revision of this book appeared under the title *From Munich to Danzig* (1939). K. Krofta, *Germany and Czechoslovakia* (2 vols., 1937), is a detailed account of the relations between the two countries prior to Munich. E. Wiskemann, *Prologue to war* (1940), is an acute analysis of the situation on the eve of the war. *The world in March, 1939,* edited by A. Toynbee and F. T. A. Gwatkin (1952), is a comprehensive picture of the months preceding the outbreak of hostilities. In *Failure of a mission: Berlin, 1937-1939* (1940) Nevile Henderson, the last British ambassador before the war, tells of his futile efforts to stop the outbreak of hostilities.

CHAPTERS 29 AND 30 *World War II*

General. *The background of our war* by Colonel H. Beukema and associates (1942) is an excellent brief survey of the early period of the war. *The pocket history of the second world war,* edited by H. S. Commager (1945), is a good brief survey of the entire war. Other surveys include R. W. Shugg and Major H. A. De Weerd, *World war II* (1946); F. T. Miller, *History of world war II* (1945); E. L. Hasluck, *The second world war* (1948); C. Falls, *The second world war* (1948); Gen. J. F. C. Fuller, *The second world war: 1939–1945* (1949); and R. M. Titmuss, *History of the second world war* (1950). The more recent surveys contain material that was not available right after the war. E. McInnis, *The war* (6 vols., 1940–1947), coordinates a bewildering amount of material in a sound, readable account. D. D. Eisenhower, *Crusade in Europe* (1948), is an intimate report by a leading general. W. P. Hall, *Iron out of Calvary* (1946), is a coherent discussion of underlying issues. J. Stern, *The hidden damage* (1947), is a popular account of certain phases of life during the war. H. Baldwin, *Great mistakes of the war* (1950), is an enlightening short discussion. B. H. Liddell Hart, *The revolution in warfare* (1947), is a discussion of new weapons and their influence on warfare. Winston Churchill has recorded his war experiences in grand and intimate terms in a series of volumes: *The gathering storm* (1948), *Their finest hour* (1949), *The grand alliance* (1950), *The hinge of fate* (1950), *Closing the ring* (1951), and *Triumph and tragedy* (1953). S. F. Bemis, "First gun of a revisionist historiography for the second world war," *Journal of modern history,* vol. 19 (1947), pp. 55–59, is a penetrating discussion of revisionist books.

Opening phases. F. O. Miksche, *Attack: a study of blitzkrieg tactics* (1942), is a good exposition of the methods employed by the Nazis. Other informative volumes on the newer methods of warfare are Major P. C. Raborg, *Mechanized might: the story of mechanized warfare* (1944), and P. W. Thompson, *Modern battle* (1941). *The Axis grand strategy: blueprints for the total war,* edited by L. Farago (1942), deals with the aims, methods, and conduct of total war. J. Hanč, *Tornado across Europe: the path of Nazi destruction from Poland to Greece* (1942), is a sound study by a student of military affairs. *The Russo-German alliance: August, 1939–June, 1941* by A. Rossi, translated by J. and M. Cullen (1949), is a concise, dispassionate account backed by painstaking research. J. T. Shotwell and M. M. Laserson, *Poland and Russia, 1919–1945* (1945), is a clear and helpful brief study. *Finland and world war II, 1939–1944,* edited by J. Wuorinen, (1948), throws much light on the Russo-Finnish war. D. J. Dallin, *Soviet Russia's foreign policy, 1939–1942,* translated by L. Dennen (1943), was written before many important documents were published. J. Langdon-Davies, *Invasion in the snow* (1941), discusses the strategy and tactics of the Finnish war.

From the invasion of Norway to the battle of Britain. *Norway: her invasion and occupation,* by Amanda Johnson (1948) is a painstaking synthesis. H. Koht, *Norway: neutral and invaded* (1941), depicts the struggles against the Nazis. C. J. Hambro, *I saw it happen in Norway* (1940), is a vivid eyewitness account. P. Paulmer, *Denmark in Nazi chains* (1942), describes the first months of Nazi occupation. The invasion of Holland is vividly described in E. N. van Kleffen, *Juggernaut over Holland* (1941). L. de

Jong and W. F. Stoppleman, *The lion rampant: the story of Holland's resistance to the Nazis* (1943), is interesting and informative. *The official account of what happened, 1939–1940* by the Belgian Ministry of Foreign Affairs (1942) tells the story of the Belgian invasion. The resistance to the Nazis is graphically depicted in L. Moens, *Under the iron heel* (1941), and J. Garis, *Belgium in bondage* (1944). A. D. Divine, *Dunkirk* (1945), and D. Williams, *Retreat from Dunkirk* (1941), are interesting accounts of the withdrawal. A. Maurois, *Why France fell,* translated from the French by D. Lindley (1941), and E. J. Bois, *Truth on the tragedy of France* (1941), try to explain the causes of the French collapse. Another enlightening description of the French débâcle is to be found in D. Vilfroy, *War in the west: the battle of France, May–June, 1940* (1942). P. Maillard, *France* (1942), is probably the best appraisement. One phase of the resistance movement is discussed in G. R. Millar, *Maquis* (1945). I. M. Gibson, "The Maginot Line," *Journal of modern history,* vol. 7 (1945) pp. 130–146, is an interesting short study. Events in Italy leading to the entry of that country are related in R. and E. Packard, *Balcony empire* (1942). There is also valuable information in *The Ciano diaries, 1939–1943,* edited by H. Gibson (1946). *The battle of Britain,* by H. A. Saunders (1941) is the official account of the British Air Ministry. Another informative volume is J. M. Spaight, *The sky's the limit: a study of British air power* (1940). Winston Churchill has written two books on the period: *Blood, sweat, and tears* (1941) and *The unrelenting struggle* (1942). The economic struggles are related in W. E. Murphy, *The British war economy, 1939–1943* (1943).

Germany. M. Seydewitz, *Civil life in wartime Germany* (1945), is a readable account of wartime conditions in the Third Reich. H. K. Smith, *The last train from Berlin* (1942), shows what it was like to live in Germany. Other interesting books by journalists are J. C. Harsh, *Germany at war* (1942), W. Deuel, *People under Hitler* (1942), and *This is the enemy* by F. C. Oechsner and others (1942). Informative books on the Nazi opposition include A. W. Dulles, *Germany's underground* (1947); H. Rotfels, *The opposition to Hitler* (1948); R. Andreas-Friedrich, *Berlin underground, 1938–1945,* translated by B. Mussey (1947); and F. von Schlabrendorff, *They almost killed Hitler* (1947). Hitler as a strategist is discussed in *Hitler directs his war,* selected and edited by F. Gilbert (1950); F. Halder, *Hitler as a war lord,* translated by P. Findlay (1950); and A. K. Martienssen, *Hitler and his admirals* (1949). *History of the German general staff,* by W. Goerlitz, translated by B. Battershaw (1953), lacks both scholarship and depth. B. H. Liddell-Hart, *The other side of the hill: Germany's generals* (1948), shows how the generals rose and fell during the period of the war. *The Goebbels diaries, 1942–1943,* edited and translated by L. P. Lochner (1948), show how Goebbels was running the country while Hitler was directing the war.

Naval and air war. Captain W. D. Puleston, *The influence of sea power in world war II* (1947) discusses sea power in the light of new weapons. The story of war under the sea during the early period of the war is told in A. M. Low, *The submarine at war* (1942), and H. S. Zim, *Submarines* (1942). W. Armstrong, *Battle of the oceans* (1944), is an account of the British merchant marine. Rear Admiral H. Cope and Captain W. Karig, *Battle submerged: submarine fighters of world war II* (1951), gives an excellent brief account of the role of the submarine in World War II. T. Roscoe, *U.S. submarine operations in world war II* (1950), is a worthwhile volume. The air war against Germany is described in A. A. Michie, *The air offensive against Germany* (1943). Asher

Lee, *The German air force* (1946), tells the story of the Luftwaffe from its secret beginnings to the fall of Germany. *Bomber offensive* by Sir Arthur Harris (1947) is the story of the British Bomber Command by its commander. *The army air force in world war II,* edited by W. F. Craven and J. L. Cate (2 vols., 1948–1949), is a careful scholarly analysis by a group of competent historians.

Invasion of Russia. John Scott, *Duel for Europe* (1942), tells how Hitler and Stalin came to blows. N. A. Voznesenskii, *Economy of the U.S.S.R. during world war II* (1949), is the official statement of the Russian war effort. A. Werth has written two interesting books on the fighting in Russia: *Moscow war diary* (1942) and *The year of Stalingrad* (1947). Stirring pictures of the fighting are to be found in B. Voyetekhov's *The last days of Sevastopol* (1943); B. Skomorovsky and E. G. Morris, *The siege of Leningrad* (1944); and T. Plievier, *Stalingrad,* translated by R. and C. Winston (1948).

United States and the war. H. Feis, *The road to Pearl Harbor* (1950), is a scholarly and well-balanced account of the events leading to the Japanese attack. *The undeclared war, 1940–1941* by W. L. Langer and S. E. Gleason (1953) offers a careful account of political and diplomatic events. Basil Rauch, *Roosevelt from Munich to Pearl Harbor: a study in the creation of a foreign policy* (1950), is a painstaking examination and a defense of the development of the Roosevelt foreign policy. E. O. Reischauer, *The United States and Japan* (1950), is a clear account by a well-known historian. C. A. Beard, *President Roosevelt and the coming of the war, 1941* (1949), is an attack on the Roosevelt foreign policy. W. H. Chamberlin, *America's second crusade* (1950), is a survey by a revisionist from the "unnatural alliance" of the United States with Russia to the "world's worst peace." In C. C. Tansill, *Back door to war: Roosevelt foreign policy, 1933–1941* (1952), another revisionist reconsiders the Roosevelt foreign policy on the basis of information gathered from the secret files of the State Department. W. Millis, *This is Pearl! The United States and Japan — 1941* (1947), is a good account of the period before Pearl Harbor. W. C. Johnstone, *The United States and Japan's new order* (1941), is an exposition of Japanese aims. *The United States at war,* prepared under the auspices of the Committee of Records of War Administration (1947), is an excellent summary.

Japan. W. C. Johnstone, *The United States and Japan's new order* (1941), is an exposition of Japanese aims. C. Crow, *Japan's dream of world empire* (1942), outlines the Japanese plan of conquest. Kate L. Mitchell, *Japan's industrial strength* (1942), and C. D. Carus and C. L. McNichols, *Japan: its resources and industries* (1944), offer much factual information. H. Lory, *Japan's military masters* (1943), discusses the organization and training of the Japanese army. H. J. van Mook, *The Netherlands Indies and Japan: battle on paper, 1940–1941* (1944), is a concrete account of Japanese machinations.

Eastern Europe and the Mediterranean area. S. Casson, *Greece against the Axis* (1943), outlines the campaign in Greece. Betty Wason, *Miracle in Hellas: the Greeks fight on* (1943), describes Greece under Axis occupation. L. S. Stavrianos, *Greece: the war and aftermath* (1947), is a useful study. L. S. Stavrianos and E. P. Panagopoulos, "Present-day Greece," *Journal of modern history,* vol. 20 (1948), pp. 49–158, is an excellent discussion of books on twentieth-century Greece. D. Martin, *Ally betrayed: the uncensored story of Tito and Mihailovich* (1946), discusses the situation in Yugoslavia. R. de Belot, *The struggle for the Mediterranean, 1939–1945,* translated by J. A. Field

(1951), is a brief but keen analysis. D. Young, *Rommel, the desert fox* (1950), is a full-length biography which makes confused military situations understandable. B. L. Montgomery, *El Alamein to the river Sangro* (1949), records the exploits of the British Eighth Army in North Africa.

Operations in the Pacific area. *History of the United States naval operations in world war II* by S. E. Morison was announced soon after the war as a series of fourteen volumes. Since that time more than half the volumes have appeared. J. Miller, Jr., *Guadalcanal: the first offensive* (1949), provides the first comprehensive account of ground operations during the Guadalcanal campaign. When read in connection with S. E. Morison's *The struggle for Guadalcanal, August, 1942–February, 1943* (1951) it offers a balanced account of the first American offensive operation in World War II. H. M. Smith and P. Finch, *Coral and brass* (1949), contains memoirs on the part played by the U.S. Marines in the Pacific. The U.S. Army had also issued a number of volumes in its gigantic historical series (99 projected volumes), the first volume being *The war in the Pacific: Okinawa, the last battle* by Roy Appleman and others (1948). Other volumes are C. W. Hoffman, *Saipan, the beginning of the end* (1950), and F. O. Hough, *The assault on Peleliu* (1950). The latter has also written *The island war* (1947). *The United States army in world war II* by R. R. Palmer, B. I. Wiley, and W. R. Keast (1948) is a mine of information. *The U.S. marines and amphibious war: its theory and its practice in the Pacific* by J. I. Isely and P. A. Crowl (1951) is a solid contribution. R. G. Hubler, *Flying leathernecks* (1944), tells the story of the Marine air corps in the Pacific. G. Cant has written three informative books on American naval action: *The war at sea* (1942), *America's navy in world war II* (1943), and *The great Pacific victory: from the Solomons to Tokyo* (1946). O. Jensen, *Carrier war* (1945), is interesting. C. V. Woodward, *The battle for Leyte Gulf* (1947), is a detailed authentic account of the great naval battle. *Admiral Halsey's story* by W. F. Halsey and J. Bryan (1947) covers the period from Guadalcanal to Tokyo. *Sink 'em all: submarine warfare in the Pacific* by Vice-Admiral C. A. Lockwood (1951) is a story of stark adventure. R. McKelvie, *The war in Burma* (1948), discusses the strategy and politics of the Burma campaign.

The last period in Europe. C. C. Wertenbaker, *Invasion* (1944), tells the story of D-Day and after. W. Millis, *The last phase: the allied victory in Europe* (1946), is a readable account of the war from the Normandy landings to the collapse of Germany. H. M. Cole, *The Lorraine campaign* (The U.S. Army in World War II) (1950), tells the story of Patton's Third Army with precise objectivity. H. Speidel, *Invasion 1944: Rommel and the Normandy campaign* (1950), tells the story of Rommel's defeat in France; propaganda for a lost cause. R. E. Merriam, *Dark December: the full account of the battle of the bulge* (1949), is a readable account based on official documents. H. R. Trevor-Roper, *The last days of Hitler* (1947), is an attempt to establish the facts regarding Hitler's death. *The fall of Mussolini: his own story* by B. Mussolini, edited by M. Ascoli (1947), is the self-revelation of a blustering adventurer. M. Hankey, *Politics, trials and errors* (1950), is a critical review of the policy of unconditional surrender.

The end of the war with Japan. In T. W. Lawson, *Thirty seconds over Tokio* (1943), a pilot who bombed Tokyo on the Doolittle raid relates his experiences. Masuo Kato, *The lost war* (1946), is a Japanese reporter's story of the events leading to the surrender of Japan. On the atom bomb see the bibliography for Chapter Sixteen.

CHAPTER 31 *The Elusive Peace*

W. L. Neumann, *Making the peace, 1941–1945: the diplomacy of the wartime conferences* (1950), is a brief survey of negotiations during the war. The conferences at Yalta and Dumbarton Oaks are discussed in Vera M. Dean, *The four cornerstones of peace* (1946). E. R. Stettinius, Jr., *Roosevelt and the Russians: the Yalta conference,* edited by W. Johnson (1949), is a defense of Roosevelt's role at Yalta. Admiral W. D. Leahy, *I was there* (1950), is a frank and outspoken volume by one who was present at many important conferences. Equally important is *Speaking frankly* by J. F. Byrnes (1947), an important figure at a number of the conferences. There is also much information in R. E. Sherwood, *Roosevelt and Hopkins: an intimate history* (1948). The text of the Italian treaty is printed in *Current history,* n.s. 12 (1947), pp. 376–425. R. Albrecht-Carrié, "Peace with Italy: an appraisal," *Political science quarterly,* vol. 62 (1947), pp. 481–503, is an enlightening discussion. All the early treaties are ably discussed in *Peace settlements of world war II,* edited by T. V. Kalijarvi (1948). E. Wittman, *History: a guide to peace* (1949), contains a great deal of historical information. J. R. Deane, *The strange alliance: the story of our efforts at wartime cooperation with Russia* (1947), shows the futility of our attempts at cooperation. No-yong Park, *The white man's peace* (1948), is an oriental view of western attempts at making peace.

CHAPTER 32 *The United Nations*

The U.N. G. Murray, *From the league to the U.N.* (1948), is a series of essays which make fascinating reading. N. D. Bentwich, *From Geneva to San Francisco* (1946), tells how the UN was set up. An excellent introductory volume is A. Vandenbosch and W. N. Hogan, *The United Nations* (1952), which explains the background, organization and functions of the UN. The history, purpose and activity of the UN is stated concisely and ably in S. S. Fenichall and P. Andrews, *United Nations* (1952). H. V. Evatt has written two valuable brief studies: *The United Nations* (1948) and *The task of the nations* (1949). E. P. Chase, *United Nations in action* (1951), is a valuable comprehensive study. *Documentary textbook on the United Nations* by J. E. Harley (1947) is an impressive contribution to an understanding of the UN. A. H. Feller, *United Nations and world community* (1952), sees the emergence of an international community as a result of the work of the UN. H. Kelsen, *Law of the United Nations* (1951), is a somewhat technical discussion of the basic problems of the UN. Two valuable specialized works are H. F. Haviland, *The political role of the general assembly* (1951), and S. M. Schwebel, *The secretary-general of the United Nations* (1952).

Korea. E. G. Meade, *American military government in Korea* (1951), throws much light on the Korean question during the period from 1945 to the withdrawal of U.S. forces. A. W. Green, *The epic of Korea* (1950), and J. C. Caldwell, *The Korean story* (1953), are critical of U.S. policy in Korea — not always convincing. G. M. McCune and A. L. Grey, *Korea today* (1950), is a valuable contribution. R. T. Oliver, *Why war came in Korea* (1950), is sympathetic to South Korea. R. B. Rigg, *Red China's fighting hordes* (1951), is a realistic discussion of the Chinese communist army by a U.S. officer. M. F. Nelson, *Korea and the old orders in eastern Asia* (1945), is a well-documented comprehensive study.

CHAPTERS 33 AND 34 *Western Europe since World War II*

General studies. On the governments at the end of World War II see *Contemporary foreign governments* by H. Beukema, W. M. Geer, and others (1946), a worthwhile book. K. Loewenstein, *Political reconstruction* (1947), is a penetrating discussion of the problem of political reconstruction. *UNRRA: the history of the United Nations relief and rehabilitation administration,* prepared under the direction of G. Woodbridge (2 vols., 1950), is a monumental work. *European recovery program,* edited by S. E. Harris (1949), is a symposium of 24 essays dealing largely with the role of the U.S. H. K. Smith, *The state of Europe* (1949), is a readable and at times brilliant survey. G. D. H. Cole, *World in transition: a guide to the shifting political and economic forces of our time* (1949), is an important volume by a British economist. J. S. Schapiro, *World in crisis* (1951), sketches the pattern of political development in the twentieth century. Barbara Ward, *The west at bay* (1948), discusses postwar problems in a provocative manner. *The defense of Europe* by Drew Middleton (1952) is an intelligent discussion of NATO. Hajo Holborn, *The political collapse of Europe* (1951), is an acute examination of the causes of the breakdown of the old political order in Europe. J. G. de Beus, *The future of the west* (1953), is optimistic about European unity.

Germany and Austria. P. E. Mosely, "The occupation of Germany," *Foreign affairs,* vol. 28 (1950), pp. 580–604, offers new information on the drawing of the zones. C. Landauer, "The allies and Germany's future," *Journal of modern history,* vol. 18 (1946), pp. 251–260, is an excellent discussion of pertinent books. *American military government in Germany* by H. Zink (1947) is interesting and informative. S. K. Padover, *Experiment in Germany: the story of an American intelligence officer* (1946), contains colorful descriptions of some phases of postwar life. Invaluable for this period is Lucius D. Clay, *Decision in Germany* (1950), an account by a top official. *Germany under occupation: illustrative materials and documents,* collected and edited by J. K. Pollock and J. H. Meisel (1947), is a useful book. Important books on the Nuremberg trials include: J. P. Kenny, *Moral aspects of Nuremberg* (1949); V. H. Bernstein, *Final judgment: the story of Nuremberg* (1947); and C. P. Calvocoressi, *Nuremberg, the facts, the law and the consequences* (1948). E. Kogon, *The theory and practice of hell: the German concentration camps and the system behind them,* translated by H. Norden (1950), is a graphic account. E. H. Buschbeck, *Austria* (1950), surveys postwar conditions. K. W. Rothschild, *The Austrian economy since 1945* (1951), is a brief analysis of the problems besetting the Austrian economy.

German problems. *This is Germany,* edited by A. Settel (1950), is a report on economic and social aspects of postwar Germany. C. J. Friedrich, "Rebuilding the German constitution," *American political science review,* vol. 43 (1949), pp. 461–482, 704–720, offers a penetrating analysis of the new constitution. *The struggle for democracy in Germany,* edited by G. A. Almond (1949), is a series of intelligent discussions by a group of historians. Drew Middleton, *Struggle for Germany* (1949), and R. Hill, *Struggle for Germany* (1947), discuss the position of Germany between Russia and the western powers. F. Meinecke, *The German catastrophe,* translated by S. B. Fay (1949), contains the reflections of one of Germany's most distinguished historians. Three useful books on

East Germany are J. P. Nettl, *The eastern zone and Soviet policy in Germany, 1945–1950* (1951); G. Schaffer, *The Russian zone of Germany* (1948); and F. Lowenthal, *News from Soviet Germany* (1950). *The Ruhr* by N. J. G. Pounds (1953) offers a compact, accurate picture of the Ruhr and what it means to the German and European economy.

France. D. M. Pickles, *France between the republics* (1946), is a useful, though often over-simplified, account. F. S. Hadsell, "Some sources of the resistance movement in France during the Nazi occupation," *Journal of modern history*, vol. 18 (1946), pp. 333–340, is a useful brief discussion. In *Our Vichy gamble* (1947) W. L. Langer discusses the relationship of the United States and France from June, 1940, to December, 1942. H. W. Ehrmann, *French labor from the popular front to the liberation* (1947), is essential to an understanding of French labor during the period. The same author has also written an excellent bibliographical discussion. "Recent writings on the French labor movement," *Journal of modern history*, vol. 22 (1950), pp. 151–158. S. K. Padover, *France: setting or rising star* (1950), is a good brief survey in the Foreign Policy Association Headline series. Gordon Wright, *The reshaping of French democracy*, with an introduction by P. Birdsall (1948), is excellent on the early years of the Fourth Republic. O. R. Taylor, *The fourth republic of France* (1951), and F. Goguel, *France under the fourth republic* (1952), are lucid discussions of government and politics. A. Rossi, *The communist party in action*, translated by W. Kendall (1950), analyzes French communism. The monetary difficulties of the Fourth Republic are briefly reviewed in P. Dieterlen and C. Rist, *The monetary problem of France* (1949). D. C. MacKay, *The United States and France* (1951), is an interesting and illuminating account of the relations between the two countries. The conflicting claims of France and Germany to the Saar are carefully and objectively treated in F. M. Russell, *The Saar: battleground and pawn* (1951), and L. G. Cowan, *France and the Saar, 1680–1948* (1951).

Britain. E. S. Watkins, *The cautious revolution* (1951), tells the story of the Labor government with grace and fairness. C. F. O. Clarke, *Britain today* (1951), presents socialist Britain in a series of lectures to an American audience with much insight. *Socialist Britain* by F. Williams (1949) surveys the policies and personalities of the Labor Party. G. D. H. Cole, *A history of the labour party from 1914* (1948), is an able study by a British historian. C. L. Mowat, "Some recent books on the British labor movement," *Journal of modern history*, vol. 17 (1945), pp. 356–366, is a useful discussion of pertinent literature. *Ordeal by planning* by J. Jewkes (1949) analyzes British economic difficulties and suggests a remedy. *The peaceful revolution* by H. Morrison (1949) is a series of addresses by one of the leaders of the Labor Party. E. Lipson, *Growth of English society* (1951), embodies the fruits of forty years of study in a brief compass. On the coronation and the new queen there are four interesting books: *Elizabeth and Philip* by G. Bocca (1953); *The young queen* by G. Winn (1953); *The story of the coronation* by R. S. Churchill (1953); and *God save the queen* by A. A. Michie (1953).

Spain and Italy. G. Brenan, *The face of Spain* (1951), is a report on the years of Franco's rule. *Report from Spain* by E. J. Hughes (1947) is a penetrating analysis of the Franco regime. S. M. O'Callaghan, *Cinderella of Europe* (1951), is a defense of the Franco regime. C. J. H. Hayes, *Wartime mission in Spain, 1942–1945* (1945), records his experiences as U.S. ambassador to Spain. More critical is Sir Samuel Hoare who was

British ambassador to Spain. His experiences are related in *Complacent dictator* (1947). An account of Franco's relations with other states may be found in H. Feis, *The Spanish story: Franco and the nations at war* (1948). *The masquerade in Spain* by C. Foltz (1948) is a reporter's report on Spain — interesting and readable. In *The last optimist* (1950) J. Alvarez del Vayo, a Spanish democrat, tells his story. Muriel Grindrod, *The new Italy* (1949), shows how Italy turned from war to peace. M. Einaudi and F. Goguel, *Christian democracy in Italy and France* (1952), contains an analysis of the Christian Democratic party in Italy. Among the better articles on postwar Italy are: M. Einaudi, "The constitution of the Italian republic," *American political science review*, August, 1948; F. A. Hermens, "Troubled Italian politics," *Current history*, May, 1951.

CHAPTER 35 *The Passing of the Old Colonialism*

General. P. H. Clyde, *The Far East: a history of the impact of the West on eastern Asia* (1948), is a lucid, authoritative study. *The revolt of Asia* by R. Payne (1947) discusses the men and forces behind the uprising. B. Lasker, *New forces in Asia* (1950), is a readable survey of the Asiatic revolt. O. Hardy and G. S. Dumke, *A history of the Pacific area in modern times* (1949), is a good general survey. *New cycle in Asia*, edited by H. R. Isaacs (1947), is a selection of documents on major developments in the Far East, 1943–1947. *Postwar governments in the Far East*, edited by T. Cole and J. H. Hallowell (1947), surveys the political life. *Southeast Asia in the world today*, edited by P. Talbot (1950), contains a series of lectures by recognized "experts." E. H. Jacoby, *Agrarian unrest in Southeast Asia* (1949) is an informed volume. K. P. Landon, *Southeast Asia: crossroad of religions* (1949), lucidly discusses the religious factor. *Modern far eastern international relations* by H. MacNair and D. Lach (1950) is a valuable study. In H. J. Van Mook, *The stakes of democracy in southeastern Asia* (1950), a Dutch historian surveys the situation. *The state of Asia* by L. K. Rosinger and associates (1951) discusses the major developments in Asia since World War II. Communist efforts to extend their sway over Asia are depicted in O. O. Trullinger, *Red banners over Asia* (1951), and R. Payne, *Red storm over Asia* (1951). H. Maurer, *Collision of East and West* (1951), discusses the collision of cultures. *Asian nationalism and the West*, edited by W. L. Holland (1953), is a series of essays by a group of historians.

Individual countries. *The birth of Indonesia* by D. Wehl (1948) is a well-informed objective study. R. McKelvie, *The war in Burma* (1948), is a good factual account. T. W. Wallbank, *India in the new era* (1951), is an able survey of the origin and development of the Indian union and Pakistan. *Social background of Indian nationalism* by A. R. Desai (1950) is an important contribution. *India, Pakistan, Ceylon*, edited by W. N. Brown (1951), is a useful symposium. P. Speer, *India, Pakistan, and the West* (1949), is a good study on the relationship of cultures. R. Symonds, *The making of Pakistan* (1950), is a valuable study. B. I. Schwartz, *Chinese communism and the rise of Mao* (1951), sketches the background of communism's success in China. The rise and decline of Nationalist China is portrayed in Ch'ien Tuan-sheng, *The government and politics of China* (1950). D. Bodde, *Peking diary: a year of revolution* (1950), records the experiences of an eyewitness. The postwar economic problems are lucidly discussed in D. K. Lieu, *China's economic stabilization and reconstruction* (1948). R. Payne, *Mao Tse-*

tung: ruler of Red China (1950), is a readable biography. P. Chang, *Agriculture and industrialization* (1949), discusses the interrelationship of the two. *Russia's race for Asia* by G. Creel (1949) argues for the thesis that Chinese communism is controlled from the Kremlin. *Mao's China: party reform documents, 1942–1944,* translated by B. Compton (1950), contribute much toward an understanding of Chinese communism. Mark Tennien, *No secret is safe behind the bamboo curtain* (1952), records the experiences of a Roman Catholic missionary in China. S. L. A. Marshall, *The river and the gauntlet* (1953), tells the story of the defeat of the Eighth Army by the Chinese communist forces.

British Commonwealth. *Changing empire: Churchill to Nehru* by E. Estorick (1950) is a readable survey of the process of recent change. *The British empire,* edited by H. Bolitho (1948), offers a series of essays on all parts of the empire. P. McGuire, *Experiment in world order* (1948), is an interesting popular account of the development of the Commonwealth.

Near East and Africa. R. Brock, *Blood, oil, and sand* (1952), is a correspondent's picture of the Near East. *Short history of the Middle East* by G. E. Kirk (1949) is a readable survey covering more than a century. R. Bullard, *Britain and the Middle East* (1951), covers the relations of Britain with this area from the earliest times to 1950. *Arabia reborn* by G. Kheirallah (1953) has some chapters on the recent period. *The Near East and the great powers,* edited by R. N. Frye (1951), is a group of short papers by specialists in Near-Eastern history. *The struggle for Palestine* by J. C. Hurewitz (1951) is penetrating and fair minded. J. W. Parke, *History of Palestine* (1949), has some readable scholarly chapters on the years after World War II. J. Dunner, *Republic of Israel: its history and its promise* (1950), is a careful study.

CHAPTER 36 *Russia and the New Soviet Imperialism*

Russia. F. C. Barghoorn, "Some recent books on Russia and the Soviet Union," *Journal of modern history,* vol. 21 (1949), pp. 115–120, offers excellent critical discussions of books on the Soviet Union published during the years immediately after World War II. W. Kirchner, *Russia: an outline history* (2nd ed., 1950), is a helpful little volume. H. Best, *The Soviet state and its inception* (1950), is a readable survey. *Russia, past and present* by A. G. Mazour (1951) is a sound and interesting treatment arranged under topical headings. *The Soviet Union: background, ideology, reality,* edited by W. Gurian (1951), is a useful symposium by a group of able historians. E. Stevens, *This is Russia — uncensored* (1950), sketches a picture which is neither all-black nor all-white. *Soviet attitudes toward authority* by Margaret Mead (1951) is a revealing discussion of the nature of Soviet leadership. B. Moore, Jr., *Soviet politics: the dilemma of power* (1950), is a careful analysis of the Soviet governmental system. *Materials for the study of the Soviet system,* edited by J. Meisel and E. Kozera (1951), contains constitutions, laws, decrees, and official statements. M. Salvadori, *The rise of modern communism* (1952), is an excellent brief survey. M. Ebon, *World communism today* (1948), is an able survey of communism in every country in which it is a political factor. E. Crankshaw, *Cracks in the*

Kremlin wall (1951), records what the author regards as the weaknesses of the Soviet regime. *The people of Great Russia: a psychological study* by G. Gorer and J. Rickman (1950) analyzes the relationship of the Russian people to their rulers. S. T. Possony, *A century of conflict: communist techniques of world revolution* (1953), is a full-length analysis of the Bolshevik concept of world revolution. G. Fischer, *Soviet opposition to Stalin* (1952), shows that Soviet opposition to Stalin was widespread during and immediately after World War II. F. Sternberg, *The end of a revolution: Soviet Russia from revolution to reaction* (1953), is useful and informative however one may disagree with the main thesis. Although there is much speculation in the book M. Ebon, *Malenkov: Stalin's successor* (1953), makes interesting and valuable reading.

Economic history. H. Schwartz, *Russia's Soviet economy* (1950), is a useful survey of the structure and operation of the Soviet economy. *The development of the Soviet economic system* by A. Baykov (1947) sums up the results of a lifetime of study. *Management in Russian industry and agriculture* by G. Brenstock, S. M. Schwarz, and A. Yugow (1947) shows how the Russian economic system works. S. M. Schwarz, *Labor in the Soviet Union* (1952), is a careful analysis of the changing wage levels and standards of living. A. K. Herling, *The Soviet slave empire* (1951), is an interesting and informative volume.

Social and intellectual. A. Inkeles, *Public opinion in Soviet Russia* (1950), is a penetrating examination of the Soviet technique of mass persuasion. S. R. Tompkins, *The Russian mind* (1953), is a worthwhile study. D. Tomasic, *The impact of Russian culture on Soviet communism* (1953), is an enlightening account of a neglected subject. R. Magidoff, *The Kremlin vs. the people: the story of the cold civil war in Stalin's Russia* (1953), describes and analyzes the enormous tensions in Soviet society. D. D. Runes, *The Soviet impact on society* (1953), is a painstaking examination of the cultural and social changes brought about by Marxist ideology. G. S. Counts and N. Lodge, *The country of the blind: the Soviet system of mind control* (1949), contains interesting information on the Soviet propaganda technique. B. Shub, *The choice* (1950), develops the thesis that mass dissatisfaction is the great weakness of the Soviet regime. The dynamics of political power in the Soviet Union are ably discussed in J. Towster, *Political power in the U.S.S.R., 1917–1947* (1947). There are good discussions of recent Soviet literature in G. Struve, *Soviet Russian literature, 1917–1950* (1951); M. Slonim, *Modern Russian literature from Chekov to the present* (1953); and G. Reavey, *Soviet literature today* (1947).

International relations. T. A. Bailey, *America faces Russia: Russian-American relations from early times to our day* (1950), is lucid and well-documented. *American-Russian relations in the Far East* by Pauline Tompkins (1950) is a careful scholarly work. H. H. Fisher, *America and Russia in the world community* (1947), is a painstaking study. E. Crankshaw, *Russia and Britain* (1951), is a readable survey by a well-known British historian. E. H. Carr, *The Soviet impact on the western world* (1947), is a brief informative sketch. G. Lenczowski, *Russia and the West in Iran, 1918–1948* (1949), is a comprehensive and invaluable study.

Soviet imperialism. E. D. Carman, *Soviet imperialism* (1950), is a brief account of the Soviet drive for world power. Two books by A. Bouscaren, *Soviet expansion and* *the West* (1949) and *Imperial communism* (1953), throw much light on the question of Soviet imperialism. W. Kolarz, *Russia and her colonies* (1953), brings into sharp focus the problem of the Soviet multinational state; explodes the myth that the Soviet Union has solved the problem of her racial and national minorities. Y. Gluckstein, *Stalin's satellites in Europe* (1952), is a somewhat rambling review of conditions in the Soviet-captive countries. *Moscow's European satellites,* edited by J. S. Rouček (1950), is an informative volume by a group of historians. *New constitutions in the Soviet sphere* by S. L. Sharp (1950) is a useful little volume. J. C. Harsch, *The curtain isn't iron* (1950), is a quick review by a correspondent of happenings in eastern Europe. L. Stowe, *Conquest by terror* (1952), is a readable report on the sovietization of eastern Europe.

Individual countries. J. Ciechanowski, *Defeat in victory* (1947), is an absorbing account of the efforts of the Polish government-in-exile. The efforts of the Poles to maintain their independence are described in S. Mikolajezk, *The rape of Poland* (1948), and A. B. Lane, *I saw Poland betrayed* (1949). J. Flournoy, *Hungary: the unwilling satellite* (1947), throws much light on the situation. *The struggle behind the iron curtain* by F. Nagy (1948) is an account of the changes by a former prime minister of Hungary. *Yugoslavia,* edited by R. J. Kerner (1949), is a useful symposium by 15 able historians. H. F. Armstrong, *Tito and Goliath* (1951), sets the background for the break with the Kremlin. V. Dedijer, *Tito* (1953), tells the fantastic tale of Tito's rise and his duel with Stalin. H. Hodgkinson, *Challenge to the Kremlin* (1953), is an interesting study of the quarrel between Stalin and Tito. L. White, *Balkan Caesar: Tito versus Stalin* (1951), is anti-Tito and anti-Stalin. S. Clissold, *Whirlwind* (1950), is a worthwhile account of Tito's rise to power. *Tito's communism* by J. Korbel (1951) analyzes the nature of Yugoslav communism. W. S. Vucinich, "Postwar Yugoslav historiography," *Journal of modern history,* vol. 23 (1951), pp. 41–57, is an excellent short discussion. R. H. Markham, *Tito's imperial communism* (1947), is a lively condemnation. The same author has also written *Rumania under the Soviet yoke* (1949), one of the strongest and best documented indictments of Soviet methods. H. L. Roberts, *Rumania: political problems of an agrarian state* (1951), is a scholarly discussion of the depressed state of the Rumanian peasantry. W. S. Vucinich, "Bulgaria: a Balkan soviet," *Current history,* n.s. vol. 20 (1951), pp. 129–135, is an informative short account. J. Stransky, *East wind over Prague* (1951), presents a vivid picture of communist methods. H. Ripka, *Czechoslovakia enslaved: the story of the communist coup d'état* (1951), is an account by a former Czech cabinet minister. D. A. Schmidt, *Anatomy of a satellite* (1953), gives us a clinical dissection of the anatomy of a Soviet satellite.

Index

INDEX

Abdul-Hamid II, 323
Abyssinia, 359; sought by Italy, 240, 258; *see also* Ethiopia
Acheson, Dean, 667, 686, 687
Adenauer, Dr. Konrad, 685, 686
Afghanistan, 359
Afifi, Dr. Hafiz, 666
Africa, exploration of, 258–260; French, British, and German colonies in, 261–262; World War II campaigns in, 599, 600–601, 619–620; revolt against colonialism in, 715–716
Age of Reason, 112
Agriculture, in Great Britain, 68, 79–84, 227–229; in France, 87–88; in Italy, 238–239, 518; in Spain, 245–246, 523, 530, 704; in Russia, 288, 296; Soviet collectivization of, 439, 442–446; in Balkans, 501; in Bulgaria, 506; in Turkey, 510
Aix-la-Chapelle, Congress of, 39–40
Akhmatova, Anna, 755
Albania, created after first Balkan war, 326; agricultural problem, 501; independence of, 506–507; occupied by Italy, 507, 583; independence restored, 718; sovietization of, 745
Albert of Saxe-Coburg, Prince Consort, 212
Alexander, King, and Queen Draga, assassination of, 244
Alexander, of Greece, 505
Alexander, of Yugoslavia, 503–504
Alexander I, of Russia, 28, 40, 42, 44; defiance of Napoleon, 21; enigmatic character, 29–30; ambition to rule Poland, 32–33; Holy Alliance created by, 38–39; liberalism recanted, 41–42; as king of Poland, 46
Alexander II, of Russia, enthusiasm for reform, 280–281; abolition of serfdom, 283–284; administrative reforms, 284; assassination of, 285
Alexander III, of Russia, 433; reactionary policies of, 285–288
Alexandra, of Russia, influence of, 297–298; in control of government, 385–386; execution of, 437–438
Alfonso XII, of Spain, 243
Alfonso XIII, of Spain, assassination attempts on, 244–245; government of, 524; resignation of, 525–526
Algeria, French colony in, 254, 258; riots in, 711

Alliances, preceding World War I, 352–356; preceding World War II, 584–586
Allies, 367; joined by Italy and Rumania, 374–375; reverses for, 375–376; naval blockade established, 378; propaganda in America, 381; joined by United States, 386; aid to White Russian armies, 435–436; *see also* World War I
Alsace-Lorraine, 352, 421; ceded to Germany, 170, 173; returned to France, 407; Germany's claim renounced, 415–416
Amadeo, of Spain, 243
American Expeditionary Force, 391–393
American Revolution, 6–7
Amiens, treaty of, 19
Anesthetics, advance in, 337–339
Anglo-French Entente Cordial, 355–356
Angola, held by Portugal, 258, 261
Annam, occupied by France, 263
Annunzio, Gabriel D', 249–250, 375, 403n, 512
Anschluss, 572, 579
Antibiotics, 344–346
Antonelli, Cardinal, 235
Apponyi, Count Albert, 312
Architecture, romanticism in, 121–122
Argentina, independence of, 42–43
Aristotle, 328
Arkwright, Richard, 70
Armaments, race before World War I, 356–358; Hague Conferences, 357; Washington Conference, 556, 560, 569
Arndt, Ernst Moritz, 41
Arnold, Matthew, 121
Art, romanticism in, 122–123; French, 147–148, 185–188; Russian, 303–304; *see also* Literature and Music
Asia, European imperialism in, 258, 262–267; nationalism in, 548–550, 707–709; *see also* China, India, Japan
Asia Minor, dominated by England, France, Germany, 258
Association Internationàle Africaine, 260
Astronomy, progress in, 333–334
Atatürk, Kemal, 429; rise of, 507; as president and dictator, 508–510; death of, 510
Ateliers nationaux. See National workshops
Ateliers sociaux (social workshops), 97
Atlantic Charter, 638, 640, 657, 709
Atlee, Clement R., at Potsdam Conference, 644; as prime minister, 697–699